1,000,000 Books

are available to read at

www.ForgottenBooks.com

Read online
Download PDF
Purchase in print

ISBN 978-0-282-93209-1
PIBN 10873400

This book is a reproduction of an important historical work. Forgotten Books uses state-of-the-art technology to digitally reconstruct the work, preserving the original format whilst repairing imperfections present in the aged copy. In rare cases, an imperfection in the original, such as a blemish or missing page, may be replicated in our edition. We do, however, repair the vast majority of imperfections successfully; any imperfections that remain are intentionally left to preserve the state of such historical works.

Forgotten Books is a registered trademark of FB &c Ltd.
Copyright © 2018 FB &c Ltd.
FB &c Ltd, Dalton House, 60 Windsor Avenue, London, SW19 2RR.
Company number 08720141. Registered in England and Wales.

For support please visit www.forgottenbooks.com

1 MONTH OF FREE READING

at

www.ForgottenBooks.com

By purchasing this book you are eligible for one month membership to ForgottenBooks.com, giving you unlimited access to our entire collection of over 1,000,000 titles via our web site and mobile apps.

To claim your free month visit:

www.forgottenbooks.com/free873400

* Offer is valid for 45 days from date of purchase. Terms and conditions apply.

English
Français
Deutsche
Italiano
Español
Português

www.forgottenbooks.com

Mythology Photography **Fiction** Fishing Christianity **Art** Cooking Essays Buddhism Freemasonry Medicine **Biology** Music **Ancient Egypt** Evolution Carpentry Physics Dance Geology **Mathematics** Fitness Shakespeare **Folklore** Yoga Marketing **Confidence** Immortality Biographies Poetry **Psychology** Witchcraft Electronics Chemistry History **Law** Accounting **Philosophy** Anthropology Alchemy Drama Quantum Mechanics Atheism Sexual Health **Ancient History Entrepreneurship** Languages Sport Paleontology Needlework Islam **Metaphysics** Investment Archaeology Parenting Statistics Criminology **Motivational**

BUREAU OF PLANT INDUSTRY—BULLETIN No. 63.

B. T. GALLOWAY, *Chief of Bureau.*

INVESTIGATIONS OF RUSTS.

BY

MARK ALFRED CARLETON,

ASSISTANT IN CHARGE OF CEREAL INVESTIGATIONS.

TABLE PATHOLOGICAL AND PHYSIOLOGICAL
INVESTIGATIONS.

ISSUED JULY 12, 1904.

WASHINGTON:
GOVERNMENT PRINTING OFFICE.
1904.

BULLETINS OF THE BUREAU OF PLANT INDUSTRY.

The Bureau of Plant Industry, which was organized July 1, 1901, includes Vegetable Pathological and Physiological Investigations, Botanical Investigations and Experiments, Grass and Forage Plant Investigations, Pomological Investigations, and Experimental Gardens and Grounds, all of which were formerly separate Divisions, and also Seed and Plant Introduction and Distribution, the Arlington Experimental Farm, Tea Culture Investigations, and Domestic Sugar Investigations.

Beginning with the date of organization of the Bureau, the several series of bulletins of the various Divisions were discontinued, and all are now published as one series of the Bureau. A list of the bulletins issued in the present series follows.

Attention is directed to the fact that "the serial, scientific, and technical publications of the United States Department of Agriculture are not for general distribution. All copies not required for official use are by law turned over to the Superintendent of Documents, who is empowered to sell them at cost." All applications for such publications should, therefore, be made to the Superintendent of Documents, Government Printing Office, Washington, D. C.

No. 1. The Relation of Lime and Magnesia to Plant Growth. 1901. Price, 10 cents.
 2. Spermatogenesis and Fecundation of Zamia. 1901. Price, 20 cents.
 3. Macaroni Wheats. 1901. Price, 20 cents.
 4. Range Improvement in Arizona. 1902. Price, 10 cents.
 5. Seeds and Plants Imported. Inventory No. 9. 1902. Price, 10 cents.
 6. A List of American Varieties of Peppers. 1902. Price, 10 cents.
 7. The Algerian Durum Wheats. 1902. Price, 15 cents.
 8. A Collection of Fungi Prepared for Distribution. 1902. Price, 10 cents.
 9. The North American Species of Spartina. 1902. Price, 10 cents.
 10. Records of Seed Distribution and Cooperative Experiments with Grasses and Forage Plants. 1902. Price, 10 cents.
 11. Johnson Grass. 1902. Price, 10 cents.
 12. Stock Ranges of Northwestern California. 1902. Price, 15 cents.
 13. Experiments in Range Improvement in Central Texas. 1902. Price, 10 cents.
 14. The Decay of Timber and Methods of Preventing It. 1902. Price, 55 cents.
 15. Forage Conditions on the Northern Border of the Great Basin. 1902. Price, 15 cents.
 16. A Preliminary Study of the Germination of the Spores of Agaricus Campestris and Other Basidiomycetous Fungi. 1902. Price, 10 cents.
 17. Some Diseases of the Cowpea. 1902. Price, 10 cents.
 18. Observations on the Mosaic Disease of Tobacco. 1902. Price, 15 cents.
 19. Kentucky Bluegrass Seed. 1902. Price, 10 cents.
 20. Manufacture of Semolina and Macaroni. 1902. Price, 15 cents.
 21. List of American Varieties of Vegetables. 1903. Price, 35 cents.
 22. Injurious Effects of Premature Pollination. 1902. Price, 10 cents.
 23. Berseem. 1902. Price, 15 cents.
 24. Unfermented Grape Must. 1902. Price, 10 cents.
 25. Miscellaneous Papers: I. The Seeds of Rescue Grass and Chess. II. Saragolla Wheat. III. Plant Introduction Notes from South Africa. IV. Congressional Seed and Plant Distribution Circulars, 1902-1903. 1903. Price, 15 cents.

[Continued on page 3 of cover]

A Perennial Rust.

(Æcidium Tuberculatum E. & K. on Callirrhoe involucrata Gr.)

U. S. DEPARTMENT OF AGRICULTURE.
BUREAU OF PLANT INDUSTRY—BULLETIN No. 63.
B. T. GALLOWAY, *Chief of Bureau.*

INVESTIGATIONS OF RUSTS.

BY

MARK ALFRED CARLETON,
CEREALIST IN CHARGE OF CEREAL INVESTIGATIONS.

VEGETABLE PATHOLOGICAL AND PHYSIOLOGICAL
INVESTIGATIONS.

ISSUED JULY 12, 1904.

WASHINGTON:
GOVERNMENT PRINTING OFFICE.
1904.

BUREAU OF PLANT INDUSTRY.

B. T. GALLOWAY, *Chief.*
J. E. ROCKWELL, *Editor.*

VEGETABLE PATHOLOGICAL AND PHYSIOLOGICAL INVESTIGATIONS.

SCIENTIFIC STAFF.

ALBERT F. WOODS, *Pathologist and Physiologist.*

ERWIN F. SMITH, *Pathologist in Charge of Laboratory of Plant Pathology.*
GEORGE T. MOORE, *Physiologist in Charge of Laboratory of Plant Physiology.*
HERBERT J. WEBBER, *Physiologist in Charge of Laboratory of Plant Breeding.*
WALTER T. SWINGLE, *Physiologist in Charge of Laboratory of Plant Life History.*
NEWTON B. PIERCE, *Pathologist in Charge of Pacific Coast Laboratory.*
M. B. WAITE, *Pathologist in Charge of Investigations of Diseases of Orchard Fruits.*
MARK ALFRED CARLETON, *Cerealist in Charge of Cereal Investigations.*
HERMANN VON SCHRENK,[a] *In Charge of Mississippi Valley Laboratory.*
P. H. ROLFS, *Pathologist in Charge of Subtropical Laboratory.*
C. O. TOWNSEND, *Pathologist in Charge of Sugar Beet Investigations.*
P. H. DORSETT, *Pathologist.*
RODNEY H. TRUE,[b] *Physiologist.*
T. H. KEARNEY, *Physiologist, Plant Breeding.*
CORNELIUS L. SHEAR, *Pathologist.*
WILLIAM A. ORTON, *Pathologist.*
W. M. SCOTT, *Pathologist.*
JOSEPH S. CHAMBERLAIN, *Physiological Chemist, Cereal Investigations.*
R. E. B. MCKENNEY, *Physiologist.*
FLORA W. PATTERSON, *Mycologist.*
CHARLES P. HARTLEY, *Assistant in Physiology, Plant Breeding.*
KARL F. KELLERMAN, *Assistant in Physiology.*
DEANE B. SWINGLE, *Assistant in Pathology.*
A. W. EDSON, *Scientific Assistant, Plant Breeding.*
JESSE B. NORTON, *Assistant in Physiology, Plant Breeding.*
JAMES B. RORER, *Assistant in Pathology.*
LLOYD S. TENNY, *Assistant in Pathology.*
GEORGE G. HEDGCOCK, *Assistant in Pathology.*
PERLEY SPAULDING, *Scientific Assistant.*
P. J. O'GARA, *Scientific Assistant.*
A. D. SHAMEL, *Scientific Assistant, Plant Breeding.*
T. RALPH ROBINSON, *Scientific Assistant, Plant Physiology.*
FLORENCE HEDGES, *Scientific Assistant, Bacteriology.*
CHARLES J. BRAND, *Scientific Assistant in Physiology, Plant Life History.*

---
[a] Detailed to the Bureau of Forestry.
[b] Detailed to Botanical Investigations and Experiments.

LETTER OF TRANSMITTAL.

U. S. DEPARTMENT OF AGRICULTURE,
BUREAU OF PLANT INDUSTRY,
OFFICE OF THE CHIEF,
Washington, D. C., April 20, 1904.

SIR: I have the honor to transmit herewith the manuscript of a technical paper entitled "Investigations of Rusts," by Mark Alfred Carleton, Cerealist in Charge of Cereal Investigations, Vegetable Pathological and Physiological Investigations, and recommend its publication as Bulletin No. 63 of the series of this Bureau.

The two illustrations accompanying the manuscript are necessary to a complete understanding of the subject-matter of this paper.

Respectfully,
B. T. GALLOWAY,
Chief of Bureau.

Hon. JAMES WILSON,
Secretary of Agriculture.

175977

PREFACE.

The experiments and observations on rusts which are the basis of the following notes were begun by Mr. Carleton several years ago, and were continued at intervals until the spring of 1900, when the pressure of other duties prevented further work of this kind up to the present time. The results obtained in many instances are still incomplete, but are of sufficient value to be recorded. Some of the species studied are of much economic importance. The investigation is a continuation of the work reported in Bulletin 16 of the Division of Vegetable Physiology and Pathology, and is concerned chiefly with the segregation of rust forms of economic importance on the common grasses and the completion of the life history of certain species. The work is to be carried on more extensively during 1904.

A. F. WOODS,
Pathologist and Physiologist.

OFFICE OF VEGETABLE PATHOLOGICAL AND
PHYSIOLOGICAL INVESTIGATIONS,
Washington, D. C., March 26, 1904.

CONTENTS.

	Page.
Additions to our knowledge of life histories	9
Euphorbia rust (*Uromyces euphorbiæ* C. and P.)	9
Sunflower rust (*Puccinia helianthi* Schw.)	11
Crown rust of oats (*Puccinia rhamni* [Pers.] Wettst.)	13
Segregation of host plants	14
Black stem rust of Agropyron and Elymus	15
Orange leaf rust of Agropyron and Elymus	17
Black stem rust of *Agrostis alba vulgaris*	17
Rust of Chloris (*Puccinia chloridis* Diet.)	18
Rusts of willow and cottonwood (Melampsora)	18
Winter resistance of the uredo	19
Uredo of Kentucky bluegrass rust (*Puccinia poarum* Niels.)	20
Uredo of *Puccinia montanensis* Ell	20
Emergency adaptations	21
Puccinia rexans Farl	22
Experiments with Lepto-uredineæ	25
Rust of cocklebur (*Puccinia xanthii* Schw.)	26
Rust of velvet leaf (*Puccinia heterospora* B. and C.)	26
Perennial species	27
Æcidium tuberculatum E. and K.	27
Rust of *Peucedanum fœniculaceum*	28
Description of plates	32

ILLUSTRATIONS.

		Page.
Plate I.	A perennial rust	Frontispiece.
II.	Rusts of Euphorbia and grama grass	32

INVESTIGATIONS OF RUSTS.

ADDITIONS TO OUR KNOWLEDGE OF LIFE HISTORIES.

In many instances, without any experimental proof, it is inferred that there is a connection between the different forms of rust occurring on the same host plant simply because of their constant association with each other. Sometimes it is afterwards demonstrated that these inferences are wrong, though they are probably correct in a majority of cases. Studies of the following species were made with the view of obtaining a more accurate knowledge of their life history.

EUPHORBIA RUST (*Uromyces euphorbiæ* C. AND P.).

Until the experiments herein described were performed it had not been demonstrated that there is any connection between the æcidial and other stages of this species, although experience naturally leads one to think that there is. They are in very close association on the same plant, the æcidium appearing first, quickly followed by the uredospores. In the spring of 1893 Mr. J. B. S. Norton, now professor of botany at the Maryland Agricultural College, while engaged in experiments in the germination of weeds in the greenhouses of the Agricultural Experiment Station at Manhattan, Kans., called the writer's attention to a very young rusted seedling of *Euphorbia dentata*. In this instance, as is usually the case with the young plants of this host, the pods were first badly affected by æcidia. This fact, taken together with the common observation that the seed pods of this host are usually affected by all stages of the rust, led at once to the thought that it was a case of rust propagation through the medium of the germinating seed of the host, something not before demonstrated for any other species in the entire group of Uredineæ, so far as the writer knows, unless we except the single instance of the experiments of Doctor Eriksson[a] with *Puccinia glumarum*.[b] The seed used by Mr.

---

[a] Vie latente et plasmatique de certaines Urédinées. Compt. Rend., 1897, pp. 475–477.

[b] T. S. Ralph, in Victorian Naturalist, Vol. VII, p. 18, describes an instance of a rust attacking the seed of *Senecio vulgaris*, stating that "with the microscope we are able to trace the fine yellow sporular matter into the covering of the seed, and into the seed itself;" but apparently it was not determined by further investigation whether or not the rust was able to reproduce itself through the germinating seed.

Norton was examined and the pods were found to be badly affected. Moreover, he stated that the seeds were planted without shelling. But the writer did not know then, as he does now, that this fact would probably make little difference, since the naked seeds are commonly affected, often showing actual peridia.

To test the theory of rust propagation above mentioned, experiments were instituted on April 22 for growing plants from rusted seed under a bell jar. The seed used bore all stages of the rust. The experiments were in five series: (1) Seeds shelled and disinfected by mercuric chlorid; (2) seeds unshelled and disinfected; (3) seeds shelled, but not disinfected; (4) seeds unshelled, not disinfected; (5) like series No. 4, but rusted mainly with æcidium. All were planted in pots in a greenhouse and the pots were kept under bell jars. On May 1 the plants began to come up. After about three months, when the plants had grown to a height of 3 to 5 inches, no rust had appeared on series 1 and 2, and only one spot on one plant of series 3. The plants of series 4 and 5 were much rusted, the æcidium appearing first, followed shortly by uredosori.

On April 25, 1893, it was attempted to germinate teleutospores of rust from the seeds used in these experiments, in water-drop cultures, which resulted in failure. On June 28, 1893, a similar culture of the fresh uredospores failed to germinate in two days.

In 1895 rusted seeds of *Euphorbia dentata*, sent from Kansas, were planted in the greenhouse of the Department of Agriculture, at Washington, D. C. From these three plants grew, which were kept under a bell jar. Soon one of these plants rusted badly, first with the æcidium, then a slight amount of the uredospores, and later the teleutospores. It should be remarked here that Euphorbia rust, so far as reported, occurs only on *E. maculata* in the vicinity of Washington, D. C., and the writer has never yet been able to obtain rusted seeds in that region.

On December 11, 1896, a third series of experiments was started at Washington, D. C. On that date rusted seeds of *Euphorbia dentata* from Kingman and Manhattan, Kans., were planted and kept under a bell jar as before. Eleven plants resulted by December 26. On March 8, 1897, spermogonia appeared in considerable amount on the young leaves of one plant, with a tendency to form a sort of hexenbesen.

On March 29 two more plants were rusted, one with spermogonia only on the young leaves, and the other with æcidia on the fruit. On April 10 still another plant showed spermogonia, making four in all, out of the eleven, that became rusted. (See Pl. II, fig. 1.)

As above stated, the proof that the rust actually penetrates the hulled seed is readily obtained, not only from microscopical demonstration, but also from the fact that the actual peridia may often be seen with the unaided eye in the seed. These experiments, however, further demonstrate the ability of the rust to propagate itself through the medium of the germinating seed of the host, and also make it seem probable that this is even the common method of reproduction in the case of its occurrence on *Euphorbia dentata*.

It will be noted also that the results of these experiments make it almost certain that the Æcidium and Uromyces appearing upon the plants are one and the same species, since in every case all stages resulted from planting the rusted seeds, the æcidium appearing first, then the uredo, and then the teleutospores. If anything was lacking, however, the proof has since been made complete by the experiments of Dr. J. C. Arthur, as reported in the Botanical Gazette,[a] in which the uredospores and teleutospores were obtained on *Euphorbia nutans* from a sowing of æcidiospores from other plants of the same host on June 20, 1899.

As is well known, the Euphorbia rust is widely distributed over the United States, occurring on numerous host species, but it is probably most abundant on *E. dentata* and *E. preslii*. It is a significant fact, bearing upon the ontogeny of the species, that it is also on these two hosts, particularly on *E. dentata*, that the æcidium is most common, and that the rust attacks the seed so severely. The seed pods are also affected considerably in the cases of *E. lata* and *E. marginata*.

On June 12, 1897, æcidiospores of this rust had germinated very well in water-drop culture after three days, and on June 22, after a two days' culture in water of both the æcidium and uredo from *Euphorbia marginata*, the latter germinated sparingly, but the former not at all. In no instance could the teleutospores be germinated, though germination was not attempted very often.

The writer has collected all three stages of this rust on *Euphorbia maculata*, *E. marginata*, *E. dentata*, *E. preslii*, *E. glyptosperma*, and *E. heterophylla*. On *E. petaloidea* and *E. serpyllifolia* only the uredo and teleuto stages were found, and on *E. lata* and what was probably *E. geyeri* even the uredo was rarely seen.

SUNFLOWER RUST (*Puccinia helianthi* SCHW.).

Although Saccardo rightly regards this species of Schweinitz as quite distinct, and includes with it the Æcidium often associated on the same host, in many herbaria the authority of Winter and Burrill is followed in making it a form of *Puccinia tanaceti*, while the Æcidium is commonly referred to *Æcidium compositarum*, a convenient dumping ground for numerous uncertain forms. The writer has always considered this disposition of the species to be without any good reason even on a purely morphological basis, and now the experiments

---

[a] Arthur, J. C., "Cultures of Uredineæ in 1899," Bot. Gaz., Vol. XXIX, No. 4, pp. 270–271, April, 1900.

here recorded make it rather certain that Schweinitz and Saccardo are correct. So far as this country is concerned, the writer is convinced that *P. tanaceti* either belongs almost entirely to *tanacetum* or does not exist at all. So far it has been utterly impossible, even in a greenhouse, to make transfers of the uredo from one to another of the numerous supposed hosts of that species, except among hosts of the same genus.[a] It is, at any rate, pretty certain that the forms occurring on Vernonia, Helianthus, Actinella, and Aplopappus, which have been referred to *P. tanaceti* at various times, should be considered distinct.

The circumstances connected with the culture experiments with this species were in themselves peculiar. Late in the autumn of 1897 at Manhattan, Kans., it was desired to obtain fresh material of the uredo for inoculating various hosts, but at that date very little else than the teleuto stage could be found. Finally, on October 29 a small amount was found on *Helianthus petiolaris*, mixed among a much larger quantity of teleutospores, and from this material sowings were made on *H. petiolaris* and *H. annuus*. On November 8 there resulted one rust spot on the latter host and three on the former. The spots were of the uredo stage, but the interesting feature accompanying this culture was the appearance first of spermogonia in one of the spots. This fact made it probable that a part of the infection resulted from the teleutospores of the inoculating material, even at this unusual season for the germination of these spores. On March 7, 1898, while stationed at the University of Nebraska, inoculations of *H. petiolaris* were again made with the teleutospores only from other plants of the same host, from which numerous spermogonia appeared in eight days, followed shortly by æcidia, which were fully developed by November 1. By these results the connection of the different stages of the rust is pretty well established. At the same time it is shown that the forms on *H. petiolaris* and *H. annuus* are identical. In all cultures made of this rust both the uredospores and teleutospores have been found to germinate easily and produce infections readily. Reverse cultures with æcidiospores were not made.

These experiments were first reported at the 1900 meeting of the Society for Plant Morphology and Physiology, at Baltimore. Since that time Drs. J. C. Arthur[b] and W. A. Kellerman[c] have made a number of such experiments, confirming these results, but also seeming to indicate a distinction of host forms on different species of sun-

---

[a] Dr. M. Voronin at first also obtained negative results in similar experiments in Russia in attempting transfers of the rust on to other hosts. (See Bot. Zeitung, vol. 30, pp. 694–698, Sept. 27, 1872.) Later he obtained infections of *Puccinia tanaceti* from *Tanacetum vulgare* on sunflower, which, however, did not produce such vigorous growth as ordinarily. (Bot. Zeitung, vol. 33, pp. 340, 341, May 14, 1875.)

[b] Botanical Gazette, vol. 35, p. 17, January, 1903; Journal of Mycology, vol. 10, pp. 12–13, January, 1904.

[c] Journal of Mycology, vol. 9, pp. 230–232, December, 1903.

flower. Doctor Voronin, in his experiments above mentioned, also found that rust of cultivated sunflower would not infect *Helianthus tuberosus*. In 1901 Ernst Jacky [a] inoculated the following hosts with teleutospores from *Helianthus annuus*: *H. annuus*, *H. cucumerifolius*, *H. californicus*, *H. tuberosus*, *H. maximiliana*, *H. multiflorus*, *H. scaberimus*, and *H. rigidus*, with resulting infections of the three first-named species, but no infection of any of the others.

The evidence from all these experiments just quoted and those of the writer shows at least that the rusts of *Helianthus annuus* (including cultivated varieties), *H. petiolaris*, and *H. mollis* are identical, with the probability that a distinct form exists on *H. tuberosus*.

Sunflower rust has been collected by the writer on the following species of Helianthus, including all stages on nearly every species: *H. annuus* (both wild and cultivated), *H. rigidus*, *H. petiolaris*, *H. tuberosus*, *H. hirsutus*, *H. maximiliana*, *H. grosse-serratus*, *H. orgyalis*, *H. mollis*, and *H. ciliaris*. The æcidium occurs rarely in comparison with the occurrence of other stages, but is to be found on a number of hosts and occasionally in considerable abundance. This rarity of its occurrence, together with the occurrence of spermogonia so often with the uredo, may be accounted for by the fact that the uredo is often produced by direct teleutosporic infection.

CROWN RUST OF OATS (*Puccinia rhamni* [PERS.] WETTST.).

In a mere note in a previous bulletin of this Department[b] it is stated that certain infections had just been made showing the connection of the crown rust of oats on *Phalaris caroliniana* and *Arrhenatherum elatius* with the æcidial form on *Rhamnus lanceolata*. No other demonstration of such a connection of forms had been reported up to that time. During the same season, however, Doctor Arthur obtained infections with the æcidium of *Rhamnus lanceolata* on oats at Lafayette, Ind.[c] The experiments of the writer are here given in detail.

On August 23, 1897, the uredo stage of a rust, supposed to be *Puccinia coronata*, was found in great abundance on *Phalaris caroliniana* at Stillwater, Okla. This host, with the rust, was transferred to a greenhouse of the Agricultural College at Manhattan, Kans., and inoculations were made on oats, wheat, and orchard grass on August 30, 1897, resulting September 7 in a good infection of oats, a poor one of the orchard grass, and no infection at all of wheat. Other inoculations were made September 1 on wheat and rye, with no result. By October 8 the teleutospores had appeared on the original plants of Phalaris

---

[a] Centralb. Bakt. Parasit. u. Infekt., 2 Abt., Bd. 9, No. 21, pp. 802-804, December, 1902.

[b] Cereal Rusts of the United States, Bul. No. 16, Div. of Veg. Phys. and Path., U. S. Dept. of Agriculture, 1899.

[c] Bul. Lab. Nat. Hist. State Univ. Iowa, Vol. IV, pp. 398-400, December, 1898.

at Stillwater and were of the crown rust type. After this date the experiments were continued at the State University laboratories at Lincoln, Nebr., all host plants then in use being transferred to that place. On November 16 the crown rust was found, in the uredo stage, on *Arrhenatherum elatius* on the State University farm, and a rusted plant was transferred to the greenhouse. On December 11 inoculations with the rust were made on oats and rye, resulting in a good infection of the former in twelve days, but with no result on the latter. Further inoculations of oats with the Phalaris rust on February 16, 1898, resulted again in a good infection in 9 days.

No species of Rhamnus is native near Lincoln, Nebr., but *Rhamnus lanceolata* is rather common at Weeping Water, about 20 miles east of Lincoln, where it is often badly rusted with Æcidium. From that place a large amount of the Æcidium was obtained fresh on June 1, 1898. A water-drop culture of the material, made the next day, gave a profuse germination of the spores in twenty-two hours. Inoculations with the æcidiospores on oats and *Phalaris caroliniana* were made June 1 and June 2, resulting in a successful infection of Phalaris on June 14 and of oats on June 18. The oat inoculations were made simply on detached portions of the plant preserved with their broken ends in water in a damp chamber. As in all other instances, these inoculations were made with the greatest of care to prevent accidental infections. The whole series of experiments proves (1) the connection of the æcidial form of Rhamnus with the crown rust of oats, and (2) the identity of the latter with the forms on *Phalaris caroliniana* and *Arrhenatherum elatius*, besides making it probable that orchard grass may also support this species.

SEGREGATION OF HOST PLANTS.

The most important economic results of the study of rusts are likely to be derived from the investigation of the relationship of the forms on our common grasses. Such work has already been carried on to some extent by the writer and partially reported in the bulletin entitled "Cereal Rusts of the United States." A more detailed account of some of this work will be given here. Because bearing upon the same question, it seems proper to mention also some experiments with the rusts of Salix and Populus. Probably the greatest confusion exists concerning the identity of the different forms on Agropyron and Elymus, though there is much uncertainty also about those occurring on Bromus and other genera.

The experiments here described were conducted at Stillwater, Okla., Manhattan, Kans., Lincoln, Nebr., and Washington, D. C., the host plants being sometimes transferred from one place to another. Of all these rusts the one receiving most attention was the black stem rust of Agropyron and Elymus.

BLACK STEM RUST OF AGROPYRON AND ELYMUS.

At least three and probably four different rusts occur on the species of these two grass genera, and are often so closely associated that their accurate identification is extremely difficult. Of the herbarium specimens of these rusts throughout the country, probably not one in fifty is identified with any certainty. The writer's experiments with these forms are still incomplete, but a few things at least have been established. When these grasses are brought under cultivation the changed conditions and proximity to other grasses and grains cause them to become much more rusted than is ordinarily the case. In the cultivated grass plats at the experiment stations in Oklahoma, Kansas, and Nebraska the rusts were found in great abundance. It was therefore easy to carry on many culture experiments. These experiments with the uredospores of black stem rust were sufficiently numerous to make it desirable to arrange them in the following table:

TABLE I.—*Culture experiments with black stem rust of Agropyron and Elymus.*

Date.	Locality.	Origin of inoculating material.	Plant inoculated.	Period of incubation in days.	Result.
Jan. 9, 1897	Washington, D. C.	Wheat	*Elymus virginicus*	10	Success.
Do	do	do	Wheat	10	Do.
Jan. 22, 1897	do	do	*Elymus virginicus*	11	Do.
Do	do	do	*Agropyron richardsoni.*	11	Do.
Do	do	do	Wheat	11	Do.
Do	do	do	*Agropyron occidentale*	11	Failure.
Sept. 13, 1897	Stillwater, Okla	*Agropyron tenerum*	Wheat	6	Success. a
Do	do	do	*Agropyron tenerum*	6	Do.
Oct. 5, 1897	Manhattan, Kans	*Agropyron occidentale*	Wheat	12	Failure.
Do	do	Wheat (originally *Agropyron tenerum*).	do	8	Success.
Do	do	do	Barley	8	(b)
Do	do	do	*Agropyron tenerum*	8	Failure. c
Oct. 21, 1897	do	do	Wheat	16	Success.
Do	do	do	Barley	16	Do.
Do	do	do	Oats	16	(d)
Do	do	do	Rye	16	Failure.
Do	do	*Agropyron occidentale*	Wheat	18	Do.
Do	do	do	Rye	18	Do.
Do	do	do	Barley	18	Do.
Do	do	do	*Agropyron tenerum*	18	Do.
Nov. 24, 1897	Lincoln, Nebr	do	*Agropyron occidentale*	15	Success.
Jan. 5, 1898	do	*Elymus canadensis glaucifolius.*	Wheat	21	Do. e
Do	do	do	Barley	21	Do.
Jan. 21, 1898	do	Wheat (originally *Elymus canadensis glaucifolius*).	Wheat	10	Do.
Do	do	do	Barley	10	Do.
Feb. 11, 1898	do	*Elymus canadensis glaucifolius.*	Wheat	14	Do. f
Do	do	do	Barley	14	Do.
Do	do	do	Rye	14	Failure.
Do	do	do	Oats	14	Do.
Do	do	do	*Elymus canadensis glaucifolius.*	14	Success.
Do	do	do	*Elymus virginicus*	14	Failure.
Do	do	do	*Elymus virginicus muticus*	14	Do.
Do	do	do	*Elymus intermedius*	14	Do.
Do	do	do	*Agropyron tenerum*	14	Do.
Do	do	do	*Agropyron occidentale.*	14	Do.

a Pustules differ in color from the original.
b 1 pustule only.
c Conditions very unfavorable, however.
d Apparently 1 pustule formed.
e Rust changes color and form of pustule.
f Rust changes color.

TABLE I.—*Culture experiments with black stem rust of Agropyron and Elymus*—Continued.

Date.	Locality.	Origin of inoculating material.	Plant inoculation.	Period of incubation in days.	Result.
Feb. 11, 1898	Lincoln, Nebr.	*Elymus virginicus*	*Elymus virginicus*	13	Success.
Do	do	do	*Elymus virginicus muticus*.	13	Do.
Do	do	do	*Elymus canadensis glaucifolius*.	13	Do.
Do	do	do	*Agropyron tenerum*	13	Do.
Do	do	do	*Agropyron occidentale*.	13	Failure.
Do	do	do	Rye	13	Do.
Do	do	do	Wheat	13	Do.
Feb. 21, 1898	do	Wheat (originally *Elymus canadensis glaucifolius*).	*Elymus canadensis*	7	Success. a
Feb. 25, 1898	do	do	*Hordeum jubatum*	11	Do.
Feb. 28, 1898	do	*Elymus canadensis glaucifolius*.	Wheat	9	Do. b

a Pustules differ in color from the original.   b Rust changes in appearance.

The results of these experiments, considered in connection with those recorded in Bulletin No. 16, Division of Vegetable Physiology and Pathology, U. S. Department of Agriculture, appear to establish two things, viz, (1) that the forms of black stem rust on wheat, barley, *Hordeum jubatum*, *Agropyron tenerum*, *A. richardsoni*, *Elymus canadensis*, and *E. canadensis glaucifolius* are identical, with the probability that those on *Elymus virginicus*, *E. virginicus muticus*, and *Holcus lanatus*[a] should be included; (2) that the black stem rust of *Agropyron occidentale*[b] is physiologically distinct from any other.[c]

A very interesting phenomenon in these experiments was the change in color and form of sorus of the rust produced by a transference to another host. In some cases after a transfer the rust was scarcely recognized. The change of color was sometimes from a bright yellow to a deep brown or orange, or the reverse. The uredo of *Agropyron tenerum*, for example, was often very yellow on the leaves, but changed to brown when transferred to wheat. On the species of Elymus the rust has a brown, waxy appearance, and the teleutospores long remain covered by the epidermis of the host.

---

[a] On January 5, 1900, quite successful infections on wheat were made with the uredospores of black stem rust of this host.

[b] Probably the most correct name of this host, which is known also as *Agropyron spicatum* and *A. glaucum*. (See Hitchcock, "Note on Nomenclature," Science, vol. 17, pp. 827–828, May 22, 1903.)

[c] The form on this host was described as a distinct species, named *Puccinia agropyri*, by Ellis and Everhart, in Journal of Mycology, Vol. VII, p. 131, March 10, 1892, a fact not noticed by the writer until after most of these experiments were made. This species includes *Aecidium clematidis* D. C. according to Doctor Dietel, the proof of relationship being the result of culture experiments. (Oesterr. Bot. Zeitschr., No. 8, 1892.)

ORANGE LEAF RUST OF AGROPYRON AND ELYMUS.

In the following table are summarized the results of inoculations with the uredoform of this rust. They were carried on simultaneously with those of the black stem rust, and the material was taken chiefly from the same individual host plants.

TABLE II.—*Culture experiments with orange leaf rust of Agropyron and Elymus.*

Date.	Locality.	Origin of inoculating material.	Plant inoculated.	Period of incubation in days.	Result.
Dec. 21, 1896	Washington, D. C.	Rye	Elymus americanus	16	Failure.
Do	do	do	Rye	16	Success.
Jan. 7, 1897	do	do	Elymus virginicus	12	Failure.
Do	do	do	Rye	12	Success.
Feb. 1, 1897	do	do	Elymus virginicus	13	Failure.
Do	do	do	Rye	13	Success.
Feb. 13, 1897	do	Wheat	Agropyron richardsoni.	18	Failure.
Do	do	do	Wheat	18	Success.
Do	do	do	Rye	18	Failure.
Feb. 20, 1897	do	Rye	Agropyron tenerum	12	Do.
Do	do	do	Triticum villosum	12	Do.
Do	do	do	Elymus canadensis	12	Do.
Do	do	do	Rye	12	Success.
Mar. 30, 1897	do	do	Agropyron caninum	26	Failure.
Do	do	do	Rye	26	Success.
Nov. 3, 1897	Manhattan, Kans.	do	Wheat	9	Failure.
Do	do	do	Barley	9	Do.
Do	do	do	Agropyron tenerum	9	Do.
Do	do	do	Rye	9	Success.
Jan. 5, 1898	Lincoln, Nebr.	do	do	21	Do.
Do	do	do	Elymus virginicus	21	Failure.
Mar. 4, 1898	do	Elymus virginicus	Wheat	18	Do.
Do	do	Elymus canadensis glaucifolius.	do	18	Do.
Mar. 12, 1898	do	Wheat	do	11	Success.
Do	do	do	Elymus canadensis	11	Failure.
Do	do	do	Elymus canadensis glaucifolius.	14	Do.
Do	do	do	Agropyron tenerum	11	Do.

The chief conclusion to be derived from the results of these cultures is that the orange leaf rust is very sharply limited in its host adaptation and differs widely in this respect from the black stem rust. Similar results are given in Bulletin No. 16 of the Division of Vegetable Physiology and Pathology, U. S. Department of Agriculture, for cultures of the forms on wheat and rye. In fact, it is quite probable that almost every distinct host species bears a distinct form of the rust. One of these forms on *Elymus virginicus* L. has recently been found by Doctor Arthur to be connected with the Æcidium on *Impatiens aurea* Muhl. and is now to be known as *Puccinia impatientis* (Schw.) Arth.[a]

BLACK STEM RUST OF AGROSTIS ALBA VULGARIS.

Culture experiments with the uredoform of this rust and observations in the field indicate that it is distinct and does not occur on other

---

[a] Botanical Gazette, vol. 35, pp. 18-19, January, 1903.

hosts.[a] The results of the culture experiments are given in the following table:

TABLE III.—*Culture experiments with black stem rust of Agrostis alba vulgaris.*

Date.	Locality.	Origin of inoculating material.	Plant inoculated.	Period of incubation in days.	Result.
Dec. 23, 1897...	Lincoln, Nebr	*Agrostis alba vulgaris.*	*Agrostis alba vulgaris.*	8	Success.
Do.........	....do	....do	Wheat...............	8	Failure.
Do.........	....do	....do	Oats	8	Do.
Jan. 24, 1898...	....do	....do	Wheat...............	12	Do.
Do.........	....do	....do	Oats	12	Do.
Feb. 11, 1898...	....do	*Elymus canadensis glaucifolius.*	*Agrostis alba vulgaris.*	14	Do.

The rust is evidently of the black stem rust group (*Puccinia graminis* of authors), but contains quite a number of abnormal teleutospores, including mesospores. Many measurements of these spores average 27–54 by 16–23μ, mostly 40–46 by 16–18μ.

RUST OF CHLORIS (*Puccinia chloridis* DIET.).

The uredoform of this rust is sometimes very abundant on *Chloris verticillata* in the Great Plains region, occurring in late summer and autumn. The sori are deep brown in color. The uredospores germinate very freely and easily. In a number of experiments made in 1898 it was found that the uredo on *C. verticillata* and *C. elegans* would readily transfer from either host to the other, but not to other grasses, in several cases which were attempted. In a watch-glass culture, made March 18, 1898, of uredospores from *C. elegans*, produced from artificial infection in a greenhouse, not only these spores germinated freely, but a number of newly formed teleutospores at the same time, an occurrence unusual except in the Lepto-uredineæ. Among thousands of cultures made by the writer only one other instance of this kind has occurred. In the summer of 1895 at the Biological Laboratory at Cold Spring Harbor, Long Island, both teleutospores and uredospores taken from the same sorus of a rust on *Luzula campestris* gave good germinations.[b]

RUSTS OF WILLOW AND COTTONWOOD (MELAMPSORA).

Both the uredospores and teleutospores of the rusts of willow and cottonwood germinate readily, the germ tubes of the latter containing always brilliant endochrome. Healthy leaves of either cottonwood or willow placed in a damp chamber have often been infected by the

---

[a] Arthur describes culture experiments made by his assistant, William Stuart, in July, 1898, in which wheat plants were infected with uredospores from this host, but the spores of the infection sori were larger than those of the original material. (Bul. Lab. Nat. Hist. State Univ. Iowa, vol. 4, No. 4, pp. 396–397, 1898.)

[b] The species was, without much doubt, *Puccinia obscura* Schroet.

writer in nine to twelve days. The incubation period is much shortened by using germinating spores in the inoculations. In the month of October, at Manhattan, Kans., an infection was produced in this way in three days.

It was attempted by numerous inoculations with the uredoform, chiefly at Washington, D. C., to transfer the rust from willow to cottonwood and the reverse, but always without success. An interesting feature of these experiments was the discovery of the fact that the cottonwood most common in Washington, known as South Carolina poplar, could not be infected by the uredoform from the common Western cottonwood, though these two poplars are classed by some as being the same species. Moreover, the rust does not occur in nature on the South Carolina poplar, but is very abundant on the Western cottonwood, and even occurs in Washington on the few individual trees of that type growing in the city.

WINTER RESISTANCE OF THE UREDO.

In another bulletin[a] the writer has given in detail the observations and culture experiments proving the successful wintering of the uredo in the orange leaf rust of both wheat and rye. In this connection it is easy to see a number of closely correlated facts, which may mutually explain each other: (1) As shown under the preceding topic, the uredo of black stem rust may infect a number of different hosts, and therefore has a manifoldly greater chance of propagation with the same number of uredospores than if there were but one possible host; (2) as also shown, the uredo of orange leaf rust is restricted in every case to but one host, or at most to but one genus, and a much greater production of uredospores is therefore necessary for the life of the species in this stage; (3) as a corresponding matter of fact it is well known that the uredo of the latter rust exists usually in very much larger quantity than that of the former; (4) on the other hand, the teleutosporic stage is the prevailing form of the stem rust, which fact makes this rust usually the more damaging of the two, as the teleutospores infest the stem chiefly, thus more directly interfering in plant nutrition; (5) the stem rust is proved to be connected with the barberry rust, thus giving it an additional chance for increased propagation, and this through the medium of the teleuto stage instead of the uredo; (6) finally, the uredo being the prevailing form of the leaf rust, and no æcidial form being known in this country,[b] it would seem necessary that this stage of that rust should be very hardy in order to endure extremes of cold and drought and preserve the life of the species. Previous investigations of the writer and others have amply proved that this is the case. In the meantime it is found that in other species

---

[a] Cereal Rusts of the United States, Bul. 16, Div. Veg. Phys. and Path., U. S. Dept. of Agriculture, pp. 21-23, and 44, 45.

[b] Except in the case of the form on *Elymus virginicus* already mentioned.

there exists a similar hardiness of the uredo, of which cases the following will be discussed here:

UREDO OF KENTUCKY BLUEGRASS RUST (*Puccinia poarum* NIELS.).

The writer has known for some time that the uredo stage of the bluegrass rust is able to pass the winter alive and in germinating condition during any season as far north as Lincoln, Nebr., but additional evidence has been obtained from time to time. At the same time it is significant that there is no record that the teleutospores have ever been found, except in one instance, at the above-named place. In fact, few, if any, uredoforms so hardy as this one exist in this country. On February 1, 1893, this uredo was still alive in the vicinity of Manhattan, Kans. Every month of the year it exists alive and growing in great abundance everywhere about Washington, D. C. On March 2, 1898, it was found fresh on green leaves of the host at Lincoln, Nebr. On the same spot of ground it was still growing and spreading rapidly on May 8 of the same year. Host plants were transplanted that day into a greenhouse, where the rust continued to increase rapidly. As would now be supposed, the rust is sharply limited to its one host, Kentucky bluegrass. The results of the following cultures may be given in evidence.

TABLE IV.—*Culture experiments with the uredo of Kentucky bluegrass.*

Date.	Locality.	Origin of inoculating material.	Plant inoculated.	Period of incubation in days.	Result.
Jan. 16, 1893	Manhattan, Kans.	*Poa pratensis*	Wheat	18	Failure.
Do	do	do	Oats	18	Do.
Dec. 21, 1896	Washington, D. C.	Rye (*Uredo rubigo-vera*).	*Poa pratensis*	16	Do.
Jan. 22, 1897	do	Wheat (*Uredo graminis*).	do	11	Do.
Do	do	do	*Poa nemoralis*	11	Do.
Feb. 1, 1897	do	Rye (*Uredo rubigo-vera*).	*Poa pratensis*	13	Do.
Do	do	do	*Poa nemoralis*	13	Do.
Feb. 18, 1897	do	Wheat (*Uredo rubigo-vera*).	*Poa pratensis*	18	Do.
Feb. 25, 1897	do	*Poa pratensis*	do	10	Success.

UREDO OF PUCCINIA MONTANENSIS ELL.

This is, in some respects, one of the most interesting of grass rusts. It is one of the "covered rusts," and is, indeed, so far covered that it is often entirely overlooked by collectors. The uredosori are very uniform in size and are exceedingly small, it being necessary often to examine them, or even find them, with a hand lens. They are elliptical in shape and placed end to end in long, narrow, yellow striæ between the veins of the leaf. The teleuto stage is so far hidden as to be detected only by a faintly darker color beneath the leaf epidermis. The rust is the most nearly like *P. glumarum* Eriks. and

Henn. yet found in this country. The known hosts are *Elymus canadensis* and *E. virginicus*, but it seems to occur on other hosts. Whether the forms on different hosts can be transferred from one to another is not yet fully determined.

The important fact now known, however, is that the uredoform is able to preserve the species over the winter without the intervention of other stages, though it is possible that extensive propagation is aided by other stages. October 28, 1897, fresh uredosori were observed on *Elymus canadensis* at Manhattan, Kans., and again in the same locality on November 2. But as early in the spring as May 26, at Lincoln Nebr., when there was yet but a small beginning of vegetation, the uredo had burst the epidermis of the host in grass plats at the University farm. Previous to this the living uredo had been observed in these plats practically every month of the winter.

In other instances the uredospores of certain species are so very abundant and the teleutospores so rare that there seems a probability that such species are carried over from summer to summer largely through the uredo stage alone, though there is no absolute proof of such a course. Two instances are particularly interesting—those of the uredos of *Puccinia cryptandri* Ell. and Barth., and *Puccinia* on *Panicum autumnale*.[a] The uredospores of these species begin to be conspicuously abundant about midsummer, but continue in considerable abundance until very late in autumn. The uredo of *Panicum autumnale* was found in germinating condition in Kansas up to November 3 in 1897. A water-drop culture of uredospores of this species gave excellent germination in ten hours August 21, 1897, at Perkins, Okla. The uredospores of *Puccinia cryptandri* were found in extreme abundance in Oklahoma until October 11, 1897, but in all cases without any accompanying teleutospores. Often the uredosori had a fresh appearance on portions of leaves that were quite dead.

EMERGENCY ADAPTATIONS.

In connection with some culture experiments conducted at Lincoln, Nebr., in the botanical laboratory of the State University, in February, 1898, a water-drop culture was made (February 3) of uredospores of the above-mentioned *Puccinia cryptandri* which had been collected on October 8, 1897, at Perkins, Okla., and kept to date as herbarium specimens. A fair germination resulted in twenty-four hours. Spores from the same collection were used on February 16 to inoculate seedlings of *Sporobolus airoides*,[b] with the result of the appearance of two rust spots by March 16. These spots may really have appeared much earlier and been overlooked, as they were very small and the host

---

[a] Perhaps a new species, needing further study.

[b] Apparently this same species of rust had already been collected on *Sporobolus airoides* in the same locality where the collection from *S. cryptandri* was made.

itself is well known to have extremely narrow leaves. Moreover, the spores were not germinated when applied, and, being from dried specimens, the incubation period would naturally be long. Seedlings of *S. cryptandri* were not at the time available. On March 16 a second water-drop culture was made from this dried material, resulting in the germination of a few spores.

Teleutospores from herbarium specimens have often been germinated, but the writer knows of no other instance of the germination of dried uredospores, such spores being able also to infect a different host. These observations and experiments indicate that we have here a second step in the perfection of the uredo stage as a means of propagating the species. The first step, the attainment of sufficien hardiness to continue alive in the green plant over winter, has just been discussed. Even in this case the uredo, although quite active, at least displaces the resting spore, and in a measure performs its part. But as the perennial host becomes more like an annual and the plant dies nearly or quite to the ground, as in this particular case of the Sporobolus (which is quite different in this respect from the evergreen *Poa pratensis*, for example), necessarily, in the absence of teleutospores, the uredospore must be able to infect after a dormant period. The uredospore therefore becomes now practically a resting spore, but retains the appearance and manner of germination of the summer spore. Such a modification in form or function of any stage of a species to correspond with an unusual change of condition of climate or of the host may be considered as an *emergency adaptation*.

It is easily understood how the change of conditions may be so severe as to necessitate still further modification of structure as well as function, simply as a means of protection. Such a development seems to have been actually reached in the species next discussed, which has resulted in the production of a distinct spore form, specialized from the uredo, leaving still, however, a true uredo stage for summer propagation.

PUCCINIA VEXANS FARL.

There are probably no other species in all the Uredineæ more interesting than this one, and certainly none that has been more perplexing. In this species there are three distinct spore forms aside from any æcidium or spermogonium that may possibly exist—true uredo and teleuto stages, and a peculiar one-celled form different from either of these. (Pl. II, figs. 2-9.) The species was at first made all the more puzzling by the rarity of the true uredo stage, which was not known to exist, or at least not reported, until 1890, when Dr. H. J. Webber, in the Catalogue of the Flora of Nebraska, reported its occurrence in that State. In certain seasons and localities the teleuto stage also is almost or entirely lacking.

The species was first described by Peck as a Uromyces (*U. brandegei* Pk.)[a] on the basis of material collected by Mr. T. S. Brandege, in which specimens contained only the third spore form. Because of the discovery afterwards of two-celled spores associated with this third spore form, even sometimes in the same sorus, Doctor Farlow described it as a Puccinia (*P. vexans* Farl.) in the Proceedings of the American Academy of Arts and Sciences, Vol. XVIII, pp. 82–83. At that time the true uredo stage had not been discovered.

This third spore form is far more prevalent than either of the others as a rule, but is sometimes entirely absent, leaving only the teleuto stage. It is distinct from either of the other forms in structure and appearance, and yet resembles both in some respects. It is larger than either of them, is strongly papillate, and has a much thicker cell wall, but on the other hand possesses the color and persistence of pedicels of teleutospores and appears to have pores like the uredospores. (Pl. II, fig. 5.) Doctor Farlow, in his description, says:

A species in which some of the sori contain only two-celled spores must certainly be held to be a Puccinia, and the perplexing question arises, are the one-celled spores a unilocular form of teleutospores similar to what is known in *P. cesatii* Schr., or are they the uredospores of this species? I have not been able to find any other spores which represent the uredo of the species; and never having seen the unicellular spores in germination, there is, so far as we yet know, no reason why they may not be the uredospores. On the other hand, their general appearance and the density of the cell wall would lead one to suppose that they were of a teleutosporic nature. Further conjecture is unnecessary, because, as the species is not at all rare in some localities, botanists who can examine the fungus on the spot ought to be able to ascertain whether the one-celled bodies produce promycelia or not, or else to discover the true uredo of the species.

A full description of all three forms is given by Arthur and Holway in Descriptions of American Uredineæ accompanying Fasicle IV of Uredineæ Exsiccatæ et Icones.[b]

After numerous unsuccessful trials during several years, the writer was finally able to germinate the third spore form, and, as suggested by Doctor Farlow, has in this way been able to determine its nature. In manner of germination it is exactly like the uredospore, the long simple germ tubes being produced through equatorial pores (Pl. II, figs 7 and 8), but is like the teleutospore in germinating only after a dormant period and exposure to extremes of weather. The uredo and teleuto forms being already present and morphologically different from this form, it must be considered distinct. Because of the dual nature of this spore form, the writer has already proposed for it the name *amphispore* in a paper read before the Baltimore meeting of the Society for Plant Morphology and Physiology in 1900, only an abstract of which was published.[c] The term has since been adopted by Arthur

---

[a] Bot. Gaz., 4: 127.
[b] Bul. Lab. Nat. Hist. State Univ. Iowa, Vol. V, pp. 329–330.
[c] Science, Vol. XIII, p. 250.

and Holway,[a] and a second instance of the occurrence of this form is described by them for *Puccinia tripsaci* Diet. and Holw. The entire series of observations and experiments with this species made by the writer will now be described.

The first cultures of amphispores were made January 15, 1894, at Manhattan, Kans. Both a water culture and one of a sterilized decoction of manure were employed, with no result, the chief cause of failure being probably that the experiment was too early in the season. Afterwards numerous other trials were made with no better success. In the meantime true uredospores were found on September 25, 1896, at Manhattan, Kans.

Finally a successful culture of the amphispores was made on March 8, 1897, at Washington, D. C. The germination was excellent. An abundance of rather long germ tubes, not promycelia, was produced in forty-two hours, but only one to each spore. These germ tubes, unlike those of most uredospores, are quite colorless and clear. A few teleutospores were present, none of which germinated. The culture was an ordinary water drop, but was made in a new form of culture cell, constructed to special order and similar to the Van Tieghem cell, except that the glass ring is quite thin and drawn out into an open tube on each of two opposite sides, with the opening plugged with cotton wool, thus admitting sterilized air. This construction may or may not have increased the chances for germination. The extreme weather conditions at the time, to which the specimens were first exposed, probably contributed most to the success of the culture. They were fastened to the roof of a near-by shed, and after several days of warm sunshine were thoroughly soaked with rain, which was followed by snow and then a severe freeze, soon after which the culture was made. It is an interesting feature of the experiment that the specimens were received from Dr. David Griffiths, then at Aberdeen, S. Dak., and had been collected in September, 1896, and kept in the herbarium until sent to Washington. It was unfortunate that seedlings of the host were not available for making inoculations with these perfectly viable spores. Such an experiment is yet to be made.

At Manhattan, Kans., in 1897, the uredo was present in considerable abundance from June until late in October in grass plats on the Experiment Station farm. On July 8 inoculations were made with the uredospores of this species and with *Aecidium cephalanthi* and *Ae. xanthoxyli* on seedlings of *Bouteloua racemosa* without result. Further inoculations with uredospores on October 4 were successful, rust spots appearing in twelve days (Pl. II, fig. 9), followed in nine more days with one sorus of amphispores. The uredosori are yellowish-brown and rather inconspicuous. On December 31 uredospores could not be found in the grass plats at Manhattan.

---

[a] Bul. Lab. Nat. Hist., State Univ. Iowa, Vol. V, p. 175.

At Lincoln, Nebr., a water-drop culture was made of *Puccinia verans* on March 15, 1898, resulting in a few germinations of the teleutospores in three days. Long promycelia were produced, but no sporidiola. None of the numerous amphispores present germinated.

On September 29, 1899, all three spore forms were again found in the grass plats at Manhattan. Living host plants were transferred to Washington, D. C., and seedlings were started for further experiments, when other duties intervened and the work could not be continued.

Certain facts concerning the relative abundance of the amphispores and teleutospores in different seasons and localities seem to harmonize quite well with the idea already expressed as to the function of the former. If it is the work of the amphispore to carry the species through unusually severe cold or drought, then this spore form should be relatively more abundant in dry periods and relatively more common to the westward and northward in the Great Plains. These conditions are just what exist. The amphispore prevails almost entirely in the Dakotas and in western Kansas, western Nebraska, and eastern Colorado, and appears to have been more common in eastern Kansas during a dry period of several years than during a wet period. At the same time westward toward the mountains there is less chance for an Æcidium to connect with the teleuto stage.

EXPERIMENTS WITH LEPTO-UREDINEÆ.

It is generally supposed that teleutospores which are followed by an æcidium germinate only after a considerable period of rest, usually in early spring. As already mentioned under the discussion of sunflower rust, the writer germinated teleutospores of this species readily in the autumn, and afterwards at different times during the winter. This readiness of germination, apparently at almost any date, is an indication in itself of an alliance to the lepto species. But, more than this, the autumn inoculations with material in which no uredospores could positively be detected nevertheless were, in some cases at least, followed first by spermogonia and then by the uredo! Of course occasional uredospores that may have been overlooked could have produced those few spots in which the presence of spermogonia was not certain. Here, then, is further evidence of the lepto tendency of the species. In addition, it is well known that the æcidium is rare and appears to have no fixed time of occurrence. Now, only the omission of the uredo is needed to make the rust a real lepto species. As it is, its position is more nearly that of a Hemi-puccinia than of an autœcious species. Experiments of this kind, united with critical field observations, thus throw much light upon classification as to group position, as well as enabling us to connect stages.

On the other hand, certain lepto species will be found to closely approach other groups, and, indeed, after further experiment, may have to be placed in some other group. The following species have given interesting results in culture experiments.

RUST OF COCKLEBUR (*Puccinia xanthii* SCHW.).

Observations and culture experiments of the writer show that the rust of cocklebur is probably limited to one host and is distinct from the species on Ambrosia, and also justify the suspicion that it lies very near the border of the Lepto-uredineæ, and may belong to another group.

On March 1, 1897, the first water-drop culture made gave an excellent germination in forty-eight hours. Long promycelia were produced, but no sporidiola. On February 13, 1897, at Washington, D. C., inoculations were made on seedlings of cocklebur and *Ambrosia trifida*, resulting in an infection of the former in eighteen days, but not of the latter. On March 12 a second experiment resulted in a large number of infections of cocklebur seedlings in fourteen days. In all these cases spermogonia preceded the teleutospores in the infected spots. On October 8 of the same year an æcidium was found on cocklebur in considerable abundance, associated with the teleutosori, at Perkins, Okla. An inoculation on cocklebur seedlings, made at Lincoln, Nebr., on February 16, 1898, resulted in the production of spermogonia in ten days. The inoculating material had been collected in October, 1897. An æcidium on cocklebur was again found in abundance at Las Cruces, N. Mex., on July 11, 1899. Attempts should be made to infect the cocklebur with this æcidium. Doctor Farlow says an æcidium on Xanthium in Massachusetts is frequently followed by *Puccinia xanthii*.[a]

The ease with which artificial infections are made with this rust is at first surprising. So long as there is warmth and moisture, germination occurs under almost any condition and at any time.

RUST OF VELVET LEAF (*Puccinia heterospora* B. AND C.).

In the last-mentioned experiments the inoculating material was taken each time from dead leaves. The same was true in one experiment with the rust of velvet leaf, November 14, 1896, at Manhattan, Kans., in which seedlings of the host were infected in twelve days. For all these experiments the average time of incubation was about twelve days. In December, 1896, the infected plants of the last experiment were transferred from Manhattan to Washington, D. C., and material from these was used to inoculate new seedlings, which resulted in an infection in nine days. It appears, therefore, that the

---

[a] Proc. Amer. Acad. Arts and Sci., Vol. XVIII, p. 75.

incubation period is shorter if inoculating material is taken from living plants, and during the summer it is probably about the same as that of infections from uredospores.

Numerous experiments were also made with other lepto species, including *Puccinia grindeliæ*, Pk., *P. variolans*, Hark., *P. lygodesmiæ*, E. and E., and *P. sherardianu*, Körn, with results similar to those above mentioned. The writer has already called attention to the phenomenon of the formation of catenulate sporidiola in two of these species, *P. grindeliæ* and *P. variolans*.[a]

PERENNIAL SPECIES.

The chance for the continued existence of a rust through winter resistance of the uredo without the intervention of another stage has been discussed. Though such a condition can only exist on a perennial host, or at least one that lives over winter, it must not be supposed that the fungus itself is necessarily or even usually perennial. As fast as the leaves of the host die the spores simply drop on to the next lower and younger leaves and produce reinfection, the mycelium not extending through the base of the infected leaf into the next leaves. If, however, the mycelium is found within the rootstock and after a dormant period during midwinter follows the new shoots upward in early spring and again produces sori at the surface of the plant, the rust is a true perennial. This condition appears to exist in the following species.

ÆCIDIUM TUBERCULATUM E. AND K.

It is now usually supposed that all æcidial forms will likely be found to be connected with other stages, though there are probably more of these forms whose connections are at present undetermined than there are of Lepto-uredineæ. If any Æcidium is more likely than another to be an independent species, certainly the probabilities are largely in favor of this species, which occurs on *Callirrhoe involucrata*,[b] for there is no need of another stage to perpetuate it, though another host might give it a wider distribution.

The striking orange-yellow color, large and otherwise conspicuous sori, and its complete attack of every portion of the host make this an unusually unique and attractive species (Pl. I, frontispiece). A note concerning the hardiness of this species was published by the writer several years ago.[c] The words are here quoted: "*Æcidium tuberculatum*

---

[a] Bot. Gaz., Vol. XVIII, pp. 455–456.

[b] Though not previously reported, this rust was found also on *Callirrhoe alcæoides* at Salina, Kans., in May, 1893.

[c] Bot. Gaz., Vol. XVIII, p. 453.

E. and K. is still producing æcidiospores on *Callirrhoe involucrata* outdoors here at Manhattan at the time of this writing (October 15, 1893), and Mr. E. Bartholomew, of Rooks County, Kans., tells me that he has seen in December æcidiospores on specimens of this host growing close by a large snowdrift. In the spring æcidiospores of this species begin forming about the first day of April." On December 20, 1893, after the above was transmitted for publication, the rust was found still alive although it had been under 4 inches of snow. In a water-drop culture of some of the material four spores germinated in twenty-four hours. Since that time, at later dates in the winter the living rust has been found, but close within the rootstock, with a faint color still, but producing no spores. The peculiar manner of growth of the rust, permeating the entire host and producing scattering sori all along the stems to their bases, as well as on the leaves, and the difficulty of germinating the spores harmonize also with the idea of a propagation by perennial mycelium. Besides the above instance other cultures of the spores were made as follows: At Manhattan, Kans., May 20, 1893, spores from *Callirrhoe alcæoides*, only a few germinations in forty-eight hours; at Manhattan, June 9, 1893, spores from *C. involucrata* germinated sparingly in twenty-five hours; at Manhattan, January 30, 1894, spores from *C. involucrata* growing in greenhouse, fair germination in sixty hours.

In the winter of 1896–97 infected plants of *C. involucrata* were obtained from Kansas and grown in a greenhouse at Washington, D. C., and on March 17, 1897, inoculations of seedlings of the following grasses with spores from these plants failed to produce infections: *Agropyron occidentale*, *A. richardsoni*, *Sitanion elymoides*, *Elymus canadensis*, and *Bouteloua racemosa*.

RUST OF PEUCEDANUM FŒNICULACEUM.

An Æcidium occurs on this host in Kansas and Nebraska which has been reported as *Æ. anisotomes* Reich., but the identity of which is not yet determined[a] satisfactorily to the writer. At certain places a Puccinia follows the Æcidium so closely that their connection is very probable. Both forms are particularly abundant at Manhattan, Kans. On April 25, 1893, at that place, it was determined by the study of many cross sections of the host plant that the mycelium of the Æcidium extends into the rootstock. It is one of the earliest rusts in the spring to appear in that locality. These facts make it probable that this rust is also perennial. On the other hand, it is possible that the teleutospores of the Puccinia may produce a very early infection at the base of the young shoots, resulting in the Æcidium, although in some localities no Puccinia has yet been found following the Æcidium.

---

[a] The species is probably *Puccinia jonesii* Pk., with the æcidial stage present.

At Lincoln, Nebr., on March 24, 1898, teleutospores of this same Puccinia germinated in a water-drop culture in twenty-four hours.

It should be noted that it is possible for a perennial rust to exist in an annual host, the mycelium of the rust being carried over winter in the seed of the host. Such an instance is practically certain in the Euphorbia rust already discussed. Granting that Doctor Eriksson's experiments were accurate, there would be another example in *Puccinia glumarum* Eriks. and Henn. on wheat.

PLATES.

DESCRIPTION OF PLATES.

PLATE I. *Frontispiece.* A perennial rust. *Ecidium tuberculatum* E. and K. on *Callirrhoe involucrata* Gr.

PLATE II. Fig. 1.—Seedling of *Euphorbia dentata* grown constantly under bell jar from rusted seed. Fig. 2.—*Puccinia vexans* Farl. on *Bouteloua racemosa*, both uredosori and amphisori being shown. (Natural size.) Fig. 3.—The same uredosori and amphisori shown in fig. 2 magnified 10 diameters. Fig. 4.—Uredospores of *Puccinia vexans* × 600. Fig. 5.—Amphispores of *Puccinia vexans* × 600. Fig. 6.—Teleutospore of *Puccinia vexans* × 600. Fig. 7.—Germinating uredospore of *Puccinia vexans* × 300. Fig. 8.—Germinating amphispores of *Puccinia vexans* × 300. Fig. 9.—Uredosori of *Puccinia vexans* on young seedling leaf of *Bouteloua racemosa* produced by artificial infection with uredospores from the same host. (Natural size).

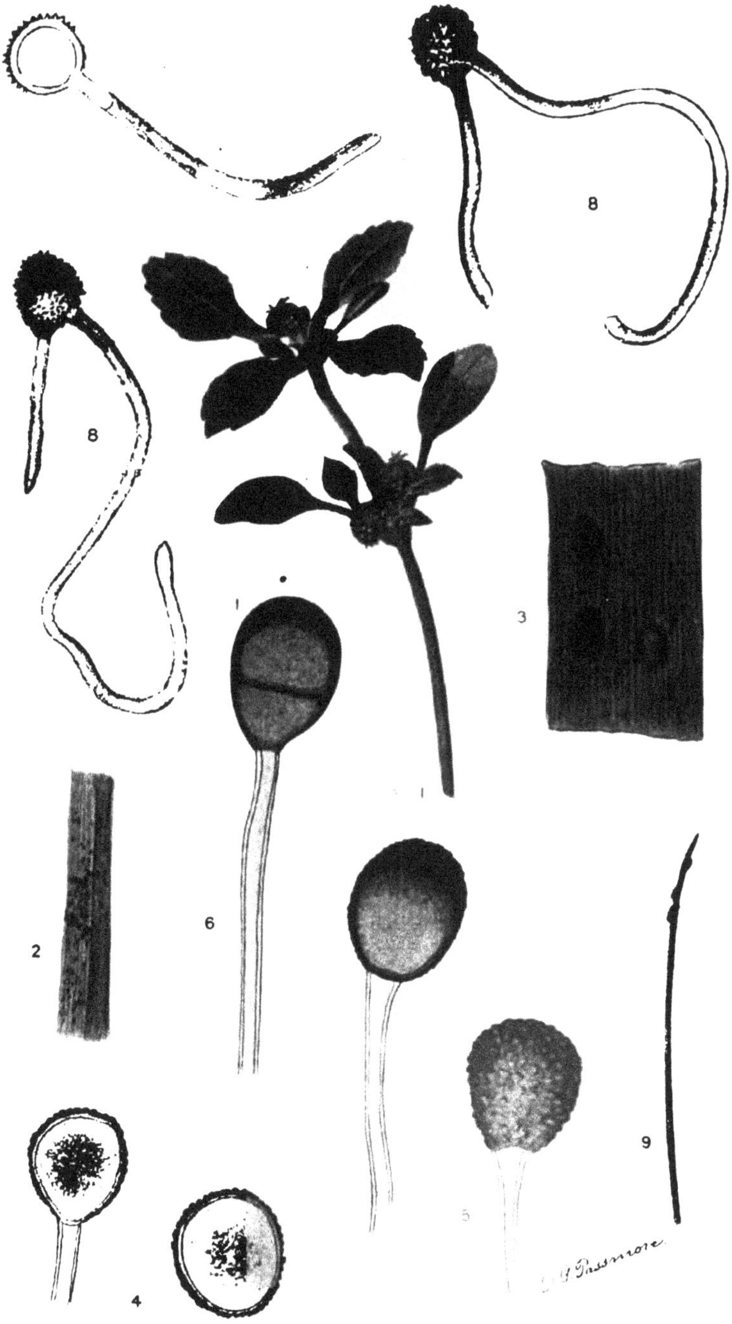

I 63, Bureau of Plant Industry, U S Dept of Agriculture. PLATE

RUSTS OF EUPHORBIA AND GRAMA GRASS.

[Continued from page 2 of cover.]

No. 26. Spanish Almonds. 1902. Price, 15 cents.
27. Letters on Agriculture in the West Indies, Spain, and the Orient. 1902. Price, 15 cents.
28. The Mango in Porto Rico. 1903. Price, 15 cents.
29. The Effect of Black Rot on Turnips. 1903. Price, 15 cents.
30. Budding the Pecan. 1902. Price, 10 cents.
31. Cultivated Forage Crops of the Northwestern States. 1902. Price, 10 cents.
32. A Disease of the White Ash Caused by Polyporus Fraxinophilus. 1903. Price, 10 cents.
33. North American Species of Leptochloa. 1903. Price, 15 cents.
34. Silkworm Food Plants. 1903. Price, 15 cents.
35. Recent Foreign Explorations, as Bearing on the Agricultural Development of the Southern States. 1903. Price, 15 cents.
36. The "Bluing" and the "Red Rot" of the Western Yellow Pine, with Special Reference to the Black Hills Forest Reserve. 1903. Price, 30 cents.
37. Formation of the Spores in the Sporangia of Rhizopus Nigricans and of Phycomyces Nitens. 1903. Price, 15 cents.
38. Forage Conditions and Problems in Eastern Washington, Eastern Oregon, etc. 1903. Price, 15 cents.
39. The Propagation of the Easter Lily from Seed. 1903. Price, 10 cents.
40. Cold Storage, with Special Reference to the Pear and Peach. 1903. Price, 15 cents.
41. The Commercial Grading of Corn. 1903. Price, 10 cents.
42. Three New Plant Introductions from Japan. 1903. Price, 10 cents.
43. Japanese Bamboos. 1903. Price, 10 cents.
44. The Bitter Rot of Apples. 1903. Price, 15 cents.
45. The Physiological Rôle of Mineral Nutrients in Plants. Price, 5 cents.
46. The Propagation of Tropical Fruit Trees and Other Plants. Price, 10 cents.
47. The Description of Wheat Varieties. 1903. Price, 10 cents.
48. The Apple in Cold Storage. 1903. Price, 15 cents.
49. The Culture of the Central American Rubber Tree. 1903. Price, 25 cents.
50. Wild Rice: Its Uses and Propagation. 1903. Price, 10 cents.
51. Miscellaneous Papers: Part I. The Wilt Disease of Tobacco and its Control. 1903. Price, 5 cents. Part II. The Work of the Community Demonstration Farm at Terrell, Tex. 1904. Price, 5 cents. Part III. Fruit Trees Frozen in 1904. 1904. Price, 5 cents.
52. Wither-Tip and Other Diseases of Citrous Trees and Fruits Caused by Colletotrichum Gloeosporioides. 1904. Price, 15 cents.
53. The Date Palm and its Utilization in the Southwestern States. 1904. Price, 25 cents.
54. Persian Gulf Dates. 1903. Price, 10 cents.
55. The Dry Rot of Potatoes Due to Fusarium Oxysporum. 1904. Price, 10 cents.
56. Nomenclature of the Apple. [In press.]
57. Methods Used for Controlling and Reclaiming Sand Dunes. 1904. Price, 10 cents.
   The Vitality and Germination of Seeds. 1904. Price, 10 cents.
   Pasture, Meadow, and Forage Crops in Nebraska. 1904. Price, 10 cents.
   A Soft Rot of the Calla Lily. [In press.]
61. The Avocado. [In press.]
62. Notes on Egyptian Agriculture. [In press.]

B. T. GALLOWAY, *Chief of Bureau.*

PATHOGENIC BACTERIA IN

GEORGE T. MOORE
BIOLOGIST AND ALGOLOGIST IN CHARGE OF LABORATORY
OF PLANT PHYSIOLOGY.

KARL F. KELLERMAN,
ASSISTANT IN PHYSIOLOGY.

PATHOLOGICAL AND PHYSIOLOGICAL
INVESTIGATIONS.

Issued May 7, 1904.

WASHINGTON:
GOVERNMENT PRINTING OFFICE.
1904.

U. S. DEPARTMENT OF AGRICULTURE.
BUREAU OF PLANT INDUSTRY—BULLETIN No. 64.
B. T. GALLOWAY, *Chief of Bureau.*

A METHOD OF DESTROYING OR PREVENTING THE GROWTH OF ALGÆ AND CERTAIN PATHOGENIC BACTERIA IN WATER SUPPLIES.

BY

GEORGE T. MOORE,
PHYSIOLOGIST AND ALGOLOGIST IN CHARGE OF LABORATORY OF PLANT PHYSIOLOGY,

AND

KARL F. KELLERMAN,
ASSISTANT IN PHYSIOLOGY.

VEGETABLE PATHOLOGICAL AND PHYSIOLOGICAL INVESTIGATIONS.

Issued May 7, 1904.

WASHINGTON:
GOVERNMENT PRINTING OFFICE
1904.

BUREAU OF PLANT INDUSTRY.

B. T. GALLOWAY, *Chief.*
J. E. ROCKWELL, *Editor.*

VEGETABLE PATHOLOGICAL AND PHYSIOLOGICAL INVESTIGATIONS.

SCIENTIFIC STAFF.

ALBERT F. WOODS, *Pathologist and Physiologist.*

ERWIN F. SMITH, *Pathologist in Charge of Laboratory of Plant Pathology.*
GEORGE T. MOORE, *Physiologist in Charge of Laboratory of Plant Physiology.*
HERBERT J WEBBER, *Physiologist in Charge of Laboratory of Plant Breeding.*
WALTER T. SWINGLE, *Physiologist in Charge of Laboratory of Plant Life History.*
NEWTON B. PIERCE, *Pathologist in Charge of Pacific Coast Laboratory.*
M. B. WAITE, *Pathologist in Charge of Investigations of Diseases of Orchard Fruits.*
MARK A. CARLETON, *Cerealist in Charge of Cereal Investigations.*
HERMANN VON SCHRENK,[a] *in Charge of Mississippi Valley Laboratory.*
P. H. ROLFS, *Pathologist in Charge of Subtropical Laboratory.*
C. O. TOWNSEND, *Pathologist in Charge of Sugar Beet Investigations.*
P. H. DORSETT, *Pathologist.*
RODNEY H. TRUE,[b] *Physiologist.*
T. H. KEARNEY, *Physiologist, Plant Breeding.*
CORNELIUS L. SHEAR, *Pathologist.*
WILLIAM A. ORTON, *Pathologist.*
W. M. SCOTT, *Pathologist.*
JOSEPH S. CHAMBERLAIN, *Physiological Chemist, Cereal Ivestigations.*
R E. B MCKENNEY, *Physiologist.*
FLORA W. PATTERSON, *Mycologist.*
CHARLES P HARTLEY, *Assistant in Physiology, Plant Breeding.*
KARL F. KELLERMAN, *Assistant in Physiology.*
DEANE B. SWINGLE, *Assistant in Pathology.*
A. W. EDSON, *Scientific Assistant, Plant Breeding.*
JESSE B. NORTON, *Assistant in Physiology, Plant Breeding.*
JAMES B. RORER, *Assistant in Pathology.*
LLOYD S. TENNY, *Assistant in Pathology.*
GEORGE G HEDGCOCK, *Assistant in Pathology.*
PERLEY SPAULDING, *Scientific Assistant.*
P. J. O'GARA, *Scientific Assistant.*
A. D. SHAMEL, *Scientific Assistant, Plant Breeding.*
T. RALPH ROBINSON, *Scientific Assistant, Plant Physiology.*
FLORENCE HEDGES, *Scientific Assistant, Bacteriology.*
CHARLES J. BRAND, *Scientific Assistant in Physiology, Plant Life History.*

---

[a] Detailed to the Bureau of Forestry.
[b] Detailed to Botanical Investigations and Experiments.

LETTER OF TRANSMITTAL.

U. S. DEPARTMENT OF AGRICULTURE,
BUREAU OF PLANT INDUSTRY,
OFFICE OF THE CHIEF,
Washington, D. C., April 30, 1904.

SIR: I have the honor to transmit herewith a paper entitled "A Method of Destroying or Preventing the Growth of Algæ and Certain Pathogenic Bacteria in Water Supplies," and to recommend that it be published as Bulletin No. 64 of the series of this Bureau.

The paper was prepared by George T. Moore, in charge of Laboratory of Plant Physiology, and Karl F. Kellerman, Assistant in Physiology, in the Office of Vegetable Pathological and Physiological Investigations, and was submitted by the Pathologist and Physiologist with a view to publication. The subject discussed in this bulletin will be of interest and value to all who have to deal with the problem of preventing algal and other contamination of water supplies.

Respectfully,
B. T. GALLOWAY,
Chief of Bureau.

Hon. JAMES WILSON,
Secretary of Agriculture.

PREFACE.

The necessity of finding some cheap and practical method of preventing or removing algal contamination of cress beds first led this Office to undertake the investigations described in this bulletin. The success of the first experiments in 1901 was so marked that it seemed wise to extend the work, and authority was, therefore, granted by Congress "to study and find methods for preventing the algal and other contaminations of water supplies."

The progress of the investigation has been noted from time to time in the annual reports of the Bureau. Though the work is not yet completed, we have been urged to publish the results already obtained for the consideration of boards of health and officers in charge of public water supplies.

Doctor Moore and Mr. Kellerman have shown that it is entirely practicable to cheaply and quickly destroy objectionable algæ in small lakes, ponds, storage reservoirs, and other similar bodies of water by the use of extremely dilute solutions of copper sulphate or of metallic copper. The fact that an extremely dilute solution (one to one hundred thousand) will also destroy the most virulent typhoid and cholera bacteria at ordinary temperatures in three hours is of great importance and significance. Solutions of copper as dilute as this are not considered injurious to man or other animals. The value of copper, especially colloidal, in preventing or treating typhoid and other related diseases should be carefully investigated by competent pathologists.

We desire it distinctly understood that, so far as bacterial contamination of water is concerned, the methods here proposed are not to take the place of, but are simply to supplement the standard methods of filtration; neither can too much stress be laid upon the importance of the consumer boiling water to be used for drinking purposes when taken from a contaminated source.

Upon application to the Department by proper authorities, information and assistance will be furnished in determining the organisms causing the trouble in cases of algal pollution, and the proper treatment will be recommended. It is earnestly hoped that no test of the method described here will be made without first consulting the Department.

As stated in the text of the bulletin—

The treatment of water supplies for the destruction of pathogenic bacteria, or any application of the copper sulphate method, which has to do with the public health is not contemplated or indeed possible by this Department. The requests of private individuals or of unauthorized bodies for information or assistance can not be granted. When State or local boards of health consider that the disinfection of a water supply is desirable and wish information upon the subject, it will be supplied as fully and freely as possible. All experiments of this kind, however, must be conducted by boards of health, and the Department can serve only in the capacity of an adviser.

We are under obligation to Dr. H. P. Wolcott and Mr. X. H. Goodnough, of the Massachusetts State Board of Health, for facilities in securing material and a temporary laboratory in the Boston State House; to the United States Bureau of Fisheries for fish used in experiments; to Dr. J. J. Kinyoun for typhoid cultures; to Dr. M. J. Rosenau for Asiatic cholera cultures, and to the Bureau of Animal Industry for cultures of typhoid and facilities for carrying on preliminary experiments.

ALBERT F. WOODS,
Pathologist and Physiologist.

OFFICE OF VEGETABLE PATHOLOGICAL
AND PHYSIOLOGICAL INVESTIGATIONS,
Washington, D. C., April 30, 1904.

CONTENTS.

	Page.
Introduction	9
Microscopical examination of drinking water	9
Wide distribution of trouble caused by algæ in water supplies	10
Methods in use for preventing bad effects due to algæ	13
Desirability of other methods	14
Determination of a physiological method	15
Effect of copper sulphate	15
Method of applying copper sulphate	25
Practical tests of the method	26
Water-cress beds	26
Water reservoirs	27
Effect of copper upon pathogenic bacteria	28
Typhoid	28
Asiatic cholera	34
Comparison of effect of other disinfectants	36
Colloidal solutions	36
Conclusions	40
Necessity of knowledge of organism and condition in reservoir	40
Application of method for destruction of pathogenic bacteria not designed to replace efficient means of filtration already in use	41
Medicinal use	42
Conditions under which the Department of Agriculture can furnish information and assistance in applying this method	42
Cost	43
Summary	43

A METHOD OF DESTROYING OR PREVENTING THE GROWTH OF ALGÆ AND CERTAIN PATHOGENIC BACTERIA IN WATER SUPPLIES.

INTRODUCTION.

The necessity and importance of maintaining by every possible means the purity and wholesomeness of public water supplies have caused those in authority to welcome a method which would in any way serve as an additional safeguard against the pollution of reservoirs or would prevent the bad effects produced by the growth of algæ and similar organisms. Although scientific men have been investigating the various problems involved for a considerable length of time, it is feared that the public has not always been in sympathy with these methods, and that, owing to the uncertainty of and disagreement among eminent authorities, the whole question of water analysis, both chemical and bacteriological, has come somewhat into disrepute.

MICROSCOPICAL EXAMINATION OF DRINKING WATER.

While the best known cases of water pollution are those due to the presence of typhoid and other germs which have given rise to serious epidemics, there are a vastly greater number of water supplies which are rendered unfit for use, not because they are dangerous to public health, but on account of the very offensive odor and taste produced in them by plants other than bacteria. For this reason, in recent years, the question of whether or not a water was fit to drink has been submitted to the biologists as well as to the chemists and bacteriologists, a biological examination being generally understood to mean the determination of the character and quantity of the microscopical plants and animals the water may contain as distinct from the bacteria.

The history of this method of examining drinking water is really confined to the last quarter of the nineteenth century, but only within ten or fifteen years have we had any accurate knowledge of the effect of these minute plants upon the water in which they live. It is probable that Dr. Hassall, of London, was the first to publish any adequate account of a thorough microscopical examination of any water supply, and this work, which appeared in 1850, was practically the only thing upon the subject for twenty-five years, when "MacDonald's Guide to the Examination of Drinking Water" was published. In the meantime various Germans had carried on investigations relating to the biology of water supplies, notably Professor Cohn, of Breslau, who, in a paper entitled the "Microscopical Analysis of Well Waters," anticipated much that has since been ascertained in regard to the effect of environment upon the character and quantity of the organism found in the water. About the time of the appearance of MacDonald's book, interest in the effect of algæ in drinking water first began to be aroused in this country, and papers by Farlow[a] and others called attention to the fact that these plants were responsible for many of the disagreeable odors and tastes in water reservoirs. By the year 1878 there was on record a list of over 60 cities and towns in the United States which had had serious trouble because of the presence of certain forms of vegetation in their reservoirs, but since then thousands of water supplies throughout the country have been rendered unfit for use by this cause alone. Early in the year 1891 the special report upon the examination and purification of water by the Massachusetts State Board of Health was published, this being the most complete treatment of the subject which had appeared up to that time. This report has been supplemented by further investigations and experiments, and the work accomplished by this board in perfecting methods for insuring a pure water supply has established the standard both in this country and abroad for similar lines of investigation.

WIDE DISTRIBUTION OF TROUBLE CAUSED BY ALGÆ IN WATER SUPPLIES.

In order to demonstrate the very wide distribution of the trouble caused by algæ in water supplies throughout the United States, a circular letter was sent to about five hundred of the leading engineers and superintendents of water companies, asking for information in regard to the deleterious effects produced by plants other than bacteria in water supplies with which they were familiar. Many instructive replies were received, indicating that those in authority were extremely anxious to be provided with some efficient remedy for preventing the bad odors and tastes in drinking water, and that they considered the

---

[a] FARLOW. Reports on Peculiar Condition of the Water Supplied to the City of Boston. Report of the Cochituate Water Board, 1876.

——— Reports on Matters connected with the Boston Water Supply. Bulletin of Bussey Inst., Jan., 1877.

——— Remarks on Some Algæ found in the Water Supplies of the City of Boston, 1877.

——— On Some Impurities of Drinking Water Caused by Vegetable Growths. Supplement to 1st Ann. Rept. Mass. State Board of Health. Boston, 1880.

——— Relations of Certain Forms of Algæ to Disagreeable Tastes and Odors. Science, II, 333, 1883.

subject worthy of most careful investigation. Quotations from some of the letters received are given, but, because there might be some objection to the naming of towns, only the State in which the trouble occurred is indicated. This is sufficient, however, to show that the difficulty is not confined to any one part of the country, and that it is the algæ alone which are responsible for most of the bad odors and tastes reported.

CALIFORNIA:
Any efforts in the direction of preventing the growth of algæ will be gratefully acknowledged. So long as the growth is healthy it is a benefit, but as soon as the algæ break up then trouble begins.

COLORADO:
We have a reservoir of water that has recently become affected through the presence of micro-organisms of the algæ type that impart to the water a disagreeable fishy odor and render its use objectionable.

DELAWARE:
A fishy taste and odor.

ILLINOIS:
The water tasted and smelled like rotten wood.

Trouble serious enough to cause general complaint by consumers on account of odor and taste.

People declared that the water was musty. The appearance of the growth is yellowish-brown, and as nearly as I can describe it the smell is musty. I certainly think the subject worthy of the best thought and work the Government can give it.

INDIANA:
The growth increased to such an extent that we were compelled to cement the bottom and 5 feet up the sides. It was as dense as a field of clover in June.

Taste was said by the people to be woody or fishy, like rotten wood or decayed fish. At one time the report got out that the body of a missing man had been found in the reservoir.

IOWA:
After certain stages in the alga's growth it seemed to die and become decomposed, thus impregnating the water, giving it a most unpleasant odor and taste.

KENTUCKY:
Fishy odor and taste, rather musty.

The odor was so strong that we had to discontinue sprinkling the streets and lawns.

Urgency in this case is great, indeed almost imperative, since the condition of the water during the past two or three summers has culminated in formal action by the authorities.

MAINE:
Trouble to such an extent as to lead us to consider, without taking definite action, whether or not the water should be filtered before being distributed. Odor is reported as exceedingly disagreeable, so that many customers avoid the use of it as far as possible and believe it injurious to health.

MASSACHUSETTS:
Trouble very serious; some years water is unfit to drink. Present year odor and taste are not so strong as last year, when it was almost impossible to drink it.

The odor was so bad that it would be almost impossible to take it as far as the mouth to taste it. Horses refused it at the street watering troughs and dogs fled from it.

MINNESOTA:
Water at times a fishy odor or taste due to decomposed vegetable matter. Experts claim it is entirely harmless.

NEW JERSEY:
Dark green gelatinous substance in water, causing a stench almost unbearable.

Have seen Uroglena so abundant that an odor could be plainly detected one-third of a mile away.

NEW YORK:
Water had a very fishy taste and smell.

So very offensive as to alarm all water takers.

It caused such a prejudice that the supply was rejected, although the pollution was of short duration.

Strong fishy odor and taste; also odor of "smartweed." Popular complaint was dead fish in water mains.

Odor and taste were fishy, popularly attributed to dead fish; but this is absurd, as the odor is that of live fish.

Odor pondy and fishy; bad water; publicly condemned. Board of health interfered, yet analysis showed that water was not unhealthful.

Very rank, water smelled bad, particularly when warmed. Tasted bad, but not injurious to health. Looked better than tasted or smelled.

Water became unfit for use, musty or cucumber taste and smell, odor very strong in hot water; water became slimy, making it exceedingly hard to filter. Odor and taste at times decidedly fishy. A bright green powder seemed to have been sprinkled on surface.

I am much interested to know that you are taking up an investigation of algæ and organisms, and I very much hope you will favor me with all circulars and information which you may issue relating to the same. I have not attempted to fill out the circular on the back of your letter, but so many cases of trouble of this kind have come to my attention that any listing of them would be very difficult.

I am devoutly thankful that science in this particular instance has got beyond the pursuit of science for recreation's sake and is doing good and endeavoring again directly to be of much use to mankind. I believe your work is the first done in line of either cure or prevention from algæ conducted in a rational manner, or so far as I know even attempted, and I have been connected with or well informed on public water supplies and their management all my professional life of some thirty-five years. The worst case I know of is at the ——— reservoir. A special commission is at this moment charged with the duty of advising whether or not property worth some two million dollars is to be abandoned on account of annual trouble from algæ.

OHIO:
Complaint from customers of a fishy taste in water like the slime from freshwater fish.

Water had a fishy taste, causing a general kick; consumers laid it to the fish in the reservoir.

All water drawn from house bibbs had an objectionable and strong odor, the popular idea being that it was due to dead fish.

The towns A— and B— both have vile water, A— all the year round, B— for six or eight weeks in the hottest part of the summer. A—'s water has a vile odor, offensively musty. All vegetables, cereals, coffee, and such edibles and drinks made with the water are scarcely endurable to the visitor.

PENNSYLVANIA:
Water had a disagreeable fishy odor.

Water smelled and tasted as if dead fish were in it.

PENNSYLVANIA—Continued.
> The growth affected the taste of the water on boiling, but was not regarded as dangerous to health.
>
> A very fishy taste and smell. I have been unable to locate, but had an idea it came from vegetation.
>
> The water during the autumn is so foul in taste and odor that it was necessary to shut off the supply. The odor is similar to that of decayed fish.
>
> The first season of using reservoir the water became so fishy that it was almost unfit for use. Since that, owing to our care of reservoir, we have had no trouble whatever.

TEXAS:
> At this time of the year algæ are fierce; some days we are on top and some days the algæ are on top. Costs us an average of $25 a month for cleaning out algæ from two reservoirs.

WISCONSIN:
> Universal complaint, caused by the odor and taste due to algæ.

METHODS IN USE FOR PREVENTING BAD EFFECTS DUE TO ALGÆ.

In order to prevent the odors and tastes above described, engineers and those in charge of water supplies have tried various remedies, none of which has been perfectly satisfactory. Since few of the algæ can develop without sunlight, the most frequent recommendation has been to cover the reservoir, and this method has proved successful in a few instances. However, the expense involved is so great as to make the remedy prohibitive in most cases, and other methods have had to be resorted to. One precaution which is now almost universally recommended as a means of preventing the growth of algæ is to remove all the organic matter possible from the reservoir and to keep the source of supply as free as can be from dead and decaying animal and vegetable matter. In one notable instance millions of dollars have been spent in the removal of earth and the substitution of gravel at the bottom of an immense new reservoir. It remains to be seen, however, whether this will be sufficient to insure permanent freedom from these troublesome plants. It is certain that attempts of this kind will delay the appearance of algæ in quantity, and, wherever it is possible to do so, every effort should be made not only to clean up the reservoir at the time of its construction, but to keep it as free as possible from organic matter after it is filled. In addition to cleanliness a direct pumping system with duplicate, in case of breakdown or repairs, has often been recommended for use with ground water, which usually produces a more luxuriant growth of algæ and similar organisms than surface water. Where it has been necessary to store such water, it has been advisable to limit the capacity of the reservoir, and frequently this storage is only intended to be used in case of fire. Even so, the cleansing of the reservoir and the frequent flushing of the water mains has been considered necessary. In storing surface water subdividing the reservoir is occasionally resorted to, and means

14 METHOD OF DESTROYING ALGÆ IN WATER SUPPLIES.

of obtaining frequent agitation are introduced wherever possible. The pumping of air into water or aerating it by means of a spraying apparatus is often of considerable value in removing foul gases which may be in solution, but the effect of aeration upon the growth of algæ in a reservoir has been very much overestimated, in some cases the quantity being actually increased by this means.

The filtration of water, both mechanically and by sand, which has proved so effective for the removal of pathogenic bacteria, has been recommended as a means of removing the odors and tastes caused by algæ, but the results obtained have not given promise of success. Perhaps the most careful experiments to determine this point have been conducted by those in charge of the Ludlow reservoir at Springfield, Mass. Here the annual trouble from algæ for the past fifteen years has been so great that every possible means has been used which offered any relief from the effects produced by these plants. On page 4 of the "Special Report on the Improvement of the Present Water Supply and an Alternative New, Independent Supply," made by the board of water commissioners to the city council of the city of Springfield, Mass., April 14, 1902, the following statement is made:

We find, as the results of the experiments of filtration, made with the sanction of your honorable body during the last fifteen months, that to purify the waters of this source by filtration would be not only doubtful as to the degree of purification, but so expensive in the cost of construction and perpetual maintenance thereafter as to make it inexpedient to attempt improvement by such a method. Your board has given constant and personal attention to the experimental work, and is convinced that the excessive growths of obnoxious fresh-water organisms, notably the Anabaena, impart to the reservoir such rank and persistent tastes and odors as to make uncertain entire removal by any method of filtration except that of the expensive kind, applicable only to the filtering of extremely small quantities of water, and requiring constant attention and adjustment.

The State board of health, in a special report (p. 84) submitted at the same time, say that the results of the experiments indicate, in the opinion of the board, that by double filtration it will be possible to purify the Ludlow reservoir; hence there seem to be differences of opinion as to the value of this treatment for the removal of odors and tastes, but on account of the expense involved there is not likely to be any very extensive use of this method.

DESIRABILITY OF OTHER METHODS.

While each of the above-mentioned methods has been used with some success, it is generally conceded by engineers that there is no known remedy which is universally applicable. It is the practice of some of the highest authorities to recommend that reservoirs frequently polluted by algæ be abandoned, and steps taken to provide an entirely new system of supply. This is, of course, the last resort, as in all such cases a large loss of money is involved. One fact is certain.

If any known method of preventing the growth of algæ was considered truly effective, it would under all circumstances be recommended.

Because of the unsatisfactory results or the prohibitive expense of the present methods recommended for ridding reservoirs of algæ, it seemed advisable that the problem be taken up from an entirely new standpoint, one that would take into consideration the biological aspect of the question and perhaps furnish a solution, through a study of the physiology of the organisms under laboratory conditions. A series of investigations were therefore undertaken to discover, if possible, some substance which, because of its extreme toxic effect upon the algæ involved, would absolutely prevent their growth in water supplies.

DETERMINATION OF A PHYSIOLOGICAL METHOD.

In determining such a physiological method of dealing with reservoirs contaminated by algæ, two conditions had to be considered: The remedy should not only be readily available and cheap enough for practical use in the largest reservoirs and by the poorest communities, but under the conditions used it must also be absolutely harmless to man; the maximum amount necessary to kill the algæ being far below the amount which could in any way affect the consumer of the water. Of the large number of substances experimented with, few gave encouraging results. Free chlorine at a dilution of 1 to 10,000, and sulphur dioxide in saturated aqueous solution at 16° C., diluted 1 to 1,000 and to 10,000, will destroy many of the common forms of algæ, but sulphur dioxide and chlorine are likewise very injurious to animal life. Silver has a very high toxicity, and were not the expense prohibitive, would undoubtedly warrant extended tests. Mercury and lead are, of course, out of the question, and zinc requires too high a concentration to be practically considered. The ordinary sodium, potassium, and ammonium salts are innocuous,[a] as are most of the acids. Loew[b] finds that magnesium sulphate is toxic in pure solution at 0.4 per cent, and that oxalates are slightly more toxic; of the acids, 0.0001 per cent oxalic kills most of the cells of *Spirogyra majuscula* in five days. Migula[c] notes the effect of many of the organic acids, but the use of these substances in the amounts requisite for treating a contaminated water supply is entirely impracticable.

EFFECT OF COPPER SULPHATE.

Reviewing the experiments carried on in the Laboratory of Plant Physiology, as well as the results obtained by other investigators, it

---

[a] Cf. Richter, Flora, 75: 4.

[b] Loew, Flora, 75: 368.

[c] Migula, Ueber den Einfluss stark verduenter Sauren auf Algenzellen, Breslau, 1888. (Original not consulted.)

seems that copper sulphate is the substance best adapted to the work in question. This salt has a very high toxicity for algæ, and experiments with a number of the forms usually found in reservoirs, and the source of much trouble, have shown that inconceivably small amounts of copper are poisonous in a high degree. These experiments demonstrated, however, that all algæ and protozoa are not equally sensitive. Among the latter *Paramæcium* is killed in three hours by a 1 to 1,000,000 solution, while *Amœba*, *Difflugia*, and *Spirostomum* die within two hours. Crustacea are more resistant, some—*Cypris* and *Daphnia* especially—requiring as much as 1 part copper sulphate to 10,000 of water to kill them. Mosquito larvæ die at a concentration varying from 10,000 to 200,000.

Quoting the results of other experimenters, Devaux[a] found that both phænogams and cryptogams were poisoned by solutions of copper diluted to the ten-millionth part or less; Coupin[b] that 1 part copper sulphate to 700,000,000 of water was sufficient to affect the growth of seedlings when applied to their roots and that this is the most injurious of the heavy metal salts tested by him; Deherain and De Moussy[c] that the development of the roots of seedlings was arrested in distilled water containing the slightest trace of copper, and they conclude from this that higher plants during germination, as well as fungi and algæ, are extremely sensitive to copper; Bain's experiments[d] indicated that 1 part of metallic copper to 25,000,000 of water was fatal to apple seedlings in one day; on the other hand, according to Raulin,[e] copper chloride does not injure *Sterigmatocystis* until a concentration of 1 to 240 is reached, although silver nitrate is toxic at 1 to 1,600,000.

In dealing with algæ, the toxic concentration varies greatly for different genera, even for different species in the same genus. Nägeli[f] demonstrated the extreme sensitiveness of *Spirogyra nitida* and *S. dubia* to the presence of copper coins in the water. *Oscillatoria*, *Cladophora*, *Œdogonium*, and the diatoms succumb in six hours to a copper sulphate solution of 1 to 20,000, and in two days to 1 to 50,000, according to Bokorny.[g] Galeotti[h] finds that a concentration between 1 to 6,300,000 and 1 to 12,600,000 is sufficient to kill *Spirogyra nitida* in two days, and that the so-called colloidal solutions at 1 to 6,300,000 are fatal in the same length of time; while in the experi-

---

[a] Devaux, Compt. Rend., **132**: 717.
[b] Coupin, Compt. Rend., **132**: 645.
[c] Deherain and De Moussy, Compt. Rend., **132**: 523.
[d] Bain, Bull. Agr. Exp. Sta. Tenn., April, 1902.
[e] Raulin, Ann. des Sc. Nat. Bot., 5e Ser., II: 93.
[f] Nägeli, Ueber oligodynamische Erscheinungen in lebenden Zellen. Neue Denkschr. d. schweizerischen Gesellsch. für die gesammten Naturwiss., **33**: 51.
[g] Bokorny, Arch. f. d. ges. Phys. d. Mensch. u. Thiere, **64**: 262.
[h] Galeotti, Biol. Centralbl., **21**: 321.

ments of Israel and Klingman[a] the presence of 60 sq. cm. of copper foil in 300 cc. of water for twenty-four hours produced plasmal cutting in *S. laxa* after one and one-fourth hours, in *S. crassa* after fifteen minutes, and in *S. majuscula* after thirty minutes. The work of Rumm[b] shows 1 to 10,000,000 solution still toxic to a few more susceptible cells of *S. longata*. According to Ono,[c] weak solutions of the salts of most of the metals encourage the growth of algæ and fungi. Mercury and copper, however, at 0.00005 per cent and 0.00001 per cent, respectively, distinctly inhibit growth. This was the case with *Stigeoclonium*, *Chroococcum*, and *Protococcus*.

In the experiments conducted in this laboratory it has not been possible as yet to include all of the organisms known to pollute water supplies. It is believed, however, that, pending the completion of more extensive work, the data at hand will be of considerable benefit to those who have to deal with contaminated reservoirs. The method of procedure in studying this question was to determine roughly the death points of the forms under consideration, using Van Tieghem cells. Accurate solutions were then made, with distilled water, and 200 cc. of each solution was pipetted into an Erlenmyer flask. The algæ, if filamentous forms, were rinsed; if free-swimming, they were concentrated by the Sedgwick-Rafter[d] method from 500 cc. to 5 cc. volume, and this 5 cc. was added to the treated water. The inaccuracy due to the addition of the 5 cc. of untreated water to the 200 cc. of treated water was disregarded. Whenever possible, a test of these concentrations, determined experimentally, was made under natural conditions by treating the pool from which the species under consideration was taken. If this was impracticable, an additional series was carried through in aquaria of 15 liters capacity, in which were kept goldfish, frogs, minnows, crustacea, and rotifers. Since in no case was there an appreciable difference in the effect of a concentration upon a particular organism under either natural or artificial conditions, no special record is made of these gross experiments.

The different species tested may, for convenience, be grouped as (1) those with death points at higher concentrations than 1 part copper sulphate to 1,000,000 parts of water; (2) those with death points between 1 to 1,000,000 and 1 to 5,000,000; and (3) those with death points at greater dilutions than 1 to 5,000,000.

---

[a] Israel and Klingman, Virchow's Archiv., **147**: 293.
[b] Rumm, Beitrage zur Wissenschaftliche Botanik, **1**: 97.
[c] Ono, Journ. of College of Sc., Imp. Univ. Tokyo, **13**: 141.
[d] Whipple, The Microscopy of Drinking Water, New York, 1899, p. 15.

Effect of various concentrations of copper sulphate upon different forms of algæ.

[d=dead; vfa=very few alive; vfd=very few dead; g=in good condition.]

GROUP 1.

CHLAMYDOMONAS PIRIFORMIS Dill.

Date.	One part copper sulphate to water, parts—						Check.
	2,000	5,000	10,000	20,000	200,000	1,000,000	
October 19–21	½d	g	g	g	g	g	g
October 21–24	1/10d	vfd	g	g	g	g	g
October 24–27	¾d	vfd	g	g	g	g	g

RAPHIDIUM POLYMORPHUM Fres.

Date.	One part copper sulphate to water, parts—						Check.
	25,000	50,000	75,000	100,000	500,000	1,000,000	
October 19–29	d	d	½d	1/10d	g	g	g
November 2–6	d	½d	½d	1/10d	g	g	g
November 16–20	d	vfa	½d	vfd	g	g	g

DESMIDIUM SWARTZII Ag.

Date.	One part copper sulphate to water, parts—						Check.
	50,000	75,000	100,000	150,000	200,000	1,000,000	
December 2–5	d	d	½d	vfd	g	g	g
January 4–7	d	d	½d	vfd	g	g	g

STIGEOCLONIUM TENUE (Ag.) Rabenh.

Date.	One part copper sulphate to water, parts—						Check.
	50,000	100,000	300,000	500,000	1,000,000	2,000,000	
December 21–24	½d	½d	½d	½d	vfd	g	g
January 2–5	½d	½d	½d	½d	vfd	g	g
January 7–11	½d	½d	½d	½d	vfd	g	g

DRAPARNALDIA GLOMERATA (Vauch.) Ag.

Date.	One part copper sulphate to water, parts—						Check.
	50,000	100,000	300,000	500,000	1,000,000	2,000,000	
December 1–8	½d	½d	¾d	¾d	vfd	g	g

NAVICULA Sp.

Date.	One part copper sulphate to water, parts—						Check.
	100,000	200,000	300,000	400,000	500,000	1,000,000	
October 20–25	d	d	½d	vfd	vfd	g	½d
January 4–9	d	vfa	½d	vfd	vfd	g	g

EFFECT OF COPPER SULPHATE.

Effect of various concentrations of copper sulphate upon different forms of algæ—Cont'd.

GROUP 1—Continued.

SCENEDESMUS QUADRICAUDA (Turp.) Breb.

Date.	One part copper sulphate to water, parts—						Check.
	100,000	200,000	300,000	400,000	500,000	1,000,000	
September 14–18	d	d	vfa	½d	g	g	g
December 7–12	d	vfa	vfa	½d	g	g	g
January 11–15	vfa	vfa	vfa	½d	g	g	g

EUGLENA VIRIDIS Ehrb.

Date.	One part copper sulphate to water, parts—						Check.
	100,000	200,000	300,000	400,000	450,000	500,000	
September 21–25	d	vfa	vfa	½d	½d	g	g
October 26–30	vfa	vfa	vfa	½d	½d	g	g
December 31–January 2	vfa	vfa	vfa	½d	½d	g	g

SPIROGYRA STRICTA (E. Bot.) Wille.

Date.	One part copper sulphate to water, parts—						Check.
	50,000	75,000	100,000	200,000	500,000	1,000,000	
December 25–30	d	vfa	½d	g	g	g	g

GROUP 2.

CONFERVA BOMBYCINUM Ag.

Date.	One part copper sulphate to water, parts—						Check.
	50,000	100,000	300,000	500,000	1,000,000	2,000,000	
October 1–4	d	d	d	d	d	g	g
October 8–11	d	d	d	vfa	vfa	g	g
October 13–17	d	d	d	vfa	vfa	g	g

CLOSTERIUM MONILIFERUM (Bory) Ehrb.

Date.	One part copper sulphate to water, parts—					Check.
	25,000	100,000	500,000	1,000,000	2,000,000	
December 14–18	d 12hrs	d 24hrs	d	d	½d	g

SYNURA UVELLA Ehrb.

Date.	One part copper sulphate to water, parts—						Check.
	250,000	500,000	666,666	750,000	1,000,000	2,500,000	
March 14	d 5–25min	d 15–30min	d 15–45min	d 15–60min	d 28–60min	g at 1hr	g at 1hr
March 18	d 5–25min	d 15–30min	d 15–45min	d 15–60min	d 28–60min	g at 1hr	g at 1hr

Effect of various concentrations of copper sulphate upon different forms of algæ—Cont'd.

GROUP 2—Continued.

ANABÆNA CIRCINALIS Raben.

Date.	One part copper sulphate to water, parts—						Check.
	50,000	100,000	500,000	1,000,000	3,000,000	5,000,000	
December 26-29	d	d	d	d	½d	vfd	g
January 4-7	d	d	d	d	½d	vfd	g

ANABÆNA FLOS-AQUÆ Breb.

Date.	One part copper sulphate to water, parts—						Check.
	50,000	100,000	500,000	1,000,000	3,000,000	5,000,000	
July 12-14	d 12hrs	d 24hrs	d 24hrs	d 36hrs	d 72hrs	½d	g
August 27-29	d 12hrs	d 24hrs	d 24hrs	d 36hrs	d 72hrs	½d	g

GROUP 3.

UROGLENA AMERICANA Calk.

Date.	One part copper sulphate to water, parts—				Check.
	1,000,000	2,500,000	5,000,000	10,000,000	
March 19, 1903	d 3-5min	d 16hrs	vfa 16hrs	vfa 16hrs	g

The foregoing tables clearly demonstrate the effectiveness of copper sulphate as an agent for the destruction of algæ, and as the cost for an amount of this salt necessary to make the strongest solution required will not exceed from 50 to 60 cents per million gallons, but one condition remains to be satisfied—that it shall be absolutely harmless to man, domestic animals, and fish under the conditions used.

In general, animal life is less susceptible to injury by copper than is plant life, though most of the higher plants, some of the fungi, and, as the preceding tables show, certain algæ will live in concentrations of copper sulphate that would be fatal in a few hours to fish and frogs. The critical concentration for game fish is higher than that for such fish as carp and catfish. Black bass in good condition have endured concentrations of 1 to 50,000 for many weeks with no apparent discomfort, while 1 to 100,000 was sufficient to kill German and mirror carp in a few hours, and 1 to 500,000 killed the most susceptible in a few days. Mud catfish are affected at practically the same concentration; goldfish at slightly greater, while yellow perch are perhaps less susceptible than goldfish. This agrees with the results of Perry and Adams,[a] who state that minnows and goldfish live indefinitely in a 1 to 200,000 solution.

---

[a] Perry & Adams, 4th Rept. River Polut. Conn., 2: 377-391.

EFFECT OF COPPER SULPHATE.

The effects of copper upon the higher animals have been studied by a large number of investigators, and the following results may be appropriately cited:

Metallic copper and its oxides, mixed with sugar, albuminoids, and fats, had no noticeable effect upon dogs; even 8 grams of fine powder (4 grams each of copper monoxide and dioxide) caused only a slight sickness. Verdigris in small amounts produced none of the violent results it is supposed to cause in man. Soluble salts of copper can be given in quantities up to 1 gram daily, but more than this has a fatal effect.[a]

Dogs that had eaten half a gram of copper acetate per day for 24 days suffered but slightly; one dog was unaffected by doses as high as 5 grams at a time.[b] Similar results were obtained by Du Moulin,[c] who gave dogs and rabbits as much as 3 to 5 grams, causing sickness but in no case death, and Hippolyte Kuborn[d] states that a dog can take 4 grams of copper sulphate with but slight effect.

Ellenberger and Hofmeister[e] experimented with sheep, giving them from 18 to 182½ grams of copper in quantities sometimes as large as 2 grams per day, with fatal results. Tschirsch[f] deduced from this that the nontoxicity of weak solutions of copper does not hold for ruminants, but this seems hardly warranted. Two grams per day can scarcely be considered a small amount, yet one sheep lived 53 days and the other 128.

Ever since copper compounds have come into general use as fungicides, the question as to their effect upon the human system has received more or less attention.[g] At times there have been vague and misleading statements in the public press, calculated to alarm those who are in the habit of using vegetables and fruits which have been subjected to treatment with Bordeaux mixture. The popular belief seems to be that copper is a poison, but it is found upon examination that the very best authorities are by no means agreed upon this point. It is true that after the question had been discussed for seven months before the Belgian Royal Academy of Medicine, in 1885, it was finally decided that copper compounds in foods were harmful, but it should be remembered that in the whole discussion, where every effort was made by one side to show that copper was an actual poison, not a

---

[a] Burcq & Ducom, Journal de Pharmacie et Chimie, 25: 546, 1877.

[b] Galippe, Journal de Pharmacie et Chimie, 23: 298.

[c] Du Moulin, Journal de Pharmacie et Chimie, 5: 189.

[d] Hippolyte Kuborn, Congrès Internationale d'Hygiène, 2: 216, 1878.

[e] Ellenberger and Hofmeister, Archiv für wissench. u. prakt. Thierheilkunde, 9: 325, 1883.

[f] Tschirsch, Das Kupfer vom Standpunkte der gerichtlichen Chemie, Toxicologie und Hygiene, Stuttgart, 1893.

[g] Spraying Fruits for Insect Pests and Fungous Diseases, with a Special Consideration of the Subject in Its Relation to the Public Health. U. S. Department of Agriculture, Farmers' Bulletin No. 7, 1892. See also Bull. No. 6, Div. Veg. Path., U. S. Dept. Agric.

single instance was given of injury to health resulting from the daily absorption of a small quantity of copper. On the other hand, many instances were cited where foods containing copper in considerable amounts were used without producing any harmful effect whatever. It should be noted also that the law prohibiting the use of copper in regreening fruits was repealed by the French authorities after the discussion before the Belgian Academy.

According to Thiemann-Gartner,[a] chronic copper poisoning has never been proved. The supposed copper colic was discussed by Burcq[b] before the Congrès Internationale d'Hygiène in 1878, and declared by him to have no existence; he even went so far as to assert an immunity against cholera for the workers in copper during various epidemics at Paris, Toulon, Marseilles, and elsewhere, but this statement he afterwards modified with reference to the epidemic of 1832. The good health of copper workers is also noted by Houlès and Pietra-Santa,[c] though they do not claim for them immunity from typhoid and cholera. Gautier[d] states that persons working in dye factories, where the hands, faces, and even hair were colored green by copper, were physically unaffected, which is true also of copper turners, who remain apparently in the best of health although constantly in an atmosphere highly charged with copper dust.

A considerable number of experiments have been made to determine the effect of copper upon man when taken into the intestinal tract. For fourteen months Galippe[e] and his family used food cooked and cooled in copper vessels, the amount of copper present in the food being sufficient to be easily determined. Kobert's experiments[f] show that a 60-kg. man can take 1 gram of copper per day with perfect safety. From his own results Lehmann[g] considers that copper to the amount of 0.1 gram in vegetables may produce bad taste, nausea, possibly colic and diarrhea, but nothing more serious. He has himself found peas containing as much as 630 mg. of copper per kilogram not distasteful, and 200 mg. consumed at a single meal was without effect. A very careful and thorough series of tests have shown that some individuals, at least, can take copper even to the amount of 400 to 500 mg. daily for weeks without detriment to their health.

Tschirsch[h] finds that 0.01 to 0.02 of copper (0.039 to 0.078 of copper sulphate) in dilute form have no effect; 0.05 to 0.2 causes only vomiting and diarrhea.

---

[a] Thiemann-Gartner, Handbuch und Beurtheilung der Untersuchung der Wasser, Braunschweig, 1895.
[b] Burcq, Congrès Internationale d'Hygiène, 1: 529, 1878.
[c] Houlès and Pietra-Santa, Journal de Pharmacie et Chimie, 5th Ser., 9: 303.
[d] Gautier, Le Cuivre et le Plomb, Paris. 1883.
[e] Galippe, Compt. Rend., 84: 718.
[f] Kobert, Lehrbuch der Intoxicationen. (Original not consulted.)
[g] Lehmann, Münch. Med. Wochensch., 38: 603.
[h] Tschirsch, l. c.

The process of regreening legumes is described by Bouchardat and Gautier,[a] showing the amount of copper thus introduced into the vegetables to be too small to produce any injurious effect. The maximum amount of this metal in regreened peas as given by Gautier[b] is 125 mg. per kilogram, in connection with which he notes that Chatin and Personne have given it as 270 mg. According to Gautier, the amount of copper ordinarily consumed in a full meal is 95 mg.

Lafar[c] attributes the green color of Lodisan and Parmesan cheese to the presence of copper, giving the maximum amount for Lodisan cheese as 215 mg. per kilogram. Chocolate[d] contains 0.005 to 0.125 gram per kilogram, cafe bourbon[e] 8 mg. per kilogram, and beef 1 mg. per kilogram. There is 0.01 gram of copper sulphate in 1½ pounds of bread,[f] 0.1 gram of copper oxide has been found in 1 kilogram of preserves, and similar amounts are normally present in a large number of commodities used for food.

Medicinal uses of copper compounds are cited by Du Moulin.[g] He has prescribed 12 to 15 cg. for scrofulous children, for cases of ophthalmia, etc., and found no ill effects. Copper sulphate in doses of 40 to 50 cg. for four or five days has proved beneficial to children with diphtheria.

Summarizing from a large number of experiments, Bernatzik[h] concludes as follows: After entering the stomach only small quantities of copper are absorbed by the blood, and toxic action occurs only when the necessary amount can accumulate in the circulation. Silver, copper, and zinc have almost the same medicinal properties, the difference being of degree rather than kind. They differ markedly from other heavy metals, having no harmful effects upon the tissues, and producing no fatal functional injuries; hence they are not poisons in the same sense as are lead, mercury, arsenic, antimony, and phosphorus. Moreover, in the case of copper, after suspension of the dose the injured functions return to the normal.

It is evident that there is still a considerable difference of opinion among eminent authorities as to the exact amount of copper which may be injurious, but as a very conservative limit we may accept 0.02 gram as the amount that may with safety be absorbed daily. According to Merck's Index, the National Dispensatory, and the United States Dispensatory, the dose of copper sulphate for tonic and astrin-

---

[a] Bouchardat and Gautier, Congres Internationale d'Hygiene, 5: 486.
[b] Gautier, l. c.
[c] Lafar, Technical Mycology, 159.
[d] Duclaux, Bull. de la Soc. Chim. de Paris, 16: 35.
[e] Sargeau, Jour. de Pharm., 18: 219, 654; 16: 507.
[f] Tschirsch, l. c.
[g] Du Moulin, Journal de Pharmacie et Chimie, 18: 189.
[h] Bernatzik, Encyclop. d. ges. Medicin., 11: 429; Encyclop. d. ges. Heilkunde, 11: 429.

gent purposes is one-fourth grain, or 0.016 gram; as an emetic, a dose of five grains, or 0.33 gram. Thus it is seen that even if the maximum concentration of copper sulphate necessary to destroy algæ in reservoirs were maintained indefinitely, the total absorption from daily use would be very far below an amount that could produce the least unpleasant effect. Taking a dilution of one to one million, which in all cases would be sufficient to prevent the growth of a polluting algal form, it would be necessary to drink something over twenty quarts of water a day before an amount which is universally recognized as harmless would be introduced into the system, while more than fifty quarts would have to be consumed before there would be danger of producing an unpleasant or undesirable effect. As will be seen from the preceding tables the use of copper sulphate at this maximum strength of one to one million would need to be resorted to only in extreme cases, and for a very short length of time, for, the reservoir once entirely free from the organisms, a very much weaker solution would be sufficient should any further application be necessary.

Perhaps the strongest argument in favor of using a chemical treatment of this kind is that even though enough copper should be added to a reservoir to make a one-millionth solution, nothing like this amount would appear in the water distributed. A very large percentage of the copper is combined with the algæ and precipitated in other ways, so that practically none would remain in solution after the first few hours.[a] Samples of water taken from a reservoir treated with sufficient copper sulphate to make a solution of one to one million, failed to show any reaction for copper after twenty-four hours, although all the algæ were killed. It is believed that the process used of evaporating down the original quantity and testing by the delicate potassium ferro-cyanide method would certainly have detected copper had it been present in the proportion of one to fifty million. Other tests were made by different chemists, but always with negative results.

In addition to the use of copper sulphate in reservoirs containing water to be used for domestic purposes, there are possibilities of its application in treating irrigation reservoirs, small pleasure lakes, fish ponds, oyster beds, etc. Here it may often be desirable to exceed the strength of solution that would represent the maximum required in a municipal water supply. This would be done not only to kill all the algæ, but to destroy or drive away reptiles and other pests, leaving the water perfectly clear and clean. The use of some such method for the destruction of mosquito larvæ also seems worthy of attention. The mere removal of the great mass of algal growths in stagnant pools undoubtedly reduces the number of larvæ by destroying this source

---

[a] Adsorption, according to True and Ogilvie (Science, N. S., **19**: 421), would materially reduce the quantity of copper in solution. See also Bull. No. 9, Veg. Phys. and Path., U. S. Dept. Agric.

of their food and depriving them of protection from fish and other enemies. This is probably the explanation of the reported[a] decrease in the number of mosquito larvæ after spraying a lily pond with Bordeaux mixture, although it is possible that the strength of the solution used may have been partly responsible for their death. It is believed that it will not be impracticable to use the amounts of copper sulphate necessary to actually destroy such larvæ. Certainly this method if effective offers considerable advantages over any now in use, and it should be thoroughly tested. Cooperative experiments are now under way with the Bureau of Entomology to determine the strength of solution necessary to kill larvæ of different species and ages under various conditions.

METHOD OF APPLYING THE COPPER SULPHATE.

The method of introducing the copper sulphate into a water supply is extremely simple. Though any plan will suffice which distributes the copper thoroughly, the one recommended and used by the Department of Agriculture is as follows: Place the required number of pounds of copper sulphate in a coarse bag—gunny-sack or some equally loose mesh—and, attaching this to the stern of a rowboat near the surface of the water, row slowly back and forth over the reservoir, on each trip keeping the boat within 10 to 20 feet of the previous path. In this manner about 100 pounds of copper sulphate can be distributed in one hour. By increasing the number of boats, and, in the case of very deep reservoirs, hanging two or three bags to each boat, the treatment of even a large reservoir may be accomplished in from four to six hours. It is necessary, of course, to reduce as much as possible the time required for applying the copper, so that for immense supplies with a capacity of several billion gallons it would probably be desirable to use a launch, carrying long projecting spars to which could be attached bags each containing several hundred pounds of copper sulphate.

In waters that have a comparatively high percentage of organic acid it is sometimes advisable to add a sufficient amount of lime or some alkali hydrate to precipitate the copper. The necessity for this will never occur in a limestone region, as in this case there will always be enough calcium hydrate or carbonate to cause the desired precipitation. The precipitation of copper does not mean the destruction of its toxicity, for experiments conducted in this laboratory have confirmed Rumm's[b] results that the insoluble salts of copper, such as the hydrate, carbonate, and phosphate, are toxic only if they are in contact with the cell, but are highly toxic in that case. In this connection it should be mentioned that Hedrick[a] has described a method for con-

---

[a] Hedrick, Gardening, 11: 295.   [b] Rumm, l. c.

trolling the growth of algal scum in lily ponds by the use of Bordeaux mixture which seems to have been temporarily effective. However, the impracticability of using such a mixture is apparent for the destruction of microscopic algæ distributed through a reservoir or a lake containing millions of gallons.

PRACTICAL TESTS OF THE METHOD.

WATER-CRESS BEDS.

The first practical test of the treatment of water for the purpose of killing out extensive growths of algæ was made in the fall of 1901 near Ben, Va., in connection with the cultivation of water cress for market. Water cress is grown there, as well as in other parts of the country, in large quantities during the winter, it being a valuable crop at that season of the year. The cress is confined in beds made by constructing dams across a small stream, which maintains a water level not too high for the growth of the plants and yet permits flooding when there is danger of a freeze. In the locality where the experiments were carried on the water was obtained from a thermal spring with a temperature the year around of about 70° F. Such a temperature was particularly favorable to the development of *Spirogyra* and similar filamentous algæ, so that when the cress was freshly cut they frequently increased to such an extent as to completely smother out a large part of the young and tender plants. The only known remedy under such conditions was to rake out the water cress and algæ and reset the entire bed. This was an expensive method, however, besides being successful only about half the time. Consequently, it was very desirable to devise some means of preventing the growth of the algæ without injuring the water cress, and the treatment by means of copper suggested itself. At first a strong solution of copper sulphate was used, spraying it on the algal covered surface of the beds, but this only destroyed the few filaments with which the copper came in contact, the large mass of algæ being practically unaffected. The method of applying the copper by means of dissolving it directly in the beds was next tried, and the success of the treatment was almost immediately evident. In this case the amount of copper added was about equal to a strength of 1 to 50,000,000 parts of water, but it is probable that by the time it reached most of the *Spirogyra* it was considerably weakened, as it was impossible to prevent a slight current of fresh water from passing through the beds at all times.

The success of the copper treatment for eradicating algæ from cress beds has been thoroughly demonstrated, and there is no reason why growers should have trouble from this cause in the future. The strength of the solution used for killing the algæ is so very much weaker than that which might affect the cress that there is no possible danger of injuring the latter if the solution is used by anyone capable of observing ordinary care. The question of how long a treatment is effective must, of course, depend upon conditions, but it is believed that the application of the proper amount of copper once or twice a year will in most cases be sufficient to keep down any algal pest. The manager of the Virginia Cress Company writes, under date of April 12, 1904:

> The "moss" has given me no trouble at all this winter. In fact I have for six months only had to resort to the copper sulphate once. * * * All the conditions were favorable last fall and early winter for a riot of "moss," but it did not appear at all until just a few days ago, and then yielded to treatment much more readily than it did when I first began to use the copper.

WATER RESERVOIRS.

The successful elimination of algæ from the cress beds of the South, under conditions which were particularly favorable to the growth of these pests, made it desirable that experiments be inaugurated calculated to demonstrate the possibility of ridding water reservoirs of the disagreeable odors and tastes caused by similar organisms. While it was realized that the popular prejudice against any chemical treatment of drinking water was strong, it was believed that the very weak solution, together with the very rapid disappearance of the salt added, would not render it a prohibitive method when applied under the direction of the proper authorities. It was also found that consumers of a water which possessed a disgusting odor and taste were not so prejudiced against the use of even a chemical method of extermination, provided it could be proved that no bodily harm would result.

In the spring of 1903 there was brought to the notice of the Department the supply of a water company in Kentucky, which promised to furnish a most satisfactory test. Ever since the construction of their reservoir it had given off an unpleasant odor. For the first two seasons this was supposed to be due to decaying vegetation, but later years demonstrated the well-known "pigpen" odor due to algæ, and this increased from year to year until it was almost unbearable.

In July, 1903, when the trial was begun, the microscopical examination demonstrated an average of—

```
Anabæna ................................................per cc..  7,400
Clathrocystis .............................................do....  1,100
Eudorina..................................................do....    200
```

There were about 25,000,000 gallons of water in the reservoir at the time of the experiment, and on account of the great number of blue-green algæ present it was decided to apply the copper at a strength of 1 to 4,000,000. About 50 pounds of copper sulphate was accordingly placed in a coarse sack and this, attached to a boat, was dragged over the surface of the reservoir, giving especial attention to the region which seemed to contain the greatest number of *Anabæna* filaments.

28 METHOD OF DESTROYING ALGÆ IN WATER SUPPLIES.

The decrease in the number of organisms as the result of this treatment during the next twenty-four hours was very decided. In two days the surface was clear and the water had lost its blue-green color, becoming brown, due to the dead organisms held in suspension. There was a slight increase in odor during the first two days after treatment, but this was followed by a gradual subsidence until it had entirely disappeared, not to appear again that season. The following list of counts made from surface examinations at one station illustrates what went on throughout the reservoir, and shows the almost immediate effect of a 1 to 4,000,000 solution of copper sulphate upon the number of filaments of *Anabæna flos-aquæ*. The treatment was made July 9.

	Filaments per cubic centimeter.
July 6	3,400
July 10	54
July 11	8
July 13	0
July 15	0
July 20	0

It remains to be seen what the condition will be during the coming summer, but it is believed it can never be any worse than at the time of treatment, and it is reasonable to suppose that there will be considerably fewer organisms this year than last. Even though an annual treatment of the reservoir prove necessary, involving a cost of from $25 to $50, the already great improvement in the quality of the water will certainly make it justifiable.

Other experiments of a similar character were carried on in different parts of the country with reservoirs of a capacity of from 10,000,000 to 600,000,000 gallons. While the results were all favorable, it is deemed best not to publish any detailed account until the effect of the treatment can be followed through another season. The summer of 1903 was cold and wet, and in some cases the decrease in the number of organisms may have been due to these factors. However, the several instances of the very sudden and rapid disappearance of forms which were present in tremendous quantity, without any reappearance, indicated that the treatment was most effective. Those in charge of these water supplies reported that they were well satisfied with the result.

EFFECT OF COPPER UPON PATHOGENIC BACTERIA.

TYPHOID.

The value of copper sulphate as an agent for the destruction of algæ polluting reservoirs suggests its use in cases where the organism is pathogenic. Since this salt is fatal to the algal growths, it seemed probable that it would also destroy bacteria, and that cholera germs and typhoid germs might succumb to its action.

The sterilization of public water supplies by chemical means has so far seemed an impossibility. Nearly every known substance has been tested, but the high concentrations required to produce the desired effect, the extreme toxicity of the agents, their cost, or the difficulty of application, have eliminated all but copper sulphate as a possibility for the present purpose. According to Semmer and Krajewski,[a] a 1 to 160 solution of this salt will inhibit action in infected blood, and septic bacteria can be destroyed with a 10 per cent solution. Bolton[b] says that 1 to 500 is toxic, but 1 to 1,000 permits the growth of cholera; 1 to 200 and 1 to 500, respectively, produce the same results with typhoid, and some of the spore-bearing forms are unaffected at 2 per cent. Green[c] gives 2½ per cent as the amount necessary to kill typhoid in two to twenty-four hours, and finds cholera only slightly less sensitive. Israel and Klingman,[d] however, find that almost infinitesimal amounts of copper in colloidal solution are fatal to typhoid, cholera, and *Bacillus coli*. There is considerable literature upon the use of copper sulphate as a disinfectant for clothing, bedding, cesspools, etc., but it is not necessary to review it at this place. Sternberg[e] found that its germicide power was decidedly superior to the corresponding salt of iron and zinc, and demonstrated that it destroyed micrococci from the pus of an acute abscess in the proportion of 1 to 200. He says, "This agent (cupric sulphate), then, is a valuable germicide and may be safely recommended for the disinfection of material not containing spores."

The high percentage of copper sulphate given by most of these authorities seems to preclude the idea of its practical use for the purpose desired. It should be remembered, however, that these investigators were working for a very different end, namely, to find concentrations destructive to bacteria in the presence of large quantities of albuminoid and fatty matter. Experiments conducted under similar circumstances have confirmed the above results, but the conditions obtaining in public water supplies are widely different. Here the amount of albuminoid matter is so small that the death point of the typhoid or cholera organism is lowered tremendously and very dilute solutions of copper are shown to be toxic. The tabulated results on the succeeding pages demonstrate this fact.

[a] Semmer and Krajewski, Arch. f. exp. Path. u. Pharmakol., **14**: 139.
[b] Bolton, Rep. of Com. on Disinfectants, Am. Pub. Health Assn., 1888, p. 153.
[c] Green, Zeit. für Hyg., **13**: 495.
[d] Israel and Klingman, Virchow's Archiv., **147**: 293.
[e] Sternberg, Rep. Com. Disinfection, Am. Pub. Health Assn., 1888, p. 38. See also Infection and Immunity, New York and London, 1903.

Effect of copper sulphate upon Bacillus typhi at different temperatures.[a]

[Determination made in tubes of bouillon. + indicates growth after 48 hours' incubation; − indicates no growth.]

Duration of exposure to action of copper sulphate.	Temperature.	Check.	1 part copper sulphate to 100,000 parts of water.	1 part copper sulphate to 200,000 parts of water.	1 part copper sulphate to 500,000 parts of water.
	°C.				
2 hours	38	+	−	+	+
	28	+	+	+	+
	23.5	+	+	+	+
	14	+	+	+	+
	4	+	+	+	+
4 hours	38	+	−	+	+
	28	+	--	+	+
	23.5	+	(?)	+	+
	14	+	+	+	+
	4	+	+	+	+
6 hours	38	+	−	−	+
	28	+	−	+	+
	23.5	+	−	+	+●
	14	+	+	+	+
	4	+	+	+	+
12 hours	38	+	−	−	+
	28	+	−	+	+
	23.5	+	−	+	+
	14	+	−	+	+
	4	+	(?)	+	+

[a] Experiment conducted in test tubes, each containing 5 cc. of sterilized water, portions of which had been previously treated with the desired amounts of copper sulphate. All tubes inoculated with a 3 mm. loop of a 24-hour culture of B. typhi.

Effect of copper sulphate upon Bacillus typhi cultures of various ages.[a]

[Determination made in tubes of bouillon. + indicates growth after 48 hours' incubation; − indicates no growth.]

Duration of exposure to action of solution of 1 part copper sulphate to 100,000 parts of water.	Culture 36 hours old.	Culture 24 hours old.	Culture 18 hours old.	Culture 12 hours old.	Culture 6 hours old.	Culture 3 hours old.
3 hours	+	+	+	+	−	−
6 hours	(?)	−	−·	−	−	−
9 hours	−	−	−	−	−	−

[a] Experiment conducted in test tubes each containing 5 cc. of sterilized water, portions of which had been previously treated with the desired amount of copper sulphate. All tubes inoculated with a 3 mm. loop of a culture of B. typhi of the proper age.

Effect of copper sulphate on Bacillus typhi at different temperatures.[a]

[Determination made in Petri dishes.]

Duration of exposure to action of copper sulphate.	Temperature.	Check.	One part copper sulphate to 100,000 parts of water.	One part copper sulphate to 200,000 parts of water.	One part copper sulphate to 500,000 parts of water.
	°C.	*Colonies.*	*Colonies.*	*Colonies.*	*Colonies.*
2 hours	5	720	315	1,440	894
2 hours	38	1,260	0	312	917
5 hours	5	155	115	495	278
5 hours	38	37	0	9	21

[a] Experiment conducted in test tubes each containing 5 cc. of sterilized water, portions of which had been previously treated with the proper amounts of copper sulphate. All tubes inoculated with a 3 mm. loop of an 18-hour culture of B. typhi.

EFFECT OF COPPER UPON PATHOGENIC BACTERIA.

Effect of copper sulphate upon Bacillus typhi at room temperature.[a]

[Determination made in Petri dishes.]

Duration of exposure to action of copper sulphate.	Check.	One part copper sulphate to—				
		100,000 parts water.	200,000 parts water.	500,000 parts water.	1,000,000 parts water.	5,000,000 parts water.
		Colonies.	Colonies.	Colonies.	Colonies.	Colonies.
½ hour	1,650	5,481	2,376	2,754	2,646	3,645
1 hour	1,836	918	2,106	2,403	1,377	1,755
1¼ hours	1,566	1,026	1,242	1,323	2,673	2,808
2 hours	1,485	864	1,296	2,835	2,430	3,024
2¼ hours	999	243	1,620	1,485	2,727	2,106
3 hours	1,134	180	1,161	1,620	1,782	756
3½ hours	1,080	156	783	918	2,079	1,242
4 hours	783	108	972	1,998	1,836	1,458
8 hours	270	0	72	405	324	459
12 hours	297	0	14	42	243	405

[a] Experiment conducted in test tubes each containing 5 cc. of sterilized water, portions of which had been previously treated with the desired amounts of copper sulphate. All tubes inoculated with a 3 mm. loop of an 18-hour culture of *B. typhi*.

Effect of copper sulphate upon Bacillus typhi at room temperature.[a]

[Determination made in Petri dishes.]

Duration of exposure to action of copper sulphate.	No. 1. Check.		No. 2. One part copper sulphate to 200,000 parts water.			No. 3. One part copper sulphate to 100,000 parts water.			No. 4. One part copper sulphate to 50,000 parts water.			No. 5. One part copper sulphate to 100,000 parts water.		
	Colonies.		Colonies.			Colonies.			Colonies.			Colonies.		
	Bacillus typhi.	Molds.	Bacillus typhi.	Molds.	Saprophytic bacteria.	Bacillus typhi.	Molds.	Saprophytic bacteria.	Bacillus typhi.	Molds.	Saprophytic bacteria.	Bacillus typhi.	Molds.	Saprophytic bacteria.
0 hour	144	4	5	108	2	7	3	1	4	3,672	0	0	234	0	5
	792	2	4	90	1	4	198	1	5	5,742	1	1	306	0	0
3 hours	14,634	2	7	11	0	5	72	3	4	0	0	0	6	0	0
	16,212	0	0	126	0	2	6	0	0	4	0	1	4	1	0
4 hours	954	0	2	0	0	1	0	0	0	0	0	0	0	2	0
	558	3	31	0	0	0	0	0	0	0	0	3	0	0	0
6 hours	24,300	2	8	0	1	1	0	0	1	0	0	0	0	0	0
	19,400	0	0	0	1	5	0	0	0	0	0	3	0	1	1
8 hours	20,484	0	0	0	0	2	0	0	1	0	0	0	0	0	0
	19,674	0	0	0	0	0	0	0	3	0	0	2	0	1	0
12 hours	6,156	0	33	0	0	0	0	0	0	0	0	0	0	0	0
	21,600	0	0	0	0	0	0	0	0	0	0	0	0	0	0

[a] Experiment conducted in 12-liter aquaria. No. 1 was untreated; copper sulphate was added to Nos. 2, 3, 4, and 5. Three cubic centimeters of a mixture of cultures of *B. typhi* were added to each jar 18 hours before treating. All small nonliquifying colonies counted as typhoid.

32 METHOD OF DESTROYING ALGÆ IN WATER SUPPLIES.

Effect of copper sulphate upon Bacillus typhi at low temperature.[a]

[Determination made in Petri dishes.]

Duration of exposure to action of copper sulphate.	Temperature.	Check.	One part copper to 100,000 parts water.
	°C.	Colonies.	Colonies.
3 hours	5	2,187	1,944
6 hours	5	2,646	881
9 hours	5	1,026	702
12 hours	5	351	98
24 hours	5	37	0

[a] Experiment conducted in test tubes each containing 5 cc. of sterilized water, part of which had been previously treated with the desired amount of copper sulphate. All tubes inoculated with a 3 mm. loop of a culture of *B. typhi* of the proper age.

Effect of copper sulphate upon Bacillus coli cultures of various ages.[a]

[Determination made in tubes of bouillon. + indicates growth after 48 hours' incubation; − indicates no growth.]

Duration of exposure to action of solution of 1 part copper sulphate to 100,000 parts water.	Culture 36 hours old.	Culture 24 hours old.	Culture 18 hours old.	Culture 12 hours old.	Culture 6 hours old.	Culture 3 hours old.
3 hours	+	+	+	+	+	−
6 hours	−	−	+	−	−	−
9 hours	−	−	+	−	−	−

[a] Experiment conducted in test tubes each containing 5 cc. of sterilized water, part of which had been previously treated with the desired amount of copper sulphate. All tubes inoculated with a 3 mm. loop of a culture of *B. coli* of the proper age.

Effect of copper sulphate upon Bacillus coli at different temperatures.[a]

[Determination made in tubes of bouillon. + indicates growth after 48 hours' incubation; − indicates no growth.]

Duration of exposure to action of copper sulphate.	Temperature.	Check.	One part copper sulphate to— 100,000 parts water.	200,000 parts water.	500,000 parts water.
	°C.				
2 hours	38	+	+	+	+
	28	+	+	+	+
	23.5	+	+	+	+
	14	+	+	+	+
	4	+	+	+	+
4 hours	38	+	−	+	+
	28	+	+	+	+
	23.5	+	+	+	+
	14	+	+	+	+
	4	+	+	+	+
6 hours	38	+	−	+	+
	28	+	+	+	+
	23.5	+	+	+	+
	14	+	+	+	+
	4	+	+	+	+

[a] Experiment conducted in test tubes each containing 5 cc. sterilized water, portions of which had been previously treated with the desired amounts of copper sulphate. All tubes inoculated with a 3-mm. loop of a 24-hour culture of *B. coli.*

Effect of copper sulphate upon Bacillus coli at room temperature.[a]

[Determination made in Petri dishes.]

Duration of exposure to action of copper sulphate.	Check.	1 part copper sulphate to—				
		100,000 parts of water.	200,000 parts of water.	500,000 parts of water.	1,000,000 parts of water.	5,000,000 parts of water.
	Colonies.	Colonies.	Colonies.	Colonies.	Colonies.	Colonies.
½ hour	3,888	5,697	4,455	8,937	5,490	6,426
1 hour	3,456	2,295	1,755	2,700	3,483	2,160
1½ hours	2,592	2,565	1,755	2,403	1,377	1,873
2 hours	2,079	1,971	3,429	1,890	3,267	3,912
2½ hours	3,969	2,835	2,296	3,456	2,214	2,349
3 hours	2,457	1,701	1,242	3,834	2,106	3,078
3½ hours	1,566	1,404	2,295	1,431	2,025	3,240
4 hours	1,323	675	1,593	2,403	1,674	1,836
8 hours	1,107	96	459	1,026	513	1,728
12 hours	297	5	43	366	513	891

[a] Experiment conducted in test tubes, each containing 5 cc. of sterilized water, portions of which had been previously treated with the desired amounts of copper sulphate. All tubes inoculated with a 3 mm. loop of an 18-hour culture of *B. coli*.

Effect of copper sulphate upon Bacillus coli at low temperature.[a]

[Determination made in Petri dishes.]

Duration of exposure to action of copper sulphate.	Temperature.	Check.	1 part copper to 100,000 parts water.
	° C.	Colonies.	Colonies.
3 hours	5	2,700	2,673
6 hours	5	3,591	1,620
9 hours	5	2,403	1,215
12 hours	5	2,106	1,431

[a] Experiment conducted in test tubes each containing 5 cc. of sterilized water, part of which had been previously treated with the desired amount of copper sulphate. All tubes inoculated with a 3 mm. loop of a culture of *B. coli* of the proper age.

Effect of copper sulphate upon paracolon cultures of various ages.[a]

[Determination made in tubes of bouillon. + indicates growth after 48 hours' incubation; — indicates no growth.]

Duration of exposure to action of solution of 1 part copper sulphate to 100,000 parts of water.	Culture 36 hours old.	Culture 24 hours old.	Culture 18 hours old.	Culture 12 hours old.	Culture 6 hours old.	Culture 3 hours old.
3 hours	+	—	?	..	—	—
6 hours	—	—	—	—	?	—
9 hours	—	—	—	—	..	..

[a] Experiment conducted in test tubes each containing 5 cc. of sterilized water, part of which had been previously treated with the desired amount of copper sulphate. All tubes inoculated with a 3 mm. loop of a culture of paracolon of the proper age.

These tables show that *Bacillus typhi* is more sensitive to copper sulphate than is *coli*, that the para group are about equally sensitive, and that temperature has a very important bearing on the toxicity of the copper in solution. At room temperature, which is near the temperature of a reservoir in summer, a dilution of 1 to 100,000 is fatal to *typhi* in three to five hours; at 5° it requires twenty-four hours for complete destruction.

The results obtained were checked in three ways:

(1) Five cubic centimeters of each of the solutions to be tested, made up with filtered hydrant water and check tubes of the same water, were sterilized in test tubes. To each of these was transferred one 3-mm. loop of a bouillon culture of the bacillus. After the proper exposure, a 3-mm. loop of the inoculated water from each tube was transferred to a sterile bouillon tube with a corresponding number. These bouillon tubes were then incubated forty-six hours at 38°, the time and concentration of the agent required to prevent growth being noted.

(2) Instead of transferring to bouillon tubes from the inoculated water, the transfer was made to gelatine tubes, and plates were poured in 10-cm. Petri dishes, thus making it possible to estimate the reduction in the number of bacteria in concentrations not sufficient to prevent growth. .

(3) Five 12-liter aquaria, two of which contained a high percentage of organic matter, also a large quantity of algæ and other aquatic plants, were inoculated, each with 3 cubic centimeters of cultures of *Bacillus typhi* of different ages, and allowed to stand eighteen hours, and two poured plates were made from each aquarium, the 3-mm. loop being used in all cases. To these aquaria were then added a 1 per cent solution of copper sulphate in sufficient quantity to produce the desired concentration. After the proper time had elapsed, another series of plates was made, this being repeated every two hours for a period of twelve hours.

The tests were made upon four distinct cultures of *Bacillus typhi*, designated respectively Wasserman, Stokes, Say, and Longcope, and except in the case of the aquaria series, upon *Bacillus coli* and some of the para forms. These organisms were obtained from the laboratory of H. K. Mulford & Co.

ASIATIC CHOLERA.

The method of procedure in determining the toxic concentration for *Microspira comma* (*Spirillum choleræ*) was identical to that employed in the case of *Bacillus typhi*. The tables on the next page show that the toxic limits of these two pathogenic organisms are very similar and that *Microspira comma* is slightly more sensitive to copper sulphate than is *Bacillus typhi*. To destroy the cholera germ requires about three hours in a 1 to 100,000 solution at a temperature above 20°. A longer exposure or a higher concentration is necessary to produce this result at lower temperatures.

Effect of copper sulphate upon Microspira comma at different temperatures. [a]

[Determination made in Petri dishes.]

Duration of exposure to action of copper sulphate.	Temperature.	Check.	One part copper sulphate to—		
			100,000 parts water.	200,000 parts water.	500,000 parts water.
	°C.	Colonies.	Colonies.	Colonies.	Colonies.
2 hours	5	1,866	1,400	566	3,366
	15	2,500	533	1,100	1,000
	26	3,500	3	100	733
	30.5	4,556	7	66	1,433
4 hours	5	1,533	133	13	766
	15	1,033	21	72	95
	26.5	1,033	0	6	11
	30.5	1,466	0	0	12
6 hours	5	2,000	32	9	700
	15	3,033	9	20	84
	26.5	3,600	0	166	533
	30.5	1,066	0	0	90

[a] Experiments conducted in test tubes, each containing 5 cc. of sterilized water, portions of which had been previously treated with the desired amounts of copper sulphate. All tubes inoculated with a 3 mm. loop of a 14-hour culture of *M. comma*.

Effect of copper sulphate upon Microspira comma at different temperatures. [a]

[Determinations made in buillon tubes. + indicates growth after 48 hours' incubation; − indicates no growth.]

Duration of exposure to action of copper sulphate.	Temperature.	Check.	1 part of copper sulphate to—		
			100,000 parts water.	200,000 parts water.	500,000 parts water.
	°C.				
2 hours	17	+	+	+	+
	24.4	+	+	+	+
	30.5	+	−	−	+
4 hours	17	+	+	+	+
	24.4	+	−	+	+
	30.5	+	−	−	+
6 hours	17	+	−	+	+
	24.4	+	−	+	−
	30.5	+	−	−	

[a] Experiment conducted in test tubes each containing 5 cc. of sterilized water, part of which had been previously treated with the desired amount of copper sulphate. All tubes inoculated with a 3 mm. loop of a 16-hour culture of *M. comma*.

It will be seen that the concentration of copper required is considerably greater than the maximum necessary for the destruction of algæ, and would, of course, be injurious to the aquatic animals normally present in a reservoir if it were allowed to act for any great length of time. Experiments in this laboratory have demonstrated, however, that the time necessary to remove *Bacillus typhi* is from three to four hours in summer, twenty-four hours in the coldest weather, and that under such conditions the solution does not injure fish and frogs or the common aquatic plants such as *Elodea*, *Myriophyllum*, and *Lemna*. To remove the copper at the desired time the method suggested in the preceding section in the case of acid and soft waters may be employed—that is, precipitate the copper by some soluble hydroxide or carbonate. This somewhat complicates the treatment, as it will be necessary to determine from the character of the water the amount of copper necessary to produce a solution of 1 to 100,000, as well as to estimate how much of the hydroxide or carbonate should be added. That such work be conducted under the constant and direct supervision of competent authorities is even more important than when treating for algal contamination.

COMPARISON OF EFFECT OF OTHER DISINFECTANTS.

A comparison of the effect of copper sulphate with certain other substances commonly used as disinfectants is instructive, and gives some idea of the great toxicity of this metal. Mercuric chloride (corrosive sublimate) is slightly more fatal to typhoid and cholera than copper sulphate acting at a lower temperature and in a shorter length of time. Carbolic acid, one hundred times as strong as the dilution found to be effective for copper sulphate, and acting eight times as long, failed to kill. The same is true of formalin used between fifteen and twenty times the strength of a 1 to 100,000 solution. Using one thousand times the amount of citric acid that would be used of copper sulphate produces death. Thymol is effective in six hours when used in a solution of 1 to 5,000, and naphthalene is five times weaker.

COLLOIDAL SOLUTIONS.

The preceding experiments have dealt with copper in solution as the salt of some acid. The effect upon water of metallic copper surfaces, producing the so-called colloidal solution of copper, deserves especial mention. As Nägeli, Galeotti, and Israel and Klingman have abundantly demonstrated, the slight amounts of copper thus brought into solution are highly toxic to many forms of algæ and bacteria.

The experiments carried on in this laboratory show that it is undoubtedly possible to exterminate *Uroglena* and some forms of *Spirogyra* by suspending in the water copper foil sufficient to give an area of about 1 sq. cm. to each 100 cc. of water. This would not be a practicable method of treating a reservoir, but it suggests the possibility of sheet copper being used as a preventive of pollution. By suspending large sheets of this metal at the intake of a reservoir, it is probable that conditions would be rendered sufficiently antagonistic to algal growth to maintain the sterility of a reservoir after it had once been thoroughly cleansed of polluting forms. It would, of course, be necessary to keep such copper sheets clean in order to prevent a reduction of the toxic action due to the formation of an insoluble or slimy coating on its surface. It is possible that some electrical method may be perfected for rapidly obtaining a strong colloidal solution, which will furnish a more convenient means of application than that of the crude salt.

In regard to the bacteria causing cholera and typhoid, the importance of the specific toxic effect of colloidal copper is probably much greater than with algæ. The following tables show the proportions of the area of copper to the quantity of water and to the time and the temperature necessary to produce the complete sterilization of water containing these pathogenic germs:

Effect upon Bacillus typhi of exposure to colloidal solution of copper at room temperature.[a]

[Determination made in tubes of bouillon. + indicates growth after 48 hours' inoculation; — indicates no growth.]

Duration of exposure to action of copper.	Check.	15 sq. mm. copper foil in 10 cc. of water.	100 sq. mm. copper foil in 10 cc. of water.	225 sq. mm. copper foil in 10 cc. of water.
10 hours	+	+	+	+
15 hours	+	+	+	..
20 hours	+	+	—	—
50 hours	+	+	—	—

[a] Experiment conducted in test tubes containing 10 cc. each of sterilized water. The copper foil was sterilized and added immediately before inoculating the tubes with the usual 3 mm. loop of a 24-hour culture of *B. typhi*. This experiment was duplicated with three separate strains of typhoid with identical results.

Effect upon Bacillus typhi of exposure to colloidal solution of copper at room temperature.[a]

[Determination made in Petri dishes.]

Duration of exposure to action of copper.	Check.	1 sq. cm. copper foil to 5 cc. of water.	4 sq. cm. copper foil to 5 cc. of water.
	Colonies.	Colonies.	Colonies.
½ hour	1,650	2,241	2,025
1 hour	1,836	1,944	2,349
1½ hours	1,566	1,620	1,188
2 hours	1,465	1,674	1,188
2½ hours	999	675	1,053
3 hours	1,134	972	918
3½ hours	1,080	1,242	621
4 hours	783	837	360
8 hours	270	216	0
12 hours	297	24	0

[a] Experiment conducted in test tubes, each containing 5 cc. of sterilized water. The copper foil was sterilized, and added immediately before inoculating the tubes with the usual 3 mm. loop of a 24-hour culture of *B. typhi*.

Effect upon Bacillus coli of exposure to colloidal solution of copper at room temperature.[a]

[Determination made in tubes of bouillon. + indicates growth after 48 hours' inoculation; − indicates no growth.]

Duration of exposure to action of copper.	Check.	15 sq. mm. copper foil in 10 cc. of water.	100 sq. mm. copper foil in 10 cc. of water.	225 sq. mm. copper foil in 10 cc. of water.
10 hours	+	+	+	+
16 hours	+	+	+	−
20 hours	+	+	+	−
50 hours	+	+	+	−

[a] Experiment conducted in test tubes containing 10 cc. each of sterilized water. The copper foil was sterilized and added immediately before inoculating the tubes with the usual 3 mm. loop of a 24-hour culture of *B. coli*.

Effect upon Bacillus coli of exposure to colloidal solution of copper at room temperature.[a]

[Determination made in Petri dishes.]

Duration of exposure to action of copper.	Check.	1 sq. cm. copper foil to 5 cc. of water.	4 sq. cm. copper foil to 5 cc. of water.
	Colonies.	*Colonies.*	*Colonies.*
½ hour	3,888	2,241	3,024
1 hour	3,456	1,971	2,025
1½ hours	2,592	1,512	2,754
2 hours	2,079	1,188	1,846
2½ hours	3,969	1,242	999
3 hours	2,457	1,242	1,593
3½ hours	1,566	1,026	2,727
4 hours	1,323	1,323	810
8 hours	1,107	702	69
12 hours	297	348	0

[a] Experiment conducted in test tubes, each containing 5 cc. of sterilized water. The copper foil was sterilized and added immediately before inoculating the tubes with the usual 3-mm. loop of a 24-hour culture of *B. coli*.

Effect upon paracolon of exposure to collodial solution of copper at room temperature.[a]

[Determination made in tubes of bouillon. + indicates growth after 48 hours' inoculation; − indicates no growth.]

Duration of exposure to action of copper.	Check.	15 sq. mm. copper foil in 10 cc. of water.	100 sq. mm. copper foil in 10 cc. of water.	225 sq. mm. copper foil in 10 cc. of water.
5 hours	+	+	+	+
10 hours	+	+	+	−
16 hours	+	+	+	−
20 hours	+	+	−	−
50 hours	+	+	−	−

[a] Experiment conducted in test tubes containing 10 cc. each of sterilized water. The copper foil was sterilized and added immediately before inoculating the tubes with the usual 3 mm. loop of a 24-hour culture of paracolon. This experiment was duplicated upon another form of paracolon with exactly the same results.

Effect upon paratyphoid of exposure to colloidal solution of copper at room temperature.[a]

[Determination made in tubes of bouillon. + indicates growth after 48 hours' inoculation; — indicates no growth.]

Duration of exposure to action of copper.	Check.	15 sq. mm. copper foil in 10 cc. of water.	100 sq. mm. copper foil in 10 cc. of water.	225 sq. mm. copper foil in 10 cc. of water.
10 hours	+	+	+	+
16 hours	+	+	+	—
20 hours	+	+	—	—
50 hours	+	+	—	—

[a] Experiment conducted in test tubes containing 10 cc. each of sterilized water. The copper foil was sterilized and added immediately before inoculating the tubes with the usual 3 mm. loop of a 24-hour culture of paratyphoid.

Effect upon Microspira comma of colloidal solution of copper at various temperatures.[a]

[Determination made in Petri dishes.]

Duration of exposure to action of copper.	Temperature.	Check. Colonies.	¼ sq. cm. copper foil to 5 cc. water. Colonies.	2 sq. cm. copper foil to 5 cc. water. Colonies.
2 hours	°C. 5	1,866	833	2,500
	15	2,500	733	2,433
	26.5	3,500	4,600	333
	30.5	4,556	1,666	533
4 hours	5	1,533	52	29
	15	1,033	633	366
	26.5	1,033	200	0
	30.5	1,466	8	30
6 hours	5	2,000	700	10
	15	3,033	45	17
	26.5	3,600	300	0
	30.5	1,066	4	8

[a] Experiments conducted in test tubes, each containing 5 cc. of sterilized water, portions of which had been previously treated with the desired amounts of copper sulphate. All tubes inoculated with a 3 mm. loop of a 14-hour culture of *M. comma*.

It is evident that the amount of surface exposed in any ordinary copper tank would far exceed the amount demanded for the above results, and it is likewise certain that after standing from 6 to 8 hours at room temperature in a *clean* copper vessel water becomes safe to drink even though it may have contained cholera and typhoid germs. It remains to be seen whether or not the application of these facts to conditions in the Tropics, where cholera is abundant, will be of any value. It would seem that the construction of canteens and other water vessels from copper might serve as an additional safeguard, if not an actual preventive of this disease, and would prove of considerable value where distillation or efficient filtration apparatus is not at hand.

CONCLUSIONS.

It is believed that the foregoing experiments demonstrate the possibility of the use of copper sulphate for the destruction or prevention of growths of algæ in water supplies, and that when used under the direction of a competent authority, it is the only practicable remedy for this trouble capable of universal application which has ever been proposed. It is, of course, probable that with the experience which must come from a wider opportunity for testing this salt, many improvements will be made in the practical application of the treatment to large bodies of water. However, it is hoped that the results already obtained, together with trials now under way, will make it possible to begin using this method within a short time upon a large scale throughout the country.

NECESSITY OF KNOWLEDGE OF ORGANISM AND CONDITION IN RESERVOIR.

It can not be too strongly emphasized, however, that harmless as the method undoubtedly is under proper control, it must always require a certain amount of definite knowledge in regard to the condition of the reservoir before any treatment can be made, even by those thoroughly able to conduct such an experiment. This is regarded as a fortunate requisite, since it will tend to prevent the irresponsible or careless dosing of reservoirs by incompetents, who are occasionally in charge of water supplies.

Before the amount of copper to be added can possibly be known, it is absolutely necessary to ascertain the exact character of the organism causing the trouble. This will make a microscopical examination of the first importance. Also, the sooner such an examination reveals the presence of the polluting form, the more effective will be the treatment. If examinations are made at short intervals during the entire year, it is possible to detect the troublesome forms at their first appearance and by prompt treatment to destroy the algæ before the consumer is aware of any difficulty. The early detection of the algæ will also make a considerable difference in the expense of the treatment, as it may require fifteen or twenty times as much copper to clean a reservoir after the bad odor and taste are evident than it would could the application have been made before the organism began to rapidly multiply. In all cases the use of copper as a preventive rather than a cure is advocated, and this can not be intelligently applied unless the microscopical examinations are thorough and frequent at the time of year the trouble is to be anticipated.

On account of the necessity of determining the nature of the organism and the time of its appearance as nearly as possible, it will become as imperative for water companies to employ some one competent to

CONCLUSIONS.

make these examinations as it now is to have a chemist or bacteriologist. In fact, in regions where the difficulty from algæ is great, the microscopical examination must take precedence of everything else as a means of keeping the water palatable and satisfactory to the consumer.

In addition to the character of the organisms and the earliest possible determination of their appearance, it has already been pointed out that the chemical constitution, the temperature, and other special conditions of the water are factors in determining the line of treatment. No specific instructions are given in this bulletin for the amount of copper sulphate which is to be used for each species of algæ which is known to affect water supplies, because it is impossible to make a definite statement without a knowledge of the conditions already mentioned. *Each reservoir must be regarded as an individual case, requiring special knowledge and a particular prescription.* It is believed that the public water supplies of this country are worthy of such special care, and it would be a matter of regret if the method proposed here should ever be regarded as a universal panacea to be used by everyone, regardless of the organism to be eradicated and the condition of the water.

APPLICATION OF METHOD FOR DESTRUCTION OF PATHOGENIC BACTERIA NOT DESIGNED TO REPLACE EFFICIENT MEANS OF FILTRATION ALREADY IN USE.

The use of copper sulphate in clearing polluted reservoirs of pathogenic bacteria, such as typhoid and cholera, is regarded as incidental to the main purpose of the investigation. There already exists a most efficient means of preventing the appearance of these organisms in water supplies, and under no circumstances can it be considered that the method as described is expected to replace or supersede slow sand or any other efficient filtration. There are conditions, however, which sometimes make it desirable to thoroughly sterilize a reservoir, and under those circumstances the use of copper sulphate is believed to offer a new and adequate way of dealing with the difficulty. Experience has demonstrated the impossibility of compelling consumers of what may be an infected water to boil it, or observe other precautionary measures, and the absence of proper filtration plants in a very great number of cities and towns in this country makes it necessary that some efficient method for destroying disease germs in water be employed until the danger from pollution be past. Up to this time no satisfactory and yet harmless method has been known that would become effective in the course of a very few hours and the cost of which was in the reach of every community. It is believed that the results of the experiments upon typhoid and cholera germs described in this bulletin indicate that it will be possible under competent direction to employ copper sulphate with perfect safety in any municipal water reservoir which may have become infected with some nonspore-forming disease germ. Its application to barnyard tanks and pools as a preventive of hog cholera may also prove to be of value. Since the selective toxicity of this salt renders it fatal to pathogenic forms peculiar to water, while the common saprophytic or beneficial bacteria are unaffected, the method is particularly well adapted for this purpose.

MEDICINAL USE.

While it is not within the province of this bulletin to discuss or recommend any line of medical treatment, reference should be made to the fact that certain eminent practitioners, after reviewing the results here published, are of the opinion that the use of copper in cases of typhoid fever and related diseases should be more thoroughly investigated than it has been heretofore. It was the testimony of several that other intestinal troubles, more recently presumed to be due to the presence of certain disease germs in drinking water and milk, had responded most favorably to copper in one form or another.

CONDITIONS UNDER WHICH THE DEPARTMENT OF AGRICULTURE CAN FURNISH INFORMATION AND ASSISTANCE IN APPLYING THIS METHOD.

The problem of destroying or preventing the growth of algæ by the method devised in the laboratory of plant physiology in water reservoirs, lakes, ponds, water-cress beds, and wherever these plants have become a pest, is one which distinctly comes within the province of the Department of Agriculture. Definite instructions as to the treatment to be followed will at all times be furnished to the proper authorities who may desire assistance, and in so far as the limited facilities of the laboratory permit, determination will be made of the organisms causing the trouble. It is earnestly hoped that no tests of the method described here will be made without first consulting with the Department. Those most intimately connected with this work are constantly gaining information and experience, and this may prove of considerable value, besides a saving of expense, to those who have occasion to exterminate algal pests.

The treatment of water supplies for the destruction of pathogenic bacteria, or any application of the copper-sulphate method which has to do with public health, is not contemplated or indeed possible by this Department. The requests of private individuals or unauthorized bodies for information or assistance can not be granted. When State or local boards of health consider that the disinfection of a water supply is desirable and wish information upon the subject it will be supplied as fully and freely as possible. All experiments of this kind, however, must be conducted by the board of health, and the Department can serve only in the capacity of an adviser.

COST.

No definite estimate of the cost of the treatment of a reservoir can be given, because of the special conditions governing each case. It is evident, however, that the maximum cost of material for exterminating algæ can not exceed 50 to 60 cents per million gallons, and will often be less than half this amount. The cost for the copper-sulphate destruction of bacteria will be from $5 to $6 per million gallons, and where lime or some soluble hydrate is used in addition the cost would be increased about one-third. The cost of labor necessary to introduce these substances will be slight, since two men can usually treat from 10,000,000 to 20,000,000 gallons in less than three hours.

SUMMARY.

The importance of maintaining all public water supplies at the highest degree of purity and wholesomeness is too well recognized to require any discussion.

The disagreeable odors and tastes so often present in drinking water are due almost exclusively to algæ, although the economic importance of studying these plants has not been recognized until recent years.

These algal forms are widely distributed, and reservoirs in many States have been rendered unfit for use by their presence.

The methods now known for preventing or removing the odors and tastes caused by algæ have proved unsatisfactory, either because of prohibitive expense or failure to accomplish result.

It is therefore desirable that some new, cheap, harmless, and effective method be devised for ridding reservoirs of these pests.

It has been found that copper sulphate in a dilution so great as to be colorless, tasteless, and harmless to man, is sufficiently toxic to the algæ to destroy or prevent their appearance.

The mode of application makes this method applicable to reservoirs of all kinds, pleasure ponds and lakes, fish ponds, oyster beds, watercress beds, etc. It is also probable that the method can be used for the destruction of mosquito larvæ.

At ordinary temperatures 1 part of copper sulphate to 100,000 parts of water destroys typhoid and cholera germs in from three to four hours. The ease with which the sulphate can then be eliminated from the water seems to offer a practical method of sterilizing large bodies of water, when this becomes necessary.

The use of copper sulphate for the prevention of disease is regarded as incidental and is not designed in any way to supplant efficient preventive measures now in use. It is believed, however, that up to this time no such satisfactory means of thoroughly, rapidly, and cheaply sterilizing a reservoir has been known. Since the selective toxicity of copper sulphate renders it fatal to pathogenic forms peculiar to water, while the saprophytic or beneficial bacteria are unaffected, the method is particularly well adapted for this purpose.

Definite knowledge in regard to what organisms are present, the constitution of the water, its temperature, and other important facts are necessary before it is possible to determine the proper amount of copper sulphate to be added. A microscopical examination thus becomes as important as a bacteriological or chemical analysis.

No rule for determining the amount of copper sulphate to be added can be given. Each body of water must be treated in the light of its special conditions.

The cost of material for exterminating algæ will not exceed 50 to 60 cents per million gallons and will usually be less. The destruction of pathogenic bacteria requires an expenditure of from $5 to $8 per million gallons, not including the cost of labor.

()

U. S. DEPARTMENT OF AGRICULTURE.
BUREAU OF PLANT INDUSTRY—BULLETIN NO. 65.
B. T. GALLOWAY, Chief of Bureau.

RECLAMATION

OF

COD SAND DUNES.

BY

J. M. WESTGATE,
ASSISTANT IN SAND-BINDING WORK.

AND FORAGE PLANT INVESTIGATIONS.

ISSUED JUNE 30, 1904.

WASHINGTON:
GOVERNMENT PRINTING OFFICE.
1904.

BULLETINS OF THE BUREAU OF PLANT INDUSTRY.

The Bureau of Plant Industry, which was organized July 1, 1901, includes Vegetable Pathological and Physiological Investigations, Botanical Investigations and Experiments, Grass and Forage Plant Investigations, Pomological Investigations, and Experimental Gardens and Grounds, all of which were formerly separate Divisions, and also Seed and Plant Introduction and Distribution, the Arlington Experimental Farm, Tea Culture Investigations, and Domestic Sugar Investigations.

Beginning with the date of organization of the Bureau, the several series of bulletins of the various Divisions were discontinued, and all are now published as one series of the Bureau. A list of the bulletins issued in the present series follows.

Attention is directed to the fact that "the serial, scientific, and technical publications of the United States Department of Agriculture are not for general distribution. All copies not required for official use are by law turned over to the Superintendent of Documents, who is empowered to sell them at cost." All applications for such publications should, therefore, be made to the Superintendent of Documents, Government Printing Office, Washington, D. C.

No. 1. The Relation of Lime and Magnesia to Plant Growth. 1901. Price, 10 cents.
2. Spermatogenesis and Fecundation of Zamia. 1901. Price, 20 cents.
3. Macaroni Wheats. 1901. Price, 20 cents.
4. Range Improvement in Arizona. 1902. Price, 10 cents.
5. Seeds and Plants Imported. Inventory No. 9. 1902. Price, 10 cents.
6. A List of American Varieties of Peppers. 1902. Price, 10 cents.
7. The Algerian Durum Wheats. 1902. Price, 15 cents.
8. A Collection of Fungi Prepared for Distribution. 1902. Price, 10 cents.
9. The North American Species of Spartina. 1902. Price, 10 cents.
10. Records of Seed Distribution and Cooperative Experiments with Grasses and Forage Plants. 1902. Price, 10 cents.
11. Johnson Grass. 1902. Price, 10 cents.
12. Stock Ranges of Northwestern California: Notes on the Grasses and Forage Plants and Range Conditions. 1902. Price, 15 cents.
13. Experiments in Range Improvement in Central Texas. 1902. Price, 10 cents.
14. The Decay of Timber and Methods of Preventing It. 1902. Price, 55 cents.
15. Forage Conditions on the Northern Border of the Great Basin. 1902. Price, 15 cents.
16. A Preliminary Study of the Germination of the Spores of Agaricus Campestris and other Basidiomycetous Fungi. 1902. Price, 10 cents.
17. Some Diseases of the Cowpea. 1902. Price, 10 cents.
18. Observations on the Mosaic Disease of Tobacco. 1902. Price, 15 cents.
19. Kentucky Bluegrass Seed: Harvesting, Curing, and Cleaning. 1902. Price, 10 cents.
20. Manufacture of Semolina and Macaroni. 1902. Price, 15 cents.
21. List of American Varieties of Vegetables. 1903. Price, 35 cents.
22. Injurious Effects of Premature Pollination. 1902. Price, 10 cents.
23. Berseem; The Great Forage and Soiling Crop of the Nile Valley. 1902. Price, 15 cents.
24. Unfermented Grape Must. 1902. Price, 10 cents.

[Continued on page 3 of cover.]

Bul. 65, Bureau of Plant Industry, U S. Dept of Agriculture.

PLATE I.

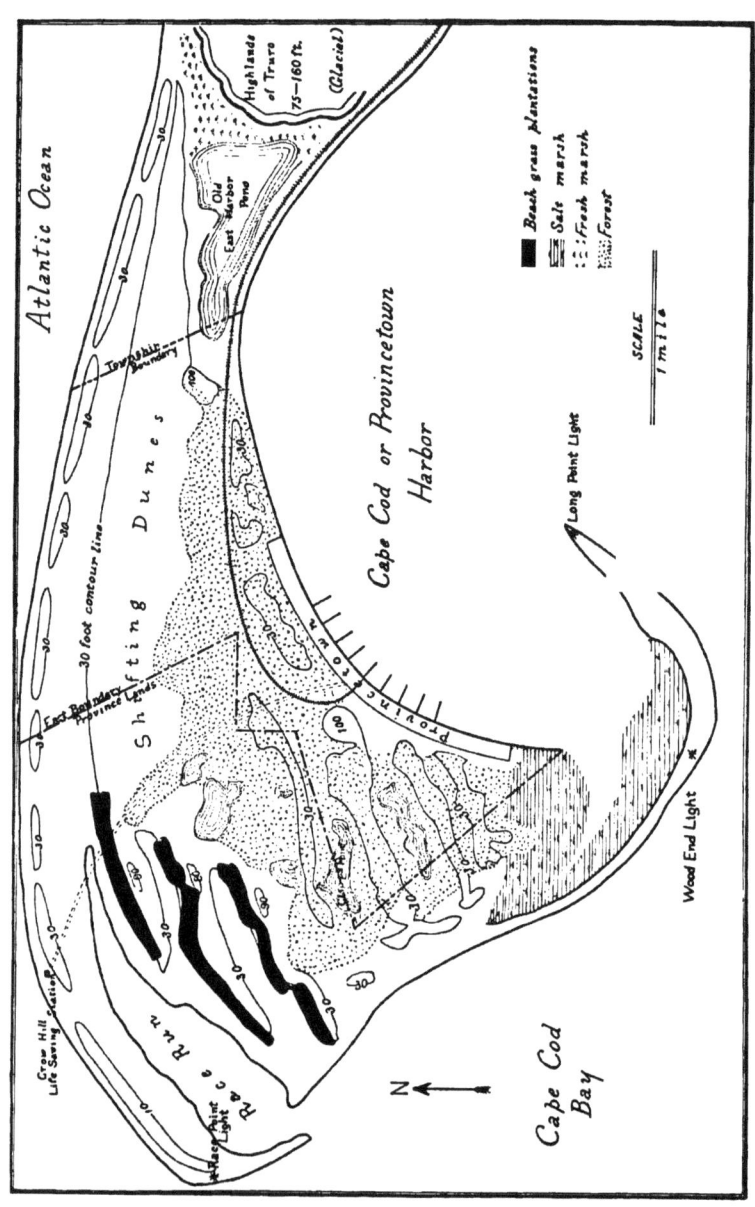

MAP OF THE SAND AREAS INCLOSING CAPE COD HARBOR.

U. S. DEPARTMENT OF AGRICULTURE.
BUREAU OF PLANT INDUSTRY—BULLETIN NO. 65.
B. T. GALLOWAY, *Chief of Bureau.*

RECLAMATION

OF

CAPE COD SAND DUNES.

BY

J. M. WESTGATE,
ASSISTANT IN SAND-BINDING WORK.

GRASS AND FORAGE PLANT INVESTIGATIONS.

ISSUED JUNE 30, 1904.

WASHINGTON:
GOVERNMENT PRINTING OFFICE.
1904.

BUREAU OF PLANT INDUSTRY.

BEVERLY T. GALLOWAY, *Chief.*
J. E. ROCKWELL, *Editor.*

GRASS AND FORAGE PLANT INVESTIGATIONS.

SCIENTIFIC STAFF.

W. J. SPILLMAN, *Agrostologist.*

A. S. HITCHCOCK, *Assistant Agrostologist, in Charge of Cooperative Experiments.*
C. V. PIPER, *Systematic Agrostologist, in Charge of Herbarium.*
C. R. BALL, *Assistant Agrostologist, in Charge of Work on Arlington Farm.*
DAVID GRIFFITHS, *Assistant Agrostologist, in Charge of Range Investigations.*
S. M. TRACY, *Special Agent, in Charge of Gulf Coast Investigations.*
P. L. RICKER, *Assistant in Herbarium.*
J. M. WESTGATE, *Assistant in Sand-Binding Work.*
BYRON HUNTER, *Assistant in Agrostology.*
MATT. A. CROSBY, *Assistant in Farm Management.*
R. A. OAKLEY, *Assistant in Agrostology.*
C. W. WARBURTON, *Assistant in Farm Management.*
AGNES CHASE, *Agrostological Artist.*

LETTER OF TRANSMITTAL.

U. S. DEPARTMENT OF AGRICULTURE,
BUREAU OF PLANT INDUSTRY,
OFFICE OF THE CHIEF,
Washington, D. C., May 10, 1904.

SIR: I have the honor to transmit herewith a paper on "Reclamation of Cape Cod Sand Dunes," and respectfully recommend that it be published as Bulletin No. 65 of the series of this Bureau.

This paper was prepared by Mr. J. M. Westgate, Assistant in Sand-Binding Work, Grass and Forage Plant Investigations, and has been submitted by the Agrostologist with a view to publication.

The six plates accompanying the paper are necessary to properly illustrate the text.

Respectfully,
B. T. GALLOWAY,
Chief of Bureau.

Hon. JAMES WILSON,
Secretary of Agriculture.

PREFACE.

The extensive areas of sand dunes which surround Cape Cod Harbor furnish the best example that this country affords of the extensive utilization of beach grass for the binding of shifting sand which would otherwise cause great damage by its encroachment on valuable property. The harbor and city alike are endangered by the shifting dunes which have been encroaching upon them since the original devastation of the forests which formerly held the sands in check.

For a century and a half beach grass has been utilized for sand-binding work upon the cape by the Commonwealth of Massachusetts and by the General Government for the purpose of protecting Cape Cod Harbor, but it was not until 1893 that the State of Massachusetts put in operation the present extensive system of reclamation, which has proved so successful. The Province lands, upon which these plantings have been made, are owned by the State, and the work itself is under the immediate supervision of Mr. James A. Small.

Since these operations are proving so successful and the methods developed there are applicable in a large measure to other similar areas in this country, Mr. J. M. Westgate, Assistant in Sand-Binding Work, was authorized to visit Cape Cod for the purpose of investigating the details of the work now in progress, and to determine, as far as possible, the causes which led to the devastation, and also the measures which have at various times been taken looking to the reclamation of the shifting dunes. The results of the investigation are presented in this bulletin.

Acknowledgments are due the authorities having the reclamation work in charge for the courtesy shown to Mr. Westgate in providing every means to facilitate his investigations.

W. J. SPILLMAN,
Agrostologist.

OFFICE OF THE AGROSTOLOGIST,
Washington, D. C., May 11, 1904.

CONTENTS.

	Page.
Introduction	9
Ecological relations of the vegetation	10
Ecological factors	10
Mode of deposition of the Cape sands	12
Development of the dune range	13
Natural reclamation	14
Areas receiving gradual accumulations of sand	15
Areas not receiving gradual accumulations of sand	16
Marshes and bogs	17
Early accounts	18
Devastation of the established dune areas	18
Early conditions incident to the devastation	19
Restrictive legislation	20
Artificial reclamation of the Cape sands	21
Early work of sand control	21
Recent work by the State	24
Preliminary operations	24
Attempts without beach grass	24
Utilization of beach grass	25
Relative merits of spring and fall planting	25
Selecting and transplanting the sets	26
Cost of planting	27
Present status of the various plantings	27
Effectiveness of brush laying	28
Efficiency of beach grass for sand binding	28
Necessity of ultimate forestation	30
Miscellaneous operations on the sand	31
Road construction	32
Reclamation of small areas	32
Commercial utilization of sand	33
Development of the protective beach ridge	34
The Province lands	34
State ownership	34
Value of the lands	35
Summary	35
Bibliography	36
Description of plates	38

ILLUSTRATIONS.

	Page.
Plate I. Map of sand areas inclosing Cape Cod Harbor .... Frontispiece.	
II. Fig. 1.—Beach grass forming protective beach ridge. Fig. 2.—Beach grass, showing method of vegetative propagation	38
III. Fig. 1.—Set of beach grass suitable for transplanting. Fig. 2.—Transplanting beach grass	38
IV. Fig. 1.—Sand dune burying forest. Fig. 2. Beach grass plantations. General view	38
V. Fig. 1.—Bayberry bushes without grass protection. Fig. 2.—Bayberry bushes with grass protection	38
VI. Fig. 1.—Wind erosion of nonprotected sand. Fig. 2.—Protecting a road through the dunes	38

RECLAMATION OF CAPE COD SAND DUNES.

INTRODUCTION.

The sand areas at the extremity of Cape Cod comprise approximately 6,000 acres, less than half of which is under the protection of forest covering. The city of Provincetown, with its extensive fishing and shipping interests, is built along a narrow strip of reclaimed land lying in the lee of the inner range of fixed dunes bordering the harbor. The peculiar shape and position of the city bring it into immediate peril should any destructive force be brought to bear upon the adjacent dune areas, or in case of the encroachment of the shifting dunes farther back but in line with the winter winds, which are by far the most efficient in sand movement. The harbor around a portion of which the city is built is even more endangered, as it is surrounded by the sand accumulations which have been washed around the head of the Cape, and the entire border on three sides is threatened with the possibilities of sand encroachment. Many houses now stand where a century ago small boats found convenient anchorage. In fact, certain areas have been filled in several hundred feet during the last half century. The value of the harbor thus endangered can hardly be overestimated. It is the home port of a large fleet of fishing vessels, while as a harbor of refuge its position, capacity, depth, excellent anchorage, and land-locked condition combine to render it one of the most important on the Atlantic coast. As many as 1,000 vessels are said to have been counted at one time in the harbor during the heavy gales which occasionally occur along the coast. The entire portion originally known as "East Harbor" has been rendered worthless by the encroaching sands, a fresh-water marsh marking its original site. Not only is the harbor of great commercial value, but in event of war its position is such as to render it of great strategic importance. During the civil war a portion of the extreme end of the Cape was ceded to the Government. Batteries were established and war vessels were at times stationed in the harbor.

The greater portion of the sand areas inclosing the harbor is owned by the State and designated "Province lands" (Pl. I). This enables the authorities to exercise a more effective surveillance than would be possible were the areas under private ownership.

The problem of controlling the drifting sands of the Cape has concerned the municipal, State, and National authorities for two hundred years, and the extensive planting of beach grass as a means of protection dates back for more than a century.

The physiographic and botanical phases of the subject presented are based upon the writer's personal observations and collections. The bibliography indicates the source of the historical features. Many of the details were derived from an examination of the statutes and town records, together with what could be deduced from local testimony and personal observation. The details of the early work of dune control were obtained from the records on file in the War Department, all the work of harbor protection on the part of the General Government having been under the supervision of that Department.

ECOLOGICAL RELATIONS OF THE VEGETATION.

ECOLOGICAL FACTORS.

The ecological factors which are of the most importance in the consideration of the sand-dune areas are light and heat, wind, soil, and moisture. The low specific heat of the sand causes it to respond very quickly to any change of temperature in the surrounding medium. The sand becomes excessively hot on the side of the dune exposed to the direct rays of the sun and for the same reason the cooling process at night is quite as marked. The extremes of temperature incident to this condition are severe upon any form of vegetation and probably constitute the chief reason for the absence of many species which might otherwise be present. The oceanic location of the area tends to produce an equable climate. The thermometer rarely registers temperatures below 2° F. in winter or above 85° F. in summer, except immediately upon the bare sand areas, where the conditions are much less equable.

The wind is an important factor for several reasons. Its effect upon transpiration, especially when augmented by the high temperatures incident to the heated layers of air at the surface of the sand, is very marked. The distortions of the trees so often noticeable along the coast are not present, as the rejuvenescence of extensive forested dunes has destroyed the woody vegetation to beyond the limits of the injurious effect of the unbroken salt-laden winds. The bombardment by the sand which the wind hurls against the vegetation is especially severe. The presence of sand as large as wheat grains (one-eighth to one-sixth inch in diameter) in great quantities on the dunes testifies to the force of the winter gales which swept it there from the beach below. The force of this bombardment may be realized when walking across a dune area during a strong wind or by examining the effect of the sand blast upon the windward side of the exposed vegetation.

The action of the wind in shifting the sand and thereby either uprooting or burying the vegetation is one of the most obvious points to be noted in a shifting dune area. The heavy winter winds, usually from the northeast or northwest, are the most effective in shifting the sand and in preventing the existence of vegetation. A much more meager vegetative covering is present on the northern than on the southern slopes of the partially established dunes.

The isolated location of the area is such as to subject it to the unbroken force of the winds. The average hourly velocity of the wind for Nantucket, where records are accessible, is 11.7 miles per hour. Gale velocities of from 50 to 60 miles per hour are not infrequent, while velocities as high as 72 miles per hour have been recorded.

The soil of the entire area is largely reassorted glacial sand, at least 95 per cent of which is light-colored quartz. The other constituents are principally magnetite, limonite, feldspar, schist, and garnet. The vigorous growth of the vegetation in the protected locations indicates that the sand is not as deficient in food salts as is sometimes supposed. The large size and angularity of the grains constitute the characteristic features of the Cape sands. It is noticeable that on the bare wind-swept slopes the dune sand has been swept away, leaving the coarser grains, which remain and act as a protective blanket, thus reducing the movement of the underlying sand by the wind.

The following table indicates the size of the two kinds of sand. No. 1 was taken from the surface of the windward slope of one of the dunes. No. 2 was taken from 8 inches beneath the surface of a typical dune and fairly represents the bulk of the Cape sands.

Diameter.	Sample No. 1.	Sample No. 2.
	Per cent.	*Per cent.*
6-2 mm	64.6	00.0
2-1 mm	27.9	16.8
1-0.5 mm	7.5	77.0
0.5-0.25 mm	0.0	5.2
0.25-0.05 mm	0.0	1.0

The moisture relations of the dune vegetation are unique. Though the upper layers of sand are usually hot and dry during the growing period except when rain is actually falling, the moisture comes to within a few inches of the surface, even during periods of protracted drought. The effect of a heavy rain is not noticeably different from that of a very light one, as in either case a few hours of sunshine suffice to remove all visible traces of the precipitation, most of which percolates at once to the lower layers of sand. For this reason the number of rainy days, which averages 96, is of greater moment than the actual annual precipitation of 43 inches, which is sufficient under proper soil conditions to produce a luxuriant vegetation. The snows which might afford considerable protection to the vegetation of the sand stretches are blown off and lodged in the lee of the dunes or within areas covered with vegetation. The humidity incident to the oceanic location of the Cape acts in favor of the existing vegetation. The average annual rainfall is 42.58 inches. The accompanying table indicates the normal monthly precipitation as compiled from the normals for neighboring stations.

	Inches.		Inches.
January	3.90	July	2.89
February	3.39	August	3.62
March	3.98	September	2.91
April	3.41	October	4.00
May	3.62	November	4.38
June	2.74	December	3.74

The factor of associated vegetation or the interrelations of individuals and species is of little importance in areas of shifting sands. The conditions do not admit of a closed formation, that is, where the vegetation completely covers the ground, and it is only when this does finally obtain that the factor assumes an important rôle in the plant society.

Mode of Deposition of the Cape Sands.

The arm of the Cape extending around Cape Cod Bay consists of glacial deposits, with the exception of about 10 square miles which is composed entirely of post-Glacial sand which has subsequently washed around the head of the Cape from the south, inclosing the harbor within a sickle-shaped sand hook.

The addition of sand to the extremity of the Cape apparently takes place in the form of successive bars, which are built up off the north shore and added to the Cape by deposition in the neck of the channels lying to the east and south, forming successive "race runs" (Pl. I), which are gradually filled in by tide and wind deposits. The sand cast up by the waves on one of these new beaches is dried and blown inland, forming a beach ridge or foredune and eventually a dune range, which, protected by the succeeding deposits, ultimately becomes covered by the forest and associated vegetation.

The above hypothesis is supported by the following observed facts: (1) Four old dune ranges now forested but badly distorted by the long-continued action of the wind; (2) three dune ranges held only by beach grass and lying north of the first-mentioned ranges, parallel with them and also with the north shore of the Cape; (3) a race run (now nearly filled in) with its flanking beach ridge fast becoming a conspicuous foredune (Pl. I and Pl. II, fig. 1); (4) a bar in present process of formation offshore and to northward of the present shore line but parallel with it; (5) the seven dune ranges indicated constitute the main body of the extremity of the Cape; (6) the presence of shingle or coarse beach deposits underlying the dunes in places, and on the same level with the present beach.

If this be the method of deposition it follows that the necessity for sand fixation will never cease unless the sand supply for the shore drift becomes exhausted. However, the process of sand accumulation is so comparatively slow as to be of little importance when compared with the more serious conditions incident to the extensive areas of only partially reclaimed sand dunes.

Development of the Dune Range.

It is probable that each of the seven dune ranges which constitute the greater portion of the extremity of the Cape was developed in a similar manner, from the successive beach ridges and ensuing foredunes, by the accumulation of the sands blown up from the beaches. The vegetation has been an important factor in their formation, and although the intermediate stages between the foredune and the forested dune range are fragmentary the general sequence of events is evident.

As soon as the sand deposited by the waves is blown up to beyond the action of the tides the beach grass, associated with the typical strand vegetation, spreads rapidly over the surface and retards the movement of the resulting beach ridge. As the sand accumulations continue, the ridge becomes a foredune. The beach grass pushes its way up through the accumulating sand by the formation of new rootstocks, thus keeping the ever-increasing area of sand comparatively well covered, as the gradual addition of sand constitutes one of the essential conditions for the ideal growth of the grass (Pl. II, fig. 1). The foredune continues to rise and other species of plants come in, but ultimately a height is reached where the unbroken winds are of sufficient force to prevent the vegetation from holding the sand. At this stage the long foredune becomes a dune range and begins to move inland, covering the preexistent vegetation in its path (Pl. IV, fig. 1). The movement continues until the dune range is sufficiently removed from the unbroken force of the ocean winds to permit the development of a vegetative covering dense enough to prevent its movement. The forested condition ultimately dominates.

The development of the succeeding beach ridge and foredune may have been rapid enough to afford some protection to the preceding dune range, and thus hasten its fixation by the vegetation which would develop more rapidly under the protection afforded by the new foredune.

This beach ridge is of two possible origins. It may be formed from the normal sand accumulations cast up by the waves along the old beach, after the dune range migrates inland, or it may develop from the sand spit or bar which is added to the mainland as first indicated.

In either case it exerts the same protective influence on the inland vegetation. It may or may not remain stationary long enough for the forest in the lee to reach its farthest possible extension seaward before its rejuvenescence causes it to begin its migration inland.

The movement inland on the part of the newly formed dune range was probably never extensive, as there is little evidence of its having encroached upon the preceding range. However, the contour of each indicates that it was shifting to some extent before its fixation. It is quite probable that the ranges were never entirely bare, as the new accumulations of sand were not so rapid as to prevent the existence of a partial vegetative covering upon the dune range.

The devastating activities within historic times have destroyed any intermediate stages which may have existed between the foredune at present in process of formation on the north shore and the forested dune ranges which lie inland from the three dune ranges which have been devastated by human agencies. It is probable that the forest was never able to develop as far as the beach, owing to the exposure to the severe north winds. However, old forest beds outcropping in places among the unforested dunes demonstrate that the forest originally extended much farther seaward than it does at the present time.

Of the seven dune ranges constituting the body of the extremity of the Cape, only the inner four are at present forested. These are badly distorted, but were probably formed as has just been indicated, as the irregularities are not greater than could be reasonably postulated when the action of the wind during the interval of time which has elapsed since their formation is considered (Pl. I). These ranges are covered with a growth of pine and oak, with an occasional beech in the more favored situations. The outer three ranges are covered with scattering growths of beach grass. The depressions between the ranges are characterized by wild or partially reclaimed cranberry bogs and the associated vegetation. It is probable that all these ranges, with the possible exception of the outer one, were at one time forested, but have been brought to their present unstable condition within historic times.

Natural Reclamation.

The natural reclamation of sand areas may be observed in the study of the series of dunes in the various stages of fixation or establishment by the native vegetation. The forest which ultimately obtains is unable to develop directly upon the bare sand areas. There are certain definite stages that must be passed through before the mesophytic conditions incident to the forest are attained. The vegetation of each stage requires more favorable conditions than did that of its predecessor and at the same time is making the conditions possible for the existence of the vegetation which characterizes the succeeding stage. Even when the forest condition is reached the cycle is not complete, for the presence of the ultimate climax forest species is possible only after the continued existence of other species of trees has gradually rendered the soil, moisture, and protection sufficiently favorable for the development of the climax type. The ultimate forested condition is the same whether the original area be a salt marsh or a shifting dune, and the sand areas under consideration show several types of reclamation which differ in the initial stages.

AREAS RECEIVING GRADUAL ACCUMULATIONS OF SAND.

These areas are confined principally to the depositing beaches and are of less relative importance at the present time than formerly. The strand plants form a zone just above the action of the tides. The sea rocket (*Cakile edentula*), beach pea (*Lathyrus maritimus*), and cocklebur (*Xanthium echinatum*) may be mentioned as typical species. These strand plants are effective in retarding the sand which is blown inland from the beach. They also act as pioneers to the succeeding vegetation which dominates when the original area has become built up sufficiently far beyond the action of the tides to permit the development of another strand or beach formation below the one just indicated. Beach grass (*Ammophila arenaria*) is the dominant species, and extends itself to well within the limit of the wave action during the winter storms (Pl. II, figs. 1 and 2). This is associated with seaside golden-rod (*Solidago sempervirens*) and sand wormwood (*Artemisia caudata*).

The bayberry (*Myrica carolinensis*), wild rose (*Rosa lucida?*), and beach plum (*Prunus maritima*) may be taken as typical of the shrub vegetation which encroaches upon these areas from the wooded stretches lying inland. These, by their presence, increase the humus content of the soil and furnish the necessary protection for the development of the seedlings of the pitch pine (*Pinus rigida*) which soon extend themselves over the partially reclaimed areas. Later the oaks (*Quercus rubra* and *Q. velutina*) become associated with the pine, and in especially favored situations the beech (*Fagus americana*) ultimately dominates. The few areas which have reached this last stage present a somewhat unusual condition. As the beech represents the extreme mesophytic type of forest growth in the northeastern United States and normally grows only in the presence of the most favorable edaphic conditions of soil, moisture, and exposure, the development of the beech formation upon the sand dune is of rare occurrence. The great bulk of the present forest covering consists of the pine and oak, although the white birch (*Betula populifera*), white oak (*Quercus alba*), and red maple (*Acer rubrum*) are to be observed in the lower areas.

The undergrowth within the timbered area consists largely of ink berry (*Ilex glabra*) and huckleberry (*Gaylussacia resinosa*). The wintergreen or checkerberry (*Gaultheria procumbens*) forms an extensive substratum below the two species just mentioned, while the hog cranberry or bearberry (*Arctostaphylos uva-ursi*) forms extensive mats where the undergrowth of shrubs is more open. The two grasses, *Agrostis hyemalis* and *Danthonia spicata*, are abundant, forming scattered clumps throughout the open woodlands. Less important but characteristic species of shrubs and vines occurring in the forests are green brier (*Smilax rotundifolia*), bayberry (*Myrica carolinensis*), service berry (*Amelanchier botryapium*), Virginia creeper (*Parthenocissus quinquefolia*), dwarf blueberry (*Vaccinium pennsylvanicum*), and coast arrowwood (*Viburnum venosum*). Several species of wild rose are to be noted in the more open places in the forest and along its borders.

AREAS NOT RECEIVING GRADUAL ACCUMULATIONS OF SAND.

If, instead of receiving the gradual accumulations of sand, an area is subjected to the eroding action of the wind or at least fails to receive additions of sand, the early stages are quite different from those which characterize the areas just mentioned. The reclamation process at first is very slow, for the heavy winds frequently destroy the work of a whole season and the reduced vigor of the plants incident to the conditions renders the process of humus accumulation extremely slow. The beach grass as before is the pioneer and continues to occupy the area for some time, although not showing a thrifty growth. The poverty grass (*Hudsonia tomentosa*) formation gradually develops and often nearly covers the ground with its procumbent herbaceous stems. This condition continues for some time before there is sufficient humus accumulation for the next members of the cycle. At this stage the bearberry or hog cranberry (*Arctostaphylos uva-ursi*) appears and extends its mat-like evergreen growth over large areas. This is associated with such species as *Polygonella articulata* and *Corema conradii*. These are followed by the bayberry and the beach plum. The ensuing development is substantially that cited for the areas receiving gradual accumulations of sand, as when the formation becomes closed in the two instances there is no further opportunity for either the addition or removal of sand, and hence the initial differences no longer obtain.

As indicated above, the succession of stages from the accumulating beach to the forest was probably the one which characterized the development of the vegetation upon the original sand areas of the Cape. As the deposition of the sand was comparatively slow the vegetation was able to keep pace with the increments, thus preventing the existence of any extensive sand wastes. The devastating influences which have been brought to bear upon the forested dune areas within historic times have resulted in the extensive areas of loosely bound sands which, with the exception of the brows of the shifting dunes, are for the most part subject to wind erosion. This renders the latter system of natural reclamation most important at the present time. It may be doubted if this system of natural reclamation would be able to reforest the extensive wastes of sand were it not for the artificial reclamation processes which have recently been inaugurated.

MARSHES AND BOGS.

The accumulation of sand incident to the formation of the sand hooks or spits has caused considerable areas of salt marshes to be developed (Pl. I). The shifting sands have prevented the establishment of any natural drainage system, and as a result there are extensive areas of ponds and marshes between the dune ranges. These two processes have been the cause of the existence of extensive marsh and bog lands throughout the area. The sand hook which exists at the extreme point of the Cape inclosing the harbor is bordered by an extensive salt marsh. The typical marginal species is saltwort (*Salicornia ambigua*). The characteristic grasses of the salt marsh are the salt reed grass (*Spartina polystachya*) and the salt meadow grass (*Spartina patens*). These grasses constitute the bulk of the salt-marsh hay cut for the local market.

The salt marsh at the head of the old race run at the northwest corner of the sand areas is being gradually filled in by tide and wind deposits. The Salicornia-Juncus-Scirpus formation gives way to extensive areas of cranberry (*Oxycoccus macrocarpus*).

Clapps Pond, one of the fresh-water ponds and marshes lying between the dune ranges, presents over a considerable portion of its surface a sphagnum bog society. Among the characteristic species may be mentioned *Sphagnum acutifolium* (?), pitcher plant (*Sarracenia purpurea*), *Kalmia angustifolia*, and *Xolisma ligustrina*. The margins of the bog are shallow and are rapidly giving way to the encroaching forest. Young pitch pines were noted as extending for a considerable distance into the margin of the bog.

In the low, moist areas between the nonforested dune ranges the cranberry is dominant, occupying large areas to the exclusion of other species. These areas are surrounded by a scattered growth of *Cyperus grayi* and *Carex silicea*. The condition indicated is not permanent, for if undisturbed the woody growth eventually dominates to the exclusion of the above-named species and the forest condition ultimately develops. The improvement and utilization of the cranberry bogs often necessitate the removal of large numbers of bushes which are present as forerunners of the forest. The order of the succession of the woody plants is practically the same as that given for the other classes of sand areas, except that the beach plum is not conspicuous. It is these low areas that constitute the nuclei of the forests, as it is here that they first develop and then gradually extend to the higher areas. This fact, as will be mentioned under the development of cranberry bogs, constitutes the chief reason for the State's objection to the utilization of these areas for this purpose, as it retards the natural development of the forested condition desired by those who have the preservation of the harbor in mind.

While it is not probable that all of these low areas will ever become entirely forested, yet it is evident that this is the stage to which the low areas, as well as the dunes, are slowly trending. The recent reclamation processes will hasten this condition as the encroachment of the dunes has been checked.

EARLY ACCOUNTS.

The early accounts of the New England coast, dating back to the earliest French and English explorers, and possibly even to the Norsemen, essentially agree in their descriptions of the general outlines and forested condition of the Cape. The wooded area appears to have been much more extensive at those dates than at present, although there has always been, at least within historic times, more or less shifting sand exposed to the action of the winds. Champlain in one of his voyages described the Cape and named it Cape Blanc on account of the white color of its sand areas.

The old forest beds, now for the most part covered with sand, but outcropping in places, demonstrate that the wooded areas, at least three times, extended much farther toward the north side of the Cape than they do at present. The tree stumps visible at low tide near Wood End light-house substantiate the local tradition that the forest extended well out on to the extreme point of the Cape a century and a half ago. It is safe to say that at least three-fourths of the non-forested sand areas of to-day were well covered with trees within historic times. However, the devastation is not so marked as it was three-quarters of a century ago, at which time extensive reclamation processes were inaugurated.

DEVASTATION OF THE ESTABLISHED DUNE AREAS.

The principal causes of the rejuvenescence of the sand areas and the incident encroachment upon the forest were the pasturing of stock and the partial destruction of the forest covering. The early statutes show many instances where these practices were forbidden under heavy penalties. Much of the injury has been due to fires, as is

DEVASTATION OF DUNE AREAS.

evidenced by the charred stumps and charcoal beds which outcrop in places among the devastated dune areas.

The forests close to the harbor were naturally assailed at an early date by the inhabitants and shipmasters, who found the timber a convenient source of certain necessary supplies. The salt factories, which originally constituted an important industry on the Cape, used wood for fuel for evaporation purposes until the beginning of the last century when the more economical method of sun evaporation was introduced. This caused the destruction of large quantities of timber, as did also the extensive production of pitch and turpentine, and the use of the wood on the part of the inhabitants for fuel, fish flakes, ship repairs, and other purposes.

The pasturing of cattle upon the scattered clumps of *Agrostis hyemalis* and *Danthonia spicata* in the more open places in the forested area and upon the beach grass on the outer dune ranges appears to have been a very potent cause of much of the rejuvenescence.

The more recent devastating influences have been much less important. It is still the custom to cut certain areas of beach grass for hay. Until recently it was the practice to cure much of the marsh hay on the adjacent beach ridge which has been artificially built up by the Government as a harbor protection. This process resulted in the killing out of much of the beach grass by smothering it in event of rain, owing to the consequent nonremoval of the marsh hay. The removal of sods for reclamation work within the city limits has caused some concern to the authorities, as has also the utilization of the low areas for the production of cranberries, but, even in the aggregate, these activities are relatively unimportant when compared with the early devastation of the established dune areas.

EARLY CONDITIONS INCIDENT TO THE DEVASTATION.

The conditions incident to the devastation of the forested areas appear to have been most severe about a century ago. Many of the houses were constructed on piles to allow the sand to sweep under rather than to accumulate and bury them. Large amounts of sand were artificially removed to prevent the burial of the houses. The sand blast was so severe at times as to completely etch the glass in the windows in a comparatively short space of time. At that time the road led along the beach at low tide and at high tide the travel was through the heavy sands farther up on the beach. The streets were of the same loose sand that everywhere abounded, and it is stated that it was not until the last century that a plank walk was constructed along one side of the principal street of the town.

The committee which was appointed in 1825 to investigate the conditions at Provincetown reported that the trees and beach grass had been cut down and destroyed on the seaward side of the Cape, allowing the sand to become loosened and driven in great quantities toward the harbor. The report also states that—

The space where a few years since existed some of the highest lands of the cape, covered with trees and bushes, now presents an extensive waste of undulating sand.

The filling up and consequent destruction of that part of the harbor known as East Harbor was the work of the drifting sands to the northward, a fresh-water marsh now marking its original site. As an instance of the effects of the rejuvenated sand areas it may be stated that several once valuable farms situated along Stouts Creek, near Truro, have been covered with sand and to-day there is no trace of even the creek to indicate the location of the original properties.

RESTRICTIVE LEGISLATION.

The devastated sand areas at the extremity of the Cape have been the object of State and local concern since the earliest days of its settlement. Accounts state that as early as 1703 local public measures were taken to prohibit the destruction of timber on the "East Harbor lands."[a] In 1714 the devastation incident to the boxing and barking of pine trees for the production of pitch and turpentine had become so extensive upon the sand areas at the extremity of the Cape as to be at that date prohibited by State statute.

It was originally the practice on the part of the inhabitants farther south along the Cape to allow a considerable number of cattle to range over the northern extremity. As the grass growing in the timbered areas was limited, the stock was forced to subsist to some extent upon the beach grass, which then as now covered considerable areas of the Cape sands. An act was passed in 1740 prohibiting this practice and providing for the impounding of the stock found at large upon the lands. In 1745 the destruction of timber within half a mile of the shore was prohibited under penalty. These acts, however, were not as effective as their framers had hoped and were reenforced at intervals.

In 1825 the devastation had become so extensive that commissioners were appointed by the State to investigate the conditions. Their suggestions resulted in an act to prevent the unrestricted pasturage of stock and the destruction of beach grass and woody growth either by pulling or cutting. The enforcement of this measure, together with the reclamation processes inaugurated at this time, materially reduced the devastation which at this period was probably the worst in the history of the Cape.

In 1838 Provincetown was required to elect annually a committee of three persons: (1) To enforce the existing laws regulating the Province lands; (2) to grant permits for the use of portions of these lands by

---

[a] Massachusetts House Doc. 339, p. 49.

various inhabitants of the town when such use was not detrimental to the safety of the harbor or the town; (3) to enter any of the Province lands, inclosed or uninclosed, for the purpose of setting out trees or beach grass. The cost of the planting was to be defrayed by the occupant of the lands if the necessity for planting resulted from his actions; otherwise the town was authorized to provide for the expenses incident to the planting operations. This was known as the "beach grass committee," and it continued in existence until 1893, when the reclamation work by the State required the appointment of a superintendent on full time.

In 1854 an act, reenforced in 1869, was passed, appointing an agent to prosecute for the penalties prescribed for the destruction of the vegetation. He was authorized to issue permits for pasturage and the removal of sod and brush where the same would work no injury to the harbor or other property. The beach grass committee was continued with the indicated curtailment of its duties. This act became practically noneffective. With the extensive population so close to the public forests and only one person to defend them, it is not surprising that the removal of timber and sod should have proceeded almost without interruption. In 1891 the agent was paid for only five days' services and he issued but four permits. No attempt was made to prosecute parties for the removal of sod without a permit. This constitutes only another instance of the difficulty of enforcing a law in the face of opposing public sentiment.

In 1893 the inhabitants of Provincetown were ceded the lands lying within and adjacent to the city limits, the State retaining possession of what to-day constitutes the Province lands (Pl. I). A superintendent of the Province lands was appointed to look after the interests of the State and to take charge of the reclamation processes at that time inaugurated.

ARTIFICIAL RECLAMATION OF THE CAPE SANDS.

Early Work of Sand Control.

Although at as early a date as the beginning of the eighteenth century there was considerable local concern for the devastation of the sand dune areas, there does not appear to have been much work, other than legislative, actually performed until after the middle of the same century. It was at this time, when the sea broke through to the cove inlet in the arm of the Cape at East Harbor and threatened to destroy the entire Cape Cod Harbor, that the extensive planting of beach grass was commenced. This grass, used in connection with brush fences, repaired the break, and in the course of a few years caused extensive accumulations of sand. It appears to have been the practice upon the part of the inhabitants of Truro to devote a specified time each year to the planting of beach grass. The aggregate effect of this regular and combined effort was quite marked, although it is always difficult to estimate the results of measures more or less protective in nature. In 1826, as a result of the report of the commission appointed by the State the preceding year to investigate the devastation of the lands surrounding the harbor, the General Government inaugurated an extensive and systematic attempt at the reclamation of the exposed sand areas by the planting of beach grass.

The operations required appropriations extending over a period of twenty-eight years and aggregating the sum of $36,350. Of this amount it is reported that $29,889.06 was spent in planting 1,403 acres of the barren sand areas with beach grass. It was soon found that it was best to first plant the areas lying farthest to the windward, as these constituted the source of the sand and the spreading of the grass by seed over the unplanted areas would be facilitated. The actual planting operations were commenced in 1830, and the bulk of the plantings was made between this date and 1839. The grass was brought from Truro in boats and planted at intervals of from two to three feet, depending upon the exposure to the winds. Most of the grass was set with the aid of a shovel, two men working together, although in the low places a pike provided with a crossbar 15 inches from the point proved an excellent tool, as deeper planting was possible and but one man was necessary. This method was found to be impracticable in dry sand, as the small holes filled with sand before the sets could be inserted. Mr. Asa S. Bowly was the superintendent during the greater portion of the time. Spring planting was the rule, and about two hundred acres were planted each season, requiring a force of fifty laborers.

In 1852 the planting was resumed, this time for the purpose of strengthening the narrow arm of the Cape separating East Harbor from the ocean. At this time there was an abundance of grass within the old plantations available for transplanting, although the grass on certain areas had been buried, while in others it had been uprooted by the wind. As a rule the grass on the higher elevations had suffered the most and it was thought best to confine the plantings to the lower areas. The spreading of the grass was facilitated by prohibiting the pasturing of cattle upon the Province lands.

The General Government has spent to June 30, 1903, the sum of $162,019.86 for the protection of the harbor. Aside from the amount expended for grass planting, this has been used for dikes, bulkheads, and groin fences to catch and hold the sand in place. It has always been the practice to plant beach grass for the purpose of accumulating sand along the dikes and bulkheads, thus increasing the protection afforded by them.

The work of the State was principally confined to legislative acts until the recent work was begun in 1893. It should be stated, however, that in 1868 the sum of $131,770.14 was expended in the construction of a dike across East Harbor for the purpose of protecting the remaining portion of the harbor from the large quantities of sand which were carried out by each ebb tide. This dike greatly facilitates the travel southward from Provincetown and is utilized by the railway and State road. The city of Provincetown was authorized to levy taxes to cover the expenses incurred by its beach-grass committee, but an examination of the general records failed to reveal any considerable expenditures by the committee, which was nominally continued until 1893. The regular annual work on the part of the inhabitants of Truro in the planting of beach grass was probably a potent factor in reducing the evil effects of the shifting sand. The independent work on the part of private citizens was on a very small scale. In one instance a number of cranberry growers combined efforts for the purpose of planting beach grass to protect their bogs from the encroaching sand.

There are not sufficient data at hand to render possible a just opinion concerning the effectiveness of the early work of sand reclamation. The devastation is much less than when reclamation processes were commenced, but it is difficult to state to what extent the natural reclamation processes, unassisted save possibly by the restraining but poorly enforced statutes, are to be credited with the change in the conditions.

The grass plantations along the bulkheads, designed to accumulate sand for the protection of the harbor from the sea, have, without apparent exception, been successful. The plan.ings to restore the breach caused by the sea breaking over into East Harbor resulted in perhaps the greatest single success of any of the earlier operations. The fact that two-thirds of the nonforested areas were covered with beach grass by the end of the last century indicates that the early plantings were probably more lasting in their effect than has been supposed (Pl. IV, fig. 2).

One criticism made is to the effect that the planting was too much confined to the high hills, where it was without protection and as a result the grass was uprooted and destroyed. The statement concerning uprooting indicates that possibly the plantings were too thin, as the plantations recently made on the same exposed places have as yet shown little tendency to be blown out. Perhaps the most just criticism that can be made of the plan of operation is that the woody plants were not introduced within the grass plantations. The life of the beach grass on the areas not receiving regular accumulations of sand seldom exceeds ten years, a period of time which, however, suffices for the establishment of a self-protecting plantation of bushes and tree seedlings which require but little subsequent attention to render the reclamation permanent.

RECENT WORK BY THE STATE.

PRELIMINARY OPERATIONS.

The artificial reclamation which had been prosecuted with more or less vigor during the first half of the last century apparently received but little attention until 1892, when the trustees of the public reservations were authorized to submit all available information concerning the status of the sand encroachments and control, together with a comprehensive plan for the reclamation of the nonforested sand areas that threatened the harbor. The committee made a careful personal examination of the land and presented, with their general report, a stenographic transcript of the proceedings of a mass meeting of the representative citizens of Provincetown and Truro, who presented such information and suggestions as they were able to give concerning the historic features of the sand areas and the most practical steps to be taken for their reclamation. As a result of the trustees' report the Province lands were placed in charge of a permanently employed superintendent, Mr. James A. Small.

The State at this time relinquished its right to the lands within and immediately adjoining the city of Provincetown, leaving but 3,290 acres under State title. Of this area approximately 2,000 acres were nonforested.

Correspondence with various authorities revealed the fact that the initial operations would have to be more or less experimental, owing to the lack of data concerning the previous reclamation operations upon similar areas. Even the available details of the extensive grass plantations made upon the same areas in the early part of the century were purely matters of local tradition.

There was expended during the ten years ending January 1, 1904, the sum of $31,929.78 for the reclamation of these lands. The following itemized statement has been furnished by the authorities:

Beach grass planting	$10,950.00
Introduction of woody growth	6,011.78
Construction and maintenance of roads	6,250.00
Superintendence	6,000.00
Incidental expenses, including survey	2,718.00
Total	31,929.78

ATTEMPTS WITHOUT BEACH GRASS.

The three great dune ranges which lie between the timbered area and the north shore of the Cape were entirely bare upon their northern slopes, and were encroaching at the rate of 15 feet per year upon the forest and toward the city and harbor from a quarter of a mile to a mile distant (Pl. IV, fig. 1). The less exposed areas were partially covered with beach grass, while the lower places were dominated by native cranberry bogs, surrounded by the characteristic low-growing vegetation. As the bare northern slopes of the dune ranges constituted the source of the sand supply, the initial attempts involved the covering of these areas with vegetation.

Extensive plantings of shrubs and tree seedlings were made upon the outer range of dunes. The result was that the heavy winter gales of the first season buried, uprooted, or killed by the sand blast so great a portion of these plantings that some other method of procedure was considered necessary. The next season the transplanting of beach grass was commenced, as the experience of the preceding season had demonstrated that some protection for the woody plants is necessary until they have made sufficient growth to be self-protecting (Pl. V, figs. 1 and 2). The beach grass was selected for this purpose as it occurs very abundantly in places immediately adjacent to the areas which required planting and had been extensively utilized in the early reclamation attempts.

UTILIZATION OF BEACH GRASS.

Grass planting operations on each range commenced on the west end and were extended eastward with more or less regularity. The following table shows the salient points concerning the various plantings, which aggregate 219 acres. The mortality percentages were calculated from a number of counts in several representative areas within each season's planting. The mortality appears to have been less among the fall plantings.

Year.	Acreage planted.		Mortality of plantings, per cent.	
	Spring.	Fall.	Spring.	Fall.
1895	11	2	50	31
1896	12	4	61	38
1897	20	22	40	35
1898	3	17	22	11
1899	13	22	6	2
1900	4.5	15.5	4	2
1901	4	21	3	2
1902	1	20	1	1
1903	2	25	0	0
Total	70.5	148.5		

RELATIVE MERITS OF SPRING AND FALL PLANTING.

The early plantings on the Province lands and the Cape generally were as a rule made in the spring, although many parties practiced fall planting. The plantings incident to the recent work of reclamation have been made for the greater part in the autumn. It is the consensus of opinion that better results follow fall planting for the following reasons: (1) In the fall the growth of the season is finished and plants are dormant for a considerable period of planting weather. (2) The new rootstocks appear to be more firmly attached than they are in the spring, and are consequently less liable to be broken off during the transplanting process. (3) The days are cooler and the incident evaporation less. (4) It is easier to distinguish prime planting stock, and the rooted nodes lying within a few inches of the surface of the sand may be readily removed by hand pulling; in the spring they are apt to be either buried or exposed by the action of the shifting sands. (5) There is an additional winter of effectual protection to be gained by fall planting, as the dormant sets suffer no deterioration the first winter.

The above table concerning the plantings of the different years and seasons shows a marked difference in favor of fall planting. However, the difference between the two seasons is so slight as to be offset by any practical reason why the spring season should be utilized for planting, as for instance the greater ease in procuring the labor or the necessity of finding nearly permanent employment for the help in order to keep it available when needed. In case the planting is extensive it can rarely be completed in one season, and the planting period is thus practically doubled if the spring as well as the fall season can be utilized.

SELECTING AND TRANSPLANTING THE SETS.

The plants selected for transplanting are vigorous and well rooted. This means in practice 2-year-old stock, as the year-old plants are not mature enough or sufficiently rooted to bear transplanting well, as do the older plants. If more than two years old the vitality is likely to be low. As a rule the 2-year-old plants may be readily pulled with the hand and still retain sufficient rootage to enable them to grow when transplanted (Pl. III, fig. 1). It should be mentioned that the hand pulling is not extensively practiced elsewhere in the country, it being the custom to use a spade or shovel in procuring the planting stock. The results indicate that it is largely a matter of opinion as to which method is the better. The plants are piled in bunches and carted to the place where the planting is in progress. Whenever they are to be exposed to the air for any length of time they are heeled in with a covering of moist sand over the roots.

When setting out the grass it is the custom for two men to work together (Pl. III, fig. 2). The one with a shovel inserts it in the sand as far as the foot can force it. A backward pull of the handle loosens the sand at the bottom of the hole, while a forward thrust produces a sufficient opening between the back of the shovel and the sand to allow the insertion of the plant by the second man, who carries an armful of the sets. The man with the shovel by one pressure of his foot packs the sand around the newly set plant. The shovel is inserted a second time at a distance of about 20 inches from the first, and all is ready for the next set. The planting proceeds quite rapidly, as two men are able to set 600 plants per hour.

COST OF PLANTING.

The cost of planting depends upon the thickness at which the grass must be set. On the more exposed areas requiring thick setting five men procuring sets, two teamsters, and eight planters, working nine hours per day, are able to cover an acre in two days. With wages at $2 per day the cost is approximately $65 per acre. This is with an abundance of planting stock growing within a mile of the areas to be covered. The thickness of the planting is responsible for the great expense of the operation, but the exposure of the northern slopes to the severe winter gales makes it probable that thinner plantings would prove ineffective, at least upon the most exposed areas. The expense is much less on the more protected areas, where thinner planting suffices, and those having the work in charge state that the 219 acres, covered with grass, have been planted at an average cost of $50 per acre.

The plantings of the first two years were made in rows ranging from 12 to 18 inches apart with the plants 12 inches or less in the row, but this method appears to be less desirable than the irregular setting which has since been used, as under the latter method there are no uninterrupted channels through which the wind might sweep. The plants are set approximately 20 inches apart, but there is evidence, however, that it is not necessary to set them so close as this, except on the most exposed areas. The thinner plantings afford more rooting area for the sets, and this helps to maintain the vigor of the transplanted sets. The increase in cost of the thick over the thin planting is not justified unless there is considerable advantage to be derived from the former. It has been the custom to protect the plantings with lateral brush hedges. The large branches are set vertically in the ground at intervals of from 2 to 3 feet and the interstices filled with smaller brush. These hedges catch great quantities of sand or in case of wind erosion prevent the uprooting of the grass (Pl. VI, fig. 1).

In some of the areas the small and isolated elevations have been covered at a considerable expense with grass. This has been thought to be an unnecessary procedure, as the wind reduces these elevations, furnishing a gradual accumulation of sand over the plantings on the associated level areas, which instead of proving a detriment to the plantations increases the vigor and vegetative propagation.

PRESENT STATUS OF THE VARIOUS PLANTINGS.

The table giving the acreage and mortality shows the salient facts concerning the plantings of the different dates and seasons. There is a uniform deterioration from the time the plants are set until they have disappeared. This is shown more clearly in Plate V, figure 2, than in the mortality table, for in the latter no account is taken of the great reduction in size and vigor which the sets have undergone. In the plantations of 1895 beach grass and poverty grass (*Hudsonia tomentosa*) from wind-scattered seed are slowly working in among the old sets. It is possible that this natural reclamation process will continue until the entire area is permanently covered with vegetation, although this same site was covered with grass in 1830 and the force of the winds prevented the natural vegetation from establishing itself among the transplanted beach grass. In the plantations of 1899 there are to be noted areas where the grass has retained its natural vigor, although there is no apparent difference between these and the areas showing a less vigorous growth.

EFFECTIVENESS OF BRUSH LAYING.

It has been the custom to cover certain areas with brush, usually those at the top of the ranges and just above the grass plantations. These areas were more or less subject to the eroding action of the wind, and it was thought that brush would answer the purpose better than beach grass. The brush was at first laid on in squares, but this proved less effective than the method of placing the brush uniformly over the entire surface; hence the latter system has been adopted. The beach grass comes in from naturally sown seed, and since the sand is not accumulating the grass is more or less depauperate; yet it is able to survive and by the time the brush decays has prepared the way for the succeeding vegetation, which, in connection with the grass, is able to hold the sand quite effectively. The laying of brush has been practiced quite extensively for the protection of roadways through the sand. The total area covered has been about 15 acres, at an approximate cost of $25 per acre. The addition of a small amount of soil to the area covered with brush has been found to greatly hasten the formation of the vegetative covering. The application need not be continuous nor at all thick. Brush cut with the leaves attached is best, as the humus content of the sand is increased and a much better protection afforded as long as the leaves remain.

EFFICIENCY OF BEACH GRASS FOR SAND BINDING.

Although many grasses have been tried at various times and places in this and foreign countries, no other has proved so effective as the beach grass. The long, tough, but flexible leaves of the beach grass enable it to endure the action of the wind with little detriment. A bunch of dead grass will withstand two seasons of wind action without becoming entirely destroyed. The statements sometimes made concerning the sand-binding power of the roots of this grass must be taken with some allowance. The principal place where the sand-binding action of the rootstocks may be observed is where an area covered with beach grass becomes rejuvenated. Here, the places most thickly overgrown with the grass are the last to be eroded by the wind. The grass stems and exposed rootstocks hanging loosely over the sides of the eroded hillock protect it to a considerable extent and retard its ultimate reduction. So far as observed the rootstocks seldom form a thick mat-like mass sufficiently near the water's edge to be of material assistance in reducing the eroding action of the waves, except in severe storms, when the wave action extends inland for a considerable distance (Pl. II, fig. 1). The chief value of the grass in this instance is the accumulation of sand induced, which, by its presence, keeps the destruction of the property adjoining the water reduced to a minimum.

Beach grass ordinarily requires a gradual accumulation of sand over its crown to induce a normal vigorous growth. It is for this reason that it is to be noted in great clumps protruding from the crest of small dunes, where it has accumulated a considerable quantity of sand each year, but at the same time not enough to cover it so deeply that the new plants are unable to develop. This is due to the fact that when the grass becomes partially buried the sand is no longer held by the protruding grass leaves and it passes over, and the grass is able to renew its growth the following year with increased vigor, since the accumulated sand is permeated with the roots of the new rootstock sent out by the half-buried clump. A healthy growth of beach grass can thrive where the burial by sand is not over a foot per year.

The areas which usually require planting are generally those from which the sand is being removed by the wind rather than those which are receiving the accumulations so essential to the vigor of the grass. For this reason the most that can be expected of the grass is that this sand removal shall be checked as long as the grass is able to survive under the unfavorable conditions, which allow of no accumulation of sand over the plants. The decrease in vigor of the sets from the time they are set out is a matter of common knowledge to those who have noted the plantations of beach grass under these conditions for a series of years. (See mortality table, p. 25.) It appears that this necessity for sand accumulation lies in the fact that it induces the development of new rootstocks by the old plant and thus occupies an unused portion of the sand which presents such a dearth of food salts that these are soon depleted and the deterioration noted must ensue unless new areas of sand are made tributary. Furthermore, there is no power of downward growth on the part of the rootstocks, and as a set rarely possesses more than two nodes the root system is very limited. The new rootstocks developed in the accumulated layers of sand constitute the only means of bringing new supplies of sand within reach of the grass plants. The old rootstock becomes buried, but continues to support to some extent the new plants until sufficiently established to be able to withstand the rather severe conditions incident to the dune areas. This process continues and the grass is thus continually rejuvenated.

Another reason for the deterioration noted above may be the fact that a single set of grass is not of indefinite existence, and unless it is induced to increase vegetatively it soon loses its vigor. There are areas in the United States where this deterioration subsequent to the transplanting is not manifested. At Grand Haven, Mich., at Coos Bay, Oregon, and at Poplar Branch, N. C., the beach grass has continued to increase in vigor since the plantations were established. This is apparently due to the fact that the plantings were made sufficiently far apart to allow most of the sand to drift through the plantations, thus enabling each set to receive a small amount of sand. This method, however, would be applicable only to limited areas on Cape Cod, as it is the eroding surfaces which require protection. However, these instances indicate that it is possible in certain areas to distribute the sand accumulation and often build up areas that are eroding, and this method should be in mind whenever a plan of attack on the dune areas is under consideration. The great reduction in the cost per acre where this thin planting can be utilized is a decided point in favor of its adoption wherever at all practicable. The cost of the Coos Bay plantations has been only $8 per acre, 64 acres having been planted in a single season with an appropriation of $500. In this place the grass was set 4 feet apart, and rather favorable climatic and edaphic conditions have been to some extent responsible for the success of such thin planting.

Trials of other sand-binding grasses have demonstrated the superiority of beach grass for sand-binding purposes under conditions which characterize the dune areas of Cape Cod. In 1901 experiments were made with the sand sedge (*Carex macrocephala*) and seaside bluegrass (*Poa macrantha*). These are very efficient sand binders upon the Pacific coast, and were obtained through the Division of Agrostology from Clatsop beach, near Fort Stevens, Oregon. Neither the seedlings nor the sets of these species proved successful. The seeds germinated well, but failed to survive the winter, as was also the case with the transplanted sets.

NECESSITY OF ULTIMATE FORESTATION.

The marked deterioration of the beach-grass plantings shows the need of introducing woody growth among the areas at as early a date as possible (Pl. V, figs. 1 and 2). The various native or imported woody plants should be set out among the grass soon after the grass has been planted, as the first years of the protection afforded by the grass are the best and are, in the aggregate, none too long to enable the shrubs and young trees to make sufficient growth and rootage to be self-protecting by the time the grass deteriorates so as to be practically valueless. It seems that it is necessary to start such a shrub or bush as the bayberry. This is not injured by the unfavorable conditions, and seedlings of pines and oaks may with safety be introduced among the bushes. Even the planting of the pine seeds and acorns has with this protection been successful.

Several species of woody plants have been tried with varying success. The following have been found to be unadapted to the conditions: Seaside pine (*Pinus maritima*), tree of heaven (*Ailanthus glandulosa*), ironwood (*Ostrya virginiana*), European birch (*Betula alba*), tamarack (*Tamarix gallica*), poplar (*Populus alba*), larch (*Larix* sp.), willow (*Salix* sp.), and privet (*Ligustrum vulgare*). Too much weight should not be given to the unsuccessful attempts with the willow and poplar, as they have made a vigorous growth on the sand within the city limits, and their behavior elsewhere, under almost as adverse conditions, appears to at least justify a more extended trial.

The successful species are comparatively few in number. Of the pines, pitch pine (*Pinus rigida*), Austrian pine (*P. laricio*), and Scotch pine (*P. sylvestris*) are proved successes. The pitch pine is used most extensively, as it grows naturally in the adjacent forests, and young trees and cones can be obtained in almost unlimited quantities. The black locust (*Robinia pseudacacia*) and the European or black alder (*Alnus glutinosa*), though not occupying extensive areas, have proved thoroughly adapted to the conditions, and it is the plan to increase the plantings of these two species. The Scotch broom (*Cytisus scoparius*) is well adapted to the conditions with the one exception of not being perfectly hardy, as many small areas have been killed by one or two excessively cold winters, though much of the original planting is still alive and vigorous. The plant does not spread readily from seed, as the severe conditions prohibit its existence in the early seedling stage, and furthermore, the seed being large and conspicuous is readily eaten by birds and small animals. The growth is very dense, and even scattered bunches would prevent the sand from shifting, but its semihardiness makes it decidedly inferior to the bayberry, which is locally abundant, perfectly hardy, and easily transplanted. The bayberry has formed the bulk of the pioneer plantings of woody growth, and used in connection with the beach grass appears to be the only necessary forerunner of the pines.

Miscellaneous Operations on the Sand.

Besides the reclamation processes leading to the ultimate reforestation of the dunes, there are a number of other operations which have ameliorated to some extent the adverse conditions incident to the sand dunes. Among these may be mentioned the construction of roads, formation of cranberry bogs, etc., the development of a sod in pastures, cemeteries, and lawns, and the accumulation of sand to form a beach ridge for harbor protection.

ROAD CONSTRUCTION.

The problem of road construction in sandy regions, and, as a rule, districts with sparse population, is a very difficult one, and is frequently not solved until the demand has long been imperative. The road leading from Provincetown south originally followed the beach at low tide, but at high water the travel was through the heavy sand farther up on the beach. The State is at present constructing a macadamized road extending from Provincetown southward, thus connecting it with the main part of the State. Before the road across the sand areas was macadamized, liberal applications of clay had facilitated the travel for many years.

There are several roads across the Province lands, and where they lead through the forested portion they are in good repair. On the shifting sand areas none but the State road has received much attention, although most of the portions where there is danger of gullying by the wind have received a protective covering of brush (Pl. VI, fig. 2).

The building of the State road across the Province lands was commenced in 1894 and completed in 1901. It extends from the city to the Peaked Hill Life-Saving Station and provides an easy means of access to the heart of the dune territory. The road was not constructed across the dunes area until the shifting sands had been brought under control. The roadbed was first graded and then covered with a layer of brush, after which it received a covering of turf sod obtained from the adjacent woods. It is still in good condition and promises with some attention to be fairly permanent, as it is subject to but little heavy teaming. The cost of construction was about 35 cents per running foot.

When the railroad was constructed the cuts were covered with brush and rubbish, which proved sufficient protection until a natural growth of beach grass developed, and no difficulty has since been experienced from gullying by the wind.

RECLAMATION OF SMALL AREAS.

Although the State holds the title to the Province lands and the public in general has had free access to its natural products, there are certain areas of the native cranberry bogs which have been staked off and improved by private parties. This was a common practice and many of the berry growers were assessed either on the land or its product. There seems to have been no serious outcome from this procedure except that it generally involved the removal of considerable brush and bushes, thus preventing the development of the forest in the immediate area. This has been the cause of some conflict of opinion with the State authorities, as it is the idea of those that have the preservation of the harbor in mind that the lands can be controlled with much less expense if the entire area be forested, and it may be said that the present State appropriations for the Cape are to this end. Fires have been started from the careless burning of the brush removed in the process of clearing the bogs. However, it appears that even with State ownership of the land the present prices of cranberries make them a source of little, if any, profit, as the soil is not adapted to producing yields comparable with those farther south along the Cape.

The pasturage of cattle upon the Province lands has long been prohibited by statute, and the pastures in use have been reclaimed from the bog lands near the city. Certain low places have been filled in, and the redtop present forms a close turf and is apparently able to withstand the usual amount of pasturing

The lee side of an established dune adjacent to the city has been terraced for the purpose of growing strawberries. The necessary substratum for the vines was obtained from the humus accumulation on the side of the dune. As there are numerous similar areas in the immediate vicinity, this indicates the possibilities if due care were taken not to rejuvenate the dunes, and there appears to be little danger of this on the lee slopes.

As with all old places, the cemetery is extensive and its uniformly good appearance is worthy of note, especially when the adverse conditions are considered. The soil rendering the bluegrass sod possible was either hauled in wagons from further south along the Cape or brought by boat from across the bay. A recent addition to the cemetery was leveled off and the bare sand protected with brush and sods, most of which came from the land leveled for the addition. The above statements may also be made concerning the lawns about the residences in the city, as the soil for these had to be imported from the same sources.

COMMERCIAL UTILIZATION OF SAND.

The sand, being of varying size, angular, and light colored, is valuable for many purposes, but its exportation appears to have been discontinued. The sand constituting an entire dune was at one time removed to Boston, the ships returning with loads of soil for use on lawns and in the cemetery. A glass factory was once in operation farther south on the Cape, but it, too, has been discontinued. The sand is valuable for polishing and cutting marble and granite, as well as for use in mortar, and in former years "Cape Cod sand" was frequently specified in important contracts for building in cities having navigable water connection with Provincetown. Sand was used in filling in the shallow water at the base of the forested dunes to form building sites for the business houses and dwellings, as originally there was very little building space along the harbor, which was so shallow near the edge as to make landing difficult.

DEVELOPMENT OF THE PROTECTIVE BEACH RIDGE.

The extensive sand flats and marshes associated with the sand hook forming one side of the harbor have always been subject to the inroads of the sea, which threatened the harbor with great incursions of sand. A protective beach ridge has been developed in all of the weaker places on the sand hook. Groin fences, in connection with beach grass, have induced extensive accumulations of sand, which are very effective in protecting the harbor and the bulkheads from the action of the sea during storms. This process of reclamation is in operation at present, the object being to build up a protective beach ridge along the salt marsh near the extreme end of the Cape south and west of Provincetown.

THE PROVINCE LANDS.

STATE OWNERSHIP.

The Province lands, situated at the extremity of Cape Cod, have had a peculiar history. When the provincial government ceased and Massachusetts became a State, all of the unoccupied lands retained the title of "Province lands," as all the land had previously been designated. It was not until 1893 that the State ceded to the inhabitants of Provincetown even their building sites, although previous to that date they had been privileged to give warranty deeds when making real estate transfers. There exist excellent reasons for State ownership of these sand areas which inclose the harbor, as it is only under such ownership that the necessary attention can be given to render the protection of the harbor efficient. The city and harbor are entirely too important to allow the half-established sand areas which endanger them to pass into the hands of private parties and to be subject to possible shortsighted policies leading to immediate profit.

It seems equally desirable that the State should also own what are known as the "Lotted lands," which constitute the sand areas lying between the Province lands and the glacial deposits comprising the original head of the Cape (see Pl. 1). The sand of this area is more loosely bound and the shifting dunes are much nearer the harbor than are the sand areas of the Province lands. The "Lotted lands" are of little economic value and title could be obtained for a nominal consideration. At the present time timber and beach-grass hay are being removed by private persons to supply the local demand for these products. In view of the importance of the property thus endangered these practices need no comment.

Value of the Lands.

Agriculturally and horticulturally the lands surrounding the harbor have little value. No field crops are raised, and the redtop pastures are very small, being for the most part reclaimed bogs with an aggregate area of approximately 25 acres. The salt marshes yield about 200 tons of hay per year, and beach-grass hay to the amount of 15 tons is annually obtained from the sand areas lying just outside of the Province lands. The cranberry bogs, while extensive, are not regarded as especially profitable holdings even with the State owning the lands.

The sylvicultural resources of the lands might possibly be turned into account. The growth of the timber is slow, but the climatic contions are favorable, and an intelligent system of forestation under existing prices would materially assist in providing for the expenses incident to the supervision of the lands.

It has been suggested that the lands might be improved and brought into the market as building lots for summer cottages, or, this failing of realization, that a game preserve might be established and a revenue derived from shooting privileges. Neither of the projects appears to have met with much favor. The chief value of the lands is as a harbor former, and all plans should conserve to this end.

The idea of converting the area into a marine park has many points in its favor, and it may be stated that those in charge of the land have this project in mind and are working to that end. The isolation, beauty of natural scenery, and oceanic location, with its 5 miles of heavy surf and an equal frontage on the bay, combine to render the locality probably without an equal on the Atlantic coast. The harbor must be protected from the loose sands on the north side of the Cape, and the forested condition necessary for a marine park is exactly what is required by the proposed plans to render the area a permanent protection to the harbor, and the money spent in reclaiming the lands, if applied along landscape-engineering lines, will ultimately produce an ideal ocean park. The successful development of the Golden Gate Park at San Francisco has demonstrated the possibilities of such sandy tracts when properly reclaimed.

SUMMARY.

The sand areas inclosing Cape Cod Harbor were originally forested, but have been extensively devastated within historic times. Restrictive legislation dating back as far as 1714 has exerted a restraining influence upon the devastating activities. In 1826 extensive reclamation processes were inaugurated, but were unsuccessful owing to the failure to introduce woody plants within the beach-grass plantations. The State in 1893 formulated an extensive plan for the reclamation of these areas. The initial plantings of woody plants were unsuccessful, owing to their having been introduced into the shifting sand areas without the protection of beach grass. Plantations of beach grass aggregating 219 acres have been made and large numbers of bayberry bushes, young pines, etc., have been introduced among the grass, which persists until the bushes and young trees have attained sufficient size to be self-protecting. The State has expended for reclamation purposes during the ten years ending January 1, 1904, $31,929.78, of which $10,950 was for grass planting. The General Government has spent $162,019.86 in its work of harbor protection, and the total amount expended upon the harbor by the State and National Governments is $325,719.78. This includes $131,770.14 expended by the State in 1868 for the construction of a dike across East Harbor.

The sand areas are of vital importance to the harbor and their control necessitates reforestation, which is at present being accomplished, the authorities having in mind the ultimate development of a marine park.

BIBLIOGRAPHY.

DWIGHT, T. Travels in New England and New York, 1796 and 1797 (1823).

Mass. Sen. Doc. No. 5 (1854).

(Being a report on Cape Cod and East harbors.)

FLINT, C. L. Grasses and forage plants (1858).

THOREAU, H. D. Cape Cod (1864).

Mass. House Doc. No. 50.

(Being a report on the condition of Long Point and East Harbor.)

Mass. Sen. Doc. No. 5 (1872).

(Being a report on the construction of the East Harbor dike in 1868.)

Annual reports of the Chief of Engineers, U. S. Army, 1876, pp. 181–190; 1879, pp. 273–275; 1886, pp. 574–577; 1903, pp. 87, 783–784.

Mass. House Doc. No. 339 (1893).

(Being a report on the Province lands authorized under chapter 420 of the acts of 1892.)

SMALL, JAMES A. Reports of the Superintendent of the Province lands. Annual reports of the Harbor and Land Commissioners, 1893–1903.

SCRIBNER, F. LAMSON-. Grasses as sand and soil binders. Reprint from the Yearbook of the U. S. Dept. Agric., 1894, pp. 421–436.

——— Sand-binding grasses. Reprint from the Yearbook of the U. S. Dept. Agric., 1898, pp. 405–420.

COWLES, H. C. Ecological relations of the vegetation on the Lake Michigan sand dunes. Reprint from the Bot. Gaz., 27 : 95 et seq.

HOLLICK, A. Geological and botanical notes: Cape Cod and Chippaquidick Island, Massachusetts. Bul. N. Y. Bot. Gard., 2 : 381–407.

PLATES.

DESCRIPTION OF PLATES.

PLATE I. (Frontispiece.) Map of the sand areas inclosing Cape Cod Harbor. The 30-foot contour lines indicate roughly the topography and general outlines of the seven dune ranges which constitute the larger portion of the sand areas surrounding the harbor. The outer three nonforested dune ranges have been covered with beach grass and are indicated in black.

PLATE II. Fig. 1.—Beach grass forming protective beach ridge. The grass is shown to extend to within the limit of wave action during the winter storms. Its peculiar habit of sending out rootstocks when buried enables it to keep the ever-increasing sand deposits well covered. The gradual accumulations of sand incident to these depositing ridges form the ideal conditions for the thrifty growth of this grass. The beach ridge indicated has increased 20 feet in height during the past twenty years. The beach grass has been the chief factor in accumulating the sands necessary for the strengthening of this portion of the sand areas protecting the harbor. Fig. 2.—Beach grass, showing method of vegetative propagation. Beach grass is efficient in the natural reclamation processes owing to the method of rapid vegetative propagation from rootstocks, which enables scattered individuals to soon cover the drifting sands with a sufficient growth to prevent the sand movement.

PLATE III. Fig. 1.—Set of beach grass suitable for transplanting. The set shows two nodes of the rootstock with attached rootlets. Two-year-old stock is most desirable for transplanting. The method of hand pulling is practiced throughout these areas. Fig. 2.—Transplanting beach grass. The gently sloping sand areas are covered with beach grass in the manner indicated. The brows of the hills are covered immediately with bayberry transplanted from the adjoining timbered areas. The steeper slopes are often reduced to an angle of 25 degrees or less before the planting is begun.

PLATE IV. Fig. 1.—Lee slope of a sand dune showing the manner in which the advancing dune buries forests lying in its path. Fig. 2.—General view of the grass plantations, looking south. Native growth in foreground. In the background the transplanted beach-grass area adjoins the sands not yet covered. Bayberry bushes have been introduced upon the crests of the dunes. Before these areas were covered with the grass, the dunes were encroaching upon the forest and city shown in the distance.

PLATE V. Fig. 1.—Bayberry bushes without grass protection. The presence of bushes alone is not sufficient to prevent the shifting of the sand. The large size of the sand grains is indicated in the foreground. Fig. 2.—Bayberry bushes with grass protection. The deterioration of the grass is evident but its duration is sufficient to enable the introduced woody growth to become self-protecting. The grass was planted in 1898 and the bayberry a year subsequently.

PLATE VI. Fig. 1.—Wind erosion of nonprotected sand. The brush line in the center marks the eastward extension of the beach grass plantings of 1898. The amount of sand erosion by the wind since the grass was introduced is clearly indicated on the eroded sand areas at the left where it appears that at least 15 feet of sand have been removed. Fig. 2.—Protecting a road through the dunes. The brush lines, logs, and bushes form an efficient protection to the sides of the cut. The roadbed consists of brush overlaid with turf sods obtained from the neighboring forest.

FIG. 1.—BEACH GRASS FORMING PROTECTIVE BEACH RIDGE.

FIG. 2.—BEACH GRASS, SHOWING METHOD OF VEGETATIVE PROPAGATION.

Bul. 65, Bureau of Plant Industry, U. S. Dept of Agriculture. PLATE III.

FIG. 1.—SET OF BEACH GRASS SUITABLE FOR TRANSPLANTING.

FIG. 2.—TRANSPLANTING BEACH GRASS.

FIG. 1.—SAND DUNES BURYING FOREST.

FIG. 2.—BEACH GRASS PLANTATIONS—GENERAL VIEW.

Fig. 1.—Bayberry Bushes Without Grass Protection.

Fig. 2.—Bayberry Bushes with Grass Protection.

Bul. 65, Bureau of Plant Industry, U. S. Dept of Agriculture PLATE VI.

FIG. 1.—WIND EROSION OF NONPROTECTED SAND.

FIG. 2.—PROTECTING A ROAD THROUGH THE DUNES.

[Continued from page 2 of cover.]

No. 27. Letters on Agriculture in the West Indies, Spain, and the Orient. 1902. Price, 15 cents.
28. The Mango in Porto Rico. 1903. Price, 15 cents.
29. The Effect of Black Rot on Turnips. 1903. Price, 15 cents.
30. Budding the Pecan. 1902. Price, 10 cents.
31. Cultivated Forage Crops of the Northwestern States. 1902. Price, 10 cents.
32. A Disease of the White Ash Caused by Polyporus Fraxinophilus. 1903. Price, 10 cents.
33. North American Species of Leptochloa. 1903. Price, 15 cents.
34. Silkworm Food Plants. 1903. Price, 15 cents.
35. Recent Foreign Explorations. 1903. Price, 15 cents.
36. The "Bluing" and the "Red Rot" of the Western Yellow Pine, with Special Reference to the Black Hills Forest Reserve. 1903. Price, 30 cents.
37. Formation of the Spores in the Sporangia of Rhizopus Nigricans and of Phycomyces Nitens. 1903. Price, 15 cents.
38. Forest Conditions and Problems in Eastern Washington, Eastern Oregon, etc. 1903. Price, 15 cents.
39. The Propagation of the Easter Lily from Seed. 1903. Price, 10 cents.
40. Cold Storage, with Special Reference to the Pear and Peach. 1903. Price, 15 cents.
41. The Commercial Grading of Corn. 1903. Price, 10 cents.
42. Three New Plant Introductions from Japan. Price, 10 cents.
43. Japanese Bamboos. 1903. Price, 10 cents.
44. The Bitter Rot of Apples. 1903. Price, 15 cents.
45. The Physiological Rôle of Mineral Nutrients in Plants. Price, 5 cents.
46. The Propagation of Tropical Fruit Trees and Other Plants. Price, 10 cents.
47. The Description of Wheat Varieties. 1903. Price, 10 cents.
48. The Apple in Cold Storage. 1903. Price, 15 cents.
49. The Culture of the Central American Rubber Tree. 1903. Price, 25 cents.
50. Wild Rice: Its Uses and Propagation. 1903. Price, 10 cents.
51. Miscellaneous Papers: Part I. The Wilt Disease of Tobacco and its Control. 1903. Price, 5 cents. Part II. The Work of the Community Demonstration Farm at Terrell, Tex. 1904. Price, 5 cents. Part III. Fruit Trees Frozen in 1904. 1904. Price, 5 cents.
52. Wither-Tip and Other Diseases of Citrous Trees and Fruits Caused by Colletotrichum Gloeosporioides. 1904. Price, 5 cents.
53. The Date Palm. Price, 20 cents.
54. Persian Gulf Dates. 1903. Price, 10 cents.
55. The Dry Rot of Potatoes Due to Fusarium Oxysporum. 1904. Price, 10 cents.
56. Nomenclature of the Apple. [In press.]
57. Methods Used for Controlling and Reclaiming Sand Dunes. 1904. Price, 10 cents.
58. The Vitality and Germination of Seeds. 1904. Price, 10 cents.
59. Pasture, Meadow, and Forage Crops in Nebraska. 1904. Price, 10 cents.
60. A Soft Rot of the Calla Lily. [In press.]
61. The Avocado: Its Propagation, Cultivation, and Marketing. [In press.]
62. Notes on Egyptian Agriculture. [In press.]
63. Further Investigations of Rusts. [In press.]
64. A Method of Destroying or Preventing the Growth of Algæ and Certain Pathogenic Bacteria in Water Supplies. 1904. Price, 5 cents.

BUREAU OF PLANT INDUSTRY—BULLETIN NO. 66.

SEEDS AND PLANTS IMPORTED

DURING THE PERIOD FROM SEPTEMBER, 1900, TO DECEMBER, 1903.

INVENTORY No. 10; Nos. 5501—9896.

SEED AND PLANT INTRODUCTION AND DISTRIBUTION.

Issued February 8, 1905.

WASHINGTON:
GOVERNMENT PRINTING OFFICE.
1905.

U. S. DEPARTMENT OF AGRICULTURE.

BUREAU OF PLANT INDUSTRY—BULLETIN NO. 66.

B. T. GALLOWAY, *Chief of Bureau.*

SEEDS AND PLANTS IMPORTED

DURING THE PERIOD FROM SEPTEMBER, 1900, TO DECEMBER, 1903.

INVENTORY No. 10; Nos. 5501—9896.

SEED AND PLANT INTRODUCTION AND DISTRIBUTION.

Issued February 8, 1905.

WASHINGTON:
GOVERNMENT PRINTING OFFICE.
1905.

BUREAU OF PLANT INDUSTRY.

B. T. GALLOWAY,
Pathologist and Physiologist, and Chief of Bureau.

VEGETABLE PATHOLOGICAL AND PHYSIOLOGICAL INVESTIGATIONS.
ALBERT F. WOODS, *Pathologist and Physiologist in Charge,
Acting Chief of Bureau in Absence of Chief.*

BOTANICAL INVESTIGATIONS AND EXPERIMENTS.
FREDERICK V. COVILLE, *Botanist in Charge.*

GRASS AND FORAGE PLANT INVESTIGATIONS.
W. J. SPILLMAN, *Agrostologist in Charge.*

POMOLOGICAL INVESTIGATIONS.
G. B. BRACKETT, *Pomologist in Charge.*

SEED AND PLANT INTRODUCTION AND DISTRIBUTION.
A. J. PIETERS, *Botanist in Charge.*

ARLINGTON EXPERIMENTAL FARM.
L. C. CORBETT, *Horticulturist in Charge.*

EXPERIMENTAL GARDENS AND GROUNDS.
E. M. BYRNES, *Superintendent.*

J. E. ROCKWELL, *Editor.*
JAMES E. JONES, *Chief Clerk.*

SEED AND PLANT INTRODUCTION AND DISTRIBUTION.

SCIENTIFIC STAFF.

A. J. PIETERS, *Botanist in Charge.*

W. W. TRACY, Sr., *Special Agent.*
S. A. KNAPP, *Special Agent.*
DAVID G. FAIRCHILD, *Agricultural Explorer.*
JOHN E. W. TRACY, *Expert.*
GEORGE W. OLIVER, *Expert.*

LETTER OF TRANSMITTAL.

U. S. DEPARTMENT OF AGRICULTURE,
BUREAU OF PLANT INDUSTRY,
OFFICE OF THE CHIEF,
Washington, D. C., May 5, 1904.

SIR: I have the honor to transmit herewith, and to recommend for publication as Bulletin No. 66 of the series of this Bureau, the accompanying manuscript entitled "Seeds and Plants Imported During the Period from September, 1900, to December, 1903."

This manuscript has been submitted by the Botanist in Charge of Seed and Plant Introduction and Distribution with a view to publication.

Respectfully, B. T. GALLOWAY,
Chief of Bureau.

Hon. JAMES WILSON,
Secretary of Agriculture.

PREFACE.

The present inventory, No. 10 of our series, covers a number of introductions almost equal to the entire number included in the previous nine inventories. It is put forth as the first part of the record of the permanent work of this office with these introductions, and shows what seeds and plants have been introduced. The completion of the record requires a report of the disposition made of these seeds and the results obtained from the experimental work done in this country. Such records will appear from time to time as our different introductions are tested and either discarded or found to be valuable additions to the plants cultivated by American farmers and gardeners.

The introductory statement by Mr. Fairchild covers the general information in regard to the sources from which these introductions have been obtained, and I wish in addition to emphasize the fact that the seeds and plants represented by this inventory have all been distributed, and that the inventory is in no sense intended as a check list to enable persons to call for seeds and plants with which they would like to experiment.

A. J. PIETERS,
Botanist in Charge.

OFFICE OF SEED AND PLANT
   INTRODUCTION AND DISTRIBUTION,
      Washington, D. C., May 4, 1904.

SEEDS AND PLANTS IMPORTED DURING THE PERIOD FROM SEPTEMBER, 1900, TO DECEMBER, 1903.

INTRODUCTORY STATEMENT.

This inventory of seeds and plants which have been collected by agricultural explorers, or received through other sources by this Office, covers the period from September, 1900, to December, 1903. It includes 4,396 accession inventory numbers. Since the last inventory was published in 1901 the explorers and special agents of this Office have continued their extensive searches after new and promising varieties of plants for introduction into this country. The notes furnished regarding the different introductions vary greatly with regard to their completeness and it is desired to point out clearly that this inventory makes no pretenses to being an embodiment of all the information we possess regarding the various seeds and plants listed. It is merely a collection, largely for use in this Office and by members of the State experiment stations, of the notes which accompanied the various seeds and plants when they were sent in. Their value will in many cases be more historical than explanatory. For some of the most important numbers, separate detailed reports have been issued in the form of bulletins or are being prepared for publication.

It will be noticed that no attempt has been made to follow the latest reforms in nomenclature, the Kew Index having been taken in most cases as a convenient guide in the spelling of the different scientific names.

The quantities of seeds or plants represented by these different numbers are, as a rule, small, and in the vast majority of cases it has been necessary to distribute them as soon as possible after arrival to competent experimenters throughout the country. It will therefore be, in most cases, impossible to furnish seeds or plants described in this inventory. If, however, special reasons can be shown by reputable experimenters why further introductions of certain species or varieties should be made, this Office will be glad to take the matter up, for it is desirous of introducing any new variety which may be called to its attention by plant breeders or others in a position to carry out consecutive and careful plant-introduction experiments.

Of the nearly 4,400 new introductions, a very large number represent work accomplished by the explorations of Mr. Barbour Lathrop, of Chicago, with whom the writer had the pleasure of being associated as Agricultural Explorer. Mr. Lathrop's explorations, which have required about four years of travel abroad, were carried out with the one practical object of making a reconnoissance of the useful plant possibilities of the world, and have successfully covered every continent and touched every important archipelago. Owing to the very out-of-the-way parts of the world visited by Mr. Lathrop, a large number of the seeds and plants secured by him are so rare that they will be exceedingly difficult to replace, and the Office considers itself extremely fortunate to have enlisted the cooperation of such a public-spirited man as Mr. Lathrop, who has conducted these various explorations almost entirely at his own expense, with no other idea than that of benefiting the American public through this branch of the work of the Department of Agriculture. No stronger evidence is needed of the practical value of plant-introduction work than that furnished by Mr. Lathrop's devotion to its study.

The collections of the several Department agricultural explorers which are represented in this inventory have also been gathered from a wide range of the earth's surface. The explorations of Dr. S. A. Knapp, the results of which are represented in the inventory, covered his second voyage to the Orient in 1901-2, and comprised a trip to Hawaii, Japan, China, Manila, the Straits Settlements, and British India in search of information bearing on the rice question of the South. Bavaria, Austria, Dalmatia, Greece, Egypt, Tunis, Algeria, and Spain were explored by the writer for brewing barleys, hops, fruits, and forage crops. Mr. C. S. Scofield made a careful survey of the leguminous fodder and green manure crops of Algeria and incidentally a study of the wheat varieties of France. Mr. M. A. Carleton made a second trip in 1900 through Austria and Roumania, into Russia and Central Asia, and returned through Turkey and Servia in search of cereals and forage crops. Mr. E. R. Lake, a specialist on American prunes, was sent in 1900 on a short trip to the prune-growing regions of France. Dr. J. N. Rose, of the U. S. National Museum, assisted us in 1901 in his botanizing trips in Mexico to secure a collection of desert plants and varieties of other plants of economic importance. Mr. Ernst A. Bessey was sent as agricultural explorer on two expeditions in search of hardy alfalfas and more resistant fruits for the Northwest. The first was through Russia to Turkestan in 1902, and the second to the Caucasus in 1903. Mr. Thomas H. Kearney and Mr. T. H. Means, the latter of the Bureau of Soils, were sent as explorers to the arid regions of Algeria, Tunis, and Egypt in search of better strains of Egyptian cotton and alkali-resistant grains and fodder plants. Mr. P. H. Rolfs, in charge of the Subtropical

Laboratory at Miami, Fla., visited for this Office in 1903 several islands in the West Indies in search of varieties of cassava and other suitable agricultural plants for southern Florida. Mr. G. Onderdonk, of Nursery, Tex., a specialist on stone fruits, made a trip to Mexico for this Office in search of varieties of this class of fruits for the Southern States.

In addition to the seeds and plants which these various exploring trips have brought in, the Office is indebted to correspondents all over the world for numerous interesting things which have been presented to it and for which credit is given in each separate instance under the various numbers.

It is desired to urge strongly in this introductory statement that the numbers which accompany these seeds and plants when they are sent out should be carefully preserved by those who receive them. By means of these inventory numbers the seeds and plants can always be identified. The machinery of the Office is so arranged that a permanent record is kept on file of all seeds and plants sent out, and the addresses of the experimenters to whom they are sent. This feature is considered essential, and unless carefully carried out there will be nothing on record to prevent reintroductions of plants which have proved by extensive trials to be unworthy of a place in American agriculture, and much annoyance and delay will be caused in the handling of those things which are successful.

While it is one of the aims of plant introduction to encourage those who can afford it to try new plants, such an object would not be gained by any attempt to supply those who—misguided, perhaps, by exaggerated newspaper accounts—apply for seeds or plants which they are not in a position to test successfully. All seeds are sent out with the idea that those who receive them are willing to take the pains to reply to queries from this Office regarding the success of their trial and to supply on request reasonable quantities of seeds, scions, or plants produced from the imported material. A failure on the part of an experimenter to respond to repeated inquiries or his refusal to assist in giving new introductions a wide distribution will affect unfavorably his standing in the list of capable experimenters which it is one of the objects of this plant introduction work to create.

DAVID G. FAIRCHILD,
Agricultural Explorer.

WASHINGTON, D. C., *April 18, 1904.*

INVENTORY.

5501 to 5512.

From Washington, D. C. Seeds from a number of crab-apple trees growing on the grounds of the Department of Agriculture. These trees were imported from Russia, by Prof. N. E. Hansen, in 1898. The numbers in parentheses are those under which the trees were received from Professor Hansen. They are as follows:

5501. PYRUS PRUNIFOLIA EDULIS. (No. 4.)

5502. PYRUS PRUNIFOLIA PURPUREA. (No. 5.)

5503. PYRUS PRUNIFOLIA. (No. 6.)
Transparent.

5504. PYRUS PRUNIFOLIA. (No. 7.)
Transparent.

5505. PYRUS PRUNIFOLIA MOSCOWIENSIS. (No. 8.)

5506. PYRUS PRUNIFOLIA PURPUREA. (No. 9.)

5507. PYRUS PRUNIFOLIA MACROCARPA. (Nos. 10 and 11.)

5508. PYRUS PRUNIFOLIA BACCATA. (No. 12.)

5509. PYRUS PRUNIFOLIA BACCATA. (No. 15.)

5510. PYRUS PRUNIFOLIA BACCATA. (No. 16.)

5511. PYRUS PRUNIFOLIA. (No. 17.)

5512. PYRUS PRUNIFOLIA. (No. 18.)

5513. AVENA SATIVA. Oat.

From Torneå, Finland. Received through Messrs. Lathrop and Fairchild (No. 435), September 27, 1900.

North Finnish Black. "This seed is from the north province of Finland, and being grown at this high latitude should be early ripening. It is not, however, of first quality because the recent crops have been very poor." (*Fairchild.*)

5514. AVENA SATIVA. Oat.

From Torneå, Finland. Presented by F. O. U. Nordberg, through Messrs. Lathrop and Fairchild (No. 435a, Aug. 6, 1900). Received September 27, 1900.

North Finnish Black. "One liter of black oats of the 1897 crop, which was so highly prized here that I could only get this small quantity. It should ripen earlier than No. 5513." (*Fairchild.*)

5515. TRITICUM VULGARE. Wheat.

From Michaux, Va. Received September 27, 1900.

Banat. Grown in Virginia from seed imported by this Department in 1899.

5516. PASSIFLORA EDULIS. **Passion flower.**

From New South Wales, Australia. Presented by Dr. N. A. Cobb. Received September 27, 1900.

"This plant grows best in good soil at some distance from the coast, where there is little frost and an annual rainfall of about 50 inches. The plants are usually trellised about 6 feet apart, grow rapidly, and bear fruit the second year." (*Cobb.*) (See No. 1906, Inventory No. 5.)

5517. GLYCINE HISPIDA. **Soy bean.**

From Macassar, Celebes. Received through Messrs. Lathrop and Fairchild (No. 336, Jan., 1900), October 8, 1900.

Katjang-Koro.

5518. PHASEOLUS MUNGO. **Gram.**

From Macassar, Celebes. Received through Messrs. Lathrop and Fairchild (No. 337, Jan., 1900), October 8, 1900.

"A small bean used in soups." (*Fairchild.*)

5519. DOLICHOS sp. **Ussi bean.**

From Lombok, Dutch East Indies. Received through Messrs. Lathrop and Fairchild (No. 338, Jan., 1900), October 8, 1900.

Katjang Ussi.

5520. CUCURBITA sp. **Squash.**

From Amboina, Dutch East Indies. Received through Messrs. Lathrop and Fairchild (No. 339 Jan. 15, 1900), October 8, 1900.

"Native-grown squash, suited to a moist, warm climate. Said to be very sweet when cooked." (*Fairchild.*)

5521. PHASEOLUS LUNATUS. **Lima bean.**

From Lombok, Dutch East Indies. Received through Messrs. Lathrop and Fairchild (No. 340, January 7, 1900), October 8, 1900.

"A peculiar white and black striped lima bean." (*Fairchild.*)

5522. ARACHIS HYPOGAEA. **Peanut.**

From Matarum, Lombok, Dutch East Indies. Received through Messrs. Lathrop and Fairchild (No. 341, January 7, 1900), October 8, 1900.

"A large rough-shelled, three-seeded peanut, having thin shells and a good flavor." (*Fairchild.*)

5523. ORYZA SATIVA. **Rice.**

From Surabaya, Java. Received through Messrs. Lathrop and Fairchild (No. 342, January, 1900), October 8, 1900.

"Short-grained Java rice." (*Fairchild.*) (Injured in transit.)

5524. CAPSICUM ANNUUM. **Red pepper.**

From Macassar, Celebes. Received through Messrs. Lathrop and Fairchild (No. 343, January 10, 1900), October 8, 1900.

"A small variety of very hot red pepper generally used green in Macassar. Probably the same as that used in Java and other parts of the Dutch East Indies." (*Fairchild.*)

5525. CAPSICUM ANNUUM. **Red pepper.**

From Macassar, Celebes. Received through Messrs. Lathrop and Fairchild (No. 344, January 10, 1900), October 8, 1900.

"A long red pepper of the shape of the so-called Guinea pepper." (*Fairchild.*)

5526. CAPSICUM ANNUUM. **Red pepper.**

From Bali Island, Dutch East Indies. Received through Messrs. Lathrop and Fairchild (No. 345, January 7, 1900), October 8, 1900.

A long red variety.

5527. SOLANUM sp.

From Bali, Dutch East Indies. Received through Messrs. Lathrop and Fairchild (No. 346, January 7, 1900), October 8, 1900.

"A white-fruited species which is used on the *Rijstafel* or rice table of Europeans. Much like an eggplant, of which it may be only a variety." (*Fairchild.*)

5528. MOMORDICA sp.

From Macassar, Celebes. Received through Messrs. Lathrop and Fairchild (No. 347, January 11, 1900), October 8, 1900.

"A fruit called Paparé here. It is eaten raw. When mature it is very showy, with bright-red endocarp. Said by Paillieux and Bois to grow well in France." (*Fairchild.*)

5529. CITRUS LIMETTA. **Lime.**

From Macassar, Celebes. Received through Messrs. Lathrop and Fairchild (No. 348, January 11, 1900), October 8, 1900.

"A very thin-skinned, juicy lime of inferior flavor." (*Fairchild.*)

5530. CAPSICUM ANNUUM. **Red pepper.**

From Macassar, Celebes. Received through Messrs. Lathrop and Fairchild (No. 349, January 11, 1900), October 8, 1900.

A long red variety.

5531. CITRUS LIMONUM. **Lemon.**

From Banda, Dutch East Indies. Received through Messrs. Lathrop and Fairchild (No. 350, February 8, 1900), October 8, 1900.

"*Sauerbier*, a very large, thin-skinned, exceedingly juicy lemon of good flavor, sent through the kindness of Mr. Sauerbier from his own garden. The fruit examined was 3 inches in diameter, with smooth skin, not over one-quarter of an inch thick, and large oil glands. The flesh is composed of large cells which are much elongated in shape and therefore easily broken by pressure. The amount of juice is exceptionally large. Nearly three-fourths of an ordinary glassful was squeezed by hand from a single fruit. Juice of good flavor, somewhat aromatic, but the fruit was too ripe to judge fairly. The tree is said to be small. This is the finest lemon seen by us on the expedition, and its discovery was made by Mr. Lathrop." (*Fairchild.*)

5532. CITRUS LIMONUM. **Lemon.**

From Banda, Dutch East Indies. Received through Messrs. Lathrop and Fairchild (No. 351, February 8, 1900), October 8, 1900.

From the garden of Mr. Sauerbier. "Seeds from the remarkable lemon described in No. 5531. Its seedlings may produce its like." (*Fairchild.*)

5533. CITRUS LIMONUM. **Lemon.**

From Banda, Dutch East Indies. Received through Messrs. Lathrop and Fairchild (No. 352, February 8, 1900), October 8, 1900.

"Seeds from lemon said to have come from the same tree as No. 5531. The fruits from which these seeds were taken were smaller, but still of unusual size and excellence." (*Fairchild.*)

5534. CANARIUM AMBOINENSE. **Amboina almond.**

From Amboina, Dutch East Indies. Received through Messrs. Lathrop and Fairchild (No. 353, February 8, 1900), October 8, 1900.

"This is possibly the stateliest avenue tree in the world and forms in the famous garden of Buitenzorg, Java, the '*Canarium Allée*,' which is noted as the most beautiful avenue in existence. A valuable table oil is made from the kernels of the fruits and these are highly prized by Europeans, being eaten like almonds. If introduced into the Philippines they might be made to pay as a secondary crop." (*Fairchild.*)

5535. SOLANUM MELONGENA. **Eggplant.**

From Amboina, Dutch East Indies. Received through Messrs. Lathrop and Fairchild (No. 354, February 8, 1900), October 8, 1900.

"Fruit long, striped with red, purple, and white." (*Fairchild.*)

5536. CAPSICUM ANNUUM. **Red pepper.**

From Amboina, Dutch East Indies. Received through Messrs. Lathrop and Fairchild (No. 355, February 14, 1900), October 8, 1900.

"An excellent variety of egg-shaped red pepper." (*Fairchild.*)

5537. CAPSICUM ANNUUM. **Red pepper.**

From Singapore. Received through Messrs. Lathrop and Fairchild (No. 356, January 24, 1900), October 8, 1900.

"A long, slender variety of red pepper." (*Fairchild.*)

5538. CAPSICUM ANNUUM. **Red pepper.**

From Macassar, Celebes. Received through Messrs. Lathrop and Fairchild (No. 357, January 11, 1900), October 8, 1900.

"A small red pepper." (*Fairchild.*)

5539. **Forest tree.**

From Boela, Ceram Island, Dutch East Indies. Received through Messrs. Lathrop and Fairchild (No. 358, January 18, 1900), October 8, 1900.

"Seeds from a single fruit of a beautiful orange-red color; borne by a small forest tree with lanceolate dark-green leaves. Fruits borne in pairs, and are pulpy, jelly-like, and almost transparent. One of the showiest fruits I have ever seen. I do not know whether or not it is edible." (*Fairchild.*)

5540. **Forest tree.**

From Boela, Ceram Island, Dutch East Indies. Received through Messrs. Lathrop and Fairchild (No. 359, January 18, 1900), October 8, 1900.

"Fruit oblate spheroid, dark green, several-seeded with hard, smooth exocarp. Flesh brown and spongy. Not known to be edible." (*Fairchild.*)

5541. **Forest tree.**

From Boela, Ceram Island, Dutch East Indies. Received through Messrs. Lathrop and Fairchild (No. 360, January 18, 1900), October 8, 1900.

"One-seeded, purple-fleshed fruit, from clearing in virgin forest. Said to be poisonous." (*Fairchild.*)

5542. VICIA FABA. **Broad bean.**

From Dutch East Indies. Received through Messrs. Lathrop and Fairchild (No. 361, January 11, 1900), October 8, 1900.

"Sample of a variety of broad bean which is canned and sent from Holland to India, where it is cooked in water and eaten as a great delicacy by Europeans. Most excellent eating." (*Fairchild.*)

5543. **Shade tree.**

From Toeal, Kei Island, Dutch East Indies. Received through Messrs. Lathrop and Fairchild (No. 362, January 20, 1900), October 8, 1900.

"A rapidly growing shade tree resembling *Albizzia lebbek*, but with long cylindrical pods of dark-brown color. Suitable for Florida, Porto Rico, or any tropical region." (*Fairchild.*)

5544. MOMORDICA sp.

From Toeal, Kei Island, Dutch East Indies. Received through Messrs. Lathrop and Fairchild (No. 363, January 20, 1900), October 8, 1900.

"A small-fruited species growing wild in the island. Said to be eaten raw by the natives." (*Fairchild.*)

5545. SOLANUM MELONGENA. **Eggplant.**

From Toeal, Kei Island, Dutch East Indies. Received through Messrs. Lathrop and Fairchild (No. 364, January 20, 1900), October 8, 1900.

"A yellow-fruited species of *Solanum*, cooked and eaten by the natives. May prove valuable for breeding purposes." (*Fairchild.*)

5546. CAPSICUM ANNUUM. **Red pepper.**

From Gisser Island (a typical atoll near Ceram), Dutch East Indies. Received through Messrs. Lathrop and Fairchild (No. 365, February 3, 1900), October 8, 1900.

"A large oblong variety of red pepper." (*Fairchild.*)

5547. CITRUS DECUMANA. **Pomelo.**

From Sekar, Dutch New Guinea. Received through Messrs. Lathrop and Fairchild (No. 366, February 1, 1900), October 8, 1900.

"Seeds of a large and very sour variety of pomelo or shaddock presented by the Radja of Sekar, a village on the coast of Dutch New Guinea. The shaddock is native of the islands of the Malay Archipelago, being more particularly abundant in the Friendly Isles and Fiji. Introduced into India from Java and into the West Indies by Captain Shaddock, hence the name *Shaddock*. It is cultivated in most tropical countries." (*Fairchild.*)

5548.

From Wetter Island, Dutch East Indies. Received through Messrs. Lathrop and Fairchild (No. 367, January 23, 1900), October 8, 1900.

"Long purple fruit found on the shore of the island of Wetter. The pulp is soft like that of a plum. It is said not to be edible." (*Fairchild.*)

5549. CONVOLVULUS sp. (?)

From Dammer Island, Dutch East Indies. Received through Messrs. Lathrop and Fairchild (No. 368, January 22, 1900), October 8, 1900.

"A large vigorous vine with curious seed pods." (*Fairchild.*)

5550. CONVOLVULUS sp. (?)

From Dammer Island, Dutch East Indies. Received through Messrs. Lathrop and Fairchild (No. 369, January 22, 1900), October 8, 1900.

"Small-fruited vine which covers low trees and shrubs." (*Fairchild.*)

5551.

From Dammer Island, Dutch East Indies. Received through Messrs. Lathrop and Fairchild (No. 370, January 22, 1900), October 8, 1900.

"From vine not in flower, but of luxuriant growth, covering trees and shrubs." (*Fairchild.*)

5552. CUCURBITA sp. (?)

From Dammer Island, Dutch East Indies. Received through Messrs. Lathrop and Fairchild (No. 371, January 22, 1900), October 8, 1900.

"A vigorous cucurbitaceous vine, covering trees and shrubs and bearing large numbers of curious dry fruits resembling *Luffa*." (*Fairchild.*)

5553. CAPSICUM ANNUUM. **Red pepper.**

From Gisser Island, Dutch East Indies. Received through Messrs. Lathrop and Fairchild (No. 372, February 4, 1900), October 8, 1900.

"A cherry-shaped red pepper." (*Fairchild.*)

5554. CITRUS LIMETTA. **Lime.**

From Gisser Island, Dutch East Indies. Received through Messrs. Lathrop and Fairchild (No. 373, February 3, 1900), October 8, 1900.

"Seeds from a lime of very peculiar shape. Long and slender, with a decided beak at the lower end. Flavor inferior." (*Fairchild.*)

5555. CAPSICUM ANNUUM. **Red pepper.**

From Gisser Island, Dutch East Indies. Received through Messrs. Lathrop and Fairchild (No. 374, February 3, 1900), October 8, 1900.

"A small red pepper."

5556. CAPSICUM ANNUUM. **Red pepper.**

From Toeal, Kei Island, Dutch East Indies. Received through Messrs. Lathrop and Fairchild (No. 375, January 31, 1900), October 8, 1900.

"A small cherry-shaped red pepper." (*Fairchild.*)

5557. CONVOLVULUS sp. (?)

From Dobbo, Aru Islands, Dutch East Indies. Received through Messrs. Lathrop and Fairchild (No. 376, January 28, 1900), October 8, 1900.

"Seed from vine growing in the mangrove swamps near the town. Ornamental." (*Fairchild.*)

5558. CONVOLVULUS sp. (?)

From Dobbo, Aru Islands, Dutch East Indies. Received through Messrs. Lathrop and Fairchild (No. 377, January 28, 1900), October 8, 1900.

"Seeds from a plant growing near mangrove swamps on sandy soil." (*Fairchild.*)

5559. CUCURBITA sp. **Squash.**

From Sekar, Dutch New Guinea. Received through Messrs. Lathrop and Fairchild (No. 378, February 2, 1900), October 8, 1900.

"Seeds from a squash presented by the Radja of Sekar, a small village on the coast of New Guinea." (*Fairchild.*)

5560. ZEA MAYS. **Maize.**

From Amboina, Dutch East Indies. Received through Messrs. Lathrop and Fairchild (No. 379, February 7, 1900), October 8, 1900.

"A variety of Indian corn which is of such superior quality that it is shipped from the island of Amboina to many other points in the archipelago. A hard flinty variety, and worthy of trial in Porto Rico, Hawaii, and the Philippines." (*Fairchild.*)

5561. ARACHIS HYPOGAEA. **Peanut.**

From the Dutch East Indies. Received through Messrs. Lathrop and Fairchild (No. 380, February 7, 1900), October 8, 1900.

"A very large peanut, one of the most delicious we have ever tasted, probably from the island of Ternate." (*Fairchild.*)

5562.
>From Letti Island, Dutch East Indies. Received through Messrs. Lathrop and Fairchild (No. 381, January 25, 1900), October 8, 1900.

"Small fruits with lemon-yellow pulp, very sour. Brought on board and sold by natives of Letti." (*Fairchild.*)

5563. CHAVICA OFFICINARUM. **Long pepper.**
>From Macassar, Celebes. Received through Messrs. Lathrop and Fairchild (No. 382, January 22, 1900), October 8, 1900.

"A sample of so-called *Tjabeh aroij*, used in the Dutch East Indies as a condiment. It is very hot, and is much used by the natives in their curries. It is also used in medicine." (*Fairchild.*)

5564. CICCA NODIFLORA.
>From Amboina, Dutch East Indies. Received through Messrs. Lathrop and Fairchild (No. 383, February 7, 1900), October 8, 1900.

"Seeds from fruit tree, the sap of which is used for poisoning arrows. The roots are used as a medicine for asthma. Syphilis is treated with a decoction of the leaves, and the sour fruits are used for making preserves. The seeds act as a purgative. The tree grows about 25 feet high." (*Fairchild.*)

5565. CAPSICUM ANNUUM. **Red pepper.**
>From Fack Fack, Dutch New Guinea. Received through Messrs. Lathrop and Fairchild (No. 384, February 1, 1900), October 8, 1900.

"Very small red pepper found growing on a bush 4 feet high." (*Fairchild.*)

5566. CALOPHYLLUM sp.
>From Saparoea Island, Dutch East Indies. Received through Messrs. Lathrop and Fairchild (No. 385, February 8, 1900), October 8, 1900.

"A giant tree growing in front of the Controlleur's house at Saparoea. One of the most beautiful shade trees I have ever seen." (*Fairchild.*)

5567. CUCUMIS SATIVUS. **Cucumber.**
>From Macassar, Dutch East Indies. Received through Messrs. Lathrop and Fairchild, October 8, 1900.

"An excellent variety of uniform size and shape, especially suited for cultivation in the Tropics." (*Fairchild.*)

5568. STUARTIA PENTAGYNA.
>From Gage, Tenn. Presented by Mr. J. H. H. Boyd, through Mr. Lyster H. Dewey, of the Division of Botany. Received October 17, 1900.

5569. HUMULUS LUPULUS. **Hop.**
>From Auscha, Bohemia. Received through Mr. E. R. Lake, October 18, 1900.

Auscha Red.

5570. HUMULUS LUPULUS. **Hop.**
>From Auscha, Bohemia. Received through Mr. E. R. Lake, October 18, 1900.

Saaz.

5571. THEA VIRIDIS. **Tea.**
>From Ceylon. Received October 30, 1900.

Highest class "Jat," a wild indigenous tea.

5572 to 5585. **Leguminous forage plants.**

From Algeria. Presented by Doctor Trabut, Government Botanist of Algeria, through Mr. W. T. Swingle. Received November 2, 1900.

"This valuable collection comprises small amounts of the seed of a number of forage plants which are cultivated by Doctor Trabut at the Algerian experiment station at Rouïba. Many of these were introduced into culture by Doctor Trabut, and are now sent out of North Africa for the first time. Some of the plants occur in other parts of the Mediterranean region, but in general the forms of these species found growing in Algeria are more resistant to drought than those obtained elsewhere. This has proved true of the common vetch from Tunis, the narrow-leaved lupine or naturalized form of the Corsican lupine. All of these species are adapted for planting in autumn in the warmer regions of the South and Southwest. Unfortunately, only a small amount of seed of these species could be obtained. It is hoped that enough can be grown in this country to give a fair trial another year. There can be no doubt that all of the native North African forage plants deserve a most careful trial in the arid and semiarid regions on the Pacific slope. All of these are winter crops and should be sown in early autumn, since at that time there is sufficient moisture in the soil to enable the seed to germinate. The climate of North Africa is very mild in winter, and probably most of these species would be injured by severe frosts. They could, however, be grown in spring in Washington State and Oregon, where the winter would probably prove too severe to permit of their being sown in autumn." (*Swingle.*)

5572. VICIA CALCARATA. **Vetch.**

"This vetch is native to the Mediterranean region. The seed of this particular sort was obtained at Boghar in Algeria where the climate is very dry. This is one of the species introduced into culture by Doctor Trabut." (*Swingle.*)

5573. VICIA HIRTA. **Vetch.**

"This plant, which is usually considered to be a hairy form of *Vicia lutea*, occurs very commonly in Algeria and has been introduced into cultivation by Doctor Trabut. It reaches a height of 16 to 18 inches at the experiment station at Rouïba." (*Swingle.*)

5574. VICIA FULGENS. **Scarlet vetch.**

"An Algerian vetch with handsome red flowers. It is an annual and grows with extraordinary vigor, reaching a height of 6 to 8 feet and yielding an abundance of excellent forage. Doctor Trabut, who introduced the species into culture, reports that at the experiment station at Rouiba, near Algiers, it yields 40 tons of green fodder to the acre. The great drawback of this most promising vetch is that the pods when ripe snap open, especially under the influence of hot winds, and scatter the seed, rendering its collection very difficult and the seed in consequence high priced. It is sown in autumn before the first rains in Algeria, either alone or with winter oats. It occasionally produces seed abundantly. It is to be hoped that some region may be found in the United States which has a sufficiently humid atmosphere during the ripening period of the pods to prevent their scattering the seeds. It might be possible to breed varieties which would hold the seed better. This vetch is most likely to succeed in the Southern States and on the Pacific slope." (*Swingle.*) (See Nos. 3825 and 4336, inventory No. 8.)

5575. VICIA SATIVA. **Common vetch.**

"Doctor Trabut has been making comparative tests of all obtainable varieties of the common vetch at the Algerian Experiment Station at Rouïba. The one which proves best adapted to Algerian conditions is the present number, which is from the dry regions of Tunis." (*Swingle.*)

5576. VICIA BENGALENSIS. **Bengal vetch.**

"This name is given by the Kew Index as a synonym of *V. nissoliana*. It is one of the best of the numerous species of vetch grown at the Algerian Experiment Station at Rouïba. It somewhat resembles the scarlet vetch, attaining a considerable height." (*Swingle.*)

5572 to 5585—Continued.

5577. VICIA FABA. **Horse bean.**

"This is a dwarf form of horse bean which Doctor Trabut reports as growing wild 25 miles south of Teniat. He considers it to be undoubtedly the wild form of the cultivated broad beans and horse beans. It is utilized by the Arabs, but is probably of little value compared with the improved form, though it may resist drought better, since it comes from a dry region in Algeria." (*Swingle.*)

5578. MELILOTUS MACROSTACHYS. **Melilot.**

"This species of melilot, native to Algeria, differs from most of the sweet clovers in having no pronounced odor. In consequence of this it is readily eaten by cattle. It has succeeded very well at the Experiment Station at Rouïba, where it attains a height of from 3 to 6 feet." (*Swingle.*)

5579. TRIGONELLA CORNICULATA. **Small fenugreek.**

"This species, which has the same strong odor as fenugreek, from which it differs, however, in having very much smaller pods and seeds, grows very vigorously at the Experiment Station at Rouïba, where it attains a height of from 3 to 5 feet. It could not be used for feeding milch cows, as the strong odor would make the milk unsalable. It is, however, used for fattening stock and as a green manure. It is said to resist drought very well." (*Swingle.*)

5580. TRIGONELLA GLADIATA. **Trigonella.**

"This plant also resembles fenugreek in odor. It has been cultivated with some success at the Experiment Station at Rouïba." (*Swingle.*)

5581. SCORPIURUS VERMICULATA. **Rabbit's ear.**

"This plant is a half-prostrate annual and grows wild all through northern Algeria. It is said to furnish an excellent forage on good land and the Arabs eat the seeds. The pods, which are bent more or less into a circle, are as large as one's finger and lie on the ground. They are eaten greedily by the sheep and constitute one of their important foods on the plains of northern Algeria." (*Swingle.*)

5582. ONONIS AVELLANA. **Ononis.**

"This is said by Doctor Trabut to be a good green manure for heavy soils. It is found only in Algeria, where it occurs in few localities on clay hills." (*Swingle.*)

5583. LUPINUS ANGUSTIFOLIUS. **Narrow-leafed lupine.**

"This species is commonly grown by the Kabyles and Arabs, and is used by them as a substitute for coffee. It is the earliest maturing species grown in North Africa and is good for green manure. It is said to dislike an excess of lime in the soil." (*Swingle.*)

5584. LUPINUS TERMIS. **Egyptian or Corsican lupine.**

"This is considered by Doctor Trabut to be the best species for culture in North Africa. It is sown at the rate of about 100 pounds to the acre, in autumn, and it grows rapidly, and in February or March can be plowed under. It much resembles the white lupine, but is said to be taller and have larger seeds. It is a very promising species for culture in California." (*Swingle.*)

5585. LATHYRUS TINGITANUS. **Tangier flat pea.**

"This species, which is a native of North Africa, is considered by Doctor Trabut to be one of the best forage plants in Africa. It reaches a height of from 3 to 4 feet and drives out all other plants. Sown in autumn it prevents the growth of all weeds, and on the 16th of May gives a crop of 3½ tons of dry hay to the acre. It is sown at the rate of about 50 pounds of seed per acre and is sometimes sown with one-third the weight of winter oats. It is a beautiful plant, very vigorous, and probably has a great future as a forage plant in the South and Southwest. (*Swingle.*)

5586. NEOWASHINGTONIA sp. **Fan palm.**

From San Diego, Cal. Presented by Mr. T. S. Brandegee; collected in Cajon de Santa Maria, near Calamaguet, on the eastern shore of Lower California.

5587. HUMULUS LUPULUS. **Hop.**

From Spalt, Bavaria, Germany. Received through Mr. D. G. Fairchild (No. 461), November 19, 1900.

Spalt City. "Cuttings or 'Fächser' of the finest Spalt hops grown in the restricted area of Spalt, Bavaria. These Spalt hops are renowned throughout Germany as next to the Saaz and Auscha, the best in the world. They are exported from here in considerable quantities to America where they are used by the large brewers in the manufacture of their finest beers. In planting these cuttings it should be remembered that they have been taken in October and transported to America and may suffer in vigor by this unusual treatment. The cuttings are planted here four or five together in one hill, being placed upright in the ground some 3 inches apart and covered about 1½ to 2 inches with soil. The hills are from 3 to 4 feet apart each way. The soil, which is the most important item of any in hop culture, must be a sandy loam. In Spalt it is a disintegrated red sandstone, similar to the soil in the Bohemian hop region of Saaz. Only in the small region about the little village of Spalt do these famous hops develop their fine aroma and valuable lupulin contents. Before planting, the soil should be carefully worked to a depth of 2¾ to 3 feet and the culture should be scrupulously clean during the season. This is not a heavy bearer, one pound per pole being a maximum. Its value lies in its superior quality of aroma. The best grade of hop from which these cuttings are taken brings this year on the Spalt market over 15 cents per pound. Great care should be taken that no male hop plants are grown near these Spalt hops, as their presence induces a heavy seed production and an immediate lowering of the quality of the yield. Harvesting, sulphuring, etc., as usual." (*Fairchild.*)

5588. HUMULUS LUPULUS. **Hop.**

From Spalt, Bavaria, Germany. Received through Mr. D. G. Fairchild (No. 462, October 24, 1900), November 19, 1900.

Seed from the best *Spalt hops*, grown in the village of Massendorf. "This variety of hop produces very few seeds indeed, and these may be of distinct value for breeding purposes and for the selection of a more vigorous strain of superlative quality." (*Fairchild.*)

5589. COCHLEARIA ARMORACIA. **Horse-radish.**

From Biersdorf, Bavaria. Received through Mr. D. G. Fairchild (No. 457, October 19, 1900), November 12, 1900.

"Cuttings of a variety of Bavarian horse-radish which ranks among the best in Europe. It is much milder in flavor than the malin variety, and its method of cultivation is different." (*Fairchild.*) (See S. P. I. Circular No. 21.)

5590. HORDEUM DISTICHUM. **Barley.**

From Kitzing, Bavaria. Received through Mr. D. G. Fairchild (No. 458), November 26, 1900.

Lower Frankish *Kitzing* brewing barley. "The most noted Bavarian variety, and one of the best brewing barleys in the world. It is a heavy, thin-skinned sort containing a large percentage of starch. It was grown on a *heavy clay soil*, and should, according to the growers in Bavaria, be tried on a *light but not too sandy soil*. A change of soil is considered essential." (*Fairchild.*)

5591. HORDEUM DISTICHUM. **Barley.**

From Kitzing, Bavaria. Received through Mr. D. G. Fairchild (No. 459, October 22, 1900), November 26, 1900.

"This is the same as No. 5590, except that it was grown on light soil, and should, therefore, be tried on heavy clay soils in America." (*Fairchild.*)

5592. HORDEUM DISTICHUM. **Barley.**

From Würzburg, Bavaria. Received through Mr. D. G. Fairchild (No. 460, October 22, 1900), November 26, 1900.

Lower Frankish brewing barley. Essentially the same as Nos. 5590 and 5591. Suited to fairly light soils.

5593. HUMULUS LUPULUS. **Hop.**

From Wolnzach, Bavaria. Received through Mr. D. G. Fairchild (No. 462, October 25, 1900), November 19, 1900.

Cuttings from the Wolnzach hops. "These are late-ripening hops of excellent quality, but not so highly prized as those from Saaz or Spalt. Cuttings from 6-year-old stocks, suited to a friable loam; yield from ¼ to ½ pound per pole; probably not so susceptible to soil conditions as the Saaz." (*Fairchild.*)

5594. HUMULUS LUPULUS. **Hop.**

From Wolnzach, Bavaria. Received through Mr. D. G. Fairchild (No. 463, October 25, 1900), November 19, 1900.

Seeds from Wolnzach hops.

5595 to 5608.

From the Government Laboratory, Georgetown, Demerara, British Guiana. Received through the Division of Chemistry, October 19, 1900.

A collection of sugar-cane arrows with fertile seeds sent by Mr. J. B. Harrison.

5595.	(J. B. H.	74.)	**5602.**	(J. B. H.	5044.)
5596.	(J. B. H.	116.)	**5603.**	(J. B. H.	5201.)
5597.	(J. B. H.	790.)	**5604.**	(J. B. H.	5443.)
5598.	(J. B. H.	1485.)	**5605.**	(J. B. H.	5444.)
5599.	(J. B. H.	1850.)	**5606.**	(J. B. H.	5454.)
5600.	(J. B. H.	2093.)	**5607.**	(J. B. H.	5717.)
5601.	(J. B. H.	5041.)	**5608.**	(J. B. H.	5774.)

5609. MELINIS MINUTIFLORA. **Molasses grass.**

From São Paulo, Brazil. Presented by the Brazilian minister, the Hon. Dr. J. F. de Assis-Brasil, through the U. S. Consul at São Paulo, September, 1900.

5610. VILLEBRUNEA INTEGRIFOLIA. **Assam rhea.**

From Calcutta, India. Presented by D. Prain, Superintendent of the Royal Botanic Garden, Calcutta. Received November 16, 1900.

(See Agric. Ledg., Calcutta, 1898, No. 15, for description of this fiber plant.)

5611. HUMULUS LUPULUS. **Hop.**

From Wolnzach, Bavaria. Received through Mr. D. G. Fairchild, November 19, 1900.

"A mixture of hop seeds from the drying room of Wolnzach." (*Fairchild.*)

5612. PASSIFLORA EDULIS. **Passion flower.**

From Auckland, New Zealand. Presented by J. P. Carolin, through Mr. George William Hill, Chief of the Division of Publications. Received November 21, 1900.

5613. ATRIPLEX LEPTOCARPA. **Saltbush.**

From Berkeley, Cal. Presented by the California Experiment Station, through Prof. Chas. H. Shinn. Received November 21, 1900.

5614. ATRIPLEX HALIMOIDES. **Saltbush.**

From Berkeley, Cal. Presented by the California Experiment Station, through Prof. Chas. H. Shinn. Received November 21, 1900.

5615. CINNAMOMUM CAMPHORA. **Camphor.**

From Berkeley, Cal. Presented by the California Experiment Station, through Prof. Chas. H. Shinn. Received November 21, 1900.

5616. VITIS VINIFERA. **Grape.**

From Saonara, Italy. Received through Mr. D. G. Fairchild, November 23, 1900, from Fratelli Sgaravatti.

Sultanina rosea.

5617 to 5621.

From Manila, P. I. Received July 1, 1900.

No descriptions furnished.

5617.	ERYTHRINA CARNEA.	Dap-dap.
5618.	BIXA ORELLANA.	Achiote.
5619.	SOLANUM MELONGENA.	Eggplant.
5620.	COIX LACHRYMA-JOBI.	Job's tears.
5621.	INGA LANCEOLATA.	

5622. HUMULUS LUPULUS. **Hop.**

From Tetschen, Bohemia. Received through Mr. D. G. Fairchild, November 30, 1900.

"Seed from wild hops growing on the grounds of the Experiment Station at Tetschen-Liebwerd." (*Fairchild.*)

5623. CLIANTHUS DAMPIERI.

From Roebourne, West Australia. Presented by Mr. W. F. Cusack. Received December 3, 1900.

"A beautiful garden flower and also good feed for stock. It will grow with 6 inches of rain per annum, or one day good rain in the year. The seed requires scorching or soaking in hot water." (*Cusack.*)

5624.

From Roebourne, West Australia. Presented by Mr. W. F. Cusack. Received December 3, 1900.

"A leguminous shrub 6 feet high. Splendid feed for horses, cattle, and sheep. It is smaller than 5623, erect instead of prostrate. A beautiful garden flower." (*Cusack.*)

5625.

From Roebourne, West Australia. Presented by Mr. W. F. Cusack. Received December 3, 1900.

Mundle bundle. "A good perennial tussock grass. Grows where the annual average rainfall is 14 inches, and the thermometer sometimes shows temperatures up to 127° F. in the shade." (*Cusack.*)

5626. **Pela.**

From Roebourne, West Australia. Presented by Mr. W. F. Cusack. Received December 3, 1900.

"A good annual. It grows on sandy soil very well with small rainfall." (*Cusack.*)

5627. RUBUS NUTKANUS. Salmon berry.

From Blaine, Wash. Presented by Mr. C. E. Flint. Received November 6, 1900.

A large red raspberry growing on the Pacific Coast of North America.

5628. TRITICUM VULGARE. Wheat.

From Portland, Oreg. Presented by Mr. R. C. Judson. Received December 4, 1900.

Yaroslaf winter wheat. Grown from No. 2792; imported from the Government of St. Petersburg, Russia, in March, 1899, by Mr. M. A. Carleton. Considered objectionable for Oregon because of bearded character.

5629. TRITICUM VULGARE. Wheat.

From Portland, Oreg. Presented by Mr. R. C. Judson. Received December 4, 1900.

Banatka winter wheat. Grown from No. 2956; imported by Mr. M. A. Carleton in March, 1899.

5630. TRITICUM VULGARE. Wheat.

From Portland, Oreg. Presented by Mr. R. C. Judson. Received December 4, 1900.

Sandomir winter wheat. Grown from No. 2958, imported by Mr. M. A. Carleton in March, 1899.

5631. HUMULUS LUPULUS. Hop.

From Schwetzingen, Germany. Received through Mr. D. G. Fairchild (No. 456, Nov. 6, 1900), December 5, 1900.

"Cuttings of the Schwetzingen hop, one of the best early varieties, ripening the middle of August. Not considered by Professor Braungart as so delicate as the 'Saaz' or 'Spalt,' and on this account may thrive better on American soils." (*Fairchild.*)

5632. CAESALPINIA BONDUCELLA.

From Manila, P. I. Received July, 1900.

This genus of leguminosæ contains some 40 species; inhabitants of the Tropics of both hemispheres. Robust, erect trees, shrubs, or woody prickly climbers; leaves large; flowers showy, yellow. In some parts of India it grows at an altitude of 2,500 feet. Oil from the seeds is useful in convulsions and palsy, debility after fever, and other diseases. Is said to soften the skin and remove pimples. The seeds are used instead of quinine, and also as an ointment. In disorders of the liver the leaves are considered very efficacious. The nuts are used for making bracelets and necklaces. The seeds are used by children in place of marbles and in other games. The root is also used for medical purposes.

5633. JUGLANS REGIA. Walnut.

From Mettmenstetten, Switzerland. Presented by Hon. A. Lieberknecht, U. S. Consul at Zürich.

5634. GARCINIA MANGOSTANA. Mangosteen.

From Ceylon. Received through Mr. D. G. Fairchild, December 7, 1900. Presented by Dr. Valentine Duke, of Newara, Eliya.

Fruits covered with a coating of paraffin to preserve the germinative power of the seeds.

5635. TRITICUM VULGARE. Wheat.

From Kurman-Kemelchi, Central Crimea. Received through Mr. M. A. Carleton, December 12, 1900.

Crimean. "A hard red winter wheat, one of the best in the world. Adapted for trial in Kansas, Oklahoma, northern Texas, Missouri, and southern portions of Iowa and Nebraska." (*Carleton.*)

5636. TRITICUM VULGARE. **Wheat.**

From Altonau, near Melitopol, in northern Taurida. Received through Mr. M. A. Carleton, December 12, 1900.

"Similar to No. 5635, but from a rather colder latitude and not ripening quite so early. Adaptation like No. 5635." (*Carleton.*)

5637. TRITICUM VULGARE. **Wheat.**

From Altonau, near Melitopol, in northern Taurida. Received through Mr. M. A. Carleton, December 12, 1900.

Girka winter wheat. "A beardless variety, soft-grained, but very hardy. Adaptation like No. 5635." (*Carleton.*)

5638. TRITICUM VULGARE. **Wheat.**

From Constantinovskol, 40 miles east of Stavropol, in north Caucasus. Received through Mr. M. A. Carleton, December 12, 1900.

Ulta. "A hard, red-grained, bearded, winter variety, very resistant to cold and drought. Adapted for trial as a winter wheat in Iowa, Nebraska, and the southern portions of Wisconsin, Minnesota, and South Dakota, and eastern Colorado. An excellent variety for all of Kansas and northern portions of Missouri and Oklahoma." (*Carleton.*)

5639. TRITICUM DURUM. **Wheat.**

From Uralsk Territory, Russia. Received through Mr. M. A. Carleton, December 12, 1900.

Kubanka. "One of the best macaroni wheats known. Sown in the spring. Admirably adapted for growing in the semiarid regions, between the one hundredth meridian and the Rocky Mountains, and North Dakota to Texas, and also in New Mexico, Arizona, Utah, eastern Oregon, and the Palouse country." (*Carleton.*)

5640. TRITICUM VULGARE. **Wheat.**

From Padi, Saratov, Russia. Received through Mr. M. A. Carleton, December 12, 1900.

Padi. "A beardless, soft, or semihard winter wheat. Adapted to all the northern winter wheat States, from New York to Kansas and southward to the thirty-fifth parallel." (*Carleton.*)

5641. TRITICUM VULGARE. **Wheat.**

From Starobelsk, Kharkof, Russia. Received through Mr. M. A. Carleton, December 12, 1900.

Kharkof. "A bearded, hard, red, winter wheat, similar to No. 5635, but coming from a region much farther north and therefore extremely hardy. Especially resistant to piercing, dry, winter winds, where there is little snowfall. Admirably adapted for trial as a winter wheat in Minnesota, South Dakota, Iowa, northern Nebraska, Wisconsin, and perhaps southern North Dakota." (*Carleton.*)

5642. TRITICUM DURUM. **Wheat.**

From Ambrocievka, 20 miles northeast of Taganrog, in the Don Territory, Russia. Received through Mr. M. A. Carleton, December 12, 1900.

Yellow Gharnovka. "A macaroni wheat similar to No. 5643, but having yellow grains. Sown in the spring. Adapted for trial in the most arid portions of the United States." (*Carleton.*)

5643. TRITICUM DURUM. **Wheat.**

From Ambrocievka, 20 miles northeast of Taganrog, in the Don Territory, Russia. Received through Mr. M. A. Carleton, December 12, 1900.

Gharnovka. "The best macaroni wheat from the vicinity of Taganrog. Sown in the spring. Adapted for trial in the most arid portions of the United States." (*Carleton.*)

SEPTEMBER, 1900, TO DECEMBER, 1903.

5644. TRITICUM DURUM. **Wheat.**

From Ambrocievka, 20 miles northeast of Taganrog, in the Don Territory, Russia. Received through Mr. M. A. Carleton, December 12, 1900.

Velvet Don. "An excellent macaroni wheat with *black beards*. Sown in the spring. Adaptation same as for No. 5643." (*Carleton.*)

5645. TRITICUM DURUM. **Wheat.**

From Ambrocievka, 20 miles northeast of Taganrog, in the Don Territory, Russia. Received through Mr. M. A. Carleton, December 12, 1900.

Black Don. "A *black-chaff* macaroni wheat. Sown in the spring. This wheat and the two preceding numbers, however, might be sown in November or December with good results in Texas, New Mexico, Arizona, and southern California. Adaptation same as for No. 5643." (*Carleton.*)

5646. TRITICUM DURUM. **Wheat.**

From Taganrog, Don Territory, Russia. Received through Mr. M. A. Carleton, December 12, 1900.

Gharnovka. "A spring wheat, but may be sown in late autumn south of the 35th parallel. This and No. 5643 are the best of the Taganrog macaroni wheats. Adaptation same as for three preceding numbers." (*Carleton.*)

5647. PANICUM MILIACEUM. **Proso.**

From Uralsk Territory, Russia. Received through Mr. M. A. Carleton, December 12, 1900.

White Ural. "The best sort for milling and extremely drought resistant. Adapted to growing in all semiarid districts west of the Mississippi River." (*Carleton.*)

5648. PANICUM MILIACEUM. **Proso.**

From Uralsk Territory, Russia. Received through Mr. M. A. Carleton, December 12, 1900.

Yellow Ural. "A variety of excellent quality, yielding heavily, and very resistant to drought. Adaptation same as No. 5647." (*Carleton.*)

5649 to 5686. PRUNUS DOMESTICA. **Prune.**

From France. Received through Mr. E. R. Lake, December 8, 1900. A collection of French grafted stock, as follows:

5649.

Cœur de bœuf. From Salvetat, Carcassonne, France. (Lake No. 1.)

5650.

Chaproni. From Vallerand, Traverny, France. (Lake No. 2.)

5651.

Giant. From Barbier, Orleans, France. (Lake No. 3.)

5652.

Iejum Erik. From Barbier, Orleans, France. (Lake No. 4.)

5653.

Des Béjonniers. From Barbier, Orleans, France. (Lake No. 5.)

5654.

Quetsche sucré. From Barbier, Orleans, France. (Lake No. 6.)

5655.

Mirabelle de Metz. From Barbier, Orleans, France. (Lake No. 7.)

5649 to 5686—Continued.

5656.
Sainte Catherine. From Barbier, Orleans, France. (Lake No. 8.)

5657.
Bleu de Belgique. From Rothberg, Gennevilliers, France. (Lake No. 9.)

5658.
Jaune d'Agen. From Rothberg, Gennevilliers, France. (Lake No. 10.)

5659.
The Czar. From Rothberg, Gennevilliers, France. (Lake No. 11.)

5660.
Grand Duc. From Rothberg, Gennevilliers, France. (Lake No. 12.)

5661.
Altesse. From Rothberg, Gennevilliers, France. (Lake No. 13.)

5662.
Big rose. From Croux et Fils, Paris, France. (Lake No. 14.)

5663.
Quetsche de Letricourt. From Croux et Fils, Paris, France. (Lake No. 15.)

5664.
Belle de Louvrain. From Croux et Fils, Paris, France. (Lake No. 16.)

5665.
Surpasse monsieur. From Croux et Fils, Paris, France. (Lake No. 17.)

5666. (Number not occupied.)

5667.
Tardive musque. From Baltet Frères, Troyes, France. (Lake No. 19.)

5668.
Mirabelle grosse. From Baltet Frères, Troyes, France. (Lake No. 20.)

5669.
Mirabelle petite. From Baltet Frères, Troyes, France. (Lake No. 21.)

5670.
Mirabelle précoce. From Baltet Frères, Troyes, France. (Lake No. 22.)

5671.
Mirabelle tardive. From Baltet Frères, Troyes, France. (Lake No. 23.)

5672.
De Norbet. From Baltet Frères, Troyes, France. (Lake No. 24.)

5673.
Monsieur hâtif. From Baltet Frères, Troyes, France. (Lake No. 25.)

5674.
Précoce de Tours. From Baltet Frères, Troyes, France. (Lake No. 26.)

5675.
Prince Englebert (strain). From Baltet Frères, Troyes, France. (Lake No. 27.)

5649 to 5686—Continued.

5676.
Reine Claude d' Ouillins. From Baltet Frères, Troyes, France. (Lake No. 28.)

5677.
R^{e}i$_i$^{le} Claude d' Althau. From Baltet Frères, Troyes, France. (Lake No. 29.)

5678.
De Montfort. From Baltet Frères, Troyes, France. (Lake No. 30.)

5679.
Iy A^{gen} améliorée. From Baltet Frères, Troyes, France. (Lake No. 31.)

5680.
Quetsche de Dorel. From Baltet Frères, Troyes, France. (Lake No. 32.)

5681.
R^{e}i$_i$^{le} des Mirabelles. From Baltet Frères, Troyes, France. (Lake No. 33.)

5682.
R^e$_{ein}$^{e} Victoria. From Fleury-Meudon, near Paris, France. (Lake No. 34.)

5683.
V^o$_{olet}$ prune. From Fleury-Meudon, near Paris, France. (Lake No. 35.)

5684.
S$_{an}$^{nois} quetsche. From Sannois, France. (Lake No. 36.)

5685.
Rein^e Claude violette (strain). From Sannois, France. (Lake No. 37.)

5686.
Gloire d' Épinay. From Epinay, France. (Lake No. 38.)

5687. PYRUS **MALUS.** **Apple.**

From France. Received through Mr. E. R. Lake, December 8, 1900.
Transparente de Croncels. (Lake No. 39.)

5688. PYRUS **MALUS.** **Apple.**

From France. Received through Mr. E. R. Lake, December 8, 1900.
Transparente de Zurich. (Lake No. 40.)

5689. VITIS **VINIFERA.** **Grape.**

From France. Received through Mr. E. R. Lake, December 8, 1900.
Gamay. (Lake No. 41.)

5690 to 5744. PYRUS **spp.** **Apple.**

From France. Received through Mr. E. R. Lake, December 8, 1900. A collection of ornamental apples, as follows:

5690.	SEROTINA.	5702.	FLAVA.
5691.	IILLENT ARGENTE.	5703.	INTERMEDIA.
5692.	OBLONGA.	5704.	TURBINATA.
5693.	JOHN DOWNIE.	5705.	COERULESCENS.
5694.	PAUL'S IMPERIAL.	5706.	HALLEANA.
5695.	SPECTABILIS IMPERIAL.	5707.	VESPER ROSE.
5696.	PULCHELLA.	5708.	MARENGO.
5697.	SPECIOSA.	5709.	TENORII CARNEA PLENA.
5698.	SULFUREA.	5710.	AMPLA.
5699.	ATROPURPUREA.	5711.	PRUNIFOLIA PENDULA.
5700.	NIVEA POLYPETALA.	5712.	MINNESOTA.
5701.	FASTIGIATA.	5713.	SPHAEROCARPA.

5690 to 5744—Continued.

5714.	GENERAL GRANT.	5730.	LONGIFOLIA.
5715.	TARDIV D'HIVER.	5731.	MAXIMA.
5716.	RINGO.	5732.	À FLEUR DOUBLE.
5717.	PULCHRA.	5733.	FASTIGIATA BIFERA.
5718.	KAIDO.	5734.	WHITNEY.
5719.	MAGNIFICA.	5735.	À FRUIT BLANC.
5720.	NIGRA.	5736.	QUAKER BEAUTY.
5721.	EDULIS.	5737.	IBRIC?
5722.	ORANGE.	5738.	SPECTABILIS IMPERIAL REVENI.
5723.	LADY ELGIN.		
5724.	TRANSLUCENS.	5739.	NIKITA FLORIBUNDA.
5725.	MONTREAL BEAUTY.	5740.	VAN WYCK.
5726.	LUTESCENS.	5741.	HYSLOP.
5727.	MAGNIFICA.	5742.	THE FAIRY.
5728.	FLAVESCENS.	5743.	TORINGO.
5729.	CIRE.	5744.	YELLOW SIBERIAN.

5745. EUCALYPTUS GLOBULUS.

From San Francisco, Cal. Received through Trumbull and Beebe, July 14, 1900.

5746 to 5750. TRIFOLIUM PRATENSE. **Red clover.**

From Hamburg, Germany. Received December 14, 1900. A collection of seeds of various European strains, as follows:

5746.	ENGLISH.	5749.	RUSSIAN.
5747.	HUNGARIAN.	5750.	SILESIAN.
5748.	ITALIAN.		

5751. ANDROPOGON RUFUS. **Jaragua.**

From Matto Grosso Province, Brazil. Presented by the Brazilian minister, Hon. J. F. de Assis-Brasil, December 1, 1900.

A native fodder grass called by the Portuguese "provisorio." Described by Mr. Assis-Brasil in his book on Brazilian agriculture. (See letter of October, 1899.)

5752. ARCTOSTAPHYLOS sp. **Pendicuas.**

From Celaya, Mexico. Presented by Prof. Felix Foëx. Received December 10, 1900.

"The brown berries of this plant are edible. When fresh they are not disagreeable, having a fresh subacid flavor. When dried they are nearly tasteless, but are used in great quantities medicinally. An infusion is used for catarrh and headaches. The tree which produces them is very ornamental." (*Foëx.*)

5753. CARICA HETEROPHYLLA. **Jarrilla.**

From Celaya, Mexico. Presented by Prof. Felix Foëx. Received December 10, 1900.

"A curious fruit, being *drunk* as one would swallow a raw egg, and not eaten. The name is *Jarrilla* or 'little pitcher,' because it is shaped like a pitcher and is always full of water. The water contained in it is fresh and slightly acid, resembling lemon juice. When the fruit is taken from the plant it acquires in a few days a bitter taste, something like lemon peel, but without its aroma. The plant is a perennial, half climber, and grows wild on the hills around Celaya." (*Foëx.*)

5754. TRITICUM DURUM. **Wheat.**

From Matagalpa, Nicaragua. Presented by Hon. Isaac A. Manning, U. S. consular agent. Received December 17, 1900.

Nicaragua. Grown at an elevation of 2,200 feet.

5755. CUCUMIS MELO. **Muskmelon.**

From Erfurt, Germany. Received December 13, 1900.

Coral Reef. This is a cantaloupe of very striking appearance, the rind being studded with warty excrescences. The melon is bright yellow, with reddish markings, small seed cavity, and greenish yellow flesh. If planted in frames in winter it ripens fruit in early summer.

5756. HORDEUM DISTICHUM. **Barley.**

From Pilsen, Austria. Received through Mr. D. G. Fairchild (No. 466, November 7, 1900), February 9, 1901.

Mixed barley used for brewing the original Pilsen beer; said by the brewing master of the great Pilsen "Urquelle" Brewery to compare favorably with *Hanna* barley.

5757. HUMULUS LUPULUS. **Hop.**

From Polepp, Bohemia. Received through Mr. D. G. Fairchild (No. 469, November 14, 1900), December 18, 1900.

Seed from the drier in Polepp of the *Semsch Red* variety.

5758. HUMULUS LUPULUS. **Hop.**

From Polepp, Bohemia. Received through Mr. D. G. Fairchild (No. 470), December 18, 1900.

Red Semsch. "This variety originated in the immediate neighborhood of Polepp. It was discovered in 1853 as a sport among the so-called 'Tschims' hops, which were then grown here in Polepp, by Wenzel Semsch, a hop grower then only 20 years of age. This hop is earlier than the Saaz variety and more productive. It is remarkably uniform in time of blooming and ripening, and has been sent all over Bohemia and Alsatia, and thousands of cuttings go every year to Saaz, where they are planted. The largest proportion of Saaz hops comes from these cuttings. The exact locality of the garden from which these cuttings were taken I can not positively affirm further than that it is in the renowned Polepp or Polepp-Platte region, which is famous through its production of a quality of hop which often in good years approaches very closely to that of the best Saaz variety. The important facts are that it is an August-ripening hop of very uniform maturity and possessed of a very fine aroma and 'bitter' (so fine in fact that it is everywhere reported as being used for mixing with Saaz hops as a substitute), and a productiveness which stands to the Saaz hop as 5 to 3 in proportion; 180 poles will yield 110 pounds of hops, while it requires about 300 poles of the Saaz to yield as much. The soil upon which these hops are grown is a dark friable loam with a subsoil of gravel, in strong contrast with the soil of Saaz or Spalt, which is so-called perm or disintegrated red sandstone. The whole Polepp region, which is the largest single stretch of hop country in Bohemia, has this dark, rich, alluvial soil. Formerly the whole valley bottom was a peat bog. Fine sand is often used to lighten the soil. It is strewn along the rows and worked in. For further particulars regarding the origin of this Semsch hop, see No. 5759." (*Fairchild.*)

5759. HUMULUS LUPULUS. **Hop.**

From Werbitz, Bohemia. Received through Mr. D. G. Fairchild (No. 471), December 18, 1900.

Semsch red. "Cuttings of the original specimen from the garden of the son of Wenzel Semsch, to whose efforts the production and distribution of this remarkable hop are due." (*Fairchild.*)

5760. HUMULUS LUPULUS. **Hop.**

From Saaz, Bohemia. Received through Mr. D. G. Fairchild (No. 475, November 19, 1900), December 18, 1900.

Saaz. One-year-old plants of the original *Saaz* hop. This variety has without doubt the finest "bitter" and best "aroma" of any known sort, but its small yield makes it an unprofitable kind to raise. It requires often from 300 to 480 plants to produce 110 pounds of hops, while 180 poles of the *Semsch red* will produce the same amount. These plants come from the city region of Saaz, where the soil is a brick-red broken-down sandstone of the Lower Permian formation.

5761. COCHLEARIA ARMORACIA. **Horse-radish.**

From Malin (Kuttenberg), Bohemia. Received through Mr. D. G. Fairchild (No. 479, November 22, 1900), December 18, 1900.

Malin. The finest flavored, sharpest horse-radish in the world, being cultivated in a different way from that generally practiced in America. The marketable shoots are only one season old instead of several. (See Circular No. 1, Section of Seed and Plant Introduction.)

5762. CYDONIA VULGARIS. **Quince.**

From Carlovitz, Slavonia. Presented by Director Hess, of the Agricultural School of Laun, Bohemia, through Mr. D. G. Fairchild (No. 473, November 15, 1900). Received December 18, 1900.

Cuttings from a tree that bore fruit weighing 14 ounces, of excellent shape, and of a deeper yellow than most quinces seen in America. Said to be an indigenous Slavonian variety.

5763. ARACHIS HYPOGAEA. **Peanut.**

From Washington, D. C. Seed of No. 4253, grown during the season of 1900 on the Potomac Flats.

5764 to 5766. GLYCINE HISPIDA. **Soy bean.**

From Washington, D. C. Three varieties of soy beans from Japan, grown during the season of 1900 on the Potomac Flats.

5764. COMMON. (S. P. I., No. 4912.)

5765. BEST WHITE. (S. P. I., No. 4913.)

5766. BEST GREEN. (S. P. I., No. 4914.)

5767. PISTACIA VERA × P. TEREBINTHUS.

From San Francisco, Cal. Presented by Mr. G. P. Rixford, through Mr. W. T. Swingle. Received December, 1900.

"This number comprises the fruits of the terebinth tree ripened near San Francisco. Most of these fruits contain no seed, although they look very plump and have a perfectly developed pit or stone. According to Mr. Rixford, the fruits which are decayed or with dark-purple exteriors are the ones which most often contain seeds. The majority of the fruits vary from wine color to pink and are more or less studded over with white specks. The flesh is very thin, probably only about one thirty-second of an inch." (*Swingle.*)

5768. HUMULUS LUPULUS. **Hop.**

From Tettnang, Bavaria. Received from Mr. J. A. Bueble, through Mr. D. G. Fairchild (No. 464, November 4, 1900), December 26, 1900.

"Sets of the earliest ripening hop variety in Europe, often maturing by the end of July. They occupy a special place on the European hop market, being used by many breweries for brewing their first summer beer." (*Fairchild.*)

SEPTEMBER, 1900, TO DECEMBER, 1903.

5769. BETA VULGARIS. **Sugar beet.**
From Paris, France. Received February, 1900.
Vilmorin's French Very Rich.

5770. BETA VULGARIS. **Sugar beet.**
From Germany. Received February, 1900.
Strandes Kleinwanzleben.

5771. BETA VULGARIS. **Sugar beet.**
From Germany. Received February, 1900.
Hoernings Kleinwanzleben.

5772. BETA VULGARIS. **Sugar beet.**
From Germany. Received February, 1900.
Dippes Kleinwanzleben Elite.

5773. BETA VULGARIS. **Sugar beet.**
From Utah. Received February, 1900.
American-grown seed. From Lehi, Utah.

5774. CUCUMIS MELO. **Winter muskmelon.**
From Arizona. Received December 29, 1900.
Seed grown at Phoenix, Ariz., from No. 149, originally imported from New Bokhara, Turkestan, by Prof. N. E. Hansen, February, 1898.

5775. VACCINIUM VITIS-IDAEA. **Foxberry.**
From Finland. Presented by Dr. Gösta Grotenfeld. Received December 31, 1900.

5776. OXYCOCCUS PALUSTRIS. **Small cranberry.**
From Finland. Presented by Dr. Gösta Grotenfeld. Received December 31, 1900.

5777. QUEBRACHIA LORENTZII. **Quebracho colorado.**
From La Plata, Argentina. Presented by Dr. Carlos Spegazzini. Received January 4, 1900.

"A magnificent slow-growing tree, with a wood like iron, containing much tannic acid. Last year's seeds from Salta Province." (*Spegazzini.*)

5778. MACHAERIUM TIPU. **Tipu.**
From La Plata, Argentina. Presented by Dr. Carlos Spegazzini. Received January 4, 1900.

"Leguminosae; beautiful tree for gardens and forest, rapid grower, producing excellent wood for building purposes." (*Spegazzini.*)

5779. ELYMUS ANDINUS. **Coiron flor.**
From La Plata, Argentina. Presented by Dr. Carlos Spegazzini. Received January 4, 1901.

5780. LIBOCEDRUS CHILENSIS.

From La Plata, Argentina. Presented by Dr. Carlos Spegazzini. Received January 8, 1901.

Cipres de Patagonia.

5781. ASPIDOSPERMA QUEBRACHO BLANCO. **Quebracho blanco.**

From La Plata, Argentina. Presented by Dr. Carlos Spegazzini. Received January 8, 1901.

"A very rapidly growing tree, with medicinal properties." (*Spegazzini.*)

5781a. GOMPHOCARPUS sp. **Buluba.**

From La Plata, Argentina. Presented by Dr. Carlos Spegazzini. Received December, 1900.

5782. LATHYRUS MAGELLANICUS.

From La Plata, Argentina. Presented by Dr. Carlos Spegazzini. Received January, 1901.

Mixed seeds of this and *Vicia macraei.*

5783. PROSOPIS DENUDANS.

From La Plata, Argentina. Presented by Dr. Carlos Spegazzini. Received January 5, 1901.

Algarroba orozii?

5784. BERBERIS DULCIS.

From La Plata, Argentina. Presented by Dr. Carlos Spegazzini. Received January 5, 1901.

Calafata parra. From Chubut.

5785. PHYSALIS FRANCHETI (?).

From Tokyo, Japan. Presented by Mr. T. Watase, of Tokyo Plant and Seed Co. A variety with very large fine fruits.

5786. GOMPHOCARPUS sp. **Buluba.**

From the Soudan, Africa. Presented by Doctor Trabut, Government Botanist of Algeria, through Mr. Lyster H. Dewey, Assistant Botanist, U. S. Department of Agriculture.

"I have cultivated this species of gomphocarpus for several years under the name 'Buluba.' It attains a large growth, and yields a beautiful fiber closely resembling silk." (*Trabut.*)

5787. HUMULUS LUPULUS. **Hop.**

From Bohemia, Austria-Hungary. Received through Mr. D. G. Fairchild (No. 483), January, 1901.

Semsch. "Cuttings of this noted hop, from the neighborhood of the most famous locality of the Platte, where it is known to yield almost as fine hops as the best Saaz variety and in much larger quantity. It is this variety which the growers of the Saaz variety have imported in large quantities into Saaz to replace the old Bohemian variety, which has so fallen off in yield that its culture no longer pays, unless a fancy price can be secured. These hops possess an aroma that is really fine. Professor Chodounsky, of the Experiment Station for Brewing Industries in Prague, one of the best-known and most careful judges of hop varieties, says of this Semsch hop:

"'This red hop, which gives a much larger yield than the old Bohemian red hop (Saaz variety), is to be reckoned among the very good hops. It has an oval form, a well-shaped spindle, and an agreeable aroma. It is considered as an intermediate type approaching the Rakonitz-Saaz hop, standing next to it as regards worth. This is probably the best yielder of all the really fine European varieties.'

"As these cuttings have been secured with great difficulty, and as it will be more and more difficult to obtain others, they should be given especial attention. In order to propagate them as rapidly as possible, the young shoots should be layered next spring and cut into lengths when rooted. These cuttings have been taken from one of the best hop gardens in the Platte region in Bohemia, but being cut during the winter they are not as thrifty as if taken in the spring. The rule in Bohemia is to place a single cutting in a hill, but if small and weak it might be better to put two together.

"These hops produce the finest aroma when planted on yellow clay soils. The vines are light yellow when grown in sandy or clayey soil, but darker when grown where the soil has more humus, or is of a peaty or swampy character—what the Germans call '*moor Erde.*'" (*Fairchild.*)

5788 to 5792. HORDEUM DISTICHUM. Barley.

From Munich, Bavaria. Received through Mr. D. G. Fairchild (No. 467), January 16, 1901.

A collection of prize-winning barleys from the Barley and Hop Exposition, 1900. Forwarded by Hon. James H. Worman, U. S. Consul at Munich, as follows:

5788. (467b.) 5791. (467f.)
5789. (467d.) 5792. (467g.)
5790. (467e.)

5793. HORDEUM DISTICHUM NUTANS. Barley.

From Kwassitz, Moravia, Austria. Received through Mr. D. G. Fairchild (No. 481), January 16, 1901.

Moravian or *Hanna*. "The noted *Hanna* brewing barley from the breeder or selecter, Emanuel Ritter von Proskowetz, of Kwassitz. This is unquestionably one of the best brewing barleys in the world and is noted for its qualities of early ripening, unusual heavy yields, and special mealiness, which latter, together with other qualities of kernel, renders it one of the great favorites among German as well as Austrian brewers. Notwithstanding a duty in Bavaria of 22 marks per German ton on brewing barleys and an increased cost of transportation, the best Bavarian breweries import this *Hanna* barley. In the Thirty-ninth Session of the Bavarian House of Deputies (1899) the purchase of these *Hanna* barleys among other foreign sorts by the famous Hofbrauhaus was made the reason of an attack upon the director of this State institution and, although the claim was not sustained that the *Hanna* barley is superior to the *best* Bavarian, the inference which is drawn is that on the average it is more satisfactory and economical from the brewer's standpoint. The former director of the Brauhaus Staubwasser claimed in his defense that the *Hanna* barley, especially that grown in Hungary, was ready for malting earlier than Bavarian varieties, which speaks for the earliness of the variety claimed by the producer. Von Proskowetz claims for the variety a *pedigree* and says that it was selected as a single plant from some barley which he knew to be of very old Moravian origin. Through careful selection he has been able to bring its productivity up to 3,700 kilos per hectare and *shorten its period of growth by over a week.* It is a light straw producer *suited especially to light or sandy loams.* Owing to its early ripening quality it is especially valuable in Hungary, where the hot season occurs the latter part of July, but after the *Hanna* barley has so far matured as to be little influenced by it. Sow in March, or earlier if possible, providing soil is in proper condition. On light soil drill in rows 5 inches apart, on heavier soils 6 to 7 inches. If it can be made to follow a beet root or potato crop so much the better. Owing to its heavy yielding capacity, earliness, and high grade as a brewing grain, this variety is driving out all other sorts in Austria and every year large quantities of seed grain are imported into Hungary. So far as I can ascertain this is the first importation of this variety ever made into America." (*Fairchild.*)

5794. HORDEUM DISTICHUM. Barley.

From Leneschitz, Bohemia. Received from Prof. Frantisek Hess, of the Laun Ag. School, through Mr. D. G. Fairchild (No. 472, November 15, 1900), January 16, 1901.

An excellent brewing barley, probably not a pure stock. A part of the same lot which took the first prize in the Austrian section of the Paris Exposition. From the estate of Josef Pisoft.

34   SEEDS AND PLANTS IMPORTED.

5795. PHASEOLUS VULGARIS.   **Adler bean.**

From Sachsenfeld, Styria, Austria. Received through Mr. D. G. Fairchild (No. 484, December 21, 1900), January 16, 1901.

Adler. A sample. "One of the finest varieties known in Austria. It is indigenous to Styria, where it is considered by connoisseurs an exceptionally fine table bean. I have eaten it and found it unusually good, though the skin is somewhat tough. It is, however, worth a trial by experiment stations." (*Fairchild.*)

5796. PAPAVER SOMNIFERUM.   **Poppy.**

From Sachsenfeld, Styria, Austria. Received through Mr. D. G. Fairchild (No. 485, December 20, 1900), January 16, 1901.

A large-podded variety of poppy, grown in Styria exclusively for the production of oil. The pods are collected in autumn, dried, their tops cut off, and the seed shaken out. The seed is then ground and an oil is pressed out of it. This oil is extensively used in cooking and as a table oil. It is said not to grow rancid, and is very highly esteemed by the Styrians. The pods are often 2 inches in diameter." (*Fairchild.*)

5797. COFFEA ARABICA.   **Coffee.**

From Macassar, Celebes. Presented by Mr. Karl Auer, U. S. consular agent, Macassar, through Messrs. Lathrop and Fairchild (No. 485a, February 11, 1900), January 22, 1901.

Patjoe or *Bonthain* coffee. "A superior local variety from south Celebes, which was formerly exported in large quantities to Europe." (*Fairchild.*)

5798. BROMELIA sp.   **Timbiriche.**

From Celaya, Mexico. Presented by Prof. Felix Foëx. Received January 22, 1901.

"Like the Jarilla (No. 5753), it is a fruit to be drunk, not eaten. It is ground or crushed in water. The Mexicans prefer this as a refreshing drink to lemonade made from lemons. It is especially valuable for improving hard water, i. e., calcareous or magnesian waters, because the acid in the fruit precipitates these salts. The fruit does not grow in this vicinity, but in an arid region higher up. The plant is said to resemble the Yucca, but I have not seen it. The fruits sell in the markets here at 1 cent each, while other fruits have no value because of their abundance." (*Foëx.*)

5799. TRITICUM POLONICUM.   **Polish wheat.**

From France. Received January 23, 1901.

Polish or *Astrakhan.*

5800. TRITICUM DURUM.   **Wheat.**

From Paris, France. Received January 23, 1901.

Belotourka.

5801. LAVANDULA VERA.   **Lavender.**

From Paris, France. Received January 23, 1901.

5802. LAVANDULA SPICA.   **Spike lavender.**

From Paris, France. Received January 23, 1901.

5803. SESAMUM INDICUM.   **Sesame.**

From Paris, France. Received January 23, 1901.

White seeded.

5804. SESAMUM INDICUM.   Sesame.

From Paris, France. Received January 23, 1901.

Yellow seeded.

5805 to 5809. ANDROPOGON SORGHUM.   Sorghum.

From Medicine Lodge, Kans. Received February, 1901. Seed of the following varieties:

5805.
Amber.

5806.
Collier.

5807.
Colman.

5808.
Kansas orange.

5809.
Minnesota early amber.

5810 to 5823. PYRUS MALUS.   Apple.

From Stockholm, Sweden. Presented by Director Axel Pihl, of the Swedish Horticultural Society, Rosendal, through Messrs. Lathrop and Fairchild (Nos. 400–413, July 18, 1900). Received February 4, 19C1.

5810.

Astrachan sparreholms (Svensk Pomologi Applen, p. 73). "Originated in 1859. Ripens late in September; not commonly cultivated even in Sweden; as good as any ripening at this time; believed to be a hybrid between White Astrakhan and Rosenhäger." (*Fairchild.*)

5811.

Bjorkvicks (Svensk Pomologi, p. 93). "A fall apple; well known; first described in 1862; original tree in middle Sweden, at Bjorkvicks." (*Fairchild.*)

5812.

Fagerö (Svensk Pomologi, p. 91). "A new sort worthy of trial. Not well known, even in Sweden." (*Fairchild.*)

5813.

Frösåkers. "A fall apple, little known, even in Sweden. Director Pihl says it is a good sort; has been introduced into Finland within the last ten years, and is cultivated there with great success." (*Fairchild.*)

5814.

Gimmersta. "Of unknown origin. Little known, even in Sweden. An excellent early (September) table apple; very hardy; a first-rate market apple." (*Fairchild.*)

5815.

Hampus. "A summer apple of the very first quality; rather small; trees hardy, but of slow growth; probably of Swedish origin; very commonly grown; one of the best known and most extensively grown sorts." (*Fairchild.*)

5816.

Oranie. "A well-known summer or early autumn sort, in color not very attractive, but in flavor next to "Humus," the best in Sweden; very heavy and early bearer; hardy; largely cultivated in Sweden. Director Pihl recommends it heartily for trial." (*Fairchild.*)

5817.

Svensk vinterpostof. "One of the oldest and commonest sorts; late autumn and early winter variety of medium quality; most used as a table apple, but is suitable for kitchen use; does not keep late into winter." (*Fairchild.*)

5810 to 5823—Continued.

5818.

Ringstads. "A showy red-cheeked table apple of excellent quality; a good market sort; largely planted in Sweden and Finland; quite hardy. Highly recommended by Director Pihl." (*Fairchild.*)

5819.

Stenkyrke. "One of the very best Swedish sorts. Excellent keeper. A very good table apple. Originated on the chalky soil of Gottland. It does well on clay soil and is heartily recommended by Director Pihl." (*Fairchild.*)

5820.

Städringe. "Late summer or early autumn variety. Ripens in September. A table apple of very fine quality. Origin unknown. Ranks very high, though it is not very commonly cultivated." (*Fairchild.*)

5821.

Säfstaholms. "Ripens in September. A most popular sort and one Director Pihl thinks would be very highly prized in America. A table sort made known by the well-known Swedish pomologist, Olof Eneroth. Quite hardy." (*Fairchild.*)

5822.

Åkerö. "This variety is considered, at the present time, to be the best of all the Swedish apples. The tree is one of the hardiest and of uncommonly strong growth. Not liable to disease. A winter table apple of excellent quality. Keeps until spring. A heavy bearer only at advanced age. Grows well in any kind of soil. The original tree is standing at Åkerö, although planted more than one hundred years ago. Much propagated in last twenty-five years." (*Fairchild.*)

5823.

Ölands Kungs. "Closely related to *Scharlakansparmän*, but is not the same. A small, very bright red table apple. Sold in very large quantities as a Christmas-tree apple, for which it is especially suited, as it keeps well until Christmas. Hardy and tolerably productive." (*Fairchild.*)

5824. PRUNUS DOMESTICA. **Plum.**

From Stockholm, Sweden. Presented by Director Axel Pihl through Messrs. Lathrop and Fairchild (No. 414, July 18, 1900). Received February 4, 1901.

Allmänna gul. "A very good cooking plum. Extremely hardy, but not a very heavy bearer. Almost always propagated by root division. Grown as far north as any plum." (*Fairchild.*)

5825. CERATONIA SILIQUA. **Carob.**

From Lissa Island, Dalmatia. Received through Mr. D. G. Fairchild (No. 499, January 7, 1901), February 5, 1901.

"Bud sticks of a variety with large sweet pods." (*Fairchild.*)

5826. LATHYRUS PLATYPHYLLUS.

From Stockholm, Sweden. Presented by Prof. V. Wittrock, director of the botanic gardens, Frescati, through Messrs. Lathrop and Fairchild (No. 441, August 11, 1900). Received February 5, 1901.

"A species of Lathyrus named by Retzius *L. platyphyllus.* Its origin is uncertain. In Professor Wittrock's garden, at Frescati, are plants which have been growing for twelve years. One of these is planted against a wall 12 feet or more high, and the plant has spread over a large surface and overtops the wall by several feet. The vigor of this plant is remarkable and the amount of fodder produced apparently great. So far no experiments with the plant have been made in the field. As it is a perennial and makes a comparatively little growth in the first three years, such experiments as have been started do not as yet show results. A few seeds only are obtainable here, as the plant seldom ripens its seeds in this latitude. Director Wittrock thinks it is quite possible that this plant is a different variety from that described by Retzius. So far as I am aware it is quite unknown as a fodder plant outside of southern Sweden, where Professor Wittrock has sent seeds. It deserves careful attention." (*Fairchild.*)

5827. BROMUS INERMIS.   **Smooth brome-grass.**

From Stockholm, Sweden. Presented by Prof. V. Wittrock through Messrs. Lathrop and Fairchild (No. 442, August 10, 1900). Received February 5, 1901.

5828. CEPHALARIA TATARICA.

From Stockholm, Sweden. Presented by Prof. V. Wittrock through Messrs. Lathrop and Fairchild (No. 443, August 10, 1900). Received February 5, 1901.

"A new fodder plant of exceptionally vigorous growth. Professor Wittrock thinks it is worthy of extensive trial." (*Fairchild.*)

5829. HEDYSARUM OBSCURUM.

From Stockholm, Sweden. Presented by Prof. V. Wittrock through Messrs. Lathrop and Fairchild (No. 445, August 10, 1900). Received February 5, 1901.

"A high Alpine fodder plant which occurs above the timber line and is especially suited to mountain climates, although growing well in deep soil in the valleys or on the plains. The root system is very long; grows readily from seed if latter has been passed through a 'preparator' or rubbed with sandpaper. Otherwise it will take one to three years to germinate. Has been grown here twelve years on same spot. Yield is good. Highly ornamental. Professor Wittrock says it is the best Alpine fodder plant he knows." (*Fairchild.*)

5830. CALAMAGROSTIS PHRAGMITOIDES.

From Stockholm, Sweden. Presented by Prof. V. Wittrock through Messrs. Lathrop and Fairchild (No. 446, August 11, 1900). Received February 5, 1901.

"An excellent fodder grass for moist localities. It very seldom seeds, but spreads rapidly when once planted. Yields a heavy, nutritious fodder." (*Fairchild.*)

5831. AMMOPHILA ARENARIA.   **Beach-grass.**

From Stockholm, Sweden. Presented by Prof. V. Wittrock through Messrs. Lathrop and Fairchild (No. 447, August 11, 1900). Received February 5, 1901.

"An excellent fodder grass for moist localities in high latitudes. The plant has a wandering habit. It dies out in one place after a few years, but spreads from a center in all directions. It yields a large quantity of valuable fodder, according to Professor Wittrock." (*Fairchild.*)

5832. GLYCERIA SPECTABLIS.

From Stockholm, Sweden. Presented by Prof. V. Wittrock through Messrs. Lathrop and Fairchild (No. 448, August 11, 1900). Received February 5, 1901.

"A forage plant grown extensively in some parts of Sweden. Adapted to moist places. Baron von Pijkull Volloesäby, of Knifsta, Sweden, has large cultures of this plant and can supply rhizomes in quantity for trial if desired." (*Fairchild.*)

5833. VERBASCUM SPECIOSUM.

From Stockholm, Sweden. Presented by Prof. V. Wittrock through Messrs. Lathrop and Fairchild (No. 449, August 11, 1900). Received February 5, 1901.

"An East European or West Asiatic biennial that has just been determined by Professor Wittrock. It is quite new, and one of the most gorgeous yellow decorative plants I have ever seen. The immense flower spikes, of which there are many branches, remain covered with blossoms for more than a month. Caution should be taken with it as, like others of the same genus, it may prove a weed. Professor Wittrock says it is very easily rooted out and will probably never be a bad weed." (*Fairchild.*)

5834. TRIFOLIUM PANNONICUM.

From Stockholm, Sweden. Presented by Prof. V. Wittrock. Received February 5, 1901.

5835. FESTUCA ARUNDINACEA.

From Stockholm, Sweden. Presented by Dr. V. Wittrock. Received February 3, 1901.

5836. HUMULUS LUPULUS. **Hop.**

From Polepp, Bohemia. Received through Mr. D. G. Fairchild (No. 470a), 1901.

Red Semsch. Same as No. 5758.

5837. COCHLEARIA ARMORACEA. **Horse-radish.**

From Polepp, Bohemia. Received through Mr. D. G. Fairchild, January, 1901.

5838. ELEUSINE CORACANA. **Ragi millet.**

From Rhodesia, South Africa. Presented by Dr. Wm. L. Thompson, of Oberlin, Ohio.

Upoka or *Ngoza.* "This is the most important food plant of the natives of Rhodesia and its yield of seed is said to be something phenomenal." (*Fairchild.*)

5839. CUCUMIS SATIVUS. **Cucumber.**

From Znaim, Austria. Received through Mr. D. G. Fairchild (No. 480), January 10, 1901.

Znaim. "A variety largely grown for salting and pickling. Said by Mr. W. W. Tracy, sr., to be a mixture of strains probably deriving its name merely from the noted locality where cucumber growing is largely practiced." (*Fairchild.*)

5840. ACTINIDIA.

From Ichang, China. Received through Mr. G. D. Brill (No. 1), December, 1900.

"Large fruited. Chinese name *Yang Tao.*" (*Brill.*)

5841. ASTRAGALUS CICER.

From Stockholm, Sweden. Presented by Dr. V. Wittrock through Messrs. Lathrop and Fairchild (No. 444, August 10, 1900). Received February 6, 1901.

"Considered by Doctor Wittrock to be a very important forage plant. It spreads with great rapidity and should be watched as it may become a weed. Suited to both sandy and clay soils. A true Steppe plant. Better for prairies than for cultivated lands." (*Fairchild.*)

5842. HORDEUM DISTICHUM. **Barley.**

From Binsbach, Bavaria. Received from Mr. D. G. Fairchild, through the kindness of Hon. James H. Worman, United States Consul at Munich, 1901.

Chevalier.

5843. HORDEUM VULGARE. **Barley.**

From Binsbach, Bavaria. Received from Mr. D. G. Fairchild, through the kindness of Hon. James H. Worman, United States Consul at Munich, 1901.

Webs.

5844. HORDEUM VULGARE. **Barley.**

From Binsbach, Bavaria. Received from Mr. D. G. Fairchild, through the kindness of Hon. James H. Worman, United States Consul at Munich, 1901.

Franken.

5845. HORDEUM DISTICHUM. **Barley.**

From Thalham, Bavaria. Received from Mr. D. G. Fairchild, through the kindness of Hon. James H. Worman, United States Consul at Munich, 1901.

Bohemian.

5846. HORDEUM DISTICHUM var. NUTANS. **Barley.**

From Binsbach, near Gonheim, Bavaria. Received through Mr. D. G. Fairchild (No. 478), February, 1901.

"This barley was awarded the gold medal as the best of 680 exhibits of brewing barley at the Bavarian Barley and Hop Exposition, held at Munich, September 29 to October 3, 1900." (*Fairchild.*)

5847 to 5899. HORDEUM DISTICHUM. **Barley.**

From Paris. Received through Mr. D. G. Fairchild, February, 1901. Samples of barley obtained at the exposition, as follows:

5847.
Kitzinger.

5848.
Pilsen.

5849.
Laniger. (No. 573.)

5850.
Kwassitzer.

5851.
Landgerste. (No. 442.)

5852.
Scottish pearl. (No. 159.)

5853.
Chevalier. (No. 47.)

5854.
Fünfstettener. (No. 551.)

5855.
Fünfstettener. (No. 63.)

5856.
Saal or Kaiser. (No. 167.)

5857.
Frankish. (No. 608.)

5858.
Common two-rowed. (No. 238.)

5859.
(No. 479.)

5860.
(No. 108.)

5861.
Lower Bavarian. (No. 476.)

5862.
Hanna. (No. 149.)

5863.
Melon. (No. 325.)

5864.
Imperial. (No. 48.)

5865.
Chevalier. (No. 64.)

5866.
Chevalier. (No. 198.)

5867.
Bohemian. (No. 135.)

5868.
Bohemian. (No. 454.)

5869.
Goldthorpe. (No. 1.)

5870.
Frankish. (No. 356.)

5847 to 5899—Continued.

 5871.
  Frankish. (No. 300.)
 5872.
  Lower Bavarian. (No. 417.)
 5873.
  Mittelgerste Thürengen. (No. 599.)
 5874.
  Christensen's Goldthorpe. (No. 43.)
 5875.
  Juwel. (No. 324.)
 5876.
  Bavarian. (No. 567.)
 5877.
  Hanna. (No. 79.)
 5878.
  Laninger. (No. 670.)
 5879.
  (No. 683.)
 5880.
  Frankish. (No. 220.)
 5881.
  Hanna. (No. 152.)
 5882.
  Webbs. (No. 191.)
 5883.
  Lower Bavarian. (No. 107.)
 5884.
  Tauber. (No. 310.)

 5885.
  (No. 3.)
 5886.
  Bohemian. (A).
 5887.
  Poppenheim.
 5888.
  (Probably not a pure variety.)
 5889.
  (No. 2.)
 5890.
  Poppenheim.
 5891.
  Hanna.
 5892.
  Kitzingen.
 5893. (Number not used.)
 5894.
  Hanna.
 5895.
  Bohemian.
 5896.
  Bohemian.
 5897.
  I Schwarzenberg.
 5898.
  II Schwarzenberg.
 5899.
  III Schwarzenberg.

5900. CUCUMIS SATIVUS.   **Cucumber.**

From Auburn, N. Y. Received through Mr. G. W. Boynton, February 6, 1901. *Aksel dwarf*, grown from No. 8, Inventory No. 1.

5901. RAPHANUS SATIVUS.   **Radish.**

From Amite City, La. Received through Mr. W. O. Posey, February 6, 1901. Seed grown from No. 1189, Inventory No. 2.

5902. CAPSICUM ANNUUM.   **Sweet pepper.**

From Anna Maria Key, Fla. Received through Mr. W. C. Berg, February 9, 1901. Seed grown from No. 3976, Inventory No. 8.

5903. HORDEUM DISTICHUM. **Barley.**

From Saaz, Bohemia. Received through Mr. D. G. Fairchild (No. 477, Nov. 20, 1900), February 9, 1901.

"Bohemian brewing barley from the estates of Prince Schwarzenberg, at Jinovic, near Saaz. From sandy loam, soil rich in lime. Much exported to Norway. This is an excellent representative Bohemian barley, though probably not a pure variety." (*Fairchild.*)

5904. CUCUMIS MELO. **Muskmelon.**

From Elgin, Utah. Received through Mr. J. F. Brown, February 9, 1901.

Khiva. Seed grown from No. 114, Inventory No. 1.

5905. SECALE CEREALE. **Rye.**

From Tenmile, W. Va. Received through Mr. F. Spiker, February 12, 1901.

Winter Ivanof, grown from No. 1342, Inventory No. 2.

5906. CUCURBITA MAXIMA. **Honey pumpkin.**

From Eden, Nebr. Received through Mr. D. J. Wood, February 14, 1901.

Seed grown from No. 14, Inventory No. 1.

5907. CHAETOCHLOA ITALICA. **Millet.**

From Brookings, S. Dak. Received through Prof. D. A. Saunders, February 15, 1901.

Seed grown from No. 2798, Inventory No. 7.

5908. CUCUMIS MELO. **Muskmelon.**

From Waterloo, Kans. Received through Mr. J. W. Riggs, February 14, 1901.

Maroussia Lessevitsky, grown from No. 27, Inventory No. 1.

5909 to 5918. VITIS VINIFERA. **Grape.**

From Lesina Island, Dalmatia. Received through Mr. D. G. Fairchild (Nos. 486–495), February 20, 1901. A collection of grape cuttings of the following varieties:

5909.

Boglich. "A dark-colored sweet table grape having a thick skin. The bunches are said to grow to a very large size, sometimes weighing as much as fourteen pounds. Suitable for limestone soils." (No. 486.) (*Fairchild.*)

5910.

Marascina. "A small light-brown translucent grape, of unusual sweetness. It is a shy bearer and subject to Peronospora. Originated near Sebenico on mainland. A high-grade dessert wine, known as *Marascina*, is made from this grape. This wine somewhat resembles Marsala, but is considered by some as superior, and sells for a much higher price than any of the other wines of this region." (No. 487.) (*Fairchild.*)

5911.

Stronzo di Gallo. "One of the three best grapes grown on this island. It is a thin-skinned white grape of a peculiar long shape and contains but one seed. It will keep until January. Suitable for poor limestone soils." (No. 488.) (*Fairchild.*)

5909 to 5918—Continued.

5912.

Kurtelaska. "A white wine grape, native of the island, producing medium-sized crowded clusters. A wine known as 'Apollo,' highly prized in Germany and Austria, is made by extracting the juice from the fresh grapes and fermenting it, separated from the skins. Suitable for limestone soils." (No. 489.) (*Fairchild.*)

5913.

Dernekusa. "The black grape from which the common wine of Lesina is made. It is a thin-skinned grape of medium size, and is said to be a fair table grape. It is a heavy producer." (No. 490.) (*Fairchild.*)

5914.

Ugava. "A white grape serving for the production of a bottled wine exported from Lesina. Only a few plantations of this variety exist on the island because the plants require a rich soil. The wine is sold for 1.20 to 1.30 florins a liter, which is high, considering that ordinary wines bring from .25 to .50 florin a liter." (No. 491.) (*Fairchild.*)

5915.

Banjoska. "A variety of wine grape brought to the island from a neighboring small island, called 'San Clementi,' according to accounts given me. It makes a strong wine, which is imported especially into Hungary. Berries small. Heavy bearer. Suitable for dry, strong, calcareous situations." (No. 492.) (*Fairchild.*)

5916.

Palarusa. "A white wine variety from which much of the Lesina wine is produced. One hundred kilos of grapes yield, it is said, 90 kilos of wine. Not particular as to soil." (No. 493.) (*Fairchild.*)

5917.

Puiska. "A thick-skinned, firm-fleshed white grape, originally from Apulia, Italy, but grown here many years. Said to be a very heavy bearer." (No. 494.) (*Fairchild.*)

5918.

Trojka. "A very large table grape of excellent flavor. It is a heavy bearer and keeps well. It is a native of Lesina and requires a rich soil." (No. 495.) (*Fairchild.*)

5919. FICUS CARICA. **Fig.**

From Lesina Island, Dalmatia. Received through Mr. D. G. Fairchild (No. 496, Jan. 7, 1901), February 20, 1901.

San Pietro. "The figs of the small island of Lesina, which lies off the Dalmatian coast, are noted in Triest as the most delicate of any which come to that port, except the high-priced Smyrna sorts. They have not the size or the flavor of the Smyrnas, but, considering the fact that they do not require fertilization with the caprifig insect, they are certainly worthy of a trial in the California fig plantations. This variety is a very early one, ripening here in June. It is also reported to be exceptionally large." (*Fairchild.*)

5920. FICUS CARICA. **Fig.**

From Lesina Island, Dalmatia. Received through Mr. D. G. Fairchild (No. 497, January 7, 1901), February 20, 1901.

Zarniza. "Cuttings of one of the ordinary figs grown on this island. Dark in color, produces crops twice a year. It is sometimes dried and packed in small barrels and exported." (*Fairchild.*)

5921. FICUS CARICA. **Fig.**

From Lesina Island, Dalmatia. Received through Mr. D. G. Fairchild (No. 498, January 7, 1901), February 20, 1901.

Zamozujić'a. "A good fig with unusually tender skin, far superior to the dried Italian or Greek figs. Many maintain that as far as tenderness of skin is concerned it is really superior to the Smyrna figs. It is not fertilized by the caprifig insect and may prove a superior sort if once fertilized seed are produced. Worthy of trial. This fig is shipped in large quantities to Triest." (*Fairchild.*)

5922. AMYGDALUS PERSICA. **Peach.**

From Lesina Island, Dalmatia. Received through Mr. D. G. Fairchild (No. 500, January 8, 1900), February 20, 1901.

Giallo. "Cuttings of one of the best peaches of Dalmatia, and, although a clingstone, is worth trying in any variety test. Suitable for stony hillsides of a calcareous nature." (*Fairchild.*)

5923. AMYGDALUS PERSICA. **Peach.**

From Lesina Island, Dalmatia. Received through Mr. D. G. Fairchild (No. 501, January 8, 1900), February 20, 1901.

Bianca. "Cuttings of a white-fleshed freestone peach of excellent quality, maturing in August. Suitable for stony hillsides of a calcareous nature." (*Fairchild.*)

5924. PYRUS COMMUNIS. **Pear.**

From Lesina Island, Dalmatia. Received through Mr. D. G. Fairchild (No. 502, January 8, 1901), February 20, 1901.

Nyoko. "Cuttings of a variety of pear said to be of superior quality. Somewhat similar to the Bartlett. Suitable for calcareous hillsides in warm climates like Arizona and southern California." (*Fairchild.*)

5925. BRASSICA OLERACEA. **Cabbage.**

From Osage, Iowa. Received through Mr. George Phillips, February 12, 1901.

Earliest white, grown from No. 6. Inventory No. 1.

5926. BRASSICA OLERACEA. **Cabbage.**

From Osage, Iowa. Received through Mr. George Phillips, February 13, 1901.

White Reval, grown from No. 4. Inventory No. 1.

5927. PHASEOLUS VULGARIS. **Bean.**

From Waynesville, N. C. Received through Dr. G. D. Green, February 13, 1901.

Flageolet, grown from No. 2069. Inventory No. 5.

5928. CICER ARIETINUM. **Garbanzo.**

From Tenino, Wash. Received through Mr. J. F. Cannon, February 25, 1901. Seed grown from No. 2376. Inventory No. 5.

5929. PHASEOLUS VULGARIS. **Bean.**

From Judsonia, Ark. Received through Mr. Jacob C. Bauer, February 23, 1901.

Soissons, grown from No. 2068. Inventory No. 5.

5930. ANDROPOGON SORGHUM. **Sorghum.**

From Scottsville, Ky. Received through Mr. Rupert Huntsman, February, 1901.

Colman, grown from No. 4308. Inventory No. 8.

5931. PRUNUS DOMESTICA. **Plum.**

From Saaz, Bohemia. Presented by Doctor Wolfram through Mr. D. G. Fairchild (No. 476, November 18, 1900). Received February 26, 1901.

Dolan. "Cuttings of a plum originated in the village of Dolan, near Saaz, and said by Doctor Wolfram, one of the best Bohemian horticulturists, to be of superior quality. The dried prunes made from this sort are said to be little, if any, inferior to the famous Bosnian prunes. They are large and sweet, and have a flat stone that separates very easily from the flesh." (*Fairchild.*)

5932. SORBUS EDULIS. **Sorb apple.**

From Saaz, Bohemia. Presented by Doctor Wolfram through Mr. D. G. Fairchild (No. 474, November 18, 1900). Received February 26, 1901.

"Cuttings of a variety of Sorb apple discovered several years ago in the forests of Moravia, and since distributed by the Austrian Government through its agricultural schools. The fruit is small, about the size of *Vaccinium vitis-idæa*, and, when cooked, the 'compot' closely resembles that made from this cranberry." (*Fairchild.*)

5933. PYRUS MALUS. **Apple.**

From Saaz, Bohemia. Received through Doctor Wolfram, February 26, 1901.

Calville Madame Lesans. "Similar to *Calville blanc*, but more resistant to fungous attacks." (*Wolfram.*)

5934. FAGOPYRUM ESCULENTUM. **Buckwheat.**

From Berlin, Conn. Received through Mr Earl Cooley, February 26, 1901.

Orenburg, grown from No. 2801. Inventory No. 7.

5935. ASTRAGALUS SINICUS. **Genge clover.**

From Yokohama, Japan. Received through Suzuki and Iida, March 2, 1901.

5936. LUPINUS PILOSUS CAERULEUS. **Lupine.**

From Paris, France. Received through Vilmorin-Andrieux & Co., February, 1901.

5937. LUPINUS PILOSUS ROSEUS. **Lupine.**

From Paris, France. Received through Vilmorin-Andrieux & Co., February, 1901.

5938. AVENA SATIVA. **Oat.**

From Proskurow, Russia. Received through Dr. S. de Mrozinski, March 6, 1901.

Sixty-day. Originated by Doctor Mrozinski.

5939. GOSSYPIUM BARBADENSE. **Egyptian cotton.**

From Mansourah, Egypt. Received through Mr. Alfred Dale, March 6, 1901.

Jannovitch.

5940. ORYZA SATIVA. **Rice.**

From Mansourah, Egypt. Received through Mr. Alfred Dale, March 6, 1901.

Fino.

5941. ORYZA SATIVA. **Rice.**

From Mansourah, Egypt. Received through Mr. Alfred Dale, March 6, 1901.

Eyne-il-Bint.

5942. LOTUS ULIGINOSUS.

From Paris, France. Received through Vilmorin-Andrieux & Co., March 9, 1901.

5943. PINUS SYLVESTRIS. **Scottish pine.**

From Paris, France. Received through Vilmorin-Andrieux & Co., March 9, 1901.

5944. PINUS SYLVESTRIS. **Scottish pine.**

From Paris, France. Received through Vilmorin-Andrieux & Co., March 9, 1901.
Var. *Rigensis.*

5945. PICEA EXCELSA. **Norway spruce.**

From Paris, France. Received through Vilmorin-Andrieux & Co., March 9, 1901.

5946 to 5957. LINUM USITATISSIMUM. **Flax.**

From Paris, France. Received through Vilmorin-Andrieux & Co., March 9, 1901.
A collection of seed of different varieties, as follows:

5946.
Common flax.

5947.
True imported *Riga.*

5948.
French-grown *Riga.*

5949.
White-flowering.

5950.
Yellow-seeded.

5951.
Pskoff.

5952.
Improved Russian imported *Pskoff.*

5953.
Winter.

5954.
Of Belgian origin.

5955.
Of Dutch origin.

5956.
Nostrana of Lombardy.

5957.
Catanian or Sicilian.

5958. CICHORIUM INTYBUS. **Chicory.**

From Görz, Austria. Received through Mr. D. G. Fairchild (No. 515, January 24, 1901), March 11, 1901.

"A white variety of this excellent winter salad plant, which is one of the specialties of Görz." (*Fairchild.*)

5959. BRASSICA OLERACEA. **Cabbage.**

From Görz, Austria. Received through Mr. D. G. Fairchild (No. 516, January 24, 1901), March 11, 1901.

"A variety of cabbage which is noted for its remarkable winter-keeping qualities. Recommended by Director Bolley, of the Görz Experiment Station, for trial in the Southern States." (*Fairchild.*)

5960. BRASSICA OLERACEA. **Cabbage.**

From Bocche di Cattaro, Dalmatia. Received through Mr. D. G. Fairchild (No. 520, February 2, 1901), March 11, 1901.

"Seed of a perennial cabbage known as *Capuzzo*, which forms the principal food of many hundreds of families in Dalmatia. Grown especially in the regions about Cattaro and Ragusa. It grows to a height of 5 feet and bears in this warm climate tender leaves throughout the winter. These are picked off singly, or the whole, rather irregular, small head is cut off. The stems sprout out again and furnish, in a few months, a second crop of edible leaves. They require little culture and are allowed to stand in the fields for three or four years. Other crops are cultivated between the rows of *Capuzzo*. The method of planting is precisely similar to that for cabbages. From the ease with which it is grown and its apparent favor among the common people this plant is worthy a trial in the Southern States." (*Fairchild.*)

5961 to 5963. NICOTIANA TABACUM. Tobacco.

From Corfu, Greece. Presented by the director of the Corfu Agricultural Experiment Station through Mr. D. G. Fairchild (Nos. 523–525, February 9, 1901). Received March 11, 1901.

"Seeds of the Turkish tobaccos from which the noted Egyptian cigarettes are made, being exported from parts of Turkey where they are grown, into Egypt where they are manufactured. Egyptian cigarettes are said to be made of blends of these three and other tobaccos." (*Fairchild.*)

5961.

Kavala, from the region in Turkey of this name. (No. 523.)

5962.

Xanthe, from the region in Turkey of this name. (No. 524.)

5963.

Trebizond, from the region in Asia Minor of this name. (No. 525.)

5964. CUPRESSUS SEMPERVIRENS. Cypress.

From Ragusa, Dalmatia. Received through Mr. D. G. Fairchild (No. 526, February 7, 1901), March 11, 1901.

"The cypresses of Ragusa and vicinity are very beautiful, and seem to be a distinct strain, much more symmetrical in shape than the common pyramidal kind grown in America." (*Fairchild.*)

5965. VICIA FABA. Broad bean.

From Corfu, Greece. Received through Mr. D. G. Fairchild (No. 527, February 9, 1901), March 11, 1901.

"Sample of a variety of broad bean originally from the island of Malta. It is a very heavy bearer and is preferred by the planters of Corfu to the native varieties." (*Fairchild.*)

5966. AVENA SATIVA. Oats.

From Proskurow, Russia. Received through Dr. S. de Mrozinski, March 8, 1901.

Polish. "Very fruitful and resistant to all changes of temperature. In spite of great drought, it gives comparatively good yields." (*Mrozinski.*)

5967. AVENA SATIVA. Oats.

From Proskurow, Russia. Received through Dr. S. de Mrozinski, March 8, 1901.

Polish. The same as No. 5966.

5968. TRIFOLIUM PRATENSE. Red clover.

From Proskurow, Russia. Received through Dr. S. de Mrozinski, March 8, 1901.

5969. TRIFOLIUM PRATENSE. **Red clover.**

From Proskurow, Russia. Received through Dr. S. de Mrozinski, March 8, 1901.

Same as No. 5968.

5970. KOCHIA SCOPARIA.

From Tokyo, Japan. Received through Mr. T. Watase, December 28, 1900.

5971. HUMULUS LUPULUS. **Hop.**

From Tettnang, Bavaria. Received through Mr. D. G. Fairchild (No. 482, December 10, 1900), March 12, 1901.

Tettnang late. Seed.

5972. VIOLA ODORATA. **Violet.**

From Görz, Austria. Received through Mr. D. G. Fairchild (No. 513, January 23, 1901), March 12, 1901.

Czar. "A single violet from Antonio Ferrant's houses that has been cultivated here for many years. It has a decided perfume, but is inferior to the double varieties." (*Fairchild.*)

5973. VIOLA ODORATA. **Violet.**

From Görz, Austria. Received through Mr. D. G. Fairchild (No. 512, January 23, 1901), March 12, 1901.

Conte de Brazza. "A double white violet originated in Italy and brought to Austria by Count de Brazza. It is said to be one of the best white varieties known." (*Fairchild.*)

5974. VIOLA ODORATA. **Violet.**

From Görz, Austria. Received through Mr. D. G. Fairchild (No. 511, January 23, 1901), March 12, 1901.

Parmensis. "An unusually large sweet-scented double violet, somewhat similar to the *Neapolitan.* The favorite market sort of Görz. A native of France, being found wild about Grasse." (*Fairchild.*)

5975. HORDEUM DISTICHUM. **Barley.**

From Leschkau bei Podersam, Bohemia. Presented by Wilhelm Hoffer & Son, through Mr. D. G. Fairchild. Received February, 1901.

Goldfoil.

5976. HORDEUM DISTICHUM. **Barley.**

From Kitzingen, Bavaria. Presented by Nathan Gerste & Son, through Mr. D. G. Fairchild, February, 1901.

Kitzing. "Of the best quality." (*Fairchild.*)

5977. UMBELLULARIA CALIFORNICA. **California laurel.**

From San Bernardino, Cal. Received through Mr. S. B. Parish, February, 1901.

5978. ACTINIDIA sp.

From Ichang, China. Received through Mr. G. D. Brill (No. 2), December, 1900.

Yang tao. "Bears a fruit resembling the gooseberry, about 1¼ inches long and 1 inch in diameter. Skin dull purple and quite tough. Eaten raw or cooked and also used for preserves. There are several species, to all of which the Chinese give the name *Yang tao.*" (*Brill.*)

48   SEEDS AND PLANTS IMPORTED.

5979. ACTINIDIA sp.

From Ichang, China. Received through Mr. G. D. Brill (No. 3), December, 1900.

Yang tao. "Fruit larger and more pointed than No. 5978. The skin is a lighter purple and thinner, and when eaten raw this has the better flavor." (*Brill.*)

5980. EUCOMMIA ULMOIDES.

From Ichang, China. Presented by Mr. E. H. Wilson, of Kew Gardens, through Mr. G. D. Brill (No. 4). Received December, 1900.

Ti Cheng. "A medium-sized tree growing wild around Ichang. It is said to be cultivated in the mountains of Hupei. The bark is used as a medicine and the glutinous seeds to adulterate silk. It is said that rubber can be extracted from the seeds. No successful experiments have, however, been made in the extraction of this supposed rubber." (*Brill.*)

5981. BENTHAMIA FRAGIFERA. **Strawberry tree.**

From Ichang, China. Received through Mr. G. D. Brill, December, 1900.

"Medium-sized tree, quite showy, fruit very palatable and used for food in some parts of China." (*Brill.*)

5982. CITRUS LIMONUM. **Lemon.**

From Bocce di Cattaro, Dalmatia. Received through Mr. D. G. Fairchild (No. 517, February 1, 1901), March 13, 1901.

Cattaro Giant. "A very large lemon, said to have originated in Mesopotamia. The trees are very vigorous and good bearers. The fruit sometimes weighs four or five pounds, and has a flesh of excellent flavor and juiciness." (*Fairchild.*)

5983. JUGLANS REGIA. **Walnut.**

From Bocce di Cattaro, Dalmatia. Received through Mr. D. G. Fairchild (No. 578, February 2, 1901), March 13, 1901.

Giant of Cattaro. "A very large English walnut of fine flavor, which brings double the price of ordinary walnuts on the Dalmatian market. Specimens, which were said to be smaller than the average, measured 2⅛ inches long by 1⅝ inches in diameter. The shell is hard and irregular. The tree grows rapidly and is a free bearer. Scions were taken from a tree on the farm of Francesco Navarin. Called to my attention by Cristoforo Spalatin of Castelnuovo." (*Fairchild.*)

5984. OLEA EUROPAEA. **Olive.**

From Bocce di Cattaro, Dalmatia. Received through Mr. D. G. Fairchild (No. 519, February 2, 1901), March 13, 1901.

Giant of Cattaro. "A very large seedling olive, specimens of which measured 1⅜ inches in length by 1 inch in diameter. From two trees growing near Castelnuovo. Called to my attention by Cristoforo Spalatin." (*Fairchild.*)

5985. VITIS VINIFERA. **Grape.**

From Corfu, Greece. Received through Mr. D. G. Fairchild (No. 521, February 7, 1901), March 13, 1901.

Sultanina. "A light-yellow, transparent, seedless raisin grape. Considered to be one of the most valuable varieties, and that from which the 'Sultanina' seedless raisins of Greece are made. These raisins must not be confused with the 'Corinths,' for they are twice as large, of a light golden color, semitransparent, and much more valuable." (*Fairchild.*)

5986. CITRUS LIMONUM. **Lemon.**

From Corfu, Greece. Received through Mr. D. G. Fairchild (No. 522, February 7, 1901), March 13, 1901.

A giant-fruited variety of lemon, probably the same as No. 5982.

SEPTEMBER, 1900, TO DECEMBER, 1903. 49

5987. PUNICA GRANATUM. **Pomegranate.**

From Patras, Greece. Presented by the British consul, Mr. F. B. Wood, through Mr. D. G. Fairchild (No. 548, February 16, 1901). Received March 14, 1901.

"A very large pomegranate, sometimes at least 6 inches in diameter. The fruit is red and attractive, and instead of being sweet as most sorts are, this is sour like a lemon." (*Fairchild.*)

5988. PUNICA GRANATUM. **Pomegranate.**

From Patras, Greece. Presented by the British consul, Mr. F. B. Wood, through Mr. D. G. Fairchild (No. 549, February 16, 1901). Received March 14, 1901.

"A large sweet-flavored pomegranate of excellent quality." (*Fairchild.*)

5989. CITRUS AURANTIUM. **Blood orange.**

From Patras, Greece. Presented by the British consul, Mr. F. B. Wood, through Mr. D. G. Fairchild (No. 550, February 16, 1901). Received March 14, 1901.

Patras blood. "A small, nearly seedless blood orange, the pulp being the most completely blood-red of any orange I have ever seen, the segment partitions especially so. Skin too thin for a good shipping variety, mottled dark and light, with many large oil glands. It is very juicy, of excellent, almost vinous flavor." (*Fairchild.*)

5990. CITRUS AURANTIUM. **Blood orange.**

From Corfu, Greece. Received through Mr. D. G. Fairchild (No. 528, February 10, 1901), March 14, 1901.

"A blood variety, the pulp of which is beautifully mottled with light red and the skin with a darker orange color." (*Fairchild.*)

5991. CITRUS LIMONUM. **Lemon.**

From Corfu, Greece. Received through Mr. D. G. Fairchild (No. 529, February 10, 1901), March 14, 1901.

"A variety of lemon which bears quite seedless fruits from the flowers which mature in October, and fruits full of seed from the spring flowers. The seedless fruits are called "mules" or "mulas," and differ in shape from the ordinary, being more globose and possessing a persistent pistil which often projects some distance beyond the circumference of the fruit. Often over 10 and sometimes even 20 per cent of the fruits on a tree are seedless, I am told. I am inclined to attribute the seedlessness to lack of fertilization." (*Fairchild.*)

5992. CORYLUS sp. **Hazelnut.**

From Corfu, Greece. Presented by Antonio Colla through Mr. D. G. Fairchild (No. 540, February 13, 1901). Received March 14, 1901.

"A large thin-shelled, full-meated hazelnut, growing wild in Corfu. The trees are vigorous and good bearers." (*Fairchild.*)

5993. CITRUS LIMONUM. **Lemon.**

From Corfu, Greece. Received through Mr. D. G. Fairchild (No. 530, February 10, 1901), March 14, 1901.

Similar to No. 5991.

5994. POPULUS ALBA (?) **Poplar.**

From Patras, Greece. Presented by the British consul, Mr. F. B. Wood, through Mr. D. G. Fairchild (No. 551, February 16, 1901). Received March 14, 1901.

"Cuttings from a poplar of remarkably rapid growth. The tree is 30 years old and over 3½ feet in diameter, while neighboring trees of about the same age are not more than half that size. The tree is very beautiful, of spreading habit." (*Fairchild.*)

5995. TRITICUM VULGARE. **Wheat.**

From San Giovanni a Teduccio, Italy. Received through Dammann & Co. (No. 1), March 12, 1901.

Scavurso.

5996. TRITICUM VULGARE. **Wheat.**

From San Giovanni a Teduccio, Italy. Received through Dammann & Co. (No. 2), March 12, 1901.

Iumilio.

5997. TRITICUM VULGARE. **Wheat.**

From San Giovanni a Teduccio, Italy. Received through Dammann & Co. (No. 3), March 12, 1901.

Biancolilla.

5998. BORONIA MEGASTIGMA.

From Melbourne, Australia. Presented by Carolin & Co. Received March, 1901.

"Sow in spring in seed pans in light, loamy soil. Plant out in autumn from 2 to 4 feet apart. Use no manure. The plants come into bearing the second year, and live six or seven years." (*Carolin.*)

5999. TRITICUM DURUM. **Wheat.**

From Proskurow, Russia. Presented by Dr. S. de Mrozinski. Received March 19, 1901.

Kubanka. A sample packet of this well-known variety of macaroni wheat.

6000 to 6110.

From Russia, Hungary, and Roumania. Received through Mr. M. A. Carleton, November, 1900.

A collection of seeds secured during the season from June to September, 1900.

6000. TRITICUM VULGARE. **Wheat.**

From Odessa, Russia. "A semihard red wheat; of good quality for milling, but not commonly exported. Adapted for cultivation in the middle States of the Plains." (*Carleton.*)

6001. TRITICUM VULGARE. **Wheat.**

From Odessa, Russia. *Ulta.* "A hard or semihard red spring wheat of excellent quality for milling, forming a large part of the wheat that is exported from the Kherson and Ekaterinoslav governments through Odessa." (*Carleton.*)

6002. TRITICUM VULGARE. **Wheat.**

From Odessa, Russia. *Ghirka.* "This is the principal beardless variety of red spring wheat grown in Russia, particularly in south Russia and the Volga River region. It differs from the usual varieties of Russian spring wheat in being beardless and not quite so hard grained. It forms a large part of the wheat exported from Russia." (*Carleton.*)

6003. TRITICUM VULGARE. **Wheat.**

From Berdiansk, Russia. *Berdiansk.* "A red, hard-grained, bearded winter wheat with white chaff, very similar to Crimean. It is grown in the region north of the Sea of Azov. It is an excellent variety for cultivation in the middle prairie States." (*Carleton.*)

6004. TRITICUM VULGARE. **Wheat.**

From Berdiansk, Russia. *Belokoloska.* "A red, hard-grained, beardless spring wheat with white chaff, very similar to No. 6001. Grown in the vicinity of the Sea of Azov." (*Carleton.*)

6000 to 6110—Continued.

6005. TRITICUM DURUM. **Wheat.**

From Berdiansk, Russia. *Arnautka.* "A very good sample of this variety of wheat commonly grown in the region just north of the Sea of Azov." (*Carleton.*)

6006. TRITICUM VULGARE. **Wheat.**

From Konstantinovskoe, Russia. *Ulta.* See No. 5638.

6007. TRITICUM VULGARE. **Wheat.**

From Tsaritsyn, Russia. *Torgova.* "A very hard-grained, hardy winter wheat grown in the extreme northern portion of Stavropol government, well adapted for trial in Iowa, Nebraska, and South Dakota." (*Carleton.*)

6008. TRITICUM DURUM. **Wheat.**

From Tsaritsyn, Russia. *Black Don or Chernokoloska.* "A very good variety of macaroni wheat, with black chaff, grown in the Don Territory near Poltava, Russia." (*Carleton.*)

6009. TRITICUM DURUM. **Wheat.**

From Tsaritsyn, Russia. *Kubanka.* "A very good sample of this variety of macaroni wheat commonly grown in south Russia." (*Carleton.*) See No. 5639.

6010. TRITICUM VULGARE. **Wheat.**

From Berdiansk, Russia. *Belokoloska.* The same as No. 6004.

6011. TRITICUM DURUM. **Wheat.**

From Saratov, Russia. *Egyptian.* "A very hard-grained variety of macaroni wheat somewhat similar to Kubanka, but having longer grains." (*Carleton.*)

6012. TRITICUM VULGARE. **Wheat.**

From Rostov-on-Don, Russia. *Beloglino.* "One of the hardiest red winter wheats known. Grown near Beloglinskaya, in the northern portion of the Stavropol Government, a region of great extremes of temperature and moisture. The grain is very hard and makes an excellent quality of flour. It is admirably adapted for trial in Iowa, Nebraska, and South Dakota." (*Carleton.*)

6013. TRITICUM VULGARE. **Wheat.**

From Rostov-on-Don, Russia. *Beloglino.* "Practically the same as No. 6012, but a poorer quality." (*Carleton.*)

6014. TRITICUM DURUM. **Wheat.**

From Taganrog, Russia. *Gharnovka.* "A representative sample of the best quality of this macaroni wheat, grown by the peasants in the region south of Taganrog." (*Carleton.*)

6015. TRITICUM VULGARE. **Wheat.**

From Ambrocievka, Russia. *Crimean.* "A very hard red winter wheat, similar to Nos. 5635 and 5636, but grown in the district about 20 miles north of Taganrog, in the Don Territory." (*Carleton.*)

6016. TRITICUM VULGARE. **Wheat.**

From Berdiansk, Russia. *Kerch.* "A hard red winter wheat, very similar to *Crimean*, grown near the Sea of Azov. It is very drought-resistant and well adapted for the middle prairie States. It will probably ripen a little earlier than the variety commonly called *Turkey*." (*Carleton.*)

6017. TRITICUM VULGARE. **Wheat.**

From Kurman-Kemelechi, Russia. *Crimean.* Same as No. 5635.

6000 to 6110—Continued.

6018. Triticum durum. **Wheat.**

From Berdiansk, Russia. *Arnautka.* "A sample of this excellent macaroni wheat, grown near Taganrog." (*Carleton.*)

6019. Triticum durum. **Wheat.**

From Berdiansk, Russia. *Arnautka.* "The same variety as No. 6018, but of better quality." (*Carleton.*)

6020. Triticum durum. **Wheat.**

From Berdiansk, Russia. *Arnautka.* "Similar to Nos. 6018 and 6019, but of better quality." (*Carleton.*)

6021. Triticum vulgare. **Wheat.**

From Stavropol, Russia. "A hard red winter wheat of excellent quality, very similar to No. 5638." (*Carleton.*)

6022. Avena sativa. **Oat.**

From near Stavropol, Russia. "A large white oat having heavy straw and large, well-filled heads." (*Carleton.*)

6023. Hordeum hexastichum. **Barley.**

From near Stavropol, Russia. *Six-rowed.* "Apparently a standard variety in this region." (*Carleton.*)

6024. Panicum miliaceum. **Proso.**

From Chaplino, Russia. *White.* "One of the varieties of millet commonly grown in the Don Territory, Russia." (*Carleton.*)

6025. Panicum miliaceum. **Proso.**

From Sarepta, Russia. *White.* "A standard variety of millet grown in the lower Volga region." (*Carleton.*)

6026. Panicum miliaceum. **Proso.**

From Sarepta, Russia. *Grey.* "This variety of millet succeeds quite well in the lower Volga region, but is not so commonly grown as other kinds." (*Carleton.*)

6027. Panicum miliaceum. **Proso.**

From Sarepta, Russia. *Yellow.* "One of the standard sorts of millet grown in the lower Volga region." (*Carleton.*)

6028. Zea mays. **Corn.**

From Bukharest, Roumania. *Red Pignoletto.* "A standard variety of Italian *Pignoletto* corn commonly grown in Roumania. *Pignoletto* is a term which perhaps belongs more properly to a group of varieties than to a single variety. It includes some of the best sorts grown in Italy and to a large extent in Roumania." (*Carleton.*)

6029. Zea mays. **Corn.**

From near Taganrog, Russia. *Czekler.* "One of the best varieties of corn grown in South Russia." (*Carleton.*)

6030. Zea mays. **Corn.**

From near Taganrog, Russia. *Bessarabian.* "This is a standard variety of corn, commonly grown in Bessarabia, where a large proportion of the entire Russian corn crop is grown." (*Carleton.*)

6000 to 6110—Continued.

6031. ZEA MAYS. **Corn.**

From near Taganrog. Russia. *Chenkvantino.* "A variety of corn grown to a considerable extent in south Russia, Roumania, Hungary, and Italy." (*Carleton.*)

6032. ZEA MAYS. **Corn.**

From near Taganrog, Russia. *Asiatic.* "A Trans-Caucasian variety of corn considered to be one of the best for south Russia." (*Carleton.*)

6033. ZEA MAYS. **Corn.**

From Ambrocievka, Russia. *Red Flint.*

6034. ZEA MAYS. **Corn.**

From Saratov, Russia. "A large-grained variety of sugar corn grown in the lower Volga region." (*Carleton.*)

6035. CANNABIS SATIVA. **Hemp.**

From Mezohegys, Hungary. "A standard variety of hemp grown in central Hungary." (*Carleton.*)

6036. CAMELINA SATIVA. **False flax.**

From Bukharest, Roumania. "A plant grown to a considerable extent in Russia and Roumania for the oil. It should be used only experimentally, as it is likely to become a bad weed. (*Carleton.*)

6037. CITRULLUS VULGARIS. **Watermelon.**

From Berdiansk, Russia. "A rather small, round, red-fleshed melon of very good flavor." (*Carleton.*)

6038. CITRULLUS VULGARIS. **Watermelon.**

From Berdiansk, Russia. "A red-fleshed melon of average size." (*Carleton.*)

6039. CITRULLUS VULGARIS. **Watermelon.**

From Taganrog, Russia. "An excellent red-fleshed melon of medium size." (*Carleton.*)

6040. CITRULLUS VULGARIS. **Watermelon.**

From Taganrog, Russia. "An excellent melon of medium size, dark-green skin, with red flesh and black seeds." (*Carleton.*)

6041. CITRULLUS VULGARIS. **Watermelon.**

From Rostov-on-Don, Russia. "A very rich melon with red flesh and black seeds." (*Carleton.*)

6042. CITRULLUS VULGARIS. **Watermelon.**

From Tikhoretskaya, Russia. "A medium or small round melon, very light green on the outside with darker green bands. Red flesh and very small black seeds; flavor, excellent." (*Carleton.*)

6043. CITRULLUS VULGARIS. **Watermelon.**

From Stavropol, Russia. "A large red-fleshed melon with black seeds. It is peculiarly colored on the outside, being light green with vertical bands of dark green." (*Carleton.*)

6044. CITRULLUS VULGARIS. **Watermelon.**

From the region about 40 miles east of Stavropol, Russia. "A melon of medium size, dark green outside with light-brown seeds, adapted for cultivation in the semiarid districts." (*Carleton.*)

6000 to 6110—Continued.

6045. CITRULLUS VULGARIS. **Watermelon.**

From Stavropol, Russia. "A melon of medium size, very light green on the outside with darker vertical stripes, red flesh, and spotted brown seeds. Adapted for cultivation in semiarid districts." (*Carleton.*)

6046. CITRULLUS VULGARIS. **Watermelon.**

From Ekaterinodar, Russia. "A rather large melon, dark green on the outside, with red flesh and large brown seeds." (*Carleton.*)

6047. CITRULLUS VULGARIS. **Watermelon.**

From Guiloyaksaiskaya, near Ekaterinodar, Russia. "An excellent melon of rather large size, dark green on the outside, with red flesh, brown seeds, and good flavor." (*Carleton.*)

6048. CITRULLUS VULGARIS. **Watermelon.**

From Tsaritsyn, Russia. "A rather large melon, very light green or nearly white on the outside, with light-green stripes, very small black seeds. This is one of the most common watermelons grown on a commercial scale in the Volga region." (*Carleton.*)

6049. CITRULLUS VULGARIS. **Watermelon.**

From Saratov, Russia. Mixed watermelon seeds.

6050. CITRULLUS VULGARIS. **Watermelon.**

From Uralsk, Russia. "A small round melon, greenish white on the outside, red flesh, red seeds, and very rich flavor. Grown by the Kirghiz on the steppes. Adapted for cultivation in very dry districts." (*Carleton.*)

6051. CITRULLUS VULGARIS. **Watermelon.**

From Uralsk, Russia. "A good melon of medium or small size, round, greenish white on the outside, with red flesh and small black seeds. Grown by the Kirghiz on the steppes. Adapted for cultivation in very dry districts." (*Carleton.*)

6052. CITRULLUS VULGARIS. **Watermelon.**

From Saratov, Russia. "An excellent melon of very large size, round, dark green on the outside, with large reddish-brown seeds. Grown in an extremely dry region, therefore adapted for cultivation in dry districts." (*Carleton.*)

6053. CITRULLUS VULGARIS. **Watermelon.**

From Novokhopersk, Russia. "A very fine rich-flavored melon of unusual appearance. It has the form of a crooked-neck squash, dark green on the outside, netted with lighter green, yellow flesh tinged with salmon-white seeds. Adapted for cultivation in very dry regions." (*Carleton.*)

6054. CITRULLUS VULGARIS. **Watermelon.**

From Blagodat, Russia. "An excellent melon of average size, green outside, with white flesh and spotted dark-brown seeds." (*Carleton.*)

6055. CITRULLUS VULGARIS. **Watermelon.**

From Ambrocievka, Russia. "An excellent melon of large size, dark green on the outside, with red flesh and light-brown seeds." (*Carleton.*)

6056. CITRULLUS VULGARIS. **Watermelon.**

From Dolinskaya, Russia. "A good melon of rather small size, peculiarly colored on the outside, gourd-shaped, with light-brown black-bordered seeds." (*Carleton.*)

6000 to 6110—Continued.

6057. CITRULLUS VULGARIS. **Watermelon.**

From Russia. "A very large rich melon, green outside, with red flesh and light-brown seeds." (*Carleton.*)

6058. CUCUMIS MELO. **Muskmelon.**

From Odessa, Russia. *Bread melon.* "An Egyptian melon of medium size, somewhat flattened vertically, prominently ribbed with a very rough surface, remaining green on the outside for a long time, but turning considerably yellow when fully ripe; flesh yellow, sometimes slightly tinged with salmon, rather firm. When fully ripe the flavor is excellent. It is sometimes called the Pineapple (*Ananas*) melon." (*Carleton.*)

6059. CUCUMIS MELO. **Muskmelon.**

From Sevastopol, Russia. "A melon of average size with greenish-yellow flesh and white seeds." (*Carleton.*)

6060. CUCUMIS MELO. **Muskmelon.**

From Berdiansk, Russia. "One of the common varieties of muskmelon grown in the region north of the Sea of Azov." (*Carleton.*)

6061. CUCUMIS MELO. **Muskmelon.**

From Berdiansk, Russia. "A round, smooth melon of medium size and fine flavor; flesh greenish yellow." (*Carleton.*)

6062. CUCUMIS MELO. **Muskmelon.**

From Taganrog, Russia. "An excellent, smooth-skinned melon; flesh greenish yellow." (*Carleton.*)

6063. CUCUMIS MELO. **Muskmelon.**

From Rostov-on-Don, Russia. "An excellent round melon of medium size; very smooth on the outside; flesh white with pink spots." (*Carleton.*)

6064. CUCUMIS MELO. **Muskmelon.**

From Rostov-on-Don, Russia. *Kochanka.* "One of the most popular melons grown in South Russia; rather small, round and smooth, yellowish white on the outside, with green bands or splotches; flesh green except near the seed, where it is salmon color; seeds rather large and almost white." (*Carleton.*)

6065. CUCUMIS MELO. **Muskmelon.**

From Ekaterinodar, Russia. "A rather large melon, yellowish green on the outside and netted; green flesh, very juicy, and of fairly good flavor." (*Carleton.*)

6066. CUCUMIS MELO. **Muskmelon.**

From Ekaterinodar, Russia. The same variety as No. 6064. Grown in North Caucasus.

6067. CUCUMIS MELO. **Muskmelon.**

From Tsaritsyn, Russia. *Kalminka.* "Name derived from the word Kalmuck. Melon netted, nearly round, yellow, mottled with green when ripe. Flesh green, very sweet, and good. Seeds light yellow." (*Carleton.*)

6068. CUCUMIS MELO. **Muskmelon.**

From Kamishin, Russia. *Krestyanka.* "A rather large, long melon, yellow, slightly netted. Flesh yellow, and fairly good. A popular sort in the north Volga region." (*Carleton.*)

6000 to 6110—Continued.

6069. Cucumis melo. **Muskmelon.**

From Astrakhan, Russia. "A large, round melon of excellent flavor. Seeds below medium size, brownish green in color, rather short and thick." (*Carleton.*)

6070. Cucumis melo. **Muskmelon.**

From Saratov, Russia. *Kalminka.* "A large, rather long melon of light orange color, netted greenish white; flesh very juicy and sweet. Large seeds. One of the best varieties in the Astrakhan government." (*Carleton.*)

6071. Cucumis melo. **Muskmelon.**

From Uralsk, Russia. *Bokhara.* "A rather large melon, yellowish green in color, and netted. Flesh green near the rind; salmon pink near the seeds, with very rich flavor. One of the best sorts grown by the Kirghis farmers on the east side of the Ural River." (*Carleton.*)

6072. Cucumis melo. **Muskmelon.**

From Uralsk, Russia. "A rather long melon, yellow, with dark-green spots; flesh greenish white." (*Carleton.*)

6073. Cucumis melo. **Muskmelon.**

From Povorino, Russia. "A very large melon, yellow, roughly netted with green. Flesh white, or slightly tinged with green, very firm. Flavor good. Seeds nearly white." (*Carleton.*)

6074. Cucumis melo. **Muskmelon.**

From Kharkof, Russia. *Ananas.* "Probably the same as No. 6058." (*Carleton.*)

6075. Cucumis melo. **Muskmelon.**

From Taganrog, Russia, "A melon of medium size, nearly round, yellow, surface considerably netted. Flesh green with very rich, sweet flavor near the rind.' (*Carleton.*)

6076. Cucumis melo. **Muskmelon.**

From Taganrog, Russia. *Ananas.* "Similar to No. 6074." (*Carleton.*)

6077. Cucumis melo. **Muskmelon.**

From Taganrog, Russia. "A small melon with smooth surface, netted yellow and green. Flesh green." (*Carleton.*)

6078. Cucumis melo. **Muskmelon.**

From Blagodat, estate of Mr. Rutchenko, about 20 miles north of Taganrog, Russia. *Rostor.* "An excellent melon of medium to large size, elongated or fairly round, smooth, almost white on the outside. Flesh green, very sweet, and juicy." (*Carleton.*)

6079. Pistacia vera. **Pistache.**

From Stavropol, Russia. "A variety said to come from Syria bearing unusually large nuts." (*Carleton.*)

6080. Cucumis sativus. **Cucumber.**

From Saratov, Russia. *Pavlovskii.* "One of the standard varieties of garden cucumbers grown in the lower Volga region of Russia." (*Carleton.*)

6081. Cucumis sativus. **Cucumber.**

From Saratov, Russia. *Moscow.* "A long, dark-green variety, grown in the lower Volga region, Russia." (*Carleton.*)

6000 to 6110—Continued.

6082. CUCUMIS SATIVUS. **Cucumber.**

From Saratov, Russia. "One of the standard varieties of cucumber grown in the lower Volga region." (*Carleton.*)

6083. CUCUMIS SATIVUS. **Cucumber.**

From Saratov, Russia. *Muron.* "A rather early variety of cucumber, grown in the lower Volga region." (*Carleton.*)

6084. RAPHANUS SATIVUS. **Radish.**

From Saratov, Russia. *Moscow.* A rather long, early, white variety, grown in the region near Moscow." (*Carleton.*)

6085. RAPHANUS SATIVUS. **Radish.**

From Saratov, Russia. *Delicesse.* "An early variety of excellent flavor, grown in the region near Moscow, Russia." (*Carleton.*)

6086. RAPHANUS SATIVUS. **Radish.**

From Saratov, Russia. *Erfurt.* "A long, white variety of winter radish, grown near Moscow, Russia." (*Carleton.*)

6087. RAPHANUS SATIVUS. **Radish.**

From Saratov, Russia. "A small, round radish of good quality grown near Moscow, Russia." (*Carleton.*)

6088. CUCURBITA MAXIMA. **Pumpkin.**

From Saratov, Russia. "A good variety, grown near Moscow, Russia." (*Carleton.*)

6089. CUCURBITA MAXIMA. **Pumpkin.**

From Saratov, Russia. *Hundred pound.* "A large yellow pumpkin." (*Carleton.*)

6090. LYCOPERSICUM ESCULENTUM. **Tomato.**

From Saratov, Russia. "A very large red tomato, grown in n... th Caucasus, "Russia." (*Carleton.*)

6091. LYCOPERSICUM ESCULENTUM. **Tomato.**

From Saratov, Russia. *Trophy.* "A large-fruited, late tomato, grown near Tsaritsyn, Russia." (*Carleton.*)

6092. PHASEOLUS VULGARIS. **Bean.**

From Jassy, Roumania. "A very large, white, kidney-shaped bean, grown in the northern part of Roumania." (*Carleton.*)

6093. HELIANTHUS ANNUUS. **Sunflower.**

From Taganrog, Russia. "A large, dark, gray-seeded variety, commonly used for eating, grown in southern and central Russia." (*Carleton.*)

6094. HELIANTHUS ANNUUS. **Sunflower.**

From the District Experimental Farm at Taganrog, Russia. "A variety of sunflower having small-sized, striped seeds which are used for oil." (*Carleton.*)

6095. HELIANTHUS ANNUUS. **Sunflower.**

From the field near Tikhoretskaya in Kuban Territory, North Caucasus, Russia. "A variety of sunflower having large, rather long, black seeds, much grown in North Caucasus, but not well known in other parts of Russia." (*Carleton.*)

6000 to 6110—Continued.

6096. PRUNUS sp. **Cherry.**

From Budapest, Hungary. "A small black cherry commonly grown in Hungary." (*Carleton.*)

6097. PRUNUS sp. **Cherry.**

From Budapest, Hungary. "Seeds of an excellent variety of white cherry grown in the vicinity of Budapest." (*Carleton.*)

6098. PRUNUS sp. **Cherry.**

From near Budapest, Hungary. *Spanish.* "Seeds of a variety of cherry commonly grown in this vicinity." (*Carleton.*)

6099. PRUNUS sp. **Cherry.**

From Budapest, Hungary. "Seeds of a large-fruited black cherry extensively grown in this region." (*Carleton.*)

6100. PRUNUS sp. **Cherry.**

From Budapest, Hungary. "Seeds of a large pink cherry grown in this vicinity." (*Carleton.*)

6101. RIBES RUBRUM. **Red currant.**

From Budapest, Hungary. "Seeds of a red currant of medium size grown in this vicinity." (*Carleton.*)

6102. PYRUS MALUS. **Apple.**

From markets of Sevastopol, Russia. *Anis.* "Seeds of one of the best and commonest varieties grown in the Crimea. A very good fruit and quite popular." (*Carleton.*)

6103. PRUNUS sp. **Plum.**

From Sevastopol, Russia. "A variety very similar to *Green Gage* and grown to a considerable extent in the Crimea." (*Carleton.*)

6104. PRUNUS sp. **Plum.**

From Sevastopol, Russia. *Ringolot.* "Seeds of one of the best varieties grown extensively in the Crimea." (*Carleton.*)

6105. PRUNUS sp. **Plum.**

From Sevastopol, Russia. *Mirabelle.* "A large plum of excellent flavor grown to a considerable extent in the Crimea. This and No. 6104 seem to be two of the best varieties in that region." (*Carleton.*)

6106. PRUNUS sp. **Plum.**

From Sevastopol, Russia. "A green sort grown to a considerable extent in the Crimea." (*Carleton.*)

6107. PRUNUS sp. **Cherry.**

From Belbek, Russia. "Seeds of a variety of sour cherry commonly grown in the Crimea." (*Carleton.*)

6108. PRUNUS sp. **Plum.**

From Rostov-on-Don, Russia. "A variety originally from the Crimea, with very large fruit of a delicious flavor when fully ripe. Possibly the same as No. 6105." (*Carleton.*)

6109. AMYGDALUS PERSICA. **Peach.**

From Rostov-on-Don, Russia. "A small Crimean variety. Fruit round, purple, and very hairy. Flesh sweet near the rind, but sour next the seed." (*Carleton.*)

6000 to 6110—Continued.

6110. PYRUS COMMUNIS. **Pear.**

From Kharkof, Russia. *Yellow Flesh.* "A pear of medium size, yellow and pink in color. Extremely juicy and having an excellent flavor. By far the best pear in the Kharkof markets." (*Carleton.*)

6111. TRITICUM VULGARE. **Wheat.**

From Proskurow, Russia. Received through Dr. S. de Mrozinski, March 19, 1901.

Podolia. An excellent variety, but not so resistant to drought as Nos. 5999 and 6112.

6112. TRITICUM VULGARE. **Wheat.**

From Proskurow, Russia. Received through Dr. S. de Mrozinski, March 19, 1901.

Poltava. "An extremely drought-resistant variety." (*Mrozinski.*)

6113. PYRUS MALUS. **Apple.**

From Corfu, Greece. Presented by Mr. Antonio Colla, through Mr. D. G. Fairchild (No. 539, February 13, 1901). Received March 20, 1901.

Corfu. "Scions of a very large and delicious apple, probably a native of the island. It should be tried in the Southern States, Porto Rico, and Hawaii." (*Fairchild.*)

6114. FICUS CARICA. **Fig.**

From Corfu, Greece. Presented by Mr. Antonio Colla, through Mr. D. G. Fairchild (No. 541, February 13, 1901.) Received March 20, 1901.

Fracatsani of Corfu. "Scions of the largest and finest flavored table fig grown on the island of Corfu. Trees vigorous. Fruit light-colored and unusually large, thin-skinned, and juicy." (*Fairchild.*)

6115. CITRUS LIMONUM. **Lemon.**

From Corfu, Greece. Presented by Mr. Antonio Colla, through Mr. D. G. Fairchild (No. 542, February 13, 1901). Received March 20, 1901.

Colla giant. "Scions from a tree bearing immense fruit, some specimens weighing 2¼ pounds. Probably the same as Nos. 5982 and 5986." (*Fairchild.*)

6116. CITRUS AURANTIUM. **Orange.**

From Corfu, Greece. Presented by Mr. Antonio Colla, through Mr. D. G. Fairchild (No. 543, February 13, 1901). Received March 20, 1901.

"Scions of a variety of seedless orange. Possibly the Maltese variety." (*Fairchild.*)

6117. CITRUS LIMONUM. **Lemon.**

From Corfu, Greece. Received through Mr. D. G. Fairchild (No. 544, February 14, 1901), March 20, 1901.

"Scions of a thin-skinned, nearly seedless lemon having salmon-colored flesh. The tree is very ornamental, the leaves being variegated." (*Fairchild.*)

6118. VITIS VINIFERA. **Grape.**

From Castelnuova, Dalmatia, Austria. Received through Mr. D. G. Fairchild (No. 545, February 14, 1901), March 20, 1901.

Marzamina. "Cuttings of a heavy-bearing excellent variety of wine grape, said to have been grown in the Bocche di Cattaro since the time of the Roman occupation; said to make one of the best of Dalmatian wines." (*Fairchild.*)

6119. VITIS VINIFERA. Grape.

From Castelnuova, Dalmatia, Austria. Received through Mr. D. G. Fairchild (No. 546, February 14, 1901), March 20, 1901.

Marzamina genuina. "Cuttings of an old variety of wine grape, probably a native of the country. It is like No. 6118, only of superior flavor and not such a heavy bearer." (*Fairchild.*)

6120. CYDONIA VULGARIS. Quince.

From Corfu, Greece. Presented by Mr. Antonio Collas, through Mr. D. G. Fairchild (No. 547, February 13, 1901). Received March 20, 1901.

Corfu. "Cuttings of a very large pear-shaped quince. The trees are handsome, vigorous, and coarse growing. The quality of the fruit is poor, but its size and color may make it a desirable sort for breeders. The flesh is milder flavored than American varieties, and can be eaten raw." (*Fairchild.*)

6121. CITRUS LIMONUM. Lemon.

From Patras, Greece. Received through Mr. D. G. Fairchild (No. 552, February 17, 1901), March 15, 1901.

"A variety of lemon which has the reputation of being very nearly seedless." (*Fairchild.*)

6122. PISTACIA VERA. Pistache.

From Aintab, Syria. Presented by Rev. A. Fuller, through Mr. W. T. Swingle. Received March 26, 1901.

Aintab. "Scions of what is here regarded as the best variety of the pistachio tree. This tree does best on dry, rocky soil on mountains or hillsides." (*Fuller.*)

6123. PISTACIA VERA. Pistache.

From Aintab, Syria. Presented by Rev. A. Fuller, through Mr. W. T. Swingle. Received April 1, 1901.

Aintab. "Scions of what is here regarded as the best variety of the pistachio tree. This tree does best on dry, rocky, deep soil on mountains or hillsides." (*Fuller.*)

6124. VITIS VINIFERA. Grape.

From Aintab, Syria. Presented by Rev. A. Fuller, through Mr. W. T. Swingle. Received April 1, 1901.

Hunisa. "A large, dark wine-colored and very beautiful table grape, slightly oblong in shape. Flesh firm and fruity; ripens late (November) and has remarkable powers of keeping. Hung in a dry, cool place it will keep perfectly until April, only slightly withering as it is kept, and the flavor rather improving with age. To my mind it is the best all-round food grape I have ever seen." (*Fuller.*)

6125 to 6130. OLEA EUROPAEA. Olive.

From Fresno, Cal. Presented by Mr. George C. Roeding, through Mr. W. T. Swingle. Received April 6, 1901.

A collection of rooted olive cuttings as follows:

6125.
Manzanillo.

6126.
Neradillo.

6127.
Rubra.

6128.
Mission.

6129.
Serillano.

6130.
Pendulina.

6131. CUCUMIS MELO. Muskmelon.

From Marseille, France. Received through Hon. Robert P. Skinner, United States Consul-General, March 21, 1901.

Cavaillon. "These seeds should be planted under glass early in the spring and subjected to the least possible change of temperature until the weather is settled and the plants have become sufficiently advanced to warrant transplanting. This melon is one of the most valued horticultural products of southern France. It might be successfully cultivated in the latitude of Washington, and certainly in our Southern States. The fruit, when ripe, is very much the color of our green watermelons; the flesh is light green in color, highly perfumed and extremely palatable." (*Skinner.*)

6132. CANAVALIA ENSIFORMIS. Halberd bean.

From Morioka, Japan. Received through Rev. E. Rothesay Miller, March 9, 1901.

Nata-Mame. "This, as a string bean eaten when young, is one of the finest I have ever tasted. It grows much like pole limas, 10 feet high, and the pods are of immense size, often over a foot long and an inch and a half broad and half an inch thick. The Japanese use them generally for pickling when young, and they are very fine for this purpose, but as a string bean they are well worth introducing into the United States. They are cultivated about like pole limas, but need a warm climate for ripening. Should do well south of the latitude of Pennsylvania." (*Miller.*)

6133. CUCURBITA sp. Crepe squash.

From Morioka, Japan. Received through Rev. E. Rothesay Miller, March 9, 1901.

Chirimen Kabucha. "This squash is rather large, of a dark-green color, changing to yellow, sometimes even to a light greenish-blue color. The appearance is like a rough muskmelon, flattened considerably. I think it comes from Shinshu, one of the central provinces of Japan, but grows well here. It is about the best of the Japanese squashes, and is quite different from the varieties commonly grown in the United States, and may be worth cultivation." (*Miller.*)

6134. BRASSICA RAPA. Turnip.

From Morioka, Japan. Received through Rev. E. Rothesay Miller, March 9, 1901.

"A large white turnip, possibly worth cultivating for stock feeding." (*Miller.*)

6135. RAPHANUS SATIVUS. Radish.

From near Tokyo, Japan. Received through Rev. E. Rothesay Miller, March 9, 1901.

Daikon. "This is the immense radish used by the Japanese for pickling and eaten by them three times a day. The seeds I send are of an especially large and fine variety which grows near Tokyo." (*Miller.*)

6136. RAPHANUS SATIVUS. Radish.

From Sakura Island, Japan. Received through Rev. E. Rothesay Miller, March 9, 1901.

Sakura-gima Daikon. "This is another variety of the 'Daikon' radish, grown on Sakura Island, in the Bay of Kagoshima. It is not long, like No. 6135, but turnip shaped, and grows to such an immense size that the natives say two of them make a horse load." (*Miller.*)

6137. RAPHANUS SATIVUS. Radish.

From Sakura Island, Japan. Received through Rev. E. Rothesay Miller, March 9, 1901.

Sakura-gima Daikon. "The same as No. 6136, but can be planted about two weeks later." (*Miller.*)

6138. CORYLUS TUBULOSA. **Hazelnut.**

From Rovigno, Austria. Received through Mr. D. G. Fairchild (No. 509, January 19, 1901), March 23, 1901.

Pignatele. "Plants of a small hazelnut, inferior in quality to No. 6139. May, however, be worthy of trial in comparison with American varieties." (*Fairchild.*)

6139. CORYLUS TUBULOSA. **Hazelnut.**

From Rovigno, Austria. Received through Mr. D. G. Fairchild (No. 508, January 19, 1901), March 23, 1901.

Noce lunghe. "Plants of the best variety of Rovigno hazelnut. This variety is grown only in the Province of Istria and because of its scarcity is not much exported. It is a variety not reproduced from seed; requires a calcareous dry soil, and is said to be a heavy bearer. The size of the nuts will recommend them to American growers. In quality of kernel I consider them inferior to those of *Corylus pontica.* The plant forms a small tree, 12 to 15 feet high, with rather handsome trunk and graceful branches; would be an ornament to any garden. This variety will stand a temperature of +14° F. easily and probably much lower. I consider it a promising addition to American nut-bearing trees, and it deserves a thorough distribution through the South. Secured through the kindness of Emil Watzke, of Rovigno." (*Fairchild.*)

6140. VITIS VINIFERA. **Grape.**

From Sebenico, Austria. Received through Mr. D. G. Fairchild (No. 505, January 17, 1901), March 23, 1901.

Marascina. "Cuttings of the delicate variety of grape from which the famous Marascina wine (not the liqueur) is made. The vines are not very hardy and are subject to Peronospora. From the region where the sort originated and the only place where the wine is still manufactured." (*Fairchild.*)

6141. PINUS BRUTIA. **Pyrenean pine.**

From Triest, Austria. Received through Mr. D. G. Fairchild (No. 506, January 18, 1901), March 23, 1901.

"Pyrenean pine, a variety especially valuable for its rapid growth and ability to endure drought. Indigenous to Syria, Asia Minor, Cyprus, Crete, and parts of Italy. This has been used with great success on the dry limestone soil of the *Karst* formation. It makes a handsome showing in from two to three years; especially recommended for planting in the warmer regions of the South on limestone soil." (*Fairchild.*)

6142. CHRYSANTHEMUM CINERARIAEFOLIUM. **Pyrethrum.**

From Milna, Brač Island, Austria. Received through Mr. D. G. Fairchild (No. 507, January 4, 1901), March 23, 1901.

"Seed from a locality noted for its continued profitable production of the Dalmatian insect powder, notwithstanding American and Australian competition." (*Fairchild.*)

6143. CERATONIA SILIQUA. **Carob.**

From Triest, Austria. Received through Mr. D. G. Fairchild (No. 510, January 20, 1901), March 10, 1901.

Carob. (See No. 3112, Inventory No. 7.)

6144. LIATRIS ODORATISSIMA. **Vanilla plant.**

From Biloxi, Miss. Received through Mr. S. M. Tracy, February, 1901.

6145. CRAMBE MARITIMA. **Sea kale.**

From Centralia, Kans. Received through Mr. A. Oberndorf, jr., March 27, 1901.

SEPTEMBER, 1900, TO DECEMBER, 1903.

6146. CUCUMIS MELO. **Muskmelon.**

From Hungary. Presented by Dr. L. Waltherr, Inanda, N. C. Received March 28, 1901.

Turkestan. "The Turkestan muskmelons were imported into Hungary by the famous linguist, Wambery, nearly fifty years ago from Turkestan, Central Asia, and the importation was a great success. The fruit is sometimes round, sometimes oblong, and weighs sometimes even 7 kilograms. The rind has a special yellow color, is sometimes netted; the flesh has a greenish yellow color, is very sweet and juicy, and so soft that it must be eaten with a spoon. It is far superior to any muskmelons of this country." (*Waltherr.*)

6147. CUCUMIS MELO. **Muskmelon.**

From Hungary. Presented by Dr. L. Waltherr, Inanda, N. C. Received March 28, 1901.

Pineapple. "A variety having fruit of the shape of a pineapple, with the same half-yellow, half-green color as that of a half-ripe pineapple, and the rind is sprinkled with small tuberous prominences from the size of a pea to the size of a hazelnut, so that it resembles a pineapple at a distance. The flesh is hard, sweet, and has a deep yellow color like an orange rind." (*Waltherr.*)

6148. CUCUMIS MELO. **Muskmelon.**

From Hungary. Presented by Dr. L. Waltherr, Inanda, N. C. Received March 28, 1901.

"A hybrid of Turkestan No. 6146, and pineapple No. 6147; delicious to eat." (*Waltherr.*)

6149 to 6159. CITRULLUS VULGARIS. **Watermelon.**

From Hungary. Presented by Dr. L. Waltherr, Inanda, N. C. Received March 28, 1901.

A collection of Hungarian varieties as follows:

6149.	6154.
6150.	6155.
"With white rind and red flesh; very fine." (*Waltherr.*)	6156. "Very fine." (*Waltherr.*)
6151.	6157. *Marsowsky.* "Finest kind in Hungary." (*Waltherr.*)
6152. "Very fine." (*Waltherr.*)	
6153. "Very fine." (*Waltherr.*)	6158.
	6159.

6160.

From Guadalupe, Mexico. Presented by Dr. L. Waltherr, Inanda, N. C. Received March 28, 1901.

Cinco palomas. "An ornamental plant, the flowers of which resemble five pigeons; hence the Mexican name 'Cinco palomas.'" (*Waltherr.*)

6161. TAXUS BACCATA. **Yew.**

From Hungary. Presented by Dr. L. Waltherr, Inanda, N. C. Received March 28, 1901.

6162. PYRUS BACCATA. **Siberian crab apple.**

From the Khabarovsk forest. Presented by the Department of Agriculture, St. Petersburg, Russia. Received April 20, 1901.

6163. SPIROSTACHIS OCCIDENTALIS.

From Byron, Cal. Received through Prof. J. Burtt Davy, April 1, 1901.

6164. CANNABIS INDICA. **Hemp.**

From Calcutta, India. Received through Prof. D. Prain, superintendent of the Sibpur Botanical Garden, April, 1901.

Hasheesh, the well-known opiate, is extracted from the resin of this plant.

6165 to 6168. BETA VULGARIS. **Chard.**

From San Giovannia a Teduccio, Italy. Received through Dammann & Co., April 1, 1901.

6165.
Chilean scarlet-ribbed.

6167.
Chilean yellow-ribbed.

6166.
Silver-ribbed (yellowish white).

6168.
Silver-ribbed, curled.

6169. RAPHANUS SATIVUS. **Radish.**

From Acneta, Cal. Received March 25, 1901. Seed grown from No. 1237, Inventory No. 2.

6170. CITRULLUS VULGARIS. **Watermelon.**

From Forestburg, S. Dak. Received through Mr. H. C. Warner, March 19, 1901. Seed grown from No. 61, Inventory No. 1.

"This was the best in quality of 80 varieties in two different seasons. Medium size, oblong, light and dark-green striped, sometimes all light. Flesh dark red, sweet, very rich, early." (*Warner.*)

6171. CITRULLUS VULGARIS. **Watermelon.**

From Forestburg, S. Dak. Received through Mr. H. C. Warner, March 19, 1901. Seed grown from No. 105, Inventory No. 1.

"Medium size, round, light and dark-green striped, flesh red, sweet; productive, early." (*Warner.*)

6172. ZEA MAYS. **Corn.**

From Summerville, S. C. Received through Mr. H. A. Jamison, March, 1901. Egyptian. Seed grown from No. 3998, Inventory No. 8.

6173. IPOMOEA BATATAS. **Sweet potato.**

From Manatee, Fla. Received through Mr. A. J. Pettigrew, March, 1901.

6174. AVENA SATIVA. **Oat.**

From Mustiala, Finland. Received through Messrs. Lathrop and Fairchild (No. 425), April 3, 1901.

North Finnish Black. "Dr. Gösta Grotenfelt, director of the Agricultural Institute of Mustiala, has grown this *Black* oat from seed imported from Torneå, Paavola, and Umeå (this latter in Sweden). He finds the seed from Torneå and Umeå very similar, but the Paavola variety is somewhat browner, not black and gray in color like the other two sorts. He has also compared the *North Finnish Black* with Canadian oats, which he got through the seed-breeding institute of Svalöf, Sweden. The comparison is as follows: *Canada* took one hundred and thirteen days to ripen, while the *North Finnish Black* took only ninety-eight days. The latter is the average for four years (1892–1895). In comparison with all sorts of foreign-grown varieties the figures for the four years stand as 98.9 : 111.8 days for ripening period. Dr. Grotenfelt says that the yield is small. For 1895, 42.4 kilos of dried straw and grain (air dried) per *are*. The foreign sorts yielded in the same year 49.1 kilos per *are*. The grain yield of the *North Finnish Black* variety was 12.6 kilos per *are*, while the foreign varieties yielded 16.4 kilos per *are*. These foreign sorts, it must be remarked, were all varieties which had been especially bred—some from Svalöf and others from the experiment station in Tystofte, in Denmark. During *six years of cultivation at Mustiala this North Finnish Black oat has lost none of its early-ripening qualities*. In good years the foreign-grown sorts here yield best, but in bad season *they yield nothing at all, while the North Finnish Black always yields about the same amount*. This variety deserves thorough trial in Alaska and the North Atlantic States, and should be used for breeding purposes wherever an early ripening variety of oat is desired. To get the best results it should be sown as early as possible. These various varieties have been analyzed in Mustiala, and it has been found that the *North Finnish Black* variety has 13.58 per cent of dry weight of *protein*, while the *South Finnish Brown* oat, for example, only 10.7 per cent, and the *South Finnish White* 11.77 per cent, and foreign oats only 11.79 per cent *protein*. Although, because of the small yield of the *North Finnish Black* variety, the actual protein quantity per *are* is smaller than that of the foreign sorts, the fact that the former is really richer in protein is an important point for plant breeders. The figures are: *North Finnish Black*, 1.54 kilos per *are;* foreign, including *Canada* variety, 1.73 per *are*. There have so far been very few experiments here in Finland *en gros*. Those few have been, however, very satisfactory." (*Fairchild*.) (See No. 5513.)

6175. HORDEUM TETRASTICHUM. Barley.

From Mustiala, Finland. Received through Messrs. Lathrop and Fairchild (No. 426, August 1, 1900), April 3, 1901.

Four-rowed Lapland. "This comes from Pillo, a town lying 30 kilometers north of the Arctic Circle. It is a stunted variety, which ripens at least 10 to 14 days earlier than South Finnish or European varieties, and although it does not produce large quantities of grain, but small kernels and in small quantity, it deserves the especial attention of plant growers in Alaska. Dr. G. Grotenfelt is at the present time busy with its culture and hopes to maintain its earliness and, by crossing, increase its productiveness. At the present time it is almost ripe here in the Doctor's experimental plats, while all other sorts (except No. 427, L. & F.) are quite green. For a very short-season locality and also for breeding purposes this may prove of considerable value where barley is grown. Secured through Dr. Grotenfelt's kindness." (*Fairchild*.)

6176. BRASSICA RAPA. Turnip.

From Mustiala, Finland. Received through Messrs. Lathrop and Fairchild (No. 428, August 1, 1900), April 3, 1901.

White Tankard Purple Top. "A Scottish variety of fodder turnip which has been grown here for fifty years. This variety, grown on Finnish soil, has proved superior to that grown from seed imported from Scotland, and it is worthy a trial in Alaska. Its growth in spring is particularly rapid, and it therefore escapes the attacks of insect enemies better than other sorts. Will be sent by Director G. Grotenfelt in November." (*Fairchild*.)

6177. FAGOPYRUM ESCULENTUM. Buckwheat.

From Mustiala, Finland. Received through Messrs. Lathrop and Fairchild (No. 430, August 1, 1900), April 3, 1901.

Finnish. "This buckwheat is for planting in Alaska. It is believed to be an early ripening variety. It is cultivated in east Finland on a large scale, but little in west Finland. It is now in bloom in Doctor Grotenfelt's experimental plats. Will be sent by Doctor Grotenfelt in November." (*Fairchild*.)

6178. BRASSICA CAMPESTRIS. Turnip.

From Mustiala, Finland. Received through Messrs. Lathrop and Fairchild (No. 429, August 1, 1900), April 3, 1901.

Mustiala. "A variety of Swedish turnip which has been originated here in Mustiala and grown for over fifteen years. It is the best sort that has been tested here and is very regular in growth and altogether to be recommended for fodder purposes in Alaska." (*Fairchild*.)

6179. BRASSICA RAPA. **Turnip.**

From Mustiala, Finland. Received through Messrs. Lathrop and Fairchild (No. 432, August 1, 1900), April 3, 1901.

Finnish Svedje. "This is one of the few originations of the old Finnish people. It is called *Svedje* because it is grown on soil that has been burned over, i. e., in new clearings. The seed was sown by the peasants by taking into the mouth and spitting out as a Chinaman sprinkles clothes. It is a small variety, said to be of superior flavor, and is baked in the oven in butter after being pulled, a little boiling water being added as the turnips become brown. It can be grown in the Arctic Circle, and is a highly prized vegetable, worthy of especial attention." (*Fairchild.*)

6180. JUGLANS REGIA. **Walnut.**

From Patras, Greece. Received through Mr. D. G. Fairchild (No. 553), April 4, 1901.

"Cuttings from a single tree on the estate of Mr. S. D. Stamo which bears nuts that are unusually large and thin shelled." (*Fairchild.*)

6181. JUGLANS REGIA. **Walnut.**

From Zante, Greece. Received through Mr. D. G. Fairchild (No. 554, February 21, 1901), April 4, 1901.

"Cuttings from a single tree on the estate of Mr. Angalotti, at Bocali, which bore nuts that are somewhat irregular in form, but of very large size, some specimens measuring 6 inches in circumference, and so thin shelled that they can be crushed in the hand; not as large nor as regular in shape, however, as No. 6182. The quality is excellent and the tree reported to be a good bearer." (*Fairchild.*)

6182. JUGLANS REGIA. **Walnut.**

From Zante, Greece. Received through Mr. D. G. Fairchild (No. 555, February 21, 1901), April 4, 1901.

"Cuttings from a single tree growing through the roof of a small shop near the house of one Sig. Machalitza, in the town of Zante. The nuts are regular in form and of very unusual size, measuring 5$\frac{11}{16}$ by 5$\frac{11}{16}$ inches in both circumferences. Heavy, and said to be well filled with an excellent flavored meat." (*Fairchild.*)

6183. CYDONIA SINENSIS. **Chinese quince.**

From Zante, Greece. Received through Mr. D. G. Fairchild (No. 556, February 21, 1901), April 4, 1901.

"Cuttings of the *scented quinces* called "musk," "citron," or "Japanese" quinces; grown in this vicinity. The fruits are very large and woody and seldom used for preserving. Their principal value is as ornamentals and as perfume fruits to store away with linen to give it an agreeable odor." (*Fairchild.*)

6184. CITRUS AURANTIUM. **Orange.**

From Zante, Greece. Received through Mr. D. G. Fairchild (No. 557, February 21, 1901) April 4, 1901.

Queen. "The trees from which these cuttings were taken are the only bearing trees of the kind on the island. The fruit is of a dark orange color, almost seedless, and of very fine flavor. It is worth trying in California and Florida orchards." (*Fairchild.*)

6185. CITRUS LIMONUM. **Lemon.**

From Zante, Greece. Received through Mr. D. G. Fairchild (No. 558, February 22, 1901) April 4, 1901.

"Cuttings of a thick-skinned, nearly seedless, variety of lemon growing in the monastery garden of Kalitero. Very juicy and extremely acid." (*Fairchild.*)

6186. CYDONIA SINENSIS. **Chinese quince.**

From Zante, Greece. Received through Mr. D. G. Fairchild (No. 559) April 4, 1901.

Cuttings from a seedling quince, possibly the same as No. 6183. *See also* No. 6362.

6187. CYDONIA VULGARIS. **Quince.**

From Zante, Greece. Received through Mr. D. G. Fairchild (No. 560, February 22, 1901) April 4, 1901.

Apple. "Cuttings of the favorite quince of Zante, used for preserves, marmalades, and as a table fruit. When fully ripe they are eaten like apples, which they resemble in shape." (*Fairchild.*)

6188. CYDONIA SINENSIS. **Chinese quince.**

From Zante, Greece. Received through Mr. D. G. Fairchild (No. 561, February 21, 1901) April 4, 1901.

"Cuttings of a small, scented quince grown for its sweet-scented fruit, which is not edible." (*Fairchild.*)

6189. PINUS PINEA. **Stone pine.**

From Zante, Greece. Presented by Count S. Lunzi through Mr. D. G. Fairchild (No. 562, February 21, 1901). Received April 4, 1901.

"The edible seeds of this pine are so thin shelled that they can be easily broken with the fingers, while the ordinary type has such hard-shelled seeds that they must be broken open with a hammer. Should be tried in the dry parts of Florida and the Southwest." (*Fairchild.*)

6190. CITRUS LIMONUM. **Lemon.**

From Zante, Greece. Presented by Mr. Geo. Sargint through Mr. D. G. Fairchild (No. 563, February 22, 1901). Received April 4, 1901.

"A young plant grown from a bud of an old lemon tree that has always borne seedless fruit." (*Fairchild.*)

6191. ERIOBOTRYA JAPONICA. **Loquat.**

From Zante, Greece. Presented by Mr. Geo. Sargint through Mr. D. G. Fairchild (No. 564, February 22, 1901). Received April 4, 1901.

"Two young plants grown by Castagnias Aristides from cuttings of an old loquat tree reported to bear only seedless fruits." (*Fairchild.*)

6192. VIOLA ODORATA. **Violet.**

From Zante, Greece. Received through Mr. D. G. Fairchild (No. 565, February 22, 1901) April 4, 1901.

Parmensis. Plants of a very large double violet exported from Zante to all parts of Greece. Lacking in perfume. Grown in the open air in Zante, not under glass.

6193. CYDONIA VULGARIS. **Quince.**

From Zante, Greece. Received through Mr. D. G. Fairchild, April 4, 1901. No data.

6194. CANNABIS SATIVA. **Hemp.**

From Yokohama, Japan. Received through L. Boehmer & Co., April 5, 1900.

6195. RHUS CORIARIA. **European sumac.**

From Paris, France. Received through Vilmorin-Andrieux & Co., April 5, 1901.

6196. SEQUOIA SEMPERVIRENS. **Redwood.**

From Berkeley, Cal. Received through Mr. Charles H. Shinn, April 6, 1901.

6197. CUCURBITA MOSCHATA. **Cushaw.**

From Oakgrove, Ind. Received through Mr. H. A. Allen, April 4, 1901.

6198. BRASSICA NAPUS. **Rape.**

From La Crosse, Wis. Received through John A. Salzer Seed Company, April, 1901.

Dwarf Victoria.

6199. LINUM USITATISSIMUM. **Flax.**

From Paris, France. Received through Vilmorin-Andrieux & Co., April 8, 1901.

Irish-grown seed.

6200 to 6220. ORYZA SATIVA. **Rice.**

From the Philippine Islands. Presented by Hon. J. Aranato, secretary of agriculture of the island of Negros. Received March 9, 1901.

A collection of native varieties of rice as follows:

6200.

Capao. An early variety, to be sown on irrigated land in May and harvested in September.

6201.

Gui-os. An early variety, sown on irrigated land in May and harvested in September.

6202.

Cabatingan. An early variety, sown on irrigated or dry land in May and June and harvested in September and October. The grains of this variety, after being boiled, cling together and are therefore adapted for use in the preparation of jellies.

6203.

Bunga-tagum. An early variety, sown on irrigated land early in June and harvested early in October. The grain is very white and highly esteemed for food.

6204.

Morado.

6205.

Cachuri. An early, "fragrant" variety, sown in April and harvested in August. Cultivated on the mountain slopes. Its principal use is for the manufacture of "Pilipig."

6206.

Mayuro. An early variety, sown on irrigated land early in June and harvested in October. The grain is very white and highly esteemed for food.

6207.

Baráo. An early variety, sown on irrigated land early in June and harvested at the end of October.

6208.

Cotsiam. An early rice, sown on irrigated land in April and May and harvested in August and September.

6200 to 6220—Continued.

6209.

Caayaá. An early variety, sown on irrigated land early in June and gathered in October. The grain is red and is valued as an article of food.

6210.

Cabunlog. A late variety sown on irrigated land at the end of June or early in July and gathered in December or early in January.

6211.

Piracút. An early variety, sown on dry land in May and gathered in September. The grains of this rice cling together after being boiled, and this substance is used in the preparation of dainties.

6212.

Lubang. An early variety, sown on either irrigated land or dry land in May or June and harvested in September or October.

6213.

Lumantao. An early variety, sown on irrigated or dry land in May or June and harvested in September or October.

6214.

Dagul-pilit. A late variety, sown on dry or irrigated lands in May and harvested in November. The grains of this rice cling together after being boiled and are used for making delicacies.

6215.

Caba. An early variety, sown on irrigated land early in June and harvested the last of October.

6216.

Tapul-pilit. A late variety, sown on irrigated land late in June or early in July and harvested in December and January.

6217.

Calanay-pilit. A late variety, sown on irrigated land late in June or the first of July and harvested in December and January.

6218.

Tupúl-pilit. An early variety, sown on dry land in May and harvested in September. The grains of this are dark, and when boiled cling together and serve for the making of delicacies.

6219.

Macau. A late variety, sown on irrigated lands late in June or early in July and harvested in December and January.

6220.

Soladong. A late variety, sown on irrigated land the last of June and first of July; harvested in December and January.

6221 to 6238.

From the Philippine Islands. Presented by Hon. J. Aranato, secretary of agriculture of the island of Negros. Received March 9, 1901.

A collection of seeds of economic plants grown by the natives, as follows:

6221. CHAETOCHLOA ITALICA. Millet.

Dana. An early-maturing grass, the seeds of which are used for making jellies.

6221 to 6238—Continued.

6222. SESAMUM INDICUM.   Sesame.

Lunga. Sown in May and harvested in October. The oil of "ojonjoli" is extracted from the seeds.

6223. DOLICHOS SINENSIS (?).   Bean.

Balatong.

6224. PHASEOLUS MUNGO.   Gram.

Mongo.

6225.   Bean.

Marayo. A black climbing bean, sown in May and harvested in October; used for pottage.

6226. PHASEOLUS CALCARATUS.   Bean.

Tajori. A yellow climbing bean, sown in May and harvested in October; used for pottage.

6227.   Pea.

Native name, *Cadios.* An undetermined variety of pea.

6228. DOLICHOS SINENSIS.   Bean.

Lestones. A climbing bean, sown in May and harvested in September; used for pottage.

6229. NICOTIANA TABACUM.   Tobacco.

6230. ZEA MAYS.   Corn.

An early variety; sown in May and harvested in August and September.

6231. ZEA MAYS.   Corn.

The first crop from American seed.

6232. ZEA MAYS.   Corn.

The second crop from American seed.

6233. ZEA MAYS.   Corn.

An early purple variety; sown in May and harvested in August and September.

6234. MUSA TEXTILIS.   Manila hemp.

Abaca-Bisaya. In the island of Negros it is the custom to sow the seed of this plant in the months of May, June, and July.

6235. MUSA TEXTILIS.   Manila hemp.

Abaca-Kinisol. In the island of Negros it is the custom to sow the seed of this plant in the months of May, June, and July.

6236. MUSA TEXTILIS.   Manila hemp.

Abaca-Moro. In the island of Negros it is the custom to sow the seed of this plant in the months of May, June, and July.

6237. MUSA TEXTILIS.   Manila hemp.

Abaca-Lono. In the island of Negros it is the custom to sow the seed of this plant in the months of May, June, and July.

6238. (Museum specimen.)

6239. MUSA TEXTILIS.   **Manila hemp.**

Museum specimen only.

6240. OLEA EUROPAEA.   **Olive.**

From Fresno, Cal. Presented by Mr. George C. Roeding, through Mr. W. T. Swingle. Received April 6, 1901.

Obliza.

6241 to 6243. FICUS CARICA.   **Caprifig.**

From Fresno, Cal. Presented by Mr. George C. Roeding, through Mr. W. T. Swingle. Received April 6, 1901.

6241.   **6243.**

Roeding's No. 1 variety.   Roeding's No. 3 variety.

6242.

Roeding's No. 2 variety.

6244. FICUS CARICA.   **Fig.**

From Fresno, Cal. Presented by Mr. George C. Roeding, through Mr. W. T. Swingle. Received April 6, 1901.

Smyrna.

6245. CITRUS AURANTIUM.   **Orange.**

From Mustapha, Algiers, Algeria. Presented by Dr. L. Trabut, Government Botanist, through Mr. W. T. Swingle. Received April 8, 1901.

6246. CITRUS DECUMANA.   **Pomelo.**

From Eustis, Fla. Presented by Mr. Frank W. Savage, through Mr. W. T. Swingle. Received April 8, 1901.

6247. CITRUS NOBILIS (?).   **Orange.**

From Eustis, Fla. Presented by Mr. Frank W. Savage, through Mr. W. T. Swingle. Received April 8, 1901.

King, or King of Siam.

6248. CITRUS AURANTIUM.   **Orange.**

From Eustis, Fla. Presented by Mr. Frank W. Savage, through Mr. W. T. Swingle. Received April 8, 1901.

Sanford Mediterranean.

6249. CITRUS AURANTIUM.   **Orange.**

From Eustis, Fla. Presented by Mr. Frank W. Savage, through Mr. W. T. Swingle. Received April 8, 1901.

Ruby blood.

6250. CITRUS DECUMANA.   **Pomelo.**

From Eustis, Fla. Presented by Mr. Frank W. Savage, through Mr. W. T. Swingle. Received April 8, 1901.

Aurantium.

6251. OLEA EUROPAEA. **Olive.**

From Mustapha, Algiers, Algeria. Presented by Dr. L. Trabut, Government Botanist, through Mr. W. T. Swingle. Received April 30, 1901.

Mascara, a variety from M. Jaubert's place at Inkermann. Thought by Mr. Swingle to be possibly the very large sort, the fruit of which sometimes weighs 17 grams. Doctor Trabut considers it the same as the variety *Bréa* of Tlemsen.

6252. PISTACIA VERA. **Pistache.**

From Mustapha, Algiers, Algeria. Presented by Dr. L. Trabut, Government Botanist, through Mr. C. S. Scofield. Received May 22, 1901.

Sfax (female). "The sort grown about Sfax, Tunis, where large quantities of pistaches were formerly produced. It is said to be a good variety and was formerly largely exported, but of late prices have declined and exports from Sfax ceased. This variety was obtained last year from the same tree and was sent through the University of California to Mr. G. P. Rixford, who succeeded in grafting it on the terebinth tree on his place in Sonoma County." (*Swingle.*)

6253. PISTACIA VERA. **Pistache.**

From Mustapha, Algiers, Algeria. Presented by Dr. L. Trabut, Government Botanist, through Mr. C. S. Scofield. Received May 22, 1901.

Sfax (male). "Scions from male tree growing in the botanical garden of the *Écoles Superieures* at Algiers." (*Scofield.*) See No. 6252.

6254. FICUS CARICA. **Caprifig.**

From Maison Carrée, near Algiers, Algeria. Presented by M. Lepiney through Mr. C. S. Scofield. Received May 28, 1901.

6255 to 6258.

(Numbers not utilized.)

6259. XIMENIA AMERICANA. **Hog plum.**

From Miami, Fla. Presented by Mr. H. C. Henricksen. Received May 21, 1901.

6260 to 6271.

A collection of Danish vegetable seed.

6260. BETA VULGARIS. **Beet.**

Yellowstone. "Yellow, bottle-shaped; is a half-breed beet of unusual yielding ability in connection with great nutritive substance; requires an early sowing, but does not make great claims as to soil. It is a comparatively new variety, which is in great demand." (*Kolle Bros.*)

6261. BETA VULGARIS. **Beet.**

McKinley. "Pink, bottle-shaped. It combines yielding power with nutritive substance, but wants a rich, warm soil. Under these conditions it is a variety of high value." (*Kolle Bros.*)

6262. BETA VULGARIS. **Beet.**

Adam. "White, cylinder-shaped variety, which ranges between the common fodder beets and fodder sugar beets. Combines good yielding power with a respectable nutritive substance. It requires a somewhat low-situated, deep-molded soil, and, thus placed, it will scarcely be exceeded by any other beet variety in regard to yielding power." (*Kolle Bros.*)

6263. BETA VULGARIS. **Beet.**

Red Oberndorfer. "This is an improved old variety which, by strict selection in field and laboratory, has attained its standing among 'bell-shaped beets.' It is particularly fit for a warm, light soil." (*Kolle Bros.*)

6260 to 6271—Continued.

6264. BETA VULGARIS. **Beet.**

Red Eckendorfer. "Like *Red Oberndorfer*, it is an old variety which by treatment has reached perfection. Its value lies in its great yielding power, while its nutritive contents are rather low. In order to attain its full development it should be sown in moldy, well-fertilized, moist soil." (*Kolle Bros.*)

6265. BRASSICA RAPA. **Turnip.**

Fiona.

6266. BRASSICA OLERACEA var. BOTRYTIS. **Cauliflower.**

Danish Mammoth. Grown on the island of Fyen, Denmark.

6267. BRASSICA OLERACEA var. BOTRYTIS. **Cauliflower.**

Extra Early Dwarf Erfurt. Grown on the farm of the royal palace, Fredricksburg.

6268. BRASSICA OLERACEA var. BOTRYTIS. **Cauliflower.**

Danish Snowball.

6269. BRASSICA OLERACEA var. BOTRYTIS. **Cauliflower.**

Extra Early Dwarf Erfurt. Grown on the island of Fyen, Denmark.

6270. BRASSICA OLERACEA var. BOTRYTIS. **Cauliflower.**

Extra Early Improved Erfurt. Grown on the island of Zealand, Denmark.

6271. BRASSICA OLERACEA var. BOTRYTIS. **Cauliflower.**

Copenhagen Snowball. Grown at Copenhagen, Denmark.

6272. TRITICUM VULGARE. **Wheat.**

From Volo, Greece. Presented by Mr. Ar. Tsakonas, of Athens, through Mr. D. G. Fairchild (No. 581, March 23, 1901). Received April 15, 1901.

Diminum. "A spring variety. The name means 'two months.' This is a semi-hard sort, used in Greece to plant after the failure of the winter wheat is known. It is not a two months' wheat, as the name implies, but matures in about three months, being planted the last of February and harvested the first of June. It is a light bearer and not very highly esteemed in Greece, except for the purpose described." (*Fairchild.*)

6273 to 6278.

From the Philippine Islands. Presented by Hon. J. Aranato, secretary of agriculture of the island of Negros. Received March 9, 1901. A collection of seeds as follows:

6273. ZEA MAYS. **Corn.**

"Early; sown in May, harvested in August and September." (*Aranato.*)

6274. THEOBROMA CACAO. **Cacao.**

6275.

Nanca. "A tree which matures at five or six years of age. The fruits, called 'Nanca,' as well as the leaves, are used as greens when young, and when mature the fruit is used as dessert." (*Aranato.*)

6276.

Dagmay. "A bulbous plant which is sown in May and harvested the January following. It grows well in light, loose, rich soil and requires to be kept well covered to produce any shoots. It is used in cooking to take the place of the sweet potato or ordinary potato." (*Aranato.*)

6273 to 6278—Continued.

6277. DIOSCOREA sp.?

Tamis. "A twining tuberous plant, which is sown in May and harvested the following January. It requires stakes about 7 feet high, grows best in a loose, well-fertilized soil, and its roots should be frequently covered with earth. It is used in cooking as a substitute for the potato and sweet potato." (*Aranato.*)

6278. COFFEA ARABICA. Coffee.

6279. PHASEOLUS sp. Bean.

From China. Received from Mr. J. Lawton Taylor, Honolulu, Hawaii, April 16, 1901.

Meru (?). "Very mealy or granular when boiled." (*Taylor.*)

6280 to 6299. VITIS sp. Grape.

From Departmental Nursery of Maine and Loire, France. Received from Mr. Louis Leroy, Angers, France, April 19, 1901.

A collection of phylloxera-resistant varieties for use as stocks.

6280.
Riparia × Rupestris 101.

6281.
Mourvedre × Rupestris 1202.

6282.
Bourrisquou × Rupestris 603.

6283.
Berlandieri × Riparia 157-11.

6284.
Chasselas × Berlandieri 41.

6285.
Colorado E.

6286.
Colomband × Rupestris 3103.

6287.
Bourrisquou × Rupestris 601.

6288.
Solonis × Riparia 1616.

6289.
Riparia grand glabre.

6290.
Pure Berlandieri.

6291.
Monticola × Riparia 554.

6292.
Riparia × Rupestris 3309.

6293.
Aramon × Rupestris 2.

6294.
Aramon × Rupestris Ganzin 1.

6296.
Rupestris du Lot.

6297.
Rupestris Martin.

6298.
Aramon × Rupestris Ganzin 1.

6299.
Riparia Gloire de Montpellier.

6300 to 6306. VITIS sp. Grape.

From Caplat. A collection of grapes, No. 6300 being Japanese and the others Chinese. Received through Mr. Louis Leroy, Angers, France, April 19, 1901.

6300.
Precoce Caplat.

6301.
Alenconnaise (new).

6302.
Romaneti trilobées.

6303.
Tisserandi, inédite de Mandchurie.

6304.
Morandi.

6305.
Pagnacci.

6306.
Romaneti.

6307 to 6339.

From the Tokyo Seed and Plant Company, Tokyo, Japan. Received April 20, 1901.

A collection of miscellaneous seeds, as follows:

6307. ORYZA SATIVA. Rice.
Sugaichi.

6308. ORYZA SATIVA. Rice.
Adzuma Nishiki.

6309. CANNABIS SATIVA. Hemp.
Shimonita.

6310. CANNABIS SATIVA. Hemp.
Hiroshima.

6311. VIGNA CATJANG. Cowpea.
Black Jurokusasage.

6312. GLYCINE HISPIDA. Soy bean.
Black Flat.

6313. VICIA FABA. Broad bean.
Large Soramame.

6314. GLYCINE HISPIDA. Soy bean.
Yoshioka.

6315. VICIA FABA. Broad bean.
Early Soramame.

6316. PISUM SATIVUM. Pea.

6317. CANNABIS SATIVA. Hemp.
Tochigi.

6318. PHASEOLUS MUNGO-RADIATUS. Gram.
Muroran.

6319. DOLICHOS LABLAB. Hyacinth bean.
White.

6320. DOLICHOS LABLAB. Hyacinth bean.
Purple.

6321. PHASEOLUS MUNGO-RADIATUS. Gram.
Yainari.

6322. CANNABIS SATIVA. Hemp.
Aidzu.

6323. CANAVALIA ENSIFORMIS. Knife bean.
White Natamame.

6307 to 6339—Continued.

6324. CANAVALIA GLADIATA. **Knife bean.**
Pink Natamame.

6325. CANNABIS SATIVA. **Hemp.**
Iwate.

6326. GLYCINE HISPIDA. **Soy bean.**
Rokugatsu.

6327. VIGNA CATJANG. **Cowpea.**
Kurakake.

6328. VIGNA CATJANG. **Cowpea.**
Kintohi.

6329. ASTRAGALUS SINICUS. **Genge clover.**
An early variety of this clover. (See No. 3725, Inventory No. 8.)

6330. ASTRAGALUS SINICUS. **Genge clover.**
A late variety of this clover. (See No. 3725, Inventory No. 8.)

6331. LESPEDEZA BICOLOR. **Bush clover.**
Hagi.

6332. PISUM SATIVUM (?). **Red fodder pea.**

6333. GLYCINE HISPIDA. **Soy bean.**
Gosha.

6334. GLYCINE HISPIDA. **Soy bean.**
Black Round.

6335. GLYCINE HISPIDA. **Soy bean.**
Green Medium.

6336. GLYCINE HISPIDA. **Soy bean.**
Bakaziro.

6337. BOEHMERIA NIVEA. **Ramie.**
No. 1.

6338. BOEHMERIA NIVEA. **Ramie.**
No. 2.

6339. BOEHMERIA NIVEA. **Ramie.**
No. 3.

6340. QUERCUS ILEX. **Holly oak.**
From Vilmorin-Andrieux & Co., Paris, France. Received April 22, 1901.

6341. CAPPARIS INERMIS. **Caper.**
From Vilmorin-Andrieux & Co., Paris, France. Received April 22, 1901.
A spineless form of caper.

6342. CERATONIA SILIQUA. **Carob.**

From Vilmorin-Andrieux & Co., Paris, France. Received April 22, 1901.

6343. QUERCUS ILEX. **Green truffle oak.**

Obtained through Vilmorin-Andrieux & Co. from Mr. A. Rousseau, Carpentras, Vaucluse, France. Received April 22, 1901.

6344. QUERCUS PUBESCENS. **White truffle oak.**

Obtained through Vilmorin-Andrieux & Co. from Mr. A. Rousseau, Carpentras, Vaucluse, France. Received April 22, 1901.

6345. QUEBRACHIA LORENTZII. **Quebracho colorado.**

From Ronaldo Tidblom, director of agriculture and animal industry, Buenos Ayres, Argentina. Received April 22, 1901.

From the semidesert territories of Chaco and Formosa.

6346. ASPIDOSPERMA QUEBRACHO-BLANCO. **Quebracho blanco.**

Presented by Ronaldo Tidblom, director of agriculture and animal industry, Buenos Ayres, Argentina. Received April 22, 1901.

From the semidesert territories of Chaco and Formosa. The name given by Sig. Tidblom was *A. quebracho* Schlect., which does not appear in the Kew Index.

6347. VACCINIUM VITIS-IDAEA. **Mountain cranberry.**

Presented by Prof. Theodor Erben, of the agricultural-botanical experiment station of Tabor, Bohemia. Received April 25, 1901.

6348. RUBUS IDAEUS. **Raspberry.**

Obtained from France by Mr. G. B. Brackett, Pomologist, U. S. Department of Agriculture.

"This belongs to the *R. idaeus* group. The plant is a strong, upright grower, everbearing in its habit. The fruit is large, red, and of excellent quality. It ripens from July to December." (*Brackett.*)

6349. PISTACIA VERA. **Pistache.**

From Athens, Greece. Received through Mr. D. G. Fairchild (No. 569, March 3, 1901), April 27, 1901.

Female trees. Three-year-old trees budded the winter of 1900-1901 and the preceding winter.

"The pistache is a valuable nut tree, well suited for culture in regions having a hot, dry climate. The nuts sell in this country from 40 cents to $1.25 a pound, wholesale. They are already extensively used in America for flavoring confectionery and ice creams, and it is confidently expected that they will be widely used as a table nut, to be served like the almond, as soon as they become better known. In the eastern Mediterranean countries, where the pistache is the best known and choicest nut, it is much more used for eating from the hand than for flavoring. These nuts are among the most delicious known, rather smaller than the almond, but more delicate in flavor and a little oilier, somewhat resembling in texture and taste the piñon of the Rocky Mountains. Unlike the piñon and almond, the pistache nut has a shell easily opened with the fingers, since it contains two thin valves, which split open and become nearly separated as the fruit dries.

"The sorts having yellow kernels are most used in oriental countries as a nut to eat from the hand, but the green sorts only are in demand for flavoring, since the public has become accustomed to associating this color with pistaches used for this purpose.

The pistache is a small tree, 15 to 30 feet high, belonging to the same family as the sumac (*Anacardiaceae*). The male and female flowers are borne on different trees, and this necessitates securing both kinds of trees for an orchard, or, what is preferable, that scions of the male sort be grafted on the female trees that bear the fruit. One male tree is said to suffice to pollinate from five to ten female trees. The best method of propagation is to graft the pistache on the terebinth tree (*Pistacia terebinthus*), a near relative of the pistache, native of the Mediterranean countries where the pistache is cultivated. It is preferable to grow the terebinth trees from seed in place in the orchard, but they can be transplanted, if necessary. The present importation comprises three-year-old trees which were grafted in nursery rows and dug up early in March.

"The pistache will endure a temperature of from 10° to 20° F. It is about as hardy as the fig and olive, possibly rather hardier. Its crop is not so liable as that of the almond to injury by late frosts, because it flowers much later in spring, a matter of great importance in the Southwest, where the almond is often injured because of its habit of blooming early. The pistache thrives best on a deep soil containing lime, but it succeeds also on other soils. A warm southern hillside is the best location. The tree is adapted especially for culture in regions having a dry summer season. It requires about the same climate as the olive, and will doubtless succeed in parts of California, Arizona, and possibly in some regions in Florida. Around the shores of the Mediterranean, where it is commonly cultivated, the tree is not irrigated. It needs about as much water as the olive, and, like it, can succeed on hillsides too dry to support most other fruit trees.

"The trees comprised under this number are female trees, and should be planted 20 to 25 feet apart, with a male tree (No. 6350) in the center of the group of females. The grafts should be cut back to two buds. The trees should be watered judiciously this season until properly started, after which no special care is necessary. Although these trees are already older than is desirable for transplanting, it is hoped that by care they can all be made to live, and that a small quantity of nuts will be produced year after next. The trees will bear full crops when they are 7 years old. The average yield is about 20 pounds." (*W. T. Swingle and D. G. Fairchild.*)

6350. PISTACIA VERA. **Pistache.**

From Athens, Greece. Received through Mr. D. G. Fairchild (No. 569, March 8, 1901), April 27, 1901.

Male trees. "Three-year-old stocks budded 1899–1900 to male scions." (*Fairchild.*)

6351. NEOWASHINGTONIA FILAMENTOSA. **Fan palm.**

Received March, 1901, through Prof. Charles H. Shinn, from Johnson & Musser Seed Company, Los Angeles, Cal.

6352. ERYTHEA EDULIS. **Guadalupe palm.**

Received March, 1901, through Prof. Charles H. Shinn, from Johnson & Musser Seed Company, Los Angeles, Cal.

6353. HUMULUS LUPULUS. **Hop.**

From Horst Brothers, Horstville, Cal. Received April 25, 1901.

A collection of American varieties.

6354. JUGLANS REGIA. **Walnut.**

From Karpenisi, Greece. Presented by Mr. Xanthopoulo, of the Agricultural Experiment Station of Patras, Greece, through Mr. D. G. Fairchild (No. 568, March, 1901). Received April 27, 1901.

"Plants of a very large, thin-shelled walnut which grows in the mountains of Karpenisi, Southern Thessaly. I did not see specimens of this nut, but heard that an unusually large one from one of these trees was sent to the Paris Exposition of 1898. It was so thin shelled that it was necessary to pack it in cotton. Mr. Xanthopoulo, who secured the plants, says he took them from the original trees in Karpenisi which bore the giant nuts sent to Paris." (*Fairchild.*)

6355. PISTACIA sp. **Pistache.**

From Athens, Greece. Received through Mr. D. G. Fairchild, April 27, 1901.

Stocks originally budded with the pistache (No. 6349), of which the scions died in transit. To be used as stocks upon which to graft the true pistache.

SEPTEMBER, 1900, TO DECEMBER, 1903. 79

6356. VITIS sp. **Grape.**

Received, through Mr. G. B. Brackett, Pomologist, U. S. Department of Agriculture, from Matthew Crawford, Cuyahoga Falls, Ohio, April 29, 1901.

6357. FICUS CARICA. **Fig.**

From T. S. Williams, Monetta, S. C. Received April 29, 1901.

6358. PYRUS BACCATA. **Siberian crab apple.**

From Troitzkosavsk, Altai Province, Siberia. Received, through A. Fischer von Waldheim, director of Imperial Botanic Gardens, St. Petersburg, Russia, April 30, 1901.

This was marked "*Pyrus baccata genuina.*"

6359. BETA VULGARIS. **Sugar beet.**

Grown in Friedrichswerth, Germany, by Ed. Meyer. Presented by Beet Sugar Gazette Co., Chicago, Ill., April 29, 1901.

Friedrichswerther Elite.

6360. CITRUS LIMONUM. **Lemon.**

From Poros Island, Greece. Received through Mr. D. G. Fairchild (No. 576), April 27, 1901.

"One of the best varieties of Poros lemons, which are noted in Greece as the finest coming to the Athens market. The scions are from trees that often bear nearly or quite seedless fruits." (*Fairchild.*)

6361. CITRUS sp.

From Canné, Crete. Received through Mr. D. G. Fairchild (No. 580, March 14, 1901), April 27, 1901.

"Grafting wood of a remarkable citrous fruit, which resembles in shape a large, somewhat pear-shaped lemon. It is Australian gold in color, with a soft, rather thin skin and a flesh as dark colored as some oranges and of a remarkably agreeable, very mild acid, slightly bitter taste. In resembles in flavor a pomelo, only it is somewhat milder. Altogether a most refreshing fruit and deserving the serious attention of all pomelo and other citrus growers. It is possibly a cross or result of several crosses, including the orange, bergamot, and lemon. There are a few weak spines, the leaf has a winged petiole, and the fruit is borne on long, swinging fruit stalks. The name *lemon pomelo* is suggested because it is shaped like a lemon and tastes something like a pomelo. There is no popular name here in Crete. It is probable, in fact, that there are not more than a half dozen trees in existence on the island." (*Fairchild.*)

6362. CYDONIA SINENSIS. **Chinese quince.**

From Zante, Greece. Received through Mr. D. G. Fairchild, April 27, 1901.

Seeds of No. 6183.

6363. CUCUMIS MELO. **Melon.**

From Zante, Greece. Received through Mr. D. G. Fairchild (No. 567, February 22, 1901), April 27, 1901.

Zante winter. "This is said to be the best of the winter melons of Zante, having a delicious sweet flavor and keeping until the opening of spring. It is cultivated like any ordinary melon, plucked before frost in autumn, and allowed to ripen in a cool place free from frost. In Zante the fruits are hung up to ripen in small fiber slings on the wall. A specimen was tasted by the writer on the 22d of February, and although it was somewhat lacking in sweetness proved a most palatable fruit. Good melon connoisseurs say that these winter melons from Zante are often deliciously sweet, even when kept until spring." (*Fairchild.*)

6364. CUCUMIS MELO. **Winter melon.**

From Zante, Greece. Received through Mr. D. G. Fairchild (No. 566, February 22, 1901), April 27, 1901.

Cephalonia. "A winter canteloupe, which is grown to perfection on the island of Cephalonia, one of the Ionian group. The melons are cultivated in the usual way and in autumn plucked and strung up in a primitive basket of rough twisted grass. Here they are left to ripen and from midwinter until April the inhabitants of both Cephalonia and Zante serve them on their tables. These winter melons have a thin rind, which is loosely attached to the flesh and can be peeled off like the skin of an orange, leaving the most beautiful ice-cream-like, greenish flesh behind. I know of no more beautiful table fruit than a half melon peeled and served in this way. It looks like a mound of pistache ice cream and would captivate any fruit lover." (*Fairchild.*)

6365. CITRUS LIMONUM. **Lemon.**

From Andros Island, Greece. Received through Mr. D. G. Fairchild, April 27, 1901.

Seed from fruits which are nearly seedless.

6366. VITIS VINIFERA. **Corinth.**

From region of Nemeo, Greece. Received through Mr. D. G. Fairchild, April 27, 1901.

Corinth. "Among the clusters of ordinary dried *Corinths*, which are usually seedless, there are generally small branches bearing larger berries. These berries have often one or more seeds in them. These seeds were taken from such berries. It may be possible, by the use of such seeds, to produce new seedless varieties." (*Fairchild.*)

6367. HORDEUM DISTICHUM ERECTUM. **Barley.**

From Patras, Greece. Received through Mr. D. G. Fairchild, April 27, 1901.

6368. MEDICAGO sp.

From mountains of Corfu, Greece. Received through Mr. D. G. Fairchild (No. 537), April 27, 1901.

"One of the numerous leguminous fodder plants which grow rankly on the island and form a large part of the excellent Corfu hay. Procured through the assistance of Mr. Antonio Collas." (*Fairchild.*)

6369. TRITICUM VULGARE. **Wheat.**

From Trieste, Austria. Received through Mr. D. G. Fairchild, April 27, 1901.

Riete Originario. "A noted winter variety, said to be resistant and a good yielder. Grown in the vicinity of Görz and Trieste, Austria." (*Fairchild.*)

6370. TRITICUM VULGARE. **Wheat.**

From Greece. Received through Mr. D. G. Fairchild, April 27, 1901.

Cologna. "A winter variety." (*Fairchild.*)

6371. TRITICUM DURUM. **Wheat.**

From Corfu, Greece. Received through Mr. D. G. Fairchild, April 27, 1901.

Sample only.

6372. TRITICUM POLONICUM? **Wheat?**

From Corfu, Greece. Received through Mr. D. G. Fairchild, April 27, 1901.

"Sample only; probably of Russian origin." (*Fairchild.*)

6373. TRITICUM VULGARE. **Wheat.**

From Greece. Received through Mr. D. G. Fairchild, April 27, 1901.

Sample only, labeled *Jucente* (?).

6374. VITIS VINIFERA. **Corinth.**

From Patras, Greece. Received through Mr. D. G. Fairchild from Cremidi Brothers, of Patras, Greece. Received April 27, 1901.

Corinth. "Large berries containing seeds. These large berries are produced, I am told, occasionally by certain branches of the plant which otherwise bear only seedless fruit. They have often many seeds in them. New varieties of the *Corinth* grape are likely to originate as seedlings from this generally seedless variety." (*Fairchild.*)

6375. NIGELLA AROMATICA. **Fennel flower.**

Grown on the Potomac Flats, District of Columbia, under the direction of W. R. Beattie, from No. 2129.

6376. HIBISCUS ESCULENTUS. **Okra.**

Grown on the Potomac Flats, District of Columbia, under the direction of W. R. Beattie, from No. 3636.

6377. DOLICHOS LABLAB. **Lablab bean.**

Grown on the Potomac Flats, District of Columbia, under the direction of W. R. Beattie, from No. 2083.

6378. PHASEOLUS MUNGO. **Gram.**

Grown on the Potomac Flats, District of Columbia, under the direction of W. R. Beattie, from No. 3868.

6379. GLYCINE HISPIDA. **Soy bean.**

Grown on the Potomac Flats, District of Columbia, under the direction of W. R. Beattie, from No. 3870.

6380. MEDICAGO TURBINATA. **Bur clover.**

Grown on the Potomac Flats, District of Columbia, under the direction of W. R. Beattie, from No. 4187.

6381. OCIMUM BASILICUM. **Sweet basil.**

Grown on the Potomac Flats, District of Columbia, under the direction of W. R. Beattie, from No. 2008.

6382. CAPSICUM ANNUUM. **Red pepper.**

Grown on the Potomac Flats, District of Columbia, under the direction of W. R. Beattie, from No. 3905.

A sweet pepper.

6383. CAPSICUM ANNUUM. **Red pepper.**

From Athens, Greece. Received through Mr. D. G. Fairchild, April 27, 1901.

"A market variety in Athens." (*Fairchild.*)

6384 to 6424.

From Pyeng Yang, Korea. A collection of seeds of economic plants which are cultivated in Korea. Presented by Rev. W. M. Baird. Received May 3, 1901.

6384. ORYZA SATIVA. **Black rice.**

"Plant in May." (*Baird.*)

6385. FAGOPYRUM ESCULENTUM. **Buckwheat.**

6386. GLYCINE HISPIDA. **Soy bean.**

Black.

6384 to 6424—Continued.

6387. CALLISTEPHUS HORTENSIS. China aster.
Red.

6388. CALLISTEPHUS HORTENSIS. China aster.
White.

6389. CHAETOCHLOA ITALICA. Millet.

6390. ALLIUM CEPA. Onion.

6391. PHASEOLUS sp. Bean.

6392. CALLISTEPHUS HORTENSIS. China aster.
Red.

6393. PERILLA sp.?

"A fine oil for the table is extracted from the seeds. Sow in April or May." (*Baird.*)

6394. BRASSICA JUNCEA. Chinese mustard.
"Plant in April." (*Baird.*)

6395. CUCUMIS SATIVA. Cucumber.
"Plant in April or May." (*Baird.*)

6396. GLYCINE HISPIDA. Soy bean.
White.

6397. GLYCINE HISPIDA. Soy bean.

6398. RAPHANUS SATIVUS. Radish.
Large. "Plant in August." (*Baird.*)

6399. HORDEUM VULGARE. Barley.
Late.

6400. GOSSYPIUM BARBADENSE. Cotton.
"Plant in May." (*Baird.*)

6401. ZEA MAYS. Corn.
Late. "Plant in April or May." (*Baird.*)

6402. CUCURBITA PEPO. Pumpkin.
April.

6403. HORDEUM VULGARE. Barley.
"A hull-less variety." (*Baird.*)

6404. ZOYSIA PUNGENS. Korean lawn grass.
Used in Korea for lawns.

6405. ZOYSIA PUNGENS. Korean lawn grass.
Used in Korea for lawns.

6406. ANDROPOGON SORGHUM. Sorghum.

"A kind of grain similar in appearance to broom corn or sugar cane. The seeds are eaten. The canes are very straight and quite useful. Planted in May." (*Baird.*)

6384 to 6424—Continued.

 6407. COIX sp.   Job's tears.

 6408. PANICUM MILIACEUM.   Broom-corn millet.

 6409. PANICUM CRUS-GALLI.   Barnyard grass.

 6410. CHAETOCHLOA ITALICA.   Foxtail millet.

 6411. ANDROPOGON SORGHUM.   Sorghum.

"Kind of grain similar in appearance to broom corn and sugar cane. The grain is eaten by Koreans. The canes are straight and valuable." (*Baird.*)

 6412. LAGENARIA VULGARIS.   Gourd.

 6413. VIGNA CATJANG.   Cowpea.

 6414. GLYCINE HISPIDA.   Soy bean.

"Plant in May." (*Baird.*)

 6415. PHASEOLUS sp.   Bean.

Black.

 6416. GLYCINE HISPIDA.   Soy bean.

Black.

 6417. PHASEOLUS MUNGO-RADIATUS (?).   Gram.

 6418. PHASEOLUS MUNGO-RADIATUS (?).   Gram.

 6419. CHRYSANTHEMUM CARINATUM.

"Very good greens for dressing with salad oil are prepared from this." (*Baird.*)

 6420. SESAMUM INDICUM.   Sesame.

"An oil is extracted from the seeds which is useful for oiling furniture, etc." (*Baird.*)

 6421. IMPATIENS BALSAMINA.   Balsam.

 6422. CELOSIA CRISTATA.   Cockscomb.

 6423. ZINNIA ELEGANS.   Zinnia.

 6424. TAGETES sp.   Marigold.

6425 to 6428.

From Stockholm, Sweden. Received through Messrs. Lathrop and Fairchild (Nos. 419, 420, 422, 423) from Lindahls Fröhandel, May 6, 1901.

A collection of vegetable seeds as follows:

 6425. CUCUMIS SATIVUS.   Cucumber.

Stockholm's Torg. "The most popular cucumber in Sweden, suitable for planting in Alaska. It is a white, very hardy variety, though said to be inferior to green sorts." (*Fairchild.*)

 6426. CUCUMIS MELO.   Muskmelon.

Stockholm's Torg. "The best Swedish market variety of cantaloupe. It is here cultivated under glass, and the melons are sold for 2 to 4 kroner, or 50 cents to $1 apiece." (*Fairchild.*)

6425 to 6428—Continued.

6427. BRASSICA OLERACEA. **Cabbage.**

Stockholm's Torg. "A native variety of Swedish cabbage, said to be a very early maturing sort. For planting in Alaska." (*Fairchild.*)

6428. PISUM SATIVUM. **Pea.**

Stensärter äkta. "An early ripening Swedish pea, suitable for Alaska and other northern localities." (*Fairchild.*)

6429. VITIS VINIFERA. Corinth.

From Panariti, Greece. Received through Mr. D. G. Fairchild (No. 575, March 6, 1901), May 9, 1901.

"The variety of grape producing the *currants* or *corinths* of commerce. These cuttings were purchased in the village of Panariti, which lies among the mountains back of Xyloncastron. This village is noted for producing some of the finest corinths in Greece. It is the custom in Greece to plant very long cuttings in the rocky soil, digging down even into the bed rock, upon which the base of the cutting is allowed to rest. In Greece the vines are planted about 5 feet apart each way, and are trained wholly without a wire or other trellis. The claim is made that the fruit is so delicate, being, as is well known, an essentially seedless grape, that it requires the dense shade made by the foliage of the low sprawling canes which spring from the low-cut, upright, main trunk of the plant. As the clusters mature, these sprawling canes are lifted from the ground and supported on short stakes to prevent the grapes from actually lying on the ground. After the petals have dropped from the flowers, i. e., when the fruit is well 'set,' the vines are ringed or girdled. This girdling is done on the main trunk of the vine, a thin quarter-inch-wide ring of bark being removed. This ringing is said to be essential to the production of a large berry. It is the belief that the berries from vines not ringed are richer in sugar, not so filled with juices, and keep better than those from ringed vines. The climate and soil in which the corinth will thrive are various. Necessary requisites are a long summer with good insolation and a not too high temperature, 95° F. being looked on as a very high temperature in the regions where these plants are cultivated. It is a popular belief that the corinth degenerates rapidly on being introduced into foreign countries, and that it even becomes a seed-bearing grape. I can not find that this belief is supported by sufficient evidence. Samples of corinths grown in Australia show that at least the plant does not produce seed there and does produce a utilizable product, which, however, is inferior in size and flavor to good Greece-grown specimens. The small size may be caused by a neglect to ring or a failure to perform this important process at the proper time, i. e., just after the fruit sets. This variety is exceedingly subject to the downy mildew (*Plasmopara viticola*), and the fields of Greece were ravaged by a frightful epidemic of this disease last year. The immediate locality from which these cuttings came was spared." (*Fairchild.*)

6430. PHASEOLUS VIRIDISSIMUS. Gram.

From Athens, Greece. Received through Mr. D. G. Fairchild (No. 571), May 9, 1901.

"One of the smallest and most delicate beans in the world. The beans are not much larger than grains of rice and of a deep green color. They are said to be most delicious when cooked alone or with rice in the national Greek dish called *Pilaff*. Their culture in Greece is a restricted one and the beans are considered a great delicacy. This is a variety which should receive a thorough distribution, as it is one worthy of trial throughout the south. I am indebted to Prof. Th. de Heldreich, of Athens University, for calling my attention to this species of which he has made a special study. Probably a variety of the *gram* of India (*Phaseolus mungo*)." (*Fairchild.*)

6431. VIGNA CATJANG. Cowpea.

From Athens, Greece. Received through Mr. D. G. Fairchild (No. 572, March 7, 1901), May 19, 1901.

"This legume is highly prized by the Greeks, who use it as we do the ordinary bean. (*Fairchild.*)

6432. Brassica oleracea var. **botrytis.** **Cauliflower.**

From Athens, Greece. Received through Mr. D. G. Fairchild (No. 573, March 7, 1901), May 5, 1901.

"An early variety of cauliflower which ripens in December in Greece. Its heads attain most unusual proportions and are of quite unusual flavor. It is sown here in August or September." (*Fairchild.*) (See No. 6434.)

6433. Lens esculenta var. **microsperma.** **Lentil.**

From Athens, Greece. Received from Dr. Th. de Heldreich through Mr. D. G. Fairchild (No. 570, March 8, 1901), May 9, 1901.

"A small-seeded, very delicate lentil which was first described by Dr. Th. de Heldreich, the noted explorer of the Grecian flora. (See *Revue des Sciences Naturelles Appliquées 37e Anné No. 15.5 Août 1890. Note sur une variété nouvelle ou peu Connue de Lentille.*) The variety is cultivated on the islands of Cephalonia and Leucade, two of the Ionian group, and differs essentially from the ordinary *Lens esculenta* Mch., having smaller elipsoid, even almost spherical, seeds which possess a marginal border very inconspicuous and obtuse. The color is pale yellow and they vary in diameter from three to five millimeters. Their ordinary lentil is lens shaped, circular, and has a sharply defined margin. This *microsperma* is said to be more tender than the ordinary sorts and much more easily cooked, and the flavor is reported to be superior, lacking that pronounced characteristic taste which makes lentils objectionable to some people. Deserves a thorough trial as a vegetable for soups and purées. A calcareous soil is essential to its cultivation. Stalks make a good fodder." (*Fairchild.*)

6434. Brassica oleracea var. **botrytis.** **Cauliflower.**

From Athens, Greece. Presented by Dr. Th. de Heldreich, of Athens University, through Mr. D. G. Fairchild (No. 574, March 7, 1901). Received May 9, 1901.

"A late variety of Grecian cauliflower which is planted in December and matures in March. Is a monster headed white variety of excellent flavor." (See No. 6432.) (*Fairchild.*)

6435. Vicia ervilia.

From Canné, Crete. Received through Mr. D. G. Fairchild (No. 594, March 16, 1901), May 17, 1901.

Orobus. "A forage plant very largely cultivated in the island of Crete. It is sown like any ordinary vetch, and the seeds are fed to the oxen and cattle. Cav. G. M. Fumis, inspector of agriculture at Canné, can secure this in quantity should it prove of sufficient interest." (*Fairchild.*)

6436. Lathyrus ochrus.

From Canné, Crete. Received through Mr. D. G. Fairchild, May 17, 1901.

Vicos. "A forage plant cultivated on the island of Crete." (*Fairchild.*)

6437. Vicia sp.

From Canné, Crete. Received through Mr. D. G. Fairchild, May 17, 1901.

Yares or *Gesu.* "A forage plant cultivated on the island of Crete." (*Fairchild.*)

6438. Phoenix dactylifera. **Date.**

From Alexandria, Egypt. Received through Mr. D. G. Fairchild (No. 582, March 30, 1901), May 11, 1901.

Hayani. "This is the earliest sort grown in the Delta region of the Nile and one of the best-known kinds there. It is a red table date, becoming black when ripe; 2 to 2½ inches long; cylindrical. It ripens in September or October. Not used as a drying date. It sells in the season for 2 piasters Turkish (10 cents) per oke (3 pounds). Matures its fruit all at once." (*Fairchild.*)

6439. PHOENIX DACTYLIFERA. **Date.**

From Alexandria, Egypt. Received through Mr. D. G. Fairchild (No. 583, March 30, 1901), May 11, 1901.

Zaglul. "A variety from the Nile Delta region. Fruits of this sort are very large, often 3 inches long. They are eaten by the Arabs when red in color and still unripe. They are table dates, but are not prized as highly by Europeans as by the Arabs, who pay a high price for them. It is a variety which hangs on late in the season." (*Fairchild.*)

6440. PHOENIX DACTYLIFERA. **Date.**

From Alexandria, Egypt. Received through Mr. D. G. Fairchild (No. 584, March 30, 1901), May 11, 1901.

Bint Aisha. "The best variety of table date in lower Egypt, at least it is so considered by many Europeans. It is not a keeping date, being so sweet and sticky that when ripe it must be eaten with a fork. A short, black, small (1½ inches long) date, ripening in December. Skin separates very easily from the flesh. Sells for 10 to 15 cents for three pounds. Stem of mature palm very slender." (*Fairchild.*)

6441. PHOENIX DACTYLIFERA. **Date.**

From Alexandria, Egypt. Received through Mr. D. G. Fairchild (No. 585, March 30, 1901), May 11, 1901.

Samani. "A variety of Delta date; large, yellow, 2 to 2¼ inches long, with a thick skin; ripening in November. It is used in making preserves, which are manufactured especially well by a Mr. Tambaco, of Alexandria, who puts them in tin cans for export after they have been stewed in sugar. They must be peeled before canning, as the skin is tough. Thought of very highly by many Europeans as a sweet characteristic preserve. Is also canned with little sugar, as Americans can plums." (*Fairchild.*)

6442. PHOENIX DACTYLIFERA. **Date.**

From Alexandria, Egypt. Received through Mr. D. G. Fairchild (No. 586, March 30, 1901), May 11, 1901.

Dakar Majahel. "A male variety which is used in the Delta for fertilizing purposes. All the varieties, of which there are at least eight in the region of Ramley alone, are fertilized with the pollen of this *Dakar Majahel.* It is claimed to be the only sort that can be used on all these eight varieties." (*Fairchild.*)

6443. ALBIZZIA LEBBEK **Lebbek.**

From Cairo, Egypt. Received through Mr. D. G. Fairchild (No. 611, April 18, 1901), May 17, 1901.

"A much used shade tree about Cairo. Owing to the inroads of a borer, however, this species is being gradually replaced in Egypt by other forms such as *Ficus nitida.*" (*Fairchild.*)

6444. KIGELIA PINNATA (?). **Sausage tree.**

From Cairo, Egypt. Received through Mr. D. G. Fairchild (No. 612, April 18, 1901), May 17, 1901.

"This sausage tree is not only a very curious species, bearing its flowers and fruit on long pendant pedicels, but it is a foliage and landscape tree of great merit, worthy of introduction into the parks of southern Florida. Its foliage is exceedingly hard and harsh and very brittle and its heavy sausage-shaped fruits are so heavy as to be dangerous when they fall from the tree. In the Ezbekieh Gardens in Cairo a beautiful specimen of this tree is to be seen." (*Fairchild.*)

6445. PHOENIX DACTYLIFERA. **Date.**

From Charkia, Cairo, Egypt. Received through Mr. D. G. Fairchild (No. 606), May 17, 1901.

Amri (fruit bought on the market). "This sort is known as the best drying date in Egypt. It is in its prime in November but keeps until May or June. A large, red date with a dry, though not unpleasant taste. Some of the specimens are two inches long. Skin rather tough and in most respects inferior to Algerian varieties. These seeds are from trees probably pollinated by some other variety, so they may not yield true *Amri* seedlings." (*Fairchild.*)

6446. ELETTARIA CARDAMOMUM. **Cardamom.**

From Heneratgoda, Ceylon. Received from J. P. William & Bros., May 17, 1901.

Malabar. "In planting cardamons, nursery beds should be prepared about 3 feet wide and 6 feet long; if the soil is poor, cow-dung manure or vegetable mold should be mixed with it (half soil and half manure). Sow the seed, covering it lightly with soil, give the young plants shade, and water them regularly once every evening. Seeds will germinate in from six to eight weeks or possibly not for twelve weeks. When the seedlings are 4 to 6 inches high they should be removed to another bed and planted about 6 to 8 inches apart. When they attain 1 to 2 feet high they are ready to plant in the field about 6 to 12 feet apart, according to the nature of the soil, and should be planted in rainy weather. In planting, the bulb of the plant only should be covered and not the stem; in poor soils, holes are necessary about 1 foot deep and 1½ feet wide which are filled with surface soil, mixed with cow-dung manure or vegetable mold. Care should be taken to keep the nursery thoroughly free from weeds." (*William.*)

6447. ERYTHROXYLON COCA. **Coca.**

From Heneratgoda, Ceylon. Received through J. P. William & Bros., May 17, 1901.

Huanuco. "This plant is a native of tropical South America; it thrives from the sea level up to 5,000 feet and over. The large leaved *Huanuco* variety is especially suited to elevations from 2,000 feet and upward." (*William.*)

6448. CROTON TIGLIUM. **Croton oil tree.**

From Heneratgoda, Ceylon. Received through J. P. William & Bros., May 17, 1901.

"This tree grows even in the poorest soil or abandoned coffee plantations from the sea level up to 3,000 feet and over. Once a week a coolie shakes the tree and picks up from the ground what pods have fallen off, then drops the pods in the sun, shells them, and gives another drying, which is all that is required. A net profit of about 1 shilling a tree per annum has been realized from full-grown trees." (*William.*)

6449. SANTALUM ALBUM. **Sandalwood.**

From Heneratgoda, Ceylon. Received through J. P. William & Bros., May 17, 1901.

"This tree yields the sandalwood of commerce. The same tree produces both the white and yellow sandalwood, the last being the inner part of the tree and very hard and fragrant, especially near the roots. The tree grows from sea level up to 5,000 feet on red and stony soils, and among rocks where the soil is good. The principal item of forest revenue in Mysore is sandalwood. The export to Europe and other countries is yearly increasing." (*William.*)

6450. ALEURITES TRILOBA. **Candle nut.**

From Heneratgoda, Ceylon. Received through J. P. William & Bros., May 17, 1901.

"Oil from the large seeds of this tree is much used for lamps under the name of 'Kekuna' oil; also in painting as a drying oil. In the manufacture of soap it replaces cocoanut oil at Othahiti. The cultivation is easy, the culture being possible from the sea level up to 2,000 feet altitude." (*William.*)

6451. ARTOCARPUS INTEGRIFOLIA. **Honey Jack.**

From Heneratgoda, Ceylon. Received through J. P. William & Bros., May 17, 1901.

"The fruits of this tree, including the seeds, are used as food in various ways, and are highly esteemed by the natives. The fruits weigh as much as 100 pounds. The timber is largely used for all kinds of furniture and building purposes. It is also largely exported to Europe. A full-grown old tree is worth £5 and upward. This is one of the best shade trees for coffee, cocoa, and cardamons, and from the sea level up to 2,000 feet its fallen leaves enrich the soil. The demand for jackwood timber is yearly increasing, as well as the price. Leaves are excellent fodder for cattle, goats, and sheep." (*William.*)

6452. SAPINDUS TRIFOLIATUS.

From Heneratgoda, Ceylon. Received through J. P. William & Bros., May 17, 1901.

6453 to 6460. ERIOBOTRYA JAPONICA. Loquat.

From Mustapha Supérieur, near Algiers, Algeria. Presented by Rev. Ewyn Arkwright, from Villa Thémely, through W. T. Swingle. Scions obtained in June, 1900. Grafted trees shipped April 13, 1901; received May 18, 1901.

"This valuable collection of loquats comprises most of the large sorts which have originated in Algeria, where much attention has been paid recently to this valuable fruit. Single fruits of some of these varieties weighed 59 grams, or something over two ounces. There are differences in the time of ripening as well as in the size and flavor of these varieties." (*Swingle.*)

6453.
Don Carlos.

6454.
Baronne Hall.

6455.
St. Michel, long.

6456.
Marcadal.

6457.
Olivier.

6458.
Scala.

6459.
St. Michel, round.

6460.
Narbonne.

6461 to 6468. FICUS CARICA. Fig.

From Rouïba, Algeria. Presented by Dr. L. Trabut, Government Botanist, through Messrs. W. T. Swingle and C. S. Scofield. Received May 17, 1901.

"This collection embraces the principal varieties of figs which are grown at Damascus, and was secured by the French consul there on February 14, 1895. They were sent to Dr. L. Trabut, Government Botanist, Algeria, who planted them at Rouïba in March, 1895. The original notes which accompanied the varieties and which, presumably, were prepared by the French consul are given under each of the numbers." (*Swingle.*)

6461.
Kaab el Ghazal. Fruit medium size, white, yellow outside, of the color of honey inside, splitting open when ripe.

6462.
Sultani. Fruit large, yellow outside, red inside, splitting open at maturity. An early variety.

6463.
Mamari (labeled *Mennoni*, probably erroneously). Fruit medium size, yellow outside, red inside, splitting open when ripe. A late variety.

6464.
Malaki blanc. Fruit large, yellow, white outside, red inside; does not split open when ripe.

SEPTEMBER, 1900, TO DECEMBER, 1903. 89

6461 to 6468—Continued.

6465.

Sultanie. Grows on dry lands. Fruit medium size, yellow outside, white inside, splitting open when ripe.

6466.

Malaki (labeled *Masaki*, probably erroneously). Fruit large, yellow outside, honey colored inside, splitting open when ripe.

6467.

Baalie. Fruit small, green outside, red inside; does not split open when ripe.

6468.

Hamari. This variety is not included in the descriptive list of varieties furnished by the French consul to Dr. Trabut.

6469 to 6471. FICUS CARICA. **Fig.**

From Kabylia, Algeria. Presented by Dr. L. Trabut, Government Botanist, through Messrs. W. T. Swingle and C. S. Scofield. Received May 17, 1901.

6469.

Abakour amellal (early white). "A fig from Kabylia, a good fig-growing region, said to produce two crops a year, brebas and figs." (*Swingle and Scofield.*)

6470.

Aberkan (black). "A fig from Kabylia, a good fig-growing region, said to produce two crops a year, brebas and figs." (*Swingle and Scofield.*)

6471.

Yousef blanche. "A fig from Kabylia found by General Yousef at time of conquest, 1830–45." (*Swingle and Scofield.*)

6472. FICUS CARICA. **Fig.**

From Rouïba, Algeria. Presented by Dr. L. Trabut, Government Botanist, through Messrs. W. T. Swingle and C. S. Scofield. Received May 17, 1901.

Figuier de Smyrne. "An unnamed Smyrna fig obtained by Doctor Trabut through the French consul some years ago. (*Swingle and Scofield.*)

6473. FICUS CARICA. **Caprifig.**

From Rouïba, Algeria. Presented by Dr. L. Trabut, Government Botanist, through Messrs. W. T. Swingle and C. S. Scofield. Received May 17, 1901.

"A wild caprifig having short flat fruits." (*Scofield.*)

6474. FICUS CARICA. **Caprifig.**

From Rouïba, Algeria. Presented by Dr. L. Trabut, Government Botanist, through Messrs. W. T. Swingle and C. S. Scofield. Received May 17, 1901.

"A wild caprifig having long fruits." (*Scofield.*)

6475. FICUS CARICA. **Caprifig.**

From Algiers, Algeria. Received through Mr. C. S. Scofield, May 17, 1901.

Hamma. "A very valuable variety growing by a stone quarry above the Jardin d'Essai du Hamma, near Algiers. Bears large quantities of winter-generation caprifigs (*mamme*). It is probably from this tree that the Blastophaga was introduced into California in 1899. It bears abundant profichi also." (*Swingle.*)

6476. FICUS CARICA. **Caprifig.**

From Algiers, Algeria. Received through Mr. C. S. Scofield, May 17, 1901.

"Growing at the stone quarry above Jardin d'Essai du Hamma, near Algiers. Did not hold winter fruits well." (*Scofield.*)

6477. FICUS CARICA. **Caprifig.**

From Biskra, Algeria. Obtained by Mr. W. T. Swingle, May 15, 1900. Grown one year at Algiers. Received May 17, 1901.

Laudi (?). "Cuttings from tree in a garden in old Biskra." (*Swingle.*)

6478. FICUS CARICA. **Caprifig.**

From Chetma oasis, near Biskra, Algeria. Obtained by Mr. W. T. Swingle, May 14, 1900. Grown one year at Algiers. Received May 17, 1901.

Bsikri. "Cuttings from a tree in a garden." (*Swingle.*)

6479. FICUS CARICA. **Caprifig.**

From Biskra, Algeria. Obtained by Mr. W. T. Swingle, May 15, 1900. Grown one year at Algiers. Received May 17, 1901.

Bsikri. "Cuttings from a tree in garden in Old Biskra." (*Swingle.*)

6480. FICUS CARICA. **Fig.**

From Biskra, Algeria. Obtained by Mr. W. T. Swingle, May 15, 1900. Grown one year at Algiers. Received May 17, 1901.

Choer. "Cuttings from a fig tree growing in the road running south along the west side of Biskra oasis. Probably of no great value." (*Swingle.*)

6481. FICUS CARICA. **Caprifig.**

From Algiers, Algeria. Presented by Dr. L. Trabut, Government Botanist, through Messrs. W. T. Swingle and C. S. Scofield. Received May 17, 1901.

Hamma. The same as No. 6475.

6482. FICUS CARICA. **Caprifig.**

From Algiers, Algeria. Presented by Dr. L. Trabut, Government Botanist, through Messrs. W. T. Swingle and C. S. Scofield. Received May 17, 1901.

Wild fig, with entire leaves from stone quarry above the Jardin d'Essai du Hamma, near Algiers.

6483. FICUS CARICA. **Caprifig.**

From Algiers, Algeria. Presented by Dr. L. Trabut, Government Botanist, through Messrs. W. T. Swingle and C. S. Scofield. Received May 17, 1901.

"A variety of caprifig from M. Eymes de Cheffi." (*Swingle and Scofield.*)

6484. FICUS CARICA. **Caprifig.**

From Algiers, Algeria. Presented by Dr. L. Trabut, Government Botanist, through Messrs. W. T. Swingle and C. S. Scofield. Received May 17, 1901.

Sultani. The same as No. 6462.

6485. FICUS CARICA. **Caprifig.**

From Algiers, Algeria. Presented by Dr. L. Trabut, Government Botanist, through Messrs. W. T. Swingle and C. S. Scofield. Received May 17, 1901.

Yousouf blanche. The same as No. 6471.

6486. FICUS CARICA. **Caprifig.**

From Algiers, Algeria. Presented by Dr. L. Trabut, Government Botanist, through Messrs. W. T. Swingle and C. S. Scofield. Received May 17, 1901.

Hamari. The same as No. 6468.

6487. FICUS CARICA. **Caprifig.**

From Algiers, Algeria. Presented by Dr. L. Trabut, Government Botanist, through Messrs. W. T. Swingle and C. S. Scofield. Received May 17, 1901.

Belamie.

6488. FICUS CARICA. **Caprifig.**

From Chetma oasis, near Biskra, Algeria. Obtained by Mr. W. T. Swingle, May 14, 1900. Grown one year at Algiers. Received May 17, 1901.

Booung. "A late sort considered of fourth quality. Cuttings from a tree in a garden." (*Swingle.*)

6489. FICUS CARICA. **Caprifig.**

From Algiers, Algeria. Presented by Dr. L. Trabut, Government Botanist, through Messrs. W. T. Swingle and C. S. Scofield. Received May 17, 1901.

Figue de l'Archipel (Archipelago fig).

6490. FICUS CARICA. **Caprifig.**

From Algiers, Algeria. Obtained by Mr. W. T. Swingle. Received May 17, 1901.

Bourlier. "A variety much prized by the Kabyle fig growers who come 15 miles or more to Reghaïa to M. Bourlier's farm to get the fruits to use in caprifying figs." (*Swingle.*)

6491. FICUS CARICA. **Caprifig.**

From Algiers, Algeria. Presented by Dr. L. Trabut, Government Botanist, through Messrs. W. T. Swingle and C. S. Scofield. Received May 17, 1901.

Malaki noir (labeled *Masaki noir*, probably erroneously). Fruit large, violet-colored without, red within, not splitting open at maturity. A late variety.

6492. IRIS UNGUICULARIS. **Iris.**

From Algiers, Algeria. Presented by Rev. Ewyn Arkwright, through Mr. C. S. Scofield. Received May 17, 1901.

Iris stylosa (white sport). "A very handsome white sport of this curious iris (also called *Iris stylosa*), which bears its fruit capsules at or just below the surface of the ground. The flowers have a tube 8 to 12 inches long which serves to support them at the level of the ends of the leaves differing widely from the ordinary species where the tubes are short and the flowers attached to two stems." (*Swingle.*)

6493. FICUS CARICA. **Fig.**

From Algiers, Algeria. Presented by Dr. L. Trabut, Government Botanist, through Messrs. W. T. Swingle and C. S. Scofield. Received May 17, 1901.

Abakour amclab(?) or *Abacour amclale.*

6494. FICUS SAKOUI. **Fig.**

From Algiers, Algeria. Presented by Dr. L. Trabut, Government Botanist, through Messrs. W. T. Swingle and C. S. Scofield. Received May 17, 1901.

6495. FICUS CARICA. **Fig.**

From Algiers, Algeria. Presented by Dr. L. Trabut, Government Botanist, through Messrs. W. T. Swingle and C. S. Scofield. Received May 17, 1901.

Abakour aberkan (early black).

6496. FICUS CARICA. **Fig.**

From Algiers, Algeria. Presented by Dr. L. Trabut, Government Botanist, through Messrs. W. T. Swingle and C. S. Scofield. Received May 17, 1901.

Yousouf. "A fig from Kabylia, found by General Yousef at the time of the French conquest, 1830–1845." (*Swingle and Scofield.*)

6497. FICUS CARICA. **Fig.**

From Algiers, Algeria. Presented by Dr. L. Trabut, Government Botanist, through Messrs. W. T. Swingle and C. S. Scofield. Received May 17, 1901.

Mamari or *Mennoni.* "An early fig from Damascus obtained by Doctor Trabut through the French consul some years ago." (See No. 6463.) (*Swingle and Scofield.*)

6498. FICUS CARICA. **Fig.**

From Algiers, Algeria. Presented by Dr. L. Trabut, Government Botanist, through Messrs. W. T. Swingle and C. S. Scofield. Received May 17, 1901.

Kaab el ghazal. See No. 6461.

6499. FICUS CARICA. **Fig.**

From Algiers, Algeria. Presented by Dr. L. Trabut, Government Botanist, through Messrs. W. T. Swingle and C. S. Scofield. Received May 17, 1901.

Aberkan or *aberkane.* "A fig from Kabylia, a good fig-growing region, said to produce two crops a year, brebas and figs." (*Swingle and Scofield.*)

6500. VITIS VINIFERA. **Grape.**

From Algiers, Algeria. Presented by Dr. L. Trabut, Government Botanist, through Messrs. W. T. Swingle and C. S. Scofield. Received May 17, 1901.

Sultanie. "A white grape bearing large bunches of fruit suitable for table use or for making a kind of port or Madeira wine." (*Scofield.*)

6501. VITIS VINIFERA. **Grape.**

From Algiers, Algeria. Presented by Dr. L. Trabut, Government Botanist, through Messrs. W. T. Swingle and C. S. Scofield. Received May 17, 1901.

Smyrna seedless raisin.

6502 and 6503.

(Numbers not utilized.)

6504. ACTINIDIA sp.

From Kuling, China. Received through Dr. G. D. Brill (No. 7), May 17, 1901.

"Will grow at an elevation of 3,500 feet and over." (*Brill.*)

6505. VITIS ROMANETI. **Wild grape.**

From Kuling, China. Received through Dr. G. D. Brill (No. 8), May 17, 1901.

"Thorny grape, which bears large clusters of good-sized, black berries." (*Brill.*)

6506.

(Number not utilized.)

6507 to 6646.

From China. Received through Dr. G. D. Brill, May 17, 1901.

A collection of seeds and plants made during an extended trip through China in 1900. The notes regarding the various numbers are copied from letters written during this period, no separate descriptive list of the various introductions having been furnished. Doctor Brill's numbers are given.

6507. PYRUS sp. Pear.

From Ichang. "Small and medium, russet colored around the half near the stem. Rest of skin covered with russet dots. Skin coarse, flesh firm." (No. 10.) (*Brill.*)

6508. PYRUS sp. Pear.

From Ichang. "Medium sized, drum-shaped, skin yellow and dotted." (No. 11.) (*Brill.*)

6509. PYRUS sp. Pear.

From Ichang. (No. 12.)

6510. PYRUS sp. Pear.

From Ichang. (No. 13.)

6511. PYRUS sp. Pear.

From the vicinity of Ichang. (No. 14.)

6512. PYRUS sp. Pear.

From the vicinity of Ichang. (No. 15.)

6513. PYRUS sp. Pear.

From the vicinity of Ichang. (No. 16.) "Fruit medium small, skin white to greenish, fruit flattened-round. Flesh dry, quality poor." (*Brill.*)

6514. PYRUS sp. Pear.

From the vicinity of Ichang. (No. 17.) "A flat pear, reddish in color." (*Brill.*)

6515. PYRUS sp. Pear.

From the vicinity of Ichang. (No. 18.) "Fruit medium small, skin white to greenish, fruit flattened-round. Flesh dry, quality poor." (*Brill.*)

6516. PYRUS sp. Pear.

From the vicinity of Ichang. (No. 19.) "Ripens in September; a longer and larger pear than the Kieffer; of similar shape, but smoother; color, rich golden yellow; quality, good; free from woody tissue; very handsome; often weighs 1½ pounds." (*Brill.*)

6517. PYRUS sp. Pear.

From the vicinity of Ichang. (No. 20.) "Large, but of poor quality; skin brown-russet color, with corky dots the size of sesame seeds; good baked." (*Brill.*)

6518. PYRUS sp. Pear.

From the vicinity of Ichang. (No. 21.) "Very large; cavity at stem deep; coarse flesh." (*Brill.*)

6519. PYRUS sp. Pear.

From the vicinity o chang. (No. 22.)

6507 to 6646—Continued.

6520. PYRUS sp.   **Pear.**

From the vicinity of Ichang. (No. 23.) "Ripens very early: small-medium; flat; color yellow-green; slightly acid." (*Brill.*)

6521. PYRUS sp.   **Pear.**

From the vicinity of Ichang. (No. 24.) "Size large; larger around at stem end than blossom end; very sweet and good; texture fine. Chinese say it is 'cooling.'" (*Brill.*)

6522. DIOSPYROS KAKI.   **Japanese persimmon.**

From the vicinity of Ichang. (No. 25.) "Small fruited." (*Brill.*)

6523. DIOSPYROS KAKI.   **Japanese persimmon.**

From the vicinity of Ichang. (No. 26.) "Large fruited." (*Brill.*)

6524. DIOSPYROS KAKI.   **Japanese persimmon.**

From Wuchang. (No. 27.) "Small, rather pointed, red; flesh firm and of good quality, not astringent." (*Brill.*)

6525. DIOSPYROS KAKI.   **Japanese persimmon.**

From Wuchang. (No. 28.) "Large, red persimmon, rather pointed. Similar to No. 6524, only three times the size." (*Brill.*)

6526. DIOSPYROS KAKI.   **Japanese persimmon.**

From Wuchang. (No. 29.) "Small, yellow; not as good as the red." (*Brill.*)

6527. DIOSPYROS KAKI.   **Japanese persimmon.**

From Wuchang. (No. 30.) "Large, flat, ridged, yellow, slightly astringent; has a crease around its greatest diameter as though a string had been tied around it before it was fully ripe." (*Brill.*)

6528. PYRUS sp.   **Apple.**

From Wuchang. (No. 31.) "Each tree has buds of three varieties. A soft mealy apple, resembling a Hyslop crab. Of good size and firm flesh. A variety cultivated for flowers." (*Brill.*)

6529. PRUNUS CERASUS.   **Cherry.**

From Wuchang. (No. 32.) "Tree small. Fruit rather small, pointed, yellowish-red. Ripens at end of April. Never allowed to attain full size before being picked." (*Brill.*)

6530. CASTANEA sp.   **Chestnut.**

From Hankow. (No. 33.) "Propagated by root cuttings. Large nuts. Tree bears very young, at from 5 to 7 feet." (*Brill.*)

6531. PRUNUS sp.

From Ichang. (No. 34.) "Came to me as a peach. Chinese name is for cherry." (*Brill.*)

6532. PYRUS sp.   **Pear.**

From the vicinity of Ichang. (No. 35.) "Same as No. 6507." (*Brill.*)

6533. CASTANEA sp.   **Chestnut.**

From Ichang. (No. 36.) "Root cuttings of a tree bearing large nuts. Bears early and the tree does not grow large." (*Brill.*)

6534. PRUNUS ARMENIACA.   **Apricot.**

From Ichang. (No. 37.) "Large and late." (*Brill.*)

6507 to 6646—Continued.

6535.
(Number not utilized.)

6536. PRUNUS sp. **Plum.**

From Sai Tseo, above Hankow. (No. 39.) "Pointed, reddish-yellow, sweet; flesh clings to the stone." (*Brill.*)

6537. PRUNUS sp. **Plum.**

From Ichang. (No. 40.)

6538. PRUNUS sp. **Plum.**

From Ichang. (No. 41.)

6539. PRUNUS sp. **Plum.**

From Ichang. (No. 42.)

6540. PRUNUS sp. **Plum.**

From Sai Tseo, above Hankow. (No. 43.)

6541. AMYGDALUS PERSICA. **Peach.**

From Sai Tseo, above Hankow. (No. 44.) "Flat, freestone, ripens in May." (*Brill.*)

6542. AMYGDALUS PERSICA. **Peach.**

From near Sai Tseo, above Hankow. (No. 45.) "White, fine fleshed, flat, freestone, ripening the middle of May." (*Brill.*)

6543. AMYGDALUS PERSICA. **Peach.**

From Sai Tseo. (No. 46.) "Long, rather pointed, red-fleshed, freestone." (*Brill.*)

6544. AMYGDALUS PERSICA. **Peach.**

From Sai Tseo. (No. 47.) "Medium size, flat, freestone, ripening in May." (*Brill.*)

6545. AMYGDALUS PERSICA. **Peach.**

From Sai Tseo. (No. 48.) "Flat, freestone, quality very good. Ripens in June." (*Brill.*)

6546. PRUNUS sp. **Plum.**

From Sai Tseo. (No. 49.) "Large, round, with deep suture down one side. Flesh, red. Ripens in August." (*Brill.*)

6547. AMYGDALUS PERSICA. **Peach.**

From Ichang. (No. 50.) "White peach." (*Brill.*)

6548. AMYGDALUS PERSICA. **Peach.**

From the mountains above Ichang. (No. 50a.)

6549. ZIZYPHUS JUJUBA. **Chinese date.**

From Ichang. (No. 50a.) "Much used for preserves by drying in sugar or sirup. Also eaten fresh." (*Brill.*)

6550. VICIA FABA. **Broad bean.**

From Hankow. (No. 51.) "Large flat bean, a few in a pod. Used for food green and dry. Planted in October or December." (*Brill.*)

6507 to 6646—Continued.

6551. PISUM SATIVUM. **Pea.**

From the valley of Hankow. (No. 52.) "Much resembles the Canadian field pea. Tender ends of shoots, pods, and the peas, green and dry, are used for food." (*Brill.*)

6552. PISUM SATIVUM. **Pea.**

From the mountains near Hankow. (No. 53.)

6553. VICIA sp. (?) **Pea.**

From Ichang. (No. 54.) "Grown 1,000 to 3,000 feet above river. Taller than the others. Much used as food by boat 'trackers.'" (*Brill.*)

6554. VICIA sp. (?)

From Chiu Niu, near Hankow. (No. 55.) "Used as a green manure for rice fields. Sown in October to November and plowed under in April. Larger than No. 6555." (*Brill.*)

6555. VICIA CRACCA. **Vetch.**

From Wusueh. (No. 56.) "Used especially as a green manure for rice fields. Sown in September to November. Often among the late rice, beans, or buckwheat." (*Brill.*)

6556. GLYCINE HISPIDA. **Soy bean.**

(No. 57.) "Much used for bean curd and oil all over central China. Probably as many of these are grown as all the other varieties together." (*Brill.*)

6557. VIGNA CATJANG. **Cowpea.**

From Hankow. (No. 58.) "Is ground with water into a paste and pressed into long strings, which are dried and boiled in water." (*Brill.*)

6558. GLYCINE HISPIDA. **Soy bean.**

From Hankow. (No. 59.) "Used for bean curd and oil. Considered better than No. 6556." (*Brill.*)

6559. GLYCINE HISPIDA. **Soy bean.**

From beyond Chiu Niu. (No. 60.) "Planted between the rows of rice and ripening late in the fall, after the rice is harvested. Used the same as No. 6556, only quality poorer. Will grow on very wet land." (*Brill.*)

6560. GLYCINE HISPIDA. **Soy bean.**

From beyond Chiu Niu. (No. 61.) "Planted and used the same as No. 6559. Planted in July or August." (*Brill.*)

6561. GLYCINE HISPIDA. **Soy bean.**

From Hankow. (No. 62.) "A black bean, used for same purposes as Nos. 6559 and 6560, but of better quality. Not planted with other crops." (*Brill.*)

6562. PHASEOLUS MUNGO-RADIATUS. **Gram.**

(No. 63.) "Planted on the banks of rice fields and in odd corners. Will grow in hard-baked soils. Used in the same way as No. 6557." (*Brill.*)

6563. VIGNA CATJANG. **Cowpea.**

(No. 64.) "Grows to a height of four feet or more. Used for food." (*Brill.*)

6564. PHASEOLUS MUNGO. **Gram.**

From Ichang. (No. 65.) "Grows on the mountains between the Indian corn. Largely takes the place of rice; is also cooked with vegetables before fully dry." (*Brill.*)

6507 to 6646—Continued.

6565. PHASEOLUS VULGARIS. Bean.

From Ichang. (No. 66.) "A climber. Used as a snap bean." (*Brill.*)

6566. VIGNA CATJANG. Cowpea.

From Hankow. (No. 67.) "These peas are often ground to a paste with water and fried in a hot kettle, forming a huge pancake." (*Brill.*)

6567. VIGNA CATJANG. Cowpea.

From Hankow. (No. 68.) "Long-podded bush bean. Used almost entirely green as a snap bean. It is planted early in the spring in cold frames after being soaked in water, then transplanted." (*Brill.*)

6568. VIGNA CATJANG. Cowpea.

From Hankow. (No. 69.) "Same as No. 6567, except a climber, trained on a trellis." (*Brill.*)

6569. DOLICHOS LABLAB. Bean.

(No. 70.) "A great trailer. Usually planted above banks or fences. A profuse bearer of flat pods, which later are used green as snap beans. Late variety." (*Brill.*)

6570. CANAVALIA ENSIFORMIS. Jack bean.

(No. 71.) "A great climber; strong grower. Often planted around the houses for shade. Pods over 1 foot long, containing about nine large beans. Pods are cut up and eaten green, and also salted. Beans are very good, but expensive." (*Brill.*)

6571. ASTRAGALUS SINICUS. Genge clover.

(No. 72.) "A cloverlike plant, sown from September to December. Plowed under in April as a green manure for rice. Grows to a height of $1\frac{1}{2}$ to $2\frac{1}{2}$ feet. Has many tubercles on the roots and will grow in very wet land. Reseeds itself on the overflowed lands." (*Brill.*)

6572. GYMNOCLADUS CHINENSIS. Soap tree.

(No. 73.) "Large tree. The pods are pounded to a paste and used as a soap. They have the smell of rancid butter. Seeds are used as a dye." (*Brill.*)

6573. ZEA MAYS. Corn.

From the mountains above Ichang. (No. 74.) "Has been grown there for 200 years or more. Originally from America. Resists drought well. Much used as food." (*Brill.*)

6574. ZEA MAYS. Corn.

From the mountains above Ichang. (No. 75.) (Same as No. 6573, except in color.)

6575. ORYZA SATIVA. Rice.

From Hankow. (No. 76.) "A glutinous rice, very much like No. 6577. It is planted a little earlier and will ripen in two weeks less time." (*Brill.*)

6576. ORYZA SATIVA. Rice.

(No. 77.) "A glutinous rice sown in May and harvested in November. Very productive." (*Brill.*)

6577. ORYZA SATIVA. Rice.

(No. 78.) "A glutinous rice with red or brown hulls, which are quite easily separated from the kernels. Rather late in ripening." (*Brill.*)

6507 to 6646—Continued.

6578. ORYZA SATIVA. Rice.

(No. 79.) "A glutinous rice, ripening a little earlier than No. 6584. The hull is very thin and gives a large proportion of hulled rice. Hulls very long. Mostly used for making candy." (*Brill.*)

6579. ORYZA SATIVA. Rice.

(No. 80.) "A hard rice that does not swell a great deal in cooking. Sown in May, transplanted in June, harvested in September. Hulls thin, giving a large per cent of clean rice." (*Brill.*)

6580. ORYZA SATIVA. Rice.

(No. 81.) "A hard rice with long awns and brown, thick chaff." (*Brill.*)

6581. ORYZA SATIVA. Rice.

(No. 82.) "A round, short-grained, glutinous rice, with small, compact heads. Ripens a week earlier than No. 6578, or about the middle of July." (*Brill.*)

6582. ORYZA SATIVA. Rice.

(No. 83.) "Straw large and coarse. Hull quite thick. Best rice of this section." (*Brill.*)

6583. ORYZA SATIVA. Rice.

(No. 84.) "A hard rice; straw short and small, but tough; hulls thin; yields well." (*Brill.*)

6584. ORYZA SATIVA. Rice.

(No. 85.) "Grows 3½ to 4 feet high. The seed is sown in March and it is ripe in July. Field is then flooded after harvest and suckers start out which produce a smaller crop in September. Yields heavy crop of good rice. More of this is sown than of any other variety around Hankow." (*Brill.*)

6585. ORYZA SATIVA. Rice.

From Ichang. (No. 86.) "A brown-hulled rice." (*Brill.*)

6586. ORYZA SATIVA. Rice.

From Ichang. (No. 87.) "It is said to ripen three months from sowing the seed." (*Brill.*)

6587. ORYZA SATIVA. Rice.

From Ichang. (No. 88.)

6588. ORYZA SATIVA. Rice.

From Shasi. (No. 89.) "A glutinous rice sown on the overflowed lands. The plants are said to stand an excess of water and to keep their heads above it better than any other variety." (*Brill.*)

6589. CHAETOCHLOA ITALICA. Millet.

From Sai Tseo. (No. 90.) "Much used by the people as porridge in place of rice in the north of the province." (*Brill.*)

6590. CHAETOCHLOA ITALICA. Millet.

From Sai Tseo. (No. 91.) "Used in same way as No. 6589." (*Brill.*)

6591. CHAETOCHLOA ITALICA. Millet.

From Ichang. (No. 92.) "Grown in the mountains and much used as a substitute for rice." (*Brill.*)

6507 to 6646—Continued.

6592. CHAETOCHLOA ITALICA. **Millet.**

From Ichang. (No. 93.) "Has the same use as No. 6591, but is said to be of a different variety." (*Brill.*)

6593. CHAETOCHLOA ITALICA. **Millet.**

From Ichang. (No. 94.) "Said to be more glutinous than Nos. 6591 and 6592." (*Brill.*)

6594. CHAETOCHLOA ITALICA. **Millet.**

From the plains above Hankow. (No. 95.)

6595. SESAMUM INDICUM. **Sesame.**

From Hankow. (No. 96.) "Black variety, much used for oil; seeds also used in candy and cake; oil is considered the best of all for cooking." (*Brill.*)

6596. SESAMUM INDICUM. **Sesame.**

(No. 97.) "White variety, used the same as No. 6595, but grown in much larger quantities. The oil is considered better than any other vegetable oil for cooking. Exported to France and Germany in large quantities." (*Brill.*)

6597. HORDEUM VULGARE. **Barley.**

From Chiu Niu, near Hankow. (No. 98.) "Boiled with rice or boiled and eaten in place of rice." (*Brill.*)

6598. TRITICUM VULGARE. **Wheat.**

From near Hankow. (No. 99.) "Fish-headed wheat, with small, compact heads." (*Brill.*)

6599. TRITICUM VULGARE. **Wheat.**

From near Hankow. (No. 100.) "Long-headed wheat." (*Brill.*)

6600. TRITICUM VULGARE. **Wheat.**

(No. 101.) "Variety most sown on the plains after the summer overflow of the river." (*Brill.*)

6601. HORDEUM VULGARE. **Barley.**

From below Hankow. (No. 102.) "Largely used here for feeding horses." (*Brill.*)

6602. FAGOPYRUM ESCULENTUM. **Buckwheat.**

(No. 103.) "Sown in August or September. Said to be different from No. 6603. Called sweet buckwheat." (*Brill.*)

6603. FAGOPYRUM ESCULENTUM. **Buckwheat.**

(No. 104.) "Sown early in the spring and called bitter buckwheat." (*Brill.*)

6604. ANDROPOGON SORGHUM. **Sorghum.**

From Hankow. (No. 105.) "Grows to a height of 12 feet or more. Planted on land too dry for rice. Used for distilling, and refuse is used for pigs and cattle. In some places used for human food." (*Brill.*)

6605. RAPHANUS SATIVUS. **Radish.**

From Hankow. (No. 106.) "Sown from September to November. Grows all winter." (*Brill.*)

6507 to 6646—Continued.

6606. ABUTILON AVICENNAE.   Chinese hemp.

From Hankow. (No. 107.) "Much used for the manufacture of rope and coarse bagging. The plant is cut, tied in small bundles, and packed in mud or water for about five days. The bark is then stripped off by hand and washed, and it is then ready for market." (*Brill.*)

6607. BRASSICA JUNCEA.   Chinese mustard.

From Wuchang. (No. 108.) "This seed is planted in August or September. Young plants are then transplanted to rows about 1 to 3 feet apart. The best is grown about Wuchang. Flower stalks are cut all winter continuously. They are eaten much like asparagus. Color, purple, but said to change to green after a season or two if the seed is planted in any other place." (*Brill.*)

6608. HOVENIA DULCIS.   Raisin tree.

From Hupeh Province. (No. 109.) "Large, handsome tree. The thickened, sweet seed stems are sold on the street, and the Chinese eat them after feasts of wine, saying they prevent the wine from making them drunk." (*Brill.*)

6609. PTEROCARYA STENOPTERA.   Wing nut.

From Hankow. (No. 100a.) "Large, quick-growing, soft-wooded tree, growing along streams. Planted on the Hankow Bend." (*Brill.*)

6610. BRASSICA PE-TSAI.   Chinese cabbage.

From Hsiang Yang. (No. 102a.) "Best cabbage of central China. Shipped down the river Han to Hankow in large quantities. Its successful growth appears limited to certain localities. Seeds sown late in April, then transplanted. A month before maturity a rice straw is often tied around the head to make it more compact." (*Brill.*)

6611. BRASSICA PE-TSAI.   Chinese cabbage.

From Hsiang Yang. (No. 103a.) "Same as No. 6610, only a larger variety." (*Brill.*)

6612. RAPHANUS SATIVUS.   Radish.

From Sui Chow. (No. 104a.) "Round, globe shaped, smooth, fine red color. Called a turnip by the Chinese and cooked in the same way." (*Brill.*)

6613. BRASSICA JUNCEA.   Chinese mustard.

From Sui Chow. (No. 105a.) "Top and root are salted much the same as sauerkraut and sold in all large towns." (*Brill.*)

6614. BRASSICA JUNCEA.   Chinese mustard.

(No. 106a.) "Produces very large leaves which are wilted in the sun and then pickled with salt. May be valuable as a food for sheep." (*Brill.*)

6615. DAUCUS CAROTA.   Carrot.

(No. 107a.) "Medium long, yellow. Sown in autumn and generally dug all winter." (*Brill.*)

6616. SPINACIA OLERACEA.   Spinach.

(No. 108a.) "Much used all winter." (*Brill.*)

6617. CHRYSANTHEMUM CORONARIUM.   Edible chrysanthemum.

(No. 109a.) "A plant much used, cooked with other vegetables." (*Brill.*)

6618. LACTUCA SATIVA.   Lettuce.

(No. 110.) "Stalk becomes much thickened and succulent, and is cooked as a vegetable. Leaves used only by very poor people. Foreign varieties are used around the ports." (*Brill.*)

6507 to 6646—Continued.

6619. ARTEMISIA sp.

(No. 111.) "Used as greens, cooked." (*Brill.*)

6620. CUCURBITA PEPO. Squash.

(No. 112.) "Long, green skinned, smooth. Flesh very white. Often weighs 65 pounds or more. Shipped to Hankow in large quantities." (*Brill.*)

6621. CUCURBITA PEPO. Squash.

(No. 113.) "Thick, fine skinned, dark yellow, very irregular in shape. Flesh thick, firm, and yellow." (*Brill.*)

6622. BRASSICA JUNCEA. Chinese mustard.

(No. 114.) "A large mustard that might have value for sheep food." (*Brill.*)

6623. INDIGOFERA TINCTORIA. Indigo.

(No. 115.)

6624. POLYGONUM sp.

(No. 116.) "Very dark color." (*Brill.*)

6625. SAPIUM SEBIFERUM. Tallow tree.

From Hankow. (No. 117.) "Seeds used for wax. Coating around the seed much harder than that in it. Tree has hard white wood, even grained. Used for carving, incense, etc. Much of the tallow is exported from Hankow." (*Brill.*)

6626. AVENA sp. Wild oat.

(No. 118.) "Grows wild or mixed with barley. Has long awns." (*Brill.*)

6627. RUBUS sp. Raspberry.

From Yang Tse Gorges, above Kuei Fu. (No. 119.) "Strong grower, prolific bearer. Fruit red, of good size and good flavor." (*Brill.*)

6628. RUBUS sp. Raspberry.

From near Kuling, near Kukiang. (No. 120.) "Said to be good as to size and quality." (*Brill.*)

6629. AMYGDALUS PERSICA. Peach.

(No. 121.) "Stones of several varieties." (*Brill.*)

6630. PRUNUS ARMENIACA. Apricot.

(No. 122.) "Stones of several varieties." (*Brill.*)

6631. PRUNUS CERASUS (?). Cherry.

(No. 123.)

6632. CANNA sp. Canna.

From Wau Hsien. (No. 124.) "Growing wild." (*Brill.*)

6633. THEA VIRIDIS. Tea.

From Yang To Seng. (No. 125.) "Seed from one of the best tea districts of China." (*Brill.*)

6634. CASTANEA sp. Chestnut.

(No. 126.) "Seed mixed, large and medium." (*Brill.*)

6507 to 6646—Continued.

6635. AMYGDALUS PERSICA. **Peach.**

From mountains near Ichang. (No. 127.) "Flowers late, fruit ripens in September. Freestone. Fruit small and quite hairy." (*Brill.*)

6636. CITRUS AURANTIUM. **Orange.**

(No. 128.) "Three varieties of orange seed." (*Brill.*)

6637. BOEHMERIA NIVEA. **Ramie.**

From near Wuchang. (No. 129.)

6638. BOEHMERIA NIVEA. **Ramie.**

From Hunan. (No. 130.) "These roots are from some brought from the best plantations of Hunan for the Viceroy Chang Chi Teng. Hunan is supposed to produce some of the best fiber of China." (*Brill.*)

6639. [Unidentified plant.]

From Loo Ho Ko, on Han River. (No. 131.) "Is cooked much as white potatoes are. Grown from pieces of the root." (*Brill.*)

6640. CITRUS AURANTIUM. **Orange.**

From Ichang. (No. 132.)

6641. CITRUS LIMONUM. **Lemon.**

From Ichang. (No. 133.) "Very juicy, fragrant, full of seeds, large, round, thick-skinned. Used by Chinese as a medicine." (*Brill.*)

6642. CITRUS NOBILIS. **Mandarin orange.**

From Wuchang. (No. 134.) "Medium size, loose-skinned orange, slightly sour." (*Brill.*)

6643. CITRUS MEDICA. **Citron.**

From Wuchang. (No. 135.) "Tight-skinned, round orange." (*Brill.*)

6644. CITRUS NOBILIS. **Mandarin orange.**

From Wuchang. (No. 136.) "Large, loose-skinned." (*Brill.*)

6645. CITRUS DECUMANA. **Pomelo.**

From Ichang. (No. 137.) "Small, white-fleshed."

6646. CITRUS DECUMANA. **Pomelo.**

From Ichang. (No. 138.) "Small, red-fleshed. Considered the best." (*Brill.*)

6647. CITRUS AURANTIUM. **Orange.**

From Corfu, Greece. Presented by Mr. Antonio Colla, through Mr. D. G. Fairchild (No. 533, February 12, 1901). Received May 21, 1901.

"A striking variety of orange which is extremely light in color, and according to Mr. Colla is called in Corfu '*Arancio con pello bianco.*' May be of value for breeders." (*Fairchild.*)

6648. FICUS CARICA. **Fig.**

From Corfu, Greece. Presented by Mr. Antonio Colla through Mr. D. G. Fairchild (No. 536, February 12, 1901). Received May 21, 1901.

"A variety of fig ripening its fruits in February when no leaves are on the tree. The fig is small, but very sweet, and it is very much relished by Europeans in Corfu. It is not a drying fig. Known in Corfu as '*Fico di Febbraio.*'" (*Fairchild.*)

6649. OLEA EUROPAEA. Olive.

From Corfu, Greece. Presented by Mr. Antonio Colla through Mr. D. G. Fairchild (No. 535, February 12, 1901). Received May 21, 1901.

"A variety of olive which is said to ripen its fruit in July instead of in October and at the same time to be a heavier yielder than the ordinary sorts grown in Corfu. Called '*Olivo di Estate*,' and I am assured by Mr. Colla, of Corfu, that this variety is known only in a small part of the island of Corfu." (*Fairchild.*)

6650. JUGLANS REGIA. Walnut.

From Corfu, Greece. Presented by Mr. Antonio Colla through Mr. D. G. Fairchild (No. 531, February 12, 1901). Received May 21, 1901.

"A very large variety of walnut grown at Paleocastritza, near the town of Corfu. The nut is of quite unusual proportions and the shell is said to be of only medium thickness. The thin skin of the kernel is also said to be less bitter than that of ordinary varieties." (*Fairchild.*)

6651. JUGLANS REGIA. Walnut.

From Corfu, Greece. Presented by Mr. Antonio Colla through Mr. D. G. Fairchild (No. 532, February 12, 1901). Received May 21, 1901.

"A variety of walnut having a shell so thin that it splits open of itself as the exocarp or outer covering dries, exposing the kernel within. An interesting house nut, but probably of little commercial value. May, however, be excellent for breeding purposes." (*Fairchild.*)

6652. JUGLANS REGIA. Walnut.

From Corfu, Greece. Received May 21, 1901.

(No data.)

6653. LINUM USITATISSIMUM. Flax.

From Kafr-el-Zayat, Egypt. Received through Mr. D. G. Fairchild (No. 607, April 18, 1901), May 21, 1901.

"The native Egyptian flax which, according to Mr. Bonaparte's experiments near Cairo, is much inferior to the Belgian imported variety. I can not say positively that this Egyptian variety used by Bonaparte was identical with this seed sent. The stems are long, not blanched near the ground, but of quite miniature and slender size compared with that from Belgian seed. For breeders only." (*Fairchild.*)

6654. CITRUS LIMONUM. Lemon.

From Cairo, Egypt. Received through Mr. D. G. Fairchild (No. 608, April 18, 1901), May 21, 1901.

Lemon beledi. "A native Egyptian lemon which is not grafted, but grown from seed. It comes true to seed, or reasonably so at any rate. It is a thin-skinned, very juicy variety and is keenly appreciated in Egypt, although a good Syrian variety is common there. This is valued for its great juiciness and wonderfully prolific character." (*Fairchild.*)

6655. GOSSYPIUM sp. Cotton.

From Cairo, Egypt. Received through Mr. D. G. Fairchild, May 21, 1901.

"Samples of a variety said to be growing wild in the Sudan, and also a sample from the Province of Tokar, in the Sudan, grown from seed sent up there from Lower Egypt last year to show the quality of Sudan-grown cotton." (*Fairchild.*)

6656. PYRUS MALUS. Apple.

Received through Hunter & Sons, Gosford, New South Wales, May 22, 1901.

Irish Peach.

6657. PAULOWNIA sp.

From China. Received through Dr. G. D. Brill (No. 101), May 17, 1901.

6658. HORDEUM VULGARE. **Barley.**

From the Han River, China. Received through Dr. G. D. Brill (No. 102½), May 17, 1901.

"From up the Han River, where it is used for food in place of rice." (*Brill.*)

6659. ACTINIDIA sp.

From China. Received through Mr. G. D. Brill, May 17, 1901.

6660. CRYPTOMERIA JAPONICA.

From Japan. Received through Tokyo Seed and Plant Company, Yokohama, May 22, 1901.

6661. DALBERGIA SISSOO.

From Cairo, Egypt. Received through Mr. D. G. Fairchild (No. 601, April 18, 1901), May 24, 1901.

"A rapidly growing, hard-wooded tree which is easily propagated by root cuttings. It is a pretty ornamental for warm regions, with delicate foliage of light green, and it is looked upon by the gardener near Cairo, Mr. Stamm, as one of the most promising avenue trees in Egypt. Personally I find that its shade-giving properties are too scanty to recommend it for this purpose. It will do well as a park or garden tree, however. It requires plenty of water and warmth." (*Fairchild.*)

6662. RHAMNUS CALIFORNICA. **Cascara sagrada.**

Presented by Prof. Jos. Burtt Davy, Berkeley, Cal. Received May 27, 1901.

The plant from which the drug cascara of commerce is secured.

6663. MAURANDIA BARCLAIANA.

Presented by Prof. Jos. Burtt Davy, Berkeley, Cal. Received May 27, 1901.

6664. MADIA SATIVA.

Presented by Prof. Jos. Burtt Davy, Berkeley, Cal. Received May 27, 1901.

6665. ELAEAGNUS LONGIPES. **Goumi.**

Presented by Prof. Jos. Burtt Davy, Berkeley, Cal. Received May 27, 1901.

6666. ACACIA RETINODES (?).

Presented by Prof. Jos. Burtt Davy, Berkeley, Cal. Received May 27, 1901.

In Kew Index synonymous with *A. neriifolia.*

6667. EUPHORBIA LATHYRIS.

Presented by Prof. Jos. Burtt Davy, Berkeley, Cal. Received May 27, 1901.

6668. STERCULIA DIVERSIFOLIA.

Presented by Prof. Jos. Burtt Davy, Berkeley, Cal. Received May 27, 1901.

6669. VICIA FABA. **Broad bean.**

Presented by Prof. Jos. Burtt Davy, Berkeley, Cal. Received May 27, 1901.

6670. VICIA GIGANTEA. **Vetch.**

Presented by Prof. Jos. Burtt Davy, Berkeley, Cal. Received May 27, 1901.

6671. CANNABIS INDICA. **Hemp.**

From Royal Botannical Garden, Sibpur, Calcutta, India. Received May 31, 1901.

6672. LARIX LEPTOLEPIS. **Japanese larch.**

From Japan. Received through Vilmorin Andrieux & Co., Paris, France, June 3, 1901.

6673 to 6678. GOSSYPIUM BARBADENSE. **Cotton.**

From Cairo, Egypt. Received through Mr. D. G. Fairchild (Nos. 600–605, April 18, 1901), June 10, 1901.

"A collection of cottons which have been selected by Christian Stamm, of Cairo, from fields of the Egyptian cotton and from his own experimental plats.

6673.

Mit Afifi. Selected cream color. First year of selection.

6674.

Very large growing variety, 2 to 2.50 meters high, bearing very large capsules. Grown in Stamm's garden in Cairo.

6675.

Jannovitch. Cream colored, selected from Stamm's own garden.

6676.

The descendant of a cross between a variety sent year before last to Mr. H. J. Webber and a variety called by Stamm "Berla." Shows tendency toward cream color.

6677.

Berla. Second generation. Selected from fields as the yellowest sort among many thousands. The yield of this sort was very high, even double that of many others grown in Stamm's garden.

6678.

"Wild cotton from Omdurman in the Sudan." (*Fairchild.*)

6679. GOSSYPIUM BARBADENSE. **Cotton.**

From Shibin-el-Kanater, Egypt. Received through Mr. D. G. Fairchild, June 10, 1901.

Mit Afifi. Ordinary variety.

6680. TRITICUM DURUM. **Wheat.**

From Minieh, Egypt. Received through Mr. D. G. Fairchild (No. 634, May 5, 1901), June 10, 1901.

Mishriki. "A very fine variety of this wheat which was exhibited last season at the Khedivial Agricultural Society's show in Cairo, and which Mr. George P. Foaden, the secretary of the society, remarked as the finest he has ever seen in Egypt. Secured through Mr. Foaden's kindness from the grower in the province of Minieh, which lies between the twenty-eighth and twenty-ninth degrees of latitude. The wheat is grown on irrigated land, and from all I can ascertain is remarkably pure, considering how mixed almost all Egyptian wheats are. This wheat will probably not withstand the cold winters of the pl- 'ns at all, but will very likely prove of great value in Texas. It is a hard wheat, whose qualities for macaroni making are quite unknown. Its yielding capacity, I believe, will prove satisfactory, although its resistance to rust, I surmise, may not equal that of other Egyptian sorts, for I notice the heads sent as samples are more or less rusted. Should be planted on soil receiving irrigation and tried as a *winter* wheat in the Southwest on good, rich, stiff soil." (*Fairchild.*) (See No. 7016.)

6681 to 6693.

From Alexandria, Egypt. Presented by the firm of B. Nathan & Co., through Mr. D. G. Fairchild. Received June 10, 1901. A collection of seeds of cultivated plants gathered in the Sudan by one of the firm.

6681. ANDROPOGON SORGHUM. Sorghum.

Kusabee, Arabic name.

6682. PANICUM MILIACEUM (?). Broom-corn millet.

"Coming from the River Dukhu." (*Fairchild.*)

6683. SESAMUM INDICUM. Sesame.

6684. GOSSYPIUM sp. Cotton.

A mixed lot of seed of different races and even species.

6685. ANDROPOGON SORGHUM. Sorghum.

"Very good quality." (*Fairchild.*)

6686. ANDROPOGON SORGHUM. Sorghum.

Aish Abou Girdeh, Arabic name.

6687. CICER ARIETINUM. Chick-pea.

Hummos, Arabic name.

6688. LUPINUS sp. Lupine.

Tirmoos, Arabic name.

6689. ANDROPOGON SORGHUM. Sorghum.

Hajiree, Arabic name.

6690. ANDROPOGON SORGHUM. Sorghum.

Hamaisee, Arabic name.

6691. ANDROPOGON SORGHUM. Sorghum.

Feterite, Arabic name.

6692. PANICUM MILIACEUM (?). Broom-corn millet.

Dukhu, Arabic name.

6693. ANDROPOGON SORGHUM. Sorghum.

Safra, Arabic name.

6694 to 6711.

From Pekin, China. Received through Dr. G. D. Brill, June 12, 1901. A collection of seeds of cultivated plants, as follows:

6694. CUCUMIS SATIVUS. Cucumber.

"This forcing cucumber is grown with heat during the winter. Many specimens were from 1 foot to 18 inches long, very crisp, and of good quality. Each had a small weight attached to it after it was an inch and a half long to keep it straight." (*Brill.*)

6695. CUCURBITA sp. Squash.

6696. SOLANUM MELONGENA. Eggplant.

"Large, purple, of very fine quality." (*Brill.*)

6697. CUCUMIS MELO. Muskmelon.

"Said to be of very good quality." (*Brill.*)

6694 to 6711—Continued.

6698. CUCURBITA sp. **Squash.**

"Flesh very white, much used by Chinese, cooked with meat or alone." (*Brill.*)

6699. RAPHANUS SATIVUS. **Radish.**

"Large, red, flat variety, resembling a turnip. Kept through the winter and much eaten raw, as well as cooked." (*Brill.*)

6700. RAPHANUS SATIVUS. **Radish.**

6701. RAPHANUS SATIVUS. **Radish.**

"A winter variety." (*Brill.*)

6702. RAPHANUS SATIVUS. **Radish.**

"A forcing variety, grown under mats or under benches in cucumber houses. It is sold in bunches when small. Globe shaped. It is also grown very thickly and the young radishes are pulled when about to send out the third leaf. For use in salads." (*Brill.*)

6703. RAPHANUS SATIVUS. **Radish.**

"Small, long, red variety." (*Brill.*)

6704. RAPHANUS SATIVUS. **Radish.**

"Long, white variety." (*Brill.*)

6705. BRASSICA OLERACEA. **Cabbage.**

"A very long-headed cabbage, 3 to 5 inches in diameter. The quality is said by foreigners to be excellent. Some say it has a very delicate flavor and can be eaten without causing indigestion by people who can not eat the 'foreign' cabbage." (*Brill.*)

6706. DAUCUS CAROTA. **Carrot.**

6707. APIUM GRAVEOLENS. **Celery.**

"Not very good in comparison with foreign varieties, but better than that of central China." (*Brill.*)

6708. CUCURBITA sp. **Gourd.**

"Hard shells used for drinking cups, etc." (*Brill.*)

6709. PANICUM MILIACEUM. **Broom-corn millet.**

"Much used in the place of rice by the people around Pekin. Cooked as porridge." (*Brill.*)

6710. ANDROPOGON SORGHUM. **Sorghum.**

"This is much grown for human food around Pekin and is considered much superior to the other varieties." (*Brill.*)

6711. PANICUM MILIACEUM. **Broom-corn millet.**

"This variety is said to withstand drought well." (*Brill.*)

6712. COFFEA ARABICA. **Coffee.**

From Macassar, Celebes, Dutch East Indies. Presented by Mr. K. Auer, U. S. Consular Agent at Macassar, through Messrs. Lathrop and Fairchild. (No. 385.) Received June 12, 1901.

Patjoe or *Bonthain*. A superior variety of coffee grown in southern Celebes.

6713 to 6730. PYRUS MALUS. **Apple.**

From Gosford, New South Wales. Received through Hunter & Sons, June 19, 1901.

A collection of varieties, as follows:

6713.
Fall Beauty.

6714.
Winter Majetin.

6715.
Autumn Tart.

6716.
Lord Wolseley.

6717.
Ruby Pearmain.

6718.
Golden Queen.

6719.
Northern Spy.

6720.
Menagerie.

6721.
Striped Beaufin.

6722.
Yarra Bank.

6723.
Chataslee.

6724.
Magg's Seedling.

6725.
Early Richmond.

6726.
Tetofsky.

6727.
Primate.

6728.
New England Pigeon.

6729.
Stubbard Codlin.

6730.
Irish Peach.

6731 to 6753. PYRUS MALUS. **Apple.**

From Emerald, Victoria. Received through Mr. C. A. Nobelius, June 19, 1901.

A collection of varieties, as follows:

6731.
Sharp's Early.

6732.
Cole's Rymer.

6733.
William Anderson.

6734.
Kooroochiang.

6735.
John Sharp.

6736.
Cliff's Seedling.

6737.
Santa Clara King.

6738.
Granny Smith.

6739.
Sharp's Late Red.

6740.
Ruby Gem.

6741.
Northern Spy.

6742.
Statesman.

6743.
Winter Majetin.

6744.
Early Richmond.

6731 to 6753—Continued.

6745.
Sharp's Nonesuch.

6746.
Ruby Pearmain.

6747.
Fall Beauty.

6748.
Irish Peach.

6749.
Magg's Seedling.

6750.
Lord Wolseley.

6751.
The Queen.

6752.
Shroeder's.

6753.
Taupaki.

6754 to 6772. PYRUS MALUS. **Apple.**

From Camden, New South Wales. Received from Ferguson & Son, June 19, 1901.
A collection of varieties, all grafted on Northern Spy stocks, as follows:

6754.
Striped Beaufin.

6755.
Golden Queen.

6756.
New England Pigeon.

6757.
Chatastee.

6758.
American Golden Pippin.

6759.
Menagerie.

6760.
Stubbart Codlin.

6761.
Ruby Pearmain.

6762.
Primate.

6763.
Lord Wolseley.

6764.
Yarra Bank.

6765.
Northern Spy.

6766.
Autumn Tart.

6767.
Winter Majetin.

6768.
Irish Peach.

6769.
Magg's Seedling.

6770.
Tetofsky.

6771.
Early Richmond.

6772.
Fall Beauty.

6773 to 6823. FICUS CARICA. **Caprifig.**

From Kabylia, Algeria. Received through Mr. C. S. Scofield, June 19, 1901.
"This collection, secured by Mr. Scofield in the spring of 1901, consists of cuttings of all the caprifig trees he observed in the vicinity of Tizi Ouzou and Fort National in the mountainous part of Kabylia to the east of the town of Algiers. No data could be secured in regard to most of the numbers and some may prove to be duplicates. All of the 50 numbers are caprifigs, with the exception of 6819, which is an ordinary

edible fig. This collection, as well as those enumerated before in this inventory, was secured in the hope of getting an assortment of caprifigs having as wide a range of climatic and soil requirements as possible, in the hope of finding varieties suited to harbor the blastophaga in all parts of California and the Southwest where fig culture is feasible. These varieties are on trial in the Department gardens, and will be distributed when their qualities have been determined." (*Swingle.*)

6773.

"Cuttings from tree No. 18, growing along road from Fort National to Tizi Ouzou." (*Scofield.*)

6774.

"Cuttings from tree No. 11, growing along road from Fort National to Tizi Ouzou." (*Scofield.*)

6775.

"Cuttings from a large tree (No. 33) in the rich bottom lands about a mile or two beyond Tizi Ouzou on the way from Fort National." (*Scofield.*)

6776.

"Cuttings from tree No. 12 along the road from Fort National to Tizi Ouzou." (*Scofield.*)

6777.

"Cuttings from a large and very fine orchard above Mr. Bankhardt's mill, 4 or 5 miles out of Tizi Ouzou on the road to Fort National." (*Scofield.*)

6778.

"Cuttings from a large and very fine orchard just above Mr. Bankhardt's mill, 4 or 5 miles out from Tizi Ouzou on the road to Fort National." (*Scofield.*)

6779.

"Cuttings from tree No. 22 along the road from Fort National to Tizi Ouzou." (*Scofield.*)

6780.

"Cuttings from tree No. 23 along the road from Fort National to Tizi Ouzou." (*Scofield.*)

6781.

"Cuttings from a tree in large and very fine orchard above the mill belonging to Mr. Bankhardt, 4 or 5 miles out from Tizi Ouzou on the road to Fort National." (*Scofield.*)

6782.

"Cuttings from tree No. 10 along the road from Fort National to Tizi Ouzou." (*Scofield.*)

6783.

"Cuttings from tree No. 14 along road from Fort National to Tizi Ouzou. (Possibly *Ghazarh, early*. Cuttings from tree in immediate vicinity of Tizi Ouzou. Label lost.)" (*Scofield.*)

6784.

"Cuttings from tree No. 21 along the road from Fort National to Tizi Ouzou." (*Scofield.*)

6785.

"Cuttings from tree No. 6 on the road from Fort National to Tizi Ouzou." (*Scofield.*)

6773 to 6823—Continued.

6786.

"Cuttings from a large and very fine orchard just above Mr. Bankhardt's mill, 4 or 5 miles out from Tizi Ouzou on the road to Fort National." (*Scofield.*)

6787.

"Cuttings from tree No. 24 along the road from Fort National to Tizi Ouzou." (*Scofield.*)

6788.

"Cuttings from tree No. 13 along the road from Fort National to Tizi Ouzou, near Fort National." (*Scofield.*)

6789.

Dhaalou, No. 1. "Cuttings from tree on north side of valley in the immediate vicinity of Tizi Ouzou." (*Scofield.*)

6790.

"Cuttings from tree No. 15 along the road from Fort National to Tizi Ouzou." (*Scofield.*)

6791.

"Cuttings from very fine large tree growing in rich bottom lands a mile or so beyond Tizi Ouzou." (*Scofield.*)

6792.

"Cuttings from tree No. 7 along the road from Fort National to Tizi Ouzou." (*Scofield.*)

6793.

Ghazar, No. 1, an early variety. "Cuttings from tree in immediate vicinity of Tizi Ouzou. (Possibly another kind, No. 14, from tree along road from Fort National to Tizi Ouzou. Label missing.)" (*Scofield.*)

6794.

"Cuttings from tree near Fort National, on the other side (from Tizi Ouzou). Tree still carried the winter fruit in considerable numbers." (*Scofield.*)

6795.

"Cuttings from tree in orchard in rich bottom lands a mile or two beyond Tizi Ouzou (from Fort National), tree of medium size." (*Scofield.*)

6796.

"Cuttings from a tree, No. 25, along the road from Fort National to Tizi Ouzou." (*Scofield.*)

6797.

"Cuttings from tree No. 4 along the road from Fort National to Tizi Ouzou." (*Scofield.*)

6798.

"Cuttings from tree No. 19 along the road from Fort National to Tizi Ouzou." (*Scofield.*)

6799.

"Cuttings from tree No. 17 along road from Fort National to Tizi Ouzou." (*Scofield.*)

6773 to 6823—Continued.

6800.

"Cuttings from tree No. 16 along road from Fort National to Tizi Ouzou." (*Scofield.*)

6801.

Ghazar, No. 3. "Cuttings obtained from large tree, south side of the valley, in immediate vicinity of Tizi Ouzou, rather late." (*Scofield.*)

6802.

"Cuttings from tree No. 8 along the road from Fort National to Tizi Ouzou." (*Scofield.*)

6803.

Texcout, No. 1. "Early variety. Cuttings from tree on north side of valley in the immediate vicinity of Tizi Ouzou." (*Scofield.*)

6804.

"Cuttings from tree on other side of Fort National from Tizi Ouzou. Worthy of mention, as they still carried the winter fruit in considerable numbers—both old and new fruits." (*Scofield.*)

6805.

"Cuttings from tree No. 20 along road from Fort National to Tizi Ouzou." (*Scofield.*)

6806.

"Cuttings from tree on south side of valley in the immediate vicinity of Tizi Ouzou. Name unknown; season medium, intermediate." (*Scofield.*)

6807.

Dhaalou, No. 2. "Cuttings from tree in immediate vicinity of Tizi Ouzou, from north side of valley." (*Scofield.*)

6808.

"Cuttings from a very fine, large tree in orchard in the rich bottom lands a mile or two beyond Tizi Ouzou from Fort National." (*Scofield.*)

6809.

Marza-Ko. "Cuttings from tree on north side of valley in the immediate vicinity of Tizi Ouzou." (*Scofield.*)

6810.

Dhaalou, No. 3. "Cuttings from tree on north side of valley in the immediate vicinity of Tizi Ouzou." (*Scofield.*)

6811.

Ahzaim (2). Late. "Cuttings from tree on north side of valley in immediate vicinity of Tizi Ouzou." (*Scofield.*)

6812.

"Cuttings from tree No. 9 along the road from Fort National to Tizi Ouzou." (*Scofield.*)

6813.

Ahzaim, No. 1. Late. "Cuttings from tree on north side of valley in immediate vicinity of Tizi Ouzou." (*Scofield.*)

6773 to 6823—Continued.

6814.

"Cuttings from tree No. 1, near Fort National, on road to Tizi Ouzou." (*Scofield.*)

6815.

Texkourt (short form). Late. "Cuttings from tree on south side of valley in the immediate vicinity of Tizi Ouzou." (*Scofield.*)

6816.

"Cuttings from tree in a large and very fine orchard just above a flour and oil mill belonging to Mr. Bankhardt. It is 4 or 5 miles out of Tizi Ouzou, on the road to Fort National." (*Scofield.*)

6817.

"Cuttings from a small, scraggy, but heavily fruited tree in orchard in the rich bottom lands a mile or two beyond Tizi Ouzou." (*Scofield.*)

6818.

"Cuttings from medium-sized trees in orchard in the rich bottom lands a mile or two beyond Tizi Ouzou." (*Scofield.*)

6819.

Bakor (not a caprifig). "Excellent tree. Cuttings from tree south of Tizi Ouzou." (*Scofield.*)

6820.

Tetouzel, No. 1. Early. (Spelled Teefouzel or Trefouzel.) "Cuttings from tree on south side of valley in the immediate vicinity of Tizi Ouzou." (*Scofield.*)

6821.

"Cuttings from tree No. 5 on the road from Fort National to Tizi Ouzou." (*Scofield.*)

6822.

"Cuttings from tree south of Tizi Ouzou." (*Scofield.*)

6823.

Ain Hjedjla. "Season medium. Cuttings from tree north of Tizi Ouzou." (*Scofield.*)

6824. PISTACIA VERA. **Pistache.**

From Smyrna, Asia Minor. Received through Mr. George C. Roeding, June 29, 1901.

"Very fine pistache nut from a Greek nurseryman in Smyrna." (*Roeding.*)

6825. TRIFOLIUM SPUMOSUM.

From Mustapha Superieur, near Algiers, Algeria. Received through Mr. C. S. Scofield, May 25, 1901.

"Seed from a plant found in the grounds of the former consulate of Denmark. They are from an especially fine plant and can not be easily replaced." (*Scofield.*)

6826. VERONIA ELEPHANTUM (?)

From Cairo, Egypt. Received through Mr. D. G. Fairchild (No. 609), May 24, 1901.

"A very pretty shade tree, suitable for planting in southern Florida or southern California. It grows and fruits well in the gardens in Cairo and is considered a desirable ornamental tree for parks." (*Fairchild.*)

114

6827. ZEA MAYS. **Corn.**

From Cairo, Egypt. Received through Mr. D. G. Fairchild (No. 624), July 1, 1901.

Secured for Mr. Fairchild by George P. Foaden, esq., secretary of the Khedivial Agricultural Society of Cairo.

Morelli. "It is a low-growing sort and does not exhaust the soil as the tall-growing American kinds do. As much as 80 bushels per acre are harvested in Egypt. It has been tested in comparison with the following American sorts and yielded heavier and twenty days earlier: *Morelli*, the Egyptian sort, yielded 12$\frac{4}{8}$ ardebs per feddan; *Tender and True*, an American variety, yielded 11$\frac{4}{8}$; *Hickory King*, also American, 10; and *Imperial Leaming* only 9 ardebs. (These are Egyptian units, given only for comparison.) It is a white variety, preferred to most others in Egypt because of its extreme earliness and great productivity. It grows scarcely half as high as the American sorts. Here in Egypt the maize is broadcasted very thickly, much as we plant fodder maize. The hill system is little known. Perhaps this and the irrigation system used in the comparative test may account for the comparatively high yield of the Egyptian. This variety should be tried in irrigated regions, such as those of southern California, and a quantity should be reserved for experiments in the Colorado Desert." (*Fairchild.*)

6828. QUEBRACHIA LORENTZII. **Quebracho colorado.**

From Tucuman, Argentina. Presented by Mr. Joel Blamey, Huasan, Andalgalá Catamarca, Argentina. Received July 5, 1901.

"Large handsome trees, 40 to 50 feet high, found in the heavy river bottom forests of Argentina and Paraguay, not yet introduced into this country. The wood is of a red color, very hard, contains from 25 to 28 per cent of tannin, and is impervious to weather conditions. Logs exposed for a hundred years are still sound. It is used in Argentina for beams in house and bridge building, railroad ties, all kinds of posts, and for tannin. There were imported into the United States in 1901 60,000 tons of extract, worth nearly $300,000. Klipstein & Co., New York, state that 240,000 tons of wood are also imported annually." (*Harrison.*)

6829. **Ebony tree.**

From Tucuman, Argentina. Received through Mr. Joel Blamey, Huasan, Andalgalá Catamarca, Argentina, July 5, 1901.

6830. **Viraris.**

From Tucuman, Argentina. Received through Mr. Joel Blamey, Huasan, Andalgalá Catamarca, Argentina, July 5, 1901.

6831. OLEA EUROPAEA. **Olive.**

From Tunis, nurseries of M. G. Castet. Presented by Dr. L. Trabut, Government Botanist of Algeria, through Mr. C. S. Scofield. Received July 2, 1901.

Chetoni or *Octonbri*. This is described by N. Minangoin as an oil olive "very common in northern Tunis at Tunis, Soliman, Tebourba, Bizerte, and Grombalia, where it enters to at least the extent of two-thirds into the composition of the olive orchards." (*Bulletin de la Direction de l'Agriculture et du Commerce, Regence de Tunis 6 No. 8, January, 1901, p. 35, pl. 6, fig. 11.*)

6832. FICUS CARICA. **Caprifig.**

From Aidin, Asia Minor. Received through Mr. George C. Roeding, July 5, 1901.

"Very large caprifig from S. G. Magnisalis, Aidin." (*Roeding.*)

6833. QUERCUS AEGILOPS. **Valonia oak.**

From Nazli, Province of Smyrna, Asia Minor. Received through Mr. George C. Roeding, July 5, 1901.

This species of evergreen oak is the one furnishing the "Valonia" of commerce, one of the best tanning materials known. The acorn cups are the parts containing the tannin.

6834. OLEA EUROPAEA. **Olive.**

From Aidin, Asia Minor. Received through George C. Roeding, July 5, 1901.

Early Aidin olive grown in the Meander Valley for oil. There must be 5,000,000 rees in this valley.

6835. FICUS CARICA. **Caprifig.**

From Aidin, Asia Minor. Received through Mr. George C. Roeding, June 5, 1901.

"Very largest and finest caprifig from S. G. Magnisalis, Aidin." (*Roeding.*)

6836. FICUS CARICA. **Caprifig.**

From Aidin, Asia Minor. Received through Mr. George C. Roeding, July 5, 1901.

"One of the largest caprifigs from S. G. Magnisalis, Aidin." (*Roeding.*)

6837. FICUS CARICA. **Caprifig.**

From Aidin, Asia Minor. Received through Mr. George C. Roeding, July 5, 1901.

"Another variety of black caprifig from S. G. Magnisalis, Aidin." (*Roeding.*)

6838. FICUS CARICA. **Caprifig.**

From Aidin, Asia Minor. Received through Mr. George C. Roeding, July 5, 1901.

"Very fine caprifig from garden of S. G. Magnisalis, Aidin." (*Roeding.*)

6839. FICUS CARICA. **Caprifig.**

From Aidin, Asia Minor. Received through Mr. George C. Roeding, July 5, 1901.

"Black caprifig from garden of S. G. Magnisalis, Aidin." (*Roeding.*)

6840. FICUS CARICA. **Caprifig.**

From Aidin, Asia Minor. Received through Mr. George C. Roeding, July 5, 1901.

"Loose sample to show method of budding, inclosed with Nos. 6838 and 6839." (*Roeding.*)

6841. PRUNUS ARMENIACA. **Apricot.**

From Aidin, Asia Minor. Received through Mr. George C. Roeding, July 5, 1901.

"A small freestone apricot, having a very sweet kernel, with a flavor like an almond." (*Roeding.*)

6842. MEIBOMIA ILLINOENSIS. **Beggar weed.**

From Manhattan, Kans. Presented by Mr. J. M. Westgate. Received July 8, 1901.

A leguminous plant, possibly of some value for forage or green manure, which grows on the prairie lands of central Kansas. Seed ripens in summer and autumn. This sample was collected in the autumn of 1900.

6843. PUNICA GRANATUM. **Pomegranate.**

From Smyrna, Asia Minor. Received through Mr. George C. Roeding, July 8, 1901.

Schekerdekses. "Seedless pomegranate." (*Roeding.*)

6844. PRUNUS ARMENIACA. **Apricot.**

From Smyrna, Asia Minor. Received through Mr. George C. Roeding, July 8, 1901.

"A very large apricot, growing in the garden of Doctor Lane, American consul, Smyrna. Kernel sweet." (*Roeding.*)

6845. PRUNUS ARMENIACA. **Apricot.**

From Smyrna, Asia Minor. Received through Mr. George C. Roeding, July 8, 1901.

"A large freestone apricot, having sweet kernels like an almond" (*Roeding.*)

6846. PHOENIX DACTYLIFERA. **Date.**

From Orleansville, Algeria. Presented by M. Yahia ben Kassem. Received May, 1901.

Deglet Noor.

6847. POPULUS sp. **Poplar.**

From Kephisia, near Athens, Greece. Received through Mr. George C. Roeding, July 17, 1901.

"A poplar resembling the silver leaf in foliage, but with smaller leaves. Tree very vigorous and of spreading habit. Superior to any poplar I have ever seen. I saw one tree 6 feet in diameter, whose estimated height was 125 feet, and which had a spread of branches of 80 feet." (*Roeding.*)

6848. MORUS sp. **Mulberry.**

From Royal Grounds, Kephisia, near Athens, Greece. Received through Mr. George C. Roeding, July 17, 1901.

"A variety of mulberry with large, dark-green, rough leaves, no gloss, and having very fine fruit." (*Roeding.*)

6849. PISTACIA VERA. **Pistache.**

From Athens, Greece. Received through Mr. George C. Roeding, July 17, 1901.

"Buds of a very fine pistache nut from the garden of the agricultural experiment station at Athens." (*Roeding.*)

6850. FICUS CARICA. **Caprifig.**

From Kephisia, near Athens, Greece. Received through Mr. George C. Roeding, July 17, 1901.

"A late fruiting variety of caprifig." (*Roeding.*)

6851 to 6912.

From Oneco, Fla. Received through the firm of Reasoner Brothers, July 5, 1901.

A collection of ornamental and economic plants (nomenclature is in the main that of the nurserymen):

    6851. ABERIA CAFFRA.   **Kei apple.**

    6852. ANACARDIUM OCCIDENTALE.   **Cashew.**

    6853. ANONA MURICATA.   **Sour sop.**

    6854. ARTOCARPUS INTEGRIFOLIA.   **Jack fruit.**

    6855. COCCOLOBA UVIFERA.   **Shore grape.**

6851 to 6912—Continued.

6856. CUPANIA SAPIDA. **Akee.**

"The fruits are said to be delicious when eaten in omelettes." (*Fairchild.*)

6857. FICUS GLOMERATA. **Cluster fig.**

6858. MALPIGHIA GLABRA. **Barbados cherry.**

6859. MELICOCCA BIJUGA. **Spanish lime.**

6860. PHYLLANTHUS EMBLICA. **Emblic myrobalan.**

"This is not the true myrobalan of commerce, although its fruits are used for tanning purposes, according to Talbot." (*Trees, Shrubs, and Woody Climbers of the Bombay Presidency*, 2d ed., p. 300.)

6861. SPONDIAS DULCIS. **Otaheite apple.**

6862. TERMINALIA CATAPPA. **Tropical almond.**

6863. RHODOMYRTUS TOMENTOSA. **Downy myrtle.**

6864. AMOMUM CARDAMOMUM. **Cardamom.**

6865. CEDRELA ODORATA. **Jamaica cedar.**

6866. CEDRELA TOONA. **Toon tree.**

6867. CINNAMOMUM CASSIA. **Chinese cinnamon.**

6868. CRESCENTIA CUJETE. **Calabash tree.**

6869. GARCINIA MORELLA. **Gamboge.**

6870. GUAIACUM OFFICINALE. **Lignum-vitæ.**

6871. LAWSONIA ALBA. **Henna.**

6872. MARANTA ARUNDINACEA. **Bermuda arrowroot.**

6873. DITTELASMA RARAK. **Indian soap berry.**

6874. SEMECARPUS ANACARDIUM. **Marking nut tree.**

6875. ZINGIBER OFFICINALE. **Ginger.**

6876. CUPRESSUS FUNEBRIS. **Funeral cypress.**

6877. ABRUS PRECATORIUS. **Crab's eye vine.**

6878. ARDISIA POLYCEPHALA.

6879. BAPHIA RACEMOSA.

6880. BAUHINIA ACUMINATA. **Mountain ebony.**

6881. BAUHINIA GALPINI.

6882. BRUNFELSIA MACROPHYLLA.

6883. BUTEA FRONDOSA. **Bastard teak.**

6884. POINCIANA REGIA. **Royal poinciana.**

6885. CAESALPINIA PULCHERRIMA. **Dwarf poinciana.**

6851 to 6912—Continued.

6886. CAESALPINIA SAPPAN. **Sappan.**

"The pods and hard wood of this plant yield the valuable red dye used in coloring silk. A native of the Asiatic tropics." .(*Talbot.*)

6887. DILLENIA INDICA. **Gunstock tree.**

"Native of India. Ripe fruit eaten in curries. Wood durable, used for gunstocks." (*Talbot.*)

6888. DRACAENA DRACO. **Dragon's blood.**

Native of the Canary Islands, where, until recently, a noted tree of great age and size was standing. A valuable and curious ornamental for parks.

6889. FICUS HISPIDA.

6890. HIBISCUS TILIACEUS.

"Fiber used in India for the manufacture of elephant timber-dragging ropes." (*Talbot.*)

6891. JACQUINIA ARMILLARIS.

6892. MABA NATALENSIS.

6893. THEVETIA NEREIFOLIA. **Trumpet flower.**

6894. ATALANTIA TRIMERA.

6895. TURRAEA FLORIBUNDA (?)

6896. TUTSIA AMBOSENSIS.

(Not in Kew Index.)

6897. TODDALIA LANCEOLATA.

6898. ACROCOMIA SCLEROCARPA.

6899. ATTALEA COHUNE.

6900. CARYOTA URENS.

6901. CHAMAEROPS HUMILIS.

6902. CHAMAEROPS HUMILIS var. SPINOSA.

6903. CHAMAEROPS FARINOSA.

(Not in Kew Index.)

6904. RHAPIDOPHYLLUM HYSTRIX.

6905. COCOS AUSTRALIS.

6906. COCOS ALPHONSEI.

6907. COCOS BONNETI.

6908. ELAEIS GUINEENSIS. **Oil palm.**

6909. BACTRIS GASIPAËS.

6910. BACTRIS UTILIS.

6911. LICUALA GRANDIS.

6912. LICUALA RUMPHII.

6913 to 6932.

From Mexico. Received through Dr. J. N. Rose, assistant curator, U. S. National Museum, July 9 and 10, 1901.

A collection of Mexican ornamentals and economic plants, many of which have not been specifically identified; made in 1901 by Dr. J. N. Rose. No further data than Doctor Rose's numbers and the generic names were at hand when this inventory was prepared.

6913. OXALIS sp. (No. 207.)

6914. OXALIS sp. (No. 208.)

6915. OXALIS sp. (No. 209.)

6916. OXALIS sp. (No. 210.)

6917. OXALIS sp. (No. 211.)

6918. OXALIS sp. (No. 212.)

6919. HYMENOCALLIS HARRISONIANA. (No. 222.)

6920. (No. 213.) **"Pepo."**

6913 to 6932—Continued.

- **6921.** Cissus sp. (No. 201.)
- **6922.** Echeveria platyphylla, Rose, n. sp. (No. 202.)
- **6923.** Echeveria maculata, Rose, n. sp. (No. 217.)
- **6924.** Fouquieria splendens. (No. 205.)
- **6925.** Zephyranthes sp. (No. 206.)
- **6926.** Zephyranthes sp. (No. 214.)
- **6927.** Ampelopsis sp. (No. 215).
- **6928.** Tradescantia crassifolia. (No. 216.)
- **6929.** Sedum sp. (No. 218.)
- **6930.** Solanum sp. (No. 219.)
- **6931.** Erythrina sp. (No. 220.)
- **6932.** Tillandsia sp. (No. 221.)

6933 to 6958.

From Malta. Received through Mr. D. G. Fairchild, July 9 and 10, 1901.

A collection of figs, loquats, pomegranates, and citrous fruits secured during a short stay in Malta in May, 1901. In most cases scions only were sent.

6933. Ficus carica. Fig.
A large white variety. (No. 685e.)

6934. Ficus carica. Fig.
(No. 685.)

6935. Punica granatum. Pomegranate.
(No. 679.)

6936. Punica granatum. Pomegranate.
(No. 677.)

6937. Punica granatum. Pomegranate.
St. Catherine. (No. 673.)

6938. Eriobotrya japonica. Loquat.
(No. 681.)

6939. Eriobotrya japonica. Loquat.
(No. 684.)

6940. Punica granatum. Pomegranate.
St. Joseph. (No. 674.)

6941. Ficus carica. Fig.
Xehba. (No. 685c.)

6942. Ficus carica. Fig.
Barnisotte. (No. 685f.)

6943. Eriobotrya japonica. Loquat.
(No. 680.)

6944. Punica granatum. Pomegranate.
Santa Rosa. (No. 675.)

6945. Eriobotrya japonica. Loquat.
(No. 682.)

6933 to 6958—Continued.

6946. FICUS CARICA. **Fig.**

Black Parsot or *Barnisotte*. (No. 685d.)

6947. CITRUS AURANTIUM. **Orange.**

"The *round* blood orange of the island of Malta. This variety has nearly always a blood-colored flesh and is one of the best strains of oranges on the island. Probably originated here or was brought here at a very early date. It is quite distinct from No. 6948 and not esteemed so highly." (*Fairchild.*)

6948. CITRUS AURANTIUM. **Orange.**

"An *oval* blood orange, said by Dr. Giovanni Borg, a specialist in citrous matters in Malta, to be the finest flavored orange on the island. Personally I find it superior to No. 6947 and unparalleled for its remarkably vinous flavor." (*Fairchild.*)

6949. ERIOBOTRYA JAPONICA. **Loquat.**

"Seeds of some very large loquats from Bosketto Gardens, Malta, collected May 22, 1901." (*Fairchild.*)

6950. CITRUS AURANTIUM. **Orange.**

Maltese *oval seedless*. "Cuttings taken from trees in the governor's palace grounds in Malta. This is the best known seedless Malta orange. My experience is that it sometimes has a few seeds or rudiments of seeds in it. By many it is thought to be the best orange in Malta." (*Fairchild.*)

6951. CITRUS LIMETTA. **Lime.**

"A variety of lime growing in the gardens of San Antonio near Valetta. The origin of this variety is unknown by Doctor Borg, the citrus specialist. The fruits are almost without exception quite seedless and attain a very considerable size for limes, being often 3 inches long by 2¼ inches in smaller diameter. Doctor Borg says that owing to the peculiar flavor (a typical lime flavor) this is not appreciated in Malta, people preferring forms *with* seeds. It is a very juicy sort, with thinnish rind, and of a good color. Possibly this is the same as that sent in by Mr. Swingle (No. 3412) from Algiers. The trees are very vigorous here, even strikingly so. They commonly bear only one crop of fruit, but occasionally two crops are produced. A single fruit yielded one-fourth of an ordinary drinking glass full of juice of good flavor. Secured through the kindness of Dr. Giovanni Borg, of San Antonio Gardens, at the governor's palace." (*Fairchild.*)

6952. FICUS CARICA. **Fig.**

Tin Baitri or *St. Johns*. "Precocious fig, two cropper." (*Fairchild.*) (No. 685h.)

6953. FICUS CARICA. **Fig.**

Tina baida. (No. 685b.)

6954. CITRUS AURANTIUM. **Orange.**

Lumi-laring. "A remarkable variety of orange otherwise known as the Sweet orange or China orange. It is *always sweet even when quite green and immature*. Doctor Bonavia, well known as a specialist on the oranges of India, speaks of this variety in a recent article in the Journal of the Royal Horticultural Society, April, 1901 (Vol. XXV, pt. 3, p. 308). He remarks: 'I am informed that in Malta there exists a unique orange of the same (Portugal orange) group, but which is never sour from beginning to end, but sweet and juicy. * * * I have never met with an orange of this description in India. It would be worth while getting hold of it for the purpose of multiplying it and bringing it into commerce. Such a unique orange, I believe, has never appeared on the English market.' In Malta this orange is not very highly esteemed, and personally I find it not nearly so agreeable as the sour varieties, but nevertheless it is far superior to an immature sour orange. It is as sweet as sugar and water, and is declared to be just as sweet when half grown as when mature. It may have a decided value commercially, and will find many

6933 to 6958—Continued.

who will appreciate it. If it proves to be early ripening enough it might be sent to market much in advance of the sour sorts, when it would surprise all buyers by its sweet flavor at a time when all other varieties were too sour to be appreciated. It is medium in size, globular in shape, skin good and of fair thickness, flesh fine color and juicy, and color medium dark orange." (*Fairchild.*)

6955. ERIOBOTRYA JAPONICA. Loquat.
(No. 683.)

6956. FICUS CARICA. Fig.
(No. 685g.)

6957. FICUS CARICA. Caprifig.
Duccar. (No. 686.)

6958. ERIOBOTRYA JAPONICA. Loquat.
Seeds of large fruits.

6959. TRITICUM sp. Wheat.

From Shibin-el-Kanatir, Egypt. Received through Mr. D. G. Fairchild (No. 653, May 11, 1901), July 11, 1901.

"A collection of selected typical races of Egyptian wheat, gathered from the fields about a small village between Zagazig and Cairo. These are the best, and they show how mixed the races of Egyptian wheat are, but at the same time how remarkably free from rust. The wheat was mostly dead ripe when gathered May 7, while American sorts grown at Cairo were several weeks behind. All grown by perennial irrigation." (*Fairchild.*)

6960. CITRUS LIMONUM. Lemon.

From Chios, Turkey. Presented by Mr. N. J. Pantelides through Mr. D. G. Fairchild (No. 590, March 23, 1901). Received July 17, 1901.

Paffa. "A variety of almost seedless lemon, grown in the island of Chios." (*Fairchild.*)

6961 to 6977.

From Rouïba, Algeria. Received through Mr. C. S. Scofield.

A collection of the root tubercles of a number of leguminous forage plants collected by Mr. C. S. Scofield in May, 1901, at Dr. L. Trabut's experimental gardens.

6961. VICIA FABA.
　　Horse bean.

6962. VICIA LUTEA.

6963. TRIGONELLA FOENUM-GRAECUM.

6964. ASTRAGALUS BOETICUS.

6965. MELILOTUS INFESTA.

6966. ONOBRYCHIS VICIAEFOLIA.
　　Sainfoin.

6967. ANTHYLLIS TETRAPHYLLA.

6968. ANTHYLLIS TETRAPHYLLA.

6969. SCORPIURUS SULCATA.

6970. LOTUS TETRAGONOLOBUS.
　　Square pea.

6971. LUPINUS ANGUSTIFOLIUS.
　　Blue lupine.

6972. LUPINUS TERMIS.

6973. LATHYRUS TINGITANUS.

6974. LATHYRUS CLYMENUM.

6975. LOTUS EDULIS.

6976. LOTUS ORNITHOPODIOIDES.

6977. ONONIS ALOPECUROIDES.

6978 to 6995.

(Numbers not utilized.)

6996. TRITICUM VULGARE. **Wheat.**

From Oklahoma Agricultural Experiment Station Farm, Stillwater, Okla. Received July 26, 1901.

Weissenburg. Box containing a few heads of wheat grown from No. 5499 during season 1900–1901.

6997. TRITICUM VULGARE. **Wheat.**

From Oklahoma Agricultural Experiment Station Farm, Stillwater, Okla. Received July 26, 1901.

Weissenburg. Bag of wheat grown from No. 5499 during season 1900–1901.

6998. MEDICAGO SATIVA. **Alfalfa.**

From Gizeh, near Cairo, Egypt. Received through Mr. D. G. Fairchild, July 1, 1901.

"A small package of dried plants of alfalfa with roots showing very few nodules. These plants were grown from Argentine seed sent to Cairo by the Office of Seed and Plant Introduction and Distribution, U. S. Department of Agriculture, and planted in the spring of 1901." (*Fairchild.*)

6999. CICER ARIETINUM. **Chick-pea.**

From Gizeh, near Cairo, Egypt. Received through Mr. D. G. Fairchild, July 1, 1901.

Package of dried plants and roots for root tubercle germ. (See No. 6961.)

7000. TRIFOLIUM ALEXANDRINUM. **Berseem.**

From Gizeh, near Cairo, Egypt. Received through Mr. D. G. Fairchild, from the agricultural society. Collected about May 1, 1901.

"Roots of berseem dried in the shade. These roots came from a field which had just been grazed over by cattle." (See No. 6961.) (*Fairchild.*)

7001. PHOENIX DACTYLIFERA. **Date.**

From Fayum, Egypt. Received through Mr. D. G. Fairchild (No. 617), July 1, 1901.

Wahi. "Twenty kilos of dried fruit of a variety of date which is said to have been brought from Siwah, a small village in the oasis of Bahriyeh. It is to my taste the sweetest drying date in Egypt—at least it is much sweeter than the Amri or any other I have tasted. It has a very peculiar mealy flesh of golden to greenish yellow. The skin is very thin and smooth and of a golden brown shade. Seed short, rather large, and clinging to the meat rather firmly. The flesh is somewhat granulated with the sugar. I can not be certain that this variety did really come from Siwah, but it certainly is a sort not commonly seen at this season in Cairo, and is superior in flavor to that which is considered the best in Egypt. The word *Wahi* signifies merely oasis, according to Mr. H. A. Rankin, of Fayum." (*Fairchild.*)

7002. PHOENIX DACTYLIFERA. **Date.**

From Fayum, Egypt. Received through Mr. D. G. Fairchild (No. 618), July 1, 1901.

"Dried dates of the common variety of the Province of Fayum. They are of fair quality as a drying date, but are not equal to the 'Wahi' or 'Amri' dates, the former of which was for sale on the same market in Fayoum. It is probable that seedlings from these seeds will be mixed, although in northern Egypt only one variety of male plant is grown." (*Fairchild.*)

7003 to 7010.

From Mexico. A collection of plants received through Dr. J. N. Rose, July 15, 1901.

Doctor Rose's numbers are appended, no further data being on hand regarding the plants.

7003. MAMMILLARIA sp. (No. 204).

7004. MAMMILLARIA sp. (No. 225).

7005. ERYNGIUM sp. (No. 227).

7006. CISSUS sp. (No. 228).

7007. MANFREDA sp. (No. 229).

7008. HYMENOCALLIS sp. (No. 230).

7009. OXALIS PRINGLEI sp. (No. 233).

7010. OXALIS sp. (No. 234).

7011. FICUS SYCOMORUS. Sycamore fig.

From Biskra, Algeria. Received through Mr. D. G. Fairchild (No. 719, June 14, 1901), July 17, 1901.

"This is the sacred fig of the Egyptians. The fruit is produced in very large numbers on the main branches and trunk of the tree, being borne in clusters. The tree is used in Egypt extensively as an avenue tree, and forms one of the characteristic landscape trees of Egypt. Along the canals it grows luxuriantly and attains large dimensions. The trunk is often 2 feet or more in diameter, and the spread of the branches makes it an excellent shade tree. The objection is made by old residents, and, I feel, quite justly, that it is a 'dirty' tree, i. e., drops continually débris of green fruit and fruit stalks which have to be cleaned up. As a fruit, it is not highly esteemed by any but Arabs, who will eat almost anything. It is dry and mealy, and personally I do not care for it. The Arabs in Biskra, and also in Egypt, have a practice of cutting off the tips of the immature figs in order to make them ripen. Mr. Columbo, of Biskra, asserts that three days after this cutting is done the cut figs become twice as large as the uncut ones and develop a not unpleasant taste. It is quite possible that in Texas and Louisiana this fig might be keenly appreciated by children and even by adults." (*Fairchild.*)

7012. QUEBRACHIA LORENTZII. Quebracho colorado.

From Terr. Nac. de Misiones, Argentina. Presented by Mr. W. G. Davis, of Cordoba. Received July 17, 1901.

"These trees are found in the central northern sections of the Republic. In the provinces of Catamarca and Rioj and San Luis the rainfall rarely exceeds 300 mm. a year. Over a large extent of the quebracho forests in Santiago del Estero the average rainfall does not exceed 200 mm." (*Davis.*) (See No. 6828.)

7013. ASPIDOSPERMA QUEBRACHO-BLANCO. Quebracho blanco.

From Terr. Nac. de Misiones, Argentina. Presented by Mr. W. G. Davis, of Cordoba. Received July 17, 1901.

See No. 6828.

7014. COLA ACUMINATA. Kola nut.

From Hope Gardens, Kingston, Jamaica. Received through the director, Dr. William Fawcett, July 18, 1901.

7015. CUCUMIS MELO. Muskmelon.

From Bassousa, Egypt. Received through Mr. D. G. Fairchild (No. 633, May 1, 1901), July 1, 1901.

Shaman. "A variety of cantaloupe said to be small, oblong, often egg-shaped, and of a peculiarly delicate flavor. Very highly spoken of by Englishmen in Egypt. Bassousa is the most noted melon-growing center of Egypt." (*Fairchild.*)

7016. TRITICUM DURUM. Wheat.

From Alexandria, Egypt. Received from George P. Foaden, esq., secretary of the Khedivial Agricultural Society at Gizeh, through Mr. D. G. Fairchild, October 10, 1901.

Mishriki. A red durum wheat, of which samples have already been sent in for inspection. (See No. 6680.)

7017. CICER ARIETINUM. Chick-pea.

From Cairo, Egypt. Received through Mr. D. G. Fairchild (No. 622, April 26, 1901), July 1, 1901.

"The Syrian variety of chick-pea grown in Egypt and considered equal to the native sort. It has better seeds, however, being plumper and better formed." (*Fairchild.*)

7018. GOSSYPIUM BARBADENSE. Cotton.

From Fayum, Egypt. Received through Mr. D. G. Fairchild (No. 613), July 1, 1901.

Ashmuni. "Unginned cotton of this variety collected where it is exclusively grown, i. e., in the oasis of Fayum. I am informed that this variety is the only one which will succeed well in this province. The *Afifi, Jannovitch,* and *Abbasi* have all been tried, although, I suspect, not thoroughly. This variety may be better suited to upland cultivation than the *Jannovitch* or *Afifi,* and may be more resistant to the wilt disease." (*Fairchild.*) (See No. 7025 for ginned seed.)

7019. GOSSYPIUM BARBADENSE. Cotton.

From Cairo, Egypt. Received through Mr. D. G. Fairchild (No. 648, May 11, 1901), July 1, 1901.

Mit Afifi. Secured by George P. Foaden, esq., of the Khedivial Agricultural Society, Cairo.

7020. VICIA FABA. Horse bean.

From Cairo, Egypt. Received through Mr. D. G. Fairchild (No. 632, April 26, 1901), July 1, 1901.

"These are the varieties which took the prizes at the Agricultural Fair in Cairo last year. They are introduced for comparative trial with the other sorts." (*Fairchild.*)

7021. CICER ARIETINUM. Chick-pea.

From Cairo, Egypt. Received through Mr. D. G. Fairchild (No. 626, April 26, 1901), July 1, 1901.

Hommos Beledi. "The native variety of chick-pea. This variety is grown usually for food. The green peas are eaten raw, while the ripe peas are cooked. In Egypt this chick-pea is planted in October or November at the rate of from 30 to 40 pounds of seed per acre, depending upon whether it is sown in drills or broadcasted. On irrigable land it is watered when sown, again when in flower, and the third time when the seeds are being formed. This plant will probably prove of value as a winter soiling crop in the Southwestern States. In parts of the country subject to frost it should be sown in May or June. In parts of Egypt the plants are dried and fed to cattle. Care must be taken, however, in using it for this purpose, as it is known sometimes to be injurious to horses and even to cattle. The seeds, however, make an excellent food for domestic animals." (*Fairchild.*)

7022. LUPINUS TERMIS. Egyptian lupine.

From Cairo, Egypt. Received through Mr. D. G. Fairchild (No. 628, April 26, 1901), July 1, 1901.

"A variety of lupine planted by the Egyptians on the dry sandy edges of the irrigation basins of Upper Egypt. The seeds are sown broadcast after the irrigation water has subsided, and no more attention is given to their culture until the lupines are harvested. It is considered a valuable crop for increasing the nitrogen in the soil and the beans are eaten by the natives after being boiled in salt water. Should be tried as a soiling crop in arid regions where a single irrigation is possible." (*Fairchild.*)

7023. GOSSYPIUM BARBADENSE. **Cotton.**

From Alexandria, Egypt. Received through Mr. D. G. Fairchild (No. 593), July 1, 1901.

Jannovitch. "This variety is said to be losing in popularity in Egypt. Its yield is lighter, at least 10 per cent, and its staple, although longer than that of *Mit Afifi*, is said to be falling off in length. It is open to the serious objection that the bolls open and allow the cotton to fall to the ground early, thus making its cleaning expensive, since the natives pick it up from the ground where it has lain and become filled with dirt." (*Fairchild.*)

7024. VICIA FABA. **Horse bean.**

From Cairo, Egypt. Received through Mr. D. G. Fairchild (No. 621), July 1, 1901.

Saida. "This important fodder crop of Egypt, which forms an article of export amounting in 1898 to over one and one-half million dollars' worth, and which seems entirely unknown in America, is worthy of the most serious attention. For the Colorado Desert region and southern Texas, Louisiana, and California, the broad bean may be of great importance. This variety comes from Upper Egypt, where the bean is grown most extensively. It is a *winter* crop in Egypt and must be fitted in to American conditions. It is killed by too cold or too hot weather." (*Fairchild.*)

7025. GOSSYPIUM BARBADENSE. **Cotton.**

From Fayoum, Egypt. Received through Mr. D. G. Fairchild (No. 614, April 21, 1901), July 1, 1901.

Ashmuni. "From the ginning mill of Theodore Bakoum, Fayum. This is probably of a mixed character. See No. 7018 for sample of staple. For trial against the root disease and on uplands. It is all grown here by irrigation and is claimed to be the only sort which pays in the Fayum oasis." (*Fairchild.*)

7026. GOSSYPIUM BARBADENSE. **Cotton.**

From Cairo, Egypt. Received through Mr. D. G. Fairchild (No. 649, May 11, 1901), July 1, 1901.

Jannovitch. "Seed from plants which have been grown on land containing from 1 to 1½ per cent of salt. It is presumed that this seed will be adapted to experiments with similar soils in America and possibly will prove more resistant to the wilt disease than the *Jannovitch* seed taken from plants growing in soil with less salt in it or without any. Secured by Mr. Foaden from the lower Delta region. In quality the fiber is said to equal that coming from plants grown on the less saline soils." (*Fairchild.*)

7027. GOSSYPIUM BARBADENSE. **Cotton.**

From Cairo, Egypt. Received through Mr. D. G. Fairchild (No. 631, April 26, 1901), July 1, 1901.

7028. ERVUM LENS. **Lentil.**

From Cairo, Egypt. Received through Mr. D. G. Fairchild (No. 627, April 26, 1901), July 1, 1901.

Saidi. "The upper Nile lentil, which is cultivated in Egypt, is an important food crop. Lentils amounting in value to over $90,000 were exported in 1898 to England, France, and Turkey. It is remarkable that America should so long neglect the culture of this most excellent food plant. For some years a very well-known invalid food, called 'Revelenta Arabica,' has been manufactured in England which consists exclusively of a flour of the Egyptian lentil. Purées of lentil and lentil soup are delicacies of the European menus quite absent, generally, from American tables. As a forage crop as well, these lentils should receive serious study. This is a typical Egyptian variety. It brings nearly $2 per hectoliter, according to custom-house returns of exports. The yield varies from 20 to 25 bushels per acre and upward. Sown at rate of 1 bushel per acre broadcasted. Grown in irrigation basins. Requires little water." (*Fairchild.*)

7029. TRIGONELLA FOENUM-GRAECUM. **Fenugreek.**

From Cairo, Egypt. Received through Mr. D. G. Fairchild (No. 623, April 26, 1901), July 1, 1901.

"*Egyptian fenugreek* or *Helba*, as it is called by the Arabs. This plant yields an important condiment and its root system is so remarkably provided with tubercles that it is worthy serious attention as a green manure crop. The seeds are also of value for feeding purposes, and a large amount of fodder is produced, which, if cut before seeds ripen, is of excellent quality. The condition powders and condiment foods which are sold in England extensively and fed to ailing horses and cattle are mixtures of the fenugreek with other meals or grains. It is sometimes planted with berseem here to give a slight purgative effect to the green fodder given so commonly in Egypt to horses and cattle." (*Fairchild.*)

7030. GOSSYPIUM BARBADENSE. **Cotton.**

From Cairo, Egypt. Received through Mr. D. G. Fairchild (No. 647, May 11, 1901), July 1, 1901.

Ashmouni. "Secured through the kindness of Mr. George P. Foaden. This should prove valuable for experiments in the hot dry uplands. It is the variety grown especially in the upper Nile region." (*Fairchild.*)

7031. TRIFOLIUM ALEXANDRINUM. **Berseem.**

From Cairo, Egypt. Received through Mr. D. G. Fairchild (No. 620, April 26, 1901), July 1, 1901.

Muscowi. "This variety, as noted in No. 4254, is the common variety of the Delta region. It is the variety from which the largest number of cuttings can be made and the one likely to prove of greatest use in America." (*Fairchild.*)

7032. HIBISCUS CANNABINUS. **Ambari hemp or Teale.**

From Cairo, Egypt. Received through Mr. D. G. Fairchild (No. 625, April 26, 1901), July 1, 1901.

"This fiber plant, which is used here as a wind-break for the cotton fields, may be worth investigating, as I am assured by Mr. George P. Foaden, of the Khedivial Agricultural Society, that the prices offered for it in the London markets are very high. This *Teale* may be quite a different variety from the ordinary Ambari hemp and better suited to culture in irrigated regions of America. Mr. Foaden intends trying several acres of it as a culture next year. It is planted at the same time as the cotton in a thickly sown row around the cotton field, forming a sort of hedge. This practice is a very old one in Egypt. Some samples of this Egyptian *Teale* were sent to London and a quotation of £20 per ton was secured by Mr. Foaden." (*Fairchild.*) (See Dodge's "Fiber Plants," pp. 192–193.)

7033. TRITICUM VULGARE. **Wheat.**

From Cairo, Egypt. Received through Mr. D. G. Fairchild (No. 629, April 26, 1901), July 1, 1901.

Mezzafannager White. "A variety of Indian wheat which has recently been introduced into Egypt and has met with unusual success, being a much heavier yielder than the native. Though small in grain and thin husked, it yielded near Cairo about 12 bushels per acre more than any native sorts. Samples sent to England were pronounced 'the finest of their kind' by experts. The yield of straw was unusually large in some preliminary tests made on the grounds of the Khedivial Agricultural Society. On the Domain's lands last year there were about 1,500 acres of this Indian wheat planted and over 5,000 acres of native wheat. The Indian averaged nearly 12 bushels an acre more than the native. Less seed is required than of ordinary varieties, as the plant stools unusually well. Starts into growth more rapidly than native sorts. A winter wheat for warm climates. For information regarding this Indian wheat apply to George P. Foaden, esq., secretary of the Khedivial Agricultural Society of Cairo, through whose kindness this sample has been secured." (*Fairchild.*)

7034. ALLIUM CEPA. Onion.

From Cairo, Egypt. Received through Mr. D. G. Fairchild (No. 630, April 26, 1901), July 1, 1901.

"A native variety of onion which is grown in immense quantities on the islands and elsewhere on the upper Nile. These are for export mostly and in 1898 over $909,000 worth were exported. Train loads are piled on the wharves in Alexandria in March and April, from which point they are shipped all over Europe and even to New York, $5,365 worth going to this latter port during the quarter ending March 31, 1901. This onion forms one of the army rations now, I am told, and these Egyptian onions are of good, even superior quality. A Texas onion specialist who tested these Egyptian onions two years ago declared them to be the finest pickle onion he had ever seen. Deserves a wide distribution wherever irrigation prevails, as it is an onion for irrigated lands." (*Fairchild.*)

7035. VICIA FABA. Horse bean.

From Cairo, Egypt. Received through Mr. D. G. Fairchild (No. 650), July 1, 1901.

Beheri. "A variety of horse bean which is grown in the province of Beheri in lower Eygpt. It is a distinct variety from the *Saida* and should be tested in comparison with it. Especially valuable for experiments in irrigated regions of California, Arizona, and Texas. Secured through Mr. George P. Foaden, of the Khedivial Agricultural Society." (*Fairchild.*)

7036. GOSSYPIUM BARBADENSE. Cotton.

From Alexandria, Egypt. Received through Mr. D. G. Fairchild (No. 592), July 1, 1901.

Mit Afifi. "This variety is now more commonly grown than any other, and the *Jannovitch* variety, so popular two years ago, is said to be a lighter yielder and, by some, to be rapidly deteriorating. The *Mit Afifi* is not a white but a cream-colored cotton, and is prized especially for the manufacture of cream-colored underwear, hosiery, etc. It is also mixed with silk and is especially suited for this purpose." (*Fairchild.*)

7037. HEDYSARUM CORONARIUM. Sulla.

From Malta. Received through Mr. D. G. Fairchild (No. 689), July 23, 1901.

Malta. "Sulla from the island of Malta. This is a late maturing sort, useful when rains are abundant. It is a heavier yielder than that from Gozzo, and hence preferred by Maltese in places where there is plenty of moisture." (*Fairchild.*)

7038 to 7045. MANGIFERA INDICA. Mango.

From Bombay, India.

A collection of grafted mango plants, arranged for by Mr. John B. Beach, of West Palmbeach, Fla., through Latham & Co., Bombay. Received July 24, 1901.

7038.
Bath.

7039.
Fernandez.

7040.
Goa Alfonso.

7041.
Kala Alfoos.

7042.
Mazagon.

7043.
Roos.

7044.
Alfonso, or Alfoos.

7045.
Cowasjee Patel.

7046. GYMNOCLADUS CANADENSIS. **Kentucky coffee tree.**

From Botanic Gardens, Washington, D. C. Received through Mr. G.W. Oliver, July 23, 1901.

7047 to 7057.

From City of Mexico, Mexico. Received through Dr. J. N. Rose, July 26, 1901.

A collection of economic and ornamental plants and seeds made in Mexico in the summer of 1901. Doctor Rose's numbers are retained for identification.

7047. ERYTHRINA sp.

(No. 5301.)

7048. VITIS sp. Grape.

"A grape the stems of which die down to the ground every year. Fruit very large." (*Rose.*) (No. 5349.)

7049. ROSA sp. Rose.

(No. 5368.)

7050. OXALIS sp.

"Has beautiful red foliage." (*Rose.*) (No. 5389.)

7051. HYPTIS sp.

"Flowers red." (*Rose.*) (No. 5412.)

7052. TRIFOLIUM sp.

"A showy clover with large heads." (*Rose.*) (No. 5486.)

7053. CARDIOSPERMUM sp.

"A vine." (*Rose.*) (No. 5490.)

7054. ALBIZZIA sp.

"A beautiful leguminous tree cultivated in Mexico at an altitude of 7,000 feet. Flowers in spikes 2 or 3 inches long." (*Rose.*) (No. 5281.)

7055. Zapote borracho.

"A cultivated fruit." (*Rose.*) (No. 252.)

7056. PASSIFLORA sp.

"Edible fruit sold in markets." (*Rose.*) (No. 254.)

7057. CULPHEA sp.

(No. 5353.)

7058. COCHLEARIA ARMORACIA. **Horse-radish.**

From Stockholm, Sweden. Received through Lindahl's seed firm, July 27, 1901. (L. & F. No. 421.)

Enköping. A variety of horse-radish grown at Enköping, near Stockholm. It is as noted a sort in Sweden as the *Maliner Kren* is in Austria, and is cultivated in a similar way.

7059. CERATONIA SILIQUA. **Carob.**

From Alicante, Spain. Received through Mr. D. G. Fairchild (No. 742), July 29, 1901.

"A male variety of carob. In this region all trees of carobs are grafted or budded with this male sort. A large branch or, oftener, a secondary trunk is trained up into the center of the tree to furnish the pollen for the female flowers. This practice, which I have not observed in Greece or Algiers in the same degree of perfection, accounts no doubt for the heavy yields obtained here. This may be what is called *La Borrera.*" (*Fairchild.*)

7060. CERATONIA SILIQUA. **Carob.**

From Alicante, Spain. Received through Mr. D. G. Fairchild (No. 744), July 29, 1901.

Vera. "This is the sweetest carob I have ever tasted." (*Fairchild.*)

7061. AMYGDALUS COMMUNIS. **Almond.**

From Alicante, Spain. Received through Mr. D. G. Fairchild (No. 740), July 29, 1901.

Mollar. "A soft-shelled variety of almond grown in Alicante for table use. Especially relished when still green. The consumption of these green almonds in Mediterranean countries is very great. They are eaten with salt. This variety is not an exporting one, but may prove an addition to the orchards of California." (*Fairchild.*)

7062. AMYGDALUS COMMUNIS. **Almond.**

From Alicante, Spain. Received through Mr. D. G. Fairchild (No. 741), July 29, 1901.

Planeta. "The great exporting almond of this part of Spain. It is the variety best known and most extensively cultivated, not because it is altogether the best, according to local taste, but because of its shipping and good marketing qualities. It is wedge-shaped in form, with *hard* shell and a flat, heart-shaped kernel with medium thin skin. The *Jordan* almond, which fetches higher prices, I am told, is not grown here in Alicante. It has a thinner skin and finer flavor. The *Planeta* is, however, one of the first-class hard-shelled almonds." (*Fairchild.*)

7063. CERATONIA SILIQUA. **Carob.**

From Alicante, Spain. Received through Mr. D. G. Fairchild (No. 743), July 29, 1901.

Negra. "The commonest variety of carob grown around Alicante. It is a variety used for horse food almost entirely, and its yields are very large and regular. Every year a tree 20 years old will yield from 50 cents' worth to a dollar's worth of fruit. The culture is suited to waste places in dry soil. Trees here 200 years old yield yearly up to $3 worth apiece. This variety has little sugar in it and the seeds are surrounded by parchment. Not for table purposes." (*Fairchild.*)

7064 to 7070.

From City of Mexico, Mexico. Received through Dr. J. N. Rose, July 29, 1901.

A collection of economic and ornamental plants made in Mexico in 1901. The numbers given by Doctor Rose are retained for identification.

7064. COTYLEDON sp.
(No. 260.)

7065. MAMILLARIA sp.
(No. 261.)

7066. SEDUM sp.
(No. 263.)

7067. SEDUM sp.
(No. 264.)

7068. RUBUS sp. **Raspberry.**

"A fine raspberry and worthy of cultivation. Obtained a root and one ripe fruit. It grows at an elevation of 10,400 feet." (*Rose.*) (No. 265.)

7069. COMMELINA sp.

"A very beautiful greenhouse plant. It grows in Alpine meadows at 10,000 feet elevation." (*Rose.*) (No. 266.)

7070. SOLANUM sp.
(No. 267.)

7071. TRIGONELLA FOENUM-GRAECUM. **Fenugreek.**

From Batna (Constantin), Algeria. Received through Mr. D. G. Fairchild (No. 720), July 31, 1901.

"Sample of fenugreek seed arranged for by Mr. C. S. Scofield, coming from the mountains of the Aurès east of the town of Batna, on the high Algerian plateau. Used, as in Tunis, by the Jewesses to induce an excessive fleshiness, which is the fashion among them. This may prove a different variety and should be reserved for breeding purposes. Sent through the kindness of Mr. John Wild, of Batna." (*Fairchild.*)

7072 to 7100.

From Mexico. Received through Dr. J. N. Rose, July 31, 1901.

A collection of economic and ornamental plants made in Mexico in 1901. Doctor Rose's numbers are retained for identification.

7072. Palm.
(No. 253.)

7073. SOLANUM sp. Potato.
(No. 257.)

7074. SEDUM sp.
(No. 248.)

7075. BEGONIA sp.
(No. 238.)

7076. SEDUM sp.
(No. 239.)

7077. BEGONIA GRACILIS.
(No. 243.)

7078. SEDUM sp.
(No. 237.)

7079. DAHLIA sp.
(No. 242.)

7080. SEDUM sp.
(No. 235.)

7081. COTYLEDON sp.
(No. 245.)

7082. COTYLEDON sp.
(No. 236.)

7083. SEDUM sp.
(No. 247.)

7084. COTYLEDON sp.
(No. 255.)

7085. CEREUS sp.
(No. 223.)

7086. CEREUS sp.
(No. 224.)

7087. AGAVE sp.
(No. 246.)

7088. TILLANDSIA BENTHAMIANA.
(No. 241.)

7089. Cactus.
(No. 226.)

7090. Cactus.
(No. 203.)

7091. SENECIO sp.
(No. 256.)

7092. SENECIO sp.
(No. 258.)

7093. TILLANDSIA sp.
(No. 232.)

7072 to 7100—Continued.

7094. Orchid.
(No. 231.)

7095. Cactus.
(No. 251.)

7096. Cactus.
(No. 250.)

7097. Nolina sp.
(No. 240.)

7099. Tigridia sp.
(No. 269.)

7098. Cotyledon sp.
(No. 244.)

7100. Dasylirion sp.
(No. 262.)

7101 to 7108. Mangifera indica. Mango.

From Bangalore, India. Received through A. Lehmann, Ph. D., July 31, 1901. A collection of grafted mangoes.

7101.
Peterpasand.

7102.
Mullgoa (Mulgoba).

7103.
Badami.

7104.
Amini.

7105.
Rajabury or *Rajpury.*

7106.
Raspbury.

7107.
Gada Mar.

7108.
Sandersha or *Sandershaw (Soondershaw).*

7109 to 7116.

From Avalon, Santa Catalina Islands, California. Received through Mrs. Blanche Trask, July, 1900.

A collection of seeds of native plants, as follows:

7109. Hosackia venusta.

7110. Hosackia traskiae.

7111. Rhus ovata.

7112. Galium catalinense.

7113. Senecio hyoni.

7114. Phacelia lyoni.

7115. Lyonothamnus floribundus.

7116. Eriogonum giganteum.

7117. Danthonia californica.

From Berkeley, Cal. Received through Miss Alice F. Crane, January, 1901.

7118 to 7129.

From Berkeley, Cal. Received through Miss Alice F. Crane, January, 1901.

A collection of seeds of native Trifoliums, as follows:

7118. Trifolium gracilentum.

7119. Trifolium bifidum.

7118 to 7129—Continued.

7120.	TRIFOLIUM CILIATUM.	**7125.**	TRIFOLIUM TRIDENTATUM.
7121.	TRIFOLIUM MACRAEI.	**7126.**	TRIFOLIUM MICROCEPHALUM.
7122.	TRIFOLIUM INVOLUCRATUM.	**7127.**	TRIFOLIUM MICRODON.
7123.	TRIFOLIUM PAUCIFLORUM.	**7128.**	TRIFOLIUM FUCATUM.
7124.	TRIFOLIUM PAUCIFLORUM.	**7129.**	TRIFOLIUM FUCATUM, var. FLAVULUM.

7130. SOLANUM MELONGENA. **Eggplant.**

From Raleigh, N. C. Received through Prof. W. F. Massey, March 18, 1901.

7131. PASSIFLORA sp.

From Melbourne, Australia. Received from Carolin & Co. through Mr. G. W. Hill, Chief of the Division of Publications, U. S. Department of Agriculture.

7132. CERATONIA SILIQUA. **Carob.**

From Alicante, Spain. Received through Mr. D. G. Fairchild (No. 744), August 3, 1901.

Vera. "This is a poor yielder, but its fruits are so full of sugar that drops of sirup run out when the pods are broken. It is too dear for horse food and is eaten by the people as a delicacy. Its flesh is very crisp and lacks the harshness of other varieties. Its seeds are of a lighter color and the pods thicker. As a shade tree it is a finer looking variety, with larger leaves, than No. 7063." (*Fairchild.*) (See also Nos. 7060 and 7461.)

7133. AMYGDALUS COMMUNIS. **Almond.**

From Alicante, Spain. Received through Mr. D. G. Fairchild (No. 745), August 3, 1901.

Castillet. "A superlative sort of hard-shelled almond which was found in a garden at Mucha Miel, near Alicante. I have not been able to learn that this sort is known on the markets, although the owner assured me it brought a higher price than the *Planeta*. It is a larger, fuller shaped almond." (*Fairchild.*)

7134. AMYGDALUS COMMUNIS. **Almond.**

From Alicante, Spain. Received through Mr. D. G. Fairchild (No. 746), August 3, 1901.

Planeta. "Taken from an orchard at Mucha Miel, near Alicante. The names of these varieties are often mixed, and this may be slightly different from No. 7062." (*Fairchild.*)

7135. AMYGDALUS COMMUNIS. **Almond.**

From Alicante, Spain. Received through Mr. D. G. Fairchild (No. 748), August 3, 1901.

Fabrica. "A smaller and inferior sort to the *Planeta*, but said to be a good bearer. It is ten to fifteen days later than the *Planeta*, ripening about the middle or last of August." (*Fairchild.*)

7136. PRUNUS ARMENIACA. **Apricot.**

From Alicante, Spain. Received through Mr. D. G. Fairchild (No. 749), August 3, 1901.

Patriarca. "One of the largest fruited varieties of apricot in eastern Spain. Said to be of excellent quality. The apricots of Spain probably were introduced from

France originally, but have undergone changes in size and character, suiting them to the drought and heat of this more southern region. This *Patriarca* is the best large variety about Alicante, and is said to be a local sort." (*Fairchild.*)

7137. AMYGDALUS COMMUNIS. **Almond.**

From Alicante, Spain. Received through Mr. D. G. Fairchild (No. 755a), August 3, 1901.

Pastaneta. "A variety differing in form very materially from the other Spanish varieties. It has a truncated apex and is more or less rectangular. This variety is not planted largely about Alicante, but is the prevailing sort grown at Murcia, I am told. It fetches as high or even a higher price than the *Planeta.*" (*Fairchild.*)

7138. TRIFOLIUM PRATENSE. **Red clover.**

From New York. Received through J. M. Thorburn & Co., August 5, 1901.

7139. CICHORIUM ENDIVIA. **Endive.**

From Cassel, Germany. Received through Mr. George C. Roeding, August 5, 1901.

Self-closing, yellow Cassel summer endive.

7140. PRUNUS ARMENIACA. **Apricot.**

From Alicante, Spain. Received through Mr. D. G. Fairchild (No. 750), August 9, 1901.

Ull blanc. "A medium sized apricot famed as the finest small fruited variety in the neighborhood of Alicante. I did not have a chance to taste it, and can not vouch for its superiority." (*Fairchild.*)

7141 to 7145. MORUS sp. **Mulberry.**

From Murcia, Spain. Received through Mr. D. G. Fairchild (No. 757), August 10, 1901.

A collection of cuttings from the gardens of the Sericultural Institute of Murcia, Spain. The nomenclature is that furnished by the head gardener.

7141.
Esteril.

7142.
Arantiana.

7143.
Common, of Italy.

7144.
Glemosa.

7145.
Colson or *Lotson*, of Italy.

7146 to 7340.

From Erfurt, Germany. Received through Haage & Schmidt, seedsmen, August 10, 1901.

A collection of seeds as follows (the nomenclature is in the main that of the seedsmen):

7146. STRELITZIA AUGUSTA.

7147. AGERATUM CONYZOIDES (?)
Prinzessin Victoria Luise.

7148. AQUILEGIA CHRYSANTHA FLORE PLENO.

7149. AGERATUM CONYZOIDES (?)

7150. CUPRESSUS FUNEBRIS.

7151. ADENANTHERA PAVONINA.

7152. ANONA MACROCARPA (?)

7153. BETA CHILENSIS.
Golden yellow.

7154. MUSA MANNII (?)

7146 to 7340—Continued.

7155. Impatiens sultani splendens.
7156. Phlox drummondii. *Brilliant.*
7157. Primula obconica grandiflora violacea.
7158. Croton sebiferum.
7159. Anona suavissima (?)
7160. Campanula persicifolia flore alba.
7161. Illicium floridanum.
7162. Begonia semperflorens hybrida flore pleno.
7163. Antirrhinium majus grandiflorum luteum.
7164. Papaver orientale hybridum.
7165. Aquilegia caerulea flore luteo.
7166. Cinchona officinalis.
7167. Acanthus mollis.
7168. Impatiens sultani nacré rosé.
7169. Strelitzia reginae.
7170. Anona reniformis (?)
7171. Cordyline australis.
7172. Phormium tenax variegata.
7173. Anona cherimolia.
7174. Anona squamosa.
7175. Torenia fournieri (edentula) compacta alba.
7176. Eucalyptus robusta.
7177. Phlox drummondi cinnabarina.
7178. Torenia fournieri grandiflora.
7179. Beta brasiliensis carmoisin-carmoisi (?)
7180. Torenia fournieri (edentula) compacta coelestina.
7181. Beta chilensis carmoisin-chamoisi.
7182. Adansonia digitata.
7183. Amaranthus caudatus.
7184. Lychnis coeli-rosa.
7185. Primula obconica grandiflora rosea.
7186. Papaver bracteatum.
7187. Torenia fournieri (edentula) grandiflora coelestina.
7188. Rheum palmatum tanguticum.
7189. Phormium tenax veitchii.
7190. Jatropha glauca (?)
7191. Ficus macrophylla.
7192. Quassia amara.
7193. Cinchona succirubra.
7194. Lindelofia spectabilis.
7195. Chrysanthemum maximum.
7196. Campanula persicifolia coerulea.
7197. Torenia fournieri speciosa. *The Bride.*
7198. Carica papaya pyriformis.
7199. Beta brasiliensis (?). White.
7200. Antirrhinum majus nanum album.
7201. Antirrhinum majus sulphureum rubro-venosum.
7202. (Blank. Omitted unintentionally.)
7203. Antirrhinum majus nigro purpureum.
7204. Antirrhinum majus insigne.
7205. Clitoria ternatea.

7146 to 7340—Continued.

7206. CAESALPINIA SAPPAN. *Sappan.*

7207. GAILLARDIA AMBLYODON.

7208. ANTIRRHINUM MAJUS GRANDIFLORUM ALBUM.

7209. CARICA PAPAYA ATROVIOLACEA ELEGANTISSIMA.

7210. STRYCHNOS NUX-VOMICA.

7211. PRIMULA OBCONICA KERMESINA.

7212. PITHECOLOBIUM PRUINOSUM.

7213. ANTIRRHINUM MAJUS. *Romeo.*

7214. RHEUM PALMATUM TYPICUM.

7215. ACANTHUS NIGER.

7216. GAILLARDIA PULCHELLA LORENZIANA.

7217. TORENIA FOURNIERI.

7218. PHLOX DRUMMONDII ALBA OCULATA SUPERBA.

7219. GAILLARDIA PULCHELLA.

7220. PAPAVER ORIENTALE.

7221. PRIMULA OBCONICA GRANDIFLORA.

7222. FICUS ELASTICA.

7223. CEDRELA ODORATA.

7224. CINCHONA LEDGERIANA.

7225. AQUILEGIA CAERULEA FLORE ALBA.

7226. EUCALYPTUS GLOBULUS.

7227. BERBERIS DARWINII.

7228. IMPATIENS sp.

7229. CINCHONA CALISAYA.

7230. AQUILEGIA CALIFORNICA HYBRIDA.

7231. BEGONIA SEMPERFLORENS VULCAN-VULCAIN.

7232. PHORMIUM TENAX IMPORTIRT GR. IMPORTEÉN.

7233. PRIMULA OBCONICA GRANDIFLORA ALBA.

7234. PHORMIUM TENAX COLENSOI ARG. var.

7235. TORENIA FOURNIERI (EDENTULA) SPECIOSA. *Violetta.*

7236. TORENIA FOURNIERI (EDENTULA) SPECIOSA.

7237. STERCULIA ACERIFOLIA.

7238. CEDRELA TOONA.

7239. EUCALYPTUS CITRIODORA.

7240. MUSA SUMATRANA.

7241. TORENIA FOURNIERI (EDENTULA) COMPACTA.

7242. AQUILEGIA CAERULEA.

7243. JATROPHA MANIHOT.

7244. CHRYSANTHEMUM sp.

7245. CINCHONA HYBRIDA.

7246. JATROPHA CURCAS.

7247. CARICA CANDAMARCENSIS.

7248. CENTAUREA AMERICANA.

7249. GAILLARDIA PICTA MARGINATA ALBA.

7250. PAPAVER ORIENTALE SEMIPLENUM.

7251. PAPAVER ORIENTALE PARKINANSII.

7252. PAPAVER ORIENTALE. *Prince of Orange.*

7253. PAPAVER BRACTAETUM NANUM SPLENDENS.

7254. STERCULIA ACERIFOLIA.

7255. PITHECOLOBIUM UNGUISCATI.

7256. CEDRELA SINENSIS.

7257. JATROPHA MULTIFIDA.

7258. AQUILEGIA CHRYSANTHA.

7146 to 7340—Continued.

7259. Musa martini (?).
7260. Musa rosacea.
7261. Musa superba.
7262. Musa rosacea.
7263. Phormium tenax.
7264. Impatiens sultani hybrida nana.
7265. Primula obconica grandiflora hybrida.
7266. Caesalpinia pulcherrima.
7267. Caesalpinia coriaria.
7268. Sterculia diversifolia.
7269. Acanthus candelabrum (?).
7270. Laurus canariensis.
7271. Pterocarya caucasica.
7272. Bombax ochroma (?).
7273. Chamaerops arborea (?).
7274. Chamaerops canariensis (?).
7275. Raphis cochinchinensis.
7276. Chamaerops elegans (?).
7277. Trachycarpus excelsus.
7278. Chamaerops farinosa.
7279. Chamaerops humilis.
7280. Chamaerops humilis argentea.
7281. Chamaerops macrocarpa.
7282. Chamaerops olivaeformis (?).
7283. Chamaerops robusta (?).
7284. Chamaerops tomentosa.
7285. Phoenix dactylifera.
7286. Jubaea spectabilis.
7287. Kentia alexandria (?).
7288. Hyphaene benguelensis.
7289. Elaesis guineensis.
7290. Raphia pedunculata.
7291. Pistacia terebinthus.
7292. Acrocomia sclerocarpa.
7293. Livistona jenkinsiana.
7294. Anacardium occidentale.
7295. Musa ensete.
7296. Phoenix reclinata.
7297. Erythea edulis.
7298. Thrinax barbadensis.
7299. Livistona australis.
7300. Chamaedorea corallina (?).
7301. Chamaedorea ernesti augusti.
7302. Chamaedorea geonomaeformis.
7303. Chamaedorea gracilis.
7304. Livistona altissima.
7305. Livistona rotundifolia.
7306. Sterculia platanifolia.
7307. Campanula persicifolia flore albo pleno.
7308. Campanula persicifolia grandiflora alba.
7309. Campanula persicifolia grandiflora alba gigantea.
7310. Campanula persicifolia caeruleo pleno.
7311. Begonia semperflorens atropurpurea compacta.
7312. Begonia semperflorens flore pleno.
Bijo des Jardin.
7313. Begonia semperflorens grandiflora atropurpurea.

7146 to 7340—Continued.

7314. PRIMULA OBCONICA GRANDIFLORA FIMBRIATA.

7315. PRIMULA OBCONICA GRANDIFLORA VIOLACEA.

7316. AQUILEGIA FLABELLATA NANA ALBA.

7317. AQUILEGIA GRANDULOSA.

7318. AQUILEGIA HAYLODGENSIS.

7319. AQUILEGIA SKINNERI.

7320. AQUILEGIA STUARTI (?)

7321. AQUILEGIA VERVAENEANA FOL. VAR.

7322. HYDRIASTELE WENDLANDIANA.

7323. THRINAX ALTISSIMA.

7324. ACANTHUS MOLLIS.

7325. CAESALPINIA SEPIARIA.

7326. PYRETHRUM ROSEUM HYBRIDUM (?)

7327. BOCCONIA FRUTESCENS.

7328. CARICA PAPAYA.

7329. ACANTHUS MOLLIS.

7330. BERBERIS WALLICHIANA.

7331. CORYPHA ELATA.

7332. LIVISTONA AUSTRALIS MACROPHYLLA.

7333. ULEX EUROPAEUS.

7334. CERATONIA SILIQUA.

7335. PISTACIA VERA. **Pistache.**

7336. PISTACIA LENTISCUS. **Mastic.**

7337. PINANGA DECORA (?)

7338. THRINAX ARGENTEA.

7339. COCOS ROMANZOFFIANA.

7340. PANDANUS AQUATICUS.

7341. LUPINUS HIRSUTUS. **Blue lupine.**

From Vomero, near Naples, Italy. Received through Mr. C. Sprenger, August 13, 1901.

Used as an ornamental plant, also valued for fodder and as a green manure.

7342 to 7365.

From London, England. Received through Mr. William Bull, August 14, 1901.

A collection of plants, as follows (the nomenclature is in the main that given by Mr. Bull):

7342. JASMINUM NITIDUM.

7343. LICUALA MUELLERI.

7344. CAMOENSIA MAXIMA.

7345. CEROPEGIA WOODI.

7346. CODIAEUM VARIEGATUM.
Croton broomfieldii.

7347. CODIAEUM VARIEGATUM.
Croton excurrens.

7348. CODIAEUM VARIEGATUM.
Croton insignis.

7349. CODIAEUM VARIEGATUM.
Croton memphis.

7350. CODIAEUM VARIEGATUM.
Croton sceptre.

7351. CODIAEUM VARIEGATUM.
Croton elysian.

7352. CODIAEUM VARIEGATUM.
Croton elvira.

7353. CODIAEUM VARIEGATUM.
Croton euterpe.

7354. CODIAEUM VARIEGATUM.
Croton hermon.

7355. FICUS RADICANS VARIEGATA.

7356. FICUS INDICA.

7342 to 7365—Continued.

7357.	CINCHONA OFFICINALIS.	**Peruvian bark.**
7358.	CALODENDRUM CAPENSIS.	**Cape chestnut.**
7359.	HIBISCUS ELATUS.	
7360.	PSYCHOTRIA (?) IPECACUANHA.	**Ipecacuanha.**
7361.	KICKSIA AFRICANA.	**Lagos rubber.**
7362.	SALVADORA PERSICA.	**Mustard tree of Scripture.**
7363.	EPIPREMNUM MIRABILE.	**Tonga.**
7364.	ANTIARIS TOXICARIA.	**Upas tree.**
7365.	STANGERIA PARADOXA.	

7366. ANANAS SATIVUS. **Pineapple.**

From West Palmbeach, Fla. Received from Mr. George C. Matthams, August 13, 1901.

Ripley Queen.

7367 to 7396.

From Mexico. Received through Dr. J. N. Rose (Nos. 270-299), August 15, 1901.

A collection of Mexican plants and bulbs, as follows (Doctor Rose's numbers are retained for identification):

7367. TILLANDSIA sp.
(No. 270.)

7368. COTYLEDON sp.
(No. 271.)

7369. COTYLEDON sp.
(No. 272.)

7370. COTYLEDON sp.
(No. 273.)

7371. AGAVE sp.
(No. 274.)

7372. AGAVE sp.
(No. 275.)

7373. COTYLEDON sp.
(No. 276.)

7374. COTYLEDON sp.
(No. 277.)

7375. (No. 278.) **Cactus.**
Flat-spined.

7376. (No. 279.) **Cactus.**
Long-spined.

7377. (No. 280.) **Cactus.**
Round.

7378. (No. 281.) **Cactus.**
Four-spined.

7379. OPUNTIA sp.
(No. 282.)

7380. MAMILLARIA sp.
(No. 283.)
Oblong.

7381. MAMILLARIA sp.
(No. 284.)
Round.

7382. (No. 285.) **Cactus.**
Tall.

7367 to 7396—Continued.

7383.	CISSUS sp. (No. 286.)	7390.	COTYLEDON sp. (No. 293.)
7384.	TILLANDSIA sp. (No. 287.)	7391.	NOLINA sp. (No. 294.)
7385.	TILLANDSIA sp. (No. 288.)	7392.	YUCCA sp. (No. 295.)
7386.	TILLANDSIA sp. (No. 289.)	7393.	ZEPHYRANTHES sp. (No. 296.)
7387.	HECHTIA sp. (No. 290.)	7394.	COTYLEDON sp. (No. 297.)
7388.	FOUQUIERIA sp. (No. 291.)		
7389.	(No. 292.)		

7395. SOLANUM sp. (No. 298.) **Potato.**

Half-wild potatoes from Mount Orizaba.

7396. SOLANUM sp. (No. 299.) **Potato.**

A small wild potato from near City of Mexico.

7397. CUCUMIS MELO. Muskmelon.

From Savannah, Ga. Received through Mr. D. G. Purse, president of the Savannah Board of Trade, August 17, 1901.

Seeds from a 32-pound muskmelon.

7398. AMYGDALUS COMMUNIS. Almond.

From Malaga, Spain. Received through Mr. D. G. Fairchild (No. 765), August 19, 1901.

Jordan. "Bud sticks of the famous *Jordan* almond of commerce, which is imported into America in large quantities every year. These bud sticks were taken before the almonds were harvested in almost all cases, and from trees still bearing the *Jordan* almonds. They were difficult to obtain, and it is hoped can be grafted this autumn. This variety is without question the finest almond of its class in the world. It is exported from Spain, largely as shelled kernels, to England and the United States, and is used extensively in these places for the manufacture of confectionery. Its typical long, plump shape distinguishes it from any other sort grown in Spain. It has a very thin, delicate skin and fine, white, highly flavored flesh. There are orchards of considerable size in Spain of this variety, but as a rule the trees are scattered irregularly over the hillsides among the Sierras back of Malaga. A famous locality for them is at Alora, a half hour's railroad ride from Malaga. No special care is given the trees and many of the orchards are quite old. The soil on which they are grown is a light gravel, not fitted for any other culture. In summer it gets exceedingly dry, but the trees seem to withstand the drought very well." (*Fairchild.*)

7399 and 7400. CERATONIA SILIQUA. Carob.

From Malaga, Spain. Received through Mr. D. G. Fairchild (No. 766), August 19, 1901.

Castillana. "One of the best varieties of carob, or St. John's bread, in Spain, and probably one of the best in the world. It is eaten by the natives in the same way that the variety *Vera* is in the region of Alicante. It has a very thick, medium-sized pod, which is very sweet. Produces abundantly and is not grafted with the male variety, as in Alicante." (*Fairchild.*) See No. 7132.

7401. AMYGDALUS COMMUNIS. Almond.

From Malaga, Spain. Received through Mr. D. G. Fairchild (No. 771), August 20, 1901.

Jordan. "Bud sticks from the garden of Cristobal Paloma, of Malaga. These are probably like the former buds of this same variety, but are forwarded to make sure of getting the best strains." (*Fairchild.*)

7402 to 7413.

From Mexico. Received through Dr. J. N. Rose, August 20, 1901.

A collection of native plants, bulbs, and seeds, as follows (the numbers given by Doctor Rose are retained for identification):

7402. ZEPHYRANTHES sp. (No. 268.)

7403. COTYLEDON sp. (No. 300.)
"Large red flowers." (*Rose.*)

7404. ARGEMONE sp. (No. 301.)
"Large white flowers." (*Rose.*)

7405. ZEPHYRANTHES sp. (No. 302.)

7406. CUCURBITA sp. (No. 5287.)

7407. RUBUS sp. (No. 5380.)
"A beautiful flowering shrub." (*Rose.*)

7408. PITHECOLOBIUM sp. (No. 5840.)
"A shrub." (*Rose.*)

7409. CUCURBITA sp. (No. 5899 ?.)

7410. SOLANUM sp. (No. 5944.)
"Large purple flowers." (*Rose.*)

7411. SPHAERALCEA sp. (No. 5945.)
"A large, beautiful flowering shrub much used in Mexican parks." (*Rose.*)

7412. OXALIS sp. (No. 5956.)

7413. [Undetermined.] (No. 303.)
"Forty-nine bulbs of a beautiful white flowering water lily. The flowers stand up above the water." (*Rose.*)

7414 to 7421.

From Naples, Italy. Received from Dammann & Co., August 20, 1901.

A collection of seeds as follows (the nomenclature is in large part Dammann's):

7414. ANACARDIUM OCCIDENTALE.

7415. INGA DULCIS.

7416. TRACHYCARPUS EXCELSUS.

7417. FICUS ELASTICA.

7418. FICUS MACROPHYLLA.

7419. GAZANIA HYBRIDA. *Nora.*

7420. GAZANIA HYBRIDA. *Diana.*

7421. GAZANIA HYBRIDA. *Blondine.*

7422. TRITICUM sp. Wheat.

From Girgeh Province, Egypt. Received through Mr. D. G. Fairchild (No. 655), August 20, 1901.

"Selected Egyptian wheat secured through the kindness of Sir William Willcocks, from typical 'basin' irrigated lands of the upper Nile. This is especially for trial in the Colorado Desert experiments. It is a winter wheat in Egypt, but matures by the first (or middle at latest) of May. Probably will be more or less mixed and contain both hard and soft varieties." (*Fairchild.*)

7423. CORYLUS AVELLANA.

From Alicante, Spain. Received through Mr. D. G. Fairchild (No. 752), August 30, 1901.

"Sample seeds of what are called here on the market 'Avellinas.' They are grown near Valencia, I am told, and are one of the common sorts of hazelnuts. It is a fairly thin-shelled nut but its skin is flakey and too heavy to make it of first quality." (*Fairchild.*)

7424. CYPERUS ESCULENTUS. **Chufas.**

From Alicante, Spain. Received through Mr. D. G. Fairchild (No. 753), August 30, 1901.

"Sample of the 'Chufa' of Spain, for planting in Louisiana and other places in the South. The culture is said to be simple and lucrative in Spain. When soaked in water the rootstocks swell up and are then very sweet and palatable. They are sold as we sell peanuts on the streets. Children are very fond of them, and they are used very extensively in the manufacture, in Madrid, of a delicious ice called '*Horchata di Chufas.*'" (*Fairchild.*)

7425. TRITICUM DURUM. **Wheat.**

From Cordova, Spain. Received through Mr. D. G. Fairchild (No. 764), August 30, 1901.

Negro. "A black-bearded durum wheat grown largely about Cordova. It is called *Negro* simply, but I believe is the *Barba Negro*, from which the *Pelissier* wheat is said to have originated. None of these wheats are much exported, and it is impossible to determine here their macaroni-making properties." (*Fairchild.*)

7426. VICIA FABA. **Broad bean.**

From Alicante, Spain. Received through Mr. D. G. Fairchild (No. 755), August 30, 1901.

Mahonesas. "A variety of broad bean, preferred for boiling purposes by Alicantians. Comes from Mahon in the Balearic Islands." (*Fairchild.*)

7427. HORDEUM TETRASTICHUM. **Barley.**

From Albacete, Spain. Received through Mr. D. G. Fairchild (No. 761). Sample received August 21, 1901; 88 kilos received January 14, 1902.

Albacete. "The barley of this dry plateau region of southeastern Spain is used for brewing purposes. Although its quality for this purpose can not compare with the best *Hanna* barley, it is a good variety and worthy of trial by breeders in the southwest." (*Fairchild.*)

7428. TRITICUM DURUM. **Wheat.**

From Albacete, Spain. Received through Mr. D. G. Fairchild (No. 758), January 14, 1902.

"This is the ordinary durum wheat of this dry plateau. It is not, I am told by a dealer in Murcia, as 'strong' a variety as the Russian so-called *Taganrog*, and hence is not exported, but from what I saw of it I judge it will prove resistant to rust in a fairly high degree. No distinctive name was discoverable. It is the only hard variety." (*Fairchild.*)

7429. TRITICUM VULGARE. **Wheat.**

From Albacete, Spain. Received through Mr. D. G. Fairchild (No. 759), January 14, 1902.

Candial. "A soft variety of wheat grown on this dry plateau in southeastern Spain. This variety is very highly esteemed as a bread-making sort for home use. It may prove valuable for our dry southern plains, for it is grown without irrigation. It is quite distinct from the variety known by the name of Candeal in South America, being a soft wheat, while the South American kind is a hard wheat." (*Fairchild.*)

7430. TRITICUM DURUM (?) **Wheat.**

From Albacete, Spain. Received through Mr. D. G. Fairchild (No. 760), January 14, 1902.

Gejar. "A semihard wheat, which is said to be the best for the manufacture of macaroni of any in Spain. It is not so 'strong' as the *Taganrog*, I am told, but has a very fine gluten, which makes it sought after by Spanish macaroni makers. It is grown on the high plateau of southeastern Spain without irrigation, and is suited for trial in the southwest." (*Fairchild.*)

7431 to 7438. MORUS sp. **Mulberry.**

From Murcia, Spain. Received through Mr. D. G. Fairchild (No. 757, f, g, h, i, j, k, l, m, n), August 21, 1901.

Various species of mulberry for silkworm feeding. All dead except:

7431. *Alba nervosa.* (757 f.)

7436. *Fertil de Italia.* (757 l.)

(See Nos. 7141 to 7145.)

7439. AGAVE UNIVITATTA. **Lechuguilla.**

From Tamaulipas, Mexico. Received through Mr. L. H. Dewey, August 31, 1901. Presented by Mr. H. Riehl.

A Tampico fiber plant.

7440. PUNICA GRANATUM. **Pomegranate.**

From the island of Chios, Turkey. Presented by Mr. N. J. Pantelides, through Mr. D. G. Fairchild. Received August 23, 1901.

"Scions of a variety of pomegranate which has seeds that are very tender coated. Probably a similar variety to that commonly cultivated on the coast of Spain and considered the best market variety there." (*Fairchild.*)

7441 to 7445.

From Nice, France. Presented by Mr. A. Robertson-Proschowsky. Received August 23, 1901.

A collection of seeds as follows:

7441. TRACHYCARPUS EXCELSUS.

7442. PHOENIX RECLINATA.

7443. PHOENIX.

Hybrid pollinated with *P. reclinata.*

7444. PHOENIX PUMILA.

Pollinated with *P. reclinata.*

7445. PSIDIUM CATTLEYANUM.

7446.

From Mexico. Received through Dr. J. N. Rose (No. 304), August 24, 1901.

7447.

From Mexico. Received through Dr. J. N. Rose (No. 305), August 24, 1901.

7448. CAPSICUM ANNUUM. **Red pepper.**

From Alicante, Spain. Received through Mr. D. G. Fairchild (No. 754), August 21, 1901.

"A very fine variety of red pepper grown at Aspra, not far from Elche, near Alicante. It forms a showy object in the market place and is grown extensively." (*Fairchild.*)

7449. PIMPINELLA ANISUM. **Anise.**

From Alicante, Spain. Received through Mr. D. G. Fairchild, August 24, 1901.

"The anise seed of southeastern Spain is noted. One firm here has exported 40,000 '*vielas*' in a single year. Used in Amsterdam for the manufacture of anisette." (*Fairchild.*)

7450. AVENA SATIVA. **Oat.**

From Alicante, Spain. Received through Mr. D. G. Fairchild, August 24, 1901.

"Sample of oats from market." (*Fairchild.*)

7451. HORDEUM VULGARE. **Barley.**

From Alicante, Spain. Received through Mr. D. G. Fairchild, August 24, 1901.

"Sample of barley from market." (*Fairchild.*)

7452 to 7458. AMYGDALUS COMMUNIS. **Almond.**

From Alicante, Spain. Received through Mr. D. G. Fairchild, August 24, 1901.

Almond fruits as follows:

7452.
Mollar. From same tree as No. 7061.

7453.
Planeta. From same tree as No. 7134.

7454.
Castillet. From same tree as No. 7133.

7455.
Fabrica. From same tree as No. 7135.

7456.
Planeta. From a grower.

7457.
Planeta. From a grower.

7458.
Pastaneta. From a grower.

7459. TRITICUM DURUM. **Wheat.**

From near Alicante, Spain. Received through Mr. D. G. Fairchild, August 24, 1901.

"Sample of wheat from threshing floor." (*Fairchild.*)

7460. CERATONIA SILIQUA. **Carob.**

From Alicante, Spain. Received through Mr. D. G. Fairchild (No. 743), August 24, 1901.

Negra. Seed pods from same tree as cuttings. (No. 7063.)

7461. CERATONIA SILIQUA. **Carob.**

From Alicante, Spain. Received through Mr. D. G. Fairchild, (No. 744) August 24, 1901.

Vera. "Seed pods. This is said to be one of the sweetest varieties known. It is planted for table use especially and is too valuable for horse food. The yield is irregular and small compared with other sorts." (*Fairchild.*)

7462. CICER ARIETINUM. **Chick-pea.**

From Cordova, Spain. Received through Mr. D. G. Fairchild, August 24, 1901.

7463. TRITICUM DURUM. **Wheat.**

From Alicante, Spain. Received through Mr. D. G. Fairchild (No. 763), August 24, 1901.

Berberisco. "A variety of wheat which was introduced into Spain many years ago from Barbary, and which has won for itself the reputation of being a larger yielder and having better grain than the durum wheat *Blanco*, No. 7464. It would be interesting to try this in comparison with Algerian wheats, which are said to have originated (part of them at least) from imported Spanish sorts." (*Fairchild.*)

7464. TRITICUM DURUM. **Wheat.**

From Cordova, Spain. Received through Mr. D. G. Fairchild (No. 762), August 24, 1901.

Blanco. "A native variety of hard wheat grown about Cordova which has the reputation of being of a fair quality and, although not so productive as the so-called *Berberisco*, it is more resistant to drought. I believe it will also prove resistant to rust in a fair degree." (*Fairchild.*)

7465. TRITICUM DURUM. **Wheat.**

From Uralsk, Russia. Received through Mr. A. A. Vannohin, August 29, 1901.

Kubanka. (See No. 5639, Inventory No. 10.)

7466. TRITICUM VULGARE. **Wheat.**

From Padui, Russia. Received through Mr. M. Narishkin, August 29, 1901.

Padui. (See No. 5640, Inventory No. 10.)

7467. TRITICUM VULGARE. **Wheat.**

From Kharkof, Russia. Received through Dr. A. Boenicke, August 29, 1901.

Kharkof. (See No. 5641, Inventory No. 10.)

7468. GARCINIA MANGOSTANA. **Mangosteen.**

From Heneratgoda, Ceylon. Received through J. P. William & Bros., August 29, 1901.

7469 to 7490.

From Mexico. Received through Dr. J. N. Rose (Nos. 306 to 327), August 30, 1901.

A collection of Mexican plants and bulbs as follows (Doctor Rose's numbers are given for purposes of identification):

7469. Orchid.
(No. 306.)

7470. Orchid.
(No. 307.)

7471. Orchid.
(No. 308.)

7472. Orchid.
(No. 309.)

7469 to 7490—Continued.

    7473.   **Orchid.**
        (No. 310.)

    7474.   **Orchid.**
        (No. 311.)

    7475.   **Orchid.**
        (No. 312.)

    7476.   **Orchid.**
        (No. 313.)

    7477.   **Orchid.**
        (No. 314.)

    7478.   **Orchid.**
        (No. 315.)

7479. COTYLEDON sp. (No. 316.)	**7484.** TILLANDSIA sp. (No. 321.)
7480. ARUM sp. (?). (No. 317.)	**7485.** ZEPHYRANTHES sp. (No. 322.)
7481. TILLANDSIA sp. (No. 318.)	**7486.** TILLANDSIA sp. (No. 323.)
7482. TILLANDSIA sp. (No. 319.)	**7487.** COTYLEDON sp. (No. 324.)
7483. TILLANDSIA sp. (No. 320.)	**7488.** AGAVE sp. (No. 325.)

    7489. SOLANUM sp.   **Potato.**
        (No. 326.)

    7490.
        (No. 327.)

7491 to 7495.

    From Mexico. Received through Dr. J. N. Rose (Nos. 6259 and 328 to 331), August 31, 1901.

    A collection of Mexican plants and bulbs, as follows:

7491. (No. 6259.)	**7494.** (No. 330.)
7492. (No. 328.)	**7495.** (No. 331.)
7493. (No. 329.)	

7496. CISSUS.

    From Eagle Pass, Tex. Received through Dr. J. N. Rose, September 5, 1901.

7497.

From Mexico. Received through Dr. J. N. Rose (No. 259), September 5, 1901.

7498. VICIA FABA. **Broad bean.**

From Vomero-Naples, Italy. Received through Mr. C. Sprenger, September 5, 1901.

St. Pantaleone. "A new variety of bean having very long pods." (*Sprenger.*)

7499. ANACARDIUM OCCIDENTALE. **Cashew.**

From Kingston, Jamaica. Received through Mr. W. Harris, assistant superintendent of the Hope Gardens, September 5, 1901.

7500. MEDICAGO SATIVA. **Alfalfa.**

From Oued Rirh oasis, northern Sahara Desert. Received through Mr. W. T. Swingle from French and Arab foremen of the European date plantations. Received May, 1901.

"An early sort, resisting drought and alkali much better than the ordinary alfalfa." (*Swingle.*)

7501. SPONDIAS sp. **Ciruela.**

From Iguala, Mexico. Received through Mr. Elmer Stearns, Los Angeles, Cal., September 10, 1901.

Dried fruit.

7502. ZEA MAYS. **Corn.**

From Tampico, Mexico. Received through Mr. Elmer Stearns, Los Angeles, Cal., September 10, 1901.

Large White Mexican.

7503. PHASEOLUS VULGARIS. **Bean.**

From City of Mexico, Mexico. Received through Mr. Elmer Stearns, Los Angeles, Cal., September 10, 1901.

Large Purple.

7504. PHASEOLUS VULGARIS. **Bean.**

From City of Mexico, Mexico. Received through Mr. Elmer Stearns, Los Angeles, Cal., September 10, 1901.

Ballo Gordo. A yellow bean.

7505. CASIMIROA EDULIS. **White sapota.**

From Guadalajara, Mexico. Received through Mr. Elmer Stearns, Los Angeles, Cal., September 10, 1901.

Zapote Blanco.

7506. (Unidentified seeds.)

From City of Mexico, Mexico. Received through Mr. Elmer Stearns, Los Angeles, Cal., September 10, 1901.

Pepita para mole verde. "Sold in roasted condition on streets of Mexico." (*Stearns.*)

7507. OPUNTIA sp.

From City of Mexico, Mexico. Received through Mr. Elmer Stearns, Los Angeles, Cal., September 10, 1901.

Tuna Colorado. "Fruit is the size of a duck's egg, and has very red flesh." (*Stearns.*)

7508. CUCURBITA sp. **Pumpkin.**

From City of Mexico, Mexico. Received through Mr. Elmer Stearns, Los Angeles, Cal., September 10, 1901.

Spargel Kurbis.

7509. CEREUS sp. (?) **Pitahaya.**

From Tampica and Guadalajara, Mexico. Received through Mr. Elmer Stearns, Los Angeles, Cal., September 10, 1901.

"Fruit pink, large, sweet, and fine eating." (See Cont. U. S. Herb., Vol. V, No. 4, pp. 220–221.)

7510. CARICA PAPAYA. **Papaw.**

From Tampico, Mexico. Received through Mr. Elmer Stearns, Los Angeles, Cal., September 10, 1901.

"Fruit very large." (*Stearns.*)

7511. CUCUMIS SATIVUS (?). **Cucumber.**

From City of Mexico, Mexico. Received through Mr. Elmer Stearns, Los Angeles, Cal., September 10, 1901.

"Fruit of fine flavor, round, the size of a large apple. Bears large crop." (*Stearns.*)

7512 to 7515. TRITICUM VULGARE. **Wheat.**

From Proskurow, Russia. Received through Dr. S. Mrozinski, September 9, 1901.

Samples of wheat as follows:

7512.

Sandomirka. "A beardless wheat grown in Podolia. It is very resistant to frost, heat, and drought. This wheat was first grown in the vicinity of Sandomir, in Poland." (*Mrozinski.*)

7513.

Plock. "A variety of wheat introduced into Podolia from Plock, Poland. It is especially noted for its resistance to the effect of rain storms." (*Mrozinski.*)

7514.

Triumph of Podolia. "An improved local species, very productive and resistant to all climatic changes." (*Mrozinski.*)

7515.

Banat. "Selected from the original Hungarian *Banat*. It is noted for not degenerating as easily as the original." (*Mrozinski.*)

7516 and 7517. AMYGDALUS COMMUNIS. **Almond.**

From Malaga, Spain. Received through Mr. D. G. Fairchild (No. 769), September 13, 1901.

Jordan. "Bought in the shell from a grower in the Sierra, at a small village called Almogia, one hour's mule ride from the well-known road of Antiquera. This is a collection as it came from the trees, small and large together, and is for purposes of seed selection. It is highly probable that new varieties (seedlings) can be secured from these seeds, and they should be distributed to breeders of *Prunus*. Almost all the trees about Malaga, where this particular variety is grown and from which place almonds are shipped in large quantities to America, are budded trees. The stock is the bitter almond, seeds of which (No. 7517) are included in the same box with the Jordans. I am told, however, that seedling plants are employed and that they bear fruit reasonably true to type. The soil on which these trees are grown is very rocky and light and at this season is quite dry and dusty. Hillsides and high-lying valleys are the favorite spots for their cultivation, and the secret of their culture seems to lie in the freedom from spring frosts. They flower in January and February, and even about Malaga a crop is often lost by a frost at flowering time. These frosts being quite local, one often hears in one valley of a total loss of the crop in a neighboring one. These seeds may prove very valuable in originating later-blooming sorts of good quality and in discovering valleys suited to their culture. The seed should be carefully inspected and all specimens with gum adhering discarded. I recommend, further, that the remaining be washed with copper sulphate or some other disinfectant and well rinsed with fresh water. The disease called *Gummosis* is a troublesome one and exists in all the orchards I have visited. It is important that this disease, if it really is one, be not introduced into California. I am unaware if it is already there and has been studied. I have seen trees that appeared to be dying of the disease. Nuts attacked by it are worthless. These seeds should be stratified and planted without cracking in rich garden earth. Budding is done here only in April." (*Fairchild.*)

7518. ROMNEYA COULTERI.   Matilija poppy.

From Los Angeles, Cal. Received through Mr. Elmer Stearns, September 20, 1901.

7519. CEREUS sp. (?)   Pitahaya.

From Guadalajara, Mexico. Received through Mr. Elmer Stearns, Los Angeles, Cal., September 20, 1901.

"Fruit three to four inches long and two inches in diameter. Skin reddish pink. Pulp white and jellylike, with the seeds distributed through it. Sweet and fine eating." (*Stearns.*)

7520 to 7534.

From Paris, France. Received through Vilmorin-Andrieux & Co., September 21, 1901.

A collection of agricultural seeds, as follows:

 7520. TRIGONELLA FOENUM-GRAECUM.   Fenugreek.

 7521. LATHYRUS CICER.   Vetch.
 Gesse jarosse.

 7522. ERVUM MONANTHOS.   Lentil.
 One-flowered lentil.

 7523. ERVUM LENS HIEMALE.   Lentil.
 Red winter lentil.

 7524. LUPINUS ALBUS.   Lupine.
 White lupine.

 7525. LUPINUS LUTEUS.   Lupine.
 Yellow lupine.

 7526. ONOBRYCHIS ONOBRYCHIS.   Sainfoin.

 7527. ONOBRYCHIS ONOBRYCHIS.   Sainfoin.
 Sainfoin à deux coupes.

 7528. HEDYSARUM CORONARIUM.   Sulla.
 Spanish Sulla.

 7529. TRIFOLIUM INCARNATUM.   Crimson clover.
 Early variety.

7520 to 7534—Continued.

7530. TRIFOLIUM INCARNATUM.   **Crimson clover.**
Very late variety, with white flowers.

7531. SECALE CEREALE.   **Rye.**
Giant winter.

7532. VICIA NARBONNENSIS.   **Narbonne vetch.**

7533. VICIA VILLOSA.   **Hairy vetch.**

7534. LATHYRUS OCHRUS.   **Vetch.**

7535. LUPINUS ANGUSTIFOLIUS.   **Blue lupine.**

From Eustis, Fla. Sent by Mr. F. W. Savage through Mr. W. T. Swingle. Received September 23, 1901.

A North African variety. Grown from No. 5583.

7536 to 7556.

From Paris, France. Received through Vilmorin Andrieux & Co., September 23, 1901.

A collection of seeds as follows:

7536. ALBIZZIA JULIBRISSIN (?)

7537. MORUS ALBA. Hat-var. MORETTI.

7538. SCHINUS MOLLE.

7539. SCHINUS TEREBINTHIFOLIUS.

7540. FICUS ELASTICA.

7541. CAESALPINIA BONDUCELLA.

7542. HURA CREPITANS.

7543. SWIETENIA MAHAGONI.

7544. COLUIFERA BALSAMINUM.

7545. ARENGA SACCHARIFERA.

7546. CYCAS NORMANBYANA.

7547. LICUALA GRANDIS.

7548. LIVISTONA JENKINSIANA.

7549. CINCHONA CALISAYA.

7550. CINCHONA LEDGERIANA.

7551. CINCHONA CALISAYA.

7552. CINCHONA SUCCI-RUBRA.

7553. LESPEDEZA SIEBOLDI.

7554. ILEX INTEGRA.

7555. ABRUS PRECATORIUS.

7556. LEUCADENDRON ARGENTEUM.

7557 to 7574.

From St. Albans, England. Received through Sander & Co., September 24, 1901.

A collection of plants as follows:

7557. RICHARDIA sp.
Calla leucoxantha.

7558. LEEA SAMBUCINA.

7561. DIANTHUS CARYOPHYLLUS.   **Carnation.**
Ivanhoe.

7559. PANAX AUREUM.

7560. PASSIFLORA PRUINOSA.

7557 to 7574—Continued.

7562. DIANTHUS CARYOPHYLLUS.   Carnation.
J. Coles.

7563. DIANTHUS CARYOPHYLLUS.   Carnation.
Lily Measures.

7564. DIANTHUS CARYOPHYLLUS.   Carnation.
Mrs. F. Sander.

7565. DIANTHUS CARYOPHYLLUS.   Carnation.
Monica.

7566. DIANTHUS CARYOPHYLLUS.   Carnation.
Mrs. Joicey.

7567. RICHARDIA sp.
Calla Elliottiana Rossii.

7568. ACANTHOPHOENIX CRINITA.

7569. BENTINCKIA NICOBARICA.

7570. COCOS CORONATA.

7571. CYRTOSTACHYS RENDA.

7572. HETEROSPATHE ELATA.

7573. PTYCHORAPHIS AUGUSTA.

7574. KENTIA SANDERIANA.

7575 and 7576. TRITICUM DURUM.   Wheat.

Grown by Oscar C. Snow, Mesilla Park, N. Mex., under contract. Distributed from the New Mexico Agricultural Experiment Station. Reported ready for delivery September, 1901.

7575. *Gharnovka*, grown from No. 5643.

7576. *Kubanka*, grown from No. 5639.

7577. PHYSALIS PERUVIANA.   Cape gooseberry.

From Lima, Peru. Received through Mr. Elmer Stearns, Los Angeles, Cal., September 26, 1901.

Naranjilla. "Plant 2 to 3 feet tall, branching, leaves large. Fruits abundant. The local name means Little Orange." (*Stearns.*)

7578. TRITICUM DURUM.   Wheat.

From province of Oran, Algeria. Received through Messrs. D. G. Fairchild and C. S. Scofield (No. 721), September 26, 1901.

Marouani. "This wheat is cultivated extensively on the elevated rolling lands in the western part of the province, and is one of the best of the types of durum wheats cultivated by the Arabs. The quantity obtained is from the estate of M. J. Labouresse, at Tessala, near Sidi-bel-Abbès. It has been carefully selected by Mr. Labouresse from year to year until a fairly pure and very vigorous stock has been obtained. The variety is very hardy, resistant to rust, and succeeds fairly well under rather droughty conditions. The grain is especially adapted for the manufacture of semolina. In the province of Oran the wheat is sown in November and ripens in June, but it might succeed as a spring wheat in the spring-wheat region of the northern United States." (*Fairchild and Scofield.*)

7579. TRITICUM DURUM.   Wheat.

From Sidi-bel-Abbès, province of Oran, Algeria. Received through Messrs. D. G. Fairchild and C. S. Scofield (No. 722), September 26, 1901.

Medeah. "This is one of the best-known macaroni wheat varieties of western Algeria. When grown on the high rolling lands in the vicinity of the city of Medeah it produces a grain with very valuable macaroni-making qualities. It was recently introduced into the vicinity of Sidi-bel-Abbès, where it gives promise of being a very valuable sort, ripening ten to fifteen days earlier than the Marouani and similar sorts grown in that vicinity. It is ordinarily sown here in November and ripens early in June, but it is worth trying as a spring wheat in the northern United States. The sample obtained is from the farm of M. J. Labouresse, of Tessala, near Sidi-bel-Abbès, which latter is one of the noted wheat growing districts of Algeria, possessing a light rich soil." (*Fairchild and Scofield.*)

7580. TRITICUM DURUM. **Wheat.**

From Batna, Constantine, Algeria. Received through Messrs. D. G. Fairchild and C. S. Scofield (No. 729), September 26, 1901.

Adjini. "This wheat is from stock grown by the Arabs on the rolling lands of the Aurès Mountains, east of Batna, where the summer temperature often reaches 100° F. and where it frequently drops to zero in winter. It is a variety highly spoken of by the macaroni manufacturers of Marseille, and, although rapidly deteriorating in quality, when cultivated there, has given very good yields when grown without irrigation on lower lands of the high plateau of the province of Constantine. The soil on these lands is excessively rich in sulphate of magnesia and is of a hard and gravelly nature. Although a winter wheat in Batna, being sown in December or January and harvested early in July, it will be worth a trial in the spring-wheat region. The seed obtained is from Arab growers, whose methods of culture are very primitive, and the Department is indebted to Mr. G. Ryf, manager of the Geneva Society of Setif, for its purchase from them." (*Fairchild and Scofield.*)

7581. TRITICUM DURUM. **Wheat.**

From El-Outaya, Constantine, Algeria. Received through Messrs. D. G. Fairchild and C. S. Scofield (No. 730), September 26, 1901.

Kahla. "This wheat will be found to differ from the *Kahla*, No. 7794, of the high plateau region, as it comes from plants grown by irrigation on the somewhat salty sands of the northern Sahara Desert. It is one of the few sorts of wheats that maintain their good quality when grown year after year in slightly alkaline soils. It is highly valued by the Arabs for its rich content of elastic gluten. It is grown on land that probably has at least 5 per cent of salt in it and the irrigation water itself with which the plants are irrigated is slightly salty, not so salty, however, as to be quite undrinkable. The wheat is planted in El-Outaya in December or January, but it might be worth trying as a spring wheat in the North. This seed is from the farm of Mr. Charles des Places at El-Outaya. As a macaroni wheat its rank is not known, but its ability to grow in alkaline soil makes it especially valuable for any experiments in the irrigated salt lands of America. We were told that a change of seed was especially beneficial on these salt lands. Quantities of wheat are brought down from the neighboring mountains to plant on these salt lands. This change of seed forbids the formation of any salt-resistant race, but does not change the interest in these wheats for other salt lands." (*Fairchild and Scofield.*)

7582. TRITICUM VULGARE. **Wheat.**

From El-Outaya, Constantine, Algeria. Received through Messrs. D. G. Fairchild and C. S. Scofield (No. 731), September 26, 1901.

Fretes. "This variety, sometimes called *Freitiss*, is one of the few soft wheats grown in Algeria. It is particularly noted for its early maturity and is often extensively planted in the Sahara Desert in seasons when the winter rains occur so late that the durum varieties usually grown would not have time to mature. When planted in November, as it is in Algeria, at the same time with durum varieties, it is said to ripen two months in advance of them. The seed obtained was grown on the rather salty desert sands in the vicinity of El-Outaya, north of Biskra, and watered with somewhat alkaline but still drinkable irrigation water. The variety is said to have originated from a shipment of Russian wheat which was made into Algeria at the time of a famine many years ago. Its early maturing qualities attracted attention, and it has been cultivated in small quantities by the Arabs ever since. The seed obtained is from the farm of Mr. Charles B. des Places." (*Fairchild and Scofield.*)

7583. HORDEUM TETRASTICHUM. **Barley.**

From El-Outaya, Constantine, Algeria. Received through Messrs. D. G. Fairchild and C. S. Scofield (No. 732), September 26, 1901.

Beldi. "This and the following variety (No. 7584) are sorts planted on the saline soils of the edge of the Sahara Desert. They are grown by irrigation, but the irrigation water itself is saline. In quality they are neither of them of superior excellence and are little used, if any, for beer-making purposes. The yield is small when compared with that of barley grown on good soils, but it nevertheless seems to pay the French colonists to grow it in these regions where very few plants of any kind succeed. The Arabs feed their horses largely on barley and even eat it themselves. Mr. des Places says, however, that on these saline soils where this barley is grown he finds a change of seed beneficial, even necessary, and he imports every year or two his seed barley and seed wheat from the mountains, because it so rapidly degenerates. These barleys are introduced for a trial on the salt lands of the Southwest. The names given are Arab ones for slightly different strains. Secured of Mr. Charles B. des Places." (*Fairchild and Scofield.*)

7584. HORDEUM TETRASTICHUM. **Barley.**

From El-Outaya, Constantine, Algeria. Received through Messrs. D. G. Fairchild and C. S. Scofield (No. 733), September 26, 1901.

Telli. "A barley for salt lands under irrigation. See No. 7583 for description." (*Fairchild and Scofield.*)

7585. TRITICUM TURGIDUM. **Wheat.**

From Oran, Algeria. Received through Messrs. D. G. Fairchild and C. S. Scofield (No. 734), September 26, 1901.

Black Poulard. "This is one of the so-called Poulard wheats, a class which is commonly grown in France on stiff or heavy soils unfavorable to the culture of less vigorous sorts. The quality of the grain is considered inferior to that of either *T. durum* or *T. vulgare*. It is particularly valuable on account of its vigorous growth and hardiness. It is usually grown as an autumn wheat, but is worthy of trial on any land too heavy or too coarse to produce ordinary wheats to good advantage. The seed was secured from M. Vermeil, professor of agriculture at Oran, who has it growing in his experimental plats under the Arabic name of 'Kahla,' a name which, however, is applied in other parts of Algeria to a quite different variety of wheat. (See Nos. 7581 and 7794.) This is not a macaroni wheat, but may be used for flour making." (*Fairchild and Scofield.*)

7586. MEDICAGO SATIVA. **Alfalfa.**

From Setif, province of Constantine, Algeria. Received through Messrs. D. G. Fairchild and C. S. Scofield (No. 735a), November 11, 1901.

"A wild variety which has been introduced into culture by Mr. G. Ryf, of Setif, who is conducting experiments, the results of which are published by the "Comice Agricole," of Setif, of which Mr. Ryf is a prominent member. This variety has been remarkable in its variation since its introduction to cultivation, and the seed should prove an excellent foundation stock from which to select varieties for special soils and conditions. In general it has been found very resistant to drought and well adapted to soils rich in phosphates. Mr. Ryf has an interesting method of cultivating it. He plants the seed in rows 39 inches apart and cultivates between the rows the first season. The following season the crops of hay are cut as rapidly as they come on, and the plants spread out, forming broad bands or rows. The season following, the space between the rows and all but a narrow band 8 inches wide of the alfalfa is plowed under and well tilled. After this cultivation a crop of wheat is sown between the rows of alfalfa, and when this is matured and removed a light cultivation is given, and the following year the rows of alfalfa are allowed to spread out and crops of hay are taken off. In this way wheat and alfalfa are alternated from year to year. Mr. Ryf finds that by following this method the perennial leguminous forage crops give much better results than annual ones. This he attributes largely to the extra amount of cultivation that this method permits. In fact he finds that for his conditions an extra cultivation of the soil gives better results in the following crop than the planting of an annual leguminous crop, with which cultivation is impossible. This is seed from a procumbent form of the plant." (*Fairchild and Scofield.*)

7587. MEDICAGO SATIVA. **Alfalfa.**

From Setif, Constantine, Algeria. Received through Messrs. D. G. Fairchild and C. S. Scofield (No. 735a), November 11, 1901.

A wild variety, with erect form. (See No. 7586.)

7588. MEDICAGO MEDIA. **Sand lucern.**

From Setif, Constantine, Algeria. Received through Messrs. D. G. Fairchild and C. S. Scofield (No. 735a+), November 11, 1901.

Luzerne rustique.

7589. BAUHINIA sp. **White bauhinia.**

From Mount Silinda, Melsetter district, Rhodesia, South Africa. Received through Dr. Wm. L. Thompson, October 1, 1901.

"Is quite rare. The flowers are large and beautiful and very abundant, but very delicate. The plant seems quite sensitive to frost and many plants have been injured by it this year." (*Thompson.*)

7590. BAUHINIA sp. **Red bauhinia.**

From Mount Silinda, Melsetter district, Rhodesia, South Africa. Received through Dr. Wm. L. Thompson, October 1, 1901.

"The red variety is very widely and generally distributed over this region." (*Thompson.*)

7591 to 7630.

From London, England. Received through James H. Veitch & Sons, October 3, 1901.

A collection of ornamental plants as follows (nomenclature is that of the seedsmen):

7591. BEGONIA sp. Begonia.
Winter Cheer.

7592. BEGONIA sp. Begonia.
Adonis.

7593. BEGONIA CARMINATA. Begonia.

7594. BEGONIA sp. Begonia.
Ensign.

7595. BEGONIA EUDOXA. Begonia.

7596. BEGONIA INCOMPARABILIS. Begonia.

7597. BEGONIA sp. Begonia.
John Heal.

7598. BEGONIA sp. Begonia.
Mrs. Heal.

7599. BEGONIA sp. Begonia.
Venus.

7600. BEGONIA sp. Begonia.
Winter Perfection.

7601. CODIAEUM VARIEGATUM. Croton.
Mrs. McLeod.

7602. CODIAEUM VARIEGATUM. Croton.
Aigburth Gem.

7603. CODIAEUM VARIEGATUM. Croton.
Mrs. Iceton.

7591 to 7630—Continued.

- 7604. CODIAEUM VARIEGATUM.   Croton.
  Princess of Wales.
- 7605. DRACAENA sp.
  Duchess of York.
- 7606. DRACAENA sp.
  Esckhantei.
- 7607. DRACAENA sp.
  The Sirdar.
- 7608. DRACAENA sp.
  Exquisite.
- 7609. DRACAENA sp.
  Donsetti.
- 7610. AMASONIA CALYCINA.
- 7611. MARANTA MAJOR.
- 7612. ALLAMANDA BLANCHETII.
- 7613. MEDINILLA BORNENSIS.
- 7614. MEDINILLA MAGNIFICA.
- 7615. MUSSAENDA GRANDIFLORA.
- 7616. ROUPALA POHLII.
- 7617. VRIESIA FENESTRALIS.
- 7618. TILLANDSIA LINDENIANA.
- 7619. GUZMANIA MUSAICA.
- 7620. URCEOLINA PENDULA.
- 7621. ZINGIBER OFFICINALE.
- 7622. RICHARDIA ELLIOTTIANA.
- 7623. RICHARDIA PENTLANDI.
- 7624. HEDYCHIUM GARDNERIANUM.
- 7625. DIANTHUS CARYOPHYLLUS.   Carnation.
  Blush White.
- 7626. DIANTHUS CARYOPHYLLUS.   Carnation.
  Lady Grimstone.
- 7627. DIANTHUS CARYOPHYLLUS.   Carnation.
  Lord Rosebery.
- 7628. DIANTHUS CARYOPHYLLUS.   Carnation.
  Trumpeter.
- 7629. DIANTHUS CARYOPHYLLUS.   Carnation.
  George Maquat.
- 7630. SEMELE ANDROGYNA.

7631 to 7636. PHOENIX DACTYLIFERA.   **Date palm.**

From Egypt. Received through Mr. D. G. Fairchild (No. 597) from Mr. Em. C. Zervudachi, Alexandria, October 2, 1901.

7631.

Amri. "One of the best varieties, of large size; color, garnet verging on black." (*Zervudachi.*)

7632.

Oga of Bedrichen. "Of medium size; color, garnet verging on black." (*Zervudachi.*)

7633.

Nagl-el-Basha. "One of the best varieties, of large size; color, yellowish." (*Zervudachi.*)

7631 to 7636—Continued.

7634.

Sultani or *Soubaa-el-Sitti.* "One of the best varieties, of medium size; color, yellowish." (*Zervudachi.*)

7635.

Birket-el-Haggi. "Of medium size; color, garnet verging on black." (*Zervudachi.*)

7636.

Am-hat. "Of small size and yellowish color." (*Zervudachi.*)

7637. LATHYRUS TINGITANUS. **Tangier scarlet pea.**

From Algeria. Received through Mr. D. G. Fairchild, September 26, 1901.

7638. CICER ARIETINUM. **Chick-pea.**

From Rouïba, Algeria. Received through Mr. D. G. Fairchild, September 26, 1901.

7639. LATHYRUS SATIVUS.

From Rouïba, Algeria. Received through Mr. D. G. Fairchild, September 26, 1901.

7640 to 7645.

From Tunis, Tunis. Received through Mr. D. G. Fairchild (Nos. 697 to 702), October 4, 1901.

Samples of miscellaneous seeds presented by the School of Agriculture of Tunis.

7640. HORDEUM VULGARE. **Naked barley.**

Chair-en Nebbi. "Originated in Tunis, but grown in the trial gardens of the college for three years." (No. 697.) (*Fairchild.*)

7641. HORDEUM VULGARE. **Naked barley.**

"From Turkestan. Grown three years in Agricultural College garden, Tunis." (No. 698.) (*Fairchild.*)

7642. TRIGONELLA FOENUM-GRAECUM. **Fenugreek.**

"The grain is eaten by the Jewish women of Tunis in large quantities in order to increase their avoirdupois, it being the fashion to weigh as much as 200 pounds or more. Primarily, however, a forage and soiling crop." (No. 699.) (*Fairchild.*)

7643. ANDROPOGON HALAPENSIS.

Sorgho d'Alep. "This is an important grain crop of north Africa. It hybridizes easily with broom corn and causes the latter to deteriorate." (No. 700.) (*Fairchild.*)

7644. CARTHAMNUS TINCTORIUS. **Safflower.**

"Grown as an oil plant." (No. 701.) (*Fairchild.*)

7645. GUIZOTIA ABYSSINICA.

"An oil-producing plant used like sesame. It is grown similarly." (No. 702.) (*Fairchild.*)

7646. PENNISETUM SPICATUM. **Pearl millet.**

From Tunis, Tunis. Received through Mr. D. G. Fairchild (No. 696), October 4, 1901.

Millet de Chandelles. "Probably grown extensively in the south of the province of Tunis, about Gabez. Arabs use it for food, Europeans for forage. May be useful for breeding. From School of Agriculture, Tunis." (*Fairchild.*)

7647. GOSSYPIUM sp. **Cotton.**

From Tunis, Tunis. Received through Mr. D. G. Fairchild (No. 695), September 26, 1901.

Coton bruine de Mallaganza. "Single boll of a brown cotton from the collection of cottons at the School of Agriculture of Tunis. Its origin is quite unknown." (*Fairchild.*)

7648. LINUM USITATISSIMUM. **Flax.**

From Oran, Tunis. Received through Mr. D. G. Fairchild (No. 717), September 26, 1901.

"Said to resist drought very well." (*Fairchild.*)

7649. LINUM USITATISSIMUM. **Flax.**

From Tunis, Tunis. Received through Mr. D. G. Fairchild (No. 716), September 26, 1901.

"Also said to be drought resistant." (*Fairchild.*)

7650 to 7653. TRITICUM DURUM. **Wheat.**

From Tunis, Tunis. Presented by the School of Agriculture of Tunis through Mr. D. G. Fairchild (Nos. 703 to 706). Received September 26, 1901.

Samples of wheat from the collection in the School of Agriculture of Tunis. They bear the following native names, for whose spelling Mr. R. Gagey, instructor at the college, is responsible:

7650.
Sba er Roumi (*Sboa-el-Roumia*). (No. 706.)

7651.
Azizi. (No. 705.)

7652.
Médeah. (No. 704.)

7653.
Abd-el-Kader. (No. 703.)

7654. CAPSICUM ANNUUM. **Red pepper.**

From Tunis, Tunis. Received through Mr. D. G. Fairchild (No. 718), September 26, 1901.

"A large, very fine, long red pepper from market of Tunis." (*Fairchild.*)

7655. CICER ARIETINUM. **Chick-pea.**

From Tunis, Tunis. Received through Mr. D. G. Fairchild (No. 707, May 27, 1901), September 26, 1901.

"The native chick-pea of Tunis for comparative tests as to nodule-producing properties and resistance to drought. From the School of Agriculture in Tunis." (*Fairchild.*)

7656. LOTUS TETRAGONOLOBUS. **Square pea.**

From Tunis, Tunis. Received through Mr. D. G. Fairchild (No. 715, May 27, 1901), September 26, 1901.

"A new forage and seed legume being tried at the Tunis Agricultural College. Its root nodules are remarkable for their size and number, and its seed-bearing capacity is extraordinary." (*Fairchild.*)

7657. TRIFOLIUM ALEXANDRINUM. **Berseem.**

From Cairo, Egypt. Received through Mr. D. G. Fairchild (No. 642, May 9, 1901), October 10, 1901.

Saida. "This variety stands somewhat intermediate in character between *Muscowi* and *Fachl.* Its long-root system enables it to withstand dry weather very well, and it is considered in Egypt as a variety of dry-land Berseem. It yields two cuttings only, and is therefore sown in such regions as can be irrigated two or three times. It should be sown in autumn, on land with a limited power of irrigation, and will yield, on an average, about 6 tons of green fodder per acre at the first cutting and 4 or 5 at the second. It makes better hay than the *Muscowi*, but can not be considered of as great importance as that variety. The root system of this variety is longer than in either of the others." (*Fairchild.*)

7658. TRIFOLIUM ALEXANDRINUM. Berseem.

From Cairo, Egypt. Received through Mr. D. G. Fairchild (No. 643, May 9, 1901), October 10, 1901.

Fachl. "This variety differs materially from the *Muscowi* (No. 7659), being used on land which is irrigated by the basin system, that is, by being overflowed for forty days in the autumn. The seed is broadcasted at the rate of a bushel an acre on the mud, and no later irrigations are found necessary, as the plant gives only one cutting. This, however, yields 9 tons of green fodder per acre and makes a better hay than the *Muscowi*. In order to secure the seed of this variety it is the practice to sow the same broadcast with wheat or barley, and the seed is separated from the grain by thrashing, it being much smaller and lighter. This variety will be limited in its use to regions where only one irrigation can be given during the winter, or possibly may prove valuable as a spring forage crop." (*Fairchild.*)

7659. TRIFOLIUM ALEXANDRINUM. Berseem.

From Cairo, Egypt. Received through Mr. D. G. Fairchild (No. 644), October 10, 1901. Secured through the kindness of the secretary of the Khedivial Agricultural Society of Egypt, Mr. George P. Foaden.

Muscowi. "The great fodder and soiling crop of Egypt. An annual, leguminous, green fodder crop, considered indispensable by the Egyptians as a half-year rotation with cotton. Its fodder-producing value, effect upon the soil in storing up nitrogen, and cleansing effect are considered exceptional. It will be best suited to irrigated lands in warm climates, but might also be tested as a spring fodder crop in the northwestern coast States. In Egypt the seed is sown generally in October, after the soil has been thoroughly irrigated to prepare a moist bed for the seed. It is sown broadcast at the rate of not less than 40 pounds per acre. Even as high as 50 to 60 pounds are sown. This is due in part to the prevalence of weevils in the seed, which sometimes destroy the germinating power of a large percentage. The seed should be harrowed into the soil lightly, and when started the young plants should be given plenty of water. In Egypt the plants grow so rapidly that if sown toward the end of October a first cutting can be made after forty-five or fifty days, but if sown later, after the cooler weather has set in, it takes a much longer time for the plants to develop. Depending upon the amount of water and the temperature, the plants yield from four to five cuttings, yielding for the first and second cuttings about 8 tons of green forage per cutting and for the third and fourth cuttings somewhat less. In order to secure seed for next year's planting the plants should be left to stand after the fourth cutting, when they will go to seed. In Egypt the seed production is larger and heavier than in the case of clover. After each cutting a sufficiently long period should elapse before the plants are irrigated again, to allow the cut surfaces of the stems to dry out; otherwise the water will rot the plants. This fodder plant deserves a thorough test in the Colorado Desert region, beet-sugar regions of the Southwest, and as a soiling crop in the orchards of California." (*Fairchild.*)

7660. TRITICUM VULGARE. Wheat.

From Cairo, Egypt. Received through Mr. D. G. Fairchild (No. 638, May 9, 1901), October 10, 1901.

Bohi. "A soft wheat which is grown popularly about Cairo, and is considered one of the best soft wheats of Egypt. This sample comes from the grounds of the Khedivial Agricultural Society and was remarkably free from *Puccinia*, although the American wheat varieties, *Henderson's Pedigreed* and *Gold Corn*, growing adjacent, were very badly rusted. This *Bohi* is an early ripening sort, at least one month earlier than above-mentioned American wheats. It is improbable that this variety will withstand a very low temperature, and it ought to do best in irrigated regions of the Southwest. It is planted about the 20th of November in Egypt and is cut the first week in May, although, from an American standpoint, it would be ripe by the last week in April. All wheat is left until dead ripe before cutting in Egypt. The temperature during the winter seldom goes below 40° F." (*Fairchild.*)

7661. SESAMUM INDICUM. **Sesame.**

From Cairo, Egypt. Received through Mr. D. G. Fairchild (No. 635, May 9, 1901), October 10, 1901.

White. "This forms an important, profitable crop on the basin irrigated lands. It should be tried as late as the beginning of July after floods of Colorado River have subsided and might mature by the end of October. The seed should be broadcasted on the mud at a rate of about a bushel per acre. If possible, two subsequent waterings should be made, one when a few inches high and another later. If mud is not fresh it would be best to plow the land and harrow in the seed. (See No. 3972, Inventory No. 8, for description of oil making.) Lord Cromer, in his last report, mentions that sesame is exported from Egypt to Europe. It is largely used for making the Turkish sweetmeat *Chacla*(?). Profits in Egypt are estimated at about $40 an acre. For use in the Colorado River experiments. Secured through the kindness of Mr. George P. Foaden, secretary of the Khedivial Agricultural Society." (*Fairchild.*)

7662. SESAMUM INDICUM. **Sesame.**

From Cairo, Egypt. Received through Mr. D. G. Fairchild (No. 636, May 9, 1901), October 10, 1901.

Brown. "I can not find that this has any advantage over the white, or vice versa, but it may prove better adapted to growth in the Colorado River flood plain. Secured through the kindness of Mr. George P. Foaden, secretary of the Khedivial Agricultural Society." (*Fairchild.*)

7663 to 7677.

From Asia Minor. Received through Mr. George C. Roeding, October 11, 1901.

A collection of economic plants secured in September, 1901, as follows:

7663. FICUS CARICA. **Caprifig.**

From Aidin. Designated "F."

7664. FICUS CARICA. **Caprifig.**

From Aidin. "*D.*" "A very large caprifig (same as No. 6832), from the garden of S. G. Magnisalis." (*Roeding.*)

7665. FICUS CARICA. **Caprifig.**

From Aidin. "*E.*" "One of the largest caprifigs from the garden of S. G. Magnisalis. (Same as No. 6836.)" (*Roeding.*)

7666. FICUS CARICA. **Caprifig.**

From Aidin. "*I.*" "A variety from the garden of S. G. Magnisalis, near the ruined mosque. This is not the variety especially mentioned by Mr. W. T. Swingle." (*Roeding.*)

7667. FICUS CARICA. **Caprifig.**

From Aidin. "*G.*" Very largest and finest caprifig from the garden of S. G. Magnisalis. Same as No. 6835." (*Roeding.*)

7668. PISTACIA VERA. **Pistache.**

From Smyrna. "From the Greek nurseryman near Smyrna." (*Roeding.*)

7669. PYRUS sp. **Pear.**

From Smyrna. "Wild pear growing near Smyrna, a good stock, valuable for clay ground." (*Roeding.*)

7670. AMYGDALUS PERSICA. **Peach.**

From Smyrna. "A yellow cling, yellow to the pit, ripening in August. From Pounar Bashi." (*Roeding.*)

7663 to 7677—Continued.

7671. VITIS VINIFERA. **Grape.**

From Smyrna. "A superior variety of Malaga called *Rezaki*. Probably *Datte de Beyrouth*." (*Roeding*.)

7672. PRUNUS ARMENIACA. **Apricot.**

From Smyrna. "From Pounar Bashi near Smyrna. An apricot with a sweet kernel like an almond." (*Roeding*.)

7673. PISTACIA TEREBINTHUS. **Terebinth.**

From Smyrna. *Karabanour.* "Buds from male pistachio terebinth." (*Roeding*.)

7674. PUNICA GRANATUM. **Pomegranate.**

From Smyrna. *Tcherkerdeksis.* "The seedless pomegranate from Pounar Bash." (*Roeding*.)

7675. OLEA EUROPAEA. **Olive.**

From Smyrna. "Pickling and oil olive from Greek nurseryman near Smyrna." (*Roeding*.)

7676. PUNICA GRANATUM. **Pomegranate.**

From Smyrna. *Feysinar.* "Pomegranate from Pounar Bashi." (*Roeding*.)

7677. PUNICA GRANATUM. **Pomegranate.**

From Smyrna. *Kadinar.* "Pomegranate from Pounar Bashi." (*Roeding*.)

7678. COFFEA ARABICA. **Coffee.**

From Macassar, Celebes. Received through Messrs. Lathrop and Fairchild (No. 386a, February 11, 1900), October 15, 1901. Sent by Hon. K. Auer, United States consul.

Menado. "The bean of this famous coffee is very large. It is one of the highest priced coffees on the market. Sells dry in Amsterdam at 70 to 80 cents Dutch per one-half kilo. Best 'Java Brown' brings no more." (*Fairchild*.)

7679. VICIA HIRTA.

From Tessala, Algeria. Obtained by Mr. C. S. Scofield, April, 1901. Received October 21, 1901.

"Dried roots and tubercles from barley field at Tessala." (*Scofield*.)

7680. LATHYRUS SATIVUS.

From Oran, Algeria. Obtained by Mr. C. S. Scofield, April, 1901. Received October 21, 1901.

"Dried roots and tubercles of the 'Pois Carré' from salt-impregnated field near Oran. Much cultivated." (*Scofield*.)

7681. LUPINUS LUTEUS. **Yellow lupine.**

From Rouïba, Algeria. Obtained by Mr. C. S. Scofield, April 10, 1901, through Dr. L. Trabut. Received October 21, 1901.

"Dried roots and tubercles. Tubercle growth considered by Doctor Trabut as pathological and characteristic of *Lupinus luteus*." (*Scofield*.)

7682. TRIFOLIUM ANGUSTIFOLIUM.

From Kabylia, Algeria. Obtained by Mr. C. S. Scofield, April, 1901. Received October 21, 1901.

"Roots and tubercles." (*Scofield*.)

7683. TRIFOLIUM PANORMITANUM.

From Rouïba, Algeria. Obtained by Mr. C. S. Scofield, April 10, 1901. Received October 21, 1901.

"Roots and tubercles." (*Scofield.*)

7684. AMYGDALUS COMMUNIS. **Almond.**

From Malaga, Spain. Received through Mr. D. G. Fairchild (No. 768, July 31, 1901), October 21, 1901.

"Supposed to be grafted plants of the famous Jordan almond. Upon arrival they proved to be only ungrafted seedlings, and not at all as per the contract made with the Spanish gardener." (*Fairchild.*)

7685. TRITICUM VULGARE. **Wheat.**

From Volo, Greece. Received through Mr. D. G. Fairchild (No. 581, March 23, 1901), September 28, 1901.

Diminum. "A variety of spring wheat called *Diminum*, meaning 'two months.' This is a semihard wheat used in Greece to plant after the failure of the winter wheat. It is not a two-month wheat, as its name implies, but matures in about three months, being planted the last ot February and harvested the first of June. It is a light bearer, not very highly esteemed in Greece except for a catch crop, as it were, when winter wheat has failed. Sent by kindness of Mr. Ar. Tsakonas, of Athens, who can secure a large quantity in June, if desired." (*Fairchild.*)

7686. NICOTIANA TABACUM. **Tobacco.**

From Godwinsville, Ga. Received through Mr. H. J. Webber, October 28, 1901.

Asmyr. A Turkish cigarette tobacco. About 6 ounces of seed obtained by Mr. Webber through Mr. Robert Viewig, who imported the original seed from Turkey and grew it at Godwinsville, Ga. A crop was grown in 1899, from which the present seed was taken. Production usually very light, but product of superior quality.

7687. VITIS sp. **Grape.**

From southern Mexico. Received through Dr. J. N. Rose (No. 5349), October 28, 1901.

"A new grape, collected in southern Mexico this past season. It is a very remarkable species in that it dies down to the ground each year, apparently arising from the big deep-set tuber or tuberous root. It produces an immense growth of vines, the internodes often being 1½ to 2 feet long. The fruit is borne in large clusters, sometimes nearly a foot long, individual grapes being about the size of the fox grape." (*Rose.*)

7688. HEERIA JALAPA.

From southern Mexico. Received through Dr. J. N. Rose (No. 6081), October 28, 1901.

"A very beautiful little trailing plant, well suited for baskets or for a carpet plant. It belongs to a genus of plants much cultivated." (*Rose.*)

7689 to 7765.

From Algeria. Secured by Mr. C. S. Scofield, April to June, 1901. Received at the Department in October, 1901. Turned over to the Office of Seed and Plant Introduction and Distribution, March 6, 1903.

"The following collection of leguminous plants was obtained by Mr. C. S. Scofield, in many cases through the kindness of Dr. L. Trabut, government botanist of Algeria. This collection represents the results of many years careful study by Doctor Trabut, who, with Doctor Battangier, published a flora of Algeria, in which some of these species were described for the first time. Doctor Trabut familiarized himself with the indigenous flora of Algeria by many expeditions to all parts of the colony, and some of the most promising species for culture were found to be very rare in a wild state, having been almost exterminated by herbivorous animals. The collection here enumerated was obtained for study and not for distribution. It is of the very greatest value and the various species are now being cultivated in a preliminary way by the Department of Agriculture to get information as to their adaptability to American conditions. As the life histories of the various species are worked out so that reasonable prognosis can be made as to the value of the plant for forage or for hay or green manure and some information can be given as to the regions where it is most likely to succeed, and where seed can be grown at a reasonable cost, then this species will be introduced into practical culture. It is likely that many plants of the greatest value for the future development of American agriculture, especially in the dry regions of the West, are included in this collection, which is the cream of what has been brought together by twenty years' study in North Africa, one of the richest regions of the world for leguminous plants suitable for field culture." (*Swingle.*)

7689. LUPINUS TERMIS. **White lupine.**

"This plant is one of the prominent lupines which has a place in general culture. It has a vigorous, upright growth." (*Scofield.*)

7690. LUPINUS ANGUSTIFOLIUS.

"Specimen found near Fort National, where the soils are evidently of marble or limestone origin." (*Scofield.*)

7691. ONONIS AVELLANA.

"This plant is too coarse for use as a forage plant; it may have a place as a soil fixer or for green manuring." (*Scofield.*)

7692. MELILOTUS MACROSTACHYS.

"Specimen obtained from trial plats at the botanical station at Rouïba. This is one of the most promising plants of this genus. It is the only one not objectionable for forage purposes on account of its odor. It has a vigorous growth, often reaching 3½ feet in height, and has a large leafy surface." (*Scofield.*)

7693. MELILOTUS SPECIOSA.

"Specimen from botanical garden at Rouïba. Several varieties of this species are under cultivation. It is a fairly good forage plant, being erect and producing an abundance of foliage." (*Scofield.*)

7694. MELILOTUS SULCATA.

"Specimen from the garden of the school of medicine of Algiers. This plant is one of the least valuable of this genus. It has rather harsh stems and does not have an abundant leaf growth. It seeds very freely." (*Scofield.*)

7695. MEDICAGO ARBOREA.

7696. CYTISUS PROLIFERUS.

"Specimen from botanical station at Rouïba. This plant has been introduced into Algeria from the Canary Islands. It is a shrub, often 12 to 14 feet high; very leafy and producing a large number of seed pods. The new shoots are often trimmed from the tree and used in the dryer countries." (*Scofield.*)

7697. CYTISUS LINIFOLIUS.

7698. SCORPIURUS VERMICULATA.

"Specimen from botanical station at Rouïba, where it is both wild and cultivated. Plant has creeping habit, rather vigorous, but seldom more than 7 or 8 inches high; fruits very freely. There are large numbers of nodules. The plant is principally for sheep pasturing and for enriching the soil in nitrogen." (*Scofield.*)

7689 to 7765—Continued.

7699. Trifolium panormitanum.

"Specimen found growing wild near botanical station at Rouïba. This plant closely resembles *T. alexandrinum* in general appearance and habit of growth. The lower tooth of the calyx is very much longer than the other four teeth, making identification simple. This plant is little or not at all cultivated as yet in Algeria, but was found to have gained possession of some wild hay fields near Tizi Ouzou. It is very vigorous and upright in habit of growth, often over 2 feet in height." (*Scofield.*)

7700. Lotus tetragonolobus. Square pea.

"Specimen found growing wild near botanical station at Rouïba. Plant has a reclining or creeping habit, seldom growing more than 10 or 12 inches in height; it is very vigorous, leaves of a very bright green color, flowers brilliant, rosy red. It fruits freely and bears large numbers of root nodules; has been introduced into America in an experimental way through the Department of Agriculture. It deserves further attention." (*Scofield.*)

7701. Vicia hirta.

"Specimen obtained from botanical station at Rouïba, where the plant grows wild. It has been tried in culture there, but has not done well enough to hold a place in competition with other species of the same genus. The stem is upright, but rather weak, sometimes reaching 2 feet in height." (*Scofield.*)

7702. Vicia faba.

7703. Vicia fulgens.

"From small plat growing at botanical station at Rouïba. This species is one of the very important ones introduced by Dr. Trabut into culture in Algeria. It seeds very freely and produces a large amount of foliage." (*Scofield.*)

7704. Vicia narbonnensis.

"Specimen from botanical station at Rouïba, where it is both wild and cultivated. This plant is erect, very succulent, and robust. It is often sown with winter oats to be cut for green forage. It seeds freely and matures early in May. A close relative of this plant, possibly a variety of the species, is often confused with it, the other variety being entirely glabrous, while the type is decidedly hispid." (*Scofield.*)

7705. Vicia bengalensis.

(This seed was never turned over to the Office of Seed and Plant Introduction and Distribution, as it was all used in experiments by the Office of Vegetable Pathological and Physiological Investigations.) (See No. 5576.)

7706. Vicia calcarata.

"Specimen found near botanical station at Rouïba, probably not from cultivated plats. This plant is commonly found along the Algerian coast, growing in hay fields and waste places. So far as known it is not at all cultivated." (*Scofield.*)

7707. Vicia sativa.
Vicia sativa de Toulouse.

7709. Vicia sativa.
Vicia sativa de Tunis.

7708. Vicia sativa.
Blanche.

7710. Hedysarum coronarium.

"Specimen found growing in the garden of the School of Medicine of Algiers. Source of seed not known. Plant very robust; stems rather weak." (*Scofield.*)

7689 to 7765—Continued.

7711. HEDYSARUM PALLIDUM.

"Specimen obtained from near Oran by Mr. D G. Fairchild. It was nearly matured. The plant is mentioned by Battandier as being perennial, having large, ornamental flowers which are white and streaked with purple; the stem fleshy, decumbent; the leaves somewhat pubescent, not as long as the flower clusters; the leaflets 10 to 20 mm. by 5 to 10; flowers in oblong flower clusters; the pod spiny, 4 to 7 articulations with vertical spines at the ends; common in salty and gypsum soils." (*Scofield.*)

7712. HEDYSARUM MAURITANICUM.

"Specimen from garden of the School of Medicine of Algiers; seed probably brought by Doctor Trabut from somewhere in the province of Oran. The plant is somewhat less vigorous than *H. coronarium;* stems reclining; plant often more than 2 feet in height." (*Scofield.*)

7713. TRIGONELLA FOENUM-GRAECUM. **Fenugreek.**

"Specimen from the garden of the School of Medicine of Algiers. This plant has an upright habit of growth, reaching 18 to 20 inches in height; has a very important place in general culture as a soil enricher and a green forage crop. It is often planted in the autumn between rows of grapevine and turned under the following spring, when the cultivation of the grapes begins. When used as a green forage crop, or when the seed is used, the fat producing effect is very noticeable. The plant has a very strong odor when dried, and animals fed on the dry grain or green forage are strongly affected by the odor. Eggs from hens fed on this plant are uneatable. Meat of animals having access to it can not be used as human food; as a horse food it is of considerable importance. The Jewish women eat a meal prepared from the grain of this plant and become enormously fat. It is already used to some extent in Virginia, and very widely cultivated throughout Persia and India. About 1,000 tons of this seed are sold annually by one dealer, Schempft & Co., in the Liverpool Stock Exchange. This seed forms an essential quality of nearly all prepared stock foods. The root bears a large number of nodules." (*Scofield.*)

7714. TRIGONELLA CORNICULATA.

7715. FESTUCA FANARA.

7716. VICIA LUTEA.

7717. VICIA SICULA.

"Specimen found growing wild near the botanical station at Algiers. So far as known, the plant is not cultivated, but is found very commonly along the Algerian coast. The stems are rather small. It is of no present value as a forage plant." (*Scofield.*)

7718. VICIA EGYPTIANA.
(Not in Kew Index.)

7719. ASTRAGALUS BOETICUS.

"Specimen found growing wild in the garden of the School of Medicine of Algiers. So far as known, this plant has not been introduced into culture. The stem is upright, though inclined to be weak, 20 to 24 inches high; rather straggling in habit of growth; plant deserves attention for improvement." (*Scofield.*)

7720. ANTHYLLIS TETRAPHYLLA.

"Specimen found in the woods above Mustapha. This plant is said to be adapted for use in arid regions. It has a creeping habit of growth, fruits very freely, and produces a large number of root nodules." (*Scofield.*)

7721. ANTHYLLIS VULNERARIA.

"Specimen found in the woods above Mustapha. This plant is not common in Algeria. It has a decidedly different habit of growth from that of *A. tetraphylla.* It grows very commonly along the bluffs above Hussien Dey." (*Scofield.*)

7689 to 7765—Continued.

7722. CERATONIA SILIQUA. Carob.

"Seeds of an improved variety from Blidah." (*Scofield*.)

7723. BRASSICA OLERACEA. Cabbage.

"A few seeds of a wild cabbage from Rouïba." (*Scofield*.)

7724. AEGILOPS OVATA.
From Bouli Bree (?)

7725. HEDYSARUM PALLIDUM.
From Oran.

7726. HIPPOCREPIS MULTISILIQUOSA.

"Specimen from the garden of the School of Medicine of Algiers. So far as known, this plant is not of great importance as a forage plant. It rarely reaches 20 inches in height, and has a straggling habit of growth. The stem is hard and produces few leaves." (*Scofield*.)

7727. HYMENOCARPUS CIRCINATA.

"This plant is described by Battandier as being velvety pubescent; stems about 1 foot in height, erect or blanched; lower leaves entire, obtuse, attenuated at the petiole, 4 to 6 cm. by 2; leaf pinnately divided with an odd leaf at the end; flowers 2 to 4 in a peduncle, umbel exceeding the leaf; pod velvety, flattened, orbiculate, sometimes spiny at the back, sometimes not, 15 mm. in diameter. This plant is extremely rare and difficult to find, but Doctor Trabut is of the opinion that it is of very great value as a forage plant, although it is not yet evident that he has experimental proof to support the belief. Secured by Mr. Fairchild from wild plants growing not far from Oran through assistance of Prof. M. Doumergue, of Oran." (*Scofield*.)

7728. LATHYRUS TINGITANUS.

"This grows from year to year in the garden of the School of Medicine of Algiers, producing a large number of flowers which are nearly or quite all fertile." (*Scofield*.)

7729. LATHYRUS NUMIDICUS.

"Specimen found growing in the garden of the School of Medicine of Algiers. The original seed was found by Doctor Trabut on the rocks near El Kantara. The plant has a creeping habit of growth; matures very early and produces a large number of well filled pods; grain rather small, round, dark gray." (*Scofield*.)

7730. LOTUS ORNITHOPODIOIDES.

"Specimen from the garden of the School of Medicine of Algiers. This plant is common in waste places near Algiers; has not very robust stems; some reclining; grows in rather poor soil; may reach a height of 15 inches. The roots bear numerous peculiarly globose nodules. The plant bears seed very freely." (*Scofield*.)

7731. LOTUS EDULIS.

"Specimen from garden of the School of Medicine of Algiers. This plant has a creeping habit of growth, and produces many pods which are fleshy, with comparatively small seeds, and the pods when green are sweet to the taste. Doctor Trabut thinks that this plant can be improved to be used as a vegetable." (*Scofield*.)

7732. LUPINUS LUTEUS.

7733. LUPINUS sp.

"A violet lupine of Spanish origin." (*Scofield*.)

7734. MEDICAGO DENTICULATA var. APICULATA.

7689 to 7765—Continued.

7735. MEDICAGO ECHINUS.

"Specimen found near Oued Smaar, Algeria. This plant is one of the important annual medicagos. It has an inclining or creeping habit of growth; is very vigorous, and produces a large number of fruits." (*Scofield.*)

7736. MEDICAGO HELIX var. RIGIDULA.

7737. MEDICAGO DENTICULATA.

7738. MEDICAGO ORBICULARIS.

7739. MEDICAGO TRUNCATULA.

7740. MEDICAGO TURBINATA.

"Specimen found in woods above Mustapha. This plant has an inclining, or sometimes upright, habit of growth. It is an annual, and deserves a trial." (*Scofield.*)

7741. MEDICAGO TRUNCATULA.

7742. MEDICAGO CILIARIS.

7743. MEDICAGO SECUNDIFLORA.

"Obtained on Ain el Hadjar Plateau." (*Scofield.*)

7744. MELILOTUS MACROCARPA.

"Specimen found near Hotel Continental, Mustapha. It is not particularly common. The plant is mentioned by Battandier as being upright, profusely branched, with bright green leaflets, very large, obovate, glaucous underneath; flowers about 6 mm. long, pale yellow, in loose bunches, exceeding the leaves. The fruit is almost as large as a small pea, ovoid, obtuse, or spherical; seeds, one or two, large, tuberculate. It is said that Arabs sometimes use these fruits as a spice, since they have the odor of the melilot in a very high degree." (*Scofield.*)

7745. ONONIS sp.

7746. ONOBRYCHIS sp.

7747. ONONIS AVELLANA.

7748. ERIOBOTRYA JAPONICA. Loquat.

(Seed never turned over to the office of Seed and Plant Introduction and Distribution.)

7749. GENISTA SPHAEROCARPA.

7750. SCORPIURUS VERMICULATA.

7751. SCORPIURUS SULCATA.

"Specimen found near Hotel Continental, Mustapha. This plant seems to be at present of very little value. Like *S. vermiculata* it never attains any considerable height, and is, if anything, less vigorous than *S. vermiculata*. It thrives, however, in very poor soil, and is a harmless weed." (*Scofield.*)

7752. TRIGONELLA GLADIATA.

"Nearly related to *T. foenum-graecum*." (*Scofield.*)

7753. TRIFOLIUM ANGUSTIFOLIUM.

"Specimen from grounds of Danish consulate, Mustapha. This plant is closely allied to *T. incarnatum*. It does not thrive well in Algeria, seldom reaching more than 1 foot in height, and producing few, if any, branches. Some very vigorous specimens were seen near Oran and west of there, where it is more common than near Algiers. It is an annual, maturing early in May." (*Scofield.*)

7689 to 7765—Continued.

7754. TRIFOLIUM LAPPACEUM.

"Specimen from the grounds of the Danish consulate, Mustapha. This plant is one of the less vigorous of the genus. It has a somewhat reclining habit of growth; stems seldom more than 12 to 15 inches long, rather soft and delicate. This plant is common in waste places in the vicinity of Algiers." (*Scofield.*)

7755. TRIFOLIUM GLOMERATUM.

"Specimen found near Oued Smaar, Algeria. This plant has a creeping, or at least an inclining habit of growth; is found on roadsides or in waste places; is as yet of no particular importance as a forage plant." (*Scofield.*)

7756. TRIFOLIUM PALLIDUM.

"Specimen from the garden of the School of Medicine of Algiers. This plant is common in the fields and waste places along the coast near Algiers; it resembles *T. pratense* somewhat in habit of growth, though it inclines to be smaller and less vigorous." (*Scofield.*)

7757. TRIFOLIUM PANORMITANUM.

7758. TRIFOLIUM REPENS.

"Specimen from nursery of Mr. Labatut, of Tizi Ouzou. It grows to a height of 8 to 10 inches from its creeping stem; produces seed freely; leaves and stems bright green; very succulent." (*Scofield.*)

7759. TRIFOLIUM SPUMOSUM.

"Specimen found growing wild near botanical station at Rouïba. The plant is an annual, vigorous and succulent, with rather weak stems, sometimes reaching a height of 20 to 24 inches under favorable conditions, i. e., in soils of limestone origin; the root nodule development is very pronounced. So far as known this plant is not yet cultivated, but it has the appearance of being of great value should it be introduced and somewhat improved by selection. It seeds very freely, producing grains somewhat larger than *T. pratense.*" (*Scofield.*)

7760. TRIFOLIUM STELLATUM.

"Specimen from near botanical station at Rouïba. This plant is very common along the roadsides and in the waste places of Algiers. It is not of great importance as a forage plant. It seldom reaches a height of more than ten inches, and the stem branches very little." (*Scofield.*)

7761. TRIFOLIUM TOMENTOSUM.

7762. VICIA SATIVA.

"Large seeded variety." (*Scofield.*)

7762a. VICIA SATIVA.

"A small seeded variety." (*Scofield.*)

7763. VICIA SATIVA.

"Specimen from the garden of the School of Medicine of Algiers. There are very many varieties of this species growing wild in Algiers." (*Scofield.*)

7764. VICIA HIRTA.

From Tessala, Algeria.

7765. VICIA SATIVA, var. MACROCARPA.

"Specimen found in grounds of Danish consulate, Mustapha Superieure. This is doubtless the variety known as 'Macrocarpa,' but very little is definitely known about the varieties of *Vicia sativa.* They grow in very large numbers, and attempts to classify them have up to the present time been fruitless." (*Scofield.*)

7766 to 7768.
(Numbers not utilized.)

7769. FRAGARIA spp. Strawberry.
From Mexico. Received through Dr. J. N. Rose, October 30, 1901.
Seeds of cultivated varieties for plant-breeding purposes.

7770. SABAL EATONIA.
From Miami, Fla. Received through Mr. H. C. Henricksen, October 26, 1901. Collected by Mr. P. H. Rolfs.

7771. THRINAX FLORIDANA.
From Miami, Fla. Received through Mr. H. C. Henricksen, October 26, 1901.

7772. SERENOA SERRULATA.
From Miami, Fla. Received through Mr. H. C. Henricksen, October 26, 1901.

7773. INODES PALMETTO.
From Miami, Fla. Received through Mr. H. C. Henricksen, October 26, 1901.

7774. COCCOTHRINAX GARBERI.
From Miami, Fla. Received through Mr. H. C. Henricksen, October 26, 1901.

7775. COFFEA ARABICA. Coffee.
From Macassar, Celebes. Received through Messrs. Lathrop and Fairchild (No. 386a, February 11, 1900), October 30, 1901. Sent by K. Auer, United States Consular Agent.

Menado. (See No. 7678.)

7776. PUNICA GRANATUM. Pomegranate.
From Oran, Algeria. Received through Messrs. D. G. Fairchild and C. S. Scofield (No. 738, June 14, 1901), October 30, 1901.

"Grafting wood of several varieties of pomegranates of Algerian origin from the *Orphelinat de Misserghin,* near Oran." (*Fairchild.*)

7777. CERATONIA SILIQUA. Carob.
From Oran, province of Oran, Algeria. Received through Messrs. D. G. Fairchild and C. S. Scofield (No. 737, June 14, 1901), October 30, 1901.

"Large fruited variety of carob, introduced into Algeria from Spain. Said to be monœcious, not requiring the presence of male trees to make it fruitful. Pods are large, thick, and of reported superior excellence." (*Fairchild.*)

7778 to 7780. AMYGDALUS COMMUNIS. Almond.
From Alicante, Spain. Received October 30, 1901.

7778.
Marcona. Nuts of this Spanish variety of almond.

7779.
Pastaneta. Nuts of this Spanish variety of almond.

7780.
Costereta. Nuts of this Spanish variety of almond.

7781. CAPSICUM ANNUUM. **Red pepper.**

From Los Angeles, Cal. Received October 26, 1901, from Mr. Elmer Stearns.

"From seed in mixed spices from Japan." (*Stearns.*)

7782. CAPSICUM ANNUUM. **Red pepper.**

From Los Angeles, Cal. Received October 26, 1901, through Mr. Elmer Stearns.

"Originally from Juarez, Mexico. Forms a bush nearly 4 feet high, with peppers erect instead of hanging." (*Stearns.*)

7783. CAPSICUM ANNUUM. **Red pepper.**

From Los Angeles, Cal. Received October 26, 1901, through Mr. Elmer Stearns.

"Originally from Juarez, Mexico." (*Stearns.*)

7784. HEDYSARUM CORONARIUM. **Sulla.**

From Malta. Received through Mr. D. G. Fairchild (No. 688, May 22, 1901), July 23, 1901.

Gozzo. "An early ripening variety of sulla from the little island of Gozzo, near Malta. This is said to be superior to the kind grown on Malta in seasons when spring rains are scanty, as it matures properly, while the Malta variety fails to ripen well. In seasons of abundant spring rainfall it is not economical, because it matures too soon. The seed in the seed pod is used in Malta, and it was not possible to get cleaned or decorticated seed. According to the literature, sulla should be planted in deep soil. This variety forms the principal fodder and soiling crop of an island where soil is not much over 6 to 8 inches deep on a bed of calcareous rock. It is sown here in July and August on the wheat or barley stubble and allowed to 'scorch' in the burning sun until the September or October rains begin to mature it, as they say. (The use of a seed scratcher might make quick germination possible and probably largely increase the stand.) It is cut here only when in full bloom, for, if left to stand, the leaves fall. The yield per acre is unusual. Some growers report 40 to 90 tons of green fodder, but no definite information on this point was obtained. It is the great green cover crop of Malta, and a rotation of wheat or oats and sulla is very common here. Everywhere the fields are filled with big stacks of the bundles of this plant. In some countries the seed is immersed for five minutes in hot water to hasten germination. The fleshy roots are often dug by peasants and fed to the hogs or horses. They are full of starch and sugar. The root tubercles are rather small and delicate, but very numerous. Attempts to cultivate the specific germ of these tubercles are being made from dried roots sent to Dr. George T. Moore from Malta." (*Fairchild.*)

7785. TRITICUM DURUM. **Wheat.**

From Vesoul-Benian, Algeria. Received through Messrs. D. G. Fairchild and C. S. Scofield (No. 723, June 20, 1901), November 6, 1901.

Pelissier. "This wheat, which is one of the best varieties of macaroni wheats grown in Algeria, is said to have been originated by selection from native Algerian durum wheats by a Mr. Pelissier, at Pont de l'Isser, a small town in western Oran. From there it was introduced into the western part of the province of Algiers. Mr. Paul Chalvin, of Vesoul-Benian, received a small quantity of seed from Doctor Trabut, botanist of the Government of Algeria, and by a rough en masse selection he has kept it almost pure. The variety under the name *Pelissier* is better known in the province of Algiers than in that of Oran, where it is said to have originated; in fact, we found no one growing it, even in Mr. Pelissier's neighborhood. Mr. Chalvin, from whom this seed was bought, sells his whole crop for seed purposes, and has practiced for four years a selection of the best ears. These are collected by his Arab foreman and thrashed by hand. About 200 kilos of this selected grain are sown, and the process is repeated every year. Last year this selection was not done. This wheat sent is about four generations from such selection. Mr. Chalvin believes the field from which it was taken will produce about 45 bushels per acre. At the Paris Exposition Mr. Chalvin took a gold medal on a sheaf of this wheat. Owing to its hardiness, vigorous growth, and large yield, this wheat is gradually replacing all other sorts in the vicinity of Vesoul-Benian, and at Doctor Trabut's botanical experiment station at Rouïba, Algiers, it has ranked among the best in yielding capacity and resistance to rust. The climate of Vesoul-Benian (altitude 700 meters) is a warm one, -25° and +23° F. being the usual minimums in winter. The snows, sometimes a foot or more deep, are of very short duration. The mean yield of this variety was about 16 to 22 bushels per acre on stiff clay soil without hardpan. It is on this stiff soil that the variety seems to do best. The resistance to drought shown by this sort is evidenced by the fact that it has proved a success in the Chelif Valley, where as early as the beginning of June the thermometer rises to 107° F., and droughts of long duration are said to occur in the spring. In Algeria the wheat is planted in November and harvested in June, but it is worth while testing it in America as a spring wheat in the northern States. The only noticeable weeds in the fields from which this seed was bought were wild anise, a wild oat (*Arena sterilis*), and a large flowered carrot, none being of a serious character except the wild anise, which ripens about the same time with the wheat. It is, however, a light seeded plant, and its seeds are easily blown out by the fanning mill." (*Fairchild and Scofield.*)

7786. TRITICUM VULGARE. Wheat.

From Kharkof, Russia. Received November 9, 1901, through Dr. A. Boenicke, president of the Kharkof Agricultural Society.

Kharkof. (Same as No. 7467.)

7787. TRITICUM VULGARE. Wheat.

From Rostov-on-Don, Russia. Received through Hon. W. R. Martin, acting United States consular agent, November 9, 1901.

Beloglina. A variety of hard winter wheat from Byelaya Glinskaya station, Don Territory. (See Nos. 6012 and 6013.)

7788. HEDYSARUM CORONARIUM ALBIDUM. Sulla.

From Setif, Province of Constantine, Algeria. Received through Messrs. D. G. Fairchild and C. S. Scofield (No. 735c), November 11, 1901.

"This variety, which differs from the type of the species by having white flowers, is found by Mr. Ryf (see No. 7586) to be much longer lived and in general preferable to the ordinary *H. coronarium* of the region. The seeds, however, are very slow in germinating and should be put through some sort of a seed-scratching device before planting." (*Fairchild and Scofield.*)

7789. HEDYSARUM NAUDINIANUM.

From Setif, Province of Constantine, Algeria. Received through Messrs. D. G. Fairchild and C. S. Scofield (No. 735b), November 11, 1901.

"This is a very hardy, narrow leaved, bushy variety, indigenous to the vicinity of Setif. It has been recently introduced into cultivation by Mr. Ryf (see No. 7586), who is trying it under the same cultural methods that he uses with his new strain of alfalfa. His experiments are not yet completed, but he has reasons to hope that this species will prove of value, especially for dry and rather poor soils." (*Fairchild and Scofield.*)

7790. HEDYSARUM CORONARIUM. Sulla.

From Setif, Province of Constantine, Algeria. Received through Messrs. D. G. Fairchild and C. S. Scofield, November 11, 1901.

Red Flowered. "This is the ordinary type which is widely grown as a forage or soiling crop in Algeria. It is perennial and yields abundant crops under favorable conditions. It is widely used in all countries bordering on the western Mediterranean. As a hay crop, its greatest weakness is that its leaves fall easily when they become dry." (*Fairchild and Scofield.*)

7791. MELILOTUS sp. Melilot.

From China. Received from Dr. C. Sprenger, Vomero, near Naples, Italy, November 1, 1901.

7792. TRITICUM DURUM. **Wheat.**

From Setif, Constantine Province, Algeria. Received through Messrs. D. G. Fairchild and C. S. Scofield (No. 724, June 20, 1901), November 6, 1901.

Mahmoudi. "This is quite similar to a well-known Algerian variety called 'Nab-el-bel.' It is one of the most highly valued wheats for the macaroni trade which Setif furnishes. The latter locality is probably the largest primary market for macaroni wheats in Algeria. The seed obtained is from that grown by the Arabs in the vicinity of Setif and the purity of type can not be guaranteed. This quantity is secured through the kindness of Mr. G. Ryf, manager for the *Société Genevoise de Sétif.* In the country of its origin, this wheat is sown in November or December and ripens late in June or early in July. It may be worth while trying it, however, in the spring-wheat regions of America, where it would be classed as one of the so-called 'goose' wheats." (*Fairchild and Scofield.*)

7793. TRITICUM DURUM. **Wheat.**

From Setif, Constantine Province, Algeria. Received through Messrs. D. G. Fairchild and C. S. Scofield (No. 725, June 20, 1901), November 6, 1901.

Mohamed ben Bachir. "This variety of wheat is one of the prominent sorts grown by both Arabs and French farmers on the high plateau of the Province of Constantine. It is one of the sorts highly prized by manufacturers of macaroni, although its name has not won for itself a reputation in the trade. It is one of the several valuable sorts commonly cultivated in this justly celebrated wheat region. The saying is that this wheat was originally brought from Mecca by the pilgrim whose name it bears. In botanical characters it is much like the *Pelissier* variety (No. 7785), and it is possible that the *Pelissier* was obtained from this stock. This seed was purchased of Mr. G. Ryf, of Setif, manager of the Geneva Company, and one of the best cultivators in the country." (*Fairchild and Scofield.*)

7794. TRITICUM DURUM. **Wheat.**

From Setif, Constantine Province, Algeria. Received through Messrs. D. G. Fairchild and C. S. Scofield (No. 726, June 20, 1901), November 6, 1901.

Kahla. "This is one of the wheats commonly grown by Arabs throughout Algeria. As the name *Kahla* signifies, this is a black-chaffed sort. It is generally considered to be one of the best of the Algerian wheats for adaptability to a wide variety of adverse conditions. When such are favorable it produces grain of excellent quality for macaroni manufacture. Under certain favorable climatic conditions the chaff loses color somewhat, but under native culture on the gravelly hills of Algeria or in the semiarid plains the purple-black of the chaff is a striking feature. This seed is furnished the Department by Mr. G. Ryf, manager of the Geneva Society of Setif. Commonly planted in November or December and harvested in June or July." (*Fairchild and Scofield.*)

7795. TRITICUM DURUM. **Wheat.**

From Setif, Constantine Province, Algeria. Received through Messrs. D. G. Fairchild and C. S. Scofield (No. 727, June 20, 1901), November 6, 1901.

Richi. "This variety is one of the best known from the Setif region, which latter is perhaps the most important wheat-growing center of Algeria. It is very highly prized for its good qualities as a macaroni-making wheat. The seed introduced was grown by Arabs in the vicinity of Setif, and it may be mixed, but a little careful selection to prominent type should give a good stock of pure seed. This wheat is a vigorous grower, often succeeding fairly well on even very poor soil. As to quality for macaroni making, it ranks very high. It is usually sown in December or January and harvested in June or July, but might be worthy of trial in the spring-wheat region of the United States. Seed was obtained through Mr. G. Ryf, of Setif. The region of Setif is on the high Algerian plateau, 3,500 feet above sea level. The winters there are more severe than in many parts of Algeria, the temperature frequently dropping to zero and snow being not infrequent." (*Fairchild and Scofield.*)

7796. HORDEUM TETRASTICHUM. **Barley.**

From Setif, Constantine Province, Algeria. Received through Messrs. D. G. Fairchild and C. S. Scofield (No. 728, June 20, 1901), November 6, 1901.

Tetcherit. "The barleys of Algeria are nearly all four-rowed or six-rowed varieties and have, as do most barleys grown in hot climates, thick glumes. A cross section shows them to be remarkably mealy, and we were told they are exported into Antwerp and Dunkirk, France, for beer-making purposes. The Belgian beer is not noted for its fine quality, and from the appearance of the grain I do not believe it will prove as good a brewing barley as many American sorts. The fact, however, that it is grown in such a warm climate and has nevertheless a certain renommé as a brewing barley, entitles it to a preliminary trial. The types will be found more or less mixed, as no process of selection has been practiced. Resistance to drought will be found one of its primary characteristics. Purchased of Mr. G. Ryf, manager of the Geneva Company of Setif. This latter place is on the high plateau, 3,500 feet above the sea, where the thermometer falls to about zero and where snows of considerable depth sometimes occur. This variety will be found to have much of the 'wild' character objectionable to barley breeders, but may show qualities of hardiness in spring droughts which will be of value. It should be tested in the Southwest and in California." (*Fairchild and Scofield.*)

7797. ANDROPOGON SORGHUM. Sorghum.

From El Outaya, Algeria. Received through Mr. C. S. Scofield, November 14, 1901. Obtained June 16, 1901.

Beshna. "White sorghum. Sample from El Outaya in the edge of the Sahara Desert, where it is used as a summer growing soiling crop. Seed probably came from Kabylie, where this crop is very generally grown. The seed is sometimes used as human food." (*Scofield.*)

7798. PHOENIX DACTYLIFERA. Date.

From Paris, France. Received through Mr. C. S. Scofield. November 13, 1901.

Deglet noor, probably. Seeds of dates bought in Paris.

7799 to 7847.

From Erfurt, Germany. Received through Haage & Schmidt, nurserymen, November 4, 1901. The nomenclature is, in the main, that of the seedsmen.

A collection of plants as follows:

7799. CALADIUM ADAMANTINUM.

7800. CALADIUM ALBANENSE.

7801. CALADIUM ASSUNGUY.

7802. CALADIUM BILANTRA.

7803. CALADIUM CACAPAVA.

7804. CALADIUM.
Comte de Germiny.

7805. CALADIUM.
Duchesse de Mortemarte.

7806. CALADIUM.
Ibis Rose.

7807. CALADIUM.
L'Insolite.

7808. CALADIUM.
Mavambeia.

7809. CALADIUM.
Mary Freeman.

7810. CALADIUM.
Ouro Fino.

7811. CALADIUM.
Rio de Janeiro.

7812. CALADIUM VENOSUM.

7813. RICHARDIA ELLIOTTIANA.

7814. RICHARDIA NELSONI.

7815. RICHARDIA PENTLANDI.

7816. EPIPREMNUM MIRABILE.

7817. PHYLLOSTACHYS AUREA.

7818. BAMBUSA AUREO-STRIATA.

7819. ARUNDINARIA JAPONICA.

7820. PHYLLOSTACHYS MITIS.

7821. BAMBUSA DISTICHA.

7822. PHYLLOSTACHYS NIGRA.

7823. ARUNDINARIA SIMONI.

7799 to 7847—Continued.

- **7824.** Phyllostachys violascens.
- **7825.** Desfontainea spinosa.
- **7826.** Sparrmannia africana.
- **7827.** Sparrmannia africana flo. pl.
- **7828.** Holbaellia latifolia.
- **7829.** Testudinaria elphantipes.
- **7830.** Cascarilla muzonensis(?)
- **7831.** Cedrela odorata.
- **7832.** Dorstenia contrajerva.
- **7833.** Dracaena draco.
- **7834.** Malpighia urens.
- **7835.** Myristica Horsfieldii.
- **7836.** Helleborus hybridus.
- **7837.** Helleborus niger.
- **7838.** Hepatica triloba fl. caerulea pl.
- **7839.** (Number not utilized.)
- **7840.** Hepatica triloba fl. rubra pl.
- **7841.** Leucanthemum uliginosum.
- **7842.** Viola odorata. *Princess Beatrix.*
- **7843.** Viola odorata. *Reine des Violettes.*
- **7844.** Viola odorata, rossica.
- **7845.** Viola odorata. *Victoria Regina.*
- **7846.** Viola odorata. *Belle de Châtenay.*
- **7847.** Viola odorata. *Mad. Millet.*

7848 to 7859. Lilium. Lily.

From Yokohama, Japan. Received from Suzuki & Iida, American agents of The Yokohama Nursery Company, November 6, 1901.

A collection of lilies as follows:

- **7848.** Lilium auratum rubra vittatum.
- **7849.** Lilium auratum platyphyllum.
- **7850.** Lilium auratum wittei.
- **7851.** Lilium maculatum.
- **7852.** Lilium browni.
- **7853.** Lilium maximowiczii.
- **7854.** Lilium longiflorum variegatum.
- **7855.** Lilium speciosum.
- **7856.** Lilium japonicum.
- **7857.** Lilium elegans. *Alice Wilson.*
- **7858.** Lilium elegans semi pleno.
- **7859.** Lilium rubellum.

7860 to 7901.

From near Berlin, Germany. Received from Mr. L. Spath, November 14, 1901.

A collection of plants as follows (nomenclature of Mr. Spath retained):

- **7860.** Actinidia arguta.
- **7861.** Amygdalus davidiana.
- **7862.** Amygdalus davidiana fl. alba pl.
- **7863.** Amygdalus persica dianthiflora pl.
- **7864.** Aymgdalus persica fl. pl.
- **7865.** Amygdalus persica fol. pur.

7860 to 7901—Continued.

7866. AMYGDALUS PERSICA.
Kaiser Friedrich III.

7867. AMYGDALUS PERSICA.
Klara Mayer.

7868. AMYGDALUS PERSICA PYRAMIDALIS.

7869. BERBERIS ILICIFOLIA.

7870. BERBERIS STENOPHYLLA.

7871. BERBERIS THUNBERGII MINOR.

7872. BUXUS HANDSWORTHIENSIS.

7873. CERATOSTIGMA PLUMBAGINOIDES.

7874. CERCIDIPHYLLUM JAPONICUM.

7875. CLEMATIS sp.
André Leroy.

7876. CLEMATIS sp.
Barillet Deschamps.

7877. CLEMATIS sp.
Belisaire.

7878. CLEMATIS sp.
Belle of Woking.

7879. CLEMATIS sp.
Blue Gem.

7880. CLEMATIS sp.
Claude de Lorraine.

7881. CLEMATIS sp.
Duchess of Edinburgh.

7882. CLEMATIS sp.
Edith Jackmann.

7883. CLEMATIS sp.
Fairy Queen.

7884. CLEMATIS sp.
Jackmani.

7885. CLEMATIS sp.
Jackmani alba.

7886. CLEMATIS sp.
La Gaule.

7887. CLEMATIS sp. LANUGINOSA.
Marie Defosse.

7888. CLEMATIS sp.
Mrs. Geo. Jackman.

7889. CLEMATIS sp.
Prince of Wales.

7890. CLEMATIS sp.
Lawsoniana.

7891. CLEMATIS sp.
Star of India.

7892. CLEMATIS sp.
Elsa Spath.

7893. CLEMATIS sp. RUBELLA.

7894. CLEMATIS sp.
Madam Granger.

7895. CLEMATIS sp.
Princess Mary.

7896. CLEMATIS sp. VELUTINA PURPUREA.

7897. LONICERA CAPRIFOLIUM.

7898. LONICERA HUMILIS.

7899. PARROTIA PERSICA.

7900. PRUNUS PANICULATA fl. ros. pl.

7901. RIBES SANGUINEUM.

7902 to 7907. THEA VIRIDIS. **Tea.**

From "Pinehurst," near Summerville, S. C. Received through Dr. Charles U. Shepard, special agent in charge of tea culture investigations, United States Department of Agriculture, November 18, 1901.

American grown tea seed as follows:

7902.
Japanese. Very hardy.

7903.
Amoy. A very hardy Chinese variety.

7904.
Darjeeling. Tender, but very fine.

7905.
Kangra. Hardy, fragrant, and dwarf.

7906.
Assam Hybrid. Good and reliable.

7907.
Chinese Dragon's Pool. Very good, but probably the plants are short lived.

7908. BETA VULGARIS. **Beet.**

From Eisleben, Saxony. Presented by Mr. Franz Jodl, of Prague, Bavaria. Received November 14, 1901.

Verbesserte Kleinwanzleben. This seed was grown by W. Ramdohr, on the Wimmelburg domain, Saxony.

7909 to 7941a. CHRYSANTHEMUM spp.

From Paris, France. Received from Vilmorin-Andrieux & Co., November 20, 1901.

A collection of 34 varieties of large-flowering chrysanthemums, planted in the Department greenhouses.

7909.
Alcon.

7910.
Alcyone.

7911.
Altair.

7912.
Antares.

7913.
Bellatrix.

7914.
Fatinie.

7915.
Henry.

7916.
Megrez.

7917.
Orves.

7918.
Perfection Rose.

7919.
Perle.

7920.
Princesse Galitzine.

7921.
Mrs. A. Barrest.

7922.
Miss Ida Barwood.

7923.
Mrs. Ch. Birch.

7924.
Alice F. Carey.

7925.
Miss Lucy Chesseman.

7926.
Col. Baden-Powell.

7909 to 7941a—Continued.

7927. *M. Hugh Crawford.*	**7935.** *James Molyneux.*
7928. *Madeline Davis.*	**7936.** *Onion.*
7929. *Lady Janet Clarke.*	**7937.** *Ralph Hatton.*
7930. *Lord Cromer.*	**7938.** *Silver Queen.*
7931. *Major Mathew.*	**7939.** *Souvenir de Marchioness of Salisbury.*
7932. *Meredith.*	**7940.** *J. R. Upton.*
7933. *Mermaid.*	**7941.** *Von Andre.*
7934. *Florence Molyneux.*	**7941a.** *Henry Weeks.*

7942 to 7945.

From Paris, France. Received through Vilmorin-Andrieux & Co., November 22, 1901.

Seeds of leguminous plants as follows (nomenclature of seed firm retained):

7942. VICIA FABA EQUINA.   **Horse bean.**
Féverole d'hiver.

7943. VICIA FABA EQUINA.   **Horse bean.**
Féverole de Loraine.

7944. AVENA SATIVA.   **Oat.**
Belgian Winter.

7945. MEDICAGO MEDIA.   **Sand lucern.**
Luzerne rustique.

7946. ERIOBOTRYA JAPONICA.   **Loquat.**

From Vomero, Naples, Italy. Received through Dr. C. Sprenger, November 27, 1901.

A seedless or one-seeded variety originated by Doctor Sprenger.

7947 and 7948.

(Numbers not utilized.)

7949. PISTACIA VERA.   **Pistache.**

From Aintab, Turkey in Asia. Received through Rev. A. Fuller, November 15, 1901.

7950. Pistacia vera × palaestina. **Butum.**

From Aintab, Turkey in Asia. Received through Rev. A. Fuller, November 15, 1901.

7951. Pistacia mutica. **Menengech.**

From Aintab, Turkey in Asia. Received through Rev. A. Fuller, November 15, 1901.

7952. Medicago getula.

From Mustapha, Algeria. Received through Dr. L. Trabut, Government Botanist, November 22, 1901.

7953. Juglans cinerea. **Butternut.**

From Biltmore, N. C. Received through Dr. C. A. Schenck, November 25, 1901.

7954. Juglans nigra. **Black walnut.**

From Biltmore, N. C. Received through Dr. C. A. Schenck, November 25, 1901.

7955 and 7956. Aberia caffra. **Kei apple.**

From Cape Town, South Africa. Presented by Prof. Peter MacOwan, botanist and horticulturist, department of agriculture of Cape Colony. Received November 26, 1901.

7955. Seeds gathered in June, 1901.

7956. Seeds gathered October 30, 1901.

7957 to 7961.

From Paris, France. Received through Vilmorin-Andrieux & Co., November 30, 1901.

A collection of asparagus seed as follows:

7957. Asparagus officinalis.
Violette de Hollande.

7958. Asparagus officinalis.
Blanche d' Allemagne.

7959. Asparagus officinalis.
Tardive d' Argenteuil.

7960. Asparagus verticillatus.
Grimpante.

7961. Asparagus sprengeri.

7962 to 7968.

From Mexico. Received through Dr. J. N. Rose (Nos. 345 to 351), U. S. National Museum, November 26, 1901.

A collection of Mexican seeds and plants as follows:

7962.

"Unknown variety of shrubby plant. Elevation nearly 6,000 feet. Flowers yellow and fine. Plant given for identification." (*Rose.*) (No. 345.)

7963. Chrysanthemum sp.

"Flowers white and very floriferous. Worthy of introduction." (*Rose.*) (No. 346.)

7964. Cosmos sp.

"Includes three or four varieties of *Cosmos* and seeds of two new plants, one of the latter tuberous rooted and valuable." (*Rose.*) (No. 347.)

7962 to 7968—Continued.

7965.
"New tuberous-rooted plant." (*Rose.*) (No. 348.)

7966. DAHLIA SILVESTRE.
"Red and yellow; single. I also send tubers." (*Rose.*) (No. 349.)

7967. DAHLIA sp.
"*Red.*" (*Rose.*) (No. 350.)

7968. DAHLIA sp.
"*Yellow.*" (*Rose.*) (No. 351.)

7969 and 7970. HORDEUM VULGARE. **Barley.**

From Smyrna, Asia Minor. Received through Mr. George C. Roeding, Fresno, Cal., from Mr. B. J. Agadjanian, of Smyrna, November 15, 1901.

7969. *White.* **7970.** *Black.*

7971. CRESCENTIA ALATA.

From Jalisco, Mexico. Received through Mr. Elmer Stearns, Los Angeles, Cal., November 15, 1901.

7972. CUCUMIS MELO. **Winter muskmelon.**

From Zante, Greece. Presented by Count N. Salamo Luazi through Mr. D. G. Fairchild. Received September 25, 1901.

Green. See No. 6363.

7973. LESPEDEZA BICOLOR. **Bush clover.**

From Japan. July, 1901. Presented by John D. Jones, esq., Augusta, Ga., through Dr. B. T. Galloway.

Said to be a fine fodder plant.

7974. CANAVALIA ENSIFORMIS. **Knife bean.**

From Japan. Received through Dr. B. T. Galloway, July, 1901.

7975 to 7984.

From Erfurt, Germany. Received through Haage & Schmidt, December 6, 1901.

A collection of seeds obtained for experimental work on rust diseases, being conducted by Mr. John L. Sheldon, of the University of Nebraska:

7975. ASPARAGUS OFFICINALIS.
Schneekopf.

7976. ASPARAGUS OFFICINALIS.
Ruhm von Braumschweig.

7977. ASPARAGUS OFFICINALIS.
Erfurt Giant.

7978. ASPARAGUS OFFICINALIS.
Burgunder Riesen.

7979. DIANTHUS ALPINUS.

7980. DIANTHUS ARENARIUS (?)

7981. DIANTHUS ARMERIA (?)

7982. DIANTHUS CHINENSIS.

7983. DIANTHUS CHINENSIS.

7984. DIANTHUS CHINENSIS.

7985 to 7989. AMYGDALUS COMMUNIS. **Almond.**

From Alicante, Spain. Received through Mr. D. G. Fairchild (Nos. 740-765), December 7, 1901.

A collection of young almond trees budded on Myrobolan stocks by M. Georges Boucher, Paris, France, with buds secured in Spain by Mr. Fairchild, as follows:

7985.
Mollar. (*Fairchild.* No. 740, July 19, 1901.)

7986.
Planeta. (*Fairchild.* No. 741, July 19, 1901.)

7987.
Castillet. (*Fairchild.* No. 745, July 20, 1901.)

7988.
Pastaneta. (*Fairchild.* No. 755a, July 19, 1901.)

7989.
Jordan. (*Fairchild.* No. 765, July 30, 1901.)

7990 and 7991. HICORIA PECAN. **Pecan.**

From Morgan City, La. Received through Mr. B. M. Young, December 7, 1901.

7990.
Frotscher. "Very large, soft shelled." (*Young.*)

7991.
Stuart. "Very large, soft shelled." (*Young.*)

7992. HORDEUM DISTICHUM. **Barley.**

From Munich, Bavaria. Received through Mr. D. G. Fairchild (No. 467, November 10, 1900), January, 1901.

"A variety of barley grown by Mich. Hartmann, of Mainstockheim, Bavaria, which took a prize at the Munich Barley and Hop Exposition, 1900." (*Fairchild.*) (See Nos. 5788-5792.)

7993 to 8071. VITIS VINIFERA. **Grape.**

From Thomery, France. Received through Etienne Salomon & Sons, December 11, 1901.

A collection of grafted grapevines, as follows:

7993. ADMIRAL DE COURTILLER on RIPARIA RUPESTRIS, 3309.

7994. AGOSTENGA on RIPARIA RUPESTRIS, 3306.

7995. BICANE on RIPARIA GLOIRE.

7996. BLACK ALICANTE on RIPARIA RUPESTRIS, 3306.

7997. BLANC D'AMBRE on RIPARIA RUPESTRIS, 3306.

7998. CHASSELAS DORÉ on RIPARIA GLOIRE.

7999. CHASSELAS CIOTAT on RIPARIA RUPESTRIS, 3306.

8000. CHASSELAS BOUCHES DU RHONE on RIPARIA RUPESTRIS, 3309.

8001. CHASSELAS BESSON on RIPARIA RUPESTRIS, 3306.

8002. CHASSELAS NEGROPONT on RIPARIA GLOIRE.

7993 to 8071—Continued.

8003. CHASSELAS DUHAMEL on ARAMON RUPESTRIS, G. No. 1.
8004. CHASSELAS MUSQUE VRAI on RUPESTRIS DU LOT.
8005. CHASSELAS NAPOLEON on RIPARIA RUPESTRIS, 3306.
8006. CHASSELAS ROSE ROYAL on ARAMON RUPESTRIS, G. No. 1.
8007. CHASSELAS TOKAY DES JARDINS on ARAMON RUPESTRIS, G. No. 1.
8008. CHASSELAS VIBERT on RIPARIA RUPESTRIS, 3306.
8009. CHASSELAS VIBERT on ARAMON RUPESTRIS, G. No. 1.
8010. CINSAULT on RIPARIA GLOIRE.
8011. CLAIRETTE GROS GRAINS on RIPARIA RUPESTRIS, 3306.
8012. CLAIRETTE MAZEL on RIPARIA GLOIRE.
8013. CLAIRETTE MAZEL on ARAMON RUPESTRIS, G. No. 1.
8014. CLAIRETTE MUSQUE TALABOT on ARAMON RUPESTRIS, G. No. 1.
8015. CORNICHON BLANC on RIPARIA GLOIRE.
8016. CORNICHON VIOLET on RIPARIA GLOIRE.
8017. CORNICHON VIOLET on ARAMON RUPESTRIS, G. No. 1.
8018. FOSTER'S WHITE SEEDLING on RIPARIA GLOIRE.
8019. FRANKENTHAL HATIF on RIPARIA RUPESTRIS, 101–114.
8020. GEN. DE LA MARMORA on RIPARIA RUPESTRIS, 3306.
8021. GOLDEN CHAMPION on ARAMON RUPESTRIS, G. No. 1.
8022. GRADISKA on RIPARIA GLOIRE.
8023. JOANNENC CHARNU on ARAMON RUPESTRIS, G. No. 1.
8024. LE COMMANDEUR on RIPARIA RUPESTRIS, 3306.
8025. MADELEINE BLANCHE on RIPARIA RUPESTRIS, 3306.
8026. MADELEINE BLANCHE DE JACQUES on ARAMON RUPESTRIS, G. No. 1.
8027. MADELEINE ROYALE on RIPARIA RUPESTRIS, 3306.
8028. MADELEINE ROSE on RIPARIA GLOIRE.
8029. MALAGA BLANC on RUPESTRIS DU LOT.
8030. MAMELON on RIPARIA RUPESTRIS, 3306.
8031. MESLIER HATIF on ARAMON RUPESTRIS, G. No. 1.
8032. MORILLON BICOLOR on RIPARIA RUPESTRIS, 3306.
8033. MUSCAT ALBARIANS on RUPESTRIS DU LOT.
8034. MUSCAT BIFERE on ARAMON RUPESTRIS, G. No. 1.
8035. MUSCAT BIFERE on RIPARIA RUPESTRIS, 3306.
8036. MUSCAT DE HAMBURGH on RUPESTRIS DU LOT.

7993 to 8071—Continued.

- **8037.** MUSCAT ROUGE DE MADERE on RIPARIA RUPESTRIS, 3306.
- **8038.** PETITE ST. JEAN on RIPARIA GLOIRE.
- **8039.** PIS DE CHEVRE DES ALPES on RIPARIA RUPESTRIS, 3306.
- **8040.** PRECOÇE DE KIENTZHEIM on RIPARIA GLOIRE.
- **8041.** ROSAKI on RIPARIA RUPESTRIS, 3306.
- **8042.** RAISIN BOISSELOT on RIPARIA RUPESTRIS, 3306.
- **8043.** ROUSSANNE on RIPARIA RUPESTRIS, 3306.
- **8044.** SAINT ANTONIO on RIPARIA GLOIRE.
- **8045.** SATINE JAUNE on RIPARIA RUPESTRIS, 3306.
- **8046.** SERVAN BLANC on RIPARIA RUPESTRIS, 3306.
- **8047.** SICILIEN on RIPARIA, G. No. 1.
- **8048.** SOUVENIR DU CONGRESS on RIPARIA RUPESTRIS, 3306.
- **8049.** SUCRE DE MARSEILLE on RIPARIA RUPESTRIS, 3306.
- **8050.** SULTANIEH ROSE on RIPARIA RUPESTRIS, 3306.
- **8051.** TENERON VAUCLUSE on RUPESTRIS DU LOT.
- **8052.** TOKAY ANGEVIN on RIPARIA GLOIRE.
- **8053.** TRENTHAM BLACK on RIPARIA RUPESTRIS, 3306.
- **8054.** CHASSELAS VIBERT on ARAMON RUPESTRIS, G. No. 1.
- **8055.** BURGRAVE DE HONGRIE on RUPESTRIS DU LOT.
- **8056.** PIS DE CHEVRE NOIR on RUPESTRIS DU LOT.
- **8057.** VERDELHO DE MADERE on RIPARIA GLOIRE.
- **8058.** SULTANINA on RUPESTRIS DU LOT.
- **8059.** LEANI ZOLO on RUPESTRIS DU LOT.
- **8060.** PRESIDENT CARDENAUX on RUPESTRIS DU LOT.
- **8061.** SAUVIGNON BLANC on RUPESTRIS DU LOT.
- **8062.** TSIEN TSIEN on MOURVEDRE RUPESTRIS, 202.
- **8063.** ULLIADE BLANCHE on RUPESTRIS DU LOT.
- **8064.** CHASSELAS BULHERY on RIPARIA GLOIRE.
- **8065.** PRECOÇE DE KIENTZHEIM on RIPARIA GLOIRE.
- **8066.** SEIBEL No. 1, AMERICAN HYBRID.
- **8067.** SEIBEL No. 2, AMERICAN HYBRID.
- **8068.** BOURRISQUOU 3907, AMERICAN HYBRID.
- **8069.** ARAMON RUPESTRIS G. No. 1, AMERICAN LOT.

7993 to 8071—Continued.

8070. OLIVIER DE SERRES on ARAMON RUPESTRIS, G. No. 1.

8071. OLIVETTE DE CADENET on RIPARIA RUPESTRIS, 3306.

(By "American Lot" is understood in France the stock on which the European Lot is grafted.)

8072 to 8121. PAEONIA MOUTAN. Tree peony.

From Yokohama, Japan. Received through the Yokohama Nursery Company, November 23, 1901.

A collection of grafted plants as follows:

8072.
Yoyo-no-homare.

8073.
Yaso-okino.

8074.
Kamadafuji.

8075.
Kumoi-dsuru.

8076.
Gioku-sho-kaku.

8077.
Aduma-saki.

8078.
Nishiki-gawa.

8079.
(Number not utilized.)

8080.
Kumoma-no-tsuki.

8081.
Fuji-araski.

8082.
Adzuma-nishiki.

8083.
Ginfukurin.

8084.
Michi-shiba.

8085.
Renkaku.

8086.
Kagurajima.

8087.
Kumo-no-nishiki.

8088.
Anyoji.

8089.
Iwato-Kagami.

8090.
Yuki-arashi.

8091.
Kokirin.

8092.
Akasho-jishi.

8093.
Hakubanrya.

8094.
Hakugan.

8095.
Hinode-dsuru.

8096.
Tokiwadsu.

8097.
Asahi-minato.

8098.
Ruriban.

8099.
Kame-asobi.

8100.
Saishoji.

8101.
Konron-koku.

8072 to 8121—Continued.

8102. *Akashi-gata.*
8103. *Bunbudo.*
8104. *Nishikishima.*
8105. *Adzumakagami.*
8106. *Fuji-no-mine.*
8107. *Hana-tachabana.*
8108. *Shishi-gashiri.*
8109. *Shi-un-ryu.*
8110. *Gabisan.*
8111. *Shoki-kaguru.*
8112. *Gioku-senshin.*
8113. *Seirin.*
8114. *O-sakadasuki.*
8115. *Fukashigi.*
8116. *Kausenden.*
8117. *Daikagura.*
8118. *Muhensai.*
8119. *Saigyo sakura.*
8120. *Momo-zono.*
8121. *Ivo-no-seki.*

8122 to 8188.

From Yokohama, Japan. Received through Suzuki & Iida, American agents of The Yokohama Nursery Company, New York, December 13, 1901.

A collection of plants as follows (the nomenclature in the main is that of the nursery company):

8122. MICHELIA COMPRESSA.
8123. CLERODENDRON SQUAMATUM.
8124. DEUTZIA SIEBOLDIANA.
8125. STYRAX JAPONICA.
8126. STYRAX OBASSIA.
8127. LIGUSTRUM CILIATUM.
8128. PITTOSPORUM TOBIRA.
8129. QUERCUS ACUTA.
8130. QUERCUS CUSPIDATA.
8131. QUERCUS DENTATA.
8132. QUERCUS DENTATA AUREA.
8133. QUERCUS GLANDULIFERA.
8134. QUERCUS GLAUCA.
8135. QUERCUS LACERA (?).
8136. QUERCUS LAEVIGATA (?).
8137. QUERCUS PHILLYREOIDES.
8138. QUERCUS PINNATIFIDA.
8139. QUERCUS SERRATA.
8140. GINKGO BILOBA VARIEGATA.
8141. CHAMAECYPARIS OBTUSA, var. KAMUKURA-HIBA.
8142. CHAMAECYPARIS OBTUSA, var. HOTARU-HIBA.

8122 to 8188—Continued.

8143. CHAMAECYPARIS OBTUSA, var. EMBI-HIBA.

8144. CHAMAECYPARIS OBTUSA, var. KANA-AMI.

8145. DAPHNE GENKWA.

8146. EDGEWORTHIA GARDNERI.

8147. KADSURA JAPONICA.

8148. KADSURA JAPONICA, spotted.

8149. KADSURA JAPONICA, white variegated.

8150. ACER TANABATA.
Various cultural varieties.

8151. ACER SANGUINEUM.

8152. ACER ATROPURPUREUM.

8153. ACER OSHIU-BENI.

8154. ACER JAPONICUM.

8155. ACER SANGUINEUM, Seigen.

8156. ACER ROSEUM.

8157. ACER VERSICOLOR.

8158. ACER OSAKA-ZUKI.

8159. ACER ATRO-DISSECTUM VARIEGATUM.

8160. ACER ATROPURPUREUM DISSECTUM.

8161. ACER RETICULATUM.

8162. ACER OKUSHIMO.

8163. ACER ATRO-DISSECTUM (green).

8164. ACER URIME.

8165. ACER KINUKASAYAMA.

8166. ACER AOBA.

8167. ACER HATSUYUKI KAIDO.

8168. ACER AUREUM.

8169. ACER SCOLOPENDRIFOLIUM RUBRUM.

8170. ACER SCOLOPENDRIFOLIUM (green).

8171. ACER ATROPURPUREUM VARIEGATUM.

8172. ACER AKIKAZE-NISHIKI.

8173. ACER ROSA-MARGINATIA.

8174. ACER CARPINIFOLIUM.

8175. ACER TRIFIDUM.

8176. ACER RUFINERVE.

8177. ACER TSUMAGAKI.

8178. ACER TSURU-NISHIKI.

8179. ACER MUSATORIYAMA.

8180. ACER PICTUM ALBUM.

8181. ACER JAPONICUM FILICIFOLIUM.

8182. ACER NISHIKIGASANE.

8183. ACER PICTUM AUREUM.

8184. ACER MURAKUMO.

8185. ACER KOMONUISHIKI.

8186. ACER JAPONICUM.

8187. ACER JAPONICUM.

8188. ACER JAPONICUM.

8189 to 8192.

From Yokohama, Japan. Received through Suzuki & Iida, American agents of the Yokohama Nursery Co., New York City, December 17, 1901.

A collection of seeds as follows:

8189. HAMAMELIS JAPONICA.

8190. STERCULIA PLATANIFOLIA.

8191. XANTHOXYLON PIPERITUM.

8192. PODOCARPUS MACROPHYLLA.

8193 to 8199.

From Lucknow, India. Received through the Government Horticultural Garden, December 16, 1901.

A collection of plants as follows:

- **8193.** BOMBAX MALABARICUM.
- **8194.** CLAUSENA EXCAVATA.
- **8195.** DILLENIA SPECIOSA.
- **8196.** FICUS INDICA.
- **8197.** STIGMAPHYLLON PERIPLOCAEFOLIUM.
- **8198.** RONDELETIA CHINENSIS.
- **8199.** RUSCUS HYPOPHYLLUM.

8200 to 8203. HICORIA PECAN. Pecan.

From Ocean Springs, Miss. Received through The Stuart Pecan Company, December 21, 1901.

8200.
Russell.

8201.
Stuart.

8202.
Jewett.

8203.
Van Deman.

8204. PISTACIA VERA × PISTACIA TEREBINTHUS.

From San Francisco, Cal. Received through Mr. W. T. Swingle from Mr. G. P. Rixford, secretary of the California Academy of Sciences, December 23, 1901.

8205 and 8206.

From Paris, France. Received through Vilmorin-Andrieux & Co., December 27, 1901.

- **8205.** CINCHONA OFFICINALIS.
- **8206.** AGATHIS AUSTRALIS.

8207. COFFEA ARABICA. Coffee.

From Macassar, Celebes. Received through Messrs. Lathrop and Fairchild from Hon. Karl Auer, United States Consul, December 28, 1901.

Timor.

8208. JUGLANS REGIA. Walnut.

From Zante, Greece. Presented by Mr. Alfred L. Crow, through Mr. D. G. Fairchild, January 6, 1902.

Large Zante.

8209. CYDONIA SINENSIS. Chinese quince.

From Zante, Greece. Presented by Mr. Alfred L. Crow, through Mr. D. G. Fairchild. Received January 6, 1902.

Scented quince.

8210. CITRUS NOBILIS × CITRUS BIGARADIA. Orange.

From Mustapha, Algiers, Algeria. Received through Dr. L. Trabut, Government Botanist, January 7, 1902. (A second packet January 14, 1902.)

Clementine. A hybrid of *Citrus nobilis* and *Citrus bigaradia sinensis salicifolia*, var. *granito.*

"Fruit very fine and beautiful. I recommend it." (*Trabut.*)

8211. COFFEA ARABICA. **Coffee.**

From Macassar, Celebes. Received through Messrs. Lathrop and Fairchild, from Hon. Karl Auer, United States Consul, January 7, 1902.

Chemnitz (?).

8212 and 8213. TRITICUM DURUM. **Wheat.**

From Uralsk, Russia. Purchased from the Ural Millers' Association. Received January 9, 1902.

8212.
Kubanka. Crop of 1900.

8213.
Kubanka. Crop of 1901.

8214. PROSOPIS JULIFLORA. **Mesquite.**

From Honolulu, Hawaiian Islands. Received through Mr. Jared G. Smith, director of the agricultural experiment station, January 10, 1902.

8215. POLYGONUM TATARICUM. **India wheat.**

From the Himalaya Mountains. Received through Dr. C. Sprenger, Vomero, near Naples, Italy, January 15, 1902.

"A large growing specimen." (*Sprenger.*)

8216 to 8218. CYPERUS ESCULENTUS. **Chufa.**

From Spain. Received through Mr. D. G. Fairchild (No. 772, Aug. 9, 1901), January 14, 1902. Secured through kindness of Hon. R. M. Bartleman, United States Consul at Valencia.

"Chufa cultivation in southeastern Spain is one of its most profitable industries; the underground tubers are used to make the *Horchata de chufas*, a favorite ice, sold very extensively in all the large cities in Spain." (*Fairchild.*)

8216.
From Alboraya.

8218.
From Algemese.

8217.
From Balasuar.

8219. CUCUMIS MELO. **Winter muskmelon.**

From Valencia, Spain. Received through Mr. D. G. Fairchild (No. 772, August 9, 1902), January 14, 1902.

8220 and 8221. TRITICUM VULGARE. **Wheat.**

From northern China. Received through Mr. G. D. Brill, January 17, 1902.

8220.
Red.

8221.
White.

8222 to 8225. AGARICUS CAMPESTRIS. **Mushroom.**

From Paris, France. Received through Dr. B. M. Duggar, January 18, 1902.

Mushroom spawn from Vilmorin-Andrieux & Co., as follows:

8222.
Triple. Virgin spawn, white variety.

8224.
Ordinaire. Virgin spawn, brown variety.

8223.
Double. Virgin spawn, brown variety.

8225.
Crop spawn, brown variety.

8226 to 8228. THEA VIRIDIS. Tea.

From Heneratgoda, Ceylon. Received through J. P. William & Bros., January 18, 1902.

Tea seed, as follows:

8226.

"Assam hybrid tea seed of highest class *Jat*, light leaf variety from Invery Estate, Dickoya, Ceylon, elevation 4,500 feet." (*William.*)

8227.

"Highest class *Jat* Assam Hybrid tea seed from Abbotsford Estate, Dimbulla, Ceylon, elevation 5,500 feet." (*William.*)

8228.

"Pure Manipuri indigenous tea seed, of highest class *Jat*, from Pen-y-len Estate, Dolosbage, Ceylon, over 4,000 feet elevation." (*William.*)

8229. BETA VULGARIS. Sugar beet.

From Wimmelburg, near Eisleben, Germany. Presented by Frantisek Jodl, Prague, Bohemia, January 18, 1902.

Kleinwanzleben improved.

8230 to 8232. TRITICUM DURUM. Wheat.

From Ambrocievka, Russia. Received from the estate of A. Michalkov, January 21, 1902.

Macaroni wheats as follows:

8230.

Yellow Gharnovka.

8232.

Black Don. (Chernokoloska.)

8231.

Velvet Don. (Chernouska.)

8233 to 8236. ERIOBOTRYA JAPONICA. Loquat.

From Mustapha, Algiers, Algeria. Received through Messrs. D. G. Fairchild and C. S. Scofield (Nos. 690 to 693), January 22, 1902.

8233.

Marcadal. "A nearly seedless variety from the Rev. Mr. Arkwright's garden." (*Fairchild.*)

8234.

Olivier. "From the Rev. Mr. Arkwright's garden. Fruits weigh over 52¾ grams apiece." (*Fairchild.*)

8235.

St. Michele. "From the Rev. Mr. Arkwright's garden. Said to weigh as much as 75 grams." (*Fairchild.*)

8236.

Meffre's No. 2. "Said by its originator, M. Henri Meffre, of El Merdj, to exceed in size any of the foregoing and to be of excellent quality." (*Fairchild.*) No. 693.

8237. MINA TRILOBATA.

From Mustapha, Algiers, Algeria. Received from Meffre & Salom Sons, January 22, 1902.

8238. BETA VULGARIS. **Sugar beet.**

From Athensleben bei Löderburg, Germany. Received through H. Bennecke & Son, January 23, 1902.

Kleinwanzlebener Nachzucht. This seed was presented to Dr. H. W. Wiley, Chief of Bureau of Chemistry, United States Department of Agriculture.

8239. SOLANUM DREGEI. **Natal thorn.**

From Los Angeles, Cal. Received through Mr. Elmer Stearns, January 24, 1902.

Grown from seed of No. 1987, Inventory No. 5.

8240. SPONDIAS LUTEA. **Ciruela amarillo.**

From Iguala, Guerrero, Mexico. Received through Mr. Elmer Stearns, Los Angeles, Cal., January 24, 1902.

8241 to 8298.

From Nice, France. Received through Mr. A. Robertson-Proschowsky, January 27, 1902.

A collection of seeds as follows: The determination of these species is that of Mr. Robertson-Proschowsky.

8241. AGAPANTHUS UMBELLATUS.

8242. AGAVE LOPHANTHA, Schiede?

8243. ALBIZZIA LOPHANTHA.

8244. ARBUTUS UNEDO.

8245. ARISTOLOCHIA ELEGANS.

8246. ARTEMISIA ARGENTEA.

8247. ARAUJIA SERICIFERA Brot.?

8248. ASPARAGUS SPRENGERI.

8249. BIGNONIA TWEEDIANA.

8250. CARDIOSPERMUM HALICACABUM.

8251. CARICA QUERCIFOLIA.

8252. CASSIA CORYMBOSA.

8253. CASSIA OCCIDENTALIS (?)

8254. CASUARINA EQUISETIFOLIA.

8255. CEANOTHUS AZUREUS Desf. (HYBRIDUS Hort.)
Gloire de Versailles.

8256. CLERODENDRON HASTATUM.

8257. CORDYLINE AUSTRALIS.
Cordyline indivisa of the trade.

8258. DOLICHOS LABLAB.

8259. EREMOCARPUS SCABER.

8260. ELAEAGNUS PUNGENS var. SIMONI.

8261. NICOTIANA GLAUCA.

8262. OLEARIA HAASTI.

8263. PASSIFLORA PRUINOSA.

8264. PERIMEDIUM DISCOLOR (?)

8265. PHOENIX RECLINATA.

8266. PHOENIX PUMILA × PHOENIX RECLINATA.

"Fruits of rather good taste when fresh. In moist climates, like Florida, other species than *Phoenix dactylifera* might in time, through selection and hybridization, produce good varieties." (*Proschowsky.*)

8267. PHORMIUM TENAX.

8268. PLECTRANTHUS STRIATUS (?).

8269. PODACHAENIUM PANICULATUM.

8270. POLYGONUM LANIGERUM.

8271. PORANA RACEMOSA (?) Roxb.

8272. PROSOPIS GLANDULOSA (?)

8241 to 8298—Continued.

8273.	RICHARDIA AFRICANA Kth.		8286.	THALIA DEALBATA.
8274.	RICHARDIA ALBO-MACULATA.		8287.	VITEX INCISA.
8275.	RICINUS COMMUNIS, var. 1.		8288.	WIGANDIA sp. (hybrid?)
8276.	RICINUS COMMUNIS, var. 2.		8289.	EUPHORBIA sp.
8277.	RUSCUS HYPOGLOSSUM.		8290.	FICUS MACROPHYLLA.
8278.	SCHINUS MOLLE.		8291.	GOMPHOCARPUS TEXTILIS.
8279.	SENECIO LONGIFOLIUS.		8292.	GLOBULARIA SALICINA Lam.
8280.	SOLANUM sp.		8293.	HEDYCHIUM GARDNERIANUM Rosc.
8281.	SOLANUM LACINIATUM Ait. (S. RECLINATUM l'Herit).		8294.	JACARANDA OVALIFOLIA.
8282.	SOLANUM MARGINATUM.		8295.	IOCHROMA TABULOSA Benth.
8283.	SOLANUM PSEUDOCAPSICUM.		8296.	LIGUSTRUM JAPONICUM.
8284.	SOLANUM WARSZEWICZII.		8297.	MESEMBRYANTHEMUM ACINACIFORME.
8285.	SOLLYA HETEROPHYLLA.			
8298.	MESPILUS GERMANICA.			**Medlar.**

8299. MEDICAGO ELEGANS.

From Mustapha, Algiers, Algeria. Received through Dr. L. Trabut, Government Botanist, January 27, 1902.

8300 to 8306. ORYZA SATIVA. **Rice.**

From Kobe, Japan. Received through Dr. S. A. Knapp, January 27, 1902.

Seed rice as follows, Japanese names being given:

8300.
Shinriki. From Hyogo district.

8301.
Shiratama. From Fukuoka district.

8302.
Komachi. From Kumamoto district.

8303.
Omase. From Kumamoto district.

8304.
Miyako. From Yamaguchi district.

8305.
From Chiugoku district.

8306.
From Chikuzen district.

8307. JUGLANS REGIA. **Walnut.**

From Aintab, Asia Minor. Received through Rev. A. Fuller, January 28, 1902. Wild Persian walnuts.

8308 to 8310. CUCUMIS MELO. **Muskmelon.**

From Lisbon, Portugal. Received through Señor Abel Fontoina da Costa, January 30, 1902.

8308.
Amarello.

8309.
Alpiaca.

8310.
Palha (Valentien).

8311. KHAYA SENEGALENSIS. **African mahogany.**

From Mount Silinda, Melsetter district, Rhodesia, South Africa. Received through Dr. Wm. L. Thompson, January 31, 1902.

Ubaba. This is one of the finest timber trees of South Africa, growing to a large size, sometimes 6 feet or more in diameter. Resists the attacks of insects and is very durable. Generally grows near streams, but is also found in other places. Called by the natives "Ubaba," from the bitter bark.

8312. SIMMONDSIA CALIFORNICA. **Jojoba.**

From Las Flores, Lower California, Mexico. Received through Mr. F. Plunk, jr., January 30, 1902.

8313 to 8329.

From Erfurt, Germany. Received through Haage & Schmidt, February 1, 1902.

A collection of seeds as follows:

8313. CARYOTA MITIS.

8314. COCOS YATAY.

8315. CHRYSALIDOCARPUS LUTESCENS.

8316. PYRETHRUM ROSEUM.

8317. LEUCADENDRON ARGENTEUM.

8318. CINNAMOMUM sp.

8319. PAPAVER BRACTEATUM.

8320. PHORMIUM TENAX.

8321. COCOS DATIL.

8322. EUTERPE EDULIS.

8323. OREODOXA REGIA.

8324. CHAMAEDOREA SARTORI.

8325. OREODOXA OLERACEA.

8326. ACANTHOPHOENIX CRINITA.

8327. KENTIOPSIS MACROCARPA.

8328. BEGONIA REX × DIADEMA.

8329. KENTIA MACARTHURI. (Horticultural variety.)

8330. AMYGDALUS PERSICA. **Peach.**

From near North Gate, Canton, China. Received through Messrs. Lathrop and Fairchild (No. 774, December 20, 1901), February 3, 1902.

"A variety of peach growing in a Chinese orchard at Ngau lan Kong. The habit of this tree resembles that of an apricot, and, although I saw none of the fruit, I believe it is quite a distinct type from the ordinary Eagle Beak peach, which is the common variety about Canton. I was not able to get a name for this variety." (*Fairchild.*)

8331 to 8334. AMYGDALUS PERSICA. **Peach.**

Eagle Beak peach from Canton, China. Received through Messrs. Lathrop and Fairchild (No. 775, December 20, 1901), February 3, 1902.

"From orchard trees growing near the Great North Gate of Canton, at Ngau lan Kong, of the *Ying tsui t'o* or Eagle Beak peach. This variety resembles the Honey closely, except that the pointed tip of the fruit is more curved, according to Dr. J. M. Swan, of the Canton Hospital. I saw no specimen myself. According to Doctor Swan's gardener this variety blooms in March and April, while other sorts here bloom in February. The peach is said to be very sweet, even inclined to be a bit mawkish in flavor. The fruit is brought to the market some time early in July. The market for peaches in Canton is a short one, being in all not over five weeks—the last three weeks of June and the first two weeks of July. The *Peen t'o* type of peach is unknown here in Canton, so far as I can ascertain. It certainly must be a rare form here if it occurs at all. These cuttings were taken from small commercial orchards, and, it being winter, I am obliged to take the identification through an interpreter that they are the Eagle Beak. To insure getting all the varieties in the orchard, I got several lots from the different parts of the orchard. These I have marked 775, a, b, c, respectively. The numbers 8331, 8332, 8333, and 8334 correspond with these numbers. This peach is not larger than the Honey, but may prove later blooming and be valuable on this account." (*Fairchild.*)

8335. MORUS MULTICAULIS. **Chinese mulberry.**

From Canton, China. Received through Messrs. Lathrop and Fairchild (No. 776), February 3, 1902.

"A variety of mulberry cultivated for its leaf, used in feeding silkworms. The method of culture is to plant the cuttings deep in the ground, leaving two buds above the soil. The plant is never allowed to make a tree, but is cut down every year to the ground. The plants are only 6 to 8 inches apart, in rows 1½ feet from one another." (*Fairchild.*)

8336. POPULUS sp. (?) **Poplar.**

From Canton, China. Received through Messrs. Lathrop and Fairchild (No. 777, December 20, 1901), February 3, 1902.

"A low growing poplar with small leaves of a peculiar, truncated shape, which color up in December here in southern China a beautiful wine red. The splashes of color which this poplar gives to the landscape are very beautiful and the species is worth growing as an ornamental for this purpose alone." (*Fairchild.*)

8337. AMYGDALUS PERSICA. **Peach.**

From Canton, China. Received through Messrs. Lathrop and Fairchild (No. 778, December 20, 1901), February 3, 1902.

Ying tsui t'o. "Eagle Beak peach from a garden at Fati, opposite the island of Shameen. Probably much the same as Nos. 8331 to 8334, but as all these peaches seem to be grown from seed and are not grafted it may be slightly different." (*Fairchild.*)

8338. PRUNUS sp. **Red plum.**

From Canton, China. Received through Messrs. Lathrop and Fairchild (No. 779, December 20, 1901), February 3, 1902.

Hung Mui. "The flower and fruit are both said to be red and the latter to be an inch or more in diameter. It flowers somewhat later than the *Tsing Mui*, which is beginning to bloom now. This is from Yat Chun garden, at Fati, near Canton. These Chinese plums are said to be good canners, but likely to have a bitter taste on standing. They are not highly prized by the Europeans, who say they are hard and have a tendency to be astringent. The trees I saw at Fati were not remarkable, except for the great vigor of some young shoots springing from the old trunk which had been cut down. I can not vouch positively for the name of the variety as I worked through an interpreter." (*Fairchild.*)

8339. PRUNUS sp. **Plum.**

From Canton, China. Received through Messrs. Lathrop and Fairchild (No. 780, December 20, 1901), February 3, 1902.

Nam Wa Li. "A variety of plum called the Southern Glorious plum, according to Dr. J. M. Swan's translation. It is a red plum, about three-fourths of an inch in diameter, quite round, skin not tough, seed small. The sauce made from this variety turns bitter if left to stand for even an hour. If the tree is given good culture it produces fruits 1½ inches in diameter. It flowers in March. The tree I saw was quite vigorous and not grafted." (*Fairchild.*)

8340. AMYGDALUS PERSICA. Peach.

From Canton, China. Received through Messrs. Lathrop and Fairchild (No. 781, December 20, 1901), February 3, 1902.

Pak Wat tim t'o. "A slightly sweet, white stone variety of rather small size, preferred by some to the *Ying tsui t'o*, which, it is said, has too sweet a flavor. It has no beak like the latter, but is a typical south Chinese shape, according to Dr. J. M. Swan, of the Canton Hospital, who very kindly described this variety." (*Fairchild.*)

8341. DIOSPYROS KAKI. Persimmon.

From Canton, China. Received through Messrs. Lathrop and Fairchild (No. 782, December 20, 1901), February 3, 1902.

Hung tsi. "A soft persimmon, of dark-red color, which is preferred by many Europeans to the hard type that is only edible after soaking in water for an hour. This is grown at Fati, near Canton." (*Fairchild.*)

8342. PRUNUS sp. Plum.

From Canton, China. Received through Messrs. Lathrop and Fairchild (No. 783, December 20, 1901), February 3, 1902.

Pak Mui. "A white plum, according to the interpreter. The tree is a fairly vigorous grower and abundant producer of flowers. It is not cultivated extensively here, so far as I can find out, and I have been unable to get a description of the variety." (*Fairchild.*)

8343. AMYGDALUS PERSICA. Peach.

From Canton, China. Received through Messrs. Lathrop and Fairchild (No. 784, December 20, 1901), February 3, 1902.

Ying tsui t'o, or the Eagle Beak peach, from Fati, near Canton. "These are from different trees than Nos. 8331 to 8334, and may prove to have superior qualities. All that I have seen are seedling trees. Few peaches seem to be grafted." (*Fairchild.*)

8344. PSIDIUM GUAJAVA. Guava.

From Canton, China. Received through Messrs. Lathrop and Fairchild (No. 785, December 20, 1901), February 3, 1902.

"A reputed large-fruited (2 inches or so in diameter) yellow guava of good quality. The guavas about Canton are grown in the same fields with the rice. A single patch is often planted to a mixture of peach and guava trees, and both are grown on low ridges about 6 to 8 feet apart each way. No name was obtained." (*Fairchild.*)

8345. PRUNUS sp. Plum.

From Canton, China. Received through Messrs. Lathrop and Fairchild (No. 786, December 20, 1901), February 3, 1902.

Tsing mui. "A white-flowered, green-fruited plum. The fruit reaches 1 inch in diameter and is round in shape. This was just beginning to flower on December 20, much earlier than the *Hung Mui* or *Nam wa li* (*li* is pronounced as if spelled 'lay' in this word)." (*Fairchild.*)

8346. FICUS sp. Milk tree.

From Canton, China. Presented by Dr. J. M. Swan, of the Canton Hospital, through Messrs. Lathrop and Fairchild (No. 802, December 20, 1901), February 3, 1902.

Nau Nai Shu. "A large entire-leaved species of *Ficus*, which bears, even when quite young, large quantities of figs, at least an inch in diameter and quite sweet. Used as a shade tree in Canton. This was taken from Doctor Swan's yard at the Canton Hospital." (*Fairchild.*)

8347. CITRUS LIMETTA (?)   **Lime.**

From Canton, China. Sent by Messrs. Lathrop and Fairchild (No. 803, December 20, 1901), February 3, 1902.

"Orange-fruited lime. Scions taken from some fruit in the market of Canton of a variety of lime about 2 inches in diameter. In color this lime is as dark orange as a blood orange from Malta, and its flesh is not light, as the lime is generally, but a deep orange. It seems like a very sour orange. It is used everywhere here in place of lemon or other kinds of lime. I did not see the trees growing, so can not describe them." (*Fairchild.*) (These scions were not received.)

8348. AMYGDALUS COMMUNIS.   **Almond.**

From Malaga, Spain. Received through Mr. D. G. Fairchild (No. 767, July 31, 1901), February 4, 1902.

Jordan. "Bud sticks sent by Francisco Borgos Himenez, of Alhaurin, a village near Cartama, one and one-half hour's ride from Malaga." (*Fairchild.*)

8349. PISTACIA VERA.   **Pistache.**

From Aintab, Syria. Received through Rev. A. Fuller.

8350 to 8352. VIOLA ODORATA.   **Violet.**

From Paris, France. Received through Vilmorin-Andrieux & Co., February 4, 1902.

A collection of violet seed for experimental work, as follows:

8350.
Perpetual.

8352.
The Czar.

8351.
Perpetual, white.

8353. VIOLA CORNUTA.   **Violet.**

From Paris, France. Received through Vilmorin-Andrieux & Co., February 4, 1902.

Blue.

8354. VIGNA CATJANG.   **Cowpea.**

From Morioka, Japan. Received through Rev. E. Rothesay Miller, February 4, 1902.

A variety of cowpea having pods 3 feet long. Cooked and eaten like string beans.

8355 to 8357. DOLICHOS LABLAB.   **Bean.**

From Morioka, Japan. Received through Rev. E. Rothesay Miller, February 4, 1902.

Edible podded beans as follows:

8355.
Green pods.

8357.
Purple pods.

8356.
Purplish pods.

8358. VICIA FABA.   **Broad bean.**

From Canton, China. Received through Messrs. Lathrop and Fairchild (No. 791, December 21, 1901), February 5, 1902.

"A green variety of broad bean found on the market of Canton. This is used for human food, and is grown extensively in Central China, and I have seen large gardens of broad beans near Shanghai." (*Fairchild.*)

8359. ORYZA SATIVA. Rice.

From Canton, China. Received through Messrs. Lathrop and Fairchild (No. 788, December 21, 1901), February 5, 1902.

Si Mu. "Rice from Ching Shieng district, Canton province, 20 miles from Canton. It is a low-growing variety. This rice is imported to America for Chinese use, and is very highly prized by the Chinese because of its fine quality and especially because of its fine aroma. The price per katty is 6 cents, while ordinary rice costs about 4. Coolies often smuggle this rice out of the country, because there is an export duty on rice in Canton and this kind is the finest known to the Cantonese." (*Fairchild.*)

8360. ORYZA SATIVA. Rice.

From Canton, China. Received through Messrs. Lathrop and Fairchild (No. 790, December 21, 1901), February 5, 1902.

No Mai. "Old man's rice, a variety used for flour and pastry making. It is said to be very tough and nutritious and satisfying. Not generally employed for boiling purposes. It is a very expensive rice, bringing 8 cents a katty. Not classed with the ordinary boiling rices." (*Fairchild.*)

8361. ORYZA SATIVA. Rice.

From Canton, China. Received through Messrs. Lathrop and Fairchild (No. 789, December 21, 1901), February 5, 1902.

Wong Chim. "A variety of rice grown in Ching Sien or Ching Shien. I am told this is, next to No. 8359, the finest rice in Canton, but is not exported. It brings only 5 cents a katty when the other brings 6 cents. Vermicelli is said to be made of it." (*Fairchild.*)

8362. CASTANEA sp. Chestnut.

From Canton, China. Received through Messrs. Lathrop and Fairchild, February 6, 1902.

8363. PRUNUS ARMENIACA. Apricot.

From Canton, China. Received through Messrs. Lathrop and Fairchild (No. 800, December 20, 1901), February 5, 1902.

"Dried apricots from the Canton market. There seem to be no apricots grown about Canton, at least none of the Europeans I have talked with have seen any, and these are probably imported from north China." (*Fairchild.*)

8364. CANARIUM ALBUM. Chinese olive.

From Canton, China. Received through Messrs. Lathrop and Fairchild (No. 798, December 20, 1901), February 5, 1902.

Pak Lam. "This is a fruit sold in China by the thousands of tons, both in the dried state and pickled, and stained a light-yellow color. The plant is grown in orchards up the river from Canton and forms a very important article of commerce. Scarcely a fruit stall of any size is without it. The methods of preparation seem to be numerous. Worthy of preliminary plantings in Florida and southern California." (*Fairchild.*)

8365. PRUNUS sp. Plum.

From Canton, China. Received through Messrs. Lathrop and Fairchild (No. 799, December 20, 1901), February 5, 1902.

"Dried plums from the market in Canton. The origin of the trees is quite uncertain, but the fruit probably came from somewhere up the West or North rivers. The dealer said they came from Foo Chow, but no reliance is to be put on this statement." (*Fairchild.*)

8366. ELEOCHARIS TUBEROSA. Water chestnut.

From Canton, China. Received through Messrs. Lathrop and Fairchild (No. 801, December 20, 1901), February 5, 1902.

"An especially fine variety of the water chestnut, which is imported in large quantities into Canton from Kwai Lam, up the river. It is larger and better than the ordinary sort and should be given a trial in California, where the Chinese already grow the ordinary variety. (See Bulletin No. 68 of the Office of Experiment Stations.) There are numerous uses to which this swamp plant is put. Worthy of consideration as a plant for cultivation in the swamps of the South." (*Fairchild.*)

8367. CITRUS NOBILIS × CITRUS BIGARADIA. **Orange.**

From Mustapha, Algiers, Algeria. Received through Dr. L. Trabut, Government Botanist, January 5, 1902.

Clementine.

8368. CITRUS NOBILIS × CITRUS DECUMANA. **Orange.**

From Mustapha, Algiers, Algeria. Received through Dr. L. Trabut, Government Botanist, January 5, 1902.

8369 to 8385.

From Erfurt, Germany. Received through Haage & Schmidt, February 5, 1902. A collection of seeds, as follows:

8369. VIOLA MUNBYANA (?).

8370. VIOLA ODORATA BARRENSTEINI.

8371. VIOLA ODORATA BARRENSTEINI, fl. ALBO.

8372. VIOLA ODORATA.
Czar.

8373. VIOLA ODORATA.
Czar fl. albo.

8374. VIOLA ODORATA.
Kaiserin Augusta.

8375. VIOLA ODORATA.
Laucheana.

8376. VIOLA ODORATA.
Reine des Violettes.

8377. VIOLA ODORATA ROSSICA.

8378. VIOLA ODORATA SEMPERFLORENS.

8379. VIOLA ODORATA SEMPERFLORENS fl. ALBO.

8380. VIOLA ODORATA SEMPERFLORENS.
Hamburger treib.

8381. VIOLA ODORATA.
Victoria Reginae.

8382. CAMPANULA MEDIUM.

8383. CODONOPSIS VIRIDIFLORA (?).

8384. DIANTHUS BARBATUS.

8385. DELPHINIUM ZALIL.

8386. THEA VIRIDIS. **Tea.**

From Tokyo, Japan. Received through The Tokyo Plant and Seed Company, February 10, 1902.

Formosa.

8387 to 8409.

From Yokohama, Japan. Received through L. Boehmer & Co., February 3, 1902.

A collection of plants and bulbs, as follows:

8387. LILIUM LONGIFLORUM.

8388. IRIS LAEVIGATA.

8389. IRIS JAPONICA.

8390. IRIS TECTORUM.
Blue.

8391. IRIS TECTORUM.
White.

8392. PAEONIA MOUTAN.

8393. CASTANEA CRENATA.
Japanese mammoth chestnut.

8394. DAPHNE ODORA.
Pink.

8395. DAPHNE ODORA.
White.

8387 to 8409—Continued.

8396. HYDRANGEA HORTENSIS var. AIGAKU.

8397. HYDRANGEA HORTENSIS var. AJISAI.

8398. HYDRANGEA HORTENSIS var. BENJAKU.

8399. HYDRANGEA HORTENSIS.

8400. MAGNOLIA PARVIFLORA ERECTA.

8401. MAGNOLIA PARVIFLORA PENDULA.

8402. MAGNOLIA GRANDIFLORA EXONIENSIS.

8403. CORNUS KOUSA.

8404. CINNAMOMUM LOUREIRII.

8405. RAPHIOLEPIS JAPONICA.

8406. RHUS SUCCEDANEA.

8407. RHUS VERNICIFERA.

8408. ZELKOVA ACUMINATA.

8409. STAUNTONIA HEXAPHYLLA.

8410. CITRULLUS VULGARIS. **Watermelon.**

From Elgin, Utah. Received through Mr. John F. Brown, February 12, 1902.

Winter. A round, white melon, which will keep in perfect condition for several months after maturing. Flesh crimson, very sweet and tender. Seeds small and black. Rind quite tough when fully ripe. The average weight of these melons is about 20 pounds, although specimens weighing 40 pounds have been grown.

8411 to 8413. MANGIFERA INDICA. **Mango.**

From Colombo, Ceylon. Presented by Dr. C. Drieberg, of the Agricultural School, Cinnamon Gardens, Colombo, through Messrs. Lathrop and Fairchild (Nos. 805 to 807), January 13, 1902. Received February 15, 1902.

Scions of three varieties of mangoes, as follows:

8411.

Jaffna. "A long-fruited, medium-sized green mango. The seed is fairly large; flesh golden yellow. It is edible even before fully ripe. A vigorous grower and good bearer. This is the best market mango in Ceylon, and is the one generally planted about the villages. The name would imply its origin in the northern province of Ceylon, but Doctor Willis, of Peradeniya Gardens, says the variety is scarcely known in that province." (*Fairchild.*) (No. 805.)

8412.

Rupee. "The largest fruited variety of mango grown in Ceylon. It is called the Rupee, or two-shilling mango, because of the price paid for a single fruit. Its origin is unknown. It is very large, sometimes 5 inches long, nearly globular, light green in color when ripe. A shy bearer. Skin tender and easily bruised, rendering it a poor shipper. Flesh a golden yellow. Seed small in proportion to the size of the fruit. A rare variety even in Ceylon. The fruits are considered a great delicacy and much sought after by those who know it. Flesh free from stringiness and flavor delicious, but only when properly and perfectly ripened. The tree is not very robust, and Doctor Drieberg does not recommend the variety for general planting." (*Fairchild.*) (No. 806.)

8411 to 8413—Continued.

8413.

Thurston. "These scions are from a single tree (there is only one on the island of Ceylon) growing directly in front of Doctor Drieberg's bungalow, at the agricultural school at Colombo (Cinnamon Gardens). This tree was planted by a Mr. Thurston, and for convenience I have given it his name. It is not a variety known elsewhere on the island. The tree is between 30 and 40 years old and is a very heavy bearer. The fruit is of medium size, short, and somewhat globular. The stone is of medium size and the skin is dark green even when ripe. It ripens well off the tree. It is a vigorous grower, has a sweet flavor, and, according to Doctor Drieberg, is acid when not fully ripe. The flesh is greenish in color near the skin and slightly fibrous." (*Fairchild.*) (No. 807.)

8414. CITRUS NOBILIS × CITRUS DECUMANA. Orange.

From Mustapha, Algiers, Algeria. Received through Dr. L. Trabut, Government Botanist, February 15, 1902.

Seeds.

8415. CITRUS AURANTIUM. Orange.

From Mustapha, Algiers, Algeria. Received through Dr. L. Trabut, Government Botanist, February 15, 1902.

Merki. A small packet of seeds of a variety of sweet orange.

8416. CERATONIA SILIQUA. Carob.

From Candia, Crete. Presented by H. B. M. consul, Walter E. Lanson, of Candia, through Mr. D. G. Fairchild (No. 579), February 17, 1902.

"Cuttings of the best variety of carob, or St. John's bread, for grafting on seedling trees. I am informed that the Candian variety of carob is one of the best in the market, bringing the highest prices. It is a tree which is being more extensively planted every year on the island of Crete, and its pods already form one of the principal exports, both of Crete and Cyprus. It is exported to England, France, and Italy, where it is used for cattle food and for a surrogate to mix with chocolate. According to the inspector of agriculture of Crete, Cavre. G. M. Fumis, this Candian variety has more sugar in it than the other sorts grown in Crete." (*Fairchild.*)

8417. CARICA PAPAYA. Papaw.

From Honolulu, Hawaii. Received through Mr. Jared G. Smith, special agent in charge of the agricultural experiment station, February 17, 1902.

Seed grown from No. 5112, Inventory No. 8.

8418. VIGNA CATJANG. Cowpea.

From Monetta, S. C. Received through Mr. T. S. Williams, December 5, 1901.

Iron. This variety of cowpea is noted for its remarkable resistance to wilt disease and root-knot.

8419 to 8421. MANGIFERA INDICA. Mango.

From Bombay, India. Received through Messrs. Lathrop and Fairchild (Nos. 810 to 812, January 21, 1902), February 24, 1902.

Scions of three varieties of mangoes, as follows:

8419.

Douglas Bennett's Alphonse. "The Bombay mangoes are noted all over the Orient, and they are generally classed as a single sort, but in reality there are numerous varieties. The Alphonse, or, in Hindustani, Alfoos, is considered by connoisseurs as the very finest. These scions are taken from a tree on the estate of Mr. Cooper, near Goregon Station, one hour's ride from Bombay, and

8419 to 8421—Continued.

represent an especially fine strain of the Alphonse mango, which was called to our attention by Mr. Douglas Bennett, superintendent of markets in Bombay, who desires that it be given his name. He says that all he knows of its origin is that over one hundred and thirty years ago it was discovered by a Parsee merchant, and that grafts were put down at Gwalia Tank Road, below Combali Hill, in Bombay, but that now very few of these are to be seen. The supply of this mango is so limited that fancy prices are paid for it, and few Europeans even have ever tasted the fruit. In size it is 3 by 4 by 2 inches and in color a golden yellow when ripe. The flesh is quite without stringiness, stone small, and flavor, according to Mr. Bennett, the best in the world. It is a large-leaved variety and forms a good-sized tree, but is of scraggly growth." (*Fairchild.*) (No. 810.) (See No. 8727.)

8420.

Bottle. "A good market sort, of Bombay. Green in color, ripening to reddish yellow. Flesh is yellowish in color and is not stringy. The fruit is long and slender, hence the name 'Bottle.' The stone is small. The fruit ripens, as do most of the Bombay mangoes, from April to May." (*Fairchild.*) (No. 811.)

8421.

Pirie. "A green, pointed-shaped variety from the Cooper estate at Goregon. Said by the owner, an inspector in the Bombay markets, to be, next to the *Alphonse*, the best of the Bombay mangoes. The seed is larger than that of the *Alphonse* and the flavor is excellent. Has the undesirable quality of being a poor keeper, losing its flavor quickly after fully ripe." (*Fairchild.*) (No. 812.)

8422 to 8424. GLYCINE HISPIDA. Soy bean.

From Yokohama, Japan. Received through Dr. S. A. Knapp, February 24, 1902.

8422.
Ita Name. Early.

8424.
Ita Name. Late.

8423.
Ita Name. Medium.

8425. JUGLANS CORDIFORMIS. Walnut.

From Yokohama, Japan. Received through Dr. S. A. Knapp, February 24, 1902.

8426. JUGLANS SIEBOLDIANA. Walnut.

From Yokohama, Japan. Received through Dr. S. A. Knapp, February 24, 1902.

8427. PHYLLOSTACHYS MITIS. Bamboo.

From Yokohama, Japan. Received through Dr. S. A. Knapp, February 24, 1902.

Moso chiku.

8428. PHYLLOSTACHYS QUILIOI. Bamboo.

From Yokohama, Japan. Received through Dr. S. A. Knapp, February 24, 1902.

Madake.

8429. JUNCUS EFFUSUS. Rush.

From Yokohama, Japan. Received through Dr. S. A. Knapp, February 24, 1902.

198   SEEDS AND PLANTS IMPORTED.

8430 to 8433. PUNICA GRANATUM. **Pomegranate.**

From Valetta, Malta. Presented by Baron Testaferrata Abela, through Mr. D. G. Fairchild. Received February 25, 1902.

Cuttings as follows:

8430.
Giuseppe. Prima quality.

8431.
Duc Colon, di S. Caterina.

8432.
Frances.

8433.
S. Rosa.

8434. ELEUSINE CORACANA. **Ragi millet or Kurakkan.**

From Colombo, Ceylon. Received through Messrs. Lathrop and Fairchild (No. 809, January 13, 1902), February 25, 1902.

"A species of millet which is planted all over Ceylon by the Singalese. It is a most important food crop for the natives, although given little attention by Europeans. Watt's Dictionary of Indian Products, 1890, Vol. III, p. 237, gives a long account of the use of this species in India, where it forms one of the great staples. Ferguson describes it as the most prolific of cultivated grasses. One variety, *E. stricta* Roxb., gives an increase of 120 fold, another 500 fold, and a single seed has been calculated to produce no less than 8,100 seeds in a single year. These seeds are very small, however. The food made from this species is coarse, though nourishing. When boiled the flour forms a sticky paste, which must be eaten with greasy gravy to be palatable. There are two varieties in this sample, mixed together, this being the way the field was sown. The two sorts are called *Hanasu Kurakkan*, or *Black Kurakkan*, and *Kiri* (White or Milk) *Kurakkan*. The seed is broadcasted and raked in or trampled in with the feet in May, in Ceylon, and the crop ripens in three months. It seems, however, to be sometimes planted at other times of the year. These varieties are suited only to irrigated lands and for trial in tropical regions with an abundance of rain. This species is a native of Ceylon, but varieties of the same species are cultivated under the native names of *Marua Kairarii* or *Kelvaragu* in continental India. This whole question of the Indian millets, many of which withstand severe dry weather, Watt says, is worthy of especial attention, and all the best varieties should be secured. Doctor Drieberg, superintendent of School Gardens, Cinnamon Gardens, Colombo, should be applied to for a larger quantity of this seed, which at this season is difficult to secure in good condition. As a chicken food this is reputed to be unsurpassed, fattening poultry with great rapidity. This is grown in a region which has 75 to 100 inches of rainfall a year." (*Fairchild.*)

8435. CITRUS DECUMANA. **Pomelo.**

From Poona, India. Received through Messrs. Lathrop and Fairchild (No. 815, January 26, 1902), February 25, 1902.

"A variety of pomelo which is said to be practically seedless, though not of first quality. It may prove useful for crossing purposes. It is medium large and has a thick skin. The flesh is too dry." (*Fairchild.*)

8436. VITIS VINIFERA. **Grape.**

From Poona, India. Received through Messrs. Lathrop and Fairchild (No. 816, January 27, 1902), February 25, 1902.

Bhokri. "A sweet, white sort, with rather tough skin, but very productive. This is one of the best varieties for general cultivation about Poona, which has a high altitude, tropical climate, temperature as high as 120°, and with 30 inches of rainfall. It is said to have originated in the north of India. It bears two crops a year, only the second one, however, being sweet." (*Fairchild.*)

8437. JASMINUM SAMBAC. **Arabian jasmine.**

From Poona, India. Received through Messrs. Lathrop and Fairchild (No. 817, January 25, 1902), February 25, 1902.

"A variety of jessamine much cultivated by the natives of India and used by them in their worship under the name of *Mogaree*. It is a vigorous growing shrub and bears an abundance of very large, double, white flowers, which are highly perfumed. Some of these flowers are said to be as large as a camelia blossom. The plant requires rich soil and is very sensitive to cold. It is strictly a tropical plant, although doing well in gardens in Cairo. The cuttings should be treated in the usual way, i. e., rooted in moist sand, and the plants can be set out in a rich border. This is the largest variety of the jessamine I know, and if not already introduced into Hawaii, southern California, or Florida, deserves to be generally propagated and distributed. From the Empress Gardens, in Poona, India." (*Fairchild.*)

8438. POINSETTIA PULCHERRIMA. Poinsettia.

From Poona, India. Received through Messrs. Lathrop and Fairchild (No. 818, January 25, 1902), February 25, 1902.

"A double poinsettia of rare beauty. Instead of the usual whorl of bright red leaves characteristic of the ordinary poinsettia this sort has from three to five such whorls. These are at their best when the green leaves have fallen and the light gray stems are quite bare. As a decorative plant for giving a splash of the brightest red to a landscape this plant is unequalled." (*Fairchild.*)

8439. CITRUS AURANTIUM. Orange.

From Poona, India. Received through Messrs. Lathrop and Fairchild (No. 819, January 26, 1902), February 25, 1902.

Kowla. "Described by Woodrow in his 'Gardening in India,' page 193, as an indifferent dessert fruit, but considered by the natives of India as well worth attention and, in fact, recommended as a good sort. A distinct variety, and hence worthy of a collection." (*Fairchild.*)

8440. MANGIFERA INDICA. Mango.

From Poona, India. Received through Messrs. Lathrop and Fairchild (No. 820, January 26, 1902), February 25, 1902.

Alphonse or *Aphoos.* "From a tree in the Empress Gardens at Poona. It may prove a different strain from Nos. 8419 and 8727. This is the best Bombay mango and is remarkable for its good shipping qualities. It can be picked when still green, laid or shipped in straw with plenty of air, and kept for six weeks. Even after ripe, fruits can be kept for a week or more. A much better shipper than the *Mulgoba* and more productive." (*Fairchild.*)

8441. CITRUS AURANTIUM. Orange.

From Poona, India. Received through Messrs. Lathrop and Fairchild (No. 821, January 26, 1902), February 25, 1902.

Ladoo. "This is a popular orange in India and is of the mandarin class, although not so fine looking in appearance. The oil glands are finer and the color is a duller orange, sometimes russet. It deserves a place in every collection of oranges as a distinct type. Woodrow, in his 'Gardening in India,' page 209, figures this variety and recommends it for planting. It is a loose-skinned sort but the skin is more nearly filled by the flesh than the ordinary mandarin and in texture it is unusually crisp and of good flavor. Very little fiber is one of its characteristics. In size it is about the average of the mandarin type. Secured by the superintendent of the Empress Gardens in Poona." (*Fairchild.*)

8442. MANGIFERA INDICA. Mango.

From Poona, India. Received through Messrs. Lathrop and Fairchild (No. 822, January 26, 1902), February 25, 1902.

Borsha. "See Woodrow, Gardening in India, page 248. Fruit weighs on an average 10 ounces. Ripens by the first of July Flesh is as dry as that of *Mulgoba* or *Alphonse* and can be cut like cheese. It is three to four weeks later in ripening than the *Alphonse* and is considered almost its equal in quality. One large tree of this variety is said to have often yielded over $150 worth of fruit in a single crop. It should be planted in alluvial soil and given plenty of bone ash. The banks of a river or irrigation canal are especially well suited to mango culture. This variety is distinguished from the *Mulgoba* by its young shoots, which are distinctly reddish in color. Mangoes are sometimes shipped from Bombay to London, which is eighteen days' or more of sea travel." (*Fairchild.*)

8443. CITRUS sp.

From Poona, India. Received through Messrs. Lathrop and Fairchild (No. 823, January 26, 1902), February 25, 1902.

Jamburee or *Jamboorce*. "A variety of *Citrus* which is used in India extensively for stocks on which the orange is grafted. Considerable discussion regarding its influence on the scions of sweet oranges will be found in Woodrow's 'Gardening in India,' pages 214 and 215. In one place Woodrow calls this a lime, in another a citron." (*Fairchild.*)

8444. MANGIFERA INDICA. Mango.

From Poona, India. Received through Messrs. Lathrop and Fairchild (No. 824, January 26, 1902), February 25, 1902.

Pakria. "Described at some length by Woodrow, page 247, in his Gardening in India, and considered by some as one of the three best mangoes in the Bombay presidency; at any rate it is a sort in big demand for planting. It ripens three or four weeks later than the *Alphonse*—i. e., from the end of May to the end of June. Secured through the kindness of Mr. Kannetkar, superintendent of Empress Gardens in Poona. (*Fairchild.*)

8445. THYSANOLAENA AGROSTIS.

From Poona, India. Received through Messrs. Lathrop and Fairchild (No. 825, January 26, 1902), February 25, 1902.

"Two pieces of rhizome of an ornamental cane from the Himalayas. It flowers profusely and remains in flower for four months. The inflorescences are steel-gray and great masses of them are produced. The plant grows to a height of 8 to 10 feet and forms large clumps like pampas grass or like some species of *Arundo*. It is altogether the handsomest cane for borders that I have ever seen. It deserves a wide distribution in Hawaii and southern California. As seeds were not procurable the experiment of sending two rhizomes in a perforated tin case by sample post has been attempted. If successful more can be had of the superintendent of the Empress Gardens in Poona. Seed may be had of the Calcutta Botanic Gardens. The plant requires good rich soil and plenty of moisture. In the Poona Gardens it is grown on irrigated land because there are only about 25 inches of yearly rainfall. The cuttings should be given such treatment as would be given the ordinary ornamental canes." (*Fairchild.*)

8446. CITRUS AURANTIUM. Orange.

From Poona, India. Received through Messrs. Lathrop and Fairchild (No. 826, January 26, 1902), February 25, 1902.

Cintra or *Suntura*. "Woodrow (Gardening in India, p. 210), says this is the finest orange in India. It weighs from 7 to 10 ounces. One sort has loose skin, the other tightly fits the pulp. It has very few seeds, and is often quite seedless. The flesh is unusually crisp and has almost no fiber, but is somewhat lacking in sweetness. The oil glands are very small and close together in the skin. The color is not so bright as that of the mandarin of Japan. This variety is of especial interest only because of its reported seedlessness and the fiberless nature of the flesh, which is quite remarkable. I am assured this is the tight-skinned variety, which is superior to the loose-skinned one. The type is distinctly a mandarin one. Through the kindness of Superintendent Kannetkar of the Empress Gardens, Poona." (*Fairchild.*)

8447. CITRULLUS VULGARIS. Watermelon.

From the Agricultural Experiment Station, Pomona, Cal. Received February 20, 1902.

Khama or *Tsamma*. This melon is very valuable for stock feeding in dry countries, as it thrives with very little water. (Grown from No. 4322.)

8448 to 8453. PYRUS MALUS. Apple.

From Misserghin, near Oran, Algeria. Received through Messrs. D. G. Fairchild and C. S. Scofield, from the Nursery of the Orphelinat de l'Annonciation, February 26, 1902.

8448 to 8453—Continued.

Apple trees and scions as follows:

8448.
Algerienne.

8449.
D'Eve.

8450.
De Chataignier.

8451.
Nain Paradis.

8452.
Precoce de Tunis.

8453.
Nain de Mahon.

8454 and 8455. CYDONIA VULGARIS. Quince

From Misserghin, near Oran, Algeria. Received through Messrs. D. G. Fairchild and C. S. Scofield from the Nursery of the Orphelinat de l'Annonciation, February 26, 1902.

Quince scions as follows:

8454.
De Laghouat.

8455.
De Mahon.

8456 to 8460.

From San Giovanni á Teduccio, Italy. Received through Dammann & Co., March 3, 1902.

8456. VIOLA CORNUTA.

8457. VIOLA CORNUTA ALBA.

8458. VIOLA CORNUTA.
Admiracion.

8459. VIOLA CORNUTA.
Blue Perfection.

8460. VIOLA ODORATA SEMPERFLORENS.

8461. LATHYRUS sp.

From the Vomero, Naples, Italy. Received through Dr. C. Sprenger, March 5, 1902.

"A native of Mexico." (*Sprenger.*)

8462. VITIS VINIFERA. Grape.

From Kurrachee, India. Received through Messrs. Lathrop and Fairchild (No. 827, February 2, 1902), March 10, 1902.

Sufetha. "An indigenous white grape, grown successfully at Kurrachee. It is one of the three best in cultivation here, where there is only 7 inches of rainfall and the temperature in summer goes to 110° F. from March to the end of June, and the soil is noticeably alkaline. Berry large and round; bunches 4½ pounds in weight; long, crowded, heavy cropper; flavor good; skin thick and leathery. It is said to be a good keeper and shipper, being shipped from Kurrachee to Bombay and Lahore. These cuttings are from the Kurrachee Public Gardens." (*Fairchild.*)

8463. VITIS VINIFERA. Grape.

From Kurrachee, India. Received through Messrs. Lathrop and Fairchild (No. 829, February 2, 1902), March 10, 1902.

Goolabie. "An indigenous variety of grape which thrives better than such forms as the *Black Hamburg*, and, according to our informant, Mr. Lester, superintendent of the public gardens of Kurrachee, it is considered superior in flavor to the *Black Hamburg*. This is the favorite grape for Kurrachee conditions, which resemble those of Tulare (California) and Arizona, being a desert where only 7 inches of rain falls and where, for the summer months, a temperature of 110° is of daily occurrence. The soil is decidedly alkaline, in fact too much so for ordinary European grapes. The variety is said to be a purple, small-berried kind, a very heavy cropper, fruiting the end of April. The bunches weigh 1½ to 2 pounds. The berry has a very thin skin and two or three seeds. The name means 'rose flavored' and the flavor is that of rose petals. It was introduced into Poona, India, but did not succeed there." (*Fairchild.*)

8464. VITIS VINIFERA. **Grape.**

From Kurrachee, India. Received through Messrs. Lathrop and Fairchild (No. 828, February 2, 1902), March 10, 1902.

Kandhari. "A long-berried, thin-skinned, white grape with very large bunches, 3 to 4 pounds in weight. It is a vigorous grower, but light bearer. An indigenous sort, of fine flavor, suited to an arid climate, and alkaline soil in a very warm climate." (*Fairchild.*)

8465 to 8475. CITRULLUS VULGARIS. **Watermelon.**

From Monetta, S. C. Received through Mr. T. S. Williams, November 5, 1901.

Seeds from hand-pollinated melons, grown from seeds imported by the Office of Seed and Plant Introduction:

8465. From No. 16.

Melon of average size with dark-green stripes. Flesh orange-colored and of very fine flavor. Vine small and not vigorous. This is an excellent melon for home use.

8466. From No. 35.

A small green melon with white spots. The flesh is deep red and very fine. The vine is small, but strong.

8467. From No. 68, which is evidently mixed seed.

A large, pale-green melon with broad, dark stripes. The flesh is orange-colored and of very fine flavor. The vine is very vigorous.

8468. From No. 68.

A medium-sized, pale-green melon with broad, dark-green stripes. The flesh is orange colored and of good flavor. The vine is very vigorous.

8469. From No. 46.

A large, light-gray melon. The flesh is deep red and of fine flavor. The vine is very vigorous.

8470. From No. 93.

A rather large, gray melon, with green stripes. The flesh is pink and of very fine flavor. The vine is vigorous.

8471. From No. 2847.

A fairly good, green melon of average size. The flesh is pale red and of good flavor. The vine is strong.

8472. From No. 2847.

A medium-sized, mottled-green melon. The flesh is red and of good flavor. The vine is strong.

8473. From No. 2848.

A large, white melon. The flesh is deep red, of fine texture and very fine flavor.

8474. From No. 2849.

A medium-sized, dark-green melon, with small white stripes. The flesh is deep red, of fine texture and delicious flavor.

8475. From No. 6151.

A very large, dark-green, striped melon. The flesh is pink, of rather coarse texture, but fine flavor.

8476. PISTACIA MUTICA. **Menengech.**

From Aintab, Syria. Presented by Rev. A. Fuller, through Mr. W. T. Swingle. Received March 10, 1902.

8477 and 8478. PISTACIA VERA. **Pistache.**

From Aintab, Syria. Presented by Rev. A. Fuller, through Mr. W. T. Swingle. Received March 10, 1902.

8477.   **8478.**
Large red.   *Large green.*

8479 to 8482. PISTACIA VERA. **Pistache.**

From Aintab, Syria. Presented by Rev. A. Fuller, through Mr. W. T. Swingle. Received March 10, 1902.

8479.
Selected mixed fresh pistache nuts from the market.

8480.
Aleppo red. Very large and fine.

8481.
A large, unnamed, green variety.

8482.
Koz. Known as the "Walnut" pistache.

8483. PISTACIA VERA × (?) **Butum.**

From Aintab, Syria. Presented by Rev. A. Fuller, through Mr. W. T. Swingle. Received March 10, 1902.

Fresh, selected "Butum" nuts.

8484. PISTACIA MUTICA. **Menengech.**

From Aintab, Syria. Presented by Rev. A. Fuller, through Mr. W. T. Swingle. Received March 10, 1902.

Selected fresh seeds.

8485. PISTACIA MUTICA. **Menengech.**

From Aintab, Syria. Presented by Rev. A. Fuller, through Mr. W. T. Swingle. Received March 10, 1902.

Ordinary seeds from the market.

8486 to 8501.

From Washington, D. C. Received March 10, 1902.

A collection of seeds grown on the Potomac Flats by Mr. W. R. Beattie from seeds furnished by the Office of Seed and Plant Introduction.

    8486. PHASEOLUS MUNGO. Grown from No. 6321.

    8487. PHASEOLUS MUNGO. Grown from No. 6417.

    8488. PHASEOLUS MUNGO. Grown from No. 6318.

    8489. GLYCINE HISPIDA. Grown from No. 6314.

    8490. GLYCINE HISPIDA. Grown from No. 6333.

    8491. GLYCINE HISPIDA. Grown from No. 6334.

8486 to 8501—Continued.

- **8492.** GLYCINE HISPIDA. Grown from No. 6386.
- **8493.** GLYCINE HISPIDA. Grown from No. 6396.
- **8494.** GLYCINE HISPIDA. Grown from No. 6336.
- **8495.** GLYCINE HISPIDA. Grown from No. 6397.
- **8496.** GLYCINE HISPIDA. Grown from No. 6416.
- **8497.** GLYCINE HISPIDA. Grown from No. 6312.
- **8498.** VIGNA CATJANG. Grown from No. 6311.
- **8499.** VIGNA CATJANG. Grown from No. 6327.
- **8500.** VIGNA CATJANG. Grown from No. 6328.
- **8501.** VIGNA CATJANG. Grown from No. 6413.

8502. MAGNOLIA KOBUS. Magnolia.

From Yokohama, Japan. Received through L. Boehmer & Co., March 13, 1902.

8503. PAEONIA MOUTAN. Tree peony.

From Yokohama, Japan. Received through L. Boehmer & Co., March 13, 1902.

8504. ZAMIA FLORIDANA. Coontie.

From Miami, Fla. Received through Prof. P. H. Rolfs, in charge of the Subtropical Laboratory of the United States Department of Agriculture.

8505. THEA VIRIDIS. Tea.

From Heneratgoda, Ceylon. Presented by Messrs. J. P. William & Bros. Received March 17, 1902.

Formosa.

8506 and 8507. FICUS CARICA. Fig.

From the island of Chios, Turkey. Presented by Mr. N. J. Pantelides, through Mr. D. G. Fairchild. Received March 19, 1902.

Fig cuttings as follows:

8506.

Figue de Chios. "Very fine when fresh." (*Pantelides.*)

8507.

Figue de Syria. Lombardica. "A very fine, large variety, blackish on the outside and bright red inside." (*Pantelides.*)

8508 to 8515. ORYZA SATIVA. Rice.

From Japan. Received through Dr. S. A. Knapp, March 19, 1902.

Seed rice as follows:

8508.

Fusakichi. From Bizen district. (I)

8509.

Mansaku bozu. From Fukuoka district. (J)

8510.

From Ise district. (K)

8511.

From Buzen district. (L)

8512.

From Iyo district. (M)

8513.

From Higo district. (N)

8514.

From Bizen district. (O)

8515.

From Banshu (?) district. (P)

8516. CANNABIS SATIVA. **Hemp.**

From Danville, Ky. Received through Mr. George Cogar, March 20, 1902.

8517 to 8520. PISTACIA VERA. **Pistache.**

From Marseille, France. Received through Mr. Claude Montel, March 21, 1902.

    8517. Grafted female pistache trees.

    8518. Grafted male pistache trees.

    8519. Female pistache scions.

    8520. Male pistache scions.

8521. PISTACIA TEREBINTHUS. **Terebinth.**

From Marseille, France. Received through Mr. Claude Montel, March 21, 1902. Terebinth stocks for grafting.

8522 and 8523. TRITICUM DURUM. **Wheat.**

From Brookings, S. Dak. Seed grown in 1901 under contract by Prof. J. H. Shepard, of the South Dakota Agricultural Experiment Station.

    8522.
    Kubanka. Grown from No. 5639.

    8523.
    Velvet Don. Grown from No. 5644.

8524 to 8529.

From Paris, France. Received from Vilmorin-Andrieux & Co., March 27, 1902.

    8524. LINUM USITATISSIMUM. **Flax.**
    Original *Riga.*

    8525. CANNABIS SATIVA. **Hemp.**
    Russian.

    8526. THYMUS VULGARIS. **Thyme.**

    8527. THYMUS SERPYLLUM. **Creeping thyme.**

    8528. LAVANDULA VERA. **Lavender.**

    8529. LAVANDULA SPICA. **Spike lavender.**

8530 to 8537.

Received from J. M. Thorburn & Co., of New York City, March 29, 1902. A collection of foreign-grown seeds of medicinal plants, for use in experimental work under the direction of Dr. R. H. True, of the Department of Agriculture.

    8530. ATROPA BELLADONNA. **Belladonna.**

    8531. ARNICA MONTANA. **Mountain tobacco, or mountain snuff.**

    8532. DIGITALIS PURPUREA. **Foxglove.**

    8533. GLYCYRRHIZA GLABRA. **Licorice.**

    8534. DATURA STRAMONIUM. **Thorn apple.**

    8535. HYOSCYAMUS NIGER. **Henbane.**

    8536. PAPAVER SOMNIFERUM. **Poppy.**

    8537. ACONITUM NAPELLUS. **Aconite.**

8538. AVENA SATIVA. **Oat.**

From Bozeman, Mont. Presented by the Director of the Agricultural Experiment Station. Received April 1, 1902.

Swedish Select. Grown from No. 2788.

8539 to 8542.

From Poona, India. Received through Dr. S. A. Knapp, April 1, 1902.

8539. PHASEOLUS ACONITIFOLIUS.

Math. "This legume is grown in the Deccan and the Gujarat as a 'kharif,' or rain crop, sown only in the rainy season. It does well on light, stony, upland soil, with an average annual rainfall of 30 inches. The usual method is to sow a mixture of 8 pounds of *Bajri* (*Pennisetum typhoideum*) and 1½ pounds of *Math* per acre in July, the crop being harvested in November or December." (*Knapp.*)

8540. PHASEOLUS MUNGO.

Mug. "This plant is largely grown as a 'kharif,' or rain crop, and also as a 'rabi' (cold-weather crop) in many parts of India. As a 'kharif' crop it is mixed with sorghum (*Jowari*), while as a 'rabi' crop it is sown after rice has been harvested. It does best in a deep, black soil, with an average rainfall of from 30 to 35 inches. It ripens in three months after sowing." (*Knapp.*)

8541. PHASEOLUS RADIATUS.

Udid. "This bean is largely cultivated in India as a subordinate crop with sorghum (*Jowari*), the usual amount sown being 6 pounds of *Jowari* and 3 pounds of *Udid.* It does best if sown in June in deep, black soil, with a rainfall of from 30 to 35 inches, being harvested in September. *Udid* is also grown in some sections as a second crop after rice." (*Knapp.*)

8542. DOLICHOS UNIFLORUS.

Kulthi. "This plant is largely grown on light soils of a strong or sandy nature, and thrives with a moderate rainfall. It is usually sown with bulrush millet (*Pennisetum typhoideum*), the rate per acre being 8 pounds of millet to 2 pounds of *Kulthi.*" (*Knapp.*)

8543 to 8547.

From Nagpur, India. Received through Dr. S. A. Knapp, April 1, 1902.

8543. ORYZA SATIVA. **Rice.**

Dhan. A quick-ripening variety.

8544. TRITICUM DURUM. **Wheat.**

Haura Gahoo.

8545. DOLICHOS LABLAB. **Lablab bean.**

Tal, Val, or *Popat.*

8546. ANDROPOGON SORGHUM. **Sorghum.**

A late variety used for forage.

8547. ANDROPOGON SORGHUM. **Sorghum.**

Used for forage.

8548 to 8552.

From Lahore, India. Received through Dr. S. A. Knapp, April 1, 1902.

A collection of wheats as follows:

8548. TRITICUM VULGARE.

Pure red wheat, grown without irrigation on land near the river. (No. 1.)

8548 to 8552—Continued.

8549. TRITICUM VULGARE.

Pure white wheat, grown on slightly salty land irrigated with canal water. (No. 2.)

8550. TRITICUM DURUM.

Round red wheat, grown on slightly salty land irrigated with canal water. (No. 3.)

8551. TRITICUM DURUM.

Round white wheat, grown on strong black soil irrigated with canal water. (No. 4.)

8552. TRITICUM DURUM.

Wadanak. Grown on light, slightly sandy soil irrigated with well water.

8553 to 8562.

From Christiania, Norway. Presented by Prof. C. Doxrud, of the Christiania School of Technology, for testing in comparison with seeds from other countries. Received April 2, 1902.

8553. PHLEUM PRATENSE. Timothy.

8554. DACTYLIS GLOMERATA. Orchard grass.

8555. TRIFOLIUM PRATENSE. Red clover.

8556. TRIFOLIUM HYBRIDUM. Alsike clover.

8557. PISUM SATIVUM. Pea.

Early.

8558. AVENA SATIVA. Oat.

8559. HORDEUM HEXASTICHUM. Barley.

8560. HORDEUM DISTICHUM. Barley.

8561. TRITICUM VULGARE. Wheat.

Red spring.

8562. PISUM SATIVUM. Pea.

Sueding.

8563 and 8564. PHOENIX DACTYLIFERA. Date.

From Kurrachee, India. Received through Messrs. Lathrop and Fairchild (No. 830, February 1, 1902), April 4, 1902.

Cupcap, Chupchap, or *Cupcup.* "This is a variety of the *Karak pokhta,* or cooked dates, and is considered one of the best of its class. These cooked dates are prepared in the following way: The fruits are picked before fully ripe, while still full, plump, and slightly astringent. They are boiled for an hour in fresh water, to which one handful of salt per gallon of water is added. After boiling they are spread out in the sun to dry. These boiled dates are sold in large quantities in India. They form an indispensable part of every marriage feast. Higher prices are paid for them in India, I am informed, than for the dates shipped to America. This sort is, when properly prepared, quite sweet, in fact, tastes quite as if candied. The slight flavor of tannin may be due to careless preparation. It is a fairly early date, coming into fruit about Maskat in July. It is also a good date to eat fresh. It keeps almost indefinitely. There are several qualities of this variety. That marked *a* came from Kurrachee, while *b* was secured in Maskat." (*Fairchild.*)

8565. CAPSICUM ANNUUM. **Red pepper.**

From Kurrachee, India. Received through Messrs. Lathrop and Fairchild (no number), April 4, 1902.

Bird's bill.

8566. CAPSICUM ANNUUM. **Red pepper.**

From Kurrachee, India. Received through Messrs. Lathrop and Fairchild (No. 828, February 6, 1902), April 4, 1902.

"The common red pepper in use in Kurrachee. It is mild in comparison with the Maskat variety. It is dark wine-red in color, and long and conical in shape. Bought in a Maskat market." (*Fairchild.*)

8567. PHOENIX DACTYLIFERA. **Date palm.**

From Kurrachee, India. Received through Messrs. Lathrop and Fairchild (no number), April 4, 1902.

"*Bagist* or *Dairi* dates, a second-class variety eaten by the common people." (*Fairchild.*)

8568. CAPSICUM ANNUUM. **Chili pepper.**

From Maskat, India. Received through Messrs. Lathrop and Fairchild (No. 837, February 6, 1902), April 4, 1902.

"A very hot orange or light-red variety of red pepper, reputed to be one of the hottest peppers on the Persian Gulf. Bought in a Maskat bazaar." (*Fairchild.*)

8569. PHOENIX DACTYLIFERA. **Date palm.**

From Maskat, India. Received through Messrs. Lathrop and Fairchild (No. 831, February 6, 1902), April 4, 1902.

Burni. "Dried dates of one of the *Karak pokhta* or cooking class. This date is also said to be a first-class drying or pressed date, but with poor keeping qualities. It is so delicate that it can not be sent successfully to America, but it is considered superior in flavor to the *Fard* date, which is the variety commonly shipped to America. It is the earliest date known at Maskat, and one of the very finest flavored sorts. It ripens in Maskat in June, but this region of Maskat has a temperature in summer of 110° and even 117° F. in the shade, so that the sort might ripen later if transplanted to a region with a cooler summer temperature. The dates sent are of the boiled sort only, the dried kind being quite unobtainable." (*Fairchild.*)

8570. PHOENIX DACTYLIFERA. **Date palm.**

From Kurrachee, India. Received through Messrs. Lathrop and Fairchild (No. 834, Feb. 2, 1902), April 4, 1902.

Jahadi. "Dried dates of one of the second quality sorts shipped into India from the Persian Gulf. This variety is probably shipped to America." (*Fairchild.*)

8571. PHOENIX DACTYLIFERA. **Date palm.**

From Maskat, India. Received through Messrs. Lathrop and Fairchild (No. 833, February 6, 1902), April 4, 1902.

Khanezi. "Dried dates of a first-class Persian Gulf sort sent largely to America. This is considered inferior to the *Fard*, but still ranks as a very good sort." (*Fairchild.*)

8572. PHOENIX DACTYLIFERA. **Date palm.**

From Kurrachee, India. Received through Messrs. Lathrop and Fairchild (No. 832, February 5, 1902), April 4, 1902.

Fard. "Dried dates of the variety most commonly shipped from the Persian Gulf to America. This is not considered the finest of the dates, but is one of the best shippers. It is a dark, medium-sized sort, of good quality. It is grown about Maskat and the southern part of the Persian Gulf. It is a medium early date, later than *Burni.*" (*Fairchild.*)

8573. Phoenix dactylifera. **Date palm.**

From Bahrein, Arabia. Received through Messrs. Lathrop and Fairchild (No. 835, February 10, 1902), April 4, 1902.

Khalasa. "Dried dates of one of the finest varieties in the Persian Gulf. These dates are so delicate that they are not shipped to America, although they may be kept several months, as is evidenced by the present samples. They are reported to suffer by the sea voyage. The date has very little fiber, being a sticky sort with a decidedly caramel-like texture. The flavor is superior to that of the best *Fard* date and the skin is soft and delicate. The stone is small, but not unusually so. It is considered the best date on the Persian Gulf by Mr. J. C. Gaskin, British consul, who has been a dealer in one of the largest date firms at Bassorah, and by Mr. S. M. Zwemer, who has traveled all over Arabia. Personally I prefer the *Pangh Ghur* date and the *Deglet Noor*, but the *Khalasa* approaches these closely for sweetness and delicacy. It is sticky, however, and might not be well suited to such style of packing as is in vogue with the French packers in Algiers. Secured through the kindness of Messrs. Gaskin and Zwemer, of Bahrein." (*Fairchild.*) (See No. 8753.)

8574. Pistacia vera. **Pistache.**

From Bunder Abbas, Persia. Received through Messrs. Lathrop and Fairchild (No. 839, February 11, 1902), April 4, 1902.

"Bought in the market of Bunder Abbas. They were said to have been brought down some nineteen days by caravan from the town of Kerman, in the interior. They were fresh in December or November. The trees were probably grafted, although no definite information on this point could be obtained. Kerman is said to have a temperate climate." (*Fairchild.*)

8575. Lagenaria sp. **Gourd.**

From Jask, Persia. Received through Messrs. Lathrop and Fairchild (No. 840, February 11, 1902), April 4, 1902.

"A white, edible gourd growing to a large size, 1½ feet long by 8 inches in diameter. It forms a pretty trellis plant in Jask, where the temperature rises to 110° F. and no rain falls. It is grown by irrigation. It may prove of value in the Colorado desert region. It is prepared by boiling in salt water like any of the squash family. The leaves are large and the flowers are white with long tubes to the corolla." (*Fairchild.*)

8576. Vitis candicans. **Mustang grape.**

From Tiger Mill, Texas. Presented by Mr. H. T. Fuchs to Hon. A. S. Burleson and by him to this Department. Received April 7, 1902.

Seeds of the finest wild grapes of Texas, according to Mr. Fuchs' letter.

8577. Carica papaya. **Papaw.**

From Mexico. Presented by Mr. Elmer Stearns, 3226 Manitou avenue, Los Angeles, Cal. Received March 29, 1902.

"These seeds were from a fruit 6 inches long by 3½ inches in diameter, grown in the hot country southwest of Guadalajara." (*Stearns.*)

8578. Opuntia sp. **Prickly pear.**

From Guadalajara, Mexico. Presented by Mr. Elmer Stearns, 3226 Manitou avenue, Los Angeles, Cal. Received March 29, 1902.

Tuna colorado. "These seeds were from a fruit 2 inches by 1½ inches in diameter." (*Stearns.*)

8579. Opuntia sp. **Prickly pear.**

From City of Mexico, Mexico. Presented by Mr. Elmer Stearns, 3226 Manitou avenue, Los Angeles, Cal. Received March 29, 1902.

Tuna amarilla.

8580. CEREUS sp. **Pitahaya.**

From Mexico. Presented by Mr. Elmer Stearns, 3226 Manitou avenue, Los Angeles, Cal. Received March 29, 1902.

"These seeds were from a fruit weighing 1 pound, grown in the foothills 75 miles west of Tampico, Mexico." (*Stearns.*)

8581 to 8583. VITIS VINIFERA. **Grape.**

From Aintab, Syria. Received through Rev. A. Fuller, April 15, 1902.

Grape cuttings as follows:

8581.

Aintab Summer (Nabodada). "A large, oblong, white grape. The flesh is rather coarse, but it is much prized for table use." (*Fuller.*)

8582.

Aintab Autumn (Kabbajuk). "A medium-sized, round, white grape, much prized for table use. It ripens in July and August." (*Fuller.*)

8583.

Aintab Winter (Hunisa). "A large, wine-colored, oblong grape. It ripens in October and November and keeps until March." (*Fuller.*)

8584 to 8589.

From Chin-kiang, China. Received through Dr. S. A. Knapp from Rev. Dr. S. P. Barchet, Shanghai, China, April 15, 1902.

8584. GLYCINE HISPIDA. **Soy bean.**

"A very prolific, nearly white variety, used for making oil and also for food. It is sometimes ground into flour and used for making cakes." (*Knapp.*)

8585. PHASEOLUS sp. **Bean.**

"Used for food and for making starch. It grows well on sandy soil." (*Knapp.*)

8586. GLYCINE HISPIDA. **Soy bean.**

"A very oily variety, used chiefly for fattening purposes. Planted in July or August." (*Knapp.*)

8587. VICIA FABA. **Broad bean.**

"A large, rank-growing variety that will stand frost. It is planted in November." (*Knapp.*)

8588. PISUM sp. **Pea.**

"A rank-growing variety used for food. It is planted in November." (*Knapp.*)

8589. TRITICUM VULGARE. **Wheat.**

"A hardy, rust-proof variety. Sown in October or November. (*Knapp.*)

8590 to 8592.

From Shanghai, China. Received through Dr. S. A. Knapp from Rev. Dr. S. P. Barchet, April 15, 1902.

8590. ORYZA SATIVA. **Rice.**

"An early variety. It is sown late in May or early in June." (*Knapp.*)

8590 to 8592—Continued.

8591. ORYZA SATIVA.   **Rice.**

"A late variety. It is sown late in June or early in July." (*Knapp.*)

8592. VICIA FABA.   **Broad bean.**

"Quite similar to No. 8587, but not so large." (*Knapp.*)

8593 and 8594. ORYZA SATIVA.   Rice.

From Kiang-si Province, China. Received through Dr. S. A. Knapp from Rev. Dr. D. W. Nichols, Nan-chang, China, April 15, 1902.

8593.

Wan Ku (late rice). "A beautiful white grain, quite flaky when cooked." (*Nichols.*)

8594.

Tsoa Ku (early rice). "A crop of this and the preceding variety can be grown on the same ground the same year." (*Nichols.*)

8595. THEA VIRIDIS.   Tea.

From Calcutta, India. Received from the Pashok Tea Company (Limited), Kilburn & Co., agents, April 15, 1902.

Pashok Darjeeling.

8596. VICIA FABA.   Broad bean.

From Sheridan, Mont. Presented by Mr. S. M. Wilson, April 15, 1902.

These beans are said by Mr. Wilson to come from northern Sweden, and to endure a degree of cold that kills other tender vegetation.

8597 and 8598.

From Erfurt, Germany. Received through Haage & Schmidt, seedsmen, April 19, 1902.

8597. CARYOTA URENS.   **Wine or toddy palm.**

8598. RAVENALA MADAGASCARIENSIS.   **Travelers' tree.**

8599. PUNICA GRANATUM.   Pomegranate.

From Bagdad, Arabia. Received through Messrs. Lathrop and Fairchild (No. 883, March 8, 1902), April 21, 1902.

Achmar or *Red.* "This variety bears fruit of a very large size. I have seen a specimen over 2 pounds in weight. The skin is thin, but there are many thick walls dividing the segments. The seeds are large, each with a deep, very juicy, wine-red arillus. Remarkable for its size and red color." (*Fairchild.*)

8600. ZIZYPHUS JUJUBA.   Jujube.

From Bagdad, Arabia. Received through Messrs. Lathrop and Fairchild (No. 887, March 8, 1902), April 21, 1902.

Nebuk or *Nabug ajam.* "A Persian variety, called the red jujube. A variety larger than the *Bagdad*, but not of as good flavor. These jujube trees, as they are grown in Mesopotamia, are the most picturesque, in fact the only conspicuous shade trees in the region, and are worthy of trial along irrigation canals. They bear enormous crops of small fruits, about the size of cherries, which are greedily sought after by the children. The fruits taste much like baked apples. There is a variety in which the seed, instead of being hard, like a date stone, is thin shelled, and one can eat it easily." (*Fairchild.*) (See No. 8702.)

8601. CITRUS LIMONUM. **Lemon.**

From Bagdad, Arabia. Received through Messrs. Lathrop and Fairchild (No. 889, March 8, 1902), April 21, 1902.

Hameth. "A Bagdad variety which is of most excellent quality and characterized by a dark orange 'blush' at the stem end, making it a peculiar and showy fruit. The skin is very thin, and the fruit very juicy and of medium size. The shape of those I saw was almost that of an egg." (*Fairchild.*)

8602. CITRUS AURANTIUM. **Orange.**

From Bagdad, Arabia. Received through Messrs. Lathrop and Fairchild (No. 890, March 8, 1902), April 21, 1902.

Portugal Asfar. "A common Bagdad orange which is in all respects, except the presence of seeds, a remarkably fine orange. It does well in the alluvial adobe soil of Bagdad, and even where there is some alkali in the soil. These scions came from the garden of Abdul Kader Kederry, at Bagdad." (*Fairchild.*)

8603. CITRUS AURANTIUM. **Orange.**

From Bagdad, Arabia. Received through Messrs. Lathrop and Fairchild (No. 891, March 8, 1902), April 21, 1902.

Aboul serra. "A navel orange, with seeds, of especially fine aroma, I am told, which is cultivated by Sheik Abdul Kader Kederry, and is worth testing as a new variety. The oranges of Bagdad are in general excellent, and this one, although I was unable to test it, may be no exception." (*Fairchild.*)

8604. CITRUS AURANTIUM. **Orange.**

From Bagdad, Arabia. Received through Messrs. Lathrop and Fairchild (No. 892, March 8, 1902), April 21, 1902.

Narinji. "A variety of orange with a 'button' at the flower end; from a tree in the garden of Sheik Abdul Kader Kederry. It has an excellent flavor and has few seeds. This is one of the common varieties of Bagdad, and is an excellent orange." (*Fairchild.*)

8605. VITIS VINIFERA. **Grape.**

From Bagdad, Arabia. Received through Messrs. Lathrop and Fairchild (No. 893, March 9, 1902), April 21, 1902.

(L. & F. No. 893 is *Citrus aurantium*, but the tube so marked contained grape cuttings without data.)

8606. CITRUS DECUMANA. **Pomelo.**

From Bagdad, Arabia. Received through Messrs. Lathrop and Fairchild (No. 894, March 9, 1902), April 21, 1902.

"A species of pomelo or shaddock, of which the skin is used for making preserves. I did not have an opportunity to taste the fruit, but presume it is of second quality." (*Fairchild.*)

8607 to 8642. CITRULLUS VULGARIS. **Watermelon.**

From Monetta, S. C. Received November 5, 1901.

A collection of seeds of hand-pollinated watermelons grown by Mr. T. S. Williams from seed furnished by the Office of Seed and Plant Introduction.

8607.	Grown from No. 18.	**8611.**	Grown from No. 39.
8608.	Grown from No. 25.	**8612.**	Grown from No. 48.
8609.	Grown from No. 26.	**8613.**	Grown from No. 55.
8610.	Grown from No. 33.	**8614.**	Grown from No. 84.

8607 to 8642—Continued.

8615.	Grown from No. 84.	**8629.**	Grown from No. 2845.
8616.	Grown from No. 85.	**8630.**	Grown from No. 106.
8617.	Grown from No. 86.	**8631.**	Grown from No. 2846.
8618.	Grown from No. 86.	**8632.**	Grown from No. 2850.
8619.	Grown from No. 87.	**8633.**	Grown from No. 3680.
8620.	Grown from No. 88.	**8634.**	Grown from No. 3680.
8621.	Grown from No. 98?	**8635.**	Grown from No. 4899.
8622.	Grown from No. 98?	**8636.**	Grown from No. 6149.
8623.	Grown from No. 102.	**8637.**	Grown from No. 6170.
8624.	Grown from No. 104.	**8638.**	Grown from No. 6038.
8625.	Grown from No. 2739.	**8639.**	Grown from No. 6039.
8626.	Grown from No. 2740.	**8640.**	Grown from No. 6046.
8627.	Grown from No. 2843.	**8641.**	Grown from No. 6052.
8628.	Grown from No. 2844.	**8642.**	Grown from No. 6056.

8643. PUNICA GRANATUM. **Pomegranate.**

From Bassorah, Arabia. Received through Messrs. Lathrop and Fairchild (No. 847, February 26, 1902), April 22, 1902.

Mellasi. "A large 'seedless' pomegranate with light-colored flesh. This is said to be the best variety in Arabia and to be quite free from seeds; i. e., the coats of the seeds are probably so delicate that they offer no resistance to the teeth when eating the fruit. Secured through the kindness of Mr. Raphael Sayegh, of Bassorah." (*Fairchild.*)

8644. PYRUS MALUS. **Apple.**

From Bassorah, Arabia. Received through Messrs. Lathrop and Fairchild (No. 848, February 26, 1902), April 22, 1902.

Persian. "This apple will grow well in a region where dates are produced and where for three months the thermometer keeps about the 100° F. mark. It is not of the best quality, but is quite edible, and should be tested in the desert regions of the Colorado River and in the dry regions of Texas. It requires irrigation." (*Fairchild.*)

8645. CYDONIA VULGARIS (?)

From Bassorah, Arabia. Received through Messrs. Lathrop and Fairchild (No. 849, February 26, 1902), April 22, 1902.

Bahamro. "A stock which is used in Arabia, especially in Mesopotamia, on which to graft apples, pears, and quinces. It is reported to be an excellent stock in this very hot region of the Tigris Valley, where the thermometer stands for three months near the 100° F. mark and where it often rises to 117° F. It is cultivated here on adobe soil under irrigation." (*Fairchild.*)

8646. PUNICA GRANATUM. **Pomegranate.**

From Bassorah, Arabia. Received through Messrs. Lathrop and Fairchild (No. 850, February 26, 1902), April 22, 1902.

Nejidi. "A red-fleshed variety of pomegranate which is considered second only to the seedless or *Mellasi* variety. The fruit is large and has a very thin skin." (*Fairchild.*)

8647. VITIS VINIFERA. **Grape.**

From Bassorah, Arabia. Presented by Hadji Abdulla Negem through Messrs. Lathrop and Fairchild (No. 854, February 25, 1902). Received April 22, 1902.

Abiat. "A white grape which is medium in time of ripening and of reputed excellent quality. It is trained from trunk to trunk of the date palms at Abu Kasib. Soil an adobe with abundant moisture in it." (*Fairchild.*)

8648. VITIS VINIFERA. **Grape.**

From Bassorah, Arabia. Received through Messrs. Lathrop and Fairchild (No. 855, February 25, 1902), April 22, 1902.

Asuad Suamee. "A black, early grape, with very large berries and rather tough skin, which is cultivated among the date groves at Abu Kassib. The quality of this sort is reported to be exceptionally good. The practice of grape growing under the palms is rapidly spreading in Mesopotamia. It is worthy of trial in Arizona and southern California." (*Fairchild.*)

8649. VITIS VINIFERA. **Grape.**

From Bassorah, Arabia. Presented by Hadji Abdulla Negem through Messrs. Lathrop and Fairchild (No. 856, February 25, 1902). Received April 22, 1902.

Bengi. "A late, black grape of superior quality, according to the report of Europeans in the region. It is said to be the best variety here in Bassorah and to be really 'as fine as the hothouse-grown *Black Hamburgh.*' Grown under the date palms at Abu Kassib." (*Fairchild.*)

8650. AVENA SATIVA. **Oat.**

From Mustiala, Finland. Received through Messrs. Lathrop and Fairchild from Mustiala Landtbruks och Mejeri-Institut, April 25, 1902.

North Finnish Black.

8651. FATSIA JAPONICA.

From Paris, France. Received through Vilmorin-Andrieux & Co., April 26, 1902.

8652. TRITICUM DICOCCUM. **Emmer.**

From Dunseith, N. Dak. Received through Mr. Arthur Hagendorf, April 29, 1902.

8653. ANONA CHERIMOLIA. **Custard apple.**

From Chile. Presented by Dr. A. W. Thornton, of Ferndale, Wash. Received April 28, 1902.

Cherimoya. Seeds of a choice variety.

8654 to 8679a.

From Ootacamund, India. Presented by R. L. Proudlock, esq., Curator of the Government Botanic Gardens. Received April 30, 1902.

8654. ACROCARPUS FRAXINIFOLIUS.

8655. CUPRESSUS TORULOSA.

8656. LASIOSIPHON ERIOCEPHALUS.

8657. MELIOSMA ARNOTTIANA.

8658. ROSA GIGANTEA.

8659. ACER OBLONGUM.

8660. CEDRELA TOONA.

8661. CLEMATIS WIGHTIANA.

8662. DALBERGIA LATIFOLIA.

8663. EXACUM BICOLOR.

8664. ILEX WIGHTIANA.

8665. PHOTINIA LINDLEYANA.

8666. PTEROCARPUS MARSUPIUM.

8654 to 8679—Continued.

8667.	RHODOMYRTUS TOMENTOSA.	8674.	PHOENIX RUPICOLA.
8668.	URCEOLA ESCULENTA.	8675.	AGAPANTHUS UMBELLATUS.
8669.	CELTIS SEROTINA.	8676.	CASSIA GRANDIS.
8670.	MICROTROPIS OVALIFOLIA.	8677.	PEDICULARIS ZEYLANICA.
8671.	TURPINIA POMIFERA.	8678.	PINUS LONGIFOLIA.
8672.	ELETTARIA CARDAMOMUM.	8679.	SANTALUM ALBUM,
8673.	MICHELIA NILAGIRICA.	8679a.	LITSEA ZEYLANICA.

8680. MANGIFERA INDICA. Mango.

From Colombo, Ceylon. Received through Messrs. Lathrop and Fairchild (No. 948, April 6, 1902), May 5, 1902.

Jaffna. "For a description of this variety see No. 8411. I have tasted this mango but find it, although not stringy, far inferior to the *Alphonse* Bombay mango. It lacks the fine aroma and dark orange colored flesh." (*Fairchild.*)

8681 and 8682.

From Heneratgoda, Ceylon. Received through J. P. William & Bros., May 5, 1902.

8681.	COFFEA LIBERICA.	Coffee.
8682.	COFFEA HYBRIDA.	Coffee.

8683. LUFFA AEGYPTIACA. Sponge gourd.

From Springfield, Mo. Presented by Mr. Joe P. Wilson. Received May 10, 1902.

Grown from No. 3982, Inventory No. 8.

8684 and 8685.

From Poona, India. Received through Dr. S. A. Knapp, May 10, 1902.

8684. TRITICUM DURUM. Wheat.

Kala Kushal.

8685. ANDROPOGON SORGHUM. Sorghum.

Hasar. Grown in Sampayam, Belyaum district.

8686 to 8692.

From Surat, India. Received through Dr. S. A. Knapp, May 10, 1902.

8686. DOLICHOS LABLAB. Bean.

Kadvá Vál or *Kadvá Wál.*

8687. VIGNA CATJANG. Cowpea.

Chowali, Chola, or *Choli.*

8688. ORYZA SATIVA. Rice.

Kamoda. From Ahmedabad, Geyarat.

8689. ORYZA SATIVA. Rice.

Sunkhavel. From Surat, Geyarat.

8690. ORYZA SATIVA. Rice.

Ambamore. From Surat, Geyarat.

8686 to 8692—Continued.

8691. ANDROPOGON SORGHUM. Sorghum.
Sholapuri.

8692. ANDROPOGON SORGHUM. Sorghum.
Perio.

8693. THEA VIRIDIS. Tea.

From Colombo, Ceylon. Received through Messrs. Lathrop and Fairchild (No. 947, April 6, 1902), May 14 and May 29, 1902.

Assam. "Sent by Mr. Hadden, of Kotiyagala, Ceylon, through Director John C. Willis, of the Peradeniya Gardens." (*Fairchild.*)

8694 to 8697.

From Santiago, Chile. Presented by Señor Federico Albert, chief of the Section of Zoological and Botanical Investigations. Received May 14, 1902.

8694. ARISTOTELIA MACQUI. Maqui.
8695. KAGENECKIA sp.
8696. TREVOA QUINQUENERVIA. Tralhuen.
8697. TREVOA TRINERVIA. Trevu.

8698. HIBISCUS SABDARIFFA. Roselle.

From Punjab, India. Presented by Abdulla Khan, clerk in the office of director of land records, through Dr. S. A. Knapp, agricultural explorer. Received May 14, 1902.

Patma. Common red.

8699. ORYZA SATIVA. Rice.

From Hongkong, China. Received through Dr. S. A. Knapp, agricultural explorer, May 16, 1902.

Simi.

8700. PRITCHARDIA GAUDICHAUDII. Fan palm.

From Honolulu, Hawaii. Presented by Mr. Jared G. Smith, director of the Hawaii Agricultural Experiment Station. Received May 22, 1902.

8701. MANGIFERA INDICA. Mango.

From Saigon, Cochin China. Received through Messrs. Lathrop and Fairchild (No. 949, April 16, 1902), May 22, 1902.

Cambodiana or *Xodi Vói.* "This is a delicious mango, of medium size, furnished with a short beak, yellow when ripe, with a faint but agreeable aroma. The flesh varies slightly from light to deep orange in color. Has an excellent, fine, delicate flavor and is never stringy. It is not as rich as the *Alphonse*, of Bombay, either in aroma or flavor, but nevertheless worthy of rank among the best mangoes I have ever eaten. Doctor Haffner, of the botanic gardens of Saigon, informs me that this sort is never grafted, but is a variety which reproduces itself from seed. This being the case, I deem it probable that out of the lot of over a hundred seeds which we are sending some remarkable ones ought to be secured. I believe there is a slight variation among the seedlings, although it is a surprisingly constant variety." (*Fairchild.*)

8702. ZIZYPHUS JUJUBA. Jujube.

From Bassorah, Arabia. Received through Messrs. Lathrop and Fairchild (No. 851, February 26, 1902), May 22, 1902.

Nabug. "The seed in this fruit, instead of being covered with a very hard shell, is like paper, giving the variety the name of being seedless. The tree is the most satisfactory shade tree in this hot region, having a spreading top with somewhat drooping branches covered with small, dark-green leaves. The plant is a most prolific bearer. The fruits when ripe are like Haws in mealiness, and they are keenly relished by the Arabs. They are about one-half to three-fourths inch in diameter. This so-called seedless sort is, paradoxically enough, propagated by seed, and is said to come true to them. It is a tree well suited to the banks of irrigation canals in the hottest regions which we have." (*Fairchild.*)

8703. ZIZYPHUS JUJUBA. Jujube.

From Bassorah, Arabia. Received through Messrs. Lathrop and Fairchild, May 22, 1902.

"Seeds of the common jujube largely grown throughout this arid country." (*Fairchild.*)

8704. QUERCUS CORNEA. Oak.

From Hongkong, China. Received through Messrs. Lathrop and Fairchild (No. 950, April 29, 1902), May 22, 1902.

"Edible acorns from a species of oak which grows in southern China, even on the island of Hongkong. The acorns have a hard, horny shell and a sweet flesh of very agreeable flavor. The acorns are sent in very large quantities to Hongkong from Canton. They are eaten by the Chinese with great pleasure, and are often roasted. They would be acceptable, I believe, to Americans, and the tree ought to do well in the Southern States. If the tree, which is a pretty one, proves a success, large quantities can be had through the botanic gardens at Hongkong, but only at this season of the year." (*Fairchild.*)

8705. PRUNUS sp. Plum.

From Hongkong, China. Received through Messrs. Lathrop and Fairchild (No. 951, April 19, 1902), May 22, 1902.

"A beautiful little plum, said to be grown in Canton. It was purchased on the Hongkong market. It is of a beautiful, transparent, wine red color, with a delicate skin which is covered with the finest, most delicate pubescence imaginable, resembling a bloom which can not be rubbed off. When ripe the fruit has a delicate, agreeable aroma, which is that of a half-ripe Japanese quince. In taste the plum is not very good, but decidedly refreshing. It is sour with a slightly bitter taste. The flesh is yellow in color and inclined to be solid and stringy. The stone is a cling, being covered with many long fibers. In shape it is pointed with a distinct keel. The skin is very delicate but in flavor is *intensely bitter.* It separates from the flesh with difficulty." (*Fairchild.*)

8706. CITRUS AURANTIUM. Orange.

From Kabylia, Algeria. Presented by Dr. L. Trabut, Government Botanist, Mustapha, Algiers, Algeria. Received May 26, 1902.

Bandja. A late, sweet orange, which reproduces itself from seed.

8707. PISTACIA MUTICA. Menengech.

From Smyrna, Asia Minor. Presented by Mr. George C. Roeding, of Fresno, Cal. Received May 26, 1902.

8708. PRITCHARDIA MARTII. Fan palm.

From Olaa, Hawaii. Presented by Mr. Jared G. Smith, special agent in charge of the Hawaii Agricultural Experiment Station at Honolulu.

From an altitude of from 2,000 to 2,500 feet.

8709. EUCOMMIA ULMOIDES.

From Paris, France. Received through Vilmorin-Andrieux & Co., May 29, 1902.

Tu Chung. Rooted cuttings of this Chinese plant. It is used medicinally. It is claimed that the leaves contain a large amount of gutta-percha.

8710 to 8726. PYRUS MALUS. **Apple.**

From New South Wales, Australia. Presented by Messrs. Hunter & Sons, of "The Penang," near Gosford, through Hon. D. C. McLachlan, undersecretary, department of mines and agriculture, Sydney, to replace trees and cuttings received in bad condition in June, 1901. Received May 29, 1902. Hunter & Sons' numbers are given.

Apple trees as follows:

8710.
Allsops early. (No. 237.)

8711.
American Golden Pippin. (No. 256.)

8712.
Carrington, Small's. (No. 238.)

8713.
Early Richmond. (No. 83.)

8714.
George Neilson. (No. 157.)

8715.
Lady Hopetown. (No. 234.)

8716.
Menagerie. (No. 220.)

8717.
Perfection, Shepherd's. (No. 4.)

8718.
Sharp's Early. (No. 232.)

8719. (Label missing.)

Apple scions as follows:

8720.
Autumn Tart.

8721.
Chestattee. (No. 221.)

8722.
Fall Beauty. (No. 80.)

8723.
Jupp's Carrington. (No. 210.)

8724.
Lord Wolseley. (No. 50.)

8725.
Ruby Pearmain. (No. 228.)

8726.
Yarra Bank. (No. 252.)

8727. MANGIFERA INDICA. **Mango.**

From Bombay, India. Received through Messrs. Lathrop and Fairchild (No. 814, January 28, 1902), June 5, 1902.

Douglas Bennett's Alphonse. "Named in honor of the superintendent of markets in Bombay, who has called our attention to this superlative strain and who has very kindly donated to the American Government the trees which he guarantees to be of this special variety. This sort should be compared with No. 8419, which latter number is composed of scions from the tree of which these are believed to be grafts." (*Fairchild.*)

8728. GOSSYPIUM BRASILIENSE (?) **Kidney cotton.**

From Ciego de Avila, Cuba. Presented by Mr. Felix M. Catala. Received June 5, 1902.

Wild Cuban kidney cotton.

8729 to 8734. MANGIFERA INDICA. **Mangoes.**

From Bombay, India. Received through Messrs. Lathrop and Fairchild (No. 944, March 30, 1902), June 7, 1902.

A collection of trees donated to the Department by Mr. J. N. Tata, of Bombay, who has a very large collection of the best mangoes from all over India. These are those he considers the finest of his whole collection, which is one of the largest in the world. These include, doubtless, some of the most valuable sorts of mangoes of all India.

8729.
Nowshirwani.

8730.
Paheri.

8731.
Ameeri.

8732.
Totafari.

8733.
Hafu or *Alphonse.*

8734.
Jamshedi.

8735. CURCUMA LONGA. Turmeric.

From Bombay, India. Received through Dr. S. A. Knapp, June 7, 1902.

8736. ZINGIBER OFFICINALE. Ginger.

From Bombay, India. Received through Dr. S. A. Knapp, June 7, 1902.

8737. TRITICUM DURUM. Wheat.

From Bombay, India. Received through Dr. S. A. Knapp, June 7, 1902.

Hansoli. Grown at Surat, in Gujarat.

8738 to 8745. PHOENIX DACTYLIFERA. Date palm.

From Bagdad, Arabia. Received through Messrs. Lathrop and Fairchild (Nos. 866 to 873, March 10, 1902), June 7, 1902.

8738.

Kustawi. "Considered one of the two best dates in the region of Bagdad. It is a variety which, though acknowledged to be far superior to the sorts which are sent to America, is not exported because of its poor shipping quality. If this date succeeds in America it can, without doubt, be easily shipped by rail, as I have eaten here in Bagdad good specimens over five months old. It is a sticky sort, as packed by the Arabs, although I believe its skin is thick enough to allow of its being packed as the *Deglet Noor* of Algiers is packed. The fruit is not over 1¼ inches long, as judged by dry specimens, and has a seed about seven-eighths inch in length by five-sixteenths inch in diameter. The flesh is not very thick, but exceedingly sweet and, like the other good dates of this region, of a decidedly gummy consistency. It is placed by the Arabs second in rank to the *Maktum*, which is richer in sugar and somewhat fleshier. I have only tasted the *Maktum* once, but I believe it superior in flavor to the *Kustawi*, owing to the fact that the region of Bagdad is much drier than that of Bassorah. This date is probably better suited to conditions prevailing in California and Arizona than the sorts grown in Bassorah. It is considered, however, one of the most delicate dates to cultivate, requiring much more care than such sorts as the *Zehedy, Ascherasi,* and *Bedraihe.* Not being a date for export the price is low, as is the case with the *Berhi* of Bassorah. It sells for about $2.60 to $3 per 210 pounds, while the *Bedraihe* brings about $4 to $4.40. This variety begins to ripen about the 1st of August in this exceedingly hot climate. It should be planted with the growing bud 2 inches above the soil. The best ground will be an adobe, like the silt of the Colorado River, or such as occurs in certain places on the experimental farm at Phoenix. This sort is said to be a good bearer, but I do not know just how heavy the yields are. There is very little fiber to the date, and it is altogether an exceptionally fine sort." (*Fairchild.*) (No. 866.)

8739.

Ascherasi. "One of the highest-priced dates on the market in Bagdad. It is, as I have seen it, always a more or less dry sort, never pressed into a conglomerate mass in the way the other sorts are. It is the sort preferred by

8738 to 8745—Continued.

Bagdadians to eat with walnuts, and is preferred by many to any other kind. Personally, I found it a very eatable date, and it has the very great advantage of not soiling the hands. The flesh is, however, even when fresh, hard enough to allow shipping. In fact the dates are even sent, when fresh, from Mundeli to Bagdad in skins. Generally, however, the fruit is allowed to dry on the tree until it becomes hard. It is not exported from Bagdad, but consumed in Mesopotamia. The price sold dry is about $3.20 to $3.60 per 100 kilos on the Bagdad market. It is suited to a region with less water than that of Bassorah. It matures about the middle of September to the 1st of October in Bagdad." (*Fairchild.*) (No. 867.)

8740.

Bedraihe. "This ripens in September and the first of October, and is allowed to dry on the trees. As sold here in the markets it is a yellow date, about 1¼ to 1½ inches long and three-fourths inch to 1 inch in diameter. The base of the date is quite dry, as I have seen it, but the tip is transparent or semitransparent and quite sweet, although at this season of too gummy a consistency to be agreeable. In Bagdad this date is generally sold dry, and brings $4 to $4.20 for 210 pounds, i. e., it is the most expensive according to weight, but the other sorts, having a great deal of water in their composition, contain proportionately less food. Many Bagdadians prefer this sort, when fresh and softer, to all other kinds. There is an immense consumption of this variety in Bagdad. I believe this date would be a success in America because it is so different from other sorts, and for the reason that it is a remarkably good keeper, and when not too old is really very good eating. It is far superior to the dry dates of Egypt, and not to be confused with dry dates in general, for it has scarcely any disagreeable fibers about the seed. It deserves attention in American plantations." (*Fairchild.*) (No. 868.)

8741.

Maktum. "Considered by the Arab sheik, Abdul Kader Kederry, of Bagdad, to be the finest date, except one, in the world, the *Mirhage* from Mandele, which it resembles, being superior. It is a date not often seen on the Bagdad market, and I was unable to get any of good quality to taste. A very fine date, which was said to be of the *Maktum* sort, which I tasted, was a richer date than the *Kustawi*, although of the same general type. The probabilities are that this is a delicate sort which produces only a small quantity of fruit. The date I tasted came from Kasimain, but the tree is cultivated up the river from Bagdad. These trees were donated to the Department by Sheik Abdul Kader Kederry, of Bagdad." (*Fairchild.*) (No. 869.)

8742.

Burni. "For a description of this date see No. 8569. I believe it properly belongs to Maskat. It being winter I am not able to verify the identification of these varieties, but must buy the plants of Arabs or others who know the sorts." (*Fairchild.*) (No. 870.)

8743.

Zehedi. "This is probably the commonest date about Bagdad. It is the *quickest to develop* and the *heaviest yielder of all the dates about Bagdad*, according to Mr. Raphael Casparkan, of Bagdad, who very kindly donated a lot of twenty-four palms to the Department, including part of these. It is a cheap date here, selling for only $1.40 to $2 per 210 pounds. The date is small, not over 1¼ inches long by three-fourths inch in diameter. It is not entirely like Egyptian dates, but is so dry that the individuals do not stick together. They have very little fiber, the stone is small, and the flesh quite sweet even when dry. When fresh this sort is packed in skins and exported to Egypt and Singapore, under the name of *Kursi*. It is often sold on the bunch when fresh and called *Zehedi Gus*, in which shape it is very highly thought of. I tasted the so-called *Kursi* and found it decidedly inferior in flavor and amount of flesh to the *Kustawi*. The variety is, however, I am assured, *the most resistant of any, so far as water is concerned, being quite drought resistant*, and although the

8738 to 8745—Continued.

product is a cheap one, the heavy yields make it a very profitable sort. It ripens about September or October. It sells in Bagdad (dry), I am told, for $1.40 to $2 per 210 pounds." (*Fairchild.*) (No. 871.)

8744.

Barban. "This date is reported to ripen in July and yield only fairly good fruits. It is the earliest ripening of the Bagdad dates, I am told, and deserves a place in the gardens for this reason. This variety is red before ripening but turns black when mature. It is not a very sweet sort, and not very highly thought of by the Bagdadians. It is rarely cultivated except outside of Bagdad. Its early ripening qualities are what make it worthy of trial in America. It is probable that this sort will not ripen so early in America because the amount of heat is probably considerably less." (*Fairchild.*) (No. 872.)

8745.

Sukeri. "A very large variety of date, said by Mr. Raphael Casparkan to be 2 inches or more in length, and when fresh, to be of good quality. Mr. Casparkan donated these to the Government, and the determinations are his, for I could not distinguish the different varieties which he selected. Worthy of trial in Arizona on account of its large size." (*Fairchild.*) (No. 873.)

8746 to 8752. PHOENIX DACTYLIFERA. **Date palm.**

From Bassorah, Arabia. Received through Messrs. Lathrop and Fairchild (Nos. 895 to 901, February 25, 1902), June 7, 1902.

8746.

Berhi. "A variety of date which, though never shipped to the American market, is said by every one in this region to be unquestionably the best date in this part of the Persian Gulf, inferior only to the *Khalasa* date of Hassa. It ripens, as do most all these Shat-el-Arab dates, in the month of September, and it is therefore likely to prove very valuable because of its superior quality and its early ripening character. It ripens in September in Bassorah, where the temperature goes to 117° F. in the shade. It is a sticky date, but nevertheless a variety with a very fine flavor, and grows well on adobe alluvial deposits. It is watered by canal irrigation as often during the year as the tide rises, viz, twice a day. I have tasted this *Berhi*, and it is superior to the *Halawi*, the principal export sort, and also to the *Taberzal*. The seed is very small." (*Fairchild.*) (No. 895.)

8747.

H'weis or *Hevezi.* "One of the best dates of the Persian Gulf. A delicate, light-colored date of medium size, with medium-sized stone. It ripens in Bassorah in September. It is very little known, even at Bassorah. Grown, as are all of the dates on the Shat-el-Arab River, in stiff clay, almost adobe soil, in raised areas surrounded by canals, which are flooded twice a day by water from the river as it is backed up by the tides, the variety is a sticky sort, but deserves the serious attention of experimenters with date palms, on account of its superior flavor and excellent color. The summer temperature of Bassorah rises to 117° and sometimes to 120° F. in the shade. In winter it drops to below 50°. The soil where the date is grown is distinctly saline. This date has not been shipped to American markets, but would be a good selling date, and for this reason it is well worth planting in southern California (Colorado Desert) and Arizona." (*Fairchild.*) (No. 896.)

8748.

Sayer or *Ustaamran.* "A variety of date darker in color than the *Halawi*, but of fair flavor. A standard sort in New York. It is said to do best on a light sandy soil, and to require less water than No. 8747. *Sayer* is a word also used to indicate a mixed lot of dates, but these trees are of a distinct long fruited dark sort. The trees are taller than those of the variety *Halawi*, and not so uniformly straight. This sort is most likely to succeed on sandy soils, or, at least, to do better on sandy than on ordinary adobe soil. It is inferior in quality to *Halawi* and *Khadrawi*, but, nevertheless, a good market date. It is grown here very extensively." (*Fairchild.*) (No. 897.)

8746 to 8752—Continued.

8749.

Gunnami. A male variety. "Considered by Hadji Abdulla Negem as the best pollen-producing male in this region. It holds its pollen best, and the latter is found to be 'stronger' than that of any other sort. One male tree suffices for 100 female trees." (*Fairchild.*) (No. 898.)

8750.

Halawi. "One of the standard sorts grown on the Shat-el-Arab River, of Arabia, and it is one of the principal dates shipped to the American market. There must be millions of trees of this variety along the river. A fairly light-colored date, short and thick, with a good-sized stone, and very little fiber about the seed. Grown under the same conditions as No. 8747, and ripens in September." (*Fairchild.*) (No. 899.)

8751.

Khadrawi. "A darker colored, longer date than the *Halawi*, and inferior to it. It is one of the standard sorts for shipment to America, but is not a delicate skinned variety; therefore an excellent packing date. It is a sticky date, and ripens in September or the first of October." (*Fairchild.*) (No. 900.)

8752.

Unnamed variety. "Sent without label from Abu Kassib, by Hadji Abdulla Negem, with Nos. 8746 to 8752, for all of which I am indebted to the kind assistance of Mr. H. P. Chalk, agent of Hills Bro. & Co., of New York." (*Fairchild.*) (No. 901.)

8753. PHOENIX DACTYLIFERA. **Date palm.**

From Hassa, Arabia. Received through Messrs. Lathrop and Fairchild (No. 905, March 17, 1902), June 7, 1902.

Khalasa or *Khalasi.* "This date is known all over the Persian Gulf as one of the three best dates. It certainly has few equals, and its only rivals are the *Maktum*, *Taberzal*, and *Berhi*, and probably also, though I have not tasted it, the *Mirhage*. Palgrave, author of 'Travels in Eastern Arabia,' 1863, says the literal translation of the name *Khalasi* is 'quintessence,' and that it 'is easily first of its kind.' The country in which it is grown is, according to Zwemer, a sandy one, with underground springs or water courses, water being reached only a few feet below the surface of the soil. This country of Hassa or El Hassa lies 60 miles or so inland from Bahrein Island, and these palms were brought by camels from that region. The climate in winter is hot in daytime, but cold at night, and in summer it is excessively hot. This variety matures its fruit, I presume, sometime in August or September, though I can not state this positively. It is a variety worthy the serious consideration of our date growers, as it will probably be better suited to our conditions than the Bassorah dates, which will require more water to bring them to full development. We are indebted to H. B. M. Vice-Consul J. C. Gaskin, of Bahrein, for securing these sets and for many other favors, and also to Mr. H. M. Zwemer for information about Hassa dates." (*Fairchild.*)

8754 to 8761. PHOENIX DACTYLIFERA. **Date palm.**

From Maskat, Arabia. Received through Messrs. Lathrop and Fairchild (Nos. 906 to 913, March 21, 1903), June 7, 1903.

8754.

Fard. "A long, large-sized, late date, of dark color but good flavor. About 1,000 tons of this date are exported from Maskat to America every year, it being the principal export date of the region of Maskat. These young palms were brought from Semail, 50 miles in the interior, where there are extensive plantations of this and other sorts. There are estimated by Vice-Consul Mackirdy, who very kindly secured these for the Department, to be half a million date trees in the Semail Valley. This date ripens in August and sells for $40 Mexican per 1,800 pounds. It is the best flavored soft packing date in the region. It is adapted to the hottest regions in America." (*Fairchild.*) (No. 906.)

8754 to 8761—Continued.

8755.

Burni. "This is a light-colored date about the same size as the *Fard*, but thinner, also from Semail. It ripens in Maskat in July. It was formerly shipped to America, but was found to be a poorer keeper than the *Fard*, and now it is no longer demanded. Because of its scarcity it sells for $50 Mexican per 1,800 pounds." (*Fairchild.*) (No. 907.)

8756.

Nagal. "An early variety from Semail, 50 miles in the interior, *ripening in June*. It is a light-colored date about 1¼ inches long and three-fourths inch in diameter. It is not as sweet as the *Fard*, but is highly prized because *it is the earliest date in the region*. It is consumed locally and only in a fresh condition. High prices are paid for it by the Arabs. It is a soft sort, resembling the *Fard*." (*Fairchild.*) (No. 908.)

8757.

Mubsali. "From Semail, 50 miles inland from Maskat. This date is a long, large, variety, which is picked before being ripe, boiled for an hour in salt water, and then spread out in the sun to dry. (See Nos. 8563 and 8564.) These dates, which are as hard as stick candy, and almost as sweet, are sold in India, where there is a big demand for them, and where higher prices are paid than for the ordinary *Fard* variety. They sell for $80 Mexican per 1,800 pounds. This belongs to the *Karak pokhta* class of dates, which are served in India at every wedding and festival. They are sometimes eaten fresh. It is the best paying date in Maskat. Suitable for dry, hot regions. It ripens in July." (*Fairchild.*) (No. 909.)

8758.

Khanezi. "From Semail, 50 miles inland from Maskat. An almost round, soft, very sweet sort, only consumed locally. It is a rare variety, ripening in July. It is eaten in the fresh state and considered one of the best of this kind in Maskat." (*Fairchild.*) (No. 910.)

8759.

Khassab. "From Semail, 50 miles inland from Maskat. A red variety when ripe, somewhat shorter in shape than the *Fard*. It ripens in August. It is a soft variety, therefore not a shipping date. It is reported to be the heaviest yielder of any, as much as 450 pounds being borne by a single tree. It is not as sweet as the *Fard*, but is still of good quality." (*Fairchild.*) (No. 911.)

8760.

Hellali. "From Semail, a date region 50 miles back of the town of Maskat. It is as round fruited as a walnut, light colored and soft. It is not a packing date but is used fresh. The bunches are exceedingly large. A rare sort even in Maskat." (*Fairchild.*) (No. 912.)

8761.

"*Fachl* or *Fahel*, meaning *male* date, from the valley of Semail, 50 miles in the interior behind Maskat. This is the variety used in this great valley, where half a million trees are grown, as the pollinator. It might be called simply *Semail Fahel*, to distinguish it from the Egyptian *Fahel* or male sent in 1900." (*Fairchild.*) (No. 913.)

8762 to 8785. PHOENIX DACTYLIFERA. Date palm.

From Kej, Baluchistan. Received through Messrs. Lathrop and Fairchild (Nos. 914 to 937, March 23, 1902), June 7, 1902.

A collection of date palms secured through the kindness of Lieutenants Grant and Maxwell, of the First Baluchistan Light Infantry, from Kej, a region six days by camel from Guadur, near the Pangh Ghur region. The soil is an adobe but mixed with small rocks. It is watered from artificial wells. The palms are as follows:

8762.

Mozati. One of the finest flavored dates in the world. It is sent in earthen jars, packed in the sirup of inferior sorts, to Kurrachee and Bombay. It is said to ripen in July. It is a large, round sort with small stone, golden brown flesh, and delicate skin. (No. 914.)

8763.
Gush. A male variety. (No. 915.)

8764.
Apdandon. (No. 916.)

8765.
Soont Gora. (No. 917.)

8766.
Hashna. (No. 918.)

8767.
Gonzelli. (No. 919.)

8768.
Jalghi. (No. 920.)

8769.
Bagum Jurghi. (No. 921.)

8770.
Shukkeri. (No. 922.)

8771.
Koroch. (No. 923.)

8772.
Hallani. (No. 924.)

8773.
Shapego. (No. 925.)

8774.
Dishtari. (No. 926.)

8775.
Chupshook. (No. 927.)

8776.
Korroo. (No. 928.)

8777.
Rogani. (No. 929.)

8778.
Churpan. (No. 930.)

8779.
Kharba. (No. 931.)

8780.
Dundari. (No. 932.)

8781.
Subzoo. (No. 933.)

8782.
Gond Gorbug. (No. 934.)

8783.
Washclont. (No. 935.)

8784.
Kalara. (No. 936.)

8785.
Hurshut. (No. 937.)

8786 to 8793. PHOENIX DACTYLIFERA. **Date.**

From the vicinity of the Persian Gulf. Received through Messrs. Lathrop and Fairchild, June 7, 1902. Samples of dried dates as follows:

8786.
Bedraihe. From Bagdad market. (No. 868.) (See No. 8740.)

8787.
A variety sold in the Kurrachee market in two-gallon earthen jars. It is said to come from the interior of Baluchistan. Its name is not known.

8788.
Kadrawi. (No. 900.) (See No. 8751.)

8786 to 8793—Continued.

8789.

Kustawi. From Bagdad market. (No. 866.) (See No. 8738.) A very fine date, though somewhat stringy.

8790.

Berhi. Dates as packed in paper cartons for European market. (No. 895.) (See No. 8746.)

8791.

Halawi. Dates as packed in paper cartons for export to all parts of the world. (No. 899.) (See No. 8750.)

8792.

Busser. From Bassorah, Arabia. An inferior variety.

8793.

Zehedi. "From Bagdad market." (*Fairchild.*) (No. 871.) (See No. 8743.)

8794. PHOENIX DACTYLIFERA. **Date.**

From Bagdad, Arabia. Received through Messrs. Lathrop and Fairchild (No. 885, March 10, 1903), June 7, 1902.

Taberzal. "Sample of dried dates. This is a rare date even at Bagdad, and I did not find it on the markets. Agha Mohammed, British consular agent at Kasimain, very kindly donated these to the Department. It is a small date 1¼ to 1⅜ inches long by about seven-eighths inch in diameter. When dry it is of an amber color. The skin is a lighter shade than the flesh, is loose, rather papery in texture, and can be removed with the fingers from the dried flesh. The flesh is never dry in the sense of being hard, but has the consistency of a chocolate caramel and is sweet and of characteristic date flavor. The seed is of medium size and fits loosely in the dry flesh. There is scarcely any fiber about the seed. The stem has a trifle too large disk (involucre), but is easily removed with the fingers. When fresh it is considered one of the most delicate dates in Bagdad, though not so fine or so large as the *Berhi* (No. 8746), which it resembles. I have not seen the *Berhi*, but take this as the opinion of a date shipper. These dates, if not pressed into skins or cases, are dry enough to be handled with the fingers. This is a point of great importance. The *Deglet Noor* of Algiers would probably be quite as unappetizing if pressed into baskets or boxes. I secured these samples too late to make it possible to secure plants, but they can be had through Vice-Consul Hürner, of Bagdad, from Agha Mohammed, who donated these." (*Fairchild.*)

8795. PHOENIX DACTYLIFERA. **Date.**

From Bagdad, Arabia. Received through Messrs. Lathrop and Fairchild, June 7, 1902.

Ascherasi. Samples of dates. (See No. 8739, L. & F. No. 867.)

8796 and 8797. VITIS VINIFERA. **Grape.**

From Kandahar, India. Received through Messrs. Lathrop and Fairchild, June 7, 1902.

Samples of raisins bought in the Kurrachee market.

8796.

Seedless. Very sweet and thoroughly candied.

8797.

A large, light-colored raisin with seeds.

8798. GOSSYPIUM sp. **Cotton.**

From Arabia. Received through Messrs. Lathrop and Fairchild, June 7, 1902.

"Probably from the garden of Abdul Kader Kederry, on the Tigris River." (*Fairchild.*)

8799. CAPSICUM ANNUUM. **Red pepper.**

From Bassorah, Arabia. Received through Messrs. Lathrop and Fairchild (No. 852, February 26, 1902), June 7, 1902.

"A lance-shaped variety of red pepper from the market of Bassorah. The fruits are not over 1 inch to 1¼ inches long." (*Fairchild.*)

8800. PISTACIA VERA × (?) **Butum.**

From Bagdad, Arabia. Received through Messrs. Lathrop and Fairchild (No. 874, March 9, 1902), June 7, 1902.

"A small packet of seeds from the market of Bagdad. These may be hardier than the European butum." (*Fairchild.*)

8801. PISTACIA MUTICA. **Menengech.**

From Bagdad, Arabia. Received through Messrs. Lathrop and Fairchild (No. 874, March 9, 1902), June 7, 1902.

"Sample of seed from Bagdad market. These may prove hardier stocks than the European sorts." (*Fairchild.*)

8802. (Undetermined.) **Sissi.**

From Bagdad, Arabia. Received through Messrs. Lathrop and Fairchild (No. 875, March 11, 1902), June 7, 1902.

"Seeds brought from the mountains of Persia beyond Mosul. They are edible and are eaten by the Arabs as the Chinese eat melon seeds. The flesh is sweet, but there is little of it. The plant which produces these fruits is said to be a shrub and likely to withstand desert conditions." (*Fairchild.*)

8803. AMARANTHUS HYPOCHONDRIACUS (?) **Chagoggee.**

From Wönsau, Korea. Presented by Mr. C. F. S. Billbrough, of Wönsau, through Messrs. Lathrop and Fairchild (No. 773), June 10, 1902.

"Used in Korea as an ornamental, having masses of bright red foliage. The plant is an annual, 6 feet high. It is used by the natives for food, being boiled like cabbage. It is, further, much relished by stock. It should be grown for identification and may prove a new thing as an ornamental or may be of use as a fodder plant." (*Fairchild.*)

8804. ORYZA SATIVA. **Rice.**

From Niuchwang, China. Presented by Hon. Henry B. Miller, United States consul, through the Department of State. Received June 10, 1902.

K'ien Tzu. "Dry land rice, sown the last of April or the first of May and harvested early in September. It grows best on low land or on rich yellow soil. It must not be flooded, but requires rain at the time the grain is forming. It will not grow on high, dry clay land." (*Miller.*)

8805. PANICUM MILIACEUM. **Broom-corn millet.**

From Bassorah, Arabia. Received through Messrs. Lathrop and Fairchild (No. 853, February 25, 1902), June 7, 1902.

Dukkhn. "A kind of millet which is sown on the mud after flooding the soil with irrigation water and left to mature its crop without further watering. It is said to produce and ripen its heads in forty days, so that two crops are generally grown each year on the same soil. This is sent for trial in the Colorado Desert region and western Texas." (*Fairchild.*)

8806. MEDICAGO SATIVA. **Alfalfa.**

From Bassorah, Arabia. Received through Messrs. Lathrop and Fairchild (No. 904, March 15, 1902), June 7, 1902.

Djet. "This is treated like any alfalfa (see No. 8823). This is given a separate number as it comes from 500 miles south of the locality whence No. 8823 was sent. Secured through the assistance of Mr. Raphael Sayegh, of Bassorah." (*Fairchild.*)

8807. CICER ARIETINUM. **Chick-pea.**

From Bassorah, Arabia. Received through Messrs. Lathrop and Fairchild (No. 903, March 15, 1902), June 7, 1902.

Humus. "Sold everywhere on the markets of Mesopotamia. It is suited to very hot regions with little water. Sent for trials in California and Arizona." (*Fairchild.*)

8808. TRITICUM DURUM. **Wheat.**

From Bassorah, Arabia. Received through Messrs. Lathrop and Fairchild (No. 902, March 16, 1902), June 7, 1902.

Karun. "A hard wheat which is grown on the river Karun in Persia. It is reported to be the best wheat coming to the Bassorah market and is grown in a region where scant rains fall and which is exposed to excessive hot weather. Suited for our dry, hot Southwest." (*Fairchild.*)

8809. HORDEUM TETRASTICHUM. **Barley.**

From Bagdad, Arabia. Received through Messrs. Lathrop and Fairchild (No. 886, March 10, 1902), June 7, 1902.

Black. "The native barley of the Tigris Valley above Bagdad. It should be suited to culture in our dry Southwest, as it is a short season variety and depends on the scanty rains in January and February for its moisture. I understand that this barley is sometimes exported to Europe." (*Fairchild.*)

8810. LATHYRUS CICER. **Pea.**

From Bagdad, Arabia. Received through Messrs. Lathrop and Fairchild (No. 880, March 9, 1902), June 7, 1902.

Hortuman. "A species of the pea family, which in the market is called *Hortuman*, but, according to the dictionaries, *Hortuman* means *oat*, and this is evidently one of the Leguminosæ. It is cultivated by planting in hills or drills, and grows, according to the very unsatisfactory information which I could pick up, to a height of about 2 feet. The grains are produced in a pod and they form the valuable product of the plant. The straw is, however, also said to be fed to cattle, but has not any great value. The grain is exceedingly hard and requires grinding before it can be used. It is then cooked with rice or boiled and eaten alone. It is grown without much water, but generally on irrigated lands. It is suitable for trial in the extremely hot regions of the Colorado Desert. Its use as a soiling crop is quite unknown, but it may be of considerable value, nevertheless, for people here are evidently quite ignorant of soiling crops. Bought in the bazar at Bagdad, where it is not at this season a very common grain." (*Fairchild.*)

8811. TRITICUM DURUM. **Wheat.**

From Bagdad, Arabia. Received through Messrs. Lathrop and Fairchild (No. 879, March 9, 1902), June 7, 1902.

Hurma. "A large-grained, hard wheat which is called *Hurma*, meaning widow, because of the large size of the grains. This sample comes from the wheat-growing region of Mosul and is cultivated without irrigation. It deserves a trial in our arid-region experiments." (*Fairchild.*)

8812. TRITICUM VULGARE. **Wheat.**

From Bagdad, Arabia. Received through Messrs. Lathrop and Fairchild (No. 878, March 9, 1902), June 7, 1902.

Kermansha. "The finest looking soft wheat to be found on the Bagdad market. It comes from Kermansha, in Persia, where it is grown without irrigation. It brings a lower price than the *Kurdistan* and *Karoon* wheats, because it is soft and has not the 'strength' of the latter, which is necessary in the making of the Arabic 'Hubus' or pancake-like bread. It is worth a trial in dry regions." (*Fairchild*.)

8813. Triticum durum. **Wheat.**

From Bagdad, Arabia. Received through Messrs. Lathrop and Fairchild (No. 877, March 9, 1902), June 7, 1902.

Kurd. "A wheat grown in Kurdistan and brought down to the Bagdad market. It is used for bread making and brings good prices, being, in fact, one of the highest priced wheats in the Bagdad market. Bread from this wheat is made in thin sheets like German pancakes and has a decided mixture of the macaroni wheat flour in it. This wheat is harder than No. 8812. The *Kurd* wheats and the *Karun* or *Karoon* wheats are considered the best sorts sold in Bagdad and I understand they are grown without irrigation, depending only upon the scanty rains. They should be tested to show their resistance to rust and drought." (*Fairchild*.)

8814. Phaseolus viridissimus. **Bean.**

From Bassorah, Arabia. Received through Messrs. Lathrop and Fairchild (No. 864, March 3, 1902), June 7, 1902.

Maash. This is grown in Mesopotamia and used as food. It is employed with rice and even boiled and eaten alone. It is planted in drills or hills, like ordinary string beans, and grows to a height of 2 feet or more. This resembles, I am informed, the *Merjemek* of Turkey. I think this is the same species as No. 6430 sent in 1901 as *Phaseolus viridissimus*, secured in Athens, Greece. This bean should be tested in the irrigated lands of the Southwest, and as a vegetable throughout the Southern States of America." (*Fairchild*.)

8815. Andropogon sorghum. **Sorghum.**

From Bassorah, Arabia. Received through Messrs. Lathrop and Fairchild (No. 863, February 25, 1902), June 7, 1902.

Edra. "A kind of sorghum like the *Dura* of the Egyptians. This is a white variety grown in this hot region where the temperature often goes to 117° F. and during the summer ranges between 85° and 99° F. day and night. No other irrigation than that of the rains is received by the plants, and yet it is said that it can be relied upon generally to give a fair crop. It is worth trying on the scorching deserts of California. The grain makes excellent second-class food." (*Fairchild*.)

8816 to 8819. Triticum. **Wheat.**

From Bassorah, Arabia. Received through Messrs. Lathrop and Fairchild (Nos. 857 to 861, February 25, 1902), June 7, 1902.

"A collection of wheats from the Euphrates, Tigris, and Karun river valleys, which are the three great wheat growing regions of Mesopotamia. These wheats are not generally grown by irrigation but depend upon the rains for their water, and as the climate is a dry and excessively hot one and the soil an adobe, inclined to be alkaline, these wheats deserve trial in similar excessively hot regions in America. Their rust-resisting qualities I know nothing about. With the exception of the Karun variety they are not especially fine wheats, but from their very long culture here in Mesopotamia they should be tried in the Colorado Desert region and on any stiff soil which is subject to droughts. Larger quantities may be had by corresponding with Mr. H. P. Chalk, of Bassorah, referring to the varieties by name. These are exposed two months to a summer shade temperature of 117° to 120° F. and stand it well. The wheats are as follows." (*Fairchild*.)

8816. Triticum durum.

Buetha. A hard wheat from Arag, on the Euphrates River. (No. 858.)

8817. Triticum vulgare.

Bagdad. A soft variety from Bagdad. (No. 859.)

8816 to 8819—Continued.

8818. TRITICUM DURUM.

Koola. A hard wheat from Kurdistan; exact origin in doubt. (No. 860.)

8819. TRITICUM DURUM.

Humera. A hard sort of dark color, from Arag, on the Euphrates River.

8820. TRITICUM DURUM. Wheat.

From Bagdad, Arabia. Received through Messrs. Lathrop and Fairchild (No. 876, March 9, 1902), June 7, 1902.

Hurma. "A hard wheat grown at Desphuli, in Persia, near the Karun River. This sample was bought on the market in Bagdad. It is grown in a region noted for its extreme summer heat and scanty rains and should be suited to arid-land conditions. Exact data were unobtainable." (*Fairchild.*)

8821. PANICUM MILIACEUM. Broom-corn millet.

From Kurrachee, India. Received through Messrs. Lathrop and Fairchild (No. 943, March 27, 1902), June 7, 1902.

San China. "Grown on the Sewage Farm at Kurrachee. It is an excellent forage crop, and should be tried, though not new to America, in the Colorado Desert region. The grain is fed to cattle and working bullocks. It is coarse, but is said to be a profitable crop. The yields are large. It is possibly a different strain from the ordinary." (*Fairchild.*)

8822. ZEA MAYS. Maize.

From Bagdad, Arabia. Received through Messrs. Lathrop and Fairchild (No. 884, March 11, 1902), June 7, 1902.

"A Mesopotamian maize, given me by Agha Mohammed, of Kasimain. It is the variety commonly grown in the region and is sent as illustrating the low condition of agriculture in this wonderful region." (*Fairchild.*)

8823. MEDICAGO SATIVA. Alfalfa.

From Bagdad, Arabia. Presented by Agha Mohammed, the Nawab at Kasimain and consular agent at that place for His British Majesty. Received through Messrs. Lathrop and Fairchild (No. 881, March 10, 1902), June 7, 1902.

Djet or *El-djet.* "A larger quantity of seed can be secured through arrangement with the American vice-consul at Bagdad, Mr. Rudolph Hürner. Although the Nawab admits this to be the best plant for horses he has ever grown, he says that he is the first in the region of Bagdad to grow it, and this, notwithstanding the fact that at Kerbella, only a day's journey away, large areas have been planted to it from ancient times. In the especially hot summers the fields are irrigated three times a month; in the cooler summers only twice. From 9 to 10 cuttings are taken each year, and the fields are manured with stable manure after each cutting. The life, i. e., profitable life, of a field of this *djet* is seven years. This variety should be admirably suited to our irrigated lands in California and Arizona, and deserves a trial in comparison with the Turkestan alfalfa. It should also be tested as to alkali resistance." (*Fairchild.*)

8824. PRUNUS sp. Plum.

From Kurrachee, India. Received through Messrs. Lathrop and Fairchild (No. 940, February 26, 1902), June 7, 1902.

Kandahar. "A peculiar dried plum sold on the market in Kurrachee and said to have come down from Kandahar. I have never eaten this plum stewed, so do not know of what quality it is. Sent for breeding purposes." (*Fairchild.*)

8825. PRUNUS ARMENIACA. **Apricot.**

From Kurrachee, India. Received through Messrs. Lathrop and Fairchild (No. 938, February 26, 1902), June 7, 1902.

"Dried apricots which were bought on the market in Kurrachee as coming from Kandahar. These apricots, when stewed and served as they are in India, have a really very delicious flavor. There is a bit of disagreeable fiber about the stone, but altogether they struck me as a novelty worthy of attention. Should they prove valuable, cuttings may be obtained by correspondence." (*Fairchild.*)

8826. PRUNUS sp. **Plum.**

From Arabia. Received through Messrs. Lathrop and Fairchild, June 7, 1902.

No data furnished.

8827. PRUNUS sp. **Plum.**

From Bassorah, Arabia. Received through Messrs. Lathrop and Fairchild (No. 865, February 26, 1902), June 7, 1902.

Aluche. "A variety sold on the markets of Bassorah as coming from Persia. A sour variety, which may be useful to breeders." (*Fairchild.*)

8828. ZIZYPHUS JUJUBA. **Jujube.**

From Bassorah, Arabia. Received through Messrs. Lathrop and Fairchild, June 7, 1902.

Samples of a variety similar to No. 8702.

8829 to 8847. FICUS CARICA. **Fig.**

From Italy. Received through Mr. W. T. Swingle (Nos. 101 to 119), June 13, 1902.

"The following collection of caprifig cuttings was obtained during the spring of 1902 at Naples, the classic ground for the study of caprifigs and caprification. Considerable attention was given to the study of the botanical characters of the caprifig trees, and detailed descriptions were drawn up of seven of the principal varieties of caprifigs occurring in this region. It was found possible to draw up a key for the determination of the different varieties of caprifig, based on these characters, which key is given below. It applies only to those of the caprifigs which were carefully studied, but it will doubtless prove useful to investigators who wish to study the caprifigs of Naples. This collection, like that included under numbers 6473 to 6491 and 6773 to 6823, has been introduced to this country in the hope of securing an assortment of caprifigs adapted to all the climatic and soil conditions occurring in California, where all of these caprifigs will be tested as soon as possible. A few varieties of figs are also included in this collection." (*Swingle.*)

KEY TO SEVEN PRINCIPAL VARIETIES OF NEAPOLITAN CAPRIFIGS.

Leaves *nearly entire* or but slightly lobed, small, short, covered with a golden pubescence; middle lobe obtuse and rounded. *Petioles short* and *very stout*, also pubescent. Veins reddish on drying. Profichi ovate with few male flowers; flower pedicels green. No. 8838.

Leaves decidedly lobed, or, if not, nearly smooth.
  Leaves *velvety pubescent, petioles short and very stout*, also pubescent. Leaves many (5–7) *lobed*. Middle lobe with obtuse and rounded apex. Veins green on drying. Lamina yellow dotted. Profichi small *oval* with many male flowers. No. 8844.
  Leaves not velvety, hairy; profichi ovate.
    Petioles very long (reaching beyond sinuses when reflexed). Sinuses very deep and narrow. Middle lobe with rounded apex. Leaf long and narrow with U-shaped base. Veins reddish on drying. No. 8829.
    Petioles short or medium in length (not reaching to sinuses if reflexed).
      Profichi depressed at apex. Flower cavity *broader than long*. Leaves with *deep and narrow sinuses;* medium sized, regular in outline; 3-lobed, middle lobe with acute straight-sided apex. Lamina decurrent on petiole. Veins drying reddish; flower pedicels purplish. No. 8834.
      Sinuses open, usually shallow. Profichi not depressed at apex. Flower cavity longer than broad.
        Middle lobe rounded and obtuse. Leaf and petiole moderately hairy. Sinuses shallow and open. Veins drying reddish. Lamina not decurrent. No. 8832.
        Middle lobe with acute, straight-sided apex.
          Leaves large, irregularly 3–5 lobed. Sinus shallow, usually very open. Lamina decurrent. Veins drying reddish. Flower pedicels purplish. No. 8845.
          Leaves medium sized. Lamina not decurrent. Veins green on drying. *Petioles and palmate veins very glabrous.* Flower pedicels green. No. 8837.

8829 to 8847—Continued.

8829.

From Naples. "A medium-sized tree in a garden on Posilipo hill on Strada Nuova di Posilipo, evidently a cultivated sort. It bore a fair number of *mamme;* full of *Blastophagæ* on April 19, and still had a few *mamme* attached on May 14. The *profichi* are abundant. Apparently a valuable late sort. Its botanical characters are as follows: *Petioles very long,* when reflexed reaching beyond base of sinuses. Leaves small, long, and narrow, smoothish, 3-lobed, with deep and narrow sinuses, sometimes closed above. Middle lobe much expanded, with a blunt rounded apex; lateral lobes unusually narrow. Base U-shaped, with decurrent lamina. Veins drying reddish. Petioles very long and slender; slightly hairy. Profichi ovate, medium sized, 45 x 30 mm. Very unlike other sorts in leaf characters. Resembles most No. 8834, but has very much longer petioles, while No. 8834 has acute, straight-sided apex and profichi depressed at tip. No. 8832 has similar U-shaped base, but differs greatly in having shallow sinuses, shorter petioles, and abruptly attached lamina." (*Swingle.*) (No. 101.)

8830.

From Naples. "A large tree in the Botanic Garden, covered with *profichi*, but destitute of *mamme.* The *profichi* were far advanced and had abundant male flowers; but one that had been injured was soft, and this may indicate that this variety has the drawback of producing *profichi* which soften as they ripen. A valuable early sort." (*Swingle.*) (No. 102.)

8831.

From Naples. "A medium-sized tree, evidently of a cultivated sort, in a garden on Posilipo hill, near Villanova. Bore both *mamme* and *profichi.*" (*Swingle.*) (No. 103.)

8832.

From Naples. "A medium-sized tree, of a cultivated sort, in a garden on Posilipo hill. It had a few *mamme* still attached and many *profichi.* Its botanical characters are as follows: *Leaf U-shaped with shallow open sinuses and rounded apex.* Leaf medium sized, slightly hairy, 3-lobed, with shallow and rather open sinuses. Base U-shaped, with abruptly joined lamina. Apex of middle segment rounded. Veins slightly reddish on drying. Petiole medium length and not very slender; somewhat hairy. Profichi ovate, 58 x 37, with abundant male flowers. Near to No. 8837, but has a rounded instead of an acute apex and more hairy petioles. See under 8829. Differs from No. 8834 with U-shaped leaves in having open shallow sinuses and rounded apex." (*Swingle.*) (No. 104.)

8833.

From Naples. "A small seedling tree, growing from a wall retaining a roadway on Posilipo hill. Floral envelopes long and nearly hiding the flowers, which were still immature on May 9, 1902. Probably a seedling fig, but possibly a very large caprifig." (*Swingle.*) (No. 105.)

8834.

From Resina, near Naples. "A large tree in Villa Amelia, bearing a few *mamme* and abundant *profichi.* Evidently a cultivated sort. The tree had been caprified with *mamme*, in spite of the presence of a fair number of *mamme* attached to the branches. Its botanical characters are as follows: *Profichi depressed at apex.* Leaves small, rounded, regular in outline, 3-lobed, slightly hairy, with deep, narrow sinuses, often closed. Middle lobe with acute, straight-sided apex. Base U-shaped, with decurrent lamina. Veins drying reddish. Petiole medium or short, slender, slightly hairy. Profichi ovate, depressed at apex, 52 x 36. Some of the flower pedicels purplish. Differs from No. 8845 in smaller leaves, regular in outline, and narrower sinus, and from No. 8837 in having reddish veins on drying and a decurrent lamina. See also under No. 8829, which has longer petioles and rounded tip." (*Swingle.*) (No. 106.)

8829 to 8847—Continued.

8835.

From Resina, near Naples. "A medium-sized tree in Villa Amelia, probably the same as No. 8834." (*Swingle.*) (No. 107.)

8836.

From San Giovanni a Teduccio, near Naples. "A large tree, which had been cut back for grafting; growing in the garden of Dammann & Co. Owing to the presence of only young trees, there were no *mamme*, but a few *profichi* with very long pedicels were seen." (*Swingle.*) (No. 108.)

8837.

From Naples. "A medium-sized tree, evidently of a cultivated sort, growing in a garden on Posilipo hill. Had a few *mamme* and abundant, very large *profichi*, with numerous male flowers. A promising sort. Its botanical characters are as follows: *Petioles almost glabrous.* Leaves medium sized, slightly hairy, 3-lobed, with rather deep and narrow sinuses. Middle lobe narrow below and bulging above, with very acute, straight-sided apex, bulging moderately. Base cordate; lamina not decurrent, broad space between margin and first palmate vein. Veins drying green. Petioles *glabrous*, or nearly so; slender. Profichi very large ovate, 71 x 42, with very many male flowers. Flower pedicels green. Principal palmate vein glabrous. Skin marked with small reddish brown specks. Resembles No. 8834, but has not decurrent lamina and has flower pedicels and veins of dried leaves green, besides petioles which are less hairy. Very like No. 8845, q. v., and No. 8832." (*Swingle.*) (No. 109.)

8838.

From Naples. "A small tree growing in a garden. No *mamme* were seen, but there were numerous medium-sized *profichi*, which had only a few male flowers. Leaves nearly entire, with golden pubescence. Its botanical characters are as follows: *Leaves nearly entire*, small, short, pubescent, with golden hairs, as are the short, thick petioles; sinuses present, shallow and open, not extending one-third way to middle. Middle lobe blunt deltoid, nearly straight-sided, over 90 mm. long. Veins reddish on drying. Base cordate; lamina abruptly attached to petiole. Ultimate veinlets very fine and visible by transmitted light. Profichi ovate, 53 x 30 mm., with few male flowers. Skin with large, nearly white spots. Resembles No. 8844 in pubescence, which is, however, *less* marked, and in having short, stout petioles. No. 8844 differs in having lobed leaves and *oval* small profichi, and yellow spots on dried leaves. Slightly resembles the slightly lobed No. 8832, but has much shallower sinuses, and No. 8832 has rounded middle lobe and longer slender petiole and smoother leaf." (*Swingle.*) (No. 110.)

8839.

From Naples. "A large tree in a garden on the hill between Arenella and Capodimonte. May be a caprifig." (*Swingle.*) (No. 111.)

8840.

From Naples. "A cultivated sort, growing near No. 8831, in garden on Posilipo hill, near Villanova." (*Swingle.*)

8841.

From Naples. "A cultivated sort, growing in garden near No. 8831, on Posilipo hill, near Villanova." (*Swingle.*) (No. 113.)

8842.

From Vico Equense, near Castellamare. "A medium-sized tree, growing in a cliff by the road between Vico Equense and Sejano. It may be a caprifig." (*Swingle.*) (No. 114.)

8829 to 8847—Continued.

8843.

From Naples. "A good-sized tree, evidently of a cultivated sort, on Posilipo hill. Probably a *brebas* tree, i. e., a sort which matures the spring generation corresponding to the profico generation of a caprifig." (*Swingle.*) (No. 115.)

8844.

From Miseno, near Pozzuoli. "*Profico bianco*, white caprifig. A small tree in the garden on the top of Mount Miseno. It had a few *mamme* and some *profichi* which showed a large number of male flowers. Evidently a cultivated sort of value. Its botanical characters are as follows: Leaves velvety hairy, petioles thick and short; also velvety pubescent. Leaves medium sized, short and thick, decidedly 3–7-lobed. Sinuses rather open, usually less than one-half way to middle. Leaves (some at least) show numerous small yellowish dots on the upper surface. Apical lobe bluntly deltoid with nearly straight sides. Base strongly cordate. Lamina abruptly attached to midrib. Veins usually drying green. Lateral lobes bulge so sinus line cuts them. Profichi very small (possibly young?) 38 x 33 oval, with many male flowers. Skin marked with large, nearly white dots." (*Swingle.*) (No. 116.)

8845.

From Naples. "A large tree of a cultivated sort, growing in a garden on Posilipo hill. It had numerous *profichi* containing many male flowers. A promising caprifig. Its botanical characters are as follows: Leaves large, irregular in outline, with very open sinuses. Leaf large, irregular in outline, somewhat hairy; 3–5-lobed sinuses, rather shallow and very open. Lateral lobes very coarsely dentate. Middle lobe thick and bulging but slightly, with an acute straight-sided apex. Base U-shaped or slightly cordate. Lamina decurrent. Veins reddish on drying; palmate veins hairy. Petioles only slightly hairy, rather long and not very slender. Profichi very large, ovate, 62 x 40, with a good number of male flowers; pedicels of flowers purplish at base. Much resembles No. 8837, but differs in having large leaf, more decurrent lamina, and more hairy petioles and veins, and flower pedicels purplish at base. Most resembles No. 8834; differs in large irregular leaf, with more open sinuses and profichi not depressed at apex." (*Swingle.*) (No. 117.)

8846.

From Naples. "A large cultivated fig in a garden on Posilipo hill, bearing a few *brebas*." (*Swingle.*) (No. 118.)

8847.

From Lago Averno, near Pozzuoli. "A large tree near the road from Arco Filice to Pozzuoli. It was covered with *brebas* figs. A promising sort of early fig." (*Swingle.*) (No. 119.)

8848 to 8886.

From Nice, France. Presented by A. Robertson-Proschowsky. Received June 13, 1902.

A collection of seeds as follows:

- **8848.** AGERATUM MEXICANUM.
- **8849.** AMORPHA FRUTICOSA.
- **8850.** ANTHOLYZA AETHIOPICA.
- **8851.** ARAUJIA SERICIFERA.
- **8852.** ARISTOLOCHIA ELEGANS.
- **8853.** BERBERIS NEPALENSIS.

8848 to 8886—Continued.

- **8854.** CARICA QUERCIFOLIA.
- **8855.** CASSIA CORYMBOSA.
- **8856.** CERATONIA SILIQUA.
  "Sweet fruited." (*Proschowsky.*)
- **8857.** CERCIS SILIQUASTRUM.
- **8858.** CORDYLINE BANKSII.
  "This may be some hybrid." (*Proschowsky.*)
- **8859.** EUPATORIUM sp.
  "It has abundant white flowers in midwinter." (*Proschowsky.*)
- **8860.** EUPATORIUM ATRORUBENS.
  "An evergreen bush with very beautiful foliage and flowers in midwinter." (*Proschowsky.*)
- **8861.** EUPATORIUM ATROVIOLACEUM.
- **8862.** FATSIA JAPONICA.
- **8863.** FREYLINIA CESTROIDES.
- **8864.** FRANSERIA ARTEMISIOIDES.
- **8865.** GLAUCIUM FLAVUM.
- **8866.** HEDERA HELIX var. AURANTIA.
- **8867.** HIBISCUS sp.
- **8868.** IPOMOEA FICIFOLIA.
- **8869.** IRIS LAEVIGATA.
- **8870.** MAYTENUS BOARIA.
- **8871.** MELALEUCA VIRIDIFLORA.
- **8872.** OLEA EUROPAEA.
  Nice. "Famous for oil. The fruit is very good for preserving in salt solution. The tree is of a very graceful weeping habit." (*Proschowsky.*)
- **8873.** OLEARIA HAASTII.
- **8874.** OREOPANAX PLATANIFOLIUM.
  "A very ornamental evergreen." (*Proschowsky.*)
- **8875.** OXALIS CORNICULATA var. ATROPURPUREA.
- **8876.** SALVIA GESNERAEFLORA.
  "A very showy winter-blooming shrub. It produces very few seeds." (*Proschowsky.*)
- **8877.** SENECIO DELTOIDES.
- **8878.** SENECIO PETASITES.
- **8879.** SENECIO GRANDIFOLIUS.
- **8880.** SOLANUM PYRACANTHUM.
- **8881.** SOLANUM SODOMAEUM.

8848 to 8886—Continued.

8882. SOLLYA HETEROPHYLLA.

"A twining evergreen shrub with very beautiful blue flowers." (*Proschowsky.*)

8883. SOPHORA JAPONICA.

8884. STERCULIA PLATANIFOLIA.

8885. TACSONIA MOLLISSIMA.

"A very beautiful climbing plant, with large rose-colored flowers and abundant fruits of a pleasant, refreshing flavor." (*Proschowsky.*)

8886. TRIGLOCHIN MARITIMUM.

8887 to 8889.

From Erfurt, Germany. Purchased from Haage & Schmidt. Received June 21, 1902.

Palm seeds as follows:

8887. RHOPALOSTYLIS SAPIDA.   **8889.** HOWEA FORSTERIANA.

8888. HOWEA BELMOREANA.

8890. ERIOBOTRYA JAPONICA. Loquat.

From Tokyo, Japan. Received through Messrs. Lathrop and Fairchild (No. 954, June 2, 1902), June 23, 1902.

Tanaka. "The largest fruited loquat in Japan. This variety originated as a seedling in the yard of Mr. Ioshio Tanaka, at 72 Kinskecho, Tokyo. Mr. Tanaka is a noted Japanese authority on economic botany, and as originator of this remarkably large loquat, his own name has appropriately been given to it. A single fruit has weighed more than 97 grams, while the largest reported in Algiers, Malta, or Spain, so far as I am aware, was only 85, and the largest I have seen was only 56 grams. This is certainly a larger sort than any of these noted African or Spanish varieties. The scions were taken from the original seedling tree in Professor Tanaka's yard in Tokyo, and it is to be hoped can be used for budding. The fruit in formalin, which Professor Tanaka showed me, was egg-shaped, and the largest loquat I have ever seen. Quality is said to be very good. Professor Tanaka delivered an address on this loquat in 1897, at Nagasaki, in which he said the range of weight is between 40 and 80 grams only. The weight of 97 grams was exceptional." (*Fairchild.*)

8891. PANICUM CRUS-GALLI. Japanese millet.

From Niuchwang, China. Presented by Hon. Henry B. Miller, United States Consul, through the State Department. Received June 23, 1902.

8892. TRITICUM VULGARE. Wheat.

From Moscow, Russia. Received through E. Immer & Son, June 27, 1902.

Romanoff Spring.

8893. NICOTIANA TABACUM. Tobacco.

From Sumatra. Received through Messrs. Lathrop and Fairchild (No. 955), July 7, 1902.

Deli. "From one of the best plantations in Deli, East Sumatra. Secured by Mr. Barbour Lathrop personally. See special letter of explanation to Dr. Galloway, June 10, 1902." (*Fairchild.*)

8894. CITRUS BIGARADIA (?) Bitter orange.

From Shidzuoka, Japan. Received through Messrs. Lathrop and Fairchild (No. 956, June 16, 1902), July 8, 1902.

Natsu dai-dai. "A flat, broad, summer variety of the Japanese bitter orange, which is a remarkable citrous fruit and deserves the study of citrus growers. It is only of fair quality, but ripens at a time when our pomelos are over, and when the craving for a sour breakfast fruit is perhaps strongest, i. e., in May and June. These scions came from a noted old citrus grower near Shidzuoka, and are a gift to the United States Government. For fuller notes on this fruit see No. 8903. Tanaka gives in his 'Useful Plants of Japan' *Citrus bigaradia* as the species name for *Dai-dai*, but does not identify the *Natsu dai-dai*." (*Fairchild*.)

8895. CITRUS BIGARADIA (?). Bitter orange.

From Shidzuoka, Japan. Received through Messrs. Lathrop and Fairchild (No. 957, June 16, 1902), July 8, 1902.

Natsu dai-dai. "A globular formed, slightly different variety of summer bitter orange from No. 8894. Donated by a famous old citrus grower near Shidzuoka, where the government is going to start an experiment station for citrous and other fruits. For a fuller description on this fruit see Nos. 8894 and 8903." (*Fairchild.*)

8896. CITRUS JAPONICA. Kumquat.

From Shidzuoka, Japan. Received through Messrs. Lathrop and Fairchild (No. 958), July 8, 1902.

Nimpo. "Scions of one of the best varieties of kumquat in Japan; with large, round fruits. These kumquats, which are small oranges, eaten skin and all, are much more common in China and Japan than in America, and are worthy of being much better known on our markets. Donated by a veteran citrus grower in Shidzuoka." (*Fairchild.*)

8897 to 8899. TRITICUM DURUM. Wheat.

From Bombay, India. Received through Messrs. Lathrop and Fairchild (No. 945, April 2, 1902), July 14, 1902.

Three varieties of hard wheat from Ralli Brothers, in Bombay, suited for macaroni making. One sack of each forwarded by Latham & Co., of Bombay.

8897.

Khata. "This variety has been tested in Nag Pur, where it proved the most rust resistant of any kind experimented with. Nag Pur is one of the hottest regions in India, and any wheat which endures the heat of that region will be likely to do well in our desert regions of Arizona and California. This *Khata* is said by Ralli Brothers to be the best of all Indian hard wheats, and whenever they can buy it cheap enough and ship it to Genoa it brings as good a price as the hard Russian wheats. This deserves the serious attention of the hard-wheat experimenters, and may prove superior to the Algerian, Russian, or Spanish varieties for our conditions." (*Fairchild.*) (No. 945a.)

8898.

Khandwa. "This is not so good from the standpoint of such big firms as Ralli Brothers, and it does not have the reputation of being as rust resistant as the *Khata.*" (*Fairchild.*) (No. 945b.)

8899.

Pila gheen. "This is not so good from the standpoint of such big firms as Ralli Brothers, and it does not have the reputation of being as rust resistant as the *Khata.*" (*Fairchild.*) (No. 945c.)

8900. GLYCINE HISPIDA. Soy bean.

From Anjo, Japan. Received through Messrs. Lathrop and Fairchild (No. 963, June 29, 1902), July 24, 1902.

"Twenty-six numbered seeds of a giant soy bean presented to the Department by Mr. K. Obata, director of the Tokai branch agricultural experiment station at Anjo, Japan, on condition that should any of the seeds prove to have inherited the characteristics of its female parent he is to have returned to him a fair quantity of the beans which it produces. All the beans have been numbered, and it is desired especially that a record of each be kept for information. This most exceptional sport from which these beans are taken measured 12½ feet in length and had a stem 1 inch in diameter at the base. It yielded about one-fifth of a gallon of beans, while ordinary plants, I am assured by Mr. Obata, give from 50 to 60 seeds only. Its root system is well developed, but whether unusual it is impossible to say, as it was dug before Mr. Obata saw it. The history of this most remarkable sport is as follows: Mr. J. Miyazaki, a descendant of a Samurai and now a second-hand clothier in the village of Okasaki, found in his small back yard a soy bean which neither he nor his wife had planted purposely, but over which they quarreled, the wife wishing to pull it up because it grew to such unusual proportions and spread over the whole yard. Mr. Miyazaki, however, found in this abnormal plant something to interest him, and when the local district fair was held in Mukada in October he dug up the plant and exhibited it there, but he unfortunately and thoughtlessly ate up most of the beans. Mr. Obata, of the experiment station at Anjo, saw the plant at the fair, visited Mr. Miyazaki's place, and rescued the remaining handful of seed. He got samples of the soil where the plant grew and has sown about 20 seeds in this soil at the experiment station. I have seen and photographed this remarkable sport and think it worthy of the most careful attention." (*Fairchild.*)

8901 and 8901a. PYRUS COMMUNIS. Pear.

From Chios Island, Turkey in Asia. Presented by Mr. N. J. Pantelides, through Mr. D. G. Fairchild. Received July 29, 1902.

8901.
Chamoyea.

8901a.
Kurania kirakia.

8902. CITRUS NOBILIS. Mandarin orange.

From Fukui, Japan. Received through Messrs. Lathrop and Fairchild (No. 959, June 24, 1902), July 21, 1902.

Unshu. "A large-fruited, thick, loose-skinned mandarin orange, which is generally quite seedless but sometimes has one or two seeds. In quality it is not quite so sweet as the common but smaller *Kishu Mikan*, which is the common mandarin orange of Japan. This seedless variety is known all over Japan, but these scions come from the coldest region in which oranges are grown in Japan, where the temperature sometimes goes down to $-10°$ C.—i. e., 14° above zero F.—and where for fifty days or so a foot of snow lies on the ground. In this region, which is a very restricted one, called Sano, near Fukui, ice forms on the rice fields to the thickness of a quarter of an inch. However, the trees are covered by large bamboo mats during December, January, and February, and even with this covering the minimum of last year, 14° above zero, did them material injury. This sort has gradually driven the ordinary seed-bearing mandarin out of the market and is now, since ten years or more ago, the most popular mandarin in Japan." (*Fairchild.*)

8903. CITRUS DECUMANA (?) Pomelo. (?)

From Fukui, Japan. Received through Messrs. Lathrop and Fairchild (No. 960, June 24, 1902), July 21, 1902.

Natsu daidai. "Large summer orange. This fruit deserves the attention of all pomelo growers, as it is a variety to be had on the Japanese market *as late as the end of June.* I saw it as early as the close of April, so that the season is two months at least. It is not as fine and juicy as our best pomelo, but is nevertheless at this season eaten with relish by everyone, both European and Japanese. It is served with sugar, as pomelos are served in America, and would pass among all but connoisseurs as a tolerably good pomelo. Further than this, it ranks as one of the hardiest citrous fruits in Japan. These scions came from a tree that was exposed last winter, with a bamboo mat shelter, to a temperature of $+14°$ F., and although it lost some of its leaves it was not killed by the low temperature. A foot of snow covered the ground about this plant for several weeks during the months of January and February." (*Fairchild.*) (See No. 8894.)

8904. CITRUS NOBILIS. Mandarin orange.

From Fukui, Japan. Received through Messrs. Lathrop and Fairchild (No. 961, June 24, 1902), July 21, 1902.

Koji. "A small-fruited variety with seeds. It is noted for its hardiness, being cultivated in a region where the thermometer drops to $+14°$ F. and where the plants are surrounded by snow as late as February. It is not an especially fine variety, but is worthy of trial in the variety gardens. See Nos. 8902 and 8903 for further descriptions of climate where it is grown." (*Fairchild.*)

8905. CITRUS NOBILIS. **Mandarin orange.**

From Fukui, Japan. Received through Messrs. Lathrop and Fairchild (No. 962, June 24, 1902), July 21, 1902.

Koji. "This is similar to No. 8904, but is said to bear larger, finer fruits. It was not the season for any of these fruits, so I can not say as to their excellence except from reports." (*Fairchild.*)

8906 to 8909.

From Nice, France. Presented by Mr. A. Robertson-Proschowsky. Received July 31, 1902.

Seeds as follows:

8906. ARISTOTELIA MACQUI.

8907. TACSONIA MOLLISSIMA.

"A variety with flowers of a darker color than the type." (*Proschowsky.*)

8908. TACSONIA MOLLISSIMA.

8909. OLEA EUROPAEA.

Nice. (See No. 8872.)

8910. CROTALARIA JUNCEA. **Sunn hemp.**

From Bombay, India. Received through Dr. S. A. Knapp, July 26, 1902.

8911 and 8912. ORYZA SATIVA. **Rice.**

From Bombay, India. Received through Dr. S. A. Knapp, July 26, 1902.

8913. PRUNUS ARMENIACA. **Apricot.**

From Coahuila, Saltillo, Mexico. Received through Miss Lelia Roberts, July 20, 1902.

8914. CERATONIA SILIQUA. **Carob.**

From Marseille, France. Received through Hon. Robert P. Skinner, United States Consul-General, August 9, 1902.

8915. VOANDZEIA SUBTERRANEA. **Woandsu (African goober).**

From Dar-es-Salam, German East Africa. Presented by Mr. D. Holtz. Received August 22, 1902.

8916 to 8975.

From Buenos Ayres, Argentina. Presented by Señor Carlos Thays, director of parks, through Mr. Frank W. Bicknell. Received August 20, 1902.

8916.	OPUNTIA DECUMANA.	**8922.**	PSIDIUM GUAJAVA.
8917.	SAMBUCUS AUSTRALIS.	**8923.**	ENTEROLOBIUM sp.
8918.	COCOS YATAY.	**8924.**	DESMODIUM UNCINATUM.
8919.	SOLANUM POCOTE.	**8925.**	TERMINALIA TRIFLORA (?).
8920.	CECROPIA PALMATA.	**8926.**	SESBANIA SANCTIPAULENSIS.
8921.	MAYTENUS BOARIA.	**8927.**	QUILLAJA SAPONARIA.

8916 to 8975—Continued.

- 8928. XANTHOXYLON sp.
- 8929. PIPTADENIA CEBIL.
- 8930. LIPPIA TURBINATA.
- 8931. PARKINSONIA ACULEATA.
- 8932. TIPUANA SPECIOSA.
- 8933. COCOS AUSTRALIS.
- 8934. GLEDITSIA AMORPHOIDES.
- 8935. CAESALPINIA GILLIESII.
- 8936. BIXA ORELLANA.
- 8937. EUGENIA sp. **Anacahuita.**
- 8938. EUGENIA MATO.
- 8939. LITHRAEA AROEIRINHA.
- 8940. ENTEROLOBIUM TIMBOUVA.
- 8941. DALBERGIA NIGRA.
- 8942. SAPINDUS TRIFOLIATUS.
- 8943. SCHINUS MOLLE.
- 8944. PSIDIUM CATTLEIANUM.
- 8945. MIMOSA SENSITIVA ARBOREA.
- 8946. TRICUSPIDARIA DEPENDENS.
- 8947. CESTRUM PSEUDO-QUINA.
- 8948. ACACIA FARNESIANA.
- 8949. COLLIGUA JABRASILIENSIS.
- 8950. TECOMA STANS.
- 8951. LUCUMA NERIIFOLIA.
- 8952. LIPPIA LYCIOIDES.
- 8953. ILEX PARAGUAYENSIS.
- 8954. BOCCONIA FRUTESCENS.
- 8955. LANTANA CAMARA.
- 8956. GRABOWSKIA GLAUCA.
- 8957. EUGENIA PUNGENS.
- 8958. HETEROPTERIS UMBELLATA.
- 8959. CESTRUM PARQUI.
- 8960. CARICA QUERCIFOLIA.
- 8961. OPUNTIA FICUS-INDICA.
- 8962. CLEMATIS HILARII.
- 8963. EUGENIA MICHELII.
- 8964. COPERNICIA CERIFERA.
- 8965. HIBISCUS ARGENTINUS.
- 8966. PSIDIUM GUAJAVA var. PYRIFERUM.
- 8967. CHORISIA CRISPIFLORA.
- 8968. MORRENIA ODORATA.
- 8969. EUGENIA EDULIS.
- 8970. SCUTIA BUXIFOLIA.
- 8971. BAUHINIA CANDICANS.
- 8972. CELTIS TALA.
- 8973. CITHAREXYLUM BARBINERVE.
- 8974. ACACIA MONILIFORMIS.
- 8975. JACARANDA CHELONIA.

8976. GARCINIA MANGOSTANA. **Mangosteen.**

From Saigon, Cochin China. Received through Messrs. Lathrop and Fairchild from Mr. M. E. Haffner, director of agriculture of Cochin China, September 3, 1902.

8977 to 9013.

From Aburi, Gold Coast, Africa. Presented by the curator of the Botanic Gardens. Received September 5, 1902.

- 8977. ABRUS PRECATORIUS.
- 8978. ACHRAS SAPOTA.
- 8979. ADENANTHERA PAVONINA.
- 8980. ANONA MURICATA.

8977 to 9013—Continued.

8981.	ANONA SQUAMOSA.	8999.	MICHELIA CHAMPACA.
8982.	ARACHIS HYPOGAEA.	9000.	PALISOTA BARTERI.
8983.	ARTOCARPUS INTEGRIFOLIA.	9001.	PERSEA GRATISSIMA.
8984.	BAUHINIA PICTA.	9002.	PIMENTA ACRIS.
8985.	BUTYROSPERMUM PARKII.	9003.	PITHECOLOBIUM SAMAN.
8986.	CAJANUS INDICUS.	9004.	POINCIANA REGIA.
8987.	CALOTROPIS GIGANTEA.	9005.	RAPHIA VINIFERA.
8988.	CASSIA ALATA.	9006.	SIDEROXYLON DULCIFICUM.
8989.	CHRYSOPHYLLUM CAINITO.	9007.	SPATHODEA CAMPANULATA.
8990.	COFFEA LIBERICA.		
8991.	CRESCENTIA CUJETE.	9008.	SPONDIAS DULCIS.
8992.	ELAEIS GUINEENSIS.	9009.	SPONDIAS LUTEA.
8993.	FUNTUMIA ELASTICA.	9010.	THEOBROMA CACAO. **Cacao.**
8994.	GARCINIA HANBURYI.		
8995.	HONCKENYA FICIFOLIA.	9011.	THEVETIA NEREIFOLIA. **Trumpet flower.**
8996.	HURA CREPITANS.		
8997.	LABRAMIA BOJERI.	9012.	THUNBERGIA ERECTA.
8998.	LEUCAENA GLAUCA.	9013.	VOANDZEIA SUBTERRANEA.

9014. PYRUS MALUS. **Apple.**

From Saltillo, Mexico. Received through Mr. G. Onderdonk, special agent of the Office of Seed and Plant Introduction, September 9, 1902.

Peron.

9015 and 9016. PRUNUS ARMENIACA. **Apricot.**

From Saltillo, Mexico. Received through Mr. G. Onderdonk, special agent, September 9, 1902.

9015.
Perry.

9016.
From a large tree at Chepultepec farm.

9017 to 9019. CITRUS DECUMANA. **Pomelo.**

From Bangkok, Siam. Secured by Dr. G. B. McFarland, and imported by Rev. G. R. Callender, at the request of Messrs. Lathrop and Fairchild. Received September 11, 1902.

"A seedless variety, or possibly three different varieties of pomelo, from the garden of Prince Mom Chow Rachawongse, of the lineage of the former Second King. The seedless pomelos, sold on the Hongkong market, which are supposed to be produced by trees of this variety, are the best pomelos in the Orient. The "seedless Bangkok" was the sort requested by us. The circumstances connected with the introduction of these pomelo plants, many months after Messrs. Lathrop and Fairchild visited Siam, were such that it is not possible to say definitely whether one single variety of the "Bangkok seedless" was represented by the three plants brought in, or whether the Prince sent one plant each of three kinds." (*Fairchild.*)

9020. CUCUMIS MELO. **Muskmelon.**

From Valencia, Spain. Presented by Hon. R. M. Bartleman, United States Consul. Received September 20, 1902.

Bronze. One of the finest Spanish varieties.

9021. TRIGONELLA FOENUM-GRAECUM. **Fenugreek.**

From New York. Received through J. M. Thorburn & Co., September 29, 1902.

This seed was grown in southern Germany.

9022. CUCUMIS MELO. **Muskmelon.**

From Valencia, Spain. Presented by Hon. R. M. Bartleman, United States Consul. Received October 2, 1902.

Bronze. (These seeds may be of the same variety as No. 9020, but as they are much lighter in color they have been given a separate number.)

9023. PSIDIUM GUAJAVA. **Guava.**

From Merritt, Fla. Presented by Mr. L. H. Gurney. Received October 6, 1902.

9024. ANONA SQUAMOSA. **Custard apple.**

From Mussoorie, united provinces of Agra and Oudh, India. Presented by Rev. H. Marston Andrews. Received October 6, 1902.

Sharifa or custard apple seed, grown in Dehra Dun, on the south side of a wall. The trees grow to a height of from 15 to 25 feet.

9025. OENOTHERA SINUATA.

From Santa Rosa, Cal. Presented by Mr. Luther Burbank, through Mr. D. G. Fairchild. Received September 30, 1902.

"Mr. Burbank thinks this a valuable ornamental." (*Fairchild.*)

9026. TRIFOLIUM RESUPINATUM. **Strawberry clover.**

From North Australia. Presented by Mr. Luther Burbank, of Santa Rosa, Cal., through Mr. D. G. Fairchild. Received September 30, 1902.

"Found in culture at Mr. Burbank's experimental gardens." (*Fairchild.*)

9027. PYRETHRUM TCHIHATCHEWII.

From Santa Rosa, Cal. Presented by Mr. Luther Burbank, through Mr. D. G. Fairchild. Received September 30, 1902.

"Said to be from Asia Minor. Should be sown in pots and transplanted. Forms a pretty mat of foliage like a lawn, and could be used for lawn purposes." (*Fairchild.*)

9028. MUSA TEXTILIS. **Manila hemp.**

From Manila, P. I. Presented by Mr. John W. Gilmore, of the Insular Bureau of Agriculture, through Mr. L. H. Dewey, Assistant Botanist of the Department of Agriculture. Received October 10, 1902.

9029. PRUNUS CERASUS. **Cherry.**

From Vladimir, Russia. Received through Mr. E. A. Bessey (No. 101, July 22, 1902), October 9, 1902.

Vladimir. "Sun-dried cherries from the garden of Feodor Gontcheroff. These cherries, which will not be picked until about July 31, are from a garden typical as to the method of cultivation (or rather lack of cultivation). The trees are propagated by shoots from the roots regardless of any order. The trees are never pruned nor is the ground ever cultivated. The young shoots are allowed to grow up with the older trees. The result is a dense thicket or jungle, almost impenetrable, of trees from 8 to 12 feet high. In spite of this lack of care the trees bear rather freely. The cherries are usually fully ripe by the 20th of July, but this year being cold only part were ripe. The cherries are black, about five-eighths to three-fourths inch in diameter, with blood-red flesh and juice. They are sweet and juicy, but still retain a pleasant, acid flavor. The general idea that this variety is propagated, as a rule, from seeds is erroneous, that method being used only rarely. However, the variety is said to come fairly true to seed." (*Bessey.*)

9030. PRUNUS CERASUS. **Cherry.**

From Dobrovka, near Vladimir, Russia. Received through Mr. E. A. Bessey (No. 103, July 22, 1902), October 9, 1902.

"From the garden of Vladimir cherries of Makar Kulikoff and Gregori Rezanoff. This tree differs from the others in being exceedingly prolific, the cherries nearly hiding the leaves. The tree is much more vigorous and less inclined to branch at the ground. The leaves are larger and darker green and more coarsely dentate. The leaves are shiny above while those of the neighboring Vladimir cherry trees are dull. The cherries are borne in clusters, those of the Vladimir being usually single or in pairs. They ripen ten days later than the Vladimir, i. e., normally about July 31, and are nearly black when ripe. The flesh is only slightly colored. The cherries are juicy and said to be sweeter than those of the true Vladimir variety. No trees were obtainable. Seeds (in the sun-dried cherries) were obtained in the hope that something valuable may be obtained. This is believed to be a seedling of the true Vladimir." (*Bessey.*)

9031 to 9039.

A miscellaneous collection of exotic plants growing in the Department grounds and greenhouses, which were turned over to the Office of Seed and Plant Introduction for distribution, October, 1902. The origin of most of them is unknown.

    9031. JACARANDA CHELONIA.

    From Argentina. Seed received May, 1901.

    9032. TECTONA GRANDIS. **Teak.**

    9033. GRABOWSKIA GLAUCA.

    From Argentina. May be a good hedge plant.

    9034. SOPHORA JAPONICA. **Pagoda tree.**

    9035. RUBUS sp.

    From Mexico. Presented by Dr. J. N. Rose (No. 194), assistant curator, U. S. National Museum. "The leaves have a metallic luster, making it a fine ornamental." (*Rose.*)

    9036. STERCULIA PLATANIFOLIA.

    9037. NUYTSIA FLORIBUNDA.

    9038. ALBIZZIA LEBBEK.

    9039. INDIGOFERA ANIL.

    From Porto Rico. Received October, 1901.

9040. CITRUS AUSTRALICA.

From Botanic Garden, Pisa, Italy. Received through Mr. W. T. Swingle (No. 120), October 16, 1902.

"A small tree, 12 feet high, with abundant foliage; trunk 4 feet high, 6 inches in diameter at base. Tree grows alongside *C. trifoliata* and, like it, seems to stand the cold at Pisa, which sometimes reaches 10° F. in winter and kills pistaches. Fruit is like a lime in Australia, and the species may prove very useful in breeding a hardy lime or lemon, or for a stock." (*Swingle.*)

9041. PHYLLOSTACHYS CASTILLONIS. **Bamboo.**

From Yokohama, Japan. Received through Messrs. Lathrop and Fairchild (No. 983, July 28, 1902), November, 1902.

Kimmei-chiku. "Plants of the 'golden' or 'striped' bamboo of Japan. This species has the most decorative culms of any of the Japanese bamboos, being of a golden yellow color striped with green. When young these stems are brilliant in their freshness and a clump of them is a most beautiful sight. This bamboo is said to have been introduced into Japan from Korea. It is by no means a common sort, even in Japan. Owing to the fact that the green stripes fade after the culms are cut, its decorative value is confined to the living stems, especially those one year old. The plant grows to a height of 15 to 16 feet, even occasionally to 39 feet, and the culms attain 10 inches in circumference. If planted in a sheltered place on rich soil which is kept well mulched it will produce in a few years a handsome clump of the golden stems. The leaves are slightly variegated. It is exceedingly variable in the variegations, both of leaf and stem, the green stripes sometimes being scarcely visible. Sprouts appear in June in Japan and are said to be edible, though I have never heard of this variety being grown for food. It is essentially an ornamental plant." (*Fairchild.*)

9042. PHYLLOSTACHYS NIGRA. **Bamboo.**

From Yokohama, Japan. Received through Messrs. Lathrop and Fairchild (No. 984, July 28, 1902), November, 1902.

Kuro-chiku, Kurodaké, or *Gomadaké.* "Plants of the Japanese black bamboo. This species is characterized by its dark brown to purple-black culms, which make it one of the handsomest species in Japan. It does not grow much over 20 feet in height, even under the best conditions of soil and climate. The shoots do not turn black until the second year, the first season being green with dark, freckle-like spots. The black bamboo formed at one time a considerable source of revenue to Japan, being largely exported to Europe and America, but of recent years the demand for it has fallen off. The growers say it is because the exporters have shipped immature culms. It is still extensively used for walking sticks, umbrella handles, etc. It grows largest on rich alluvial soil, needs plenty of phosphoric acid and potash, and the ground should be heavily mulched so that it will not dry out." (*Fairchild.*)

9043. PHYLLOSTACHYS HENONIS, var. MADARADAKE. **Bamboo.**

From Yokohama, Japan. Received through Messrs. Lathrop and Fairchild (No. 985, July 28, 1902), November, 1902.

Madaradake or *Ummon-chiku.* "Plants of the mottled bamboo from Hakone, province of Omi, arranged for through the assistance of Professor Hirase, a well-known Japanese botanist. This variety is characterized by having distinct blotches (possibly of fungus origin) on its culms. These blotches are of a dark-brown color, sometimes with concentric rings of a darker hue. The mottled culms are especially prized for fancy furniture making, as the mottling is permanent. The plant resembles *Phyllostachys henonis* in growth, and under favorable conditions attains a height of over 15 feet. The blotches on this bamboo do not make their appearance until the third or fourth year, and are more pronounced in the shady parts of the grove. If exposed to bright sunshine it is said the blotches fail to appear. This variety should be given especial attention, not planted in very small clumps, and grown on rich, well-drained soil in locations well sheltered from the wind. It is probably not so hardy as some other sorts and until well established should be protected with a heavy mulch of straw in the winter. The soil should not be allowed to dry out, but should be kept moist by an inch of good mulch during the summer as well." (*Fairchild.*)

9044. PHYLLOSTACHYS BAMBUSOIDES. **Bamboo.**

From Yokohama, Japan. Received through Messrs. Lathrop and Fairchild (No. 986, July 29, 1902), November, 1902.

Yadake. "The arrow bamboo, from whose culms the Japanese archers of feudal times had their shafts prepared. The culms are especially suited to this purpose, for they are straight, extremely hard, and of about the proper diameter. The arrows of present-day archers in Japan are also made of this bamboo. The sort was first introduced into England in 1894, Mitford says, and is consequently a comparatively new kind. In Japan it is not so common as many other types, being seen rarely in cultivated ground. It is pronounced hardy in England by Mitford, and a valuable acquisition. In habit it is cespitose, and its clumps are tall and closely set with the culms. Its broad leaves give it a very decorative appearance, individual leaves being as much as 11 inches long by 1¾ inches broad. It is sometimes used as a hedge plant in Japan, and its wood finds uses in the manufacture of tea sieves, baskets, etc. In general appearance it is quite unlike the ordinary bamboos, most of the leaves being borne only on the upper portion of the culms." (*Fairchild.*)

9045. PHYLLOSTACHYS MITIS. **Bamboo.**

From Yokohama, Japan. Received through Messrs. Lathrop and Fairchild (No. 987, July 29, 1902), November, 1902.

Moso-chiku or *Mouso-chiku.* "Plants of the edible bamboo of Japan. This variety, which Japanese historians say was introduced into Japan from China a century and a half ago, is not the species best suited for timber purposes, although the largest in size of any of the hardy sorts in Japan. Its culms are sold, it is true, and used in the manufacture of dippers, pots, vases, water troughs, etc., but the wood is softer and more brittle than that of the *Madake*, No. 9046. As a vegetable it is cultivated in small forests near the principal cities, and is given great care. Its young, tender shoots, like giant asparagus shoots, form one of the favorite spring vegetables of all classes in Japan. European and American residents in Japan are, many of them, fond of this vegetable, some even being passionately so. Its cultivation for the purpose of shoot production, therefore, is alone worthy the consideration of truck growers in the extreme South. A market can probably be created for the shoots as soon as a large enough supply can be insured to make the effort worth while. On the other hand, the value of the culms for use in fence making, basket making, and the production of a host of farm and garden conveniences, makes it worth a place in the back yard of every farmer in those regions suited to its growth. It is one of the hardy sorts, and so far as beauty is concerned it is, according to Mitford, 'the noblest of all the bamboos generally cultivated in England.' The severe winter of 1895 in England cut the culms down to the ground, but during that season the thermometer dropped below zero Fahrenheit. Even after this severe freeze the roots remained alive. It is not to be expected that this form will attain so large -dimensions in the colder, drier climate of America, but the size of the culms of bamboos depends so much upon the richness of the soil and the methods of culture that, with proper nourishment, there is no reason why large-sized culms, over 2 inches in diameter, should not be produced in America. I have measured a shoot in Japan which was 1 foot 7¾ inches in circumference, and there are records of culms nearly 3 feet in circumference. These large culms were over 40 feet in height. A forest of these large bamboos forms one of the most beautiful sights in the world. In planting for its edible shoots about 120 plants are set out to the acre, but if for forest purposes at least 200 plants should be used. The balls of earth and roots should be more carefully set than those of deciduous trees, as the rhizomes, if injured, stop growing, and the spreading of the plant is checked. The fibrous roots are very brittle after planting and a heavy mulch of straw and loose earth should be kept on the field, so that the surface soil will not dry out. A sheltered situation is essential to the growth of this species, and rich, alluvial soil is what it likes best. Standing water beneath the soil kills it, and much gravel prevents its rapidly spreading. A sufficient number should be planted in a clump to enable the young plants, after a few years, to effectually shade the ground, otherwise, no tall, straight culms will be produced. Judicious thinning out of the small shoots, while still young, tends to make the plant produce larger culms." (*Fairchild.*)

9046. PHYLLOSTACHYS QUILIOI. **Bamboo.**

From Yokohama, Japan. Received through Messrs. Lathrop and Fairchild (No. 988, July 29, 1902), November, 1902.

Madake. "This is the great timber-producing bamboo of Japan. It is grown in large plantations or forests near the large cities of Japan, and its culture is said to be among the most profitable of any plant culture in the country. There are extensive wild forests south of Kobe, but the finest culms come from the cultivated forests; these culms are more regular in size and of better shape. The wood of this species is said to be superior in elasticity and durability to either that of the *Moso*, No. 9045, or *Hachiku*, No. 9047. Its extensive uses are too numerous to mention, for they would form a list as long as that of an enumeration of the uses of the white pine in America. The cultivation of this bamboo is not a difficult one, and forests of it should be started in all regions having a suitable climate. The species is one of the hardiest of the large-sized kinds in Japan and thrives in England, proving hardier than *Moso*, No. 9045. It never attains the same dimensions as this species, but often, however, grows to a height of 30 to 40 feet, and culms having a diameter of 2½ to 3 inches are not unusual. Even 4-inch culms are described by the books. The size of these culms depends largely upon the method of culture and how carefully the forests are thinned out and manured. About 300 plants should be set to an acre, in such a way that their spreading rhizomes will not interfere with each other at the start. The soil should be worked over to a depth of 18 inches several months before planting, and if of a heavy clay, should be lightened by working in straw and litter from the barnyard. After planting, the ground should be heavily mulched to prevent the top soil from drying out, and every means should be taken to insure that the ground is soon shaded by the growing shoots. The soil about the bases of the culms should be kept in semiobscurity. This object is only obtained by moderately thick planting and judicious thinning. Small clumps are not so likely to produce large stems as quickly as large patches, for the reason that the soil is more exposed to the drying effect of the sun. Only rich, alluvial, well-drained soil is likely to prove suitable for a bamboo forest of this species. The thickness of the pipes of this sort of bamboo is greater than that of any of the other common kinds, and this characteristic makes the culms more rigid and more serviceable for many purposes. It is of great importance that a young forest of bamboos be protected from the wind, for the young, tender shoots are easily injured. Wind-breaks of conifers are used in Japan even where the winds are anything but severe. A sheltered valley, or the base of a mountain slope, is sometimes chosen as offering such a sheltered situation. In setting young plants out great care should be taken not to injure the buds on the rhizomes or to break off the fibrous roots by packing down the soil too roughly about them. This species is likely to prove the most valuable of any of the Japanese hardy bamboos." (*Fairchild.*)

9047. PHYLLOSTACHYS HENONIS.   Bamboo.

From Yokohama, Japan. Received through Messrs. Lathrop and Fairchild (No. 989, July 29, 1902), November, 1902.

Hachiku. "The second most important timber bamboo of Japan. Its method of culture is exactly similar to that of the *Madake*, No. 9046, and often it is cultivated side by side with this species. The brittleness of its joints, I am told, prevents its being used for many purposes, such as barrel hoops, for which the *Madake* is better adapted. On the other hand, the fine bamboo ribs of Japanese paper lanterns are generally made from this species. The height of this species is little inferior to that of the *Madake*, but it may be easily distinguished from it by the absence of dark spots on the sheath in young shoots. The sheaths are a solid light-straw color. The pseudophyll has a wavy outline. As an ornamental, this species is singled out by Mitford as the most beautiful of all the Japanese bamboos. In hardiness in Japan it ranks about the same as *Phyllostachys quilioi*. Mitford says it is one of the hardiest species in England, retaining its green color through the winter, the leaves not being injured by the cold. It should be given good soil and protection for the first few winters, or until thoroughly established." (*Fairchild.*)

9048. PHYLLOSTACHYS MARLIACEA.   Bamboo.

From Yokohama, Japan. Received through Messrs. Lathrop and Fairchild (No. 990, August, 1902), November, 1902.

Shibo-chiku or *Shiwa-chiku.* "Plants of the wrinkled bamboo, perfectly hardy in England, characterized by having the base of the culm fluted or covered with longitudinal grooves and ridges. The stems of this species are especially prized for use in the woodwork of the special tea-ceremony rooms of old Japanese houses. An uncommon form in England and very decorative. Hard to get in quantity, even in Japan. It should be given the same treatment as that given to *Phyllostachys quilioi.*" (*Fairchild.*)

9049. BAMBUSA QUADRANGULARIS.   Bamboo.

From Yokohama, Japan. Received through Messrs. Lathrop and Fairchild (No. 991, August, 1902), November, 1902.

Shiho-chiku or *Shikaku-daké.* "Plants of the square bamboo. This is not considered as hardy as the previously mentioned species, *Phyllostachys quilioi*, and it will be advisable to give it especial care upon arrival. The plants should be potted and kept in a cool house over winter; not planted out at once. The culms of this species are square only when large. The small culms are round like any other kind. It produces its young shoots in Japan as early as February or March, I am told, and this feature may make it difficult to acclimate. Mitford says its rootstock is very vigorous, and, from clumps which I have seen near Yokohama, I judge it to be capable of producing small forests of culms 20 to 30 feet high. It is a beautiful form and its stems are much used for all classes of ornamental woodwork. It is not, however, very largely cultivated in Japan." (*Fairchild.*)

9050. ARUNDINARIA SIMONI. Bamboo.

From Yokohama, Japan. Received through Messrs. Lathrop and Fairchild (No. 992, August, 1902), November, 1902.

Narihiradaké. "One of the hardiest and tallest of the Japanese bamboos, perfectly hardy in England, where it is very commonly grown. It is mainly an ornamental and should be planted in small clumps. Its peculiar attraction lies in the large, persistent, or semipersistent sheaths, which do not fall off until the shoots are mature. It spreads rapidly, but for several years the young shoots are likely to be small. In Kew, Mitford says, this species has grown to a height of 18 feet, and I have seen specimens in Japan 20 feet high. It is a very showy form and one which is worthy a place in any collection of bamboos. It is not a forest type, and should be planted in clumps of three or four plants. So far as I know, little use is made of this species in Japan. It should be planted in sheltered locations, in fertile, mellow soil, and given especial care for the first two or three winters." (*Fairchild.*)

9051. PHYLLOSTACHYS RUSCIFOLIA. Bamboo.

From Yokohama, Japan. Received through Messrs. Lathrop and Fairchild (No. 994, August, 1902), November, 1902.

Bungozasa. "A small species of bamboo, not over 2 feet high. The plants sent are designed for trial along the banks of irrigation canals in California and elsewhere. The species is said to be an excellent sand binder and capable of forming a thick mat of pretty green foliage and an indestructible mass of interwoven roots and rhizomes. Plant 6 feet apart each way on the slopes of the canal bank and give attention until well established. This may prove of considerable value for making the banks of canals permanent. It will probably withstand considerable drought, and it forms a very pretty mat of foliage on slopes or under the shade of conifers in parks. It is not an uncommon species in England, and is also slightly known in America." (*Fairchild.*)

9052. PHYLLOSTACHYS AUREA. Bamboo.

From Yokohama, Japan. Received through Messrs. Lathrop and Fairchild. (No. 995, August, 1902), November, 1902.

Hotei-chiku or *Horai-chiku.* "The so-called 'golden' bamboo; a misnomer, as the culms are no more deep yellow in color than those of other sorts. It is distinguished by the short internodes at the base of the culm. It is an ornamental and the species most used for canes and fishing rods. It should be planted in clumps of not less than 15 plants for ornamental effect or for propagation. It is hardier than *Phyllostachys mitis* and probably one of the hardiest species in Japan. The sprouts are said to be of a better flavor than those of the real edible species, though this fact is not commonly known. In England this species grows to a height of 14 feet 6 inches, Mitford says. It is a much smaller species than *P. mitis, P. quilioi,* or *P. henonis*, but worthy of a place in every bamboo collection." (*Fairchild.*)

9053. BAMBUSA VEITCHII. Bamboo.

From Yokohama, Japan. Received through Messrs. Lathrop and Fairchild (No. 997, August, 1902), November, 1902.

Kuma-zasa. "A bamboo eminently suited for planting under conifers on lawns to form a dense mass of foliage. The edges of the leaves in this species die in winter and turn light yellow, giving them a striking landscape effect. Worth trying on embankments of canals in California. Not less than 50 plants should be planted in a place, say, 2 feet apart each way. For the slopes of embankments or roadways it produces remarkably pretty effects. It is used here in Japan very extensively for this purpose, and is also said to be a very good sand binder, but will probably not stand drought or salt water. It spreads very rapidly, but if it threatens to become troublesome by spreading, a ditch 2 feet wide by 2 feet deep, kept open by occasional redigging, will prevent its getting beyond control. A species whose value is in its decorative and sand-binding character. It is said to be quite hardy in England." (*Fairchild.*)

9054. Bamboo.

From Yokohama, Japan. Received through Messrs. Lathrop and Fairchild (No. 998, August, 1902), November, 1902.

Shakutan. "A broad-leaved species of bamboo which resembles in habit *Bambusa veitchii*, only the stems are much taller and the leaves are larger. It is suited for planting on embankments and under trees on a lawn to form a decorative mass of foliage. It is said to come from the Hokkaido and to be very hardy. It should be planted in lots of ten or more. In the Hokkaido the culms are used for pipe stems and a host of other objects where a small, hard, flinty pipe is desired. I can not find that this is commonly known in Europe under this name, though it comes near Mitford's description of *Bambusa palmata*, which he says is a striking ornamental species and evidently hardy; at least he says nothing to the contrary. It grows to a height of 5 feet." (*Fairchild.*)

9055. BAMBUSA VULGARIS. Bamboo.

From Yokohama, Japan. Received through Messrs. Lathrop and Fairchild (No. 999, August, 1902), November, 1902.

Taisau-chiku (?). "A tender variety of bamboo for Florida. This species comes from the hottest part of Japan and is the only species of the shipment not hardy. Its wood is said to be useful, though inferior to that of the hardy species. This may prove a different variety from those already in Florida under this specific name. Should be planted in lots of at least five." (*Fairchild.*)

9056. BAMBUSA ALPHONSE KARRI. Bamboo.

From Yokohama, Japan. Received through Messrs. Lathrop and Fairchild (No. 1000, August 9, 1902), November, 1902.

Suwochiku, or *Suochiku*. "A species of striped bamboo which is considered by Mitford as tender in England. It is an exceedingly pretty species and worthy of trial in clumps in Florida and southern California, where it should grow to a height of 10 feet. When young the culms appear in autumn of a purplish color, traversed with green stripes. This should be distributed in lots of at least 10 plants." (*Fairchild.*)

9057. ARUNDINARIA HINDSII. Bamboo.

From Yokohama, Japan. Received through Messrs. Lathrop and Fairchild (No. 1001, August, 1902), November, 1902.

Kanzan-chiku. "A species of bamboo which is commonly grown in clumps near the houses of the peasants in Japan. It forms a very pretty clump from 12 to 17 feet high and, although Mitford says his specimens were cut down to the ground by a severe winter, they grew up again, showing the species is not really tender. Should be tried in Florida, Arizona, or southern California. So far as I know, no use is made of this species except that of broom making." (*Fairchild.*)

9058. ARUNDINARIA HINDSII var. GRAMINEA. Bamboo.

From Yokohama, Japan. Received through Messrs. Lathrop and Fairchild (No. 1010, August, 1902), November, 1902.

Taimin-chiku. "A very decorative, narrow-leaved species of bamboo which is used in Japan for hedges and ornamental clumps. It grows 10 to 12 feet high and forms a dense thicket of slender stems. The foliage is narrow and grasslike and resembles, though it is narrower, that of *Arundinaria hindsii*, No. 9057. It is a very common form and is used for making baskets used in pressing oil from various seeds. It is probably less hardy than other forms like *Phyllostachys quilioi*." (*Fairchild.*)

9059. SOLANUM TUBEROSUM. **Potato.**

From Callao, Peru. Secured by Mr. Joseph C. Cree, United States vice-consul, October, 1902.

Papas amarillas. One-half bushel of native yellow potatoes.

9060. MYRICA FAYA.

From Fayal, Azores Islands. Presented by Hon. Moyses Benarus, United States consular agent.

This shrub or small tree grows on the sandy shores of these and other subtropical islands.

9061 to 9082.

From Buenos Ayres, Argentina. Presented by Señor Carlos D. Girola, chief of the division of agriculture. Received September 15, 1902.

A collection of seeds, as follows:

9061. CAREX DARWINII.
9062. CAREX DECIDUA.
9063. CAREX HAEMATORRHYNCA.
9064. CAREX MACLOVIANA.
9065. CAREX PSEUDOCYPERUS.
9066. JACARANDA CUSPIDIFOLIA.
9067. LIBOCEDRUS CHILENSIS.
9068. SCHINUS DENTATUS.
9069. SCHINUS DEPENDENS var. PATAGONICA.
9070. SCHINUS MONTANA.
9071. TECOMA sp.
9072. ARISTOTELIA MACQUI.
9073. CHORISIA INSIGNIS.
9074. COCOS AUSTRALIS.
9075. COCOS YATAY.
9076. ENTEROLOBIUM TIMBOUVA.
9077. ENTEROLOBIUM TIMBOUVA.
9078. FEIJOA SELLOWIANA.
9079. LARREA NITIDA.
9080. MACHAERIUM FERTILE.
9081. PROSOPIS DENUDANS.
9082. PIPTADENIA MACROCARPA.

9083 to 9122.

From Nice, France. Presented by Mr. A. Robertson-Proschowsky. Received October 24, 1902.

A collection of seeds, as follows:

9083. ACACIA ARMATA.
9084. ACACIA CYANOPHYLLA.
9085. ACACIA FARNESIANA.
9086. ALBIZZIA MOLUCCANA.
9087. ALBIZZIA ODORATISSIMA.
9088. ANCHUSA ITALICA.
9089. ASYSTASIA BELLA.
9090. CEANOTHUS AZUREUS.
9091. COBAEA SCANDENS.
9092. COMMELINA COELESTIS.
9093. CORONILLA ATLANTICA.
9094. CUPHEA IGNEA.
9095. CUPHEA SELENOIDES.
9096. CUPRESSUS SEMPERVIRENS.
9097. CYPERUS PAPYRUS.
9098. DIOTIS CANDIDISSIMA.
9099. ERIOBOTRYA JAPONICA.
"From large fruits of very good quality." (*Proschowsky.*)
9100. ERYNGIUM AGAVEFOLIUM.

9083 to 9122—Continued.

9101. EUPATORIUM ATRORUBENS.
"Very remarkable leaves and flowers." (*Proschowsky.*)

9102. GENISTA MONOSPERMA.
"A very ornamental bush." (*Proschowsky.*)

9103. IRIS GERMANICA.
Varieties.

9104. IRIS SIBERICA.
Varieties.

9105. KNIPHOFIA ALOIDES var. NOBILIS.

9106. LANTANA RADULA.

9107. LESPEDEZA BICOLOR.

9108. LINARIA SAXATILIS (?).

9109. MALVA SYLVESTRIS.

9110. MARISCUS NATALENSIS.

9111. MELALEUCA LEUCADENDRON.

9112. NOTOCHAETE HAMOSA.

9113. OPUNTIA GYMNOCARPA.
"A very large and ornamental cactus with delicious fruit." (*Proschowsky.*)

9114. OSYRIS ALBA.

9115. PELARGONIUM ZONALE.
Varieties.

9116. PHORMIUM TENAX.
"Foliage variegated, very beautiful." (*Proschowsky.*)

9117. PHYGELIUS CAPENSIS.

9118. PODACHAENIUM PANICULATUM.
"Very ornamental." (*Proschowsky.*)

9119. RIVINA HUMILIS.

9120. SOLANUM ERYTHROCARPUM.

9121. SOLANUM sp.

9122. STERCULIA ACERIFOLIA.

9123 and 9124.

From Paris, France. Received through Vilmorin-Andrieux & Co., November 3, 1902.

9123. OLEA LAURIFOLIA.   9124. OLEA VERRUCOSA.

9125. TRITICUM VULGARE.   **Wheat.**

From Kharkof, in the Starobelsk district, Russia. Received through Mr. E. A. Bessey (No. 108, July 25, 1902), November 4, 1902.

Kharkof. "Red, bearded, hard winter wheat from the Starobelsk district of the government of Kharkof. This is similar to the *Kharkof* wheat obtained last year, but from a region where the winters are much drier." (*Bessey.*)

9126. BALSAMORHIZA SAGITTATA.

From Bridges Peak, Mont. Received through Mr. V. K. Chesnut, of this Department, November 5, 1902.

9127 and 9128.

From Santiago, Chile. Presented by Señor Federico Albert, chief of the section of zoological and botanical investigations, department of industries and public works. Received November 12, 1902.

9127. LITHRAEA AROERINHA.

9128. PERSEA LINGUE.

9129. TRITICUM VULGARE. **Wheat.**

From Padi, Saratov government, Russia. Received through Mr. E. A. Bessey (No. 109, July 25, 1902), November 15, 1902.

Winter wheat. "A softish, light-colored wheat, with smooth heads. Said to have been originally grown from the Hungarian Banat, but is somewhat darker colored and harder." (*Bessey.*)

9130. TRITICUM DURUM. **Wheat.**

From Naples, Italy. Received through Messrs. Lathrop and Fairchild (No. 1076). Sample received by mail November 28, 1902; 300 kilos received December 10, 1902.

Saragolla. "Wheat grown in the province of Apulia, along the Adriatic coast of southern Italy. This wheat is esteemed by the producers of the famous Gragnano macaroni as the best in the world for the production of a delicate, fine-flavored product. It has not the strength of the Taganrog varieties, which, owing to the small quantity of native wheat securable, are imported into Italy for semola-making purposes. It has, however, a better flavor, I am told, and the yield of semola from it is greater per weight of grain than from any of the imported hard wheats. It, therefore, sells from 1.25 to 1.75 lire per quintal (100 kilos) higher than imported wheats, which have to pay an import duty as well. Macaroni made from this variety of wheat will not keep as long as that made from Taganrog sorts and is more liable to the attacks of insects, but for quick consumption (three to six months) it is considered superior, and the gourmets of Naples order their macaroni made of the *Saragolla* wheat. The climate of the region about Foggia, where the best of this variety is said to be grown, is one of the driest in Italy—only 18 inches of rainfall in the year—and the soil is said to be stiff but impregnated with lime—i. e., calcareous. This variety deserves the attention of American macaroni-wheat growers. As it comes from a region where the winters are mild, it will probably not prove hardy as a winter wheat north of the thirty-fifth parallel of latitude. The summer temperature of Apulia is high, but not commonly over 100° F. The heavy rains occur in autumn, spring, and winter." (*Fairchild.*)

9131. TRITICUM VULGARE. **Wheat.**

From Dzhizak, a town about 100 miles northwest of Samarcand, on the railroad. Obtained through the Samarcand representatives of Mr. H. W. Dürrschmidt by Mr. E. A. Bessey (No. 118, August 30, 1902). Received December 1, 1902.

Chul bidai (or *bugdai*), meaning *steppe wheat.* "This grain is grown on the Steppes without irrigation. The grains are hard, but it is not *T. durum* (according to Mr. Schifron). This variety yields two harvests a year, for it can be sown as either a winter or spring wheat. If the former, the harvest comes in July; if the latter, the harvest comes in September. If sown in the spring, it is sown just as soon as the snow melts. The spring-sown is the most certain to yield a good crop, for the fall-sown must depend upon the rather uncertain snows. This seed, however, is from the fall-sown seed, being obtained in July. It is selected from over 1,000 poods offered for sale and is remarkably clean and free from foreign seeds for this region." (*Bessey.*)

9132. CITRUS NOBILIS × CITRUS BIGARADIA. **Tangerine.**

From Mustapha, Algiers, Algeria. Presented by Dr. L. Trabut, Government Botanist. Received December 3, 1902.

Clementine.

9133. HORDEUM DISTICHUM NUTANS. **Barley.**

From Fort Atkinson, Wis. Received through Ex-Governor W. D. Hoard, December 5, 1902.

Hanna. Grown from No. 5793.

9134. MUSA TEXTILIS. **Manila hemp.**

From Manila, P. I. Presented by Mr. W. S. Lyon, of the Insular Bureau of Agriculture, to Mr. L. H. Dewey, Assistant Botanist, United States Department of Agriculture. Received December 15, 1902.

9135 to 9146. OPUNTIA sp. **Tuna.**

From Mexico. Received through Dr. Edward Palmer (Nos. 1 to 12), December 19, 1902.

A collection of seeds as follows:

9135.

Amarillos. "One of the finest of the Mansa forms of tuna and well suited to the use of travelers, being large and containing sufficient water to quench the thirst. Outside it is amber-yellow in color; inside it is decidedly amber or with orange patches. Very productive fruit of this form will be found in the market up to December. The flesh is firm, with the flavor of boiled carrots with a large admixture of sugar." (*Palmer.*) (No. 1.)

9136.

Cardona. "Nine pears of this variety sold in the San Luis Potosi market for 1 cent. It is a small, rich, sweet fruit. The flesh is blotched with maroon and red. The commonest and most useful of all the tunas, yielding a fair supply in December. This fruit is much used in making a summer drink known as 'colonche,' which is largely in use. *Queso de tuna*, tuna cheese, is a round cake made from *Tuna cardo*. The fruit is divested of its jacket and then rubbed through an earthenware strainer and the resulting mass is cooked six hours, then worked (like candy) until all the heat is expelled, and then put into round frames to harden. This is a commercial article all over Mexico. The tuna *Cardona* contains sugar enough to preserve it." (*Palmer.*) (No. 2.)

9137.

Durasnillo Blanco (little white peach tuna). "Sold in the market of San Luis Potosi, 25 for 1 cent. This tuna is eaten entire, not having its rind removed. The seeds are compacted in a wad to resemble a peach stone. It is but a second class fruit. Inside it resembles a white freestone peach, firm, acid-sweet, with water-colored pulp. Its rind is canary-colored outside. I think this tuna would make a good pickle." (*Palmer.*) (No. 3.)

9138.

Durasnillo Colorado, or little red peach tuna. "Sold 25 for 1 cent in the market of San Luis Potosi. The fruit is eaten entire. Fine acid-sweet, much relished by some. Has the flavor of some late freestone peaches. It is rose-colored on the outside and a rose-pink inside (with a fleecy white spot near the base and also at the apex of the fruit). The seeds are compacted inside in a mass to resemble a peach stone. I think this would make a good pickle." (*Palmer.*) (No. 4.)

9139.

Cuejas. "Sold 30 for 1 cent in the market at San Luis Potosi. A remarkably juicy fruit, with a delightful acid taste, which might make it suitable for wine and a fine jelly. The fruit is first dark mauve, then rich maroon, a color fine for wine and jelly. It is considered but a second-class fruit; nevertheless all that come to the market are consumed." (*Palmer.*) (No. 5.)

9140.

Cameosa. "A Mansa form, sold in the market of San Luis Potosi 9 for 1 cent. A fine rich fruit with a watermelon flavor, and very juicy, making it fine for a breakfast fruit. Inside it has white patches intermixed with its mealy, tempting pulp, which is rich reddish crimson in color. The exterior is a pink crimson. This much prized fruit is abundant until the end of October." (*Palmer.*) (No. 6.)

9141.

Mansa Colorado. "Sold in the market of San Luis Potosi 4 for 1 cent. Old fruit is a dark mauve on the outside and bright maroon inside. A juicy, agreeable fruit which might make a good wine. At the base is a white patch, and at the apex under the skin is a circle of rose color. Many consider this equal in quality to any tuna. Disappears from market at the end of October." (*Palmer.*) (No. 7.)

9135 to 9146—Continued.

9142.

Blanca mansa. "Sold in the market of San Luis Potosi in piles of 7 for 1 cent. The fruit is greenish-white outside and a lighter white (with an icy look) inside. An agreeable juicy flavor renders it fine for early meals. It has rather a thin skin, and is one of the choicest tunas. Out of season at end of October." (*Palmer.*) (No. 8.)

9143.

Toconostle. "Fruit resembling a peach, with seed compacted in the center to represent the stone. The outside is a soft green when the fruit is young and of a salmon color when it is older. The flesh is solid and has an acid taste. Marmalade is made of it by removing the rind and seed core, boiling in water to remove the sourness, and cooking in sugar in the usual manner for marmalade. The fruit is also eaten chopped up and fried. Good pickles are said to be made of it. It is also cut into pieces and put into soups or boiled with vegetables and meats, and can be preserved in the ordinary way. It is also candied to represent white Smyrna figs, being first boiled in water (after the seeds have been removed from the apex) and then in sugar the usual way for candied fruit." (*Palmer.*) (No. 9.)

9144.

Chavaña. "Sold 10 for 1 cent in the market of San Luis Potosi. The fruit is a dark-mauve color outside and lighter colored inside. The rind is rather thick. The fleshy parts represent lines of white circles, which contain the seeds, and between which are lines of light mauve pulp. The core is decidedly white. The flesh has a rich, sweet, juicy taste like no other tuna; may be nearest to a rich, juicy apple. This is a wild variety. Can be used for preserves and marmalade. It seems to be next to *Cardona* in the amount of sugar it contains." (*Palmer.*) (No. 10.)

9145.

Castilla Colorado. "In the market of San Luis Potosi 10 of these large, magnificent fruits can be bought for 1 cent. Purple-mauve on the outside, rich crimson inside, but the two ends of the fruit are inclined to be carmine at first, but in the fully mature fruit of a rich claret hue. The juice might pass for claret wine. One of the largest, showiest, and richest flavored, and perhaps equal in flavor to the richest pear. It is one of the rarest tunas, and is soon out of the market." (*Palmer.*) (No. 11.)

9146.

Blanca Castalina. "Four sold in the market of San Luis Potosi for 1 cent. Yellow-white on the outside, but of an icy whiteness inside. Flesh solid, not as moist as some of the *Mansas*, and with a very agreeable watermelon taste. It is large, and has a rather thin skin. There seems to be considerable sugar in the fruit. Abundant in the market until the end of October, when it begins to disappear." (*Palmer.*) (No. 12.)

9147 to 9160. PHASEOLUS sp. **Bean.**

From San Luis Potosi, Mexico. Received through Dr. Edward Palmer, December 19, 1902.

A collection of selected "frijoles" as follows:

9147.

Amarillo. "A third-class bean, said to be of good flavor. For trial in New Mexico, Arizona, and southern California." (*Palmer.*)

9148.

Ballo. "A first-class bean, the leader in quality, and greatly admired, particularly by the rich. It is a good producer, fair sized, and light in color, which latter quality should warrant its trial in the United States. It should be tried in New Mexico, Arizona, and southern California." (*Palmer.*)

9147 to 9160—Continued.

9149.

Berendo. "A second-class bean; not without merit, however, as it has a large number of purchasers. When the beans are old they are much darker than when new. Plant just before a rain. For trial in New Mexico, Arizona, and southern California." (*Palmer.*)

9150.

Blanco bolador. "A third-class bean, but may improve with cultivation. Only two lots were seen on the markets. It is generally eaten when no better bean can be had. After being boiled it is sometimes fried in lard. It resembles our lima bean. It should be tried in New Mexico, Arizona, and southern California." (*Palmer.*)

9151.

Borado. "Rated as a second-class bean, though it is good when fried. It has many purchasers. The variations shown in the piles in the market prove that it crosses freely. For trial in New Mexico, Arizona, and southern California." (*Palmer.*)

9152.

Blanco. "A third-class bean which does not seem to be a favorite. It closely resembles the white bean of the United States, and I refused to eat it if any colored beans were on hand. Grows with a small amount of water. For trial in New Mexico, Arizona, and southern California." (*Palmer.*)

9153.

Ballo almo halla (*Cacaguate*, peanut bean). "This bean resembles the kernel of a peanut. It is a first-class bean, relished by many for its flavor, and as it is of a light color may be a good one to cultivate. Try in New Mexico, Arizona, and southern California." (*Palmer.*)

9154.

Color de Rosa. "A second-class bean, and yet there are many who prefer it. It seems to cross freely, judging from the 'half castes' in the piles of beans on the market. Should be tried in New Mexico, Arizona, and southern California." (*Palmer.*)

9155.

Garbansillo. "A first-class bean preferred by many, as it has a rich flavor. It is white, and on that account might claim recognition by those who like no other color, however high the quality. It grows freely on the table-lands of Mexico, and therefore might grow upon our plains and surpass our white bean in quality and productiveness. Should succeed in Utah." (*Palmer.*)

9156.

Grullito. "A first-class bean in every respect, and has only the *Ballo* as a rival according to most people. It is said to yield bountifully. It should be tried in New Mexico, Arizona, and southern California." (*Palmer.*)

9157.

Gruyo. "A second-class bean which seems to be a good producer. For trial in New Mexico, Arizona, and southern California." (*Palmer.*)

9158.

Guevo de Vieja. "A second-class bean, not abundant in the market. For trial in New Mexico, Arizona, and southern California." (*Palmer.*)

9159.

Negro. "Rated as a third-class bean. It is grown only in the tropics, where no other bean thrives well. There it is appreciated. This sample came from Veracruz and was the purest in the market, either as regards adulteration or crossing. As a personal choice for permanent food, I should select this bean, as it has a satisfying quality to it. For trial in southern part of Florida." (*Palmer.*)

9147 to 9160—Continued.

9160.

Siguino. "A second-class bean, used a great deal. For trial in New Mexico, Arizona, and southern California." (*Palmer.*)

9161. PYRUS LONGIPES.

From Mustapha, Algiers, Algeria. Presented by Dr. L. Trabut, Government Botanist. Received December 23, 1902.

9162. EDGEWORTHIA GARDNERI. **Paper plant.**

From Shizuoka, Japan. Received through Messrs. Lathrop and Fairchild (No. 1008, August, 1902), January 6, 1903.

Mitsumata. "The paper plant, from which some of the finest Japanese paper is made. This fine paper is imported in large and increasing quantities into America, where it is used for legal paper, stocks and bonds, deeds, diplomas, etc. This plant requires especial attention, and a bulletin on its culture has appeared—B. P. I. Bulletin No. 42. In Japan the seeds are kept in bags of palm sheath fiber in a shallow hole in the floor of a house or shed, which is covered with boards to keep it dark. In planting in the spring, sow in rows in rich garden soil, and when several inches high transplant to nursery rows, and cultivate until large enough to plant out in permanent locations. It may, however, be planted out when only 8 to 9 inches high. The plant is semihardy, but is often given protection, even in Japan. A frost of 6 or more degrees will not kill it, as it is a deciduous plant. It seems to adapt itself to a variety of soils, and I believe it can be grown in arid regions by irrigation; at least it is worthy of trial in them. The paper pulp yielded by the bark is four times as valuable as ordinary wood pulp in Japan, and makes a quality of paper which for many uses is immeasurably superior to our wood pulp or even rag papers. This whole question of producing a bast paper in America is one worthy the serious consideration of our cultivators in the South. In Japan the cultivation of this species is increasing rapidly, I am told, and the consumption by foreigners of these fine *Mitsumata* papers is larger every year. The attempt to find out where the plant will grow should be made by the distribution of small potted plants rather than of seeds, and one of the main objects of this first importation of seeds is to discover how far north the plant will prove hardy. The bush grows about 6 feet high, is decorative, and is sometimes planted for its pretty yellow flowers." (*Fairchild.*)

9163. EDGEWORTHIA GARDNERI. **Paper plant.**

From Yokohama, Japan. Received through Messrs. Lathrop and Fairchild (No. 1011, August, 1902), January 6, 1903, and February 28, 1903.

(See No. 9162 for description.)

9164. MYRICA NAGI.

From Yokohama, Japan. Received through Messrs. Lathrop and Fairchild (No. 1009, August, 1902), January 6, 1903.

Yama momo. "Plants of the best variety of this fruit species. (See No. 9314.) The best kind, i. e., that producing the largest fruit, has serrated leaves, I am informed. Entire leaved forms produce smaller, scarcely edible fruits. This is a very slow-growing tree, which will not produce fruit for six or seven years. Possibly a few fruits will be produced in four years from these trees." (*Fairchild.*)

9165. WICKSTROEMIA CANESCENS. **Paper plant.**

From Yokohama, Japan. Received through Messrs. Lathrop and Fairchild (No. 1012, August, 1902), January 6, 1903.

Gampi. "A species of tree from which the noted *Gampi* paper is made. This plant has never been cultivated in Japan, but grows wild in the mountains of the provinces of Yamato, Ise, Mino, etc. The demand for the bark is so great that the plant is being killed out. The paper made from its bark is the toughest, finest, silkiest paper in the world, and is used for the manufacture of letter press-copying books, etc. In America many of these Japanese letter books are in use, and the export of this *Gampi* paper is an important one for Japan. The plant will probably do best in the mountains of the South, and the young plants should be distributed to such persons as can give them a trial by setting them out, a few in a place, to ascertain how hardy the species is. The plant is easily propagated by root cuttings, and this method should be used to secure a small forest of it. The species runs readily by means of shoots from the root, and trees 2 inches in diameter were not unusual before the big demand set up for this delicate *Gampi* paper. Now it is difficult, it is said, to find trees of more than a few feet in height. If this species can be brought into forest cultivation it will add to the market a paper pulp of the greatest value." (*Fairchild.*)

9166. ARALIA CORDATA. Udo.

From Yokohama, Japan. Received through Messrs. Lathrop and Fairchild (No. 1013, August, 1902), February 28, 1903.

Kan Udo. "Seed of a new salad plant called *Udo*. This is described in B. P. I. Bulletin No. 42. It is a delicate, new salad which should find a most acceptable place on the tables of well-to-do Americans, for it comes into season in October and November. It is as crisp as celery, and has a refreshing flavor quite its own." (*Fairchild.*)

9167. ARALIA CORDATA. Udo.

From Yokohama, Japan. Received through Messrs. Lathrop and Fairchild (No. 1014, August, 1902), January 6, 1903.

Kan Udo. "Roots of the same variety of *Udo* as No. 9166. For description see B. P. I. Bulletin No. 42. This variety should be given a different treatment from that given to No. 9168, *Moyashi Udo.*" (*Fairchild.*)

9168. ARALIA CORDATA. Udo.

From Yokohama, Japan. Received through Messrs. Lathrop and Fairchild (No. 1016, August, 1902), January 6, 1903.

Moyashi Udo. "Young roots of the forcing *Udo*, a new salad plant of great promise. These roots should be kept packed in straw, where they will not dry out nor mold, in a cool storage place until next spring, when they should be planted out in rows 2 by 3 feet apart, and cultivated all summer as potatoes are cultivated. In the autumn, after the leaves die, the old roots are dug and packed closely together in the bottom of a trench 2 feet deep, and covered with leaf-mold and rich loam to force them into growth. The blanched shoots, 2-3 feet long and as big as a man's thumb, are as tender as celery, and make a delicious salad if shaved and served with a French dressing. This forcing variety is likely to be useful throughout the South. See B. P. I. Bulletin No. 42." (*Fairchild.*)

9169. ARALIA CORDATA. Udo.

From Yokohama, Japan. Received through Messrs. Lathrop and Fairchild (No. 1016a, August, 1902), January 6, 1903.

Moyashi Udo. "Old roots, which should be planted out next spring in rows 2 by 3 feet apart, cultivated all the season, and next winter forced by burying in a trench, as has been described for No. 9168. These old roots will produce good-sized shoots the first winter's forcing, while young roots will produce only a few small ones." (*Fairchild.*)

9170 to 9199. PRUNUS PSEUDO-CERASUS var. HORTENSIS.
Flowering cherries.

From Yokohama, Japan. Received through Messrs. Lathrop and Fairchild (No. 1017, August, 1902), January 6, 1903.

"A collection of the different varieties of flowering cherries from a noted grower in Tokyo—Mr. Takagi. There are hundreds of slightly different sorts of this flowering cherry, which is, as is well known, the favorite flower of the Japanese. It is inconceivable that Europeans and Americans have not followed the example of this race of flower lovers and planted long avenues or whole hillsides with this superbly beautiful plant. As an avenue tree in summer, the cherry would not be a success except when mingled with some other sort, but its beauty during the spring months warrants its being planted in big masses in our large parks instead of as single, isolated trees. The beauty of the cherry trees of Japan lies in the fact that there are miles of them or acres of them in bloom at once. Great care should be taken to keep the names of the varieties straight, to enable other plants to be ordered if desired later. These flowering cherries can be grafted on our wild cherry or on any good cherry stock. Single, double, and weeping sorts are included in this shipment. A list follows." (*Fairchild.*)

9170.
Nara Sakura.

9171.
Oshiogun.

9172.
Chioshiu hisakura.

9173.
Oyama fugin.

9174.
Yokihi.

9175.
Kuramayama.

9176.
Ito Kukuri.

9177.
Surugadai nioi.

9178.
Ogasa yama.

9179.
Gozanoma.

9180.
Ichio.

9181.
Daijen.

9182.
Botun sakura

9183.
Ochiochin.

9184.
Omanogawa.

9185.
Horinshi.

9186.
Amayadori.

9187.
Yedosakura.

9188.
Ouchisakura.

9189.
Shiogama.

9190.
Higurashi.

9191.
Bauriko.

9192.
Rui arashi.

9193.
Tamamari.

9194.
Ukon.

9195.
Kangosan.

9196.
Murasaki sakura.

9197.
Gayeakehono.

9198.
Shirofugin.

9199.
Sikigan.

9200. PRUNUS MUME. **Japanese plum.**

From Yokohama, Japan. Received through Messrs. Lathrop and Fairchild (No. 1018, August, 1902), January 6, 1903.

Rinshiu. "The favorite variety used for stocks by the Japanese nurserymen. This is worthy of trial as a vigorous, resistant stock upon which to bud both European and American varieties of plum. It should be tried by nurserymen interested in the question of the influence of the stock on the scion. The fruit of the Japanese apricot is used principally for pickling purposes. The trees are unusually vigorous growers, heavy bearers, and are considered the best commercial plum trees of the *Ume* class in the nursery region of Ikeda, Japan." (*Fairchild.*)

9201. PRUNUS TOMENTOSA. **Japanese cherry.**

From Tokyo, Japan. Received through Messrs. Lathrop and Fairchild (No. 1015, August, 1902), February 28, 1903.

"A decorative cherry with fruits the size of a large pea and sessile, or nearly so, on the long, slender branches. The fruits are edible, but not of good quality. For breeders and as an ornamental species. The fruits have a considerable amount of pulp on them and are much more delicate than those of the American choke cherry." (*Fairchild.*)

9202 to 9210. PRUNUS TRIFLORA. **Japanese plum.**

From Yokohama, Japan. Received through Messrs. Lathrop and Fairchild (No. 1019, August, 1902), January 6, 1903.

"Fruiting plums of the *Hatankyo* class. Great confusion exists in the nomenclature of these Japanese plums. The *Hatankyo* class is often confused with the *Botankyo*. The early ripening sorts are sometimes called *Hatankyo*; the late ripening kinds *Botankyo*. They are the largest of the true plums of Japan, and have a smooth skin like the European species. Said to be shy bearers and not as profitable for commercial purposes as the *Sumomo* class of small-sized, thin-skinned, soft-fleshed fruit. These *Hatankyos* or *Hatankios* are somewhat like the *Burbank* and *Wickson* in type. They are hard fleshed, and make the best stewed plums I have ever eaten. A list of the varieties follows." (*Fairchild.*) (See also Nos. 9222 and 9223.)

9202.	9207.
Okutsmo.	*Ohatankyo.*
9203.	9208.
Furugiya.	*Ringotane.*
9204.	9209.
Nakatesumomo.	*Hakubotan.*
9205.	9210.
Hachioji.	*Benibotan.*
9206.	
Suikamomo.	

9211 to 9216. PRUNUS MUME. **Japanese plum.**

From Yokohama, Japan. Received through Messrs. Lathrop and Fairchild (No. 1020, August, 1902), January 6, 1903.

"One-year-old plants of the *Ume* class of Japanese plums. These are quite different from European and American plum varieties, having a short but distinct pubescence. The fruit is exceedingly sour and is not designed for table use, except in the form of pickles. These pickles are the sourest things I have ever tasted, and are consumed in large quantities in Japan, being pickled with the leaves of a labiate, *Perilla arguta*, which give the plums a reddish color and aromatic taste. They are not much relished by Europeans, because of their intensely sour flavor. This class of plums is well known in America among breeders, but a collection of the different varieties will doubtless be acceptable for purposes of comparison. It is more like the apricot plum than anything else." (*Fairchild.*)

9217 to 9220. AMYGDALUS PERSICA. **Japanese peach.**

From Yokohama, Japan. Received through Messrs. Lathrop and Fairchild (No. 1021, August, 1902), January 6, 1903.

"A collection of one-year-old plants of Japanese peach varieties. There are a number of distinct varieties of these Japanese peaches, and some are fairly sweet and many are unusually juicy. It is not possible for me to say how recently these sorts may have been introduced into Japan from China. A list of the varieties follows." (*Fairchild.*)

9217.
Hanbei.

9218.
Nasehi maru.

9219.
Kintoki.

9220.
Mizumito.

9221. AMYGDALUS PERSICA. **Nectarine.**

From Yokohama, Japan. Received through Messrs. Lathrop and Fairchild (No. 1022, August, 1902), January 6, 1903.

Chosen or Korean nectarine. "A freestone variety, with smooth, almost greasy skin, which is sold everywhere in the markets in July in Japan. It is a juicy, white-fleshed sort, bitter near the stone, but with a decided and agreeable peach flavor." (*Fairchild.*)

9222 and 9223. PRUNUS TRIFLORA. **Japanese plum.**

From Yokohama, Japan. Received through Messrs. Lathrop and Fairchild (No. 1019, August, 1902), January 6, 1903.

(These two varieties were incorrectly labeled "L. & F., No. 1017," and packed with that lot.) (See Nos. 9202 to 9210.)

9222.
Kowase.

9223.
Yome momo.

9224. ARALIA CORDATA. **Udo.**

From Yokohama, Japan. Received through Messrs. Lathrop and Fairchild (No. 1016, August, 1902), January 6, 1903.

Moyashi udo. A new salad plant of great promise. (See No. 9168.)

9225. VICIA GEMELLA.

From Yokohama, Japan. Secured by Messrs. Lathrop and Fairchild (not numbered) through the Yokohama Nursery Company. Received February 28, 1903.

9226. LAGENARIA sp. **Gourd.**

From Yokohama, Japan. Presented by the Yokohama Nursery Company. Packed with seeds secured by Messrs. Lathrop and Fairchild. Received February 28, 1903.

Kanpio gourd.

9227. PUERARIA THUNBERGIANA. **Kudzu.**

From Yokohama, Japan. Received through Messrs. Lathrop and Fairchild (No. 1023, August, 1902), February 28, 1903.

Kudzu. "This broad-leaved, perennial, leguminous climber is well known in America, being often seen in private gardens where it is used as an arbor plant or to produce tropical effects by allowing it to grow over the tops of bushes or low-growing trees. For this purpose alone it is a valuable plant. In Japan the fleshy roots are used for starch making and the foliage is cut and fed to cattle for fodder. Whole hillsides are sometimes covered with this plant in Japan, where it grows wild, and in these regions its foliage is utilized for fodder purposes and a fine quality of starch is made from its roots. It should be tested as a fodder-producing plant in waste places. The seed should be sown in a seed bed and the young plants set out in rich soil. I am told it does not withstand much drought." (*Fairchild.*)

9228. PUERARIA THUNBERGIANA. **Kudzu.**

From Yokohama, Japan. Received through Messrs. Lathrop and Fairchild (No. 1024, August, 1902), January 6, 1903.

"*Kudzu* roots for trial as a fodder plant. These roots should be planted in a single plat about 5 feet apart each way and the vines allowed to grow over the ground in all directions. It is possible that by repeatedly cutting the shoots back before they are too tough a continuous supply of fodder may be secured. The plant is a leguminous one and may be of service for breeders." (*Fairchild.*)

9229. MEDICAGO DENTICULATA.

From Yokohama, Japan. Received through Messrs. Lathrop and Fairchild (No. 1025, August, 1902), January 6, 1903.

Uma goyashi. "A biennial wild-fodder *Medicago* with yellow flowers, which grows 2 feet in height. Its stems are said to be highly relished by horses, which eat them greedily in the spring. So far as I have observed the plant is not cultivated." (*Fairchild.*)

9230. LESPEDEZA BUERGERI.

From Yokohama, Japan. Received through Messrs. Lathrop and Fairchild (No. 1026, August, 1902), February 28, 1903.

No Hagi. "The species of *Hagi* in Japan are especially prized for ornamental purposes and their summer and autumn flowers are used extensively for decoration. This species, the *No Hagi*, is said to be a good fodder plant, but how it is used I have been unable to discover. It is a low, bushy, hardy perennial." (*Fairchild.*)

9231. JUGLANS REGIA. **Walnut.**

From Shanghai, China. Received through Messrs. Lathrop and Fairchild (No. 953, May 10, 1902), January 6, 1903.

"A variety of walnut bought on the market in Shanghai. This variety is said to be eaten all the year round by the Chinese. I could not find from which province it came." (*Fairchild.*)

9232. JUGLANS REGIA. **Walnut.**

From Hongkong, China. Received through Messrs. Lathrop and Fairchild, January 6, 1903.

These few nuts are from a lot secured by Mr. H. Suzuki, of the Yokohama Nursery Company, Yokohama, Japan, and may be slightly different from No. 9231.

9233. PRUNUS TRIFLORA. **Japanese plum.**

From Ikeda, Japan. Received through Messrs. Lathrop and Fairchild (No. 968), January 6, 1903.

Hatankyo. "A special sort of this common variety of plum. This fruit has a decided red blush upon it and is not of that translucent yellow which is said to characterize the sort in other parts of Japan. In flavor it leaves a good deal to be desired." (*Fairchild.*)

9234. THERMOPSIS FABACEA.

From Yokohama, Japan. Received through Messrs. Lathrop and Fairchild (No. 1030), from the Yokohama Nursery Company. Received February 28, 1903.

Sendai Hagi. "Seed of this yellow flowered variety, 1 foot high, perennial, said to be very showy." (*Fairchild.*)

9235. PRUNUS TRIFLORA? **Japanese plum.**

From Ikeda, Japan. Received through Messrs. Lathrop and Fairchild (No. 969), January 6, 1903.

Guanji. "A small fruited sort, 1 inch in diameter, bought in the orchard. Though differing little from No. 9236, it seems well to keep them apart. This is a vinous flavored variety, flattened in shape, with thin, sour skin, rich flavored flesh, and altogether the most delicate plum I have eaten in Japan, though not to be compared with a good variety of *Prunus domestica*. It is said to be the best paying plum in Ikeda, the plum-growing center of Japan." (*Fairchild.*)

9236. PRUNUS TRIFLORA? **Japanese plum.**

From Ikeda, Japan. Received through Messrs. Lathrop and Fairchild (No. 970, July 5, 1902), January 6, 1903.

Guanji. "Seeds bought on the market. This is essentially the same as No. 9235, though the fruit is somewhat larger and not quite so sweet. It is evidently one of the principal market plums, for one sees it everywhere, whether under this or some other name." (*Fairchild.*)

9237. VICIA HIRSUTA.

From Yokohama, Japan. Received through Messrs. Lathrop and Fairchild (No. 1033, August, 1902), February 28, 1903.

Suzumeno yendo. "A leguminous plant worthy of investigation as a possible fodder plant or for breeding experiments, as it is said to be occasionally used in Japan for fodder. I was unable to see this species growing." (*Fairchild.*)

9238. DESMODIUM PODOCARPUM var. JAPONICUM.

From Yokohama, Japan. Received through Messrs. Lathrop and Fairchild (No. 1034, August, 1902), February 28, 1903.

Nusubito Hagi. "A species of Leguminosæ of possible use in breeding experiments with leguminous fodder plants. I did not see the plant growing." (*Fairchild.*)

9239 to 9243. PYRUS SINENSIS. **Japanese pear.**

From Yokohama, Japan. Received through Messrs. Lathrop and Fairchild (No. 1035, August, 1902), January 6, 1903.

"This collection will include, according to contract, some sorts which keep until July and even longer, and some very large-fruited kinds, which originated in the north of Japan. I have eaten many varieties of pear in Japan and, while none are as good as our pears, they are, nevertheless, refreshing fruits. I believe they should be advertised as a fruit for poor people, since the trees are heavy bearers and the fruit will keep well. In Japan nearly all the trees seen were trained upon overhead trellises, and it seems to be the popular idea that they will not bear well unless so trained. The selection of these varieties has been left to Mr. H. Suzuki, of the Yokohama Nursery Company, whose friend at Kawasaki is a specialist in Japan pears. A list follows." (*Fairchild.*)

9239.
Waseaka.

9240.
Ofurugawa.

9241. (Label missing.)

9242.
Tai haka.

9243.
Chiojuro.

9244 to 9247. ERIOBOTRYA JAPONICA. **Loquat.**

From Yokohama, Japan. Received through Messrs. Lathrop and Fairchild (No. 1036, August, 1902), January 6, 1903.

Japanese loquats, called *Biwas* in Japan, as follows:

9244.
Tanaka. (See No. 8890.)

9245.
Long fruit.

9246.
Variegated.

9247.
Maruni.

9248 to 9267. NELUMBIUM SPECIOSUM. **Lotus.**

From Tokyo, Japan. Received through Messrs. Lathrop and Fairchild (No. 1039, August, 1902), January 6, 1903.

"A collection of pot lotuses for cultivation under water in large shallow pots of 2 feet in diameter and a foot deep. These plants are from a noted lotus grower in Tokyo, who claims to have hundreds of varieties and whose lotus show in late August is said to be unusually fine. The rhizomes of these pot lotuses are kept in a cool place over winter and in spring set out in 6 to 8 inches of rich mud at the bottom of the pots, which are kept filled to within an inch of the brim with water. The second year these rhizomes should bloom and produce a beautiful show of flowers. Judging from water-color sketches, which I saw in the Tokyo Botanic Gardens, the variety of form and color among these lotuses must be something quite unusual. All shades of pink, yellow, and green, and many variegated forms were represented. The pots should never be allowed to dry out, but the mud must be kept continually covered with water. The varieties are as follows." (*Fairchild.*)

9248.
Inazuma.

9249.
Shiro Shakuyaku.

9250.
Beni botan.

9251.
Sakuralen.

9252.
Kayo.

9253.
Tokalen.

9254.
Kinshi.

9255.
Nishikilen.

9256.
Mangitsu.

9257.
Itten kobai.

9258.
Tenjiku len.

9259.
Hakubotan.

9260.
Usuyo.

9261.
Shokan.

9262.
Giosan.

9263.
Nankin kuchibin.

9264.
Ashimaru.

9265.
Myiyo.

9266.
Beni Tinshi.

9267.
Tamausagi.

9268. CITRUS BIGARADIA? **Bitter orange.**

From Yokohama, Japan. Received through Messrs. Lathrop and Fairchild (No. 1040, August, 1902), January 6, 1903.

Natsu Mikan or *Natsu Shiro.* "An especially fine variety of the bitter orange. This is a remarkable fruit and worthy the serious attention of citrus growers. It is not of such fine flavor as our pomelo, but still is sufficiently palatable to serve the same purpose, and it matures at a different time of the year. *This fruit is common on the market from April until the middle of August* in Japan and, although in August it is a poor fruit, it still serves very well as a morning appetizer. This is the commonest, often the only citrous fruit to be seen on the Japanese markets in July, and I judge the number of tons consumed every year is very large. The tree is said to be a vigorous-growing one and a good bearer. This variety is also one of the hardiest citrus sorts in Japan, withstanding a temperature of + 12° F. on the west coast of the main island. An important point in the culture of this variety is to leave the fruit hanging as long a time as possible on the trees, not picking it green and allowing it to ripen." (*Fairchild.*)

9269. CITRUS DECUMANA. **Pomelo.**

From Yokohama, Japan. Received through Messrs. Lathrop and Fairchild (No. 1041, August, 1902), January 6, 1903.

Asa hikan. "I understand this is a summer-ripening pomelo." (*Fairchild.*)

9270. PRUNUS TRIFLORA. **Japanese plum.**

From Ikeda, Japan. Received through Messrs. Lathrop and Fairchild (No. 971, July 5, 1902), January 6, 1903.

Obeni. "A flattened variety, looking much like a large *Guanji* (see No. 9236), though lacking its flavor. The skin and flesh are intensely sour even when nearly ripe. Never sweet enough to be good eating. These fruits were bought on the market." (*Fairchild.*)

9271. CITRUS NOBILIS. **Mandarin orange.**

From Yokohama, Japan. Received through Messrs. Lathrop and Fairchild (No. 1043, August, 1902), January 6, 1903.

Unshu or *Unshiu Mikan.* "This is the best Japanese mandarin orange. It is said to be quite seedless and very juicy. I do not believe it is the equal of our best mandarin oranges, but its seedless character makes it valuable. It is grown extensively all over middle Japan, especially in the Province of Kii. It is already known in America." (*Fairchild.*)

9272. CITRUS DECUMANA. **Pomelo.**

From Yokohama, Japan. Received through Messrs. Lathrop and Fairchild (No. 1044, August, 1902), January 6, 1903.

Aya buntan. "A red-fleshed variety of pomelo which is eaten with great relish by the Japanese. It is doubtless inferior in flavor to our best pomelos, but its red flesh is a character of value." (*Fairchild.*)

9273. PRUNUS TRIFLORA. **Japanese plum.**

From Ikeda, Japan. Received through Messrs. Lathrop and Fairchild (No. 972, July 5, 1902), January 6, 1903.

Obeni. "These fruits came direct from orchard trees which are noted for producing especially fine fruits. They were certainly much larger and finer than those bought on the market, and I believe this is a different strain from No. 9270." (*Fairchild.*)

9274 and 9275. CITRUS JAPONICA. **Kumquat.**

Received through Messrs. Lathrop and Fairchild (Nos. 1046 and 1047, August, 1902), January 6, 1903.

Nagami-kinkan. "Two varieties of these kumquats were ordered, but the Yokohama Nursery Company sent only the one sort marked *Nagami-kinkan*, which is said to be an elliptical or obovate fruited kind." (*Fairchild.*)

9276. MYRICA FAYA.

From Madeira. Presented by Mr. J. B. Blandy, of Funchal. Received February 21, 1903.

9277. CELTIS SINENSIS.

From Yokohama, Japan. Received through Messrs. Lathrop and Fairchild (No. 1049, August, 1902), February 28, 1903.

"One of the prettiest shade trees in Japan, suitable for avenues or private gardens, parks, etc. It resembles *C. australis* which is so commonly used in Algiers and southern Spain, but does not attain the large size of this species, so far as I have observed. It should be tried in the Southwest as a shade tree." (*Fairchild.*)

9278. CORYLUS ROSTRATA. **Hazelnut.**

From Yokohama, Japan. Received through Messrs. Lathrop and Fairchild (No. 1050, August, 1902), February 28, 1903.

Hashibami. "Seeds of this wild species of hazelnut which may prove valuable for breeding purposes. The nut is not highly prized in Japan, and is nowhere given the attention that the hazelnut gets along the Black Sea or in Istria." (*Fairchild.*)

9279. PRUNUS TRIFLORA. **Japanese plum.**

From Kobe, Japan. Received through Messrs. Lathrop and Fairchild (No. 973), January 6, 1903.

Obeni. "Seed, originally from Ikeda, that was bought on the market in Kobe. It is very much like No. 9270. It is evidently one of the favorite market plums of this region. It resembles the American wild-goose plum. The trees are reported to be regular and heavy bearers." (*Fairchild.*)

9280. JUGLANS CORDIFORMIS. **Walnut.**

From Yokohama, Japan. Received through Messrs. Lathrop and Fairchild (No. 1052, August, 1902), January 6, 1903.

Himegurumi. "A long, pointed walnut which is a narrower and slenderer type than that called in Japan *Otafuku.* Probably both seed variations of the same species." (*Fairchild.*)

9281. PRUNUS TRIFLORA. **Japanese plum.**

From Kobe, Japan. Received through Messrs. Lathrop and Fairchild (No. 974, July 7, 1902), January 6, 1903.

Sumomo of Awaji Island. "A delicate variety, like our wild-goose plums in quality. A thin-skinned, juicy, sour-fleshed, bright-red, translucent variety, with small stone, and a slightly bitter taste near the stone." (*Fairchild.*)

9282. PERILLA OCYMOIDES.

From Yokohama, Japan. Received through Messrs. Lathrop and Fairchild (No. 1054, August, 1902), February 28, 1902.

"Seed of a labiate which is grown extensively in Japan for oil-producing purposes. The oil expressed from the seed is considered the best known for the manufacture of the remarkable oil and leather papers of Japan. It takes the place of linseed, which, I am informed, is not so good for this purpose. The plant can be grown very easily by irrigation or without it in regions where soil is cheap, and there is a possibility that it could be produced cheaply enough to make it a profitable article of export. It should be tried in the irrigated regions of the Southwest. I am informed that Australia imports the oil and the seed also from Japan. In Japan the seed is sown in a nursery bed in the middle of June, and the young plants are transplanted about the 1st of July into rows 2 to 3 feet apart and set 6 inches apart in the row. The ordinary methods of cultivation to keep down the weeds are all that are necessary. It is not grown here on irrigated land. The seed ripens in November. In America it could probably be planted earlier and harvested earlier. According to the owner of an oil mill in Yamada, 100 plants of Perilla yield 1 sho = 0.39 gallon of seed, 17 per cent of which by volume is oil. The price of this oil in Japan, as quoted by the oil mill owner, is 45 yen per koku (1 koku = 39.7 gallons; 1 yen = 50 cents). The seeds are likely to fall out of the dry calyx if left until overripe, and I am told the yield is therefore best in wet seasons. The crop is a variable one, and the price therefore quite variable. Land is so valuable in Japan that this crop does not rank as a good paying one, but if grown on cheap land, in Washington State, for example, it might be produced so cheaply as to pay very well. It is worth a trial at least in the wet regions of Washington." (*Fairchild.*)

9283. RICINUS COMMUNIS. **Castor oil bean.**

From Yokohama, Japan. Received through Messrs. Lathrop and Fairchild (No. 1055, August, 1902), January 7, 1903.

"For breeding purposes. By request." (*Fairchild.*)

9284. AMYGDALUS PERSICA.   **Japanese nectarine.**

From Kobe, Japan. Received through Messrs. Lathrop and Fairchild (No. 975, July 7, 1902), January 6, 1903.

Zumbai momo. "The only variety of nectarines said to be seen on the Kobe market." (*Fairchild.*)

9285. AMYGDALUS PERSICA.   **Japanese peach.**

From Kobe, Japan. Received through Messrs. Lathrop and Fairchild (No. 976, July 7, 1902), January 6, 1903.

Taruya. "A typical honey peach, an old va.iety on the Kobe market. Least valuable and least abundant here." (*Fairchild.*)

9286. TRICHOSANTHES CUCUMEROIDES.

From Yokohama, Japan. Received through Messrs. Lathrop and Fairchild (No. 1058, August, 1902), February 28, 1903.

"Seed of a wild perennial vine of the cucurbit family, which has large, dark-green leaves of unusually beautiful velvet texture. I have never seen such beautiful foliage except on some tropical aroids. This vine I have only seen growing in the shade or semishade of Cryptomeria trees, but I am assured it will grow well in the bright sunlight. If this is true it promises to be an interesting addition to our arbor plants, and deserves to be given the widest possible distribution. Its flowers are said to be very pretty, while its fruit, about the size of a duck's egg, is showy and useful, in Japan at least, where it takes the place of soap. The roots are used for starch production. The seed should be planted in the same way that cucumber seeds are planted. The roots will probably prove hardy all over the United States, but during the first winter some of them should be dug up and kept in a cold house." (*Fairchild.*)

9287. TRICHOSANTHES CUCUMEROIDES.

From Yokohama, Japan. Received through Messrs. Lathrop and Fairchild (No. 1059, August, 1902), February 28, 1902.

"Roots of No. 9286 for immediate trial. They should be planted out next spring after being kept like dahlia roots through the winter." (*Fairchild.*)

9288. TRICHOSANTHES JAPONICA.

From Yokohama, Japan. Received through Messrs. Lathrop and Fairchild (No. 1060, August, 1902), February 28, 1903.

"Seed of a species of cucurbit, related to Nos. 9286 and 9287, but with broader, larger leaves, which have not such a velvety texture. It is said to have fruit twice the size of the latter. These fruits are eaten after preserving in soy or salt. Starch is made from the roots. For trial as an arbor plant." (*Fairchild.*)

9289. SOLANUM sp. (?)   **"Kiswaheli" tomato.**

From Tanga, German East Africa. Received through Messrs. Lathrop and Fairchild (No. 1085, January 18, 1903), March 3, 1903.

Ngogwe or *Njanja*: "A native tomato grown by the Kiswahelis of the Tanga region. The fruit is 1½ inches in diameter, egg-shaped, brilliant light red, thick skinned, and with rough protuberances at its apex. The flesh is scanty and with little flavor, placentæ tough, and with many seeds. The negroes say it is a perennial plant, grown everywhere, about 4 feet high." (*Fairchild.*)

9290. TAMARIX CHINENSIS.

From Yokohama, Japan. Received through Messrs. Lathrop and Fairchild (No. 1062, August, 1902), January 6, 1903.

"A species of *Tamarix* which has finer and more delicate foliage than *T. gallica.* It should be tried in Florida and California along the seashore drives in comparison with the ordinary species." (*Fairchild.*)

9291. XANTHOXYLON PIPERITUM. Japanese pepper.

From Yokohama, Japan. Received through Messrs. Lathrop and Fairchild (No. 1063, August, 1902), February 28, 1903.

"A small shrub, the leaves of which are very agreeably aromatic and are used most effectively by Japanese housewives and by Europeans in Japan as a garniture. It would form a very acceptable variation from the conventional parsley. The small round fruits, flower buds, and leaves are boiled with meat dishes to give them a flavor, and the fruits are always served after eels as a digestive." (*Fairchild.*)

9292. TROCHODENDRON ARALIOIDES. Birdlime tree.

From Yokohama, Japan. Received through The Yokohama Nursery Company, February 28, 1903.

(This seed was apparently substituted by the Nursery Company for L. and F. No. 1064, *Ilex integra.*) (See 9293.)

9293. TROCHODENDRON ARALIOIDES. Birdlime tree.

From Yokohama, Japan. Received through Messrs. Lathrop and Fairchild (No. 1065, August, 1902), January 6, 1903.

"A species of tree the bark of which is macerated and made into birdlime in Japan. This tree produces the best birdlime in the country, it is said, and there is an export of the article to Europe." (*Fairchild.*)

9294. FAGOPYRUM ESCULENTUM. Buckwheat.

From Yokohama, Japan. Received through Messrs. Lathrop and Fairchild (No. 1066, August, 1902), January 6, 1903.

Sando Soba. From Nagano. "This Nagano buckwheat is famous in Japan, where all sorts of cakes, macaroni, and tarts are made from its flour. The question of the uses of buckwheat in Japan would form a very interesting and profitable study, for there are a hundred ways, I imagine, in which the buckwheat is employed, whereas we know of only a few." (*Fairchild.*)

9295. FAGOPYRUM ESCULENTUM. Buckwheat.

From Yokohama, Japan. Received through Messrs. Lathrop and Fairchild (No. 1067, August, 1902), January 6, 1903.

"A species of *Fagopyrum* which is said to be inferior to *F. esculentum*, but is cultivated and may be of interest for breeding purposes." (*Fairchild.*)

9296. JUNIPERUS CHINENSIS var. PROCUMBENS.

From Yokohama, Japan. Received through Messrs. Lathrop and Fairchild (No. 1068, August, 1902), January 6, 1903.

"A beautiful procumbent juniper which is used most effectively as a substitute for lawns on sloping embankments. It covers them with a mass of luxuriant foliage which is strikingly effective. In the Tokyo Botanic Gardens there is a very attractive lawn made in this way. The plants should be set about 3 feet apart each way and allowed to run freely in all directions until they completely cover the ground with a thick mat 12 to 18 inches deep. It will probably prove hardy about Washington." (*Fairchild.*)

9297 and 9298. SOLANUM MELONGENA. Eggplant.

From Yokohama, Japan. Received through Messrs. Lathrop and Fairchild (No. 1069, August, 1902), January 6, 1903.

9297.

Naga nasu. "Considered the best variety in Japan, where eggplants are very largely eaten. They are even used for candying purposes. A candied eggplant is very delicate indeed, tasting something like a fig." (*Fairchild.*)

9298.

Maru nasu. "A round, black variety of eggplant, sold everywhere in the markets of Japan." (*Fairchild.*)

9299. ZOYSIA PUNGENS. **Japanese lawn grass.**

From Yokohama, Japan. Received through Messrs. Lathrop and Fairchild (No. 1071, August, 1902), January 6, 1903.

Birodoshiba. "A very fine-leaved lawn grass which forms a most beautiful velvet-like turf. The plant is said to have originated in southern Japan, to be sensitive to frost, but to be one of the prettiest lawn grasses in the country. It should be tested in California and Florida, where good lawn grasses are desired." (*Fairchild.*)

9300. ZOYSIA PUNGENS. **Japanese lawn grass.**

From Yokohama, Japan. Received through Messrs. Lathrop and Fairchild (No. 1072, August, 1902), January 6, 1903.

"A coarser leaved species of lawn grass than No. 9299, but otherwise of similar habit. These potted plants should be split up into a large number of small pieces and set out as is usually done with lawn grasses not grown from seed. It is said to be hardier than No. 9299." (*Fairchild.*)

9301. ALLIUM FISTULOSUM. **Forcing onion.**

From Yokohama, Japan. Received through Messrs. Lathrop and Fairchild (No. 1073, August, 1902), January 6, 1903.

"The seed is sown in spring and the young onions are dug in July and inclined in long deep trenches, where they are gradually covered with earth almost to their tops. This covering of earth bleaches them and makes a length of about 14 inches of leaf edible. Sometimes the seed is sown in autumn and the transplanting to trenches done in the spring." (*Fairchild.*)

9302. AMYGDALUS PERSICA. **Peach.**

From Kobe, Japan. Received through Messrs. Lathrop and Fairchild (No. 977, July 7, 1902), January 6, 1903.

Samomo. "This is the earliest ripening peach on the Kobe market. It is not very sweet but is of attractive color. It is an old sort in Kobe." (*Fairchild.*)

9303. MEDICAGO SATIVA. **Alfalfa.**

From Limache, Peru. Presented by Mr. Adolfo Eastman Cox. Received October 20, 1903.

Seed of the native Peruvian alfalfa. Secured in Peru by Beéche, Duval & Co., and shipped through their house in New York.

"This variety has the following advantages over the Chilean: The stems are hollow and more succulent; the growth commences earlier in spring and continues later in the autumn, materially increasing the yield per acre, and it grows taller. On the other hand care has to be taken in feeding stock on it as it is apt to produce hoven (heaves)." (*Cox.*)

9304. AMYGDALUS PERSICA. **Peach.**

From Kobe, Japan. Received through Messrs. Lathrop and Fairchild (No. 978, July 7, 1902), January 6, 1903.

Tinsin Suimitsuto. "One of the favorite sorts on the Kobe market, although too light in color to be very attractive. It is of large size and has been, it is said, recently introduced into southern Japan. According to nurserymen in Saitama Prefecture this can not be what they call the *Tinsin Suimitsuto* for that has red flesh, even before wholly ripe." (*Fairchild.*)

9305. AMYGDALUS PERSICA. **Peach.**

From Kobe, Japan. Received through Messrs. Lathrop and Fairchild (No. 979, July 7, 1902), January 6, 1903.

Suimitsuto. "One of the earliest sorts and one of the sweetest of the peaches in the Kobe market. It differs in shape from the *Honey* type, being more like the *Persian*. It comes from the province of Sanuki, Japan." (*Fairchild.*)

9306. Prunus triflora. **Plum.**

From Kobe, Japan. Received through Messrs. Lathrop and Fairchild (No. 980, July 7, 1902), January 6, 1903.

Botankyo. "A light-colored variety of Hatankyo. A large-fruited plum, with very juicy flesh and thin skin." (*Fairchild.*) (See Nos. 9202–9210.)

9307. Vicia faba. **Broad bean.**

From Yokohama, Japan. Received through Messrs. Lathrop and Fairchild (No. 1031, August, 1902), January 6, 1903.

Otafuku. "Said to be remarkable for its size and good quality. The young beans of this variety are said to be especially delicious." (*Fairchild.*)

9308 to 9312. Vicia faba. **Broad bean.**

From Yokohama, Japan. Received through Messrs. Lathrop and Fairchild (No. 1032, August, 1902), January 6, 1903.

"Five sorts of the Japanese broad bean or *Sora mame*, as follows:

9308.
Chiu otafuku.

9309.
Isun mame.

9310.
Kotsubu.

9311.
Yatanbusa.

9312.
Tsunashimam ame.

"The broad bean plays an important rôle in Japan, being grown extensively in ground which is later used for paddy rice. It is particularly abundant on the coast of the Japan Sea and in the colder parts of Japan. Almost exclusively used for human food." (*Fairchild.*)

9313. Prunus triflora **Plum.**

From Kobe, Japan. Received through Messrs. Lathrop and Fairchild (No. 981, July 7, 1902), January 6, 1903.

Hatankyo. "This is like the variety *Satsuma* in America and may be the same, though I am not familiar enough with the American type to say. The flesh is a blood or claret red color, very juicy, and not very sweet." (*Fairchild.*) (See No. 9202.)

9314. Myrica nagi.

From Kobe, Japan. Received through Messrs. Lathrop and Fairchild (No. 982, July 7, 1902), January 6, 1903.

Yama momo. "This fruit is said to be cultivated in the province of Kii. The beautiful fruits look something like raspberries, but resemble most in shape small fruits of *Arbutus unedo*, the strawberry tree of Italy. Their flesh is deep wine red, mildly acid, and refreshing. A very decorative fruit for fruit dishes, but not of great value for other purposes. Mr. Tanaka says it grows wild in the warm regions of Japan and forms a tree 20 feet high. The bark furnishes a tanning material." (*Fairchild.*)

9315. Panicum trypheron. **Guinea grass.**

From Sabana Grande, Porto Rico. Presented by Mr. Frank D. Gardner, special agent in charge of the Porto Rico Experiment Station. Received January 10, February 3, and February 9, 1903.

One of the best fodder grasses of the Tropics.

9316. Myrica faya.

From St. Michael, Azores. Presented by Mr. F. S. Chaves. Received January 12, 1903.

9317. OPUNTIA FICUS-INDICA. **Prickly pear.**

From Taormina, Sicily. Received through Messrs. Lathrop and Fairchild (No. 1079, November 24, 1902), January 17, 1903.

"A prickly pear which bears fruit containing comparatively few seeds. The variety is a white-fleshed one of medium size. The thallus is very spiny indeed, and the fruit is covered with small spines. This sort is considered more delicious than the ordinary kinds, and having but few seeds is in this respect entitled to the consideration of growers. A comparatively small number of plants of this variety are grown about Taormina, because the fruit is not a good market one, neither is it a very heavy cropper, but as the starting point for a seedless-fruited cactus it should appeal to any breeder of this very important and much neglected group of useful plants." (*Fairchild.*)

9318. ALLIUM CEPA. **Onion.**

From Valencia, Spain. Received through Hon. R. M. Bartleman, United States Consul, January 26, 1903.

"This large, mild-flavored onion is a native of Denia and the whole Valencia region. Attempts to grow these onions in other parts of Europe have not been successful, as they generally lose their mild flavor after the first season. The size of the onion is regulated by the farmers to suit the taste of the foreign buyers. Those shipped to the United States are the largest grown, and those intended for British markets the smallest. The seed is planted in beds from the middle of January until the first week in February, and transplanted when sufficiently developed. When large onions are desired, the plants are placed about 10 inches apart and plied with fertilizers and large quantities of water. When smaller ones are desired the plants are placed close together." (*Bartleman.*)

C. C. Morse & Co., of Santa Clara, Cal., state that this onion is without doubt the progenitor of Maule's "Prize Taker."

9319. PRUNUS ARMENIACA. **Apricot.**

From San Luis Potosi, Mexico. Received through Mr. G. Onderdonk, of Nursery, Tex., special agent of this Department, October, 1902.

9320. AMYGDALUS PERSICA. **Peach.**

From San Luis Potosi, Mexico. Received through Mr. G. Onderdonk, of Nursery, Tex., special agent of this Department, October, 1902.

9321. AMYGDALUS PERSICA. **Peach.**

From Saltillo, Mexico. Received through Mr. G. Onderdonk, of Nursery, Tex., special agent of this Department, October, 1902.

9322. MEDICAGO SATIVA. **Alfalfa.**

From Tuggurt, Algeria. Received through Mr. Thomas H. Kearney, December 8, 1902.

An alkali-resistant variety. Crop of 1902.

9323. MEDICAGO SATIVA. **Alfalfa.**

From Tuggurt, Algeria. Received through Mr. Thomas H. Kearney, December 8, 1902.

An alkali-resistant variety. Crop of 1901.

9324. TRITICUM DURUM. **Wheat.**

From Relizane, Algeria. Received through Mr. Thomas H. Kearney, December 8, 1902.

Marouani. An alkali-resistant variety.

9325. PISTACIA ATLANTICA. **Afsie or Betoom.**

From Duperré, Algeria. Received through Mr. W. T. Swingle (No. 122) from Dr. L. Trabut, Government Botanist of Algeria. Collected by Mr. Frank Joly. Received January 10, 1903.

"A large tree, reaching 40 to 50 feet in height and 4½ feet in diameter. The leaves produce a gall 'Afs-el-betoom,' which is an article of considerable commercial importance in Tripoli and Tunis. It is the only tree of any size growing in the northern Sahara, where it occupies the 'dayas' or depressions in the plateaus. Of much promise as a drought and alkali resistant stock for the pistache. A deciduous tree, not so resistant to cold as the Chicudia." (*Swingle.*)

9326 to 9341. ORYZA SATIVA. **Rice.**

From Lake Charles, La. Received through Dr. S. A. Knapp, January 19, 1903.

9326.

Shinriki. Grown from No. 8300. From Hyogo district, Japan. Doctor Knapp considers this the best early Japan rice.

9327.

Shiratamo. Grown from No. 8301. From Fukuoka district, Japan. A very good early variety.

9328.

Komachi. Grown from No. 8302. From Kumamoto district, Japan. This is a medium late variety of no great value.

9329.

Omase. Grown from No. 8303. From Kumamoto district, Japan. One of the best medium varieties.

9330.

Miyako. Grown from No. 8304. From Yamaguchi district, Japan. A medium early variety that may be of value.

9331.

An unnamed variety. Grown from No. 8305. From Chiugoku district, Japan. This is not so early as No. 9326, but has many good qualities.

9332.

An unnamed variety. Grown from No. 8306. From Chikuzen district, Japan. One of the best medium varieties. Practically the same as *Kiushu.*

9333.

Fusakichi. Grown from No. 8508. From Bizen district, Japan. A medium early variety of remarkable quality. The seeds are exceptionally large, and on suitable land, with plenty of water, this will probably be one of the very best varieties.

9334.

Mansaku bozu. Grown from No. 8509. From Fukuoka district, Japan. This is one of the best medium varieties.

9335.

An unnamed variety. Grown from No. 8310. From Ise district, Japan. This is a medium variety and may become valuable.

9336.

An unnamed variety. Grown from No. 8511. From Buzen district, Japan. This is a medium variety and may prove valuable.

9326 to 9341—Continued.

9337.
An unnamed variety. Grown from No. 8512. From Iyo district, Japan. This is a medium late variety of extra vigor and fairly good yield.

9338.
An unnamed variety. Grown from No. 8513. From Higo district, Japan. This is one of the best late varieties.

9339.
An unnamed variety. Grown from No. 8514. From Bizen district, Japan. This is a late variety that may prove valuable.

9340.
An unnamed variety. Grown from No. 8515. From Banshu district, Japan. This is the best late variety.

9341.
Honduras rice. One of the standard varieties, grown for comparison.

9342. ORYZA SATIVA. **Rice.**

From Kin-hua, China. Secured by Dr. S. P. Barchet, of the United States consulate, Shanghai, China, at the request of Dr. S. A. Knapp. Received January 22, 1903.

A late variety sown in May.

9343. ORYZA SATIVA. **Rice.**

From Ki-ni, Kin-hua, China. Secured by Dr. S. P. Barchet, of the United States consulate, Shanghai, China, at the request of Dr. S. A. Knapp. Received January 22, 1903.

Glutinous rice. Sown in May.

9344. GLYCINE HISPIDA. **Soy bean.**

From Chiu-hua, China. Secured by Dr. S. P. Barchet, of the United States consulate, Shanghai, China, at the request of Dr. S. A. Knapp. Received January 22, 1903.

Chiu-hua. "In case of future reference to the bean, if you call this the *Chiu-hua* bean I shall know what is meant, in the absence of a botanical name, as I have not seen this bean anywhere else. It is sown broadcast in paddy fields before the rice is harvested. The moist ground favors the sprouting, and the standing grain shields the sprouting plant from the sun. By the time the rice is harvested the beans have taken firm roots and require no further care. Horses and cattle are very fond of them green or in the ripe state. The bean also makes a good food for man. This bean I think well worth a trial in the Southern States." (*Barchet.*)

9345. AMYGDALUS COMMUNIS. **Almond.**

From Mustapha, Algiers, Algeria. Presented by Dr. L. Trabut, Government Botanist. Received January 26, 1903.

Cuttings of the wild almond of the mountains of Algeria, said to be excellent for stock.

9346. PRUNUS DOMESTICA. **Plum.**

From Mustapha, Algiers, Algeria. Presented by Dr. L. Trabut, Government Botanist. Received January 26, 1903.

Reine Claude Rouge. Cuttings of this plum. Marked by Doctor Trabut "Glorion Vincent."

9347. LINUM USITATISSIMUM. **Flax.**

From Rotterdam, Holland. Received through F. Dutilh & Co., January 29, 1903.

Dutch Riga-Child. Extra picked. From crop of 1902.

9348 to 9351. AMYGDALUS COMMUNIS. **Almond**

From Alicante, Spain. Received through Mr. D. G. Fairchild (Nos. 740, 741, 745, 755a, July 19 and 20, 1901), January 30, 1903.

A collection of young almond trees budded on myrobalan stocks by Mr. Georges Boucher, Paris, France, with buds secured by Mr. Fairchild in Spain.

9348.
Mollar. (No. 740.)

9349.
Planeta. (No. 741.)

9350.
Castillet. (No. 745.)

9351.
Pastaneta. (No. 755a.)

(See Nos. 7985 to 7989 and 9458 to 9462.)

9352. OPUNTIA FICUS-INDICA. **Prickly pear.**

From Malta. Received through Messrs. Lathrop and Fairchild (No. 1082, December 27, 1902), January 31, 1903.

"Fruits from the plants of this variety contain less than 12 seeds, according to Dr. Giovanni Borg, of Malta, who kindly presents them to the Department. These seeds are very small and not at all objectionable. The fruit inside and out is yellowish orange in color, of good flavor, Doctor Borg says, and of the size of a goose egg. The thallus is nearly spineless. It is a rare plant even in Malta. These fruits came from plants growing in a garden in Siggiewi." (*Fairchild.*)

9353. OPUNTIA FICUS-INDICA. **Prickly pear.**

From Malta. Received through Messrs. Lathrop and Fairchild (No. 1083, December 27, 1902), January 31, 1903.

"This variety resembles No. 9352 closely, but the fruits are much smaller, being only the size of a hen's egg. Seedless or at least with very few seeds. The thallus is nearly spineless. The minute bristles on the fruit, according to Dr. Giovanni Borg, can be removed by washing the fruits in a basin of water with a whisk broom. The water loosens up the small cushions of bristles and they are easily brushed away into the water. This variety is not as promising as No. 9352, but is worthy a place in the breeder's collection. The fact of its seedlessness and spinelessness makes it a valuable variety of *Opuntia* for any economic studies on the subject. From Professor Pisani's villa at Maurisi, near Zeitun, Malta." (*Fairchild.*)

9354. FICUS CARICA. **Fig.**

From Malta. Received through Messrs. Lathrop and Fairchild (No. 1084, December 28, 1902), January 31, 1903.

St. Anthony. "Dr. Giovanni Borg, director of the botanic garden, says this is one of the most delicious figs he has ever eaten. It ripens one crop of figs in June and a second in September or October. The regular late crop is red in color. No caprification is deemed necessary for this sort, which Doctor Borg thinks could be used for drying purposes. It is an uncommon variety." (*Fairchild.*)

9355. ARACHIS HYPOGAEA. **Peanut.**

From Tanegashima, Japan. Presented by Mr. H. E. Amoore. Received February 2, 1903.

29861—No. 66—05——18

9356 and 9357. ZEA MAYS. **Corn.**

From Forestburg, S. Dak. Presented by Mr. H. C. Warner. Grown from S. P. I. No. 13, which was found to be a mixture of types.

9356.
Malakoff sugar corn. White type.

9357.
Amber type.

9358. TRITICUM VULGARE. **Wheat.**

From the estate of Mr. Bezouglov, near Byeloglinskaya, Don Territory, Russia. Obtained by Mr. E. A. Bessey (No. 110, August 4, 1902), through the Theodore N. Solodov Milling Company, Rostov-on-Don, Russia. Received February 3, 1903.

Beloglino. "A hard, red, winter wheat from the crop of 1902. This has just been harvested and thrashed at this date and is of very good quality, far exceeding that of last year." (*Bessey.*)

9359. MEDICAGO SATIVA. **Alfalfa.**

From Erivan, Caucasia. Obtained by Mr. E. A. Bessey (No. 236, October 7, 1902), through Mr. N. P. Taratinoff, of Tiflis. Received February 3, 1903.

"Alfalfa from Erivan Province, the hottest and driest province in summer and coldest in winter (reaching $-22°$ F.). It should prove valuable in cold regions." (*Bessey.*)

9360 to 9402.

From Tiflis, Russian Caucasus. Presented by Mr. A. Rolloff, director of the botanic garden, through Mr. E. A. Bessey. Received February 3, 1902.

9360. PYRUS COMMUNIS. Pear.
Sini. (No. 209.)

9361. PYRUS COMMUNIS. Pear.
Nana-armud. (No. 210.)

9362. PRUNUS DOMESTICA. Plum.
Vazirali. (No. 211.)

9363. PRUNUS DOMESTICA. Plum.
Tchantchuri. (No. 212.)

9364. PRUNUS ARMENIACA. Apricot.
Agdzhanabad. (No. 213.)

9365. PRUNUS ARMENIACA. Apricot.
Achrerdi. (No. 214.)

9366. PRUNUS ARMENIACA. Apricot.
Badam-arik. (No. 215.)

9367. PRUNUS ARMENIACA. Apricot.
Norrast. (No. 216.)

9368. PRUNUS ARMENIACA. Apricot.
Tabarzei. (No. 217.)

9369. PRUNUS ARMENIACA. Apricot.
Bairam-ali. From Turkestan. (No. 218.)

9360 to 9402—Continued.

9370. Prunus armeniaca. Apricot.
Red Yusup-Khan. From Turkestan. (No. 219.)

9371. Prunus armeniaca. Apricot.
White Yusup-Khan. From Turkestan. (No. 220.)

9372. Amygdalus persica. Peach.
Zafrani. (No. 221.)

9373. Amygdalus persica. Peach.
Nazli. (No. 222.)

9374. Amygdalus persica. Peach.
Norrast-huli. (No. 223.)

9375. Amygdalus persica. Peach.
Salami. (No. 224.)

9376. Amygdalus persica. Peach.
Narindzhi. (No. 225.)

9377. Amygdalus persica. Peach.
Sachrari. (No. 226.)

9378. Amygdalus persica. Peach.
Arabuli. (No. 227.)

9379. Amygdalus persica. Peach.
Tibatvica. (No. 228.)

9380. Amygdalus persica. Peach.
Gandzhuri. (No. 229.)

9381. Ficus carica. Fig.
Tschapla. (No. 230.)

9382. Elaeagnus angustifolia.
Matna-pshat. (No. 231.)

9383. Elaeagnus angustifolia.
Unab-pshat. (No. 232.)

9384. Morus alba.
Gandzha. (No. 233.)

9385. Punica granatum.
Krmzi-kabuck. (No. 234.)

9386. Punica granatum.
Shirin-nar. (No. 235.)

9387. Mixture of seeds of Pyrus salicifolia and P. elaeagrifolia. (Nos. 203 and 204.)

9388. Pyrus communis. Pear.
Wild pear. (No. 202.)

9360 to 9402—Continued.

9389. AMYGDALUS PERSICA. **Peach.**
Wild peach.

9390. PRUNUS ARMENIACA. **Apricot.**
Wild apricot. (No. 205.)

Seeds of cultivated varieties of peaches as follows:

9391. AMYGDALUS PERSICA. **Peach.**
Narindschi. (No. 206.)

9392.
Guli. (No. 208.)

9395.
Spitak.

9393.
Zafrani. (No. 207.)

9396.
Lodz.

9394.
Norrast.

Seeds of cultivated sorts of apricots, as follows:

9397. PRUNUS ARMENIACA. **Apricot.**
Schalogi.

9398.
Agdschanabad.

9401.
Gevondi.

9399.
Chosrof-schack.

9402.
Gegdschanabad.

9400.
Badam-arik.

9403. STRYPHNODENDRON BARBATIMAO.
From São Paulo, Brazil. Presented by Dr. Alberto Löfgren, director of the Botanic Garden. Received February 2, 1903.
"The bark of this tree contains considerable tannin." (*Löfgren.*)

9404 and 9405. PHASEOLUS sp. **Bean.**
From São Paulo, Brazil. Presented by Dr. H. M. Lane. Received February 4, 1903.

9404. **Brown bean.**
Feijão mulato.

9405. **Black bean.**
Feijão preto.

9406. ARACHIS HYPOGAEA. **Peanut.**
From São Paulo, Brazil. Presented by Dr. H. M. Lane. Received February 4, 1903.
Ordinary variety.

9407 to 9418. GLYCINE HISPIDA. **Soy bean.**

A collection of soy beans grown by Mr. W. R. Beattie on the experimental grounds on the Potomac Flats, from introduced seed.

9407.
Grown in 1902 from S. P. I. No. 4912.

9408.
Grown in 1902 from S. P. I. No. 4913.

9409.
Grown in 1902 from S. P. I. No. 4914.

9410.
Grown in 1901 and 1902 from S. P. I. No. 6312.

9411.
Grown in 1901 and 1902 from S. P. I. No. 6333.

9412.
Grown in 1901 and 1902 from S. P. I. No. 6334.

9413.
Grown in 1901 and 1902 from S. P. I. No. 6336.

9414.
Grown in 1901 and 1902 from S. P. I. No. 6386.

9415.
Grown in 1901 and 1902 from S. P. I. No. 6396.

9416.
Grown in 1901 and 1902 from S. P. I. No. 6397.

9417.
Grown in 1901 and 1902 from S. P. I. No. 6414.

9418.
Grown in 1901 and 1902 from S. P. I. No. 6416.

9419. PHASEOLUS MUNGO-RADIATUS (?). **Gram.**

Grown on Potomac Flats in 1902 by Mr. W. R. Beattie from S. P. I. No. 6417.

9420. AMYGDALUS PERSICA. **Peach.**

From Pomona, N. C. Presented by Mr. J. Van Lindley. Received February 6, 1903.

Natural peach seed from the seedling peach orchards, for growing as stocks in comparison with Mexican seed.

9421. LINUM USITATISSIMUM. **Flax.**

From Perwez, Belgium. Received through Emile Mathy, February 8, 1903.

First choice.

9422. AVENA SATIVA. **Oat.**

From Moscow, Russia. Received through Mr. E. A. Bessey, from Immer & Sons (No. 104, July 22, 1902), February 10, 1903.

Swedish Select. "This excellent variety has proven exceptionally good for the dry Steppe region. This is a selection made in Sweden of the Ligowo oat and bred up by Immer & Sons. It originally came from Ladoga, near St. Petersburg. This year's crop." (*Bessey.*)

9423 to 9425. PANICUM MILIACEUM. **Proso.**

From Moscow, Russia. Received through Mr. E. A. Bessey, from Immer & Sons. (Nos. 105 to 107, July 22, 1902.)

9423.
Red Orenburg. Crop of 1902. Received February 10, 1903. (No. 105.)

9424.
Red Vorónezh. Crop of 1902. Received May 22, 1903. (No. 106.)

9425.
Black Vorónezh. Crop of 1902. Received May 22, 1903. (No. 107.)

9426. PISTACIA LENTISCUS. **Mastic.**

From the rocky cliffs along the seashore, between Leghorn and Castiglioncello, Italy. Collected by Mr. W. T. Swingle (No. 123, January 14, 1903). Received February 17, 1903.

"The lentisk or mastic tree is found chiefly in the immediate vicinity of the sea in the Mediterranean region wherever the winters are not too severe (it is decidedly less hardy than the terebinth). Its northern limit is about the January isotherm of 42.8° to 46.4° F. It is a small evergreen tree (other species of *Pistacia* are deciduous) or more often a shrub, branching profusely from the ground. When growing in tree form it sometimes reaches a height of 20 to 25 feet, and a diameter of 8 inches to one foot. *It prefers silicious soils and avoids those decidedly calcareous* in nature, being just the opposite of the terebinth, so the two are very rarely seen growing together in a wild state. The leaves are rich in tannin (11.5 per cent), and are collected and sold in Tunis as a substitute for sumac for tanning. The seeds are much liked by pigs, goats, and wild boars in Tunis, and are an important source of food in dry years when the fruit is apt to be unusually abundant, while other forage is scarce. In Chios a grafted variety yields *mastic*, a soft resin much prized in the Orient for chewing gum and for flavoring liquors. This is a promising stock on which to graft the pistache, especially on silicious or slightly acid soils near the sea. It is said not to be so long lived as the terebinth, and the pistache, when grafted on the lentisk, is said to live only forty years, whereas it lives one or two centuries on the terebinth. It is probably a dwarf stock and pistaches grafted on it should be set out at smaller distances apart than on other stocks. On sandy soil with moderate bottom heat, there should be no difficulty in starting the cuttings." (*Swingle.*)

9427 to 9436.

From Nice, France. Presented by Mr. A. Robertson-Proschowsky. Received January 12, 1903.

A collection of seeds as follows:

9427. ARISTOLOCHIA ELEGANS.

9428. CESTRUM ELEGANS.

9429. CISTUS ALBIDUS.

9430. CLEOME ARBOREA (?)

9431. DOLICHOS LABLAB.

9432. ECHINOCACTUS SCHUMANNIANUS.

9433. PHLOMIS FRUTICOSA.

9434. SUTHERLANDIA FRUTESCENS.

9435. PITTOSPORUM UNDULATUM.

9436. TACSONIA MANICATA.

9437. CITRUS AURANTIUM. **Orange.**

From Mustapha, Algiers, Algeria. Presented by Dr. L. Trabut, Government Botanist. Received February 16, 1903.

Seeds of the *Condja* (?) orange. Fruit very large and sweet, four hundred grams or more, resembling the *Jaffna*. One or two seeds of each fruit. It reproduces true to seed.

9438 to 9444. PHASEOLUS sp. **Bean.**

From Mexico. Received through Dr. Edward Palmer, February 21, 1903. A collection of different varieties of beans, as follows:

9438.

Garbansillo. From Saltillo. "First-class bean and seems a little different from the one at San Luis Potosi of the same name (No. 9155). When the bean from San Luis Potosi is brought to Saltillo for sale it is objected to because it is said to take more fuel for cooking, and fuel is an object. This is probably due to the fact that the water at San Luis Potosi is hard, while that at Saltillo is soft. This bean is very prolific in this section of the table-lands and is the choice of all who can afford to purchase it. Bought from Jesus Santos Grande, Saltillo, Mexico." (*Palmer.*)

9439.

Vayo-gordo. From Saltillo. "A first-class bean and a great favorite with the rich. It is said to be very productive in this section, and as it is not very dark in color it might claim recognition in the United States." (*Palmer.*)

9440.

Frijol para la sopa. From San Luis Potosi. "Not of very good quality, but much used for soups. Apparently a poor quality of *Blanco bolador.*" (*Palmer.*)

9441.

Canelo Gordo. From Saltillo. "A first-class bean which can be had in large quantities at the markets." (*Palmer.*)

9442.

Canelo Chico. From Saltillo. "A first-class bean; plentiful in the markets. It is used extensively." (*Palmer.*)

9443.

Guadalupano. From Saltillo. "A bean not much seen on the markets, somewhat resembling the *Borrado*. It is a second-class bean." (*Palmer.*)

9444.

Bolador de Color. From Saltillo. "A third-class bean, and only eaten when others can not be obtained, and then only after boiling and frying in lard." (*Palmer.*)

9445. SOLANUM sp. **Pepper.**

From San Luis Potosi, Mexico. Received through Dr. Edward Palmer, February 21, 1903.

Chili guipin. "Sold in the markets of San Luis Potosi and commonly eaten by the well-to-do. A very hot pepper. Eaten before and with soups." (*Palmer.*)

9446. PISTACIA LENTISCUS. **Mastic.**

From rocky cliff near seashore, opposite Castello Sonnino, between Leghorn and Castiglioncella, Italy. Received through Mr. W. T. Swingle (No. 124), February 20, 1903.

9447. ANACARDIUM OCCIDENTALE. **Cashew.**

From Beira, East Africa. Presented by Mr. Arthur W. H. Glenny, United States consular agent at Beira, through Messrs. Lathrop and Fairchild (No. 1092, January 28, 1903), March, 1903.

"Seed of the West Indian cashew, which came from trees growing in Rhodesia that seem unusually hardy and grow at an altitude of several thousand feet, where occasional frosts are said to occur. Worthy of trial in Florida and Porto Rico." (*Fairchild.*)

9448. PHYSALIS sp.

From Saltillo, Mexico. Received through Dr. Edward Palmer, February 21, 1903.

"A large, dark plum-colored variety, used in soups and stews. Also fried with beefsteak and sometimes used in dressings for fowls. Fruits secured in November, 1902, were sound February 6, 1903, when the seeds were removed." (*Palmer.*)

9449. ZEA MAYS. **Corn.**

From Ravenna, Ohio. Presented by the Ford Seed Company. Received February 24, 1903.

Malakhoff sugar. Grown from S. P. I. No. 13.

9450. MEDICAGO SATIVA. **Alfalfa.**

From Askhabad, Trans-Caspian Territory, Turkestan. Received through Mr. E. A. Bessey (No. 113, August 23, 1902), from Sadik-Bek Agabekov, acting governor of the district of Askhabad. February 28, 1903.

"The sort of alfalfa grown by the natives (*Tekins*) from time immemorial. Apparently well adapted to a very hot climate of low humidity and mild winters. This variety will probably not be suited for northern climates, but will thrive, when irrigated, in the very hottest, driest regions, as Askhabad is almost the hottest point in Turkestan." (*Bessey.*)

9451. MEDICAGO SATIVA. **Alfalfa.**

From Sairam, near Chimkent, Russia. Received through Mr. E. A. Bessey, from Mr. H. W. Dürrschmidt, of Tashkent (No. 150, September 29, 1902), February 28, 1903.

"The alfalfa of this region (and also around Karabulák, 24 miles northwest of Sairam) is considered to be about the best in Turkestan. It is grown in considerable quantities throughout the whole region. This is probably the coldest region in Turkestan where alfalfa is grown in such large quantities. This ought to be good for cool regions." (*Bessey.*)

9452. MEDICAGO SATIVA. **Alfalfa.**

From Karabulák, 25 miles north of Chimkent, Russia. Received through Mr. E. A. Bessey, from Mr. H. W. Dürrschmidt, of Tashkent (No. 151, September 29, 1902), February 28, 1903.

"The same methods of culture as in Sairam, only in slightly larger fields. As in Sairam, it is grown with the aid of irrigation. Sent for trial in cool regions." (*Bessey.*)

9453. MEDICAGO SATIVA. **Alfalfa.**

From Bokhara, Turkestan. Received through Mr. E. A. Bessey, from Mr. H. W. Dürrschmidt, of Tashkent (No. 152, September 29, 1902), February 28, 1903.

"Bokhara is a region containing much alkali land; the soil has a white crust when dry. Large fields of various crops are destroyed by alkali. This seed is not especially resistant to cold. It is sent for trial in alkali regions." (*Bessey.*)

9454. MEDICAGO SATIVA. **Alfalfa.**

From Khiva, Turkestan. Received through Mr. E. A. Bessey, from Mr. H. W. Dürrschmidt, of Tashkent (No. 153a, November 6, 1902, numbered in sack 153), February 28, 1903.

"Khiva is one of the driest regions in Turkestan, the average rainfall being less than 3 inches a year. It is correspondingly hot in summer, but rather cold in winter; much colder than Bokhara, Askhabad, or Karshi. Alfalfa is grown only by irrigation. It is fertilized abundantly, at least with fresh soil if not with animal manure." (*Bessey.*)

9455. MEDICAGO SATIVA. **Alfalfa.**

From Karshi, Turkestan. Received through Mr. E. A. Bessey, from Mr. H. W. Dürrschmidt, of Tashkent (No. 154a, November 6, 1902, numbered in sacks 154), February 28, 1903.

"Karshi lies about 80 miles southwest of Samarcand and about as far southeast of Bokhara. It is in the edge of the mountains and much cooler than Bokhara." (*Bessey.*)

9456. QUERCUS SUBER. **Cork oak.**

From Paris, France. Received through Vilmorin-Andrieux & Co., March 5, 1903.

9457. LINUM USITATISSIMUM. **Flax.**

From Riga, Russia. Received through the United States consul, from A. Sellmar, March 6, 1903.

Best Riga.

9458 to 9462. AMYGDALUS COMMUNIS. **Almond.**

Received through Mr. J. W. Kerr, Denton, Md. Grown by Mr. Kerr from buds furnished by this Department. Received March 7, 1903.

9458.
Castillet. Grown from S. P. I. No. 7133.

9459.
Fabrica. Grown from S. P. I. No. 7135.

9460.
Jordan. Grown from S. P. I. Nos. 7398 and 7401, mixed.

9461.
Mollar. Grown from S. P. I. No. 7061.

9462.
Planeta. Grown from S. P. I. No. 7062.

See Nos. 7985 to 7989 and 9348 to 9351. Budded on peach stocks.

9463 and 9464. PRUNUS ARMENIACA. **Apricot.**

Received through Mr. J. W. Kerr, Denton, Md. Grown by Mr. Kerr from buds furnished by this Department. Received March 7, 1903.

9463.
Patriarca. Grown from S. P. I. 7136.

9464.
Grown from S. P. I. No. 6844.

9465. Rosa sp. **Rose.**

From Cannes, France. Received through Mr. J. B. Cognet, United States consular agent, March 9, 1903.

The true perfume rose.

9466. ANONA CHERIMOLIA.

Plants grown in Department greenhouse from seed presented by Capt. J. J. Haden, Cocoanut Grove, Fla., April 16, 1902. Plants numbered March 11, 1903.

9467. ERIOBOTRYA JAPONICA. **Loquat.**

Seedling plants grown in Department greenhouse from seeds of large loquat tree in orange house. Plants numbered March 11, 1903.

9468. ERIODENDRON ANFRACTUOSUM. **Kapok.**

From Marseille, France. Presented by the United States Consulate. Received February 14, 1903. Turned over to the Office of Seed and Plant Introduction by Mr. L. H. Dewey, Assistant Botanist.

9469 and 9470. PYRUS MALUS. **Apple.**

From Naples, Italy. Presented by Prof. L. Savastano through Messrs. Lathrop and Fairchild (Nos. 1077 and 1078). Received March 14, 1903.

9469.

Annurco. "The leading market apple of the region about Naples. It is a showy red apple, with yellow streaks, and has an unusually high flavor for a variety grown so far south. It should be tested in the Southern States. Obtained through the kindness of Professor Savastano, of the agricultural school at Portici." (*Fairchild.*)

9470.

Limoncelli. "A lemon-yellow fruited variety; one of the best market varieties of southern Italy. It has a hard, crisp, slightly tough flesh, subacid and highly flavored. It is not as good as No. 9469, but I believe is a better keeper. Obtained through the kindness of Professor Savastano, of the agricultural school at Portici." (*Fairchild.*)

9471. PYRUS MALUS. **Apple.**

From Portici (Naples), Italy. Presented by Prof. L. Savastano through Messrs. Lathrop and Fairchild. Received March 14, 1903.

Melo gelato. "Grows well in the warm region about Naples. In cold countries the yield is poor. It does best in calcareous soil." (*Fairchild.*)

9472. **Palm.**

From Black River, Honduras. Presented by Mr. Frank Dean through Dr. H. J. Webber of this Department. Received March 16, 1903.

Two ounces of seed of a small, pinnate-leaved palm 6 feet high. Foliage dark green. Fine for conservatories.

9473. ATTALEA COHUNE (?) **Palm.**

From Black River, Honduras. Presented by Mr. Frank Dean through Dr. H. J. Webber of this Department. Received March 16, 1903.

Coquito. A large pinnate-leaved palm.

9474. PISTACIA MUTICA (?)

From Smyrna, Turkey in Asia. Purchased from Mr. B. J. Agadjanian, at the request of Mr. W. T. Swingle (No. 121). Received March 21, 1903.

"The celebrated turpentine tree of Chios, from which a kind of turpentine is extracted by making incisions in the bark. It grows to a large size, reaching a diameter of 5 feet 2½ inches and a height of 40 to 60 feet. The seeds yield an oil used for culinary purposes and in making toilet soaps. This tree is of great promise for use as a stock on which to graft the pistache, especially for semiarid regions in the Southwest, where this tree would be able to grow without irrigation. Worthy of trial as a shade and timber tree in warm dry regions. It is deciduous." (*Swingle.*)

9475. CAPSICUM ANNUUM. **Red pepper.**

From Pasadena, Cal. Presented by Capt. C. W. Livermore. Received March 21, 1903.

Paprica.

9476. MYRICA FAYA.

From St. Michaels, Azores Islands. Presented by Hon. George H. Pickerell, United States consul. Received March 21, 1903.

9477. PISTACIA VERA. **Pistache.**

From Catania, Italy. Presented by Hon. Alexander Heingartner, United States consul, at the request of Mr. W. T. Swingle. Received March 16, 1903.

Sicilian. "From grafted pistache trees at Bronte, on the slopes of Mount Etna. The only sort likely to succeed in America for commercial purposes. Not large, with a bright-green kernel." (*Swingle.*)

9478 and 9479. TRITICUM DURUM. **Wheat.**

From Brookings, S. Dak. Received through Mr. James H. Shepard, March 14, 1903. Grown from seed originally imported from Russia.

9478. **9479.**

Kubanka. *Velvet Don.*

9480. CITRUS NOBILIS × CITRUS BIGARADIA. **Tangerine.**

From Mustapha, Algiers, Algeria. Presented by Dr. L. Trabut, Government Botanist. Received March 19, 1903.

Clementine.

9481. CUCURBITA sp. **Squash.**

From Mustapha, Algiers, Algeria. Presented by Dr. L. Trabut, Government Botanist. Received March 21, 1903.

Courge bedouine.

9482. TRICHILIA DREGEI.

From Delagoa Bay, Portuguese East Africa. Received through Messrs. Lathrop and Fairchild (No. 1094, February 1, 1903), March 13 and 21, 1903.

Freda. "A handsome shade tree which is being used for avenue planting and which deserves trial as a shade tree in tropical gardens and also in Florida. It grows in almost pure sand, but requires water. Its seeds may be objectionable when they fall, as they are abundant and covered with a red arillus." (*Fairchild.*)

9483.

From Johannesburg, Transvaal. Received through Messrs. Lathrop and Fairchild (No. 1108, February 18, 1903), March 24, 1903.

"An undetermined species of the sunflower family which, according to Mr. R. W. Odlam, superintendent of the Municipal Garden at Johannesburg, bears very pretty pale-yellow flowers and is worthy of being brought into cultivation. These seeds were collected by him on the high veld for the purpose of planting in his garden. They should be sown immediately upon arrival." (*Fairchild.*)

9484. GERBERA JAMESONI. **Barberton or Transvaal daisy.**

From Johannesburg, Transvaal. Received through Messrs. Lathrop and Fairchild (No. 1106, February 18, 1903), March 24, 1903.

"This showy perennial is half hardy and can be grown in the open in California and the Southwest but will probably succeed as a potted plant, if set out in the summer time, even as far north as Chicago. Its flowers, which are daisy-like in shape and very large, are of a beautiful scarlet color. They are not borne in great abundance but are nevertheless very showy. The foliage, resembling slightly that of the dandelion in shape, is a deep, dark green, and the flower scapes, which rise out of a dense mass of it, are long and slender. The flower is a brilliant, attractive thing and well worthy of attention. The seeds are very short lived and should be planted at once in rich, sandy potting soil. Should germinate in ten to twelve days. The plants require plenty of water and sunshine." (*Fairchild.*)

9485. ANANAS SATIVUS. **Pineapple.**

From Durban, Natal. Received through Messrs. Lathrop and Fairchild (No. 1109, February 19, 1903), March 30, 1903.

Natal. "Sets taken from the tops of two most delicious pineapples of the common cultivated variety of Natal. More sets would be sent were it not for a disease which is prevalent among the Natal pines and which we fear to introduce into America. This disease is said to be fungous in character and to be caused by a species of Mucor which gets into the fruit through places attacked by a red mite. These two plants should be watched closely and the sets carefully examined before planting, for although they came from perfectly sound fruit they may harbor this Mucor. The Natal pineapple is a small sort of most unusual uniformity of flavor and texture and surpasses in sweetness, crispness, and freedom from fiber or seeds any other pineapple which we have ever eaten. Its small, convenient size and tenderness of flesh suit it better than any variety we have ever seen for general table use, and its excellent shipping qualities must recommend it to American growers. It has scarcely any core, and from the standpoint of the consumer it is a great pineapple. It is said to thrive with very little attention in Natal." (*Fairchild.*)

9486. MANGIFERA INDICA. **Mango.**

From Beira, Portuguese East Africa. Received through Messrs. Lathrop and Fairchild (No. 1091, January 28, 1903), April 2, 1903.

Lathrop. "The single fruit from which one of these two seeds came, and from which the following description is made, was the only one obtainable during our short stop in Beira. It was $15\frac{3}{5}$ inches in largest circumference and of a peculiar, characteristic shape; being in outline (seen from the stem end) very broadly elliptical (14 inches in circumference at base) while, seen in profile, it was heart shaped with a decided oblique tendency. It resembled in shape a Sour Sop and was nearly as large as a medium-sized specimen of this species of Anona. The skin was, when ripe, a light golden yellow and of a peculiar texture, not common to other varieties of mangoes that I have seen. It was not quite smooth but suggested the roughness of a pomelo skin. It was about one-eighth inch thick and quite tough, and on the inside it was lined with a number of long, strong fibers which did not penetrate into the flesh but adhered closely to the skin. The flesh, from this skin quite down to the short fibers attached to the seed, was entirely devoid of stringiness of any kind and had the texture of a firm custard and was of a deep golden color. In aroma it lacked very little of being as pronounced and agreeable as that of the best *Alphonse* variety of Bombay and its flesh had the indescribably rich flavor which characterizes the best varieties of this tropical fruit. The seed was small ($3\frac{3}{4}$ by $2\frac{3}{4}$ by $1\frac{1}{4}$) in proportion to the size of the fruit and the fibers attached to it are mostly about one-fourth inch long. A small bundle of fibers at one edge is 1 inch in length. This is one of the great mangoes of the world and would command fancy prices in America at any time of the year. It is fitting to name this after Mr. Barbour Lathrop, who first called it to the attention of the American public and who first introduced it into Florida. See No. 9669." (*Fairchild.*)

9487. RAPHANUS SATIVUS. Radish.

From Erfurt, Germany. Received through F. C. Heinemann, April 4, 1903.

Erfurt Crimson Giant. Heinemann's tender forcing radish.

9488. CITRUS HYBRIDA.

From Mustapha, Algiers, Algeria. Presented by Dr. L. Trabut, Government Botanist. Received April 11, 1903.

"Seed of a hybrid said to be of very good quality. Fruit nearly round, clear, yellow, sweet, and very juicy. Late." (*Trabut.*)

9489. CITRUS AURANTIUM × CITRUS BERGAMIA.

From Mustapha, Algiers, Algeria. Presented by Dr. L. Trabut, Government Botanist. Received April 11, 1903.

Seeds of a hybrid called by Doctor Trabut *Limorange*. A hybrid of the orange and mellarose. Said to be very good. Skin white. See No. 9554 for bud wood of same.

9490. PISTACIA VERA. Pistache.

From Baku, Trans-Caspian Province, Russia. Received through Mr. E. A. Bessey (October 9, 1902), April 13, 1903.

"The price of these nuts at retail in the market is 60 kopecks per pound; wholesale, 40 kopecks per pound." (*Bessey.*)

9491. PISTACIA VERA. Pistache.

From Tunis. Received through Mr. Walter T. Swingle (No. 125), February 21, 1903.

9492 to 9500.

From Japan. Presented by T. Tamura, of the agricultural experiment station at Okitsumachi, Shizuoka, Japan, through Messrs. Lathrop and Fairchild. Received April 16, 1903.

A collection of bud wood of Japanese fruits, as follows:

9492. PYRUS COMMUNIS. Pear.

9493. CITRUS JAPONICA. Kumquat.
Marukinkan.

9494. CITRUS JAPONICA. Kumquat.
Nagakinkan.

9495. CITRUS NOBILIS. Mandarin orange.
Aisomikan.

9496. CITRUS NOBILIS. Mandarin orange.
Kawahata Mikan.

9497. CITRUS sp.

Oshima Kunenbo or *Seedless Kunenbo*. "Grown on the island of Oshima, province of Osumi, prefecture Kagoshima. Fruit medium, flattened, but much larger than the common Kunenbo and very coarse. Rind thick, deep, brilliant reddish-orange color. Very fragrant. Pulp sweet, juicy, and delicious. Very good for table use and of good keeping quality." (*Tamura.*)

9492 to 9500—Continued.

9498. CITRUS AURANTIUM. **Orange.**

T. Tamura's summer orange. Originated by T. Tamura in the district of Shingai, province of Gosa, prefecture Kochi. "Fruit conical, weighing from 1¼ to 2 pounds. Skin pale white and somewhat rough. Color bright yellow in the first year, changing to dull yellow the second. Fruit remains on the tree during July and August the second season. Pulp very sweet and juicy, melting and rich in fragrance, and is very palatable, although small in quantity. Contains 20 to 25 large seeds." (*Tamura.*)

9499. CITRUS NOBILIS. **Mandarin orange.**

Tamura Unshiu, or seedless mandarin orange, originated by T. Tamura, in the district of Shingai, province of Tosa. "Fruit roundish, oblate, rind thin, somewhat rough, of a bright reddish color. Pulp sweet, subacid, juicy, and seedless. This orange will not keep as well as the true sweet orange, but is one of the best for table use. The quality is very fine." (*Tamura.*)

9500. CITRUS DECUMANA. **Pomelo.**

Kawaguchi's Buntan, or seedless pomelo. Produced only in the district of Higashimorokata, in the province of Hiuga, Prefecture Miyazaki. "Fruit medium to large, very oblate, rind thin, smooth, and pale yellow. Pulp sweet, subacid, juicy, of a dull-purplish or light-reddish color, and seedless. Quality good. Excellent for table use and a good keeper." (*Tamura.*) (No. 967, July 5, 1902.)

9501 to 9503. MESEMBRYANTHEMUM sp.

From Cape Town, South Africa. Received through Messrs. Lathrop and Fairchild (Nos. 1140 to 1142, March 11, 1903), April 17, 1903.

A collection of plants presented by Mr. Eustace Pillans, of Rosebank, near Cape Town. The species were undetermined by Mr. Pillans.

9501.

"A strikingly ornamental variety with vivid orange flowers. From Mr. Eustace Pillan's garden at Rosebank." (*Fairchild.*)

9502.

"A variety with striking magenta-colored flowers. A very strong grower. Especially adapted for borders. Flowers in the early South African spring." (*Fairchild.*)

9503.

"A tricolored sort, orange, maroon, and red. Said to be very rare. It has a most striking dewlike sheen on plant and flowers. Is a strong grower." (*Fairchild.*)

9504 to 9553. MANGIFERA INDICA. **Mango.**

From Saharanpur, united provinces of Agra and Oudh, India. Received through Mr. W. Gollan, director of the Saharanpur Botanic Garden, April 17, 1903.

A collection of small grafted mango plants as follows, one plant of each variety:

9504.
Arbuthnot.

9505.
Bhabaurea.

9506.
Brindabani. (Dead on arrival.)

9507.
Bombay, green. (Dead on arrival.)

9508.
Bombay, yellow.

9509.
Gopalbhog. (Dead on arrival.)

9504 to 9553—Continued.

9510. Khapariah.

9511. Langra.

9512. Malda.

9513. Salibunda. (Dead on arrival.)

9514. Stalkart.

9515. Strawberry.

9516. Sufaida.

9517. Alfonso.

9518. Bhurdas.

9519. Bulbulchasm.

9520. Calcuttia amin. (Dead on arrival.)

9521. Chickna.

9522. Davy's Favorite.

9523. Faizan.

9524. Fajri, long.

9525. Fajri, round.

9526. Faqirmala.

9527. Gola.

9528. Hatijhul.

9529. Kachmahua.

9530. Kakaria.

9531. Kala.

9532. Krishnabhog.

9533. Khajya.

9534. Samar Chisht.

9535. Salamar.

9536. Kistapal.

9537. Lamba Bhadra.

9538. Langra Hardoi.

9539. Langra, large.

9540. Maebias.

9541. Maradabadi amin.

9542. Nijibabadi.

9543. Nayale.

9544. Nucha.

9545. Pyasee.

9546. Ramani. (Dead on arrival.)

9547. Sanduria.

9504 to 9553—Continued.

9548.
Sharbati, brown.

9549.
Sharbati, black.

9550.
Singapur.

9551.
Sunahra.

9552.
Surkha.

9553.
Tamancha.

9554. CITRUS AURANTIUM × CITRUS BERGAMIA.

From Mustapha, Algiers, Algeria. Presented by Dr. L. Trabut, Government Botanist. Received April 18, 1903.

Scions of a white orange, a hybrid of the mellarose and orange, said by Dr. Trabut to be of excellent quality. A description of this is published in the "Revue Hort.," of Paris; exact reference not given.

9555 to 9558. BOUGAINVILLEA spp.

From Cape Town, South Africa. Received through Messrs. Lathrop and Fairchild (Nos. 1144 to 1147, March 11, 1903), April 20, 1903.

"Four different varieties of this superb creeper have been collected by Mr. Ardern and planted on his place called the 'Hill,' at Claremont. These differ in their habit of flowering, color of bracts, and vigor, and although probably not new to America, the set is sent for comparison with sorts already known in the gardens of California." (*Fairchild.*)

9555. BOUGAINVILLEA LATERESIA (?).

Has brick-red bracts and is a vigorous grower. No. 1144.

9556. BOUGAINVILLEA SPECTABILIS.

Has very dark purple bracts. A wonderfully vigorous grower, said to excel the others in its masses of bloom, which are borne for a short period only. No. 1145.

9557. BOUGAINVILLEA GLABRA.

Has very pale, purple bracts, much more so than the two other purple varieties.

9558. BOUGAINVILLEA SANDERIANA.

"A purple-flowered kind, remarkable for its free-flowering habit. It remains in flower much of the year, and although it is not so beautiful as *B. spectabilis* when the latter is in flower, it is preferable because of its constant blooming habit." (*Fairchild.*)

9559. OLEA VERRUCOSA (?). **Wild olive.**

From Cape Town, South Africa. Received through Messrs. Lathrop and Fairchild (No. 1148, March 11, 1903), April 20, 1903.

"The native wild olive of South Africa. These cuttings were taken from a tree growing in Mr. Ardern's garden at Claremont. It may be useful for breeding or as a stock in California." (*Fairchild.*)

9560 to 9568. VITIS VINIFERA. **Grape.**

From Khodjent, Russian Central Asia. Received through Mr. E. A. Bessey, from Mr. Valneff, April 20, 1903.

A collection of grape cuttings, as follows:

9560.
Khusaine.

9561.
Sheker-Angur.

9560 to 9568—Continued.

9562.
Kadu-Khusaine.

9563.
Darai.

9564.
Chelaki.

9565.
Shuvargani.

9566.
Tagobi.

9567.
Khusaine Surkh.

9568.
Bobaki.

9569. GARCINIA sp. (?).

From Delagoa Bay, East Africa. Received through Messrs. Lathrop and Fairchild (No. 1191, February, 1903), March 21, 1903.

"Seed of a large shade tree growing everywhere about and in the town of Delagoa Bay. The tree is a pretty shade tree, vigorous grower, and an enormous fruit producer. I have seldom seen any wild fruit tree which was so loaded down as the trees of this species are with their small egg-shaped green fruits. I was not able to determine the species of this tree, but according to the surmise of Mr. J. Medley Wood, of the Botanic Gardens of Durban, it is a *Garcinia*, and for that reason, as well as for its value as a shade tree, this is worth introducing into the tropical and subtropical gardens of America. It may be possible to cross this with the mangosteen, although the difference between the species seems very great. From the sour pulp of the fruit the Kaffirs prepare a variety of fermented liquor which they keenly relish. They also eat the fruit pulp fresh." (*Fairchild.*)

9570. SOLANUM MURICATUM. **Pepino.**

From Las Palmas, Canary Islands. Received through Messrs. Lathrop and Fairchild (No. 1166, April 6, 1903), April 24, 1903.

Pera Melone. "A seedless fruit plant which is grown on the terraces of Grand Canary and the other islands of the group and on Madeira as well. The fruit tastes like a canteloupe, is the shape of an egg, and when ripe is yellow, striped with splashes of purple. The texture of the yellow flesh resembles that of a ripe pear. The hotel visitors are very fond of this fruit, and it brings a good price in the markets of the island. Here the plants are grown by irrigation and bear in nine months after being planted as cuttings. Artificial fertilizers are used in their culture and the soil is a volcanic one. The fruit may be picked before it is ripe and ripened off the bush. Small shipments have been made to London, which arrived in good condition. This was introduced into California several years ago by Dr. Gustav Eisen and is now grown there." (*Fairchild.*)

9571. AVENA sp. **Mapstone oats.**

From Pietermaritzburg, South Africa. Received through Messrs. Lathrop and Fairchild (No. 1104), April 14, 1903.

"A variety of oat which has been a very prolific yielder in numerous trials at Mapstone farm in Natal." (*Fairchild.*)

9572 to 9574.

From Brookings, S. Dak. Presented by Prof. N. E. Hansen, horticulturist of the South Dakota Agricultural Experiment Station. Received April 17, 1903.

9572. CITRULLUS VULGARIS. **Watermelon.**

Grown from S. P. I. No. 23. Named *South Dakota* by Professor Hansen.

9573. ZEA MAYS. **Corn.**

Malakoff sugar corn. Grown from seed imported by Professor Hansen from Moscow, Russia, in 1902.

9574. DAUCUS CAROTA. **Carrot.**

Kuldja carrot. Grown from S. P. I. No. 1254.

9575. MUSA SAPIENTUM.

From Las Palmas, Canary Islands. Received through Messrs. Lathrop and Fairchild (No. 1168, April 12, 1903), April 27 and May 6, 1903.

Datile. "Young buds from the base of some banana plants in Mr. Nelson's garden in Las Palmas, which the gardener says came from Cuba several years ago. The fruit of this 'date' banana is very small, not over an inch or so long, it is said, but of unusual sweetness, though inclined to be dry. This may be of use for breeding purposes. The plants are small in size and do not seem very vigorous." (*Fairchild.*)

9576. VITIS VINIFERA. Grape.

From Old Bokhara, Turkestan. Received through Mr. E. A. Bessey from Mr. Voronov, the representative of Mr. H. W. Dürrschmidt (No. 114, August 27, 1902), April 29, 1903.

Kishmish. "A white (i. e., very light green) seedless grape, considered to be the best of the sorts grown near Bokhara. The berry is rather small, with a slight amount of bloom, short elliptical in outline, about one-half inch long and three-eighths inch wide, very thin skinned, with a moderately firm, juicy flesh and sweet taste, modified by the presence of sufficient acid to prevent its being insipid. The bunch is large, firm, and compact, and weighs one-half a pound to a pound. I fear that if once attacked by Anthracnose, *Plasmopara*, or Black Rot, the berries are so closely packed that the whole bunch would be destroyed, as without great care in spraying it would be impossible to properly reach the inner berries of the bunch. This variety was also seen in Ashkabad, where it is said to be of Persian origin. It s rather rare here." (*Bessey.*)

9577. VITIS VINIFERA. Grape.

From Old Bokhara, Turkestan. Received through Mr. E. A. Bessey from Mr. Voronov, the representative of Mr. H. W. Dürrschmidt (No. 115, August 27, 1902), April 29, 1903.

Khuśaini (Khoosá-eenee). "A light-green grape, considered to be one of the best, but inferior in quality to *Kishmish*, No. 9576, and *Ok Uziúm*, No. 9578. One of the most abundant varieties on the market. Very productive. Berries light green, without bloom, often tinged with a very faint red color on the sunny side, elongated elliptical in outline, an inch to 1¼ inches long by one-half to five-eighths inch in short diameter. Usually truncated at the base and shortly rounded at the apex. Often slightly larger near the base. Seeds usually only two, situated about one-third of the distance from the base to apex (rarely central). Skin thin and tender; flesh juicy and tender, but firm. Sweet and slightly acid—too little acid for some people's taste. Bunches large (three-fourths to 1 pound or more), loose, rather long; would be easy to spray." (*Bessey.*)

9578. VITIS VINIFERA. Grape.

From Old Bokhara, Turkestan. Received through Mr. E. A. Bessey from Mr. Voronov, the representative of Mr. H. W. Dürrschmidt (No. 116, August 27, 1902), April 29, 1903.

Ok Uziúm (meaning *White grape*). "A white (i. e., light green) grape, very abundant on the markets of Old Bokhara. Considered by some to be of better quality than *Khuśaini*, No. 9577, but I consider it inferior. Berries light green, with bloom, round, five-eighths to three-fourths inch in diameter, with usually three rather small seeds. Skin thin but tough, and with a slightly astringent taste, which makes it necessary to avoid chewing the skin much. Flesh firm but tender and juicy, sweet but with slight acid flavor, and superior in this respect to that of *Khuśaini*, if care is taken not to chew the skin. Bunches large (1 to 1½ pounds), very compact, with a pronounced shoulder. Apparently would be difficult to spray properly, but not so difficult as *Kishmish*, No. 9576." (*Bessey.*)

9579. VITIS VINIFERA. Grape.

From Old Bokhara, Turkestan. Received through Mr. E. A. Bessey from Mr. Voronov, the representative of Mr. H. W. Dürrschmidt (No. 117, August 27, 1902), April 29, 1903.

Shuborgónyi. "An almost black grape with a faint bloom. Quite rare in the markets. Considered inferior to *Kishmish*, No. 9576, and *Ok Uziúm*, No. 9578. Berries elliptical, small to medium, usually one-half to five-eighths inch long by three-eighths inch thick, sometimes larger. Flesh actually almost colorless, but appearing dark on cutting open, because of the dark skin and colored layer immediately below it. Skin rather tender; only very slightly, or not at all, astringent. Flesh quite firm, juicy, and sweet. Seeds none or, if present, so tender that they are not noticeable on chewing, having no hard coat. Bunches rather small, not over one-half pound, with a pronounced shoulder, rather loose, and easy to spray. Except that it stains the fingers and mouth, I consider this variety superior to *Ok Uziúm*, No. 9578, and *Kishmish*, No. 9576." (*Bessey*.)

9580. SALSOLA ARBUSCULA.

From Chardjui, Russian Central Asia. Received through Mr. E. A. Bessey from Mr. V. Paletzky, forester, of Chardjui (No. 194, October 3, 1902), May 1, 1903.

"This plant is one of the best sand binders in this region. It forms a large shrub, or even small tree, 15 to 20 feet high. It grows without irrigation in sand in a very hot region where no rain falls from April to November. In the winter it endures severe cold. This plant can be propagated either by seed (sown from January to March) or cuttings (also planted in early spring). In either case a stand of about 40 per cent is obtained. If grown along with *Aristida pennata* var. *Karelini*, No. 9582, it seeds itself in the tufts of the latter, and soon is able to take care of its own dissemination." (*Bessey*.)

9581. HALOXYLON AMMODENDRON.

From Chardjui, Russian Central Asia. Received through Mr. E. A. Bessey from Mr. V. Paletzky, forester, of Chardjui (No. 195, October 3, 1902), May 1, 1903.

"This plant often becomes a tree 20 to even 30 feet high, with a trunk 15 to 18 inches in diameter near the base. It requires a clay subsoil which holds some moisture. It is very hard to establish, but when once started is valuable as a sand binder. It will not endure salt." (*Bessey*.)

9582. ARISTIDA PENNATA var. KARELINI.

From Chardjui, Russian Central Asia. Received through Mr. E. A. Bessey from Mr. V. Paletzky, forester, of Chardjui (No. 196, October 3, 1902), May 1, 1903.

"This grass, itself valuable as a sand binder, is especially valuable from the fact that its tufts act as shelters in which the seeds of *Salsola arbuscula* (No. 9580) and *Calligonum* sp. (Nos. 9583 to 9594) lodge and grow. Nearly every bunch of this grass will be found to have growing in it a young plant of Salsola or Calligonum. The seeds are sown in holes in the sand and covered with sand by the workman's foot, or are mixed at the rate of 1 pound to 200 or 300 pounds of sand and sown broadcast; the former method is, however, preferable. It is sown in the hollows between the sand dunes, and requires only one seeding, as the following year it reseeds itself." (*Bessey*.)

9583 to 9594. CALLIGONUM sp.

From Chardjui, Russian Central Asia. Received through Mr. E. A. Bessey from Mr. V. Paletzky, forester, of Chardjui (No. 197, October 3, 1902), May 1, 1903.

9583. CALLIGONUM ARBORESCENS and C. CAPUT-MEDUSAE.

"A mixture of these two species. These two are the best of the Calligonums for sand-binding purposes. They form small trees. They are superior to *Salsola arbuscula* in that when planted from seeds or from cuttings 90 per cent grow, inferior in that they do not reseed themselves very well." (*Bessey*.) (No. 197, October 3, 1902.)

Additional species sent by Mr. Paletzky.

9584. CALLIGONUM ACANTHOPTERUM, Borsc. var. SETOSA.

9583 to 9594—Continued.

9584a. CALLIGONUM ACANTHOPTERUM, Borscz. var. SETOSA.

9584b. CALLIGONUM ACANTHOPTERUM, Borscz. var. SETOSA.

(These three packages were kept separate because of a slight variation in the appearance of the seeds.)

9585. CALLIGONUM ARBORESCENS, sp. nov.

9586. CALLIGONUM ARBORESCENS × C. ACANTHOPTERUM.

9587. CALLIGONUM CALLIPHYSA.

9588. CALLIGONUM CAPUT-MEDUSAE.

9588a. CALLIGONUM CAPUT-MEDUSAE var. RUBICUNDA.

9589. CALLIGONUM COMOSUM.

9590. CALLIGONUM DENSUM.

9591. CALLIGONUM ERIOPODUM.

9592. CALLIGONUM MICROCARPUM.

9593. CALLIGONUM PALLASII.

9594. CALLIGONUM ROTULA.

9595. CITRUS AURANTIUM. **Orange.**

From Las Palmas, Canary Islands. Received through Messrs. Lathrop and Fairchild (No. 1171, April 14, 1903), May 1, 1903.

Telde. "Considered the finest variety in Grand Canary and superior to those grown in the central part of the island. These latter, it may be remarked, are considered by Mr. Lathrop and myself some of the finest flavored oranges which we have ever eaten, being characterized by a freedom from fiber, a crisp texture of flesh, and an indescribably vinous flavor. The variety is medium in size, thin skinned and seeded. The color of the flesh varies, but in the best specimens is a shade of dark orange. The juiciness is phenomenal, and though the fruit varies greatly in flavor and color it is uniformly good and sweet. Any collection should be glad to get this variety. Its origin is unknown as far as I can discover. The name is that of the village where the fruit is grown, some 8 miles from Las Palmas." (*Fairchild.*)

9596. CITRUS AURANTIUM. **Orange.**

From Las Palmas, Canary Islands. Received through Messrs. Lathrop and Fairchild (No. 1172, April 14, 1903), May 1, 1903.

Canary seedless. "Scions from two trees which are growing on the estate of Don Juan Rodriguez, in the famous orange region along the *Barranco de la Higuera de Canaria.* These trees are reputed to produce only fruit that is absolutely seedless, and though they are very old trees they have never, so far as we could learn, produced fruits with more than the rudiments of seeds in them. No fruits were on the trees when these cuttings were taken, so the statement as to their seedlessness is that of the renter of the place, Sig. Rivero. If this orange is seedless, as claimed, and of a quality equal to the other varieties of the same locality, as is affirmed by the cultivator, the sort is well worth thorough investigation and comparison with the navel orange now grown in California. It is, I believe, a smaller sort, and may prove superior in flavor. The excellence of these oranges from this region, which is the most noted in the islands, is attested by Mr. Lathrop, who thinks them equal to the best." (*Fairchild.*)

9597. CITRUS AURANTIUM. **Orange.**

From Las Palmas, Canary Islands. Received through Messrs. Lathrop and Fairchild (No. 1172a, April 14, 1903), May 1, 1903.

Canary seedless. "Scions of a variety of seedless orange likely to prove the same as No. 9596, but taken from a much younger tree than the latter that grew a short distance away from the two old trees mentioned under No. 9596. We have taken the liberty of naming this and the previous variety the *Canary seedless.*" (*Fairchild.*)

9598. PLOCAMA PENDULA.

From Las Palmas, Grand Canary, Canary Islands. Received through Messrs. Lathrop and Fairchild (No. 1173, April 14, 1903), May 1, 1903.

"A species of low-growing shrub which occurs wild on the slopes of the arid hillside near the road from Las Palmas to Telde. It has a most beautiful weeping habit, giving the plants the appearance of tiny weeping willows. It is not over 2½ to 3 feet high. This would be very beautiful as a cover for dry hillsides overlooking the sea. It has already been brought into greenhouse culture. I believe it will withstand severe drought." (*Fairchild.*)

9599. MANGIFERA INDICA. **Mango.**

From the Philippine Islands. Received through Prof. W. S. Lyon, in charge of seed and plant introduction, Insular Bureau of Agriculture, Manila, May 4, 1903.

"One seed of mango No. 2. The fruit from which this seed was taken weighed 16 ounces. When still wet and fresh the seed weighed only 1 ounce, making more than 93 per cent of the flesh available, exclusive of a very thin and light rind." (*Lyon.*)

9600. PHOENIX DACTYLIFERA. **Date.**

From Marseille, France. Received through Champagne Bros., Ltd, May 4, 1903, 264 pounds dried Deglet Noor dates, purchased at the request of Mr. W. T. Swingle. (No. 130.)

"Dry Deglet Noor dates from the Sahara suitable for planting. Planting is best done after the ground gets warm in April or May on alkali-free soil with abundant irrigation. This superb variety can be propagated with certainty only by means of offshoots, but as these are now very difficult to obtain, it is desirable to grow seedlings in the hope of securing some that will prove equal to the parent sort in quality. About half the seedlings are generally males and one in ten can be counted on to yield good dates. It is not unreasonable to expect that some of the seedlings may be as good as the Deglet Noor, and ripen earlier, which will permit of their culture in the Salt River Valley, Arizona." (*Swingle.*)

9601. IRIS sp.

From Monte, Grand Canary, Canary Islands. Received through Messrs. Lathrop and Fairchild (No. 1174, April 17, 1903), May 4, 1903.

"A very beautiful white iris of unusual size (5 inches in diameter), which is fragrant. This grows wild in certain barrancos of Grand Canary, and Mr. Alaricus Delmard, of Monte, called it to our attention. He sent plants to English florists who declared it was new, but the plants failed to live. Its great size and the purity of its white color and its delicate perfume, like that of a lily, make it a desirable introduction, although specifically it may not be new to America." (*Fairchild.*)

9602. HEDERA HELIX var. CANARIENSIS. **Ivy.**

From Monte, Grand Canary, Canary Islands. Received through Messrs. Lathrop and Fairchild (No. 1175, April 17, 1903), May 4, 1903.

"An exceedingly vigorous, very large-leaved variety of ivy, which grows wild in the Canary Islands. The leaves are sometimes 6 to 8 inches across. It may not retain this character of large leaves, but it is worthy of trial or for breeding purposes." (*Fairchild.*)

9603. DRACUNCULUS CANARIENSIS.

From Monte, Grand Canary, Canary Islands. Received through Messrs. Lathrop and Fairchild (No. 1176, April 17, 1903), May 4, 1903.

"A giant aroid with spathes sometimes 14 to 16 inches long. Yellowish or greenish in color. Leaves deeply lobed and ornamental. Grows 6 to 8 feet in height in moist places in the mountains of Grand Canary. Might prove useful for breeders of the calla lily because of its large size. This was called to our attention by Mr. A. Delmard, of Monte." (*Fairchild.*)

9604. PORTULACARIA AFRA. Spek-boom.

From Cape Town, South Africa. Received through Messrs. Lathrop and Fairchild (No. 1130, March 8, 1903), May 6, 1903.

Spek-boom. "This bush, which grows sometimes 12 to 15 feet high, forms one of the most valuable fodder elements of the northeastern Karroo, in Cape Colony. It is a succulent-leaved species, greedily eaten by horned stock, and well worth thorough trial in the frostless, dry lands of our southwestern States. The cuttings should be placed in the hands of the gardeners of a few interested ranch owners and at the experiment stations in the States where the plant is likely to prove of value, with the understanding that they are to be grown and multiplied and small patches of mother plants started from which cuttings can be taken. The cuttings and young plants must be protected from gophers, rats, mice, or prairie dogs until several years old. At least the mother plantations should be so protected. This is not a desert plant, but simply a species which has the power to withstand a long, dry season, and because of the avidity with which live stock eat its leaves and stems it is worth acclimatizing in the frostless regions of America. It thrives best on rocky slopes and needs protection from the wind by wind-breaks. These cuttings were made from a tree growing in the grounds of the South African Museum, in Cape Town, which tree was planted many years ago by Professor MacOwan. They are a gift to the American ranchman from this veteran Cape botanist who has done so much to call attention to the good qualities of the *Spek-boom*. The climate of the region in which the tree lives is illustrated by these figures: Absolute maximum temperature for ten years (1881-1890), 108° F., absolute minimum, 21° F. Rainfall average for ten years, 18.76 inches per annum, occurring in the warm season." (*Fairchild.*)

9605. PORTULACARIA AFRA.

From Oatlands, South Africa. Received through Messrs. Lathrop and Fairchild (No. 1155, March 16, 1903), May 6, 1903.

Spek-boom. "These cuttings came from the typical Karroo, where the plant is highly prized for fodder purposes. It may prove slightly different from those taken from a tree in Cape Town, No. 9604. These cuttings were collected by Mr. Nash, of the Cape department of agriculture, and secured through Mr. Davison, chief sheep inspector of the department." (*Fairchild.*) (For description see No. 9604.)

9606. ANANAS SATIVUS. Pineapple.

From Lower Albany, Trapps Valley, South Africa. Received through Messrs. Lathrop and Fairchild (No. 1154, March 16, 1903), May 6, 1903.

Natal. "This is evidently the same variety of pineapple as No. 9485. Fresh pineapples from this region which we tested were not as fine flavored as those we ate in Natal, but the fact that they had been picked green should be taken into consideration. Should it grow as well in Florida as it does here it would prove a great success. Secured through the kindness of Mr. Eustace Pillans, agricultural assistant of Cape department of agriculture, from C. J. Ansley, Trapps Valley, Cape Colony." (*Fairchild.*)

9607. VITIS RUPESTRIS var. METALLICA. Grape.

From Cape Town, South Africa. Presented by the Cape department of agriculture through Messrs. Lathrop and Fairchild (No. 1137, March 10, 1903). Received May 6, 1903.

"A resistant American stock of South African origin, which has proved itself most admirably suited to the conditions at the Cape, and especially adapted to 'any loose soil, loam, gravel, or sand, and also in dry, open heavy soils; it can, besides, stand a fair amount of moisture in loose soils. It forms an excellent graft-bearer for all varieties of European vines, except *Hanepoot*, and possibly also other members of the *Muscat* family.' (cf. J. P. de Waal, in the Agricultural Journal, Cape of Good Hope, December 19, 1901, p. 838.) This variety, I am informed by Mr. Eustace Pillans, is the best of all the resistant stocks yet tried at the Cape, as its ease of grafting, great vigor, suitability to different kinds of soil, and grafting affinity for all but varieties of the *Muscat* type, make it a general stock of great value. Even those who do not claim that it exceeds in vigor any other sort, admit that it is the easiest grafted of any of the American stocks. The stock originated at Groot Constantia Wine Farm in a lot of seedlings from seed sown in 1886. It is uncertain whether the seed came direct from America or from France. This is entirely distinct, according to Mr. J. Bioletti (formerly of Berkeley University, California, now at Elsenburg Agricultural School), from the *Metallica* of French vineyardists. Its name applies to the luster of its foliage. The seedling was picked out in 1894, and by quick propagation in 1901 yielded 687,000 cuttings, and in 1902, 864,000 cuttings were distributed. It has been tested side by side with many French stocks, such as *Aramon rupestris, Riparia Gloire de Montpellier*, etc., and takes its place as their equal in all points and their superior as regards ease of propagation and suitability to the varieties of soil mentioned. Mr. Pillans goes so far as to predict that it will drive all other stocks out of South Africa, except for *Muscat* sorts. He claims for it a remarkable yield-giving power, extreme vigor, and resistance to the phylloxera. Mr. Bioletti admits its excellent qualities and practical growers are enthusiastic over it. This is well worth the serious consideration of Californian vine growers. The originators of this remarkable seedling are Messrs. J. P. de Waal and Eustace Pillans, of the Cape of Good Hope department of agriculture, and its trial in California should be made at once. We are indebted to Mr. Pillans for the plants sent." (*Fairchild*.)

9608. CHLORIS VIRGATA. **Rhodes grass.**

From Cape Town, South Africa. Received through Messrs. Lathrop and Fairchild (No. 1131, March 8, 1903), May 6, 1903.

"A species of pasture grass that, although scattered widely through the Tropics of both hemispheres (according to the books), has probably not before been brought into culture. Mr. Cecil Rhodes had the seed of this plant collected several years ago and sown in large patches on his place near Cape Town, called 'Groote Schur.' The grass has done well there, forming heavy sods of a good herbage, and the manager of Mr. Rhodes's farm has had the seed collected and distributed among the planters of the colony, by whom it is called 'Rhodes grass.' From what I saw of these patches on the slopes of a hillside, I do not believe this is a drought resistant form; at least it is not able to withstand very severe dry weather. It has the typical finger-like inflorescence of the genus and its strong, tough, creeping stems lie flat on the ground. When given sufficient moisture the grass is said to produce a mass of forage over 2 feet high, but what it would do if subjected to severe drought has yet to be found out. I saw a single patch which had been sown with the seed and had failed to take, and it was evident that the drought-resisting powers of the plant are quite limited. However, a grass which has attracted the attention of so keen a cultivator as Mr. Rhodes and is meeting with favorable comment from many practical men here at the Cape deserves a thorough trial in America. As the species is a perennial it need only be tested in frostless or nearly frostless regions. Its fodder value will be much inferior to alfalfa, but it will thrive on soil with little lime in it. This seed was given Mr. Lathrop for distribution in America by the steward of Mr. Rhodes's estate, and in case it succeeds, the Chartered South African Company, at Cape Town, should be notified of the success it attains." (*Fairchild*.)

9609. TRITICUM JUNCEUM.

From Cape Town, South Africa. Received through Messrs. Lathrop and Fairchild (No. 1136, March 9, 1903), May 6, 1903.

"A grass which is a native of North Africa and Europe, and is used as a sand binder here in Cape Colony. Mr. Hutchins, conservator of forests of the colony, to whom we are indebted for the seed, has found this species especially serviceable in experiments near the seashore. Von Müller remarks that it is one of the best grasses to keep rolling sand ridges together. Probably this has already been tried in America, but this South African seed may be of a different strain." (*Fairchild*.)

9610. MUSA SAPIENTUM. **Banana.**

From Las Palmas, Grand Canary, Canary Islands. Received through Messrs. Lathrop and Fairchild (No. 1169, April 12, 1903), May 6, 1903.

Manzana or *Silver*. "Young shoots from the base of a few plants of the *Silver* banana of Madeira, which variety is thought by the residents of this island to be a very superior sort and to have originated in Madeira. The fruits which we tasted were good, but not remarkable. They had an acid flavor, were juicy, had light-colored flesh, and though very refreshing as a change from the ordinary type of banana, were not especially to be recommended." (*Fairchild.*)

9611. STRYCHNOS SPINOSA (?) **Kafir orange.**

From Mozambique, East Africa. Received through Messrs. Lathrop and Fairchild (No. 1103, February 8, 1903), May 6, 1903.

"Seed (*poisonous*) of the Kafir orange, a native fruit of Portuguese East Africa. The tree is grown in Delagoa Bay only occasionally, and the Kafirs crack open the calabash-like fruit and eat the brown, plum-like flesh which surrounds the many flat angular seeds. These seeds are *said to be very poisonous*, but the flesh is quite refreshing. That of the specimen which we tasted was like a brandied peach into which cloves had been stuck. The spicy aroma of the fruit is perceptible before the hard shell has been broken open and forms one of its best characteristics. The fruits are cannon ball shaped and very heavy, and the green shell is so hard that it has to be broken with a heavy blow. It is in many ways a remarkable fruit, and although the data regarding it are meager it is well worth a place in Porto Rico, Florida, and Hawaiian gardens." (*Fairchild.*)

9612. CARISSA ARDUINA.

From Cape Town, South Africa. Received through Messrs. Lathrop and Fairchild (No. 1110, February 26, 1903), May 6, 1903.

"A beautiful, thorny, evergreen shrub, suited to frostless regions. It would be suited for hedge making and as an ornamental, for its white flowers and oblong, bright red fruits show off strikingly against its dark-green foliage. Like *Carissa grandiflora*, its fruits, resembling a large barberry fruit, are good to eat, having a sweet, fresh, but somewhat characterless taste. Standing alone this species produces a prettier shaped shrub than *C. grandiflora* and is well worth the attention of gardeners in California and Florida. These seeds are from fruit gathered in the municipal gardens in Cape Town. Breeders should be encouraged to try crossing these two species. There are other representatives of the genus in South Africa which might be used in breeding experiments. *C. acuminata*, A. D. C., is listed for Natal by J. Medley Wood in his 'Indigenous Plants of Natal;' von Mueller lists *C. brownii*, F. V. M., from East Australia, and *C. carandas* L., from India to China. All these species have edible fruits." (*Fairchild.*)

9613. MEDICAGO ARBOREA. **Tree lucern.**

From Cape Town, South Africa. Received through Messrs. Lathrop and Fairchild (No. 1111, March 3, 1903), May 6, 1903.

"Seed of the *Tree lucern*, which is said to occur in southern Europe, especially in Greece. It is, according to von Mueller in his 'Extra Tropical Plants,' page 300, the 'Cytisus' of the ancient Greeks and Romans. The plant forms a shrub 7 to 8 feet high with thick, woody stems 3 inches in diameter, which sprawl more or less over the ground. These seeds are from a single specimen in the Municipal Gardens at Cape Town, and Professor MacOwan informs me that the plant has not attracted much attention here as a fodder plant, though it grows well. For plant breeders only who are at work on the genus *Medicago*." (*Fairchild.*)

9614. SOLANUM sp.

From Cape Town, South Africa. Received through Messrs. Lathrop and Fairchild (No. 1112, March 3, 1903), May 6, 1903.

"Seed of a tree *Solanum*, of decided ornamental value, which is growing in the Municipal Gardens at Cape Town and which has never been specifically determined.

Its origin also is not known, according to Professor MacOwan. It should be sent for trial to the frostless regions of America and distributed among the superintendents of parks and public gardens and private ornamental plant growers. Its upright stem, spiny, broad leaves, and horizontal branches make it effective." (*Fairchild.*)

9615. PORTULACARIA AFRA.

From Cape Town, South Africa. Presented by Prof. P. MacOwan, Government Botanist, through Messrs. Lathrop and Fairchild (No. 1113. Received March 3, 1903), May 6, 1903.

Spek-boom. "Seed of this interesting fodder plant. (See Nos. 9604, 9605.)" (*Fairchild.*)

9616. HARPEPHYLLUM CAFFRUM. Kafir plum.

From Cape Town, South Africa. Presented by Prof. P. MacOwan, Government Botanist, through Messrs. Lathrop and Fairchild (No. 1114, March 5, 1903). Received May 6, 1903.

"One of the prettiest evergreen shade trees to be seen in the gardens of Cape Town. Prof. P. MacOwan has planted a row of these trees in a very windy situation near the parliament buildings in Cape Town and they are admirably suited to such a trying situation, where they are whipped by continuous winds which blow from various directions. Professor Sim remarks that its timber resembles mahogany and is used for wagon making, being called *eschenhout* by the Dutch. The red, showy drupes are suitable for preserves, but in the Cape they are apparently not popular though they have a pleasant acid taste, but little pulp. The branches are sometimes planted as fence poles and these large 'cuttings' take root and form trees. [*Sim.*] Professor MacOwan recommends this heartily as a shade tree for windy situations, where its beautiful dark green foliage forms a dense shade. The tree will thrive in the frostless belt of California and Florida and is sure to be appreciated by owners of parks as an avenue plant. The seeds should be sown in a seed bed and plants transplanted to situations desired. It is not a desert plant, but will stand some drought. This tree is worthy a prominent place in the gardens and parks of California and Florida." (*Fairchild.*)

9617. SOLANUM ACULEASTRUM. Natal thorn.

From Cape Town, South Africa. Presented by Prof. P. MacOwan, Government Botanist, through Messrs. Lathrop and Fairchild (No. 1115, March 8, 1903). Received May 6, 1903.

"An ornamental species with very large fruits, grows 6 feet high if grown singly or 4 to 4½ feet if in a hedge, for which latter purpose it is used by the farmers. Very acutely hook-thorned, rather disposed to use up too much space if left alone. The fruit is the size of a mandarin orange. It will not bear more than a short and slight frost. To be sent to Texas, Arizona, and California gardens." (*Fairchild.*)

9618. PASPALUM DIGITARIA.

From Cape Town, South Africa. Presented by Prof. P. MacOwan, Government Botanist, through Messrs. Lathrop and Fairchild (No. 1128, March 8, 1903). Received May 6, 1903.

"Seed of a grass, which, according to Prof. P. MacOwan, is promising for moist bottom land. It will not endure cold weather, but is suited to subtropical conditions." (*Fairchild.*)

9619. PENTZIA VIRGATA.

From Cape Town, South Africa. Presented by Prof. P. MacOwan, Government Botanist, through Messrs. Lathrop and Fairchild (No. 1129, March 9, 1903). Received May 6, 1903.

"Old seed of the fodder bush called the *Goed Karroo*. This is the best plant in the Karroo for sheep pasturage, for it furnishes good fodder, binds the sand, preventing gullying, and withstands drought. (*Fairchild.*)

9620. EUCLEA RACEMOSA.

From Cape Town, South Africa. Presented by Prof. P. MacOwan, Government Botanist, through Messrs. Lathrop and Fairchild (No. 1132, March 9, 1903). Received May 6, 1903.

"A shrub with dense, dark-green foliage, of distinctly ornamental appearance, which is especially suited for plantings near the sea that are exposed to salt spray, with the purpose of lifting the wind from the surface of the soil and checking the shifting of the sands. In experiments of fixing sand dunes this plant may prove of decided value, not so much through the action of its roots as by the formation of a cover for the sand, which will lift the wind above its surface. Strongly recommended by Professor MacOwan in his recommendations to the Cape government on the rebushing of an overstocked island off the coast called Robbin Island. This seed should be planted in a seed bed and the young plants set out when of sufficient size to bear transplanting well." (*Fairchild.*)

9621. MYOPORUM INSULARE.

From Cape Town, South Africa. Presented by Prof. P. MacOwan, Government Botanist, through Messrs. Lathrop and Fairchild (No. 1133, March 8, 1903). Received May 6, 1903.

"An extra tropical Australian tree called in South Africa *Australian blueberry*, and used there as a hedge plant or as an ornamental tree. It is proof against sea breezes, can be propagated by cuttings, grows rapidly, and will thrive down to high-tide mark. It is one of the few trees which will grow in wet saline soil. The wood is close grained and good for cabinet making. (*Fairchild.*)

9622. COTYLEDON TERETIFOLIA.

From Cape Town, South Africa. Presented by Prof. P. MacOwan, Government Botanist, through Messrs. Lathrop and Fairchild (No. 1134, March 8, 1903). Received May 6, 1903.

"Seeds of a *Cotyledon* from Grahamstown, Great Kirch River. This is a hothouse plant." (*Fairchild.*)

9623. CEPHALANDRA QUINQUILOBA.

From Cape Town, South Africa. Received through Messrs. Lathrop and Fairchild (No. 1135, March 8, 1903), May 6, 1903.

"A cucurbitaceous plant of ornamental value, running over the ground and bearing pretty yellow flowers and red fruits. It should be tried in southern California as an arbor plant mixed with other more dense shade-giving species. Probably a tender species." (*Fairchild.*)

9624. EUCALYPTUS FICIFOLIA.

From Cape Town, South Africa. Received through Messrs. Lathrop and Fairchild (No. 1157, March 16, 1903), May 6, 1903.

"Seed from some trees growing on Cecil Rhodes's place, Groote Schur. I have never seen in any landscape more gorgeous dashes of color than those produced by these trees when in bloom. The colors vary from salmon or pale pink to deep scarlet. This tree is probably known in California, perhaps under another specific name." (*Fairchild.*)

9625. PITTOSPORUM PENDULUM.

From Cape Town, South Africa. Received through Messrs. Lathrop and Fairchild (No. 1158, March 16, 1903), May 6, 1903.

"Seed of a remarkably grotesque tree growing in the municipal gardens at Cape Town. It has long slender branches which hang like those of a weeping willow. Its trunks are weird and irregular in form and give to the tree a most singular appearance. This is worthy of trial in such parks as the Golden Gate Park, of San Francisco." (*Fairchild.*)

9626. CUCURBITA MELANOSPERMA. Squash.

From San Antonio, Malta. Received through Messrs. Lathrop and Fairchild (No. 1159, December 27, 1902), May 6, 1903.

"Dr. Giovanni Borg, director of the gardens at San Antonio, called our attention to this squash as the best one for soups and as a vegetable which he had ever tested on the island. The plant also grows luxuriantly in Madeira, where it is highly prized as a vegetable. Doctor Grabham, of Funchal, remarked that it formed one of the principal foods of the native poor people. It should be given a good test by seedsmen." (*Fairchild.*)

9627. LUPINUS ALBUS (?).

From Tripoli or Tunis. Received through Messrs. Lathrop and Fairchild (No. 1160, December 1902), May 6, 1903.

"A few peculiar lupines picked up either in Tunis or Tripoli. They may be of interest to those experimenting with this plant as a green manure crop." (*Fairchild.*)

9628 to 9631. Ornamentals.

From Cape Town, South Africa. Received through Messrs. Lathrop and Fairchild (Nos. 1162 to 1165, March 16, 1903), May 6, 1903.

Seed of several ornamentals presented by Mr. H. J. Chalvin, superintendent of the municipal gardens at Cape Town, as follows:

9628. COTYLEDON sp.

Various species. Mixed seed. (No. 1162.)

9629. ASPARAGUS PLUMOSUS.

(No. 1163.)

9630. GASTERIA CROUCHERI.

(No. 1164.)

9631. MORAEA PAVONIA.

(No. 1165.)

9632 and 9633.

From Port Elizabeth district, South Africa. Received through Messrs. Lathrop and Fairchild, May 6, 1903.

9632. EUPHORBIA CORONATA.

A few seeds.

9633. LEUCADENDRON ARGENTEUM. Silver tree.

"Planted in a pot closely and allowed to grow up thickly, the silver tree is said to form a very pretty pot plant. Difficult to transplant." (*Fairchild.*)

9634. ANANAS SATIVUS. Pineapple.

From Trapps Valley, South Africa. Received through Messrs. Lathrop and Fairchild (No. 1156, March 16, 1903), May 15, 1903.

Natal. "These are probably in no way different from No. 9606, and were intended to be shipped with them, but arrived too late. Secured through the kindness of Prof. C. P. Lounsbury, entomologist of the Cape department of agriculture, from a plantation near Trapps Valley.

9635 to 9660. GOSSYPIUM BARBADENSE. Egyptian cotton.

From Egypt. Received through Mr. Thomas H. Kearney, May 16, 1903.

9635.

Extra Fine Mit Afifi. Purchased from Robin Carver, Kafr-el-Zayat.

9636.

Ashmuni. Purchased from Carver Brothers & Co., Beni-Suef.

9635 to 9660—Continued.

9637 to 9660.

Purchased from Choremi Benachi & Co., Alexandria.

9637.
Mit Afifi. First picking, from Behera Province.

9638.
Mit Afifi. Second picking, from Behera Province.

9639.
Mit Afifi. From Charkieh Province.

9640.
Mit Afifi. From Dakahlieh Province.

9641.
Mit Afifi. From Kalioubieh Province.

9642.
Mit Afifi. First picking, from Kaliuobieh Province.

9643.
Mit Afifi. First picking, from Gharbieh Province.

9644.
Mit Afifi. Second picking, from Gharbieh Province.

9645.
Mit Afifi. First picking, from Menufieh Province.

9646.
Jannovitch. First picking, from Behera Province.

9647.
Jannovitch. From Charkieh Province.

9648.
Jannovitch. From Dakahlieh Province.

9649.
Jannovitch. First picking, from Gharbieh Province.

9650.
Jannovitch. Second picking, from Gharbieh Province.

9651.
Abbasi. First picking, from Behera Province.

9652.
Abbasi. Third picking, from Behera Province.

9653.
Abbasi. From Charkieh Province.

9654.
Abbasi. From Dakahlieh Province

9635 to 9660—Continued.
    9637 to 9660—Continued.
        9655.
            Abbasi. Third picking, from Kalioubieh Province.
        9656.
            Abbasi. Second picking, from Kalioubieh Province.
        9657.
            Abbasi. First picking, from Gharbieh Province.
        9658.
            Abbasi. Second picking, from Gharbieh Province.
        9659.
            Abbasi. First picking, from Menufieh Province.
        9660.
            Abbasi. Second picking, from Menufieh Province.

9661 and 9662.   **Ornamentals.**

    From Funchal, Madeira. Received through Messrs. Lathrop and Fairchild (Nos. 1177 and 1178, April 21, 1903), May 18, 1903.

        9661. STREPTOSOLON JAMESONII.

    "This is one of the showiest flowering shrubs I have ever seen. It is a native of South Africa and there and in Madeira the bushes are covered with dense masses of yellow and orange colored blooms. Already known in California." (*Fairchild.*) (No. 1177.)

        9662. BIGNONIA CHAMBERLAYNII.

    "A beautiful lemon yellow flowering species, which grows to perfection here on walls and trellises. It is covered with masses of big trumpet-shaped flowers." (*Fairchild.*) (No. 1178.)

9663. PERESKIA ACULEATA.

    From Funchal, Madeira. Received through Messrs. Lathrop and Fairchild (No. 1183, April, 1903), May 18, 1903.

    "Cuttings of this member of the cactus family, which is used for a stock on which to graft cacti. As a stock it is well known, but as an ornamental climber probably less well known. In Funchal a single plant, 3 years old, had covered the front fence of a private house with a wealth of beautiful foliage. It was loaded with one-seeded fruits, which, though edible, had little taste. Already known in California." (*Fairchild.*)

9664. CANARINA CANARIENSIS (?).

    From Funchal, Madeira. Received through Messrs. Lathrop and Fairchild (No. 1185, April, 1903), May 16, 1903.

    "Seed of a pretty creeper, native of the Canaries and deriving its generic name from the islands. It has luxuriant light-green foliage and bears bell-shaped orange-red flowers which are quite showy. It requires much moisture and grows naturally in shaded valleys of the Canaries. These seed came from the villa of Mr. Reid, some distance above the town of Funchal, in Madeira. Should thrive in Florida and possibly in southern California. Sometimes grown as a hothouse plant." (*Fairchild.*)

9665. CANNABIS SATIVA.   **Hemp.**

    From Yokohama, Japan. Received through The Yokohama Nursery Company, 21-35 Nakamura, Yokohama, Japan, May 20, 1903.

    Aizu.

9666 and 9667.

From Surat Government farm, India. Received May 11, 1903.

9666.
Unnamed seed.

9667. ORYZA SATIVA. **Rice.**

9668. HELIANTHUS ANNUUS. **Sunflower.**

From Moscow, Russia. Received through Mr. E. A. Bessey from E. Immer & Son, May 22, 1903.
White-seeded variety, grown for oil making.

9669. MANGIFERA INDICA. **Mango.**

From Beira, Portuguese East Africa. Received through Messrs. Lathrop and Fairchild (No. 1089, January 28, 1903), May 25, 1903.

Lathrop. "During a trip down this East African coast seven years ago, Mr. Lathrop found at Beira a few mangoes of such extraordinarily fine quality that he has often spoken of them as a possibly valuable present to the mango growers of America. We reached Beira at the end of the season for this mango and could only secure one fruit of it to test and one seed of another fruit. The fruit eaten, which was given us by the American consul, Mr. Glenny, was of exquisite flavor and as free from fiber as a firm custard. The seed of this fruit and the other seed of the same variety are labeled No. 1091, L. & F., S. P. I. No. 9486. The following scanty information was obtainable about this mango: On the island of Chiloane, some 60 miles south of Beira, a monastery was established by the Portuguese several centuries ago. This monastery has been abandoned for many years, a century or more, we are told. Long after that time some fishermen found mango trees growing in the abandoned garden of the once monastery and brought the fruit to Beira. Since then small lots of this fruit are brought from Chiloane by any fishing boat passing during the mango season. The repute of this mango has spread along the African coast as being far superior to any other variety grown there. So far as we could learn no effort has been made to introduce the plant to the mainland, except in the instance of a single young tree in Beira grown from a seed. The sample we ate was delicious in flavor, delicate in texture, and of large size. This variety was named after Mr. Barbour Lathrop, its discoverer and first introducer into America." (*Fairchild.*)

9670 to 9699. MANIHOT sp. **Cassava.**

From Robert Thomson, Half Way Tree, Jamaica. Purchased on the recommendation of Prof. P. H. Rolfs. Received May 7, 1903.

9670.
Pacho No. 1.

9671.
Pacho No. 2.

9672.
Pacho No. 3.

9673.
Pacho No. 4.

9674.
Heleda No. 1.

9675.
Heleda No. 2.

9676.
Heleda No. 3.

9677.
Heleda No. 4.

9678.
Heleda No. 5.

9679.
Heleda No. 6.

9680.
Heleda No. 7.

9681.
Rio (Piet) de Paloma.

9682.
Negrita No. 1.

9683.
Negrita No. 2.

9670 to 9699—Continued.

9684.
Negrita No.

9685.
Negrita No. 4.

9686.
Blancita.

9687.
Cajon amarilla.

9688.
Notoseves.

9689.
Cabaza dura.

9690.
Pie de perdig.

9691.
Cenaguera.

9692.
Chingele.

9693.
Manteca.

9694.
Lingua de Venada.

9695.
Solita amarilla.

9696.
Mantera.

9697.
Cantabriera.

9698.
Solita blanca.

9699.
Bitter.

9700 to 9732.

From Jamaica. Received through Prof. P. H. Rolfs, May 7, 1903.

A collection of scions as follows:

9700. CITRUS AURANTIUM.   **Tangerine.**

"A tangerine seedling, secured at Porus, Jamaica. An extra large variety, nearly as large and equally as good flavored as the *King*, ripening earlier, and of a much finer color." (*Rolfs.*)

9701. CITRUS AURANTIUM.   **Tangerine.**

"A tangerine very similar to No. 9700, but ripening somewhat later." (*Rolfs.*)

9702. CITRUS AURANTIUM.   **Navel tangerine.**

"Similar to No. 9700 in size, color, and general make-up of the fruit, but being seedless and producing a small accessory orange, as in the case of the Washington navel; otherwise being of the distinct tangerine type." (*Rolfs.*)

9703. MANGIFERA INDICA.   **Mango.**

Alfoos. "This mango was introduced from India to Jamaica about fifteen years ago, and is considered to be one of the finest of the East Indian varieties." (*Rolfs.*)

9704. MANGIFERA INDICA.   **Mango.**

Bombay. "The tree from which the scions were obtained was ripening fruit in winter. The fruit weighed about three-fourths of a pound. Very luscious and producing very little fiber. Altogether a superior mango." (*Rolfs.*)

Cuttings as follows:

9705. HIBISCUS SINENSIS.

"A beautiful ornamental of unusual appearance, producing a rose-colored flower." (*Rolfs.*)

9700 to 9732—Continued.

9706. HIBISCUS SINENSIS.

"Another beautiful *Hibiscus* with very dark center and yellow outer portions of the petal." (*Rolfs.*)

9707. BOUGAINVILLEA SPECTABILIS var. LATERITIA (?).

"One of the most showy decorative plants for the lawn. The orange-colored bracts produce a very pleasing contrast with the dark-green background." (*Rolfs.*)

9708. THUNBERGIA GRANDIFLORA.

"A large flowering vine, very useful for arbor and house decoration." (*Rolfs.*)

9709. THUNBERGIA HARRISSII.

"A beautiful arbor plant." (*Rolfs.*)

9710. THUNBERGIA LAURIFOLIA.

"A beautiful plant for covering arbors and sides of houses." (*Rolfs.*)

9711. RUPPELIA GRATA.

"An ornamental, producing very striking and pleasing effects on an arbor." (*Rolfs.*)

9712. POINSETTIA sp.

"An especially fine extra double race of this variety." (*Rolfs.*)

9713. PASSIFLORA QUADRANGULARIS.

"The granadilla of the Tropics, bearing large fruit the size of an ostrich egg, the inner pulp of which has a very pleasant subacid flavor." (*Rolfs.*)

9714. PETREA VOLUBILIS.

"An arbor ornamental of extra good qualities, making a dense shade and producing a profusion of flowers." (*Rolfs.*)

9715. BEAUMONTIA GRANDIFLORA.

"A vine of large proportions, producing an immense white bloom, the tips of the corolla being pink. A valuable climbing plant for out-of-doors." (*Rolfs.*)

Seeds as follows:

9716. COFFEA ARABICA.

"A variety of this species growing in a higher altitude and producing fruit of an extraordinarily good quality." (*Rolfs.*)

9717. CLITORIA sp.

"A peculiarly crested form of this plant which makes an excellent plant for covering a lattice." (*Rolfs.*)

9718. LUFFA AEGYPTICA.

"A dishcloth gourd, the inner parts of which produce a fibrous material useful for various culinary purposes." (*Rolfs.*)

9719. CANANGA ODORATA (?).   **Ilang-Ilang.**

"Seed produced from tree growing in Jamaica." (*Rolfs.*)

9720. HURA CREPITANS.   **Sand box.**

"Useful for shade and ornamental purposes." (*Rolfs.*)

9721. ACROCOMIA sp.

"This species produces nuts that are used like hickory nuts and are most excellent." (*Rolfs.*)

9700 to 9732—Continued.

9722. OREODOXA OLERACEA. **Mountain palm of Jamaica.**
"A very handsome ornamental plant." (*Rolfs.*)

9723. SABAL sp. **Cuban sabal.**
"A very sturdy, big-trunked tree." (*Rolfs.*)

9724. LIVISTONA HOOGENDORPII.
"An ornamental palm." (*Rolfs.*)

9725. SABAL ADANSONI.
"A dwarf palmetto." (*Rolfs.*)

9726. PANDANUS VANDERMESCHII.

9727. ARECA ALICAE.

9728. COCOS BOTRYOPHORA.

9729. LIVISTONA ROTUNDIFOLIA.

9730. PANDANUS UTILIS.

9731. ROYSTONIA REGIA.
"Is supposed to be distinct from the Porto Rico and Florida royal palm, making a tree of much grander stature." (*Rolfs.*)

9732. ANANAS SATIVUS. **Pineapple.**
"Seedling pineapple plants." (*Rolfs.*)

9733. SECHIUM EDULE. **Chayote.**
From San Juan, P. R. Presented by Miss Jennie H. Ericson. Received June 1, 1903.

9734 to 9749. MEDICAGO spp.
From Madrid, Spain. Received through Messrs. Lathrop and Fairchild (No. 1189, a to p, May, 1903), June 1, 1903.

"The Botanic Gardens of Madrid have represented in their collection a large number of grasses and fodder plants, and the head gardener, Mr. Luis Aterido, has kindly furnished us with a collection of seeds of sixteen species of *Medicagos*, some of which may prove of value for breeding purposes. They are as follows:

9734.	MEDICAGO LUPULINA.	**9742.**	MEDICAGO TUBERCULATA.
9735.	MEDICAGO RIGIDULA.	**9743.**	MEDICAGO MUREX.
9736.	MEDICAGO GERARDI.	**9744.**	MEDICAGO PRAECOX.
9737.	MEDICAGO LACINIATA.	**9745.**	MEDICAGO SUFFRUTICOSA.
9738.	MEDICAGO INTERTEXTA.	**9746.**	MEDICAGO RADIATA.
9739.	MEDICAGO DISCIFORMIS.	**9747.**	MEDICAGO CILIARIS.
9740.	MEDICAGO ORBICULARIS.	**9748.**	MEDICAGO FALCATA.
9741.	MEDICAGO TENOREANA.	**9749.**	MEDICAGO SCUTELLATA.

"Among these, several are indigenous to Spain and all of them have a greater or less value as fodder plants. They are mostly annuals, however, and are therefore limited in value for direct use." (*Fairchild.*)

9750 to 9774. TRIFOLIUM spp.

From Madrid, Spain. Received through Messrs. Lathrop and Fairchild (No. 1190, May, 1903), June 1, 1903.

"Small packets of seeds from the Botanic Gardens of Madrid (see Nos. 9734 to 9749). These are for the use of anyone who is especially interested in breeding *Trifoliums*." (*Fairchild.*) They are as follows:

9750. TRIFOLIUM ANGUSTIFOLIUM.
9751. TRIFOLIUM ARVENSE.
9752. TRIFOLIUM BONANII.
9753. TRIFOLIUM CHERLERI.
9754. TRIFOLIUM DIFFUSUM.
9755. TRIFOLIUM FRAGIFERUM.
9756. TRIFOLIUM GLOMERATUM.
9757. TRIFOLIUM HISPIDUM.
9758. TRIFOLIUM INCARNATUM.
9759. TRIFOLIUM LAPPACEUM.
9760. TRIFOLIUM MARITIMUM.
9761. TRIFOLIUM MEDIUM.
9762. TRIFOLIUM MONTANUM.
9763. TRIFOLIUM OCHROLEUCUM.
9764. TRIFOLIUM PANORMITANUM.
9765. TRIFOLIUM PRATENSE.
9766. TRIFOLIUM REPENS.
9767. TRIFOLIUM RESUPINATUM.
9768. TRIFOLIUM RUBENS.
9769. TRIFOLIUM SPUMOSUM.
9770. TRIFOLIUM STRIATUM.
9771. TRIFOLIUM STRICTUM.
9772. TRIFOLIUM SUBTERRANEUM.
9773. TRIFOLIUM TOMENTOSUM.
9774. TRIFOLIUM VESICULOSUM.

9775.

From Honduras. Presented by Mr. Frank Dean, Black River. Received June 1, 1903.

"One large seed of Oracco; a fine fruit, like the Maumee sapota." (*Dean.*)

9776. Palm.

From Honduras. Presented by Mr. Frank Dean, Black River. Received June 1, 1903.

"Seeds of the Coyol palm. A large variety, growing to a height of 40 feet. Produces wine and vinegar. Seeds good for cattle and hogs." (*Dean.*)

9777.

From Honduras. Presented by Mr. Frank Dean, Black River. Received June 1, 1903.

"A climber, with flowers like the *Allamanda;* yellow, with red center. Fine plant. Name unknown." (*Dean.*)

9778 to 9789.

From Khojend, Russian Central Asia. Presented by Mr. E. M. Valneff, of Khojend, through Mr. E. A. Bessey. Received June 17, 1903.

A collection of seeds, as follows:

9778. PISTACIA VERA. Pistache.

From Hissar, Bokhara. Crop of 1902.

9779. ANDROPOGON SORGHUM. Sorghum.

Djougara.

9778 to 9789—Continued.

9780. SESAMUM INDICUM.   Sesame.
Seed of mixed colors.

9781. TRITICUM VULGARE.   Wheat.
Winter wheat.

9782. TRITICUM VULGARE.   Wheat.
Spring wheat.

9783. HORDEUM VULGARE.   Barley.
Spring barley.

9784. CHAETOCHLOA ITALICA.   Millet.

9785. PANICUM MILIACEUM.   Broom-corn millet.

9786. PHASEOLUS MUNGO.   Mung bean.

9787. CARTHAMUS TINCTORIUS.   Safflower.

9788. MEDICAGO SATIVA.   Alfalfa.

9789. LINUM USITATISSIMUM.   Flax.
Grown for oil making.

9790 to 9800.

From Tashkent, Russian Central Asia. Presented by Mr. H. W. Dürrschmidt, seedsman, of Tashkent, through Mr. E. A. Bessey. Received June 17, 1903. A collection of seeds, as follows:

9790. TRITICUM VULGARE.   Wheat.
Alabjurag winter wheat.

9791. TRITICUM VULGARE.   Wheat.
Iantagbay or *Yantagbay*.

9792. TRITICUM VULGARE.   Wheat.
Kisilbugday.

9793. TRITICUM VULGARE.   Wheat.
Tschulbugday. Grown in winter on irrigated land.

9794. TRITICUM VULGARE.   Wheat.
Aulieata. Grown in winter on unirrigated land.

9795. ZEA MAYS.   Corn.
Kukurusa.

9796. ANDROPOGON SORGHUM.   Sorghum.
Dshugara Balchá.

9797. SESAMUM INDICUM.   Sesame.
Mixed brown and white.

9798. PANICUM MILIACEUM.   Broom-corn millet.

9790 to 9800—Continued.

9799. CHAETOCHLOA ITALICA. **Millet.**

Kunak.

9800. CARTHAMUS TINCTORIUS. **Safflower.**

9801. ERIOBOTRYA JAPONICA. **Loquat.**

From Yokohama, Japan. Presented by the Yokohama Nursery Company at the request of Messrs. Lathrop and Fairchild. Received June 5, 1903.

Formosa. Seed of the Formosan loquat.

9802. NEPHELIUM LITCHI. **Leitchee.**

From Canton, China. Received through Messrs. Lathrop and Fairchild (No. 792, December 20, 1901), January 30, 1902.

Hak Ip, black leaved. "This is one of the best varieties grown about Canton, China. It is said to be a large-fruited sort, of excellent flavor, but with medium-sized stone. The dried leitchees of the market here are mostly of this form. The plant is not reproduced from seed but is grafted or inarched." (*Fairchild.*)

9803. NEPHELIUM LITCHI. **Leitchee.**

From Canton, China. Received through Messrs. Lathrop and Fairchild (No. 793, December 20, 1901), January 30, 1902.

No Mai, "tender rice" leitchee. "This is a small-seeded, very superior sort, one of the favorites on the Canton market where four or five different varieties are known and where the sale of this fruit is a very important one. Dr. J. M. Swan, of the Canton Hospital, pronounces this one of the two or three best varieties known to him." (*Fairchild.*)

9804. DIOSPYROS KAKI. **Japanese persimmon.**

From Canton, China. Received through Messrs. Lathrop and Fairchild (No. 794, December 20, 1901), January 30, 1902.

Hung tsz, large red persimmon. "This is a soft variety of medium to large size, round to oblate spheroid, dark in color, and reported to be very sweet in flavor. It is imported as being probably a Chinese variety and worthy of trial in comparison with the Japanese sorts." (*Fairchild.*)

9805. AMYGDALUS PERSICA. **Peach.**

From Canton, China. Received through Messrs. Lathrop and Fairchild (No. 795, December 20, 1901), January 30, 1902.

Hung Wat tim. "A variety of the 'Honey' type, reported to be good for preserves and not so sweet as the *Ying tsui* or Eagle Beak variety. It is medium early. Worthy of trial as coming from the south China region, though probably not of superior excellence." (*Fairchild.*)

9806. PRUNUS sp. **Plum.**

From Canton, China. Received through Messrs. Lathrop and Fairchild (No. 796, December 20, 1901), January 30, 1902.

Hung Mui. "A large red plum, fairly sweet, but of the hard-fleshed type. Like the other Chinese plums about Canton it is said to have a somewhat bitter taste when cooked and allowed to stand for an hour or so. Europeans in Canton do not prize these Chinese plums very highly. This variety blooms in February or March." (*Fairchild.*)

9807. BAMBUSA sp. **Bamboo.**

From Canton, China. Received through Messrs. Lathrop and Fairchild (No. 797, December 20, 1901), January 30, 1902.

Kam Chuk, golden bamboo. "The most beautiful of all the bamboos about Canton, a golden-stemmed sort, with stripes of green. It is rather rare on the island of Hongkong, I am told by Mr. Ford, and it is not very common about Canton. It is worthy of trial in Florida and southern California." (*Fairchild.*)

9808. MANGIFERA INDICA. **Mango.**

From Mussorie, India. Presented by Rev. H. Marston Andrews, principal of Woodstock College. Received August 8, 1903.

Malda. Said to be of very large size and spicy flavor.

9809. VITIS RUPESTRIS var. METALLICA. **Grape.**

From Cape Town, South Africa. Presented by the Cape Colony department of agriculture, through Messrs. Lathrop and Fairchild (No. 1137, March 10, 1903). Received August 10, 1903.

"Plants of a South African originated variety of resistant American stock, which has proved itself most admirably suited to the conditions at the Cape and especially adapted to 'any loose soil, loam, gravel, or sand, and also in dry, open, heavy soils. It can, besides, stand a fair amount of moisture in loose soils. It forms an excellent graft bearer for all varieties of European vines except *Hanepoot* and possibly also the members of the Muscat family.' (Cf. J. P. de Waal, in the Ag. Jour. Cape of Good Hope, December 19, 1901, p. 838.) This variety, Mr. Pillans says, is the best of all the resistant stocks yet tried at the Cape, as its ease of grafting, great vigor, suitability to different kinds of soil, and grafting affinity for all but varieties of the Muscat type make it a general stock of great value. Even those who do not claim that it exceeds in vigor any other sort, admit that *it is the easiest grafted of any of the American stocks.* The stock originated at Great Constantia Wine Farm, in a lot of seedlings from seed sown in 1886. It is uncertain whether the seed came direct from America or from France. This is entirely distinct, according to F. J. Bioletti (formerly of the experiment station at Berkeley, Cal., now at the Elsenburg Agricultural School), from the *metallica* of French vineyardists. Its name applies to the luster of its foliage. The seedling was picked out in 1894, and by quick propagation in 1901 yielded 687,000 cuttings. In 1902, 864,000 cuttings were distributed. It has been tested side by side with many French stocks, such as *Aramon rupestris, Riparia Gloire de Montpellier,* and takes its place as their equals in all points and their superior as regards ease of propagation and suitability to the varieties of soils mentioned. Mr. Pillans goes so far as to predict that it will drive all other sorts out except for Muscat sorts. He claims for it a remarkable yield-giving power, extreme vigor, and resistance to the phylloxera. Mr. Bioletti admits its excellent qualities, and practical growers are enthusiastic about it. This is well worth the serious consideration of California vine growers. The originators of this remarkable seedling are Messrs. J. P. de Waal and Eustace Pillans, of the Cape of Good Hope department of agriculture, and its trial in California should be made at once. We are indebted to Mr. Pillans for the plants sent. See No. 9607, the identical variety." (*Fairchild.*)

9810 to 9814. VITIS sp. **Grape.**

From Cape Town, South Africa. Presented by the Cape Colony department of agriculture, through Messrs. Lathrop and Fairchild (No. 1149 to 1151, and 1153, March, 1903). Received August 10, 1903.

9810. VITIS VINIFERA.

Red Hanepoot. "A variety of table grape that is believed to have originated in South Africa and which, according to Mr. Bioletti, formerly vine expert of the California Experiment Station, at Berkeley, is not known in America. The variety belongs to the *Muscat* type and may be described as a *Muscat* with the red color of the *Flaming Tokay.* It is one of the most popular of the South African varieties and is exported to England. It is an excellent shipper and a showy table sort. Sent by Mr. Eustace Pillans, from the Government vineyard at Constantia." (*Fairchild.*) (No. 1149.)

9811. VITIS VINIFERA.

Hermitage. "This is the grape from which the Cape claret is made. It is said by experts to rank high as a claret maker and not to have been tested in California. Mr. Bioletti, formerly of the California Experiment Station at Berkeley, Cal., remarks (in the Cape Journal of Agriculture, Vol. XX, No. 12, p. 696), that the Cape *Hermitage* is distinct from the sort grown in the Hermitage vineyards of France and is not so good as the *Shiraz* or *Sirah* grape, which is well known to Californians." (*Fairchild.*) (No. 1150.)

9810 to 9814—Continued.

9812. VITIS RUPESTRIS.

Le Roux. "A variety of American phylloxera-resistant stock which, according to de Waal (in the Cape Agricultural Journal, Vol. XIX, No. 13, p. 839), originated from a seedling, selected by Mr. J. G. Le Roux, of Klein, Drakenstein, Paarl. It requires a loose loam, gravel, or sand, and also grows in dry, open, heavy soils as well. *It is especially suitable as a stock for the Hanepoot and very likely also for the other Muscat varieties*, and is a good general grafting stock. Mr. Bioletti, formerly of the California Experiment Station at Berkeley, Cal., thinks this sort will be keenly appreciated in California for a stock for Muscat varieties." (*Fairchild.*) (No. 1151.)

9813. VITIS RUPESTRIS.

Pillans. "A variety of resistant American stock which has been selected by Mr. Eustace Pillans, agricultural assistant in charge of the Government wine farm at Constantia. Mr. Pillans thinks this will prove an excellent stock for the Muscat varieties of grape and, although it has not yet been thoroughly tested, he predicts its general use for this class of vines. The *Hanepoot*, which is of the *Muscat* type, does well on it. These cuttings are sent by Mr. Pillans himself." (*Fairchild.*) (No. 1153.)

9814. VITIS VINIFERA.

White Hanepoot. "Probably descended from the *White Muscat.*" (*Fairchild.*)

9815. AMYGDALUS PERSICA. Peach.

From Constantia, South Africa. Presented by the Cape Colony department of agriculture through Messrs. Lathrop and Fairchild (No. 1152, March 16, 1903). Received August 10, 1903.

Constantia. "A variety of peach which originated at Constantia. It is said by Mr. Eustace Pillans to be an excellent shipping variety, of good quality and one of the best sorts grown in Cape Colony. It deserves a trial in the collections of California and Georgia, but may not prove hardy enough for Maryland, Delaware, or Michigan. Sent by the Cape department of agriculture." (*Fairchild.*)

9816. MEDICAGO SATIVA. Alfalfa.

From Willard, Utah. Received through Mr. P. A. Nebeker, June 9, 1903.

Turkestan alfalfa seed grown by Mr. Nebeker under agreement with the Department of Agriculture from imported seed (S. P. I. No. 991), furnished him in 1900.

9817. TRIFOLIUM PANNONICUM.

From Erfurt, Germany. Received through Haage & Schmidt, July 17, 1903.

Seed from the 1902 crop.

9818 to 9823.

From Heneratgoda, Ceylon. Received through J. P. William & Bros., July 31, 1903.

Seeds of trees for arid regions, as follows:

9818. CASUARINA EQUISETIFOLIA.

9819. DALBERGIA SISSOO.

9820. ALBIZZIA PROCERA.

9821. ALBIZZIA LUCIDA.

9822. ALBIZZIA JULIBRISSIN.

9823. EUCALYPTUS GLOBULUS.

9824 to 9826.

From Santiago, Chile. Presented by Federico Albert, of the ministry of industry and public works. Received July 9, 1903.

Seeds as follows:

9824. ARAUCARIA IMBRICATA. **9826.** BELLOTA MIERSII.

9825. JUBAEA SPECTABILIS.

9827. PINUS PINEA. Umbrella pine.

From Rome, Italy. Presented by Hon. Hector de Castro, United States Consul-General. Received August 7, 1903.

9828 to 9830.

From Monte, Grand Canary, Canary Islands. Presented by Mr. Alaricus Delmard, through Messrs. Lathrop and Fairchild. Received August 14, 1903.

Seeds as follows:

9828. CANARINA CAMPANULA var. CANARIENSIS.

9829. PAPAVER sp.

9830. PINUS CANARIENSIS.

9831 to 9850.

From Mexico. Secured by Mr. G. Onderdonk, special agent of this Department, and sent to G. L. Taber, Glen St. Mary, Fla., for propagation.

9831 to 9846. PRUNUS ARMENIACA. Apricot.

9831. Onderdonk's No. 1, Taber's No. 1.

From garden of Crispin Mariscal, Coyoacan, Distrito Federal. Freestone; 4 inches in circumference; blush; rich; sweet; season, May.

9832. Onderdonk's No. 2, Taber's No. 2.

From garden of Crispin Mariscal, Coyoacan, Distrito Federal. Freestone; 4½ inches in circumference; blush; rich; sweet; season, May.

9833. Onderdonk's No. 3, Taber's No. 3.

From garden of Crispin Mariscal, Coyoacan, Distrito Federal. Freestone; 4½ inches in circumference; blush; rich; sweet; season, May.

9834. Onderdonk's No. 4, Taber's No. 4.

From garden of Crispin Mariscal, Coyoacan, Distrito Federal. Clingstone; 3¾ inches in circumference; blush; rich; sweet; season, May.

9835. Onderdonk's No. 5, Taber's No. 5.

From garden of Crispin Mariscal, Coyoacan, Distrito Federal. Freestone; 4½ inches in circumference; blush; rich; sweet; season, May.

9836. Onderdonk's No. 6, Taber's No. 6.

From garden of Crispin Mariscal, Coyoacan, Distrito Federal. Fruit not yet grown. Season, August 1.

9837. Onderdonk's No. 7, Taber's No. 7.

From garden of Carlos Ortero, San Angel, Distrito Federal. Fruits not fully grown; 5 inches in circumference; fine; season, June. Twelve buds inserted, all dead July 15, 1903. Mr. Onderdonk states that the trees do not make a vigorous growth, literally bearing themselves to death. He promised to furnish Mr. Ortero a tree if any lived, as he was permitted to take all the bud wood there was on the tree. Wood altogether too young when taken. Freestone; yellow; blush.

9831 to 9850—Continued.

9831 to 9846—Continued.

9838. Onderdonk's No. 8, Taber's No. 8.

From garden of Martin Velasco, San Angel, Distrito Federal. Freestone; 4¼ inches in circumference; cream yellow; blush; season, June 1.

9839. Onderdonk's No. 9, Taber's No. 9.

From garden of Hilario Abilo, Contreras, Distrito Federal. Freestone; 6¾ inches in circumference; cream colored; blush; sweet; season, May 25 to June 1.

9840. Onderdonk's No. 10, Taber's No. "A."

From J. R. Silliman, Saltillo, Coahuila. Variety, *Perry*. Unripe fruit six inches in circumference; cream colored; blush.

9841. Onderdonk's No. 11, Taber's No. "B."

From Santa Anita gardens, near Saltillo. Fruit 4½ inches in circumference; yellow; blush; sweet; season, May.

9842. Onderdonk's No. 12 (or 13), Taber's No. "C."

From Santa Anita gardens, near Saltillo. Fruit 5¼ inches in circumference when not fully grown; yellow; blush; season, June 5.

9843. Onderdonk's No. 13 (or 12), Taber's No. "D."

From J. R. Silliman, Saltillo, Coahuila. Unripe, 4½ inches in diameter; highly recommended by Mr. Silliman; season, July. Mr. Taber writes that the packages containing these last two numbers were both marked 12, so that it is not possible to tell which should be 12 and which 13.

9844. Onderdonk's No. 15, Taber's No. 15.

Probably from garden of J. R. Silliman, Saltillo, Coahuila. A very fine apricot, 5¾ inches in circumference; yellow; blush; season, May 25; named *Nellie* for owner's daughter.

9845. Onderdonk's No. 16, Taber's No. 16.

Probably from garden of J. R. Silliman, Saltillo, Coahuila. A very fine apricot; 5¼ inches in circumference; yellow; blush; season, June 1; named *Dorah* for owner's daughter.

9846. Onderdonk's No. 17, Taber's No. 17.

From garden of Henrique Maas, Saltillo, Coahuila. Said to be a very fine large variety. Season about July 5.

9847. PRUNUS CERASUS.   Cherry.

Onderdonk's No. 14, Taber's No. 14. Mr. Onderdonk writes that this is the Capulin cherry but does not state where the buds were secured.

9848 to 9850. AMYGDALUS PERSICA.   Peach.

9848. Onderdonk's No. 11, Taber's No. 11.

From garden of Carlos Ortero, San Angel, Distrito Federal. A large, yellow, blush, clingstone.

9849. Onderdonk's No. 12, Taber's No. 12.

From garden of Carlos Ortero, San Angel, Distrito Federal. A yellow, blush, freestone.

9850. Onderdonk's No. 13, Taber's No. 13.

From garden of Martin Velasco, San Angel, Distrito Federal. A large, white, blush, clingstone.

9851. PRUNUS CERASUS (?). **Cherry.**

From Mexico. Received through Mr. G. Onderdonk, June 29, 1903, by Mr. W. A. Taylor, pomologist in charge of field investigations.

Capulin.

9852. ANDROPOGON SORGHUM. **Kafir corn.**

From Durban, Natal. Presented by Mr. Claude Fuller, Government Entomologist, through Messrs. Lathrop and Fairchild (No. 1193a, August 5, 1903). Received August 31, 1903.

Mahele or *Mapele.* "This variety has proved more resistant than any other to a species of aphis which injures all the common sorts." (*Fairchild.*)

9853 and 9854. TRITICUM DURUM. **Wheat.**

From Poona Farm, Kirki, India. Sent by the superintendent through Latham & Co., Bombay, India, addressed to Dr. S. A. Knapp. Received July 23, 1903.

9853.　　　　　　　　　　　　**9854.**

Piola Karte. From Shuedrager (?).　　*Shet Gahu.* From Poona.

9855 and 9856. ANDROPOGON SORGHUM. **Sorghum.**

From Poona Farm, Kirki, India. Sent by the superintendent through Latham & Co., Bombay, India, addressed to Dr. S. A. Knapp. Received July 13, 1903.

9855.　　　　　　　　　　　　**9856.**

Gidgep Jowar.　　　　　　　　*Dagdi Jowar.*

9857. CASTILLA sp. nov.

From Costa Rica. Presented by Mr. Guy N. Collins, of the Department of Agriculture, June 16, 1903.

Seed of a new species of great promise as a rubber producer.

9858. THEOBROMA sp. nov. **Cacao.**

From Costa Rica. Presented by Mr. Guy N. Collins, of the Department of Agriculture, June 16, 1903.

Seeds of a new species.

9859. CASSIA AURICULATA. **Avaram.**

From Manamadura, South India. Presented by Rev. Edward P. Holton, through Miss Nina G. Holton, of this Department. Received September 5, 1903.

Grown and used extensively in South India; the bark for tanning, the leaves, twigs, and seed pods as a fertilizer for salt lands, wet cultivation. Habit, low and brushy like a blueberry bush on rocky, sandy, dry, waste lands.

9860. CYPERUS NUTANS. **Matting rush.**

From Japan. Received through Mr. R. H. Sawyer, Kennebunk, Me., July 23, 1903.

Cultivated in the rice fields of Japan. Straw dried and used in the manufacture of the coarser, cheaper grades of Japanese matting.

9861. CYPERUS TEGETIFORMIS. **Matting rush.**

From China. Received through Mr. R. H. Sawyer, Kennebunk, Me., July 23, 1903.

Native in salt marshes along the coast of China. Three-cornered rush split, dried, and used in manufacture of Chinese floor matting.

9862. ANDROPOGON SORGHUM. **Sorghum.**

From the Sudan, Africa. Presented by Dr. L. Trabut, Government Botanist, 7 Rue des Fontaines, Mustapha, Algiers, Algeria. Received September 14, 1903.

A few seeds of a strain originated in the Sudan. Recommended by Doctor Trabut as of extraordinary size and quality.

9863. PYRUS MALUS. **Apple.**

From Stockholm, Sweden. Presented by Mr. Axel Pihl, secretary of the Swedish Pomological Society, through Messrs. Lathrop and Fairchild. Received September 22, 1903.

Salems. "A newly-discovered variety, promising because of its hardiness and ability to live on poor soils." (*Fairchild.*)

9864. TRIFOLIUM PANNONICUM.

From Erfurt, Germany. Received through Haage & Schmidt September 26, 1903.

9865. SECALE CEREALE. **Rye.**

From Stockholm, Sweden. Received through Mr. J. E. W. Tracy, of this Department, August 17, 1903.

Wasa. Three small samples, from different seed houses. As the bags containing two of the samples were broken and the seed mixed, it was decided to give but one number to the three samples. (1 sample from Sellberg & Co., Stockholm; 1 sample from Öhmans, Söner & Co., Stockholm; 1 sample from another seed house.)

9866. EUPHORBIA PULCHERRIMA var. PLENISSIMA. **Poinsettia.**

From Hope Gardens, Kingston, Jamaica. Presented by Prof. William Fawcett, director, through Messrs. Lathrop and Fairchild. Received October 8, 1903.

"In 1898 Mr. Barbour Lathrop noticed a single plant of this variety growing in the Hope Botanic Gardens, of Kingston, Jamaica. Although he had seen the double variety of this plant in many places in the Tropics and in greenhouses, nowhere had he observed a plant with such unusually full whorls of colored bracts. The plant in its full glory was a perfect blaze of color, forming one of the handsomest decorative shrubs for landscape purposes that we have ever seen. The writer is inclined to believe that this is a strain from the ordinary double poinsettia, and that it can be propagated from cuttings. Its special beauty may possibly have been, however, produced by specially favorable soil conditions in Jamaica. If the former presumption is true, this will probably prove a very valuable strain for park use in those regions of the South where it will grow, and it may even prove superior to the ordinary type for greenhouse culture. It is worthy of a serious trial, both out of doors and under glass. Under notes L. and F., No. 56, in 1898, the Department's attention was called to this variety." (*Fairchild.*)

9867. PRUNUS LAURO-CERASUS. **Cherry laurel.**

From Trebizond, Turkey. Presented by Mrs. Julia F. Parmelee. Received October 9, 1903.

Kara yemish. Five plants brought by Mrs. Parmelee from Trebizond to Dunkirk, N. Y. Given to the Department through Mr. W. A. Taylor, pomologist in charge of field investigations.

9868. OCIMUM VIRIDE.

From Kew, England. Presented by the director of the Royal Botanic Gardens, Kew. Received October 9, 1903.

Obtained at the request of Dr. L. O. Howard, Entomologist of this Department, for experiments on the effect of this plant upon mosquitoes.

9869. GARCINIA MANGOSTANA. Mangosteen.

From Heneratgoda, Ceylon. Received through J. P. William & Bros., October 19, 1903.

"One thousand seeds of this most delicious of tropical fruits, which, it is believed, will prove of great commercial value to the fruit-growing interests of Porto Rico." (*Fairchild.*)

9870. PERSEA INDICA.

From Madeira. Presented by Mr. J. B. Blandy, through Mr. D. G. Fairchild. Received October 15, 1903.

"This tree is a native of the Canary Islands, and is hardier than the alligator pear. It is introduced for the purpose of testing it as a stock upon which to graft *Persea gratissima*. According to the statement of one of the principal growers in Florida, such a stock is especially desired, because the trunk of the young alligator pear is its weakest part." (*Fairchild.*)

9871. TRITICUM VULGARE. Wheat.

From Erivan, Caucasus, Asiatic Russia. Received through Mr. E. A. Bessey (No. 300, August 24, 1903), October 21, 1903.

"Red wheat from the mountains near Erivan. It is grown without irrigation and is sown in March. It should be tried in dry mountain regions." (*Bessey.*)

9872. TRITICUM DURUM. Wheat.

From Erivan, Caucasus, Asiatic Russia. Received through Mr. E. A. Bessey (No. 301, August 24, 1903), October 21, 1903.

Galgalos. "A variety of macaroni wheat which is said to be very good. It is prized for flour. It brings 30 kopecks a pood more than No. 9871. It is also grown without irrigation in the mountains. It is mostly grown as a winter wheat, being sown in October. It is also sown early in March." (*Bessey.*)

9873. JUNCUS EFFUSUS. Matting rush.

From Kobe, Japan. Presented by Dr. A. G. Boyer, of the United States consulate at Kobe. Received October 25, 1903.

Seed of the round Japanese matting rush. This seed was picked from the plants which are growing for next year's crop of matting grass, i. e., from roots that are 2 years old. The seed ripens in July.

9874 to 9876. TRIFOLIUM ALEXANDRINUM. Berseem.

From Cairo, Egypt. Secured through the courtesy of Mr. George P. Foaden, of the Khedivial Agricultural Society. Received November 7, 1903.

9874.
Muscowi.

9876.
Saida.

9875.
Fachl.

9877. HORDEUM VULGARE. Barley.

From Cairo, Egypt. Secured through the courtesy of Mr. George P. Foaden, of the Khedivial Agricultural Society. Received November 7, 1903.

Mariut.

9878. AVENA SATIVA. Oat.

From Paris, France. Received through Vilmorin-Andrieux & Co., November 9, 1903.

Belgian winter.

9879. GARCINIA COCHINCHINENSIS.

From Saigon, Cochin China. Presented by M. E. Haffner, director of agriculture of Cochin China, through Messrs. Lathrop and Fairchild. Received November 11, 1903.

"A species of *Garcinia* which is closely related to the mangosteen, and upon which it is hoped this delicious fruit tree can be grafted. This species is said to be much less limited in its range of soil and climatic conditions, and it may prove a valuable stock for the mangosteen." (*Fairchild.*)

9880. GARCINIA FERREA.

From Saigon, Cochin China. Presented by M. E. Haffner, director of agriculture of Cochin China. Received November 11, 1903.

"A species of *Garcinia* introduced for the same purpose as No. 9879, as a stock for the mangosteen." (*Fairchild.*)

9881. GARCINIA MANGOSTANA. **Mangosteen.**

From Heneratgoda, Ceylon. Received through J. P. William & Bros., November 11, 1903. Shipped from Ceylon August 31, 1903. A wardian case full of plants of this delicious tropical fruit.

9882. AMYGDALUS PERSICA var. NECTARINA. **Nectarine.**

From Marplan, Turkestan. Presented by Prof. Ralph Pumpelly. Received November 11, 1903.

Five seeds of a variety of nectarine which Professor Pumpelly describes as a very delicious, large sort, which was abundant in that portion of Turkestan. Professor Pumpelly's first impression was that this was a smooth-skinned peach, thinking that the nectarine would not be likely to occur in that portion of Turkestan.

9883. CLERODENDRON FOETIDUM.

From Cape Town, South Africa. Presented by Prof. P. MacOwan, of the Cape department of agriculture. Received November 9, 1903.

A hardy, ornamental bush 3 to 6 feet in height, said to be hardy in the Middle and Southern States and not new to this country.

9884 to 9886.

From Guadalajara, Mexico. Presented by Mr. Federico Chisolm. Received November 16, 1903.

Seeds of native Mexican plants as follows:

9884. DAHLIA sp. **Wild dahlia.**

Dwarf, leaves very thickly covered with fine prickly hairs, flowers on stem 24 to 48 inches tall, have a diameter of 1½ to 2 inches, petals blood red, with very high glaze, center yellow.

9885. **Tuberose (?)**

Chicalam. Small bulb, one or two slender, round leaves 12 to 36 inches long. Flowers exquisite, colored like a fuchsia, in clusters on slender, round stem 12 to 40 inches high. Blooms July, August, and September. (Doctor Rose says this is probably a tuberose.)

9886.

Bulb with leathery leaves splotched with brown. Flowers green, not valuable, August. Leaves sometimes 12 inches long by 4 inches broad. May be useful for foliage. Doctor Rose says probably *Amole* (*Chlorogalum pomeridianum* or *Agave americanum*).

9887. SECALE CEREALE. **Rye.**

From North Watergap, Pa. Received through Mr. M. L. Michael, November 14, 1903.

Winter Ivanof. Grown in 1903 from S. P. I. No. 1342.

9888. TRICHOLAENA ROSEA.

From Honolulu, Hawaii. Presented by Mr. Jared G. Smith, special agent in charge of the Hawaiian agricultural experiment station. Received November 23, 1903.

9889 and 9890. PHASEOLUS VIRIDISSIMUS. **Bean.**

Grown from S. P. I. No. 6430, in 1903.

9889. Received through Mrs. Hattie L. Asseltine, Fruithurst, Ala., November 28, 1903.

9890. Received through Mr. John J. Dean, Moneta, Cal., December 4, 1903.

The California grown seed is noticeably larger than that grown in Alabama.

9891. EUTREMA WASABI. **Japanese horse-radish.**

From Yokohama, Japan. Presented by Mr. H. Suzuki, of the Yokohama Nursery Company, through Messrs. Lathrop and Fairchild. Received December 7, 1903.

"Described in B. P. I. Bulletin No. 42. The Japanese horse-radish, which is eaten with raw fish as commonly in Japan as ordinary horse-radish is eaten in America with raw oysters." (*Fairchild.*)

9892. ATRIPLEX LEPTOCARPA. **Saltbush.**

From Sydney, Australia. Received through Anderson & Co., December 5, 1903.

9893. DESMODIUM TRIFLORA.

From Mayaguez, Porto Rico. Sent by Mr. G. N. Collins, of the Department of Agriculture, through Mr. D. G. Fairchild. Received December 14, 1903.

This plant is used as a soil covering on the coffee plantations in Porto Rico.

9894 to 9896.

From Tanegashima, Japan. Presented by Mr. R. Chester, through Mr. R. B. Handy, of this Department. Received December 12, 1903.

Native Japanese seeds, as follows:

9894. **Red jessamine.**

One-half ounce of seed that looks like four-o'clocks.

9895. **Lily.**

Very decorative.

9896.

A few seeds, without name or other data.

INDEX OF COMMON AND SCIENTIFIC NAMES.

Abaca. (*See* Hemp, manila.)
Aberia caffra, 6851, 7955, 7956.
Abrus precatorius, 6877, 7555, 8977.
Abutilon avicennae, 6606.
Acacia armata, 9083.
    cibaria, 5385.
    cyanophylla, 9084.
    farnesiana, 8948, 9085.
    moniliformis, 8974.
    retinioides, 6666.
Acanthophoenix crinita, 7568, 8326.
Acanthus candelabrum, 7269.
    mollis, 7167, 7324, 7329.
    niger, 7215.
Acer japonicum, 8150 to 8188.
    oblongum, 8659.
Achiote, 5658.
Achras sapota, 8978.
Aconite, 8537.
Aconitum napellus, 8537.
Acrocarpus fraxinifolia, 8654.
Acrocomia sp., 9721.
    sclerocarpa, 6898, 7292.
Actinidia sp., 5840, 5978, 5979, 6504, 6659.
    arguta, 7860.
Adansonia digitata, 7182.
Adenanthera pavonina, 7151, 8979.
Aegilops ovata, 7724.
Afsie, 9325.
Agapanthus umbellatus, 8241, 8675.
Agaricus campestris, 8222 to 8225.
Agathis australis, 8206.
Agave sp., 7087, 7371, 7372, 7488, 8242.
    univittata, 7439.
Ageratum conyzoides, 7147, 7149.
    mexicanum, 8848.
Akee, 6856.
Albizzia sp., 7054.
    julibrissin, 7536, 9822.
    lebbek, 6443, 9038.
    lophantha, 8243.
    lucida, 9821.
    moluccana, 9086.
    odoratissima, 9087.
    procera, 9820.
Aleurites triloba, 6450.
Alfalfa, 6998, 7500, 7586 to 7588, 8806, 8823, 9303, 9322, 9323, 9359, 9450 to 9455, 9788, 9816.
    Turkestan, 9451 to 9455, 9788, 9816.
Algaroba, see Carob, and Mesquite.
Allamanda blanchetii, 7612.

Allium cepa, 6390, 7034, 9318.
    fistulosum, 9301.
Almond, 7061, 7062, 7133 to 7135, 7137, 7398, 7401, 7452 to 7458, 7516, 7517, 7684, 7778 to 7780, 7985 to 7989, 8348, 9345, 9348 to 9351, 9458 to 9462.
    amboina, 5534.
    tropical, 6862.
Amaranthus caudatus, 7183.
    hypochondriacus, 8803.
Amasonia calycina, 7610.
Ammophila arenaria, 5831.
Amomum cardamomum, 6864.
Amorpha fruticosa, 8849.
Ampelopsis sp., 6827.
Amygdalus communis, 7061, 7062, 7133 to 7135, 7137, 7398, 7401, 7452 to 7458, 7516, 7517, 7684, 7778 to 7780, 7985 to 7989, 8348, 9345, 9348 to 9351, 9458 to 9462.
    davidiana, 7861, 7862.
    persica, 5922, 5923, 6109, 6541 to 6545, 6547, 6548, 6629, 6635, 7670, 7863 to 7868, 8330 to 8334, 8337, 8340, 8343, 9217 to 9220, 9221, 9284, 9285, 9302, 9304, 9305, 9320, 9321, 9372 to 9380, 9389, 9391 to 9396, 9420, 9805, 9815, 9848 to 9850, 9882.
Anacardium occidentale, 6852, 7294, 7414, 7499, 9447.
Ananas sativus, 7366, 9485, 9606, 9634, 9732.
Anchusa italica, 9088.
Andropogon halepensis, 7643.
    rufus, 5751.
    sorghum, 8505 to 5809, 5930, 6406, 6411, 6604, 6681, 6685, 6686, 6689 to 6691, 6693, 6710, 7797, 8546, 8547, 8685, 8691, 8692, 8815, 9779, 9796, 9852, 9855, 9856, 9862.
Anise, 7449.
Anona cherimolia, 7173, 8653, 9466.
    macrocarpa (Hort.), 7152.
    muricata, 6853, 8980.
    reniformis (Hort.), 7170.
    squamosa, 7174, 8981, 9024.
    suavissima (Hort.), 7159.

Antholyza aethiopica, 8850.
Anthyllis tetraphylla, 6967, 6968, 7720.
  vulneraria, 7721.
Antiaris toxicaria, 7364.
Antirrhinum majus, 7163, 7200, 7201, 7203, 7204, 7208, 7213.
Apium graveolens, 6707.
Apple, 5687, 5688, 5690 to 5744, 5810 to 5823, 5933, 6102, 6113, 6528, 6656, 6713 to 6772, 8448 to 8453, 8644, 8710 to 8726, 9014, 9469 to 9471, 9863.
  crab, 5501 to 5512, 6162, 6358.
  custard, 8653, 9024.
  Kei, 6851, 7955, 7956.
  Otaheite, 6861.
  sorb, 5932.
  thorn, 8534.
Apricot, 6534, 6630, 6841, 6844, 6845, 7136, 7140, 7672, 8363, 8825, 8913, 9015, 9016, 9319, 9364 to 9371, 9390, 9397 to 9402, 9463, 9464, 9831 to 9846.
  Japanese, 9200, 9211 to 9216.
Aquilegia caerulea, 7165, 7225, 7242.
  californica, 7230.
  chrysantha, 7148, 7258.
  flabellata, 7316.
  glandulosa, 7317.
  haylodgensis, 7318.
  skinneri, 7319.
  stuarti, 7320.
  vervaeneana, 7321.
Arachis hypogaea, 5522, 5561, 5763, 8982, 9355, 9406.
Aralia cordata, 9166 to 9169, 9224.
Araucaria imbricata, 9824.
Araujia sericifera, 8247, 8851.
Arbutus unedo, 8244.
Arctostaphylos sp., 5752.
Ardisia polycephala, 6878.
Areca alicae, 9727.
Arenga saccharifera, 7545.
Argemone sp., 7404.
Aristida pennata var. *Karelini*, 9582.
Aristolochia elegans, 8245, 8852, 9427.
Aristotelia macqui, 8694, 8906, 9072.
Arnica montana, 8531.
Arrowroot, Bermuda, 6872.
Artemisia sp., 6619.
  argentea, 8246.
Artocarpus integrifolia, 6451, 6854, 8983.
Arum sp., 7480.
Arundinaria hindsii, 9057, 9058.
  japonica, 7819.
  simoni, 7823, 9050.
Asparagus officinalis, 7957 to 7959, 7975 to 7977.
  plumosus, 9629.
  sprengeri, 7961, 8248.
  verticillatus, 7960.
Aspidosperma quebracho, 5781, 6346, 7013.
Assam rhea, 5610.
Aster, China, 6387, 6388, 6392.
Astragalus boeticus, 6964, 7719.
  cicer, 5841.

Astragalus onobrychis, see Onobrychis onobrychis.
  sinicus, 5935, 6329, 6330, 6571.
Asystasia bella, 9089.
Atalantia trimera, 6894.
Atriplex halimoides, 5614.
  leptocarpa, 5613, 9892.
Atropa belladonna, 8530.
Attalea cohune, 6899, 9473 (?).
Avaram, 9859.
Avena sp., 6626, 9571.
  sativa, 5513, 5514, 5938, 5966, 5967, 6022, 6174, 7450, 7944, 8538, 8558, 8650, 9422, 9878.

Bactris gasipaës, 6909.
  utilis, 6910.
Balatong, 6223.
Balsam, 6421.
Balsamorhiza sagittata, 9126.
Bamboo, 8717 to 7824, 8427, 8428, 9041 to 9058, 8907.
Bambusa sp., 9807.
  alphonse karri, 9056.
  aureo-striata, 7818.
  disticha, 7821.
  quadrangularis, 9049.
  reitchii, 9053.
  vulgaris, 9055.
Banana, 9485, 9575, 9610.
Baphia racemosa, 6879.
Barley, 5590 to 5592, 5756, 5788 to 5794, 5842 to 5899, 5903, 5975, 5976, 6023, 6175, 6367, 6399, 6403, 6597, 6601, 6658, 7427, 7451, 7583, 7584, 7640, 7641, 7796, 7969, 7970, 7992, 8559, 8560, 8809, 9133, 9783, 9877.
Barnyard grass, 6409, 8891.
Basil, sweet, 6381.
Bast, 7359.
Bauhinia sp., 7589, 7590.
  acuminata, 6880.
  candicans, 8971.
  galpinii, 6881.
  picta, 8984.
Beach-grass, 5831.
Bean, 5517, 5519, 5927, 5929, 6092, 6132, 6223, 6225, 6226, 6228, 6279, 6319, 6320, 6323, 6324, 6377, 6391, 6415, 6430, 6560, 6565, 6569, 6570, 7503, 7504, 7974, 8355 to 8357, 8545, 8585, 8686, 8814, 9147 to 9160, 9404, 9405, 9431, 9438 to 9444, 9889, 9890.
  Adler, 5795.
  broad, 5542, 5965, 6313, 6315, 6550, 6669, 7426, 7462, 7498, 8358, 8587, 8592, 8596, 9307 to 9312.
  castor, 8275, 8276, 9283.
  horse, 5577, 6961, 7020, 7024, 7035, 7942, 7943.
  hyacinth, 6319, 6320.
  lima, 5521.
  mung, 5518, 6224, 6318, 6321, 6378, 6417, 6418, 6562, 6564, 8486 to 8488, 9419, 9786.
  perennial, 6565.

INDEX OF COMMON AND SCIENTIFIC NAMES. 319

Bean, soy, 5764 to 5766, 6312, 6314, 6326, 6333 to 6336, 6379, 6386, 6396, 6397, 6414, 6416, 6556, 6558 to 6561, 8422 to 8424, 8489 to 8497. 8584, 8586, 8900, 9344, 9407, 9418.
Beaumontia grandiflora, 9715.
Beet, 6260 to 6264.
    sugar, 5769 to 5773, 6359, 7908, 8229, 8238.
Beggar weed, 6842.
Begonia, sp., 7075, 7591 to 7600.
    gracilis, 7077.
    rex × *Begonia diadema*, 8328.
    semperflorens, 7162, 7231, 7311 to 7313.
Belladonna, 8530.
Bellota miersii, 9826.
Benthamia fragifera, 5981.
Bentinckia nicobarica, 7569.
Berberis darwini, 7227.
    dulcis, 5784.
    ilicifolia, 7869.
    nepalensis, 8853.
    stenophylla, 7870.
    thunbergii, 7871.
    wallichiana, 7330.
Berseem. (*See* Clover, Egyptian.)
Beta brasiliensis, 7179, 7199.
    chilensis, 7153, 7181.
    vulgaris, 5769 to 5773, 6165 to 6168, 6260 to 6264, 6359, 7908, 8229, 8238.
Betoom, 9325.
Bignonia chamberlaynii, 9662.
    tweediana, 8249.
Birdlime, 9292, 9293.
Bixa orellana, 5618, 8936.
Blighia sapida, 6856.
Bocconia frutescens, 7327, 8954.
Boehmeria nivea, 6337, 6338.
Bombax malabaricum, 8193.
    ochroma, 7272.
Boronia megastigma, 5998.
Bougainvillea sp., 9555 to 9558.
    spectabilis, 9556, 9707.
Brachychiton.
Brassica campestris, 6178.
    juncea, 6394, 6607, 6613, 6614, 6622.
    napus, 6198.
    oleracea, 5925, 5926, 5959, 5960, 6427, 6705, 7723.
        botrytis, 6266 to 6271, 6432, 6434.
    pe-tsai, 6610, 6611.
    rapa, 6134, 6176, 6179, 6265.
Broccoli, see Cauliflower.
Brome-grass, smooth, 5827.
Bromelia sp., 5798.
Bromus inermis, 5827.
Brunfelsia macrophylla, 6882.
Buckthorn, California, 6662.
Buckwheat, 5934, 6177, 6385, 6602, 6603, 9294, 9295.
Buluba, 5781a, 5786.
Butea frondosa, 6883.
Butternut, 7953.
Butum, 7950, 8483, 8800.

Butyrospermum parkii, 8985.
Buxus handsworthiensis, 7872.

Cabbage, 5925, 5926, 5959, 5960, 6427, 6705, 7723.
    Chinese, 6610, 6611.
    Stockholm Torg, 6427.
Cacao, 6274, 9858, 9010.
Cactus, 7089, 7090, 7095, 7096, 7375 to 7378, 7382.
Caesalpinia bonducella, 5632, 7541.
    coriaria, 7267.
    gilliesii, 8935.
    pulcherrima, 6885, 7266.
    sappan, 6886, 7206.
    sepiaria, 7325.
Cajanus indicus, 8986.
Calabash tree, 6868.
Caladium sp., 7799 to 7812.
Calamagrostis phragmitoides, 5830.
Calla, 7557, 7567.
Calligonum sp., 9583 to 9594.
Callistephus hortensis, 6387, 6388, 6392.
Calodendrum capensis, 7358.
Calophyllum sp., 5566.
Calotropis gigantea, 8987.
Camelina sativa, 6036.
Camoensia maxima, 7344.
Campanula medium, 8382.
    persicifolia, 7160, 7196, 7307 to 7310.
Camphor, 5615.
Cananga odorata, 9719.
Canarina campanula, var. *canariensis*, 9828.
    canariensis (?), 9664.
Canarium album, 8364.
    amboinense, 5534.
Canavalia ensiformis, 6132, 6323, 6570, 7974.
    gladiata, 6324.
Candle nut, 6450.
Canna sp., 6632.
Cannabis indica, 6164, 6671.
    sativa, 6035, 6194, 6309, 6310, 6317, 6322, 6325, 8516, 8525, 9665.
Cantaloupe, 7015.
Canterbury bells, 8382.
Caper, spineless, 6341.
Capparis inermis, 6341.
Caprifig, 6241 to 6243, 6254, 6473 to 6479, 6481 to 6491, 6773 to 6818, 6820 to 6823, 6832, 6835 to 6840, 6850, 6957, 7663 to 7667, 8829 to 8832, 8834 to 8838, 8840, 8841, 8844, 8845.
Capsicum annuum, 5524 to 5526, 5530, 5536 to 5538, 5546, 5553, 5555, 5556, 5565, 5902, 6382, 6383, 7448, 7654, 7781 to 7783, 8565, 8566, 8568, 8799, 9475.
Cardamom, 6446, 6864.
Cardiospermum sp., 7053.
    halicacabum, 8250.
Carex darwinii, 9061.
    decidua, 9062.
    haematorrhynca, 9063.
    macloviana, 9064.
    pseudo-cyperus, 9065.

Carica candamarcensis, 7247.
  papaya, 7198, 7209, 7328, 7510, 8417, 8577.
  quercifolia, 8251, 8854, 8960.
  heterophylla, 5753.
Carissa arduina, 9612.
Carnation, 7561 to 7566, 7625 to 7629.
Carob, 5825, 6143, 6342, 7059, 7060, 7063, 7132, 7399, 7400, 7460, 7461, 7722, 7777, 8416, 8856, 8914.
Carrot, 6615, 6706, 9574.
Carthamus tinctorius, 7644, 9787, 9800.
Caryota mitis, 8313.
  urens, 6900, 8597.
Cascara sagrada, 6662.
Cascarilla muzonensis, 7830.
Cashew, 6852, 7294, 7414, 7499, 9447.
Casimiroa edulis, 7505.
Cassava, 9670 to 9699.
Cassia alata, 8988.
  auriculata, 9859.
  corymbosa, 8252, 8855.
  grandis, 8676.
  occidentalis, 8253.
Castanea sp., 6530, 6533, 6634, 8362.
  crenata, 8393.
Castilla sp. nov., 9857.
Casuarina equisetifolia, 8254, 9818.
Cauliflower, 6266 to 6271, 6432, 6434.
Ceanothus azureus, 8255, 9090.
Cecropia palmata, 8920.
Cedar, bastard, 6866.
  Jamaica, 6865.
  Japanese, 6660.
Cedrela odorata, 6865, 7223, 7831.
  sinensis, 7256.
  toona, 6866, 7238, 8660.
Celery, 6707.
Celosia cristata, 6422.
Celtis serotina, 8669.
  sinensis, 9277.
  tala, 8972.
Centaurea americana, 7248.
Cephalandra quinqueloba, 9623.
Cephalaria tatarica, 5828.
Ceratonia siliqua, 5825, 6143, 6342, 7059, 7060, 7063, 7132, 7334, 7399, 7400, 7460, 7461, 7722, 7777, 8416, 8856, 8914.
Ceratostigma plumbaginoides, 7873.
Cercidiphyllum japonicum, 7874.
Cercis siliquastrum, 8857.
Cereus sp., 7085, 7086, 7509, 7519, 8580.
Ceropegia woodii, 7345.
Cestrum elegans, 9428.
  parqui, 8959.
  pseudo-quina, 8947.
Chaetochloa italica, 5907, 6221, 6389, 6410, 6589 to 6594, 9784, 9799.
Chagoggee, 8803.
Chamaecyparis obtusa, 8141 to 8144.
Chamaedorea corallina, 7300.
  ernesti-augusti, 7301.
  geonomaeformis, 7302.
  gracilis, 7303.
  sartorii, 8324.
Chamaerops arborea (?), 7273.
  canariensis (?), 7274.

Chamaerops elegans (?), 7276.
  farinosa (?), 6903, 7278.
  humilis, 6901, 6902, 7279, 7280, 7416.
  macrocarpa, 7281.
  olivaeformis (?), 7282.
  robusta (?), 7283.
  tomentosa, 7284.
Chard, 6165 to 6168.
Charica officinarum, 5563.
Chayote, 9733.
Cherimoya, 8653, 9466.
Cherry, 6096 to 6100, 6107, 6529, 6631, 9029, 9030, 9170 to 9199, 9847, 9851.
  Barbados, 6858.
  Japanese, 9201.
  flowering, 7900, 9170 to 9199.
Cherry laurel, 9867.
Chestnut, 6530, 6533, 6634, 8362.
  Cape, 7358.
  Japanese, 8393.
  water, 8366.
Chicalam, 9885.
Chick-pea, 5928, 6687, 6999, 7017, 7021, 7462, 7638, 7655, 8807.
Chicory, 5958.
Chili guipin, 9445.
China grass. (*See* Ramie.)
Chloris virgata, 9608.
Cho-cho. (*See Sechium edule*.)
Chorisia crispiflora, 8967.
  insignis, 9073.
Chowali, 8687.
Chrysalidocarpus lutescens, 8315.
Chrysanthemum sp., 7244, 7909 to 7941a, 7963.
  carinatum, 6419.
  cinerariaefolium, 6142.
  coronarium, 6617.
  edible, 6419, 6617.
  maximum, 7195.
Chrysophyllum cainito, 8989.
Chufa, 7424, 8216 to 8218.
Cicca nodiflora, 5564.
Cicer arietinum, 5928, 6687, 6999, 7017, 7021, 7462, 7638, 7655, 8807.
Cichorium endivia, 7139.
  intybus, 5958.
Cinchona calisaya, 7229, 7549, 7551.
  hybrida, 7245.
  ledgeriana, 7224, 7550.
  officinalis, 7166, 7357, 8205.
  succirubra, 7193, 7552.
Cinco palomas, 6160.
Cinnamomum sp., 8318.
  camphora, 5615.
  cassia, 6867.
  loureirii, 8404.
Cinnamon, Chinese, 6867.
Ciruela, 7501, 8240.
Cissus sp., 6921, 7006, 7383, 7496.
Cistus albidus, 9429.
Citharexylum barbinerve, 8973.
Citron, 8643.
Citrullus vulgaris, 6037 to 6057, 6149 to 6159, 6170, 6171, 8410, 8447, 8465 to 8475, 8607 to 8642, 9572.

INDEX OF COMMON AND SCIENTIFIC NAMES. 321

Citrus sp., 8443, 9497, 9700 to 9702.
  aurantium, 5989, 5990, 6116, 6184, 6245, 6248, 6249, 6636, 6640, 6647, 6947, 6948, 6950, 6954, 8415, 8439, 8441, 8446, 8602 to 8604, 8706, 9437, 9498, 9595 to 9597, 9700 to 9702.
  × *bergamia*, 9489, 9554.
  australica, 9040.
  bigaradia (?) 8894, 8895, 9268.
  decumana, 5547, 6246, 6250, 6645, 6646, 8435, 8606, 8903, 9017 to 9019, 9269, 9272, 9500.
  hybrida, 8210, 9488.
  japonica, 8896, 9274, 9275, 9493, 9494.
  limetta, 5529, 5554, 6951, 8347.
  limonum, 5531 to 5533, 5982, 5986, 5991, 5993, 6115, 6117, 6121, 6185, 6190, 6360, 6361, 6365, 6641, 6654, 6960, 8443, 8601.
  medica, 6643.
  nobilis, 6247, 6642, 6644, 8902, 8904, 8905, 9271, 9495, 9496, 9499.
    × *C. bigaradia*, 8210, 8367, 9132, 9480.
    × *C. decumana*, 8368, 8414.
Clausena excavata, 8194.
Clematis sp., 7875 to 7896.
  hilarii, 8962.
  jackmani, 7884.
  rubella, 7893.
  wightiana, 8661.
Cleome arborea, 9430.
Clerodendron foetidum, 9883.
            hastatum, 8256.
            squamatum, 8123.
Clianthus dampieri, 5623.
Clitoria sp., 9717.
  ternatea, 7205.
Clover, alsike, 8556.
  bur, 6380.
  bush, 6331, 7973.
  crimson, 7529, 7530.
  Egyptian, 7000, 7031, 7657 to 7659, 9874 to 9876.
  genge, 5935, 6329, 6330, 6571.
  red, 5746 to 5750, 5968, 5969, 7138, 8555.
  strawberry, 9026.
Cobaea scandens, 9091.
Coca, 6447.
Coccoloba uvifera, 6855.
Coccothrinax garberi, 7774.
Cochlearia armoracia, 5589, 5761, 5837, 7058.
Cockscomb, 6422.
Cocos alphonsei, 6906.
  australis, 6905, 8933, 9074.
  bonneti, 6907.
  botryophora, 9728.
  coronata, 7570.
  datil, 8321.

Cocos romanzoffiana, 7339.
  yatay, 8314, 8918, 9075.
Codiaeum variegatum, 7346 to 7354, 7601 to 7604.
Codonopsis viridiflora, 8383.
Coffea arabica, 5797, 6278, 6712, 7678, 7775, 8207, 8211, 9716.
  hybrida, 8682.
  liberica, 8681, 8990.
Coffee, 5797, 6278, 6712, 7678, 7775, 8207, 8211, 8681, 8682, 8990, 9716.
  tree, Kentucky, 7046.
Coiron flor, 5779.
Coix sp., 6407.
  lachryma-jobi, 5620.
Cola acuminata, 7014.
Colliguaja brasiliensis, 8949.
Commelina sp., 7069.
  coelestis, 9092.
Convolvulus sp., 5549, 5550, 5557, 5558.
Coontie, 8504.
Copernicia cerifera, 8964.
Cordyline australis, 7171, 8257.
  banksii, 8858.
Corinth, 6366, 6374, 6429.
Corn, 5560, 6028 to 6034, 6172, 6230 to 6233, 6273, 6401, 6573, 6574, 6827, 7502, 8822, 9356, 9357, 9449, 9573, 9795.
  Kafir, 9852.
Cornus kousa, 8403.
Coronilla atlantica, 9093.
Corylus sp., 5992.
  avellana, 7423.
  rostrata, 9278.
  tubulosa, 6138, 6139.
Corypha elata, 7331.
Cosmos sp., 7964.
Cotton, 6400, 6655, 6684, 7647, 8728, 8798.
  Egyptian, 5939, 6673 to 6679, 7018, 7019, 7023, 7025 to 7027, 7030, 7036, 9635 to 9660.
Cotyledon sp., 7064, 7081, 7082, 7084, 7098, 7368 to 7370, 7373, 7374, 7390, 7394, 7403, 7479, 7487, 9628.
  teretifolia, 9622.
Cowpea, 6311, 6327, 6328, 6413, 6431, 6563, 6566 to 6568, 8354, 8418, 8498 to 8501, 8687.
Crab's eyes, 6877.
Crambe maritima, 6145.
Cranberry, 6347.
Crescentia alata, 7971.
  cujete, 6868, 8991.
Crotalaria juncea, 8910.
Croton. (See *Codiaeum variegatum*.)
Croton sebiferum, 7158.
  tiglium, 6448.
Cryptomeria japonica, 6660.
Cucumber, 5587, 5839, 5900, 6080 to 6083, 6395, 6425, 6694, 7511.
Cucumis sp., 7511.

Cucumis melo, 5755, 5774, 5904, 5908, 6058 to 6078, 6131, 6146 to 6148, 6363, 6364, 6426, 6697, 7015, 7397, 7972, 8219, 8308 to 8310, 9020, 9022.
 metuliferus, 5179.
 sativus, 5567, 5839, 5900, 6080 to 6083, 6395, 6425, 6694, 7511.
Cucurbita sp., 5520, 5552, 5559, 6133, 6695, 6698, 6708, 7406, 7409, 7508, 9481.
 maxima, 5906, 6088, 6089.
 melanosperma, 9626.
 moschata, 6197.
 pepo, 6402, 6620, 6621.
Cupania sapida, 6856.
Cuphea, sp., 7057.
 ignea, 9094.
 selenoides, 9095.
Cupressus funebris, 6876, 7150.
 sempervirens, 5964, 9096.
 torulosa, 8655.
Curcuma longa, 8935.
Currant, red, 6101.
Cushaw, 6197.
Cycas normanbyana, 7546.
Cydonia sp., 8645.
 sinensis, 6183, 6186, 6188, 6362, 8209.
 vulgaris, 5762, 6120, 6187, 6193, 8454, 8455.
Cyperus esculentus, 7424, 8216 to 8218.
 nutans, 9860.
 papyrus, 9097.
 tegetiformis, 9861.
Cypress, 5964, 9096.
 funeral, 6876.
Cyrtostachys renda, 7571.
Cytisus linifolium, 7697.
 proliferus, 7696.

Dactylis glomerata, 8554.
Dagmay, 6276.
Dahlia sp., 7079, 7967, 7968, 9884.
 silvestre, 7966.
Daisy, Transvaal or Barberton, 9484.
Dalbergia latifolia, 8662.
 nigra, 8941.
 sissoo, 6661, 9819.
Dana, 6221.
Danthonia californica, 7117.
Dap-dap, 5617.
Daphne genkwa, 8145.
 odora, 8394, 8395.
Dasylirion sp., 7100.
Date, 6438 to 6442, 6445, 6846, 7001, 7002, 7631 to 7636, 7798, 8563, 8564, 8567, 8569 to 8573, 8738 to 8795, 9600.
 Chinese. (*See* Jujube.)
Datura stramonium, 8534.
Daucus carota, 6615, 6706, 9574.
Delphinium zalil, 8385.
Desfontainea spinosa, 7825.
Desmodium illinoense, 6842.
 podocarpum, 9238.

Desmodium triflorum, 9893.
 uncinatum, 8924.
Deutzia sieboldiana, 8124.
Dianthus alpinus, 7979.
 arenarius, 7980.
 armeria, 7981.
 barbatus, 8384.
 caryophyllus, 7561 to 7566, 7625 to 7629.
 chinensis, 7982 to 7984.
Digitalis purpurea, 8532.
Dillenia indica, 6887.
 speciosa, 8195.
Dioscorea sp., 6277.
Diospyros kaki, 6522 to 6527, 8341, 9804.
Diotis candidissima, 9098.
Dittelasma rarak, 6873.
Dolichos sp., 5519.
 lablab, 6319, 6320, 6377, 6569, 8258, 8355 to 8357, 8545, 8686, 9431.
 melanophthalmus, 6431.
 sinensis, 6223, 6228.
 uniflorus, 8542.
Dorstenia contrajerva, 7832.
Dracaena sp., 7605 to 7609.
 draco, 6888, 7833.
Dracunculus canariensis, 9603.
Dragon's blood, 6888, 7833.
Dye plant, 6879.

Ebony, mountain, 6880.
Ebony tree, 6829.
Eccremocarpus scaber, 8259.
Echeveria maculata, 6923.
 platyphylla, 6922.
Echinocactus schumannianus, 9432.
Edgeworthia gardneri, 8146, 9162, 9163.
Eggplant, 5535, 5545, 5619, 6696, 7130, 9297, 9298.
Elaeagnus angustifolia, 9382, 9383.
 longipes, 6665.
 pungens, 8260.
Elaeis guineensis, 6908, 7289, 8992.
Eleocharis tuberosa, 8366.
Elettaria cardamomum, 6446, 8672.
Eleusine coracana, 5838, 8434.
Elymus andinus, 5779.
Emmer, 8652.
Endive, 7139.
Enterolobium sp., 8923.
 timbouva, 8940, 9076, 9077.
Epipremnum mirabile, 7363, 7816.
Eriobotrya japonica, 6191, 6453 to 6460, 6938, 6939, 6943, 6945, 6949, 6955, 6958, 7748, 7946, 8233, to 8236, 8890, 9099, 9244 to 9247, 9467, 9801.
Eriodendron anfractuosum, 9468.
Eriogonum giganteum, 7116.
Ervum lens, 7028.
 hiemale, 7523.
 microsperma, 6433.
 monanthos, 7522.
Eryngium sp., 7005.
 agavefolium, 9100.
Erythea edulis, 6352, 7297.
Erythrina sp., 6931, 7047.

INDEX OF COMMON AND SCIENTIFIC NAMES. 323

Erythrina carnea, 5617.
Erythroxylon coca, 6447.
Esparsette, *see* Sainfoin.
Eucalyptus citriodora, 7239.
　ficifolia, 9624.
　globulus, 5745, 7226, 9823.
　robusta, 7176.
Euclea racemosa, 9620.
Eucommia ulmoides, 5980, 8709.
Eugenia sp., 8937.
　edulis, 8969.
　mato, 8938.
　michelii, 8963.
　pungens, 8957.
Eupatorium sp., 8859.
　atrorubens, 8860, 9101.
　atroviolaceum, 8861.
Euphorbia sp., 8289.
　coronata, 9632.
　lathyris, 6667.
　pulcherrima, 9866.
Euterpe edulis, 8322.
Eutrema wasabi, 9891.
Exacum bicolor, 8663.

Fagopyrum esculentum, 5934, 6177, 6385, 6602, 6603, 9294, 9295.
Fatsia japonica, 8651, 8862.
Feijoa sellowiana, 9078.
Fennel flower, 6375.
Fenugreek, 6963, 7029, 7071, 7520, 7642, 7713, 9021.
　small, 5579.
Festuca arundinacea, 5835.
　fanara, 7715.
Ficus sp., 8346.
　carica, 5919 to 5921, 6114, 6241 to 6244, 6254, 6357, 6461 to 6491, 6493 to 6499, 6648, 6773 to 6823, 6832, 6835 to 6840, 6850, 6933, 6934, 6941, 6942, 6946, 6952, 6953, 6956, 6957, 7663 to 7667, 8506, 8507, 8829 to 8847, 9354, 9381.
　elastica, 7222, 7417, 7540.
　glomeratus, 6857.
　hispida, 6889.
　indica, 7356, 8196.
　macrophylla, 7191, 7418, 8290.
　radicans, 7355.
　sakoni, 6494.
　sycomorus, 7011.
Fig (*see also* Capriflg), 5919 to 5921, 6114, 6244, 6357, 6461 to 6491, 6493 to 6499, 6648, 6819, 6933, 6934, 6941, 6942, 6946, 6952, 6953, 6956, 8346, 8506, 8507, 8829 to 8847, 9354, 9381.
　cluster, 6857.
　Sycamore, 7011.
Filbert, 7423.
Flax, 5946 to 5957, 6199, 6653, 7648, 7649, 8525, 9347, 9421, 9457, 9789.
　false, 6036.
　white-flowered, 5949.
Fouquieria sp., 7388.
　splendens, 6924.
Foxberry, 5775.
Foxglove, 8532.

Fragraria sp., 7769.
Franseria artemisioides, 8864.
Freda, 9482.
Freylinia cestroides, 8863.
Frijole, 9147 to 9160.
Funtumia elastica, 8993.

Gaillardia amblyodon, 7207.
　pulchella, 7216, 7219, 7249.
Galium catalinense, 7112.
Gamboge tree, 6869.
"Gampi" paper plant, 8165.
Garbanzo, *see* Chick-pea.
Garcinia sp. (?), 9569.
　cochinchinensis, 9879.
　ferrea, 9880.
　hanburyi, 8994.
　mangostana, 5634, 7468, 8976, 9869, 9881.
　morella, 6869.
Gasteria croucheri, 9630.
Gazania hybrida, 7419 to 7421.
Genista monosperma, 9102.
　sphaerocarpa, 7749.
Gerbera jamesonii, 9484.
Ginger, 6875, 7621, 8736.
Ginkgo biloba, 8140.
Glaucium flavum, 8865.
Gleditsia amorphoides, 8934.
Globularia salicina, 8292.
Glyceria spectabilis, 5832.
Glycine hispida, 5764 to 5766, 6312, 6314, 6326, 6333 to 6336, 6379, 6386, 6396, 6397, 6414, 6416, 6556, 6558 to 6561, 8422 to 8424, 8489 to 8497, 8584, 8586, 8900, 9344, 9407 to 9418.
Glycyrrhiza glabra, 8533.
Gomphocarpus sp., 5781a, 5786.
　textilis, 8291.
Gossypium sp., 6655, 6684, 7647, 8728, 8798.
　barbadense, 5939, 6400, 6673 to 6679, 9018, 7019, 7023, 7025 to 7027, 7030, 7036, 9635 to 9660.
　brasiliense (?), 8728.
Goumi, 6865.
Gourd, 5528, 5544, 6412, 6708, 8575, 9226.
　sponge, 8683.
Grabowskia glauca, 8956, 9033.
Gram, green, *see* Bean, mung.
Grape, 5616, 5689, 5909 to 5918, 5985, 6118, 6119, 6124, 6140, 6280 to 6306, 6356, 6366, 6374, 6429, 6500, 6501, 7048, 7671, 7687, 7993 to 8071, 8436, 8462 to 8464, 8581 to 8583, 8605, 8647 to 8649, 8796, 8797, 9560 to 9568, 9576 to 9579, 9607, 9809 to 9814.
　mustang, 8576.
　shore, 6855.
　wild, 6505.
Grape fruit. (*See* Pomelo.)
Green gram. (*See* Bean, mung.)
Guaiacum officinale, 6870.
Guava, 8344, 9023.
Guinea grass, 9315.
Guizotia abyssinica, 7645.

Guzmania musaica, 7619.
Gymnocladus canadensis, 7046.
   chinensis, 6572.

Haloxylon ammodendron, 9581.
Hamamelis japonica, 8189.
Harpephyllum caffrum, 9616.
Hazelnut, 5992, 6138, 6139, 9278.
Hechtia sp., 7387.
Hedera helix, 8866, 9602.
Hedychium gardnerianum, 7624, 8293.
Hedysarum coronarium, 7037, 7528, 7710, 7784, 7788, 7790.
   mauritanicum, 7712.
   naudinianum, 7789.
   obscurum, 5829.
   pallidum, 7711, 7725.
Heeria sp., 7688.
Helianthus annuus, 6093 to 6095, 9668.
Helleborus hybridus, 7836.
   niger, 7837.
Hemp, 6035, 6164, 6194, 6309, 6310, 6317, 6322, 6325, 6606, 6671, 8516, 8525, 9665.
  ambari, 7032.
  manila, 6234 to 6237, 6239, 9028, 9134.
  sunn, 8910.
Henbane, 8535.
Henna, 6871.
Hepatica triloba, 7838, 7840.
Heteropteris umbellata, 8958.
Heterospathe elata, 7572.
Hibiscus sp., 8867.
   argentinus, 8965.
   cannabinus, 7032.
   elatus, 7359.
   esculentus, 6376.
   sabdariffa, 8698.
   sinensis, 9705, 9706.
   tiliaceus, 6890.
Hicoria pecan, 7990, 7991, 8200 to 8203.
Hippocrepis multisiliquosa, 7726.
Holboellia latifolia, 7828.
Honckenya ficifolia, 8995.
Honey Jack, 6451.
Hop, 5569, 5570, 5587, 5588, 5593, 5594, 5611, 5622, 5631. 5757 to 5760, 5768, 5787, 5836, 5971, 6353.
Hordeum distichum, 5590 to 5592, 5756, 5788 to 5792, 5794, 5842, 5845, 5847 to 5899, 5903, 5975, 5976, 7992, 8560.
   erectum, 6367.
   nutans, 5793, 5846, 9133.
   hexastichum, 6023, 8559.
   tetrastichum, 6175, 7427, 7583, 7584, 7796, 8809.
   vulgare, 5843, 5844, 6399, 6403, 6597, 6601, 6658, 7451, 7640, 7641, 7969, 7970, 9783, 9877.
Horse-radish, 5589, 5761, 5837, 7058.
  Japanese, 9891.
Hosackia traskiae, 7110.
   venusta, 7109.

Hovenia dulcis, 6608.
Howea belmoreana, 8888.
   forsteriana, 8889.
Humulus lupulus, 5569, 5570, 5587, 5588, 5593, 5594, 5611, 5622, 5631, 5757 to 5760, 5768, 5787, 5836, 5971, 6353.
Hura crepitans, 7542, 8996, 9720.
Hydrangea hortensis, 8396 to 8399.
Hydriastele wendlandiana, 7322.
Hymenocallis sp., 7008.
   harrisiana, 6919.
Hymenocarpus circinata, 7727.
Hyoscyamus niger, 8535.
Hyphaene benguelensis, 7288.
Hyptis sp., 7051.

Igna lanceolata, 5621.
Ilang-ilang, 9719.
Ilex integra, 7554.
  paraguayensis, 8953.
  wightiana, 8664.
Illicium floridanum, 7161.
Impatiens sp., 7228.
  balsamina, 6421.
  sultani, 7155, 7168, 7264.
India wheat, 8215.
Indigo, 6623.
Indigofera anil, 9039.
  tinctoria, 6623.
Inga dulcis, 7415.
Inodes palmetto, 7773.
Iochroma tubulosa, 8295.
Ipecacuanha, 7360.
Ipomoea batatas, 6173.
  ficifolia, 8868.
Iris sp., 9601.
  germanica, 9103.
  japonica, 8389.
  laevigata, 8388, 8869.
  sibirica, 9104.
  tectorum, 8390, 8391.
  unguicularis, 6492.
Ivy, 9602.

Jacaranda chelonia, 8975, 9031.
  cuspidifolia, 9066.
  ovalifolia, 8294.
Jack fruit, 6854.
Jacquinia armillaris, 6891.
Japanese horse-radish, 9891.
Jaragua, 5751.
Jarilla, 5753.
Jasmine, Arabian, 8437.
Jasminum nitidum, 7342.
  sambac, 8437.
Jatropha curcas, 7246.
  glauca, 7190.
  manihot, 7243.
  multifida, 7257.
Jessamine, red, 9894.
Job's tears, 5620, 6407.
Johnson grass, 7643.
Jojoba, 8312.
Jubaea spectabilis, 7286, 9825.
Juglans cinerea, 7953.
  cordiformis, 8425, 9280.
  nigra, 7954.

INDEX OF COMMON AND SCIENTIFIC NAMES. 325

Juglans regia, 5633, 5983, 6180 to 6182, 6354, 6650 to 6652, 8208, 8307, 9231, 9232.
    sieboldiana, 8426.
Jujube, 6549, 8600, 8702, 8703, 8828.
Juncus effusus, 8429, 9873.
Juniperus chinensis, 9296.

Kadsura japonica, 8147 to 8149.
Kafir orange, 9611.
    plum, 9616.
Kageneckia sp., 8695.
Kale, sea, 6145.
Kapok, 9468.
Kentia alexandria, 7287.
    macarthuri (Hort.), 8329.
    sanderiana, 7574.
Kentiopsis macrocarpa, 8327.
Khaya senegalensis, 8311.
Kicksia africana, 7361.
Kigelia pinnata, 6444.
Kniphofia aloides, 9105.
Kochia scoparia, 5970.
Kola, 7014.
Korean lawn grass, 6404, 6405.
Kudzu, 9227, 9228.
Kulthi, 8542.
Kumquat, 8896, 9274, 9275, 9493, 9494.
Kunenbo, 9497.

Labramia bojeri, 8997.
Lacolaco, 6238.
Lac tree, 6883.
Lactuca sativa, 6618.
Lagenaria sp., 8575, 9226.
    vulgaris, 6412.
Lantana camara, 8955.
    radula, 9106.
Larch, Japanese, 6672.
Larix leptolepis, 6672.
Larrea nitida, 9079.
Lasiosiphon eriocephalus, 8656.
Lathyrus sp., 8461.
    cicer, 7521, 8810.
    clymenus, 6974.
    magellanicus, 5782.
    numidicus, 7729.
    ochrus, 6436, 7534.
    platyphyllus, 5826.
    sativus, 7639, 7680.
    tingitanus, 5585, 6973, 7637, 7728.
Laurel, California, 5977.
Laurus canariensis, 7270.
Lavender, 5801, 8528.
    spike, 5802, 8529.
Lavandula spica, 5802, 8529.
    vera, 5801, 8528.
Lawsonia alba, 6871.
Lebbek, 6443, 9038.
Lechuguilla, 7439.
Leea sambucina, 7558.
Leitchee, 9802, 9803.
Lemon, 5531 to 5533, 5982, 5986, 5991, 5993, 6115, 6117, 6121, 6185, 6190, 6360, 6361, 6365, 6641, 6654, 6960, 8443, 8601.
Lens esculenta. (*See Ervum lens*.)
Lentil, 6433, 7028.

Lentil, one-flowered, 7522.
    winter, 7523.
Lespedeza bicolor, 6331, 7973, 9107.
    buergeri, 9230.
    sieboldi, 7553.
Lettuce, 6618.
Leucadendron argenteum, 7556, 8317, 9633.
Leucaena glauca, 8998.
Leucanthemum uliginosum, 7841.
Liatris odoratissima, 6144.
Libocedrus chilensis, 6870, 9067.
Licorice, 8533.
Licuala grandis, 6911, 7547.
    muelleri, 7343.
    rumphii, 6912.
Lignum-vitæ, 6870.
Ligustrum ciliatum, 8127.
    japonicum, 8296.
Lilium auratum, 7848 to 7850.
    browni, 7852.
    elegans, 7857, 7858.
    joponicum, 7856.
    longiflorum, 7854, 8387.
    maculatum, 7851.
    maximowiczii, 7853.
    rubellum, 7859.
    speciosum, 7855.
Lily, 7848 to 7859, 9895.
    water, 7413.
Lime, 5529, 5554, 6951, 8347.
    Spanish, 6859.
Linaria saxatilis, 9108.
Lindelofia spectabilis, 7194.
Linum usitatissimum, 5946 to 5957, 6199, 6653, 7648, 7649, 8524, 9347, 9421, 9457, 9789.
Lippia lycioides, 8952.
    turbinata, 8930.
Lithraea aroeirinha, 8939.
    molle, 9127.
Litsea zeylanica, 8679a.
Livistona altissima, 7304.
    australis, 7299, 7332.
    hoogendorpii, 9724.
    jenkinsiana, 7293, 7548.
    rotundifolia, 7305, 9729.
Lonicera caprifolium, 7897.
    humilis, 7898.
Loquat, 6191, 6453 to 6460, 6938, 6959, 6943, 6945, 6949, 6955, 6958, 7748, 7946, 8233 to 8236, 8890, 9099, 9244 to 9247, 9467, 9801.
Loseosiphon eriocephalus, 8656.
Lotus, 9248 to 9267.
Lotus edulis, 6975, 7731.
    ornithopodioides, 6976, 7730.
    tetragonolobus, 6970, 7656, 7700.
    uliginosus, 5942.
Lucern, sand, 7945.
    tree, 9613.
Lucuma neriifolia, 8951.
Luffa aegyptiaca, 8683, 9718.
Lunga, 6222.
Lupine, 5936, 5937, 6688.
    blue, 5583, 6971, 7341, 7535.
    Egyptian or Corsican, 5584, 7022.
    narrow-leaved, 5583.

Lupine, white, 7524, 7689.
    yellow, 7525, 7681.
Lupinus, sp., 6688, 7733.
    albus, 7524, 9627.
    angustifolius, 5583, 6971, 7535, 7690.
    hirsutus, 7341.
    luteus, 7525, 7681, 7732.
    pilosus caeruleus, 5936.
        roseus, 5937.
    termis, 5584, 6972, 7022, 7689.
Lychnis coeli-rosa, 7184.
Lycopersicum esculentum, 6090, 6091.
Lyonothamnus floribundus, 7115.

Maba natalensis, 6892.
Machaerium fertile, 9080.
        tipu (Benth.). (*See Tipuana speciosa.*)
Madia sativa, 6664.
Magnolia grandiflora, 8402.
    kobus, 8502.
    parviflora, 8400, 8401.
Mahogany, 7543.
        African, 8311.
Maize. (*See* Corn.)
Malpighia glabra, 6858.
    urens, 7834.
Malva sylvestris, 9109.
Mammillaria sp., 7003, 7004, 7065, 7380, 7381.
Mandarin. (*See* Orange, Mandarin.)
Manfreda sp., 7007, 7087.
Mangifera indica, 7038 to 7045, 7101 to 7108, 8411 to 8413, 8419 to 8421, 8440, 8442, 8444, 8680, 8701, 8727, 8729 to 8734, 9486, 9504 to 9553, 9599, 9669, 9703, 9704, 9808.
Mango, 7038 to 7045, 7101 to 7108, 8411 to 8413, 8419 to 8421, 8440, 8442, 8444, 8680, 8701, 8727, 8729 to 8734, 9486, 9504 to 9553, 9599, 9669, 9703, 9704, 9808.
Mangosteen, 5634, 7468, 8976, 9869, 9881.
Manihot sp., 9670 to 9699.
Maple, Japanese, 8150 to 8188.
Maqui, 8694.
Maranta arundinacea, 6872.
    major, 7611.
Mariscus natalensis, 9110.
Marking nut tree, 6874.
Mastic, 7336, 9426, 9446.
Math, 8539.
Maurandia barclaiana, 6663.
Maytenus boaria, 8870, 8921.
Medicago sp., 6368.
    arborea, 7695, 9613.
    ciliaris, 7742, 9747.
    denticulata, 7734, 7737, 9229.
    disciformis, 9739.
    echinus, 7735.
    elegans, 8299.
    falcata, 9748.
    gerardi, 9736.
    getula, 7952.
    helix, 7736.
    intertexta, 9738.
    laciniata, 9737.

Medicago lupulina, 9734.
    media, 7588, 7945.
    murex, 9743.
    orbicularis, 7738, 9740.
    praecox, 9744.
    radiata, 9746.
    rigidula, 9735.
    sativa, 6998, 7500, 7586 to 7588, 8806, 8823, 9303, 9322, 9323, 9359, 9450, 9788, 9816.
        var. *turkestanica*, 9451 to to 9455, 9877, 9816.
    scutellata, 9749.
    secundiflora, 7743.
    suffruticosa, 9745.
    tenoreana, 9741.
    truncatula, 7739, 7741.
    tuberculata, 9742.
    turbinata, 6380, 7740.
Medinilla bornensis, 7613.
    magnifica, 7614.
Medlar, 8298.
Melaleuca leucadendron, 9111.
    viridiflora, 8871.
Melicocca bijuga, 6859.
Melilot, 5578, 7791.
Melilotus sp., 7791.
    infesta, 6965.
    macrostachys, 5578, 7692, 7744.
    speciosa, 7693.
    sulcata, 7694.
Melinis minutiflora, 5609.
Meliosma arnottiana, 8657.
Menengech, 7951, 8476, 8484, 8485, 8707, 8801.
Mesembryanthemum sp., 9501 to 9503.
    acinaciforme, 8297.
Mespilus germanica, 8298.
Mesquite, 8214.
Michelia champaca, 8999.
    compressa, 8122.
    nilagirica, 8673.
Microtropis ovalifolia, 8670.
Milk tree, 8346.
Millet, 5907, 6221, 6389, 6410, 6589 to 6594, 9784, 9798, 9799.
    African, 5838, 8434.
    Barbados, 6604.
    broom-corn, 5647, 5648, 6024 to 6027, 6408, 6682, 6692, 6709, 6711, 8805, 8821, 9423 to 9425, 9785, 9798.
    Japanese. (*See Panicum crusgalli.*)
    pearl, 7646.
    Ragi, 5838.
Mimosa sensitiva, 8945.
Mina trilobata, 8237.
Mitsumata paper plant, 9162, 9163.
Molasses grass, 5609.
Momordica sp., 5528, 5544.
Moraea pavonia, 9631.
Morrenia odorata, 8968.
Morus sp., 6848, 7141 to 7145, 7431 to 7438.
    alba, 7537, 9384.
    multicaulis, 8335.

INDEX OF COMMON AND SCIENTIFIC NAMES. 327

Mountain tobacco, 8531.
Mug, 8540.
Mulberry, 6848, 7141 to 7145, 7431 to 7438, 9384.
    Chinese, 8335.
Mundle bundle, 5625.
Musa ensete, 7295.
    mannii, 7154.
    martini, 7259.
    rosacea, 7260, 7262.
    sapientum, 9575, 9610.
    sumatrana, 7240.
    superba, 7261.
    textilis, 6234 to 6237, 6239, 9028, 9134.
Mushroom, 8222 to 8225.
Muskmelon, 5755, 5774, 5904, 5908, 6058 to 6078, 6131, 6146 to 6148, 6363, 6364, 6426, 6697, 7015, 7397, 7972, 8219, 8308 to 8310, 9020, 9022.
Mussaenda grandiflora, 7615.
Mustard, Chinese, 6394, 6607, 6613, 6614, 6622.
    tree of Scripture, 7362.
Myoporum insulare, 9621.
Myrica faya, 9060, 9276, 9316, 9476.
    nagi, 9164, 9314.
Myristica horsfieldii, 7835.
Myrobalan emblic, 6860.
Myrtle, downy, 6863.

Nanca, 6275.
Natal thorn, 8239, 9617.
Nectarine, 9221, 9284, 9882.
Nelumbium speciosum, 9248 to 9267.
Neowashingtonia sp., 5586.
    filamentosa, 6351.
Nephelium litchi, 9802, 9803.
Nicotiana glauca, 8261.
    tabacum, 5961 to 5963, 6229, 7686, 8893.
Nigella aromatica, 6375.
Nolina sp., 7097, 7391.
Notochaena hamosa, 9112.
Nuytsia floribunda, 9037.

Oak, 8704.
    cork, 9456.
    holly, 6340, 6343, 6344.
    Valonia, 6833.
Oat, 5513, 5514, 5938, 5966, 5967, 6022, 6174, 6626, 7450, 7944, 8538, 8558, 8650, 9422, 9571, 9878.
    Mapstone, 9571.
    wild, 6626.
Ocimum basilicum, 6381.
    viride, 9868.
Oenothera sp., 9025.
Oil plant, 7644 to 7646.
Okra, 6376.
Olea europaea, 5984, 6125 to 6130, 6240, 6251, 6649, 6831, 6834, 7675, 8872, 8909.
    laurifolia, 9123.
    verrucosa, 9124, 9559.
Oleander, yellow, 6893.
Olearia haastii, 8262, 8873.

Olive, 5984, 6125 to 6130, 6240, 6251, 6649, 6831, 6834, 7675, 8872, 8909, 9124, 9559.
    Chinese, 8364.
Onion, 6390, 7034, 9301, 9318.
Onobrychis sp., 7746.
    onobrychis, 7526, 7527.
    viciaefolia, 6966.
Ononis sp., 7745.
    alopecuroides, 6977.
    arellana, 5582, 7691, 7747.
Opuntia sp., 7379, 7507, 8578, 8579, 9135 to 9140.
    decumana, 8916.
    ficus-indica, 8961, 9317, 9352, 9353.
    gymnocarpa, 9113.
Oracco, 9775.
Orange, 5989, 5990, 6116, 6184, 6245, 6247 to 6249, 6636, 6640, 6642, 6644, 6647, 6950, 6954, 8210, 8367, 8368, 8414, 8415, 8439, 8441, 8446, 8602 to 8604, 8706, 8896, 8902, 8904, 8905, 9132, 9271, 9274, 9275, 9437, 9480, 9488, 9493 to 9499, 9595 to 9597.
    bitter, 8894, 8895, 9268.
    kumquat, 8896, 9274, 9275, 9493, 9494.
    Mandarin, 6247, 6642, 6644, 8902, 8904, 8905, 9271, 9495, 9496, 9499.
Orchard grass, 8554.
Orchid, 7094, 7469 to 7478.
Oreodoxa oleracea, 8325, 9722.
    regia, 8323.
Oreopanax platanifolium, 8874.
Orobus, 6435.
Oryza sativa, 5523, 5940, 5941, 6200 to 6220, 6307, 6308, 6384, 6575 to 6588, 8300 to 8306, 8359 to 8361, 8508 to 8515, 8543, 8590, 8591, 8593, 8594, 8688 to 8690, 8699, 8804, 8911, 8912, 9326 to 9343, 9667.
Osyris alba, 9114.
Oxalis sp., 6913 to 6918, 7010, 7050, 7412.
    corniculata, 8875.
    pringlei, 7009.
Oxycoccus palustris, 5776.

Paeonia moutan, 8072 to 8121, 8392, 8503.
Pagoda tree, 9034.
Palisota barteri, 9000.
Palm, 5586, 6351, 6908, 7072, 8700, 8708, 9472, 9473, 9776.
    date. (*See* Date.)
Panax aureum, 7559.
Pandanus aquaticus, 7340.
    utilis, 9730.
    vandermechii, 9726.
Panicum crus-galli, 6409, 8891.
    miliaceum, 5647, 5648, 6024 to 6027, 6408, 6682, 6692, 6709, 6711, 8805, 8821, 9423 to 9425, 9785, 9798.
    trypheron, 9315.
Papas amarillas, 9059.
Papaver sp., 9829.

Papaver bracteatum, 7186, 7253, 8319.
　　　　orientale, 7164, 7220, 7250 to 7252.
　　　　somniferum, 5796, 8536.
Papaw, 7510, 8417, 8577.
Paper plant, 9162, 9163, 9165.
Paprica, 9475.
Paraguay tea, 8935.
Parkinsonia aculeata, 8931.
Parrotia persica, 7899.
Paspalum digitaria, 9618.
Passiflora sp., 7056, 7131.
　　　　edulis, 5516, 5612.
　　　　pruinosa, 7560, 8263.
　　　　quadrangularis, 9713.
Passion flower, 5516, 5612, 7056, 7131.
Paulownia sp., 6657.
Pea, 6227, 6316, 6332, 6428, 6551 to 6554, 8557, 8562, 8588, 8810.
　　flat Tangier, 5585.
　　square, 6970, 7656, 7700.
Peach, 5922, 5923, 6109, 6541 to 6545, 6547, 6548, 6629, 6635, 7670, 8330 to 8334, 8337, 8340, 8343, 9217 to 9220, 9285, 9302, 9304, 9305, 9320, 9321, 9372 to 9380, 9389, 9391 to 9396, 9420, 9805, 9815, 9848 to 9850.
　　ornamental, 7863 to 7868.
Peanut, 5522, 5561, 5763, 8982, 9355, 9406.
Pear, 5924, 6110, 6507 to 6521, 6532, 7669, 8901, 8901a, 9360, 9361, 9388, 9492.
　　Japanese, 9239 to 9243.
　　melon, 9570.
　　prickly, 9317, 9352, 9353.
Pecan, 7990, 7991, 8200 to 8203.
Pedicularis zeylanica, 8677.
Pela, 5626.
Pelargonium zonale, 9115.
Pendicuas, 5752.
Pennisetum spicatum, 7646.
Pentzia virgata, 9619.
Peony, tree, 8072 to 8121, 8392, 8503.
Pepino, 9570.
Pepo, 6920.
Pepper, 5524 to 5526, 5530, 5536 to 5538, 5546, 5553, 5555, 5556, 5565, 5902, 6382, 6383, 7448, 7654, 7781 to 7783, 8565, 8566, 8568, 8799, 9445, 9475.
Pereskia aculeata, 9663.
Perilla sp., 6393.
　　　　ocymoides, 9282.
Perimedium discolor, 8264.
Persea gratissima, 9001.
　　　　indica, 9870.
　　　　lingue, 9128.
Persimmon, Japanese, 6522 to 6527, 8341, 9804.
Peruvian bark, 7357.
Petrea volubilis, 9714.
Pe-tsai. (*See* Cabbage, Chinese.)
Phacelia lyoni, 7114.
Phaseolus sp., 5517, 6279, 6391, 6415, 6560, 8585, 9147 to 9160, 9404, 9405, 9438 to 9444.
　　　　aconitifolius, 8539.
　　　　calcaratus, 6226.
　　　　lunatus, 5521.

Phaseolus mungo, 5518, 6224, 6378, 6564, 8486 to 8488, 8540, 9786.
　　　　mungo-radiatus, 6318, 6321, 6417, 6418, 6562, 9419.
　　　　radiatus, 8541.
　　　　viridissimus, 6430, 8814, 9889, 9890.
　　　　vulgaris, 5795, 5927, 5929, 6092, 6565, 7503, 7504.
Phleum pratense, 8553.
Phlomis fruticosa, 9433.
Phlox drummondii, 7156, 7177, 7218.
Phoenix dactylifera, 6438 to 6442, 6445, 6846, 7001, 7002, 7285, 7631 to 7636, 7798, 8563, 8564, 8567, 8569 to 8573, 8738 to 8795, 9600.
　　　　hybrid × reclinata, 7443.
　　　　pumila × reclinata, 7444, 8266.
　　　　reclinata, 7296, 7442, 8265.
　　　　rupicola, 8674.
Phormium tenax, 7172, 7189, 7232, 7234, 7263, 8267, 8320, 9116.
Photinia lindleyana, 8665.
Phygelius capensis, 9117.
Phyllanthus emblica, 6860.
Phyllostachys aurea, 7817, 9052.
　　　　bambusoides, 9044.
　　　　castillonis, 9041.
　　　　henonis, 9043, 9047.
　　　　marliacea, 9048.
　　　　mitis, 7820, 8427, 9045.
　　　　nigra, 7822, 9042.
　　　　quilioi, 8428, 9046.
　　　　ruscifolia, 9051.
　　　　violascens, 7824.
Physalis sp., 9448.
　　　　francheti, 5785.
　　　　peruviana, 7577.
Picea excelsa, 5945.
Pimenta acris, 9002.
Pimpinella anisum, 7449.
Pinanga decora, 7337.
Pine, Pyrenean, 6141.
　　Scottish, 5943, 5944.
　　stone, 6189.
　　umbrella, 9827.
Pineapple, 7366, 9485, 9606, 9634, 9732.
Pinus brutia, 6141.
　　　　canariensis, 9830.
　　　　longifolia, 8678.
　　　　pinea, 6189, 9827.
　　　　sylvestris, 5943, 5944.
Piptadenia cebil, 8929.
　　　　macrocarpa, 9082.
Pistache, 6079, 6122, 6123, 6252, 6253, 6349, 6350, 6355, 6824, 6849, 7335, 7668, 7949, 8349, 8477 to 8482, 8517 to 8520, 8574, 9477, 9490, 9491, 9778.
Pistacia sp., 6355.
　　　　atlantica, 9325.
　　　　lentiscus, 7336, 9426, 9446.
　　　　mutica, 7951, 8476, 8484, 8485, 8707, 8801, 9474 (?).
　　　　terebinthus, 7291, 7673, 8521.

INDEX OF COMMON AND SCIENTIFIC NAMES. 329

Pistacia vera, 6079, 6122, 6123, 6252, 6253, 6349, 6350, 6824, 6849, 7335, 7668, 7949, 8349, 8477 to 8482, 8517 to 8520, 8574, 9477, 9490, 9491, 9778.
    × (?) (Butum), 8483, 8800.
    × *palaestina*, 7950.
    × *terebinthus*, 5767, 8204.
Pisum sp., 6553, 6554, 8588.
    sativum, 6316, 6332, 6428, 6551, 6552, 8557, 8562.
Pitahaya, 7509, 7519, 8580.
Pithecolobium sp., 7408.
    pruinosum, 7212.
    saman, 9003.
    unguis-cati, 7255.
Pittosporum pendulum, 9625.
    tobira, 8128.
    undulatum, 9435.
Plectranthus striatus, 8268.
Plocama pendula, 9598.
Plum, 5824, 5931, 6103 to 6106, 6108, 6536 to 6540, 6546, 8338, 8339, 8342, 8345, 8365, 8705, 8824, 8826, 8827, 9222, 9223, 9279, 9281, 9346, 9362, 9363, 9806.
    hog, 6259.
    Japanese, 9202 to 9210, 9233, 9235, 9236, 9270, 9273, 9306, 9313.
Podachaenium paniculatum, 8269, 9118.
Podocarpus macrophylla, 8192.
Poinciana, dwarf, 6885.
Poinciana regia, 6884, 9004.
Poinsettia, 8438, 9712, 9866.
Poinsettia sp., 9712.
    pulcherrima, 8438.
Polygonum sp., 6624.
    lanigerum, 8270.
    tataricum, 8215.
Pomegranate, 5987, 5988, 6843, 6935 to 6937, 6940, 6944, 7440, 7674, 7676, 7677, 7776, 8430 to 8433, 8599, 8643, 8646, 9385, 9386.
Pomelo, 5547, 6246, 6250, 6645, 6646, 8435, 8606, 8895, 8903, 9017 to 9019, 9268, 9269, 9272, 9500.
Popat, 8545.
Poplar, 5994, 6847, 8336.
Poppy, 5796, 8536, 9829.
    Matilija, 7518.
Populus sp., 6847, 8336.
    alba, 5994.
Porana racemosa, 8271.
Portulacaria afra, 9604, 9605, 9615.
Potato, 7073, 7395, 7396, 7489, 9059.
    sweet, 6173.
Primula obconica 7157, 7185, 7211, 7221, 7233, 7265, 7314, 7315.
Prince's feather, 8803.
Pritchardia gaudichaudii, 8700.
    martii, 8708.
Proso. (See *Panicum miliaceum*.)
Prosopis denudans, 5783, 9081.
    glandulosa, 8272.
    juliflora, 8214.
Prune, 5649 to 5686.

Prunus sp., 6096 to 6100, 6103 to 6108, 6531, 6536 to 6540, 6546, 8338, 8339, 8342, 8345, 8365, 8705, 8824, 8826, 8827, 9806.
    armeniaca, 6534, 6630, 6841, 6844, 6845, 7136, 7140, 7672, 8363, 8825, 8913, 9015, 9016, 9319, 9364 to 9371, 9390, 9397 to 9402, 9463, 9464, 9831 to 9846.
    cerasus, 6529, 6631, 9029, 9030, 9847, 9851.
    triflora Huds., 9233, 9235, 9236, 9270, 9273.
    domestica, 5649 to 5686, 5824, 5931, 9346, 9362, 9363.
    laurocerasus, 9867.
    mume, 9200, 9211 to 9216.
    Pseudo-Cerasus var. *hortensis*, 7900, 9170 to 9199.
    tomentosa, 9201.
    triflora, 9202 to 9210, 9222, 9223, 9279, 9281, 9306, 9313.
Psidium cattleianum, 7445, 8944.
    guajava, 8344, 8922, 8966, 9023.
Psychotria ipecacuanha, 7360.
Pterocarpus marsupium, 8666.
Pterocarya caucasica, 7271.
    stenoptera, 6609.
Ptychoraphis augusta, 7573.
Pueraria thunbergiana, 9227, 9228.
Pumpkin, 5906, 6088, 6089, 6402, 7505.
Punica granatum, 5987, 5988, 6843, 6935 to 6937, 6940, 6944, 7440, 7674, 7676, 7677, 7776, 8430 to 8433, 8599, 8643, 8646, 9385, 9386.
Pyrethrum, 6142.
    roseum, 7244, 7326, 8316.
    tchihatchewii, 9027.
Pyrus sp., 6507 to 6521, 6528, 6532, 7669.
    baccata, 6162, 6358.
    communis, 5924, 6110, 8901, 8901a, 9360, 9361, 9388, 9492.
    elaeagrifolia, 9387.
    longipes, 9161.
    malus, 5687, 5688, 5690 to 5744, 5810 to 5823, 5933, 6102, 6113, 6656, 6713 to 6772, 8448 to 8453, 8644, 8710 to 8726, 9014, 9469 to 9471, 9863.
    prunifolia, 5501 to 5512.
    salicifolia, 9387.
    sinensis, 9239 to 9243.

Quassia amara, 7192.
Quebrachia lorentzii, 5777, 6345, 6828, 7012.
Quebracho blanco, 5781, 6346, 7013.
    colorado, 5777, 6345, 6828, 7012.
Quercus acuta, 8129.
    aegilops, 6833.
    cornea, 8704.
    cuspidata, 8130.
    dentata, 8131, 8132.
    glandulifera, 8133.
    glauca, 8134.
    ilex, 6340, 6343.
    lacera, 8135.
    laevigata, 8136.

Quercus phillyraeoides, 8137.
    pinnatifida, 8138.
    pubescens, 6344.
    serrata, 8139.
    suber, 9456.
Quillaja saponaria, 8927.
Quince, 5762, 6120, 6187, 6193, 8454, 8455, 8645.
    Chinese, 6183, 6186, 6188, 6362, 8209.

Rabbit's ear, 5581.
Radish, 5901, 6084 to 6087, 6135 to 6137, 6169, 6398, 6605, 6612, 6699 to 6704, 9487.
Raisin tree, 6608.
Ramie, 6337, 6338.
Rape, 6198.
Raphanus sativus, 5901, 6084 to 6087, 6135 to 6137, 6169, 6398, 6605, 6612, 6699 to 6704, 9487.
Raphia pedunculata, 7290.
    vinifera, 9005.
Raphiolepis japonica, 8405.
Raspberry, 6348, 6627, 6628, 7068.
Ravenala madagascariensis, 8598.
Recina de Nato, 6238.
Red dye, 6886.
Redwood, 6196.
Rhamnus californica, 6662.
Rhapidophyllum hystrix, 6904.
Rhapis cochinchinensis, 7275.
Rheum palmatum, 7188, 7214.
Rhodes grass, 9608.
Rhodomyrtus tomentosa, 6863, 8667.
Rhopalostylis sapida, 8887.
Rhus coriaria, 6195.
Rhus ovata, 7111.
    succedanea, 8406.
    vernicifera, 8407.
Ribes rubrum, 6101.
    sanguineum, 7901.
Rice, 5523, 5940, 5941, 6200 to 6220, 6307, 6308, 6384, 6575 to 6588, 8300 to 8306, 8359 to 8361, 8508 to 8515, 8543, 8590, 8591, 8593, 8594, 8688 to 8690, 8699, 8804, 8911, 8912, 9326 to 9343, 9667.
Richardia sp., 7557, 7567, 7622, 7623, 7814.
    africana, 8273.
    albo-maculata, 8274.
    elliottiana, 7622, 7813.
    nelsoni, 7814.
    pentlandi, 7623, 7815.
Ricinus communis, 8275, 8276, 9283.
Rivina humilis, 9119.
Romneya coulteri, 7518.
Rondeletia chinensis, 8198.
Rosa sp., 7049, 9465.
    gigantea, 8658.
Rose, 7059, 9465.
Roselle, 8698.
Roupala pohlii, 7616.
Roystonea regia, 9731.
Rubber, Lagos, 7361.
Rubus sp., 6627, 6628, 7068, 7407, 9035.
    idaeus, 6348.
Rubus nutkanus, 5627.

Ruppelia grata, 9711.
Ruscus hypoglossum, 8277.
Ruscus hypophyllum, 8199.
Rush, 8429, 9860, 9861, 9873.
Rye, 5905, 7531, 9865, 9887.

Sabal sp., 9723.
    adansoni, 9725.
    eatonia, 7770.
Saccharum officinarum, 5595 to 5608.
Safflower, 7644, 9787, 9800.
Sainfoin, 6966, 7526, 7527.
St. John's bread. (*See* Carob.)
Salmon berry, 5627.
Salsola arbuscula, 9580.
Saltbush, 5613, 5614, 9892.
Salvadora persica, 7362.
Salvia gesneraeflora, 8876.
Sambucus australis, 8917.
Sandalwood, 6449.
Sand box, 9720.
Santalum album, 6449, 8679.
Sapindus trifoliatus, 6452, 8942.
Sapium sebiferum, 6625, 7158.
Sapota, white, 7505.
Sappan, 6886, 7206.
Sausage tree, 6444.
Schinus dentata, 9068.
    dependens, 9069.
    molle, 7538, 8278, 8943.
    montana, 9070.
    terebinthifolius, 7539.
Scorpiurus sulcata, 6969, 7751.
    vermiculata, 5581, 7698, 7750.
Scutia buxifolia, 8970.
Secale cereale, 5905, 7531, 9865, 9887.
Sechium edule, 9733.
Sedum sp., 6929, 7066, 7067, 7074, 7076, 7078, 7080, 7083.
Semecarpus anacardium, 6874.
Semele androgyna, 7630.
Senecio sp., 7091, 7092.
    deltoides, 8877.
    grandifolius, 8879.
    hyoni, 7113.
    longifolius, 8279.
    petasites, 8878.
Sequoia sempervirens, 6196.
Serenoa serrulata, 7772.
Sesame, 5803, 5804, 6222, 6420, 6595, 6596, 6683, 7661, 7662, 9780, 9797.
Sesamum indicum, 5803, 5804, 6222, 6420, 6595, 6596, 6683, 7661, 7662, 9780, 9797.
Sesbania sanctipaulensis, 8926.
Sideroxylon dulcificum, 9006.
Simmondsia californica, 8312.
Siris. (*See* Lebbek.)
Sissi, 8802.
Soap berry, Indian, 6873.
Soap tree, 6572.
Solanum sp., 5527, 6930, 7070, 7073, 7395, 7396, 7410, 7489, 8280, 9121, 9289, 9445, 9614.
    aculeastrum, 9617.
    dregei, 8239.
    erythrocarpum, 9120.
    laciniatum, 8281.

INDEX OF COMMON AND SCIENTIFIC NAMES. 331

Solanum marginatum, 8282.
 melongena, 5535, 5545, 5619, 6696, 7130, 9297, 9298.
 muricatum, 9570.
 pocote, 8919.
 pseudococapsicum, 8283.
 pyracanthum, 8880.
 sodomaeum, 8881.
 tuberosum, 9059.
 warszewiczii, 8284.
Sollya heterophylla, 8285, 8882.
Sophora japonica, 8883, 9034.
Sorbus edulis, 5932.
Sorghum, 5805 to 5809, 5930, 6406, 6411, 6604, 6681, 6685, 6686, 6689 to 6691, 6693, 6710, 7797, 8546, 8547, 8685, 8691, 8692, 8815, 9779, 9796, 9855, 9856, 9862.
Sorghum halepense, see *Andropogon halepensis*.
 vulgare, see *Andropogon sorghum*.
Sour sop, 6853.
Spargel kurbis, 7508.
Sparrmania africana, 7826, 7827.
Spathodea campanulata, 9007.
Spek-boom, 8604, 9605, 9615.
Sphaeralcea sp., 7411.
Spinach, 6616.
Spinacia oleracea, 6616.
Spirostachis occidentalis, 6163.
Spondias sp., 7501.
 dulcis, 6861, 9008.
 lutea, 8240, 9009.
Spruce, Norway, 5945.
Squash, 5520, 5559, 6133, 6620, 6621, 6695, 6698, 9481, 9626.
Stangeria paradoxa, 7365.
Stauntonia hexaphylla, 8409.
Sterculia acerifolia, 7237, 7254, 9122.
 acuminata, see *Cola acuminata*.
 diversifolia, 6668, 7268.
 platanifolia, 7306, 8190, 8884, 9036.
Stigmaphyllon periplocaefolium, 8197.
Strawberry, 7769.
 tree, 5981.
Strelitzia augusta, 7146.
 reginae, 7169.
Streptosolom jamesonii, 9661.
Strychnos nux-vomica, 7210.
 spinosa (?), 9611.
Stryphnodendron barbatimam, 9403.
Stuartia pentagyna, 5568.
Styrax japonica, 8125.
 obassia, 8126.
Sugar cane, 5595 to 5608.
Sulla, 7037, 7528, 7710, 7784, 7788, 7790.
Sumac, 6195.
Sunflower, 6093 to 6095, 9668.
Sutherlandia frutescens, 9434.
Swietenia mahogani, 7543.
Sycamore, 7011.

Tacsonia manicata, 9436.
 mollissima, 8885, 8907, 8908.
Tagetes sp., 6424.
Tal, 8545.

Tallow tree, 6625, 7158.
Tamarix chinensis, 9290.
Tamil avaria, 9859.
Tamis, 6277.
Tangerine, 9132, 9480, 9700 to 9702.
Taxus baccata, 6161.
Tea, 5571, 6633, 7902 to 7907, 8226 to 8228, 8386, 8505, 8595, 8693.
Teak, 9032.
 bastard, 6883.
Tecoma sp., 9071.
 stans, 8950.
Tectona grandis, 9032.
Terebinth, 5767, 7673, 8521.
Terminalia catappa, 6862.
 triflora, 8925.
Testudinaria elephantipes, 7829.
Thalia dealbata, 8286.
Thea viridis, 5571, 6633, 7902 to 7907, 8226 to 8228, 8386, 8505, 8595, 8693.
Theobroma sp. nov., 9858.
 cacao, 6274, 9010.
Thermopsis fabacea, 9234.
Thevetia nereifolia, 6893, 9011.
Thrinax altissima, 7323.
 argentea, 7338.
 barbadensis, 7298.
 floridana, 7771.
Thunbergia erecta, 9012.
 grandiflora, 9708.
 harrissii, 9709.
 laurifolia, 9710.
Thyme, 8526.
 creeping, 8527.
Thymus serpyllum, 8527.
 vulgaris, 8526.
Thysanolaena agrostis, 8445.
Ti cheng, 5980.
Tigridia sp., 7099.
Tillandsia sp., 6932, 7093, 7367, 7384 to 7386, 7481 to 7484, 7486.
 benthamiana, 7088.
 lindeniana, 7618.
Timbirichi, 5798.
Timothy, 8553.
Tipu, 5778.
Tipuana speciosa, 5778, 8932.
Tobacco, 5961 to 5963, 6229, 7686, 8893.
Toddalia lanceolata, 6897.
Toluifera balsaminum, 7544.
Tomato, 6090, 6091.
 "Kiswaheli," 9289.
Tonga, 7363.
Toon tree, 6866.
Torenia fournieri, 7175, 7178, 7180, 7187, 7197, 7217, 7235, 7236, 7241.
Trachycarpus excelsus, 7277, 7416, 7441.
Tradescantia crassifolia, 6928.
Tralhuen, 8696.
Trevoa quinquenervia, 8696.
 trinervia, 8697.
Trevu, 8697.
Trichilia dregei, 9482.
Tricholaena rosea, 9888.
Trichosanthes cucumeroides, 9286, 9287.
 japonica, 9288.
Tricuspidaria dependens, 8946.

Trifolium sp., 7052.
    alexandrinum, 7000, 7031, 7657 to 7659, 9874 to 9876.
    angustifolium, 7682, 7753, 9750.
    arvense, 9751.
    bifidum, 7119.
    bonanii, 9752.
    cherleri, 9753.
    ciliatum, 7120.
    diffusum, 9754.
    fragiferum, 9755.
    fucatum, 7128, 7129.
    glomeratum, 7755, 9756.
    gracilentum, 7118.
    hispidum, 9757.
    hybridum, 8556.
    incarnatum, 7529, 7530, 9758.
    involucratum, 7122.
    lappaceum, 7754, 9759.
    macraei, 7121.
    maritimum, 9760.
    medium, 9761.
    microcephalum, 7126.
    microdon, 7127.
    montanum, 9762.
    ochroleucum, 9763.
    pallidum, 7756.
    pannonicum, 5834, 9817, 9864.
    panormitanum, 7683, 7699, 7757, 9764.
    pauciflorum, 7123, 7124.
    pratense, 5746 to 5750, 5968, 5969, 7138, 8555, 9765.
    repens, 7758, 9766.
    resupinatum, 9026, 9767.
    rubens, 9768.
    spumosum, 6825, 7759, 9769.
    stellatum, 7760.
    striatum, 9770.
    strictum, 9771.
    subterraneum, 9772.
    tomentosum, 7761, 9773.
    tridentatum, 7125.
    vesiculosum, 9774.
Triglochin maritimum, 8886.
Trigonella corniculata, 5579, 7714.
    foenum-graecum, 6963, 7029, 7071, 7520, 7642, 7713, 9021.
    gladiata, 5580, 7752.
Triticum (mixed), 6959, 7422.
    dicoccum, 8652.
    durum, 5639, 5642 to 5646, 5754, 5800, 5999, 6005, 6008, 6009, 6011, 6014, 6018 to 6020, 6272, 6371, 6680, 7016, 7425, 7428, 7430, 7459, 7463 to 7465, 7575, 7576, 7578 to 7581, 7650 to 7653, 7785, 7792 to 7795, 8212, 8213, 8230 to 8232, 8522, 8523, 8544, 8550 to 8552, 8684, 8737, 8808, 8811, 8813, 8816, 8818 to 8820, 8897 to 8899, 9130, 9324, 9478, 9479, 9853, 9854, 9872.
    junceum, 9609.
    polonicum, 5799, 6372.
    turgidum, 7585.

Triticum vulgare, 5515, 5628 to 5630, 5635 to 5638, 5640, 5641, 5995 to 5997, 6000 to 6004, 6006, 6007, 6010, 6012, 6013, 6015 to 6017, 6021, 6111, 6112, 6272, 6369, 6370, 6373, 6598 to 6600, 6996, 6997, 7033, 7429, 7466, 7467, 7512 to 7515, 7582, 7660, 7685, 7786, 7787, 8220, 8221, 8548, 8549, 8561, 8589, 8812, 8817, 8892, 9125, 9129, 9131, 9358, 9781, 9782, 9790 to 9794, 9871.

Trochodendron aralioides, 9292, 9293.
Trumpet flower, 6893, 9011.
Tuberose, 9885.
Tu Chung, 5980, 8709.
Tuna, 7507, 8578, 8579, 9135 to 9146.
Turmeric, 8735.
Turnip, 6134, 6176, 6178, 6179, 6265.
Turpinia pomifera, 8671.
Turraea floribunda, 6895.
Tutsia ambosensis, 6896.

Ubaba, 8311.
Udid, 8541.
Udo, 9166 to 9169, 9224.
Ulex europaeus, 7333.
Umbellularia californica, 5977.
Upas tree, 7364.
Urceola esculenta, 8668.
Urceolina pendula, 7620.

Vaccinium vitis-idaea, 5775, 6347.
Val, 8545.
Verbascum speciosum, 5833.
Veronia elephantum, 6826.
Vetch, 5572, 5573, 5575, 6555, 6670, 7521, 7534.
    Bengal, 5576.
    hairy, 7533.
    Narbonne, 7532.
    sand, see Vetch, hairy.
    scarlet, 5574.
Vicia sp., 6437, 6555.
    bengalensis, 5576, 7705.
    calcarata, 5572, 7706.
    cracca, 6555.
    egyptiana, 7718.
    ervilia, 6435.
    faba, 5542, 5577, 5965, 6313, 6315, 6550, 6669, 6961, 7020, 7024, 7035, 7426, 7462, 7498, 7702, 8358, 8587, 8592, 8596, 9307 to 9312.
    equina, 7942, 7943.
    fulgens, 5574, 7703.
    gemella, 9225.
    gigentea, 6670.
    hirsuta, 9237.
    hirta, 5573, 7679, 7701, 7764.
    lutea, 6962, 7716.
    narbonnensis, 7532, 7704.
    sativa, 5575, 7707, 7708, 7709, 7762, 7762a, 7763, 7765.
        var. *macrocarpa*, 7765.

Vicia sicula, 7717.
　　rillosa, 7533.
Vicos, 6436.
Vigna catjang, 6311, 6327, 6328, 6413, 6431, 6557, 6563, 6566, to 6568, 8354, 8418, 8498 to 8501, 8687.
Villebrunea integrifolia, 5610.
Viola cornuta, 8353, 8456 to 8459.
　　munbyana, 8369.
　　odorata, 5972 to 5974, 6192, 7842 to 7847, 8350 to 8352, 8370 to 8381, 8460.
Violet, 5972 to 5974, 6192, 7842 to 7847 8350 to 8353, 8369 to 8381, 8456 to 8460.
Viraris, 6830.
Vitex incisa, 8287.
Vitis sp., 6280 to 6306, 6356, 7048, 7687.
　　candicans, 8576.
　　romaneti, 6505.
　　rupestris, 9812, 9813.
　　　　var. *metallica*, 9607, 9809.
　　vinifera, 5616, 5689, 5909 to 5918, 5985, 6118, 6119, 6124, 6140, 6366, 6374, 6429, 6500, 6501, 7671, 7993 to 8071, 8436, 8462 to 8464, 8581 to 8583, 8605, 8647 to 8649, 8796, 8797, 9560 to 9568, 9576 to 9579, 9810, 9811, 9814.
Voandzeia subterranea, 8915, 9013.
Vriesia fenestralis, 7617.

Wal, 8686.
Walnut, 5633, 5983, 6180 to 6182, 6354, 6650 to 6652, 8208, 8307, 8425, 8426, 9231, 9232, 9280.
　　black, 7954.
Watermelon, 6037 to 6057, 6149 to 6159, 6170, 6171, 8410, 8447, 8465 to 8475, 8607 to 8642, 9572.

Wheat, 5515, 5628 to 5630, 5635 to 5646, 5754, 5799, 5800, 5995 to 5997, 5999 to 6021, 6111, 6112, 6272, 6369 to 6373, 6598 to 6600, 6680, 6959, 6996, 6997, 7016, 7033, 7422, 7425, 7428 to 7430, 7459, 7463 to 7467, 7512 to 7515, 7575, 7576, 7578 to 7582, 7585, 7650 to 7653, 7660, 7685, 7785 to 7787, 7792 to 7795, 8212, 8213, 8220, 8221, 8230 to 8232, 8522, 8523, 8544, 8548 to 8552, 8561, 8589, 8684, 8737, 8808, 8811 to 8813, 8816 to 8820, 8892, 8897 to 8899, 9125, 9129, 9130, 9131, 9324, 9358, 9478, 9479, 9781, 9782, 9790 to 9794, 9853, 9854, 9871, 9872.
Wigandia sp., 8288.
Wikstroemia canescens, 9165.
Wing nut, 6609.
Woandsu, 8915, 9013.

Xanthoxylon sp., 8928.
　　　　piperitum, 8191, 9291.
Ximenia americana, 6259.

Yang tao, 5840, 5978, 5979.
Yew, 6161.
Yucca sp., 7392.

Zamia floridana, 8504.
Zapote borracho, 7055.
Zea mays, 5560, 6028 to 6034, 6172, 6230 to 6233, 6273, 6401, 6573, 6574, 6827, 7502, 8822, 9356, 9357, 9449, 9573, 9795.
Zelkova acuminata, 8408.
Zephyranthes sp., 6925, 6926, 7393, 7402, 7405, 7485.
Zingiber officinale, 6875, 7621, 8736.
Zinnia elegans, 6423.
Zizyphus jujuba, 6549, 8600, 8702, 8703, 8828.
Zoysia pungens, 6404, 6405, 9299, 9300.

O

33. North American Species of Leptoxchies. 1903. Price, 15 cents.
34. Silkworm Food Plants. 1903. Price, 15 cents.
35. Recent Foreign Explorations. 1903. Price, 15 cents.
36. The "Bluing" and the "Red Rot" of the Western Yellow Pine, with Special Reference to the Black Hills Forest Reserve. 1903. Price, 30 cents.
37. Formation of the Spores in the Sporangia of Rhizopus Nigricans and of Phycomyces Nitens. 1903. Price, 15 cents.
38. Forest Conditions and Problems in Eastern Washington, Eastern Oregon, etc. 1903. Price, 15 cents.
39. The Propagation of the Easter Lily from Seed. 1903. Price, 10 cents.
40. Cold Storage, with Special Reference to the Pear and Peach. 1903. Price, 15 cents.
41. The Commercial Grading of Corn. 1903. Price, 10 cents.
42. Three New Plant Introductions from Japan. 1903. Price, 10 cents.
43. Japanese Bamboos. 1903. Price, 10 cents.
44. The Bitter Rot of Apples. 1903. Price, 15 cents.
45. The Physiological Rôle of Mineral Nutrients in Plants. 1903. Price, 5 cents.
46. The Propagation of Tropical Fruit Trees and Other Plants. 1903. Price, 10 cents.
47. The Description of Wheat Varieties. 1903. Price, 10 cents.
48. The Apple in Cold Storage. 1903. Price, 15 cents.
49. The Culture of the Central American Rubber Tree. 1903. Price, 25 cents.
50. Wild Rice: Its Uses and Propagation. 1903. Price, 10 cents.
51. Miscellaneous Papers: Part I. The Wilt Disease of Tobacco and Its Control. 1903. Price, 5 cents. Part II. The Work of the Community Demonstration Farm at Terrell, Tex. 1904. Price, 5 cents. Part III. Fruit Trees Frozen in 1904. 1904. Price, 5 cents.
52. Wither-Tip and Other Diseases of Citrous Trees and Fruits Caused by Colletotrichum Gloeosporioides. 1904. Price, 5 cents.
53. The Date Palm. 1904. Price, 20 cents.
54. Persian Gulf Dates. 1903. Price, 10 cents.
55. The Dry Rot of Potatoes Due to Fusarium Oxysporum. 1904. Price, 10 cents.
56. Nomenclature of the Apple. [In press.]
57. Methods Used for Controlling and Reclaiming Sand Dunes. 1904. Price, 10 cents.
58. The Vitality and Germination of Seeds. 1904. Price, 10 cents.
59. Pasture, Meadow, and Forage Crops in Nebraska. 1904. Price, 10 cents.
60. A Soft Rot of the Calla Lily. 1904. Price, 10 cents.
61. The Avocado in Florida. 1904. Price, 5 cents.
62. Notes on Egyptian Agriculture. 1904. Price, 10 cents.
63. Investigations of Rusts. 1904. Price, 10 cents.
64. A Method of Destroying or Preventing the Growth of Algae and Certain Pathogenic Bacteria in Water Supplies. 1904. Price, 5 cents.
65. Reclamation of Cape Cod Sand Dunes. 1904. Price, 10 cents.

B. T. GALLOWAY, *Chief of Bureau.*

RANGE INVESTIGATIONS IN ARIZONA.

BY

DAVID GRIFFITHS,
Assistant in Charge of Range Investigations.

GRASS AND FORAGE PLANT INVESTIGATIONS.

Issued October 6, 1904.

WASHINGTON:
GOVERNMENT PRINTING OFFICE.
1904.

Bul. 67, Bureau of Plant Industry, U. S. Dept. of Agriculture. PLATE I.

LAOSA, A TYPICAL SOUTHERN ARIZONA RANCH.

U. S. DEPARTMENT OF AGRICULTURE.
BUREAU OF PLANT INDUSTRY—BULLETIN NO. 67.
B. T. GALLOWAY, *Chief of Bureau.*

RANGE INVESTIGATIONS IN ARIZONA.

BY

DAVID GRIFFITHS,
Assistant in Charge of Range Investigations.

GRASS AND FORAGE PLANT INVESTIGATIONS.

Issued October 6, 1904.

WASHINGTON:
GOVERNMENT PRINTING OFFICE.
1904.

BUREAU OF PLANT INDUSTRY.

B. T. GALLOWAY, *Chief.*

J. E. ROCKWELL, *Editor.*

GRASS AND FORAGE PLANT INVESTIGATIONS.

SCIENTIFIC STAFF.

W. J. SPILLMAN, *Agrostologist.*

A. S. HITCHCOCK, *Assistant Agrostologist in Charge of Alfalfa and Clover Investigations.*
C. V. PIPER, *Systematic Agrostologist in Charge of Herbarium.*
DAVID GRIFFITHS, *Assistant Agrostologist in Charge of Range Investigations.*
C. R. BALL, *Assistant Agrostologist in Charge of Work on Arlington Farm.*
S. M. TRACY, *Special Agent in Charge of Gulf Coast Investigations.*
D. A. BRODIE, *Assistant Agrostologist in Charge of Cooperative Work.*
P. L. RICKER, *Assistant in Herbarium.*
J. M. WESTGATE, *Assistant in Sand-Binding Work.*
BYRON HUNTER, *Assistant in Charge of Pacific Coast Investigations.*
R. A. OAKLEY, *Assistant in Domestication of Wild Grasses.*
C. W. WARBURTON, *Assistant in Fodder Plant and Millet Investigations.*
M. A. CROSBY, *Assistant in Southern Forage Plant Investigations.*
J. S. COTTON, *Assistant in Range Investigations.*
LESLIE F. PAULL, *Assistant in Investigations at Arlington Farm.*
HAROLD T. NIELSEN, *Assistant in Alfalfa and Clover Investigations.*
AGNES CHASE, *Agrostological Artist.*

LETTER OF TRANSMITTAL.

U. S. Department of Agriculture,
Bureau of Plant Industry,
Office of the Chief,
Washington, D. C., July 1, 1904.

Sir: I have the honor to transmit herewith the manuscript of a paper on Range Investigations in Arizona, which embodies a report upon investigations conducted in cooperation with the experiment station of the University of Arizona.

The paper is a valuable contribution to our knowledge of improvement of range lands, and I respectfully recommend that it be issued as Bulletin No. 67 of the regular Bureau series.

Respectfully,

B. T. Galloway,
Chief of Bureau.

Hon. James Wilson,
Secretary of Agriculture.

PREFACE.

The main features of the range problem have been reduced to two: The carrying capacity of the range, and the best methods of managing the range so as to secure the largest amount of feed from it without permanent injury to the food plants that furnish the covering of the soil. The principles of management may be reduced to the following: A proper control of the amount of stock upon a given range and the time of the year at which they are allowed upon the various subdivisions of it; the protection of such native plants as are of value, and, particularly. the saving of seeds of such plants and scattering them upon the range; lastly, the introduction upon the range of such new forage plants as experience has shown can be thus introduced.

A knowledge of the carrying capacity of the ranges is of the utmost importance, for it must form the basis of any intelligent legislation relating to the range question. This knowledge determines the rental and sale value of range lands and should also determine the size of the minimum lease or homestead for range purposes in case laws are passed providing for such disposal of the public ranges.

The present report includes a general study of range problems in southern Arizona, but is devoted more particularly to the investigations conducted in cooperation between the United States Department of Agriculture and the Arizona Experiment Station on two tracts of land situated on the Santa Rita Forest Reserve in the Territory of Arizona. The work upon one of these tracts, consisting of a fenced area of 58 square miles, has been conducted under the immediate supervision of Dr. David Griffiths, of this Office. The work upon the other area, which is also fenced and consists of some 240 acres of land, has been conducted under the supervision of Prof. R. H. Forbes, Director of the Arizona Experiment Station, by Prof. J. J. Thornbur of that station, since August, 1901. Previous to that time Doctor Griffiths was a member of the station staff at Tucson, and conducted the work on the small tract also. Once each year the Department has furnished the Arizona Experiment Station with a report of the work done by its officers upon the large tract, while the officers of the station have furnished to the Department a similar report of the work on the small tract. Particular attention is called to the study of the amount of vegetation produced upon the large tract since it was fenced nearly two years ago. It will be noted that deductions concerning the carrying capacity of this range made from this study agree in a most satisfactory manner with actual practice. It is proposed in the near future to determine by actual trial the amount of stock this fenced area will carry without deteriorating.

Acknowledgments are due to Mr. Howell Jones, of the Santa Fe railway system, for much assistance in prosecuting the investigations reported in this bulletin.

W. J. SPILLMAN, *Agrostologist.*

OFFICE OF GRASS AND FORAGE PLANT INVESTIGATIONS,
Washington, D. C., June 29, 1904.

CONTENTS.

	Page.
Introduction	9
The small inclosure	10
The large inclosure	16
Topography	16
Soil	18
Brush and timber	19
Forage plants	21
Amount of feed produced	24
Carrying capacity	32
Water for stock	34
The seasons	38
Erosion	44
The prairie dog	46
Range feed	46
The grasses	46
Pigweed family	50
The clovers	52
Alfilerilla	53
Miscellaneous winter and spring annuals	54
Miscellaneous browse plants	56
Hay crops	57
Weeds	58
Plants injurious to stock	59
Summary	60
Description of plates	62

ILLUSTRATIONS.

PLATES.

	Page.
PLATE I. Laosa, a typical southern Arizona ranch .... Frontispiece.	
II. Contrast between dry and wet seasons in foothills range: Fig. 1.—Live oak belt, upper foothills, eastern slope of Huachuca Mountains, before the rainy season began. Fig. 2.—Upper foothills, northern slope, Santa Rita Mountains, at the close of the rainy season..	62
III. The large inclosure: Fig. 1.—Pyramid Hill; horses digging for water in the sands of an arroyo. Fig. 2.—Looking south from the top of Pyramid Hill, showing general character of fenced area	62
IV. Saltbushes: Fig. 1.—*Atriplex lentiformis*, the largest of our native saltbushes, Tempe, Ariz. Fig. 2.—*Atriplex elegans;* large inclosure, northern foothills, Santa Rita Mountains	62
V. Fig. 1.—Hay meadow, Salt River Valley. Fig. 2.—Erosion along Pantano wash, east of Santa Rita Mountains	62
VI. Alfilerilla range: Fig. 1.—Alfilerilla and Indian wheat near Dudleyville. Fig. 2.—Alfilerilla and Indian wheat near Oracle	62
VII. Two phases of the range question: Fig. 1.—Goats and the oak brush upon which they live. Fig. 2.—The remains of thirteen head of cattle in a space of 30 feet along a small arroyo near Arivaca	62
VIII. Haying scenes in southern Arizona: Fig. 1.—Mexicans at Sopori stacking "celite" (*Amaranthus palmeri*). Fig. 2.—A Mexican packing hay from the mountains	62
IX. Native pasture lands in southern Arizona: Fig. 1.—Galleta (*Hilaria mutica*) in a swale south of Vail Station. Fig. 2.—A round-up in the northern foothills of the Santa Rita Mountains	62
X. Fig. 1.—An ocotilla forest about 4 miles northeast of the large inclosure. Fig. 2.—The work of prairie dogs upon the northern slope of the White Mountains	62

TEXT FIGURE.

FIG. 1. Diagram of the large inclosure in the northern foothills of the Santa Rita Mountains	17

RANGE INVESTIGATIONS IN ARIZONA.

INTRODUCTION.

The discussions of the following pages are based upon experimental work and observations made in the Territory of Arizona between the months of August, 1900, and November, 1903, in cooperation with the Arizona Experiment Station. The experimental work thus far has been conducted upon the small inclosure near Tucson, a discussion of which was the main feature of Bulletin 4 of this series. Such data regarding this work as were not included in that publication are discussed here. The opportunities of the writer for observation of the conditions obtaining throughout the main grazing areas have been very good, especially during a residence of an academic year at Tucson in 1900-1901 and during the spring, summer, and autumn of 1903.

Besides visiting the region within 60 miles of Tucson at all seasons of the year, the following list of trips over the different portions of the range country is appended for the purpose of fixing more definitely the time at which these observations were made, as well as to make the data accompanying the rather large collections of forage and other plants secured upon these several journeys and afterwards deposited in various herbaria more complete:

October 6 to 19, 1900. Tucson to Wilcox via Benson, and return via Pearce and Tombstone.

December 6 to 23, 1900. Maricopa to Tempe, and return to Picacho via Mesa and Florence.

March 17 to 22, 1903. Tucson to Laosa via Sopori and Arivaca, and return via Babuquivari Mountains and Robles.

March 24 to 30, 1903. Tucson to Dudleyville via Willow Spring Mountains, and return via San Pedro and across the Rincon Mountains to Tanque Verde.

April 7 to 15, 1903. Tucson to Nogales, and return to Phoenix via Arivaca, Coyote, Santa Rosa, and Casagrande.

May 15 to 18, 1903. Williams to Bright Angel and return.

June 29 to July 8, 1903. Huachuca Mountains to Cannanea, Sonora, Mexico.

July 16 to 17, 1903. Prescott to Mayer.

July 18 to 19, 1903. Ash Fork and Williams.

July 20 to 23, 1903. Flagstaff and south to Mogollon Mountains.

July 25 to 26, 1903. Winslow and Holbrook.

August 8 to 17, 1903. Adamana to Fort Apache via Long H ranch and St. Johns, returning via Showlow.

September 12 to 22, 1903. Adamana to Chin Lee, and return via Navajo.
September 24 to 25, 1903. Prescott to Mayer.
October 6 to 11, 1903. Tucson to Patagonia via Greaterville and Cottonwood, and return via Sopori, Arivaca, Babuquivari Mountains, and Robles.

This rather formal list takes no cognizance of the work done between trains and on short stops at various places along the lines of railroad, especially on the main line of the Santa Fe system, the Santa Fe, Prescott and Phoenix, and the Santa Fe, Prescott and Eastern railways, between Needles and Gallup and between Phoenix and Ash Fork.

Arizona has a total area of 72,332,800 acres, of which only 254,521 acres are improved; but there are reserved 19,724,717 acres, according to Governor Brodie's report to the Secretary of the Interior in 1902. A part of this reserve land is available for grazing purposes under certain restrictions, grazing being allowed upon all the forest reserves excepting the Grand Canyon, and of course the Indians raise a great deal of stock upon their reservations. Taking everything into consideration, there are probably upward of 65,000,000 acres available for stock raising.

According to the Twelfth Census (1900), there were in the Territory 1,033,634 units of stock, sheep and goats being calculated at the rate of 6 to 1 bovine animal in relation to pasture consumption. Unfortunately no distinction was made in these Census reports between range and farm stock, so that it is impossible to determine from the lists the number of stock supported on native pastures. All that can be said is that there was in the Territory in 1900 one animal unit to approximately every 65 acres of land available for stock purposes. This includes farm animals as well as range stock. It is interesting to compare these figures with those given by Mr. C. W. Gordon in the statistics of the Tenth Census. Here Mr. Gordon, who made an elaborate report upon the conditions, as well as the number of animals, estimated that in 1880 there were 229,062 units of stock, occupying 43,750 square miles of range lands, or 1 unit to 122.24 acres.

THE SMALL INCLOSURE.

A full description of the small inclosure was given in Bulletin No. 4 of this series, after the first planting was made in the winter of 1901. It will not be necessary, therefore, to enter into the details of the work on this area any further than to discuss briefly the results which have been secured by the experiments which were suggested at that time, and which have been carried on since with such modifications and changes as further light and experience have shown to be necessary.

As stated in Bulletin No. 4, some sixty species of forage plants were sown, the work being begun on the 10th and finished on the 23d of January, 1901. These plants were given various forms of treatment, the seed of some being covered by a disk harrow and of others by a smoothing harrow; in some cases the ground was harrowed or disked before planting, and in others the seed was sown on the uncultivated mesa. Besides the seed sown, *Lippia repens*, recommended as a soil binder for arid situations, was planted on one of the embankments. This plant is still living and has covered the spaces between the hills in a few places; but it can hardly be considered promising for situations which do not receive more rainfall than these mesas. Plantings of this species subsequently made have failed entirely.

The vast majority of the plantings of grasses made the first year were a failure from the start; that is, the seed did not germinate at all. There were some good rains following closely upon the completion of the seeding, furnishing ideal conditions for the germination of such grasses and other forage plants as are adapted to the prevailing conditions at that season. The following are the mean temperatures for the early months of 1901 at the university, 5 miles distant: January, 51° F.; February, 52° F.; March, 55.6° F.; April, 61.7° F.

As will be seen from an examination of the lists published in Bulletin No. 4 of the Bureau of Plant Industry, some of the seed planted was from the Northwestern States, but the greater part of it was native seed gathered the previous autumn. A considerable quantity which might be considered native was nevertheless from a very different situation from that in which it was planted upon the mesas surrounding Tucson. As examples may be mentioned the seed secured in Sulphur Spring Valley, Arizona, and in Silver City, N. Mex., all of which grew at high elevations. A comparison of the northern and southern seed during the two following months was very interesting indeed. It was the seed from the northwest which gave promise of success during February and early March. Several species from the north germinated remarkably well, while the vast majority of the native species did nothing, as was to be expected, for they make their growth during the hot, moist weather from July to September. To this general rule, however, there were some marked exceptions. *Bouteloua oligostachya*, for instance, germinated well and there was a good stand of it on plots 43 and 69 in March. Upon these plots native seed was sown, but it was secured from an altitude of about 5,000 feet. Seed of this species received from the north did not germinate, possibly owing to its being old or poorly matured. Many of the native species which did nothing upon the range germinated in the grass garden a few days later in the season, as discussed in the text and tables given below. Rescue grass (*Bromus unioloides*) purchased from seedsmen and of unknown origin germinated well enough to make a good stand had it been able to combat the drought of spring and early summer. It would have succeeded much better, no doubt, if it had been planted in early autumn.

The following tabular statement in connection with Bulletin No. 4

will serve to emphasize the fact that it was the northern-grown seed which germinated to best advantage upon the range plots during the cool weather of spring:

Record of germination upon range plots, spring of 1901.

Name of plant.	Number of plot.[a]	Origin of the seed.	Date of germination.	Condition.
Agropyron spicatum	6	Walla Walla, Wash	Feb. 9	Good stand.
Agropyron occidentale	7 and 68	....do	....do...	Thin stand.
Atriplex canescens	33	Tucson, Ariz	Mar. 4	Good stand.
Atriplex halimoides	40	California	Mar. 8	Very thin stand.
Atriplex semibaccata	43	....do	Feb. 9	Good stand.
Bouteloua oligostachya	48 and 69	Cochise, Ariz	Mar. 8	Do.
Elymus canadensis	61	Silver City, N. Mex	....do...	Thin stand.
Elymus ambiguus ?	63	Walla Walla, Wash	Feb. 21	Very thin stand.
Elymus condensatus	64	Washington	Mar. 8	Thin stand.
Elymus virginicus submuticus.	65	Walla Walla, Wash	....do...	Very thin stand.
Agropyron tenerum	66	....do	....do...	Thin stand.
Agropyron spicatum	67	....do	Feb. 9	Good stand.
Bromus polyanthus paniculatus.	74	Silver City, N. Mex	Mar. 8	Do.
Phleum asperum	75	Walla Walla, Wash	....do...	Do.

[a] For information as to the location of the plots and methods of culture, see Bul. No. 4, Bureau of Plant Industry, 1901.

Shortly after completing the seeding on the range plots, a small grass garden was established on the university campus in rather a protected place behind the main building. This was designed for purely scientific study, but it served nevertheless as a very instructive check upon the species planted on the range. The planting was done here on the 13th and 14th of February and the plots were irrigated by well water when they needed it. The saltbushes were planted in a plot by themselves at some distance from the building, and consequently in a more exposed place.

The following tabular statement lists all the plants sown upon the range which germinated under irrigation and did not do so under the natural mesa conditions. The two tables, therefore, include all species, the seed of which was of known origin, planted on the mesa, which germinated in the spring; but the last table does not give a complete record of the grass-garden germinations, for there were many things planted in the grass garden that were not at hand in sufficient quantity to be sown upon the mesa:

Record of germination upon irrigated grass garden, spring of 1901.

Name.	Number of plot.[a]	Date of germination.	Source of seed.	Condition.
Sporobolus cryptandrus	6	Nov. 15	Tucson, Ariz	Thin stand.
Sporobolus wrightii	7	Mar. 4	....do	Good stand.
Chloris elegans	11	Mar. 22	....do	Very thin stand.
Muhlenbergia gracilis	13	Mar. 4	Cochise, Ariz	Thin stand.
Hilaria cenchroides	17	Mar. 22	New Mexico	Very thin stand.
Poa fendleriana	31	Mar. 15	Silver City, N. Mex	Good stand.
Phaseolus retusus	38	Mar. 22	New Mexico	Do.
Andropogon saccharoides	39	Mar. 6	Cochise, Ariz	Thin stand.
Bouteloua rothrockii [b]	40	Apr. 13	....do	Very thin stand.
Atriplex lentiformis	62	Mar. 15	Tempe, Ariz	Thin stand.
Atriplex polycarpa	69	....do	....do	Do.

[a] These are numbers of plots in the grass garden and have no reference to previously published numbers.

[b] This was incorrectly called *B. polystachya* in Bul. No. 4 of the Bureau of Plant Industry in referring to plots 26, 31, and 70. Throughout that publication these two species were not segregated.

By the middle of May there was nothing which had been planted upon the range plots alive, except a little *Lippia repens*, which had been placed upon one of the embankments thrown up across an old roadway, and a few scattered plants of shad scale (*Atriplex canescens*) on area F. Everything else had succumbed to the drought which invariably prevails in this region from March to June.

During the rainy season of the following August several plants which were sown in the winter germinated and made some growth. The most conspicuous of these was Metcalfe's bean (*Phaseolus retusus*), which germinated and grew beautifully through August, but died out completely by the middle of September. *Andropogon saccharoides* and *Chloris elegans* made a very small growth, but nothing commensurate with the quantity of seed sown and the labor involved.

During the autumn of 1903 there was nothing to show for the plantings of 1901 except a few stray plants of *Andropogon saccharoides* in the southeastern corner of the field, a similar growth of shad scale on portions of area F, and a small strip of *Lippia repens* on one of the embankments. None of these, however, gave promise of success.

In June, 1901, the writer discontinued his connection with the Arizona Experiment Station to accept his present position in the United States Department of Agriculture. The work upon the small tract was placed under the immediate supervision of Prof. J. J. Thornbur, of that station. During the summer of 1902 cooperative arrangements were entered into by the Department of Agriculture and the Arizona station whereby the investigations on the small tract were to be continued and those upon the large tract, discussed later, were to be instituted. Since that time Professor Thornbur has had charge of the work upon the small tract and the writer that upon the large tract.

The following paragraphs relating to the work upon the small tract are based upon data obtained from reports furnished this office by Professor Thornbur.

Since the winter of 1900–1901 considerable work has been performed on this area in an attempt to conserve storm waters by the erection of embankments and by the introduction of forage plants which will thrive under the advantages afforded by the dams. It is believed that the perennial plants which have been sown thus far can not be successfully established upon these mesas without careful attention to the soil and conservation of the waters, both of which entail considerable expense.

The dams built were thrown up across the water courses as in the winter of 1901, but their forms have been slightly changed because it was found that the diversion of the water did not suffice to spread it out very much nor to check its flow sufficiently to allow it to penetrate the ground as much as necessary. This is especially true with reference to the summer rains. The precipitation during the winter months, although causing considerable run-off, is much more gentle and penetrates the ground more readily.

The work done thus far seems to indicate that the most efficient dam for a gently sloping mesa is one which is so constructed that it will spill around the ends when the water has reached a height of not more than 12 inches. This requirement demands that the dam be constructed nearly on contour lines,[a] except at the ends, which are turned so as to retain water up to the desired depth and spread it over as much ground as possible. Besides the two dams mentioned in Bulletin No. 4, seven additional ones were built in January, 1902. These vary in length from 270 to 600 feet and in height from 12 to 24 inches, and are built at an average cost of a little more than $13.

In January, 1902, some seeding was done, but only in favored places, mostly above the embankments. Fewer species were planted than the previous year, and only two made any growth at all. Egyptian clover (*Trifolium alexandrinum*) and *Panicum texanum* were sown in the same dam, the first in the lower situation. The Egyptian clover germinated beautifully early in August, but all died in a very short time. *Panicum texanum* produced only a few plants, which made no seed.

Besides the above, seeds of the following species were planted: *Hilaria mutica, Bouteloua rothrockii, Atriplex coronata, A. elegans, A. nuttallii, A. canescens, A. bracteosa, A. polycarpa, A. nummularia, A. halimoides, A. leptocarpa, A. semibaccata, A. eremicola, Rhagodia inermis*, and *R. linifolia*. No seedlings of any of these species were observed.

During the last week in June, 1903, a third seeding was done. As in the second operation, the seed was sown in the vicinity of the dams

---

[a] This form of dam was first suggested by Prof. S. M. Woodward.

and the ground was prepared to receive it. In some cases, however, seed was sown below the dams, as well as above them. The following species were planted: *Panicum texanum, Andropogon saccharoides, Bouteloua curtipendula, B. rothrockii, B. oligostachya, B. hirsuta, B. aristidoides, Eriochloa punctata, Sporobolus wrightii, S. stricta, S. cryptandrus, Phaseolus retusus, Astragalus nuttallianus, Chætochloa composita, Pappophorum apertum, Chloris elegans, Elymus glabrifolius, Epicampes rigens,* and *Leptochloa dubia.*

In all cases the seed was sown very thick. Had all grown, the plants would have been entirely too numerous upon the ground. In many cases four times as much seed was sown as would produce a good stand if it all grew. Experience has shown that a good deal of the native seed is of very low germinating quality, and must often be sown excessively thick in order to even approximate a stand.

Many of the seeds of plants sown this time made considerable growth, but only in two or three cases was there anything like a stand secured. *Andropogon saccharoides, Bouteloua curtipendula, B. oligostachya, B. hirsuta,* and *Leptochloa dubia* all made thin stands. *Bouteloua rothrockii* made a scattering growth in one situation and quite a fair stand in another, but nowhere was there a better stand where it was sown than on favorable situations upon the uncultivated and undisturbed mesa in the immediate vicinity. The best stands and the best growth were secured with *Panicum texanum* and *Chloris elegans.* The former was especially good in places, but very uneven on account of having been sown partially in the depressions in the dams where the surface soil had been removed for the construction of the embankments and partially upon ordinary weathered soil. The lower depressions doubtless held water a little too long after the summer rains for the best development of the grass. In one of the dams there was considerably less than one-half acre which would cut at the rate of 1 ton of dry feed per acre. There was about a quarter of an acre of *Chloris elegans* in one of the dams which would yield at the rate of one-fourth ton of dry feed per acre. *Panicum texanum* has yielded by far the most promising results of anything tried thus far. It is an annual, however, and can not be used except in some such way as the common cultivated millets. There is little doubt that this grass is capable of considerable application in forage-plant culture in this region. If the seed could be secured at reasonable prices it might be sown upon barley fields for the production of summer and fall grazing and possibly for a small crop of hay in October. It matured this year in about ninety days after being sown.

The behavior of some of the native grasses was very interesting this year, especially when considered from the standpoint of seed habits. Usually perennial grasses do not mature much seed the year they are planted. The case is very different with species from this region. Some of them, although distinctly perennial in habit, mature seed in abundance in three months after being sown. This was especially the case with *Andropogon saccharoides*, *Bouteloua hirsuta*, and *B. oligostachya*, and less conspicuously true of *B. curtipendula*. *Bouteloua rothrockii* and *Leptochloa dubia* produced mature heads from practically every plant which grew. *Bouteloua rothrockii* produced fine, large bunches, with an abundance of mature seed. It should be noted that the latter is but a short-lived perennial at best. It is therefore not so surprising that it should produce an abundance of seed the first season. *Trichloris fasciculata* often produces two crops of seed—one in May and the other in September—in neglected spots and fence corners in the Salt River Valley.

THE LARGE INCLOSURE.

During the spring of 1903 arrangements were made for enlarging the work begun upon the mesas near Tucson in 1900. Permission having been granted by the Department of the Interior, an irregular tract of land upon the Santa Rita Forest Reserve, containing 49.2 square miles, or 31,488 acres, in the four townships Nos. 18 and 19, in ranges 14 and 15 east, Gila and Salt River meridian, was inclosed by a four-wire fence, completed early in June (fig. 1). Practically all stock was excluded from the tract by the 10th of June. This area differs very materially from the desert mesas upon which the small inclosure is situated, as will be seen from the descriptions given below. Much of it is situated within the altitude where perennial grasses are produced, and it is therefore capable of sustaining much more stock than the small inclosure upon the mesa.

TOPOGRAPHY.

The portion of the Santa Rita Forest Reserve which, after a preliminary survey, it was decided to fence is located in the northern foothills of the Santa Rita Mountains. It has a general northwesterly slope toward the Santa Cruz River (Pl. III, fig. 2). All of the region is well drained and there is consequently no accumulation of alkali at any point. Considerable quantities of water flow over portions of the area at certain seasons of the year. The presence of *Atriplex canescens* in the northwestern portion does not necessarily indicate that there are accumulations of soluble salts in the soil at this point.

The field, as a whole, contains typical foothill pasture lands of the region at this altitude. Along the eastern side there are rocky, steep bluffs rising 500 to 800 feet above the general level of the area. To the west and south of this point there are gently sloping areas free from brush. On the west half of the north side there occurs a considerable area of "washed country," while the east half of this side is a typical arid, creosote-bush area where no grass of any consequence ever grows. None of the higher mountain areas has been included on account of the difficulty and expense of fencing. Neither are any bottom lands included, for none of the typical river bottoms lies within the reserve. The bluffs spoken of above, however, answer very well for the mountain area, for they have upon them some of the more valuable mountain grasses; but they possess the disadvantage of not

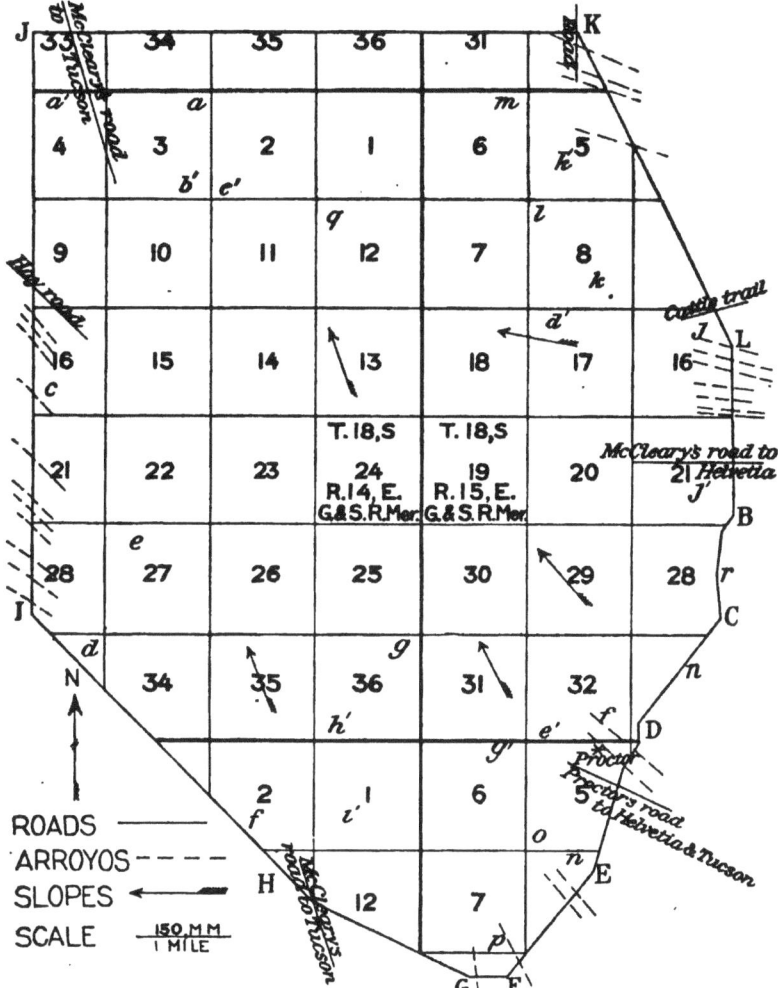

FIG. 1.—Diagram of the large inclosure in the northern foothills of the Santa Rita Mountains.

getting the rainfall of the higher mountains. It is to be regretted that no bottom land could have been fenced; but after all, in some respects, this would not be very much of an advantage, because the vacant river bottom lands in this vicinity are not, as a rule, productive, and do not figure at all conspicuously in the range feed supply.

The entire tract is more or less cut up by arroyos. These are usually steep, rugged, and rocky close to the mountains, but become wider and more shallow northward. The water which they carry during flood time is consequently spread over larger areas on the north side of the field. The surface water which goes down to the north side, however, is small in quantity and of short duration, but the sands of the arroyos carry an underground supply of water for several days after a rain. This supply of moisture to the shrubby vegetation is very considerable along these temporary water courses, but the areas between them receive only such moisture as happens to fall at those points. During the violent summer showers much of this runs off.

As stated above, the southern portion of the area is a comparatively open region, being cut by frequent arroyos, as indicated on fig. 1 between points L and G. The largest of these is the one which runs close to Proctor. At this point it is from 150 to 200 feet deep and 800 feet wide from bank to bank. Here the bottom of the arroyo is on solid rock, which accounts for the appearance of water at the surface. In general, however, it, like the others, is of coarse sand and like them widens out to the northward, its banks becoming lower and less rocky. Between the points L and B on fig. 1 on the fence line there are a number of small steep arroyos, and the same condition exists on the southern half of the west line, but the latter are less pronounced than the former. All of the arroyos are more rocky close to the mountains, and gradually spread out to the northwest, making the whole area a sloping plain, cut at frequent intervals by usually shallow washes to the northward and by deeper arroyos and canyons to the south. Besides the above water courses there are numerous gullies cut by the flood waters. These usually occur as laterals to the main arroyos, and extend into the broad gentle slopes which exist between the main water courses. The condition is a difficult one to portray, for the cuts are made by the flood waters, whose action is explained only when considered in connection with a surveyor's level and with the chemical and physical conditions of the soil. One can drive with a light rig over the entire field by picking his way slowly, but in many places he is obliged to travel considerable distances in order to get around the arroyos. This is especially true of the southern half of the field.

SOIL.

But little discussion of the subject of soil can or need be entered into. In general it may be said that the soil is of a light-brown color and composed of very fine particles intermixed with a large amount of coarse sand and gravel. On the south side it is much looser in texture, has more gravel in its composition, and packs less firmly upon drying than on the north side. On this account the sloping areas between the arroyos are not so badly washed, which condition, together with a more abundant supply of moisture, accounts for the more luxuriant vegetation and evenly distributed grassy covering. On the whole the soil does not differ from that which obtains throughout the entire region in similar situations. The area is well drained, but the soil softens very much more upon being moistened than would be expected. It is true, however, that it is very seldom that the moisture penetrates to great depths. In October, 1902, it was with great difficulty that 1-inch stakes of redwood or Oregon pine could be driven into the ground to a depth of 6 inches with an ax, yet, when the heavy rains of November came, these fell down of their own weight and could be driven into the ground their entire length by the pressure of the hand.

When the fence was built a peculiar condition of soil was observed along the middle of the northern fence line. The post-hole work was purposely done at a time when the ground was wet, and consequently, easily dug over the greater portion of the tract. In the above locality, however, to our astonishment, a heavy rainfall had not penetrated more than 2 or 3 inches, although the soil received the drainage of the entire Box Canyon region. On the greater part of the fence line, however, the winter and spring rains had penetrated to a depth of 2 feet or more. This area is known here as "washed country," which simply signifies that the upper strata of sandy loam has been removed, leaving the very closely packed, nonabsorbent subsoil exposed.

Underlying portions of the ground is a deposit of caliche, a calcareous hardpan, of variable thickness. All the arroyos, canyons, and washes are covered with a clean, coarse sand, while the steeper areas are coarse gravel and rocks. The soil particles are only slightly washed, as would be expected. Prof. W. P. Blake[a] considers the caliche to be derived from long-continued evaporations of subterranean waters raised by capillary action.

The soil of the general area is derived for the most part from the disintegration of the granitic rocks of the Santa Rita Mountain upheaval.

BRUSH AND TIMBER.

The greater part of the area is covered with a scattering growth of various shrubs and small trees. The northern and western portions contain much more shrubbery than the southern and eastern parts. A line drawn from corner L to corner I, figure 1, represents approximately the dividing line between the heavier and lighter brush. Upon the southern half there are large stretches which have practically no brush at all. Along the washes and arroyos, however, there are invariably found numerous shrubs, some of which attain to the dignity of trees, although very scraggy. A close examination of the broad,

---

[a] Transactions American Institute of Mining Engineers, Richmond meeting, February, 1901.

gentle, grassy slopes between the arroyos in this vicinity reveals a very scattering growth of mesquite (*Prosopis velutina*), which is in the form of twigs 2 to 3 feet high, with an occasional larger shrub in some of the more favorable localities. Without more critical data regarding the previous history of the region than it is possible to secure at the present time, one can not tell whether this growth indicates that this shrub is spreading or not. The present condition rather suggests this possibility. It would not be at all surprising, for there appears to be abundant evidence that such is the case under the influence of stock grazing in portions of Texas, where a closely related mesquite grows in abundance.

By far the most important shrub is the mesquite, which, like the majority of the other shrubs, is especially at home from the line LI, figure 1, northward and along the arroyos in the southern half of the inclosure. In many localities in the southern half cat-claw (*Acacia greggii*) is nearly as abundant as the mesquite at the present time. This, however, is better protected than the mesquite, and the wood choppers have generally avoided it on this account. The other smaller species of acacia (*A. constricta*) is less abundant, but is also confined to the arroyos. The blue palo verde (*Parkinsonia torreyana*), which rivals the mesquite in size, grows in similar localities. The desert willow (*Chilopsis linearis*), cottonwood (*Populus fremontii*), hackberry (*Celtis reticulata*), soapberry (*Sapindus marginatus*), and walnut (*Juglans californica*) grow sparingly in some of the upper canyons. A large part of the northwestern portion of the field is badly infested with *Isocoma coronopifolia*. The line LI, figure 1, passes through a very conspicuous growth of large bunches of *Ziziphus lycioides*, which is of as little value as the creosote bush (*Covillea tridentata*), which occupies some of the southeastern portion of the field. The greater part of the latter was avoided, however, in the final fencing, a very large area being found immediately north of the eastern portion of the inclosure. The upper edges of it are included in the northeastern portion of the field and in places along the northern portion of the McCleary road to Tucson. The line LI also represents the most profuse growth of the Cactaceæ, the main species of which are prickly pear (*Opuntia engelmanni*), cholla (*Opuntia fulgida*), and *Opuntia spinosior*. These, together with the sewarah (*Cereus giganteus*), are the most conspicuous of the cacti within the inclosure. The biznaga (*Echinocactus wislizeni*) occurs in scattering individuals over the entire tract.

Of the other cacti little need be said. *Opuntia arbuscula* grows scatteringly on the northern portion, while *Cereus fendleriana* and *C. greggii* are occasionally found in the same region. On the rocky banks and higher bluffs are numerous other inconspicuous species, such as *Mammillaria grahami*, *M. arizonica*, *Cereus rigidissimus*, and

C. caespitosus. Upon the higher elevations there are scattered plants of *Yucca baccata, Agave applanata,* and *A. schottii,* while *Yucca radiosa* is scattered along the northeastern fence line in rather limited numbers. *Nolina microcarpa* and *Dasylirion wheeleri* are conspicuous, especially on the northern slopes of the hills, while thickets of ocotilla (*Fouquiera splendens*) are frequent on the southern slopes. Scattered at rather frequent intervals all over the brushy area are to be found clumps of Brigham's tea (*Ephedra trifurca*). Besides these there are a great many other usually smaller shrubs scattered over various portions of the inclosure, some of them of considerable economic importance. They will be discussed under another head.

The area contains typical foothills, and does not differ materially from similar regions in the foothills of the Huachuca, Santa Catalina, and Babuquivari mountains in this same general region. As a rule, there are large, gently sloping, grassy areas comparatively free from brush between the brushy mesas and the sparsely timbered mountains, not only in southern Arizona, but in New Mexico as well.

FORAGE PLANTS.

This inclosed area contains three typical and natural subdivisions of the grazing lands of this portion of the Southwest, and the cattleman would look upon it as an average grazing proposition, not the best, nor yet by far the poorest. The first subdivision may be described as an arid desert mesa; the second, adjoining the first, may very properly be designated as open, gently sloping foothills, comparatively free from rocks; and the third, as rough, rocky bluffs and arroyo banks.

The arid mesa portion of the inclosure occupies approximately half of the field, and we may accept a line drawn from corner L to corner I, figure 1, as the division between this region and the open foothills. This division line would in all probability be more accurate if it were described as extending from L to a point about 1½ miles north of I on the west fence line. It will be seen that the upper edge of the heavy brush (*heavy* is used in a purely relative sense) corresponds roughly with the lower edge of the grassy area. North of this line there is but little grass, the main forage plants being various desert herbs and shrubs to be described later. In a favorable season there are areas of considerable magnitude of six weeks' grass (*Bouteloua aristidoides*) along the arroyos and on the higher levels of the west side, as far north as section 9, township 18, range 14; and there is usually more or less *Triodia pulchella* and six weeks' grass upon the rocky ridges in the northwest part of the pasture. These two grasses, however, are of little forage value here. They never, so far as experience since 1890 teaches, occur here except scatteringly. At times there are tufts of such perennial grasses as *Leptochloa dubia, Chaetochloa composita,*

Andropogon saccharoides, and *Bouteloua rothrockii*, together with the annual *Bouteloua polystachya*.

By far the greater part of the feed here is produced by the winter and spring annuals and the browse plants. The first of these are mainly Indian wheat (*Plantago fastigiata*), *Pectocarya linearis*, *Sophia pinnata*, *S. incisa*, *Thelypodium lasiophyllum*, *Monolepis nuttalliana*, *Phacelia arizonica*, *Ellisia chrysanthemifolia*, *Sphærostigma chamænerioides*, and several species of Gilia and Linanthus. There are also extensive areas of *Atriplex elegans*, often growing to the exclusion of all else and producing from 200 to 500 or more pounds of dry herbage per acre. This plant, although an annual, usually germinates in the spring and matures in autumn, passing through the dry season in the vegetative state.

The list of shrubby plants which occur here and which are of more or less forage value is quite large. The majority of them have been mentioned under another heading. The mesquite is by far the most important. Cat-claw (*Acacia greggii*), *A. constricta*, *Parkinsonia torreyana*, and *Ephedra trifurca* are also abundant. *Baccharis brachyphylla*, *B. bigelovii*, and *Anisacanthus thurberi*, while common in the shrubby mesa region, are much more abundant along the arroyos in the southern half of the field. During late spring the annual groundsel (*Senecio longilobus*), is a very conspicuous plant upon portions of the lower areas, and purslane (*Portulaca retusa*), forms a loose cover in many places in the fall. The former is probably of no forage value, while the latter furnishes good feed. In places in autumn two other species of purslane (*P. stelliformis* and *P. pilosa*) are of some value on the east side of the field.

It is to the open foothills that the greatest interest attaches, for it is here that the perennial grasses become numerous enough to be reckoned with in the range ration. The six weeks' grama (*Bouteloua aristidoides*) is by far the most abundant grass over the greater portion of this area, being especially abundant in the *Ziziphus lycioides* areas in the neighborhood of the line LI, fig. 1. In the same locality are also to be found large quantities of *Aristida americana* and its variety *humboldtiana*, the latter being usually found surrounding ant hills. *Bouteloua rothrockii* makes a tall, thin stand on the better portions of the gently sloping stretches between the arroyos, where in favorable years it makes a very conspicuous growth, but can not be said ever to take possession, for mixed with it are invariably found much six-weeks' grama and *Aristida americana*. Growing in similar situations, and in some seasons covering large areas, are to be found *Bouteloua bromoides*, *B. eriopoda*, and *B. havardii*, which, however, are the main grasses on the majority of the rocky banks and bluffs along the arroyos. In the latter situations are also to be found *Andropogon contortus*, either in solid patches or scattering bunches, and *Andropogon saccha-*

roides at slightly lower levels. Confined mainly to the loose sands in the vicinity of the washes, but also at times extending over portions of the rocky hillsides, is a scattering growth of *Bouteloua vestita*, while *Muhlenbergia porteri*, the black grama of this region, is invariably limited to the protection of cat-claw and other spiny or thorny shrubs. The rough grama (*Bouteloua hirsuta*) is usually found upon all of the rocky banks, but it is at home in the higher bluffs and mountains beyond the inclosure. The same may be said of the side-oat grama (*Bouteloua curtipendula*). Growing under the protection of bushes along the arroyos in this section is always to be found more or less *Panicum lachnanthum*.

In the spring these open, grassy foothills are a veritable flower garden of magnificent proportions, so conspicuous in the neighborhood of section 24, township 18, range 15, as to be plainly visible from Tucson, a distance of from twenty-five to thirty miles away. The poppies (*Eschscholtzia mexicana*) in this place develop a little later than upon the mesa near Tucson or in the foothills of the Tucson Mountains. This is explained by the difference in altitude and exposure, and at times may be influenced by variation in rainfall as well, although the rainfall of the winter is more evenly distributed than that of the summer season. Other plants which are abundant enough to influence the vernal landscape by their floral colors are *Linanthus aurea*, *Phacelia arizonica*, *P. crenulata*, *Orthocarpus purpurascens palmeri*, *Baileya multiradiata*, *Lupinus leptophyllus*, *Eriophyllum lanosum*, and *Baeria gracilis*. None of these are altogether without forage value, although the poppies and one or two of the other species mentioned are not eaten when there are other plants of greater palatability. The other vernal vegetation consists of such small plants as "patota" (*Pectocarya linearis*), *Plagiobothrys arizonicus*, *Eremocarya micrantha*, *Lotus humistratus*, *L. humilis*, *Astragalus nuttallii*, Indian wheat (*Plantago fastigiata* and *P. ignota*), all of which are of forage value. To these should also be added covena (*Brodiaea capitata*) and the mustards (*Lesquerella gordonii*, *Sophia pinnata*, *S. incisa*, and *Thelypodium lasiophyllum*).

The spring grasses on the open foothills amount to little in the average season. The perennials mentioned above, especially the gramas, make a slight growth of root leaves in a favorable season, and *Aristida americana* sometimes develops to the point of seed production. *Festuca octoflora* is common throughout the area, but it is never abundant enough to make any feed. *Poa bigelovii* often furnishes quite a little grazing around the bases of bushes and in other protected areas in the arroyos, where *Chaetochloa grisebachii* is of some value in the fall. In autumn there is usually considerable feed produced by lamb's-quarters (*Chenopodium fremontii*).

An enumeration of the main forage plants upon the rougher portion of the inclosure has necessarily been made in the previous paragraphs. All of the perennial-species mentioned above grow here in scattering clumps. Besides those mentioned, of which the gramas (*Bouteloua bromoides*, *B. eriopoda*, *B. curtipendula*, and *B. hirsuta*), *Andropogon saccharoides* and *A. contortus* are the most important, *Muhlenbergia vaseyana*, *Hilaria cenchroides*, *Aristida divergens*, *A. schiedeana*, *Eragrostis lugens*, *Chætochloa composita*, *Trachypogon montufari*, *Leptochloa dubia*, *Epicampes rigens*, together with a little *Hilaria mutica* in a few places, are of importance. *Panicum lachnanthum* usually grows under the protection of shrubs, as stated above, but it sometimes covers considerable areas of open land, as shown in Pl. II, fig. 2. In 1902 and 1903, *Pappophorum apertum* made a very conspicuous growth upon the top of Pyramid Hill, where it and *Nicotiana trigonophylla* were the only conspicuous plants.

The blue grama (*Bouteloua oligostachya*), although of great importance on the opposite side of the mountains, does not occur here, at least not in sufficient quantities to be of any consequence. The same is true of *Chloris elegans*.

A part of the forage upon the inclosure is produced by the Eriogonums, which are not distantly related botanically to the docks, one of which, the canaigre (*Rumex hymenosepalus*), is very common along all of the arroyos. The most important species is *Eriogonum microthecum*, which grows to best advantage on some of the rougher foothills of the regions south and west of Proctor. It makes its best development here upon the higher lands beyond the fence line. Many of the annual species are also grazed by stock, and *E. thurberi*, *E. trichopodium*, *E. cernuum*, *E. abertianum*, and *E. divaricatum* are abundant enough to influence the general aspect of portions of the field at certain seasons of the year. Besides the above species, *E. polycladon*, *E. thomasii*, *E. pharnaceoides*, and *E. watsoni* (?) are common in some localities. *Eriogonum trichopodium* is so abundant at times in the region between the bushy and open foothills and farther north as to give its characteristic yellow color to large areas of ground.

AMOUNT OF FEED PRODUCED.

It seems highly desirable to secure as accurate an estimate as possible of the amount of herbaceous feed produced upon this inclosure at the present time. This is desirable not only for an estimate of the amount of stock that can be carried upon these lands, but also as a basis for comparison as to the value of protection and systematic grazing when observations shall have been made and data secured upon such points. In view of this fact an attempt was made to secure at the most opportune times during the two vegetative seasons as accurate an estimate as possible of the amount of growth which occurred upon the inclosure during the seasons of 1903. The estimate was secured by measuring the yield of all vegetation excepting the shrubs upon representative areas carefully selected from the different divisions of the tract. The positions of the plots measured are indicated by letters upon the diagram (fig. 1). A to Q represent those areas measured between the 1st and 20th of April, and A' to K' between the 29th of September and 2d of October, 1903.

It will be noticed that but few perennials, aside from the grasses included in the fall reckoning, are listed. It was the intention to estimate only the grasses and other annual plants, but it was decided after the work was begun to include a few perennial species other than the grasses. It might appear better to have made quantitative measurements upon those plants of forage value only; but it is exceedingly difficult to decide which species are and which are not forage plants. It often happens that nearly all plants that grow are eaten. What is grazed depends largely upon what is available for stock to eat within walking distance of water. It was deemed better, therefore, to measure the entire growth exclusive of the shrubbery, and to estimate the nonforage plants by deducting from the totals thus obtained such a percentage as seems justifiable, based upon personal observations as well as the testimony of stockmen.

In these measurements a unit area 3 feet by 7 feet was adopted, and in the majority of cases the areas were measured by a frame of the dimensions stated constructed for this purpose. In a few cases the areas were measured with a tapeline. All plants within the frame were pulled up, counted, cleaned, the roots cut off at the surface of the ground, and the plants thoroughly dried and subsequently weighed. In some instances where the number of plants was very large and the distribution uniform, one-half of the plot only was used for the estimate, although the tables given below are based upon areas of 3 feet by 7 feet for the sake of uniformity in tabulation. In four instances plants were discarded—that is, no records of them are made in these tables. They were so small and of such insignificant weight that they would amount to only about 1 pound per acre. The annotations in the last column of the tables mention these.

While making the measurements in the spring it was found that in some of the plots there was a number of very small seedlings which it was decided not to include at that time on account of the fact that they would necessarily have to be included in the autumnal measurements. This avoided counting the same plants twice. It was decided to include *Atriplex elegans* in both spring and autumnal measurements, because of the better growth made by it than by the others, and on account of the great loss which the plant would sustain during the long dry season from April to the first of July. This loss, it is thought, will in a large measure correct the error incurred by the double estimate of this plant. The measurements were made when it was believed the maximum yield for the season would be secured. It was impossible, of course, to select a time when the maximum for each plant could be obtained on account of the difference in the date of maturity and the difference in the resistance to the drought of late spring.

Tabular statement of plot measurements.

[Each plot contains 21 square feet.]

Name of plant.	Number of plants.	Height of plants.	Condition of plants.	Weight.	Condition of plot.
Plot A.		*Inches.*		*Grains.*	
Eschscholtzia mexicana	4	5	In bloom	26	
Atriplex elegans	9	3	Very young	76	
Gilia floccosa	9	4	Under bloom	20	
Lotus humilis	1	2	In fruit	2	
Pectocarya linearis	10	2	....do	104	A broad, nearly level area from which some surface soil has been removed by erosion. Sparsely covered with shrubbery.
Sphærostigma chamæneri-oides	4	5	In bloom	2	
Lepidium montanum	5	7	....do	80	
Filago californica	1	1	....do	3	
Triodia pulchella	1	2	....do	2	
Phacelia arizonica	5	4	In fruit	28	
Lotus humistratus	4	2	In bloom	21	
Caucalis microcarpa	9	4	....do	6	
Plot B.					
Monolepis nuttalliana	57	3½	In fruit	1,631	A broad, shallow depression, from which nearly all brush has been cut and the surface soil removed by erosion.
Atriplex elegans	5	5	Very young	94	
Onagra trichocalyx	1	1	In bloom	10	
Plot C.					
Filago californica	2	1½	In bloom	1	
Lotus humistratus	1	1½	....do	2	On a stony ridge in an area cut with steep, shallow ravines.
Sphærostigma chamæneri-oides	1	3½	....do	4	
Gilia floccosa	1	3	Under bloom	2	
Eriogonum abertianum	4	3	In bloom	10	
Plot D.					
Aristida americana	24	6	Under bloom	297	On the southern exposure of a stony knoll containing an unusually good growth of Aristida. Besides the list there are 223 seedling *Eriocarpum gracilis* less than 1 inch high.
Lupinus leptophyllus	3	5	Early bloom	56	
Lotus humistratus	20	2	In bloom	63	
Plot E.					
Lotus humistratus	183	3 to 4	In fruit	555	A gently sloping, grassy area at the upper edge of the heavier mesquite brush. Besides the plants listed there are two small seedlings of *Gærtneria tenuifolia*, and ten plants of *Bouteloua rothrockii* beginning to grow.
Pectocarya linearis	116	2½	....do	611	
Astragalus nuttallii	7	2 to 4	In bloom	11	
Plantago ignota	26	4	Early bloom	53	
Gilia floccosa	8	5	....do	11	
Plagiobothrys sp	71	3 to 4	In fruit	469	
Plot F.					
Plantago ignota	595	1 to 4	Early bloom	245	Very similar to E. No brush excepting an occasional mesquite from 2 to 3 feet in height. There is considerable old grass of *Bouteloua rothrockii*, *B. aristidoides*, and *Aristida americana* from last season.
Lotus humistratus	189	1	Full bloom	126	
Plagiobothrys arizonicus	35	6	Late bloom	147	
Pectocarya linearis	371	1 to 3	In fruit	318	
Orthocarpus purpurascens palmeri	37	5	In bloom	93	
Gilia floccosa	38	2 to 3½	Early bloom	56	

Tabular statement of plot measurements—Continued.

Name of plant.	Number of plants.	Height of plants.	Condition of plants.	Weight.	Condition of plot.
PLOT G.		Inches.		Grains.	
Plagiobothrys sp	14	4	In fruit	101	
Lupinus concinnus	190	1 to 8	Early bloom	999	
Calandrinia menziesii	276	1¼	In fruit	700	
Plagiobothrys arizonicus	17	3 to 12	....do	116	
Lotus humistratus	94	1 to 1¼	In bloom	56	Differing but little from Plot F. Besides the plants listed there are 12 small seedlings of *Eriocarpum gracilis* to be included in the autumnal reckoning.
Baeria gracilis	53	3 to 4	Full bloom	53	
Linanthus aureus	4	3 to 4	....do	2	
Plantago ignota	49	2 to 4	Under bloom	35	
Festuca octoflora	84	1¼ to 4	....do	14	
Filago californica	35	1 to 3	In bloom	14	
Phacelia arizonica	6	2	Early bloom	15	
Eremocarya micrantha	49	1 to 1¼	In fruit	21	
PLOT H.					
Eriogonum thurberi	97	1 to 2	In bloom	77	In the bottom of Box Canyon, upon a coarse, sandy alluvium, which has not been disturbed for several years.
Eremocarya micrantha	21	1 to 2	....do	8	
Lupinus leptophyllus	21	4 to 8	....do	102	
PLOT I.					
Lotus humistratus	67	1 to 5	In fruit	56	Upon a stony, southern exposure bordering Box Canyon. Besides the plants listed there are 30 plants of perennial grasses just beginning to develop. *Opuntia engelmanni* is very conspicuous here.
Plantago ignota	38	1 to 3	Early bloom	57	
Erodium texanum	7	3	In fruit	78	
Eriophyllum lanosum	19	1 to 2	Full bloom	9	
Phacelia crenulata	10	2 to 6	In bloom	23	
Astragalus nuttallii	34	3	In fruit	259	
PLOT J.					
Eschscholtzia mexicana	343	1 to 9	In fruit	542½	Broad, open, gently sloping foothill region which produced a large crop of *Bouteloua aristidoides* last year.
Plantago ignota	291	1 to 2	Early bloom	70	
Lotus humistratus	32	(a)	Full bloom	101	
Eremocarya micrantha	115	1 to 2	....do	14	
Erodium cicutarium	3	2	Early fruit	6	
Eriophyllum lanosum	5	1 to 2	Full bloom	4	
Stylocline micropodes	35	1 to 2	In bloom	7	
Pectocarya linearis	24	1 to 2	In fruit	5	
PLOT K.					
Pectocarya linearis	310	1 to 4	In fruit	878	On a rocky hillside among steep, stony, bare arroyos. *Zizyphus lycioides* is conspicuous here. *Bouteloua aristidoides* was the chief crop last fall.
Lotus humistratus	2	1¼	In bloom	10	
Lotus humilis	8	1½	In fruit	36	
Erodium texanum	3	3 to 4	....do	6	
Lepidium lasiocarpum	1	4	....do	18	
Eriophyllum lanosum	80	2 to 3	In bloom	105	
PLOT L.					
Lotus humilis	226	1	In bloom	180	Similar to K, but farther from arroyo. Besides the list, there is one plant each of *Plagiobothrys arizonicus*, *Baeria gracilis*, *Filago californica*, and *Eremocarya micrantha*. All would weigh less than 2 grains.
Linanthus bigelovii	13	2 to 3	....do	6	
Linanthus aureus	2	3½	....do	4	
Gilia floccosa	5	2 to 3	Under bloom	3	
Caucalis microcarpa	5	5	In bloom	.6	

a Prostrate.

Tabular statement of plot measurements—Continued.

Name of plant.	Number of plants.	Height of plant.	Condition of plants.	Weight.	Condition of plot.
PLOT M.		Inches.		Grains.	
Thelypodium lasiophyllum.	7	10 to 18	In fruit........	79	About one-third of plot situated under a Zizyphus bush, where the vegetation is much more abundant than in the remainder of the area, but it represents an average for this kind of situation.
Cryptanthe intermedia....		5 to 8	In bloom.......	31	
Pectocarya linearis........		1 to 3	....do.........	20	
Caucalis microcarpa.......		2 to 3	In fruit........	2	
Sphærostigma chamænerioides.	5	3 to 12	Early bloom....	18	
Ellisia chrysanthemifolia.	1	6	Late bloom.....	6	
Sophia pinnata............	12	10 to 14	....do.........	95	
PLOT N.					
Lotus humistratus........	490	1 to 3	Full fruit.......	1,053½	Gently sloping open foothills. Eschscholtzia mexicana very abundant a short distance away, but comparatively few plants within 20 rods of the plot. Besides the plants listed there are 31 seedlings of Gærtneria tenuifolia and 10 bunches of perennial grasses.
Plagiobothrys sp..........	2	1 to 2	In fruit........	4	
Plagiobothrys arizonicus..	9	3 to 5	Late fruit......	22	
Linanthus aureus.........	8	1 to 3	Late bloom.....	2	
Pectocarya linearis........	8	2 to 4	Late fruit......	8	
Eremocarya micrantha....	32	1 to 1½	....do.........	5½	
Plantago ignota...........	374	1 to 3	In fruit........	283	
PLOT O.					
Mentzelia albicaulis.......	1	6	In fruit........	3	On a sandy, gravelly wash which has not been disturbed for about two years. The plants in situations like this habitually grow much larger than in other places. They are, however, much fewer in number.
Phacelia crenulata........	2	4	In bloom.......	4	
Lupinus leptophyllus......	1	4	In fruit........	27	
Gilia inconspicua..........	6	8 to 12	....do.........	92	
Gilia floccosa..............	3	3 to 4	....do.........	27	
Eschscholtzia mexicana...	1	5	Late bloom.....	2	
Plantago ignota...........	1	5	In fruit........	26	
Eremocarya micrantha....	2	2 to 4	....do.........	10	
Lupinus concinnus........	2	3 to 5	....do.........	101	
Pectocarya linearis........	1	3	....do.........	8	
PLOT P.					
Plagiobothrys arizonicus..	56	5 to 10	In fruit........	1,905	Typical representation of the uneroded lands just above the washes and below the rocky bluffs on either side. It is between areas of this nature and the sandy washes that trees and shrubs grow in this part of the inclosure.
Lupinus concinnus........	4	3 to 4	Late bloom.....	116	
Malacothrix fendleri......	1	4	In bloom.......	8	
Gilia floccosa..............	2	3½	....do.........	21	
Linanthus aureus.........	2	3	Full bloom.....	6	
Gilia inconspicua?........	11	7 to 11	In fruit........	81	
Phacelia arizonica........	1	3½	Late bloom.....	10	
Astragalus nuttallii.......	1	3	In fruit........	2	
Eremocarya micrantha....	11	1 to 2	....do.........	18	
PLOT Q.					
Ellisia chrysanthemifolia..	4,612	3 to 7	In bloom.......	1,008	Typical development in the protection of bushes.
PLOT A'.					
Atriplex elegans..........	10	12	Mature.........	968	Uneroded. In other respects not different from Plot A.
PLOT B'.					
Atriplex elegans..........	72	4 to 6	....do.........	1,614	Surface soil partially removed by erosion.
Portulaca retusa...........	106	3	In bloom.......	126	
Bouteloua aristidoides....	2	4	Mature.........	1	
PLOT C'.					
Atriplex elegans..........	82	14	Mature.........	4,479	Surface soil largely removed by flood waters.

*Tabular statement of plot measurements—*Continued.

Name of plant.	Number of plants.	Height of plants.	Condition of plants.	Weight.	Condition of plot.
PLOT D'.		Inches.		Grains.	
Bouteloua rothrockii	82	18 to 24	Mature	1,560	
Allionia incarnata	1	1 to 2	In fruit	81	
Bouteloua havardii	1	12	Mature	106	
Machaeranthera sp	22	3 to 7	Late bloom	204	In the upper end of a small stony arroyo.
Aristida americana	2,604	4 to 9	Mature	504	
Eriocarpum gracilis	10	7	Late fruit	36	
Gærtneria tenuifolia	5	16	In fruit	136	
PLOT E'.					
Bouteloua bromoides	130	5 to 8	Mature	4,910	
Aristida americana	15	4	....do	1	On the bank of a small stony arroyo.
Bouteloua havardii	26	5 to 9	....do	172	
Eriocarpum gracilis	18	3 to 5	Overmature	42	
PLOT F'.					
Bouteloua aristidoides	1,148	6 to 8	Mature	2,305	On a sandy alluvial bank about 8 feet above the shifting sands.
Tribulus grandiflorus	30	4	Overmature	128	
Amaranthus palmeri	4	6	Mature	22	
PLOT G'.					
Bouteloua bromoides	158	6 to 10	Mature	1,326	
Aristida americana	903	2 to 4	Overmature	84	
Aristida americana bromoides.	3	12 to 18	Mature	82	On the broad upper end of a shallow wash west of Proctor.
Eriocarpum gracilis	6	3 to 5	Late bloom	60	
Eriogonum polycladon	15	7 to 24	Full bloom	450	
PLOT H'.					
Bouteloua bromoides	4	6 to 7	Mature	38	
Bouteloua eriopoda	20	8 to 12	....do	154	On a rocky western exposure. *Calliandra eriophylla* very abundant, there being 15 small plants upon the plot.
Bouteloua havardii	16	6 to 10	....do	120	
Eriocarpum gracilis	72	3	Overmature	122	
Bouteloua hirsuta	5	8 to 12	Mature	70	
PLOT I'.					
Panicum arizonicum	1	3	Overmature	1	
Bouteloua aristidoides	88	1¼ to 5	....do	28	On a sandy wash. The soil has been undisturbed for about one year.
Eriocarpum gracilis	2	10 to 12	....do	33	
Bouteloua rothrockii	1	18	Mature	33	
Eriogonum polycladon	1	24	Full bloom	139	
PLOT J'.					
Bouteloua artistidoides	7,854	3 to 4	Mature	1,890	A distinctly six weeks' grass (*Bouteloua aristidoides*) area.
Aristida americana	168	6 to 8	....do	42	
Bouteloua eriopoda	1	10 to 12	....do	32	
Eriocarpum gracilis	42	6	Overmature	336	
PLOT K'.					
Machaeranthera sp	3	4	Late bloom	173	Upon a gravelly knoll where it requires an exceptionally favorable year to produce any feed.
Bahia absinthifolia	1	5	Early bloom	1,467	

The following table giving totals computed from the preceding tables is more convenient of reference and shows in connection with figure 1 the relative productivity of different portions of the field:

Totals compiled from previous tables.

Plot.	Total number of plants on 21 square feet.	Weight of plants on 21 square feet.	Average weight of plants.	Computed dry weight upon 1 acre.
		Grains.	Grains.	Pounds.
A	62	370	5.97	109
B	63	1,815	28.81	537
C	9	51	5.66	15
D	47	416	8.85	123
E	411	1,710	4.16	507
F	390	985	2.58	291
G	442	2,126	4.81	629
H	139	187	1.35	55
I	175	482	2.75	143
J	303	749	2.47	221
K	347	1,053	3.03	312
L	251	199	.79	58
M	41	251	6.12	74
N	297	1,378	4.64	408
O	20	300	15.00	88
P	42	2,455	58.45	727
Q	172	1,008	5.86	298
A'	10	968	96.80	286
B'	91	1,741	19.13	515
C'	82	4,479	54.62	1,327
D'	188	2,577	13.71	763
E'	102	5,155	50.54	1,529
F'	142	2,695	18.98	798
G'	146	1,902	13.03	562
H'	81	504	6.22	149
I'	49	234	4.78	69
J'	385	2,300	5.97	1,150
K'	4	1,640	410.00	486

The last column of this table is of special interest. It shows a wide variation in the quantity of vegetation which is produced even in areas situated near each other. It must be borne in mind that the most productive plots represent comparatively small areas. The tables also show a greater average of summer growth, the average for the spring being 270 pounds per acre and for the summer season 799 pounds, or an average for the entire year of 1,069 pounds per acre.

In interpreting these figures it must be remembered that they represent very closely the total herbaceous growth and that some of the plants listed are not eaten by stock when there is more palatable feed to be had, while others are eaten only in part. In estimating the amount of stock feed, therefore, it is necessary to make a liberal deduction from the above figures. The method of making the estimate must also be taken into account. Every plant upon the plots was pulled up and the roots cut off at the surface of the ground. The weights given, therefore, include all of the plant which grows above ground. It is needless to say that it would be impracticable, indeed impossible, to take the vegetation off the ground as closely as this by grazing. Furthermore, the method practiced in obtaining these estimates removes all vegetation, leaving no seed for annual species and no cover for the roots of the perennials. Another very important factor to be considered is the fact that so many of the annuals which make good feed while green are of practically no value when once they are dried. As an example of this may be mentioned *Pectocarya linearis* and the majority of the other borages. Even if it were possible to utilize the entire development of vegetation except what should remain for seed, it would have to be done to a very large extent, especially in the case of the spring annuals, before they ripened. Attention is called especially to the fact that it would be impossible for cattle to secure the same amount of feed that is indicated in the above totals. The above apparent large yields must be considered in connection with what is actually secured from pastures under proper grazing methods in more productive parts of the country. Where blue-grass pastures are properly grazed, and upon closely cut lawns, there is not less than 1,500 to 2,000 pounds of material left upon the ground continually, and a timothy meadow from which 2 tons of hay per acre has been removed has not less than this number of pounds remaining in the stubble. It will be seen from these measurements, therefore, that the entire herbaceous development upon this tract is not over two-thirds of what remains upon the ground, ungrazed and uncut, in good pastures and meadows.

To carry the computations and comparisons still farther, we can say that as a general rule one-third of the hay and pasture plants are left in the stubble. From the yields obtained here for the plants which are not eaten by stock, or only eaten in part, 50 per cent should probably be deducted. Deducting therefore 50 per cent for plants not eaten, and an additional 33⅓ per cent for the quantity which should be left upon the ground for the protection of the roots mainly, in the case of perennials and for reseeding in the case of annuals, we have left in round numbers an average of 350 pounds per acre as the total herbaceous production available for stock feed. From this 350 pounds per acre another large deduction must be made for plants which are of forage value for only a short time during the season and therefore are capable of only partial consumption. The borages have been mentioned in this connection, and a score of others might be enumerated. Even Indian wheat is of little value after it has dried up, for the seed falls to the ground very soon after maturity, and the remainder of the plant is not eaten in the dry condition. In the same category belong the annual grasses *Bouteloua aristidoides* and *Aristida americana*, which without doubt produce as many pounds of growth upon the inclosure as all other grasses combined. It is very doubtful if these are eaten except under enforced conditions after the seed begins to ripen. Their period of usefulness as stock feed is therefore very short. Fifty per cent more should be deducted from the total available for stock feed for plants of this kind which are of little or no value when dry and therefore are not capable of complete consumption. The two species of lotus enumerated in the record of plot measurements and Pectocarya are from their habits of growth not grazed to any extent, by cattle especially, until they begin to fruit, on account of their lying flat on the ground until this time. Their period of usefulness is therefore very short. When this deduction is made, and it is believed that all of these deductions are conservative, we have left 176 pounds of dry feed per acre to be utilized under necessarily wasteful pasture practices, where green feed is present for about five months, and the season of grass production in July to September is often closely followed by a few light showers of rain, which greatly decrease the value of the cured forage. This remainder of 176 pounds is increased somewhat by the browse plants, which have not entered into our calculation.

If we consider 18 pounds per day of well-cured hay sufficient for the maintenance of a mature idle animal without adding anything to its weight, it will require 37 acres to support such an animal one year. This calculation considers the native feed equivalent to well-cured hay and allows nothing for increase in weight. Neither does it allow anything for labor performed by the animal in gathering its food and walking a distance of 5 to 10 miles for water. When additional allowances are made for these factors, the number of acres required to pasture one animal is very materially increased and approaches very closely the 50-acre estimate given upon a previous page.

CARRYING CAPACITY.

Before any rational adjustment for the proper control of public grazing lands to meet the evident pressing demands for a change in this direction can be made, much should be definitely known regarding the amount of stock that these lands will carry profitably year after year. This must form the basis of all equitable allotments. To secure such information is a most difficult task in a region where the seasons, the altitude, the slope, and the rainfall are so variable. It can be determined very easily in the Great Plains region, where conditions are uniform and reasonably constant, and indeed it is very definitely known there; but here the case is very different. There is in the Territory comparatively little native pasture land under fence, and that which is fenced is usually the better land, representing a much higher carrying capacity than the average. Even in cases where the land is fenced the areas are irregular, and therefore of uncertain acreage, with no record of the amount of grazing secured from them. The estimates below are given, therefore, reservedly, but with a feeling that they are approximately accurate for the specific areas mentioned.

Mr. W. B. McCleary has 200 acres fenced at the base of Mount Wrightson, at an altitude of approximately 4,000 feet. The conditions are approximately the same as those in the southernmost part of the area recently inclosed by the Department, except that a portion of Mr. McCleary's holding is occupied by a large wash heavily covered with brush and trees. When first fenced, it was necessary to feed some hay to the four head of stock which are carried on the land, but at the present time the area furnishes sufficient feed for this number. Mesquite beans and browse furnish no small part of the feed, and in general the area represents about an average carrying capacity for the foothill-mountain areas. It furnishes rather more browse and mesquite beans but less grass than some of the neighboring localities. In the estimate of this pasture, if the data which it furnishes be correct, the carrying capacity for the best pasture lands in the foothill-mountain areas of this region is about 1 head to 50 acres. This is probably not far from the proportion which should govern grazing upon these lands. It should be stated that this estimate is based upon the better lands, which are proportionally smaller in area than desert mesas and unproductive lands at lower altitudes.

Much effort was made to get an estimate of the carrying capacity of the land in the northern part of the Territory, where the task is even more difficult than it is farther south. The figures given for this region are purely estimates based upon the judgment of ranchers who operate in the region. A great many ranchers were consulted and their opinions secured, but the two or three quoted below seem to be based upon the most definite data.

Some information received from Mr. George L. Brooks, manager for a cattle company, shows the extent to which the country has been overgrazed in past years. The lands of this company are located from Aztec west to Angel and south to the limit of the old Atlantic and Pacific grant. This strip of country contains a little more than 1,500,000 acres. Mr. Brooks, who necessarily made a very careful study of the matter, estimates that there were upon this area for a number of years an equivalent of upward of 44,000 bovine animals, or about 1 steer to 34 acres. The loss of cattle through starvation was tremendous for several winters, and the country became so badly damaged as to compel the company to go out of the cattle business. Their losses from theft, no doubt, were considerable, but the land could not maintain stock at the above ratio. At the present time there is very little grazing on this territory except by sheep during the winter season.

A rancher near Ashfork, who pastures 1,000 head of cattle, this number of stock now having the entire run of land composing nearly eight townships, thinks that they could be carried with perfect safety on four townships. This gives 92 acres to 1 head, which seems to be a liberal allowance, and the lands would probably carry stock at the ratio of 1 bovine animal to 100 acres indefinitely.

The higher lands in the San Francisco Mountains of course produce much more abundantly than the bench lands at lower altitudes or in the valleys of the Colorado and the Little Colorado. Practically no grazing is done here, however, except in the summer season, and an estimate of the carrying capacity must, therefore, be made on an entirely different basis. The better lands here would probably support 1 sheep to 5 acres during the grazing season from May to November. This, according to the usual method of calculation, would mean 1 steer to 30 acres for the same season.

Twice during the past season the goat ranch of Mr. Joe Mayer, at Mayer, Yavapai County, Ariz. (Pl. VII, fig. 1), was visited. Mr. Mayer has run goats for a number of years on the same territory, and his estimate of the carrying capacity of this ranch is probably as accurate as can be obtained at the present time. During the course of a conversation in July Mr. Mayer stated that, as nearly as he could judge, he is using between 3 and 4 acres of land for each animal. The estimate obtained from one of the herders of the area grazed during the season gives a somewhat higher allowance for each animal. It should be borne in mind that this estimate can not be reduced to terms of bovine animals very safely, because goats thrive upon vegetation which is not eaten by cattle or, if eaten, upon which they can subsist but a short time. The ranch is located in the mountains where scrub live oak abounds, upon which the animals live exclusively for a large part of the year.

WATER FOR STOCK.

One of the most perplexing problems of the ranchmen throughout the Territory is that of the proper distribution of water for stock purposes, and every contrivance known is employed to secure this most important adjunct of the stock business. Besides the natural supplies of springs and streams, wells and surface tanks are commonly used. Many regions are so remote from available water supplies that they are not grazed except during the cooler or more moist portions of the year, when stock can endure long periods without water, or when there is temporary water in the rivers, arroyos, and natural tanks. Water is so difficult to secure in many places that the lands can not be grazed even during this season. This condition is especially true of the higher mesas remote from both mountain ranges and river valleys where neither short streams nor small springs of the mountain valleys nor the underground water supply are available.

Central Pima County, embracing Avra, Altar, Santa Rosa, and Babuquivari valleys, is especially noted for its deep wells furnished with steam pumps. The ranches in this region are very sparse, and consequently these always furnish water for the pasturing of very large areas. Some of these wells are upward of 800 feet in depth. The fuel used for pumping is almost entirely mesquite from the immediate vicinity. The supply of water at these depths appears to be inexhaustible.

The ranches situated higher in the foothills and mountains depend upon springs and shallow wells operated by windmills. The supply of water from these shallow wells, however, often varies greatly from season to season, the difference sometimes being as high as 30 feet between the level of the water in moist and dry seasons. Upon the river bottoms the natural flow of the rivers is supplemented by wells during the dry season. These are operated by steam, horse, or wind power. On account of the absence of streams and the great difficulty of obtaining well water, a large part of the northern portion of the Territory is obliged to resort to surface tanks built of earth as the only available means of supplying water to stock. Upon the higher areas in the San Francisco and contiguous mountain ranges water is abundant enough in the average season for all purposes, but upon the lower plateaus the case is very different. Here the prospective rancher is often deterred from entering the stock business on account of the great expense involved in securing water. Under a system of more stable tenure the expense might not be prohibitive, for it is estimated that tanks which hold water for one year can be built for about $500. The clay soils so common here are admirably adapted to the construction of tanks of this kind, for they hold water almost perfectly when once thoroughly tramped and compacted. In some places natural tanks are found which need only to be filled by having water conducted into them by ditches or embankments.

Another consideration which renders water relatively expensive is the low carrying capacity of the land, which decreases the number of stock which can be profitably watered in one place, making the returns for outlays much smaller than they would be under more productive conditions of soil and rainfall. Every rancher who develops water here in any form of course owns the land upon which the water is situated, but even this ownership counts for but little under the present uncertain tenure of the surrounding areas. In short, water development being expensive and the carrying capacity of the land low at best, a large acreage is necessary to furnish a livelihood.

So far as cattle especially are concerned, Arizona is essentially a breeding ground for animals which are fattened elsewhere. It would seem, however, that this would not be the case long, for the present irrigation projects, when developed, will greatly increase the feeding facilities of the Salt and other river valleys, so that many more cattle can be matured. At present, and for a long time past, practically no cattle leave the Territory in condition for the markets. This, however, is true at the present time of nearly all the native pasture regions in the United States.

Throughout the Territory, excepting in the vicinity of the irrigated regions of the Salt and Gila valleys, no hay or other feed is furnished stock. They live upon the native vegetation, consisting of grass, weeds, or browse, depending upon the locality or the season of the year. The main concern of the rancher is with branding, preventing theft, and furnishing water. It will not be long, however, under the present management of the live stock sanitary board, before thieving, which has obtained so commonly and has been the means of ruining a great many stockmen, will be a thing of the past. The scarcity of water, coupled with the small carrying capacity of the ranges, compels cattle to travel long distances. These distances would be considered prohibitive upon the native pasture lands of the Great Plains; but the development of water at intervals of 2 or 3 miles, such as is advocated and practiced there, could not be thought of here on account of the great expense and proportionally small returns.

The readiness with which stock of all kinds adapt themselves to the enforced conditions of shortage of water is remarkable. It is not, however, without great loss at certain seasons, and it is those who make the best provision for watering who are the most successful in the business. The influence of a good supply of wholesome water is very noticeable during the dry season from April to July. Abundant opportunity was had during the past year for observation on this point, inasmuch as the greater part of the dry season was spent in the southern portion of the Territory. It was evident that cattle having plenty of water and living upon mesquite and cat-claw browse were able to live through this period in better condition than those upon better pastures but with inconvenient water supply.

It is not to be supposed that cattle go to water even once a day when feeding grounds are so remote. Indeed, the habits of cattle have been so often observed by so many people that it is well known that they very often, even during the hottest weather of summer, go to water regularly only every second or sometimes every third day, if the distance is very great between water and feed. Mr. Truax, foreman of a cattle company of Apache County, relates some of his experiences in this matter. A few days before arrival at his ranch, on the 9th of August, he followed a bunch of cattle which watered at the corral at daylight in the morning. About the middle of the afternoon they were 8 miles from the ranch. He further states that his cattle often go 10 or 15 miles away from water. It hardly seems probable, however, that cattle can accustom themselves to living over twenty-four hours without suffering in the extreme heat of summer, although they thrive for a much longer period, as shown by the following signed statement, which was recently furnished at my request:

HELVETIA, ARIZ., *July 13, 1903.*

In the month of July, 1900, in building a fence for a pasture, we inclosed a 3-year-old steer. The fence was completed on the 5th of July, and the steer to our knowledge was in our pasture thirteen days without water. We will state further that there was no grass in the pasture, but there was plenty of mesquite and cat-claw browse.

W. B. MCCLEARY.
J. MARTIN.

Mr. Truax relates a still more remarkable instance than this one, in which he states that his men accidentally inclosed a cow and calf in a dry pasture in the month of July, where they remained for a period of fifteen days before being discovered. The calf at the end of the period was in apparently good condition, but the cow could not have lived much longer. These extreme cases are quoted to show that it is not at all impossible for stock to live regularly even under this subtropical heat with but two or three waterings per week, although the practice can not be upheld where there is any possibility of supplying water at shorter intervals and more convenient distances.

In many countries where sheep are extensively raised they are almost never watered, but in dry regions water must be supplied, although at rather less frequent intervals than is the case with cattle. Upon the high plateau of the Ash Fork and Seligman regions herders informed the writer during the past season that they do not water more often than once every eighty hours in the hottest weather. They remain three nights away from water with both sheep and pack burros. In this way they are able to graze an area around the water supply with a radius of about 6 miles, or about 72,000 acres. Even with this remarkable utility of water there are large areas where grazing can not be done except during the rainy season or in winter when there is snow upon the higher elevations. During a large part of the winter, when grazing is done upon alfilerilla and Indian wheat, sheep live without water for months. Little or no water is needed even in summer when feed is green.

Goats need water more often than sheep, and it is usually claimed that they can not get along without water once every twenty-four hours. They are much better travelers than sheep, however, and on this account fully as large an area can be grazed from one watering place as with sheep. Mr. J. F. Burns reports that his 500 Angoras traveled 14 miles each day for about two weeks one year with no apparent inconvenience. This means that nearly 150,000 acres could be grazed from one watering place. This amount of travel, however, is excessive, and without doubt could not be profitably continued. Mr. Mayer's herders report that their flocks do not travel over 5 miles per day, but they think that there would be no evil effect from driving them farther than this. Considering the necessity of watering more often, it is probable that no greater area can be grazed with goats than with sheep.

Horses have no difficulty in traveling 20 miles to water, it is claimed. Some portions of Arizona are overrun with cayuses of little value, a large number of which are unbranded and badly inbred. They are claimed, of course, and, being upon public range, can not be gotten rid of. Horses and burros have a decided advantage over cattle, not only from the fact that they are better travelers, but because they are able to dig for water in the sands of the arroyos. It is a novel sight to the uninitiated to see a horse or burro up to its knees in the loose sand pawing for water. During the summer rains the water level is high in the arroyo sand for some time after a shower, although there may be no running or standing water for miles around. Horses and burros very commonly supply themselves with water during the summer season in this way, and are, therefore, able to graze upon lands that cattle or even sheep can not reach. Plate III, figure 1, shows horses digging for water in a small arroyo at the western base of Pyramid Hill, within the present inclosed area on the Santa Rita Forest Reserve.

By far the greater number of sheep and goats are summered in the great highland region of the San Francisco, Mogollon, and White mountains, and wintered upon the deserts of the Salt, Colorado, and Little Colorado river valleys. This statement should be modified by the assertion that the Navajo and Moqui sheep are not included. The rainfall is so variable, however, that there is no regularity in the migrations. The exact locality where a man winters depends entirely upon the distribution of the rainfall of the late autumn of that particular season.

THE SEASONS.

There are in southern Arizona two distinct seasons of feed production; in other words, two seasons of plant growth. They are totally different in the class of plants which they produce; indeed, one can almost recognize three seasons of growth if he takes into consideration those plants which grow well during the hot weather of May and June upon the moisture which they have stored up during the winter.

The first season draws to a close with the advent of the April drought, which continues to the first of July. The second begins with the summer rains of July and terminates early in October. The spring season is largely dependent upon fall rains to start the vegetation, which grows very slowly during the winter and matures in the spring. Of course not all of the spring plants germinate in the autumn, but there is a large class of very conspicuous and important things which do germinate as early as the latter part of September, make a good growth before the cold weather sets in, grow very slowly during the cold weather, and mature in the spring. This cycle is entirely dependent, however, upon the distribution of moisture. If the months of September and October are dry no germination takes place until moisture comes in late winter. If this continues long enough in the spring a crop matures; but if not, as is usually the case, these plants dry up and there is no more feed produced until the summer rains come again.

From April to June, although it is very dry, there is a considerable development of plants which have some special provision for retaining or securing a supply of moisture. The development of these is usually not perceptible until the season of drought. Indeed, it is after the dry hot season begins that they begin their growth. Attention should be called here to the fact that it is only those plants which have means of supplying themselves with water that grow during the dry season. Those plants protected by varnish, or by having power to discard their leaves, etc., use these contrivances to enable them to live, not grow, during the dry season. The case is very different with the majority of the cacti, which store vast quantities of water in their tissues. They grow without apparent hindrance through the dry season of early summer. They are of value as food for stock, and would be closely grazed were it not for their offensive spines. The native gourds, devil's claw, the native night-blooming cereus (*Cereus greggii*), one of the ground plums (*Physalis* sp.), birthwort (*Aristolochia brevipes*), and numerous others that might be enumerated, have storage reservoirs in the form of enlarged roots. These plants, however, are of little forage value. The mesquite, on the contrary, is able to thrive through a long period of drought with no appreciable storage of water, but it is a very deep-rooted plant, and growing to best advantage along river courses and arroyos it gets water from the deeper strata there much longer than the shallow-rooted plants, and is therefore able to grow well into the summer dry season, if not fully through it into the moist summer season without being checked. During the past year this tree was in full bloom about the middle of May upon the northwestern part of the large inclosure, and it was almost completely defoliated by a lepidopterous larva by the last of the month. On the 26th of June it was again in full bloom and had nearly recovered from the effects of the defoliation. During the period from April to June there had been 2.9 inches of rain at McCleary's camp, and but 0.42 inch at Tucson. The rainfall in the mountains at

McCleary's did not reach the area in question, and as nearly as can be judged the rainfall here at this period was little if any greater than at Tucson. The effect upon the deep sands of the washes, however, was considerable, no doubt, and the deep roots of the shrubs were able to profit by it.

The winter season is characterized by an abundant (relative) growth of short-lived annuals. Some of these, as before stated, start their growth in October, or even September, at the close of the summer rainy season. Among these may be mentioned *Pectocarya linearis*, alfilerilla, Indian wheat, and a large number of boraginaceous plants which furnish a great deal of feed. Between this time and the 1st of February (it is not definitely known at what time, and, indeed, the time varies owing to the variation in precipitation) there appear a host of other short-lived plants, a large number of which are of some forage value. These are ephemeral, especially in their effect upon the landscape and in their forage utility, although they are really in the vegetative state a considerable period. The time of maturity of these winter and spring annuals in the same season is very variable, there being from two to three weeks' difference between the mesas about Tucson and the northern slope of the Santa Rita Mountains or the eastern slope of the Babuquivaris. This vernal development is mostly confined to altitudes below 4,000 feet in southern Arizona, the regions above this having really but one prominent vegetative season. The cause of this is mainly the lower temperatures of the higher altitudes, there being too low a temperature for the growth of the annuals at a time when the winter and early spring moisture is present. By the time the temperature is high enough for plant growth the moist conditions have disappeared, and there is practically no growth of vegetation, except during the summer rainy season. A very large part of the best pasture lands of this section, therefore, has but one season of plant growth.

The summer season is characterized by the production of grasses of a great variety of species. Upon the lowlands the greatest development is upon the flooded areas, which were much more abundant formerly than they are now, owing to the excessive erosion which has taken place during recent years. Upon the mesas there is but little development of perennial grasses as a usual thing, unless these mesas be high. In favorable places and in favorable seasons there are a few perennials which make considerable feed. Upon the mesa swales galleta (*Hilaria mutica*) is an important grass, while upon the less favorable situations species of grama grass sometimes make a thin growth. It is on the foothills and mountains that the grasses make their best and most pronounced growth. Here the rainfall is more abundant during the summer season than upon the lower areas, although there may not be such a difference in the winter rainy season, and the growth of grasses is proportionately larger. Nearly all grasses are in bunches and often grow 2 or 3 feet high, but always scattering. It is only in favorable depressions, where the land gets an increased quantity of moisture that there is a sufficient amount of development to produce a complete ground cover. The summer season of growth depends not only on the amount of rainfall, but upon its distribution during the period from July to September.

The following table of rainfall, prepared from Weather Bureau observations at Tuscon during the years 1902 and 1903, illustrates very nicely the difference between what are considered years of plenty and years of famine in the range business in this region:

Table showing difference in amount and distribution of precipitation in a good and in a poor season.

[Precipitation expressed in inches.]

Month.	Year.	1.	2.	3.	4.	5.	6.	7.	8.	9.	10.	11.	12.	13.	14.	15.	16.
January...	1902																
	1903																
February..	1902																
	1903		0.20	0.11		0.14	0.31			0.02					0.08	0.25	
March.....	1902										0.01						
	1903		.03	.01	0.01	T.											
April......	1902																
	1903																
May.......	1902							T.							T.		
	1903			T.	.07				T.						T.	.13	T.
June.......	1902									T.							
	1903									T.	T.	0.22					
July.......	1902										.01				.10	.04	
	1903						.16		0.23		T.	T.	T.	0.01	.08	.11	0.67
August	1902		T.		.46		T.	0.07	.05	T.		.53					
	1903			T.	.04	T.	.11	.97	.03	.20		.07					
September.	1902				T.			.06	T.			.17			T.	.16	
	1903					.05	.14		.01								
October....	1902																
	1903																
November.	1902										.21	.29					
	1903																
December.	1902												0.50	.91	.42	T.	
	1903						.10	.14	.03			.01					

Table showing difference in amount and distribution of precipitation in a good and in a poor season—Continued.

Month.	Year.	17.	18.	19.	20.	21.	22.	23.	24.	25.	26.	27.	28.	29.	30.	31.	Total.
January	1902									0.10	0.09	T.		0.20	0.14		0.53
	1903																
February	1902										T.						
	1903										T.						1.11
March	1902			0.02					0.41			T.					.44
	1903								.03	1.42	.13	T.					1.63
April	1902				T.												T.
	1903																
May	1902																T
	1903																.20
June	1902				T.								0.09	.03	.07		.19
	1903																.22
July	1902					0.05	0.21	0.01			T.						.42
	1903				0.04	.01		.02		.15	.04						1.52
August	1902	0.05			T.		T.	.15				T.		T.			1.31
	1903									.01	.99			.25			2.67
September	1902		0.09	.01	.09												.58
	1903					T.	T.			T.		0.96	.01				1.17
October	1902													1.64			1.64
	1903																
November	1902				T.	.46	.02	T.						.40			1.34
	1903																
December	1902															1.32	2.15
	1903																.28

Several important points should be noted in connection with this table of rainfall. Although arranged by calendar years, it should not be studied according to this division, although this might be done in other regions. The total rainfall of these two years was practically the same, but the good rains of October and November, 1902, with the rainfall of March and April, 1903, were the means of producing good feed during the early part of the latter year, while the rainfall of the latter half of the year 1902, although above normal, produced very poor summer feed on account of its improper distribution. It fell mainly between the 29th of October and the 14th of December, too late for the proper development of the grasses, which thrive here only under intense heat and considerable moisture. The precipitation during July, August, and September, 1903, was good and well distributed, but the fall during the last three months of the year was too light to augur very auspiciously for the winter of 1904, although the good rainfall of September was sufficient to start the annuals beautifully. It should be stated that these conditions do not bear much generalization, they apply locally where the observations on precipitation were made very well, but they may not apply at all in localities somewhat removed. For instance, the feed upon the inclosure in the Santa Rita Mountains was much better in the summer of 1902 than in the same season of 1903. This, of course, was due to a difference in conditions, which is shown by the following table, in which it will be seen that the rainfall of July was just twice as great at McCleary's camp as at Tucson, slightly less in August, but still a good amount, and decidedly more in September:

Comparison of monthly totals of precipitation at Tucson and McCleary's camp.[a]

Month.	Tucson.			McCleary's camp.		
	1902.	1903.	Average.	1902.	1903.	Average.
	Inches.	Inches.	Inches.	Inches.	Inches.	Inches.
January	0.53	0.00	0.24	0.67	0.10	0.38
February	.00	1.11	.55	.00	1.48	.74
March	.44	1.63	1.02	.85	1.59	1.22
April	.00	.00	.00	.11	.00	.06
May	.00	.20	.10	.15	.99	.57
June	.19	.22	.20	.50	1.10	.80
July	.42	1.52	.99	.90	3.04	1.97
August	1.31	2.67	1.96	3.07	2.45	2.76
September	.58	1.17	.70	3.45	1.99	2.72
October	1.64	.00	.82	.15	.00	.07
November	1.34	.00	.71	2.72	.00	1.36
December	2.15	.28	.71	1.05	.12	.58
Yearly total	8.60	8.88	8.74	13.62	12.86	13.24

[a] Observations at Tucson from U. S. Weather Bureau records, and at McCleary's camp by Mr. W. B. McCleary.

The unproductive condition of the present public lands is often attributed to drought during recent years. It is a very common thing to hear ranchers speak of the prolonged droughts during the last few years, and attribute to these the shortage in feed and the consequent decrease in the cattle industry. The majority of ranchers, however, agree that the carrying capacity of the lands is necessarily small and always has been, but that they were led to believe in the early history of the cattle business and at a time when the old vegetation upon the ground was an accumulation of long standing that the carrying capacity was much greater than it really is. This old vegetation having been eaten off and tramped out by more stock than ever should have been placed upon the land, coupled with the evil effects of erosion, described elsewhere, account for the present conditions.

The following table shows that the precipitation during the past five years has been somewhat less than during the previous four years, and that the average for the past five years has been but 0.95 inch less than the average for the past fourteen years. This table, prepared from Weather Bureau observations at Tucson, shows the total of precipitation by months and years for the past fourteen years.

Monthly totals of precipitation at Tucson, Ariz., for fourteen years.

Year.	Jan.	Feb.	Mar.	Apr.	May.	June.	July.	Aug.	Sept.	Oct.	Nov.	Dec.	Total.
	In.	In.	In.	In.	In.	In.	In.	In.	In.	In.	In.	In.	In.
1890	0.53	0.52	0.62	0.59	0.75	0.83	0.88	0.83	0.77	0.86	0.60	0.52	8.30
1891	.12	2.08	.17	.00	.18	.22	.70	2.26	.65	.00	.00	.23	6.61
1892	1.52	2.63	.98	.18	.17	.10	1.00	2.14	.37	.27	T.	.25	9.61
1893	.27	.82	1.16	T.	.75	.00	2.78	5.40	1.02	.00	.43	.49	13.12
1894	.11	1.04	1.17	T.	.05	T.	1.60	1.01	.12	.31	.00	1.88	7.29
1895	.56	T.	.00	T.	.09	.02	.11	4.48	.75	.68	4.30	.08	11.07
1896	.53	.08	.27	.12	T.	.19	3.45	1.25	1.13	3.31	.30	.76	11.39
1897	1.79	.08	.13	.00	.00	.00	1.98	3.42	2.71	.54	.00	.11	10.96
1898	1.10	T.	.63	1.05	.00	.20	3.22	3.94	.10	.00	.85	1.63	12.72
1899	.78	.39	.37	.62	T.	1.27	1.87	1.82	.08	.67	.56	T.	8.38
1900	.16	.49	.54	1.12	T.	.17	.65	.95	.86	.41	2.45	*T.	7.79
1901	1.15	1.38	.64	.04	.41	.00	2.57	1.99	.28	1.18	.08	.00	9.72
1902	.53	T.	.44	T.	T.	.19	.42	1.31	.58	1.64	1.34	2.15	8.60
1903	.00	1.11	1.63	.00	.20	.22	1.52	2.67	1.17	.00	.08	.28	8.80
Mean	9.15	10.62	8.75	3.72	2.60	3.41	22.75	2.39	.75	.71	.78	.60	9.60

EROSION.

The entire absence of a sod, a soil very slowly permeable when once thoroughly dried, steep grades, violent windstorms, and torrential rainfalls of short duration are the elements which are calculated to produce erosion in its most violent forms. Coupled with these natural conditions, excessive stocking, with scarcity of water, compelling cattle to travel long distances to feeding grounds over surfaces easily pulverized, enhances very much the erosive action of the natural elements. There always were deep gorges, cuts, arroyos, and washes in the foothills, mesas, and other sections having steep grades; but the cutting of the river channels into deep gorges which effectually drain the bottoms instead of allowing the water to spread over the broad, fertile lands is a distinctly modern condition, directly traceable to the effect of the white man's operations. (Pl. V, fig. 2.)

One of the most serious questions which confronts the rancher to-day is how to prevent this gullying. While the loss of the land itself is not, the loss of the water is a serious matter. The flood waters which once spread over the river bottoms with practically no channel are now sunken from a few feet to 20 feet below the surface, and are carried off, together with all the rich sediment which they contain.

Several ranchers whom the writer has met have been obliged, within recent years, to devise means to mitigate this evil. It is often impossible or impracticable to do anything in those cases where the cutting has progressed very far, but on the other hand it is not at all impossible nor impracticable to prevent further depredation by attacking the matter at the most advantageous point. The difficulty with work of this kind is its expense compared with the productivity of the land when no water is present for irrigation.

Two general processes are in vogue for counteracting the effect of the sinking of the water channels. The first consists in planting some soil-binding grass in such situations for the purpose of preventing further difficulty. This is usually a remedial measure which does not get at the root of the matter and is capable of but limited application after the destruction is well under way. It can be applied in this region in situations which receive flood waters from higher localities. The soils where it is attempted must already be reasonably stable in order to allow the grass to get a foothold. Mr. Harry L. Heffner, manager of the Empire Cattle Company, has experimented a great deal in this matter. The plan which he has adopted has been to establish plantations of Johnson grass upon the lands near the ends of the deep, narrow gorges and washes which approach the Pantano Wash, between the Santa Rita and Whetstone mountains. In these situations considerable areas of comparatively level lands are flooded one to three times during the year. Were three irrigations certain each year, the establishment of Johnson grass on such areas would be a comparatively easy matter. Indeed, two thorough floodings, together with the light showers that normally occur, would insure the establishment of this grass. It has been found that the most successful method of establishing a wash-resistant covering of this grass in such situations is by planting cuttings. Sections of the underground stems, from 8 to 12 inches in length, are inserted in the ground in rows across the wash, about 3 feet apart. In planting, a spade or bar is used to prepare the opening in the soil, and simply the pressure of the foot completes the operation when the cutting has been inserted. This operation is not so slow and tedious as would seem. The cuttings are easily dug or plowed up from fields which are in reasonably good tilth, and the planting is accomplished very expeditiously. Bermuda grass has also been tried in the more moist situations, but with very indifferent success thus far. This grass requires more moisture than it is possible to secure for it here, except where irrigation is practiced.

The second method in vogue to check and repair the damage done by flood waters is by the erection of embankments across the cuts, the object in all cases being to turn the water from its course on to higher lands and compel it to spread out over them instead of following the regular channel. Brush, stone, and earth are used in the formation of these embankments, which must be strong enough to withstand a great pressure until the course of the waters is once turned. When once the flow has been checked the filling up and leveling off of the gullies for some distance above the dams is quickly accomplished by the waters, which contain large volumes of sediment. The filling up process below the dam is a slow one, but the turning of the water from its course prevents further erosive action. Several small works of this nature have been observed in the valleys of the Little Colorado and White rivers and some are under contemplation by Messrs. Vail & Wakefield in the Altar Valley near the Mexican border.

THE PRAIRIE DOG.

This little animal, which has caused such devastation throughout the plains region since its enemies have been killed by the rancher and his herdsmen, is without doubt migrating into new territory. The destruction wrought by it is more pronounced east and north of the divide of the San Francisco and White mountains than anywhere else in Arizona. Large areas have been completely overrun in the vicinity of Flagstaff. In August a trip was taken through a very badly infested area between Adamana and the White Mountains. Pl. X, fig. 2, shows an infested area on the northern slope of the White Mountains, which represents in some respects the greatest injury that has been observed in any region in the Territory. It is seldom that one can secure a photographic representation of the work of the prairie dog, but here the lime pebbles—or rather the lime-covered malpais rocks and pebbles—thrown out of the burrows furnish a sufficient contrast to the black malpais rocks and bare ground to give a fairly good representation of the extent of the operations carried on by these animals. There were no perennial grasses in the infested area, and but little vegetation of any kind. No area which has been visited within the Territory is so badly overrun by these animals as that in the vicinity of the old Twenty-four Ranch and southward to the base of these mountains.

RANGE FEED.

There is without doubt no part of the country where the character of the native feed is so variable as it is in the Southwest; and this in spite of the fact that the aggregate yield per acre is very low, and that two crops are produced each year upon a large part of the range country. We have a carrying capacity here varying from one animal to 40 or 50 acres to one animal to 100 acres, as compared with one to 15 acres in portions of the Great Plains. At the same time, the grasses, which are practically the only forage plants in the latter region, are much less numerous there than in the Southwest—much less numerous in point of species. Some of the most important groups of forage plants are discussed below.

THE GRASSES.

While it may be stated in general that of the forage production of the Territory as a whole the grasses form the most important part, yet the grass production is confined to the summer season of rain, and consequently there is a large part of the year during which all stock is obliged to subsist on other things. The grasses furnish good feed from July to the 1st of January, but after that date, if the normal winter precipitation occurs, what is left of them is quite well bleached out. The value of grass for winter feeding always depends upon its being dry cured. When the winter rains come, therefore, stock begin to shun the old grass in proportion as the succulent annual stuff develops. During this cold winter and spring moist season there are, however, a few grasses which are of some importance in the forage ration upon the range. The most important of these are *Bromus carinatus*, *Poa longipedunculata*, *P. fendleriana*, *P. bigelovii*, and *Festuca octoflora*. Occasionally, however, the winter rains are prolonged into the warm spring season sufficiently to allow the perennial grasses, of which the gramas upon the open foothills are the most important, to get a start. In such a season there is some good feed produced by these in the spring, but this condition is an exceptional one, and we may say that as a general rule the perennial grasses which furnish the feed of midsummer to winter season do not grow at all in the spring. There is abundant evidence, however, that they would furnish two crops if the moisture and temperature conditions were favorable.

The most important of the grasses belong to the group known popularly as gramas (*Bouteloua* spp.), some of which are perennial and some annual. The perennials grow in the higher altitudes, and are mainly *Bouteloua oligostachya*, *B. curtipendula*, *B. bromoides*, *B. rothrockii*, *B. hirsuta*, *B. eriopoda*, and *B. havardii*, with considerable areas of *B. trifida* upon some stony, bare, high foothills. These furnish the best and most important range feed. *Bouteloua rothrockii* extends to lower altitudes than the others, and at times is strictly a mesa plant, furnishing upon favorable places and in favorable seasons a thin stand of large bunches. It is in the open foothills, however, that this species reaches its best development. Here, together with other species of lesser importance, it often makes sufficient growth for hay. The open foothills of the Whetstone, Huachuca, Santa Rita, and Babuquivari mountains, the Sulphur Spring Valley, and the high mesas between the Santa Catalina and Willow Spring mountains furnish extensive areas of this grass in favorable seasons. It is interesting to compare this distribution with similar situations in the Mesilla Valley of New Mexico, where Professor Wooton states that *Bouteloua eriopoda*, which is never an exclusive crop in southern Arizona, is often cut for hay. All of these species occur in the southern part of Arizona, but it is the blue grama (*Bouteloua oligostachya*) that is of the greatest importance in the northern part. Here it is by far the most important grass upon the high plateau surrounding the San Francisco and contiguous divides. Many of the juniper ridges so characteristic here have practically no other grass, and even this makes only a thin, short growth very different from its habit in the southern part of the Territory, where it assumes a more erect and robust character. The northeastern part of Arizona, especially from Navajo to Chin Lee. and southward to the Long H Ranch and St. Johns does not differ materially in the higher elevations from the lower juniper areas of the plateau region. The three annual species of grama (*Bouteloua aristidoides*, *B. polystachya*, and *B. prostrata*) furnish feed of a poorer quality and shorter duration than the perennial ones. The first two species are found most abundantly from the lower areas to the higher foothills in the southern part of the Territory, *Bouteloua polystachya* furnishing much the better feed of the two, but the quantity is smaller. The third or prostrate grama is an important forage plant all through the pine region in the general highland of the White, Mogollon, and San Francisco mountains. At times it also reaches favorable situations along the Little Colorado.

The main grass in the lower areas in the valley of the Little Colorado is *Sporobolus airoides*. This valley has much in common, so far as its vegetation is concerned, with the valley of the Rio Grande farther east. *Sporobolus airoides* and salt grass (*Distichlis spicata*) furnish the greatest amount of feed here, but they never yield so abundantly as they do in the Rio Grande Valley. The former is known here as saccaton, but is very different from *Sporobolus wrightii*, which makes such a magnificent growth on some of the river bottoms in the southern part of the Territory.

Galleta (*Hilaria mutica*) is an important grass throughout Arizona, although not by any means so palatable as the gramas. It nearly always occupies swales or depressions in the mesas, and for its best development gets one or more irrigations by flood water during the year. In the past season there were small areas upon the mesas south and east of Tucson that would cut one-fourth of a ton of hay to the acre of this grass. In the northern portion of the Territory, especially near Ashfork, upon the Navajo Reservation, and along the main line of the Santa Fe from the plateau region east, except in the lower areas along the Little Colorado, this must be considered one of the most important grasses. It is often grazed to the ground continuously. Curly mesquite (*Hilaria cenchroides*), a closely related species, is of great importance upon the high, open foothills, and *Hilaria rigida* is characteristic on some of the deserts along the Gila and Salt rivers.

The great highland region of the San Francisco and White mountains furnish as good summer feed as any in the Territory, and where properly pastured the parks and open places are quite productive. Here a fescue (*Festuca arizonica*) is probably the most abundant grass, although sheep men sometimes claim that it is inferior in quality to *Sporobolus interruptus*, which also grows to the exclusion of all other vegetation over quite extensive areas upon thinly wooded plateaus. Indeed, *Festuca arizonica* and *Muhlenbergia gracilis*, which occupy large areas, are not considered such good sheep feed as *Spo-*

robolus interruptus. However, they are all grazed, and thousands of sheep live on practically nothing else for a large part of the summer. Sheep fescue (*Festuca ovina* var.) is common in portions of the mountains, but it is not so abundant nor so valuable as the other species. Strange as it may seem, the bluestem of the great plains region (*Agropyron occidentale*) produces a very important part of the range feed here. In open depressions there are often pure stands of it, which, during the past season, would cut as high as one-half ton to the acre. *Aristida purpurea* is another grass which, though not considered the best of feed, is very abundant in places, and furnishes fairly good grazing when young. Among other grasses of importance here should be mentioned *Koeleria cristata*, *Sporobolus depauperatus*, *S. pringlei*, *Schedonnardus texanus*, *Agrostis hyemalis*, *Sitanion longifolium*, *S. molle*, *Blepharoneuron tricholepis*, and *Epicampes ligulata*. As would be expected the grass flora here is varied, but the species mentioned, together with the blue grama, are the most important from the stockman's standpoint.

Upon the bottom lands in the southern part of the Territory saccaton (*Sporobolus wrightii*) is without doubt the most important, and it was much more abundant formerly than now. Its place is taken on the saltier bottoms in the Salt, Gila, Little Colorado, and Sulphur Spring valleys by *Sporobolus airoides*.

The bluejoint grasses are of special importance in the southern part of Arizona, and furnish a great deal of the summer feed in the foothills and mountains. They are usually grazed to the ground. The most important species are *Andropogon saccharoides*, *A. contortus*, and *A. hirtiflorus feënsis*. The first of these often makes a good crop on usually limited highland depressions. The other two are common on rocky hillsides.

There are a number of annuals aside from those noted above which are of much value and often make comparatively large yields on limited areas. Without doubt the most important of these is *Chloris elegans*, which in favorable seasons will sometimes cut a ton of hay to the acre in situations which receive an overflow. It is also an important constituent of the foothills range feed in some localities. It was especially abundant in the Sulphur Spring Valley in 1900, and upon the eastern slope of the Santa Rita Mountains in 1902 and 1903. *Eriochloa punctata* is also an important annual, with about the same habits as the former species, and in the same connection should be mentioned *Eragrostis neo-mexicana*. The triple-awn grass (*Aristida americana*) is abundant in similar situations to the six weeks' grama. While the awns render this of little value after maturity, it nevertheless furnishes some grazing early in the rainy season upon the lower foothills throughout the southern part of the Territory.

Of the perennial species not previously mentioned there is a large number which, although not of great importance in themselves, in the aggregate furnish considerable feed. *Pappophorum wrightii* occurs in places in the open foothills and is of a great deal of importance, and the closely related species *P. vaginatum* is generally found in depressions where water accumulates. In the protection of bushes almost exclusively at the present time is to be found the so-called black grama of this region (*Muhlenbergia porteri*), which is said to have been very plentiful at one time upon open ground. This is a very interesting species, inasmuch as it is one of the few grasses of the region which has perennial culms. Confined as it is to the protection of shrubbery, it, together with a large amount of other vegetation, is left unmolested during the fall, while the grasses on the open ground are grazed off. During the winter, however, this, as well as *Panicum lachnanthum* and other grasses which tend to seek this protection, are grazed off clean, even when they form a tangled mass with cat-claw, mesquite, and cacti. It is very interesting to note that the grasses are not injured by this form of grazing nearly so much as in the open spaces. These protected areas under shrubbery, concerning which considerable has been said during recent years, are often grazed as closely as any other, but the grazing comes after the maturity of the grasses. Vegetation growing in these protected areas has several advantages. The ground is not trampled by stock, and is kept in better condition by the gophers, which almost invariably burrow here. The leaves and twigs of the bushes and joints of the cacti also furnish some protection to them. Upon the sandy bottom *Chætochloa composita* and *Sporobolus strictus* furnish some feed, while *Trichloris fasciculata* makes a thin growth on moist areas and heavier soil. It is the mountain areas that furnish the greatest quantity of valuable feed in southern Arizona. The most important grasses are the perennial gramas, bluejoints, *Leptochloa dubia*, *Lycurus phleoides*, and several species of *Muhlenbergia*. All of these are well mixed and produce a very tall growth, ranging from one-half foot to 3 feet high, but the stand is always very thin, except in the most favorable situations where water and sediment are deposited in the more gently sloping ravines where the steep mountains break off into open foothills.

Upon the sand hills in the valley of the Little Colorado there are several characteristic grasses, of which sand grass (*Calamovilfa longifolia*), drop-seed, (*Sporobolus giganteus*), and *Muhlenbergia pungens* are the most important.

PIGWEED FAMILY.

A large quantity of feed is produced by the different plants which belong to the large natural group of pigweeds. While much of it is browse, there is nevertheless some herbaceous feed furnished by the common pigweeds, several of which are closely related to the lamb's-quarters.

Without doubt the saltbushes furnish the largest amount of feed in this natural order and are abundantly distributed in many situations, some upon alkaline soil and some upon land with but little or no salt content. In the southern part of Arizona shad scale (*Atriplex canescens*), *A. polycarpa*, *A. lentiformis*, and *A. linearis* are the most abundant of the shrubby species. These are all known to the Mexicans as chamiso. The first is not so prominently a salt-loving plant as the others, although it often occurs upon somewhat alkaline soils. In the Tucson region all but the third of these occur abundantly and are invariably grazed.[a] Shad scale occurs in the valleys throughout the Territory, but the other three mentioned above are of most importance in the alkaline valleys north and west of the Tucson region. They are especially abundant in the valleys of the Gila and Salt rivers and their tributaries. *Atriplex lentiformis* is the most rapidly growing species of this genus with which the writer is familiar. Its remarkable development is well illustrated by observations made in the vicinity of Tempe in 1900, where plants which had sprung up on newly subdued land after the removal of the first crop of wheat were 5½ feet high by the 1st of December. This growth had been made between the month of June and that date.[b] Near Tempe and Phoenix it does not appear to be grazed very much, but upon the ranges along the Gila River it is not uncommon to see canes one-fourth of an inch in diameter grazed off. Having about the same range as the above are two annual species, *Atriplex elegans*, growing almost exclusively upon nonalkaline soil, and the salt-loving species, *A. bracteosa*. Both of these are grazed when feed is scarce. During the past season they were quite closely cropped along the Santa Cruz River south of Tucson. *Atriplex elegans* is a very interesting species in many ways on account of its habit of maturing seed at the close of the winter rainy season and again in midsummer. It therefore, although an annual, lives through the hot dry weather of early summer in the vegetative condition. It should be noted that there are some slight differences between the spring and summer forms, and the collections of the writer, although extensive, fail to show one of the common autumnal fruit forms at all in the spring.

The valley of the Little Colorado is especially noted for its abundance of saltbushes, some of which do not grow elsewhere in the Territory, so far as known. The saltbush flora of this region resembles that of the valley of the Rio Grande in many respects. Here that most valuable species, the spiny saltbush (*Atriplex confertifolia*), so

---

[a] See Bul. 25, Division of Agrostology, U. S. Department of Agriculture, 1891, Pl. XXVI.
[b] See Pl. IV, fig. 1.

abundant in the Great Basin, is perfectly adapted; and *Atriplex greggii* covers very extensive areas on many of the saline bottoms with an almost pure growth, especially from Corn Creek southeastward through the Holbrook, Adamana, and St. Johns regions. Upon the Navajo and Moqui Reservation, and indeed throughout the valley of the Little Colorado, shad scale fills a very important place upon both mesas and bottom lands. In the petrified forest areas there occurs a shrubby species of *Atriplex* (No. 5085), which appears to be undescribed. This is said to be grazed during the winter. In this same region *Atriplex powelli*, an annual species, covers many areas of washed lands, while *Atriplex expansa* is abundant in some localities.

Next in importance to the saltbushes should be mentioned the white sage (*Eurotia lanata*), which occupies very extensive areas upon the highlands in the northern part of the Territory. It is especially important, as a winter feed only, in the great highland region north and east of the main divide of the San Francisco and contiguous mountains. It is common in places in the higher situations in the southern part of the Territory also, but never abundant enough to be seriously considered in the range ration. It is common in the Sulphur Spring Valley and has been collected upon the Santa Rita Forest Reserve. Greasewood (*Sarcobatus vermiculatus*) makes much winter feed in all the alkaline bottoms of the Gila, Salt, and Little Colorado valleys. Red sage (*Kochia americana*) is abundant enough to furnish some winter feed in the valley of the Little Colorado.

The common lamb's-quarters of the East is represented in Arizona by several species, which are of economic importance. In southern Arizona they are of more importance in the upper foothills than elsewhere, but in the northern higher altitudes they occupy the areas under the junipers upon the mesas and ridges, and sometimes cover large depressions with an almost pure growth. They furnish good summer feed, for sheep and goats especially. The species which grow here are *Chenopodium leptophyllum*, *C. incanum*, *C. fremontii*, and *C. olidum*? (No. 5841). A small annual, *Monolepis nuttalliana*, belonging to this natural group makes a carpet in shallow depressions in the southern part of the Territory during the spring season. This is one of the plants to which the Mexicans apply the name *patota*. It is considered good feed for cattle.

THE CLOVERS.

There are but few situations in Arizona where the clovers are of much importance, but there are suggestions that they may become more abundant as time goes on. In the northern mountains *Trifolium involucratum* and *T. longipes* cover small areas in moist situations. In the canyon bottoms of the southern mountains, which are devoid of meadows in the ordinary acceptance, there grows a species which, although limited in quantity, makes dense mats over small areas. It is to two small annual species, *Trifolium gracilentum* and *T. tridentatum*, that the greatest interest attaches, for there are indications that these are introduced species which are just beginning to assert themselves in the southern part of Arizona. In March, 1903, there was good feed produced by these species in several localities in the Willow Spring Mountains. Being associated here with alfilerilla and in the direct path of the early sheep migrations from California, it is quite probable that these have been introduced in wool from California and western Great Basin points, where they occur in considerable profusion. It is interesting to note that the maturity of these two species occurs about two months earlier in these mountains than in the Sierra Nevada Mountains east of Fresno, Cal. There is a bare possibility that a systematic effort to distribute these to other mountain ranges, either by securing the seed from the situations where it is produced most abundantly or by systematic herding in the season when the clovers are ripening, may result in establishing them, thereby increasing the feed in the foothills and lower mountains. It is quite certain that they will be of value only in the foothills, below the limit of winter annuals.

ALFILERILLA.[a]

Upon the areas where the alfilerilla is thoroughly established there is no other plant, unless it be Indian wheat, which can compare with it in the quantity of feed which it produces upon the desert mesas for winter and spring grazing. There appears to be no doubt that it was introduced into Arizona by sheep from California points. It is now well distributed as far south as the northern slope of the Santa Catalina Mountains and up the San Pedro Valley as far as Benson. It has not spread very much east of the San Pedro River. From here it extends northward and westward through the desert areas and high into the plateau regions on the north and west sides of the Prescott highlands; thence westward into California. There are scattering plants of it all over the Territory, but it is in the region indicated that it is of importance. It even occurs commonly upon the San Francisco Mountains at an altitude of 7,000 feet, but it is never abundant enough to be of any importance. It is much more abundant in the vicinity of Prescott (5,320 feet), but does not produce as much feed as upon the west side of the Prescott highlands, where it extends up to Iron Springs (6,032 feet). In this region it is well established all the way from Wickenburg (2,067 feet) to Iron Springs, in the edge of the pines. It appears to be perfectly at home in the scrub-oak area below the pines, where it remained green during the season of 1903 as late as the last of May.

---

[a] See Plate VI.

According to the opinions of stockmen, it is spreading slowly, and is said to have been first observed near Willow Springs. There is a popular belief that it will thrive only on granitic soils. But this does not account for its peculiar distribution in the Tucson region. Here, as stated above, it makes a good crop in an average year on the northern slope of the Santa Catalina Mountains; but while distributed in scattering individuals all over the Santa Cruz Valley, it is never abundant enough to be of any consequence. There are a few small areas upon the northern slope of the Santa Ritas, where it is as thick upon the ground as it is upon the northern slope of the Santa Catalinas, but these areas are very limited, and therefore do not figure conspicuously in the total feed production. There is a good stand of it upon the east side of the Santa Catalina Mountains, and it is well distributed over the San Pedro Valley as far west as the top of the Rincon Mountains on the Tanque Verde road, but it does not extend in any quantity into the Santa Cruz Valley.

Some systematic attempts have been made to spread the plant. Messrs. Maish & Driscol some years ago sent a force of men to the Canyon del Oro district to gather large quantities of it, to be scattered on their Canoa property. They raked up the plant when the seed was ripening and scattered it upon their land. They have not been able to observe any material benefit. Mr. C. H. Bayless believes that it can be scattered most successfully by systematic herding of sheep at the time that the plant is maturing its seed. His plan is to herd sheep first upon land well seeded, and then upon contiguous unseeded areas. It is thought by those who have observed it that it is gradually spreading southward, and that it will eventually be as abundant in the valley south of Tucson as it is in the Oracle and Willow Springs region now. There certainly appears to be no good reason for holding a contrary view.

MISCELLANEOUS WINTER AND SPRING ANNUALS.

Under the designation "Indian wheat" the rancher recognizes a group of important forage plants belonging to the botanical genus Plantago. There are two important species, both of which make their first appearance in the autumn and mature in the spring. *Plantago fastigiata* occurs mainly upon the mesas and lower areas, and *Plantago ignota* upon the foothills. The mesas in the Tucson and Phoenix region are especially noted for the magnificent growths of *Plantago fastigiata*, which, together with alfilerilla in the latter locality, feeds the largest number of sheep in the Territory during the winter and spring seasons. Next in importance to Indian wheat should be noted patota (*Pectocarya linearis*, *P. setosa*, and *P. pencillata*), the first being much the most abundant, and indeed the only one that need be considered from a forage standpoint. These plants furnish feed up to the time of ripening, but are of no value after that date, because of their extreme harshness. Belonging to the same family as the latter is a very large group of borages, which are of importance as sheep feed. The most abundant of these are *Plagiobothrys arizonicus*, *P. tenellus*, *Amsinkia tessellata*, *Cryptanthe cylloptera*, *C. intermedia*, *C. angustifolia*, and *Eremocarya micrantha*. The water-leaf family is represented by a large number of very conspicuous plants which are of more or less forage value for a short time. The most numerous of these belong to the genus Phacelia (*Phacelia arizonica*, *P. crenulata*, *P. tanacetifolia*, and *P. ramosa*), which will seem rather peculiar forage plants to many, but they, as well as *Ellisia chrysanthemifolia*, must be listed here as of some forage value, although not grazed except when feed is scarce. Of somewhat more value than the above are numerous plants related to the cultivated phlox, of which the most important are *Linanthus bigelovii*, *L. aurea*, and *Gilia inconspicua* (?). Mexican poppy (*Eschscholtzia mexicana*) is reported by many to be of some value. Mr. Ed. Vail and others assert that their vaqueros report that stock live largely upon this poppy, Indian wheat, and jojoba (*Simondsia californica*), during winter and spring on the west side of the Babuquivari Mountains. The observations of the writer do not entirely confirm these views, but it should be stated that wherever observed other feed has been abundant enough, so that it has not been necessary for stock to graze poppies. *Malvastrum exile* makes a large amount of feed on many of the river bottoms. During the past season it was abundant and extensively grazed in the lower San Pedro, Gila, and Santa Rosa valleys.

The native mustards, *Sophia incisa*, *S. pinnata*, *Lesquerella gordonii*, *Thelypodium lasiophyllum* and pepperwort (*Lepidium lasiocarpum*) form a small but important and interesting group of forage plants in the southern part of Arizona. With the exception of *Lesquerella gordonii* they are not grazed much while green, but after they are ripe the pods and oily seeds are greatly relished, by range horses especially. Horses have never been observed in better condition upon the range than they were upon the mesas south of Tucson in May, 1903. An abundant opportunity was had to observe what they were feeding upon. They appeared to be subsisting entirely upon seeds of these cruciferous plants, which grew mainly in the protection of shrubs, where they are scarcely molested until they are ripe. During the early part of the dry season, however, they were cleaned up about as completely as the grasses in similar situations in autumn.

Quite a number of leguminous annuals are of importance in the southern part of the Territory. Upon the mesas and foothills two species of lotus (*Lotus humistratus* and *L. humilis*) and vetch (*Astragalus nuttallii*) are the most important. A glance at the tables (pp. 26–29) will show the relative importance of these to the other vernal forage plants upon the northern slope of the Santa Rita Mountains. The lupines are very conspicuous upon the higher mesas and foothills, and are often grazed a little, but they are not relished like the species of lotus. Two species are very common. *Lupinus leptophyllus* often gives its characteristic purple to large areas in steep ravines and hillsides, while *L. concinnus* is fully as abundant in places.

Miscellaneous species such as *Baeria gracilis* and *Baileya multiradiata* are abundant enough to impart their characteristic golden color to the landscape at times. *Calyptridium monandrum* and *Sphærostigma chamænerioides* both contribute to the forage ration. The two first mentioned in this paragraph are composites, and are grazed by horses, especially when they are in bloom. Very little aside from the heads is eaten. *Chænactis stevioides*, another composite annual, is much more abundant in many places than these, but it is seldom eaten. In the spring of 1903 cattle in the vicinity of Santa Rosa, where the country was white with it, were grazing upon it a little. Mr. Charles Howard, of Ashfork, reports that his flocks subsist for weeks upon *Gymnolomia annua*, which is a particularly conspicuous thing upon these highlands.

MISCELLANEOUS BROWSE PLANTS.

Besides the saltbushes and their relatives, the majority of which are browse plants, a large number of other shrubs furnish feed for stock. These plants are especially valuable during the two seasons of short feed. The value of the mesquite is proverbial, on account of the large quantity of beans which it furnishes for winter and fall feed; but it is also grazed during the summer dry season. The cat-claw (*Acacia greggii*) and *Acacia constricta* are second in importance only to the mesquite as browse plants, but their fruit is of practically no value to stock. The twigs of the blue palo verde (*Parkinsonia torreyana*) and bigota (*P. aculeata*) also make winter feed of considerable importance. Jojoba (*Simondsia californica*), abundant in the foothills and lower mountain areas, appears to be the most important browse plant in these situations. The central foreground of Plate VI, figure 1, shows how this shrub, which is normally 4 or more feet high, was grazed during the past season near Dudleyville. Mr. Ed. Vail reports this one of the most important browse plants in the valleys west of the Babuquivari Mountains. *Eriogonum microthecum* and *Calliandra eriophylla* are also of much importance in the higher foothills and lower mountains. There are large areas on the east and southeast of the Huachuca Mountains, where the first has practically taken possession. It appears to spread with excessive grazing in this locality, and it is therefore very fortunate that it is of some forage value. These shrubs are especially characteristic of the southern regions.

The scrub live oaks of the entire Territory of Arizona form a class by themselves, and deserve more attention as forage plants than is usually accorded them. White oak (*Quercus arizonicus*) is probably the most important species in the southern part of Arizona, where it has even been known to be cut and fed to cattle. The black oak (*Quercus emoryi*) is said not to be touched by cattle, a statement which it has not been possible to verify. *Quercus turbinella* furnishes more feed in places in the Prescott and Bradshaw mountains than all other forage plants combined, goats and even sheep having little else to eat at some seasons.

Brigham's tea (*Ephedra trifurca*, *E. nevadensis*, and *E. torreyana*) is very commonly grazed. The first species is confined to southern Arizona mesas and foothills, while the other two are most common in the central and northern portions of the Territory. The three-leaved sumacs (*Rhus trilobata* and *R. emoryi*) are commonly browsed. Upon the highlands of the central portion of the Territory *Cowania mexicana* and *Falugia paradoxa* are grazed wherever found. Upon the mesas and foothills in the Tucson region there are two species of composite shrubs, *Baccharis brachyphylla* and *B. bigelovii*, which are invariably grazed.

Upon all the sandy ridges in the valley of the Little Colorado there is more or less sage (*Artemisia filifolia*), which is said to make valuable winter feed.

HAY CROPS.

No more than a very brief mention of the cultivated forage crops is necessary here. Alfalfa is of course the staple wherever water for irrigation is obtainable, and there is no region where more profitable returns are obtained than in the river valleys of the Territory. It is a common practice to cut a crop of barley with the first crop of hay each year upon poorly established meadows; but strange as it may seem, the bearded variety is usually sown, although the objectionable feature of this could be very easily dispensed with by sowing the beardless form instead. It is a common practice where alfalfa meadows are pastured to cut the first crop, for two purposes. One is to get rid of the weeds and the other is to give the plants a chance to recuperate from the close pasturage by this season of growth.

Barley and wheat are very largely grown for hay as winter crops, and are frequently sown for pasturage also. The Mexican population cut a large amount of this winter grain crop, bind it up in small sheaves 6 to 10 inches in diameter, and sell it in the green state in the cities and mining camps, where there is a small market for this class of roughage. These sheaves sell at the rate of about 20 for 25 cents. Sorghum is commonly grown in the summer rainy season, supplemented by light irrigations, upon the lands which produce the winter crop of barley.

Mention has been made in previous pages of the use of *Bouteloua rothrockii* as a hay plant, but with it are always cut a large variety of other species, a specific mention of which is not necessary. Sometimes saccaton (*Sporobolus wrightii*) is cut, along with such other species as grow upon the lowlands. Upon the east side of the Santa Rita Mountains blue grama (*Bouteloua oligostachya*) and bluejoint (*Andropogon saccharoides*) together with *Chloris elegans*, often make a small crop of hay. In many situations Johnson grass makes an important addition to the native hay plants upon overflowed areas.

The Mexican population makes use of a number of weedy plants, the most important of which is *Amaranthus palmeri*. In the vicinity of Tumacacori and Sopori during the past season there were large quantities of this plant put up for winter use. The crop was invariably obtained upon land from which a crop of barley had been removed in the late spring or early summer. The barley crop in this region is often the only one grown. The lands therefore lie idle from May to October, when they are plowed again for the fall seeding. During the summer they furnish some weedy pasturage, and from favorable situations a large volunteer crop of this weed is obtained. Plate VIII, figure 1, shows Mexicans stacking a large volunteer crop of this plant about the 1st of October. The yield was not far from 3 tons per acre in the field which was being harvested. These men report it to be good hay for horses, but rather poor for cattle.

WEEDS.

In a region of such small production it is not to be expected that weeds have a very detrimental influence upon native pasture lands. The weeds, as a general rule, furnish feed when other things fail. The use that is made of alfilerilla is a striking example of this.

In a few instances, however, absolutely worthless weeds flourish upon the most productive of the range lands. The alluvial bottoms which were once covered with either annual or perennial grasses have suffered great injury during recent years on account of the establishment of the cockle bur (*Xanthium canadense*). Hundreds of acres of the very best and most productive lands in the higher valleys of southern Arizona have been absolutely taken possession of by this plant during recent years. It is hoped that Johnson grass will be the means of reclaiming these areas. It is the only plant known which can compete successfully with this weed.

Along the main line of the Santa Fe Railway, for a distance of 20 or more miles on each side of the road, the Russian thistle is well established. In the valley of the Little Colorado it appears to be quite at home upon the dry mesa land, and will doubtless become more conspicuous as time goes on. While it will cause trouble upon the cultivated areas, it is not thought that it will ever injure the range lands; indeed, it may be a decided benefit. So far as known, it does not occur in the southern part of Arizona at all.

Cleome serrata has become very conspicuous upon the poorly grassed areas of overflowed depressions throughout the northern highlands. By some this plant is said to be relished by sheep, but evidences of this have not been seen. It is especially abundant in the vicinity of Flagstaff and upon the northern slope of the White Mountains.

In the southern portion of Arizona there are two perennial weeds related to the golden rods which it is claimed are spreading rapidly. These are *Isocoma coronopifolia* and *Gutierrezia microcephala*. They are very abundant in portions of the Santa Cruz and Altar valleys.

Upon the cultivated meadows the squirrel-tail grass is very troublesome and unsightly in irrigated districts. In pastures, however, it is of little or no detriment, for it is usually prevented from becoming conspicuous by the close grazing which is usually practiced upon the alfalfa pastures. It is interesting to note that in the Salt and Gila valleys *Hordeum murinum* is the prevalent species, while *H. jubatum*, which has such a bad record in the Plains region, has not been observed. In the valley of the Little Colorado, however, this species is nearly if not quite absent, while *Hordeum jubatum* is very common and even troublesome in the cultivated fields.

PLANTS INJURIOUS TO STOCK.

There are times during years of short feed when the creosote bush (*Covillea tridentata*) causes a good deal of injury to sheep. No stock of any kind eat this shrub ordinarily, but when feed is scarce sheep are sometimes forced to feed upon it. According to a recent report from Mr. E. S. Gosney, of Flagstaff, the animals, after feeding upon this shrub for a time, run about in an unsteady fashion, and are very likely to run into any obstacle which happens to be in their way. They are said to very often run toward the herder, or even his dogs, as though seeking protection. Mr. W. H. Campbell, also of Flagstaff, who has had a good deal of experience upon the deserts north of Phoenix, states that the greatest mortality occurs among pregnant ewes.

Upon the San Francisco and contiguous highlands there occurs a great deal of loco (*Aragallus lambertii*), and in some cases in the same region areas are said to have been abandoned as sheep grazing grounds on account of the preponderance of *Asclepiodora decumbens*.

Mechanical injury is sometimes done by six weeks' grass (*Bouteloua aristidoides*) and triple-awned grass (*Aristida americana*). When matured the seeds of these two species are very annoying, to say the least, to both men and animals. The sharp-pointed seeds work into both the fleece and the feet of sheep, but are more especially injurious to the latter. They accumulate between the hoofs of the animals to such an extent as to disable them. The areas of these grasses are avoided during the time of their ripening until the seed has fallen off and partially disappeared into the soil.

SUMMARY.

The carrying capacity of the lands in Arizona varies from the rate of one bovine animal to 50 acres to one to 100 acres.

Johnson grass appears to be the best adapted for preventing erosion, and will thrive in favorable situations which receive two or more irrigations by flood waters during the year. Bermuda grass does not appear to be promising without irrigation.

The valley of the Little Colorado, so far as much of its vegetation is concerned, resembles the valley of the Rio Grande, but the yield of feed is very much smaller.

From the stockman's point of view, the seasons upon the lower southern areas are four in number, each differing from the others in the character of the feed which is available. The two seasons of feed production alternate with two seasons of short feed.

(1) Middle of February to middle of April or first of May, characterized by a growth of annual weedy plants, which furnish feed for a short time.

(2) First of May to middle of July or first of August, having little growth except of shrubby plants, upon which stock largely subsist.

(3) Middle of July to first of December, which is the season of the best feed, being characterized by growth of perennial grasses and many other forage plants.

(4) First of December to middle of February, which is the hardest season of the year upon all stock.

The growth of winter and spring annuals occurs mainly below an altitude of 4,000 feet. The best pasture lands are located principally above an altitude of 3,000 feet.

In southern Arizona a large part of the feed upon the lower unoccupied lands is furnished by shrubby plants. The remainder of the feed upon these areas, as well as upon the mesas below 3,000 or 3,500 feet, is furnished by annual weedy plants in the spring, together with annual and a few perennial grasses in the summer, and in the higher foothills and mountains by perennial grasses.

Goat raising is on the increase, and it is believed that this industry will continue to develop.

The total annual precipitation can not serve as an index of the character of the feed upon the range, its distribution during the hot summer season being of paramount importance.

It is common for cattle to travel 10 miles from water to feeding grounds, and sheep are often herded 6 miles away, making a total travel between waterings of 20 miles for cattle and 12 miles for sheep. Horses travel a much greater distance.

The prairie dog is doing a large amount of damage in the north and northeastern portions of the Territory.

Beardless barley should be more extensively substituted for the bearded form for supplementing the first cutting of alfalfa.

The Russian thistle, while widely distributed in the northern part of Arizona, has not yet appeared in the southern part to any extent at least.

There appears to be abundant evidence that the creosote bush is injurious to sheep, which are sometimes forced to eat it on account of a scarcity of feed.

The average total available feed which it is practicable to utilize upon the large inclosure is believed to be between 150 and 200 pounds of air-dry substance per acre.

Alfilerilla, one of the most important forage plants of the Territory, which was probably introduced from California in the wool of sheep, is spreading. It is believed that two species of clover were introduced in the same way.

Experimental work carried on thus far in attempting to introduce perennial forage plants upon the mesas has given very little encouragement. *Panicum texanum*, an annual, has given the best results of anything thus far introduced, and it is believed that more success will be secured with annuals than with perennials. They are not as good feed, but short-lived plants with good seed habits now furnish the main feed upon the mesas.

The following tabulation showing the relative weight of desert annuals and certain of their reproductive portions will be of interest in this connection:

Plant.	Number of plants.	Fruit or seed.	Weight of seed or fruit.	Weight of plant less seed or fruit	Condition of plants.
			Grains.	Grains.	
Pectocarya linearis	2	Seed	15½	20	Fully mature.
Lotus humilis	1	Pods	19	12	Half of pods mature.
Monolepis nuttalliana	1	Seed	49	40	10 per cent of seed not mature.

This table shows, so far as this amount of data can show, that the seed production of these three characteristic desert annuals is large when compared with the total weight of the plants. *Lotus humilis* produced, in the condition indicated, 7 grains of clean seed. Two plants of *Bouteloua aristidoides*, weighing 48 grains, produced 27 grains of spikelets. It is believed that there is a suggestion here regarding the nature of the plants which will be most successful upon these arid mesa lands. Alfilerilla is already widely introduced. It has good seed habits and special provision for burying its seed. Of course perennial forage plants would furnish better feed than the annuals, but there is little hope of establishing them without greater expense than the economic benefit seems to warrant. It may be possible to establish some of the hardier perennial species upon the foothills. This, however, is a matter for experimental work to determine.

DESCRIPTION OF PLATES.

PLATE I. (*Frontispiece.*) Laosa, a typical southern Arizona ranch.

PLATE II. Contrast between dry and wet seasons in foothills range. Fig. 1.—Live-oak belt, upper foothills, eastern slope of Huachuca Mountains, July 1, 1903, before the rainy season began. Last year's crop of grass has all been eaten off. Fig. 2.—Upper foothills, northern slope, Santa Rita Mountains, just below the oak belt, showing *Panicum lachnanthum*, grama, and mesquite at the close of the rainy season.

PLATE III. The large inclosure. Fig. 1.—Pyramid Hill, section 18, township 18, range 15. Horses digging for water in the sands of an arroyo. September, 1902. Fig. 2.—Looking south from the top of Pyramid Hill, showing the general character of the fenced area. October, 1902.

PLATE IV. Saltbushes. Fig. 1.—*Atriplex lentiformis*, the largest of our native saltbushes. Tempe, Ariz., November, 1902. Fig. 2.—*Atriplex elegans* in large inclosure, northern foothills, Santa Rita Mountains, September, 1903.

PLATE V. Fig. 1.—Hay meadow, Salt River Valley. First crop of alfalfa with winter barley, which greatly increases the yield. Phoenix, April, 1903. Fig. 2.—Erosion along Pantano Wash, east of Santa Rita Mountains, October, 1902.

PLATE VI. Alfilerilla range. Fig. 1.—Alfilerilla and Indian wheat near Dudleyville. In the central foreground are shown closely grazed bushes of "jojoba" (*Simondsia californica*). Fig. 2.—Alfilerilla and Indian wheat near Oracle. *Opuntia engelmanni*, *Yucca radiosa*, and mesquite are the conspicuous plants.

PLATE VII. Two phases of the range question. Fig. 1.—Goats and the oak brush upon which they live. Mayer, September, 1903. Fig. 2.—The remains of thirteen head of cattle in a space of 30 feet along a small arroyo near Arivaca, as the result of too great distance between feed and water. April, 1903.

PLATE VIII. Haying scenes in southern Arizona. Fig. 1.—Mexicans at Sopori stacking "celite" (*Amaranthus palmeri*), which makes a large volunteer crop after the winter crop of grain hay has been removed. October, 1903. Fig. 2.—A Mexican packing hay from the mountains. Santa Rita Mountains, July, 1903.

PLATE IX. Native pasture lands in southern Arizona. Fig. 1.—Galleta (*Hilaria mutica*) in a swale south of Vail Station. September, 1902. Old grass, there being practically no growth this year. Fig. 2.—A round-up in the northern foothills of the Santa Rita Mountains, April, 1903, when the large area was being inclosed.

PLATE X. Fig. 1.—An ocotilla forest about 4 miles northeast of the large inclosure. September, 1902. Practically no feed is produced here. Fig. 2.—The work of prairie dogs upon the northern slope of the White Mountains. Large areas of grass are destroyed by these animals. July, 1903.

O

Bul. 67, Bureau of Plant Industry, U. S. Dept. of Agriculture. PLATE II.

FIG. 1.—LIVE-OAK BELT, UPPER FOOTHILLS, EASTERN SLOPE OF HUACHUCA MOUNTAINS, FIRST OF JULY, 1903, BEFORE THE RAINY SEASON BEGAN; LAST YEAR'S CROP OF GRASS ALL EATEN OFF.

FIG. 2.—UPPER FOOTHILLS, NORTHERN SLOPE, SANTA RITA MOUNTAINS, JUST BELOW THE OAK BELT, SHOWING PANICUM MACHNANTHUM, GRAMA, AND MESQUITE AT THE CLOSE OF THE RAINY SEASON.

CONTRAST BETWEEN DRY AND WET SEASONS IN FOOTHILLS RANGE.

Bul. 67, Bureau of Plant Industry, U. S. Dept. of Agriculture. PLATE III.

FIG. 1.—PYRAMID HILL, SEC. 18, T. 18, R. 15. HORSES DIGGING FOR WATER IN THE SANDS OF AN ARROYO, SEPTEMBER, 1902.

FIG. 2.—LOOKING SOUTH FROM THE TOP OF PYRAMID HILL, SHOWING GENERAL CHARACTER OF FENCED AREA, OCTOBER, 1902.

THE LARGE INCLOSURE.

FIG. 1.—ATRIPLEX LENTIFORMIS, THE LARGEST OF OUR NATIVE SALTBUSHES, TEMPE, ARIZ., NOVEMBER, 1902.

FIG. 2.—ATRIPLEX ELEGANS. LARGE INCLOSURE, NORTHERN FOOTHILLS, SANTA RITA MOUNTAINS, SEPTEMBER, 1903.

SALTBUSHES.

Bul. 67, Bureau of Plant Industry, U S Dept. of Agriculture. PLATE V.

FIG. 1.—HAY MEADOW, SALT RIVER VALLEY. FIRST CROP OF ALFALFA WITH WINTER BARLEY, WHICH GREATLY INCREASES THE YIELD. PHOENIX, APRIL, 1903.

FIG. 2.—EROSION ALONG PANTANO WASH, EAST OF SANTA RITA MOUNTAINS, OCTOBER, 1902.

Bul 67, Bureau of Plant Industry, U. S. Dept. of Agriculture.   PLATE VI.

FIG. 1.—ALFILERILLA AND INDIAN WHEAT NEAR DUDLEYVILLE. IN THE CENTRAL FOREGROUND IS SHOWN CLOSELY GRAZED BUSHES OF "JOJOBA" (SIMONDSIA CALIFORNICA).

FIG. 2.—ALFILERILLA AND INDIAN WHEAT NEAR ORACLE. OPUNTIA ENGELMANNI, YUCCA RADIOSA, AND MESQUITE (PROSOPIS VELUTINA) ARE THE CONSPICUOUS PLANTS.

ALFILERILLA RANGE.

Fig. 1.—Goats and the Oak Brush Upon which They Live, Mayer, Ariz., September, 1903.

Fig. 2.—The Remains of 13 Head of Cattle in a Space of 30 Feet Along a Small Arroyo near Arivaca, the Result of too Great Distance Between Feed and Water. April, 1903.

TWO PHASES OF THE RANGE QUESTION.

Bul. 67, Bureau of Plant Industry, U S Dept of Agriculture. PLATE VIII.

FIG. 1.—MEXICANS AT SOPORI STACKING "CELITE" (AMARANTHUS PALMERI), WHICH MAKES A LARGE VOLUNTEER CROP AFTER THE WINTER CROP OF GRAIN HAY HAS BEEN REMOVED. OCTOBER, 1903.

FIG. 2.—A MEXICAN PACKING HAY FROM THE MOUNTAINS, SANTA RITA MOUNTAINS, JULY, 1903.

HAYING SCENES IN SOUTHERN ARIZONA.

Fig. 1.—Galleta (Hilaria mutica) in a Swale South of Vail Station, September, 1902. Old Grass, there Being Practically no Growth.

Fig. 2.—A Round-up in the Northern Foothills of the Santa Rita Mountains, April, 1903, when the Large Area was Being Inclosed.

NATIVE PASTURE LANDS IN SOUTHERN ARIZONA.

Fig. 1.—An Ocotilla Forest About 4 Miles Northeast of the Large Inclosure, September, 1902. Practically no Feed Produced Here.

Fig. 2.—The Work of Prairie Dogs Upon the Northern Slope of the White Mountains, July, 1903. Large Areas of Grass Lands are Destroyed by this Animal.

41.

46. The Propagation of Tropical Fruit Trees and Other Plants. 1903. 10 cents.

48. The Apple in Cold Storage. 1903. Price, 15 cents.

Wild Rice: Its Uses and Propagation. 1903. Price, 10 cents.

1903. Price, 5 cents. Part II. The Work of the Community tion Farm at Terrell, Tex. 1904. Price, 5 cents. Part III. Frozen in 1904. 1904. Price, 5 cents.

52. Wither-Tip and Other Diseases of Citrous Trees and Fruits Caused by Colletotrichum Gloeosporioides. 1904. Price, 5 cents.
53. The Date Palm. 1904. Price, 20 cents.
Persian Gulf Dates. 1903. Price, 10 cents.
The Dry Rot of Potatoes Due to Fusarium Oxysporum. 1904. Price, 10

56. Nomenclature of the Apple. [In press.]
57. Methods Used for Controlling and Reclaiming Sand Dunes. 1904. Price, 10 cents.
58. The Vitality and Germination of Seeds. 1904. Price, 10
59. Pasture, Meadow, and Forage Crops in Nebraska. 1904. Price, 10 cents.
A Soft Rot of the Calla Lily. 1904. Price, 10 cents.
The Avocado in Florida: Its Propagation, Cultivation, and

U. S. DEPARTMENT OF AGRICULTURE.

BUREAU OF PLANT INDUSTRY—BULLETIN NO. 68.

B. T. GALLOWAY, Chief of Bureau.

NORTH AMERICAN SPECIES OF AGROSTIS.

BY

A. S. HITCHCOCK,

SYSTEMATIC AGROSTOLOGIST IN CHARGE OF HERBARIUM.

GRASS AND FORAGE PLANT INVESTIGATIONS.

Issued April 29, 1905.

WASHINGTON:
GOVERNMENT PRINTING OFFICE.
1905.

BULLETINS OF THE BUREAU OF PLANT INDUSTRY.

The Bureau of Plant Industry, which was organized July 1, 1901, includes Vegetable Pathological and Physiological Investigations, Botanical Investigations and Experiments, Grass and Forage Plant Investigations, Pomological Investigations, and Experimental Gardens and Grounds, all of which were formerly separate Divisions, and also Seed and Plant Introduction and Distribution, the Arlington Experimental Farm, Tea Culture Investigations, and Domestic Sugar Investigations.

Beginning with the date of organization of the Bureau, the several series of bulletins of the various Divisions were discontinued, and all are now published as one series of the Bureau. A list of the bulletins issued in the present series follows.

Attention is directed to the fact that "the serial, scientific, and technical publications of the United States Department of Agriculture are not for general distribution. All copies not required for official use are by law turned over to the Superintendent of Documents, who is empowered to sell them at cost." All applications for such publications should, therefore, be made to the Superintendent of Documents, Government Printing Office, Washington, D. C.

No. 1. The Relation of Lime and Magnesia to Plant Growth. 1901. Price, 10 cents.
2. Spermatogenesis and Fecundation of Zamia. 1901. Price, 20 cents.
3. Macaroni Wheats. 1901. Price, 20 cents.
4. Range Improvement in Arizona. 1902. Price, 10 cents.
5. Seeds and Plants Imported. Inventory No. 9. 1902. Price, 10 cents.
6. A List of American Varieties of Peppers. 1902. Price, 10 cents.
7. The Algerian Durum Wheats. 1902. Price, 15 cents.
8. A Collection of Fungi Prepared for Distribution. 1902. Price, 10 cents.
9. The North American Species of Spartina. 1902. Price, 10 cents.
10. Records of Seed Distribution and Cooperative Experiments with Grasses and Forage Plants. 1902. Price, 10 cents.
11. Johnson Grass. 1902. Price, 10 cents.
12. Stock Ranges of Northwestern California. 1902. Price, 15 cents.
13. Experiments in Range Improvement in Central Texas. 1902. Price, 10 cents.
14. The Decay of Timber and Methods of Preventing It. 1902. Price, 55 cents.
15. Forage Conditions on the Northern Border of the Great Basin. 1902. Price, 15 cents.
16. A Preliminary Study of the Germination of the Spores of Agaricus Campestris and Other Basidiomycetous Fungi. 1902. Price, 10 cents.
17. Some Diseases of the Cowpea. 1902. Price, 10 cents.
18. Observations on the Mosaic Disease of Tobacco. 1902. Price, 15 cents.
19. Kentucky Bluegrass Seed. 1902. Price, 10 cents.
20. Manufacture of Semolina and Macaroni. 1902. Price, 15 cents.
21. List of American Varieties of Vegetables. 1903. Price, 35 cents.
22. Injurious Effects of Premature Pollination. 1902. Price, 10 cents.
23. Berseem. 1902. Price, 15 cents.
24. Unfermented Grape Must. 1902. Price, 10 cents.
25. Miscellaneous Papers: I. The Seeds of Rescue Grass and Chess. II. Saragolla Wheat. III. Plant Introduction Notes from South Africa. IV. Congressional Seed and Plant Distribution Circulars, 1899-1900. 1903. Price, 15 cents.
26. Spanish Almonds. 1902. Price, 15 cents.
27. Letters on Agriculture in the West Indies, Spain, and the Orient. 1902. Price, 15 cents.
28. The Mango in Porto Rico. 1903. Price, 15 cents.

[Continued on page 3 of cover.]

U. S. DEPARTMENT OF AGRICULTURE.

BUREAU OF PLANT INDUSTRY—BULLETIN NO. 68.

B. T. GALLOWAY, *Chief of Bureau.*

TH AMERICAN SPECIES OF AGROSTIS.

BY

A. S. HITCHCOCK,

SYSTEMATIC AGROSTOLOGIST IN CHARGE OF HERBARIUM.

GRASS AND FORAGE PLANT INVESTIGATIONS.

ISSUED APRIL 29, 1905.

WASHINGTON:
GOVERNMENT PRINTING OFFICE.
1905.

BUREAU OF PLANT INDUSTRY.

B. T. GALLOWAY,
Pathologist and Physiologist, and Chief of Bureau.

VEGETABLE PATHOLOGICAL AND PHYSIOLOGICAL INVESTIGATIONS.
ALBERT F. WOODS, *Pathologist and Physiologist in Charge.*
Acting Chief of Bureau in Absence of Chief.

BOTANICAL INVESTIGATIONS AND EXPERIMENTS.
FREDERICK V. COVILLE, *Botanist in Charge.*

GRASS AND FORAGE PLANT INVESTIGATIONS.
W. J. SPILLMAN, *Agrostologist in Charge.*

POMOLOGICAL INVESTIGATIONS.
G. B. BRACKETT, *Pomologist in Charge.*

SEED AND PLANT INTRODUCTION AND DISTRIBUTION.
A. J. PIETERS, *Botanist in Charge.*

ARLINGTON EXPERIMENTAL FARM.
L. C. CORBETT, *Horticulturist in Charge.*

EXPERIMENTAL GARDENS AND GROUNDS.
E. M. BYRNES, *Superintendent.*

J. E. ROCKWELL, *Editor.*
JAMES E. JONES, *Chief Clerk.*

GRASS AND FORAGE PLANT INVESTIGATIONS.

SCIENTIFIC STAFF.

W. J. SPILLMAN, *Agrostologist.*

A. S. HITCHCOCK, *Systematic Agrostologist in Charge of Herbarium.*
C. V. PIPER, *Agrostologist in Charge of Introduction of Grasses and Forage Plants.*
DAVID GRIFFITHS, *Assistant Agrostologist in Charge of Range Investigations.*
C. R. BALL, *Assistant Agrostologist in Charge of Work on Arlington Farm.*
S. M. TRACY, *Special Agent in Charge of Gulf Coast Investigations.*
D. A. BRODIE, *Assistant Agrostologist in Charge of Cooperative Work.*
P. L. RICKER, *Assistant in Herbarium.*
J. M. WESTGATE, *Assistant in Sand-Binding Work.*
BYRON HUNTER, *Assistant in Charge of Pacific Coast Investigations.*
R. A. OAKLEY, *Assistant in Domestication of Wild Grasses.*
C. W. WARBURTON, *Assistant in Fodder Plant and Millet Investigations.*
M. A. CROSBY, *Assistant in Southern Forage Plant Investigations.*
J. S. COTTON, *Assistant in Range Investigations.*
LESLIE F. PAULL, *Assistant in Investigations at Arlington Farm.*
HAROLD T. NIELSEN, *Assistant in Alfalfa and Clover Investigations.*
AGNES CHASE, *Agrostological Artist.*

LETTER OF TRANSMITTAL.

U. S. DEPARTMENT OF AGRICULTURE,
BUREAU OF PLANT INDUSTRY,
OFFICE OF THE CHIEF,
Washington, D. C., December 15, 1904.

SIR: I have the honor to transmit herewith a paper on "North American Species of Agrostis," and to recommend that it be published as Bulletin No. 68 of the series of this Bureau.

This paper was prepared by Mr. A. S. Hitchcock, Assistant Agrostologist, Grass and Forage Plant Investigations, and has been submitted by the Agrostologist with a view to publication.

The thirty-seven plates and two text figures accompanying the paper are necessary to a proper understanding of the text.

Respectfully,
B. T. GALLOWAY,
Chief of Bureau.

Hon. JAMES WILSON,
Secretary of Agriculture.

PREFACE.

For several years the specimens of grasses in the National Herbarium have been accumulating at a rapid rate. In order to classify our knowledge of this mass of material, bring it up to date, and make it available for other workers along these lines, it has been thought desirable to issue from time to time monographs treating of the larger genera. In conformity with this plan the following monograph of the genus Agrostis has been prepared by Mr. A. S. Hitchcock, of this office. While pursuing his investigations along economic lines, which have taken him into all parts of the United States. Mr. Hitchcock has taken field notes which have aided him in solving the taxonomic problems. Realizing the necessity of consulting the type specimens, many of which are in foreign herbaria, advantage was taken of his presence in Europe while investigating certain economic problems to visit the larger herbaria and take notes upon these original specimens, and thus be the better able to solve the nomenclatorial problems.

The genus Agrostis comprises about 100 species, distributed over both hemispheres, but mostly in temperate regions. Many of them are forage grasses, and a few are cultivated for this purpose. The most important of these is redtop (*A. alba*) or fiorin, as it is called in England. In some parts of this country it is called herd's grass. This is a valuable grass for wet meadows or pastures and also does well when mixed with other grasses upon drier soil. Certain forms or subspecies of this are used as lawn grasses. *A. alba vulgaris*, being small and fine, is especially useful for this purpose. One form of this, known as creeping bent, has decumbent rooting stems, which aid it in forming a thick, firm sod. Creeping bent is especially useful in the vicinity of Washington and similar localities where the conditions are not suited to either Kentucky bluegrass or Bermuda grass, being too far south for the former and too far north for the latter. Another species (*A. canina*) is used for lawns under the name of Rhode Island bent. Much of the seed sold under this name is *A. alba vulgaris*. The awned form of the last is difficult to distinguish from *A. canina* except by the presence of the palet.

Acknowledgment is made to the directors of the various herbaria in this country and Europe for numerous courtesies extended to Mr. Hitchcock, who, in some cases, was allowed to take for deposit in the National Herbarium portions of the type specimens.

W. J. SPILLMAN,
Agrostologist.

OFFICE OF GRASS AND FORAGE PLANT INVESTIGATIONS,
Washington, D. C., November 8, 1904.

CONTENTS.

	Page.
Introduction	11
Taxonomy	11
Nomenclature	12
Plates	14
Specimens listed	14
History of the genus	15
Generic description	20
Key to species	21
Description of species	22
Species excluded	55
Notes on Mexican species	57
Index to species and synonyms	61
Description of plates	66

ILLUSTRATIONS.

PLATES.

	Page.
PLATE I. Fig. 1.—*Agrostis thurberiana* Hitchc. Fig. 2.—*Agrostis æquivalvis* Trin	68
II. *Agrostis alba* L	68
III. Fig. 1.—*Agrostis alba vulgaris* (With.) Thurb. Fig. 2.—*Agrostis alba aristata* Gray	68
IV. *Agrostis alba maritima* (Lam.) Meyer	68
V. Fig. 1.—*Agrostis depressa* Vasey. (Type.) Fig. 2.—*Agrostis stolonifera* L	68
VI. *Agrostis depressa* Vasey. Oregon	68
VII. Fig. 1.—*Agrostis infla ta* Scribn. Fig. 2.—*Agrostis densiflora* Vasey	68
VIII. Fig. 1.—*Agrostis humilis* Vasey. Fig. 2.—*Agrostis exigua* Thurb.	68
IX. Fig. 1.—*Agrostis elliottiana* Schult. Fig. 2.—*Agrostis canina* L.	68
X. Fig. 1.—*Agrostis hallii californica* Vasey. Fig. 2.—*Agrostis hallii* Vasey	68
XI. *Agrostis daryi* Scribn. and spikelets of *Agrostis occidentalis* Scribn. and Merrill	68
XII. *Agrostis pringlei* Scribn	68
XIII. Fig. 1.—*Agrostis pallens* Trin. Fig. 2.—*Agrostis attenuata* Vasey.	68
XIV. Fig. 1.—*Agrostis foliosa* Vasey. Fig. 2.—*Agrostis oregonensis* Vasey	68
XV. *Agrostis pallens foliosa* (Vasey) Hitchc. (Awned form.)	68
XVI. Fig. 1.—*Agrostis pallens foliosa* (Vasey) Hitchc. (Slender form.) Fig. 2.—*Agrostis scouleri* Trin	68
XVII. *Agrostis diegoensis* Vasey	68
XVIII. *Agrostis breviculmis* Hitchc	68
XIX. Fig. 1.—*Agrostis microphylla major* Vasey. Fig. 2.—*Agrostis microphylla* Steud	68
XX. *Agrostis ampla* Hitchc	68
XXI. Fig. 1.—*Agrostis exarata* Trin. (Alaska.) Fig. 2.—*Agrostis asperifolia* Trin	68
XXII. *Agrostis grandis* Trin	68
XXIII. *Agrostis exarata* Trin. (A California form.)	68
XXIV. Fig 1.—*Agrostis rossæ* Vasey. Fig. 2.—*Agrostis varians* Trin.	68
XXV. *Agrostis howellii* Scribn	68
XXVI. Fig. 1.—*Agrostis hiemalis* (Walt.) B. S. P. (Common form.) Fig. 2.—*Agrostis hiemalis.* (Mountain form.)	68
XXVII. Types referred to *Agrostis hiemalis* (Walt.) B. S. P	68
XXVIII. Fig. 1.—*Agrostis geminata* Trin. Fig. 2.—*Agrostis geminata* Trin. (Awnless form.)	68

ILLUSTRATIONS.

	Page.
PLATE XXIX. Fig. 1.—*Agrostis idahoensis* Nash. Fig. 2.—*Agrostis tenuis* Vasey	68
XXX. *Agrostis schiedeana* Trin	68
XXXI. *Agrostis perennans* (Walt.) Tuckerm	68
XXXII. *Agrostis perennans æstivalis* Vasey	68
XXXIII. *Agrostis perennans elata* (Pursh) Hitchc	68
XXXIV. Fig. 1.—*Agrostis borealis* Hartm. (White Mountains.) Fig. 2.—*Agrostis borealis* Hartm. (Labrador.)	68
XXXV. Fig. 1.—*Agrostis mertensii* Trin. Fig. 2.—*Agrostis borealis* Hartm. (Sweden.)	68
XXXVI. Fig. 1.—*Agrostis aenea* Trin. Fig. 2.—*Agrostis aenea* Trin. Fig. 3.—*Agrostis longiligula* Hitchc	68
XXXVII. Mexican species of *Agrostis*	68

TEXT FIGURES.

FIG. 1. *Agrostis rosei* Scribn	30
2. *Agrostis paludosa* Scribn	54

NORTH AMERICAN SPECIES OF AGROSTIS.

INTRODUCTION.

The present paper is an attempt to classify our knowledge concerning one of our most perplexing genera of grasses. It deals chiefly with those species found north of Mexico, but includes a few notes on the Mexican species. The preparatory study naturally divided itself into two rather distinct lines—the classification of the species, or taxonomy, and the history of the species, or nomenclature. Each line presents difficulties, a few of which are discussed below.

TAXONOMY.

The division into species is largely subjective, and different people arrive at different results with the same material. There is a large amount of material in the National Herbarium, and in addition I have had the privilege of examining that in all the larger herbaria in this country and in Europe. The National Herbarium is by far the richest in this respect, disregarding for the moment the historical aspect. It is true that specimens representing the extremes of certain groups seem distinct, but an examination of a large suite of specimens often shows that the extremes are connected by numerous intermediate specimens. Some of these perplexing questions I have been able to answer by field observations. Some of my conclusions based on herbarium specimens may be modified by further study in the field.

On account of the simple structure of the spikelet there are few salient characters upon which to base classification. It is easy to set off the subgenus Podagrostis by the prolongation of the rachilla. The primary divisions of Euagrostis, based upon the presence or absence of a 2-nerved palet, seem also to be definite. I have used vegetative characters sparingly, as there is evidently great variation in the same species. The presence or absence of a creeping rootstock to separate the *pallens* group and the *exarata* group is satisfactory, but unfortunately much herbarium material does not show the complete base of the plant.

Considerable weight has been given by some authors to the awn as a character. After a careful examination of much material I believe it can not be relied on in such large groups as *A. alba*, *A. hiemalis*, and *A. pallens foliosa*. In some other cases it is usually a good character and can be depended upon in connection with other characters. I think the insertion of the awn is of more importance than its length. Likewise the palet varies considerably in the same species or even in the same plant. In some cases I have been forced to fall back on such unsatisfactory characters as the shape of the panicle or the length and arrangement of its branches. Even with the classification as finally presented there are a few intermediate specimens, but such are relatively rare. In any attempt to separate the large groups, such as *A. alba* or *A. hiemalis*, into smaller and definite species I was invariably confronted by such a large number of intermediates that I was convinced that no such separation could be made.

This leads me to speak of a point which I have attempted to emphasize. There are two classes of synonyms—those based upon the same type (typonyms) and those based upon different types but nevertheless considered by the author to be the same species. Authors do not often indicate this difference in their monographs. In bringing together the synonyms I have indicated briefly the basis upon which I have made the union. I hope this will aid others who differ from me in their ideas upon the limitations of the species, and who may wish to readjust the forms, to do so without finding it necessary again to consult the original sources.

NOMENCLATURE.

I have intended to follow the recommendations of the recent Code of Botanical Nomenclature, prepared by the nomenclature commission appointed by the Botanical Club of the American Association for the Advancement of Science (1904). One of the important canons is that so far as possible species should be based upon definite specimens. Much confusion has arisen from the fact that some authors have described what they supposed were new species without becoming acquainted with the species already published. There is some excuse for this, for the descriptions may have been published in inaccessible works and the older types are deposited for the most part in the European herbaria, which few of those describing grasses have taken the trouble to visit.

During my study of the genus Agrostis I have fortunately had the opportunity of visiting all the large European herbaria and have been able to examine nearly all the type specimens of our North American species. The specimens of this genus were examined in the following herbaria:

London.—The herbarium at the British Museum, in the natural history section at South Kensington, in charge of Mr. James Britten. Walter's herbarium is deposited here. The plants are mostly fragmentary and are mounted in a large folio volume. There are a few grasses, but mostly without names, and I found no types of Agrostis (*Cornucopiæ* Walt.). Other collections of importance to American botanists are those of Sloane and Gronovius. The largest collection of plants in the world is the herbarium of the Botanical Garden at Kew. One other important collection is the Linnæan herbarium at the rooms of the Linnæan Society.

Paris.—The most important herbarium is that at the Museum of Natural History in the Jardin des Plantes. In this herbarium are to be found the types of Lamarck. The very important Michaux herbarium is kept separate. There are two other large herbaria at Paris, those of Cosson and Drake, but there are few types from America.

Geneva.—There are four large herbaria here—that of De Candolle, at his residence; the Barbey herbarium, in one of the suburbs; the herbarium of the university, in charge of Professor Chodat, and the herbarium of the botanical garden, in charge of Mr. Briquet.

Vienna.—Here are the herbaria at the Hofmuseum, in charge of Doctor Zahlbruckner, and at the Botanical Garden, in charge of Doctor Wettstein.

St. Pölten.—This town is about one hour's ride west of Vienna. Here is the important herbarium of Doctor Hackel,[a] the eminent agrostologist.

Prague.—The herbarium at the Botanical Garden, where are deposited the types of Presl, is in charge of Doctor Beck.

Berlin.—The herbarium of the Botanical Garden is in charge of Doctor Engler. The Willdenow plants are kept separate.

Copenhagen.—The herbarium at the Botanical Garden is in charge of Doctor Warming. This collection is especially rich in arctic material.

St. Petersburg.—There are two large herbaria here—one at the Botanical Garden and one at the rooms of the Academy of Sciences. At the latter is deposited the Trinius herbarium, which is kept separate. The plants of the Trinius collection are unmounted and are kept in large species covers. The director, Doctor Litwinow, very kindly allowed me to take portions of the specimens for deposit in the National Herbarium when the material was sufficiently abundant.

In examining the types I took photographs and in some cases was allowed to take a few spikelets; but in this genus the spikelets are likely to be of less importance than the photographs showing habit and the notes concerning critical characters.

The types in America are more easily accessible. A large number are in the National Herbarium, including those of Vasey and of Scribner. The herbarium of the Philadelphia Academy of Natural

---

[a] Doctor Hackel has since removed to Graz.

Sciences contains the types of Muhlenberg and the types or duplicate types of Nuttall. The types of Elliott are at the College of Charleston. I have not seen these, but they were examined and reported upon by Mr. Elmer D. Merrill (U. S. Department of Agriculture, Division of Agrostology, Circular No. 29, 1901). A few types of Agrostis are in the Torrey herbarium at the New York Botanical Garden and in the Gray herbarium at Cambridge.

In discussing the types under each species I have indicated where the type specimen is to be found, and in the few cases where I have not seen this the fact is so stated.

As previously stated, I have followed the rules as published in the recent Code of Botanical Nomenclature. In applying these to the selection of type specimens I have given my reasons in each case. By adhering to these rules I have been able to present the historical data in a more satisfactory manner than by assuming the idea of a species as indicated by evolutionary development. It not infrequently happens that this idea gradually changes because authors do not have a definite type in mind. The result is often similar to that reached by a child in using a copy book, where he each time looks at the last line written instead of at the original. Again, there has been confusion because an author has wished to separate a composite group into what he thinks are species. He retains the old name for one portion and gives new names to the other portions. If he has not consulted the type he may have applied the original name to the wrong division, as the original description may not have mentioned the characters which he uses in making the separation.

PLATES.

So far as possible the drawings were made from type specimens. The artist has faithfully reproduced all the technical details of the spikelets as shown in the particular specimen at hand. But it has not been practicable to show the variation in the characters in different specimens, although it is largely upon these variations that I have based my judgment of specific differences.

SPECIMENS LISTED.

In general the specimens listed are confined to those deposited in the National Herbarium. In a few cases, where the species is rare, or on account of some peculiarity, specimens from other herbaria are mentioned. It was not thought advisable to give a complete list of specimens, but only enough to illustrate the distribution. In the case of species of limited distribution a proportionately larger number, or perhaps all, are given.

HISTORY OF THE GENUS.

The genus was established by Linnæus in the first edition of the Genera Plantarum (p. 19, No. 54, 1737), though the name was mentioned without description a little earlier (Syst. Nat., ed. 1, 1735). The description—" Cal. gluma uniflora, bivalvis, acuminata. Cor. bivalvis, acuminata, vix longitudine calycis, altera majore aristata "—is retained through all the editions of this work, except that in the sixth edition " aristata " is omitted, apparently inadvertently. It is based on " Scheuch., 3: 11.9." This citation, which follows the name in the first edition, is dropped in the fifth edition (No. 74, 1754).

Scheuchzer's Plate III, figure 11, cited by Linnæus, includes three figures, *A*, *B*, and *C*. The first two, *A* and *B*, refer to the description given on page 146, and are two figures of the same plant, *A* being a cluster of four spikelets, and *B* a single flower. The plant here described is *Stipa calamagrostis* Wahl. Plate III, figure 11, *C*, referred to on page 148 of the publication mentioned, is *Milium lendigerum* L. (*Gastridium australe* Beauv.). The second citation given by Linnæus from Scheuchzer, Plate III, figure 9, includes five figures, *A*, *B*, *C*, *D*, and *E*. The first two, *A* and *B*, accompany the description on page 139, "Arista articulata et recurva prodeunte ex alterutrius glumæ dorso, prope ejusdem basin." There are two forms described under this according to Trinius (Clavis Agrostographiæ); the first, of which the diagnosis is " Gramen parvum, paniculatum, alpinum, panicula spadicea, aristatum," is *Agrostis alpina* Scop., and the second, " Gramen paniculatum, capillaceo folio, locustis parvis spadiceo-fuscis, aristatis," is *A. rupestris* All. Figure *B*, which represents a single flower, shows a palet, which neither of the above-mentioned species possesses, but too much weight must not be attached to this discrepancy, as in many cases the presence of a palet seems to have been assumed. The third figure, *C*, is, according to Trinius, *A. canina*, while *D* and *E* refer to *A. vineale* With.

Linnæus seems to have included these various forms in one genus because they all had small one-flowered spikelets with a projecting awn. The statement " cor. bivalvis " applies only to the first-cited plants, *Stipa calamagrostis* and *Gastridium*, yet the other figures show a palet, and Linnæus probably examined the plates rather than the plants.

Although Linnæus's idea of the genus changes in the Species Plantarum, the text of Agrostis in the later editions of the Genera remains the same, although the fifth and sixth are published after 1753.

In the Species Plantarum (1: 61, 1753), Linnæus describes the following species:

Aristatæ.

1. *A. spica-venti=Apera spica-venti* Beauv.
2. *A. miliacea=Oryzopsis miliacea* Richt.
3. *A. arundinacea=Deyeuxia sylvatica* Kunth.
4. *A. rubra.* [Not identifiable. See note under *A. borealis.*]
5. *A. canina.*
6. *A. paradoxa=Oryzopsis paradoxa* Nutt.

Muticæ.

7. *A. stolonifera.*
8. *A. capillaris.*
9. *A. alba.*
10. *A. minima=Mibora verna* Beauv.
11. *A. virginica=Sporobolus virginicus* Kunth.
12. *A. indica=Sporobolus indicus* R. Br.

In the tenth edition of the Systema (2: 872, 1759) the following are added:

A. *A. sepium.* "A. petalo exteriore arista terminali recta stricta longitudine ipsius floris, panicula patula." This species was not taken up in later works and its identity is uncertain. No locality or references are given.
B. *A. interrupta=Apera interrupta* Beauv.
C. *A. calamagrostis=Stipa calamagrostis* Wahl.
D. *A. cruciata=Chloris cruciata* Sw.
E. *A. radiata=Chloris radiata* Sw.

A. paradoxa is transferred to Milium.

In the second edition of the Species (1: 91, 1762) no change is made except to omit *A. sepium* and (in the Appendix, 2: 1665, 1763) to add *A. sylvatica* (= *A. alba* L. teratological form).

Six more species are added in the Mantissa Plantarum (1: 30, 1767):

A. bromoides=Stipa aristella L.
A. australis=Gastridium australe Beauv.
A. serotina=Diplachne serotina Link. Transferred from Festuca Sp. II, although the spikelets are described as 4-flowered.
A. matrella=Zoysia pungens Willd.
A. pumila=A. alba L.
A. mexicana=Muhlenbergia mexicana Trin.

All the species mentioned appear in the twelfth edition of the Systema Naturæ (1767) except *A. sepium* and *A. matrella.*

Historically it is rather difficult to establish the type of the genus. Of the twenty-four species described by Linnæus only seven would be referred to the genus Agrostis as now limited. The first figure cited in the original description of the genus refers to *Stipa calamagrostis*, which was not included in those described in the first edition of the Species Plantarum, but was added later. In the Species Plantarum there is nothing to indicate what Linnæus considers the type of his genus.

Later writers have segregated various species, and the name Agrostis has been applied to what was left.

Adanson (Pl. Fam., 1763) changes the name. His Agrostis based upon Scheuch. 57 is Saccharum, while he gives a new name, Vilfa, to Linnæus's Agrostis, founded on Bauhin's "Gramen caninum supinum minus," which is *A. stolonifera* L. (i. e., *A. alba* L.) according to Trinius. Adanson also takes out Linnæus's first species of Agrostis as the type of Apera; the tenth species, as type of Mibora.

Walter (Fl. Carol., 1788) describes three new species under the genus Cornucopiæ, the chief generic character being the absence of the palet, "cor. 1-valvis." These are *C. hiemalis*, *C. perennans*, and *C. altissima*. He retains the name Agrostis for *A. indica* and *A. virginica*.

Michaux (Fl. Bor. Am., 1803) gives the name Trichodium to Walter's genus Cornucopiæ and describes the first two species under the new names *T. laxiflorum* and *T. decumbens*. He omits the third. He retains Agrostis (" cal. 2-valvis, gluma major "), describing:

A. indica L.=*Sporobolus indica* R. Br.
A. juncea=*Sporobolus junceus* Kunth.
A. dispar=*A. alba* L.
A. aspera=*Sporobolus asper* Kunth.
A. lateriflora=*Muhlenbergia mexicana* Trin.
A. racemosa=*M. racemosa* B. S. P.

The seventh edition of the Genera Plantarum, by Reichard, 1778, has " Cal. gluma uniflora, bivalvis acuminata, corolla paulo minor," which is followed in the eighth edition (Schreber, 1789) and ninth edition (Haenke, 1791). In the tenth edition (Sprengel, 1830) we find the characters changed to agree more nearly with the modern Agrostis: " Cal. bivalvis, acutiusculus, muticus, corollam æquans vel superans. Cor. bivalvis, callo sæpe insidens aut basi pilis brevibus suffulta; valva altera sæpe obsoleta aut nulla, altera arista vel mutica."

Jussieu (Gen. Pl., 1789) retains the old description, " Calix [corolla of Linnæus] 2-valvis gluma major."

Without taking up each authority we may glance at a few of the handbooks to note the tendency to change into what might be called the modern idea of the genus.

Gmelin (Syst. Veg., 1: 168, 1796) describes forty-one species under the limitation " Cal. 2-valvis, 1-florus, corolla paulo minor."

Willdenow (Spec. Pl., 1: 361, 1797) describes forty-six species. The genus characters are as given by Gmelin; that is, that the empty glumes are two, and a little shorter than the single flowering glume, which applies better to Sporobolus.

Persoon (Syn. Pl., 1805) agrees with his predecessors, but says "cor. 2-valvis," omitting the statement that the "calyx" is shorter than the "corolla."

Willdenow (Enum. Pl., 1809) keeps Agrostis and Trichodium separate. Agrostis is described as "Cor. 2-valvis, calyce plerumque minor, valvula major aristata seu mutica."

Brown (Prod., 1810) separates the species having the flowering glume awnless and longer than the empty glumes under a new name, Sporobolus, describing three species, one of which is *Agrostis indica* L., but he includes *A. virginica* L. in Agrostis. The distinction is not clear and Brown states that the genus Agrostis is artificial.

Beauvois (Agrost., 1812) describes Agraulus with "Glumæ palea longiores. Palea apici emarginata, infra medium aristata" to include "*Agrostis canina* L. and *A. alpina* L.," etc.; Trichodium with one palet, which is awnless; Vilfa, following Adanson in applying the name to species with two palets shorter than the glumes. His genus Agrostis is founded on *A. rubra* L., of which he gives a plate, showing a small palet with four teeth. This is the chief difference between Agrostis and Agraulus. Beauvois intends to include in Agrostis species with two palets and an awn. He recognizes Sporobolus R. Br., Muhlenbergia Schreb., and Apera Adans.

Pursh (Flora, 1814) describes fifteen American species, including species now referred to Sporobolus and Muhlenbergia, but under the generic diagnosis "Cal. 2-valvis; valvis acutis corolla brevioribus. Cor. 2-valvis." Although the genus is described as having the calyx shorter than the corolla, certain species (e. g., *A. stricta* and *A. vulgaris*) are described as having the corolla (flower) shorter than the calyx. The same is true of Muhlenberg (Gram., 1817) and of Elliott (Sketch, 1816).

Koeler (Gram., 1802) gives a consistent description of the genus, inasmuch as he states that the corolla may be smaller, equal to, or larger than the calyx, and that the awn when present may be terminal, dorsal or attached near the base. Nuttall (Gen., 1818) also makes the generic description agree with the species included.

Roemer and Schultes (Syst. Veg., 1817) describe ninety-seven species of Agrostis, but they unite several groups or sections under the generic characters: Corolla larger or smaller than the calyx, stipitate at base with one or two fascicles of hairs, larger valve awned or awnless. The sections are Vilfa (of Beauvois, which is our Agrostis, 62 species), Achnatherum (including *A. calamagrostis*, *A. sobolifera* Muhl., etc., 5 species), Agrostis (which includes *A. tolucensis* and *A. virescens* H. B. K., 8 species), Sporobolus (including *S. indica;* but some of our species are included under section Vilfa), Apera, and Cinna. Besides these there are described sixteen species of Trichodium, which includes the species with 1-valved corolla, either awned (Agraulus Beauv.) or awnless (Trichodium).

Sprengel (Syst. Veg., 1825) describes eighty-five species. He arranges them thus:

* Corollæ muticæ: valva calycis inferior minor: Vilfa Adans. Includes *A. alba* and its allies, *Sporobolus indica*, etc.
** Valva corollæ altera minutissima vel obsoleta, Trichodium Mx.
  † Corollæ aristatæ. *A. canina*, etc.
  †† Corollæ muticæ. *A. laxa* Schreb. (*A. hiemalis* Walt.) and its allies.
*** Valvæ corollinæ subæquales, altera aristata.
  † Sine rudamento alterius floris. Calycis corolla plerumque breviores.
  †† Cum rudimento cylindrico alterius corollæ. Apera Beauv.

Kunth (Enum. Pl., 1833) describes ninety species of Agrostis. In this work the genus is limited about as at present, so far as his "Species genuinæ" are concerned. He includes under "Species anomalæ" *Apera spica-venti* and *A. interrupta*, and under "Species dubiæ" a number of diverse forms. Sporobolus, Cinna, Muhlenbergia, etc., are kept separate.

Trinius (Fund., 1820) lays the foundation for the modern conception of the genera of grasses. Agrostis is characterized as having the calyx longer than the corolla, the latter 2-valved, the lower valve awned or awnless, the upper often small or obsolete. He recognizes three divisions:

(*a*) Upper valve distinct. Agrostis, *A. vulgaris*, etc.
(*b*) Upper valve minute or obsolete, awnless. Trichodium, *A. elegans*, etc.
(*c*) As above, but awned. Agraulus, *A. canina*, etc.

Muhlenbergia, Cinna, and Vilfa are recognized, the last being the same as Sporobolus R. Br. Vilfa Adans. is based on *A. stolonifera* L., but Trinius uses this name for Sporobolus R. Br.

A perusal of the history of the genus Agrostis, as accepted by modern authors since Trinius, shows that the name has not been applied in accordance with any rule.

If the name goes with the first plate cited when the genus was established in 1737, it should be applied to what is now *Stipa calamagrostis*, which would become the type.

If we start with the first edition of the Species Plantarum and take the first species described, *Apera spica-venti* Beauv. becomes the type.

If we take the first of the species described in the Species Plantarum which has not been removed as the type of a monotypic genus, *Oryzopsis miliacea* Richt. becomes the type of Agrostis.

If we take the first identifiable species of Linnæus which has not been segregated under some other genus, *A. canina* becomes the type.

If we accept the genus as indicated in the Species Plantarum and follow its subdivision we find that Adanson split up the genus, applying the name Vilfa to our Agrostis and Agrostis to Saccharum; then Agrostis would disappear, as Saccharum is a good genus.

Walter appears to be the first author who separates the species with no palet, wrongly referring them to Cornucopiæ. Michaux gives a new name, Trichodium, to this group, retaining the name Agrostis for the species with a palet. This segregation would make *A. stolonifera* the first Linnæan species to fall in Agrostis.

It would seem best to accept the evolution that has actually taken place and follow Trinius and others in applying the name, as has been done by all modern authors, including Bentham and Hooker (Gen. Pl., 1883) and Engler and Prantl (Pflanzenfamilien).

Following the provisions of canon 15, section *f*, of the recent Code of Botanical Nomenclature (Bul. Torr. Bot. Club **31**: 249), I have selected as the type species of the genus Agrostis, *A. alba* L.

GENERIC DESCRIPTIO

Spikelets small, 1-flowered, hermaphrodite, arranged in open or contracted panicles; empty glumes 2, equal or somewhat unequal, persistent (or sometimes with age deciduous from the pedicel), usually acute, sometimes acuminate or awn-pointed, carinate, usually scabrous on the keel and sometimes on the back; flower articulated above the empty glumes, the rachilla not produced except in section Podagrostis; flowering glume shorter than the empty glumes or sometimes nearly as long, thinner in texture than these, awnless, or dorsally awned below the apex, often provided with a minute tuft of hairs at base; palet two-keeled, smaller than the flowering glume, rarely of the same length, often a minute nerveless scale, or obsolete; stamens usually 3; styles distinct, stigmas plumose. Annual or perennial grasses, with culms glabrous, low or tall, erect, geniculate or creeping at base, cespitose or provided with running rootstocks; leaf blades flat or involute, usually scabrous; sheaths usually striate, often scabrous; panicle terminal, rarely also from axillary branches, open and diffuse, with capillary branches, or more or less contracted, or even spikelike.

Sporobolus differs in having the flowering glume and palet of a firmer texture and longer than the empty glumes.

Muhlenbergia differs in having the flowering glume as long or longer than the empty glumes and the awn when present terminal.

Calamagrostis differs in having a conspicuous tuft of hairs at base of flowering glume, and in having larger spikelets and stouter culms. The difference between these two genera is, however, quite artificial. In *Agrostis hallii* the hairs at the base of the flower are as long as in Calamagrostis, but the culms are not so stout.

Cinna differs in its 1-nerved palet and single stamen.

Apera differs in having the rachilla produced, the palet as long as flowering glume, the latter awned just below the apex.

Agrostis, section Podagrostis, connects those two genera, differing only in the absence of the awn and somewhat in habit.

KEY TO SPECIES.

Rachilla prolonged behind the palet.
    Spikelets 3 mm. long, usually purple .... 1. *æquivalvis*.
    Spikelets 2 mm. long, usually pale .... 2. *thurberiana*.
Rachilla not prolonged behind the palet.
    Palet evident, 2-nerved.
        Palet as much as one-half the length of the flowering glume.
            Panicle contracted or open, but not diffuse.
                Panicle contracted and lobed or verticillate; empty glumes equal, 2 mm. long, scabrous on keel and back; flowering glume one-half as long. 3. *stolonifera*.
                Panicle more open; empty glumes scabrous on keel, but smooth on back; flowering glume longer than in the preceding.
                    Plants erect or decumbent, but not provided with extensive stolons.
                        Plants of wide range; usually over 30 cm. in height .... 4. *alba*.
                        Plants of alpine region; dwarf .... 5. *humilis*.
                    Plants provided with extensive creeping stolons, the leaves on these being short and spreading. Western .... 6. *depressa*.
            Panicle diffuse; plant low .... 7. *rosei*.
        Palet about one-fourth the length of the flowering glume; panicle contracted .... 8. *glomerata*.
    Palet wanting, or a small nerveless scale.
        Flowering glume provided with a very slender awn about 5 mm. long. Delicate annuals.
            Awn straight. California .... 9. *exigua*.
            Awn flexuous. Southeastern States .... 10. *elliottiana*.
        Flowering glume awnless, or short-awned. Perennials.
            Plants spreading by rhizomes.
                Tuft of hairs at base of flowering glume 1-2 mm. long .... 11. *hallii*.
                Tuft of hairs minute or wanting .... 12. *pallens*.
            Plants tufted but not producing rhizomes.
                Panicle narrow, usually a part of the lower branches spikelet bearing from the base.
                    Panicle strict, branches very short and appressed. A low cespitose plant. California .... 13. *breviculmis*.
                    Panicle narrow but not strict. Some of the lower branches 2 cm. or more long. Group of *A. exarata*. Western.
                      Flowering glume with an exserted awn.
                        Outer glumes awn-pointed; panicle narrow and rather compact. 14. *microphylla*.
                        Outer glumes acute but not awn-pointed; panicle more open and verticillate .... 15. *ampla*.
                    Flowering glume awnless, or the awn included.
                        Panicle 5-30 cm. long; a taller plant of low altitudes .. 16. *exarata*.
                        Panicle short, 3-6 cm. long; a dwarf plant of high altitudes. 17. *rossæ*.

Rachilla not prolonged behind the palet.
  Palet wanting, or a small nerveless scale.
    Flowering glume awnless, or short-awned. Perennials.
      Plants tufted but not producing rhizomes.
        Panicle open, sometimes diffusely spreading; usually no short branches in lower whorls of branches.
          Awn of flowering glume attached near the base........... 18. *howellii*.
          Awn, if present, attached at or above the middle of the glume.
            Panicle very diffuse, with very scabrous capillary primary branches, these branching above the middle; spikelets clustered toward the ends of the smaller branches. In arctic and Alpine forms these characters are less plainly shown. In the subspecies *geminata* the branches are shorter and divaricate................... 19. *hiemalis*.
            Panicle open but not conspicuously diffuse; branches more or less capillary.
              Flowering glume awnless. Occasional specimens are awned.
                Plant delicate, 10–30 cm. high, growing at high altitudes; spikelets small, about 1.5 mm........................ 20. *idahoensis*.
                Plants tall and often stout, mostly over 50 cm. high. In some forms of *A. perennans* the culms are lax and decumbent.
                  Panicle pyramidal, dark purple. Oregon and Washington. 21. *oregonensis*.
                  Panicle elongated, oblong; lower branches several in distinct verticils, ascending. Pacific slope........... 22. *schiedeana*.
                  Panicle pyramidal to elongated oblong, pale; branches more flexuous or drooping, not usually stiffly ascending. Eastern States..............:.......................... 23. *perennans*.
              Flowering glume awned. Awnless individuals occur.
                Spikelets 2 mm. long. Introduced.................... 24. *canina*.
                Spikelets 2.5–3 mm. long.
                  Awn straight, included or slightly exserted .... 25. *melaleuca*.
                  Awn exserted, geniculate.
                    Branches of panicle nearly smooth; ligule 2–3 mm. long. 26. *borealis*.
                    Branches of panicle very scabrous; ligule usually 5–8 mm. long... 27. *longiligula*.

DESCRIPTION OF SPECIES.

Section 1. **Podagrostis** *Griseb. in Ledeb. Fl. Ross.* 4: *436. 1853. Flowering glume equaling the empty glumes; palet nearly as long as the flowering glume; rachilla prolonged behind the palet, naked or minutely pubescent.*

This section differs from Agrostis proper in having the rachilla prolonged, but agrees in habit. It differs from Calamagrostis in the absence of the callus hairs and in habit.

1. A. æquivalvis (Trin.) Trin.

A. canina æquivalvis Trin., in Bong. Mem. Acad. Sci. St. Petersb., Ser. VI, **1**: 171. 1832.[a] Veg. Sitcha. This is generally credited to Bongard, but in the preface to this article Bongard states that the grasses were worked up by Trinius, and the latter cites himself as authority for this variety in his Agrostidea. For the original description see *A. aenea* Trin. under *A. melaleuca*

---

[a] According to Mr. M. L. Fernald, who has seen the original signature cover of this publication at Kew, the date is given thereon as August, 1832.—P. L. RICKER.

Trinius suspects this variety to be a good species and points out the differences between this and *canina.*
The type specimen was collected at Sitka, Alaska, by Mertens in 1829, and is deposited in the herbarium of the Academy of Sciences at St. Petersburg. A part of the type specimen is in the National Herbarium. (Pl. I, fig. 2, *A.*)
In the original description no type is indicated, but the description is included in an article upon plants from Sitka, and the statement is made in the introduction that the plants were collected by Doctor Mertens. When the variety is raised to specific rank the author gives two localities—Sitka and Unalaska. The specimen in the National Herbarium is a single culm 30 cm. high, with a short decumbent base; culm leaves 2; panicle 4 cm. long, with the lower branch 2.5 cm. long, the branches bearing 2-3 spikelets near the end.

A. æquivalvis Trin. Mem. Acad. St. Petersb., Ser. VI. 6^2 : 362 (Agrostidea, II: 116). 1841. " Sitcha, Unalaschka, inter muscos (Mertens fil.)."

Deyeuxia æquivalvis Vasey, Contr. U. S. Natl. Herb. 8: 77, 1892. This binomial is generally credited to Bentham (Journ. Linn. Soc. 19: 91. 1881), but Bentham does not actually make this combination. He says, under the genus Deyeuxia: " In Achæta Fourn., two Mexican species, the awn appears to be deficient, but all the other characters are those of the typical Deyeuxiæ with a hairy rachilla to which I would also refer the *Agrostis æquivalvis* Trin., forming Grisebach's section Podagrostis."

Culms tufted, slender, smooth, 30-60 cm. high. Blades narrow and upright, 1 mm. wide, somewhat scabrous, those of the stem only 1 or 2 and appressed, usually 4-6 cm. long; ligule semicircular, 2 mm. long. Panicle open, 5-15 cm. long; branches slender, somewhat scabrous. Spikelets about 3 mm. long, usually purplish; empty glumes equal, sharp pointed, minutely scabrous below tip of keel; flowering glume obtuse; about as long as empty glumes; palet nearly as long as glume; rudiment minutely pubescent, one-fifth to one-half the length of the flower. (Pl. I, fig. 2.)

DISTRIBUTION: Alaska to Labrador and the mountains of Oregon.

ALASKA: Sitka, *Mertens* (type); *Wright* 1579; *Piper* 4620; Unalaska, *Kellogg* 119; Helm Bay, *Flett* 2015; Yes Bay, *Howell* 1712, *Gorman* 92; Latouche, *Piper* 4621. VANCOUVER ISLAND: *Rosendahl and Brand* 121. OREGON: Paulina Lake, Crook County, *Leiberg* 588 (this agrees with the others, but the spikelets are only 2.5 mm. long). LABRADOR: *Allen* 22½ (in part).

2. **A. thurberiana**, sp. nov.

Culms tufted, slender, 20-40 cm. high, somewhat decumbent at base. Basal leaves rather numerous, the blades lax, light green, slightly scabrous, about 10 cm. long and 2 mm. wide; culm leaves 2 or 3, the uppermost about the middle of the culm, the blade only about 5 cm. long; ligule semicircular, 6 mm. long. Panicle narrow and lax, more or less drooping, 5-8 cm. long; branches few, slightly scabrous, 2-4 in each whorl, flower-bearing from about the middle. Spikelets green or pale, rarely purple, 2 mm. long; empty glumes equal, acute but scarcely pointed; flowering glume nearly as long as the empty glumes, obtuse, faintly 5-nerved; palet about 1.3 mm. long; rudiment usually about ½ mm. long, minutely hairy; callus very minutely hairy.

The above description is based upon the type specimen. In other specimens the width of the leaves may be 2-4 mm. and the panicle may be as much as 15 cm. long; the palet varies from ½ to ⅔ the length of the flowering glume.

A. thurberiana differs from *A. æquivalvis* Trin. in the wider, more numerous, and more lax leaves, smaller spikelets, shorter palet and pedicel, and the usually narrower and less spreading panicle.

The species was first mentioned as a nomen nudum in a list of grasses by Doctor Bolander: "*Agrostis Hillebrandii* (Thurb.), Sierras (Doctor Hillebrand). Little known as yet."—Bolander, Trans. Calif. State Agric. Soc. for 1864 and 1865 (1866). The name also appears in the Index Kewensis as a synonym of *A. æquivalvis* Trin. As the name was first mentioned as a nomen nudum and later as a synonym it seems advisable to publish the species under a different name.

The type specimen of *A. thurberiana* was collected by W. N. Suksdorf (No. 1021) in wet places on mountains, Skamania County, Wash., August 28, 1890. (Pl. I, fig. 1.)

DISTRIBUTION: British Columbia and Montana to California and Utah.

BRITISH COLUMBIA: Chilliwack Valley, *Macoun* 26042, 26043; Asulkan Glacier, Selkirk Mountains, *Macoun* 3. WASHINGTON: Mount Adams, *Suksdorf* 24, 194; Nason Creek, *Sandberg and Leiberg* 676. OREGON: Mount Hood, *Hall* 618; Eagle Creek, *Cusick* 1069. MONTANA: Gallatin River, *Tweedy* 1019. WYOMING: Teton Forest Reserve, *Tweedy* 30. UTAH: Alta, Wasatch Mountains, *Jones* 1275; Salt Lake City, *Jones* 1008. CALIFORNIA: Pine Creek, *Davy;* Lake Chiquita, *Congdon* 16; (without locality) *Bolander* 6102; Lassen County, *Baker and Nutting;* Fresno County, *Hall and Chandler* 604; Blue Canyon, *Greene* in 1895.

Section 2. **Euagrostis**. *Rachilla not prolonged.*

**Palet evident, 2-nerved.*

†*Palet as much as one-half the length of the flowering glume. Species group of A. alba.*

3. A. stolonifera L.

A. stolonifera L., Sp. Pl. 62. 1753. It is best to consider as the type of this species the specimen in the Linnæan herbarium, although the name has been applied erroneously to a stoloniferous form of *A. alba* L. The Linnæan specimen is marked by Linnæus *A. stolonifera*, but is what has been called *A. verticillata* Vill. by later authors. For detailed notes upon this and reasons for considering the Linnæan specimen as the type, see Botanical Gazette **38**: 139, 1904. In this article I stated that the Linnæan specimen was from "Attica." Mr. Theo. Holm has called my attention to a statement by Hartmann (K. V. Ak. Hand., 1849), who examined this specimen and says that the characters which I interpreted as *Atica* are △ *tica*, the meaning of which he is unable to guess.

A. verticillata Vill., Prosp. 16. 1779. "Agrostis panicula subsecunda subspicata, verticillis in penicillum confertioribus. Flores virides, numerosissimi; corolla minim." Mr. C. de Candolle has kindly sent me the transcript of the description. I do not know where the type of this is located.

A. decumbens Muhl., in Ell. Sk. Bot. S. C. and Ga., **1**: 136. 1816.[a] "Grows around Charleston; rare, perhaps imported. I should have referred it to *A. dispar* Michx., but its size and almost equal valves of the corolla forbade." Mr. E. D. Merrill has examined the type specimen in Elliott's herbarium, and states that it is *A. verticillata* Vill. (U. S. Dept. Agr., Div. Agros., Circ. **29**: 10, 1901). *A. decumbens* Muhl., as described in his Catalogue, is probably a form of *A. alba*.

A. leptos Steud., Syn. Pl. Glum. **1**: 169, 1854. I have not seen this, but it doubtless must be referred to *A. stolonifera* L. "Louisiana" is given as the type locality.

A. aquatica Buckley, Proc. Acad. Nat. Sci., Phila., **1862**: 90. 1863. There appears to be no type of this in existence. There is none at the Philadelphia Academy of Natural Sciences, and Doctor Gray, in his review of Buckley's plants, states that no specimen of this was communicated to him (l. c., 332). The description applies to *A. stolonifera* L. "On small floating islands in the mill pond or large spring at San Saba, the capital of San Saba County" (Texas).

In addition to the synonyms given above there are several in the literature of European plants, such as *A. stolonifera dulcis* Pers., Syn. **1**: 75, 1805; *Vilfa dulcis* Beauv., Agrost. 16, 1812; *A. dulcis* Sibthorp in Pers., l. c., and Kunth Enum. **1**: 218, 1833; *A. alba verticillata* Pers., l. c.

---

[a] Date should be December, 1816, instead of 1817, fide Barnhart in Bul. Torr. Bot. Club, **28**: 687, 1901.—P. L. RICKER.

Culms usually decumbent at base, 20-80 cm. high, sometimes with long creeping and rooting stolons. Leaves numerous, light or glaucous green; blades lanceolate, rather short and narrowed from below the middle to the acute apex, usually 3-4 mm. wide and 5-10 cm. long. Panicle contracted, lobed or verticillate, especially at base, 3-10 cm. long, light green or rarely purplish; branches flower-bearing from base. Empty glumes equal, obtuse, or barely acute, scabrous on back and keel, 2 mm. long; flowering glume half as long, awnless, truncate and toothed at apex; palet nearly as long as its glume. (Pl. V, fig. 2.)

DISTRIBUTION: California to Texas, Mexico, and the warmer parts of South America; also in the warmer regions of the Old World, from France to India.

It grows in moist places, especially along irrigating ditches. In the United States this appears like an introduced species either from the Old World or from farther south. We have specimens from Portland, Oreg. (*Leckenby* 10), Walla Walla, Wash. (*Leckenby* 32, probably cultivated), and the species occasionally occurs in the Southeastern States. The following specimens will illustrate the range in the Southwestern States and Mexico where the species is common.

CALIFORNIA: San Bernardino Mountains, *Parish* 3284; Monterey, *Dary* 7516. ARIZONA: Grand Canyon, *Leiberg* 5947; Tucson, *Toumey* 771. NEW MEXICO: *Wright* 1984; Roswell, *Earle* 500; Rio Arriba County, *Heller* 3762. UTAH: Rockville, *Jones* 5224. TEXAS: *Lindheimer* 558; Austin, *Hall* 764. MEXICO: Valley of Mexico, *Pringle* 9596; Guadalajara, *Palmer* 230; Mexico, *Bourgeau* 224; Oaxaca, *Nelson* 1305.

We have specimens also from Guatemala (*J. D. Smith* 2702) and Bolivia (*Rusby* 40), and the species is probably common in Central America and the warmer parts of South America.

4. A. alba L.

A. alba L., Sp. Pl. 63. 1753. Placed under the section *Muticœ*. "Agrostis panicula laxa, calycibus muticis æqualibus. Roy. Lugdb. 59. Habitat in Europæ nemoribus." There are five sheets in the Linnæan herbarium marked *A. alba*, but I have considered as the type the plant thus labeled in the handwriting of Linnæus. It has a long ligule and a rather large and compact panicle.

A. dispar Michx., Fl. Bor. Am. 1: 52. 1803. "In Carolina inferiore." The type is in Michaux's herbarium deposited in the Museum of Natural History at Paris. It is the ordinary form of *A. alba*. This has often been referred to *A. altissima*.

Vilfa dispar Beauv., Agrost. 16. 1812. Transfers *A. dispar* Michx.

A. vulgaris alba Vasey, Descr. Cat. 47. 1885.

The synonymy given in European literature is very extensive. I have included here only the names by which the species has been commonly known in this country.

Culms erect or with a decumbent or rooting base, 20-150 cm. high, arising from a tufted clump of roots and sending out rootstocks or stolon-like stems, which arise into culms. Leaf blades numerous, in some forms stiff and upright, in others lax and partially twisted, scabrous, and sometimes glaucous, varying in width according to the size and vigor of the plant; ligule varying from long and acute (5 mm.) to short and obtuse. Panicle upright, 5-30 cm. long, with numerous, usually loose and spreading (not diffuse) but sometimes contracted, branches, at least the lower in whorls. Spikelets 2-3 mm. long, pale or purple; empty glumes equal, acute, somewhat scabrous on the upper part of keel, but not conspicuously so; flowering glume a little shorter than the empty glumes, sometimes only $\frac{2}{3}$ as long, obtuse, rarely awned on the back; palet $\frac{1}{2}$-$\frac{2}{3}$ as long as the flowering glume. (Pl. II.)

DISTRIBUTION: Native across the northern part of the continent and southward in the mountains. Extensively cultivated as a meadow grass under the name of redtop, and a more stoloniferous form as a lawn grass under the name of creeping bent. It has escaped from cultivation and is well established throughout the United States, though rare in the extreme South. The stoloniferous form used for lawns has been generally known as var. *stolonifera*, but it is not *A. stolonifera* L. which is *A. verticillata* Vill.

A. alba vulgaris (With.) Thurb.

A. vulgaris With., Bot. Arr. Br. Pl., Ed. III, 132. 1796. This form was first distinguished by Smith (Icones Pl., 54. 1789), but no name was given. Withering calls attention to this and supplies a name. The latter at the end of his description states: "*A. capillaris* Huds. and Bot. Arr., Ed. II. Very common, but chiefly grows on poor dry and sandy land." There is no type of *A. vulgaris* in existence.

A. alba vulgaris Thurb., in Gray Man., Ed. VI, 647. 1890. " Nat. from Europe and cultivated, also perhaps indigenous." Reduces *A. vulgaris* to a variety of *A. alba* and gives a description.

A. alba minor Vasey, Contrib. U. S. Natl. Herb., 3: 78. 1892. No type is indicated nor is there a specimen in the National Herbarium which is thus marked by Doctor Vasey. There is, however, a specimen which is labeled "*Agrostis vulgaris*, a low form, Washington. Waste ground. Dr. Geo. Vasey." This corresponds exactly to the description and may be considered the type.

This subspecies can be separated only arbitrarily from the species, as there are so many intermediate forms. Characteristic specimens as found in the United States differ from *A. alba* as follows: The culms are upright, rather slender, 20–40 cm. high, and often tufted, the rhizomes at base short or none; leaf blades short, ascending, 5–10 cm. long and 1–2 mm. wide; ligule short, 1–2 mm. long, and obtuse; panicle loose, 5–10 cm. long, the branches few, spreading, giving it a divaricate appearance. (Pl. III, fig. 1.) The descriptions of the European plant state that the panicle remains spreading after flowering, while in *A. alba* the panicle contracts. I have not observed this to be a diagnostic character. The form here described is common in New England and less so farther south, and seems fairly distinct through this region. But in the Western States, especially in the mountain region, the forms intergrade, causing great perplexity.

It is difficult to determine with the data at hand where these forms may be native in this country. The species is widely cultivated and readily escapes. It appears to be native in the northern portion of our range and in the Rocky Mountains, but the forms which give most evidence of being native are those which would be referred to *A. alba vulgaris*. The form found evidently introduced through a large part of the United States is the large plant which I have referred to *A. alba*. This has taller stems, wider leaf blades which may droop, larger, more dense panicles, the branches often spikelet-bearing nearly to the base, ligules larger, and the stolon-like rhizomes often long and stout.

The following specimens represent fairly well the smaller form, *A. alba vulgaris*:

LABRADOR: *Waghorne* 34. NEWFOUNDLAND: *Waghorne* 3, 4, 6, 17, 23, 31, 38, *Robinson and Schrenk*. August 16, 1894. NEW BRUNSWICK: St. Andrews, *Fowler*, July 24, 1900, July 30, 1901. ONTARIO: Ottawa, *Macoun* 12999. MAINE: East Auburn, *Merrill* 20; Van Buren, *Fernald* 179, 179a; Orono, *Fernald* 532. NEW HAMPSHIRE: Mount Washington, *Hitchcock*, July, 1902. VERMONT: Burlington, Herb. Univ. 40. MASSACHUSETTS: Provincetown, *Hitchcock*, July, 1902. CONNECTICUT: Greens Farms, *Pollard* 111. PENNSYLVANIA: Somerset County, *Saunders* 4. DISTRICT OF COLUMBIA: *Hitchcock*, September 20, 1903. MICHIGAN: Kewanee County, *Farwell* 571. A specimen collected at Sitka, Alaska, by Evans (266) has a palet and is referred to this species.

A teratological form of this is common in New England.[a] The floral parts are abnormally elongated. The most important synonymy of this is as follows:

A. sylvatica L., Sp. Pl., Ed. II, 2: 1665. 1763. "Habitat in Angliæ sylvis humosis."

A. alba sylvatica Scribn., Mem. Torr. Bot. Club, 5: 40. 1894. Reduces A. sylvatica L. to variety.

A. polymorpha vivipara Trin., Unifl., 200. 1824. Trinius gives an extended classification of the varieties of A. polymorpha Huds. [A. alba L.] and includes this form (A. sylvatica L.) under "monstrosa."

A. alba aristata Gray.

A. stricta Willd., Sp. Pl. 1: 366. 1797. (Not of several other authors.) "A. panicula elongata, stricta, corollis calyce minoribus: arista e basi petali, tortila, flore longiore." "Habitat in America boreali." The type of this is in the Willdenow herbarium at the Botanical Garden in Berlin.

A. stricta Muhl., Gram. 65. 1817. From the description this appears to be the same as the above. There is no specimen in Muhlenberg's herbarium at the Philadelphia Academy of Natural Sciences.

A. alba aristata Gray, Man., Ed. I, 578. 1848. Gives short description and cites A. stricta as a synonym.

A. neogœa Steud., Syn. Pl. Glum. 1: 17. 1854 "Hrbr Despreaux. Terra nova." From the description this appears to be the awned form of A. alba.

Panicle spreading; flowering glume with an exserted dorsal awn from near the base. Culm slender and rather delicate; resembling A. canina, from which it differs in having a palet about half as long as the glume.

This is scarcely more than a form of A. alba vulgaris, as the awn is often present only on a part of the spikelets of a panicle. However, the awned forms seem always to be comparatively small and delicate. (Pl. III, fig. 2.)

DISTRIBUTION: Northeastern United States.

MAINE: Greenville, Fernald 266; Southport, Fernald 533; Fort Preble, Gayle 786. RHODE ISLAND: Providence, Olney. CONNECTICUT: New Haven, Allen in 1878. NEW JERSEY: Wildwood, Pollard, July 4, 1897. DELAWARE: Faulkland, Commons; Centerville, Commons 351. WEST VIRGINIA: Wyoming County, Morris 1197; Morgantown, Millspaugh 244. DISTRICT OF COLUMBIA: Hitchcock, September 20, 1903. VIRGINIA: Portsmouth, Noyes 4.

A. aristata Sincl. is mentioned in Steud. Nom., Ed. II, 1: 39, 1840, as a synonym of A. alba, but without description; hence is not technically published, and does not interfere with the use of A. alba aristata Gray.

A specimen from meadows, Cedar Hill, Vancouver Island, British Columbia (Macoun 40, June 16, 1887), resembles many of the mountain forms of A. alba, approaching variety vulgaris, but the flowering glume is awned. The culms are taller than usual for variety aristata (being about 60 cm. high). This is mentioned in Macoun's Catalogue of Canadian Plants 2: 198, 1888, and 5: 392, 1890, under other names, but both are nomina nuda.

A. alba maritima (Lam.) Meyer.

A. maritima Lam., Encycl. 1: 61. 1783. "Cette plante croît dans les lieux sabloneux et maritimes des environs de Narbonne, et m'a été communiquée par M. l'abbé Pourret (v. s.)." I have not examined the type of this, but it is probably in the herbarium of the Jardin des Plantes at Paris.

A. alba maritima Meyer, Chloris Hanov. 656, 1836, fide Aschers. & Graebn. Synops., 2: 176. 1899.

This plant has been described in European floras under several names. The New England plant was referred to A. coarctata Ehrh. (Hoffm. Deutsch. Fl.,

---

[a] An examination of one of these specimens (White Mountains, Hitchcock, July, 1903) shows that this condition is due to the presence of nematodes (a species of Tylenchus) in the aborted ovaries.—ERNST A. BESSEY.

Ed. II, 1: 37, 1800) in Britton & Brown, Ill. Fl. and in Britton, Man. This was reduced to a variety, *A. alba coarctata* Scribn., in Rand & Redfield, Fl. Mt. Des., 177, 1894.

Culms in large tufts, often decumbent and rooting at the base. Leaves short, ascending, and rather thick. Panicle contracted, sometimes almost spikelike. (Pl. IV.)

DISTRIBUTION: Delaware and northward, mostly near the coast in brackish marshes or on sand dunes.

NEWFOUNDLAND: *Waghorne* 1, 2, 6, 14, 17, 22, 54. NOVA SCOTIA: Canso *Fowler*, August 8, 1901. NEW BRUNSWICK: Bass River, *Fowler*, July 16, 1875. MAINE: Cape Elizabeth, *Scribner*, July 26, 1895; *Gayle*, October 17, 1896; Edgartown, *Burgess*, July 17, 1893. MASSACHUSETTS: Revere, *Churchill* in 1898, *Young* in 1892, *Sears* in 1883; Nantucket, *Hitchcock*, July, 1902. CONNECTICUT: Storrs, *Hitchcock*, July, 1902; Groton, *Graves*, 243; Southington, *Bissell* in 1895. PENNSYLVANIA: Philadelphia, ballast, *Heritage* 10. NEW YORK: Amagansett, L. I., *Peck* 2. NEW JERSEY: Wildwood, *Pollard*, July 4, 1897. DELAWARE: Slaughter Beach, 95; Greenbank, 96; Faulkland, July 9, 1879—all by *Commons*.

5. A. humilis Vasey.

A. humilis Vasey, Bul. Torr. Bot Club, **10**: 21. 1883. "Has the appearance of *A. varians*, but that species has no palet. Found by W. N. Suksdorf on Mount Paddo, Washington Territory, and by Mr. Howell on Mount Adams." The type collected by Suksdorf on Mount Paddo (now called Mount Adams) is in the National Herbarium. (Pl. VIII, fig. 1.)

Culms slender, tufted, from a perennial root, erect, 10–40 cm. high. Leaves mostly basal, the blades 2–10 cm. long, 2 mm. or less wide, flat and thin, or in dwarf specimens conduplicate or filiform. Panicles 2–8 cm. long; in the taller specimens rather open and loosely flowered, in dwarf plants narrow and almost spikelike. Spikelets usually purple, 1½–2 mm. long; empty glumes equal, rather broad, and abruptly pointed, smooth or slightly scabrous on upper part of keel; flowering glume nearly as long as empty glumes, awnless; palet usually about two-thirds as long as flowering glume, or rarely shorter.

The dwarf forms can scarcely be distinguished from *A. rossæ* except by the presence of a palet. The larger forms appear to pass into *A. alba vulgaris*, but the spikelets are somewhat smaller.

DISTRIBUTION: British Columbia to Oregon and Colorado at high altitudes.

BRITISH COLUMBIA: Selkirk Mountains, *Canby* 4; Chilliwack valley, *Macoun* 26033. WASHINGTON: Mount Rainier, *Piper* 1975, 1977, *Allen* C; Olympic Mountains, *Elmer* 1951; Mount Adams, *Suksdorf* 25, 602, *Howell* 85; Skamania County, *Suksdorf* 1079; Okanogan County, *Elmer* 677. OREGON: Eagle Creek Mountains, *Cusick* 1066, 1070. IDAHO: Bitter Root Forest Reserve, *Leiberg* 2948, 2969; Mill Creek, *Henderson* 3927. WYOMING: Yellowstone Park, *Rose* 700, *Tweedy* 603; Teton Mountains, *Tweedy* 24, 26, *Merrill and Wilcox* 335, 344; Carbon County, *Nelson* 4014; Albany County, *Nelson* 1814, 5202; Dome Lake, *Nelson* 2413; Bighorn County, *Nelson* 415, *Williams* 2952. COLORADO: Buffalo Pass, *Shear and Bessey* 1447, 1452, 1460, 1461, 1478, 1479, 1486; Silver Plume, *Rydberg* 2456; Rocky Mountains, *Hall and Harbour* 673; Denver, *Eastwood*; Marshall Pass, *Clements* 213. I have also referred to this species Pringle's No. 4251, collected in the State of Mexico, at an altitude of 12,000 feet.

6. A. depressa Vasey.

A. depressa Vasey, Bul. Torr. Bot. Club, **13**: 54. 1886.

The following is the original description: "Culms decumbent and geniculate at the base, becoming erect, 6 to 10 inches high, slender, leafy below; leaves short and narrow, plain, 1 to 2 inches long, one-half line wide, acute; ligule conspicuous, about one line long, obtuse and ciliate at apex; sheaths smooth, striate, the lower ones loose; panicle narrow, 1 to 2 inches long, or in age broader and more spreading; the branches short, variable in number, 2 to 5 at the lower joints and unequal; pedicels scabrous, about as long as the spikelets, empty glumes nearly equal, about 1 line long, ovate-lanceolate, acute, roughish on the keel above; flowering glume one-third shorter, narrowly oblong, obtuse or minutely dentate at the apex; palet narrow, half as long as its glume. Collected in Clear Creek Canyon, Colo., by H. N. Patterson, 1885." (Pl. V, fig. 1.)

This rests upon a single collection, the type specimen being in the National Herbarium. What I take to be the same species occurs on the Pacific coast and was named *A. exarata stolonifera* Vasey, Bul. Torr. Bot. Club, 13: 54, 1886 (following *A. depressa*). "Bottom lands of the Columbia River, collected by Mr. W. N. Suksdorf." The type of this is also deposited in the National Herbarium. The original description is appended: "*Agrostis exarata* var. *stolonifera* V. Cespitose; culms 8 to 12 inches high from a decumbent base, with numerous short leaves, which are seldom more than an inch long, narrow, acuminate; the radical leaves also short and abundant; ligule membranaceous, conspicuous, obtuse; panicle 1½ to 2 inches long, purplish, narrow; branches very short and clustered, mostly flowering to the base, some of the lowest longer and naked below; spikelets about 1 line long, sometimes two-flowered; empty glumes nearly equal, acute, hispid on the keel; flowering glumes one-third shorter, oblong-ovate, toothed at the apex, sometimes with a short awn, palet small, equaling the ovary; long, leafy stolons, sometimes a foot long, are often emitted from the base, the joints 1 to 2 inches apart. Bottom lands of the Columbia River, collected by Mr. W. N. Suksdorf. Perhaps a good species."

This species is characterized by its tufted geniculate culms; short, narrow upright culm leaves, which are very scabrous on both surfaces; the conspicuous ligule 2–3 mm. long; and the narrow spikelike panicles. The flowering glume bears a minute prickle on the back below the tip which represents the excurrent keel. (Pl. VI.)

DISTRIBUTION: Colorado, Washington to California.

WASHINGTON: Klikitat County, *Suksdorf* 40, 140. OREGON: Astoria, *Leckenby;* Gearhart, *Hitchcock;* Fort Stevens, *Hitchcock.* CALIFORNIA: Mendocino County, *Davy and Blasdale* 6124. COLORADO: *Patterson* 46.

Suksdorf's plants have numerous 2-flowered spikelets seemingly staminate, each with palet ⅓–⅔ the length of the flowering glume, and his 140 has some of the spikelets awned.

A. depressa is connected with *A. alba* through *A. alba maritima.*

I have observed *A. depressa* growing on the sand dunes near the coast at Gearhart and Fort Stevens, Oreg. The tufts send out stoloniferous stems which creep over the sand for several feet. The sheaths on these runners are somewhat inflated and the blades are only 1–2 cm. long. The runners often end in an ascending flower culm. When the plant grows in sand, rhizomes are formed. The type specimens do not show these stolons, but in other particulars they are similar. This species is quite common along the coast of Oregon, but apparently is quite rare in the interior, as shown by the single collection from Colorado.

It is unfortunate that a species well known in one locality should have as its type a specimen from a widely separated locality and a specimen also which does not show the characteristic habit of the more western form. It is to be hoped that intermediate collections of the species may be made which will throw light upon this question of range.

7. A. rosei Scribn. & Merrill.

A. rosei Scribn. & Merrill, U. S. Dept. Agr., Div. Agros., Bul. **24**: 21. 1901.
The following is a copy of the original description:

"A slender, erect perennial, 4 to 5 dm. high, with short, flat leaves and very open, capillary panicles, 1 to 1.5 dm. long. Culms glabrous, somewhat geniculate at the lower nodes; sheaths shorter than the internodes, smooth, striate; ligule hyaline, obtuse, 2 mm. long; leaf blades linear, acuminate, 5 to 8 cm. long, 2 to 3 mm. wide, scabrous on both sides and on the margins. Panicle very open, pale or purplish, the branches capillary, the lower ones verticillate, the upper ones opposite, spreading, dichotomously or verticillately branching, somewhat scabrous, the lower ones 5 to 6 cm. long; pedicels elongated, flexuous. Spikelets about 2 mm. long; empty glumes ovate-lanceolate, acute, subequal, thin, slightly scabrous on the keel above; flowering glume slightly shorter than the empty glumes, obtuse, often with 2 or 3 blunt teeth at the apex; awn attached near the base, equaling or slightly exceeding the glume, finely scabrous, straight or slightly bent near the middle. Palea very thin, hyaline, lanceolate, obtuse, nearly three-fourths as long as the flowering glume. Grain lanceolate, about 1.5 mm. long."

Type specimen collected on Sierra Madre Mountains, State of Zacatecas, Mexico, J. N. Rose 2373, August 18, 1897.

In addition to the type we have one specimen: NEW MEXICO: Cloverdale, *Mearns* 462, July 15, 1892.

FIG. 1.—*Agrostis rosei* Scribn. & Merrill; *a*, a spikelet; *b*, the awned flowering glume and palea; *c*, the grain.

††*Palet about one-fourth the length of the flowering glume. Panicle contracted.*

8. A. glomerata (Presl) Kunth.

Vilfa glomerata Presl, Rel. Haenk **1**: 239. 1830. "Hab. in montanis Peruviæ huanoccensibus." The type specimen is in the Presl herbarium at Prague. It is a single plant with a narrow panicle, somewhat interrupted below, short palet and awnless flowering glume. Presl describes the palet as being as long as the flowering glume ("Paleæ æquilongæ") and places it in the genus *Vilfa*, but the type specimen has the palet only about one-fifth as long as the flowering glume.

A. glomerata Kunth, Enum. **1**: 219. 1833. "Peruvia." Transfers *Vilfa glomerata* Presl, and gives description.

Agrostis californica Trin., Mem. Acad. St. Petersb., Ser. VI. **6²**: 359. 1841. (Agrostidea **II**: 113.) Trinius cites *Vilfa glomerata* Presl as a synonym, but gives as the locality "California. In montanis Peruviæ huanoccensibus." The type specimen is in the herbarium of the St. Petersburg Academy of Sciences.

A few spikelets from the type are deposited in the National Herbarium. Trinius describes the flowering glume and palet as being equal ("Valvulæ æquales, glabræ"), but in the type specimen the palet is one-fourth the flowering glume. The type specimen has scabrous, somewhat inflated sheaths, panicle 4 inches long, dense and interrupted, and no awn to the flowering glume.

A densiflora Vasey, Contr. U. S. Natl. Herb. 8: 72. 1892. "Santa Cruz, Cal. (Dr. C. L. Anderson)." The type specimen is in the National Herbarium. (Pl. VII. fig. 2.)

A. densiflora arenaria Vasey, Contr. U. S. Natl. Herb. 8: 72. 1892. "Seashore Mendocino County (C. G. Pringle, in 1882)." The type specimen is in the National Herbarium. It is more decumbent and spreading at base and the panicles are somewhat narrower but other specimens connect this with *A. densiflora* Vasey.

A. arenaria Scribn. is mentioned as a synonym under *A. densiflora arenaria* Vasey (l. c.), and consequently has the same type.

A. inflata Scribn., in Beal, Grasses 2: 325. 1896. "British Columbia (Vancouver Island), Macoun 258 in 1893." Type specimen in the herbarium of Prof. W. J. Beal, Agricultural College, Michigan (No. 258).

Macoun's No. 259 is in the National Herbarium and is probably the plant to which Scribner gave the name. Mr. Macoun writes that No. 258 was collected June 9, 1893, and No. 259 about August 7 of the same year. They were not collected at quite the same locality, but he considers them evidently the same species and growing under the same conditions. It is to be noted that No. 258 has the empty glumes awned, while in No. 259 they are only slender-acuminate. (Pl. VII. fig. 1.)

This differs from *A. densiflora* Vasey in being dwarf (less than 10 cm. high) and in having the flowering glume provided with a bent, exserted awn.

Culms erect or ascending, usually 20–30 cm. high, stout, more or less scabrous below the panicle. Leaves with conspicuously striate, often inflated, sheaths, rather thick, striate, scabrous, blades abruptly pointed or boat-shaped at apex, 2–8 mm. wide, 3–7 cm. long. Panicles close and spikelike, 2–7 cm. long, 5–15 mm. thick, in the larger forms more or less lobed. Spikelets about 3 mm. long; empty glumes equal, scabrous on keel and somewhat on back, sharp-pointed, but usually not awned; flowering glume 2 mm. long, awnless or with a straight or bent awn from the middle of the back; callus hairs short; palet about .5 mm. long, 2-nerved.

DISTRIBUTION: British Columbia to Peru, along the seacoast. VANCOUVER ISLAND: *Macoun* 259. OREGON: Cape Foulweather, *Lake* in 1890. CALIFORNIA: Mendocino County, *Davy and Blasdale* 6025, 6167, 6135, *Pringle* in 1882, *Congdon* in 1902; Point Reyes, *Davy* 6755, 6792, 6793; Santa Cruz, *Anderson;* (without locality) *Kellogg and Hartford, Bigelow* in 1853–54; *Bolander* 6466 in part.

This is evidently the *A. mucronata* of Thurber in Botany of California 2: 272. 1880. The description applies, and there is a specimen in Mr. Nash's herbarium "Mendocino Co., California, Seacoast, Bolander 6466." (See note on *A. nana* under *A. breviculmis.*) This specimen is small and resembles the type of *A. inflata* Scribn.

The root of *A. glomerata* is described by Vasey, Beal, and others as annual and by Trinius as perennial. I am unable to determine certainly from the specimens whether or not the species is perennial. There is no indication of more than one year's growth, but the base of the stem seems too robust for an annual. The awn is variable. Although the type is awnless most of our specimens have awns of varying length and in the same specimen the awn may be present or absent.

A. mucronata Presl has been cited by some authors as a synonym of this. I examined this plant at Prague and do not think it occurs in the United States. It differs from *A. glomerata* in having the finer leaves mostly basal, the panicle contracted but loose and fine in appearance, and the empty glumes awn-pointed.

** *Palet wanting or a small nerveless scale.*

† *Flowering glume provided with a very slender awn about 5 mm. long. Delicate annuals.*

9. A. exigua Thurb.

A. exigua Thurb., in Brewer and Watson, Bot. Calif. 2: 275. 1880.

"Annual; culm (including panicle) 1 to 4 inches high, erect, flattened, very slightly scabrous toward the nodes, sometimes branching from near the base; leaves from an inch to 2 lines long or less, those upon the branches sometimes with the blade reduced to a mere point, mostly convolute, roughened on both sides and margins, especially near the apex; ligule about a line long, acute; sheaths very loose, strongly striate and minutely scabrous; panicle half the length of the plant, included and at first narrow, at length open; lower rays about 5, the others in pairs, the longer about an inch in length, bearing 1–5 flowers above the middle, scabrous; spikelets three-fourths of a line long, the pedicels much enlarged just below; glumes not pointed, the lower slightly longer, aculeolate on the keel and with minute scattered hairs all over, especially at the apex, generally tinged with purple; floret of but 1 palet, equaling the glumes, the callus very minute, with a few hairs; palet 5-nerved, scabrous with few minute hairs, very acute at apex, the midnerve prolonged into a roughish awn 4 lines longer than itself, inserted about one-fifth below the tip of the palet, which is split down to that point forming 2 setae; upper palet not manifest or a mere scale; stamens (1)?

"Foothills of the Sierras, Bolander. The specimens accompanied a much reduced form of *A. exarata*, from which it is abundantly distinct, as it also is from *A. canina*." (Pl. VIII, fig. 2.)

At the Gray herbarium I have examined Bolander's specimen, a portion of which is deposited in the National Herbarium, and am unable to identify it with any other species of the United States. It is unusual to have a species so rare as is indicated by a single collection in a region so well known as California, and I suspect that the species is either introduced or occurs farther to the south in Mexico or Central America, the species of which region are not sufficiently well known.

Mr. Thurber at first referred this to *A. elliottiana*, which it resembles in habit. But it differs from that species in having the flowering glumes as long as the empty glumes, the lobes extending into two awned teeth, and in the stouter straight awn. The empty glumes are only slightly acute, 1.5 mm. long, equal, slightly scabrous on back. Awn scabrous, straight, 5–6 mm. long.

10. A. elliottiana Schult.

A. arachnoides Ell., Sk. 1: 134. 1816. "From specimens collected near Orangeburg, by Mr. I. S. Bennett." Not *A. arachnoidea* Poir., Suppl. 1: 249, 1810. The type of *A. arachnoides* Ell. is in Elliott's herbarium, and has been examined by Mr. E. D. Merrill (U. S. Dept. Agr., Div. Agros., Circ. 29: 10. 1901).

A. elliottiana Schult., Mant. 2: 372. 1824. Name changed from the preceding.

Annual. Culms slender and delicate, 10–40 cm. high. Blades small, slender, and soft. Panicle diffuse, branches slender and spreading, scabrous, spikelet bearing toward the extremity. Empty glumes equal, acute, scabrous on keel, 1.5 mm. long; flowering glume about 1 mm. long, very thin and delicate, short-hairy at base, with a very delicate sinuous awn about 5 mm. long, attached on the back below the apex (sometimes unawned); palet none. (Pl. IX, fig. 1.)

DISTRIBUTION: South Carolina to Missouri and Texas.

SOUTH CAROLINA: Orangeburg, *Hitchcock.* GEORGIA: Stone Mountain, *Small* 765, *Curtiss* 6771; Rome, *Chapman.* ALABAMA: Tuskegee, *Carver* 56; Mobile, *Mohr.* TENNESSEE: Kingston Springs, *Gattinger* 3391 (Curtiss N. A. Plants).

ILLINOIS: Johnson County, *Evelyn Ridgway*. MISSOURI: Chadwick, *Bush* 48; Eagle Rock, *Bush* 258; Jefferson County, *Eggert* 161. ARKANSAS: Benton County, *Plank* 90. MISSISSIPPI: Biloxi, *Tracy* 4554. LOUISIANA: (without locality) *Bush* 33; *Carpenter*. TEXAS: Houston, *Hall* 762, 763; Gillespie County, *Jermy* 6220; Galveston, *Plank* 94; Columbia, *Bush* 120; Dallas, *Reverchon* 1039; Gregory, *Heller* 1565.

††*Flowering glume awnless or provided with a short awn. Perennials.*

‡*Plants spreading by rhizomes.*

=*Flowering glume provided at base with a tuft of hairs, 1–2 mm. long.*

11. A. hallii Vasey.

A. hallii Vasey, Contr. U. S. Natl. Herb. **8**: 74. 1892. The original description is as follows: "Culms erect, stout, 2 to 3 feet high, smooth, not stoloniferous; lower leaves narrow, inclined to be involute, the upper ones flat, 3 to 6 inches long, 1 to 2 lines wide, scabrous; ligules 2 to 3 lines long, acute; panicle 6 to 9 inches long, the rays erect, spreading, the lower in clusters of 5 to many, unequal, the longer ones 2 to 3 inches, branching above the middle; spikelets 1½ lines long, somewhat appressed and crowded; empty glumes acute, 1½ to 2 lines long, scabrous on the keel; the floral glume nearly as long, with 2 tufts of hairs at the base; palet wanting. Oregon, Washington, and California."

The type specimen was collected in Oregon by E. Hall in 1871 and is marked "A. Hallii" in Doctor Vasey's handwriting. It is deposited in the National Herbarium. (Pl. X, fig. 2.)

The description quoted above is evidently based upon several specimens and probably includes more than one species. The description states that the plants are not stoloniferous, but the type specimen does not show the base of the plant. The composite nature of the description is also indicated by the latitude given in the measurements and in the range.

A. davyi Scribn., U. S. Dept. Agr., Div. Agros., Circ. **30**: 3. 1901. "In brush on hillsides near Point Arena, Mendocino County, Cal. No. 6062 Davy and Blasdale." The type specimen is deposited in the National Herbarium. Mr. Davy has added a note that this was collected near mouth of Albion River. (Pl. XI.)

A. occidentalis Scribn. & Merrill, Bul. Torr. Bot. Club, **29**: 466. 1902. "Type specimen collected by C. L. Shear, No. 1644, in a moist glade, McMinnville, Yamhill County, Oreg., July 20, 1899." Type specimen deposited in the National Herbarium. (Pl. XI A.)

The ligules in the type specimen of *A. hallii* are in a rather unsatisfactory condition and are only three in number, but are proportionately shorter than in most of the specimens referred to here. In this respect Henderson 7 and Hall 619, both from Oregon, agree with the type.

Culms about 1 m. high, leafy. Blades 3–5 mm. wide, 10–15 cm. long; ligule usually conspicuous, often nearly 1 cm. long. Panicles 10–12 cm. long, narrow or somewhat spreading. Spikelets pale, the lower glume acuminate, about 4 mm. long, the upper a little shorter; flowering glume 3 mm. long, with a tuft of hairs at base about 1.5 mm. long; no awn or palet.

DISTRIBUTION: Oregon and California, from Santa Cruz northward.

OREGON: Yamhill County, *Howell* 67; Yoquina Bay, *Lake* 8; (without locality) *Hall* 619; *Henderson* 7. CALIFORNIA: Del Norte County, *Davy and Blasdale* 5918; Humboldt County, *Davy and Blasdale* 5493, 5723, 5873, 6175; Mendocino County, *Davy and Blasdale* 6051, 6054, 6062, 6122; *Heller* 5848; Sonoma County, *Bioletti* 110; Mount Tamalpais, *Congdon;* Alameda County, *Davy* 4252, *Blankinship* 4, *Michener and Bioletti* 128; Santa Cruz, *Anderson* in 1886.

A. hallii pringlei (Scribn.) comb. nov.

A. pringlei Scribn., U. S. Dept. Agr., Div. Agros., Bul. **7**: 156. 1897. "Plains, Mendocino County, Cal. (Pringle), and northward to Oregon (?)." Type specimen deposited in the National Herbarium. (Pl. XII.)

Differs from *A. hallii* in narrower and more compact panicles, narrower and more involute leaves, and the whole foliage more stramineous in appearance.

CALIFORNIA: Mendocino County, *Pringle* in 1882, *Congdon* in 1901, *Davy and Blasdale* 6030, 6075.

The type specimen was first named in the herbarium *A. repens* Scribn., and this name is mentioned as a synonym under *A. scouleri* Vasey (Contr. U. S. Natl. Herb., 8 : 73. 1892).

== *Tufts of hairs at base of flowering glume minute or wanting.*

12. A. pallens Trin.

A. pallens Trin., Mem. Acad. St. Petersb., Ser. VI, 6²: 328. 1841. (Agrostidea II : 82.) "Amer-borealis? (Hooker)." The type specimen is in the herbarium of the St. Petersburg Academy of Sciences. It is marked " T. 243," as are other specimens received from Hooker. In the National Herbarium are a few spikelets from the type specimen and also a photograph of the plant, which is a single erect culm with a few narrow root leaves, one culm leaf and a contracted panicle.

A. exarata littoralis Vasey, Bul. Torr. Bot. Club, 13: 55. 1886. " Found by Mr. T. J. Howell on the sandy seashore in Oregon." Type specimen in the National Herbarium, labeled " No. 64, Seashore, Tillamook Bay, Oregon. T. J. Howell, July 14, 1882."

Culms rather stiffly upright from creeping rhizomes, 20–40 cm. high, glabrous. Blades erect, 1–3 mm. wide, 5–10 cm. long. Panicles contracted, almost spikelike, 5–10 cm. long, 5–10 mm. wide. Spikelets 2.5–3 mm. long, empty glumes equal, slightly scabrous on keel, but smooth on back; flowering glumes a little shorter, awnless; palet minute. (Pl. XIII, fig. 1.)

DISTRIBUTION: Washington to California, near the seashore.

WASHINGTON: Westport, *Henderson* 2116. OREGON: Tillamook Bay, *Howell* 64; Seaside County, *Shear and Scribner* 1701, 1723, *Hitchcock* in 1901. CALIFORNIA: (without locality) *Bolander* 18, 5064, *Lemmon* in 1875; Del Norte County, *Davy and Blasdale* in 1899; Point Reyes, *Davy* 6682, 6839.

A. pallens foliosa (Vasey) comb. nov.

A. foliosa Vasey, Bul. Torr. Bot. Club, 13: 55. April, 1886. " Culms 1½ feet high, erect, smooth; culm leaves 4 or 5, erect, somewhat rigid, 4 to 6 inches long, 1½ to 2 lines wide, long pointed; ligule about 2 lines long, lacerate at apex; panicle 4 to 5 inches long, open and loose, the lower branches mostly in fives, unequal, the lower 1 inch long or more, somewhat spreading, capillary, rather few-flowered, mostly naked below; spikelets little more than 1 line long, lanceolate, abruptly acute; flowering glume nearly as long as the outer ones, 5-nerved, obtuse and shortly 4 or 5 toothed at apex; palet wanting. Collected in Oregon by T. J. Howell. The panicle much like a short branched *A. alba*."

This name appeared first as a nomen nudum (Bul. Torr. Bot. Club, 10: 63, 1883) in Professor Scribner's " List of Grasses from Washington Territory," thus, "*Agrostis foliosa* Vasey ined. equals Nos. 1 and 47 of Howell's Oregon coll."

Doctor Vasey published a second description in the Botanical Gazette for December, 1886, page 337. "'Collected in Oregon by Thomas Howell and by Dr. H. N. Bolander."

I have taken, as the type of this, one of the specimens collected in Oregon by T. J. Howell in 1881, labeled *A. foliosa* in Doctor Vasey's handwriting and designated as " No. 1." This specimen is unawned. (Pl. XIV, fig. 1.)

There is an *A. foliosa* Hortul. in Kunth., Enum., 1: 207, 1833, but it has no standing, as it is mentioned only as a synonym under *Cinna filiformis*.

The Washington and Oregon specimens have mostly a rather loose panicle. Southward into California the panicle tends to be narrower and the branches more appressed.

A. diegoensis Vasey, Bul. Torr. Bot. Club, **18**: 55. 1886. " Culms erect, stout, 2 to 3 feet or more high, smooth, leaves 4 to 7 inches long, 1 to 2 lines wide, erect, those of the culm with long sheaths (the upper ones 8 or 9 inches long) ; ligule about 2 lines long, acute; panicle 6 to 8 inches long, lanceolate, the joints rather distant (the lower 1½ to 2 inches) ; branches numerous, unequal, erect, the longer ones about 2 inches long, and floriferous above the middle, the shorter floriferous to the base, the flowers numerous; spikelets light green, 1½ to 2 lines long, outer glumes acute, scabrous on the keel; flowering glume one-third shorter, oblong, obtuse, the midnerve terminating about the middle, with or without a minute awn ; palet none. Collected at San Diego, Cal., by C. R. Orcutt. The panicle resembles that of *A. alba*, but is narrower, stouter, and more closely flowered."

There are several specimens in the National Herbarium, collected in the vicinity of San Diego by Mr. C. R. Orcutt. I have considered the type to be among those collected at the earliest date (1884), and marked *A. diegoensis* in Doctor Vasey's handwriting. Of these I have arbitrarily selected one sheet as the type specimen. This is marked " *B*," and is from Smith's Mountain. This was selected because it is a more perfect specimen. (Pl. XVII.) It happens that this plant has the awn better developed than many of the others, but I am unable to connect the presence of the awn with other characters. Only two or three of these specimens show rootstocks, but the others appear to have been broken off at the surface of the soil.

A. multiculmis Vasey ." in numerous distributions," given as a synonym under *A. diegoensis* in Beal's Grasses, N. A., **2**: 328. 1896.

Culms erect or nearly so, usually rather firm or stiff, or in the slender forms wiry, more or less tufted, but provided with creeping rootstocks, 50–120 cm. tall. Blades varying from very narrow to 3 mm. wide, usually stiff and appressed, but sometimes more lax, the lower ones often pale, straw-colored or brown at time of flowering; ligule short and rounded or acutish. Panicle pale green or rarely purplish, usually narrow, with appressed or at least stiff branches, 10–30 cm. long, some of the branches bare on lower portion, other shorter ones spikelet-bearing from base; in some forms the panicle is more open and spreading. Empty glumes nearly equal, more or less scabrous on keel and sometimes minutely so on back, 2–3 mm. long; flowering glume nearly as long as outer glumes, or only three-fourths as long, hairs at base minute; awn absent or short and straight or rarely bent; palet none. (Pl. XV, and Pl. XVI, fig. 1.)

DISTRIBUTION : British Columbia to California.

In the following specimens the awn is evident though not always exserted:

WASHINGTON : Stony places, Cape Horn, Skamania County, *Suksdorf* 2332. OREGON : Near the glacier on Mount Hood, *Henderson* 7; Mount Hood, *Howell* 42; Cascades of the Columbia, *Howell* 197; in springy places along the Applegate, *Howell* 221 in 1887 ; Portland, *Bolander* in 1886 ; (without locality), *Cusick* 1153, *Howell* 1, 4, 10, 48, 84. CALIFORNIA : *Lemmon* in 1882.

In the following specimens the awn is wanting or is only a short dorsal prickle :

BRITISH COLUMBIA : Vancouver Island, *Macoun* 30136. WASHINGTON : Cascade Mountains, *Vasey* in 1889 ; Mason County, *Piper* 949, 950 ; Falcon Valley, *Suksdorf* 131, 200, 908 ; Skamania County, *Suksdorf* 2331, 2658 ; Klickitat County, *Suksdorf* 199 ; Whitman County, *Vasey* in 1892, *Vasey* (jr.) 3054, 3057, *Piper* 1929, 3043, *Elmer* 1026. IDAHO : *Henderson* 3061 ; Moscow, *Henderson* 4641. OREGON : *Henderson* 10 ; Portland, *Howell* 51 ; Roseburg, *Howell* 219 ; Multnomah Falls, *Bolander* in 1866 ; Soda Springs, *Jones* 306. CALIFORNIA : Mount Shasta, *Palmer* 2660 ; Eagle Lake, *Davy* in 1894 ; Humboldt County, *Davy and Blasdale* 6216 ; Placer County, *Carpenter* in 1892 ; Marin County, *Davy* 6832, 6837 ; San Francisco, *Bolander;* Amador County, *Hansen* 611, 620, 1738, 1741, 1818, 1987 ; Monterey County, *Davy* 7701, 7702 ; Santa Cruz, *Anderson;* Santa Catalina Island, *Brandegee* 50 ; Santa Rosa Island, *Brandegee* 66 ;

San Diego, *Cleveland* 5, 73; *Orcutt*, several specimens collected in 1884 and two in 1890.

This variety intergrades with the species, differing chiefly in habit, the culms being taller, the foliage more lax, and the panicle more open. The form which happened to be described first, and hence is taken as the species, is confined to the sandy seacoast, and, like other seacoast forms, has a more compact panicle, more conspicuous rhizomes, and stiffer foliage. The type specimen of *A. foliosa* is unawned, but other specimens which resemble it in other respects have the flowering glume provided with a dorsal awn varying from a mere prickle to an exserted awn.

A few of the Orcutt specimens from San Diego have larger spikelets, varying from 3.5–4.5 mm. in length, and the culms are tall and stout, but I am unable to distinguish them otherwise.

‡‡ *Planta tufted, but not producing rhizomes.*

= *Panicle narrow, usually a part of the lower branches spikelet-bearing from the base.*

a. *Panicle strict; branches very short and appressed. A low cespitose plant.*

13. A. breviculmis nom. nov.

Trichodium nanum Presl, Rel. Haenk. 1: 243. 1830. "Hab. in Peruvia?" Presl's type specimen of *Trichodium nanum* is at Prague. It is the same as figured by Scribner, Ann. Rep. Mo. Bot. Gard. 10: 54, 58, pl. 34, fig. 2, 3. 1899. A discussion of the identity of our plant with Presl's is given in U. S. Dept. Agr., Div. Agros., Circ. 80: 2, 1901.

A. nana Kunth, Enum. 1: 226. 1833. "Peruviæ?" Transfers *Trichodium nanum* and gives a description.

According to the strict application of the rules of priority, a new name must be given to this plant on account of *A. nana* Delarbre, Fl. Anverg., Ed. 2, 1800. This is a form of *A. alba* and seems not to have been taken up by later authors.

Culms short, 10–15 cm. high, densely cespitose. Blades narrow and rigid, conduplicate or filiform, scabrous on margins, 2–4 cm. long, scarcely more than 1 mm. wide. Panicles strict and narrow, 2–3 cm. long, branches closely appressed, scabrous, not more than 1 cm. long. Spikelets 2½–3 mm. long, the first glume a little longer than the second, both acute and scabrous on the back, especially on the keels, pale and of firm texture; flowering glume about 1.8 mm. or a little less, awnless or with a very short awn just above the middle; palet minute, about .3 mm. long, nerveless. (Pl. XVIII.)

DISTRIBUTION: California to Peru.

CALIFORNIA: Near Fort Bragg, Mendocino County, *Bolander* 6466 in part, on cliffs, *Davy and Blasdale* 6159. NEW GRENADA: *Spruce* 5936. PERU: *Wilkes Exped.*

A. nana Kunth is described by Scribner and Merrill as having a perennial root, and in Davy and Blasdale's specimens this appears to be so, although this is not certain.

In the Gray herbarium is a specimen from the seacoast, Fort Bragg (Mendocino County), Cal., Bolander, No. 6466. This does not agree with Thurber's description of *A. mucronata* Presl in Botany of California, and hence there has been great confusion. (See note under *A. glomerata*.) Thurber's description applies to *A. glomerata* Kunth (*A. californica* Trin., *A. densiflora* Vasey), and in the herbarium of Mr. George V. Nash is a specimen of this from Mendocino County, Cal., ticketed "Bolander, 6466." Thus there were two species collected by Bolander under the same number, *A. glomerata* Kunth and *A. nana* Presl, and the latter was sent to the Gray herbarium. In the note in Botany of

California Mr. Bolander mentions collecting "at the same time what is apparently a much weatherworn awnless form of it, but it is too imperfect for determination." This is *A. nana* Kunth, the slender form in Mr. Nash's herbarium.

Mr. Nash has sent to the National Herbarium culms from his specimens of Bolander 6466, representing both species. The slender form has a small palet scarcely ½ mm. long and is identical with Davy and Blasdale, 6159. This is *A. nana*. It has the short truncate flowering glume, with denticulate apex. It is the same as the specimen in the Gray herbarium.

The stouter form looks much like the above, but has an awn below the apex of the longer and acute flowering glume, and the palet is about one-fourth the length of the flowering glume. Awn short, barely exserted. This is *A. glomerata*, though it is much smaller and the panicle narrower than most of our specimens, thus closely resembling *A. inflata* Scribn.

aa. Panicle narrow but not strict; some of the lower branches 2 cm. or more long. Group of A. exarata.

b. Flowering glume with an exserted awn.

14. A. microphylla Steud.

A. microphylla Steud., Syn. Pl. Glum. 1: 164. 1854. "Agraulus brevifoliis Nees Mpt. Douglas legit in Am. Sptr." I have not seen the type of this, but I think there is little doubt that it is the form with short spikelike inflorescence.
Polypogon alopecuroides Buckley, Proc. Acad. Nat. Sci., Phila. 1862: 88. 1863. "Columbia Plains, Oregon, Nuttall." Gray states in his criticism of Buckley's species (l. c., 332) that this was distributed as *Deyeuxia alopecuroides* by Nuttall, and consequently, if it is distinct from *A. exarata*, to which he refers it, the name should be *Agrostis alopecuroides*. Gray thus mentions two synonyms. Nuttall's plant is in the herbarium of the Philadelphia Academy of Natural Sciences.
A. virescens microphylla Scribn., U. S. Dept. Agr., Div. Agros., Circ. 30: 2 1901. Reduces *A. microphylla* Steud. to a variety.
A. microphylla major Vasey, Contr. Natl. Herb. 3: 72. 1892. Vasey quotes as synonym "(*Agrostis exarata* var. *microphylla* Watson)." The description includes several forms and no specimens or definite localities are cited, only "with the same range as the typical form." As Vasey cites an unpublished name of Watson, I have assumed that Watson's plant is the type of this variety. (Pl. XIX, fig. 1.) Watson describes his plant (Bot. King's Exp. 377, 1871) as a variety of *A. exarata*, "Var. (*A. microphylla*, Steud. Syn. Gram. 164. Torrey, .Pac. R. R. Surv. 4: 154)," and cites as localities, "On the Truckee River and in the West Humboldt Mountains, Nevada." No. "(1284)." The first cited specimen which is from Truckee valley, Nevada, collected at 4,000 feet altitude, in July, 1867, is taken as the type. Specimens from both localities were distributed under No. 1284. I find no specimens marked in Vasey's handwriting *A. microphylla major*. The specimen is more robust than the type of *A. microphylla*, but there are all gradations connecting the two.

Culms tall and often stout, 50–100 cm. or more or sometimes reduced. Blades flat and scabrous, elongated, in the larger forms as much as 7 mm., but usually 2–3 mm., wide. Panicle narrow, close, and spikelike or rather loose, 10–30 cm. long, branches scabrous, flower-bearing nearly to base. Empty glumes nearly equal, 2.5–3 mm. long, scabrous on keel and usually also on back, acuminate or setaceously pointed; flowering glume about one-third shorter, awned; awn attached about the middle of the back, exserted and bent; palet none. (Pl. XIX, fig. 2.)

DISTRIBUTION: British Columbia to California.

WASHINGTON: *Heller* 4010. OREGON: *Howell, Hall* 614, *Shear* 1645, 1648. CALIFORNIA: *Bolander* 4648, *Orcutt* 1176, *Davy and Blasdale* 5142, *Davy* 6662. LOWER CALIFORNIA: *Orcutt*. VANCOUVER ISLAND: *Dawson* 56; *Macoun* 31. WASHINGTON: Falcon Valley, *Pringle* in 1881; *Suksdorf* 1, 47; Douglas County,

Sandberg and Leiberg 327; Seattle, *Piper* 828; Chehalis County, *Heller* 4010. OREGON: *Hall* 614; Yamhill County, *Shear* 1645, 1648, 1650; Grants Pass, *Howell* in 1884; Roseburg, *Howell* 223; Washington County, *Howell* 55; White Horse Ranch, *Griffiths and Morris* 469. NEVADA: Truckee valley, *Watson* 1284, September 1867. CALIFORNIA: *Bolander* 4648, 6078; Mendocino County, *Pringle* in 1882, *Davy* 6573, *Davy and Blasdale* 5142; San Francisco, *Bolander* 19; Point Reyes, *Davy* 6777; Monterey County, *Davy* 7725; Santa Cruz, *Anderson* in 1886; Middle Tule River, *Purpus* 5638; San Diego, *Orcutt* 518, 1173, 1176; Contra Costa County, *Davy* 6662.

The type of this species represents a dwarf form. Of the specimens cited the following are similar to Steudel's plant, the others being like the Watson plant or intermediate:

OREGON: Grants Pass, *Howell* in 1884; CALIFORNIA: *Orcutt* 1176; Mendocino County, *Davy and Blasdale* 5142, *Davy* 6573; (without locality) *Bolander* 4648.

15. A. ampla sp. nov.

Culm erect from a slightly decumbent base, stout, 75 cm. high. Blades 5–8 mm. broad, about 15 cm. long, scabrous: ligule 5–6 mm. long, rounded. Panicle large and spreading, 20–25 cm. long; branches numerous, verticillate, many shorter ones spikelet-bearing from base, the longer 5–7 cm. long. Spikelets pale or purplish; lower empty glume 4 mm., upper 3.2 mm. long, acuminate, but not awn-pointed, hispidulous on keel and slightly and very minutely papillate on back, but not scabrous; flowering glume 2.3–2.5 mm. long, awned; awn inserted about the middle of the back, bent at the middle or nearly straight, 4–5 mm. long; palet a minute nerveless scale about .3 mm. long.

The type specimen is Suksdorf 135, collected on wet rocks near Rooster Rock, Multnomah County, Oreg., July 16, 1885. This is in the National Herbarium. (Pl. XX.)

DISTRIBUTION: British Columbia to Arizona.

VANCOUVER ISLAND: *Macoun* 82. WASHINGTON: Clallam County, *Elmer* 1953. Falcon valley, *Suksdorf* 132; Seattle, *Henderson* 2113 (this specimen has a decumbent and rooting base); Whatcom County, *Suksdorf* 1184; Bingen, *Suksdorf* 2829. OREGON: Yamhill County, *Shear* 1033, 1636, 1639, 1643, 1646; Roseburg, *Howell* 216, 217 in 1887; Portland, *Bolander* in 1886; Umpqua valley, *Howell* 218; Washington County, Howell 53 in 1881. CALIFORNIA: *Bolander* 4801, 6079; Mendocino County, *Davy and Blasdale* 5199, 5262, 6118; *Brown* 779; Placer County, *Palmer* 2420; Middle Tule River, *Purpus* 5638. ARIZONA: Santa Rita Mountains, *Pringle* in 1884.

Many of the specimens referred here have a more dense panicle than the type but differ from the large forms of *A. microphylla* in having a more verticillately lobed panicle and less awn-pointed glumes. From *A. exarata* this species differs in possessing the awn and in the less scabrous glumes. A few specimens seem to be intermediate between this and the other two species. From *A. longiligula* it differs in the shorter ligule and in the short flower-bearing branches of the panicle.

This species appears to be the *A. virescens* of Thurber in Botany of California, page 274, but differs from *A. virescens* H. B. K. in the longer awn, more spreading panicle, and stouter culms.

bb. Flowering glume awnless or the awn included.

16. A. exarata Trin.

A. exarata Trin., Gram. Unifl. 207. 1824. "(Paniculae contractiusculae) radiis 3, 4, a basi floriferis, hispidis; perianthio mutico glumis acuminatis ⅓ breviori: valvula superiore parva; foliis lanceolato-linearibus, planis. V. spp. ex Unalaschka, unde retulit cl. Dr. Eschholz. (Valvula inferior dorso exarata.)"

In the Trinius herbarium there are three specimens of *A. exarata*, parts of all of which are deposited in the National Herbarium; one collected by Kostalsky in Unalaska in 1829 (Pl. XXI, fig 1), one collected at Sitka by Mertens in 1829, and one collected at Sitka by Eschholz in 1826. None of these is the type specimen that was collected in Unalaska by Eschholz before 1824. If the type is in the Trinius herbarium I overlooked it. The specimens indicated above are mentioned in his subsequent work, Agrostidea II.

A. grandis Trin., Mem. Acad. St. Petersb., Ser. VI, 6^2: 316. 1841. (Agrostidea II: 70.) "Columbia (Hooker)." This is based upon a large panicle only. This form is common. The panicle is stout, long, and rather dense, usually interrupted below, as much as a foot long. The plant is stout, with leaves 6 or 8 mm. wide. In the National Herbarium are spikelets from Trinius' specimen in the herbarium of the St. Petersburg Academy and also a photograph of the single panicle, which I examined in the Trinius herbarium, labeled "Columbia N. W. Amer., No. 376, of Hook. Cat." The empty glumes are 2 mm. long, slightly unequal, acuminate, scabrous on keel. The flowering glume is about two-thirds of the length of the outer glumes, unawned. (Pl. XXII.)

A. asperifolia Trin., Mem. Acad. St. Petersb., Ser. VI, 6^2: 317. 1841. (Agrostidea II: 71.) In the Trinius herbarium there is a single culm representing the upper part of the plant, which is labeled " T. 182." This represents a somewhat larger panicled form than *A. exarata*, but does not differ in essentials. (Pl. XXI, fig. 2.)

A. exarata asperifolia Vasey, U. S. Dept. Agr., Div. Bot., Bul. 18: No. 31. 1892. Described as a form, but with no reference to synonyms. "California to Washington."

A. exarata minor Hook., Fl. Bor. Am. 2: 239. 1840. "Perianthro univalvi *A. drummondi* Torrey, mst. Valleys of the Rocky Mountains on the east and on the west side of the dividing ridge. Drummond. Douglas." I have examined the specimens of Drummond and Douglas in the herbarium of Kew, and take them to be only small forms of *A. exarata*. These two specimens are further referred to in Hooker, Flora Antarctica 2: 373, 1847, in a note on *A. tenuifolia* Bieb. var. *Fretensis*. "Intermediate between them is a common Rocky Mountain species, collected by Douglas and described as *A. exarata* in the 'Flora Boreali-Americana' (vol. 2, p. 239). There are, however, two forms of *A. exarata*; one from the east side of the Rocky Mountains, which has the scabrid broader leaves of the true *A. exarata* and a distinct upper palea (this is the *A. drummondii* Torrey Ms.); the other (or Douglas') from the west side of the dividing ridge is smaller, more slender, with small locustae, and no upper palea. It agrees closely with the Magellanic plant in size and foliage, and bears the name of *A. tenuifolia* ? Bieb., appended to it by Doctor Torrey." Duplicates of the same, mounted on one sheet, are deposited in the Torrey herbarium at the New York Botanical Garden.

A. scouleri Trin., Mem. Acad. Sci. St. Petersb., Ser. VI, 6^2: 323. 1841. (Agrostidea II: 83.) "Nutka Sund. (Hooker)." The type specimen is in the herbarium of the St. Petersburg Academy of Sciences. It consists of a single culm, with a small panicle, labeled "Nutka Sound T. 145." This species has been much misunderstood by American botanists, and the name has usually been applied to some form of *A. pallens*, from which it differs in the presence of the small palet. Trinius' statement that "valvula * * * superior ovarium aequante" has been questioned, but his type specimen shows a small palet. The type shows no rhizome and an awnless flowering glume. (Pl. XVI, fig. 2.)

A. albicans Buckley, Proc. Acad. Nat. Sci. Phila. 1862: 91. 1863. "Oregon Columbia Woods Nuttall." Type seen in herbarium of the Philadelphia Academy of Natural Sciences, but Doctor Gray, in his remarks upon Buckley's plants (Proc. Acad. Nat. Sci. Phila., 1862, p. 334), says that this was "named by Nuttall *A. oregonensis*," slightly altering the name from what it appears on Nuttall's label.

A. tenuifolia Bieb. This name was mentioned by Prof. F. L. Scribner in an article on some grasses collected by Frank Tweedy ("A List of Grasses from Washington Terr.," Bul. Torr. Bot. Club, 10: 63, 1883) as follows: "*Agrostis tenuifolia*, Bieb., Trin. Icon. 3. t. 65. This appears like a slender, narrow-leaved awnless form of *Agrostis exarata*, and has been so referred (No. 1127 Kellogg & Hartford). It seems to be a well-marked species, however, and so well accords with Trinius' figure of *A. tenuifolia* that I have little hesitation in referring it to that species. As I understand *A. exarata*, I am not prepared to unite this species with it." Tweedy's specimen is *A. exarata*. I have referred doubtfully to *A. exarata* a specimen collected by Pringle at Summit Valley, Sierra Nevada Mountains, California, September 22, 1882, at au altitude of 8.000 feet, and which closely resembles Trinius' figure of *A. tenuifolia*. The whole plant is tufted and delicate, with narrow, flat leaves. *A. tenuifolia* is described as having involute leaves.

Culms erect, from 20 to 30 cm. to 1.5 m. in height, tufted but without rhizomes. Blades short, narrow, and upright, or long, wide (5 mm. or even more) and lax, very scabrous. Panicle erect, 5-30 cm. long, contracted and spikelike or loose and somewhat spreading, but the branches almost always densely flowered, very scabrous, spikelet-bearing nearly to base. Spikelets pale, rarely purple; empty glumes equal or the lower slightly longer, acute, acuminate or sometimes sharp-pointed, 2.5-3.5 mm. long, ciliate-scabrous on the keels and often scabrous on back; flowering glume about 2 mm. long, the midnerve usually excurrent above the middle as a tiny point or prickle, rarely with a short, straight awn; palet small, about .3 mm. long. (Pl. XXIII.)

Besides the form with robust panicle described by Trinius under *A. grandis* is one with panicle close and spikelike resembling *Muhlenbergia racemosa* Michx.) B. S. P. of the Eastern States. (Pl. XXIII. A.) However, these forms are all connected by numerous transition specimens so that it is impossible to segregate them even as subspecies.

DISTRIBUTION: Alaska to Mexico. The following are a few specimens to represent distribution:

ALASKA: Yes Bay, *Howell* 1710; Unalaska, *Evans* 518; Juneau, *Coville and Kearney* 2473. BRITISH COLUMBIA: Chilliwack valley, *Macoun* 26038; Alberta, *Macoun* 18612. WASHINGTON: Montesano, *Heller* 3967, Pullman, *Piper* 1759. OREGON: Blue Mountains, *Shear* 1692, *Howell* 217, *Cusick* 804. IDAHO: Halley, *Henderson* 3269. MONTANA: Black Hawk, *Rydberg* 3275; Helena, *Shear* 385. WYOMING: Bear Lodge Mountains, *Williams* 2663; Albany County, *E. Nelson* 472. NEBRASKA: Thomas County, *Rydberg* 1492. COLORADO: Silverton, *Shear* 1227; Pagosa Peak, *Baker* 147; Mancas, *Tracy* 4325. UTAH: Aquarius Plateau, *Ward* 742; Ogden, *Tracy* 324. NEVADA: Humboldt Mountains, *Watson* 1283; Reno, *Tracy* 226. CALIFORNIA: Mount Shasta, *Palmer* 2634; Santa Rosa, *Heller* 5654; New York Falls, *Hansen* 613. ARIZONA: *Toumey* 135; *Lemmon* 3159. NEW MEXICO: *Wright* 1969, 1970; Santa Fe, *Vasey*. MEXICO: State of Chihuahua, *Pringle* 1421. It has also been collected in Wisconsin, but this is out of its range and is probably an accidental specimen.

A. grandis is well represented by—CALIFORNIA: *Hansen* 1826; *Davy and Blasdale* 6053. WASHINGTON: *Elmer* 1952. COLORADO: *Shear and Bessey* 1441. The form with spikelike panicle by—CALIFORNIA: *Palmer* 2634. NEVADA, *Tracy* 218. OREGON, *Griffiths and Morris* 907. WASHINGTON, *Piper* 1759.

17. A. rossæ Vasey.

A. varians Trin., Mem. Acad. St. Petersb., Ser. VI, 6²: 314. 1841. (Agrostidea II: 68.) "America borenl? (Hoocker 217)." Not *A. varians* Thuill., Fl. Paris 1790, which Trinius refers to *A. canina* L. The type specimen is in the Trinius herbarium in the St. Petersburg Academy of Sciences, and is labeled " T. 217." A portion of the type is deposited in the National Herbarium. In the Torrey herbarium is a duplicate type collected on summit of Grass Hill, Rocky Mountains, by Hooker, No. 217. (Pl. XXIV, fig. 2.)

Trinius, in his description of *A. varians*, seems to have included *A. humilis*, as he describes the palet as being absent, or, if present, nearly as long or about half as long as the flowering glume. The type specimen, however, shows only a very minute palet.

A. rossæ Vasey, Contr. U. S. Natl. Herb. **3**: 76. 1892. " Collected in the Yellowstone Park, Wyo., by Miss Edith A. Ross." There are but two sheets of this (the type specimen) in the National Herbarium, collected July, 1890, but I do not see that the plants differ essentially from *A. varians* Trin. (Pl. XXIV, fig. 1.)

The type *A. rossæ* differs from the type of *A. varians* in having more scabrous panicle branches and wider scabrous leaves. More material may show that these forms may be kept separate. There is considerable variation in what I have referred to *A. varians*, in the width of the leaves and the roughness of the panicle. Furthermore it is difficult to separate *A. varians* from *A. exarata*. Both these species are found commonly in the Yellowstone Park, from which comes the only specimen we have seen of *A. rossæ*. For these reasons I have united *A. varians* and *A. rossæ*, taking up the latter name because the former is untenable.

A. variabilis Rydb., Mem. N. Y. Bot. Gard. **1**: 32. 1900. Gives a new name to *A. varians* Trin.

Culms low but comparatively stout, 10–20 cm. high or rarely more, usually densely tufted from a perennial root, but without rhizomes. Blades short, 1 or 2 on the culm, and numerous at the base, 2–5 cm. long or sometimes more, 1–2 mm. wide, flat or conduplicate; sheaths rather conspicuous, especially the basal. Panicle contracted, 3–6 cm. long, about 5 mm. wide, branches appressed, the lower sometimes 2–2.5 cm. long, but usually short. Spikelets green or purple, 2 mm. long; empty glumes nearly equal, acute, scabrous on keel and somewhat on back; flowering glume 1.5 mm. long, awnless, a few short hairs at base; palet very minute. (Pl. XXIV, fig. 2.)

DISTRIBUTION: Washington to California and Wyoming at high altitudes.

WASHINGTON: Mount Rainier, *Piper* 1978, 1980, 2559; Olympic Mountains, *Elmer* 1948; Mount Adams, *Suksdorf* 14, 139; Skamania County, *Suksdorf* 1020; Okanogan County, *Elmer* 730; Nason Creek, *Sandberg and Leiberg* 656. OREGON: Stein's Mountains, *Griffiths and Morris* 562, 595, 615; Ashland Butte, *Howell*, 224; Eagle Creek Mountains, *Cusick* 1073; Wallowa Lake, *Shear* 1709. CALIFORNIA: Soda Springs, *Jones* 323; Summit valley, *Pringle* in 1882; San Bernardino Mountains, *Parish* 3302; (without locality), *Bolander* 5070. IDAHO: Bear Creek, *Leiberg* 2958. UTAH: Rabbit valley, *Ward* 741. WYOMING: Ten Sleep Lakes, *Williams* 2952½, 2964, 2967; Yellowstone Park, *Tweedy* 605; Battle Creek Mountain, *Nelson* 4070.

This may be only an alpine variety of *A. exarata* into which it seems to pass. The panicle, however, does not always have the numerous short branches spikelet-bearing at the base, although it is quite narrow. The outer glumes are not scabrous on the back as is usually the case with *A. exarata*, nor is it so conspicuously hispidulous on the keel. Transitions to *A. exarata* are shown by such forms as the specimens from Stein's Mountains, Oregon, collected by Griffiths and Morris.

== *Panicle open, sometimes diffusely spreading.*

a. *Awn of flowering glume attached near the base.*

18. A. howellii Scribn.

A. howellii Scribn., Contr., U. S. Natl. Herb. **3**: 76. 1892. "Near Hood River, Oregon (No. 198, Howell)." The type specimen is in the National Herbarium, collected August 5, 1886 (Pl. XXV.)

Culms erect or decumbent at base, 40–60 cm. high. Blades lax, very long, 3–5 mm. wide, as much as 30 cm. long. Panicle loose and spreading, scabrous, 10–30 cm. long. Spikelets pale, clustered toward the ends of the branches,

Empty glumes equal, acuminate, rather narrow and firm in texture, somewhat scabrous on keel, 3 mm. long; flowering glume 2.5 mm. long, acute, awned; awn attached to back near base, exserted, bent, about 6 mm. long; palet none.

DISTRIBUTION: OREGON, *Howell* 198; Bridal Veil, *Suksdorf* 134.

The Suksdorf specimens have a more compact panicle, resembling *A. foliosa*, but agree in having the awn inserted near base of glume. This species is not sufficiently known.

aa. *Awn, if present, attached at or above the middle of the glume.*

b. *Panicle very diffuse; branches capillary, very scabrous, the primary branching above the middle; spikelets clustered toward the ends of the smaller branches. In arctic and alpine forms the characters are less plainly shown.*

19. A. hiemalis (Walt.) B. S. P.

Cornucopiæ hyemalis Walt., Fl. Car. 73. 1788. "Culmo erecto panicula diffusa verticillata, foliis angustis suberectibus." The description scarcely suffices to identify the species, but Michaux (Flora 1: 41, 1803) states that this is the same as his *Trichodium laxiflorum*. Furthermore, Walter describes two other species, *C. perennans* and *C. altissima*, so that there is little doubt that *C. hiemalis* is the common *A. scabra* Willd. The plant is not represented in Walter's herbarium and consequently there is probably no type specimen in existence.

A. scabra Willd., Sp. Pl. 1: 370. 1798. "Habitat in America-boreali." The type specimen is in the herbarium of the Botanical Garden of Berlin. There are three panicles representing the ordinary form.

Trichodium laxiflorum Michx., Fl. 1: 42. 1803. "Hab. in humidis et pratensibus a sinu Hudsonis ad Floridam." There is a good plate of this. *Cornucopiæ hiemalis* Walt. is cited as a synonym. The type specimen is in the Michaux herbarium of the Museum of Natural History at Paris. There are the upper portions of several plants of the usual eastern form. (Pl. XXVII, 3.)

A. laxiflora Poiret, Encycl. Suppl. 1: 255. 1810. "Cette plante croît dans la Caroline, où elle a été recuillé par M. Bosc." I found the type of this in M. Cosson's herbarium, Paris.

Trichodium scabrum Muhl., Cat. Pl. 10. 1813. "Pens. fl. Jun. Cher." There is a mixture of specimens in Muhlenberg's herbarium, but since he gives as synonym *A. scabra* Willd. his name must go here, though the description in his Descriptio Graminum seems to apply to *A. perennans*.

A. laxa Schreber "Gram." is given as a synonym of *Trichodium laxiflorum* by Pursh Flora 1: 61, 1814, and hence must apply to this species regardless of the plants so labeled in the Berlin Herbarium.

A. sericea Ell., Sk. 1: 135. 1816. The description applies to a *Muhlenbergia* (*M. capillaris* Kunth), but Mr. E. D. Merrill states that the specimen in Elliott's herbarium is *A. hiemalis* (U. S. Dept. Agr., Div. Agros., Circ. 29, 1901). In such cases the specimen should not be taken as the type.

A. laxiflora Richardson, Franklin Voy. 731 (App. 3). 1823. Transfers *Trichodium laxiflorum* Michx. Richardson's specimen is in the herbarium of the British Museum, labeled "Lake Winipeg and Superior."

A. michauxii Trin. Unifl. 206. 1824. var. (see under *A. perennans*). "Panicula breviori, radiis brevioribus hispidulis." Under this are given two subvarieties, both of which are probably *A. hiemalis*. "α Panicula patente, foliis linearibus," based on *Trichodium laxiflorum* Michx. "β Panicula contractiuscula, foliis latioribus: *Agrostis* (Trichod.) *clavata* Tr. in Spreng. n. Entd. II, p. 55. V. spp. Camtsch." This last form was made a species later, *Trichodium clavatum* Schult., Mant. 8:556, 1827. In the Trinius herbarium there is a specimen of this collected by Kostalsky in 1829, marked "A michauxii m. b. A. clavata Trin. ap. Spreng. N. Entd. II." A portion of this is deposited in the National Herbarium. (Pl. XXVII, 2.)

A. abakanensis Lessing is mentioned as a synonym under *A. michauxii* by Trinius, Mem. Acad. St. Petersb. Ser. VI, 6²: 325. 1841.

Trichodium laxum Schult., Mant. 2: 157, 1824. Based on Muhlenberg's *Trichodium laxiflorum*, which name Schultes changes because of *T. laxiflorum* Michx., which he considers different. He also wishes to take up the specific name *laxa* (*Agrostis laxa* Schreb.). The culm is described as erect and the "habitat

DESCRIPTION OF SPECIES.

in arvis siccis, floret Maio." An examination of Muhlenberg's herbarium shows the following as to the species of Trichodium described by him in his Descriptio Uberior Graminum:
1. *Trichodium laxiflorum*=*A. hiemalis.*
2. *Trichodium decumbens*=*A. perennans*, the weak form.
3. *Trichodium scabrum*=*A. hiemalis* (as to name). In the herbarium there is a mixture of several grasses, one of which is *A. hiemalis.*
4. *Trichodium* (no specific name). I have been unable to determine from his herbarium what grass was referred to, but it is probably the stout form of *A. perennans.*

A. scabra tenuis Tuckerm., Amer. Jour. Sci. **45**: 45. 1843. "Vaginis scabris panicula tenui ramis erectis." "A small delicate form with a very slender panicle. Rocks of the Flume, Lincoln, N. H."
A. laxiflora cæspitosa, Torr. Fl., N. Y., **2**: 442. 1843.
A. scabriuscula Buckl., Proc. Acad. Nat. Sci. Phila. **1862**: 90. 1863. The type specimen is in the herbarium of the Philadelphia Academy of Natural Sciences. Doctor Gray in his remarks upon Buckley's plants (l. c., 334) states that this was "ticketed by Nuttall *Agrostis scabrata.*"
A. hiemalis B. S. P., Prel. Cat N. Y. 68. 1888. Gives new combination with reference to synonym *A. scabra* Willd.

Culms slender, tufted or scattered, 20–80 cm. high. Blades narrow and usually short, sometimes 2–3 mm. wide, but often very narrow, almost setaceous; sheaths striate, the upper usually somewhat inflated and inclosing the base of the panicle; panicle large and very diffuse, in the larger forms 50–60 cm. long, the branches long and capillary, very scabrous. Spikelets crowded toward the tips of the branchlets, pale or usually purple; empty glumes nearly equal or the lower slightly longer, 1.5–2 mm. long, acute or acuminate, scabrous on keels, especially the lower; flowering glume obtuse two-thirds to three-fourths as long as empty glumes, usually awnless; palet, none or minute. (Pl. XXVI, fig. 2.)

In typical forms the panicle is in flower and wide spreading at the upper part, while the base is still inclosed in the upper sheath, the branches of the lower exserted portion being numerous and appressed-ascending; later the entire panicle is exserted and the branches wide spreading; at maturity the panicle breaks away from the plant and rolls before the wind. (Pl. XXVI, fig. 1.)

DISTRIBUTION: Throughout North America from the arctic regions southward into Mexico.

In the mountains of New England is a form which has awned spikelets. I have examined this form in the White Mountains of New Hampshire and am unable to separate it as a species. At higher altitudes there is a tendency to form tufts with numerous slender radical leaves, but these characters are not at all constant. The awn when present varies in length and springs from the back of the flowering glume. (Pl. XXVII, 5.) This form has been named—

Trichodium montanum Torr., Comp. 50. 1826. "Mountains." Torrey's specimen is in the Torrey herbarium at the New York Botanical Garden. It has the tuft of setaceous leaves at base, but the flowering glume is awnless. Type specimen collected on "summit of the New Beacon Fishkill."
A. oreophila Trin., Mem. Acad. St. Petersb., Ser. VI, **6**^{2}: 323. 1841. (Agrostidea II:77.) "Bethlehem Pensylvaniæ (Moser)." Trinius gives as synonym *Trichodium montanum* Torr. This disposition is also made by Doctor Gray (Manual, Ed. 1). The species in the Trinius herbarium is, however, a small erect form of *A. perennans* Tuckerm. Trinius's description agrees with this specimen. Hence *A. oreophila* Trin. should be considered as a synonym of *A. perennans* Tuckerm., and the citation of *Trichodium montanum* Torr. was an error, arising from the fact that the specimen was sent to him under the last-mentioned name. Trinius probably intended to change the name on account of a previous *A. montanum.*
A. laxiflora montana Tuckerm., Am. Jour. Sci. **45**:43. April to June, 1843. Not *A. montana* Krock., Fl. Siles. **1**: 110, 1787, nor R. Br. **1**: 171, 1810. Tuckerman's specimen is in the Gray herbarium.

A. torreyi Tuckerm., Hovey's Mag. Hort. 9:143. April, 1843. Not *A. torreyi* Kunth, Enum. 1: 226, 1833, which is a *Muhlenbergia*.

Other specimens occur, mostly from the Eastern States, in which the flowering glume is awned, but in which this is not co-ordinated with other characters by which the specimens may be referred to any particular form or subspecies. Certain plants from Labrador (Waghorne 37 and Allen 23) resemble Tuckerman's *A. torreyi*.

A robust leafy form occurs especially in the Western States, from Washington to Arizona Territory. This passes into the following subspecies:

A. hiemalis subrepens subsp. nov.

Culms erect, tall and robust, about 1 m. high, provided with rhizomes. Panicles with relatively shorter branches. Spikelets 2.5 mm. long; flowering glume 1.6 mm. long; palet minute (.2 mm. long).

Type specimen in National Herbarium collected by C. G. Pringle in wet places, pine plains, base of Sierra Madre Mountains, State of Chihuahua, Mexico, September 28, 1887 (No. 1420).

I have referred the following to this, although the specimens do not in all cases show rhizomes or decumbent rooting bases on account of scanty material.

NEW MEXICO: Near Cloverdale, *Mearns* 490. NEVADA: Ruby Valley, *Watson* 1282. ARIZONA: Santa Catalina Mountains, *Toumey* 5 in 1894; *Pringle* in 1881; Rincon Mountains, *Nealley* 175; Tucson, *Toumey* in 1892. MEXICO: Chihuahua, *Townsend and Baker* 276. VENEZUELA: *Fendler* 2541.

A. hiemalis geminata (Trin.) comb. nov.

A. geminata Trin., Gram. Unifl. 207. 1824. "V. spp. ex Unalaschka, unde retulit cl. Dr. Eschholz." The type specimen of this is in the Trinius herbarium. A portion is deposited in the National Herbarium. The plate in Trinius's Spec. Gram. 1: 28 is characteristic.

In the type specimen the culm is 20 cm. high, panicle loose but not diffuse, 5 cm. long, divaricately branching, flowering glume provided with a scarcely exserted straight awn. In all other particulars it agrees with *A. hiemalis*. (Pl. XXVIII, fig 1.)

Unalaska, Eschholz (type). Specimens from Juneau, *Brewer and Coe* 574, and *Piper* 4622 at Kadiak and 4623 at Sitka, nearly match this, but all the other specimens have a large and more diffuse panicle, thus approaching *A. hiemalis*. Those from Alaska are: Juneau, *Cole* in 1899, *Trelease and Saunders* 2900; *Coville and Kearney* 2461, 2500. A specimen from Chilliwack valley, British Columbia (*Macoun* 26036), and another from Pagosa Pass, Colorado (*Baker* 37), have the awn, but a more diffuse panicle.

Closely agreeing with *A. geminata*, but flowering glume awnless, is a specimen collected at Ratz Harbor, Prince of Wales Island, No. 2014, J. B. Flett, July 31, 1901, "growing in moss on old logs projecting into a lake." (Pl. XXVIII, fig. 2.)

The following specimens may be placed here, although they are connected with *A. hiemalis* by a series of intergrades:

BRITISH COLUMBIA: Rogers Pass, *Macoun* 2 in 1890; Chilliwack valley, *Macoun* 26041. WASHINGTON: Mount Rainier, *Allen* in 1894. MONTANA: Little Belt Mountains, *Rydberg* 3390; Crazy Mountains, *Rydberg* 3444. WYOMING: Yellowstone Park, *Merrill* 141, 142, *Tweedy* 607, *Ross* in 1890; *Williams* 2938. CALIFORNIA: Lassens Peak, *Jones* in 1897; Kern River, *Rothrock* 323. COLORADO: Pagosa Peak, *Baker* 40 c; Buffalo Pass, *Shear and Bessey* 1453.

A form of *A. hiemalis* occurring from Alaska to Newfoundland has been described as:

Trichodium album Presl, Rel. Haenk. **1**: 244. 1830. "Hab. in sinu Nutkaensis." The type specimen is in the Presl herbarium at Prague. There are three plants mounted on the sheet; one is the ordinary form of *A. hiemalis;* a second is *A. exarata;* while the third is a taller form of *A. hiemalis* with the branches of the panicle appressed and the culm decumbent at base. This is the same as has been distributed to other herbaria under the name of *Trichodium album* and is the specimen that I take as the type. (Pl. XXVII, fig. 1.)

A. nutkaensis Kunth, Enum. **1**:222. 1833. "Sinus nutkaensis." Based on *Trichodium album* Presl. The spelling was changed by Trinius (Mem. Acad. St. Petersb., Ser. VI, **6**²: 326, 1841. Agrostidea **II**: 80) to *A. nootkaensis.*

The following specimens can be referred to this form fairly well:

ALASKA: Unalaska, *Piper* 4625; Kadiak Island, *Trelease,* 2901, 2902, 2904; *Evans,* 454, *Piper,* 4624; Yes Bay, *Howell,* 1711; Popof Islands, *Saunders* in 1899, *Kincaid* in 1899; Fort Sampson, *Kellogg,* 103; Kenai, *Nielson,* 51. NEWFOUNDLAND: *Waghorne,* 11, 12. LABRADOR: *Waghorne,* 23, 36.

In the National Herbarium are several dwarf specimens from Newfoundland, Labrador, and Alpine regions of the western mountains which appear to be *A. hiemalis,* but can not be definitely referred to any form above mentioned; for example, Waghorne 25, Newfoundland. (Pl. XXVII, fig. 4.)

bb. *Panicle open, but not conspicuously diffuse; branches more or less capillary.*

c. *Flowering glume awnless.*

20. A. idahoensis Nash.

A. tenuis Vasey, Bul. Torr. Bot. Club, **10**: 21. 1883. Not *A. tenuis* Sibth., 1794. "Collected on the San Bernardino Mountains, California, by the Parish brothers." The type specimen (No. 1085) is in the National Herbarium. (Pl. XXIX, fig. 2.)

A. idahoensis Nash, Bul. Torr. Bot. Club, **24**: 42. 1897. "Collected by A. A. and E. Gertrude Heller, at Forest, Nez Perces County, Idaho." The type specimen is the one from which Mr. Nash drew up the description, and is probably at the New York Botanical Garden. Duplicate types are in the National Herbarium and in several other herbaria. The one in the National Herbarium was collected July 16, 1896, at an altitude of 3,500 feet (No. 3431). This is about intermediate between *A. tenuis* Vasey and the subspecies *recta.* (Pl. XXIX, fig. 1.)

A. tenuiculmis Nash, Mem. N. Y. Bot. Gard. **1**: 32. 1900. Those who give the legal aspect prominence may insist that there is not sufficient evidence for citing Nash as the author of *A. tenuiculmis,* but it is evident that he intended to change the name. It is based upon the following, in Rydberg's Flora of Montana (Mem. N. Y. Bot. Garden **1**:32) : "*Agrostis tenuiculmis recta* Nash; *Agrostis tenuis erecta* Vasey, mss: not *A. erecta* Spreng. *Agrostis tenuis* Vasey, Bul. Torr. Bot. Club, **10**: 21 is antedated by *A. tenuis* Sibth. 1794, consequently both the specific and varietal name must be changed. It is a small plant with a small panicle and erect or ascending rays and no palet."

Furthermore, *A. tenuis erecta* Vasey is a manuscript name and hence *A. tenuiculmis recta* Nash rests upon the brief description cited above. But, compared with the species *A. tenuiculmis,* the variety is a taller plant with upright stem and longer panicle.

A. tenuiculmis recta Nash. Mem. N. Y. Bot. Gard. **1**: 32. 1900. Several localities are given in Montana and Yellowstone Park. Of the two specimens in the National Herbarium, probably named by Doctor Vasey *A. tenuis erecta,* one is from Washington State, collected by Suksdorf, 1883. The other from Oregon, Cusick, No. 1070, has a palet, and, though it looks similar to this, should be referred to *A. humilis.* I have therefore taken as the type of *A. tenuiculmis recta* Nash the Suksdorf specimen, which is numbered 48. This is a larger form, which differs in its taller culms, broader leaves, and often larger spikelets, but seems scarcely worth recognizing as a subspecies.

Culms slender, tufted from a perennial root, erect or geniculate at base, 10–30 cm. high. Blades narrow, one or two on the culm (1–6 cm. long), but mostly basal, when they may be as much as 10 cm. long in the taller forms. Panicles loosely spreading, 5-10 cm. long, branches capillary, minutely scabrous. Spikelets about 1.5 mm. long, pale or purplish; lower glume slightly longer and more acute than the upper, scabrous on keel; flowering glume 1 mm. long, truncate, awnless; palet minute, not more than .2 mm. long.

DISTRIBUTION: Washington to Colorado and California.

CALIFORNIA: Placer County, *Carpenter* in 1892; Fresno County, *Hall and Chandler* 603; *Palmer* 238 in 1888; Merced River, *Torrey* 567 in 1865; Mariposa County, *Congdon* in 1898; Lincoln Valley, *Kennedy and Doten* 195; Bear River, *Hansen* 2079; San Jacinto Mountains, *Hall* 784, 2363. WYOMING: Yellowstone Park, *Rydberg and Bessey* 3571, *Nelson* 6080, *Merrill* 148, 148½, *Rose* 690, *Tweedy* 33, 606. MONTANA: *Knowlton* in 1887.

The following are more robust and have been referred by some authors to *A. tenuiculmis recta* Nash:

WASHINGTON: *Suksdorf* 48. OREGON: Umatilla, *Shear* 1661, 1664½. IDAHO: St. Marys River, *Leiberg* 1130. MONTANA: Belt Pass, *Rydberg* 3327½. WYOMING: Yellowstone Park, *Merrill* 130, 143, 147, *Rydberg and Bessey* 3572. COLORADO: Pagosa Peak, *Baker* 150. This last specimen is yet more robust and there is a short straight awn on the flowering glume.

21. A. oregonensis Vasey.

A. oregonensis Vasey, Bul. Torr. Bot. Club 18:55. April, 1886. " Root fibrous (annual?); culms about 2 feet high, somewhat slender, radical leaves filiform; culm leaves distant, narrow, soon tapering to a long, slender point, 3 to 4 inches long; ligule short; panicle 4 to 5 inches long, nodding and flexuous, open but not spreading; branches capillary, unequal, mostly in fives below, above in twos or threes, the longer about 2 inches long, all naked below, and rather numerously flowered above; pedicles slender, as long as, to two or three times as long as, the spikelets, which are about 1½ lines long, narrowly lanceolate, and gradually tapering to the acute point, slightly scabrous on the keel, rather thin and purple; flowering glume a little shorter than the empty ones, narrowly lanceolate, five-nerved, apex rather obtuse; palet wanting. The panicle has a rich purple color, and it approaches the *A. scabra*, but is shorter, and with much shorter and erect branches and a firmer culm." Collected in Oregon by Mr. Howell." Type specimen in the National Herbarium, Howell 49. Panicle purple. Palet present as a very small scale .2-.4 mm. long. (Pl. XIV, fig. 2.)

DISTRIBUTION: WASHINGTON: Marsh, Kittitas County, *Henderson* 2123; wet meadows, Skamania County, July 25, 1886, *Suksdorf* 198, 907; Copalis, Chehalis County, *Conard* 47; Clallam County, *Lawrence* 318. OREGON: *Howell* 3, 49. I have also referred here Tweedy's 36 from Teton Forest Reserve, Wyoming. We have not sufficient material of this species and it may be that it is only a form of some other species. It differs from *A. longiligula* in the shorter ligule and the absence of the awn. It seems to be too robust for *A. idahoensis*, and I find no indication of rootstocks except in Henderson's No. 2123, which shows at least a rooting decumbent stem. The absence of rootstocks separates it from *A. pallens foliosa*.

There is an *A. oregonensis* Nutt., but this name has no valid standing. Doctor Gray, in his review of Buckley's new species says (Proc. Acad. Nat. Sci. Phila. 1862: 334, 1863): "*Agrostis albicans* is founded on a slender form of *A. exarata* Trin., named by Nuttall *A. oregonensis*."

To *A. oregonensis* I have also referred:

A. attenuata Vasey, Bot. Gaz. 2:337. December, 1886. " Culms slender, smooth, erect, attenuated, 2 to 3 feet long; radical leaves narrowly linear, 2 to 4 inches long; culm leaves 3, distant, sheaths shorter than the internodes, smooth; ligule membranaceous, conspicuous, 2 to 3 lines long; blade 2 to 3 inches long, narrow, acuminate; panicle 3 to 4 inches long, pyramidal, lower branches in threes or fives, somewhat unequal, 1 to 2 inches long, capillary, few-flowered, pedicels mostly longer than the spikelets, which are about 1½ lines long;

empty glumes equal, oblong-lanceolate, acute, scabrous on the keel; flowering glume nearly as long; palet wanting. Found by Mr. Thomas Howell near Mount Hood, Oregon. It belongs to the scabra group, but is well distinguished as a species."

The type specimen is in the National Herbarium and was collected in the swamps, south side of Mount Hood (No. 210) by Thomas Howell, October 1, 1886. (Pl. XIII, fig. 2.) This has a slightly different aspect from *A. oregonensis*, but I am unable to find essential characters upon which to make a separation. The panicle is stramineous, probably due to age. The most noteworthy character is that the spikelets disarticulate below the glumes, but the specimen is past maturity. In the National Herbarium there is but one other specimen agreeing with this, Coville and Applegate 753, Salmon Prairie, Clackamas County, Oreg., September 3, 1897.

22. A. schiedeana Trin.

A. schiedeana Trin., Mem. Acad. St. Petersb.; Ser. VI, 6^2: 327. 1841. (Agrostidea II: 81.) "Mexico, (Schrader)." The type specimen of this is probably in the Trinius herbarium, but I neglected to search for it.
A. hallii californica Vasey, Contr. U. S. Natl. Herb. **3**: 74. 1892. This is based upon *A. elata* of the Botany of California (Watson, Bot. Calif. **2**: 274. 1880.) The type specimen is, therefore, Bolander's 6103, which is in the National Herbarium. (Pl. X, fig. 1.) Torrey's plant from Lake Washoe, Nevada, may be the same, but our specimen shows only the upper part.

Culms tall, 60–100 cm., erect or slightly decumbent at base. Blades rather narrow, 2–3 mm. wide, upright, 10–15 cm. long. Panicle oblong, 10–30 cm. long, open, the branches in verticils, rather stiff and ascending, the lower whorls often numerous, the longer 5–10 cm. long and branching above the middle. Spikelets 2.5–3 mm. long; flowering glume 1.5–1.8 long; palet small, .2–.6 mm. long. (Pl. XXX.)

DISTRIBUTION: British Columbia to Mexico, in wet meadows.

BRITISH COLUMBIA: Vancouver Island, *Macoun* 81. WASHINGTON: Falcon Valley, *Suksdorf* 50, 189, 189a, 906; Lewis River, *Henderson* 2131. OREGON: White Horse Ranch, *Griffiths and Morris* 466. NEVADA: Quinn River Crossing, *Griffiths and Morris* 14 (grown in Grass Garden at Washington from seed). CALIFORNIA: Sierra Nevada Mountains, *Lemmon* in 1875; Bear Valley, San Bernardino Mountains, *Parish brothers* 1560. MEXICO: State of Mexico, *Pringle* 4485; Durango, *Palmer* 190. A specimen from Kadiak Island, Alaska (*Georgeson* 1 in 1898), appears to be this species. The spikelets are 3 mm. long. Another specimen from Bozeman, Mont., *Rydberg* 2218, has the flowering glume provided with an exserted bent awn.

This species has gone under the names of *A. hallii*, *A. scabra*, and *A. elata* on the Pacific coast. I may be wrong in referring our plants to *A. schiedeana*, as I have not seen the type, but the plants agree with Trinius's description. Pringle's and Palmer's specimens from Mexico have a palet about .6 mm. long, but it is a nerveless scale. (Pl. XXX, A.) The spikelets vary from 2.2 mm. to 2.7 mm. or even 3 mm. in the Alaska specimens. The specimens agree, however, in the shape of the panicle and the absence of rhizomes.

23. A. perennans (Walt.) Tuckerm.

Cornucopiæ perennans Walt., Fl. Car. 74. 1788. "Culmis subdecumbentibus; follis latioribus; panicula longa diffusa, ramis trichotomis verticillatis. Gramen undique laeve, saccharinum, aestatem sustinens, in hyeme vigens, radicibus geniculisque se cito propagans. Donum inaestimabile, conditore ad hanc diem, reservatum, hoc aevum, me instrumento, locupletatum."
A. cornucopiæ Fraser, Gentleman's Magazine **59**: 873. 1789. "Gathered in

South Carolina by Mr. Thomas Walter; even 500 miles up the country, Fraser. Sent to Linnæus from Canada by Professor Kalm." The article is entitled "Fraser's Carolina grass." A plate accompanies the description. As synonym is given *Cornucopiæ perennans* Walt. It is interesting to note that this was sent to Linnæus by Mr. Kalm, but I have not been able to find a reference to this in Linnæus's works. It seems strange that Linnæus did not describe either this or *A. hiemalis*, both of which are common in the Eastern States.

I have not seen the type specimen of this, and there probably is none in existence. In the herbarium of Mr. de Candolle at Geneva I saw a specimen labeled *Agrostis cornucopiæ* from "Carol. merid.," sent by Fraser. This may be taken as a duplicate type. It is the stout leafy form with rather large and heavy panicle and a decumbent base. There is a similar specimen in the herbarium of the Philadelphia Academy of Natural Sciences. Since Fraser was familiar with Walter's plants and states that this was collected in South Carolina by Walter, there seems to be no doubt that this is the same as *Cornucopiæ perennans* of Walter.

A. anomala Willd., Sp. Pl. 1:370. 1798. "Habitat in America boreali." Based on Walter's *Cornucopiæ perennans*.

Alopecurus carolinianus Spreng., Nach. Bot. Gart. Halle, 10, 1801. A specimen of this is in the Trinius herbarium labeled "*Alopecurus carolinianus* Spreng. ab ipso missus" and another labeled "alluvial banks Kentucky River, Robert Peter, M. D., Lexington, Ky." (Pl. XXXI, *B*.) I have not seen the type specimen.

Trichodium decumbens Michx., Fl. 1 : 42. 1803. "Hab. a Virginia maritima ad Floridam, præsertim ad ripas amnium, solo limoso hieme inundato." Type specimen in the Michaux herbarium at the Museum of Natural History at Paris. It is the common stout form and the label states that it is *Cornucopiæ perennans* Walt. The specimen does not show the base, but the description states that it is decumbent. (Pl. XXXII, *B*.)

Pursh's specimen of *Trichodium decumbens* Michx. in the Kew Herbarium is the small lax form.

Trichodium perennans Ell., Sk. 1: 99. 1816. "Grows in damp, shaded places." Elliott gives as synonym *Cornucopiæ perennans* Walt., but Mr. E. D. Merrill, who has examined the specimen in Elliott's herbarium, says it is "a form of the grass now referred to *Agrostis altissima* (Walt.) Tuckerm." (U. S. Dept. Agr., Div. Agros., Circ. 29, 1901.) This disposition depends upon the identity of the latter plant. As Elliott's species is based on *Cornucopiæ perennans* Walt., I should refer this back to Walter's plant as interpreted by Fraser.

Trichodium muhlenbergianum Schult., Mant. 2: 159. 1824. Based on Muhlenberg's Trichodium No. 4, which is probably some form of *A. perennans*.

A. michauxii Trin., Unifl. 206. 1824. Under this Trinius places three varieties. Var. α "Paniculæ longæ, amplioris, radiis elongatis, hispidissimis." This would be insufficient to identify the species, but he gives *Trichodium decumbens* Michx. as synonym.

A. noveboracensis Spreng., Syst. 1 : 260. 1825. "Sylvæ Nov. Eboræ Torr." The description seems to apply better to *A. perennans* than to *A. hiemalis*. I have not seen the type specimen.

A. schweinitzii Trin., Mem. Acad. St. Petersb., Ser. VI, 6²: 311. 1841. (Agrostidea, II: 65.) "*Trichodium clatum* Pursh (Schweinitz in hbio Martii) Pennsylvan." The specimen in the Trinius herbarium (Pl. XXXI, *A*) is not *T. elatum* of Pursh, but a lax form of *A. perennans*. However, since Trinius cites *Trichodium clatum* as synonym it might be claimed that this should be the type rather than the specimen in his herbarium. It is to be noted, however, that Trinius gives *Trichodium clatum* Pursh as a synonym of his *Agrostis elata*, described on page 71 of the same work. I therefore take as the type of *A. schweinitzii* the specimen in the Trinius herbarium. It is quite probable that Trinius means to say in the quotation above that his *A. schweinitzii* is the plant collected by Schweinitz and labeled (incorrectly) *Trichodium clatum* Pursh. This specimen appears to be the small form of this species, though only the upper part of the plant is present.

A. oreophila Trin., l. c. 323 (Agrostidea II: 77). Trinius cites *Trichodium montanum* Torr. as a synonym, but the type specimen in the Trinius herbarium is a rather small but erect form of *A. perennans*. It is from Bethlehem, Pa., sent by Moser. (Pl. XXXII, *A*.) See note on this under *A. hiemalis*.

A. perennans Tuckerm., Am. Jour. Sci. 45 : 44. 1843. "Hab. Carolina, Walter, Fraser, Elliott, Curtis; Pennsylvania, Darlington; Columbus, Ohio, Sulli-

DESCRIPTION OF SPECIES. 49

vant. The habit of this species is very marked, and it is pronounced 'quite distinct' by Doctor Darlington. It is probable that it does not occur very far to the north." As this is primarily a change of name, it is a typonym of *Cornucopiæ perennans* Walt.

I have been unable to find the specimens upon which Tuckerman based his descriptions of *A. perennans* and *A. novæ-angliæ*. The name *A. perennans* Tuckerm. should rest upon *Cornucopiæ perennans* Walt., but the description seems to refer to another form. As stated below, the species varies from the large upright stout form to a smaller lax decumbent form. These extremes seem quite distinct. From the description I think that Mr. Tuckerman had in mind the small form when he described *A. perennans* ("Culmis fere decumbentibus basi geniculatis ramosis glabris"). This was published in the American Journal of Science, July, 1843, in an article on the Trichodium section of Agrostis. In the same place he publishes *A. altissima* based on *Cornucopiæ altissima* Walt., to which he adds variety *laxa*. This is the stout large-panicled form which is described as *A. novæ-angliæ* in Hovey's Magazine of Horticulture, April, 1843.

A. novæ-angliæ Tuckerm., Hovey's Mag. 9 : 143, 1843. Not *A. novæ-angliæ* Vasey, Contr. Natl. Herb. 3 : 76, 1892, which is *A. borealis* Hartm. Tuckerman says "a stout, coarse grass of mountain brooks and wet rocks in the Notch of the White Mountains. It is wholly different from our other New England species, *A. laxiflora* and *A. scabra;* but the flowers agree so nearly with those of *A. altissima*, a southern species, that I have thought it was a variety of that plant. It differs, however, strikingly in habit." In his review of Trichodium section of Agrostis (Am. Jour. Sci. 45 : 44, 1843) Tuckerman says under *Agrostis altissima*, "β laxa (mihi) ; panicula laxiori ramis longioribus viridi. *A. novæ-angliæ* (mihi MSS.)." This would seem to indicate that the article in the American Journal of Science was written before that in Hovey's Magazine, although published a few weeks later. This is the large, leafy form found from New England to North Carolina, but it passes imperceptibly into the ordinary form and I am unable to distinguish it even as a subspecies.

A. campyla Tuckerm., Am. Journ. Sci., Ser. II, 6: 231, 1848. "Hab. New England, New York, Torrey. Pennsylvania, Muhl." Tuckerman's specimen in the Gray herbarium is the erect stout form.

A. aphanes Trin., Mem. Acad. St. Petersb., Ser VI, 6²: 346. 1841. (Agrostidea II : 100.) "Terra nova. (Lapylaie, Kunth)." From the description this appears to be *A. perennans*.

A. perennans æstivalis Vasey, Contr. Natl. Herb. 3: 76. 1892. Type specimen collected by E. Hall at Athens, Ill., September, 1864. No specimen is indicated in the original description, but the range is given as Illinois, Tennessee, and westward. There are two specimens marked by Dr. Vasey, one from Illinois and one from Tennessee (Doctor Gattinger). I have taken the former as the type. (Pl. XXXII.) This is the small form. If this form is to be distinguished by a name it is probably best to take up *æstivalis* on account of the uncertainty of *A. schweinitzii* Trin.

A intermedia Scribn., Bul. Torr. Bot. Club, 20:476. 1893.

This species is described in a footnote accompanying an account of the flora of southeastern Kentucky. Appended to this article is a list of specimens. Two numbers are mentioned with *A. intermedia*, 39 and 174. The first would be the type. This was collected on the summit of Pine Mountain, Harlan County, Tenn., by T. H. Kearney, in 1893. Professor Scribner states that this species is intermediate between *A. elata* and *A. perennans*, his idea of the latter being the small, decumbent form. I have been unable to locate the type of this, but a duplicate type is in the National Herbarium.

The citation for *A. intermedia* has generally been given as Univ. Tenn. Agr. Exp. Sta. Bul. 7: 76. 1894. (Grasses of Tennessee, Pt. II.)

A. pseudointermedia Farwell, Ann. Rept. Com. Parks and Boulevards, Detroit, Mich., 11: 46. 1900. Gives new name to *Agrostis intermedia* Scribn. on account of *A. intermedia* Balb., Elencho 85. 1802.

A. scribneriana Nash, in Small Flora S. E. States, 126. 1903. Gives a new name to *A. intermedia* on account of *A. intermedia* Balb., but overlooks *A. pseudointermedia* Farwell.

Culms erect or more or less decumbent at base, varying from weak and lax to stout and tall, 30–100 cm. tall. Leaves rather numerous, the blades lax or stiffly upright, corresponding to the culms, 1–6 mm. wide, 10–20 cm. long.

Panicle open, oblong, branches ascending, branching again about the middle. Spikelets 2-3 mm. long; empty glumes nearly equal, acute or acuminate; flowering glume 1.5-2 mm. long, awnless; palet none or minute. (Pl. XXXI.)

In habit this species is quite variable. It is common in the Middle Atlantic States in autumn. It flowers later than any other species of Agrostis in the Eastern States (September to November). In open ground the culms are tufted, stout, and erect, with stiff, ascending branches of the panicle. In woodlands the culms are likely to be decumbent at base, while in deep shade or along brooks the culms and foliage are weak and lax, the former decumbent and spreading. The panicles in this form are more open, with fewer branches, which are sometimes conspicuously divaricately branched. In the large suite of specimens examined there are all gradations between these forms.

DISTRIBUTION: Maine and Minnesota to Florida and Texas. I have also referred to this species Liebmann 714 from Mirador, Mexico. A specimen from Wolf Creek, Tenn. (Kearney No. 953), has the flowering glume awned.

The plants we have from Japan labeled *A. perennans* differ from ours in having the panicle more compact, narrower, the branches shorter and more erect.

A. perennans elata (Pursh) comb. nov.

Cornucopiæ altissima Walt., Fl. Carol. 74. 1788. " Culmo erecto, duro; panicula coarctata; flor. magnis." This description is scarcely sufficient to identify the species, which is not represented in Walter's herbarium. The plant which I have referred to *A. elata* is quite rare and there are few specimens from the Carolinas, the region covered by Walter's Flora, and it certainly is not common. There does not seem sufficient evidence for taking up Walter's name, nor is it likely to be any better known in the future. The name is inserted here because later authors have assumed that this was *Trichodium elatum* Pursh. It is more likely to have been *Agrostis alba* L.

Trichodium elatum Pursh, Fl. 1: 61. 1814. "In sandy deep swamps; New Jersey, Carolina, etc." The type specimen, or at least one collected by Pursh, is in the herbarium at Kew.

A. elata Trin., Mem. Acad. St. Petersb., Ser. VI, 6^2: 317. 1841. (Agrostidea II: 71.) "Nov. Cæsar. (Gray et Greville.)"

The type specimen is in the Trinius herbarium at St. Petersburg. There are two plants mounted on the sheet, one from pine barrens of New Jersey, collected by Doctor Torrey and sent by Greville, in 1835. The other, also from New Jersey ("Nov. Cæsar"), sent by Doctor Gray, 1835. The second would be the type, as it is the one first mentioned by Trinius. (Pl. XXXIII A.) Both specimens agree with Pursh's type. It may be best to consider this primarily a change of name, in which case the type is Pursh's plant.

A. altissima Tuckerm., Am. Jour. Sci. 45: 44. 1843. "Hab. Carolina, Walter, Curtis; New Jersey, Pursh, Torrey." Tuckerman refers to this, " T. n. 4 (anon.) Muhl. Gram., p. 52 (fide Torr.)." I should consider this primarily a change of name and that Tuckerman wished to take up Walter's *Cornucopiæ altissima* and transfer it to the genus Agrostis.

This differs from *A. perennans* in the more slender and elongated culms, often decumbent at base, but particularly in the crowding of the spikelets toward the ends of the branches, which gives them a more drooping appearance. (Pl. XXXIII.)

DISTRIBUTION: Swamps, New Jersey to Mississippi.

NEW JERSEY: *Scribner* in 1881; Pines, *Leggett* in 1873; Atlantic County, *Gross* in 1883; Tom's River, *Porter* in 1870; Egg Harbor, *Vasey* in 1884. MARYLAND: Brackish marsh, Ocean City, *Hitchcock* in 1902. VIRGINIA: Low ground, burntover pine lands, *Warburton* in 1903. NORTH CAROLINA: *M. A. Curtis* (Torrey herb.). SOUTH CAROLINA: *M. A. Curtis* in 1851 (Torrey herb.). ALABAMA: Gateswood, *Tracy* 8371. MISSISSIPPI: Biloxi, *Tracy* 3864, 4555; in pine woods clearing, Pass Christian, *Langlois* in 1882; among bushes in open marshes,

Waynesboro, *Kearney* 137; growing in hummocks in shaded pine barren bog, Nicholsen, *Kearney* 382.

cc. Flowering glume awned.

24. A. canina L.

A. canina L., Sp. Pl. 62. 1753. "Habitat in Europæ pascuis humidiusculis." Type specimen in the Linnæan herbarium. *Agraulus caninus* Beauv., Agrost. 5. 1812. Refers *A. canina* L. to this new genus. *Trichodium caninum* Schrad., Fl. Germ. 1: 198. 1806. Gives description and cites *A. canina* L. ex Willd. as synonym. Gives six varieties.

Culms tufted, 30–50 cm. tall. Blades mostly short and narrow, those of the culm 3–6 cm. long, usually not over 2 mm. wide. Panicle loose and spreading, mostly 5–10 cm. long. Empty glumes equal, acute, 2 mm. long, lower minutely scabrous on keel; flowering glume a little shorter than the empty glumes, awned on the back about the middle, awn exserted, bent, callus minutely hairy: palet none. (Pl. IX, fig. 2.)

This species is apparently not native in this country. It is in cultivation under the name of Rhode Island bent and has escaped along roadsides and fields. Our specimens in the National Herbarium are all from the Northeastern States. This species resembles the awned forms of *A. alba*, from which it differs by the absence of the palet.

25. A. melaleuca (Trin.) comb. nov.

A. canina aenea Trin., in Bong. Mem. Acad. Sci. St. Petersb. Ser. VI, 1: 170. 1832. Veg. Sitcha. Not *A. aenea* Spreng., Syst. Cur. Post. 337, 1827. For note concerning date see *A. æquivalvis*. The original descriptions of this and some other species appear in this work under *A. canina*, as follows: "191. *Agrostis canina* L., Tr. lc, p. 208. *Trichodium caninum* Schrad., Roem. et Schult. II, p. 277. Planta nostrati ex toto simillima, præterquam quod spiculas nonnihil majores habeat. Sed in regionibus illis boreali-orientalibus et aliæ Agrostidis formæ inveniuntur, quæ, etsi partim florallum evolutione singulæ varient, tamen altera in alteram adeo transeunt, ut, quantumcumque extremæ tandem a primitivo *caninæ* typo recedant, nihilominus ejusdem varietates potius, quam totidem species peculiares constituere nobis videantur. In eo enim cunctæ conveniunt, quod folia radicalia angustissima, plerumque pl. min. capillaria, culmea latiora, plana, callum, ut in genuina *canina*, subepilem s. obsolete barbatum, radicem denique pl. min. repentem habeant; tametsi et *Agr. canina* nostras minime raro radice mere fibrosa inveniatur. Harum varietatum Sitchensium altera, genuinæ proxima, quam obfiurum colorem.

α *aeneam* vocabimus, caninæ quidem floris structura, h. e. perianthbo glumis paulo breviori, valvula superiori subobsoleta, saepissimeque arista longa et geniculata gaudens, tamen in aliis speciminibus hac aut penitus caret, aut illius loco setulam perbrevem tantum emittit, floresque adeo magnos (genuina *canina* fere duplo majores) habet, ut eam primo intuitu cum var. γ. confunderes. Alia est varietas, quæ, ob glumas purpurascendo-atras et valvulas albas.

β *melaleuca* dici poterit. Radix huic distinctius repens quam in α, et γ. Perianthium, in aliis ejusdem speciminibus, glumis paulo brevius, in allis easdem æquans: in *illis* valvula inferior paulo supra medium emittit aristulam glumas vix excedentem, valvula superior autem, ut solet, minima est; in *his* valvula inferior mutica, superior adeo evoluta, ut inferiorem fere æquet. Utramque autem rem, aristam nimirum aut abbreviatam aut nullam, et in *Agr. canina* nostrate inveniri, valvulam superiorem vero etiam in *Agr. alpina, exarata* aliisque Trichodiis non raro fere in longitudinem valvulæ inferioris protractam esse, plurimæ observationes nos edocuerunt. Tertiam denique, (γ) *æquivalvem* dicendam, reapse, qualis pro se exstat, speciem propriam sistere quis non dixerit? Huic enim, præterquam quod culmum cum foliis robustiorem et paniculæ radios glumasque prorsus laeves habeat, perianthium est in floribus genuina *canina* fere duplo majoribus æquivalve, glumas æquans et muticum."

The type specimen collected at Sitka by Doctor Mertens in 1829 is in the **Trinius** herbarium. (Pl. XXXVI, fig. 2.) A portion is deposited in the

National Herbarium, as is also a portion of Mertens's specimen from Unalaska. (Pl. XXXVI, fig. 1.) I have selected the Sitka specimen as the type, because this locality is first mentioned under *A. aenea* below. No specimen or locality is mentioned by Bongard.

A. aenea Trin., Mem. Acad. St. Petersb., Ser. VI, 6²: 332. 1841. (Agrostidea II: 86). "Sitka, Unalaschka." Trinius refers to this the Alaskan forms that he had previously included under *A. canina aenea*, and *melaleuca* in *Bongard*, l. c.

A. exarata aenea Griseb., in Ledeb. Fl. Ross. 4: 441. 1853. "Hab. in insulis Unalaschka (Trin.) et Sitchka! (Bong.)" Variety *melaleuca* is included here by Grisebach.

A. canina melaleuca Trin. Mem. Acad. St. Petersb., Ser. VI, 2: 170. 1832.

The original description of this is given above in full. I have been unable to find the type specimen. From the description we see that Trinius includes two forms, the first of which has the perianth (flowering glume) a little shorter than the glumes, the superior valve (palet) very small, and has the inferior valve (flowering glume) bearing a scarcely exserted awn a little above the middle.

The second form would, from the description, belong to *A. aequivalvis*, but the name *melaleuca* should rest upon the first form, which applies to *A. aenea*. It is to be noted that Trinius himself revises his disposition of these forms when he raises *A. canina aenea* to specific rank (Agrostidea II: 86), for, allowing his diagnosis of the species, he says "*Agrostis canina, aenea et melaleuca* (utraque partim) Trin. in Bongard. Florula Sitchensis in Act. Petropol. 1832, p. 170." It is for these reasons that I have taken up *melaleuca* for the untenable name *aenea*.

Differs from *A. borealis* in having the panicle oblong rather than pyramidal, and in having the awn straight and included or slightly exserted rather than exserted and geniculate. The culms are usually tall (30–50 cm.) and more leafy than in *A. borealis*. The latter is sometimes as tall, but then has proportionately larger and more diffuse panicle. The culms of *A. melaleuca* occur as isolated plants rather than tufted, and the spikelets are copper-colored. The characteristic habitat of this species is sphagnum swamps.

DISTRIBUTION: ALASKA, Kadiak Island, *Georgeson* 2, 3, *Coville and Kearney* 2348; Sitka, *Evans* 254, *Wright* 1579; Unalaska, *Kellogg* 119; Nagai Island, *Harrington;* Attu Island, *Geol. Surv. Can.* 32, 126; *Piper,* Yakutat, 4628, 4630, Sitka 4629, Seldovia 4627, and Ankow 4626. BRITISH COLUMBIA: Rogers Pass, Selkirk Mountains, 7,000 feet, *Geol. Surv. Can.* 5. COLORADO: Silver Plume, *Rydberg* 2425; Mount Massive, 12,000 feet, *Holm,* August, 1899.

This includes most of the material that has been referred to *A. canina* and *A. rubra*. It may be that the two Alaska specimens included under *A. borealis* should go here.

26. A. borealis Hartm.

A. rubra L., Sp. Pl. 62. 1753. This name has been commonly used for our plant, but since the Linnæan plant can not be identified it seems best to take up the next name which can be definitely connected with the species here considered. My reasons for this course are given in detail in another place (Bot. Gaz. 88: 141. 1904). Briefly, they are these: There is no type specimen; the plant in Linnæus's herbarium labeled *A. rubra* is Sporobolus, and there is evidently an error. The description is insufficient and incorrect, in so far as the awn is described as terminal, while *A. canina* is said to have a dorsal awn. The citations or references to plates are based upon *Gastridium australe*. While it is true that later authors have fixed the name *A. rubra* to a definite plant, it seems best for the sake of stability to discard the name *A. rubra* L.

A. borealis Hartm., Scand. Fl., Ed. III, 17. 1838. Mr. C. H. Ostenfeld of the Copenhagen Botanical Museum, has transcribed and translated Hartmann's description for me, as follows: "Panicle pyramidal, with few-flowered, somewhat scabrous branches; awn as in the foregoing (*A. canina*); basal leaves narrower.

"Mountains in wet places (Lapland). Resembles the foregoing (*A. canina*) with regard to the flower, the following (*A. vulgaris*) with regard to the appearance in general."

A. mertensii Trin., Mem. Acad. St. Petersb. Ser. VI, 6^2: 331. 1841. (Agrostidea 11:85). " Unalaschka (Mertens.—foliis flaccidioribus et mollioribus)." *A. laxiflora mertensii* Griseb., in Ledeb. Fl. Ross. 4: 442. 1853. " Hab. in insula Unalaschka (Mertens ap Trin.)." The type specimen of *A. mertensii* is in the Trinius herbarium. A portion of this is deposited in the National Herbarium. It was collected in Unalaska by Doctor Mertens in 1829. (Pl. XXXV, fig. 1.) It differs from the Flett (1689) and the Wright (1584) specimens in having more acuminate empty glumes. The Piper (4617, 4618) specimens agree well with the type, but are more robust. It seems, however, scarcely worthy of specific or even subspecific rank. *A. inconspicuum* Kunze is mentioned under this as a synonym by Trinius.

A. canina alpina Oakes, Cat. Pl. Ver. 32. 1842. "*A. rupestris* Gray in Sill. Jour., vol. 42. On the summit of .Camel's Hump Mountain, Robbins, Tuckerman, and Macrae, July. This variety is common on the White Mountains and is connected with the common variety, which is abundant in Essex County, Mass., by several intermediate forms found at the base and on the sides of the White Mountains." *A. rupestris* Gray is a nomen nudum, as Gray in the article referred to only mentions finding *Agrostis rupestris* on Roan Mountain. (Notes of a Botanical Excursion to the Mountains of North Carolina, etc., p. 42.) I have examined the specimen of Oakes in the Gray herbarium, which is probably a duplicate, and also the specimen collected by Gray on Roan Mountain, upon which is based *A. rupestris* of Chapman's Flora, etc.

A. canina var.? *tenella* Torr., Fl. N. Y. 2: 443. 1843. "Mountains in the northern part of the State. This grass differs from *A. canina* in its less diffuse panicle, narrow glumes, and flat leaves, and yet I know of no other species to which it is more nearly allied."

A. pickeringii Tuckerm., Hovey's Mag. Hort. 9: 143. April, 1843. Also Am. Journ. Sci. 45: 42. 1843, probably later than the above, as the signature title reads "Apr.–June." In the first article the description is in English. In the second is given the equivalent in Latin, but there is added a variety *rupicola* with smaller contracted panicle and purplish white flowers from White Mountains, Pickering and Oakes, and from Camel's Hump, Vermont. *A. canina* var. *alpina* Oakes is given as a synonym of the variety. In the first the locality is " White Mountains;" the second, " White Mountains, Great Haystack." The type specimen is in the Gray herbarium.

A. concinna Tuckerm., l. c., published in both articles as above. From the first we have " Hab. White Mountains. Quite distinct from *A. alpina, A. rupestris,* and *A. canina.*" From the second article, " Hab. White Mountains, stony alpine moor on Mount Monroe, with *Carex scirpoidea* and *Potentilla minima.* Somewhat resembling *A. alpina* in habit, but that is remarkable for the two bristles at the top of the inferior palea, and the awn at its base. It is quite different from *A. rupestris* and *A. canina.*" The type specimen is in the Gray herbarium. It is possible that Tuckerman's specimens in the Gray herbarium should be considered as duplicate types.

A. rubra americana Scribn., in Macoun Cat. Pl. Can. 2: 391. 1890. " It is the same as *A. rupestris* Chapm. (non All.), found on Roan Mountain, North Carolina. The same plant grows on the White Mountains of New Hampshire (*A. canina* var. *alpina* Oakes), together with the true *A. rupestris* All." Macoun's specimens are from Mount Albert, Quebec.

A. novæ-angliæ Vasey, Contr. U. S. Natl. Herb. 8: 76. 1892. Not *A. novaangliæ* Tuckerm. Vasey cites *A. scabra* var. *montana* Tuckerm. as a synonym, but the description and the plants in the National Herbarium which Vasey studied and marked are *A. borealis.* I take as the type of this a specimen collected by C. G. Pringle in 1877 on Mount Washington, New Hampshire.

A. paludosa Scribn., U. S. Dept. Agr., Div. Agros., Bul. 11: 49. 1898. " Blanc Sablon, Labrador (Rev. A. Waghorne, September 25, 1893)." The type specimen is in the National Herbarium. This belongs to the group of dwarf forms which are intermediate between *A. hiemalis* and *A. borealis.* The type specimen resembles Macoun's No. 57, from Anticosti Island. It has the floret as long as the outer glumes and no palet. A specimen from Unalaska resembles this, but has the glumes abnormally elongated (Everman 129). I have placed this form with *A. borealis* until more material can be examined. It appears to differ only in the absence of the awn. Its apparent rarity is an indication that it may be only an awnless form of *A. borealis.*

Culms tufted, 20–40 cm. tall, or, in alpine or high northern plants, dwarf. Leaves tufted at base, few on culm; blades narrow and mostly upright, 1–2 or sometimes 3 mm. wide, 5-10 cm. long. Panicle pyramidal, 5-15 cm. long; the lower branches whorled and spreading, upper ascending or contracted, slightly scabrous or nearly smooth. Empty glumes usually purple, equal, 2.5-3 mm. long, acute, very minutely scabrous on keel toward tip; flowering glume a little shorter than the empty glumes, awn usually bent and exserted 1-3 mm. beyond the spikelet, attached about the middle of the back; in some forms the awn is shorter or even obsolete; palet none or minute. (Pl. XXXIV, fig. 1, and Pl. XXXV, fig. 2.)

DISTRIBUTION: Alaska to Labrador, and the mountains of New York and New England; also mountains of North Carolina. ALASKA: Unalaska, *Mertens* in 1829, *Piper* 4618; Kadiak, *Piper* 4617; Sitka, *Wright* 1584; Nome City, *Flett* 1689. LABRADOR: Ungava Bay, *Geol. Surv. Can.* 12981; St. Nicholls, *Waghorne* 23a; Cartridge Bight, *Waghorne* in 1891. QUEBEC: Mount Albert, *Macoun* 22, 24. NEWFOUNDLAND: *Waghorne* in 1892; Battle Harbor, *Waghorne* in 1891; Grand Lake, *Waghorne* 10. MAINE: Mount Bigelow, *Fernald and Strong* 487; Mount Katahdin, *Briggs* 32, 536, *Fernald*, July, 1900. NEW HAMPSHIRE: White Mountains, *Oakes, Pringle, Chickering, Churchill, Hitchcock, Faxon*, 4, 5, 6, 19, 20, 21, 22. VERMONT: Camel's Hump, *Pringle;* Mount Mansfield, Eggleston. NORTH CAROLINA: Roan Mountain, *Scribner, Vasey, Chickering*. A dwarf form which I have referred here is represented by: LABRADOR, *Allen* 22 (Pl. XXXIV, fig. 2), *Waghorne;* NEWFOUNDLAND, *Waghorne*.

FIG. 2.—*Agrostis paludosa* Scribn.: *a*, empty glumes: *b*, flowering glume, showing a small palet and three stamens.

Two specimens collected at Cartwright, Labrador, by *Waghorne* (34, 38) are doubtful. They differ from *A. borealis* in the leafy stem and short straight awn, and from *A. melaleuca* in the tufted habit.

A. borealis differs from the dwarf form of *A. hiemalis geminata* in the less scabrous branches of the panicle.

27. **A. longiligula** sp. nov.

Culms erect, tall, 70 cm in height. Leaves several: blades 10-15 cm. long, 3-4 mm. wide, scabrous; ligule elongated and decurrent, 5-6 mm. long. Panicle bronze-purple, 10-18 cm. long, rather densely flowered: branches very scabrous. Empty glumes acute, scabrous on the keel and minutely hispidulous on the back, lower nearly 4 mm. long, upper about 3.5 mm.; flowering glume about 2.5 mm. long, the upper portions of the nerves minutely scabrous, awned; awn rising from the middle of the back, exserted, 2-2.5 mm. long, bent at the middle; callus hairs very short; palet minute, about .2 mm. long.

The type specimen in the National Herbarium was collected near Fort Bragg, Mendocino County, Cal., in water of a meadow, by Davy and Blasdale (No. 6110), in 1899. (Pl. XXXVI, fig. 3.) The same collectors found it in other localities in this county (Nos. 6088, 6095, 6096, 6105, 6106, 6107, 6131, 6140). There is also a specimen without locality collected in California by Bolander in 1866 (No. 6472)).

This species is allied to *A. borealis*, but differs in the more scabrous branches of the panicle, in the oblong panicle, and in the long ligule.

Davy and Blasdale 6131, collected in dense brush, is tall, but very slender, and with numerous lax leaves and a diffuse green panicle. The ligules are conspicuously elongated (8 mm.).

SPECIES EXCLUDED.

The following list has been prepared by Mr. P. L. Ricker. Mr. E. D. Merrill has examined the grasses of Muhlenberg in the herbarium of the Philadelphia Academy of Natural Sciences (see U. S. Dept. Agr., Div. Agros., Circ. 27) and of Elliott in the herbarium of the College of Charleston (see Circ. 29, l. c.) and has recorded, in manuscript, notes upon the synonymy of other species. These synonyms, however, have not been given critical study and are here given only as a matter of convenience in tracing the various species of our North American flora which may have been assigned at one time or another to Agrostis, but are excluded in the present limitation of the genus.

A. affinis Schult., Mant. 2: 195. 1824. Based on Agrostis No. 17, Muhl. Descr. 75. 1817=*Sporobolus ? affinis* (Schult.) Kunth.

A. airoides Torr., Ann. Lyc. N. Y. 1: 151. 1824=*Sporobolus airoides* (Torr.) Torr.

A. aspera Michx., Fl. Bor. Am. 1: 52. 1803=*Sporobolus asper* (Michx.) Kunth.

A. australis L., Mant. Pl. 1: 30. 1767=*Gastridium lendigerum* (L.) Gaud. (*G. australe* (L.) Beauv.)

A. barbatis Buckl. ex A. Gray, Proc. Acad. Nat. Sci. Phila. 1862: 334. 1863=*Muhlenbergia texana* Buckl. fide Merrill mss.

A. barbata Pers., Syn. 1: 75. 1805=*Sporobolus asper* (Michx.) Kunth fide Spreng. sub *Agrostis aspera* Michx.

A. brevifolia Nutt., Gen. 1: 44. 1818=*Sporobolus brevifolius* (Nutt.) Scribn.

A. cæspitosa Torr., Ann. Lyc. N. Y. 1: 152. 1824=*Muhlenbergia sylvatica* Torr.?

A. cinna Lam. ex Pursh, Fl. Am. Sept. 1: 64. 1814=*Cinna arundinacea* Walt.!

A. clandestina Spreng. ex Muhl., Descr. 73. 1817=*Sporobolus asper* (Michx.) Kunth fide Merrill mss.

A. composita Poir. ex Lam., Encycl. Suppl. 1: 254. 1810=*Sporobolus compositus* (Poir.) Merrill.

A. compressa Torr., Cat. Pl. N. Y. 91. 1819 not Poir. 1810=*Sporobolus torreyanus* (R. & S.) Nash, fide Britt. Man. 107.

A. compressa Poir. ex Lam., Encycl. Supp. 1: 258. 1810=*Sporobolus asper* (Michx.) Kunth fide Merrill mss. ex descr.

A. cryptandra Torr., Ann. Lyc. N. Y. 1: 151. 1824=*Sporobolus cryptandrus* (Torr.) A. Gray.

A. debilis (H. B. K.) Spreng., Syst. 1: 262. 1825=*Muhlenbergia debilis* (H. B. K.) Trin.

A. diffusa Muhl., Descr. 46. 1817 not Host.=*Muhlenbergia sylvatica* Torr. fide Merrill mss.

A. domingensis Schult., Mant. 3: 570. 1827=*Sporobolus domingensis* (Schult.) Kunth.

A. erecta (Schreb.) Spreng., Syst. 1: 264. 1825=*Brachyelytrum erectum* (Schreb.) Beauv.

A. festucoides Muhl. ex R. & S., Syst. 1: 326. 1817 as syn.=*Muhlenbergia racemosa* (Michx.) B. S. P. fide Merrill mss.

A. filiformis Willd., Enum. 95. 1809=*Muhlenbergia mexicana* (L.) Trin. fide Ind. Kew.

A.? glauca Muhl. Descr. 76. 1817=*Calamagrostis cinnoides* (Muhl.) Barton fide Merrill mss.

A. gracilis Willd. ex Trin., in Mem. Acad. St. Petersb. VI. 6²: 302. 1841 as syn.=*Muhlenbergia gracilis* (H. B. K.) Trin.

A. grœnlandica Steud., Syn. Pl. Glum. 1: 175. 1854. Apparently not an Agrostis.

A. indica L., Sp. Pl. 63. 1753=*Sporobolus indicus* (L.) R. Br.

A. involuta Muhl., Descr. 72. 1817=*Sporobolus compositus* (Poir.) Merrill fide Merrill mss.

A. juncea Michx., Fl. Bor. Am. 1: 52. 1803=*Sporobolus junceus* (Michx.) Kunth.

A. lateriflora Michx., Fl. Bor. Am. 1: 53. 1803=*Muhlenbergia mexicana* (L.) Trin. fide Ind. Kew.

A. latifolia Trev., Beschr. Bot. Gart. Bresl. 82. 1830=*Cinna latifolia* (Trev.) Griseb.

A. lendigera DC.=*Gastridium lendigerum* (L.) Gaud.

A. littoralis Lam., Tab. Encyc. 1: 161. 1791=*Sporobolus asper* (Michx.) Kunth fide Spreng. sub Agrostis.

A. littoralis With., Bot. Arr. Brit. Pl. 23. 1776=*Polypogon littoralis* (With.) J. E. Smith.

A. longifolia Torr., Fl. U. S. 1: 90. 1824=*Sporobolus compositus* (Poir.) Merrill fide Merrill mss.

A. matrella L., Mant. 185. 1771=*Osterdamia matrella* (L.) Kuntze.

A. mexicana L., Mant. 81=*Muhlenbergia mexicana* (L.) Trin.

A. mexicana Pers., Syn. 1: 76. 1805=*Calamagrostis canadensis* L.?

A. microsperma Lag., Gen. et Sp. Pl. 2. 1816=*Muhlenbergia debilis* Trin.

A. miliacea L., Sp. Pl. 61. 1753=*Oryzopsis miliacea* (L.) Richt.

A. minutissima Steud., Syn. Pl. Glum. 1: 171. 1854=*Sporobolus ramulosus* Kunth.

A. nutans Poir. ex Lam., Encyc. Suppl. 1: 255. 1810=*Panicum anceps* Michx.?

A. oligantha R. & S., Syst. 2: 372. 1817=*Muhlenbergia tenuiflora* fide Merrill mss.

A. paradoxa L., Sp. Pl. 62. 1753=*Oryzopsis paradoxa* (L.) Nutt.

A. paradoxa R. Br. in Ross. Voy. Ed. II 2: 192. 1819 nom. nud.=*Arctagrostis latifolia* (R. Br.) Griseb. fide Ind. Kew.

A. pauciflora Pursh, Fl. Am. Sept. 2: 63. 1814=*Muhlenbergia tenuiflora pauciflora* (Pursh) Scribn.

A. polystachya Bosc, ex Lam., Encycl. Suppl. 1: 254. 1810, as syn.=*Sporobolus compositus* (Poir.) Merrill.

A. punctata (L.) Lam. Encycl. 1: 58. 1783=*Eriochloa punctata* (L.) W. Hamilt.

A. pungens Pursh, Fl. Am. Sept. 1: 64. 1814=*Sporobolus pungens* (Pursh) Kunth.=*S. virginicus* (L.) Kunth fide Hook. Fl. Brit. Ind. 7: 249. 1896.

A. racemosa Michx., Fl. Bor. Am. 1: 53. 1803=*Muhlenbergia racemosa* (Michx.) B.S. P.

A. ramosa Poir., in Lam. Encycl. Suppl. 1: 257. 1810=*Eriochloa annulata* (Flugge) Kunth fide Ind. Kew.

A. rubicunda Bosc, in DC. Hort. Monsp. 151. 1813, as syn.=*Muhlenbergia expansa* (Poir.) Trin.

A. sericea Muhl., Descr. 64. 1817=*Muhlenbergia capillaris* (Lam.) Trin. fide Merrill.

A. serotina Torr., Fl. U. S. 1: 88. 1824=*Sporobolus uniflorus* (Muhl.) Scrib. & Merrill fide Merrill mss.

A. setosa Spreng., Syst. 1: 262. 1825=*Muhlenbergia debilis* Trin. fide Merrill mss.

A. setosa Muhl., Descr. 68. 1817=*Muhlenbergia racemosa* (Michx.) B. S. P. fide Merrill mss.
A. sobolifera Muhl., in Willd. Enum. 95. 1809=*Muhlenbergia sobolifera* (Muhl.) Trin.
A. spica-venti L., Sp. Pl. 61. 1753=*Apera spica-venti* (L.) Beauv.
A. suaveolens Blytt, Mag. Naturv., 1837=*Cinna latifolia* (Trev.) Griseb. fide Ind. Kew.
A. sylvatica Torr., Fl. U. S. 87. 1824 not L. 1762=*Muhlenbergia sylvatica* (Torr.) Torr.
A. tenuiflora Willd., Sp. Pl. 1: 364. 1797=*Muhlenbergia tenuiflora* (Willd.) B. S. P.
A. tenuiflora Ell., Sk. 1: 134. 1816=*Muhlenbergia diffusa* Schreb. fide Merrill.
A. thyrsoides Bosc, in Mem. Acad. St. Petersb. Ser. VI. 6^2: 76. 1840, as syn. of *Vilfa fulvescens* Trin.
A. torreyana Schult., Mant. 2: 263. 1824=*Sporobolus torreyanus* (R. & S.) Nash.
A. trichantha Schrank, Regensb. Denksch., 2: 5, ex Steud., Syn. Pl. Glum. 1: 175. 1854. Apparently not an Agrostis.
A. trichopodes Ell., Sk. 1: 135. 1817=*Muhlenbergia expansa* Trin. fide Merrill.
A. vaginæflora Torr., in Gray Man. 576=*Sporobolus vaginæflorus* (Torr.) Wood.
A. virginica L. Sp. Pl. 63. 1753=*Sporobolus virginicus* (L.) Kunth.
A. virginica Muhl., Descr. 74. 1817=*Sporobolus vaginæflorus* (Torr.) Wood fide Merrill mss.

NOTES ON MEXICAN SPECIES.

Fournier has described several species of Agrostis, but unfortunately I have not been able thus far to identify all of these satisfactorily. It is quite possible that many of his new species will later be reduced to synonymy. Below I give transcripts of the original descriptions of Fournier's species, as published in his Mexicanas Plantas, Gramineæ, 1881.

A. tolucensis H. B. K., Nov. Gen. 1: 135. 1815.

I have not seen the type specimen of this, but we have Liebmann's No. 701 from Orizaba, which is one of the specimens cited by Fournier. I take Pringle's No. 4219, from the State of Mexico, Mexico, to be this species. (Pl. XXXVII.) A specimen from Costa Rica (Pittier 3373) also agrees with this. Pringle No. 5202, from the State of Mexico, Mexico, is a dwarf form. All agree in having the awn attached below the middle of the glume.

A. virescens H. B. K., l. c.

The type specimen is in the herbarium of the Museum of Paris. (Pl. XXXVII, B.) This has a looser panicle and the awn is attached above the middle of the flowering glume. It may be a form of *A. tolucensis* H. B. K.

"*A. schaffneri* Fourn., l. c., 94.

"Culmo glabro, 2-3 pedali; vaginis laxis, foliis planis latis mollibus, ligula longa fissa; folio ultimo paniculam longe invaginante, etiam superante; panicula longa composita, fere pedali, nitide virenti, radiis erecto-appressis basi nudis; spiculis angustis glabris; glumis nitidis florem superantibus, secus carinam scabris, inferiore longiore acuta; palea inferiore integra, involuta, arista gracili recta e medio orta florem superante; palea superiore deficiente. antheris 3.

"Tacubaya (Schaffn. n. 86 et 308 in herb. Franq.).

" Var. β. *mutica*.

"Tacubaya (Schaffn. n. 1 in herb. Franq.)."

I have seen no specimen of this. From the description it may be *A. pallens foliosa*.

"*A. tacubayensis*, Fourn., l. c., 95.

"Culmo pedali; foliis planis, fasciculorum setaceis; panicula 4-pollicari, effusa, radiis solitariis longis inæqualibus circiter a medio floriferis; glumis violaceis inæqualibus, flosculo fere dimidio breviore quam gluma inferior.

"Pr. Tacubaya, julio (Schaffn. n. 91)."

I have seen no specimens. It may be some form of *A. hiemalis*.

"*A. bourgœi* Fourn., l. c., 95.

"Culmo plus quam bipedali; foliis planis 3" longis, 2"' latis, ligula acuta laciniata bilineali, panicula acuta 3–4 pollicari, radiis hispidis brevibus remote verticillatis erecto-appressis a medio circiter floriferis, glumis atro-violaceis inæqualibus acutis in carina hispido-aculeatis, flosculo mutico paulo breviore quam gluma superior.

"Pedregal pr. Tizapan in valle Mexicensi, augusto (Bourg. n. 682)."

The type specimen is in the herbarium of the Museum of Paris. I should refer this to *A. schiedeana* Trin. as represented by Pringle 4485. There is a small palet. (Pl. XXXVII, *D*.)

"*A. virletii* Fourn., l. c., 96.

"Planta cæspitosa robusta, culmo valido, vaginis latis marcescentibus, foliis 3'" latis, planis, acutis, ligula longa amplexicauli laciniata; panicula 4–5 pollicari, invaginata, lucida, radiis erecto-appressis scabris a medio dense floriferis, ut maximum, sesquipollicaribus; glumis violaceis, scabris, acuminatis, inferiore præsertim, demum patentibus, flosculo mutico æquante glumam superiorem.

"Var. α—Palea superiore ⅔ inferioris æquante.

"San Luis de Potosi (Virl. n. 1345).

"Var. β—Palea superiore ½ paleæ inferioris æquante.

"Cum typo.

"Var. γ—Palea superiore lata ovarium cingente et squamulas lineares æquante.

"Absque loco (Schaffn. in meo herbario); pr. Tacubaya (Schaffn. n. 307 in herb. Franq. junio); pr. Guazimalpan (Schaffn. n. 4 in herb. Franq.)."

The type specimen is in the herbarium of the Museum of Paris. The palet is about two-thirds the length of the flowering glume. (Pl. XXXVII, *A*.)

"*A. berlandieri* Fourn., l. c., 96.

"Culmo sesquipedali, glabro; foliis caulinis et fasciculorem planis lineam latis, subulatis, ligula hyalina fissa sesquilineali, panicula invaginata 3–4 pollicari, contractiuscula, radiis subverticillatis imis a basi, longioribus a medio floriferis; glumis lævibis inæqualibus, palea solitaria glumas æquante.

"Totoniho (Berl. n. 531).

"Obs.—Differt ab *A. pulchella* Kunth glumis lævibus non secus carinam aculeato-hispidis, palea glumas æquante."

"*A. chinantlæ* Fourn., l. c., 96.

"Culmo pedali v. plus quam pedali, simplici, foliis setaceis, infra fasciculatis, ligula amplexicauli prominente; panicula parva 3–4 pollicari, contractiuscula, radiis partim a basi, partim a medio floriferis; spiculis secus radios densis; glumis post anthesim late apertis, flosculo mutico solitario, paulo breviore quam gluma superior.

"Chinantla (Liebm. n. 709, maio)."

"*A. setifolia* Fourn., l. c., 97.

"Culmo sesquipedali, gracili; foliis involutis subulatis; ligula amplexicauli acuta laciniata; panicula brevi depauperata laxiflora, radiis flexuosis basi longe nudis; glumis æqualibus acutis; palea solitaria paulo breviore; arista basilari longa geniculata flosculum duplum superante.

"In monte Orizabensi, 10000' (Liebm. n. 712)."

There are two specimens in the National Herbarium—Sierra de San Felipe, Oaxaca, Pringle 4895; Smith 922.

"*A. ghiesbreghtii* Fourn., l. c., 97.

"Foliis plurimis radicalibus semipedalibus setaceis rigidis pungentibus sicut et culmeis paucis; vaginis longis; ligula obtusa; panicula decomposita ovali patente, ramis repetito-verticillatis; glumis subæqualibus in carina ciliolatis, flosculo solitario tertia parte breviore quam glumæ; arista e medio oriente recta, flosculum duplum æquante.

"Oajaca (Ghiesbreght)."

Type specimen in herbarium of Museum of Paris. It closely resembles Pringle's 4895 from Mexico, but the leaves are mostly basal rather than scattered along the stem. Fournier distinguishes this from *A. setifolia* Fourn. by the straight awn, but in the Paris specimen the awn is geniculate. This is probably only a form of *A. setifolia* Fourn.

A. fasciculata (H. B. K.) R. & S., Syst. **2**: 362. 1817 (*Vilfa fasciculata* H. B. K., Nov. Gen. **1**: 139. 1815), is reported from Mexico. The type specimen from Ecuador is in the Paris Museum. (Pl. XXXVII, *C*.)

INDEX TO SPECIES AND SYNONYMS.

[Synonyms are printed in italics.]

	Page.
Agraulus caninus Beauv	51
Agrostis abakanensis Lessing	42
aenea Spreng	51
Trin	52
æquivalvis (Trin.) Trin	22
alba L	25
aristata Gray	27
coarctata Scribn	27
maritima (Lam.) Meyer	27
minor Vasey	26
sylvatica Scribn	27
verticillata Pers	24
vulgaris (With.) Thurb	26
albicans Buckl	39
alopecuroides Gray	37
altissima Tuckerm	50
ampla Hitchc	38
anomala Willd	48
aphanes Trin	49
aquatica Buckl	24
arachnoides Ell	32
arenaria Scribn	31
aristata Sincl	27
asperifolia Trin	39
attenuata Vasey	46
berlandieri Fourn	58
borealis Hartm	52
bourgæi Fourn	58
breviculmis Hitchc	36
californica Trin	30
campyla Tuckerm	49
canina L	51
aenea Trin	52
aequivalvis Trin	22
alpina Oakes	53
melaleuca Trin	52
tenella Torr	53
chinantlæ Fourn	58
clavata Trin	42
coarctata Ehrh	27
concinna Tuckerm	53
cornucopœi Fraser	47
davyi Scribn	33

	Page.
Agrostis decumbens Muhl	24
densiflora Vasey	31
arenaria Vasey	31
depressa Vasey	28
diegoensis Vasey	35
dispar Michx	25
drummondii Torr	39
dulcis Sibth	24
elata Trin	47, 50
elliottiana Schult	32
erecta Spreng	45
exarata Trin	38
aenea Griseb	52
asperifolia Vasey	39
littoralis Vasey	34
microphylla Wats	37
minor Hook	39
stolonifera Vasey	29
exigua Thurb	32
fasciculata (H. B. K.) R. & S	59
foliosa Hortul	34
foliosa Vasey	34
geminata Trin	44
ghiesbreghtii Fourn	59
glomerata (Presl) Kunth	30
grandis Trin	39
hallii Vasey	33
californica Vasey	47
pringlei (Scribn.) Hitchc	33
hiemalis (Walt.) B. S. P	42
geminata (Trin.) Hitchc	44
subrepens Hitchc	44
hillebrandii Thurb	28
howellii Scribn	41
humilis Vasey	28
idahoensis Nash	45
inconspicuum Kunze	53
inflata Scribn	31
intermedia Balb	49
Scribn	49
laxa Schreb	42
laxiflora Poir	42
Richards	42
caespitosa Torr	43
mertensii Griseb	53
montana Tuckerm	43
leptos Steud	24
longiligula Hitchc	54
maritima Lam	27
melaleuca (Trin.) Hitchc	51
mertensii Trin	53
michauxii Trin	42, 48

INDEX TO SPECIES AND SYNONYMS.

	Page.
Agrostis microphylla Steud	37
major Vasey	37
montana Krock	43
mucronata Presl	31, 36
multiculmis Vasey	35
nana Kunth	36
neogœa Steud	27
nootkaensis Trin	45
novæ-angliæ Tuckerm	49
Vasey	53
noveboracensis Spreng	48
nutkaensis Kunth	45
occidentalis Scribn. & Merrill	33
oregonensis Nutt	39
oregonensis Vasey	46
oreophila Trin	43, 48
pallens Trin	34
foliosa (Vasey) Hitchc	34
paludosa Scribn	53
perennans (Walt.) Tuckerm	47
œstivalis Vasey	49
elata (Pursh) Hitchc	50
pickeringii Tuckerm	53
rupicola Tuckerm	53
polymorpha Huds	27
vivipara Trin	27
pringlei Scribn	33
pseudointermedia Farwell	49
repens Scribn	34
rosei Scribn. & Merrill	30
rossæ Vasey	40
rubra L	52
americana Scribn	53
rupestris Gray	53
scabra Willd	42
tenuis Tuckerm	43
scabrata Nutt	43
scabriuscula Buckl	43
schaffneri Fourn	57
mutica Fourn	57
schiedeana Trin	47
schweinitzii Trin	48
scouleri Trin	39
scribneriana Nash	49
sericea Ell	42
setifolia Fourn	58
stolonifera L	24
dulcis Pers	24
stricta Willd	27
sylvatica L	27
tacubayensis Fourn	58

		Page.
Agrostis tenuiculmis Nash		45
recta Nash		45
tenuifolia Bieb		39
tenuis Sibth		45
Vasey		45
erecta Vasey		45
thurberiana Hitchc		23
tolucensis H. B. K		57
torreyi Kunth		44
Tuckerm		44
variabilis Rydb		41
varians Thuill		40
Trin		40
verticillata Vill		24
virescens H. B. K		38, 57
microphylla Scribn		37
virletii Fourn		58
vulgaris With		26
alba Vasey		25
Alopecurus carolinianus Spreng		48
Cornucopiæ altissima Walt		50
hyemalis Walt		42
perennans Walt		47
Deyeuxia æquivalvis Benth		23
alopecuroides Nutt		37
Polypogon alopecuroides Buckl		37
Trichodium album Presl		45
caninum Schrad		51
clavatum Schult		42
decumbens Michx		48
elatum Pursh		50
laxiflorum Michx		42
laxum Schult		42
montanum Torr		43
muhlenbergianum Schult		48
nanum Presl		36
perennans Ell		48
scabrum Muhl		43
Vilfa dispar Beauv		25
dulcis Beauv		24
fasciculata H. B. K		59
glomerata Presl		30

PLATES.

DESCRIPTION OF PLATES.

In all the plates the plants, panicles, or branches of panicles are drawn one-half natural size; the ligules are enlarged five times; the spikelets and florets are enlarged ten times.

PLATE I. Fig. 1.—*Agrostis thurberiana* Hitchc. Type specimen, Suksdorf 1021. Plant, ligule, spikelet, and two views of floret, showing prolonged rachilla and the palet. Fig. 2.—*Agrostis æquivalvis* Trin. Yes Bay, Alaska, Howell 1712. *A*.—Spikelet and floret, from type specimen in the Trinius herbarium, collected by Mertens.

PLATE II. *Agrostis alba* L. College Hill, Easton, Pa., T. C. Porter, July 2, 1897. Plant, ligule, spikelet, and two views of floret; rootstock and stolon from Macoun 26032 collected at Niagara Falls, Ontario, 1901.

PLATE III. Fig. 1.—*Agrostis alba vulgaris* (With.) Thurb. Apsey Beach, Newfoundland, Waghorne 23. Plant, ligule, spikelet, and two views of floret. Fig. 2.—*Agrostis alba aristata* Gray. Fort ·Preble, Maine, Gayle 786. Plant, ligule, spikelet, and two views of floret.

PLATE IV. *Agrostis alba maritima* (Lam.) Meyer. Nantucket, Mass., Hitchcock in 1902. Plant, ligule, spikelet, and two views of floret.

PLATE V. Fig. 1.—*Agrostis depressa* Vasey. Type specimen, Colorado, Patterson 46. Plant, ligule, spikelet, and two views of floret. Fig. 2.—*Agrostis stolonifera* L. Kerrville, Tex., Heller 1742. Plant, ligule, spikelet, floret, and dorsal view of flowering glume.

PLATE VI. *Agrostis depressa* Vasey. The Oregon form showing stolons, Astoria, Oreg., Leckenby in 1897. Plant, ligule, spikelet, and two views of floret.

PLATE VII. Fig. 1.—*Agrostis inflata* Scribn. Victoria, British Columbia, Macoun 259. Plant, ligule, spikelet, and two views of floret. *A*.—Spikelet and two views of floret from type specimen, Macoun 258. Fig. 2.—*Agrostis densiflora* Vasey. Type specimen, Santa Cruz, Cal., Anderson. Plant, ligule, spikelet, floret, and two flowering glumes. One flowering glume shows the mid-nerve vanishing about the middle and the other shows the mid-nerve extending into a thin awn.

PLATE VIII. Fig. 1.—*Agrostis humilis* Vasey. Type specimen, Mount Adams, Washington, Suksdorf. Plant, ligule, spikelet, and two views of floret. Fig. 2.—*Agrostis exigua* Thurb. Type specimen, California, Bolander. Plant, ligule, spikelet, and two views of floret.

PLATE IX. Fig. 1.—*Agrostis elliottiana* Schult. Collected by L. C. Johnson in Mississippi in 1886. Plant (the spikelets were unawned), ligule, spikelet, and two views of floret; an awned ·spikelet from Reverchon's No. 3391, Texas. Fig. 2.—*Agrostis canina* L. Delaware, Commons 99. Plant, ligule, spikelet, and two views of floret.

PLATE X. Fig. 1.—*Agrostis hallii californica* Vasey. Type specimen, Bolander 6103. Plant, ligule, spikelet, and two views of floret. Fig. 2.—*Agrostis hallii* Vasey. Type specimen, Oregon, Hall. Plant, ligule, spikelet, and two views of floret.

PLATE XI. *Agrostis davyi* Scribn. Type specimen, Davy and Blasdale 6062. Plant, ligule, spikelet, and two views of floret (in center). *A*.—Spikelet and two views of floret from type specimen of *Agrostis occidentalis* Scribn. & Merrill, Shear 1044.

PLATE XII. *Agrostis pringlei* Scribn. Type specimen, California, Pringle in 1882. Plant, ligule, spikelet, and two views of floret.

DESCRIPTION OF PLATES.

PLATE XIII. Fig. 1.—*Agrostis pallens* Trin. Oregon, Howell in 1882. Plant, ligule, spikelet, and two views of floret. A.—Spikelet and two views of floret from type specimen in the Trinius herbarium. Fig. 2.—*Agrostis attenuata* Vasey. Type specimen, Howell 210. Plant, ligule, spikelet, and two views of floret.

PLATE XIV. Fig. 1.—*Agrostis foliosa* Vasey. Type specimen, Oregon, Howell, in 1881. Plant, ligule, spikelet, and two views of floret. Fig. 2.—*Agrostis oregonensis* Vasey. Type specimen, Howell in 1881. Plant, ligule, spikelet, and two views of floret.

PLATE XV. *Agrostis pallens foliosa* (Vasey) Hitchc. Mount Hood, Oregon, Henderson, 7. Plant, ligule, spikelet, and two views of floret. This is a form with open, oblong panicles resembling the type of *A. foliosa* Vasey, but with spikelets awned.

PLATE XVI. Fig. 1.—*Agrostis pallens foliosa* (Vasey) Hitchc. Klickitat County, Wash., Suksdorf 199. Plant, ligule, spikelet, and two views of floret. A common form with narrow panicle. Fig 2.—*Agrostis scouleri* Trin. Type speciment, Nutka Sound, Alaska, Scouler. Plant (from photograph), spikelet, and two views of floret. This is a portion of the type from the Trinius herbarium deposited in the National Herbarium.

PLATE XVII. *Agrostis diegoensis* Vasey. Type specimen, San Diego, Cal., Orcutt in 1884. Plant, ligule, spikelet, and two views of floret.

PLATE XVIII. *Agrostis breviculmis* Hitchc. Fort Bragg, Cal., Davy and Blasdale 6159. Plant, ligule, spikelet, and two views of floret.

PLATE XIX. Fig. 1.—*Agrostis microphylla major* Vasey. Truckee valley, Nev., Watson 1284. Plant, ligule, spikelet, and two views of floret. Fig. 2.—*Agrostis microphylla* Steud. Mendocino County, Cal., Davy and Blasdale 5142. Plant, ligule, spikelet, and two views of floret. A.—Yamhill County, Oreg., Shear 1650. Panicle.

PLATE XX. *Agrostis ampla* Hitchc. Multnomah County, Oreg., Suksdorf 135. Plant, ligule, spikelet, and two views of floret.

PLATE XXI. Fig. 1.—*Agrostis exarata* Trin. Specimen from the Trinius herbarium deposited in National Herbarium; Unalaska, Kostalsky in 1829. Plant, ligule, spikelet, and two views of floret. Fig. 2.—*Agrostis asperifolia* Trin. Type specimen from the Trinius herbarium deposited in the National Herbarium. Plant, spikelet, and two views of floret.

PLATE XXII. *Agrostis grandis* Trin. Sequoia region, Cal., Hansen 1826. Plant, ligule, spikelet, and two views of floret. A common large form of *A. exarata* which matches the type specimen in the Trinius herbarium. A.—Spikelet and two views of floret from type specimen in the Trinius herbarium from Columbia region, Hooker.

PLATE XXIII. *Agrostis exarata* Trin. Amador County, Cal., Hansen 613. Plant, ligule, spikelet, and two views of floret. A common form with elongated, somewhat open panicle. A.—A panicle from plant collected at Reno, Nev., by Tracy, No. 218. A form with narrow, compact, and somewhat glomerate panicle.

PLATE XXIV. Fig. 1.—*Agrostis rossæ* Vasey. Type specimen, Yellowstone Park, Ross in 1890. Plant, ligule, spikelet, and two views of floret. Fig. 2.—Plant at left: *Agrostis varians* Trin. Type specimen from the Trinius herbarium deposited in National Herbarium. Plant, ligule. spikelet, and two views of floret. Plant at right: *A. variabilis* Rydb. Wyoming, Williams 2952½.

PLATE XXV. *Agrostis howellii* Scribn. Type specimen, Hood River, Oreg., Howell in 1886. Plant, ligule, spikelet, and two views of floret.

PLATE XXVI. Fig. 1.—*Agrostis hiemalis* (Walt.) B. S. P. Bush 554. Panicle, ligule, spikelet, and two views of floret. The common eastern form with very diffuse capillary panicle and small spikelets. In this plant the panicle is shown at maturity. Fig. 2.—A form with less diffuse panicle, common in the Rocky Mountain regions. Wyoming, Nelson 3947. Plant, spikelet, and two views of floret.

PLATE XXVII. Types referred to *Agrostis hiemalis* (Walt.) B. S. P. 1.—*Trichodium album* Presl. From specimen in the Trinius herbarium sent by Presl in 1834. Branch of panicle, spikelet, and three views of floret. 2.—From specimen of *Agrostis clavata* Trin. in the Trinius herbarium, collected by Kostalsky in 1829. Branch of panicle, spikelet, and two views of floret. 3.—From type specimen of *Trichodium laxiflorum*, in Michaux herbarium in Museum of Paris. Branch of panicle, spikelet, and two views of floret. 4.—Dwarf form of *Agrostis hiemalis* from Newfoundland. Waghorne 25. Plant, ligule, spikelet, and two views of floret. 5.—Awned form of *Agrostis hiemalis*, White Mountains, Hitchcock in 1902. Branch of panicle, spikelet, and two views of floret.

PLATE XXVIII. Fig. 1.—*Agrostis geminata* Trin. Type specimen from the Trinius herbarium, collected in Unalaska by Eschscholtz. Plant, ligule, spikelet and two views of floret. Fig. 2.—An awnless form, collected in Alaska by Flett (No. 2014). Plant, ligule, spikelet, and two views of floret.

PLATE XXIX. Fig. 1.—*Agrostis idahoensis* Nash. Duplicate type, Heller 3431. Plant, ligule, spikelet, and two views of floret. Fig. 2.—*Agrostis tenuis* Vasey. Type specimen, San Bernardino Mountains, Cal., Parish brothers 1085. Plant, ligule, spikelet, and two views of floret.

PLATE XXX. *Agrostis schiedeana* Trin. Falcon valley, Wash., Suksdorf in 1886. Plant, ligule, spikelet, and two views of floret. *A.*—Spikelet and two views of floret from Pringle No. 4485, collected in Mexico.

PLATE XXXI. *Agrostis perennans* (Walt.) Tuckerm. Washington, D. C., Hitchcock in 1903. Plant, ligule, spikelet, and two views of floret. The common upright form of open ground. *A.*—*Agrostis schweinitzii* Trin., from type specimen in the Trinius herbarium. *B.*—*Alopecurus carolinianus* Spreng., from specimen in the Triulus herbarium from Peter, Lexington, Ky.

PLATE XXXII. *Agrostis perennans aestivalis* Vasey. Athens, Ill., Hall in 1864. Type specimen. Plant, ligule, spikelet, and two views of floret. The weak decumbent form of moist, shady situations. *A.*—From type specimen of *Agrostis oreophila* Trin., in the Trinius herbarium, collected by Moser at Bethlehem, Pa. *B.*—From type specimen of *Trichodium decumbens* Michx., in Michaux herbarium in Museum of Paris.

PLATE XXXIII. *Agrostis perennans elata* (Pursh) Hitchc. Egg Harbor, N. J., Vasey in 1884. Plant, ligule, spikelet, and two views of floret. *A.*—From type specimen of *Agrostis elata* Trin. in the Trinius herbarium. Spikelet and two views of floret.

PLATE XXXIV. Fig. 1.—*Agrostis borealis* Hartm. Mount Washington, N. H., Faxon 19. The common form of the White Mountains. Plant, ligule, spikelet, and two views of floret. Fig. 2.—*Agrostis borealis* Hartm. Labrador, Allen 22. A common dwarf form. Plant, ligule, spikelet, and two views of floret.

PLATE XXXV. Fig. 1.—*Agrostis mertensii* Trin. Type specimen, Unalaska, Mertens in 1829, from the Trinius herbarium. Plant, ligule, spikelet, and two views of floret. Fig. 2.—*Agrostis borealis* Hartm. Sweden; collected by Oldberg. Plant, ligule, spikelet, and two views of floret.

PLATE XXXVI. Fig.1.—*Agrostis aenea* Trin. Unalaska, Mertens in 1829. Plant. Fig. 2.—*Agrostis aenea* Trin. Type specimen, Sitka, Mertens in 1829. Plant, spikelet, and two views of floret. Fig. 3.—*Agrostis longiligula* Hitchc. Type specimen, Mendocino County, Cal., Davy and Blasdale 6110. Plant, ligule (with fig. 2), spikelet, and two views of floret.

PLATE XXXVII. *Agrostis tolucensis* H. B. K. State of Mexico, Mexico, Pringle 4219. Plant, ligule, spikelet, and two views of floret. *A.*—Spikelet and two views of floret from type specimen of *A. virletii* Fourn. *B.*—Spikelet and two views of floret from type specimen of *A. virescens* H. B. K. *C.*—Spikelet and two views of floret from type specimen of *Vilfa fasciculata* H. B. K., from Paris Museum. *D.*—Spikelet and two views of floret from type specimen of *A. bourgaei* Fourn.

Fig. 1.—Agrostis Thurberiana Hitchc. Fig. 2.—Agrostis æquivalvis Trin.

AGROSTIS ALBA L.

Fig. 1.—Agrostis alba vulgaris (With.) Thurb.   Fig. 2.—Agrostis alba aristata Gray.

AGROSTIS ALBA MARITIMA (LAM.) MEYER.

Fig. 1.—Agrostis depressa Vasey (Type Specimen). Fig. 2.—Agrostis stolonifera L.

AGROSTIS DEPRESSA VASEY (OREGON).

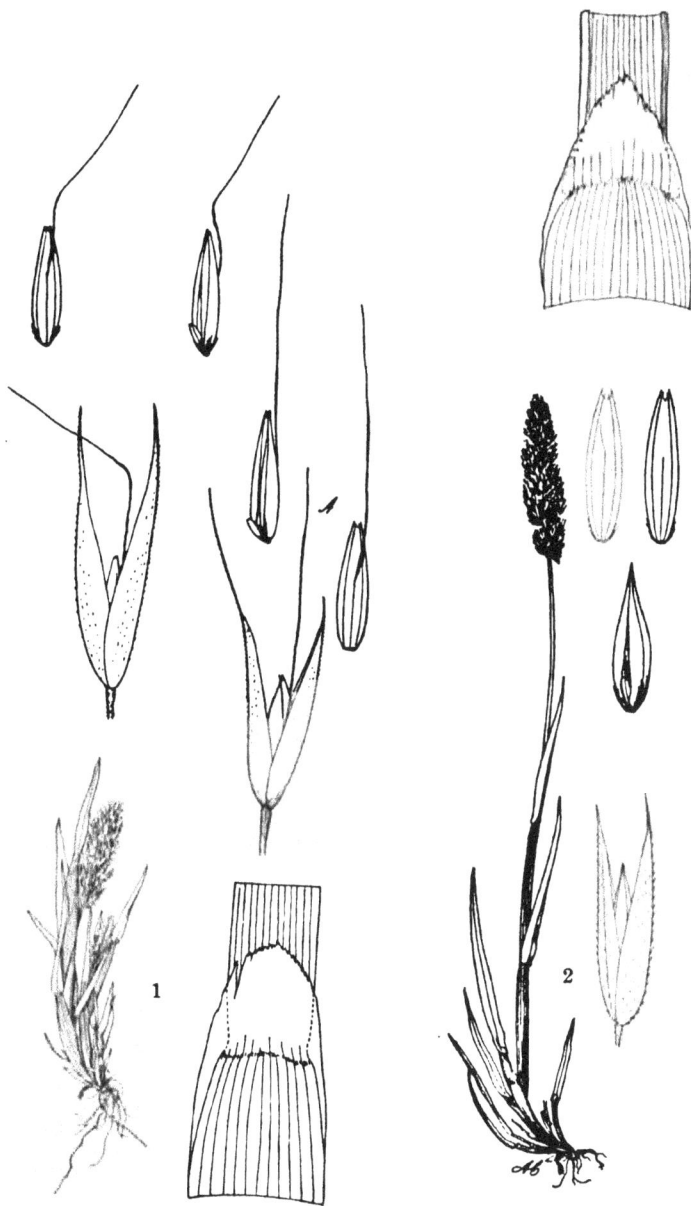

Fig. 1.—Agrostis inflata Scribn. Fig. 2.—Agrostis densiflora Vasey.

Fig. 1.—Agrostis humilis Vasey. Fig. 2.—Agrostis exigua Thurb.

Fig. 1.—Agrostis elliottiana Schult. Fig. 2.—Agrostis canina L.

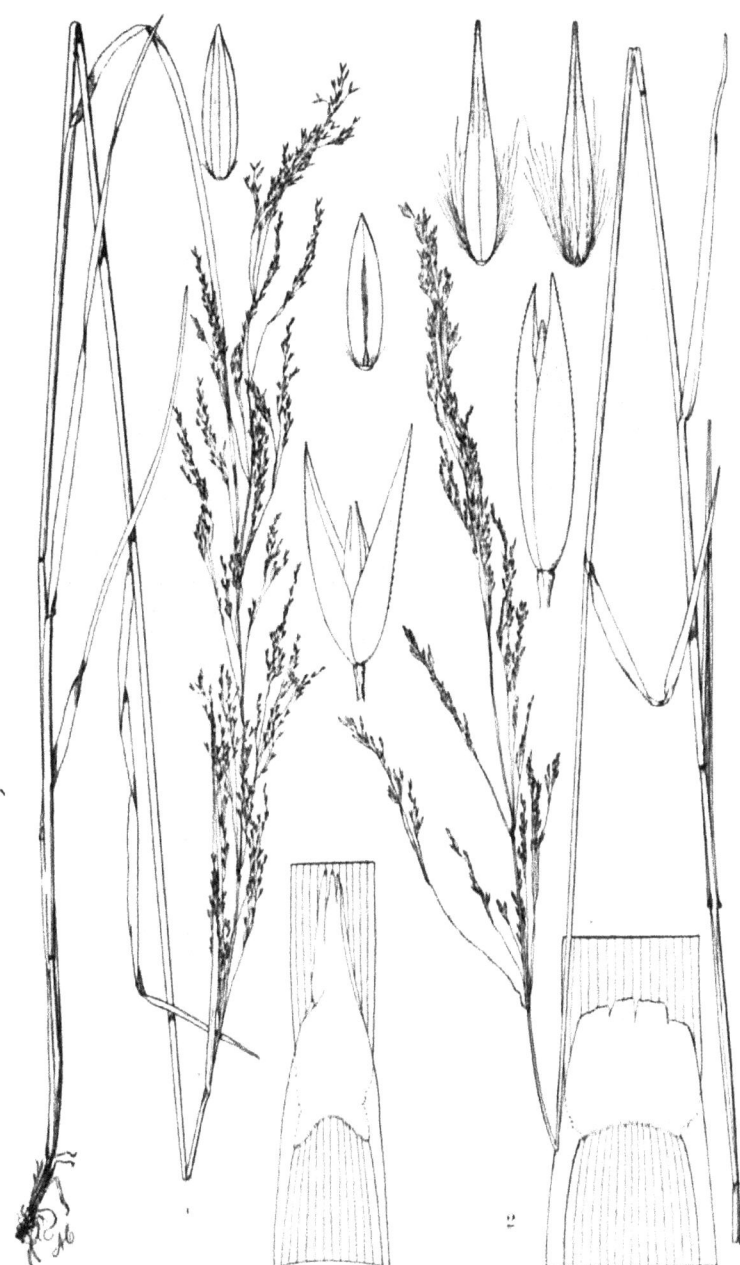

Fig. 1.—Agrostis hallii californica Vasey. Fig. 2.—Agrostis hallii Vasey.

AGROSTIS DAVYI SCRIBN. AND (A) SPIKELET OF A. OCCIDENTALIS SCRIBN. & MERRILL.

AGROSTIS PRINGLEI SCRIBN.

Fig. 1.—Agrostis pallens Trin.   Fig. 2.—Agrostis attenuata Vasey.

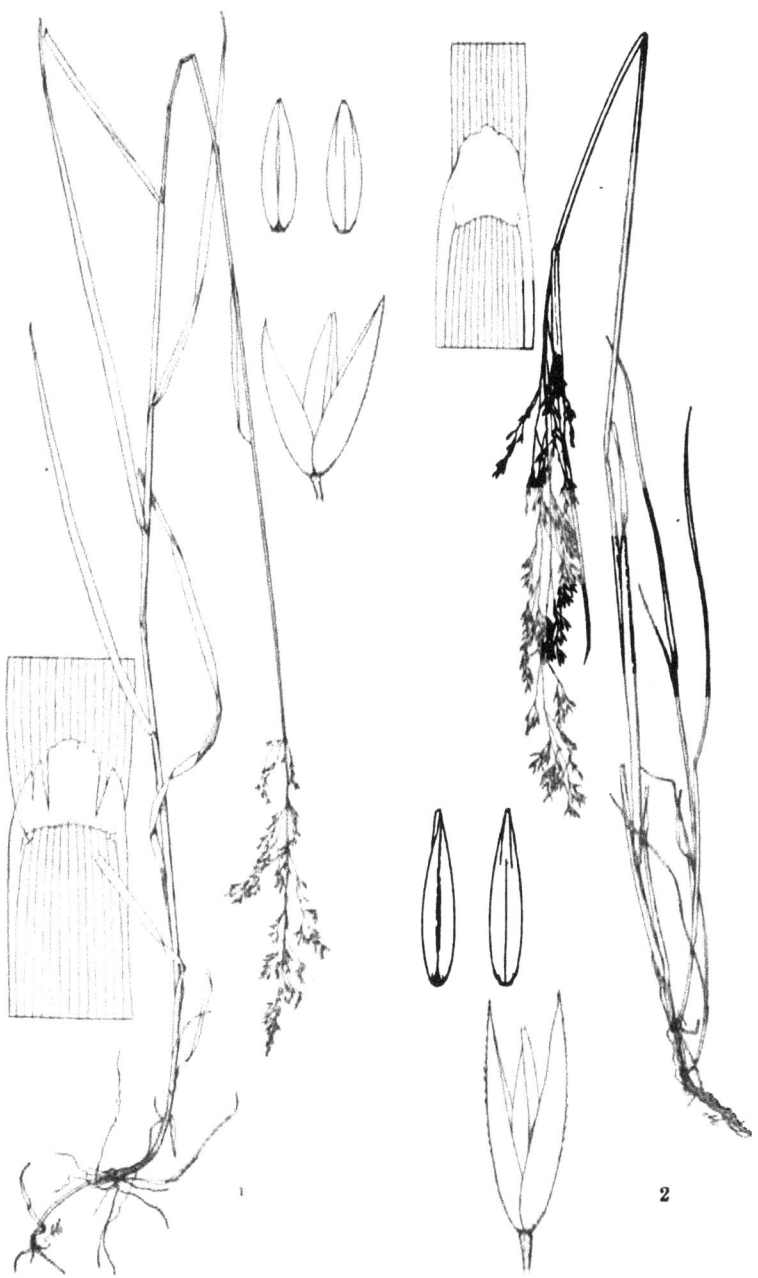

FIG. 1.—AGROSTIS FOLIOSA VASEY.   FIG. 2.—AGROSTIS OREGONENSIS VASEY.

AGROSTIS PALLENS FOLIOSA (VASEY) HITCHC. (AWNED FORM).

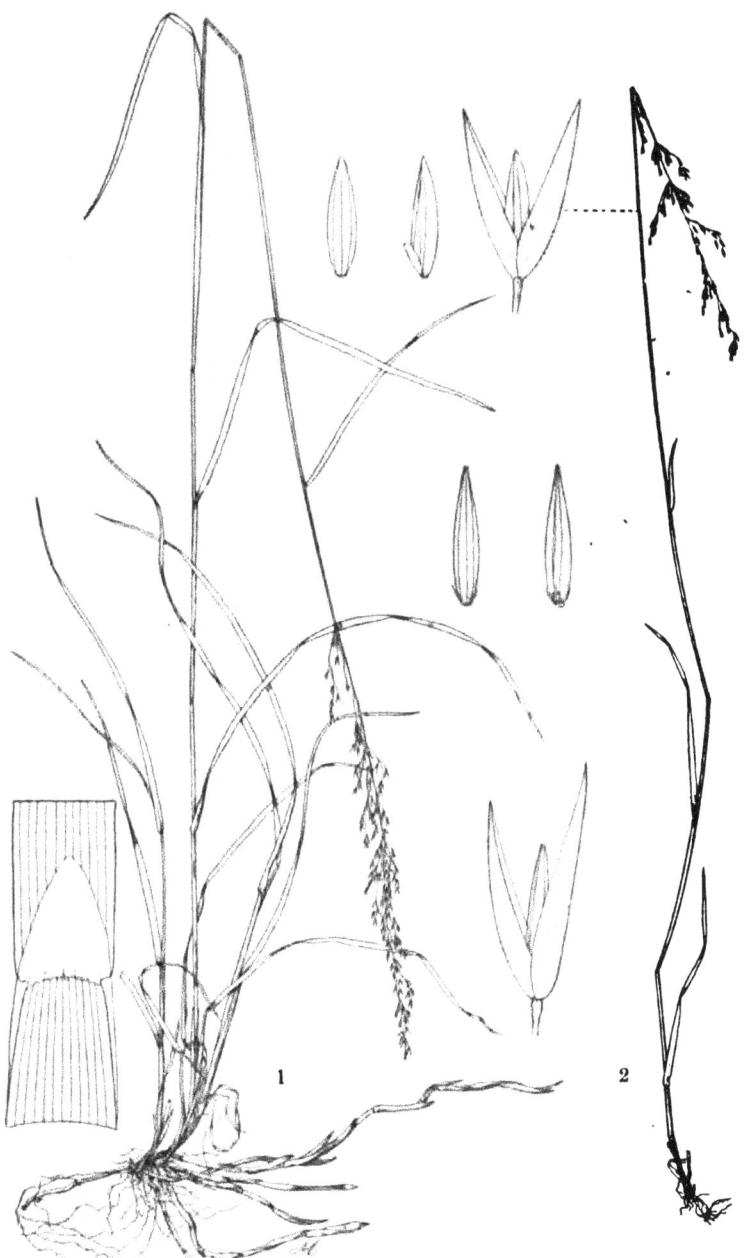

Fig. 1.—Agrostis pallens foliosa (Vasey) Hitchc. (Slender Form).
Fig. 2.—Agrostis scouleri Trin.

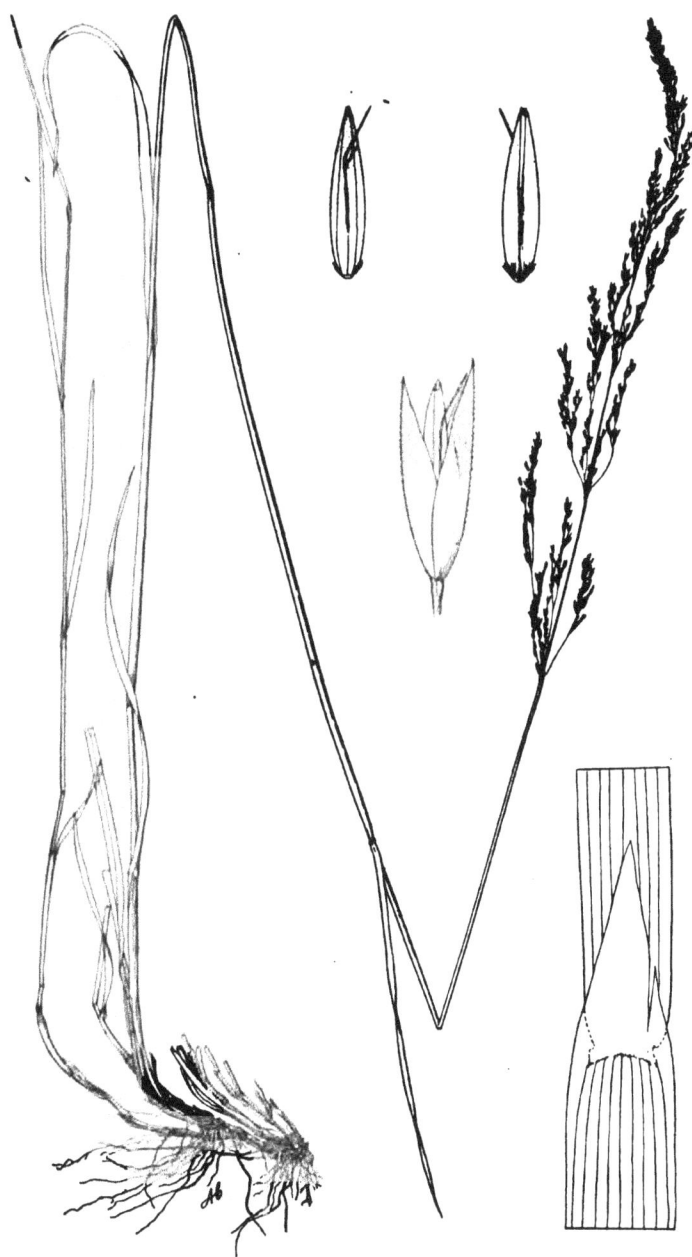

AGROSTIS DIEGOENSIS VASEY.

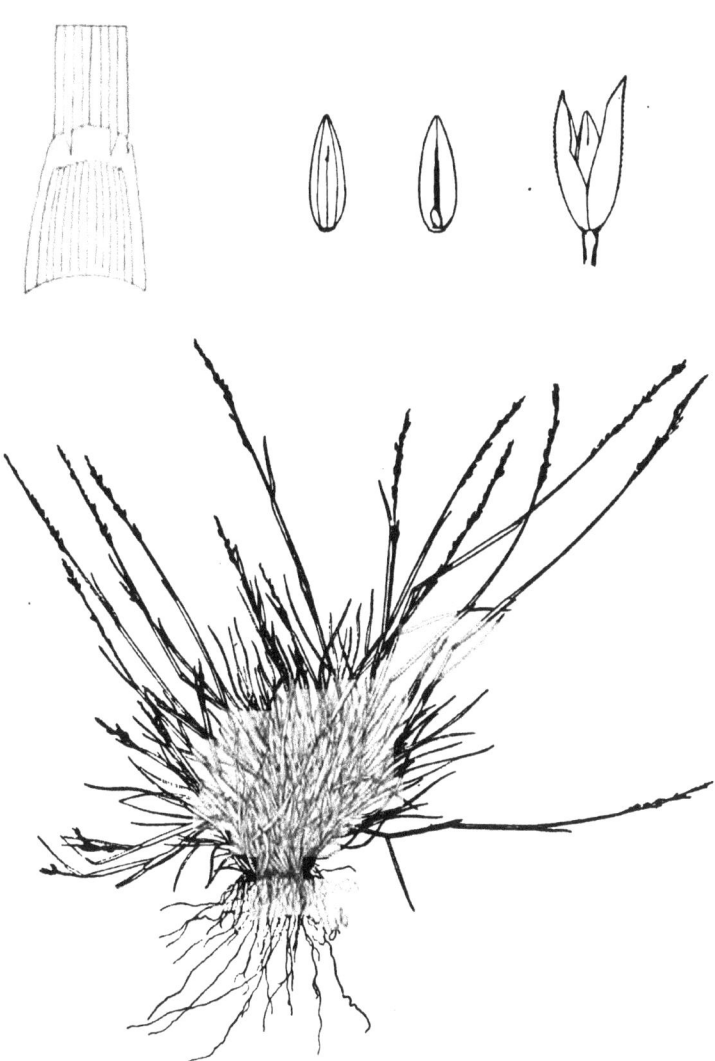

AGROSTIS BREVICULMIS HITCHC.

Fig. 1.—Agrostis microphylla major Vasey.   Fig. 2.—Agrostis microphylla Steud.

AGROSTIS AMPLA HITCHC.

Fig. 1.—Agrostis exarata Trin. (Alaska). Fig. 2.—Agrostis asperifolia Trin.

AGROSTIS GRANDIS TRIN.

AGROSTIS EXARATA TRIN.

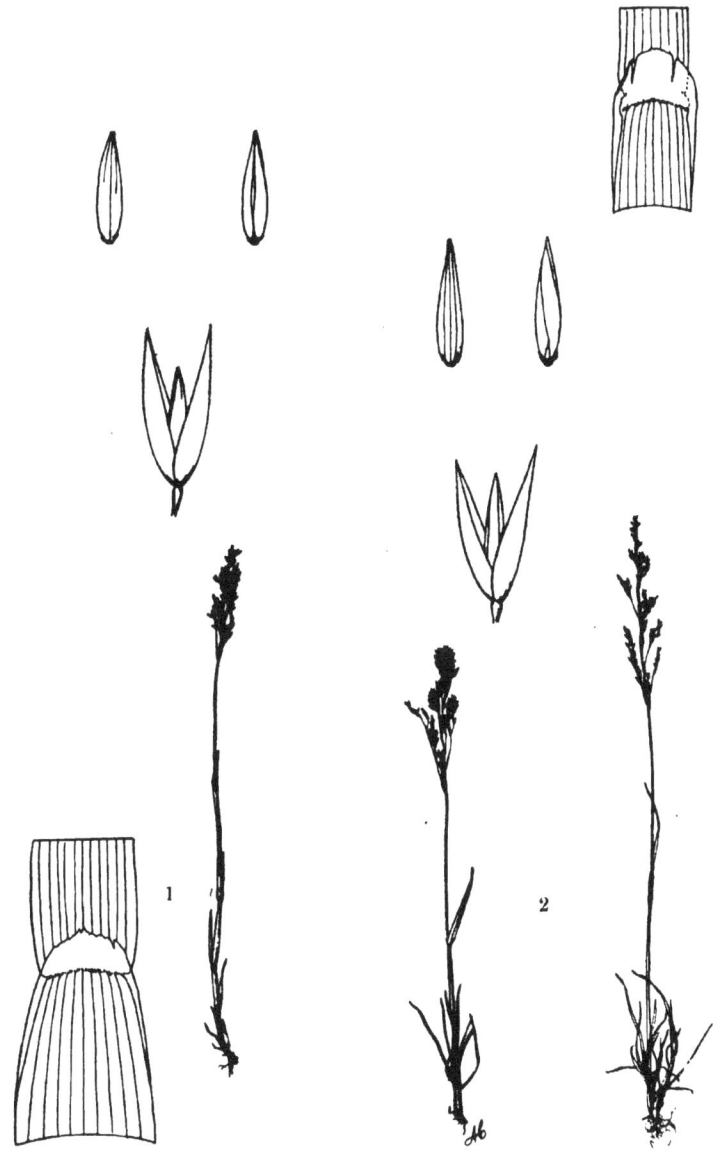

Fig. 1.—Agrostis rossæ Vasey. Fig. 2.—Agrostis varians Trin.

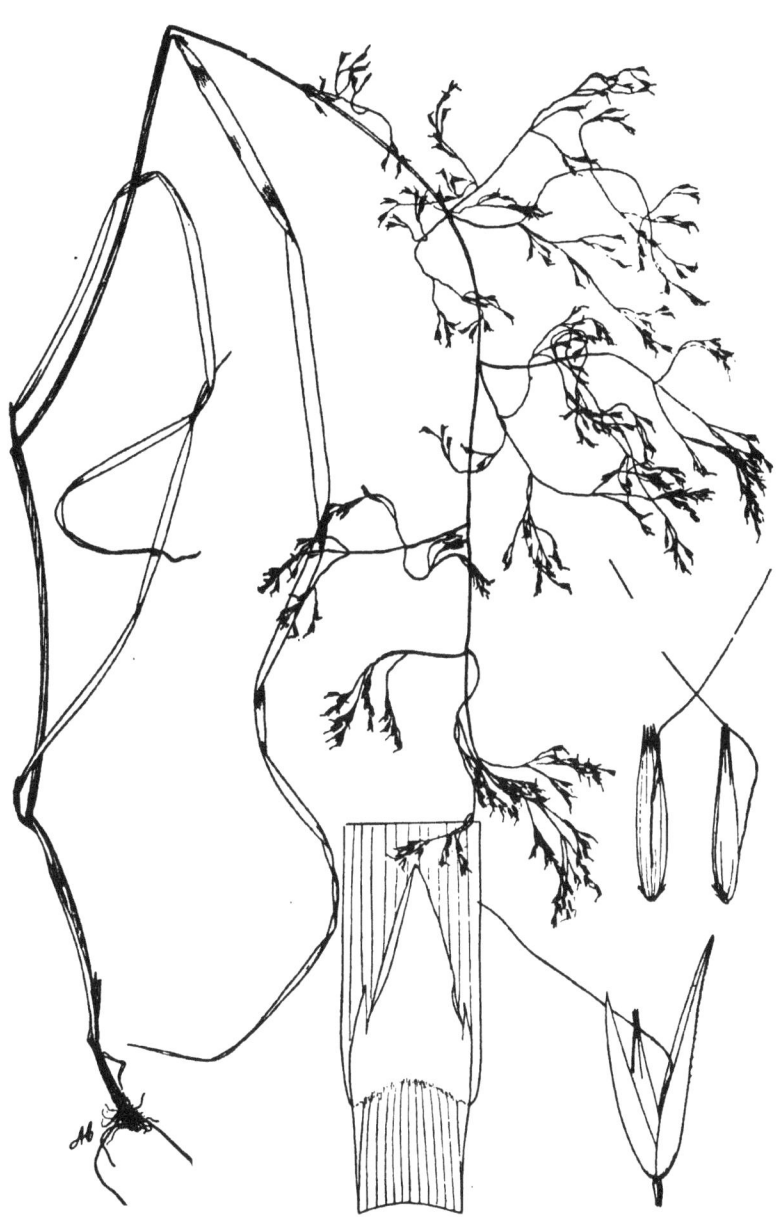

AGROSTIS HOWELLII SCRIBN.

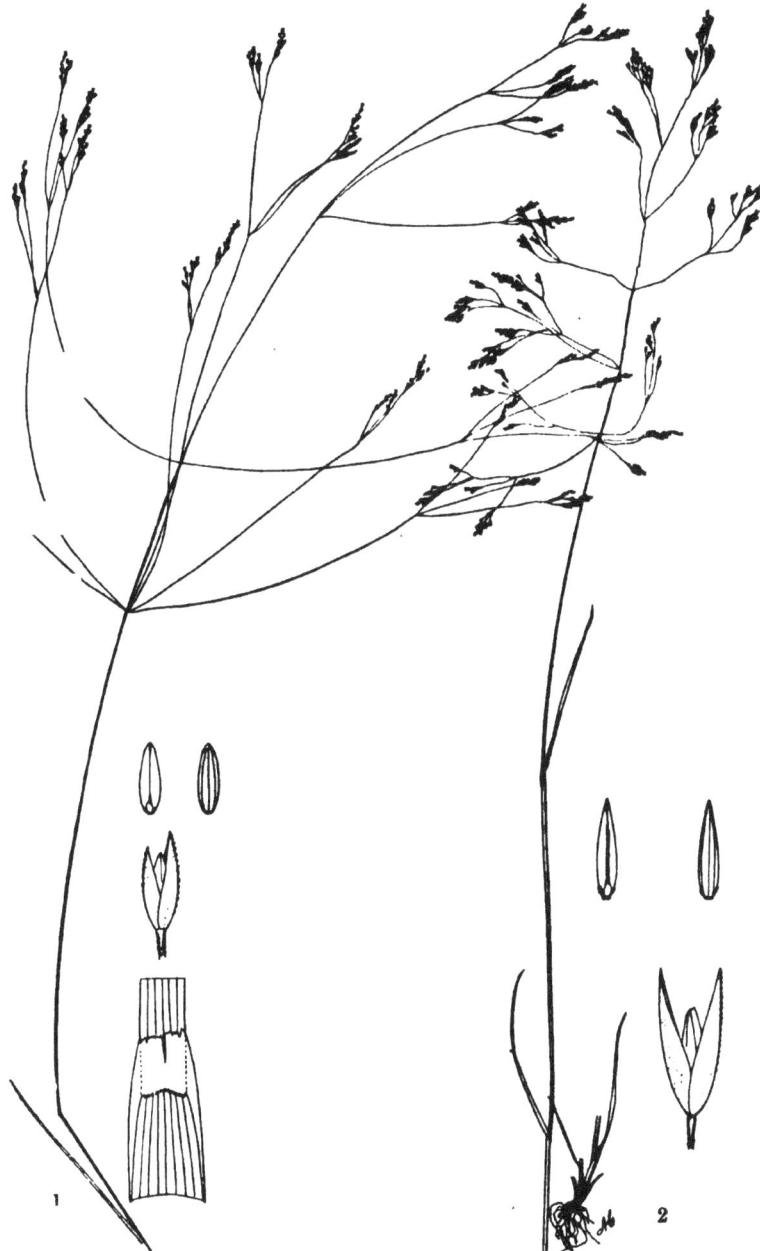

Fig. 1.—Agrostis hiemalis (Walt.) B. S. P. (Common Form). Fig. 2.—Agrostis hiemalis (Mountain Form).

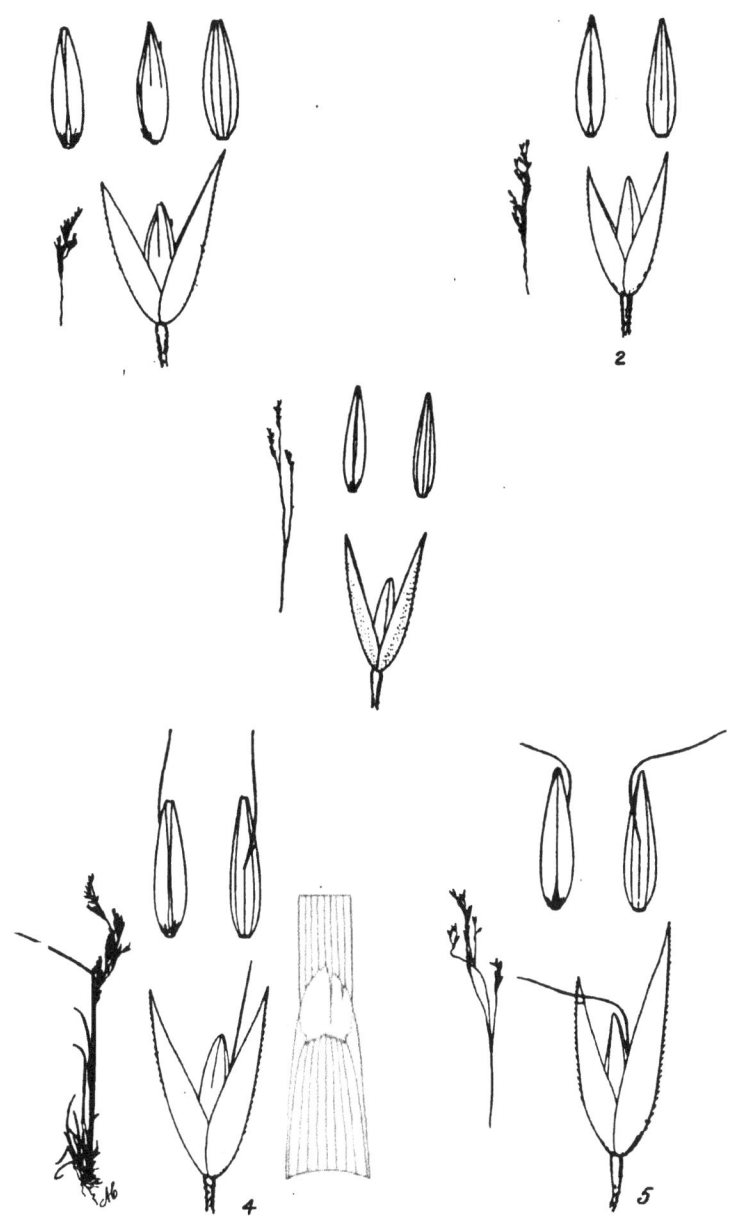

Types referred to Agrostis hiemalis (Walt.) B. S. P.

Fig. 1.—Agrostis geminata Trin.   Fig. 2.—Agrostis geminata Trin. (Awnless Form).

Fig. 1.—Agrostis idahoensis Nash.   Fig. 2.—Agrostis tenuis Vasey.

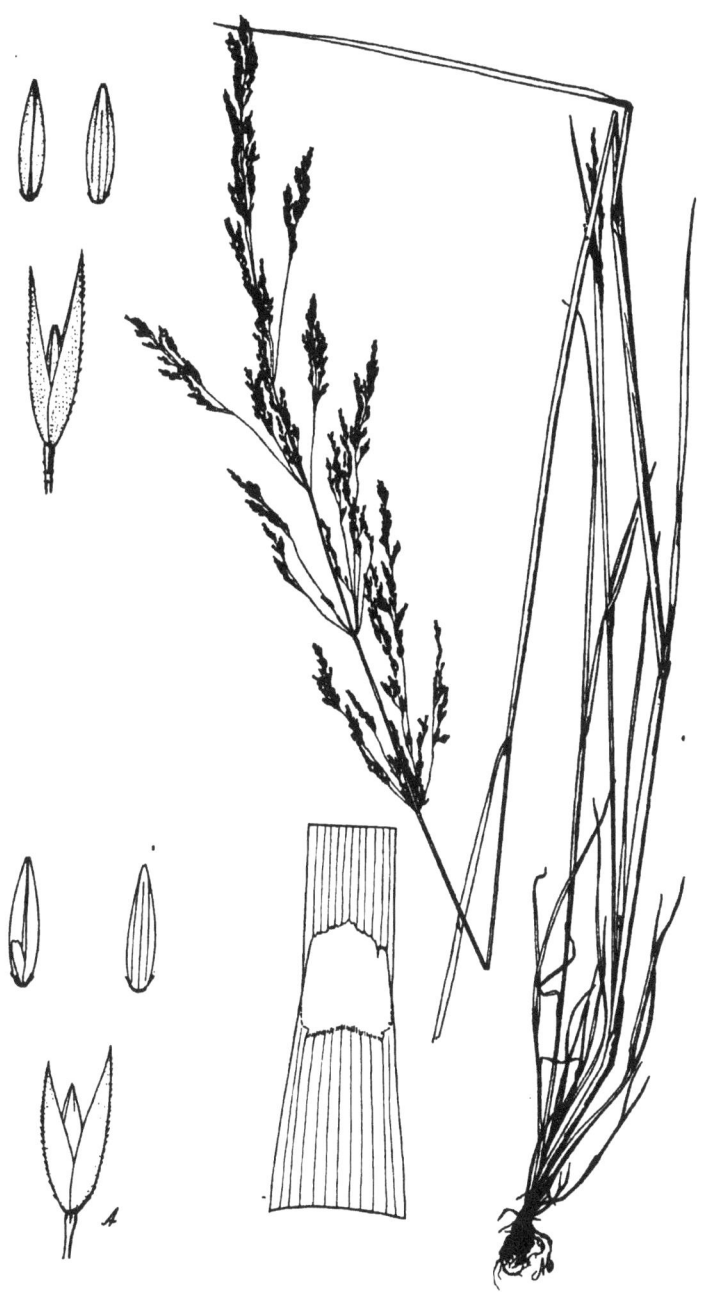

AGROSTIS SCHIEDEANA TRIN.

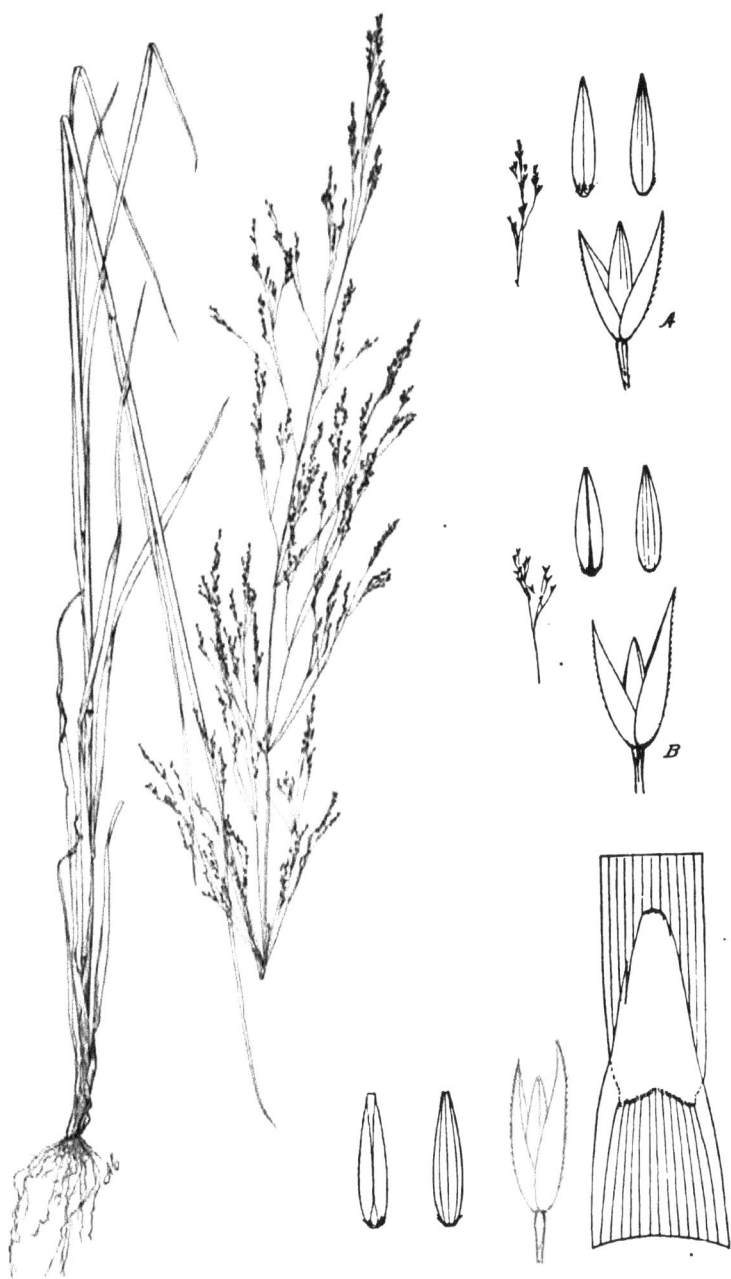

AGROSTIS PERENNANS (WALT.) TUCKERM.

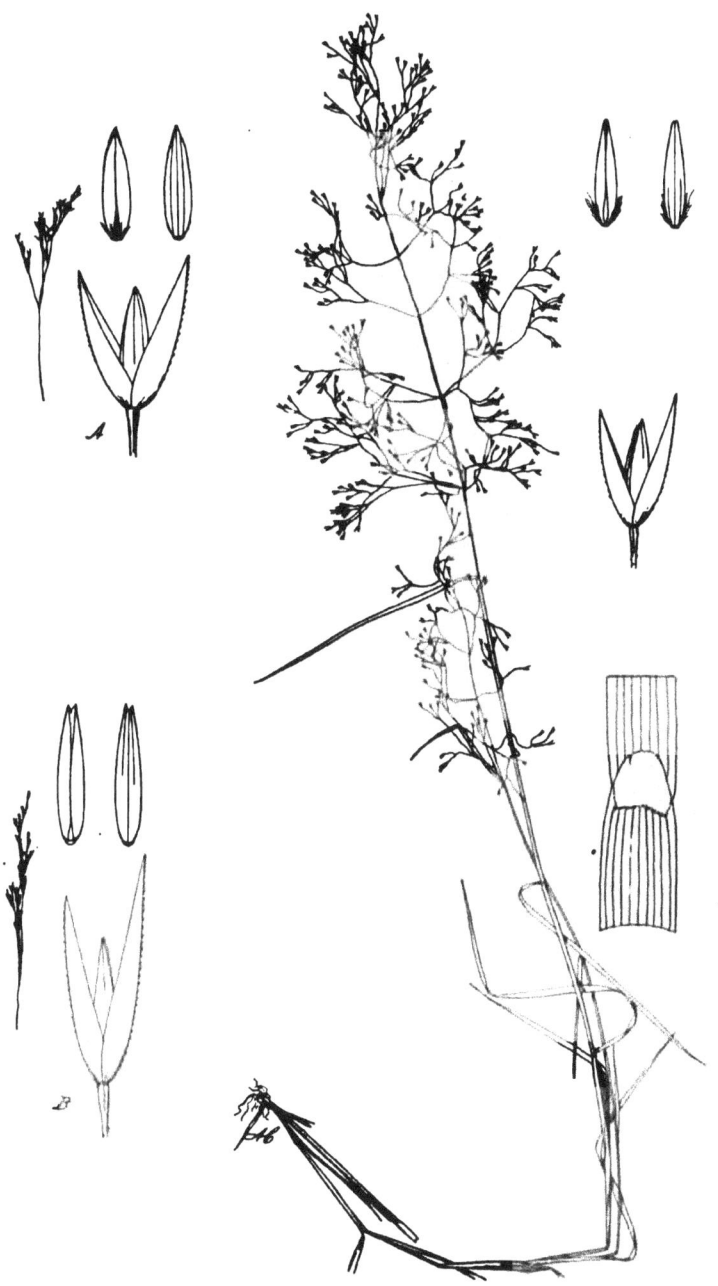

AGROSTIS PERENNANS ÆSTIVALIS VASEY.

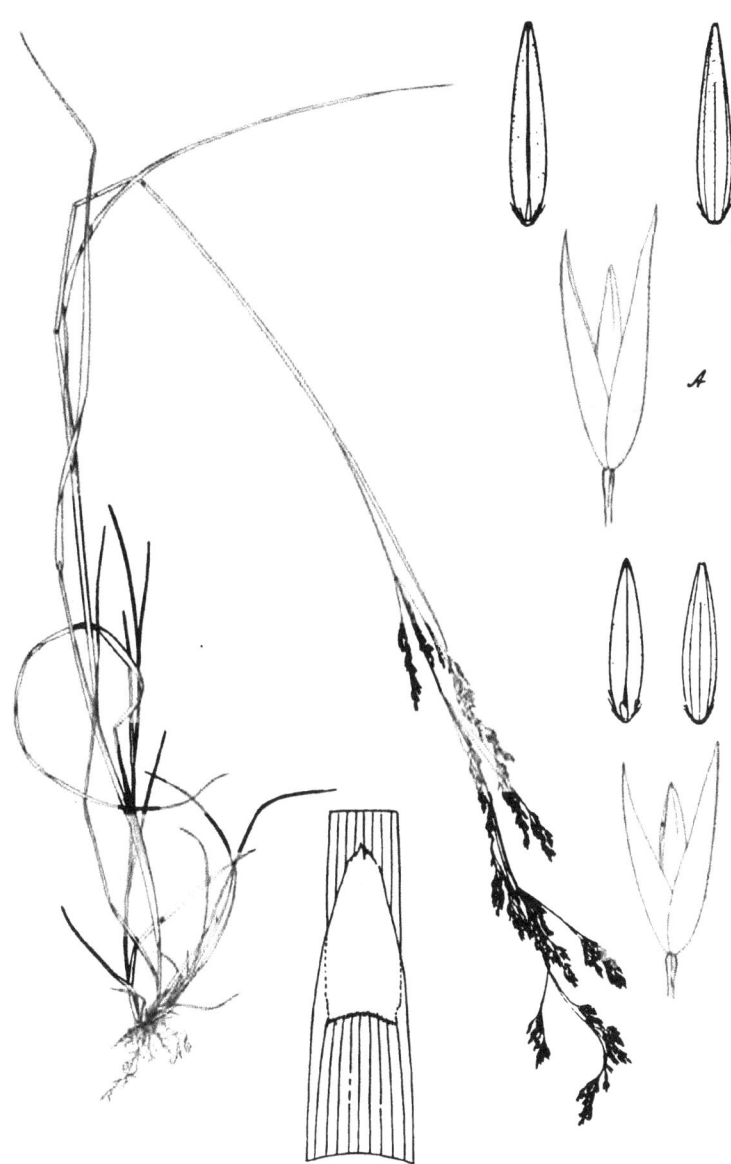

AGROSTIS PERENNANS ELATA (PURSH) HITCHC.

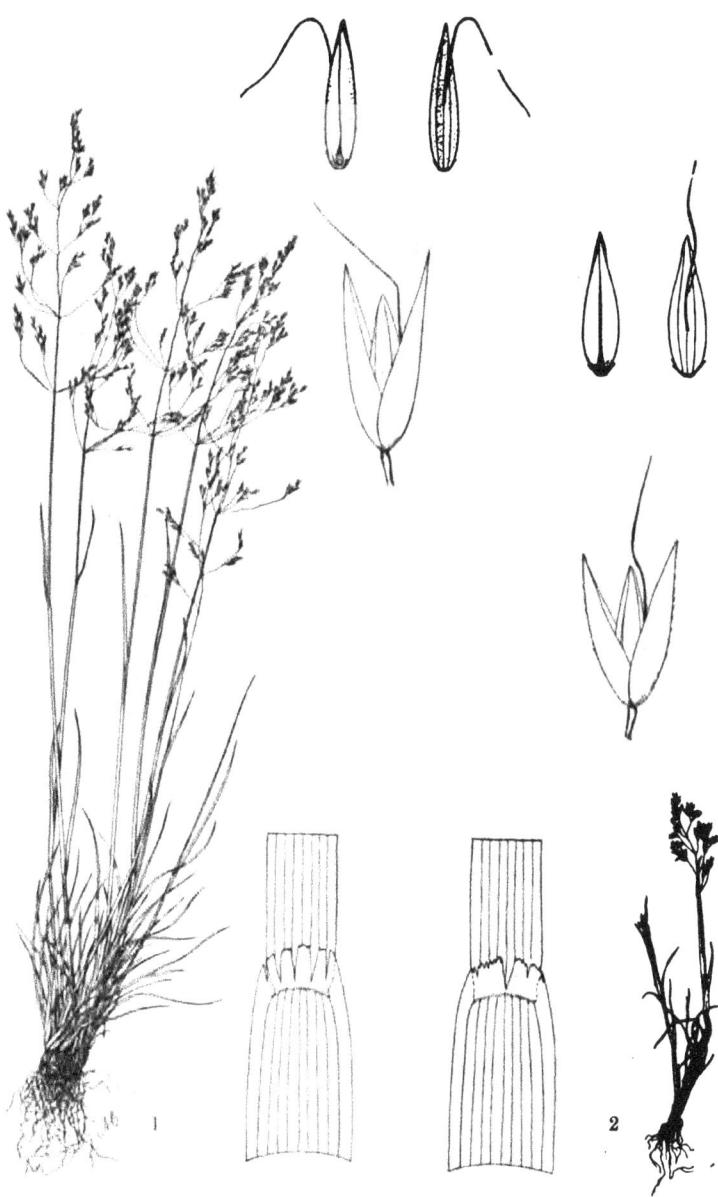

FIG. 1.—AGROSTIS BOREALIS HARTM. (WHITE MOUNTAINS). FIG. 2.—AGROSTIS BOREALIS HARTM. (LABRADOR).

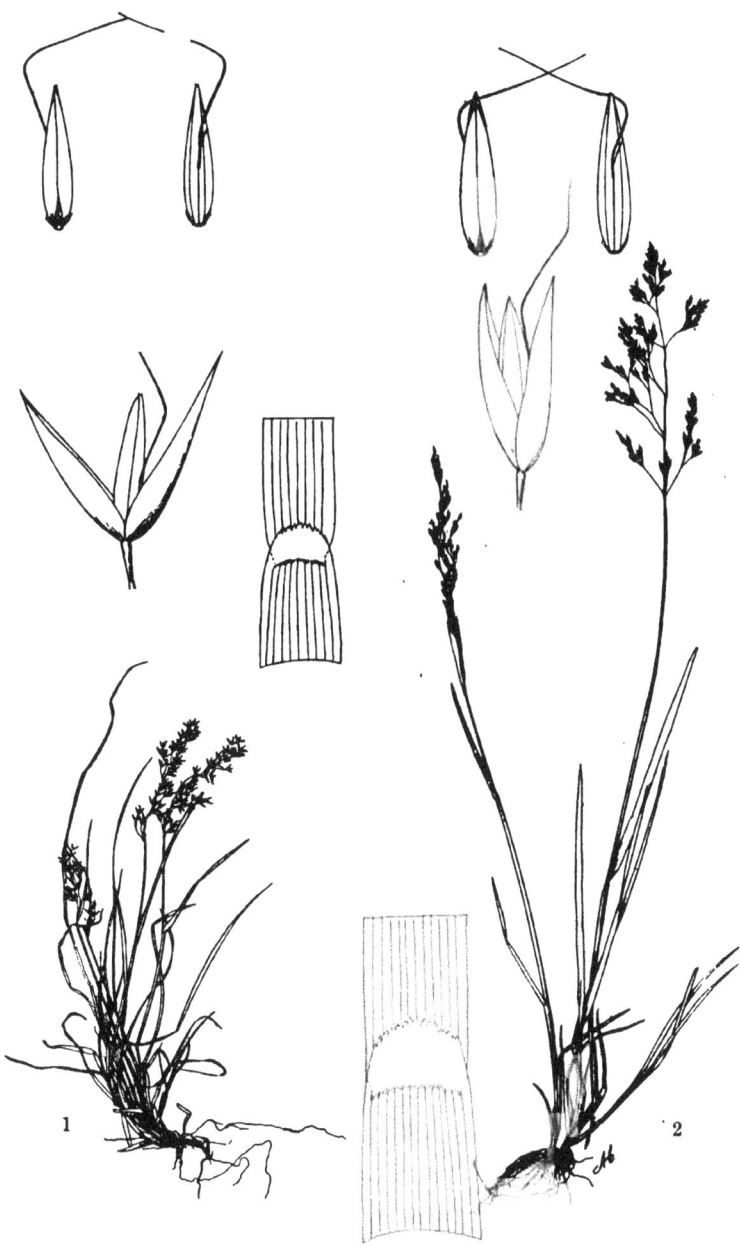

Fig. 1.—Agrostis mertensii Trin. Fig. 2.—Agrostis borealis Hartm. (Sweden).

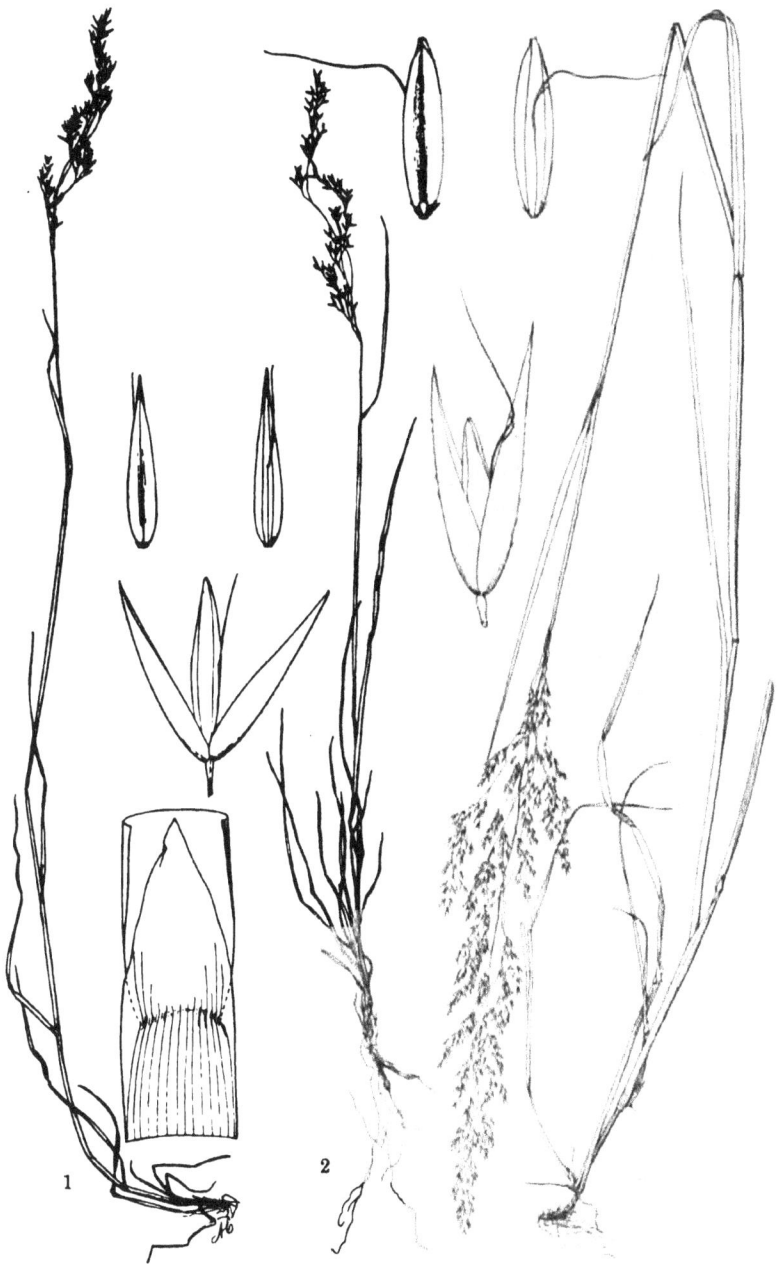

Fig. 1.—Agrostis aenea Trin. Fig. 2.—Agrostis aenea Trin. Fig. 3.—Agrostis longiligula Hitchc.

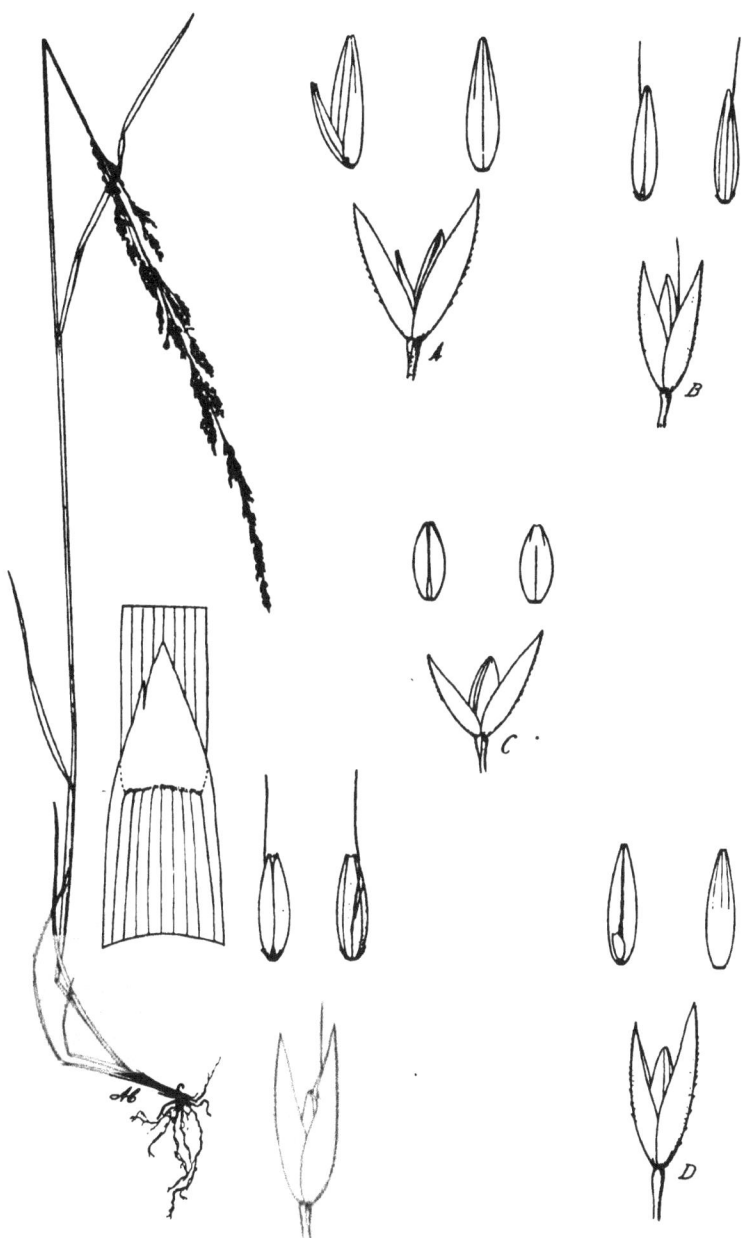

MEXICAN SPECIES OF AGROSTIS.

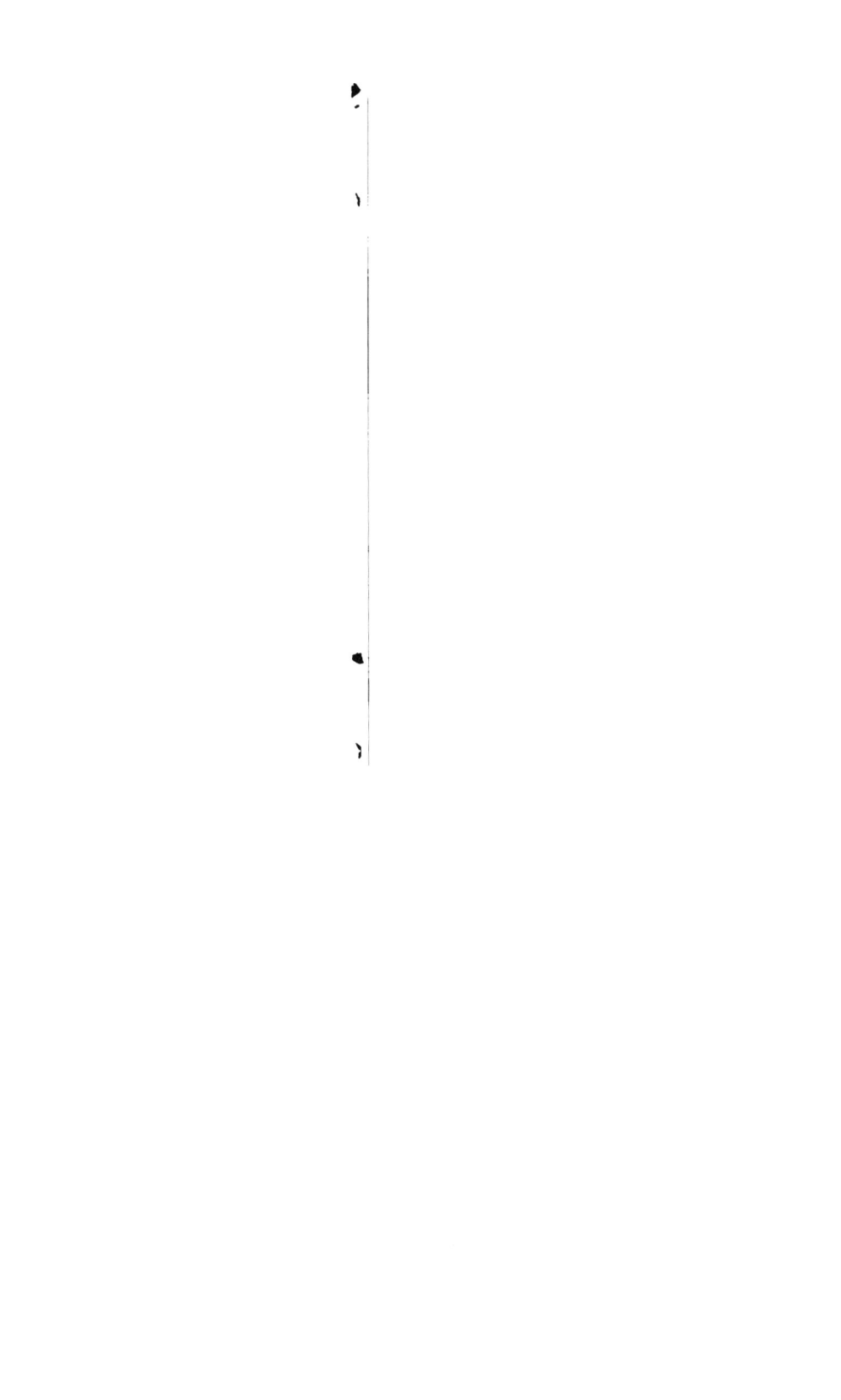

[Continued from page 2 of cover.]

No. 29. of Black Rot on 1903. Price, 15 cents.

1902. Price, 10

32. A Disease of the White Ash. 1903. Price, 10 cents.
33. North American Species of Leptochloa. 1903. Price, 15 cents.
34. Silkworm Food Plants. 1903. Price, 15 cents.
35. Recent Foreign Explorations. 1903. Price, 15 cents.
36. The "Bluing" and the "Red Rot" of the Western Yellow Pine, with Special Reference to the Black Hills Forest Reserve. 1903. Price, 30 cents.
37.

42.
43.

47.
48.

used by

1904. Price,

Certain

BUREAU OF PLANT INDUSTRY—BULLETIN NO. 69.

AMERICAN

WASHINGTON:
GOVERNMENT PRINTING OFFICE.
1904.

U. S. DEPARTMENT OF AGRICULTURE
BUREAU OF PLANT INDUSTRY—BULLETIN NO. 69.
B. T. GALLOWAY, *Chief of Bureau.*

AMERICAN VARIETIES OF LETTUCE.

BY

W. W. TRACY, Jr., Assistant, Variety Trials.

BOTANICAL INVESTIGATIONS AND EXPERIMENTS.

Issued December 23, 1904.

WASHINGTON:
GOVERNMENT PRINTING OFFICE.
1904.

BUREAU OF PLANT INDUSTRY.

B. T. GALLOWAY,
Pathologist and Physiologist, and Chief of Bureau.

VEGETABLE PATHOLOGICAL AND PHYSIOLOGICAL INVESTIGATIONS.

ALBERT F. WOODS, *Pathologist and Physiologist in Charge, Acting Chief of Bureau in Absence of Chief.*

BOTANICAL INVESTIGATIONS AND EXPERIMENTS.
FREDERICK V. COVILLE, *Botanist in Charge.*

GRASS AND FORAGE PLANT INVESTIGATIONS.
W. J. SPILLMAN, *Agrostologist in Charge.*

POMOLOGICAL INVESTIGATIONS.
G. B. BRACKETT, *Pomologist in Charge.*

SEED AND PLANT INTRODUCTION AND DISTRIBUTION.
A. J. PIETERS, *Botanist in Charge.*

ARLINGTON EXPERIMENTAL FARM.
L. C. CORBETT, *Horticulturist in Charge.*

EXPERIMENTAL GARDENS AND GROUNDS.
E. M. BYRNES, *Superintendent.*

J. E. ROCKWELL, *Editor.*
JAMES E. JONES, *Chief Clerk.*

BOTANICAL INVESTIGATIONS AND EXPERIMENTS.

SCIENTIFIC STAFF.

FREDERICK V. COVILLE, *Botanist.*

O. F. COOK, *Botanist in Charge of Investigations in Tropical Agriculture.*
RODNEY H. TRUE, *Physiologist, Drug and Medicinal Plant Investigations.*
LYSTER H. DEWEY, *Botanist in Charge of Investigations of Fiber Plants.*
EDGAR BROWN, *Botanist in Charge of Seed Laboratory.*
CARL S. SCOFIELD, *Botanist in Charge of Grain Grade Investigations.*
G. N. COLLINS, *Assistant Botanist, Tropical Agriculture.*
A. C. CRAWFORD, *Pharmacologist, Poisonous Plant Investigations.*
WILLIAM E. SAFFORD, *Assistant Curator, Tropical Agriculture.*
F. H. HILLMAN, *Assistant Botanist, Seed Herbarium.*
J. W. T. DUVEL, *Assistant, Seed Laboratory.*
W. W. TRACY, Jr., *Assistant, Variety Trials.*
W. F. WIGHT, *Assistant, Geographic Botany.*
W. O. RICHTMANN, *Pharmacognostical Expert.*
ALICE HENKEL, *Assistant, Drug and Medicinal Plant Investigations.*
W. W. STOCKBERGER, *Expert, Drug and Medicinal Plant Investigations.*

LETTER OF TRANSMITTAL.

U. S. DEPARTMENT OF AGRICULTURE,
BUREAU OF PLANT INDUSTRY,
OFFICE OF THE CHIEF,
Washington, D. C., July 22, 1904.

SIR: I have the honor to transmit herewith, and to recommend for publication as Bulletin No. 69 of the series of this Bureau, the accompanying manuscript entitled "American Varieties of Lettuce." This paper was prepared by W. W. Tracy, jr., Assistant in Botanical Investigations and Experiments, and has been submitted by the Botanist with a view to its publication.

The twenty-seven half-tone plates illustrating the varieties are necessary to a complete understanding of the text of this bulletin.

Respectfully,

B. T. GALLOWAY,
Chief of Bureau.

Hon. JAMES WILSON,
Secretary of Agriculture.

PREFACE

For an experimental horticulturist, perhaps no knowledge is more fundamental than that of the characteristics of the plant varieties with which he is dealing, yet for most kinds of garden and field vegetables it is impossible to get this information in authoritative printed form. There is such looseness of nomenclatorial practice, and such inadequacy of description regarding the varieties of vegetables, that growers, especially owners of private gardens, have much difficulty in getting the varieties best suited to their purposes. The lettuce variety known as Tennis Ball Black-Seeded is advertised by seedsmen under thirty-seven different names.

In Bulletin No. 21 of the Bureau of Plant Industry, entitled "List of American Varieties of Vegetables for the Years 1901 and 1902," were given about five thousand names of varieties of vegetables offered for sale in those years in American seed catalogues. No attempt was made to say which of these varieties were identical and which were in reality distinct, except where synonyms were given in the catalogues themselves. It had already been determined, however, to take up the various kinds of vegetables one by one and, after a careful series of trials, to publish the results, with descriptions and synonyms. Lettuce is the first vegetable to which this critical study has been given. It will be of interest, therefore, to record a statement regarding those features of the method pursued in the investigation which are novel as applied to this class of objects.

The main idea was to apply to a horticultural subject the methods of systematic botany. The particular features of this application may be itemized as follows:

1. The descriptive terms used have been defined with precision. Where a verbal description is insufficient to convey an exact idea of form, such as the degree of curliness of leaves, reference is made to an illustration. When it is desired to designate a particular kind of green color, reference is made to a well-known variety of lettuce which exhibits that color.

2. In addition to an outline of classification intended to show the relationship of the varieties, an artificial key has been given, arranged on the convenient dichotomous system and making use of the most conspicuous characters, by which the identification of varieties is very greatly facilitated.

PREFACE.

3. The varieties sufficiently different to be distinguishable by their form have been illustrated from photographs. A picture of the differences thus brought out could be conveyed by no amount of verbal description alone.

The groundwork upon which these botanical methods were applied was that of long experience and modern training in horticultural procedure, and intimate familiarity with the plants themselves.

Tentative trials were made in the years 1897, 1898, and 1899, and extensive trials were conducted in each of the four years from 1900 to 1903. Altogether 2,934 samples of lettuce seeds were secured, chiefly by purchase from seedsmen, and grown in the trials. These samples represented 444 variety names recognized by American seedsmen. The trials were conducted under Mr. Tracy's immediate direction from 1897 to 1899, at Kensington, Md., and in the succeeding years on the Potomac Flats at Washington. In addition, Mr. Tracy visited the extensive trial grounds maintained by five large seed houses, as well as seven seed farms in California, where lettuce seed is grown.

Mr. Tracy concludes that of the 404 varieties named in seedsmen's catalogues 107 represent really distinct varieties, while the others are merely these same varieties under different names. In adopting a single name for a much-named variety, the most suitable of the trade names has been chosen. No new names have been proposed by the author, even when the best of the trade names is long and cumbersome.

FREDERICK V. COVILLE,
Botanist.

OFFICE OF BOTANICAL INVESTIGATIONS AND EXPERIMENTS,
Washington, D. C., June 11, 1904.

CONTENTS.

	Page.
Introduction	9
Varieties and their description	9
Nomenclature	9
Environment and selection	10
Source of seed	11
Cultural peculiarities	11
Terms used in description	12
Classes	12
Size	13
Maturity	14
Shooting to seed	14
Habit	15
Leaves	16
Color	18
Seeds	18
Seedling plants	19
Varieties suited to different conditions and requirements	19
Table of varieties	21
Classification of varieties	23
Key to varieties	24
Description of varieties classed as distinct	28
Catalogue of variety names	80

ILLUSTRATIONS.

TYPICAL MATURE PLANTS.

	Page.
Plate I. Fig. 1.—Black-Seeded Simpson. Fig. 2.—Hanson	104
II. Fig. 1.—Tyrolese. Fig. 2.—Golden Heart	104
III. Fig. 1.—Green-Fringed. Fig. 2.—Bath Cos	104
IV. Fig. 1.—American Gathering. Fig. 2.—Early Curled Simpson	104
V. Fig. 1.—Big Boston. Fig. 2.—Prize Head	104
VI. Fig. 1.—Onondaga. Fig. 2.—Grand Rapids	104
VII. Fig. 1.—Density. Fig. 2.—Boston Curled. Fig. 3.—Mignonette. Fig. 4.—White Forcing	104
VIII. Fig. 1.—Earliest Cutting. Fig. 2.—California Cream Butter	104
IX. Fig. 1.—Emperor William. Fig. 2.—Yellow Winter. Fig. 3.—Detroit Market Gardener's Forcing	104
X. Fig. 1.—Hubbard's Market. Fig. 2.—Deacon	104
XI. Fig. 1.—Maximum (upper view). Fig. 2.—Maximum (side view)	104
XII. Fig. 1.—Malta. Fig. 2.—Italian Ice	104
XIII. Fig. 1.—Red Besson. Fig. 2.—Asparagus Lobed-Leaved	104
XIV. Fig. 1.—Asparagus. Fig. 2.—Red Winter Cos	104
XV. Fig. 1.—Lancaster. Fig. 2.—Express Cos. Fig. 3.—Baltimore Oak-Leaved	104
XVI. Fig. 1.—Oak-Leaved. Fig. 2.—Tom Thumb. Fig. 3.—Reichner	104
XVII. Sugar Loaf	104
XVIII. Fig. 1.—Half Century. Fig. 2.—Speckled Dutch Butter. Fig. 3.—Mette's Forcing	104

TYPICAL MATURE PLANTS (LONGITUDINAL SECTIONS).

XIX. Fig. 1.—Tom Thumb. Fig. 2.—Mette's Forcing. Fig. 3.—Paris White Cos. Fig. 4.—Lancaster. Fig. 5.—Hartford Bronzed Head.	104
XX. Fig. 1.—Speckled Dutch Butter. Fig. 2.—Matador. Fig. 3.—Hanson	104
XXI. Fig. 1.—Prize Head. Fig. 2.—White Star	104

TYPICAL YOUNG PLANTS.

XXII. Fig. 1.—Nansen. Fig. 2.—Tomhannock. Fig. 3.—Big Boston. Fig. 4.—Hanson. Fig. 5.—All Seasons. Fig. 6.—Passion	104

TYPICAL OUTER LEAVES.

XXIII. Fig. 1.—Boston Curled. Fig. 2.—Green-Fringed. Fig. 3.—Earliest Cutting. Fig. 4.—Speckled Dutch Butter. Fig. 5.—Tennis Ball Black-Seeded. Fig. 6.—Deacon	104
XXIV. Fig. 1.—Lancaster (back view). Fig. 2.—Lancaster (front view). Fig. 3.—Oak-Leaved. Fig. 4.—Yellow Winter. Fig. 5.—Baltimore Oak-Leaved. Fig. 6.—Big Boston	104
XXV. Fig. 1.—Early Curled Simpson. Fig. 2.—Giant Glacier. Fig. 3.—Grand Rapids	104
XXVI. Fig. 1.—Denver Market. Fig. 2.—Asparagus Lobed-Leaved and Express Cos. Fig. 3.—Hanson	104
XXVII. Fig. 1.—Asparagus. Fig. 2.—Bath Cos. Fig. 3.—Paris White Cos. Fig. 4.—Giant White Cos. Fig. 5.—Red Winter Cos	104

AMERICAN VARIETIES OF LETTUCE.

INTRODUCTION.

Lettuce is our most important salad plant and one of the most varied of our cultivated vegetables. In this country alone it is listed under more than three hundred varietal names and represents more than a hundred really distinct varieties. Being in demand at all seasons of the year, it is probably grown under more varied outdoor and indoor conditions than any other vegetable. Five hundred acres, producing about 250,000 pounds of seed, are planted in California every year for seed alone. More than 8,000 pounds of one variety have been used in a single year by one American seed house.

VARIETIES AND THEIR DESCRIPTIO .

In order to form a basis for a classification and description of American cultivated varieties it becomes necessary to decide several questions as to the proper use of names and the right methods of work. The following are the methods and terms adopted by the Department of Agriculture in conducting lettuce trials and making descriptions.

NOMENCLATURE.

The simplification of varietal nomenclature is a work of first importance. After the distinct varieties are determined it becomes necessary to decide which of the many names applied by seedsmen to a particular type shall be adopted as the one by which that type shall be known. Generally the name which was first used should be the one adopted, but it is not always practicable to do this because that name may have gone out of general use. Many of our varietal names are so firmly established that it would be almost as difficult to change a language as to change some of those whose origins are traced to a renaming of types. Even though it were possible to decide which was the name first used there would yet remain to be determined whether the name at the present time represents the same type as when first used. Another type may have been adopted, as, for example, an improved strain may have appeared in the type and this may have been given a new name and called a new variety. In the course of time seedsmen in receiving requests for the old variety may be led to fill all their orders from this new strain instead of using the original type. This is what seems to have occurred with the Early Curled Silesia lettuce, so that instead of having the old type we have now the new one, called Early Curled Simpson, which was developed from Early Curled Silesia.

Besides determining whether a name is the one first adopted, or the one in most general use at the present time, there needs to be considered also whether a name be so similar to other names as to be confusing and whether it be a many-worded one which can be shortened to one more simple. In regard to the latter question it is a safe rule to drop all such words as improved, selected, perfected, extra, select, choice, superior, celebrated, fine, and true from varietal names, and names of persons in the possessive case may often be omitted.

For the above reasons there seems, therefore, to be no hard and fast rule for the naming of varieties. In the following lettuce descriptions those names included in the list of distinct varieties have been chosen to designate the different types, and where confusing names exist among the list of subsidiary varieties the name which is preferred has been designated in some way.

ENVIRONMENT AND SELECTION.

The description of cultivated varieties becomes a particularly difficult matter because of differences due to environment and selection. All horticulturists have occasion to observe how color, shape, size, and quality are affected by the former and what great differences there are between well-selected and neglected stocks. Our cultivated varieties are quite different in this respect from our native flora, and in the matter of selection our cultivated vegetables which are propagated by seed are quite different from our fruit varieties, which are increased by cuttings. In the latter case there is simply a periodical multiplication of a single original plant or unit; in the former, a yearly aggregation of new units.

Too often the ideal formed of a variety in making selections is simply a general idea of a good plant rather than strict adherence to certain points of a variety which may not be attractive in some ways, but which are essential to its usefulness and value as a distinct sort. This lack of thoroughness in selection is not so marked in lettuce as in vegetables like corn, where, as a result of careless selection, the varieties tend to run very much together. Selection has the most marked influence on a variety when stocks are bred up from single plants. The variety is changed for good or bad more quickly in that way, but if a number of plants are selected and propagated together the checks on one another are very numerous and the average run or tendency of the variety is generally maintained, even when the selections have not been well made.

SOURCE OF SEED.

It is very important that the source of seed be mentioned in all variety descriptions. This is necessary, not so much to indicate the various stocks handled by different seedsmen as it is to show whether there be a total difference in type. It sometimes happens that varieties are changed in the seed store or labels misplaced in the field, the mistake not being discovered for several years perhaps, while in the meantime the wrong seeds may not only have been sent out from the store, but also have been planted in the field. All those who have worked on a seed farm and know what a great number of stocks are grown on such a place, will realize how easily these mistakes may occur. But the use of the wrong type is due not so much to this cause as it is to the confusion resulting from the similarity of many varietal names. Generally, when varietal names are similar, they refer to one and the same type, but there are many cases where such is not the fact, and the seed grower or seedsman not knowing all these distinctions fills the order from the wrong type.

Were the writer to relate in the following descriptions all cases where the seed of a wrong variety has been supplied, or in deciding upon the right type were he to give equal weight to all samples regardless of the reputation of the different seed houses or their ability to obtain the right type, there would result from such a course a confusion rather than a clearing up of the subject. A record of such mistakes would be of little service to the reader. It would not even illustrate the reliability of the different seed houses, for the samples in any particular case would not be numerous enough to prove anything along this line. Where there is an apparent effort on the part of a seed house to supply a certain lettuce type for a particular variety no mistakes have been mentioned in the following descriptions, but where the wrong type is regularly supplied by a seedsman or where there is no effort to supply a certain type for a particular variety it becomes worthy of publication.

CULTURAL PECULIARITIES.

Lettuce is a cool-weather plant which succeeds best when grown in the spring and autumn. It succumbs to frost and cold if previously grown in warm weather, but stands severe weather if gradually hardened to it, so much so that gardeners even as far north as Long Island sometimes sow the seed in September and winter the plants over outdoors either entirely unprotected or with only a slight covering of brush. Under favorable conditions the seed sprouts within three or four days, but it may sometimes be greatly delayed. When the weather is dry or cold, seed planted in September may not sprout until the next spring. Self-sown lettuce is common and inferior seed is sometimes obtained from such crops. Practically all the seed used in this country is raised in California. Only a very small part of it is imported, though perhaps not farther back than 1880 the larger part of it came from abroad, California having first produced seed about six years previous to that date.

Lettuce does not readily cross-fertilize in the field and different varieties are planted side by side with little danger of mixture. The plants are generally grown for seed in the same way as for market. Sometimes they are left so close together that no heads are formed, and this is said to produce inferior seed. It requires from 30 to 60 plants to produce a pound of seed.

TERMS USED IN DESCRIPTION.

Lettuce varies so greatly, whether grown under cover or outdoors, that it becomes necessary to decide upon one or the other condition for making comparison of varieties. For purposes of description and classification outdoor-grown lettuce is more satisfactory than greenhouse-grown specimens. They show greater differences in color and habit than plants grown under glass, and the following descriptions are, therefore, made from them. It will sometimes be found difficult to identify indoor-grown plants from such descriptions, and for this reason it will be necessary to bear constantly in mind that greenhouse lettuce grows much looser, more upright in habit, and is much more solid green in color than lettuce grown in the open.

CLASSES.

Cultivated lettuce is known technically to botanists as *Lactuca sativa* Linn. The species to which this name is given has not been found in the wild state, and it is generally supposed that it has been derived from *L. virosa* Linn. or *L. scariola* Linn.

The classes to be made of lettuce in the following descriptions are those recognized by most seedsmen and horticultural writers, namely, the *cos*, distinguished by their upright habit, long, loaf-shaped heads, and spatulate leaves; the *butter*, distinguished by their buttery flavor, and the *crisp*, distinguished by their hard, crisp texture. Express Cos, on Plates XV and XXVI, Paris White Cos, on Plate XIX, and the five types of leaves on Plate XXVII are good examples of the cos class; California Cream Butter, on Plate VIII, Maximum, on Plate XI, Hartford Bronzed Head, on Plate XIX, and Tennis Ball Black-Seeded, on Plate XXIII, of the butter class; while Green-Fringed, on Plate III, Malta, on Plate XII, White Star, on Plate XXI, and Grand Rapids, on

Plate XXV, show the characteristics of the crisp class. There is no difficulty in identifying the cos varieties, but certain of the crisp and butter varieties are much alike. The latter are generally more delicately flavored, softer, and more pliable in texture. The crisp varieties are coarser veined and larger ribbed than the butter sorts but not more so than the cos varieties. Their borders are also more developed than other parts of the leaf and the cotyledons of the young seedlings are generally longer than those of the butter sorts. On account of their much developed borders they are sometimes called frilled lettuce.

These three classes of lettuce are each again separated into two subclasses. The cos are divided into those which are *self-closing* or comprise kinds which form well blanched heads without tying up, and the *loose-closing*, or those open sorts, which will not form well blanched heads without tying. Express Cos, on Plate XV, and Paris White Cos, on Plate XIX, are good examples of the self-closing, and Bath Cos, on Plate III, of the loose-closing varieties.

The butter and crisp classes are separated alike into *cabbage-heading* and *bunching*, the former referring to plants whose leaves overlap one another in such a smooth, regular way as to form a head like a cabbage, and the latter to those whose heads are open, clustered, or bunched in arrangement, or if overlapping one another at all doing so at the heart only, all the outer or visible portions remaining more or less loose leaved. Hanson, on Plates I and XX, and Big Boston, on Plate V, are good examples of the cabbage-heading varieties, and Early Curled Simpson, on Plate IV, Prize Head, on Plate XXI, and Lancaster, on Plate XIX, of the bunching varieties. Under the latter subclass are embraced all degrees of clustered growth from varieties loose leaved like an endive and represented by Boston Curled and Green-Fringed to those densely bunched and represented by Black-Seeded Simpson and White Star.

The term "cutting" has been used by a few writers in the United States and by Vilmorin, of France, to embrace only varieties of the former mode of growth, but in this country it is generally made to include all bunching varieties and is used simply as another name for bunching. Vilmorin has also classified lettuces into *spring*, *summer*, and *winter*, but such a division has little value in a climate like ours, and has never been used in this country.

SIZE.

Lettuce varieties may be divided as to size into seven divisions. Examples of each are: *Very small* (White Forcing, on Pl. VII), *small* (Boston Curled, on Pl. VII), *small-medium* (Mignonette, on Pl. VII), *medium* (Reichner, on Pl. XVI), *large-medium* (Hubbard's Market, on Pl. X), *large* (California Cream Butter, on Pl. VIII), and *very large*

(Hanson, on Pl. I). The size of lettuce plants varies so much under different conditions of growth that it is not possible to give equivalents of these in figures, and they are employed only to give an idea of the relative size of varieties. They are not based wholly on either weight or total spread of plant, because some hard-headed varieties weigh more than larger but softer-headed sorts, and, on the other hand, a plant often develops in height rather than spread.

MATURITY.

The following terms may be used in lettuce descriptions to express different periods of maturity: *Very early* (meaning plants requiring from 54 to 60 days to mature from sowing of the seed), *early* (61 to 66 days), *early intermediate* (67 to 72 days), *intermediate* (73 to 76 days), *late intermediate* (77 to 80 days), *late* (81 to 85 days), *very late* (86 to 90 days). These figures are based upon trials conducted at Washington, D. C., during the spring and autumn months. They presuppose a quick germination, the plants appearing above the surface within four days after sowing the seed, and a good continuous average growth afterwards. If grown during spring in the Santa Clara Valley of California or in other similar places, or under unfavorable conditions, or in greenhouses during winter when the sun is not strong and the days are short, it may require a materially longer time to reach the same development; but if grown outdoors under similar conditions as those obtained at Washington these figures will answer for most parts of our country. It should be mentioned also that these dates are based upon the full maturity of the plant, or to the time when about one-fourth of the plants are at their prime. They do not refer to varieties when first usable, and for this reason some bunching sorts like Prize Head are not given as early a season as most seedsmen claim for them.

SHOOTING TO SEED.

The expression "shooting to seed" is used to denote the first appearance of a seed stalk. In cabbage varieties it is the same as the bursting of the head; in all varieties it is when the lettuce first becomes bitter and unusable. When plants have grown very poorly and in inferior stocks, the seed stalk sometimes develops immediately, so that no considerable head or cluster of leaves is formed. In well-grown plants of the firm cabbage-heading varieties the seed stalk is so tightly bound by the overlapping leaves that it becomes necessary to cut open the plant before the tender shoot can break through the head. This opening of the leaves is very necessary where lettuce is grown for seed. Unless it is done, the plant "heats," soon afterwards rots, and no seed stalk develops. The forcing varieties and most of the extra early and early sorts shoot to seed under the least provocation when grown outdoors in the ordinary way, and so susceptible are they to the heat and strong sun of early or middle summer that they are seldom successfully grown outdoors unless forced or started very early and transplanted. The time at which lettuce varieties shoot to seed is so variable and depends so much upon conditions that it is impossible to give exact periods for the different varieties. Moreover, a variety can remain for weeks in the autumn without shooting to seed, whereas if planted in the spring the strong sun of early summer comes at the end rather than the beginning of its growth and forces the seed stalk to develop within a few days, while the extra early sorts which may have been planted on the same day will have arrived at their maturity earlier in the season when the influences forcing the seed stalk to grow are not so strong.

The terms used to express differences in shooting to seed are as follows:

Very quickly, meaning so susceptible to heat and strong sun as to be useless for summer growing. Such varieties are rarely successful outdoors in spring, are suitable only for forcing or indoor culture, and form no head in summer and very poor ones outdoors in spring. Examples are White Forcing and Emperor Forcing.

Quickly, meaning so susceptible to heat and strong sun as to form very poor heads in summer but sometimes good ones in spring. With the exceptions of Green-Fringed, Boston Curled, and Asparagus Cos, the varieties included in this division are to be classed as strictly forcing sorts. Examples are Tennis Ball White-Seeded and Hothouse.

Intermediate, meaning quickly shooting to seed in summer if the weather is unusually warm or the sun unusually strong. Because of earliness, varieties included in this division may be classed as excellent spring and sometimes also as good summer sorts, there being with good culture and favorable conditions little premature shooting to seed in spring or early summer. Examples are Hubbard's Market and Matador.

Slow, meaning such resistance to sun and strong heat that even in the hottest weather of midsummer the plants can be left for at least five days after maturing without danger of bursting their heads. Examples are Deacon and California Cream Butter.

Very slow, meaning fit to use for an unusually long time, even under influences of the strongest sun or most intense heat. Examples are Hanson and New York.

The time at which the different varieties developed seed stalks in the Department of Agriculture trials is given in the table on page 21.

HABIT.

In describing the habit of a plant we speak of it as *compact* (White Forcing, on Pl. VII) when the growth is confined to a small compass and the leaves are well gathered together. A *spreading* plant (Red

Besson, on Pl. XIII) is one whose growth extends over much ground and whose leaves grow so flatly outward that they become well separated from the middle portion of the plant. An *upright* growth is not necessarily compact, for the middle or head part of the plant may be very upright while the outer leaves may grow very loosely outward and cover much ground.

Solidity refers only to the head or middle part of the plant, the terms *hard*, *firm*, *soft*, *loose*, and *open* being used to express the different degrees of this quality, Hanson, Tennis Ball Black-Seeded, Red Besson, Onondaga, and Golden Heart standing, respectively, as examples of each. *Hard* refers to those cabbage varieties which approach a cabbage in solidity. *Firm* refers to those cos and softer leaved cabbage varieties which are so distinctly less solid than a cabbage as to bear little comparison with it for solidity but still to be regarded as decidedly solid for a lettuce. It includes also the most solid and dense varieties of the bunching sorts or those which at their heart are as solid as the firm cabbage varieties. *Soft* refers to those varieties which are so lacking in solidity as to be easily compressed, though they have no decided spaces between the leaves of the head or cluster. *Loose* refers to those varieties which are not only easily compressed but have decided spaces between the leaves of their head or cluster. *Open* refers to those varieties of a free, spreading growth with little or no denser middle part. The blanching of a lettuce depends largely upon its solidity, and it is really unnecessary to describe both these qualities, though it has been done in the following descriptions so as to point out these important qualities more directly.

Other important considerations in the habit of a plant are the arrangement of the leaves, whether *regular* (Deacon, on Pl. X), *irregular* (Speckled Dutch Butter, on Pl. XVIII), *formal* (Bath Cos, on Pl. III), or *twisted* (Nansen, on Pl. XXII), or whether the head leaves overlap one another *closely* (Deacon, on Pl. X), turn back and twist at their borders (Mette's Forcing, on Pl. XIX), meet at their margins only (Yellow Winter, on Pl. IX), fold well over one another past the middle of the head (Hanson, on Pl. I), grow together uprightly (Half Century, on Pl. XVIII) or curve inward and overlap one another in a complete cabbagelike manner (Deacon, on Pl. X).

LEAVES.

The leaves of lettuce vary so much in shape, character, and color, whether they be from the outside or center of the plant or from young, mature, seed-producing, summer, spring, or greenhouse specimens, that it becomes necessary to decide upon one kind of leaf for making comparisons. Accordingly, the leaves referred to in the following descriptions are always, except where otherwise noted, the largest leaves of prime, outdoor plants, or those just outside the head or body of a mature specimen.

Shape.—Such great variations exist in the shape of lettuce leaves that but little can be written regarding the identification of varieties from the shape of their leaves. They may be either *broad* (Deacon, on Pl. XXIII) or *spatulate* (Early Curled Simpson, on Pl. XXV), the latter term referring to varieties with leaves gradually narrowed downward from a rounded summit. Those which curve inward are said to be *cup-shaped* (Earliest Cutting, on Pl. XXIII). The first early leaves of most varieties are spatulate. Some kinds, such as Early Curled Simpson, are of this shape when mature, but the largest middle leaves of mature plants of most varieties are as broad as long. Greenhouse-grown lettuces are more spatulate leaved than outdoor-grown specimens, and summer-grown plants are longer leaved than spring-grown ones.

Surface.—A leaf is said to be *blistered* when it has small elevations and depressions between its veins, and *crumpled* when such formations are large or consist of considerable folds and excessive developments of its growth. Grand Rapids, on Plate XXV, and Denver Market, on Plate XXVI, are good examples of leaves which are both blistered and crumpled; Express Cos, on Plate XXVI, and Green-Fringed, on Plate XXIII, of leaves which are blistered but not crumpled, and Asparagus, on Plate XXVII, of a leaf which is neither blistered nor crumpled. The very young leaves of all lettuce varieties are never crumpled and are seldom blistered. All varieties forming a head show both the crumpled and blistered character at the inner heart leaves, and it is only in the largest leaves just outside the head of a mature plant where marked variety characteristics in the surface of a leaf are found.

Margin.—The *margin* of a leaf is the line describing its contour. In lettuce it may be *entire*, i. e., without toothing or division; *serrate*, i. e., having teeth pointing forward; or *crenate*, i. e., scalloped by even, rounded notches. The serrate and crenate character is sometimes not developed until the plant is almost mature, and whenever the margin is mentioned it is the upper part which is referred to, never the lower portion, which is generally more or less jagged and does not show much character. Deacon and Earliest Cutting, on Plate XXIII, are good examples of leaves with entire margins; Big Boston, on Plates V, XXII, and XXIV, of leaves with obscurely crenate margins, and Hanson, on Plates I, XXII, and XXVI, of leaves with serrate margins.

Border.—The *border* of a leaf is that portion of the blade adjacent to the margin. In nearly all butter varieties this part is flat or blistered. In nearly all crisp lettuces it is *frilled*, by which is meant that the border is much more developed than other parts of the leaf so that it forms sharp folds. In a few varieties of both the crisp and butter sorts this part of the leaf is *undulate*, by which is meant that the border is somewhat more developed than other parts of the leaf, so that it becomes wavy and forms rounded folds. The frilled and undulate character is sometimes not developed until the plant is mature, and whenever the margin is mentioned it is the upper part to which reference is made, never the lower portion, which is generally flat and does not show much character. Lancaster, on Plate XXIV, is a good example of a flat border, and Boston Curled and Green-Fringed, on Plate XXIII, of a frilled border. The undulate borders are so obscure in lettuce plants that it is difficult to illustrate them, but those of Big Boston, on Plates V, XXII, and XXIV, White Forcing, on Plate VII, and Speckled Dutch Butter, on Plate XVIII, are perhaps the best examples which can be given.

COLOR.

There are various differences in the color of nearly all distinct varieties of lettuces which the expert seedsman makes use of in identifying varieties in the field, but which on account of their minuteness and great variation under different conditions of weather become of little use in written descriptions. In the following varieties, instead of attempting to classify the different colors, all lettuces are simply referred to as brown or green. No attempt is made to divide them, as some writers have done, into bronze, red, pink, brown, and bronzed red, though a division has been made of the different shades of green and brown, as shown in the following examples: *Very light green*, Golden Queen; *light green*, Tennis Ball Black-Seeded; *medium green*, Hubbard's Market; *dark green*, White Chavigne; *very dark green*, New York; *dull green*, Tennis Ball White-Seeded; *glossy green*, Thick Head Yellow; *light brown*, Matador; *bright brown*, Prize Head; *dark brown*, Hartford Bronzed Head; *very dark brown*, Mignonette; *dull brown*, Brown Dutch Black-Seeded.

It should be borne in mind that the color description of these different varieties is based upon outdoor-grown plants. Sorts like Onondaga which are almost solid brown out of doors become almost solid green when grown in greenhouses.

SEEDS.

The seeds of lettuce varieties differ in color, size, and shape. Color is the most important quality and is the only variation commonly mentioned in descriptions. It is referred to in the following pages as whitish, blackish, or yellowish, and the seed of Red Winter Cos is described as brownish in color. The more common terms white, black, yellow, and brown are not used because these colors are never very decided and vary greatly with age and with the methods of harvesting the seed. Those described as blackish may have a grayish tinge, as in Brown Genoa, or a brownish cast, as in California Cream Butter. The size of lettuce seed varies according to the locality in which it is grown, California seed being especially large. The crisp sorts are generally larger seeded than the butter varieties. The large crisp varieties have unusually large seeds. Some of the lettuce samples which have been examined are narrower in shape than others, a few are very pointed, but no uniform varietal differences have as yet been detected in these respects except that the Defiance variety is distinctly broader than other sorts.

SEEDLING PLANTS.

The seedling plants of the different lettuce varieties show more or less variation in the color, shape, and size of their first seed leaves, and furnish an interesting study for the botanist. These differences are, however, too slight and unimportant to be mentioned in describing varieties, and they need only be referred to by giving a few general rules in regard to them. Perhaps the most important of these is that the color of the mature plant is more or less clearly indicated by that of the young seedling, especially if the mature plant be brownish. When the brown tinge in the young seedling is so slight that it seems impossible to say whether there be any brown present, the seedling plant may in that case be cut off at its stem, and if, after withering somewhat, the stem becomes colored where it was cut, this seems to be, so far as has been observed, a sign that the plant is brownish when mature. If the stem remains green after being cut, the mature plant is probably wholly green in color. The seedlings of the cos varieties are known by their very long slender seed leaves and seem almost to be possessed of a leaf stem. The crisp varieties are uniformly narrower leaved than the butter varieties. Excepting in the case of Malta, Giant Glacier, and a few others, they are not, however, as long leaved as the cos varieties. The seed leaves of the butter varieties are generally more glossy green than the crisp and cos sorts.

VARIETIES SUITED TO DIFFERENT CONDITIONS AND REQUIREMENTS.

There are many important factors which determine the variety best suited for particular purposes. Some of these are:

(1) *Differences in soil and climate.*—The cos varieties, for example, succeed much better in England than in our country, and everywhere market gardeners find that certain kinds are best adapted for their conditions of soil and climate.

(2) *The season at which the plants are grown.*—Some kinds succeed well in the spring, but shoot to seed at once in hot weather and are of little use for summer planting. Certain kinds are very hardy to cold,

and winter successfully outdoors unprotected, while other varieties, especially the crisp sorts, are failures for this purpose.

(3) *Methods of growing, whether in greenhouses, hotbeds, or cold frames, and whether transplanted into the open or sown directly in place outdoors.*—In field culture, where time and space are not so important as in greenhouses, it is more profitable to grow the large varieties, which are much later in season than those commonly grown under glass.

(4) *The tastes of consumers or the requirements of the market.*— Some prefer the soft, delicate-flavored butter varieties, which are used for serving on the table with dressing; others are more accustomed to the hard texture of the crisp sorts; while still others think there is nothing superior to the coarse but sweet leaves of the cos lettuces, and a change from one to the other of these different types is agreeable to most persons. In some markets the light green lettuces are demanded and there is little sale for brown-colored sorts. In our eastern markets the head lettuces are most in demand during winter, while in the West the more easily grown bunching sorts of the Grand Rapids type are the kinds most used for forcing.

On account of differences due to the requirements mentioned, it is impossible to select a definite list of the best varieties. The following may be recommended as some of the best for the purposes named:

Home use.—Deacon, Hartford Bronzed Head, New York, Prize Head, Mignonette, Black-Seeded Simpson, Paris White Cos, California Cream Butter, Iceberg, Tennis Ball Black-Seeded.

Market gardening outdoors.—Big Boston, Tennis Ball Black-Seeded, Black-Seeded Simpson, Hanson, Reichner, California Cream Butter, Paris White Cos, Mammoth Black-Seeded Butter, Hubbard's Market, White Chavigne.

Market gardening under glass.—Grand Rapids, Crumpled-Leaved, Hothouse, Black-Seeded Simpson, Golden Queen, Mette's Forcing, White Star, Hubbard's Market, Tennis Ball White-Seeded, Detroit Market Gardener's Forcing.

Quality.—Half Century, Hartford Bronzed Head, Deacon, Paris White Cos, Mignonette, New York, Tennis Ball Black-Seeded, California Cream Butter, Hubbard's Market, Golden Queen.

Most largely planted in order named.—Prize Head, Hanson, Black-Seeded Simpson, Tennis Ball Black-Seeded, Big Boston, California Cream Butter, Early Curled Simpson, Mammoth Black-Seeded Butter, Deacon, Grand Rapids.

Desirable new or little-known varieties.—Mette's Forcing, Express Cos, Matador, Crumpled-Leaved, Unrivaled, White Chavigne, White Loaf, Bon Ton.

TABLE OF VARIETIES.

The measurements and dates given in the following table are based upon trials conducted at Washington, D. C., during the spring and autumn of 1903. They presuppose both a quick germination, where the plants appear above the surface within four days after sowing the seed, and a good average growth afterwards.

Variety.	Maturity from sowing seed.	First appearance of seed stalk after sowing seed.	Weight of mature plant.	Diameter of mature plant.
	Days.	Days.	Ounces.	Inches.
All Seasons	77	96	13¼	11½
American Gathering	76	96	14¼	14¼
Asiatic	77	96	13½	11¼
Asparagus	67	76	10	6¼
Asparagus Lobed-Leaved	78	91	12¼	14
Baltimore Oak-Leaved	72	96	7⅞	10¼
Bath Cos	90	109	18	11
Big Boston	78	96	16¼	11¼
Black-Seeded Simpson	78	100	20	14
Blonde Block Head	86	110	23	16¼
Bon Ton	80	105	21¼	14¼
Boston Curled	67	75	4¼	8¼
Briggs' Forcing and Garden	64	74	8	10¼
Brittle Ice	87	100	16¼	14
Brown Dutch Black-Seeded	78	93	12⅞	11¼
Brown Dutch White-Seeded	78	93	12	11¼
Brown Genoa	78	93	12¼	12
Brown Head	83	101	10¼	12
Burpee's Butter Head	82	100	16	11¼
Buttercup	79	96	6¼	9
California Cream Butter	77	94	15¼	11¼
Chartier	84	104	15¼	13
Chicago Forcing	64	69	6¼	10
Cold Frame White Cabbage	70	82	7¼	9¼
Crumpled-Leaved	62	72	8¼	9¼
Dammann's Ice	87	100	16¼	14
Deacon	73	90	9⅞	11
Defiance	79	102	8¼	12
Density	59	72	4¼	5¼
Denver Market	80	104	9⅞	12
Detroit Market Gardener's Forcing	78	96	16⅞	13¼
Dwarf White Heart Cos	79	97	20⅞	10
Earliest Cutting	70	86	6⅞	10
Emperor Forcing	54	59	5	5¼
Emperor William	74	77	8⅞	12¼
Eureka	89	107	13	14¼
Express Cos	71	83	12	7¼
German Early Head	68	78	6¼	7¼
German Incomparable	74	77	8⅞	11
Giant Glacier	88	111	12¼	17
Giant White Cos	88	107	30	12
Golden Curled	84	104	16	13
Golden Heart	72	82	11¼	14

Variety.	Maturity from sowing seed.	First appearance of seed stalk after sowing seed.	Weight of mature plant.	Diameter of mature plant.
	Days.	*Drys.*	*Ounces.*	*Inches.*
Golden Queen	65	75	6¾	7½
Golden Spotted	78	94	6	9½
Grand Rapids	69	79	12½	14
Green Cos	82	102	26¾	10
Green-Fringed	71	81	4½	10½
Half Century	69	81	7¾	8¾
Hanson	86	110	23	16½
Harbinger	69	81	7½	10½
Hardy Green Hammersmith	82	97	5¾	9½
Hartford Bronzed Head	76	96	8¾	10
Hero	89	107	11¾	13½
Hothouse	58	66	6¾	8½
Hubbard's Market	69	84	9¾	10½
Iceberg	82	108	20	14
Italian Ice	86	112	20¼	13½
Lancaster	72	89	5¾	9½
Large Yellow Market	82	98	16	13½
Lee's Market Forcing	63	73	5¾	7½
Limagne Cos	82	101	22	10
Malta	87	104	16¾	15
Mammoth Black-Seeded Butter	78	90	11¾	11½
Marblehead Mammoth	82	103	18½	14
Matador	63	75	6¾	10
Maximum	84	102	16¾	14½
Mette's Forcing	60	69	6¼	8½
Middletowner	67	75	10½	11½
Mignonette	68	83	7¾	7½
Milly	72	86	7¾	9½
Morse	80	104	22½	14
Nansen	65	72	8¾	10½
New York	87	111	25½	16½
Oak-Leaved	72	96	5¾	10½
Onondaga	73	96	7¾	11½
Paris Sugar	82	100	16	11½
Paris White Cos	82	102	26¾	10
Passion	86	103	12¼	11½
Philadelphia Butter	65	76	8	10½
Prince of Wales Cos	86	112	33¾	10½
Prize Head	76	96	14½	14
Red Besson	78	84	11½	12½
Red Winter Cos	83	105	20¾	10
Reichner	65	72	8½	10½
St. Louis Black-Seeded Forcing	67	77	8¾	12
Shotwell's Brown Head	74	92	7¾	10
Shotwell's Brown Head (Bridgeman)	74	84	7¾	10
Silver Ball	64	72	8½	10½
Speckled Dutch Butter	67	84	9¾	8½
Sugar Loaf	89	106	18	13½
Sutton's Giant Cabbage	84	102	16¾	14½
Tennis Ball Black-Seeded	71	82	11½	10½
Tennis Ball White-Seeded	57	65	6¾	8½
Thick Head Yellow	82	99	10½	13

TABLE OF VARIETIES.

Variety.	Maturity from sowing seed.	First appearance of seed stalk after sowing seed.	Weight of mature plant.	Diameter of mature plant.
	Days.	Days.	Ounces.	Inches.
Tomhanhock	76	96	13¼	13
Tom Thumb	66	82	6½	7
Trout	84	99	7½	10
Tyrolese	86	109	15½	16
Unrivaled	78	96	16¾	11¼
Victoria Red-Edged	72	86	8¾	10
White Chavigne	78	95	15¼	11¼
White Forcing	55	60	5¾	5¼
White Giant	84	100	12	12¼
White Loaf	66	78	9¼	11
White-Seeded Simpson	74	92	12¾	13¼
White Star	84	104	18¾	15
White Summer Cabbage	72	87	10¼	11¾
Yellow-Seeded Butter	80	100	9	10¼
Yellow Winter	71	85	6¾	9¼

CLASSIFICATION OF VARIETIES.

[w=whitish seeds, b=blackish seeds, y=yellowish seeds, br=brownish seeds.]

CLASS I.—Butter varieties.
  SUBCLASS I.—Cabbage-heading varieties.
    COLOR DIVISION I.—Plants wholly green.
    Advancer (w).
    All Seasons (b).
    Briggs' Forcing and Garden (w).
    Burpee's Butter Head (w).
    Buttercup (w).
    Deacon (w).
    Emperor Forcing (w).
    German Early Head. (w).
    Golden Queen (w).
    Harbinger (w).
    Hardy Green Hammersmith (w).
    Hubbard's Market (w).
    Large Yellow Market (w).
    Lee's Market Forcing (w).
    Mammoth Black-Seeded Butter (b).
    Mette's Forcing (w).
    Nansen (w).
    Paris Sugar (w).
    Philadelphia Butter (w).
    Reichner (w).
    Silver Ball (w).
    Tennis Ball Black-Seeded (b).
    Thick Head Yellow (w).
    Tom Thumb (b).
    Unrivaled (w).
    White Chavigne (w).
    White Forcing (w).
    White Giant (b).
    White Loaf (w).
    White Summer Cabbage (w).
    Yellow-Seeded Butter (y).

CLASS I.—Butter varieties—Continued.
  SUBCLASS I.—Cabbage-heading varieties—Continued.
    COLOR DIVISION II.—Plants tinged brownish, larger part green.
    Big Boston (w).
    Brown Dutch Black-Seeded (b).
    Brown Dutch White-Seeded (w).
    Brown Genoa (b).
    California Cream Butter (b).
    Cold Frame White Cabbage (w).
    Crumpled-Leaved (w).
    Defiance (w).
    Emperor William (b).
    German Incomparable (b).
    Half Century (b).
    Hothouse (w).
    Maximum (b).
    Milly (w).
    Passion (b).
    St. Louis Black-Seeded Forcing (b).
    Shotwell's Brown Head (b).
    Speckled Dutch Butter (w).
    Sutton's Giant Cabbage (y).
    Tennis Ball White-Seeded (w).
    Victoria Red-Edged (w).
    Yellow Winter (w).
    COLOR DIVISION III.—Plants brownish, small portion only greenish.
    Brown Head (w).
    Eureka (y).
    Golden Spotted (w).
    Hartford Bronzed Head (b).
    Hero (b).
    Matador (w).
    Red Besson (b).

CLASS I.— Butter varieties—Continued.
  SUBCLASS I.—Cabbage-heading varieties—Continued.
    COLOR DIVISION III.—Plants brownish, small portion only greenish—Continued.
      Shotwell's Brown Head (Bridgeman) (b).
      Sugar Loaf (w).
      Trout (w).
  SUBCLASS II.—Bunching varieties.
    COLOR DIVISION I.—Plants wholly green.
      Baltimore Oak-Leaved (w).
      Earliest Cutting (w).
      Golden Heart (w).
      Lancaster (w).
      Oak-Leaved (w).
    COLOR DIVISION II.—Plants brownish.
      Hero (b).
CLASS II.—Crisp varieties.
  SUBCLASS I.—Cabbage-heading varieties.
    COLOR DIVISION I.—Plants wholly green.
      Blonde Block Head (w).
      Brittle Ice (w).
      Dammann's Ice (w).
      Denver Market (w).
      Detroit Market Gardener's Forcing (w).
      Giant Glacier (w).
      Golden Curled (w).
      Hanson (w).
      Italian Ice (w).
      Malta (w).
      New York (w).
    COLOR DIVISION II.—Plants tinged brownish, large part greenish.
      Density (w).
      Iceberg (w).
      Marblehead Mammoth (w).
      Tyrolese (w).
    COLOR DIVISION III.—Plants brownish, small part only greenish.
      Chartier (w).
      Mignonette (b).
      Sugar Loaf (w).

CLASS II.—Crisp varieties—Continued.
  SUBCLASS II.—Bunching varieties.
    COLOR DIVISION I.—Plants wholly green.
      Black-Seeded Simpson (b).
      Bon Ton (b).
      Boston Curled (b).
      Chicago Forcing (b).
      Detroit Market Gardener's Forcing (w).
      Golden Curled (w).
      Grand Rapids (b).
      Green-Fringed (w).
      Middletowner (w).
      Morse (w).
      White-Seeded Simpson (w).
      White Star (w).
    COLOR DIVISION II.—Plants brownish, small part only greenish.
      American Gathering (w).
      Chartier (w).
      Onondaga (w).
      Prize Head (w).
      Tomhannock (w).
CLASS III.—Cos varieties.
  SUBCLASS I.—Spatulate-leaved varieties.
    HEADING DIVISION I.—Self-closing.
      COLOR DIVISION I.—Plants wholly green.
        Dwarf White Heart Cos (w).
        Express Cos (w).
        Giant White Cos (w).
        Green Cos (w).
        Limagne Cos (w).
        Paris White Cos (w).
        Prince of Wales Cos (w).
      COLOR DIVISION II.—Plants brownish.
        Red Winter Cos (br).
    HEADING DIVISION II.—Loose-closing.
      Bath Cos (b).
  SUBCLASS II.—Lanceolate-leaved varieties.
    Asparagus (b).
  SUBCLASS III.—Lobed-leaved varieties.
    Asparagus Lobed-Leaved (b).

KEY TO VARIETIES.

[Applicable only to outdoor-grown specimens.]

1. Leaves distinctly lanceolate .... *Asparagus*
1. Leaves spatulate, oval to roundish, sometimes lobed, always rounded at summit 2
2. Leaves distinctly lobed and entire 3
2. Leaves entire, serrate, or crenate at upper part, sometimes deeply cut at base but never distinctly lobed in any part 5
3. Lobes terminating mostly at base of leaf .... *Lancaster*
3. Lobes terminating mostly along midrib of leaf 4
4. Seeds blackish .... *Asparagus Lobed-Leaved*
4. Seeds whitish .... *Baltimore Oak-Leaved, Oak-Leaved*

KEY TO VARIETIES.

5. Leaves always either spatulate or oval in shape, sometimes blistered but neither outside nor inner heart leaves ever crumpled, these leaves always straight and stiff, never thin and soft. Excepting *Asparagus* and *Asparagus Lobed-Leaved* includes all lettuces commonly called cos 6
5. Leaves generally broad in shape, rarely long, never narrower than broadly spatulate, more or less blistered or crumpled or both, the inner heart leaves always crumpled and somewhat soft, never decidedly stiff and flat. Excepting the lobed-leaved varieties includes lettuces variously known as crisp, butter, cabbaging, bunching, and cutting.............. 9
6. Plant brownish.. 7
6. Plant wholly green.. 8
7. Plant washed with dull brown and seeds blackish .... *Bath Cos*
7. Plant almost solid bright brown and seeds brownish .... *Red Winter Cos*
8. Plant very early and small for a cos variety, early-intermediate in season, medium in size compared to most butter and crisp varieties........ *Express Cos*
8. Plant very late and large compared to most butter and crisp varieties...... *Dwarf White Heart Cos, Giant White Cos, Green Cos, Limagne Cos, Paris White Cos, Prince of Wales Cos*
9. Leaves serrate... 10
9. Leaves entire to crenate... 26
10. Seeds blackish.. 11
10. Seeds whitish.. 14
11. Plant brownish and cabbaging .... *Mignonette*
11. Plant wholly green and bunching..................................... 12
12. Plant dense bunching and seeds germinating readily .... *Black-Seeded Simpson, Bon Ton*
12. Plant loose bunching and seeds hard to germinate 13
13. Plant small, of a very wild, coarse quality and flavor; suitable only for garnishing .... *Boston Curled*
13. Plant never smaller than medium, not delicate in quality, but generally much liked and never wild flavored............ *Chicago Forcing, Grand Rapids*
14. Plant cabbaging 15
14. Plant bunching... 22
15. Plant more or less brownish... 16
15. Plant wholly green 19
16. Plant distinctly vase-shaped and tall, head oval in shape............. *Sugar Loaf*
16. Plant not distinctly vase-shaped and tall, head globular.................. 17
17. Plant very small and very early..................................... *Density*
17. Plant large, or very large, late..................................... 18
18. Small part only of plant brownish........ *Iceberg, Marblehead Mammoth, Tyrolese*
18. Larger part of plant brownish .... *Chartier*
19. Plant very dark green... *New York*
19. Plant light green... 20
20. Parts of leaf margin crenate.................... *Brittle Ice, Dammann's Ice, Malta*
20. All parts of leaf margins plainly serrate, no part crenate or entire........ 21
21. Plant always very distinctly cabbaging............... *Blonde Block Head, Hanson*
21. Plant generally bunching but sometimes cabbaging..... *Detroit Market Gardener's Forcing, Golden Curled*
22. Plant very brownish 23
22. Plant wholly green 25
23. Bunching when not well grown, decidedly cabbage heading when at its best .... *Chartier*
23. Always decidedly bunching 24

24. Plant treelike in appearance or with large, long stem, elevating plant high from ground .... *Tomhannock*
24. Plant not treelike in appearance, or at least not elevated high from ground, and stem not long .... *American Gathering, Onondaga, Prize Head*
25. Plant small, and although borders of leaves are enormously developed and much frilled, their surfaces are quite smooth and never crumpled but sometimes sparingly blistered .... *Green-Fringed*
25. Plant medium to very large, leaves frilled at borders and their surfaces never smooth, always more or less blistered and crumpled ...... *Early Curled Silesia, Golden Curled, Middletowner, Morse, White-Seeded Simpson*
26. Plant bunching 27
26. Plant cabbage heading 31
27. Seeds blackish ....*Hero*
27. Seeds whitish 28
28. Plant brownish .... *Sugar Loaf*
28. Plant wholly green 29
29. Plant dense bunching and leaf margins crenate .... *White Star*
29. Plant loose bunching and leaf margins entire 30
30. Leaves decidedly cup-shaped and quite smooth .... *Earliest Cutting*
30. Leaves never cup-shaped nor incurved, very much blistered and crumpled, never smooth .... *Golden Heart*
31. Seeds yellowish 32
31. Seeds whitish or blackish 34
32. Plant wholly green .... *Yellow-Seeded Butter*
32. Plant brownish 33
33. Plant largely green, brownish in spots or in blotches only ... *Sutton's Giant Cabbage*
33. Plant largely brownish, little or no green on exposed parts .... *Eureka*
34. Seeds blackish 35
34. Seeds whitish 45
35. Plant wholly green 36
35. Plant more or less brownish 38
36. Plant small-medium, early, and very dark green .... *Tom Thumb*
36. Plant medium in size or larger, intermediate or later in season, and light or very light green 37
37. Leaves very little blistered and very thick .... *All Seasons*
37. Leaves much blistered and thin .... *Mammoth Black-Seeded Butter, Tennis Ball Black-Seeded, White Giant*
38. Plant a deep, almost solid brown 39
38. Plant largely green or sometimes becoming dull greenish brown, never dark brown 40
39. Plant large in size .... *Red Besson*
39. Plant medium in size .... *Hartford Bronzed Head, Shotwell's Brown Head*
40. Plant spotted (very faintly and sparingly in Half Century) 41
40. Plant not spotted 44
41. Inner heart leaves spotted .... *Brown Genoa, Shotwell's Brown Head (Bridgeman)*
41. Inner heart leaves never spotted 42
42. Margins conspicuously fringed with hairlike bristles .... *Maximum*
42. Bristles at margin none or very obscure 43
43. Plant very dark green, sparingly and faintly spotted .... *Half Century*
43. Plant dark green or of medium green color, freely and distinctly spotted .. *California Cream Butter, Emperor William*

KEY TO VARIETIES.

44. Plant when in prime marketable condition plainly colored at base of midribs and stem of plant.................................*Brown Dutch Black-Seeded*
44. Plant when in prime marketable condition never colored at base of midribs nor stem of plant...................................*German Incomparable, Passion, St. Louis Black-Seeded Forcing*
45. Plant more or less brownish... 46
45. Plant wholly green 55
46. Plant distinctly spotted 47
46. Plant not distinctly spotted; if spotted at all very sparingly and faintly so. 50
47. Margins obscurely crenate and borders undulate............*Speckled Dutch Butter*
47. Margins entire and borders flat 48
48. Seeds very wide and plant mostly green............................*Defiance*
48. Seeds average in width and plant mostly brownish....................... 49
49. Spots large and well separated..................................... *Golden Spotted*
49. Spots fine and close together..*Trout*
50. Plant largely brownish... 51
50. Plant largely green, brownish only in places or spots...................... 52
51. Plant late and very spreading ....*Brown Head*
51. Plant early and compact ....*Matador*
52. Leaves obscurely crenate at margins and undulate at borders 53
52. Leaves entire at margins and flat at borders 54
53. Planted indoors only, a strictly forcing sort ....*Crumpled-Leaved*
53. Sometimes planted indoors, but more largely planted outdoors ....*Big Boston*
54. Large-medium in size and not suitable for forcing.....*Brown Dutch White-Seeded*
54. Small-medium in size and suitable for forcing.........*Cold Frame White Cabbage, Hothouse, Milly, Victoria Red-Edged, Tennis Ball White-Seeded, Yellow Winter*
55. Plant of the crisp class, margins obscurely crenate ....*Italian Ice*
55. Plant of the butter class, margins obscurely crenate or entire 56
56. Margins obscurely crenate and borders undulate.......................... 57
56. Margins entire and borders flat 58
57. Plant large and late-intermediate in season.............................*Unrivaled*
57. Plant small-medium or smaller and early or very early in season.........*German Early Head, Golden Queen, Lee's Market Forcing, White Forcing*
58. Plant dark green...*White Chavigne*
58. Plant not darker than medium green....................................... 59
59. Plant golden green, the lightest green in color of any lettuce...........*Buttercup*
59. Plant often very light green, but never decidedly golden green 60
60. Heads decidedly long when first forming and leaves very thick...*Asiatic, Deacon*
60. Heads generally globular, sometimes long, but leaves of such plants never thicker than medium 61
61. Plants suitable for forcing...*Advancer, Briggs' Forcing and Garden, Emperor Forcing, Harbinger, Hubbard's Market, Lee's Market Forcing, Nansen, Philadelphia Butter, Reichner, Silver Ball, White Loaf, White Summer Cabbage*
61. Plant not suitable for forcing 62
62. Leaves stiff and of poor quality, plant not suited for summer growing ....*Hardy Green Hammersmith*
62. Leaves soft rather than stiff, good quality, and succeeding well in summer .... *Burpee's Butter Head, Large Yellow Market, Paris Sugar, Thick Head Yellow*

DESCRIPTION OF VARIETIES CLASSED AS DISTINCT.

Vegetable varieties may be considered for convenience in classification and description as either distinct or subsidiary. The former class includes those representing the different types or kinds which can be identified from one another because of more or less well-defined and distinct characters. The latter is made up of renamed or so-called varieties which are plainly identical with the distinct sorts or are simply superior or deteriorated strains of them, or, if of distinct origin, are so much like the distinct varieties as to be practically identical with and indistinguishable from them.

The following list is supposed to include all the really distinct varieties sold to-day by American seedsmen. The figures following the variety name indicate the number of seedsmen who mention that name in their lists of varieties for the year 1903. The seedsmen mentioned after the figures are those from whom the seed was obtained, and upon these samples the descriptions are largely based. Besides these tests the writer has examined the lettuce fields and trial grounds of our principal seedsmen and based his descriptions also upon the correspondence and conversations which he has had with American seed growers and dealers. An effort has been made to give the exact standing of all the varieties tested. It is, however, impossible to do this in every case, and the list of synonyms which is here included is not given as an absolute one. The sorts named appeared identical at Washington and in other places where the writer has observed them, but a few of the varieties named may prove to be distinct in some other soils and under other conditions.

ADVANCER.

Listed by one seedsman. Seeds tested: Michell, 1901–1903.

Comparison.—Little known or planted. Same general character and usefulness as Hubbard's Market and Hanson and possibly identical with one of them, but further trials are necessary before this can be definitely determined.

History.—Named and introduced in this country in 1901 by Henry F. Michell, who writes that the variety was obtained from F. Spittel, Arnstadt, Germany.

ALL SEASONS.

Listed by eight seedsmen. Seeds tested: Vaughan, 1899–1903.

Description.—A decidedly butter variety, strictly cabbage-heading, large, late-intermediate in season, slow to shoot to seed, young plant very spreading, regular in growth, its leaves very straight and extending flatly over the ground. Mature plant fairly compact. Head elongated when first forming, but flattened or sometimes globular when fully developed, fairly firm, well defined, extremely well blanched, its leaves very completely but loosely overlapping one another, but outer ones of plant well separated from the head proper, the latter thereby left very bare or exposed. Leaves broad in shape, peculiarly smooth, very little blistered, crumpled, or twisted, unusually thick in appearance, but soft and limp rather than stiff; margins entire and fringed with hair-like bristles; borders flat. Color characteristic light grayish green, never spotted nor brownish in any part. Quality excellent;

sweet, decidedly buttery, and with thick, soft leaves of much substance. Seeds very blackish.

Comparison.—Scarce and little planted. A valuable new variety of the same general character and usefulness as the well-known Deacon, differing principally in being a little larger and later and may in some gardens prove a more satisfactory variety. Highly recommended for trial wherever Deacon is successful. The variety is also similar to Asiatic, and next to these two sorts perhaps most like Reichner and Silver Ball. It is readily identified by its bristled margins and blackish seeds.

Synonym.—Vaughan's All Seasons.

History.—Named and introduced into this country in 1897 by J. C. Vaughan, who states that the variety was imported from France about ten years ago under the name of Denaiff.

Illustrations.—A young plant of the variety is shown on Plate XXII. Other views which answer to illustrate the type fairly well are shown by Deacon, on Plates X and XXIII. The longitudinal section of Matador, on Plate XX, illustrates the solidity of the heads.

AMERICAN GATHERING.

Listed by fourteen seedsmen. Seeds tested: Landreth, 1900–1901; Rawson, 1901; Thorburn, 1901–1903.

Description.—A decidedly crisp variety, strictly bunching, large, early marketable, but late-intermediate in its fullest development, slow to shoot to seed. Plant very spreading, of unusually low growth, and consisting of a loose, flattened, or slightly rounded cluster of leaves, always more or less opened or spread out at the center, and therefore never in the least cabbage-like nor heading, though, nevertheless, the inner part of the plant is well blanched. Leaves short spatulate in shape, excessively blistered and crumpled, very little twisted, fairly rigid, but not stiff; finely serrate at at margins, excessively developed, much frilled at borders. Color bright brown, varying to bright green in less exposed parts and center of plant; borders of leaves no more colored than other parts, while stem of plant, base of midribs, and inner heart leaves are wholly green; no part of plant distinctly spotted. Quality good; sweet in flavor, very tender and crisp in texture, but leaf thin and lacking substance. Seeds large, whitish.

Comparison.—One of the lesser grown sorts. Usefulness and value same as Prize Head, and not sufficiently different from that well-known sort to be a very important variety. It differs in being slightly lower growing, more blistered and crumpled in the leaves, and more brownish in color.

Synonym.—Prize Head is often used in filling orders for this variety.

History.—Apparently of American origin, and known in this country for at least twenty-five years.

Illustrations.—A mature plant of the variety is shown on Plate IV. Other views which answer to illustrate the type fairly well are Hanson, on Plates XXII and XXVI, and Prize Head, on Plate XXI. The leaf of the variety, however, is considerably more crumpled than shown on Plate XXVI, or somewhat approaches that of Grand Rapids, on Plate XXV.

ASIATIC.

Listed by one seedsman. Seeds tested: Dallwig, 1900–1903.

Description.—Excepting large in size and late-intermediate in season, the description is the same as given of Deacon.

Comparison.—Scarce and rarely planted. Usefulness and value similar to Deacon. At Washington not so reliable a header, and, excepting for being little larger in size and later in season, not sufficiently different from that variety to become an important lettuce, although under some exceptional conditions it may prove more satisfactory than Deacon. The two varieties are sometimes identified by differences in color or in the shape of the heads. Asiatic is similar also to All Seasons.

History.—Apparently first listed in 1893 by W. E. Dallwig, who writes that the seed was obtained from Germany.

Illustrations.—The general character of the variety is shown by Deacon, on Plates X and XXIII, and All Seasons, on Plate XXII. The solidity of the heads is illustrated by Mette's Forcing, on Plate XIX.

ASPARAGUS.

Listed by five seedsmen. Seeds tested: Alneer, 1902; Buckbee, 1901-1902; Childs, 1899-1900; Ewing, 1901; Graham, 1902; Simmers, 1901-1902.

Description.—A peculiar cos sort, wholly different from other cultivated varieties, and more resembling a chicory than a lettuce plant. Medium in size, early-intermediate in season, shoots to seed quickly, wilts very soon after being pulled. Plant compact, composed of many lanceolate, erect, straight-growing leaves forming a long pointed cluster, yet more or less open at the center, or at least the leaves never close enough to blanch to any extent. Leaves wholly smooth, never in the least blistered, crumpled, nor twisted, entire at the upper margins, sometimes serrate at lower parts, flat at the borders, fairly thick and stiff, though a few of the outer leaves weak or wilting and falling away limply from the plant. Midrib of leaf very hard, large, and prominent. Color very dark green, never spotted nor brownish in any part. Quality very poor; tough and hard in texture and of a rank, wild flavor, excepting the midrib, which, if used at the proper stage, is very brittle, sweet, and of a peculiar flavor and texture. Seeds blackish.

Comparison.—Scarce and rarely planted. Its leaves are said to be cooked and served like asparagus, but the writer doubts whether such a use of them can be recommended. The midribs, being hard and less hollow and pithy than other sorts, make a more satisfactory dish to serve like celery than other varieties. However, for this purpose it is suitable for a few days only, as the leaves soon become bitter when the weather is at all warm or the conditions the least unfavorable for its growth. Not recommended except to amateurs in an experimental way for the purpose named.

History.—Listed by a dozen or more American seedsmen about eight years ago, and described at that time as a new variety of French origin.

Illustrations.—See Plates XIV and XXVII.

ASPARAGUS LOBED-LEAVED.

Listed by one seedsman. Seeds tested: Ewing, 1902-1903.

Description.—Classed with the cos varieties, but really as much bunching in habit as cos-like. Large, late-intermediate in season, and shooting to seed at an intermediate date. Plant very spreading, occupying much space, vase-shaped in form, with a depressed or unfilled center, the leaves growing very straight, regular, and never close enough for blanching to any extent. Leaves long and narrow in form, rounded at top, deeply lobed from top to bottom, like an oak leaf, the lower part sometimes separated into large divisions. Surface very smooth or occasionally slightly blistered, leaves never in the least crumpled nor twisted, but rather flat, stiff, and thick, and with a large protruding midrib; margins entire and borders flat. Color very dark green, never spotted nor brownish in any part. Quality very poor; tough and hard in texture, and of a rank, wild flavor, excepting the midrib, which, if used at the proper stage, is very brittle, sweet, and of a peculiar flavor and texture. Seeds blackish.

Comparison.—Scarce and rarely planted. Suitable for the same purpose as Asparagus and possessing the same faults but in a less degree. Larger, later, slower to shoot to seed, furnishing a great many more leaves, and probably better in every way than that variety, but it can not be recommended except to amateurs in an experimental way.

History.—First introduced in America in 1900 by William Ewing & Co. under the name of New Asparagus. It must not be confused with New Asparagus listed by other seedsmen, which is a lanceolate-leaved variety.

Illustrations.—See Plates XIII and XXVI.

BALTIMORE OAK-LEAVED.

Listed by three seedsmen. Seeds tested: Burpee, 1902; Griffith & Turner, 1903; Johnson & Stokes, 1899, 1900, 1903.

Description.—A butter variety, strictly bunching, medium in size, early-intermediate in season, extremely slow to shoot to seed. Plant growing very close to the ground and consisting of a low, very well rounded, symmetrical, remarkably compact, firm cluster of leaves neither well opened nor spread out at its center nor heading in habit, though inner part becomes fairly well blanched. Leaves very much twisted together in the head, broad, deeply lobed, like an oak leaf, especially the inner and larger leaves, these being sometimes almost divided and the lobes so excessively developed as to make the leaf appear like several grown together. Leaves smooth, thick, stiff, entire at margins, flat at the borders, and generally with distinct glands near the base of outer part of the midribs, one on each side. Color very bright green, never spotted nor brownish in any part. Quality poor; hard in texture, and decidedly lacking in flavor, sweetness, and delicacy. Seeds whitish.

Comparison.—Very little planted. Best known around Baltimore, Washington, Philadelphia, and in the South. A very novel, beautiful golden-green lettuce of fine form, and valuable because remarkably slow to shoot to seed and making attractive heads during the hottest summer weather, no other variety probably growing so well at this time of the year. In quality one of the poorest of all varieties, and therefore not recommended for home use. Not used for forcing. Decidedly more compact and attractive and a better lettuce in every way than the old form known as Oak-Leaved. It is more like that variety than any other, and next most like Lancaster. These three varieties are very different from other kinds, and are peculiar for the glands present at the base of their leaves.

Synonyms.—None have so far been identified. The sorts known as American Oak-Leaved and Southern Blunt Point Oak-Leaved have, however, not yet been tested by the writer.

History.—No information in regard to the history of this variety has yet been obtained excepting only that Griffith & Turner listed the variety in 1895.

Illustrations.—The variety is shown on Plates XV and XXIV. The general character of the cross section is illustrated by Lancaster on Plate XIX.

BATH COS.

Listed by three seedsmen. Seeds tested: Gregory, 1899; Rawson, 1901-1903.

Description.—A typical cos variety of the open kind, large in comparison to either the crisp or butter sorts, but only large-medium for this group. Very late in season and slow to shoot to seed. Young plant extremely regular or formal in growth, fairly spreading, its leaves many and extending almost flatly over the ground. Mature plant of a straight, upright-growing habit, but with many outer spreading leaves and therefore never really compact, though its innermost leaves form a well defined, loaf-shaped, fairly well blanched, soft head, and close loosely toward one another, their upper parts meeting at the margins instead of overlapping one another at the top of the head. Leaves oval to slightly spatulate, truncate, very smooth, never blistered, crumpled, nor twisted, very straight and flat in growth, even the inner head leaves but slightly spoon-shaped; margins shallow serrate; borders finely frilled. Color dull greenish brown and very even throughout, that is, never colored unevenly in definite areas or blotches, excepting border more colored than other parts, but even this part marked by no sharp colored edge. No part of plant distinctly spotted, stem of plant, however, and midribs of leaves to their very base plainly colored; inner head leaves wholly green. Quality fair; sweet in flavor, hard but not coarse in texture. Seeds blackish.

Comparison.—Popular in Europe, but little known and rarely planted in this country. A poor sort at Washington, generally open-growing in habit and forming no head. Too late, spreading, and unattractive for use when other sorts like Paris White Cos succeed so much better. Wholly different in habit and usefulness from any other American variety. The color, which is a dull brown, is somewhat similar to that of Brown Dutch Black-Seeded.

History.—A well-known European sort and sold in the United States for at least forty years.

Illustrations.—A mature and somewhat imperfectly developed plant of the variety is shown on Plate III. This illustrates, nevertheless, about the way the variety generally grows in this country, though when given just the right conditions it will grow decidedly taller and closer. A leaf of the variety is shown on Plate XXVII.

BIG BOSTON.

Listed by one hundred and forty-nine seedsmen. Seeds tested: Buist, 1901; Burpee, 1901; Burwell, 1900; Ferry, 1900, 1901; Griffith & Turner, 1901; Henderson, 1900, 1901; Landreth, 1899, 1901; Thorburn, 1899, 1901, 1903.

Description.—A fairly butter variety, strictly cabbage-heading, large, late-intermediate in season, slow to shoot to seed. Young plant with leaves very upright and twisted, often appearing like several specimens growing together. Mature plant very compact and forming a well-defined, broad, slightly pointed, hard, well blanched head, with outside leaves characteristically turned and twisted backward at their uppermost borders, but otherwise very tightly and completely overlapping one another. Leaves very broad, mostly smooth, slightly blistered and crumpled, fairly twisted, thick, and stiff, hard, and not easily torn, obscurely crenate at margins, undulate at borders. Color, light dull green, excepting an extremely narrow, sharply defined, light brown border, no part of leaf spotted, and inner head leaves and stem of plant never colored. Quality poor to fair; slightly buttery in flavor, hard in texture, and lacking the delicacy, sweetness, and tenderness of strictly butter varieties. Seeds whitish.

Comparison.—Probably one of the five most largely grown varieties of the United States. Adapted to all parts of the country and grown everywhere, but especially in the South by market gardeners to ship North during the winter, for which purpose it is probably grown more than any other. Succeeds especially well in late autumn and is a favorite in the East and North for growing at that time of the year. Also a good summer variety. It is a very large lettuce for forcing, and is used to some extent for growing under glass, requiring, it is said, a very cool temperature to do well in greenhouses. Distinctly a market gardener's variety and although generally satisfactory for home use other sorts of better quality are recommended to private gardeners. A splendid shipper, sure header, reliable, and hardy. Excepting in color this lettuce is the same as Unrivaled and is more like that sort than any other. Aside from this variety it does not closely resemble any other, but is perhaps more like Crumpled-Leaved than most other varieties, though very different in usefulness and value. The young plant is similar in habit to Speckled Dutch Butter.

Synonyms.—Henderson's Big Boston, Holmes's Big Boston, Big Head (Griffith & Turner), California Giant White Forcing, Giant White Forcing, Chesterfield, Houston Market, All Right, Myers' All Right, New Lettuce No. 1, Relish, Trocadero.

DESCRIPTION OF VARIETIES.

Confusing names.—Boston Market, Large Boston Market, Boston Curled, Boston Glasshouse, Boston Hothouse, Boston Forcing, and Tennis Ball White-Seeded, all different types from Big Boston.

History.—Named and introduced by Peter Henderson & Co. about fourteen years ago.

Illustrations.—Different views of the variety are given on Plates V, XXII, and XXIV. The solidity of the head is about the same as that of Matador, on Plate XX.

BLACK-SEEDED SIMPSON.

Listed by one hundred and seventy seedsmen. Seeds tested: Burpee, 1901; Farquhar, 1901; Ferry, 1900–1902; Henderson, 1901; Johnson & Stokes, 1901; Landreth, 1899, 1901; Livingston, 1900; McMillan, 1900; Thorburn, 1899, 1901, 1903.

Description.—A decidedly crisp variety, bunching, but sometimes tending to a cabbage-like growth, large, early marketable, but late-intermediate in attaining fullest development, slow to shoot to seed. Plant fairly compact and consisting of a firm, well blanched, rounded to elongated and V-shaped cluster of leaves, closely drawn together, but rarely in a way to make a visible or distinct cabbage head, though innermost heart leaves curving inward over one another generally present a half-formed concealed cabbage-like head. Leaves very broad, much blistered, crumpled and twisted, extremely thick, stiff, and coarse, with large protruding midribs, serrate margins, and much developed and excessively frilled borders. Color very light green, never spotted nor brownish in any part. Quality fair; sweet, somewhat hard and coarse in texture. Seeds large, blackish.

Comparison.—Probably one of the four most largely planted varieties of the United States. Adapted to all parts of the country and grown everywhere, but less in the South than other sections. An especial favorite with Detroit, Chicago, and other western gardeners, who probably grow this variety more than any other. Distinctly a market gardener's sort, and, though of coarse quality, it is often the most satisfactory sort for home use, because no lettuce is more reliable and easily grown. It succeeds during summer when other sorts of more delicate quality are failures. A good shipper and formerly used extensively in the West for forcing, but now largely superseded for this purpose by Grand Rapids. Like this variety it is easily grown in greenhouses, and will stand a great deal of neglect in watering and ventilation. Black-Seeded Simpson is the same in usefulness and value as Bon Ton and Morse, and sometimes can not be identified unless grown by the side of them. Similar also to Early Curled Simpson, differing principally in being larger, lighter green, more dense in growth, and more attractive in appearance.

Synonyms.—Large Black-Seeded Simpson, Curled Black-Seeded Simpson, Early Black-Seeded Simpson, Early Curled Black-Seeded Simpson, Buckbee's Earliest Forcing, Longstreth's Earliest, Salzer's Earliest, Earliest Forcing, Earliest of All, First Early, Constitution.

Confusing names.—Early Curled Simpson, which is the same as White-Seeded Simpson.

History.—First listed by American seedsmen about twenty-four years ago. Peter Henderson & Co. claim to have first introduced the variety.

Illustrations.—A mature plant is shown on Plate I. The character of the leaf is shown by Early Curled Simpson, on Plate XXV, except that the size and shape are similar to Hanson, on Plate XXVI. The young plant is similar to Hanson, on Plate XXII, and the longitudinal section to White Star, on Plate XXI, except not quite so solid.

BLONDE BLOCK HEAD.

Listed by fifteen seedsmen. Seeds tested: Burpee, 1899–1903; Farquhar, 1901; Weeber & Don, 1900.

Comparison.—Little known or planted. Excepting slightly darker in color, sometimes upright in habit when young, and often forming an oval head, the description as well as usefulness and value seem to be the same as that of Hanson, and not sufficiently different from that well-known sort to be a very important variety.

Synonyms.—Blonde Beauty, Sunset, Golden Sunset.

Confusing names.—Golden Beauty, which is a wholly different type of lettuce.

History.—Introduced by Vilmorin-Andrieux & Co., of Paris, France, and first listed in this country about fourteen years ago.

Illustrations.—Same as for Hanson.

BON TON.

Listed by one seedsman. Seeds tested: Josiah Livingston, 1899, 1900; Livingston, 1901–1903.

Comparison.—Little known or planted. Description same as Black-Seeded Simpson, and sometimes hardly distinguishable from it unless carefully compared. It is evidently a selection from that variety and superior to it in evenness of type, but also more solid, compact, lighter colored, smoother leaved, coarser frilled at borders, slower to shoot to seed, and at Washington larger in size, though reports of it from California and Michigan state it to be smaller. Usefulness and value same as Black-Seeded Simpson. Highly recommended for trial to both amateurs and market gardeners wherever Black-Seeded Simpson is liked, because for many soils and gardens it is undoubtedly a better variety.

Synonyms.—Livingston's Bon Ton.

History.—Named and introduced in 1896 by the Josiah Livingston Seed Co. After this firm discontinued business the variety was next first listed by Livingston Seed Store, of Columbus, Ohio.

Illustrations.—Same as for Black-Seeded Simpson.

BOSTON CURLED.

Listed by forty-six seedsmen. Seeds tested: Burpee, 1901–1903; Henderson, 1901; Landreth, 1899, 1900.

Description.—A decidedly crisp variety, strictly bunching, small, early-intermediate in season, wilts at once upon being pulled, shoots quickly to seed. Plant fairly compact, growing close to the ground and forming a very loose, rounded, or slightly flattened, very regular cluster of leaves, also somewhat opened or spread out in the center and never dense enough for blanching to any extent. Leaves broad and very regular in form, rarely blistered, never crumpled nor twisted, exceedingly thick, stiff, and hard. Veins many, coarse and conspicuous, margins finely serrate, borders excessively frilled and embracing nearly the whole of the visible portion of the plant. Color, medium green, never spotted nor brownish in any part. Quality very poor; tough in texture, and of a rank, wild flavor, wholly lacking sweetness. Seeds small, very blackish.

Comparison.—Very little planted. A novel and very pretty fringed lettuce, curly like an endive, but on account of its poor quality, small size, and its wilting immediately upon being pulled, it is of little use except for garnishing or ornament. One of the first varieties to shoot to seed in hot weather, but remaining fit for use a long time in the autumn or in cool weather. Stands more cold than any other variety, excepting possibly Green-Fringed. By far the most deeply fringed and curly lettuce in cultivation. Grand Rapids is perhaps most like it in these qualities and in habit of growth, but very different in usefulness and value. Like that variety, the seeds are very hard to germinate.

Synonyms.—Boston Early Curled, Boston Fine Curled, Boston Extra Fine Curled.

Confusing names.—Big Boston, Boston Market, Large Boston Market, Boston Hothouse, Boston Glasshouse, Boston Forcing, and Boston Forcing Tennis Ball White-Seeded, all different types from Boston Curled.

History.—James J. H. Gregory & Son claim to have first introduced this variety. It has been listed by them for at least thirty-nine years.

Illustrations.—The variety is shown on Plates VII and XXIII.

BRIGGS' FORCING AND GARDEN.

Listed by one seedsman. Seeds tested: Briggs, 1901–1903.

Description.—A decidedly butter variety, strictly cabbage-heading, medium in size, early in season, and quickly shooting to seed. Plant compact and forming a globular or sometimes slightly elongated, firm, well-defined, well-blanched head, with leaves very flatly overlapping one another. Leaves broad in shape, fairly blistered, crumpled, and twisted, thin and soft, their margins entire and borders flat. Color, light green; never spotted nor brownish in any part. Quality good; soft in texture, mild, delicate, buttery in flavor. Seeds whitish.

Comparison.—Little known or planted. Very similar to Reichner and Philadelphia Butter, and sometimes hardly distinguishable from them. A strictly forcing sort of apparent merit, though at Washington it has not proved as reliable as the above varieties, and it is not sufficiently different from them to be a very important lettuce.

History.—Apparently named and first listed by Briggs Bros. & Co. The name seems never to have been used by other seedsmen except in 1902 by J. M. Thorburn & Co.

Illustrations.—Same as for Reichner.

BRITTLE ICE.

Listed by one seedsman. Seeds tested: Burpee, 1903.

Comparison.—New, and as yet grown in this country only in an experimental way. Same general character and usefulness as Malta. Further trials are necessary before it can be determined in what respect, if any, it differs from that variety or other similar sorts like Dammann's Ice.

History.—Named and first introduced in this country in 1903 by W. Atlee Burpee & Co., who state the lettuce came from Australia.

Illustrations.—Same as for Malta.

BROWN DUTCH BLACK-SEEDED.

Listed by forty seedsmen. Seeds tested: Ferry, 1900–1903; Landreth, 1899, 1901; Thorburn, 1901.

Description.—A decidedly butter variety, strictly cabbage-heading, medium-large in size, late-intermediate in season and in time of shooting to seed. Young plant very regular in habit, its leaves very straight and extending flatly over the ground. Mature plant low growing, very spreading, and forming a globular, fairly defined, firm, well-blanched head with leaves closely overlapping one another. Leaves broad in shape, fairly blistered, crumpled, twisted, thick, and stiff, entire at margins, flat at borders. Color medium dull green, tinged with dull faint brown and sometimes colored a decided brown in well-defined blotches but never distinctly spotted; border no more colored than other parts, inner head leaves wholly green, stem and base of midribs plainly colored. Quality fair; sweet and decidedly buttery in flavor, fairly tender. Seeds blackish.

Comparison.—One of the lesser grown varieties. Not generally valuable and best known for its extreme hardiness to cold. Long recognized as one of the best for wintering over outdoors. Though not quick to shoot to seed it never seems to grow well during summer or hot weather. At Washington it has done well in the autumn, but very poorly in the spring. Not recommended except under special circumstances or in an experimental way. More like Brown Genoa than other varieties, differing from it in no pronounced respect except freedom from spots. Similar also to Brown Dutch White-Seeded and Shotwell's Brown Head (Bridgeman). It differs principally from the former in being more brownish in color, slightly larger, and more spreading, and from the latter in being free of spots. The dull brownish color of these four sorts is quite distinct.

Synonym.—Batavian Brown Dutch.

History.—One of the oldest American varieties. Known in this country for at least ninety-eight years.

Illustrations.—A well-grown plant will make a head as solid as Emperor William, on Plate IX, or even nearly as perfect as California Cream Butter, on Plate VIII, but generally the plants are more loose in habit than shown in these illustrations. A leaf would be fairly represented by that of Deacon, on Plate XXIII, only more crumpled and blistered. A young plant is almost as spreading as that of All Seasons, on Plate XXII.

BROWN DUTCH WHITE-SEEDED.

Listed by one seedsman. Seeds tested: Farquhar, 1901–1903.

Comparison.—Scarce, and little known or planted. Usefulness and value same as Brown Dutch Black-Seeded, and not sufficiently different from it to be an important variety. Excepting in color of seeds, the description already given of the latter variety applies also to this lettuce, though Brown Dutch White-Seeded is not quite so brown in color nor so large in size, and somewhat more compact in habit and blistered in the leaves.

History.—Known in this country for at least fifty-three years.

Illustrations.—Same as for Brown Dutch Black-Seeded.

BROWN GENOA.

Listed by one seedsman. Seeds tested: Gregory, 1899–1903.

Comparison.—Scarce, and little known or planted. Usefulness and value same as Brown Dutch Black-Seeded, and not sufficiently different from that well-known sort to be an important variety. The description is the same, except that Brown Genoa is distinctly spotted on the outside and sparingly so on the inside leaves. It is also distinguished from Brown Dutch Black-Seeded in being not quite so brownish in color, a little larger in size, and more spreading in habit.

History.—Listed in 1874 by James J. H. Gregory & Son, who write that the variety probably came from Vilmorin-Andrieux & Co., of France.

Illustrations.—Same as for Brown Dutch Black-Seeded.

BROWN HEAD.

Listed by three seedsmen. Seeds tested: Dallwig, 1899–1903; Koerner, 1900; Rawson, 1900–1903; Weber, 1903.

Description.—A decidedly buttery variety, strictly cabbage-heading, large, medium in size, late, slow to shoot to seed. Plant loose, very spreading, and forming a globular, fairly defined, soft, well-blanched head with leaves completely but very loosely overlapping one another. Leaves unusually broad, cup-shaped when young, much blistered and crumpled, slightly twisted, somewhat thin and limp, entire at margins, flat at border. Color bright brown, interspersed in a very striking manner with bright green in less exposed or depressed parts and thereby exhibiting to good advantage the blistered character of the plant; inner head leaves, stem of plant, and base of midrib wholly green; no part of plant plainly spotted. Quality good; sweet and buttery in flavor, soft in texture, but leaves thin and lacking substance. Seeds whitish.

Comparison.—One of the lesser grown varities. Suitable for summer. Wholly unfit for forcing, too deep brown in color, loose in habit, and too soft a head to be recommended for market gardeners. Sometimes attractive to amateurs on account of its brilliant color and showy heads and, except Red Besson, the most brilliant red-colored lettuce known in America. It is more like Red Besson than any other and differs principally in being less colored, thicker leaved, and smaller. It next most resembles Shotwell's Brown Head (brownish or common type).

Synonyms.—Weber's Brown Head, Hard Head, Burpee's Hard Head, Buckbee's Surprise, Surprise.

Confusing names.—Shotwell's Brown Head, Batavian Brown Head, Bronzed Head, Hartford Bronzed Head, Bronzed Curled, Bronzed Red, Brown Curled, and Beckert's Brown Curled, all different types from Brown Head.

History.—Listed by W. E. Dallwig for at least eleven years and by W. W. Rawson & Co. in 1898.

Illustrations.—The habit of the mature plant is well shown by Red Besson, on Plate XIII; the leaf by Tennis Ball Black-Seeded, on Plate XXIII, and, excepting for being much softer, the longitudinal section by Matador, on Plate XX.

BURPEE'S BUTTER HEAD.

Listed by one seedsman. Seeds tested: Burpee, 1903.

Description.—New and as yet grown in this country only in an experimental way. Same general character and usefulness as Large Yellow Market and Paris Sugar and possibly identical with one of them. Further trials are necessary before the differences can be fully made out. The originator describes the plants to be fully as large as Maximum and often 12 inches in diameter.

History.—Named and introduced in 1903 by W. Atlee Burpee & Co., and said by them to have originated in England.

Illustrations.—Same as for Large Yellow Market.

BUTTERCUP.

Listed by thirty-five seedsmen. Seeds tested: Farquhar, 1901; Ferry, 1900, 1901, 1903; Plant, 1899, 1900; Schisler-Corneli, 1899; Thorburn, 1899, 1901, 1902; Vaughan, 1901.

Description.—A decidedly butter variety, strictly cabbage-heading, small-medium in size, late-intermediate in season, very slow to shoot to seed. Plant fairly compact and forming a globular, firm, well-defined, well-blanched head with leaves closely overlapping one another. Leaves broad in shape, fairly blistered and crumpled, slightly twisted, thin, almost loose and limp, entire at margins, flat at borders. Color very light green, sometimes described as golden green, never spotted nor brownish in any part. Quality fair; delicate, sweet, buttery flavor, soft texture. Seeds whitish.

Comparison.—One of the lesser grown varieties and not generally valuable, but it is sometimes attractive to amateurs because of its beautiful color, which is the lightest green and most yellow of any lettuce in cultivation. Makes good heads in some localities and seasons, but not generally doing so at Washington or most other places. In hot weather the outside leaves often change to a faded, sickly yellow, so that the color is sometimes one of its bad features rather than its principal merit. The general character of its leaves and habit of growth is the same as the Tennis

Ball Black-Seeded. Excepting a foreign sort known as Blonde de Berlin there seems to be no other variety like it in color, and for this reason it is seldom confounded with other types.

Synonyms.—Golden Buttercup, Golden Ball, Northrup, King & Co.'s Golden Ball, Michell's Very Best, Rudolph's Favorite.

History.—First listed by American seedsmen about eighteen years ago and said to be of German origin.

Illustrations.—The mature plant is similar in habit to that of California Cream Butter, on Plate VIII, differing from it in being much smaller, more blistered in the leaves, and with heads much less developed. The leaf is similar to that of Tennis Ball Black-Seeded, on Plate XXIII, and the longitudinal section to Mette's Forcing, on Plate XIX, excepting not nearly so solid or perfect a head.

CALIFORNIA ALL HEART.

Listed by five seedsmen. Seeds tested: Alneer, 1899–1901, 1903.

Reputed to be distinct when first listed about ten years ago, but now very rarely catalogued by seedsmen, and as received here never the same in any one year, the samples obtained being identified as Chartier, Hanson, or Early Curled Simpson. The original and correct type is described as a coarse, crisp head, similar to Denver Market.

Confusing names.—All Heart as introduced by Henry A. Dreer and sometimes sold as Dreer's All Heart is a different type from California All Heart.

History.—Said to have originated with a seed grower of Santa Clara, Cal., about fourteen years ago.

CALIFORNIA CREAM BUTTER.

Listed by ninety-seven seedsmen. Seeds tested: Burpee, 1900–1902; Ferry, 1900, 1901; Germain, 1901; Johnson & Stokes, 1900; Landreth, 1899, 1901; Rice, 1903; Thorburn, 1903

Description.—A decidedly butter variety, strictly cabbage-heading, large, late-intermediate in season, slow to shoot to seed. Plant fairly compact and forming a globular, very firm, well-defined, well-blanched head, with leaves very closely overlapping one another. Leaves broad in shape, blistered, and crumpled, slightly twisted, fairly stiff, very thick, entire at margins, flat, or partly blistered at borders. Color dark, rich, glossy green, freely and distinctly spotted with deep brown as well as partly tinged in places, especially at or near the border of leaves. Stem of plant and inner head leaves never colored. Quality excellent; very buttery, fairly sweet, and with thick soft leaves of much substance. Seeds blackish, generally more brownish black than other blackish-seeded sorts and seeds often described as brown.

Comparison.—One of the ten most largely grown varieties of the United States. Planted in all parts of the country, but more especially in California and the South. This variety and Big Boston are the kinds used almost exclusively by southern gardeners to grow during winter for shipment to northern markets. Succeeds well everywhere and at all times of the year. A good shipper, very hardy to cold, stands over winter well, and is especially good for summer, but not suited for indoor culture. Recommended to private gardeners as one of the most buttery flavored and best in quality of all varieties and to market gardeners as one of the best for their purpose also. Similar in color to Tennis Ball White-Seeded and Victoria Red-Edged. In places where Passion does well it closely resembles that variety. Same habit and general value as White Chavigne.

Synonyms.—Cox's California Cream Butter, Cream Butter, German Butter, Maule's Philadelphia Butter, Bolgiano's Early Spring, Early Spring, New Orleans Large Passion, Summer Drum Head, Treasure.

Confusing names.—California All Heart, California Curled, California Giant White Forcing, California Passion, all different types from California Cream Butter.

History.—Named and introduced by W. Atlee Burpee & Co. in 1888. It is evidently the variety which was well known about that time in California as Royal Summer Cabbage.

Illustrations.—A mature plant of the variety is shown on Plate VIII. The longitudinal section is similar to that of Matador, on Plate XX, differing principally in being much larger and more solid. The leaf is about between that of Tennis Ball Black-Seeded and Deacon, both shown on Plate XXIII.

CHARTIER.

Listed by four seedsmen. Seeds tested: Ebeling, 1900, 1901; Leonard, 1901, 1902; Scott, 1899, 1900, 1903; Vaughan, 1899–1901.

Description.—A decidedly crisp variety, cabbage-heading, large, late in season, and time of shooting to seed. Plant long-stemmed, somewhat spreading and loose, and forming a globular, well-defined, firm, well-blanched, showy head, with leaves closely overlapping one another. Leaves broad in shape, fairly blistered, and crumpled, thick, and stiff, very little twisted, serrate at margins, frilled at borders. Color a distinct medium bright brown, varying to bright green in less exposed parts and top of head; border plainly marked with deeper brown than other parts of leaves, no part of plant, however, distinctly spotted; inner head leaves and stem of plant wholly green. Quality fair; very crisp, hard in texture, decidedly lacking in sweetness and delicacy. Seeds large, whitish.

Comparison.—Very little grown. At one time highly recommended at Pittsburg and Chicago, but now it seems to be little heard of. Suitable as a summer or market gardener's sort for certain soils and climates. In some places and seasons it makes an immense, showy head, but it is a very uncertain variety and the head is often soft or even bunched in growth. It sometimes forms a head as large and as showy as Hanson, but never so solid or hard; wholly unfit for forcing. Other sorts of better quality are recommended for home use. Market gardeners are advised to test it before making very large plantings. The color of the plants is perhaps most like Onondaga or Prize Head. The brown is not so abundant nor so dark as in these varieties. The leaves are similar, also, but decidedly less blistered, crumpled, and frilled in character.

Synonyms.—Brown Chartier, Pink Chartier, Brown Curled, Beckert's Brown Curled, Bronzed Curled.

History.—Listed by W. C. Beckert for at least thirteen years.

Illustrations.—When well grown the plant may resemble Hanson, on Plate I. The young plant and leaf are similar to Hanson, on Plates XXII and XXVI, respectively.

CHICAGO FORCING.

Listed by one seedsman. Seeds tested: Vaughan, 1899–1901.

Comparison.—Of same class as Grand Rapids, differing in being much earlier, smaller, finer blistered, crumpled, and frilled, and running to seed at once when planted outdoors. Formerly used for growing under glass in the same way as Grand Rapids, but not now often listed by seedsmen. Apparently almost wholly gone out of use.

History.—Introduced about 1885 by Vaughan's Seed Store but not listed by that house after 1899. It is said to have originated with a Mr. Walters, who is described as a careful grower of lettuce under cold frames.

COLD FRAME WHITE CABBAGE.

Listed by five seedsmen. Seeds tested: Thorburn, 1901–1903; Weeber & Don, 1902, 1903.

Description.—A decidedly butter variety, strictly cabbage-heading, medium in size, early-intermediate in season, and shooting to seed at an intermediate date. Plant somewhat compact and forming a globular, well-defined, firm, well-blanched head, with its leaves closely overlapping one another. Leaves somewhat cup-shaped when young, broad when mature, fairly blistered, crumpled, thick, and stiff, entire at margins, flat at borders. Color medium green, fairly tinged in places with light brown, never spotted, and inner head leaves and stem of plant never colored. Quality good; sweet, very buttery, soft in texture. Seeds whitish.

Comparison.—Very little known and planted. Strictly a market gardeners' sort and excellent for forcing, early spring, or late fall planting. Not suited for summer. Perhaps more like Victoria Red-Edged than any other variety; in fact, at times the two seem identical. Also similar to Yellow Winter, St. Louis Black-Seeded Forcing, and Tennis Ball White-Seeded.

History.—Apparently named and introduced by J. M. Thorburn & Co., who have listed it for at least ten years.

Illustrations.—The habit of the mature plant is fairly represented by that of California Cream Butter on Plate VIII, the longitudinal section by Matador, on Plate XX, and the leaf between that of Deacon and Tennis Ball Black-Seeded, both shown on Plate XXIII.

CRUMPLED-LEAVED.

Listed by five seedsmen. Seeds tested: Burwell, 1900; Rawson, 1899, 1901–1903.

Description.—A decidedly butter variety, strictly cabbage-heading, early-medium in size, and shooting to seed at an early-intermediate date. Plant very compact and forming a globular, somewhat indistinctly defined, firm, well-blanched head, with its leaves closely overlapping one another except their borders characteristically twisted and turned backward, and leaf arrangement very irregular. Leaves broad in shape, fairly blistered, crumpled, thick, and stiff, obscurely crenate at margins, undulate at borders. Color very dull medium green, tinged with brown in places, sometimes over large areas and in distinct blotches, but never distinctly spotted, and inner head leaves and stem of plant wholly green. Quality good; sweet and buttery in flavor, soft in texture. Seeds whitish.

Comparison.—One of the lesser-grown varieties of the United States. Little used or planted except around Boston and in New England, where it is largely planted in greenhouses. Suitable only for forcing. The largest of the large type of lettuce now used by New England and other greenhouse men who formerly grew only the smaller Boston Market variety for inside culture. Undoubtedly a most valuable sort and highly recommended. It is claimed for it that decay in the heart is almost unknown, and that it is a fine shipper, sure header, and very reliable. Quite different in appearance from any other sort, but perhaps more like Big Boston than any other. Tennis Ball White-Seeded, Hittenger's Belmont, and Hothouse are closely related sorts.

Synonyms.—Rawson's Crumpled-Leaved.

History.—Named and introduced by W. W. Rawson & Co. in 1899, and said to have originated in their greenhouses at Arlington, Mass.

Illustrations.—The mature plant is not well represented by any of the following illustrations, but is perhaps best shown by Big Boston, on Plate V, and California Cream Butter, on Plate VIII. The leaf is most like Big Boston, on Plate XXIV. The longitudinal section is almost as solid as that represented by Mette's Forcing, on Plate XIX, though in habit it somewhat resembles Tom Thumb, on the same plate.

DAMMANN'S ICE.

Listed by one seedsman. Seeds tested: Ewing, 1902, 1903.
Comparison.—Listed in America only by Canadian seedsmen. Not known or sold in the United States. Same general character and usefulness as Malta and hardly distinguishable from it. Further trials are necessary before the exact differences can be fully determined.
History.—Apparently first listed in America by Wm. Ewing & Co. in 1902.
Illustrations.—Same as for Malta.

DEACON.

Listed by one hundred seedsmen. Seeds tested: Burpee, 1899–1901; Robert Evans, 1899; Farquhar, 1901; Ferry, 1900, 1901; Henderson, 1900, 1901; Landreth, 1901; Thorburn, 1901–1903.
Description.—A decidedly butter variety, strictly cabbage-heading, large-medium in size, intermediate in season, slow to shoot to seed. Young plant very spreading, regular in growth, its leaves very straight and extending flatly over the ground. Mature plant fairly compact. Head elongated when first forming, globular or even flattened when fully developed, fairly firm, well defined, very well blanched, and its leaves very completely but loosely overlapping one another, but outer ones of plant well separated from the head proper, the latter thereby left very bare or exposed. Leaves broad, peculiarly smooth, though sometimes slightly blistered and crumpled, never twisted, unusually thick in appearance, but soft and limp rather than stiff, entire at margins, flat at borders. Color a peculiar light grayish green, never spotted nor brownish in any part. Quality excellent; sweet, decidedly buttery in flavor, and with thick, soft leaves of much substance. Seeds whitish.
Comparison.—One of the ten most largely planted varieties of the United States and grown everywhere. Especially popular with the market gardeners of St. Louis, Chicago, and the West, where it is largely sold as St. Louis Butter. Stands summer well, sure heading, very reliable, and always attractive. A few greenhouse men have tried it in a small experimental way under glass and reported it as the best of the cabbage-heading varieties for forcing, and as more free from rot than any other, though we have never known of its being used in a commercial way for forcing. It is a splendid market gardener's lettuce and, because of its high quality and easy culture, one of the very best for home use. Peculiarly light grayish green in color and not likely to be confounded with other variety types, except All Seasons and Asiatic, both of which it closely resembles. Reichner, Silver Ball, and Philadelphia Butter are also similar sorts. The variety belongs to the same class and possesses the same general value as California Cream Butter, White Summer Cabbage, and Tennis Ball Black-Seeded.
Synonyms.—Australian White Triumph, Big Head, Bolgiano's Big Head, Bolgiano's Golden Heart, Colossal, Tait's Colossal, Largest of All, Large Drum Head, Golden Gate, Summer Gem, Moore's Summer Gem, San Francisco Market, Sunlight, St. Louis Butter, Salzer's Sunlight, Summer Queen Drum Head, Triumph, White Russian, Russian.
History.—Named and introduced by the Joseph Harris Co. in 1879.
Illustrations.—A mature plant and leaf of the variety are shown on Plates X and XXIII, respectively. The longitudinal section is similar to that of Matador, on Plate XX, and the young plant to All Seasons, on Plate XXII.

DEFIANCE.

Listed by thirty-two seedsmen. Seeds tested: Dallwig, 1903; Dreer, 1903; Farquhar, 1901, 1903; Gregory, 1900, 1903; Johnson & Stokes, 1899, 1901; Leonard, 1903; Livingston, 1901; Michell, 1901, 1903; Rawson, 1903; Rice, 1902; Vaughan, 1900.

Description.—A decidedly butter variety, strictly cabbage-heading, large, medium in size, late-intermediate in season, very slow to shoot to seed. Young plant very upright growing, with long spatulate-shaped, twisted leaves of loose and limp growth. Mature plant slightly spreading and forming a globular, imperfectly defined, firm, well-blanched head, with its leaves very loosely and irregularly overlapping one another. Leaves of mature plant also broad in shape, fairly blistered, crumpled, thick, and stiff, entire at margins, flat at borders. Color medium green, freely spotted, tinged light brown in places, but inner head leaves, stem of plant, and base of midrib wholly green. Quality good; very buttery, fairly sweet in flavor, soft in texture. Seeds very broad, whitish.

Comparison.—One of the lesser grown varieties of the United States. Excellent for summer growing, but not as reliable for this purpose as some other cabbage sorts, like California Cream Butter and Black-Seeded Tennis Ball. The head is too irregular in shape and imperfect to be attractive, and the variety can not be very highly recommended except for its heat-resisting qualities. Not suited for forcing. Very similar to Emperor William, German Incomparable, and St. Louis Black-Seeded Forcing. The exact differences between Defiance and Emperor William have not yet been made out by the writer, except that the latter variety is dullest green in color.

Synonyms.—Always Ready, Perpignan, Plant Seed Company's Standwell, Standwell, Slow Seeder, Stubborn Seeder.

Confusing name.—Manns' Defiance Summer, a very different type of lettuce.

History.—First listed by American seedsmen about sixteen years ago and described at that time as an improvement on Perpignan.

Illustrations.—The habit of the mature plant is similar to that shown of Emperor William on Plate IX, and the leaf is perhaps most like Tennis Ball Black-Seeded of the kinds illustrated.

DENSITY.

Listed by one seedsman. Seeds tested: Henderson, 1902, 1903.

Description.—A fairly crisp variety, strictly cabbage-heading, very small, very early, and soon forming a seed stalk, but for an extra early sort very slow to shoot to seed. Plant remarkably compact and forming a globular, extremely hard, very well blanched head, with its leaves tightly drawn over one another, but their borders so twisted and turned as to produce a torn effect or bursted-like head; no distinct separation between head proper and outer leaves of plant, the whole being nearly all head. Leaves broad in shape, excessively blistered, crumpled, and twisted, very thick and stiff, finely serrate at margins, frilled at borders. Color dark dull green, with a narrow, faint dull brown border, and generally sparingly tinged with faint dull brown in exposed parts; never spotted; inner head leaves and stem of plant wholly green. Quality excellent; exceedingly sweet, tender, and fine flavored. Seeds small, whitish.

Comparison.—New and as yet used in this country for experimental plantings only. Of the very best in quality and slower to shoot to seed than other varieties of equal earliness, but too small to be of much value, except, perhaps, for forcing in frames. Amateurs may find the variety interesting, but for real usefulness the Mignonette variety is decidedly better. Excepting for color and size, it is very much like Mignonette, but otherwise it is very distinct and not easily confounded with that or any other variety.

Synonym.—Miniature.

History.—Named and first introduced by Peter Henderson & Co. in 1902.

Illustrations.—A mature plant of the variety is shown on Plate VII. The side view of Mignonette on the same plate also illustrates the type. The longitudinal section resembles that of Tom Thumb on Plate XIX.

DENVER MARKET.

Listed by one hundred and twenty-three seedsmen. Seeds tested: Barteldes, 1902; Burpee, 1901-1903; Ferry, 1899-1901; Thorburn, 1901-1903.

Description.—A decidedly crisp variety, fairly cabbage-heading, large, medium in size, late-intermediate in season, very slow to shoot to seed. Plant compact or slightly spreading, upright in habit, and forming an oval, firm, or somewhat soft, well blanched, well defined head, with its leaves closely overlapping one another, while the outer leaves of the plant are often so separated from the head proper as to leave the latter very bare or exposed. Leaves short spatulate in shape, excessively blistered and crumpled, fairly twisted and stiff, very thick, finely serrate at margins, excessively frilled at borders. Color very light green, never spotted nor brownish in any part. Quality poor; hard in texture, coarse and rank in flavor, or at least lacking sweetness and delicacy. Seeds large, whitish.

Comparison.—A popular variety in the United States, though not one of the ten most largely grown sorts. Best known in the Middle West, where it is a favorite for forcing, but not now so largely grown under glass as formerly. A satisfactory market gardener's lettuce, and good for summer. On account of its poor quality not recommended to private gardeners. The most blistered and crumpled leaved of all varieties, and this, together with its beautiful color, makes it one of the most handsome lettuces in cultivation. Very distinct and hardly comparable with other varieties. Perhaps more like Hanson than any other variety, but not closely resembling it, as sometimes described.

Synonyms.—Denver Market Forcing, Barteldes Denver Market, Kansas City Market, Kansas City White-Seeded Forcing, Dayton Market, Cincinnati Market, Early Ohio, Ohio Cabbage, Golden Forcing, Sutton's Favorite, Ritter's Forcing, Weber's Curled.

History.—Introduced by F. Barteldes & Co. in 1890.

Illustrations.—The mature plant is not well shown by any of the illustrations, but the habit may be described as between that of Hanson and Black-Seeded Simpson on Plate I, though the variety is much more blistered in the leaf and the heads are more elongated than shown in either of these illustrations. A leaf of the variety is shown on Plate XXVI. The young plant is similar to that shown of Hanson, on Plate XXII.

DETROIT MARKET GARDENER'S FORCING.

Listed by three seedsmen. Seeds tested: Burpee, 1901; Ferry, 1899-1903.

Description.—A decidedly crisp variety, bunching under glass, but semicabbage-heading outdoors, large, late-intermediate in season, slow to shoot to seed. Plant compact, upright in habit, sometimes forming a tallish, dense bunch of leaves, but more generally when well grown outdoors forming an oval, somewhat pointed head, hard and well blanched, its outside leaves tightly and flatly overlapping one another at their lower part, but turning loosely outward at their uppermost portion, and thereby surrounding the head with a loose leaf growth and much obscuring it. Leaves broad in shape, fairly blistered, crumpled and twisted, very thick, stiff, and coarse in appearance, with heavy veins and a large protruding midrib, finely serrate margins, and excessively frilled borders. Color a distinct very light green, never spotted nor brownish in any part. Quality good; crisp and firm in texture, sweet in flavor. Seeds large, whitish.

Comparison.—Popular around Detroit and parts of Michigan, but little planted or known elsewhere. With Grand Rapids, Black-Seeded Simpson, and White Star it comprises one of the four most largely grown varieties used for forcing around Detroit. Claimed to stand more heat and to be forced quicker to maturity than any other variety of the same size. Three crops are raised in the time required for growing two of other sorts. Strictly a market gardener's variety and good for summer growing. Not recommended for home use. When grown under glass it is very similar to Black-Seeded Simpson and Grand Rapids Forcing, but outdoors the habit is very distinct, and perhaps more like Hanson than any other. The color also is peculiar, and perhaps the lightest green of the crisp sorts.

Synonyms.—Engel's Forcing, Wallbaurer.

History.—Named and introduced by D. M. Ferry & Co. in 1895.

Illustrations.—A mature plant of the variety is shown on Plate IX. The young plant and leaf are similar to those shown of Hanson on Plates XXII and XXVI, respectively.

DWARF WHITE HEART COS.

Listed by six seedsmen. Seeds tested: Burpee, 1899, 1901–1903.

Comparison.—Scarce and rarely planted. Except that it is more dwarf in habit, very similar to Paris White Cos, and probably the same in usefulness and value. Further trials are necessary before all the differences can be definitely stated.

History.—Named and introduced into this country in 1895 by W. Atlee Burpee & Co. It is said by them to be a foreign sort.

Illustrations.—Similar to that of Paris White Cos.

EARLIEST CUTTING.

Listed by one seedsman. Seeds tested: Dallwig, 1900–1903.

Description.—A decidedly butter variety, strictly bunching, small-medium in size, early-intermediate in season, shooting to seed at an intermediate date. Plant decidedly loose and straggling and leaves too few for blanching to any extent. Leaves spatulate in form, decidely cup-shaped, very smooth, never blistered, crumpled, nor twisted, fairly thick, very limp, entire at margins, flat at borders. Color light green, never spotted nor brownish in any part. Quality fair; slightly buttery, soft in texture, but much lacking in delicacy and sweetness. Seeds whitish.

Comparison.—Scarce and rarely planted in the United States. One of the most loose-leaved, straggling, unattractive varieties tested at Washington. It furnished only a few leaves and seemed wholly undesirable in every way. Possibly a good sort in other countries, but wholly undesirable in this locality. Very distinct and hardly comparable with any other variety. The most loose-leaved of the cabbage varieties and its leaves more incurved than any other lettuce.

Confusing names.—Earliest of All and Earliest Forcing, both different types from Earliest Cutting.

History.—First listed in this country by W. E. Dallwig, who states the seed was obtained in Germany.

Illustrations.—A mature plant and leaf of the variety are shown on Plates VIII and XXIII, respectively.

EARLY CURLED SILESIA.

Listed by one hundred seedsmen. Seeds tested: Barteldes, 1901; Bowen, 1901; Buist, 1901; Burpee, 1900–1902; Ferry, 1899; Johnson & Stokes, 1901; Landreth, 1899, 1902; J. M. McCullough, 1901; Price & Reed, 1901; Thorburn, 1903; Vaughan, 1901.

Description.—As known in this country about fifteen years ago, this variety was distinct from Early Curled Simpson, being narrow-leaved and more open in habit, but to-day the latter variety seems to be used almost wholly in filling orders for Early Curled Silesia, so that the type as formerly known seems to be very scarce or possibly wholly gone out of use.

History.—Known in this country for at least seventy-four years and in European countries for a much longer time. Apparently one of the first varieties cultivated.

EARLY CURLED SIMPSON.

Listed by one hundred and forty seedsmen. Seeds tested: Barteldes, 1901; Buist, 1901; Burpee, 1901; Farquhar, 1901; Ferry, 1900, 1901; Henderson, 1901; Johnson & Stokes, 1899; Landreth, 1903; Price, 1901; Tait, 1901; Thorburn, 1899, 1901, 1903.

Description.—A decidedly crisp variety, strictly bunching, large-medium in size, early marketable but intermediate in time of attaining fullest development, slow to shoot to seed. Plant spreading and forming a rounded to low V-shaped, well-blanched, fairly dense cluster of leaves, more or less open or spread out at the center and never cabbage-like, though sometimes very dense. Leaves short spatulate to broad, much blistered and crumpled, fairly twisted, thick and stiff, serrate at margins, much developed and frilled at borders. Color, very light green; never spotted nor brownish in any part. Quality fair; sweet in flavor, somewhat hard and coarse in texture. Seeds large, whitish.

Comparison.—Under this or some other name one of the ten most largely used lettuce types of the United States. About thirty years ago more largely planted than any other. Grown in all parts of this country, but less in the South than other parts, and more used in the West than in other sections. Its wide use is due to its reliability, as it is certain, even under hard treatment, to make some good leaves. For this reason it is often one of the most satisfactory varieties for home use, though where lettuce can be well grown other sorts of more delicate flavor are recommended to the amateur. Possibly under some conditions more satisfactory than Black-Seeded Simpson or any other variety of its class, but for general use the former variety or Morse is more satistactory. These two varieties and Golden Curled more closely resemble it than other sorts.

Synonyms.—Early Curled White-Seeded Simpson, Early White-Seeded Simpson, White-Seeded Simpson, Perpetual, Crisp and Tender, La Crosse Market.

Confusing names.—Black-Seeded Simpson, Early Curled Black-Seeded Simpson.

History.—Listed by seedsmen in this country for at least thirty-nine years. Said to have originated with Mr. Simpson, a market gardener near Brooklyn, N. Y.

Illustrations.—A mature plant and leaf of the variety are shown on Plates IV and XXV, respectively. The young plant is similar to that of Hanson, on Plate XXII.

EMPEROR FORCING.

Listed by five seedsmen. Seeds tested: Bridgeman, 1901; Michell, 1900; Thorburn, 1899–1903.

Description.—A decidedly butter variety, strictly cabbage-heading, very small, extremely early, and shooting to seed at once in hot weather. Plant very compact and forming a globular, firm, well-defined, well-blanched head, with its leaves flatly and completely overlapping one another. Leaves broad in shape, blistered, crumpled, little twisted, fairly stiff and thick, entire at margins, flat or partly blistered at borders. Color, medium green; never spotted nor brownish in any part. Quality good; sweet, buttery in flavor, soft in texture. Seeds very small, whitish.

Comparison.—Little known or planted. Suitable only for forcing and being the earliest, smallest, and most compact of all varieties except perhaps White Forcing it would seem to be the best suited for cold frames or hotbed culture, but decidedly too small for general greenhouse use. Wholly unfit for amateurs or for outdoor culture. The plant may be described as a miniature Hubbard's Market. Same exactly as that variety in habit and also similar to Lee's Market Forcing.

Synonym.—Precocity.

Confusing name.—Emperor William, which is a very different type of lettuce.

History.—Apparently first listed in this country in 1881 by James J. H. Gregory & Son, who described it in their catalogue of that year as of German origin.

Illustrations.—The habit of the variety is well illustrated by California Cream Butter, on Plate VIII, but the size is about same as White Forcing, on Plate VII. The longitudinal section is similar to Mette's Forcing, on Plate XIX, and the leaf to Tennis Ball Black-Seeded, on Plate XXIII, but less blistered.

EMPEROR WILLIAM.

Listed by two seedsmen. Seeds tested: Stumpp & Walter, 1902; Thorburn, 1902, 1903.

Description.—A decidedly butter variety, strictly cabbage-heading, large-medium in size, intermediate in season, slow to shoot to seed. Plant spreading, loose, and forming a gobular, imperfectly defined, somewhat firm, well blanched head, with leaves very imperfectly and loosely overlapping one another. Leaves broad in shape, fairly blistered, crumpled, thick, and stiff, entire at margins, flat at borders. Color medium dull green, fairly spotted, sparingly tinged in places with faint brown, inner head leaves and stem of plant wholly green. Quality good; very buttery, fairly sweet, soft in texture. Seeds blackish.

Comparison.—New and probably not yet planted in this country except in an experimental way. Its value for our climate has not yet been proved at Washington nor in any other place so far as known by the writer. It seems to be useful in the same way as Defiance, and more closely resembles that sort than any other. Similar also to German Incomparable and St. Louis Black-Seeded Forcing.

Confusing name.—Emperor Forcing, a very different type of lettuce.

History.—First introduced in this country by J. M. Thorburn & Co. and Stumpp & Walter, who describe it as of European origin.

Illustrations.—A mature plant of the variety is shown on Plate IX. The leaf is similar to but less blistered than that shown of Tennis Ball Black-Seeded, on Plate XXIII.

EUREKA.

Listed by one seedsman. Seeds tested: Crosman, 1900–1903.

Description.—A decidedly butter variety, cabbage-heading, very large, unusually late, slow to shoot to seed. Plant extremely loose, very spreading, and forming a globular, fairly-defined, very soft, well-blanched head, with leaves regularly and completely overlapping one another, but with loose spaces between them. Leaves broad in shape, much blistered and crumpled, little twisted, thin, almost limp, obscurely crenate at margins, broadly undulate at borders. Color very bright brown, of a distinct shade, and interspersed with light green in less exposed parts, most deeply colored at borders, very sparingly spotted, stem of plant and base of midrib light pink in color, inner heart leaves sparingly spotted but not otherwise colored. Quality fair; sweet, buttery, fairly soft in texture. Seeds yellowish.

Comparison.—Scarce and rarely planted. It forms a large, showy head when well grown, but is very unreliable, sometimes more open in growth than any other butter variety and making no head whatever. Even at its best very loose in habit and heads always very soft. Of little practical value, but attractive to some amateurs because of its occasional large, showy heads and peculiar brilliant red color. Perhaps more like Vick's Hero than other American varieties, though far more even and reliable than that sort.

Synonyms.—Copper Head, Pan-American.

History.—Apparently named and first listed by Crosman Brothers, about twenty-three years ago.

EXPRESS COS.

Listed by two seedsmen. Seeds tested: Henderson, 1902, 1903; Vaughan, 1903.

Description.—A typical cos variety, strictly self-closing, medium in size, early-intermediate in season compared to the butter or crisp sorts, but very small in size and extremely early for this group; intermediate in time of shooting to seed. Plant very compact, decidedly upright in habit, its leaves when young growing straight and flat, but when older the innermost ones becoming decidedly spoon-shaped and making a well-defined, firm head of decidedly loaf-shaped form and roundish top, its leaves completely but not tightly overlapping one another, but with the outside ones so well separated from the head proper as to leave it somewhat bare or exposed. Leaves oval to slightly spatulate, outermost ones with smooth surface, and flat, innermost ones sparingly blistered and more or less cup-shaped, both, however, exceedingly regular in form, and thick, stiff, and coarse, but never in the least twisted nor crumpled, and always with coarse, hard veins, large, hard midribs, entire margins, and flat borders. Color very dark green, never spotted nor brownish in any part. Quality excellent; very hard in texture, but exceedingly sweet and crisp. Seeds whitish.

Comparison.—New and very little known or planted. Previous to the introduction of this variety the cos lettuces were not obtainable till late in the season, but with the advent of this new sort, which is decidedly earlier than any other cos variety, the season of this valuable class of lettuce has been greatly extended. Its quality is the very best or about the same as Paris White Cos, while it is also reliable and as self-closing as any other cos variety. Excellent either for the home or market gardener. It is similar to Paris White Cos, only half its size, much earlier, and darker green, or about the same shade of green as Green Cos.

History.—First introduced into this country in 1902 by Peter Henderson & Co. and Vaughan's Seed Store.

Illustrations.—A mature plant and leaf of the variety are shown on Plates XV and XXVI, respectively. The longitudinal section is similar to that given of Paris White Cos on Plate XIX.

GERMAN EARLY HEAD.

Listed by one seedsman. Seeds tested: Bridgeman, 1899–1903.

Description.—A fairly butter variety, strictly cabbage-heading, small-medium in size, early-intermediate in season, and shooting to seed quickly in hot weather. Plant extremely compact and forming a globular, well-defined, firm, well-blanched head, with leaves closely overlapping one another. Leaves broad in shape, fairly blistered and crumpled, little twisted, medium thick and stiff, obscurely crenate at margins, plainly undulate at borders. Color, light green, sometimes described as golden green; never spotted nor brownish in any part. Quality good; very sweet and slightly buttery in flavor, of a crisp, firm texture and distinct quality, quite different from most butter sorts, or somewhat approaching that of the crisp varieties. Seeds small, whitish.

Comparison.—Scarce and little planted. Reports as to its usefulness and value for this country have not come to our notice. It has always done well at Washington and appears to be a desirable variety, useful in the same way as Golden Queen, and suitable only as a market gardener's lettuce and for forcing or early planting outdoors. More like Golden Queen than any other sort, differing principally in that the shape of the head is decidedly globular, the color darker green, and margins of leaves more pronouncedly crenate.

Confusing name.—German Butter Head, a very different type of lettuce.

History.—Apparently never catalogued in this country, except by Alfred Bridgeman & Co., who have listed it for at least eight years.

Illustrations.—No good examples of the variety are offered in the accompanying illustrations, but the type is similar to that represented by White Forcing, on Plate VII.

GERMAN INCOMPARABLE.

Listed by one seedsman. Seeds tested: Dallwig, 1902, 1903.

Comparison.—Scarce and little grown. Usefulness and value apparently same as Emperor William, and except that its leaves are not spotted it is practically the same in appearance also.

History.—Apparently never catalogued in this country except by W. E. Dallwig, who first listed it in 1902.

Illustrations.—Same as for Emperor William.

GIANT GLACIER.

Listed by four seedsmen. Seeds tested: Burpee, 1901, 1903.

Description.—A decidedly crisp variety, cabbage-heading, very late, large, slow to shoot to seed. Plant extremely loose and spreading, central part somewhat upright, especially when young. Stem large and long. Head globular to short oval in shape, well defined, well blanched, its leaves regularly overlapping one another but with loose spaces between them, and head, therefore, soft, although the leaves composing it are very thick and stiff. Leaves short, spatulate in shape, though sometimes as broad as long, slightly but coarsely blistered and crumpled, little twisted, very coarse in appearance, and with prominent heavy veins and a large protruding midrib; margins deeply serrate; borders frilled. Color very light green, never spotted, nor brownish in any part. Quality fair; coarse and hard in texture, but of a sweetness and firmness which are often much liked. Seeds large, whitish.

Comparison.—New and little known. As yet planted in this country only in an experimental way. Highly recommended by introducers, but at Washington it made a late, loose, soft head, and was too spreading in habit to be recommended for market gardening or as a very useful variety for any other purpose. Other sorts, like Hanson, are decidedly preferable and more reliable. Attractive to some amateurs as an immense showy lettuce and capable, perhaps, of growing to a greater size than any other cabbage-heading variety. Possibly more like Drumhead than any other lettuce, but the color is brighter green, habit lower growing, and heads more globular. Except for color, very similar to Tyrolese.

Synonyms.—Burpee's Giant Glacier, Maule's Silver Anniversary, Silver Anniversary.

History.—Introduced in 1900 by W. Atlee Burpee & Co., who state that the variety originally came from Italy.

Illustrations.—A leaf of the variety is shown on Plate XXV. The general type of the plant is perhaps better illustrated by Tyrolese, on Plate II, and Malta, on Plate XII, than by any of the accompanying illustrations.

GIANT WHITE COS.

Listed by five seedsmen. Seeds tested: Burpee, 1899, 1901, 1902.

Comparison.—Scarce and rarely planted. Of the same general character as Paris White Cos, but less reliable and self-closing in habit and not so desirable for this country as that variety. The leaves are distinctly different from those of Paris White Cos, or more grayish green, flatter, and smoother, as well as conspicuously widest at top, prominently shouldered at upper part and jagged at margins.

History.—First introduced into this country by W. Atlee Burpee & Co., who state it to be of foreign origin. It was listed by them in 1882 as Carter's Giant White Cos.

Illustrations.—A leaf of the variety is shown on Plate XXVII. The general type of the plant is best illustrated by Express Cos, on Plate XV, and Paris White Cos, on Plate XIX.

GOLDEN CURLED.

Listed by eight seedsmen. Seeds tested: Beckert, 1899, 1900, 1903; Landreth, 1899, 1901, 1903; Scott, 1901.

Comparison.—One of the lesser grown varieties. Except for being very light solid green, the same as Chartier, already described, and but for difference in color identical also in usefulness and value.

Synonyms.—Beckert's Golden Curled, Alaska, White Chartier.

History.—Listed by above seedsmen for at least thirteen years.

Illustrations.—Same as for Chartier.

GOLDEN HEART.

Listed by two seedsmen. Seeds tested: Childs, 1899, 1900, 1902.

Description.—A decidedly butter variety, strictly bunching, very large, early-intermediate, quickly shooting to seed. Plant very spreading, and composed of a loose cluster of leaves very open at the center, extending flatly over the ground, too loose for blanching to any extent, and occupying a great amount of space. Leaves spatulate in shape, much blistered and crumpled, but flat and regular in form, never twisted, very loose, thin and limp, entire at margins, flat or partly blistered at borders. Color medium green, never spotted nor brownish in any part. Quality poor; of a somewhat bitter, rank, wild flavor, almost wholly lacking in sweetness. Seeds whitish.

Comparison.—Scarce and rarely planted. When first introduced this variety seems to have been highly recommended and was probably a useful sort; but the type appears to have degenerated or changed since then, for, as received here, it was a very spreading wild lettuce and one of the least to be recommended of all the kinds on trial. It is especially useless in hot weather and shoots to seed quicker than almost any other variety. It compares more favorably with other varieties in remaining fit for use in cool weather, but is of little value even under these conditions, because so spreading and requiring an immense amount of room to grow. Quite distinct from other sorts, but plainly more like Middletowner than any other, especially the wider-leaved plants. It is very similar to the wild plants which sometimes appear in Deacon, White Summer Cabbage, and other butter varieties.

Confusing names.—Golden Head, Golden Butter, Golden Curled, all different types from Golden Heart.

History.—Named and introduced by W. Atlee Burpee & Co., in 1884, as Burpee's Golden Heart, but not catalogued by them after 1890.

Illustrations.—A mature plant of the variety is shown on Plate II. The leaf is similar to that of Tennis Ball Black-Seeded, on Plate XXIII, except that it is more spatulate in form.

GOLDEN QUEEN.

Listed by twenty-seven seedsmen. Seeds tested: Bridgeman, 1900, 1901; Burpee 1900, 1901; Dreer, 1903; Henderson, 1899–1901, 1903; Michell, 1900; Thorburn, 1901, 1902; Weeber & Don, 1903.

Description.—A fairly butter variety, strictly cabbage-heading, small-medium in size, early, shooting to seed quickly in hot weather. Plant extremely compact, and forming a heart-shaped, somewhat pointed, fairly defined, firm, well blanched head, with leaves completely overlapping one another, except turned characteristically backward at their borders, somewhat like the petals of a rose, and the head thereby somewhat obscured. Leaves broad in shape, blistered, crumpled, twisted, thick, stiff, entire or obscurely crenate at margins, flat or slightly undulate at borders. Color a beautiful, rich, very light green, sometimes described as golden green, never brownish nor spotted in any part. Quality excellent; very sweet and slightly buttery in flavor but of a crisp, firm texture and distinct quality quite different from other butter varieties or somewhat approaching that of the crisp lettuces. Seeds whitish, small or medium in size.

Comparison.—One of the popular varieties óf the United States, though not one of the ten most largely grown sorts. Planted everywhere in the East and North. A superior forcing variety, especially for cold frames or hotbeds, and good for early planting outdoors, but not suitable for summer growing. A valuable market gardener's lettuce, but not recommended to amateurs for planting outdoors unless started early and well grown. For a rich, golden yellow color no variety is more beautiful or desirable than this one. More like German Early Head than any other lettuce. Very similar, also, to Lee's Market Forcing and White Forcing.

Synonyms.—Henderson's Golden Queen, Golden Queen, Stone Head Golden Yellow.

Confusing names.—Faust's Queen and Yellow Queen, both very different types from Golden Queen.

History.—First introduced by Peter Henderson & Co. about fourteen years ago.

Illustrations.—The type is perhaps best illustrated by White Forcing, on Plate VII, though about twice as large as that variety. The longitudinal section is similar in solidity to Matador, on Plate XX.

GOLDEN SPOTTED.

Listed by one seedsman. Seeds tested: Dallwig, 1900–1903.

Description.—A decidedly butter variety, strictly cabbage-heading, small-medium in size, late-intermediate in season, shooting to seed at an intermediate date. Plant compact and forming a globular, fairly defined, slightly firm, well-blanched head, with leaves closely overlapping one another. Leaves broad in shape, fairly blistered, crumpled and thick, little twisted, entire at margins, flat at borders. Color bright green, thickly spotted with bright brown. Spots very striking, evenly distributed over the plant, distinct and well separated from one another, not so fine or so massed together as to produce the effect of blotching or a single color; inside head leaves also spotted, and stem of plant and base of midrib plainly colored. Quality good; buttery, sweet, soft in texture. Seeds whitish.

Comparison.—Scarce and rarely planted. Too small, late, and unreliable a header to be generally useful, but very attractive because so beautifully spotted, no other variety comparing with it in this respect. The inner heart leaves, or those which are served for use, are not, however, very distinctly or thickly spotted; and for serving on the table the Trout variety will be found more attractive than this one. Only about one-half the plants are brightly spotted; the others approach a solid brown. The habit is the same as Tennis Ball Black-Seeded.

History.—W. E. Dallwig is at present the only American seedsman cataloguing this variety. It was listed by him first in 1888, but it seems that W. Atlee Burpee & Co. and others had listed it several years before.

Illustrations.—The general habit is illustrated by California Cream Butter, on Plate VIII, though the variety is far from being so solid or so perfect as represented in this figure.

GRAND RAPIDS.

Listed by one hundred and sixty-four seedsmen. Seeds tested: Burpee, 1901; Ferry, 1900—1902; Landreth, 1899, 1901; Thorburn, 1899, 1901, 1903; Vaughan, 1901, 1903.

Description.—A decidedly crisp variety, strictly bunching, early-intermediate in season, quickly shooting to seed. Plant very spreading when young, but becoming fairly compact when mature, and forming a loose, rounded cluster of leaves, growing close enough together for blanching to only a small extent, but when well grown never spread out or opened at the center. Leaves short spatulate in shape, excessively blistered and crumpled, slightly twisted, very thick and heavy, with coarse veins, large protruding midribs, serrate margins and with borders so excessively frilled and largely developed as to comprise the larger portion of the visible part of the plant. Color very light green, never spotted nor brownish in any part. Quality poor; crisp, but hard in texture; coarse and rank in flavor, or at least decidedly lacking in sweetness and delicacy. Seeds very blackish; extremely hard to germinate.

Comparison.—Probably one of the ten most largely grown varieties of the United States. The favorite for forcing in the West and other markets where hothouse lettuce is sold by weight and whose markets accept a bunching variety. It has largely replaced Black-Seeded Simpson for this purpose. At Washington it does not succeed well outdoors, and is not recommended farther south than this latitude. More easily grown in greenhouses than almost any other variety. Stands a great deal of neglect in watering and ventilation. A splendid shipper, and with many gardeners by far the best and most profitable sort for growing under glass. One of the coarser varieties, poor in quality when grown outdoors, but becoming tender and sweet when grown in greenhouses. More like Black-Seeded Simpson than any other, not only in appearance, but also in usefulness and value. Its fringed leaves and general habit are most like Boston Curled. The young plants are hardly distinguishable from Hanson and Black-Seeded Simpson. Grown in greenhouses the variety is very tall and upright in habit, not as described in the above notes which apply only to outdoor specimens.

Synonyms.—Grand Rapids Forcing, Grand Rapids Early Forcing, Mills' Earliest.

History.—Catalogued by D. M. Ferry & Co. in 1890, but known in Grand Rapids, Mich., ten or more years before that time. It is said to have originated with Mr. Eugene Davis, of Grand Rapids, and to be the result of more than fifteen years' selection of Black-Seeded Simpson.

Illustrations.—A mature plant and leaf are shown on Plates VI and XXV, respectively. The young plant is similar to Hanson, on Plate XXII. The general character of the longitudinal section is illustrated by Prize Head, on Plate XXI.

GREEN COS.

Listed by ten seedsmen. Seeds tested: Landreth, 1899, 1901, 1902; Rennie, 1903.

Comparison.—Scarce and rarely planted. Except that it is very dark green in color, its description, usefulness, and value are the same as given for Paris White Cos.

Illustrations.—Same as for Paris White Cos.

GREEN-FRINGED.

Listed by twenty-four seedsmen. Seeds tested: Burpee, 1899—1903; Templin, 1899; Vaughan, 1901.

Description.—A decidedly crisp variety, strictly bunching, small, early-intermediate in season, wilting at once upon being pulled, quickly shooting to seed. Plant growing close to the ground and composed of a loose, spreading, very regular, rosette-like cluster of leaves, very much opened or spread out at its center and growing flatly outward, never in the least upright nor clustered in growth, never blanched. Leaves broad, very regular in form, strictly smooth, rarely blistered, never crumpled nor twisted, exceedingly thick, stiff, and hard, veins many, large, coarse, and conspicuous, margins finely serrate, borders excessively frilled and so enormously developed as to embrace a large part of the visible portion of the plant. Color very dull green, never spotted nor brownish in any part. Quality very poor; tough in texture and of a rank, wild flavor. Seeds whitish.

Comparison.—Little known and rarely planted. A novel and very pretty fringed lettuce, but on account of its poor quality, small size, and its wilting immediately upon being pulled, of little use except for garnishing or ornament. Wholly unfit for marketing. One of the first to shoot to seed in hot weather but slow to do so in the autumn or in cool weather. Not suited for summer growing. More hardy to extreme cold than any other variety except perhaps Boston Curled. Very distinct and not comparable with other sorts. The thickest and hardest veined leaved lettuce in cultivation.

Synonyms.—California Curled.

History.—Catalogued by American seedsmen for at least fifteen years.

Illustrations.—A mature plant and leaf of the variety are shown on Plates III and XXIII, respectively.

HALF CENTURY.

Listed by one seedsman. Seeds tested: Childs, 1899—1903.

Description.—A decidedly butter variety, cabbage-heading, medium in size, early-intermediate in season, shooting to seed at an intermediate date. Young plant loose and spreading. Mature plant fairly compact when well developed, and forming a globular head, with leaves closely compacted uprightly and irregularly together, with little tendency to curve inward or lay flatly over one another, but nevertheless producing a firm, well blanched, but somewhat bursted-like, indistinctly defined head. Leaves short spatulate in shape, strictly smooth, never blistered nor crumpled, much twisted, exceedingly thick, fairly stiff, entire at margins, flat at borders. Color very dark green, plainly brownish at border, tinged in places during sunny weather but very little or not at all during cloudy weather, very sparingly spotted under the latter conditions and appearing as if wholly green unless very closely examined. Quality excellent; fairly buttery in flavor, exceedingly sweet, delicate, and tender, and with enormously thick leaves of great substance. Seeds blackish.

Comparison.—Scarce and rarely planted. At Washington decidedly the most tender and delicate flavored of all varieties tested. It is recommended to amateurs who want a lettuce of the very best quality. On account of its unattractive dark color, uneven shape, and tender leaves, which break upon the least handling, it becomes wholly unfit for market gardening; also an uncertain header and unreliable unless given good care. Very distinct and not easily compared with other varieties. Well-grown specimens sometimes resemble California Cream Butter.

Synonym.—Childs' Half Century.

History.—Named and first introduced in this country about 1890 by John Lewis Childs, who states that the seed was sent to him by Mrs. Belle Nance, Newmarket, Ala., in whose family it had been grown for more than fifty years.

Illustrations.—A mature plant is shown on Plate XVIII. The leaves are sometimes incurved, similar to those of Yellow Winter, on Plate XXIV.

HANSON.

Listed by one hundred and ninety-five seedsmen. Seeds tested: Burpee, 1901—1902; Dreer, 1900, 1901; Farquhar, 1901; Ferry, 1900, 1901; Henderson, 1901; Landreth, 1899; Maule, 1901; Thorburn, 1899, 1901—1903.

Description.—A decidedly crisp variety, strictly cabbage-heading, very large, very late, extremely slow to shoot to seed. Plant spreading, but not loose in habit and forming a globular, extremely hard, well-defined, well-blanched head, with leaves very flatly and tightly overlapping one another. Leaves very broad in shape, fairly blistered, crumpled and twisted, very thick, stiff and coarse in appearance, with heavy veins and a large protruding midrib; margins serrate; borders finely frilled. Color very light green, of a shining metallic surface rather than rich and glossy, never spotted nor brownish in any part. Quality good; exceedingly crisp and firm in texture, and very sweet. Seeds large, whitish.

Comparison.—Probably one of the three most largely grown varieties of the United States. Succeeds well everywhere and is largely planted in every part of this country. The standard summer cabbage-heading variety for either the home or market gardener. Sure header and reliable. Wholly unsuited for wintering over or growing indoors. More like Blonde Block Head than any other sort. Iceberg, Giant Glacier, and New York are other closely related varieties.

Synonyms.—Maule's Hanson, Dreer's Hanson, Bruce's Nonpareil, Simon's Nonpareil, Nonpareil, Los Angeles Market, Montreal Market, Hamilton Market, Evans' Hamilton Market, Toronto Market, Toronto Gem, Mastodon, Excelsior, Gardener's Friend, Gardener's Favorite.

History.—Apparently introduced by Henry A. Dreer about thirty years ago.

Illustrations.—A mature plant, a longitudinal section, a young plant, and a leaf of the variety are shown on Plates I, XX, XXII, and XXVI, respectively.

HARBINGER.

Listed by one seedsman. Seeds tested: Livingston, 1903.

Comparison.—New, and so far used in this country for experimental planting only. The trials at Washington have not yet been sufficient to determine its usefulness and value nor to make it possible to say which one of our varieties it most closely resembles. It is evidently a distinct sort, similar to Tennis Ball Black-Seeded, Reichner, and Briggs' Forcing and Garden, but at Washington not nearly so reliable for outdoors as these varieties. Its seeds are whitish.

History.—First introduced into this country by George A. Weaver & Co. in 1900, but not catalogued by them in any other year.

HARDY GREEN HAMMERSMITH.

Listed by four seedsmen. Seeds tested: Thorburn, 1899–1900; Weeber & Don, 1901–1903.

Description.—A butter variety, imperfectly cabbage-heading, small-medium in size, late, shooting to seed at an intermediate season. Plant compact, generally forming no real head, but if well grown, making an indistinctly defined head of somewhat elongated shape and fairly well blanched and firm, its leaves imperfectly overlapping one another and their borders somewhat twisted backward. Leaves broad in shape, much blistered, crumpled, and twisted, very thick and stiff, entire at margins, flat or slightly blistered at borders. Color, medium green, of a grayish, very dull, unattractive shade; never spotted nor brownish in any part. Quality poor; slightly buttery, but coarse and almost wholly lacking in delicacy and sweetness. Seeds whitish.

Comparison.—Very little grown and of little value except for its hardiness to cold. Long known as one of the best sorts to winter over outdoors, for which purpose only it is recommended. One of the poorest of all varieties in quality, and although not quick to shoot to seed in hot weather it never grows well in summer, and has always been a failure at Washington, even when planted very early. Succeeds better in the autumn than in the spring, but rarely makes really good heads under any circumstances. Very distinct, but if a comparison is made it might be said to be more like Tennis Ball Black-Seeded than any other lettuce.

Synonyms.—Hammersmith, Hardy Green Winter.

History.—One of the oldest of all varieties. Known in this country for at least one hundred years.

HARTFORD BRONZED HEAD.

Listed by one seedsman. Seeds tested: Cadwell & Jones, 1899–1902.

Description.—A decidedly butter variety, strictly cabbage-heading, small-medium in size, intermediate in season, slow to shoot to seed. Plant very compact and forming a slightly elongated, somewhat pointed, indefinitely defined, very firm, well-blanched head, with leaves very closely overlapping one another, except their uppermost borders, which are characteristically turned and twisted backward. This habit of growth, as well as the close way in which the outer leaves are drawn toward the plant, almost completely obscures the head; no distinct separation between head proper and outer leaves of plant. Leaves very broad, fairly blistered, crumpled and twisted, very thick and stiff, entire at margins, flat at borders. Color a dark, almost solid brown during summer weather, but bright green in less-exposed parts during spring or cloudy weather; stem of plant and base of midribs plainly colored; inner head leaves sparingly spotted and often rusty colored at their base. Quality excellent; buttery, exceedingly tender and sweet. Seeds blackish.

Comparison.—One of the lesser-grown varieties. More widely known under the name of Crisp as Ice. Too dark brown for a good market gardener's sort, but one of the best for home use, as it is perhaps not surpassed by any except Half Century in delicate flavor and tender quality. Good for summer, sure header, and reliable, but very late in season for so small a variety. More like Shotwell's Brown Head than any other, and so much like it as often considered to be the same; in fact, that type has frequently been sold for Crisp as Ice. After this variety it most resembles Trout.

Synonyms.—Bronzed Head, Crisp as Ice.

Confusing Names.—Batavian Brown Head, Shotwell's Brown Head, Brown Curled, Bronzed Red, Bronzed Curled, all different types from Hartford Bronzed Head.

History.—Named and introduced in 1888 by Cadwell & Jones, who state that the variety originated with the market gardeners of Hartford, Conn.

Illustrations.—A longitudinal section is shown on Plate XIX. The crumpled habit of the leaf is similar to that of Tennis Ball Black-Seeded, on Plate XXIII.

HERO.

Listed by one seedsman. Seeds tested: Vick, 1899–1901, 1903.

Description.—A butter variety, naturally cabbage-heading when at its best, but bunching under ordinary conditions, large-medium in size, very late in season, slow to shoot to seed. Plant loose, very spreading, and forming when well grown a globular, well-defined, very soft, fairly blanched head, with leaves very flatly but loosely overlapping one another, and with open spaces between them, though under ordinary conditions forming a very open cluster, with leaves spreading flatly over the ground and never growing close enough for blanching to any extent. Leaves spatulate, smooth, very little blistered, crumpled and twisted, somewhat thin, obscurely crenate to entire at margins, broadly undulate at borders. Color a peculiar light brown, no more colored at border than in other parts. Very different in color from any other variety. Quality poor; hard in texture, decidedly lacking in sweetness and flavor. Seeds blackish.

Comparison.—Scarce and rarely planted. Unreliable and too loose in habit and requiring too much skill and care for growing well to be recommended as a useful variety. Wholly unfit for market gardening, but attractive to some amateur gardeners because of its peculiarly brilliant color and very showy heads when well grown. Very distinct and hardly comparable with any other sort, except, on account of its color, sometimes associated with Eureka.

Synonym.—Vick's Hero.

History.—Named and introduced in 1898 by James Vick's Sons, who state that the seed originally came from Germany.

DESCRIPTION OF VARIETIES.

HOTHOUSE.

Listed by thirteen seedsmen. Seeds tested: Rennie & Pino, 1903.

Comparison.—Well known and extensively used in the East to grow under glass, for which purpose it is probably planted in New England more than any other variety, though it is not one of the more largely grown lettuces of the United States. A favorite with large commercial growers and superseding the smaller Tennis Ball White-Seeded variety, which for years has been the only sort used in New England for forcing. It is strictly a market gardener's forcing variety and is wholly unsuited for amateurs or for outdoor planting. When grown under glass Hothouse is decidedly larger, a little later to mature, and duller green in color than Tennis Ball White-Seeded, but outdoors the description given of the latter variety applies also to this one. The only certain distinction between the two when grown outdoors is in the color of the plants.

Synonyms.—Elliott's Hothouse, Rawson's Hothouse, Johnson & Stokes's Hothouse, Rennie & Pino's Hothouse, Hotbed, Glasshouse, Thorburn's Glasshouse, Boston Glasshouse, Noll's Boston Glasshouse, Boston Forcing Tennis Ball White-Seeded, Boston Forcing, Hittinger's Belmont, Hittinger's Forcing, Superb.

History.—Introduced about thirteen years ago. W. W. Rawson & Co. listed it in 1891 as Rawson's Hothouse.

Illustrations.—The general type of the plant is shown by California Cream Butter, on Plate VIII, the solidity of the heads by Mette's Forcing, on Plate XVIII, and the leaf, except for being less blistered, by Tennis Ball Black-Seeded, on Plate XXIII.

HUBBARD'S MARKET.

Listed by twenty-six seedsmen. Seeds tested: Ferry, 1900, 1901; Harvey, 1899; Landreth, 1899; Thorburn, 1899–1901, 1903.

Description.—A decidedly butter variety, strictly cabbage-heading, large-medium in size, early-intermediate in season, and shooting to seed at an intermediate date. Plant compact and forming a globular, very firm, fairly defined, well-blanched head, with leaves very closely overlapping one another, but more inclined to meet at their margins than to fold over past the center of the head. Leaves broad in shape, fairly blistered, crumpled, twisted, thick and stiff, entire at margins, flat at borders. Color medium green, never spotted nor brownish in any part. Quality excellent; sweet and very buttery in flavor, soft in texture. Seeds whitish.

Comparison.—One of the popular varieties of the United States, though not one of the ten most largely grown sorts. Well known in the eastern markets, but largely grown and succeeding well in all parts of the country, including the extreme South. An all-round variety, good for forcing, wintering over outdoors, and early spring, late fall, or summer growing, for all of which it is largely used. One of the best either for the private or market gardener. More like White Summer Cabbage than any other, in fact, as sometimes sold, it seems identical with that sort. Very similar to Tennis Ball Black-Seeded, differing from it principally in being a little darker green, smoother, and thicker leaved, and with head leaves not reaching over the center so completely.

History.—Named and introduced about 1875 by Chase Brothers, nurserymen, who were handling seeds at that time. It is said to have originated with a Mr. Hubbard, of Chautauqua County, N. Y.

Synonyms.—Hubbard's Forcing, Early Cabbage, Early White Cabbage, Early White Butter, Wood's Cabbage, Simon's Early White Cabbage, Early Market, Eichling's Early Market, French Market, Steckler's French Market, Dickmann's St. Louis Market, Memphis, Schindler's Early Market, Early Challenge, Gold Nugget.

Illustrations.—A mature plant of the variety is shown on Plate X. The solidity of the heads is shown by Matador on Plate XX, and the leaves are between those of Tennis Ball Black-Seeded and Deacon, both on Plate XXIII.

ICEBERG.

Listed by seventy-four seedsmen. Seeds tested: Beckert, 1900; Burpee, 1899–1903; Darch & Hunter, 1900; Livingston, 1901; Thorburn, 1903.

Description.—A decidedly crisp variety, strictly cabbage-heading, large, late, slow to shoot to seed. Plant spreading, but not loose in habit, and forming a globular, well-defined, sometimes very exposed or bare, extremely hard, well-blanched head, with leaves very completely and tightly overlapping one another. Leaves unusually broad in shape, fairly blistered, crumpled, and twisted, very thick, stiff, coarse in appearance, with heavy veins and a large protruding midrib; margins serrate; borders finely frilled. Color light green, excepting faint brown along extreme border and occasionally barely tinged in other parts, never spotted, and inner head leaves and stem of plant never colored. Quality good; exceedingly crisp and firm in texture, very sweet but not buttery in flavor. Seeds large, whitish.

Comparison.—Well known and largely planted in all parts of the United States, though not one of the ten most largely grown sorts. A standard summer cabbage-heading lettuce of the very best crisp quality, sure header, and very reliable. Suitable either for the market or private gardener, especially the latter. This type of lettuce is generally considered unsuited for forcing, but some have tried it in a small way in greenhouses and reported it a success. Very similar to, and possibly identical with, Marblehead Mammoth. Except that it is smaller and different in color, very much like Hanson and New York.

Synonyms.—Burpee's Iceberg, Curled India, Large India, Weaver's Market Gardener's.

History.—Named and introduced into this country in 1894 by W. Atlee Burpee & Co., who state that the variety is of foreign origin.

Illustrations.—Same as for Hanson.

ITALIAN ICE.

Listed by one seedsman. Seeds tested: Koerner, 1900, 1901, 1903.

Description.—The seeds of this variety as sold in the United States for the past five years have always been very poor and weak. Its germination at Washington has been uniformly unsatisfactory and no good tests of it have been obtained. For this reason it is impossible at this time to furnish a description or to state its identity. It is plainly distinct from any other variety, and the description of Hanson probably will apply very nearly to it except only that the margins of Italian Ice are obscurely crenate and its borders plainly undulate. Its seeds are whitish.

History.—Listed by W. Atlee Burpee & Co. in 1897, but never afterwards.

Illustrations.—A mature plant of the variety is shown on Plate XII.

LACINIATED BEAUREGARD.

Listed by one seedsman. Seeds tested: Salzer, 1901–1903.

Description.—The correct type of this variety as known in Europe is a very loose-bunching, deeply cut-leaved lettuce, but the sample received for trial in 1900 was Deacon, and those of the other years were Tennis Ball Black-Seeded, both of which are as different from the type as it is possible for a lettuce to be.

Comparison.—Probably suitable only for garnishing or ornament, and useful in the same way as Green-Fringed and Boston Curled.

History.—Listed by W. Atlee Burpee & Co. in 1884 and James J. H. Gregory in 1886, and figured in the former seedsman's catalogue of the year mentioned.

LANCASTER.

Listed by one seedsman. Seeds tested: Burpee, 1899–1903.

Description.—A medium butter variety, strictly bunching, medium in size, early intermediate in season, extremely slow to shoot to seed. Plant growing very close to the ground and consisting of a very well-rounded, symmetrical, remarkably compact, somewhat firm, well-blanched cluster of leaves, never opened nor spread out at the center, and only slightly more dense in the middle than in other parts. Leaves very much twisted together in the head, and general form broad, but also divided, or at least deeply lobed, the separations terminating at the base and central part consisting of one large lobe comprising the larger part of leaf, while the lobes themselves are so excessively developed as to make the leaf appear like several growing together. Leaves entirely smooth, thick, stiff, entire at margins, flat at borders, and generally with distinct glands near the base of the outer part of the midribs, one on each side. Color very light green, never spotted nor brownish in any part. Quality fair to poor; hard in texture and somewhat lacking in flavor, sweetness, and delicacy. Seeds whitish.

Comparison.—Scarce and rarely planted. The real usefulness and value of this novel variety seem to be little known. Under canvas it did better at Washington than any other sort, but outdoors the Baltimore Oak-Leaved has always grown larger and proved to be decidedly the best of the lobed-leaved varieties. Attractive because of its beautiful light-green color and fine form. More like Baltimore Oak-Leaved than any other variety. Next to this most like Oak-Leaved. Outside of these two sorts, wholly different from other varieties.

History.—Named and first introduced in 1898, by W. Atlee Burpee & Co., who state that the seed was received from Mrs. Mary E. Ringaman, Stonycreek Mills, Pa., in 1894.

Illustrations.—The variety is illustrated on Plates XV, XIX, and XXIV.

LARGE YELLOW MARKET.

Listed by two seedsmen. Seeds tested: Buist, 1900–1902; Godden, 1902.

Description.—A decidedly butter variety, strictly cabbage-heading, very large, late, slow to shoot to seed. Plant very spreading, loose in habit, and forming a globular, well-defined, soft, or slightly firm, well-blanched head, with leaves flatly but loosely overlapping one another. Leaves very broad in shape, much blistered and crumpled, little twisted, somewhat thin, almost limp, entire at margins, flat or partly blistered at borders. Color light green, never spotted nor brownish in any part. Quality excellent; mild, delicate, sweet, buttery flavor, soft texture. Seeds whitish.

Comparison.—Scarce and little planted. Probably the best of the very large, light green cabbage-heading varieties, and especially attractive to amateurs who desire an immense showy lettuce of this kind. Good for either private or market gardeners. Wholly unsuited for forcing. Very similar to and possibly identical with Paris Sugar and Burpee's Butter Head. Also resembles Thick Head Yellow and Mammoth Black-Seeded Butter.

History.—A foreign sort first listed by American seedsmen about fourteen years ago and more largely catalogued at that time than at present.

Illustrations.—The variety is not well shown in any of the following illustrations. That of California Cream Butter, on Plate VIII, perhaps represents the type as well as any, though the variety is much looser in habit, or approaches that of Red Besson, on Plate XIII. The solidity of the heads resembles Matador, on Plate XX. The leaf is similar to Tennis Ball Black-Seeded, on Plate XXIII.

LEE'S MARKET FORCING.

Listed by one seedsman. Seeds tested: Lee, 1903.

Description.—A decidedly butter variety, strictly cabbage-heading, small, early, and shooting to seed quickly in hot weather. Plant compact and forming a slightly heart-shaped or globular, well-defined, firm, well-blanched head, with leaves closely overlapping one another except their borders turned slightly backward. Leaves broad in shape, blistered, crumpled, thick, and stiff, entire or rarely obscurely crenate at margins, flat or slightly undulate at borders. Color medium green, never spotted nor brownish in any part. Quality good; sweet, buttery in flavor, soft in texture. Seeds whitish.

Comparison.—Scarce and little known or planted, but highly recommended for trial to market gardeners. Its usefulness and value seem to be the same as Golden Queen and it is more like that variety in appearance than any other. Also resembles Emperor Forcing and German Early Head.

History.—Named and first listed by Lee Pioneer Seed Company.

Illustrations.—The variety is not well shown by any of the following illustrations. Hubbard's Market, on Plate X, and White Forcing, on Plate VII, represent the type as well as any.

LIMAGNE COS.

Listed by one seedsman. Seeds tested: Maule, 1901–1903.

Description.—New and little known or planted. Same general character and usefulness as Paris White Cos. Further trials are necessary before the differences between the two can be fully determined. The variety is said to be a great favorite in the Paris markets.

History.—Introduced into this country by William Henry Maule in 1901.

Illustrations.—Same as for Paris White Cos.

MALTA.

Listed by twelve seedsmen. Seeds tested: Comstock, Ferre & Co., 1901; Simmers, 1900.

Description.—A decidedly crisp variety, cabbage-heading, very late, very large, shooting to seed at an intermediate date. Plant loose but not spreading in habit, very upright and tree-like in growth when young. Head decidedly oval in shape, fairly defined, well blanched, its leaves regularly overlapping one another, but with loose spaces between them, and head therefore soft, though the leaves composing it are very stiff and thick. Outer leaves of plant many and completely surrounding and much obscuring the head except at the top, which portion is more or less exposed. Leaves short spatulate in shape, slightly but very coarsely blistered and crumpled, fairly twisted, very coarse in appearance, with prominent, heavy veins, and a large, protruding midrib; margins serrate to obscurely crenate; borders coarsely frilled to coarsely undulate. Color very light green, never spotted nor brownish in any part. Quality poor; decidedly coarse and hard in texture, but of a firmness, and slightly sweet flavor, which is much liked by some. Seeds whitish.

Comparison.—Well known but little planted. Value very limited, its chief recommendation being immense size. Giant Glacier, Hanson, or New York are, however, generally preferable for a lettuce of this kind, and both private and market gardeners are advised to test this variety in their gardens before planting it very largely. The habit is decidedly too loose and the head too soft to be generally valuable. Habit of growth very similar to Tyrolese. Color most like Hanson.

Synonyms.—Drum Head, Ice Drum Head.

History.—A foreign sort. Known in this country for at least forty-four years.

Illustration.—A mature plant of the variety is shown on Plate XII.

MAMMOTH BLACK-SEEDED BUTTER.

Listed by thirty-three seedsmen. Seeds tested: Burpee, 1900–1903; Ferry, 1900, 1901; Henderson, 1901.

Description.—A decidedly butter variety, strictly cabbage-heading, large, intermediate in season, late-intermediate in time of shooting to seed. Plant spreading and forming a slightly oval, firm, or somewhat soft, well-defined, well-blanched head, with leaves very closely overlapping one another. Stem of plant very long, and head therefore held high above ground, thereby making the oval shape and bare or exposed appearance of the latter very pronounced. Leaves broad, much blistered and crumpled, little twisted, thin, almost loose and limp; entire at margins, flat or partly blistered at borders. Color light green, never spotted nor brownish in any part. Quality excellent; delicate, sweet, buttery in flavor, soft in texture, but leaf thin and lacking substance. Seeds blackish.

Comparison.—One of the ten most largely grown varieties of the United States. Planted largely in the East and North, especially by New York City market gardeners, who recommend it as one of the best for fall sowing. Sure header and reliable. Suitable for private as well as market gardeners. Stands summer well, but not suited for forcing. More like Tennis Ball Black-Seeded than any other variety.

Synonyms.—All Right Spring and Autumn, All Right Spring and Summer, Michell's All Right Spring and Autumn, Michell's All Right Spring and Summer, California All Head, Mammoth Large Yellow Butter, Vaughan's Mammoth Cabbage Head.

Confusing names.—Black-Seeded Butter, a different type from Mammoth Black-Seeded Butter.

History.—Apparently named and introduced by J. M. Thorburn & Co., about fourteen years ago.

Illustrations.—The general character of the variety is shown by California Cream Butter, on Plate VIII, though the type is much looser than in that figure, or somewhat approaching that of Red Besson, on Plate XIII. The solidity of the heads is illustrated by Matador, on Plate XX, and the character of the leaf by Tennis Ball Black-Seeded, on Plate XXIII.

MARBLEHEAD MAMMOTH.

Listed by nine seedsmen. Seeds tested: Livingston, 1900, 1901; Schlegel & Fottler, 1901; Gregory, 1899, 1900; Hastings, 1901.

Comparison.—One of the lesser grown varieties of the United States. Usefulness and value same as Iceberg and possibly identical with it. Further trials are necessary, however, before this can be definitely determined. The differences, if there be any, are very slight and unimportant.

Synonyms.—Shumway's Mammoth, Tender Leaf.

History.—Named and first introduced in 1886 by James J. H. Gregory & Son, who state that the variety originally came from Illinois.

Illustrations.—Same as for Hanson.

MATADOR.

Listed by one seedsman. Seeds tested: Henderson, 1903.

Description.—A decidedly butter variety, strictly cabbage-heading, medium in size, early, shooting to seed at an intermediate date. Plant compact and forming a globular, very well-defined, firm, well-blanched head, with leaves very closely overlapping one another. Leaves cup-shaped when young, very broad when full size, fairly blistered and crumpled, little twisted, somewhat thin; entire at margins, flat or partly blistered at borders. Color a beautiful light-brown and bright-green distributed in large blotches over the plant, apparently not spotted, but in sunny weather a few faint spots are evident on close examination; stem of plant, base of midribs, and inner heart leaves wholly green. Quality good; sweet, very buttery in flavor, soft in texture. Seeds whitish.

Comparison.—Very little known or planted. A most excellent variety and highly recommended to both market and private gardeners as one of the best of the sure heading, reliable, early, cabbage-heading butter sorts for fall or early spring planting. No reports of its use for forcing have yet come to our notice, but judging from our trials it is apparently an admirable variety for that purpose. In some places it may not answer as a market gardeners' variety because of its brown color. Not suited for summer growing. Usefulness and value much the same as Victoria Red-Edged Cabbage and perhaps as much like that variety as any other. In respect to color alone it is most like Brown Head.

Synonym.—First Crop.

History.—Named and first introduced into this country by Peter Henderson & Co., in 1903.

Illustrations.—A longitudinal section of the variety is shown on Plate XX. The habit of the plant is illustrated by California Cream Butter, on Plate VIII, and the character of the leaves by Tennis Ball Black-Seeded, on Plate XXIII.

MAXIMUM.

Listed by eleven seedsmen. Seeds tested: Thorburn, 1899–1901; Vaughan, 1900–1901.

Description.—A decidedly butter variety, strictly cabbage-heading, very large, late, slow to shoot to seed. Young plant spreading, very regular in habit, its leaves straight and extending flatly over the ground. Mature plant very loose, spreading, and occupying much space. Head globular or oval under some conditions, soft to somewhat firm, very well blanched, its leaves very flatly but loosely overlapping one another, while the outer leaves of plant are well separated from the head proper, thereby leaving the latter quite bare or exposed. Leaves broad in shape, fairly smooth, slightly blistered, crumpled and twisted, and on account of their great size and weight, outer leaves of plant often falling loosely away from the head proper and appearing loose and limp, though really thick and fairly stiff; margins entire and fringed with hair-like bristles; borders flat. Color dull dark green, freely spotted with dark brown, tinged faintly in places with medium brown, especially along the border, but never colored in distinct or sharp blotches, and inner head leaves and stem of plant wholly green. Quality good; fairly sweet, very buttery in flavor, and with thick, soft leaves of much substance. Seeds blackish, slightly more brownish than most blackish-seeded sorts and sometimes described as brown.

Comparison.—New and as yet not extensively planted, but rapidly coming into favor as a reliable summer variety and excellent also for spring or autumn. Not suited for forcing. Claimed by introducer to make a larger and more showy head than any other butter variety. Its dull dark color is one of its objectionable features in some markets. More like Sutton's Giant than any other variety. Next to this most like California Cream Butter. In color and first early growth very much like Passion.

Synonyms.—Thorburn's Maximum, Elliott's Leviathan, Leviathan, Hastings's Superba, Superba, Matchless, Michell's Matchless, Midsummer, Tait's Midsummer, Immensity, Henderson's Immensity, Summerlead, Johnson & Stokes's Summerlead.

History.—Named and first introduced into this country in 1898 by J. M. Thorburn & Co., who state that the variety was obtained in France.

Illustrations.—Two mature plants of the variety are shown on Plate XI. The solidity of the heads is illustrated by Matador on Plate XX, the habit of the young plants by Passion on Plate XXII, and the character of the leaves by Tennis Ball Black-Seeded on Plate XXIII.

METTE'S FORCING.

Listed by one seedsman. Seeds tested: Dallwig, 1899–1903.

Description.—A decidedly butter variety, strictly cabbage-heading, small, very early, shooting to seed at once in hot weather. Plant very compact and forming a globular, very firm, well-defined, well-blanched head, with leaves closely overlapping one another except their borders very characteristically twisted and turned backward. Leaves broad, always very regular in shape, peculiarly spoon-shaped when young, fairly blistered, crumpled, thick and stiff, entire at margins, flat at borders. Color medium green, never spotted nor brownish in any part. Quality good; fairly sweet and buttery in flavor, soft in texture. Seeds whitish, small to medium in size.

Comparison.—This little known variety is highly recommended to market gardeners as an excellent forcing sort of the butter class. It may not suit those who prefer a large-sized variety, but for a lettuce of its size no variety grew better at Washington than this one. For compactness, solidity, and fine form no variety is more desirable. Not recommended to private gardeners and unsuited for summer growing. More like Emperor Forcing than any other variety. Its habit is similar to Hubbard's Market. Best distinguished from these two sorts by its peculiar twisted borders.

Synonym.—New Forcing.

History.—Apparently never catalogued in this country except by W. E. Dallwig, who has listed it for at least eleven years. The name was changed in 1902 to New Forcing, which is very unfortunate, as under such a designation it is likely to be confused with other names.

Illustrations.—The variety is illustrated on Plates XVIII and XIX.

MIDDLETOWNER.

Listed by one seedsman. Seeds tested: Weber, 1903.

Description.—A butter variety, strictly bunching, medium in size, early intermediate in season, quickly shooting to seed in hot weather. Plant very spreading and consisting of a low-growing, flattened cluster of leaves, very open and spread out at the center, never in the least heading in habit and too open in growth for blanching to any extent. Leaves spatulate in shape, fairly blistered and crumpled, never twisted, somewhat thin, serrate at margins, frilled at borders. Color very light green, never spotted nor brownish in any part. Quality decidedly poor; hard and coarse in texture, rank and wild in flavor. Seeds whitish.

Comparison.—This scarce and little planted variety is recommended by the introducer as standing more cloudy and cold weather without rot or injury than any other lettuce and succeeding during winter in hotbeds when other sorts could not be raised or offered for sale. No other reports of its value in this or other respects have come to our notice, but at Washington last autumn it was no more hardy to cold than our common butter varieties, while for outdoor use during spring, summer, and fall it was more wild in appearance, spreading in growth, required more room to grow and perhaps proved to be the least to be recommended of all varieties tested. Very distinct and not well compared with other varieties. It resembles the wild plants sometimes found in Hanson, Black-Seeded Simpson, and Early Curled Silesia, and is similar in habit to Golden Heart.

Synonym.—Norwood.

History.—Named and first introduced by C. H. W. Weber, who states it originated with market gardeners of Middletown, Ohio.

MIGNONETTE.

Listed by twenty-four seedsmen. Seeds tested: Burpee, 1899–1901; Henderson, 1901–1903; Thorburn, 1901–1903.

Description.—A fairly crisp variety, strictly cabbage-heading, small-medium in size, early-intermediate in season, slow to shoot to seed for so early a sort. Plant remarkably compact and forming a globular, extremely hard, very well-blanched head, with leaves tightly drawn, but their borders so twisted as to produce a torn effect or bursted-like head; no distinct separation between head proper and outer part of plant, the whole being nearly all head. Leaves broad in shape, excessively blistered, crumpled, and twisted, very thick and stiff, finely serrate at margins, frilled at borders. Color dull, very dark brown with dull dark green in less exposed parts, darkest brown at borders of leaves, never distinctly spotted, inner head leaves and stem of plant wholly green. Quality excellent; exceedingly tender, crisp, and sweet. Seeds very blackish, small to medium in size.

Comparison.—One of the lesser grown varieties. An excellent sort for family use, but too small and dark brown in color for a market gardener's lettuce. Probably the most delicate in flavor and tender in texture of the crisp varieties. Very reliable for spring and fall sowing, and one of the most compact and hardest heading of all lettuces. Excepting for color probably a good forcing variety, but not recommended for summer. Similar to Density, differing in size, earliness, and color, but not closely resembling any other variety. The darkest, dullest green of all lettuces. More like Hartford Bronzed Head in color than any other.

Synonym.—Delicate.

History.—Named and first introduced by Peter Henderson & Co. in 1895.

Illustrations.—A side view of the variety is shown on Plate VII. The upper view is very similar to Density, on the same plate. The solidity of the heads is illustrated by Tom Thumb on Plate XIX.

MILLY.

Listed by two seedsmen. Seeds tested: Vaughan, 1901–1903.

Comparison.—Scarce and little grown. Very similar to Victoria Red-Edged Cabbage, and possibly identical with it. Further trials are necessary before the differences, if any, can be fully determined.

History.—Apparently introduced in 1901 by J. C. Vaughan, who states that the variety was obtained from Vilmorin-Andrieux & Co., of France.

Illustrations.—The type of the plant and solidity of the heads are illustrated by California Cream Butter and Matador, respectively, the former shown on Plate VIII and the latter on Plate XX.

MORSE.

Listed by twenty seedsmen. Seeds tested: Burpee, 1899–1903; Johnson & Stokes, 1901; Maule, 1900; Vaughan, 1900–1901.

Comparison.—One of the lesser grown varieties. Sometimes called a white-seeded Black-Seeded Simpson, and excepting in color of seed the description of the varieties is the same. Morse is, however, more blistered in the leaves, finer frilled at the borders, more compact in habit, more inclined toward forming a cabbage-like head, and is a different shade of green. The two varieties sometimes can not be distinguished unless placed side by side. Their usefulness and value are almost the same, but for some soils and conditions Morse is the better variety, and is therefore recommended for trial to both amateurs and market gardeners.

Synonym.—Hammond's Earliest Forcing.

History.—Originated by Mr. Lester Morse, of Santa Ciara, Cal., from some white seeds selected in 1892 out of Black-Seeded Simpson. It was named and introduced by W. Atlee Burpee & Co. in 1895.

Illustrations.—Same as for Black-Seeded Simpson.

NANSEN.

Listed by five seedsmen. Seeds tested: Burpee, 1901–1903; Germain, 1901.

Description.—A decidedly butter variety, strictly cabbage-heading, medium in size, early and shooting to seed at an early intermediate date. Young plant with leaves so very upright and irregularly twisted as often to appear like several plants growing together. Mature plant compact and forming a globular head, with leaves closely compacted together uprightly and irregularly, or with little tendency to curve inward and fold flatly over one another, but nevertheless producing a firm, well-blanched, though somewhat indefinitely defined head. Leaves broad, at first wholly smooth, but at maturity slightly blistered and crumpled, also much twisted, fairly thick and stiff, entire at margins, flat at borders. Color, light green; never spotted nor brownish in any part. Quality excellent; mild, delicate, sweet, buttery in flavor, soft in texture. Seeds whitish.

Comparison.—New and little known or planted. An excellent, early butter cabbage-heading variety of the best quality. Suitable for forcing, early spring or fall growing, and adapted for either the private or market gardener. Not so well suited for summer growing as Deacon and Hubbard's Market. Said to stand a great deal of frost and cold. Very similar to Hubbard's Market and Reichner.

Synonyms.—Forty Day, North Pole.

History.—Introduced into this country by Germain Seed Company in 1898. It is said to be of German origin.

Illustrations.—A young plant of the variety is shown on Plate XXII. The mature plant is perhaps best illustrated by Hubbard's Market, on Plate —, though the leaves do not overlap one another so completely as in that variety.

NEW YORK.

Listed by eighty-one seedsmen. Seeds tested: Buckbee, 1899; Farquhar, 1901; Henderson, 1900, 1901; Landreth, 1901; Thorburn, 1899, 1903.

Description.—A decidedly crisp variety, strictly cabbage-heading, very large, late, extremely slow to shoot to seed. Young plant spreading, though central portion upright and immature head decidedly long. Mature plant also spreading and forming a globular or slightly oval, very hard, well-blanched, well-defined head, its leaves very flatly and tightly overlapping one another. Leaves broad in shape, fairly blistered, crumpled and twisted, thick, stiff, and coarse in appearance, with heavy veins and a large protruding midrib; margins finely serrate; borders frilled. Color dark green, never spotted nor brownish in any part. Quality good, exceedingly crisp and firm in texture, very sweet but never buttery in flavor. Seeds large, whitish.

Comparison.—One of the popular varieties of the United States, succeeding everywhere and extensively planted in all parts of the country. Being an excellent shipper it is a favorite variety with market gardeners about New York City, and especially in California. Its dull dark green color, however, does not commend it to some markets. A reliable, sure-heading, standard summer variety for either the private or market gardener, and of the best quality. Wholly unfit for forcing or wintering over. Very similar in habit to Blonde Block Head. Excepting in color much like Hanson and Iceberg, and distinguished also from these two sorts by its upright habit when young.

Synonyms.—New York Market, Henderson's New York, Bonanza, Schwill's Bonanza, Queen, Faust's Queen, Farmer Seed Company's New Ice, Sterling, Hastings's Drum Head, Wonderful, Wheeler's Wonderful, Webb's Wonderful, Neapolitan.

Confusing names.—New York Black-Seeded Butter, New York Cold Frame White Cabbage, New York Market Gardener's Private Stock, all types different from New York.

History.—Named and introduced by Peter Henderson & Co. in 1896.

Illustrations.—Same as for Hanson.

OAK-LEAVED.

Listed by twenty-one seedsmen. Seeds tested: Maule, 1899, 1900.

Comparison.—Scarce and rarely planted. Now largely replaced by the improved variety known as Baltimore Oak-Leaved, which is more compact and dense and with leaves more developed. The true type of Oak-Leaved is difficult to obtain, as the improved variety seems to be used almost exclusively in filling orders for Oak-Leaved.

History.—First listed by American seedsmen about twenty years ago and described at that time as a new lettuce.

Illustrations.—A mature plant and leaf of the variety are shown on Plates XVI and XXIV, respectively. A longitudinal section is similar to that of Lancaster on Plate XIX only more loose and open.

ONONDAGA.

Listed by five seedsmen. Seeds tested: Burpee, 1899–1903; Ebeling, 1901.

Description.—A decidedly crisp variety, strictly bunching, intermediate in size and season, slow to shoot to seed. Plant low growing, remarkably compact, and consisting of a loose, beautifully well-rounded, very symmetrical cluster of leaves, never opened nor spread out at the middle, and never in the least cabbagelike nor solid at the center, though nevertheless the inner part is well blanched. Leaves broad, short, well rounded, very regular in form, little twisted, much blistered and crumpled, somewhat thin but not limp, very finely serrate at margins, excessively frilled and much developed at borders. Color bright brown, varying to bright green in less exposed parts and center of plant, deepest colored at borders; inner heart leaves, base of midribs, and stem of plant wholly green and no part of plant distinctly spotted. Quality good; sweet in flavor, tender, and crisp in texture. Seeds whitish.

Comparison.—Popular with some market gardeners in Onondaga County, N. Y., but apparently rarely planted in other places. Claimed by introducers to be one of the best for forcing and shipping; also easily grown in greenhouses and standing a great deal of neglect in watering and ventilation. The brown color is said to give place to light green when the lettuce is grown under glass during winter. More like Prize Head than any other variety. Being brighter colored, more rounded in form, and earlier, it is more attractive outdoors than that variety, but not so useful, because smaller and less reliable.

Synonym.—Syracuse Greenhouse.

History.—First introduced into this country by F. H. Ebeling in 1888. Said to have originated in Onondaga County, N. Y.

Illustrations.—A mature plant of the variety is shown on Plate VI. A longitudinal section is similar to that of Prize Head on Plate XXI, a young plant to that of Hanson on Plate XXII, and a leaf between that of Grand Rapids on Plate XXV, and Hanson on Plate XXVI.

PARIS SUGAR.

Listed by one seedsman. Seeds tested: Dallwig, 1900–1903.

Description.—Scarce and rarely planted. Same general character and usefulness as Burpee's Butterhead and Large Yellow Market. The differences between the three are very slight. At Washington the leaves of Large Yellow Market seemed more blistered than those of the other two, but further trials are necessary before the differences between the three can be definitely stated.

History.—W. E. Dallwig, who listed this variety in 1893, claims to have first introduced it into this country. It is described as of German origin.

Illustrations.—Same as for Large Yellow Market.

PARIS WHITE COS.

Listed by eighty seedsmen. Seeds tested: Bridgeman, 1900; Burpee, 1899, 1901; Farquhar, 1901; Henderson, 1901; Moore & Simon, 1900.

Description.—A typical cos variety, stricly self-closing, extremely large in comparison with either the butter or crisp sorts—large even for this group; late in season, and slow to shoot to seed. Plant fairly compact, decidedly upright, its leaves when young growing straight and flat, but when older inner ones becoming decidedly spoon-shaped and making a well-defined, well-blanched, firm head, decidedly loaf-shaped in form, rounded at top, and with leaves closely but not tightly overlapping one another. Leaves oval to slightly spatulate in shape, outermost ones smooth at surface and flat, innermost ones sparingly blistered and more or less cup-shaped, both, however, exceedingly regular in form, and thick, stiff, and coarse, but never in the least twisted nor crumpled in any part, and always with coarse hard veins, very large, hard midribs, entire margins, and flat borders. Color very dark green, never spotted nor brownish in any part. Quality excellent; very hard in texture, but exceedingly crisp, sweet, and of a quality and decided firmness, which makes a pleasant change from the soft buttery lettuces. Seeds whitish.

Comparison.—One of the popular varieties of the United States, though not one of the ten most largely grown sorts. Varieties of this class are very largely grown in Europe, but in America these lettuces do not seem to succeed as well as the butter and crisp varieties, and are not much grown. Many consider them the best of all in quality. They are hard and coarse in texture, but are very sweet, and possess a freshness and distinct quality which is often much liked and make a pleasant change from other varieties. Those who have never grown this class of lettuce should try a few plants. It may not be possible to grow them as well as they are grown in Europe, but they are generally satisfactory whenever tried, especially this variety, which is perhaps as self-closing and certainly as good in quality as any cos variety sold in this country. It is really the only cos sort planted to any extent in this country, and is certainly the best for either the private or market gardener. It succeeds very well in summer and can be grown to an immense size. Vilmorin states that plants weighing 6 pounds have been grown. It is similar to Prince of Wales, Green Cos, and Limagne Cos.

Synonyms.—White Cos, White Self-Folding Cos, Early White Self-Folding Cos, Heat-Resisting Cos, Landreth's Heat-Resisting Cos, Celery Cos, Romaine Cos, Trianon Cos.

History.—Listed by American seedsmen for at least forty years.

Illustrations.—A longitudinal section of the variety is shown on Plate XIX and an outside leaf on Plate XXVII. The inner head leaves of the variety are similar to that of Express Cos, on Plate XXVI, and the general character of the plant is illustrated by Express Cos, on Plate XV.

PASSION.

Listed by twenty-nine seedsmen. Seeds tested: Vincent, 1901–1903.

Description.—A decidedly butter variety, strictly cabbage-heading, large, very late, slow to shoot to seed. Young plant spreading and regular in growth, with leaves very straight and extending flatly over the ground. Mature plant spreading and forming a globular, firm, well-defined, well-blanched head, with leaves closely overlapping one another. Leaves broad in shape, somewhat blistered, crumpled, and twisted, fairly stiff, very thick, entire at margins, flat at borders. Color dark green, faintly tinged at borders and somewhat blotched in other parts with dull brown, no part of plant distinctly spotted, and stem, base of midrib, and inner head leaves wholly green. Quality good; very buttery, fairly sweet, and with thick, soft leaves of much substance. Seeds blackish, generally slightly more brownish than most black-seeded sorts and sometimes described as brown.

Comparison.—Although old and well known this variety seems to be little grown except in California and the South. In the former section it is largely used by Italian gardeners, and in the latter it is a good sort for fall and winter growing. Although not quick to shoot to seed it never seems to do well in summer or when the weather is at all warm. Not recommended except for the localities named. Never a success at Washington, even when planted early in the spring. Wholly unsuited for forcing. Some seedsmen sell another strain of this variety, which is the same as this one except that the plants are somewhat duller green in color when young, and in some localities apparently not growing so large in size. The brighter colored strain seems to be the one preferred by most market gardeners. Both are similar to California Cream Butter. Next to these they are most like Maximum and hardly distinguishable from that variety when the plants are young.

Synonyms.—California Passion, San Francisco Passion, Southern Heart, Vincent's Passion.

History.—The oldest variety on the Pacific coast. First introduced there about 1870, from France, by Sevin, Vincent & Co.

Illustrations.—Same as for California Cream Butter.

PHILADELPHIA BUTTER.

Listed by forty-two seedsmen. Seeds tested: Bowen, 1901–1903; Burpee, 1899; Ferry, 1903; Thos. Griswold, 1903; Hastings, 1903; Livingston, 1903; Rice, 1902, 1903; Texas, 1901, 1903.

Comparison.—A popular variety of the United States, but not one of the ten most largely grown sorts. Extensively planted in all parts of this country. A great favorite with Philadelphia market gardeners for early spring sowing. The exact type has not yet been demonstrated by the Department trials. The description for the above samples is the same as that given for Reichner, and most of them appeared identical with that variety. A few were very slightly different in color, habits, or shape of head, though all were the same in usefulness and value. In other samples not included above the variety was plainly more globular in shape of head and more blistered and twisted in the leaf, or with a general appearance approaching Hubbard's Market.

Synonyms.—White Head and possibly Reichner.

Confusing names.—Maule's Philadelphia Butter, Philadelphia Speckled Dutch Butter, Philadelphia Dutch Butter, all different types from Philadelphia Butter.

History.—Listed by seedsmen in this country for at least twenty years.

Illustrations.—Same as for Reichner.

DESCRIPTION OF VARIETIES. 67

PRINCE OF WALES COS.

Listed by one seedsman. Seeds tested: Graham, 1903.
Comparison.—Listed in America by Canadian seedsmen only. Not sold nor grown in this country. Except for being a little later in season, somewhat larger in size and habit of growth, and proportionately broader in shape of heads, this variety is the same as Paris White Cos, and sometimes hardly distinguishable from it even in these respects. The usefulness and value of the two are probably the same. With the possible exception of Giant White Cos, unquestionably the largest of the cos varieties sold either in this country or Canada.
History.—First listed in America by Graham Bros., who state that the seed was obtained from Cooper, Taber & Co., of England, and has been grown in that country for many years.
Illustrations.—Same as for Paris White Cos.

PRIZE HEAD.

Listed by one hundred and forty-two seedsmen. Seeds tested: Farquhar, 1900, 1901; Landreth, 1899–1901; Ritter, 1899; Thorburn, 1899; Wernich, 1900.
Description.—A decidedly crisp variety, strictly bunching, large, early marketable, but intermediate in time of attaining fullest development, slow to shoot to seed. Plant spreading, low-growing, and consisting of a loose, rounded, or slightly flattened cluster of leaves, generally more or less open or spread out at the center and therefore never in the least cabbage-like nor solid, though nevertheless the inner part of plant is well blanched. Leaves short spatulate in shape, much blistered and crumpled, very little twisted, fairly rigid but not stiff, finely serrate at margins, excessively developed and much frilled at borders. Color bright brown, varying to bright green in less exposed parts and center of plant. Border of leaves no more colored than other parts, while stem of plant, base of midribs, and inner heart leaves are wholly green, and no part of plant is distinctly spotted. Quality good; sweet in flavor, very tender and crisp in texture, but leaf thin and lacking substance. Seeds large, whitish.
Comparison.—Probably planted more largely in the United States than any other variety, thirty acres of it being grown for seed in a single year by one seed grower. Grown everywhere, but most largely planted in the West. An excellent home variety and planted extensively for family use, but thin-leaved, soon wilting, not suited for shipping, and little planted by market gardeners. A very reliable summer variety. Not adapted for forcing and never used for that purpose. The seed is lighter in weight than any other of our standard varieties. More like American Gathering than any other sort; in fact, sometimes hardly distinguishable from that variety, and often used in filling orders for it. Other similar sorts are Onondaga and Tomhannock.
Synonyms.—Briggs' Prize Head, Burpee's Prize Head, Currie's Prize Head, Ferry's Early Prize Head, Wernich's Prize Head, Early Prize Head, Peer of All, Emerald, Cincinnati Market Gardener's Brown Curled, Salzer's Peer of All, Buckbee's Ice Drum Head.
History.—Apparently named and first introduced by D. M. Ferry & Co., about twenty-five years ago.
Illustrations.—Two views of mature plants are shown on Plates V and XXI. The young plant is similar to that of Hanson, on Plate XXII, and the leaf is between that of Grand Rapids and Hanson, on Plates XXV and XXVI, respectively.

RED BESSON.

Listed by one seedsman. Seeds tested: Gregory, 1899–1902; R. H. Johnson, 1903.

Description.—A decidedly butter variety, strictly cabbage-heading, large, late-intermediate in season, slow to shoot to seed. Plant extremely loose, very spreading, and forming a globular or slightly oval, fairly defined, soft, well-blanched head, with leaves flatly but very loosely overlapping one another. Leaves very broad, cup-shaped when young, excessively blistered and crumpled, fairly twisted, very thin, soft and limp, entire at margins, flat or blistered at borders. Color very brilliant brown, interspersed with bright green in depressed or less exposed parts, the two colors being in very strong contrast and showing off in a striking manner the blistered character of the leaves. Stem of plant and base of midribs pink in color, inner heart leaves spotted, but not otherwise colored; spotted on outside or exposed parts but not appearing so unless closely examined. Quality good; sweet and very buttery in flavor, soft in texture, but leaves thin and lacking substance. Seeds blackish.

Comparison.—Scarce and little planted. Peculiar as the most solid, brilliant brown-colored lettuce in cultivation, and for this reason attractive to amateurs, but of little use to market gardeners except for limited sale as a novelty. Too spreading in habit and too soft a head to be generally valuable. Wholly unsuited for forcing. It makes large, very showy heads, and possesses real merit also as a fine summer variety. More like Brown Head than any other lettuce, especially in color.

Synonyms.—Bronzed Red, Continuity.

History.—Listed by American seedsmen for at least twenty-four years.

Illustrations.—A mature plant of the variety is shown on Plate XIII, and the character of the leaf is illustrated by that of Tennis Ball Black-Seeded, on Plate XXIII.

RED WINTER COS.

Listed by one seedsman. Seeds tested: Germain, 1900–1903.

Description.—A typical cos variety, fairly self-closing, large in comparison with either the crisp or butter sorts, but only large medium for this group. Late in season, slow to shoot to seed. Plant fairly compact, peculiarly upright in growth, and forming a well-defined, long loaf-shaped, well-blanched but soft head, its leaves loosely overlapping one another, and their upper parts meeting at the margins only, or but slightly overlapping at top of head. Leaves oval to slightly spatulate in shape, slightly emarginate, very smooth and flat, never blistered, crumpled, nor twisted, but because of their limp nature often rolled back at borders or falling loosely away from the plant. Thin leaved for a cos, but thick for a crisp or butter sort; margins entire and borders flat. Color deep bright brown, the deepest color being at borders, especially with inner leaves; unexposed parts of leaf bright green, the line between exposed and unexposed parts often marked by a sharp color difference; stem of plant and midrib of all leaves to their very base plainly colored, very distinctly spotted on inner head leaves. Because so deep brown on exposed parts of plant the spots there are not evident unless closely examined. Quality good; sweet, crisp, soft in texture for a cos sort. Seeds dark brown.

Comparison.—Scarce and rarely planted. By far the deepest red-colored cos variety, and possessing the distinction also of being remarkably hardy to cold and very constant in character, probably no other cos comparing with it in these respects. Other than for these qualities the variety can not be recommended in any way. On account of its color and soft, limp leaves it would seem to be unsuited for market gardeners. Wholly unlike any other cos known in this country.

History.—Listed by American seedsmen for at least forty years but not by the Germain Fruit Company till 1898.

Illustrations.—A mature plant of the variety is shown on Plate XIV and an outside leaf on Plate XXVII.

REICHNER.

Listed by seven seedsmen. Seeds tested: Johnson & Stokes, 1899, 1901; Thorburn, 1899-1903.

Description.—A decidedly butter variety, strictly cabbage-heading, medium in size, early, shooting to seed at an early intermediate date. Young plant very upright in habit, with leaves sometimes so much twisted as to make the plant appear like several plants grown together. Mature plant very compact and forming a globular or slightly elongated, firm, well-defined, well-blanched head, with leaves closely overlapping one another except outside ones which are characteristically turned and twisted backward at their uppermost borders. Head peculiarly long and pointed when first forming, the twisted habit of the leaves most pronounced at this period of growth. Leaves broad, fairly blistered and crumpled, much twisted at their uppermost part, fairly thick but inclined to be slightly loose and limp rather than stiff; margins entire and borders flat. Color light green, never spotted nor brownish in any part. Quality good; delicate, sweet, buttery in flavor, soft in texture. Seeds whitish.

Comparison.—Under this or some other name, one of the popular lettuces of the United States, though not one of the ten most largely grown types. A favorite with Philadelphia gardeners. An exceedingly valuable sort for the market gardeners to sow in the autumn or in early spring. Excellent also for forcing in frames and one of the best for wintering over outdoors. In some places it grows so well under the aforesaid conditions that no variety compares with it for beautiful, solid heads. Rarely suited for private gardens. Wholly unsuited for summer growing. Very similar to Philadelphia Butter and Silver Ball, and possibly identical with one or both of them. Next to these varieties most like White Loaf.

Synonyms.—Reichner's Forcing, Reichner's White Butter, Reichner's Early White Butter, Florida Header, Waldorf, Henderson's Waldorf, Neapolitan Sash, Simon's Neapolitan Sash, Stringer's Early White Butter, Rochester Market, Ridge, Yellow Queen, Mongolian.

History.—Named and first listed in 1893 by Johnson & Stokes. It is said by them to have originated with the Reichners, who are described as prominent market gardeners of Philadelphia.

Illustrations.—A mature plant of the variety is shown on Plate XVI. The solidity of the head is illustrated by Mette's Forcing and Hartford Bronzed Head, on Plate XIX, and the character of the young plant by Nansen, on Plate XXII.

ST. LOUIS BLACK-SEEDED FORCING.

Listed by six seedsmen. Seeds tested: Dickmann-Dusard, 1899, 1900, 1902; plant, 1901-1903; Schisler-Corneli, 1902.

Description.—A decidedly butter variety, strictly cabbage-heading, large medium in size, early-intermediate in season, quickly shooting to seed. Plant spreading, loose, and forming a globular, fairly defined, somewhat firm, well-blanched head, with leaves loosely overlapping one another. Leaves broad in shape, blistered and crumpled, slightly twisted, fairly stiff and thick, entire at margins, flat at borders. Color medium green, of a somewhat dull grayish shade, and tinged with brown in places, no part of leaf distinctly spotted; border no more colored than other parts, and inner head leaves and stem of plant wholly green. Quality good; fairly sweet, decidedly buttery in flavor, soft in texture. Seeds very blackish.

Comparison.—One of the lesser grown varieties. Said by the introducers to be the leading variety for forcing with St. Louis market gardeners. Not yet tested in Washington in greenhouses, but for outdoors both there and in other places it seems to be unreliable and unsatisfactory. An unusually large and loose-leaved variety for forcing. Described as a very large, loose, black-seeded Boston Market, but possibly more like Emperor William, German Incomparable, and Defiance than that variety.

Synonyms.—Favorite, Saunders.
Confusing names.—St. Louis Butter, St. Louis Market, both different types from St. Louis Black-Seeded Forcing.
History.—Introduced by Plant Seed Company in 1892.

SHOTWELL'S BROWN HEAD.

Listed by five seedsmen. Seeds tested: Thorburn, 1900; Wood, Stubbs & Co., 1903.

Description.—The above samples, which refer only to the common and apparently correct type of this variety, are described as follows: A decidedly butter variety, strictly cabbage-heading, medium in size, intermediate in season, slow to shoot to seed. Plant somewhat loose and spreading, forming a globular or slightly oval, well defined, soft, or slightly firm, well blanched head, with leaves flatly but loosely overlapping one another. Leaves cup-shaped when young, broad when full size, much blistered and crumpled, fairly twisted, somewhat thin, soft, and limp, entire at margins, flat at borders. Color bright brown, interspersed with bright green in depressed or less exposed parts, stem of plant and base of midribs faintly colored, inner head leaves sparingly spotted but not otherwise colored, outside of plant also spotted but the exposed parts of leaf such a deep brown color that spots are almost same color as rest of leaf and not evident unless closely examined. Quality, good; sweet and very buttery in flavor, soft in texture, but leaves thin and lacking substance. Seeds blackish.

Comparison.—One of the lesser grown varieties and rare. On account of its dark color not suited for market gardeners nor to be recommended to amateurs when other sorts like Hartford Bronzed Head, of similar color and character, are so much better for the purpose. A good summer variety, and succeeding especially well in the autumn. Most like Hartford Bronzed Head, in fact so much like it in appearance as often to be sold for that variety or its synonyms. Some seedsmen claim the two are identical, but such is a serious mistake. Shotwell's Brown Head is similar in color to Brown Head.

Confusing names.—Batavian Brown Head, Brown Head, Bronzed Head, Hartford Bronzed Head, all different types from Shotwell's Brown Head.

History.—Apparently introduced by J. M. Thorburn & Co., who have listed it for at least nineteen years.

Illustrations.—The habit of the mature plant is not well shown by any of the following illustrations, but is perhaps best illustrated by Yellow Winter, on Plate IX, though head is longer in shape and leaves less cup-shaped. The solidity of the heads is illustrated by Hartford Bronzed Head on Plate XIX.

SHOTWELL'S BROWN HEAD (Bridgeman).

Listed by one seedsman. Seeds tested: Bridgeman, 1901–1903.

Description.—A decidedly butter variety, strictly cabbage-heading, medium in size, intermediate in season and time of shooting to seed. Young plant very regular in growth, with leaves growing very straight and extending flatly over the ground. Mature plant somewhat spreading, low growing, and forming a globular, fairly defined, firm, well blanched head, with leaves closely and flatly overlapping one another. Leaves broad in shape, fairly blistered, crumpled and twisted, thick and stiff, entire at margins, flat at borders. Color medium dull green, tinged throughout with very faint dull brown, rarely, however, becoming brownish in defined areas or blotches, freely and distinctly spotted on outside leaves, and sparingly so on inner heart leaves, border no more colored than other parts of leaf. Stem of plant and base of midribs plainly colored and inner leaves also spotted but not otherwise colored. Quality, fair; sweet, decidedly buttery in flavor, fairly tender. Seeds blackish.

Comparison.—Scarce and little planted. Too late, unreliable, dull green in color, and possessing no specially good qualities to recommend it as superior to other sorts for either private or market gardening. Wholly unfit for forcing. Though not quick to shoot to seed, it never seems to do well during summer. Succeeded best at Washington in the autumn. More like Brown Genoa than any other variety. Much larger, later, and more spreading than the brown or common type generally sold by seedsmen.

Illustration.—Same as for Brown Genoa.

SILVER BALL.

Listed by thirty-nine seedsmen. Seeds tested: Burpee, 1899–1902; Buist, 1901; Comstock-Ferre, 1903; Ferry, 1903; Dreer, 1903; Johnson & Stokes, 1903; Livingston, 1901; Moore & Simon, 1901; Michell, 1903; J. M. McCullough, 1903.

Comparison.—A popular variety of the United States, though not one of the ten most largely grown sorts. The exact type has not yet been fully demonstrated by the Department trials. Some of the samples appeared to be the same as Reichner, but more often they were not quite so even and contained plants approaching those of Deacon. Another type resembling Large Yellow Market, but not included in any of the above samples, has also been sold by seedsmen and caused further confusion.

Synonyms.—Burpee's Silver Ball, Early Silver Ball.

History.—Introduced in 1884 by W. Atlee Burpee & Co., who state that the variety originally came from France.

Illustrations.—Same as for Reichner.

SPECKLED DUTCH BUTTER.

Listed by twenty-six seedsmen. Seeds tested: Landreth, 1899–1901; Livingston, 1900; Moore & Simon, 1901.

Description.—A medium butter variety, fairly cabbage-heading, medium in size, early-intermediate in season and time of shooting to seed. Young plant with leaves fairly upright and twisted, sometimes so much so as to resemble several plants growing together. Mature plant compact, low growing, very flattened at top, and forming a solid, well blanched though indistinctly defined head, with leaves so much twisted and irregularly compacted together as to produce a torn effect or bursted-like head; no distinct separation between head proper and outer part of plant. Leaves broad in shape, crumpled and twisted, fairly thick and stiff, hard and not easily torn, obscurely crenate at margins, undulate at borders. Color medium green, freely and distinctly spotted, faintly tinged in places, especially at border, inner head leaves and stem of plant wholly green. Quality fair; hard in texture, slightly buttery in flavor, but lacking delicacy and sweetness. Seeds small, whitish.

Comparison.—One of the lesser grown varieties. Not planted to any extent except in the vicinity of Philadelphia, where it is perhaps more largely grown in early spring and in cold frames than any other lettuce. Very hardy, reliable, and an admirable sort for market gardeners, but not suited for summer growing. Distinctly a market gardener's sort, but for private gardeners other sorts of better quality are recommended. Very distinct and not well compared to other varieties. Its habit is similar to Tom Thumb, its color to Big Boston, while its usefulness and value are about the same as Golden Queen.

Synonyms.—Speckled Early Dutch Butter, Simon's Speckled Dutch Butter, Michell's Early Speckled Dutch Butter, Philadelphia Dutch Butter, Hornberger's Dutch Butter, Early Dutch Butter, Dutch Butter, Brown Speckled Dutch Butter, Stringer's Early White Butter, Virginia Solid Header.

History.—The D. Landreth Seed Company claim to have first introduced this variety in 1848 and describe it as the result of a greenhouse hybridization between the old Hammersmith and Madeira.

Illustrations.—A mature plant of the variety is shown on Plate XVIII and a leaf on Plate XXIII. A longitudinal section is similar to that of Tom Thumb, on Plate XIX, and a young plant to that of Big Boston, on Plate XXII.

SUGAR LOAF.

Listed by one seedsman. Seeds tested: Gregory, 1899–1903.

Description.—Classed as a crisp sort and cabbage-heading, though really somewhat resembling the butter varieties and often bunching in habit. Very large and late. Slow to shoot to seed. Plant spreading and consisting of a vase-shaped cluster of leaves, very regular and formal in arrangement, the middle part of which when young is much hollowed or undeveloped, but when mature, becomes filled with a firm, well-blanched, incomplete cabbage-like head, the large part of the plant, however, consisting of the outer, nonheading, looser portion. Leaves broad in shape, little blistered, crumpled and twisted, very much turned backward at borders and thereby conforming to the vase form of the plant; also thick, stiff, and coarse, their margins varying from serrate to obscurely crenate and borders from frilled to undulate. Color largely brownish green, but with some portions a full brown and less exposed parts and center of plant light green, no part of plant spotted; stem of plant, inner head leaves, and base of midribs wholly green. Quality fair; hard in texture, fairly sweet, slightly buttery in flavor. Seeds whitish.

Comparison.—Little known or planted. Used mostly in New England. Too late and unreliable, as well as too brown in color and poor in quality, to be recommended either to private or market gardeners, except only in special soils or under conditions where, upon trial, it may be found to succeed well. More like Tyrolese than any other lettuce, not only in appearance but in usefulness and value as well. The habit is similar to Malta.

Confusing names.—White Loaf, Large White Loaf, Bolgiano's White Loaf, all different from Sugar Loaf.

History.—Named and introduced in 1882, by James J. H. Gregory & Son, who state that the variety was received from a customer in Illinois in the spring of 1879.

Illustrations.—Two mature plants of the variety are shown on Plate XVII.

SUTTON'S GIANT CABBAGE.

Seeds tested: Michell, 1899–1901.

Comparison.—Same as Maximum, except that seeds are yellowish. Usefulness and value probably also the same.

History.—Sold in this country only during 1900 and 1901 by Henry F. Michell in the original sealed packets received from Sutton, of England.

Illustrations.—Same as for Maximum.

TENNIS BALL BLACK-SEEDED.

Listed by one hundred and sixteen seedsmen. Seeds tested: Burpee, 1900–1903; Burwell, 1899; Farquhar, 1901; Henderson, 1901; Landreth, 1899, 1901; Northrup-King, 1903; Rawson, 1900, 1901; Thorburn, 1899–1901.

Description.—A decidedly butter variety, strictly cabbage-heading, large-medium in size, early-intermediate in season, shooting to seed at an intermediate date. Plant compact or slightly spreading and forming a globular, firm, very well-defined, well-blanched head, with leaves very closely overlapping one another. Plant when in flower sends out many side stems instead of one large main stem. Leaves broad, excessively blistered and crumpled, little twisted, thin, almost limp and loose, entire at margins, blistered or flat at borders. Color light green, never spotted nor brownish in any part. Quality excellent; delicate, sweet, buttery in flavor, soft in texture, but leaf thin and lacking substance. Seeds blackish, rarely very black.

Comparison.—One of the four most largely grown varieties of the United States. Succeeds everywhere and at all seasons. Under this or some other name largely planted in all parts of this country, especially the East. In the vicinity of Boston, New York, Philadelphia, Baltimore, and Washington it is more largely grown by market gardeners in summer than any other variety. Except that it is too loose in habit for forcing, an all-round variety. Its adaptability for all purposes is shown by the descriptive character of its synonyms given below. No other variety has been so largely renamed. Good for spring, summer, or autumn, and stands wintering over outdoors at Washington as well as any other variety. Highly recommended to both private and market gardeners. Sure header, very reliable, hardy, excellent shipper, and good seller. Very similar to Yellow-Seeded Butter, Thick Head Yellow, and Hubbard's Market. It is distinguished from the latter by its thinner and more crumpled leaves and its lighter green color.

Synonyms.—Early Tennis Ball Black-Seeded, Arlington Tennis Ball Black-Seeded, All Heart, Dreer's All Heart, All the Year Round, Baltimore Cabbage, Black-Seeded Butter, Black-Seeded Summer, Bolgiano's Black-Seeded Summer, Griffith & Turner's Black-Seeded Summer, Bloomsdale Butter, Bloomsdale Reliable, Crosman's Improved, Dickmann's Private Stock, Market Gardener's Private Stock, Thorburn's Market Gardener's Private Stock, Eclipse, Everlasting, Everett's Everlasting, Farquhar's Long-Standing, Frankfort Head Black-Seeded, Lapp's Head, Large Butter Head, Long Island Winter, Ninety and Nine, Twentieth Century, White Peach, Sensation, Moore's Magnum Bonum, Salamander, Perfected Salamander, Market Gardener's Salamander, Satisfaction Black-Seeded, Price & Knickerbocker's Mammoth Head, New York Black-Seeded Butter, Schwill's Hard Head.

History.—A very old variety of European origin and known in this country for at least forty-eight years.

Illustrations.—A leaf of the variety is shown on Plate XXIII. The general habit of the mature plant is illustrated by California Cream Butter, on Plate VIII, and the solidity of the heads by Mette's Forcing, on Plate XIX.

TENNIS BALL WHITE-SEEDED.

Listed by ninety-seven seedsmen. Seeds tested: Buckbee, 1901; Burpee, 1901; Burwell, 1899; Farquhar, 1900; Johnson & Stokes, 1899; Landreth, 1899–1901; Rawson, 1901; Thorburn, 1899–1901, 1903.

Description.—A decidedly butter variety, strictly cabbage-heading, small-medium in size, very early in season, and shooting to seed at once in hot weather. Plant very compact and forming a globular, firm, well-defined, well-blanched head, with leaves very closely overlapping one another. Leaves broad in shape, blistered, crumpled, slightly twisted, fairly stiff and thick, entire at margins, flat or partly blistered at borders. Color dull medium green, sometimes brownish over large areas and in distinct blotches, but never distinctly spotted, and inner head leaves and stem of plant wholly green. Quality good; sweet, buttery in flavor, soft in texture. Seeds whitish.

Comparison.—A popular variety of the United States, though not one of the ten most largely grown sorts. For years almost the only variety used in the East for forcing in greenhouses. About fifteen years ago larger sorts came into favor and to-day the largest growers do not seem to plant this variety. Wholly unsuited for summer growing, not recommended as reliable for growing outdoors, and not suited for private gardeners. A splendid shipper and distinctly a market gardener's forcing variety. More like Hothouse than any other lettuce. Except for differences in size and season, very similar to Victoria Red-Edged and Milly.

Synonyms.—Arlington Tennis Ball White-Seeded, Godden's White-Seeded Forcing, Boston Market, Buckbee's Ideal, Frankfort Head White-Seeded.

History.—A very old variety of European origin and known in this county for at least forty-two years.

Illustrations.—The general habit of the variety is illustrated by California Cream Butter, on Plate VIII; the leaf by Tennis Ball Black-Seeded, on Plate XXIII, and the solidity of the heads by Matador, on Plate XX.

THICK HEAD YELLOW.

Listed by six seedsmen. Seeds tested: Burpee, 1902, 1903.

Description.—A decidedly butter variety, strictly cabbage-heading, large, late, fairly slow to shoot to seed. Plant spreading, very loose in habit, and forming a globular, well-defined, soft, or slightly firm, well-blanched head, with the leaves flatly but loosely overlapping one another. Leaves very broad in shape, excessively and very coarsely blistered and crumpled, little twisted, somewhat thin, almost limp, entire at margins, flat, partly blistered, or somewhat inclined to undulate at borders. Color light green, very glossy and rich, never spotted nor brownish in any part. Quality excellent; mild, delicate, sweet, buttery in flavor, soft in texture. Seeds whitish.

Comparison.—Scarce and little planted. Not suitable for forcing, but a good variety for outdoors, though not as reliable for this purpose as Tennis Ball Black-Seeded. Being one of the most crumpled and blistered in leaf and most glossy light green in color of all the varieties, it becomes in some respects one of the most attractive lettuces in cultivation. Recommended for trial to both private and market gardners. More like Tennis Ball Black-Seeded than any other, differing principally in larger size, softer head, looser habit, and brighter, more glossy green color.

Synonyms.—Erfurt Large Thick Head Yellow, Mammoth Erfurt Yellow.

History.—First listed by American seedmen about twelve years ago, and described at that time as a new German variety.

Illustrations.—The habit is between that of California Cream Butter, on Plate VIII, and Red Besson, on Plate XIII. The general character of the leaf is illustrated by that of Tennis Ball Black-Seeded, on Plate XXIII, and the solidity of the heads by Matador, on Plate XX.

TOMHANNOCK.

Listed by thirty-nine seedsmen. Seeds tested; Burpee, 1899–1901, 1903.

Description.—A decidedly crisp variety, strictly bunching, large, early marketable but intermediate in attaining fullest development, slow to shoot to seed. Plant very spreading and consisting of a few but very large leaves gathered into a loose cluster at the top of an enormously thick, long stem, the growth somewhat tree-like and the cluster somewhat flattened in shape, more or less open or spread out at center and never in the least cabbage-like nor dense, though the inner part is well blanched. Leaves spatulate in shape, much blistered and crumpled, very little twisted, fairly rigid but not stiff, finely serrate at margins, excessively frilled and much developed at borders. Color almost solid deep bright brown, varying to bright green in less exposed parts and center of plant, borders of leaves no more colored than other parts, stem of plant, base of midribs and inner heart leaves wholly green, and no part of plant distinctly spotted. Quality good; sweet in flavor, very tender and crisp in texture, but leaf thin and lacking substance. Seeds large, whitish.

Comparison.—Scarce and little planted. Not suited for forcing and rarely as satisfactory for outdoors as Prize Head or other varieties of similar color and character. The largest stemmed of all varieties except, perhaps, Malta, and this, together with its tree-like habit and enormous leaves, gives it a very striking appearance, but unfits it for marketing. Probably of little value to market gardeners. More like Prize Head than any other lettuce, being like it in color, but different in habit.

Synonyms.—Burpee's Tomhannock, Bronzed Tomhannock.

History.—Introduced in 1886 by W. Atlee Burpee & Co., and said by them to have originated in northern New York.

Illustrations.—A young plant of the variety is shown on Plate XXII. The habit of the mature plant is illustrated by that of Prize Head on Plate V, and the character of the leaf is about between that of Grand Rapids and Hanson, on Plates XXV and XXVI, respectively.

TOM THUMB.

Listed by nine seedsmen. Seeds tested; Burpee, 1899–1903; Farquhar, 1900–1903.

Description.—Neither a strictly crisp nor butter sort, but perhaps most properly placed with the latter; decidedly cabbage-heading, small, medium in size, early, and shooting to seed unusually slowly for an early variety. Plant extremely compact, low growing, flattened on top and forming a hard, well-blanched but indefinitely defined head, with leaves so twisted at their borders and irregularly compacted together as to produce a torn effect or burst like head; no distinct separation between head proper and outer part of plant, the whole being nearly all head. Leaves broad in shape, very much blistered, crumpled, and twisted, very thick and stiff, obscurely crenate at margins, slightly undulate at borders. Color very dark green, never spotted nor brownish in any part. Quality good; fairly sweet, hard in texture, between the butter and crisp varieties in flavor and firmness. Seeds blackish, small to medium in size.

Comparison.—One of the lesser grown varieties and scarce. Said to be a favorite in England for hotbed and pot culture. Recommended by seedsmen in this country as a good greenhouse sort. A few instances of its successful use for this purpose have come to notice, but for most gardeners it is decidedly too small, although reliable, easily grown, and exceedingly compact. Not adapted for general summer growing, but may be planted outdoors successfully in autumn or early spring. Suited for both the amateur and market gardener. Very distinct and not well compared to other varieties. Its color is even darker green than New York. The habit is somewhat similar to Speckled Dutch Butter and Mignonette, and its usefulness and value about the same as Golden Queen:

Synonyms.—Wheeler's Tom Thumb, Landreth's Forcing.

History.—First introduced in England by H. Wheeler & Son, and first listed by American seedsmen a few years later as Wheeler's Tom Thumb.

Illustrations.—A mature plant of the variety is shown on Plate XVI, and a longitudinal section on Plate XIX. The general character of the leaf is the same as that shown of Speckled Dutch Butter, on Plate XXIII.

TROUT.

Listed by one seedsman. Seeds tested: Farquhar, 1899–1903.

Description.—A decidedly butter variety, strictly cabbage-heading, small medium in size, late, slow to shoot to seed. Plant compact and forming a globular or slightly pointed, somewhat imperfectly defined, firm, well-blanched head and except for being turned back at their extreme top the leaves of the head closely overlap one another. Leaves broad, fairly blistered, crumpled, twisted, thick and stiff, entire at margins, flat at borders. Outside of plant completely spotted with dark brown, but spots so numerous, minute, and blended together as really to make the plant solid dark brown in color. Inside head leaves very distinctly spotted, the spots here being large and well separated. Stem of plant and base of midribs plainly colored. Quality good; sweet, buttery, soft in texture. Seeds whitish.

Comparison.—Scarce and little known or planted. So much smaller, later, and less reliable than other sorts of like habit and character that it can not be recommended except to amateurs, who will find it attractive because of its beautifully spotted inner heart leaves. For serving on the table it makes a novel and attractive dish, no other variety comparing with it for distinctly spotted inner heart leaves. Golden Spotted is more distinctly and brightly spotted on the outside leaves, but less so on the inner leaves than this one. Succeeds fairly well in Summer. The habit is quite similar to Hartford Bronzed Head and the color much like Shotwell's Brown Head.

History.—Listed by R. & J. Farquhar & Co. for at least twenty years.

Illustrations.—A longitudinal section of the plant is similar to that of Hartford Bronzed Head, on Plate XIX, except that the plant is less compact and does not make so perfect a head. The leaf is similar to that of Tennis Ball Black Seeded, on Plate XIII.

TYROLESE.

Listed by one seedsman. Seeds tested: Saul, 1903.

Description.—A decidedly crisp variety, cabbage-heading, very late, very large, slow to shoot to seed. Plant loose, spreading, central part somewhat upright, especially when young. Stem of plant very large and long. Head globular to short oval in shape, well defined, well blanched, and its leaves regularly overlapping one another but with loose spaces between them, and head therefore soft, though the leaves composing it are very thick and stiff. Leaves short spatulate in shape, sometimes as broad as long, slightly but coarsely blistered and crumpled, little twisted, very coarse in appearance, with prominent, heavy veins, and large protruding midrib; margins deeply serrate, borders frilled. Color dull green, faintly and indistinctly blotched with dull brown in places, border green or at least not distinctly brownish; inner head leaves wholly green but stem of plant and base of midribs plainly colored, no part of plant spotted. Quality fair; coarse, and hard in texture, but of a sweetness and firmness which are often much liked. Seeds large, whitish.

Comparison.—Very little known or planted. Too late, loose, and spreading in habit and head too soft to be recommended to market gardeners or as a very useful variety for amateurs. Other varieties like Hanson are decidedly preferable and more reliable. Possibly attractive to some amateurs because of the immense size to which the plants can be grown. Succeeds well in summer. More like Sugar Loaf than any other lettuce, differing principally in color and being less vase-shaped in form.

Illustrations.—A mature plant of the variety is shown on Plate II.

UNRIVALED.

Listed by six seedsmen. Seeds tested: Bruce, 1902, 1903; Plant, 1902; Thorburn, 1903.

Comparison.—Little known or planted, but rapidly coming into favor with market gardeners in places where the Big Boston variety does well. Its usefulness and value are exactly the same as that variety, but it is preferred by some gardeners because solid green in color and, except for being slightly lighter green and without the brownish tinge at the borders, it is the same as Big Boston. Its claim for recognition is based wholly on this difference. For description see Big Boston.

Synonyms.—Universal, Unsurpassed, Landreth's Unsurpassed.

History.—First introduced into America by John A. Bruce & Co. and J. A. Simmers in 1902 and first listed by seedsmen in this country a year later. Evidently the same variety listed by Vilmorin-Andrieux & Co., of France, as Sans Rivaled.

VICTORIA RED-EDGED.

Listed by thirteen seedsmen. Seeds tested: Buckbee, 1899; Graham, 1903; Simmers, 1899, 1900; Steele, Briggs & Co., 1901, 1903.

Description.—A decidedly butter variety, medium in size, early-intermediate in season, and shooting to seed at an intermediate date. Plant compact and forming a globular, firm, well-defined, well-blanched head, with leaves closely overlapping one another. Leaves broad in shape, blistered and crumpled, slightly twisted, fairly thick and stiff, entire at margins, flat or partly blistered at borders. Color medium green, tinged with brown in places, sometimes over large areas and in distinct blotches but never distinctly spotted, and inner head leaves and stalks never colored. Quality good; sweet, buttery in flavor, soft in texture. Seeds whitish.

Comparison.—Scarce in this country and very little planted. Strictly a market gardener's sort. Excellent for forcing, early spring, or late fall sowing, but not well adapted for summer. More like Milly than any other lettuce, and possibly identical with it. After this variety the most like Tennis Ball White-Seeded and California Cream Butter.

Synonyms.—There seems to be considerable misunderstanding regarding this variety. The Jerome B. Rice Seed Company and the Chesmore-Eastlake Seed Company mention it as the same as Prize Head, and in years past it was catalogued by a considerable number of seedsmen as Large Drum Head, both of which are quite different from the original type, which is the one described above.

History.—Listed by American seedsmen for at least twenty-seven years. Of foreign origin.

Illustrations.—The habit of the mature plant is illustrated by that of California Cream Butter, on Plate VIII, the solidity of the heads by that of Matador, on Plate XX, and the character of the leaf by that of Tennis Ball Black-Seeded, on Plate XXIII.

WHITE CHAVIGNE.

Listed by four seedsmen. Seeds tested: Ferry, 1903; Harmon, 1901, 1903; Tilton, 1900, 1901; Veitch, 1899.

Description.—A decidedly butter variety, strictly cabbage-heading, large, late-intermediate in season, slow to shoot to seed. Plant fairly compact and forming a globular, very firm, well-defined, well-blanched head, with leaves closely overlapping one another. Leaves broad in shape, blistered and crumpled, slightly twisted, fairly stiff, very thick, entire at margins, flat or partly blistered at borders. Color dark green, never spotted nor brownish in any part. Quality excellent; sweet, very buttery in flavor, and with soft, thick leaves of much substance. Seeds whitish.

Comparison.—Little planted in this country, but rapidly becoming known as a reliable summer variety. Claimed by some to make better heads during summer than any other lettuce. Its usefulness and value for our country have been well proved and it is highly recommended to both market gardeners and amateurs. Very hardy to cold and a good sort to winter over outdoors. Not adapted for forcing. Except for difference in color it is very similar in appearance to California Cream Butter and is a good sort to grow wherever that variety does well. Very similar also to Hubbard's Market, though larger and darker green in color.

Synonyms.—Rosette, Maule's Rosette, Farmer's Pride, Bolgiano's Farmer's Pride, White-Seeded Summer, Griffith & Turner's White-Seeded Summer, Kendel's Excelsior Head.

History.—Recently listed by American seedsmen as a new French variety, though the name has been in use by American seedsmen for at least twenty-one years. Tests of it made by experimenters about eighteen years ago report it to be similar to Deacon and Silver Ball and the type recognized at that time seems to be quite different from the one which is now being advertised by seedsmen.

Illustrations.—Same as for California Cream Butter.

WHITE FORCING.

Listed by three seedsmen. Seeds tested: Buist, 1899–1901; Bolgiano, 1899–1903.

Description.—A fairly butter variety, strictly cabbage-heading, very small, extremely early, and shooting to seed at once when grown outdoors. Plant extremely compact, and forming a heart-shaped or somewhat pointed, well-defined, firm, well-blanched head, with leaves closely overlapping one another, except that their borders are turned characteristically backward somewhat like the petals of a rose, the head thereby presenting a looser leaf growth and being somewhat obscured. Leaves broad in shape, blistered, crumpled, twisted, thick, stiff, obscurely crenate at margins, slightly undulate at borders. Color a beautiful light green, never spotted nor brownish in any part. Quality excellent; very sweet and slightly buttery in flavor, but of a crisp, firm texture and distinct quality, different from most butter sorts and somewhat approaching the crisp varieties. Seeds very small, whitish.

Comparison.—One of the lesser grown varieties. Suitable only for forcing and being the earliest, smallest, and most compact of all varieties except perhaps Emperor Forcing and Density, it would seem to be the best suited for cold frames or hotbeds, but it is decidedly too small for general greenhouse use. Wholly unfit for the amateur or for outdoor culture. More like Golden Queen than any other lettuce, differing in no important respects except size and earliness.

Synonyms.—Bolgiano's White Forcing, Perfection Early White Forcing, Buist's Perfection White Forcing.

Confusing names.—California Giant White Forcing, Giant White Forcing, Godden's White-Seeded Forcing, all different types from White Forcing.

History.—Listed by American seedsmen for at least seventeen years.

Illustrations.—A mature plant of the variety is shown on Plate VII. The solidity of the heads is illustrated by that of Matador, on Plate XX.

WHITE GIANT.

Listed by two seedsmen. Seeds tested: Ewing, 1902, 1903.

Comparison.—So far this new variety has been used in this country and Canada for experimental planting only. The trials of it at Washington have not yet been sufficient to determine its exact usefulness and value nor to say which of our varieties it most closely resembles. It is evidently a distinct sort, similar in appearance to Tennis Ball Black-Seeded, but very late in season, mammoth in size, and very spreading in habit. At Washington it has done very poorly, being a very uncertain header and unreliable, but in California it seems to grow well. Wholly unfit for forcing. Seeds blackish.

History.—Listed first in America by Wm. Ewing & Co.

WHITE LOAF.

Listed by four seedsmen. Seeds tested: F. W. Bolgiano & Co., 1899, 1900, 1902; J. Bolgiano & Son, 1903; Griffith & Turner, 1899–1903.

Comparison.—A favorite with Washington and Baltimore market gardeners, but apparently not known nor planted elsewhere. In the vicinity of these cities it is largely used for early spring sowing and is almost the only sort planted for wintering over outdoors. For the last three years stocks of this variety have been very much mixed, but if the pure strain is obtained this is a most excellent variety and is highly recommended to both amateurs and market gardeners. Usefulness and value much the same as Reichner and, except that it is large-medium in size, the description is the same as given for that variety. White Loaf is, however, a little later to mature and is slower to shoot to seed, as well as more crumpled, but less twisted, in its leaves.

Synonyms.—Large White Loaf, Bolgiano's White Loaf, Large Loaf, Loaf.
Confusing name.—Sugar Loaf, which is a very different type from White Loaf.
History.—Apparently named and first introduced by J. Bolgiano & Son about ten years ago.
Illustrations.—The general habit of the mature plant is illustrated by that of Reichner, on Plate XVI; the young plant by that of Nansen, on Plate XXII, and the solidity of the heads by that of Matador, on Plate XX.

WHITE STAR.

Listed by thirty seedsmen. Seeds tested: Ferry, 1899, 1901; Tilton, 1901.

Description.—A crisp variety, sometimes cabbage-like in growth, but generally decidedly more bunching than cabbaging; marketable at an intermediate season, but late outdoors in attaining fullest development; very large; slow to shoot to seed. Plant fairly compact for so large a sort, and consisting of a dense, well-blanched cluster of leaves, rounded to broadly V-shaped in form, its innermost heart leaves generally curving over one another and forming an incomplete concealed cabbage-like head, partly visible at the top of the plant. Leaves very broad, excessively blistered, crumpled, and twisted into large, coarse folds; also very thick and stiff and with heavy veins and large, protruding midrib; broadly but shallow crenate at margins; decidedly undulate at borders. Color very light green, never spotted nor brownish in any part. Quality poor; hard and coarse in texture, and decidedly lacking in sweetness, delicacy, and flavor. Seeds large, whitish.

Comparison.—A popular variety of the United States, though not one of the ten m os largely grown sorts. With Grand Rapids, Detroit Market Gardeners' Forcing, and Black-Seeded Simpson it forms the four varieties most largely grown under glass around Detroit. It is an excellent variety for summer, and in some outdoor trials at Washington it made the largest and most showy plants of any. In California it does not grow to a large size. A fine shipper and reliable. An excellent variety for market gardeners and highly recommended to them for trial as being possibly better than any other for certain soils and gardens. On account of its poor quality, not recommended for private gardeners. Very distinct, but perhaps more like Morse than any other lettuce.

Synonyms.—Tilton's White Star, Buckeye, Golden Beauty.
History.—Introduced by A. Tilton & Son in 1889.
Illustrations.—A longitudinal section of the variety is shown on Plate XXI. The general habit of the plant is illustrated by that of Black-Seeded Simpson, on Plate I.

WHITE SUMMER CABBAGE.

Listed by fifty-five seedsmen. Seeds tested: Bridgeman, 1900, 1901; Ferry, 1900, 1901; Henderson, 1900, 1901; Vaughan, 1901.

Comparison.—Same general character and usefulness as Hubbard's Market and almost identical with it. As received in Washington a little larger, more spreading in habit, and not quite so even in type nor as desirable as that variety. For description see Hubbard's Market.

Synonyms.—Large White Summer, White Cabbage.
History.—Known in this country for at least twenty-three years.
Illustrations.—Same as for Hubbard's Market.

YELLOW-SEEDED BUTTER.

Listed by thirty seedsmen. Seeds tested: Burpee, 1899–1901; Ferry, 1901, 1902; Henderson, 1901–1903.

Description.—A decidedly butter variety, strictly cabbage-heading, medium in size, late-intermediate in season, slow to shoot to seed. Plant compact and forming a globular, firm, very well defined, well blanched head, with leaves very closely overlapping one another. Leaves broad, much blistered and crumpled, little twisted, fairly thick, entire at margins, flat or partly blistered at borders. Color light green, never spotted nor brownish in any part. Quality good; sweet, buttery in flavor, soft in texture. Seeds yellowish.

Comparison.—A popular variety of the United States, though not one of the ten most largely grown sorts. Useful in the same way as Tennis Ball Black-Seeded, but later in season and probably not as sure heading nor reliable. More like that variety in appearance than any other. Also similar to Hubbard's Market and White Summer Cabbage.

Synonyms.—Gray-Seeded Butter, Bloomsdale Early Summer, Champion, Champion Spring and Summer, Moore's Champion Spring and Summer, Denham's Mammoth Green, Solid Header.

History.—Introduced by Peter Henderson & Co., about twenty-two years ago.

Illustrations.—Same as for Tennis Ball Black-Seeded.

YELLOW WINTER.

Listed by one seedsman. Seeds tested: Thorburn, 1900-1902.

Description.—A decidedly butter variety, strictly cabbage-heading, medium in size, early-intermediate in season, fairly slow to shoot to seed. Plant compact and forming a globular, soft to somewhat firm, well defined, well blanched head. Leaves uniformly cup-shaped and upright, especially when young, and very closely overlapping one another, but meeting at the margins only, not folding past one another over the top of head, the whole growth peculiarly regular and formal. Leaves broad in shape, fairly blistered, crumpled, thick and stiff, never twisted, entire at margins, flat or slightly blistered at borders. Color medium green, slightly tinged light brown in places, apparently not spotted but occasional spots distinguishable on close examination; stem of plant and inner head leaves wholly green. Quality fair; medium buttery and sweet in flavor, fairly tender. Seeds whitish.

Comparison.—Scarce and little planted. Recommended for growing in frames, starting early and transplanting outdoors in spring, or for late fall sowing or wintering over outdoors. Not suited for summer. A strictly market gardener's sort. Usefulness and value same as Cold Frame White Cabbage and probably more like that variety in appearance than any other.

Synonyms.—Thorburn's Yellow Winter.

History.—Introduced in 1900 by J. M. Thorburn & Co., who state that it is of European origin.

Illustrations.—A mature plant of the variety is shown on Plate IX and a leaf on Plate XXIV. The solidity of the heads is illustrated by Matador on Plate XX.

CATALOGUE OF VARIETY NAMES.

The following list embraces nearly all varieties catalogued to-day by American seedsmen. Those which are omitted embrace kinds of which the tests were unsatisfactory or the seed not obtainable. Both distinct and subsidiary sorts are included in this list, the former embracing those preferred names mentioned in the preceding list of real varieties and the latter those so-called varieties which, upon trial, have been found to be strains, synonyms, or sorts practically identical with the true varieties already described. Following each variety is given the number of seedsmen who mention that variety in their seed list for the year 1903. Where such data are omitted, the name has been regarded as equivalent to some other similar name, and the number of seedsmen who catalogue it has been counted with those of the preferred name. The seedsmen mentioned after these statements are those from whom seed was obtained, and upon whose samples the descriptions are largely based.

Advancer. (*See* p. 28.)

Alaska. (Listed by one seedsman. Seeds tested: Bailey, 1901.)
Same as Golden Curled. Named and introduced as a new variety in 1895 by Sunset Seed Company.

All Cream. (Listed by eight seedsmen. Seeds tested: May, 1899–1903; Salzer, 1899, 1900, 1903.)
Prize Head, Hanson, New York, Buttercup, and Chartier were received in response to orders for this variety. Most of the samples from Salzer have been Prize Head and those from May have generally been Hanson. Named and introduced as a novelty in 1892 by John A. Salzer.

All Heart. (Listed by two seedsmen. Seeds tested: Dreer, 1900–1902.)
Same as Tennis Ball Black-Seeded. Named and introduced as a new variety in 1900 by Henry A. Dreer. The type is quite different from that of California All Heart.

All Right Spring and Autumn. (Listed by two seedsmen. Seeds tested: Michell, 1900–1903.)
Same as Mammoth Black-Seeded Butter. Named and introduced as a new variety in 1900 by Henry F. Michell under the name of Michell's All Right Spring and Summer, but changed in 1902 to Michell's All Right Spring and Autumn. The type is quite different from that of Myer's All Right.

All Right Spring and Summer. (Seeds tested: Michell, 1900–1901.)
See All Right Spring and Autumn.

All Seasons. (*See* p. 28.)

All the Year Round. (Listed by forty-five seedsmen. Seeds tested: Gregory, 1900; Henderson, 1899, 1900, 1902.)
The type universally sold in the United States under this name is Tennis Ball Black-Seeded, but in England another type is said to be in use. The variety is of foreign origin and has been listed by American seedsmen for at least twenty-eight years.

Always Ready. (Seeds tested: Landreth, 1899.)
Same as Defiance. Named and first listed in 1894 by D. Landreth Seed Company, but not catalogued after 1899. The name seems to have wholly gone out of use.

American Gathering. (*See* p. 29.)

Arlington Tennis Ball Black-Seeded. (Listed by one seedsman. Seeds tested: Burwell, 1899.)
Same as Tennis Ball Black-Seeded. The word Arlington is attached to the common name because the variety is popular with gardeners at Arlington, Mass., but sometimes it is added to indicate also that the stock seed is grown at that place.

Arlington Tennis Ball White-Seeded. (Listed by four seedsmen. Seeds tested: Burwell, 1899; Johnson & Stokes, 1899.)
Same as Tennis Ball White-Seeded. The word Arlington is attached to the common name because the variety is popular with gardeners at Arlington, Mass., but sometimes it is added to indicate also that the stock seed is grown at that place.

Asiatic. (*See* p. 29.)

Asparagus. (*See* p. 30.)

Asparagus Lobed-Leaved. (*See* p. 30.)

Atlanta Market. (Listed by one seedsman. Seeds tested: McMillan, 1901–1903.)
As received here this variety has been very different every year, the samples of the various years being identified as Denver Market, Deacon, and New York. Named and first listed by McMillan Seed Company in 1900, but it seems that before this time it was listed as McMillan's Cabbage.

Australian White Triumph. (Listed by one seedsman. Seeds tested: Moore & Simon, 1901, 1903.)
Same as Deacon. Named and introduced in 1900 by Moore & Simon, who state the variety was received from a market gardener in Australia. The type is quite different from the Triumph catalogued by other seedsmen.

Balloon Cos. (Seeds tested: Bridgeman, 1899, 1900; Evans, 1901; R. H. Johnson, 1903.)
This variety, which is a well-known foreign sort, is not now catalogued by seedsmen of the United States. It was listed by W. Atlee Burpee & Co. in 1884. Very similar to, possibly identical with, Paris White Cos.

Baltimore Cabbage. (Listed by two seedsmen. Seeds tested: Griffith & Turner, 1899–1901.)
Same as Tennis Ball Black-Seeded. Named and introduced by Griffith & Turner in 1892. The name is well known in the vicinity of Baltimore, but is little heard of elsewhere.

Baltimore Oak-Leaved. (*See* p. 31.)

Batavian Brown Dutch. (Seeds tested: Ebeling, 1899, 1900.)
Same as Brown Dutch Black-Seeded.

Bath Cos. (*See* p. 31.)

Beckert's Brown Curled. (Seeds tested: Beckert, 1899, 1900, 1902, 1903.)
Described under Brown Curled.

Beckert's Golden Curled. (Seeds tested: Beckert, 1899, 1900, 1903.)
Described under Golden Curled.

Big Boston. (*See* p. 32.)

Big Head. (Listed by four seedsmen. Seeds tested: F. W. Bolgiano & Co., 1900, 1901; J. Bolgiano & Son, 1903; Griffith & Turner, 1899–1901; Salzer, 1900.)
Identical with Deacon as received from F. W. Bolgiano & Co. and J. Bolgiano & Son, Big Boston as received from Griffith & Turner, and Denver Market as received from John A. Salzer. The name was apparently first used by J. Bolgiano & Son and is well known in the vicinity of Baltimore and Washington, but little heard of elsewhere.

Black-Seeded Butter. (Listed by fourteen seedsmen. Seeds tested: Burpee, 1899–1901, 1903; Henderson, 1901.)
Same as Tennis Ball Black-Seeded. Listed by American seedsmen for at least twenty years. Sometimes described as larger than Tennis Ball Black-Seeded. The type is a different one from that of Mammoth Black-Seeded Butter.

Black-Seeded Simpson. (*See* p. 33.)

Black-Seeded Summer. (Listed by four seedsmen. Seeds tested: F. W. Bolgiano & Co., 1902; Griffith & Turner, 1899, 1900.)
Same as Tennis Ball Black-Seeded. Named and introduced in 1898 by Griffith & Turner. The name is well known in the vicinity of Baltimore and Washington, but is little heard of elsewhere. In the latter place it is about the only sort used for summer growing.

Blonde Beauty. (Listed by six seedsmen. Seeds tested: Vaughan, 1899–1901.)
Recognized everywhere as the same as Blonde Block Head. Introduced from France about 1890 by several American seedsmen. The type is quite different from Golden Beauty.

Blonde Block Head. (*See* p. 34.)

Bloomsdale Butter. (Listed by three seedsmen. Seeds tested: Landreth, 1899–1901.)
Same as Tennis Ball Black-Seeded. Named and introduced by D. Landreth Seed Company, who have listed the variety for at least twenty years.

Bloomsdale Early Summer. (Listed by two seedsmen. Seeds tested: Dallwig, 1901; Landreth, 1899–1901.)
Same as Yellow-Seeded Butter. Named and introduced as a new variety in 1860 by D. Landreth Seed Company, who state that it is the result of a hybridization between the French Perpignan and English Imperial. Said to be known as Creole in the vicinity of New Orleans. The type is quite different from that of Bloomsdale Butter and Bloomsdale Reliable.

Bloomsdale Reliable. (Listed by two seedsmen. Seeds tested: Landreth, 1899–1901.)
Same as Tennis Ball Black-Seeded. Named and introduced as a new variety in 1860 by D. Landreth Seed Company, who state that it is the result of a hybridization between the French Perpignan and English Imperial. The type is quite different from that of Bloomsdale Early Summer.

Bolgiano's Black-Seeded Summer. (Seeds tested: F. W. Bolgiano & Co., 1901, 1902.)
Described under Black-Seeded Summer.

Bolgiano's Big Head. (Seeds tested: F. W. Bolgiano & Co., 1900, 1901; J. Bolgiano & Son, 1903.)
Described under Big Head.

Bolgiano's Early Spring. (Seeds tested: F. W. Bolgiano & Co., 1899–1903.)
Described under Early Spring.

Bolgiano's Farmer's Pride. (Seeds tested: J. Bolgiano & Son, 1903.)
Described under Farmer's Pride. The name seems to be known only in the vicinity of Baltimore and Washington.

Bolgiano's Golden Heart. (Listed by one seedsman. Seeds tested: J. Bolgiano & Son, 1903.)
Same as Deacon, and different from that usually sold as Golden Heart.

Bolgiano's White Forcing. (Seeds tested: F. W. Bolgiano & Co., 1899–1903.)
Described under White Forcing.

Bolgiano's White Loaf. (Seeds tested: F. W. Bolgiano & Co., 1899, 1900, 1902; J. Bolgiano & Son, 1903.)
Described under White Loaf.

Bonanza. (Listed by one seedsman. Seeds tested: Schwill, 1899–1901.)
Same as New York. Named and introduced in 1900 by Otto Schwill & Co., as Schwill's Bonanza.

Bon Ton. (*See* p. 34.)

Boston Curled. (*See* p. 34.)

Boston Fine Curled. (Listed by four seedsmen. Seeds tested: Farquhar, 1899–1901.)
Same as Boston Curled.

Boston Forcing. (Listed by one seedsman. Seeds tested: Vick, 1903.)
Same as Hothouse. The type is quite different from that of Big Boston, Boston Curled, and Boston Market.

Boston Forcing Tennis Ball White-Seeded. (Listed by one seedsman. Seed tested: Farquhar, 1901–1903.)
Same as Hothouse. The type is quite different from that of Boston Market, Big Boston, and Boston Curled.

Boston Glasshouse. (Seeds tested: Noll, 1901.)
Same as Hothouse. It should not be confounded with Big Boston, Boston Market, and Boston Curled.

Boston Market. (Listed by ninety-three seedsmen. Seeds tested: Buckbee, 1901; Burpee, 1901; Henderson, 1901, 1902; Michell, 1899; Thorburn, 1899–1901.)
Accepted everywhere as the same as Tennis Ball White-Seeded. The name Boston Market has been used for twenty-five or more years because this lettuce is so largely planted by Boston market gardeners. The type is different from that of Big Boston, Large Boston Market, Boston Curled, Boston Glasshouse, Boston Hothouse, and Boston Forcing.

Briggs' Forcing and Garden. (*See* p. 35.)

Brittle Ice. (*See* p. 35.)

Bronzed Curled. (Listed by one seedsman. Seeds tested: Landreth, 1899–1902.)
Same as Chartier. Named and introduced as a new variety in 1893 by D. Landreth Seed Company. The type is quite different from that of Bronzed Head, Hartford Bronzed Head, Brown Head, Shotwell's Brown Head, Batavian Brown Head, and Bronzed Red.

Bronzed Head. (Listed by one seedsman. Seeds tested: Veitch, 1899.)
Same as Hartford Bronzed Head. The type is quite different from that of Brown Head, Shotwell's Brown Head, Batavian Brown Head, Bronzed Curled, and Brown Curled.

Bronzed Red. (Listed by one seedsman. Seeds tested: Eastman, 1899–1902.)
Same as Red Besson. Named and introduced by the above seedsman, who states that it is a chance seedling or sport. The type is quite different from that of Bronzed Curled, Brown Curled, Bronzed Head, Hartford Bronzed Head, and Shotwell's Brown Head.

Brown Chartier. (Listed by one seedsman. Seeds tested: Scott, 1899—1903.)
Same as Chartier. The word "Brown" is applied by the above seedsman to distinguish the variety from White Chartier.

Brown Curled. (Listed by two seedsmen. Seeds tested: Beckert, 1899, 1900, 1902, 1903; Comstock, Ferre & Co., 1901, 1902.)
Same as Chartier. The type is quite different from that of Bronzed Head, Brown Head, and Shotwell's Brown Head.

Brown Dutch Black-Seeded. (*See* p. 35.)

Brown Dutch White-Seeded. (*See* p. 36.)

Brown Genoa. (*See* p. 36.)

Brown Head. (*See* p. 36.)

Buckbee's Earliest Forcing. (Listed by one seedsman. Seeds tested: Buckbee, 1899—1901.)
Same as Black-Seeded Simpson. Named and introduced in 1897 by H. W. Buckbee. The variety should not be confounded with Earliest Cutting, as sold by W. E. Dallwig.

Buckbee's Ice Drum Head. (Listed by one seedsman. Seeds tested: Buckbee, 1899—1901.)
Same as Prize Head. A decidedly bunching sort; not cabbage heading, as the name would seem to indicate.

Buckbee's Ideal. (Listed by one seedsman. Seeds tested: Buckbee, 1900.)
Same as Tennis Ball White-Seeded. Named and first listed by H. W. Buckbee, in 1900.

Buckbee's Superb. (Listed by one seedsman. Seeds tested: Buckbee, 1901.)
Same as Hothouse. Apparently named and first listed by above seedsman. The type is quite different from that of Hastings' Superba.

Buckbee's Surprise. (Seeds tested: Buckbee, 1903.)
Described under Surprise.

Buckeye. (Listed by one seedsman. Seeds tested: Tilton, 1901.)
Same as White Star. Named and first listed in 1901 by A. Tilton & Son.

Burpee's Butter Head. (*See* p. 37.)

Burpee's Hard Head. (Seeds tested: Burpee, 1899—1903.)
Described under Hard Head.

Burpee's Prize Head. (Seeds tested: Farquhar, 1900, 1901.)
Described under Prize Head.

Burpee's Silver Ball. (Seeds tested: Burpee, 1899—1902.)
Described under Silver Ball.

Burpee's Tomhannock. (Seeds tested: Burpee, 1899—1901, 1903.)
Described under Tomhannock.

Buttercup. (*See* p. 37.)

CATALOGUE OF VARIETY NAMES. 85

California All Head. (Listed by one seedsman. Seeds tested: R. H. Johnson, 1901.)
Same as Mammoth Black-Seeded Butter. The type is quite different from that of California All Heart.

California All Heart. (See p. 38.)

California Cabbage. (Listed by one seedsman. Seeds tested: Shumway, 1900, 1901.)
Same as California Cream Butter in 1900 and Deacon in 1901. Named and first listed by above seedsman.

California Cream Butter. (See p. 38.)

California Giant White Forcing. (Listed by one seedsman. Seeds tested: Moore & Simon, 1900, 1903.)
Same as Big Boston. Named and introduced as a new variety in 1892 by Moore & Simon, under name of Large White Forcing, but changed by them in 1895 to California Giant White Forcing. The type is quite different from that of White Forcing and Perfection White Forcing.

Celery Cos. (Listed by fourteen seedsmen. Seeds tested: Livingston, 1899, 1900.)
Same as Paris White Cos.

Champion. (Listed by one seedsman. Seeds tested: Burwell, 1899—1901.)
Same as Yellow-Seeded Butter.

Champion Spring and Summer. (Listed by three seedsmen. Seeds tested: Johnson & Stokes, 1899—1902; Moore & Simon, 1900, 1901.)
Same as Yellow-Seeded Butter. Named and introduced as a new variety in 1891 by Johnson & Stokes. The type is quite different from that of All Right Spring and Autumn.

Chartier. (See p. 39.)

Chesterfield. (Seeds tested: Wood, 1901.)
Same as Big Boston. Named and introduced as a new variety in 1901 by T. W. Wood & Son, but not listed by them or any other seed house after that year.

Chicago Forcing. (See p. 39.)

Childs' Half Century. (Seeds tested: Childs, 1899—1903.)
Described under Half Century, on page 52.

Cincinnati Market. (Listed by three seedsmen. Seeds tested: J. C. McCullough, 1902, 1903.)
Same as Denver Market.

Cincinnati Market Gardener's Brown Curled. (Listed by one seedsman. Seeds tested: Weber, 1903.)
Same as Prize Head. The type is quite different from that of Brown Curled or Bronzed Curled.

Cold Frame White Cabbage. (See p. 40.)

Constitution. (Listed by one seedsman. Seeds tested: Great Northern Seed Company, 1901, 1903.)
Same as Black-Seeded Simpson. Named and introduced as a new variety in 1901 by the above seedsmen.

Continuity. (Listed by five seedsmen. Seeds tested: Burpee, 1901—1903; Thorburn, 1903.)
Same as Red Besson. Introduced from England as a new variety by W. Atlee Burpee & Co. in 1901.

Copper Head. (Listed by one seedsman. Seeds tested: Johnson & Stokes, 1902, 1903.)
Same as Eureka. Named and introduced as a new variety in 1902 by above seedsmen.

Cream Butter. (Listed by four seedsmen. Seeds tested: Childs, 1899—1901.)
Same as California Cream Butter.

Crisp as Ice. (Listed by six seedsmen. Seeds tested: Burpee, 1901; Livingston, 1900—1902; Maule, 1899—1901.)
Same as Hartford Bronzed Head. Named and introduced as a new variety in 1894 by Livingston Seed Company.

Crisp and Tender. (Listed by one seedsman. Seeds tested, Buckbee; 1901.)
Same as White-Seeded Simpson. Named and first listed by above seedsman.

Crosman's Golden King. (Seeds tested: Crosman, 1899, 1900.)
Described under Golden King.

Crosman's Improved. (Listed by one seedsman. Seeds tested: Crosman, 1900, 1901.)
Same as Tennis Ball Black-Seeded. Named and first listed by above seedsman.

Crumpled-Leaved. (*See* p. 40.)

Curled India. (Listed by nine seedsmen. Seeds tested: Landreth, 1899, 1900, 1901.)
Same as Iceberg. A very old name known to American seedsmen for at least forty years, but now nearly gone out of use. It is also sold as India, Large Curled India, and Large India. The name is best known in New England.

Cut and Come Again. (Listed by one seedsman. Seeds tested: Moore & Simon, 1900–1903.)
Same as Black-Seeded Simpson. Named and introduced as a new variety in 1895 by above seedsmen.

Dammann's Ice. (*See* p. 41.)

Daybreak. (Listed by one seedsman. Seeds tested: Buckbee, 1903.)
Same as Black-Seeded Simpson. Named and first listed in 1903 by H. W. Buckbee.

Dayton Market. (Listed by one seedsman. Seeds tested: Ritter, 1899.)
Same as Denver Market. Apparently first named by above seedsman, who states it is very popular with the market gardeners of Dayton, Ohio, and that it has been grown in the vicinity of that city for more than thirty-five years.

Deacon. (*See* p. 41.)

Defiance. (*See* p. 41.)

Delicate. (Listed by one seedsman. Seeds tested: Page, 1901.)
Same as Mignonette. Named and first listed in 1901 by Page Seed Company.

Denham's Mammoth Green. (Listed by one seedsman. Seeds tested: Harvey 1899, 1901, 1902.)
Same as Yellow-Seeded Butter. The name was apparently first used by above seedsman.

Density. (*See* p. 42.)

Denver Market. (*See* p. 43.)

Detroit Market Gardener's Forcing. (*See* p. 43.)

Dickmann's Early White Butter. (Seeds tested: Dickmann, 1899.)
Described under Early White Butter.

Dickmann's Private Stock. (Seeds tested: Dickmann, 1899, 1900.)
Same as Tennis Ball Black-Seeded.

Dickmann's St. Louis Market. (Seeds tested: Dickmann, 1899, 1901.)
Same as Hubbard's Market. The type is quite different from that of St. Louis Butter and St. Louis Black-Seeded Forcing.

Dreer's Hanson. (Seeds tested: Dreer, 1900, 1901.)
Described under Hanson.

Drum Head. (Listed by twenty-four seedsmen. Seeds tested: Comstock, Ferre & Co., 1901; Farquhar, 1901; Steckler, 1901.)
Same as Malta. The words Drum Head, either alone or in connection with other words, have been used in this country for at least thirty-eight years to form names of a great number of different types of lettuce. Therefore, when this name is used it is uncertain which type is referred to. Drum Head seems to have been first applied to the Malta lettuce and is to-day probably most correctly applied to that type. Malta, Deacon, California Cream Butter, and Hubbard's Market seem to be the types most sold under the name of Drum Head.

Dwarf White Heart Cos. (*See* p. 44.)

Earliest Cutting. (*See* p. 44.)

Earliest of All. (Seeds tested: Sioux Falls Seed Company, 1899, 1900.)
Same as Black-Seeded Simpson. Named and first listed by above seedsmen. The type is quite different from that of Earliest Cutting.

Early Butter. (Listed by two seedsmen. Seeds tested: Gregory, 1899–1901; Weeber and Don, 1900, 1901.)
Same as Philadelphia Butter as received from the former and Tennis Ball Black-Seeded from the latter seedsmen. A very uncertain name and likely to be taken for either of the above types or for Hubbard's Market.

Early Cabbage. (Listed by nine seedsmen. Seeds tested: McMillan, 1900, 1901.)
Same as Hubbard's Market. The use of this ambiguous name is discouraged. It is often taken to refer to a number of similar named types of wholly different character.

Early Challenge. (Listed by one seedsman. Seeds tested: May, 1899, 1900.)
Same as Hubbard's Market. Named and first listed about seven years ago by the above seedsman.

Early Curled Silesia. (*See* p. 44.)

Early Curled Simpson. (*See* p. 45.)

Early Drum Head. (Seeds tested: Schisler-Corneli, 1903.)
Same as Hubbard's Market. See Drum Head.

Early Dutch Butter. (Seeds tested: Buist, 1899, 1900.)
Same as Speckled Dutch Butter.

Early Market. (Listed by three seedsmen. Seeds tested: Eichling, 1900, 1901; May, 1899, 1900, 1903; Schindler, 1903.)
Same as Hubbard's Market.

Early Ohio. (Listed by four seedsmen. Seeds tested: Bruce, 1899, 1900; Robert Evans, 1901; Lee, 1903.)
Same as Denver Market. The Robert Evans Seed Company claims to have first introduced this variety. It was listed in this country as a new variety about sixteen years ago.

Early Prize Head. (Seeds tested: Buckbee, 1901; Burpee, 1900–1903; Ferry, 1900, 1901; Henderson, 1901.)
Same as Prize Head.

Early Silver Ball. (Seeds tested: Johnson & Stokes, 1901.)
Same as Silver Ball.

Early Spring. (Listed by two seedsmen. Seeds tested: F. W. Bolgiano, 1899–1903.)
Same as California Cream Butter. The name was probably first used by above seedsman or by J. Bolgiano & Son, and seems to be known only in the vicinity of Washington and Baltimore.

Early Tennis Ball Black-Seeded. (Seeds tested: Ferry, 1900, 1901.)
Same as Tennis Ball Black-Seeded.

Early White Butter. (Listed by four seedsmen. Seeds tested: Buist, 1899; Dusard, 1899; Michell, 1899.)
Same as Hubbard's Market.

Early White Cabbage. (Listed by fourteen seedsmen. Seeds tested: Dreer, 1901 Michell, 1899; Moore & Simon, 1900; Steckler, 1901.)
Same as Hubbard's Market as received from Henry F. Michell and Reichner as received from the other seedsmen mentioned above.

Early White Self-Folding Cos. (Seeds tested: Ferry, 1899, 1901.)
Same as Paris White Cos.

Eclipse. (Listed by one seedsman. Seeds tested: Great Northern, 1903.)
Same as Tennis Ball Black-Seeded. Named and introduced as a new variety in 1902 by Great Northern Seed Company.

Eichling's Early Market. (Seeds tested: Eichling, 1900, 1901.)
Described under Early Market.

Elliott's Leviathan. (Seeds tested: Elliott, 1901.) Described under Leviathan.

Emerald. (Listed by one seedsman. Seeds tested: Great Northern, 1900.)
Same as Prize Head. Named and introduced as a new variety in 1900 by Great Northern Seed Company.

Emperor Forcing. (*See* p. 45.)

Emperor William. (*See* p. 46.)

Engel's Forcing. (Listed by one seedsman.)
Same as Detroit Market Gardener's Forcing. A local name used by Lohrman Seed Company, of Detroit, Mich.

Erfurt Large Thick Head Yellow. (Seeds tested: Dallwig, 1899, 1900.)
Same as Thick Head Yellow.

Eureka. (*See* p. 46.)

Evans' Hamilton Market. (Seeds tested: Robert Evans, 1901.)
Same as Hanson. Described under Hamilton Market.

Everlasting. (Listed by one seedsman. Seeds tested: Everitt, 1899, 1900, 1903.)
Same as Tennis Ball Black-Seeded. Listed by above seedsman for at least eight years, but apparently never listed by other seed houses.

Excelsior. (Listed by one seedsman. Seeds tested: Ewing, 1900, 1903.)
Same as Hanson. Apparently first named and listed by above seedsman. The type is quite different from that of Kendel's Excelsior Head.

Express Cos. (*See* p. 46.)

Farmer Seed Co.'s New Ice. (Listed by one seedsman. Seeds tested: Farmer Seed Company, 1903.)
Same as New York. Named and introduced as a new variety in 1903 by Farmer Seed Company.

Farmer's Pride. (Listed by two seedsmen. Seeds tested: J. Bolgiano & Son, 1903.)
Same as White Chavigne.

Farquhar's Long-Standing. (Listed by one seedsman. Seeds tested: Farquhar, 1899–1901.)
Same as Tennis Ball Black-Seeded. Named by above seedsman, but other similar names, like Long-Standing Cabbage, listed by W. Atlee Burpee in 1886, Long-Standing-Bronze Head, listed by Johnson & Stokes in 1893, and Long-Standing White Cos, listed by Germain Seed Company in 1896, have formerly been in use, though all seem to be very different from this type.

Faust's Queen. (Seeds tested: Faust, 1899, 1900.)
Described under Queen.

Favorite. (Seeds tested: Schisler-Corneli, 1901.)
Same as St. Louis Black-Seeded Forcing. Named and introduced in 1900 by above seedsmen, but not now listed by them or any other seed house. The type is quite different from that of Rudolph's Favorite, Sutton's Favorite, Gardener's Favorite, and Florida Favorite.

Ferry's Early Prize Head. (Seeds tested: Ferry, 1900, 1901.)
Same as Prize Head.

First Crop. (Listed by one seedsman. Seeds tested: Weaver, 1903.)
Same as Matador. Named and introduced as a new variety in 1903 by the above seedsman. The type is quite different from that of First Early.

First Early. (Listed by one seedsman. Seeds tested: Great Northern Seed Company, 1900, 1901.)
Same as Black-Seeded Simpson. Named and first listed by Great Northern Seed Company. The type is quite different from that of First Crop.

Florida Header. (Listed by one seedsman. Seeds tested: Crosman, 1900, 1901; Hastings, 1901.)
Same as Reichner.

Forty Day. (Listed by one seedsman. Seeds tested: Maule, 1902, 1903.)
Same as Nansen. Named and introduced as a new variety in 1902 by William Henry Maule.

Frankfort Head Black-Seeded. (Listed by six seedsmen. Seeds tested: Brinker, 1899, 1901; Kendel, 1901.)
Same as Tennis Ball Black-Seeded. A very old name, known in this country for at least thirty-seven years.

Frankfort Head White-Seeded. (Listed by one seedsman. Seeds tested: Brinker, 1899.)
Same as Tennis Ball White-Seeded. A very old name, known in this country for at least thirty-seven years.

French Market. (Listed by one seedsman. Seeds tested: Steckler, 1900, 1901, 1903.)
Same as Hubbard's Market. Named and introduced as a new variety in 1899 by J. Steckler Seed Company and described by them as a great improvement on Hubbard or Large Green Royal.

Frotscher's New Orleans Large Passion. (Seeds tested: Steckler, 1899, 1901.)
Described under New Orleans Large Passion.

Gardener's Favorite. (Listed by two seedsmen. Seeds tested: Bruce, 1901; Simmers, 1899–1901.)
Same as Hanson. Apparently named and first listed by John A. Bruce & Co. The type is quite different from that of Florida Favorite, Sutton's Favorite, and Rudolph's Favorite.

Gardener's Friend. (Listed by one seedsman. Seeds tested: Darch & Hunter, 1903.)
Same as Hanson. Named and first listed in 1903 by Darch & Hunter.

German Butter. (Listed by one seedsman. Seeds tested: Salzer, 1899–1901, 1903.)
Same as California Cream Butter. Named and first listed in 1895 by John A. Salzer.

German Early Head. (*See* p 47.)

German Incomparable. (*See* p. 48.)

Giant Crystal Head. (Listed by twelve seedsmen. Seeds tested: Michell, 1901; Thorburn, 1901, 1903.)
Introduced into this country from Germany by American seedsmen in 1901. It is described as a cross between Hanson and Salamander and was sent out by Chris. Lorenz, of Germany, as a new lettuce, but in Department trials indistinguishable from Iceberg even when grown by the side of it.

Giant Glacier. (*See* p. 48.)

Giant Golden Heart. (Listed by three seedsmen. Seeds tested: Breck, 1903.)
The samples tested were indistinguishable from Iceberg or Giant Crystal Head, though the variety is described by Beckert and Weaver as dark green in color. The above seedsman, who first listed it in this country in 1903, describes it as a sport from Giant Crystal Head and to closely resemble it.

Giant White Cos. (*See* p. 48.)

Giant White Forcing. (Listed by one seedsman. Seeds tested: Tait, 1903.)
Same as Big Boston. Said by above seedsman to be an improvement on Big Boston. The type is quite different from that of White Forcing, Bolgiano's White Forcing, and Perfection White Forcing.

Glasshouse. (Listed by three seedsmen. Seeds tested: Thorburn, 1900–1903.)
Same as Hothouse. Named and first listed by above seedsman as Thorburn's Glasshouse.

Godden's White-Seeded Forcing. (Listed by one seedsman. Seeds tested: Godden, 1901, 1902.)
Same as Tennis Ball White-Seeded. The name is evidently used only by above seedsman. The type is quite different from that of White Forcing, Perfection White Forcing, Giant White Forcing, and California Giant White Forcing.

Golden Ball. (Listed by seven seedsmen. Seeds tested: Northrup, King & Co., 1900, 1901; Ritter, 1899; Hopkins, 1901; Nebraska, 1901; Springfield, 1901.)

Same as Buttercup as received from first two and Hubbard's Market from last three seedsmen above. Listed as a novelty by American seedsmen about twenty-five years ago and described as of Russian origin. The original and correct type seems to be Buttercup, which is quite different from that of Golden Heart, Golden Head, Golden Forcing, Golden Beauty, Golden King, and Golden Gate.

Golden Curled. (*See* p. 49.)

Golden Beauty. (Listed by one seedsman. Seeds tested: Tilton, 1899–1901, 1903.)

Same as White Star. Named and introduced in 1892 by A. Tilton & Son. It is claimed by them to be an improvement on White Star in being of larger growth. The type is quite different from that of Blonde Beauty.

Golden Buttercup. (Seeds tested: Schisler-Corneli, 1899.)
Same as Buttercup.

Golden Forcing. (Seeds tested: Landreth, 1899.)

Same as Denver Market. Named and first listed by D. Landreth Seed Company in 1899, but never afterwards, and the name seems now to have wholly gone out of use. The type is quite different from that of Golden Head, Golden Ball, Golden Nugget, Golden Stone Head, Golden Heart, Golden Sunset, Golden King, and Golden Gate.

Golden Gate. (Listed by eight seedsmen. Seeds tested: Johnson & Stokes, 1900, 1901.

Same as Deacon. Named and introduced as a new variety in 1900 by above seedsmen.

Golden Head. (Listed by one seedsman. Seeds tested: Templin, 1899–1901.)

No one type seems to be recognized for this variety. The samples received were the same as Prize Head in 1899, Golden Queen in 1900, Philadelphia Butter in 1901. Described by above seedsman as cabbage heading. Formerly listed by Livingston Seed Company as Livingston's Golden Head. The variety should not be confounded with Golden Forcing, Golden Curled, Golden Heart, Golden Ball, Golden Buttercup, Gold Nugget, Golden Queen, Golden Beauty, nor Golden Gate.

Golden Heart. (*See* p. 49.)

Golden King. (Listed by one seedsman. Seeds tested: Crosman, 1899, 1900.)

Same as Buttercup in 1899 and Reichner in 1900. Named and first listed by above seed house.

Golden Queen. (*See* p. 49.)

Golden Spotted. (*See* p. 50.)

Gold Nugget. (Listed by six seedsmen. Seeds tested: Burpee, 1899, 1900, 1902; Stumpp & Walter, 1903.)

Same as Hubbard's Market. First listed by W. Atlee Burpee & Co. in 1899. The type is quite different from that of Golden Ball, Golden Buttercup, Golden Head, Golden Curled, Golden Heart, and Golden Stone Head.

Grand Rapids. (*See* p. 50.)

Gray-Seeded Butter. (Listed by three seedsmen. Seeds tested: Thorburn, 1899–1901.)
Same as Yellow-Seeded Butter.

Green Cos. (*See* p. 51.)

Green-Fringed. (*See* p. 51.)

Griffith & Turner's Black-Seeded Summer. (Seeds tested: 1899, 1900.)
Described under Black-Seeded Summer.

Griffith & Turner's White-Seeded Summer. (Seeds tested: Griffith & Turner, 1899, 1900, 1902.)
Described under White-Seeded Summer.

Half Century. (*See* p. 52.)

Hamilton Market. (Listed by two seedsmen. Seeds tested: Bruce, 1899–1901; Robert Evans, 1901.)

Same as Hanson. Said to have been named and first listed by Robert Evans Seed Company, but catalogued also by American seedsmen for at least twenty years.

CATALOGUE OF VARIETY NAMES. 91

Hammond's Earliest Forcing. (Listed by one seedsman. Seeds tested: Hammond, 1901.)
Same as Morse. Named and first listed by Harry N. Hammond Seed Company. The type is quite different from that of Earliest Cutting as sent out by W. E. Dallwig.

Hanson. (*See* p. 52.)

Harbinger. (*See* p. 53.)

Hard Head. (Listed by eight seedsmen. Seeds tested: Burpee, 1899, 1903; Childs, 1900.)
Same as Brown Head. Named and introduced as a new variety in 1887 by W. Atlee Burpee & Co. under the name of Burpee's Hard Head and said by them to have originated with a German seed grower. The name is very misleading, as the variety is anything but a hard head.

Hardy Green Hammersmith. (*See* p. 53.)

Hardy Green Winter. (Listed by eight seedsmen. Seeds tested: Bridgeman, 1901; Plant, 1900; Thorburn, 1903; Vick, 1899–1903.)
Same as Hardy Green Hammersmith. One of the oldest of all lettuce names. Known in this country for at least fifty-seven years.

Hartford Bronzed Head. (*See* p. 54.)

Hastings' Drum Head. (Listed by one seedsman. Seeds tested: Hastings, 1901.)
Same as New York. The name is very misleading, as Drum Head is more generally applied to Malta and several other types described under Drum Head.

Hastings' Superba. (Listed by one seedsman. Seeds tested: Hastings, 1903.)
Same as Maximum. Named and first listed by above seedsman in 1903. The type is quite different from that of Buckbee's Superb.

Heat-Resisting Cos. (Listed by five seedsmen. Seeds tested: Landreth, 1899.)
Same as Paris White Cos. Listed for at least twenty-five years by above seed house as Landreth's Heat-Resisting Cos.

Heavy Weight. (Listed by one seedsman. Seeds tested: Salzer, 1899–1901, 1903.)
Same as Big Boston as received the first two and New York the last two years. Named and introduced as a new variety in 1895 by above seedsman under the name of Salzer's Heavy Weight.

Henderson's New York. (Seeds tested: Farquhar, 1901; Henderson, 1900, 1901.)
Described under New York.

Hero. (*See* p. 54.)

Hittinger's Belmont. (Listed by seventeen seedsmen. Seeds tested: Burpee, 1900, 1902; Farquhar, 1900, 1901.)
Same as Hothouse. Named and introduced as a new variety in 1891 by Schlegel & Fottler, who state that it originated with Hittinger Brothers, of Belmont, Mass. The name is best known in the East.

Hornberger's Dutch Butter. (Listed by two seedsmen. Seeds tested: Johnson & Stokes, 1899–1902.)
Same as Speckled Dutch Butter. Named and introduced in 1896 by Johnson & Stokes as an improvement on Speckled Dutch Butter.

Hothouse. (*See* p. 55.)

Houston Market. (Listed by one seedsman. Seeds tested: Reichardt & Schulte, 1903; Thompson, 1902.)
Same as Big Boston. Apparently named and first listed by J. H. Thompson Seed and Rice Milling Company, the predecessors of Reichardt & Schulte.

Hubbard's Forcing. (Seeds tested: Harvey, 1899.)
Same as Hubbard's Market.

Hubbard's Market. (*See* p. 55.)

Iceberg. (*See* p. 56.)

Ice Drum Head. (Listed by seven seedsmen. Seeds tested: Bridgeman, 1901, 1903; Vincent, 1901.)
Same as Malta. The type is quite different from that of Buckbee's Ice Drum Head as sent out by H. W. Buckbee.

92   AMERICAN VARIETIES OF LETTUCE.

Ice Head. (Listed by one seedsman. Seeds tested: Godden, 1901.)
Same as Reichner. Apparently named and first listed by above seedsman.

Immensity. (Listed by ten seedsmen. Seeds tested: Henderson, 1901-1903.)
Same as Maximum. Named and first listed by Peter Henderson & Co.

Imperial. (Listed by five seedsmen. Seeds tested: Landreth, 1899-1903; Tait, 1901, 1903; Vick, 1899-1903; Wood, Stubbs & Co., 1903.)
A very old name which has been recognized in this country for at least one hundred years. A number of different types seem to be sold under this name. The samples mentioned above were identified as California Cream Butter, Deacon, Hubbard's Market, Malta, Mammoth Black-Seeded Butter, Middletowner, and Reichner. Probably Deacon and Hubbard's Market are at present the ones most used for Imperial. The name is not often used, and the misunderstanding arising from its use is therefore not very common.

Italian Ice. (*See* p. 56.)

Johnson & Stokes' Hothouse. (Seeds tested: Johnson & Stokes, 1900.)
Described under Hothouse.

Johnson & Stokes' Summerlead. (Seeds tested: Johnson & Stokes, 1901.)
Described under Summerlead.

Kaiser Wilhelm. (Listed by one seedsman. Seeds tested: Salzer, 1899, 1901, 1903.)
No one type seems to be recognized for this variety. The above samples were identified as Deacon, Denver Market, and Early Curled Simpson. Named and first listed by John A. Salzer in 1899.

Kansas City White-Seeded Forcing. (Listed by two seedsmen. Seeds tested: Plant Seed Co., 1899—1901.)
Same as Denver Market. Apparently named and first listed in 1899 by above seedsmen, though it is said to have been used by gardeners of Kansas City since 1865.

Kendel's Excelsior Head. (Listed by one seedsman. Seeds tested: Kendel, 1900, 1901.)
Same as White Chavigne. Named and first listed in 1898 by A. C. Kendel. The type is quite different from that of Excelsior as sold by other seedsmen.

Laciniated Beauregard. (*See* p. 56.)

La Crosse Market. (Listed by one seedsman. Seeds tested: Salzer, 1903.)
Same as Early Curled Simpson. Named and introduced as a new variety in 1902 by above seedsman.

Lancaster. (*See* p. 57.)

Landreth Forcing. (Listed by two seedsmen. Seeds tested: Landreth, 1899-1902.)
Same as Tom Thumb. Named and first listed in 1896 by above seed house.

Landreth's Heat-Resisting Cos. (Seeds tested: Landreth, 1899.)
Described under Heat-Resisting Cos.

Landreth's Unsurpassed. (Seeds tested: Landreth, 1902.)
Described under Unsurpassed.

Lapp's Head. (Seeds tested: Barnard, 1899.)
Same as Tennis Ball Black-Seeded. The name was formerly used by above seedsman, but apparently has now wholly gone out of use.

Large Boston Market. (Listed by one seedsman. Seeds tested: Thorburn, 1899, 1901.)
It seems this name was originally intended to separate the old Boston Market from the new variety developed from it about thirteen years ago and sold as Hothouse and Hittinger's Belmont, but that its use has often been misunderstood and the old Boston Market, as well as Big Boston, has sometimes been sold under its name. The above seedsman's samples appeared to be Boston Market.

Large Butter Head. (Listed by two seedsmen. Seeds tested: Bridgeman, 1900.)
Same as Tennis Ball Black-Seeded.

Large Drum Head. (Seeds tested: Ferry, 1899; Lamberson, 1901.)
Same as Deacon from former and Hubbard's Market from latter seedsman. See Drum Head.

Large India. (Seeds tested: Cadwell & Jones, 1899; Comstock, Ferre & Co., 1901; Weeber & Don, 1901.)
Same as Iceberg.

Large Loaf. (Seeds tested: Griffith & Turner, 1901.)
Same as White Loaf. The type is quite different from that of Sugar Loaf.

Large Passion. (Seeds tested: Bowen, 1903; Buist, 1899–1900; Texas Seed Company, 1903.)
The samples from the first two seedsmen above were the duller-leaved strain of Passion, and those from the latter seed house the glossy-leaved strain.

Largest of All. (Listed by two seedsmen. Seeds tested: Johnson & Stokes, 1900; Landreth, 1899–1901; Weber, 1903.)
Same as Deacon. Named and introduced as a new variety in 1868 by D. Landreth Seed Company, and said by them to be a trial-bed hybridization accidently accomplished between Malta and Mogul.

Large White Loaf. (Seeds tested: F. W. Bolgiano & Co., 1901–1903; Griffith & Turner, 1901; Manns, 1901.)
Same as White Loaf. The type is quite different from that of Sugar Loaf.

Large White Summer. (Seeds tested: Henderson, 1899, 1901, 1903; Thorburn, 1899, 1901, 1903.)
Same as White Summer Cabbage.

Large Yellow Market. (*See* p. 57.)

Lee's Market Forcing. (*See* p. 58.)

Leviathan. (Listed by one seedsman. Seeds tested: Elliott, 1901.)
Same as Maximum. Named and first listed by Elliott in 1901.

Limagne Cos. (*See* p. 58.)

Livingston's Bon Ton. (Listed by one seedsman. Seeds tested: Livingston, 1901–1903.)
Described under Bon Ton.

Loaf. (Seeds tested: Griffith & Turner, 1899.)
Described under White Loaf.

Long Island Winter. (Listed by one seedsman. Seeds tested: Landreth, 1899–1901.)
Same as Tennis Ball Black-Seeded. Named and first listed in 1898 by D. Landreth Seed Company.

Long-Standing. (Listed by one seedsman. Seeds tested: Farquhar, 1899–1901.)
Described under Farquhar's Long-Standing.

Longstreth's Earliest. (Listed by one seedsman. Seeds tested: Longstreth, 1899–1901.)
Same as Black-Seeded Simpson. Named and first listed by the above seedsman. The type is quite different from that of Earliest Cutting as sold by W. E. Dallwig.

Los Angeles Market. (Listed by one seedsman. Seeds tested: Johnson & Musser, 1901.)
Same as Hanson. Named and first listed by above seedsmen.

Luxury. (Listed by one seedsman. Seeds tested: Missouri Valley Seed Company, 1903.)
Same as Hartford Bronzed Head, though above seed house's description states that it is medium green in color, and with a large, loose, crisp, curly head. Named and introduced as a new variety in 1903 by Missouri Valley Seed Company.

Magnum Bonum. (Listed by two seedsmen. Seeds tested: Moore & Simon, 1900, 1901, 1903.)
Named and introduced as a new variety in 1895 by Moore & Simon under the name of Moore's Magnum Bonum. The samples received were the same as Tennis Ball Black-Seeded, but the above seedsmen describe it as similar to or possibly identical with Mammoth Black-Seeded Butter, while in England a similar lettuce of a very different character is known under name of Magnum Bonum Cos, and seems also to have been known in this country about seventy-six years ago.

Malta. (*See* p. 58.)

Mammoth. (*See* Price & Knickerbocker's Mammoth Head and Shumway's Mammoth.)

Mammoth Black-Seeded Butter. (*See* p. 59.)

Mammoth Erfurt Yellow. (Listed by one seedsman. Seeds tested: Dallwig, 1902–1903.)
Same as Thick Head Yellow. Listed by W. E. Dallwig in 1893 as Erfurt Large Yellow Thick Head, under which name it is said to have been known in Germany. Changed by above firm in 1900 to its present name.

Mammoth Large Yellow Butter. (Seeds tested: Thorburn, 1899–1901.)
Same as Mammoth Black-Seeded Butter. Named and introduced by J. M. Thorburn & Co., about fourteen years ago, but changed by them in 1904 to Mammoth Black-Seeded Butter.

Mammoth Salamander. (Seeds tested: Johnson & Stokes, 1899–1901.)
Same as Mammoth Black-Seeded Butter. Named and introduced by above seedsmen as a new variety in 1898.

Marblehead Mammoth. (*See* p. 59.)

Market Gardener's Salamander. (Seeds tested: Burwell, 1899.)
Same as Tennis Ball Black-Seeded. Named and first listed by E. E. Burwell in 1897.

Market Gardener's Forcing. (Listed by one seedsman. Seeds tested: Alneer, 1901.)
Same as Morse. The type is quite different from that of Market Gardener's Private Stock and Detroit Market Gardener's Forcing.

Market Gardener's Private Stock. (Listed by eighteen seedsmen. Seeds tested: Burpee, 1901; Ferry, 1900–1901; Landreth, 1899–1901; Thorburn, 1899–1903; Weeber & Don, 1902.)
Same as Tennis Ball Black-Seeded. Named and first listed about twelve years ago by J. M. Thorburn & Co. under the name of Thorburn's Market Gardener's Private Stock. The name is well known, especially in the vicinity of New York.

Mastodon. (Listed by one seedsman. Seeds tested: Archias, 1903.)
Same as Hanson. Named and introduced as a new variety in 1902 by L. E. Archias Seed Company.

Matador. (*See* p. 59.)

Matchless. (Listed by one seedsman. Seeds tested: Michell, 1903.)
Same as Maximum. First listed and named in 1903 by Henry F. Michell as Michell's Matchless.

Maule's Hanson. (Seeds tested: Maule, 1901.)
Same as Hanson.

Maule's Philadelphia Butter. (Listed by one seedsman. Seeds tested: Maule, 1900–1902.)
Same as California Cream Butter. Listed by above seedsman for at least fifteen years. The name is very misleading, because Philadelphia Butter as usually sold by seedsmen refers to a lettuce quite different from this type. It should not be confounded with Philadelphia Speckled Dutch Butter, which is still another type.

Maule's Rosette. (Seeds tested: Maule, 1901–1903.)
Same as White Chavigne. Named and introduced as a new variety in 1902 by William Henry Maule.

Maule's Silver Anniversary. (Seeds tested: Maule, 1903.)
Described under Silver Anniversary.

Maximum. (*See* p. 60.)

Memphis. (Seeds tested: Ullathorne Seed Company, 1899.)
Same as Hubbard's Market. Apparently never listed except by above seed house.

Mette's Forcing. (*See* p. 61.)

Michell's All Right Spring and Summer. (Seeds tested: Michell, 1900–1902.)
Described under All Right Spring and Autumn.

Michell's Early Speckled Dutch Butter. (Seeds tested: Michell, 1899–1900.)
Described under Speckled Dutch Butter.

CATALOGUE OF VARIETY NAMES. 95

Michell's Very Best. (Seeds tested: Michell, 1899–1901.)
Same as Buttercup. Named and first listed in 1899 by Henry F. Michell, but not catalogued by him or any other seed house after 1901.

Middletowner. (See p. 61.)

Midsummer. (Listed by one seedsman. Seeds tested: Tait, 1901–1903.)
Same as Maximum. As Tait's Midsummer this variety was apparently named and first listed by the above seedsman, but from 1889 to 1891 W. Atlee Burpee & Co. listed a German variety under the name of Midsummer or Genezzano, which was a lettuce identical or similar to Brown Head and very different from this one.

Mignonette. (See p. 62.)

Mills' Earliest. (Listed by one seedsman. Seeds tested: Mills, 1899–1902.)
Same as Grand Rapids. Named and first listed in 1897 by above seedsman.

Milly. (See p. 62.)

Miniature. (Listed by two seedsmen. Seeds tested: Thorburn, 1903.)
Same as Density. First listed in 1903 by both W. Atlee Burpee & Co. and J. M. Thorburn & Co. Said to have originated some three or four years before with Chris. Lorenz, of Erfurt, Germany.

Mongolian. (Listed by one seedsman. Seeds tested: Johnson & Stokes, 1901–1903.).
Same as Reichner. Named and introduced as a new variety in 1902 by Johnson & Stokes.

Montreal Market. (Seeds tested: Wm. Evans, 1900; Ewing, 1899.)
Same as Hanson from the former and Deacon from the latter seedsman. Apparently not listed after 1900.

Morse. (See p. 62.)

Moore's Champion Spring and Summer. (Seeds tested: Moore & Simon, 1900, 1901.)
Described under Champion Spring and Summer.

Moore's Magnum Bonum. (Seeds tested: Moore & Simon, 1900, 1901.)
Described under Magnum Bonum.

Moore's Summer Gem. (Seeds tested: Moore & Simon, 1900, 1901.)
Described under Summer Gem.

Myers' All Right. (Listed by six seedsmen. Seeds tested: Johnson & Stokes, 1899, 1900.)
Same as Big Boston. Named and introduced as a new variety in 1888 by Johnson & Stokes, who state it originated with Mr. Henry Myers, a prominent Philadelphia market gardener. The type is quite different from that of All Right Spring and Autumn.

Nansen. (See p. 63.)

Neapolitan Cabbage. (Listed by one seedsman.)
A very old name known in this country for at least thirty-nine years. The variety seems to have had its origin in France. It has not yet been tested on the Department grounds, but reports of it from other places state it to be the same as Sibley's Genesee of twenty years ago, Chou de Naples of Italian seedsmen, and New York of the present day. The type is quite different from that of Neapolitan Sash listed by Moore & Simon.

Neapolitan Sash. (Listed by one seedsman. Seeds tested: Moore & Simon, 1900–1903.)
Same as Reichner. Named and first listed in 1895 by above seedsmen as Simon's Neapolitan Sash. The Neapolitan Cabbage, a very old sort of foreign origin and catalogued about thirty-eight years ago by seedsmen in this country, but now listed only by George A. Weaver Company, is a very different lettuce from Neapolitan Sash.

New Asparagus. (Listed by two seedsmen. Seeds tested: Buckbee, 1901, 1902; Ewing, 1902, 1903.)
The former seedsman's samples were the same as the lanceolate-leaved type of Asparagus described on page 30, and the latter seedsman's samples the same as the lobed-leaved type of Asparagus also described on page 30.

New Lettuce No. 1. (Listed by one seedsman. Seeds tested: Moore & Simon, 1900, 1901, 1903.)
Same as Big Boston. Named and first listed in 1900 by Moore & Simon, who state they obtained the variety from Mr. John Norbeck, a Philadelphia market gardener.

New Orleans Large Passion. (Listed by four seedsmen. Seeds tested: Steckler 1899–1902.)
Same as California Cream Butter.

New York. (*See* p. 63.)

Ninety and Nine. (Listed by one seedsman. Seeds tested: Crosman, 1900, 1901; Vaughan, 1899.)
Same as Tennis Ball Black-Seeded. Listed about nine years ago by a few seedsmen in this country, but the name seems now to have wholly gone out of use.

Nonsuch. (Seeds tested: Pearce, 1899.)
Same as Deacon. Apparently named and first listed by the above seedsman the predecessor of Darch & Hunter.

Noll's Boston Glasshouse. (Seeds tested: Noll, 1901.)
Described under Boston Glasshouse.

Nonpareil. (Listed by twelve seedsmen. Seeds tested: J. M. McCullough, 1901; Simmers, 1899–1901.)
Same as Hanson. Listed by John A. Bruce & Co. for at least fifty years.

Norfolk Royal. (Seeds tested: Landreth, 1901.)
Same as Deacon. Apparently named and first listed by above seedsman.

North Pole. (Listed by three seedsmen. Seeds tested: Burpee, 1901–1903; Germain, 1901.)
Same as Nansen. First listed in this country by Germain Seed Company in 1898 as synonymous with Nansen. Said to be of German origin.

Northrup, King & Co.'s Golden Ball. (Seeds tested: Northrup, King & Co., 1900, 1901.)
Described under Golden Ball.

Norwood. (Listed by one seedsman. Seeds tested: J. M. McCullough, 1902, 1903.)
Same as Middletowner. Named and first listed in 1902 by above seedsman.

Oak-Leaved. (*See* p. 64.)

Ohio Cabbage. (Listed by one seedsman. Seeds tested: Steele, Briggs & Co., 1901; Tilton, 1901.)
Same as Denver Market.

Onondaga. (*See* p. 64.)

Pan-American. (Listed by one seedsman. Seeds tested: Mills, 1902.)
Same as Eureka. Named and first listed in 1901 by above seedsman.

Paris Sugar. (*See* p. 65.)

Paris White Cos. (*See* p. 65.)

Passion. (*See* p. 66.)

Peer of All. (Listed by one seedsman. Seeds tested: Salzer, 1899–1901, 1903.)
Same as Prize Head in 1899 and 1901, and Chartier in 1900 and 1903. Named and first listed by above seedsman, who has listed it for at least nine years.

Perfected Salamander. (Seeds tested: Henderson, 1900–1902.)
Described under Salamander.

Perfection Early White Forcing. (Seeds tested: Buist, 1899–1901.)
Same as White Forcing. Named and first listed in 1887 by Robert Buist Company, under name of Buist's Perfection White Forcing. The type is quite different from that of Godden's White-Seeded Forcing, Giant White Forcing, and California Giant White Forcing.

Perpetual. (Listed by nine seedsmen. Seeds tested: Chesmore-Eastlake, 1902; Huntington & Page, 1901; Johnson & Stokes, 1899, 1900; Livingston, 1900; Rice, 1901.)
Same as Early Curled Simpson. Listed in 1880 by James J. H. Gregory & Son as Nellis' Perpetual, but apparently named and first listed by other seedsmen.

Perpignan. (Listed by ten seedsmen. Seeds tested: Vaughan, 1899, 1900.)
Same as Defiance. An old variety of German origin listed by seedsmen in this country for at least thirty-seven years. A lettuce similar to Deacon and very distinct from this type seems to have formerly been largely sold under this name.

Philadelphia Butter. (*See* p. 66.)

Philadelphia Dutch Butter. (Seeds tested: Burpee, 1899-1901, 1903.)
Same as Speckled Dutch Butter. The type is quite different from that of Philadelphia Butter and Maule's Philadelphia Butter.

Philadelphia Early White Cabbage. (Listed by five seedsmen. Seeds tested: Burpee, 1899—1903; Johnson & Stokes, 1901, 1903.)
In some trials the above samples appeared the same as Philadelphia Butter; at other times the same as Reichner. The variety is probably identical with one of them.

Pink Chartier. (Seeds tested: Vaughan, 1899-1901.)
Same as Chartier. A name formerly applied to Chartier by above seedsman, but not now used by him or any other seedsman.

Plant Seed Company's Standwell. (Seeds tested: Plant, 1901.)
Described under Standwell.

Precocity. (Listed by one seedsman. Seeds tested: Henderson, 1902, 1903.)
Same as Emperor Forcing. Named and first listed in 1902 by above seedsman.

Premium Cabbage. (Listed by ten seedsmen. Seeds tested: Chesmore-Eastlake, 1903; Manns, 1901; Rice, 1900, 1901; Vick, 1901-1903.
In some trials the above samples appeared the same as Philadelphia Butter; at other times the same as Reichner, or Hubbard's Market. The variety is probably the same as one of these sorts. Apparently named and introduced in 1875 by James Vick's Sons under the name of Vick's Premium Cabbage. They state that Mr. Hubbard, of Chautauqua County, N. Y., was the originator, and sold some of his seed to their seed house and also to Chase Brothers, nurserymen, who were handling seed at that time. The latter are said to have introduced the lettuce as Hubbard's Market.

Price & Knickerbocker's Mammoth Head. (Listed by one seedsman. Seeds tested: Price, 1899-1901.)
Same as Tennis Ball Black-Seeded. Named and first listed by above seedsman in 1876.

Prince of Wales Cos. (*See* p. 67.)

Prize Head. (*See* p. 67.)

Queen. (Seeds tested: Faust, 1899, 1900.)
Same as New York. Named and first listed as Faust's Queen by above seedsman. The type is quite different from that of Golden Queen and Yellow Queen.

Rawson's Crumpled-Leaved. (Seeds tested: Rawson, 1899, 1901.)
Described under Crumpled-Leaved.

Rawson's Hothouse. (Seeds tested: Rawson, 1900, 1901; Vaughan, 1900; Vick, 1901.)
Described under Hothouse.

Red Besson. (*See* p. 68.)

Red Winter Cos. (*See* p. 68.)

Reichner. (*See* p. 69.)

Reichner's Early White Butter. (Seeds tested: Johnson & Stokes, 1899-1901.)
Same as Reichner.

Relish. (Listed by one seedsman. Seeds tested: Iowa Seed Company, 1899, 1902, 1903.)
Same as Big Boston. Named and introduced as a new variety in 1900 by above seed house.

Rennie & Pino's Hothouse. (Seeds tested: Rennie & Pino, 1903.)
Described under Hothouse.

Ridge. (Listed by one seedsman. Seeds tested: Johnson & Stokes, 1900.)
Same as Reichner. Named and first listed by above seedsmen.

Rochester Market. (Seeds tested: Glass, 1901, 1903.)
Same as Reichner. Apparently named and first listed about five years ago by above seedsman.

Romaine Cos. (Listed by twenty-six seedsmen Seeds tested: Landreth, 1901; Moore & Simon, 1900, 1901.)
Same as Paris White Cos. A very old name. Sometimes used to designate the cos class of lettuce, but whenever applied in this country to designate a variety it is generally Paris White Cos which is referred to.

Rosedale. (Listed by one seedsman. Seeds tested: Darch & Hunter, 1899–1901, 1903.)
Same as Denver Market the first two years and Defiance the last two. Apparently first listed by John A. Pearce, the predecessor of the above seedsmen.

Rosette. (Listed by one seedsman. Seeds tested: Maule, 1901–1903.)
Described under Maule's Rosette.

Royal Cabbage. (Listed by thirty-two seedsmen. Seeds tested: Buist, 1900, 1901; Dusard, 1899, 1900; Robert Evans, 1899; Landreth, 1899; Plant, 1900; Steckler, 1901; Tait, 1901; Vick, 1899–1903.)
A name known in this country for at least thirty-eight years and much misused. Applied to a number of different lettuce types, but principally to Hubbard's Market and California Cream Butter. The above samples were all the former variety except those from Michell, which were California Cream Butter. The name has been used for many years in California to designate California Cream Butter; in fact, was in use many years before California Cream Butter was known.

Rudolph's Favorite. (Listed by three seedsmen. Seeds tested: Iowa, 1901; Vaughan, 1899–1901.)
Same as Buttercup. Of foreign origin. First listed in this country by Vaughan's Seed Store in 1894. The type is quite different from that of Gardener's Favorite, Sutton's Favorite, and Florida Favorite.

St. Louis Black-Seeded Forcing. (*See* p. 69.)

St. Louis Butter. (Listed by eleven seedsmen. Seeds tested: Currie, 1903; Landreth, 1902; Scott, 1899, 1900; Vaughan, 1899–1901.)
Same as Deacon. The name has been used in this country at least sixteen years, and is well known in Chicago, St. Louis, and the West. The type is quite different from that of St. Louis Market and St. Louis Black-Seeded Forcing.

St. Louis Market. (Listed by eight seedsmen. Seeds tested: Dusard, 1899–1902; Eber, 1903; Plant, 1901, 1903; Schisler-Corneli, 1903.)
It seems this name is used by most seedsmen to represent a type identical with Hubbard's Market, but that some others take it to refer to St. Louis Butter. All of the above samples were the former variety. In no case should it be confounded with St. Louis Black-Seeded Forcing, as that is unquestionably a different type from either of these two varieties.

Salamander. (Listed by one hundred and seventeen seedsmen. Seeds tested: Burpee, 1903; Burwell, 1899, 1900; Farquhar, 1901; Ferry, 1900, 1901; Henderson, 1900–1902; Johnson & Stokes, 1899, 1900, 1903; Landreth, 1899, 1901; Thorburn, 1899, 1901.)
Same as Tennis Ball Black-Seeded. Named and introduced as a new variety in 1882 by Peter Henderson & Co., who state that it originated with Hudson County, N. Y., market gardeners. In 1895 another strain was listed by these seedsmen and called Perfected Salamander. Commonly considered to be larger than Tennis Ball Black-Seeded, but it has not proved so at Washington nor in other trials which the writer has examined. It is one of the best known of all lettuce names.

Salzer's Colossal. (Listed by one seedsman. Seeds tested: Salzer, 1899, 1901, 1903.)
Same as Deacon. Named and introduced in 1899 by above seedsman. The type is quite different from that of Tait's Colossal.

Salzer's Earliest. (Listed by one seedsman. Seeds tested: Salzer, 1899, 1901.)
Same as Black-Seeded Simpson. Named and first listed by above seedsman, who has catalogued it for at least nine years. It should not be confounded with Earliest Cutting as sent out by W. E. Dallwig.

Salzer's Peer of All. (Seeds tested: Salzer, 1899–1901, 1903.)
Described under Peer of All.

Salzer's Sunlight. (Seeds tested: Salzer, 1900, 1901, 1903.)
Described under Sunlight.

San Francisco Market. (Listed by twelve seedsmen. Seeds tested: Burpee, 1901–1903.
Same as Deacon. Apparently named and first listed in 1897 by W. Atlee Burpee & Co., not, however, as a new variety, but as another name for Deacon. It should not be confounded with San Francisco Passion.

San Francisco Passion. (Listed by one seedsman. Seeds tested: Buist, 1901.)
Same as Passion. The type is quite different from that of San Francisco Market.

Satisfaction Black-Seeded. (Listed by twenty-five seedsmen. Seeds tested: Farquhar, 1900; Gregory, 1900; Plant, 1899.)
Same as Tennis Ball Black-Seeded. An English variety listed by seedsmen in this country for at least twenty-six years.

Saunders. (Seeds tested: Beckert, 1899, 1900, 1902.)
Same as St. Louis Black-Seeded Forcing. Named and first listed in 1891 by above seedsman, who states that the variety is named after a local market gardener in whose possession it had remained for a number of years.

Schindler's Early Market. (Seeds tested: Schindler, 1903.)
Described under Early Market.

Schwill's Bonanza. (Seeds tested: Schwill, 1899.)
Described under Bonanza.

Sensation. (Listed by twenty-seven seedsmen. Seeds tested: Johnson & Stokes, 1899–1901; Thorburn, 1900, 1901.
Same as Tennis Ball Black-Seeded. Named and introduced by Johnson & Stokes from France in 1892.

Shotwell's Brown Head. (*See* p. 70.)

Shotwell's Brown Head (Bridgeman). (*See* p. 70.)

Shumway's Mammoth. (Listed by one seedsman. Seeds tested: Shumway, 1899–1901.)
Same as Marblehead Mammoth. Named and first listed by above seedsman.

Silver Anniversary. (Listed by one seedsman. Seeds tested: Maule, 1903.)
Same as Giant Glacier. Named and introduced in 1902 by William Henry Maule as Maule's Silver Anniversary.

Silver Ball. (*See* p. 71.)

Simmers' Nonpareil. (Seeds tested: Simmers, 1899, 1901.)
Described under Nonpareil.

Simon's Early White Cabbage. (Seeds tested: Moore & Simon, 1900.)
Described under Early White Cabbage.

Simon's Neapolitan Sash. (Seeds tested: Moore & Simon, 1900—1903.)
Described under Neapolitan Sash.

Simon's Speckled Dutch Butter. (Seeds tested: Moore & Simon, 1901.)
Described under Speckled Dutch Butter.

Slow Seeder. (Listed by one seedsman. Seeds tested: Landreth, 1899—1901.)
Same as Defiance. Apparently named and first listed in 1894 by above seed house.

Solid Header. (Listed by one seedsman. Seeds tested: Briggs, 1901.)
Same as Yellow-Seeded Butter.

Southern Heart. (Listed by one seedsman. Seeds tested: Salzer, 1901.)
Same as Passion. The above seedsman first used this name in 1901, but it may have been used by others before that date.

Speckled Dutch Butter. (*See* p. 71.)

Speckled Early Dutch Butter. (Seeds tested: Dreer, 1899; Michell, 1899, 1900.)
Same as Speckled Dutch Butter.

Standwell. (Listed by one seedsman. Seeds tested: Plant Seed Company, 1900, 1901.)
Same as Defiance. Listed by above seed house for at least ten years, and in 1886 by Johnson & Stokes as Johnson's Standwell.

Steckler's French Market. (Seeds tested: Steckler, 1900, 1901, 1903.)
Described under French Market.

Sterling. (Listed by one seedsman. Seeds tested: Northrup King & Co., 1900, 1901.)
Same as New York. Named and introduced as a new variety in 1900 by above seedsmen.

Stone Head Golden Yellow. (Listed by thirty-two seedsmen. Seeds tested: Bridgeman, 1900, 1901, 1903; Dallwig, 1900, 1901; Ebeling, 1900; Eber, 1901; Ewing, 1901; Gregory, 1900, 1902, 1903; Thorburn, 1901, 1902.)
As generally sold in the United States this variety seems to be the same as Golden Queen. All the above samples proved to be of the latter variety, and as imported into this country from Germany about twenty-five years ago it seems to have been of this type at that time also. There seems to be much misunderstanding, however, in the use of the name, as orders for this variety have been filled by seeds which proved to be Yellow-Seeded Butter, Golden Heart, Hubbard's Market, Emperor Forcing, Buttercup, and Tennis Ball Black-Seeded, while still another type, very different from these and similar to Golden Queen, but larger and later, appears to be sometimes used for Stone Head Golden Yellow.

Stringer's Early White Butter. (Listed by one seedsman. Seeds tested: Moore & Simon, 1901.)
Same as Reichner. Listed by above seedsman in 1891, but it is not known whether others had previously used the name.

Stubborn Seeder. (Listed by one seedsman. Seeds tested: Maule, 1899—1901, 1903.)
Same as Defiance. Apparently named and first listed by above seedsman, who has used the name for at least fifteen years.

Sugar Loaf. (See p. 72.)

Summer Drum Head. (Seeds tested: Michell, 1900, 1901; Texas Seed Company, 1903.)
Same as California Cream Butter from the former and Hubbard's Market from latter seed house. (See Drum Head.)

Summer Gem. (Listed by one seedsman. Seeds tested: Moore & Simon, 1900, 1903.)
Same as Deacon. Named and first listed as Moore's Summer Gem in 1892 by above seedsmen. The type is quite different from that of Toronto Gem.

Summerlead. (Listed by one seedsman. Seeds tested: Johnson & Stokes, 1901.)
Same as Maximum. Named and first listed in 1901 by above seedsmen.

Summer Queen Drum Head. (Listed by one seedsman. Seeds tested: Moore & Simon, 1903.)
Same as Deacon. Apparently named and first listed in 1892 by above seedsmen as Simon's Summer Queen Drum Head. See Drum Head.

Sunlight. (Listed by one seedsman. Seeds tested: Salzer, 1900, 1901, 1903.)
Same as Deacon. Apparently named and first listed by above seedsman as Salzer's Sunlight, under which name it has been catalogued for at least nine years.

Sunset. (Listed by one seedsman. Seeds tested: Ford, 1901.)
Same as Blonde Block Head. It seems that this lettuce was introduced as a new variety about fourteen years ago. It is universally regarded by seedsmen to be the same as Blonde Block Head.

Surprise. (Seeds tested: Buckbee, 1903.)
Same as Brown Head. Named and first listed in 1902 by above seedsman.

Sutton's Favorite. (Seeds tested: Michell, 1899, 1900.)
Same as Denver Market. Listed by above seedsman in 1900 and 1901, who sold the variety during these years in the original seed packets obtained from Sutton, of England. The type is quite different from that of Favorite, Rudolph's Favorite, Gardener's Favorite, and Florida Favorite.

Sutton's Giant Cabbage. (See p. 72.)

CATALOGUE OF VARIETY NAMES.

Tait's Colossal. (Listed by one seedsman. Seeds tested: Tait, 1903.)
Same as Deacon. The type is quite different from that of Salzer's Colossal.

Tait's Imperial. (Seeds tested: Tait, 1901, 1903.)
Described under Imperial.

Tait's Midsummer. (Seeds tested: Tait, 1901.)
Described under Midsummer.

Tait's Royal Cabbage. (Seeds tested: Tait, 1904.)
Described under Royal Cabbage.

Tender Leaf. (Seeds tested: Shumway, 1901.)
Same as Marblehead Mammoth. Named and first listed by above seedsman.

Tennis Ball Black-Seeded. (See p. 72.)

Tennis Ball White-Seeded. (See p. 73.)

Thick Head Yellow. (See p. 74.)

Thorburn's Glasshouse. (Seeds tested: Thorburn, 1900—1902.)
Described under Glasshouse.

Thorburn's Market Gardener's Private Stock. (Seeds tested: Thorburn, 1899, 1900, 1903.)
Described under Market Gardener's Private Stock.

Thorburn's Maximum. (Seeds tested: Thorburn, 1899—1901.)
Described under Maximum.

Thorburn's Yellow Winter. (Seeds tested: Thorburn, 1900—1903.)
Described under Yellow Winter.

Tilton's White Star. (Seeds tested: Ferry, 1899—1902; Maule, 1900; Templin, 1900; Tilton, 1900, 1904; Thorburn, 1903.)
Described under White Star.

Tomhannock. (See p. 74.)

Tom Thumb. (See p. 75.)

Toronto Gem. (Listed by one seedsman. Seeds tested: Steele, Briggs & Co., 1899—1901.)
Same as Hanson. Named and introduced in 1888 by above seedsmen. The type is quite different from that of Summer Gem.

Toronto Market. (Listed by two seedsmen. Seeds tested: Simmers; 1899—1901.)
Same as Hanson. Apparently named and first listed by above seedsman, who has catalogued it for at least seven years.

Treasure. (Listed by two seedsmen. Seeds tested: Johnson & Stokes, 1899—1901.)
Same as California Cream Butter. Named and introduced in 1895 by above seedsmen.

Trianon Cos. (Listed by fifty-seven seedsmen. Seeds tested: Farquhar, 1901; Henderson, 1901; Johnson & Stokes, 1899; Rawson, 1901; Thorburn, 1899—1901.)
Same as Paris White Cos.

Triumph. (Listed by one seedsman. Seeds tested: Manns, 1901, 1903.)
Same as Deacon. Named and introduced as a new variety in 1900 by above seedsman. The type is quite different from that of Australian White Triumph.

Trocadero. (Listed by twelve seedsmen. Seeds tested: Thorburn, 1899, 1900, 1902.)
Same as Big Boston. A well-known French variety listed by seedsmen in this country for at least twenty years.

Trout. (See p. 75.)

Twentieth Century. (Listed by one seedsman. Seeds tested: Noll, 1900—1903.)
Same as Tennis Ball Black-Seeded. Named and first listed as a new variety about five years ago by above seedsman.

Tyrolese. (See p. 76.)

Universal. (Listed by one seedsman. Seeds tested: Livingston, 1903.)
Same as Unrivaled. Named and first listed in 1903 by above seedsman.

Unrivaled. (*See* p. 76.)

Unsurpassed. (Listed by one seedsman. Seeds tested: Landreth, 1902.)
Same as Unrivaled. Named and first listed in 1902 by above seed house.

Vaughan's All Seasons. (Seeds tested: Vaughan, 1903.)
Described under All Seasons.

Vaughan's Mammoth Cabbage Head. (Seeds tested: Vaughan, 1899–1901.)
Same as Mammoth Black-Seeded Butter. Named and first listed in 1901 by above seedsman but not catalogued by any seed house after 1901.

Vick's Hero. (Seeds tested: Vick, 1899–1903.)
Described under Hero.

Vick's Premium Cabbage. (Seeds tested: Vick, 1903.)
Described under Premium Cabbage.

Vick's Royal Cabbage. (Seeds tested: Vick, 1899–1903.)
Described under Royal Cabbage.

Victoria Red-Edged. (*See* p. 77.)

Vincent's Passion. (Seeds tested: Vincent, 1901, 1903.)
Described under Passion.

Virginia Solid Header. (Listed by seven seedsmen. Seeds tested: Koerner, 1900; Landreth, 1899, 1900, 1902; Mark W. Johnson, 1900.)
Same as Speckled Dutch Butter. Named and introduced in 1865 by D. Landreth Seed Company.

Waldorf. (Listed by two seedsmen. Seeds tested: Henderson, 1901–1903.)
Same as Reichner. Named and introduced as a new variety in 1898 by above seedsmen.

Weaver's Market Gardener's. (Listed by one seedsman. Seeds tested: Weaver, 1903.)
Same as Iceberg. Named and first listed in 1903 by George A. Weaver Seed Company. The type is quite different from that of Market Gardener's Private Stock.

Webb's Wonderful. (Seeds tested: Burpee, 1901, 1902.)
Described under Wonderful.

Weber's Brown Head. (Listed by one seedsman. Seeds tested: Weber, 1903.)
Described under Brown Head.

Weber's Curled. (Listed by one seedsman. Seeds tested: Weber, 1903.)
Same as Denver Market. Apparently named and first listed by above seedsman.

Wernich's Prize Head. (Seeds tested: Wernich, 1900.)
Described under Prize Head.

Wheeler's Tom Thumb. (Seeds tested: Burpee, 1900, 1901.)
Described under Tom Thumb.

Wheeler's Wonderful. (Seeds tested: Wheeler, 1903.)
Described under Wonderful.

White Cabbage. (Seeds tested: Vaughan, 1900, 1901.)
Same as White Summer Cabbage. A very old name.

White Chartier. (Listed by one seedsman. Seeds tested: Scott, 1899–1903.)
A name which has been applied by above seedsman to Golden Curled, the word *white* being attached to distinguish it from Chartier, which is a brown-colored lettuce.

White Chavigne. (*See* p. 77.)

White Cos. (Listed by seventeen seedsmen. Seeds tested: Landreth, 1899, 1901, 1902; Thorburn, 1899, 1901.)
Same as Paris White Cos.

White Forcing. (*See* p. 78.)

White Giant. (*See* p. 78.)

White Head. (Listed by five seedsmen. Seeds tested: Ferry, 1900.)
Same as Philadelphia Butter. A name which has been used for at least sixteen years by above seedsman as synonymous with Philadelphia Butter.

White Loaf. (*See* p. 78.)

White Peach. (Listed by one seedsman. Seeds tested: Moore & Simon, 1900, 1901, 1903.)
Same as Tennis Ball Black-Seeded. Named and first listed in 1892 by above seedsmen.

White Russian. (Listed by six seedsmen. Seeds tested: Johnson & Stokes, 1899.)
Same as Deacon.

White-Seeded Simpson. (Listed by thirteen seedsmen. Seeds tested: Johnson & Stokes, 1900.)
A very old variety, known in this country for at least forty years. It is said to be derived from Early Curled Silesia and to have originated with Mr. Simpson, a market gardener near Brooklyn, N. Y.

White-Seeded Summer. (Listed by two seedsmen. Seeds tested: Griffith & Turner, 1899, 1900, 1902.)
Same as White Chavigne. Named and first listed by Baltimore and Washington seedsmen, about seven years ago.

White Self-Folding Cos. (Seeds tested: Ferry, 1900.)
Same as Paris White Cos.

White Star. (*See* p. 79.)

White Summer Cabbage. (*See* p. 79.)

Wonderful. (Listed by forty-six seedsmen. Seeds tested: Burpee, 1901, 1902; Dreer, 1899–1901; Farquhar, 1901; Wheeler, 1903.)
Same as New York. An English variety first listed in this country by Henry A. Dreer in 1897.

Wood's Cabbage. (Listed by two seedsmen. Seeds tested: Wood, 1899–1902.)
Same as Hubbard's Market. Named and first listed in 1894 by above seedsman.

Yellow Queen. (Listed by one seedsman. Seeds tested: May, 1901, 1903.)
Same as Reichner. Apparently named and first listed in 1901 by above seedsman. The type is quite different from that of Faust's Queen and Golden Queen.

Yellow-Seeded Butter. (*See* p. 79.)

Yellow Winter. (*See* p. 80.)

O

FIG. 1.—BLACK-SEEDED SIMPSON.

FIG. 2.—HANSON

TYPICAL MATURE PLANTS.

(About one-fifth natural size.)

Fig. 1.—Tyrolese.

Fig. 2.—Golden Heart.

TYPICAL MATURE PLANTS.

(About one-fifth natural size.)

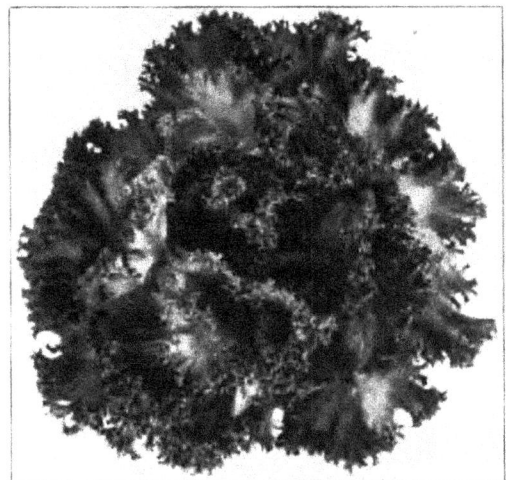

Fig. 1.—Green-Fringed.

Fig. 2.—Bath Cos.

TYPICAL MATURE PLANTS.

(About one-fifth natural size.)

Fig. 1.—American Gathering.

Fig. 2.—Early Curled Simpson.

TYPICAL MATURE PLANTS.

(About one-fifth natural size.)

Fig. 1.—Big Boston.

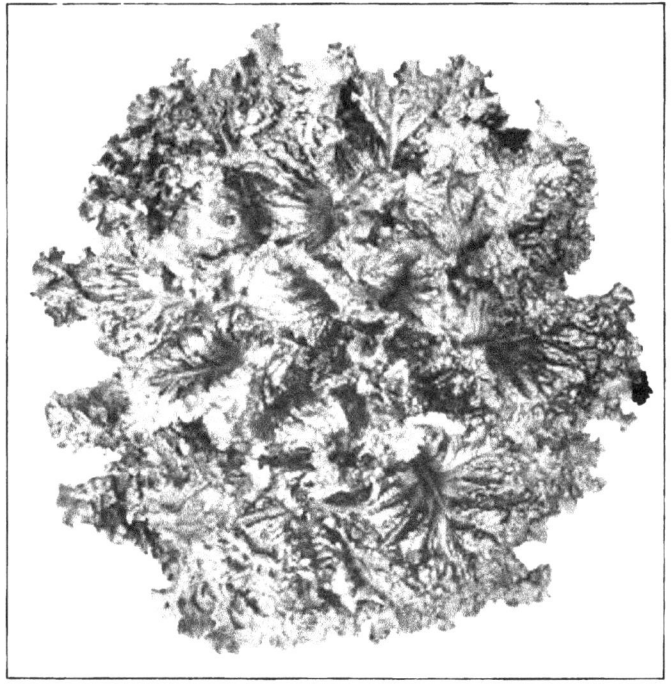

Fig. 2.—Prize Head.

TYPICAL MATURE PLANTS.

(About one-fifth natural size.)

Bul. 69, Bureau of Plant Industry, U. S. Dept. of Agriculture.　　　　　　　　PLATE VI.

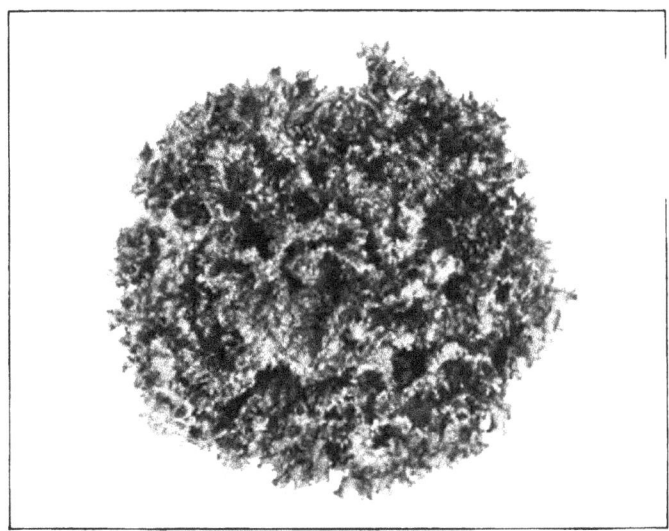

FIG. 1.—ONONDAGA.

FIG. 2.—GRAND RAPIDS.

TYPICAL MATURE PLANTS.

(About one-fifth natural size.)

Bul. 69, Bureau of Plant Industry, U. S. Dept. of Agriculture.　　　　　　　　　　　PLATE VII.

FIG. 1.—DENSITY.

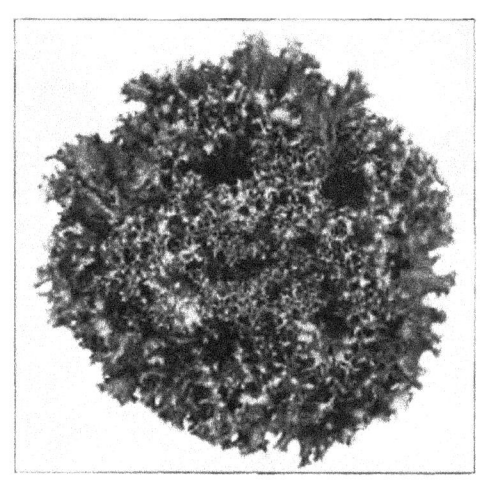

FIG. 2.—BOSTON CURLED.

FIG. 3.—MIGNONETTE.

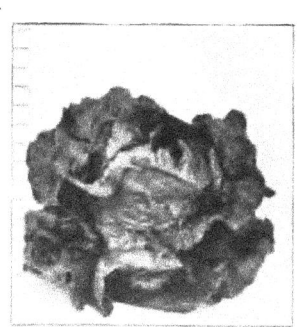

FIG 4.—WHITE FORCING.

TYPICAL MATURE PLANTS.
(About one-fifth natural size.)

Fig. 1.—Earliest Cutting.

Fig. 2.—California Cream Butter.

TYPICAL MATURE PLANTS.

(About one-fifth natural size.)

Fig. 1.—Emperor William.

Fig. 2.—Yellow Winter.

Fig. 3.—Detroit Market Gardener's Forcing.

TYPICAL MATURE PLANTS.

(About one-fifth natural size.)

Bul. 69, Bureau of Plant Industry, U. S. Dept. of Agriculture. PLATE X.

FIG. 1.—HUBBARD'S MARKET.

FIG. 2.—DEACON.

TYPICAL MATURE PLANTS.

(About one-fifth natural size.)

Fig. 1.—Maximum (upper view)

Fig. 2.—Maximum (side view).

TYPICAL MATURE PLANTS.
(About one-fifth natural size.)

Fig. 1.—Malta.

Fig. 2.—Italian Ice.

TYPICAL MATURE PLANTS.

(About one-fifth natural size.)

Fig. 1.—Red Besson.

Fig. 2.—Asparagus Lobed-Leaved.

TYPICAL MATURE PLANTS.

(About one-fifth natural size.)

Fig. 1.—Asparagus.

Fig. 2.—Red Winter Cos.

TYPICAL MATURE PLANTS.

(About one-fifth natural size.)

Fig. 1.—Lancaster.

Fig. 2.—Express Cos.

Fig. 3.—Baltimore Oak-Leaved.

TYPICAL MATURE PLANTS.
(About one-fifth natural size.)

Fig. 1.—Oak-Leaved.

Fig. 2.—Tom Thumb.

Fig. 3.—Reichner.

TYPICAL MATURE PLANTS.
(About one-fifth natural size.)

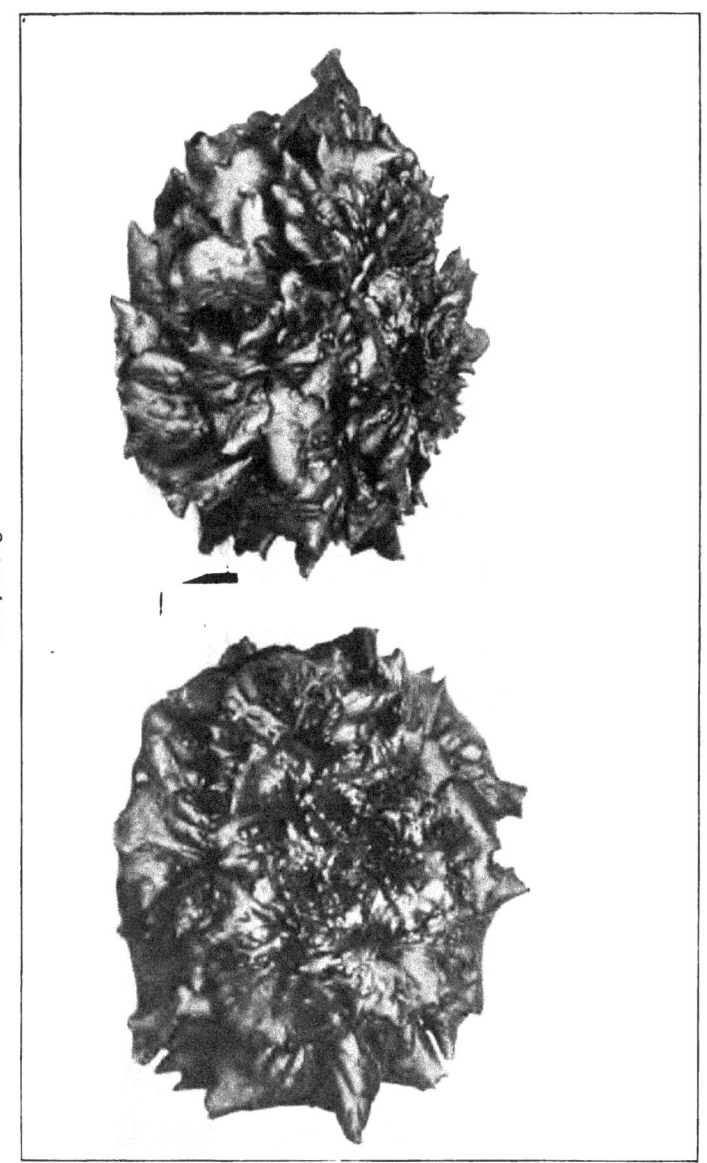

Bul. 69, Bureau of Plant Industry, U. S. Dept. of Agriculture. PLATE XVII.

SUGAR LOAF.
TYPICAL MATURE PLANTS.
(About one-fifth natural size.)

Fig. 1.—Half Century.

Fig. 2.—Speckled Dutch Butter

TYPICAL MATURE PLANTS.
(About one-fifth natural size.)

Fig. 3.—Mette's Forcing.

Bul. 69, Bureau of Plant Industry, U. S. Dept. of Agriculture. PLATE XVIII.

FIG. 1.—HALF CENTURY.

FIG. 2.—SPECKLED DUTCH BUTTER

FIG. 3.—METTE'S FORCING.

TYPICAL MATURE PLANTS.
(About one-fifth natural size.)

Bul. 69, Bureau of Plant Industry, U. S. Dept. of Agriculture. PLATE XIX.

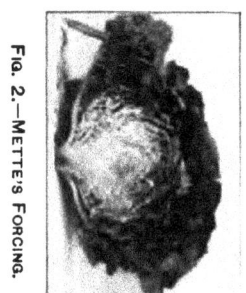

Fig. 1.—Tom Thumb.

Fig. 2.—Mette's Forcing.

Fig. 3.—Paris White Cos.

Fig. 4.—Lancaster.

Fig. 5.—Hartford Bronzed Head.

TYPICAL MATURE PLANTS (LONGITUDINAL SECTIONS).
(About one-fifth natural size.)

Fig. 1.—Speckled Dutch Butter.

Fig. 2.—Matador.

Fig. 3.—Hanson.

TYPICAL MATURE PLANTS (LONGITUDINAL SECTIONS).

(About one-fifth natural size.)

Fig. 1.—Prize Head.

Fig. 2.—White Star.

TYPICAL MATURE PLANTS (LONGITUDINAL SECTIONS).

(About one-fifth natural size.)

Fig. 1.—Nansen.

Fig. 2.—Tomhannock.

Fig. 3.—Big Boston.

Fig. 4.—Hanson.

Fig. 5.—All Seasons.

Fig. 6.—Passion.

TYPICAL YOUNG PLANTS.
(About two-fifths natural size.)

Fig. 1.—Boston Curled.

Fig. 2.—Green-Fringed.

Fig. 3.—Earliest Cutting.

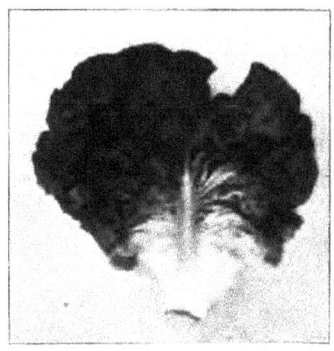
Fig. 4.—Speckled Dutch Butter.

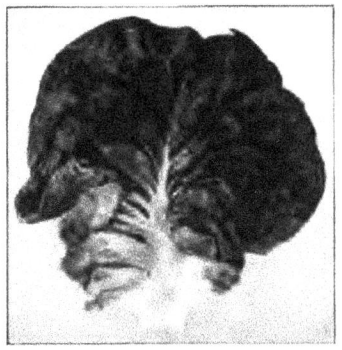
Fig. 5.—Tennis Ball Black-Seeded.

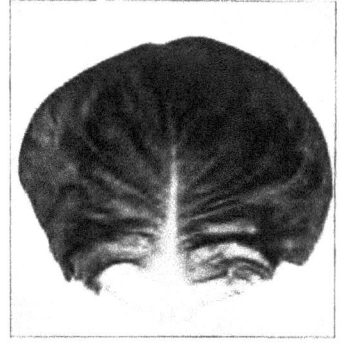
Fig. 6.—Deacon.

TYPICAL OUTER LEAVES.
(About one-fourth natural size.)

Fig. 1.—Lancaster (back view).

Fig. 2.—Lancaster (front view).

Fig. 3.—Oak-Leaved.

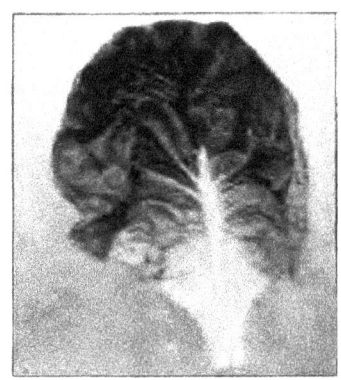
Fig. 4.—Yellow Winter.

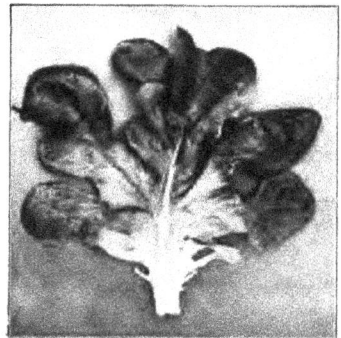
Fig. 5.—Baltimore Oak-Leaved.

Fig. 6.—Big Boston.

TYPICAL OUTER LEAVES.
(About one-fourth natural size.)

Fig. 1.—Early Curled Simpson.

Fig. 2.—Giant Glacier.

Fig. 3. Grand Rapids.

TYPICAL OUTER LEAVES.
(About one-fifth natural size.)

Fig. 1.—Denver Market.

Fig. 2.—Asparagus Lobed-Leaved and Express Cos

TYPICAL OUTER LEAVES.
(About one-fourth natural size.)

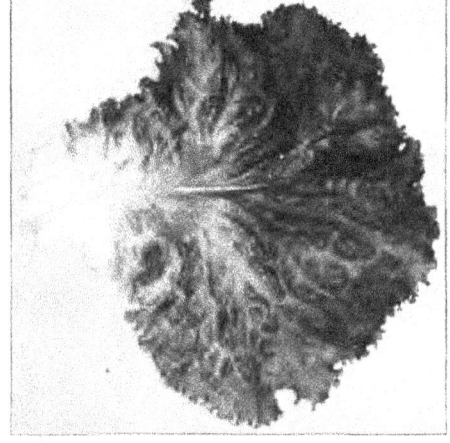

Fig. 3.—Hanson.

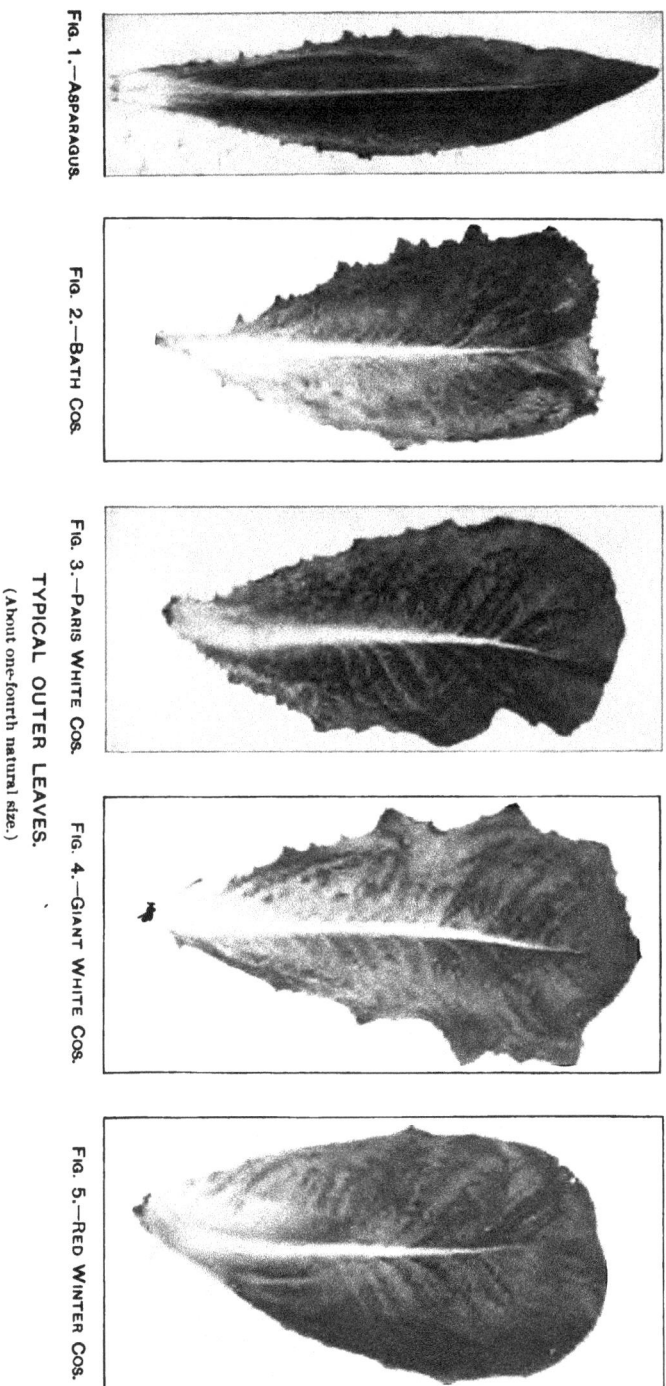

TYPICAL OUTER LEAVES.
(About one-fourth natural size.)

[Continued from page 2 of cover.]

No. 25. Miscellaneous Papers: I. The Seeds of Rescue Grass and Chess. II. Saragolla Wheat. III. Plant Introduction Notes from South Africa. IV. Congressional Seed and Plant Distribution Circulars, 1902–1903. 1903. Price, 15 cents.
26. Spanish Almonds. 1903. Price, 15 cents.
27. Letters on Agriculture in the West Indies, Spain, and the Orient. 1902. Price, 15 cents.
28. The Mango in Porto Rico. 1903. Price, 15 cents.
29. The Effect of Black Rot on Turnips. 1903. Price, 15 cents.
30. Budding the Pecan. 1902. Price, 10 cents.
31. Cultivated Forage Crops of the Northwestern States. 1902. Price, 10 cents.
32. A Disease of the White Ash Caused by Polyporus Fraxinophilus. 1903. Price, 10 cents.
33. North American Species of Leptochloa. 1903. Price, 15 cents.
34. Silkworm Food Plants. 1903. Price, 15 cents.
35. Recent Foreign Explorations, as Bearing on the Agricultural Development of the Southern States. 1903. Price, 10 cents.
36. The "Bluing" and the "Red Rot" of the Western Yellow Pine, with Special Reference to the Black Hills Forest Reserve. 1903. Price, 30 cents.
37. Formation of the Spores in the Sporangia of Rhizopus Nigricans and of Phycomyces Nitens. 1903. Price, 15 cents.
38. Forest Conditions and Problems in Eastern Washington, Eastern Oregon, etc. 1903. Price, 15 cents.
39. The Propagation of the Easter Lily from Seed. 1903. Price, 10 cents.
40. Cold Storage, with Special Reference to the Pear and Peach. 1903. Price, 15 cents.
41. The Commercial Grading of Corn. 1904. Price, 10 cents.
42. Three New Plant Introductions from Japan. 1903. Price, 10 cents.
43. Japanese Bamboos. 1903. Price, 10 cents.
44. The Bitter Rot of Apples. 1903. Price, 15 cents.
45. The Physiological Rôle of Mineral Nutrients in Plants. 1903. Price, 5 cents.
46. The Propagation of Tropical Fruit Trees and Other Plants. 1903. Price, 10 cents.
47. The Description of Wheat Varieties. 1903. Price, 10 cents.
48. The Apple in Cold Storage. 1903. Price, 15 cents.
49. The Culture of the Central American Rubber Tree. 1903. Price, 25 cents.
50. Wild Rice: Its Uses and Propagation. 1903. Price, 10 cents.
51. Miscellaneous Papers: Part I. The Wilt Disease of Tobacco and Its Control. 1903. Price, 5 cents. Part II. The Work of the Community Demonstration Farm at Terrell, Tex. 1904. Price, 5 cents. Part III. Fruit Trees Frozen in 1904. 1904. Price, 5 cents. Part IV. The Cultivation of the Australian Wattle. 1904. Price, 5 cents. Part V. Legal and Customary Weights per Bushel of Seeds. 1904. Price, 5 cents.
52. Wither-Tip and Other Diseases of Citrous Trees and Fruits Caused by Colletotrichum Gloesporioides. 1904. Price, 15 cents.
53. The Date Palm. 1904. Price, 20 cents.
54. Persian Gulf Dates. 1903. Price, 10 cents.
55. The Dry Rot of Potatoes Due to Fusarium Oxysporum. 1904. Price, 10 cents.
56. Nomenclature of the Apple. [In press.]
57. Methods Used for Controlling and Reclaiming Sand Dunes. 1904. Price, 10 cents.
58. The Vitality and Germination of Seeds. 1904. Price, 10 cents.
59. Pasture, Meadow, and Forage Crops in Nebraska. 1904. Price, 10 cents.
60. A Soft Rot of the Calla Lily. 1904. Price, 10 cents.
61. The Avocado in Florida. 1904. Price, 5 cents.
62. Notes on Egyptian Agriculture. 1904. Price, 10 cents.
63. Investigations of Rusts. 1904. Price, 10 cents.
64. A Method of Destroying or Preventing the Growth of Algæ and Certain Pathogenic Bacteria in Water Supplies. 1904. Price, 5 cents.
65. Reclamation of Cape Cod Sand Dunes. 1904. Price, 10 cents.
66. Inventory No. 10 of the Office of Seed and Plant Introduction and Distribution. [In press.]
67. Range Investigations in Arizona. 1904. Price, 15 cents.
68. North American Species of Agrostis. [In press.]

Lightning Source UK Ltd.
Milton Keynes UK
UKHW040311060119
335017UK00009B/350/P